COST ACCOUNTING

COST ACCOUNTING

LANE K. ANDERSON, Ph.D., CPA, CMA
Ernst & Young Professor of Accounting

DONALD K. CLANCY, Ph.D.
Professor of Accounting and Peat Marwick Faculty Fellow

Both of
Texas Tech University

...inewood, IL 60430
Boston, MA 02116

Cover and part image: L'Horloge du Musée d'Orsay by André Renoux
Courtesy of Editions André Roussard

Material from the Uniform CPA Examination Questions and Unofficial Answers, copyright © 1987 by the American Institute of Certified Public Accountants, Inc., is reprinted (or adapted) with permission.

Material from the Certified Management Accountant Examination Questions and Unofficial Answers, copyright © 1974, 1975, 1976, 1977, 1981, 1983, 1984, 1985, 1986, and 1987 by the Institute of Certified Management Accountants, is reprinted (or adapted) with permission.

Sponsoring editor:	Michael Reynolds
Developmental editor:	Diane M. Van Bakel
Project editor:	Lynne Basler
Production manager:	Irene H. Sotiroff
Designer:	Lucy Lesiak Design
Artist:	John Foote
Compositor:	Arcata Graphics/Kingsport
Typeface:	10/12 Times Roman
Printer:	Von Hoffmann Press, Inc.

Library of Congress Cataloging-in-Publication Data

Anderson, Lane K.
    Cost Accounting/Lane K. Anderson, Donald K. Clancy.
      p.   cm.
    Includes bibliographical references.
    ISBN 0-256-08683-4
     1. Cost accounting. I. Clancy, Donald K. II. Title.
HF5686.C8A6843 1991
657'.42—dc20   90–33271
                                    CIP

We dedicate this book to our spouses,
Dianne Anderson and Diana Denchfield Clancy, and our children.
With their support and encouragement over several years,
we pressed onward to complete this text.

About the Authors

Lane K. Anderson is the Ernst & Young Professor of Accounting at Texas Tech University. He received both an M.B.A and a Ph.D. in Accounting at the University of Wisconsin–Madison, and a Master of Accountancy at Brigham Young University. He is a CMA, having been awarded a Robert Beyer Gold medal in the CMA examination, and is a holder of a CPA certificate in Utah. Professor Anderson is a member of the National Association of Accountants, the American Institute of Certified Public Accountants, the American Accounting Association, and the National Contract Management Association.

Professor Anderson has many years of business experience with CPA firms, government, and industry. He was a staff auditor with Arthur Andersen & Company and a special consultant in the government contract services practice of Ernst & Young. He also served for four years on the staff of the Cost Accounting Standards Board (CASB), three of those years as an assistant director of the CASB staff. Professor Anderson continues active consulting with major aerospace and defense contractors on cost accounting matters related to government contracts.

In addition to active participation in the business community, Professor Anderson is an experienced teacher and has been honored as an outstanding teacher by several student organizations. He has taught graduate and undergraduate courses in cost and managerial accounting and accounting systems at Texas Tech University, the University of Maryland, and Brigham Young University. He conducts training programs in cost accounting subjects for major corporations and CPA firms, and instructs a number of professional continuing education courses. With over 20 years of teaching experience, he is acutely sensitive to student needs and knows how to help students maximize their learning experiences.

Professor Anderson is an active writer. His articles appear in the *Journal of Accountancy, Management Accounting,* the *Journal of Accounting Education,* and in a number of other journals. In addition, he authored *Accounting for Government Contracts: Cost Accounting Standards* and is editor for *Accounting for Government Contracts: Federal Acquisition Regulation.*

Donald K. Clancy is the Peat Marwick Faculty Fellow and a Professor of Accounting at Texas Tech University. In addition, he holds an appointment as Adjunct Professor of Health Care Organization Management with the Texas Tech School of Medicine. He received the M.B.A and Ph.D. degrees in Accounting at Pennsylvania State University. He has taught cost accounting and accounting systems for 20 years at Pennsylvania State University, the University of New Mexico, and Texas Tech University.

Professor Clancy has had several years experience as a cost analyst in industry and as a staff auditor in public accounting. He has also been a consultant to industry and service organizations, especially health care organizations, on the design of internal management accounting systems. Professor Clancy was recently the president of the management accounting section of the American Accounting Association, which is an international organization of over 1,500 professors interested in teaching and research in the field of managerial accounting. He is active with the *Journal of Management Accounting Research* as a reviewer of contributions on current research in the field of management accounting. He coedited, with Robert Capettini, *Cost Accounting, Robotics, and the New Manufacturing Environment* and prepared the reference work *Annotated Management Accounting Readings* for the Management Accounting Section. He is currently serving on the Council of the American Accounting Association.

Professor Clancy has written over 25 articles that have appeared in such journals as *Management Accounting, Cost and Management, Accounting, Organizations, and Society, Abacus, Journal of Accounting and Business, Advances in Accounting, Journal of Systems Management, Accounting and Business Research, Financial Analysts Journal* and *International Journal of Management.*

Preface

Cost Accounting is about change and taking risks. It reflects the current and foreseeable environment of companies of all sizes struggling to become more competitive in price, quality, and service. The marketplace is fluid, and management cannot successfully battle the ebb and flow of worldwide markets without the appropriate applications of cost accounting principles and practices. Accountants are spending more of their time in identifying activities that generate costs, in designing cost systems that better trace costs to products and services, in assisting managers in cost management, and in developing traditional, as well as new, performance measures. *Cost Accounting* is not radically different, but it identifies where, how, and why accountants should apply cost accounting principles and practices within current and future operations.

APPROACH

Four fundamental building blocks form the foundation of *Cost Accounting*. Each one is important in its own right, but together they have helped shape this text into a powerful learning tool.

Conceptual Framework

Each subject area is set in a framework that shows you where the pieces fit and why each one is important. In this context, an identification of the *what, how,* and *why* flows logically from concept to application. Each topic covers important systems design aspects and appropriate computer applications, and identifies how management at various levels plays a role. This means you will have the conceptual framework to understand why you are doing certain work, rather than merely applying procedures.

Cost Systems Design

Cost accounting literature and industry leaders are calling for a move from internal accounting systems designed around external requirements to multiple cost systems and ultimately to integrated cost systems. We hear of *activity costing* as the new wave in better costing of products and services. Activity costing is extolled as the means of establishing performance measures that will lead to improvement in quality and customer service. *Cost Accounting* emphasizes the important design concepts that implement activity costing in the appropriate areas, although the term *activity costing* is not always mentioned. This systems design material is not intended to substitute for a complete course in accounting systems.

Applications across Industries and Organizations

Although cost accounting finds its origin in a manufacturing setting, the concepts are applicable to a broad spectrum of companies and organizations. Applications in manufacturing, service, merchandising, and not-for-profit organizations are interwoven throughout each chapter and the assignments. To bring breadth to your education, we include real-world illustrations in the chapters and real-world problems in the end-of-chapter material that explore cost accounting issues in a wide variety of industries and geographical locations. In addition, you will learn the importance of cost accounting concepts as they relate to careers in public accounting, service-oriented businesses, manufacturing companies, merchandising companies, and not-for-profit organizations.

Integration of Materials

Cost Accounting covers the major issues affecting cost accounting systems, such as cost drivers, activity costing, the international marketplace, and human behavioral implications. Instead of compartmentalizing such issues in an individual chapter, they are interwoven with the concepts to which they apply. For example, although activity costing is covered in Chapters 8 and 25, it is also a part of the concepts discussed in a number of the other chapters. Therefore, we discuss significant issues in the dual context of understanding both the concepts and the implementation concerns.

CONTENT AND ORGANIZATION

Overall Organization

Cost Accounting consists of 26 chapters and 13 teaching appendixes. These materials are organized into seven parts to provide greater flexibility for selecting and organizing topic coverage.

Part I: Basic Concepts. The four chapters in Part I are the essential or core materials that support the remaining chapters. These topics bring perspective to cost accounting and serve as a foundation for appropriately applying later materials.

Part II: Accounting for Production Costs. Part II provides the characteristics that differentiate a job order and process cost system and a description of changes in the production environment. It also covers the accounting issues related to the three major cost elements: materials, labor, and overhead.

Part III: Accounting for Specialized Production Environments. The three chapters in Part III look at special situations and their related concerns. Here, process costing and joint production are discussed in depth. Although the accounting community is pressing for the elimination of non-value added activities that generate waste and scrap, spoilage and defective units, the costs of such activities must be accounted for. Those concerns are addressed here.

Part IV: Planning and Control of Activities. Part IV builds on the earlier parts as it discusses standard costs and budgeting systems. The budgeting area is somewhat unique in that it provides the planning process in terms of how entities should organize for budgeting activities within the master budget framework. Special emphasis is placed on the estimation and planning of cash flows.

Part V: Performance Measurement and Investigation. This part brings together six areas that relate to performance evaluation and control topics. The materials on variance investigation and models for process control are unique to a cost accounting course.

Part VI: Decision Support Processes. Part VI covers the short- and long-term decision making. The short-term operational decisions are presented in a traditional manner. We hope to bring a new perspective to long-term capital budgeting decisions by introducing you to a number of techniques for including uncertainty in developing estimates for investments and future cash flows.

Part VII: Concepts for Designing Costs Systems. This part covers specific areas of cost systems design. Chapter 25 handles the concepts and issues of cost allocation that apply to determining costs for products and services, identifying costs in planning and decision making, and the use of costs in control and performance evaluation. Chapter 26 is unique and unlike material in other cost accounting textbooks. It is integrative, pulling together most of the text from the perspective of the management accounting systems design responsibility of the chief financial officer functioning as a member of the management team.

Glossary. The end-of-book glossary will help you look up meanings of terms without having to find the chapters where they are discussed. In addition, each term has a chapter indication if you want to go to that chapter for additional discussion.

Chapter Highlights

Each chapter has been carefully structured to make learning easier. The major elements of this structure follow:

Business Problem. Each chapter begins with a realistic business situation or problem that focuses on material covered in the chapter. In many chapters, this problem is the central illustration throughout the chapter, and in others it becomes the problem for review at the end of the chapter.

Learning Objectives. Learning objectives identify the chapter contents and what you should be able to do upon completing the end-of-chapter materials. They serve as a guide to your study.

Summary. A brief synopsis of each chapter helps you organize, review, and integrate key concepts.

Summary of Formulas. A summary of formulas used in such chapters as cost-volume-profit analysis is presented at the end of the chapter for quick reference.

Problem for Review. Problems with suggested solutions enable you to test your knowledge of chapter material and obtain immediate feedback regarding appropriate answers.

Key Terms and Concepts. Important terms and concepts are defined and set in bold type throughout each chapter. They are also listed at the end of the chapter and referenced by page.

Additional Readings. This text is a survey of the topics in cost and managerial accounting. Should you desire to pursue refinements or expand beyond the text, a list of additional reading material is provided at the end of each chapter.

Appendixes. There are 13 teaching appendixes in the book. In some cases, the appendix includes review topics that are taught in other courses, but which may complement this text's material. Other appendixes discuss advanced topics that can easily be integrated with the basic topic coverage. Each appendix is organized as a self-contained teaching and learning unit: learning objectives, questions, exercises, and problems.

End-of-Chapter Materials

The assignment material at the end of each chapter permits you to review and apply the concepts of the chapter. This material includes review questions, discussion questions, exercises, problems, and extended applications.

Because you may be preparing for professional examinations, several problems within appropriate chapters are taken from the Certified Management Accounting (CMA) and CPA examinations, with more material from the CMA examination because it has a broader emphasis on cost and managerial accounting issues.

Review Questions. Review questions provide a review of the chapter concepts in simple implementation situations.

Discussion Questions. Thought-provoking questions relate to chapter content but include complexities not discussed in the chapter. They are intended to stimulate thinking about issues related to the subject matter. These questions can be used to spark class discussion or provide the themes for written reports.

Exercises. Exercises are usually one or two simple concepts with basic computations. They provide a good review of chapter materials without a lot of complexity.

Problems. Problems include either more than one issue, challenging situations, or complex computations. Each problem is based on a real-life type of situation. Personal computers with spreadsheet capabilities are required to complete some problems.

Extended Applications. Extended applications have still greater depth and complexity. They are designed to help students integrate various concepts within the chapter and across chapters. The extended applications require creativity in arriving at solutions to help students develop their skills in using computer spreadsheets or in report writing.

Flowchart of Chapter Relationships

Although considerable flexibility exists for sequencing chapters for study, there is an order based on prerequisite text and problem materials. The flowchart on the next page shows those chapters that must come before others.

SUPPLEMENTS

Supporting materials are required for both the instructor and student. The following ancillary materials are available.

For the Instructor

Instructor's Resource Guide. This important guide serves several purposes. It gives suggestions for presenting the concepts in a logical flow, and guides the selection of exercise and problem material by providing expected completion times and levels of difficulty. It helps extend the topical material beyond the basic chapter content. The resource guide was prepared by Professor Jay S. Holmen of the University of Wisconsin, Eau Claire.

Solutions Manual. The solutions manual contains solutions to all review and discussion questions, exercises, problems, and extended applications. Additional clarifying notes and suggestions are presented where appropriate.

Solutions Transparencies. These transparencies include selected exercises, problems, and extended applications.

Test Bank. A test bank includes a variety of questions and short problems. The questions within each category range from simple to complex to provide several alternative combinations to select from. The test bank was prepared by Professor Jay S. Holmen and has been designed to assure that test questions are compatible and consistent with the text material.

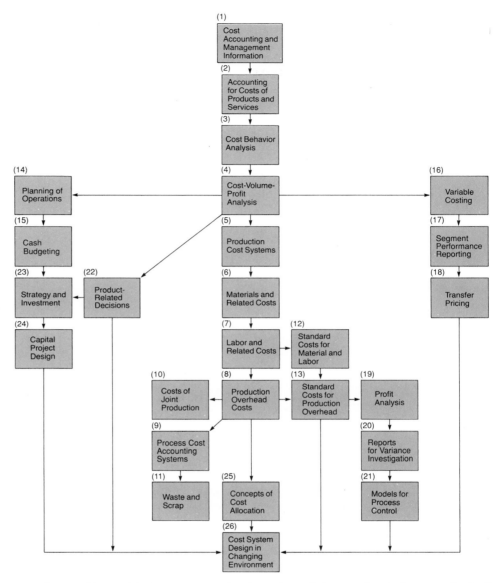

CompuTest. This is a computerized version of the test bank that permits individualizing each examination to your own circumstances.

For the Student

Study Guide. A study guide assists you in reviewing each chapter's content, in checking your progress in understanding concepts, and in preparing for examinations. The study guide was prepared by Professor Lamont F. Steedle of Towson State University.

Spreadsheet Applications Template Software (SPATS). Approximately 60 problems have templates prepared for electronic spreadsheets, eliminating the long setup time usually required for a complex problem. The problems involved are keyed in the margin with the following spreadsheet symbol:

ACKNOWLEDGMENTS

This text was completed with the input and assistance of many people. To list by name all of those who provided insights, improvements, or encouragement would be an impossible task as there were many who were influential. We owe a debt of gratitude and feel it important to recognize some special people, even with the risk that we may have forgotten someone.

First, we thank the hundreds of students at Texas Tech University, who used the manuscript in classes over a two-year period. Their response demonstrated that the text is comprehensive, clearly written, has an even-handed approach, and is appropriate for the level intended. They gave innumerable suggestions for improving clarity, reorganizing for better understanding, and for illustrating concepts. Also, there are the many students who contributed ideas for exercise and problem material. We have recognized those students whose problem ideas were adapted by showing their names in parentheses next to the exercise or problem.

Second, we thank the many reviewers who provided comments that enhanced the quality of this work. These reviewers include:

Robert J. Campbell, Miami University; Ronald L. Clark, University of Georgia; Michael F. Cornick, University of North Carolina–Charlotte; Paul Dierks, Wake Forest University; James M. Emig, Villanova University; Jay S. Holmen, University of Wisconsin–Eau Claire; Lyle Jacobsen, California State University–Hayward; Phillip A. Jones, Sr., University of Richmond; David E. Keys, Northern Illinois University; Patrick B. McKenzie, Arizona State University; Roland A. Minch, State University of New York–Albany; John H. Salter, University of Central Florida; Melkote K. Shivaswamy, Ball State University; Gwen Totterdale, San Diego State University; Glenn Vent, University of Nevada–Las Vegas; and Stephen L. Woehrle, Mankato State University.

Third, we thank Benson Wier and Edward Sikes for their efforts in working every problem in the text and checking the solutions. They gave many suggestions for improving solution presentation.

We are indebted to those people at Richard D. Irwin, Inc., who provided editorial, development, and production assistance. We thank John Black, the acquisitions editor who got us moving and kept the yoke on us over the years as we moved toward completion. Then, a special person gets our thanks because she pushed us through the final stages and helped with the inevitable frustrations of completion. She is Diane Van Bakel, our developmental editor. Finally, we thank Lynne Basler in production, who worked all the fine details of converting manuscript to final print.

Permission has been received from the Institute of Certified Management Accountants of the National Association of Accountants to use questions and/or unofficial answers from past Certificate in Management Accounting (CMA) examinations. Also, our appreciation is extended to the American Institute of Certified Public Accountants for permission to use (or to adapt) selected problems from their examinations. These problems bear the notations CMA and CPA, respectively.

A FINAL COMMENT

This textbook is meant to be helpful to instructors and students of cost accounting. We certainly welcome any suggestions from you that will enhance future editions of the text. We welcome comments, either written or by telephone. We can be reached at the Area of Accounting, College of Business Administration, Texas Tech University, Lubbock, Texas 79409: (806) 742-3181.

Lane K. Anderson
Donald K. Clancy

Brief Contents

Contents

xix

PART II

ACCOUNTING FOR PRODUCTION COSTS   151

PART III

ACCOUNTING FOR SPECIALIZED PRODUCTION ENVIRONMENTS   319

9   PROCESS COST ACCOUNTING SYSTEMS   321

10   COSTS OF JOINT PRODUCTION   378

I

Basic Concepts

Cost Accounting and Management Information

■

MAIN STREET AMERICA

Every community has its main street; no two main streets are the same, yet all have certain things in common. There are the convenience store, a supermarket, a bakery or doughnut shop, a drugstore, a hardware store, some kind of department store, a flower and gift shop, a jewelry store, a camera shop, a variety store, a sporting goods store, a TV and appliance repair shop, and, perhaps a farm implement store. Automobile drivers see the various car dealerships, service stations, a garage with its reliable mechanic, a tire store, and an auto parts store. For those desiring to get out in the evening, there are an ice cream shop and restaurants of many varieties. At least one motel has a vacancy for the tired traveler. An office building houses offices of a travel agency, an insurance agency, an attorney, a certified public accountant, and, occasionally, a barber.

Similar too are the community services available. The municipal building has offices for its police, mayor, and other administrators. There are a library, a fire station, a power company, a post office, different schools, and hidden somewhere on the outer fringes of the community is a sewage disposal plant. Of course, there are a bank, a savings and loan, doctors and dentists, clinics and a hospital, a bus depot, and an airport. Lest we forget, one or two places of worship stand stately or are hidden in a landscape of trees and shrubs.

Industrial areas are important in larger cities. They might include a salvage yard, a tire factory, a toy factory, a heavy equipment manufacturer, a refinery, a chemical plant, a food-processing plant, a concrete-mix company, or a research laboratory.

There will be warehouses to hold production of the factories and plants. On the outskirts of many towns, expect to see farms of various sizes.

What does this meandering through town have to do with cost accounting? The stores, services, or industries, regardless of size, have a common need: internal accounting information. For example, banks analyze the cost of services in order to charge customers appropriately. Churches evaluate actions against plans if they are to survive on the voluntary contributions from members. Motels track occupancy rates and the costs of bedding and cleaning if they are to realize a profit. Even the operations of the airport require careful analysis if the city council tries to increase fees or taxes to support the airport.

Although cost accounting was first developed in a manufacturing environment, its concepts and methods are being extended to every type of organization. Whether it manufactures a product, provides a service, or acts as a distributor of products, an organization has accounting information needs. This text is dedicated to explaining the internal accounting needs of organizations and to describing how systems are designed to provide information to satisfy those needs.

LEARNING OBJECTIVES

After studying this chapter, you should be able to:

1. Explain the interrelationships among management accounting, financial accounting, and cost accounting.
2. Distinguish among cost determination, planning and decision-making, and control and performance evaluation.
3. Describe the accounting information needs of top, middle, and lower management.
4. Describe the differences among manufacturing, merchandising, and service organizations.
5. List the primary responsibilities of the controller and treasurer.
6. Identify the major professional and governmental organizations that influence cost accounting.

INTERNAL ACCOUNTING

Economic activity is represented by events occurring in the organizations that make up our economy. During our stroll along main street, we saw the variety of products and services provided by a broad range of organizations. They all have needs for accounting information, whether for use by the managers of internal activities within the organization or to meet the requirements and interests of external parties. Management accounting, in a broad sense, deals with both internal and external accounting needs.

Management Accounting

Management accounting has gained acceptance as a body of accounting knowledge. The National Association of Accountants defines **management accounting** as follows:

> Management Accounting is the process of identification, measurement, accumulation, analysis preparation, interpretation, and communication of financial information used by

management to plan, evaluate, and control within an organization and to assure appropriate use of and accountability for its resources. Management accounting also comprises the preparation of financial reports for nonmanagement groups such as shareholders, creditors, regulatory agencies, and tax authorities.[1]

The definition is sufficiently broad to conclude that management accounting embraces just about everything that corporate accountants do, with the exception of the independent audit function. For our purposes, management accounting is the underlying framework for all accounting information needs of an organization. Two major subsets of this framework are financial accounting and cost accounting, as shown below:

Internal Accounting Information

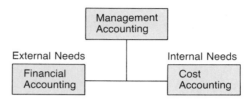

Financial Accounting

The primary purpose of **financial accounting** is to provide information to outsiders on (1) the results of company operations and (2) the company's financial position. Financial statements, if audited by a certified public accountant, must conform to generally accepted accounting principles that are established by the Financial Accounting Standards Board. Information contained in the statements is in large part directed to external parties for investment, compliance, or tax-collection purposes. The groups having an interest, demanding disclosures, or placing requirements on the organization are:

- Owners and creditors
- Taxing authorities, such as the Internal Revenue Service
- Government regulatory agencies
- Industry associations
- Managers and employees
- General public

Cost Accounting

The primary purpose of **cost accounting** is to provide internal, primarily financial, information for the management of the company. Although the original information provided by cost accounting was limited to finding the costs of products and activities, the subject matter has evolved to include financial planning, controlling operations, and investment topics.

Management accounting encompasses a body of concepts and techniques shared by both financial and cost accounting. Beyond this sharing, cost accounting connects the detailed operations with the external financial reports. Cost accounting plays a significant role in financial accounting for two important reasons. First, allocations are needed to arrive at the various dollar amounts that must be disclosed as part of financial statement preparation. Second, product costs are the values used in inventory pricing, and inventories are often a major component in determining operating results and financial position for manufacturing and merchandising organizations.

Cost accounting is well known for its emphasis on cost determination and cost-

---

[1] NAA, *Objectives of Management Accounting,* ''Statements on Management Accounting,'' Statement No. 1B (June 17, 1982), p. 1.

allocation methods. However, it includes much more, such as planning operations, measuring performance, and many decision-making techniques.

Cost management is a new term coined to reflect changes that are occurring in the role of cost accounting. **Cost management** is the process of managing the activities that cause costs in organizations. The primary purpose of cost management is to maintain, meet, or beat the competition on selling price and profits. Thus, in cost management, emphasis is placed on measuring, planning, and evaluating activities that cause or drive costs. During the 1980s, management accountants became more aware of and involved with cost management.

Most practicing accountants use the terms *management accounting* and *cost accounting* interchangeably. We view management accounting as an all-encompassing framework; cost accounting deals primarily with three important areas: cost determination, planning and decision-making, and control and performance measurement. Although some structure is implied by these three areas, the function of cost accounting is to serve the internal accounting information needs of management, whatever those needs happen to be.

INTERNALLY REPORTED INFORMATION

Managers need many types of accounting information. We classify these needs into three major categories:

1. Cost determination, or inventory valuation and income determination (also called *product costing*).
2. Short-term and long-term planning and decision-making.
3. Control and performance measurement.

Accounting systems that are consistent with and support these informational requirements are needed. Therefore, cost accounting also deals to some extent with information systems development.

Cost Determination

The process of finding the costs of something is called **cost determination.** These things can be products or services. For example, costs may be needed for products and supplies in inventory, an X-ray treatment in a hospital, the preparation of a tax return for a client, a rock concert at a state fair, a continuing education course at a local university, a checking account at a bank, or a local office of a state welfare program. Cost determination looks for the costs directly traceable or specifically identifiable with the object of interest plus a share of the other related costs.

Planning and Decision-Making

The survival of any organization depends greatly on the quality of the short-term and long-term planning and decision-making taking place within the organization. Although the two terms are shown separately, planning and decision-making are intertwined: planning involves decision-making and decision-making assumes planning. Some accountants use *planning* for short-term situations and *decision-making* for long-term cases. We find it difficult to differentiate between the two terms, so we will use *planning* in this section to cover both.

Planning is the formulation of short-term and long-term goals and objectives, predictions of potential results under alternative ways of achieving them, and decisions of how to attain the desired results. The decisions affect resources in areas such as:

1. Sales prices and volume.
2. Product profitability.
3. Addition or deletion of products or services.

4. Make or buy decisions regarding component parts.
5. Purchase commitments.
6. Facilities expansion or contraction.
7. Capital expenditures.

The accountant is assumed to be able to provide reasonably accurate cost estimates for each of these areas.

Control and Performance Measurement

Control is a process of comparing actions against plans. It maintains the specific steps taken by management to achieve its goals and objectives and to use resources effectively and efficiently. **Effectiveness** measures whether an object was achieved or not. **Efficiency** measures how resources were used to achieve the objective. Feedback from the accountant to management provides information about how well the actions represent the plans and identifies where managers may need to make corrections or adjustments in future planning and controlling activities. We call this feedback **performance measurement.**

The two major accounting tools for helping managers with their control responsibilities are budgets and performance reports. A **budget** is a quantitative expression of a plan of action. It is an aid to coordination and implementation of the actions by the responsible management. **Performance reports** are measurements of activities. They often consist of comparisons of actual with budgeted results. The differences are variances subject to possible managerial review.

Internal accounting information takes many forms, and the primary emphasis is placed on the relevance of the information to the interested party. Timeliness is very important. Thus, special analyses may be performed with data and reports that have been tailored to specific managers and the decisions that they have to make.

Interested Parties

The primary interested parties of internal reporting are top, middle, and lower management. This does not mean that outsiders have little desire for the information, but the organization is under no obligation to release it to outsiders. In fact, most organizations fear that internal information in the hands of outsiders destroys a competitive advantage or increases an officer's risk of liability when projections are not met.

Top, middle, and lower management each require different types of information. There is a rough correspondence between a manager's level in the organization and the type of accounting information needed.

Top Management. Top managers identify the goals and objectives for the organization. They set the guidelines for the major programs and indicate the direction the organization will pursue and how resources will be allocated. The process followed usually goes by the term **strategic planning.**[2]

These high-level managers face unstructured or semistructured problems that cover decisions on which products or services to provide and the development of new markets. They consider also how the economy, competitors, availability of resources, and other outside factors may affect the organization. For this reason, some of the information used is from external sources. Top management's accounting information is usually highly summarized, encompasses a long time period, is future oriented, and deals with a number of variables.

---

[2] The concepts of strategic planning, management control, and process control are attributed to Robert Anthony of the Harvard Business School in "Management Control," Chapter 1 of *Management Control Systems* (Homewood, Ill.: Richard D. Irwin, Inc., 1965).

Middle Management.   Middle managers address semistructured problems relating primarily to obtaining and using resources effectively and efficiently. The process followed by middle managers is known as **management control;** it involves controlling the day-to-day activities of the organization. Since control systems are implemented to monitor activities, managers need output from the accounting system that provides performance measurement information. Managers want information that will help them in formulating standards and operating budgets, planning working capital, choosing product improvements, planning staff levels, measuring and improving performance of subordinates, and similar decisions. Middle management requires accounting information on a regular basis in a somewhat summarized form.

Lower Management.   Lower management follows a management process called **operating control** that provides the mechanism needed to see that individual jobs or projects are carried out within a specified framework. Therefore, lower-level managers face semistructured or structured problems that deal with specific tasks. Each manager typically has authority to operate within a particular department or category of work. The types of decision are usually known, and the required information and decision rules are usually identified explicitly, perhaps in the organization's operating manual. Lower management needs information that is detailed, accurate, short term in nature, and provided frequently and routinely. Such information is obtained mainly from sources within the organization.

In addition to the various levels of management, the types of organizations are important in a properly functioning accounting information system.

ORGANIZATIONAL ENVIRONMENT

The foundation of our economy has changed dramatically in the last 40 years from a manufacturing base to a service base. In 1950, well over half of U.S. workers were employed in basic industries. Less than 20 percent were working in service businesses. By the early 1990s, however, over half of the workers held positions related to service activities. Examples of these positions include bank tellers, librarians, systems analysts and designers, accountants, lawyers, secretaries, nurses, journalists, salespersons, and public relations specialists.

For purposes of the following discussion, we categorize organizations as production, merchandising, and service.

Production and Merchandising Organizations

Most people easily distinguish between companies that make products and those that distribute the products to customers. For example, manufacturers have needs for information that differ from those of merchandisers. Material, work in process, and finished goods inventories usually represent a significant element of the company's assets, so cost determination is important. Manufacturers must carefully plan production capacity that meets the needs of their chosen markets. Survival depends upon producing a quality product at a total cost that beats the competition.

Merchandising includes more than the typical retail store. It includes consumer cooperatives, wholesale buying clubs, network marketing groups, and a number of other approaches for moving products from manufacturer to consumer. Merchandising organizations are concerned about investment in and management of inventories and control of operating expenses. Cost determination for products is relatively simple because it is the purchase price of inventories adjusted for various discounts and credits. The real key for the merchandiser is controlling the costs of human resources, marketing, and facilities that require planning and controlling activities. The key to survival depends on maintaining the mix of products, prices, and promotional efforts.

The major changes in organizations have come in the rapid expansion of the service industries. These organizations are discussed in more detail in the next section.

Service Organizations

Service organizations are of two basic types: public service and internal service. Examples of the organizations that provide service to the public are government agencies, schools and universities, research laboratories, hospitals, banks, hotels, public utilities, sports teams, airlines, labor unions, and professional practices.

Examples of internal service groups include accounting departments, research departments, planning groups, information systems groups, and staffs of various administrative functions. All of these internal service organizations support the economic performance and the purpose of the business. Although they operate within an economic institution, they do not sell to outside customers. However, managers often compare the cost of internal service with the cost of obtaining that service outside the institution.

Service organizations have found that the markets for their services have become more competitive during the past decade. Competition is based on the amount of time required to perform the service and its quality. Although manufacturing organizations place significant emphasis on inventory management, service organizations cannot inventory their services. Their inventories are primarily office and incidental supplies that will not constitute a large proportion of the cost of the services the organization renders. Accounting in service organizations most often involves planning, developing, and controlling human resources.

CHANGES IN WORLD MARKETS

During the late 1970s and early 1980s, the profitability of many U.S. industries deteriorated rapidly. Many U.S. companies were no longer competitive in quality or price in world markets. Companies in high technology fields, for example, electronics or aviation, no longer had the best technology. Basic industries, such as steel and automobiles, produced lower-quality products at a higher cost than their counterparts in other countries.

During the 1980s and into the 1990s, American industry has been reshaped dramatically to meet the challenges of world competition. Emphasis has shifted from earning short-run profits to producing goods with high quality that can be sold at a competitive price.

In order to make profits at a competitive price in world markets, the cost of the product or service must be carefully planned and managed. Consequently, there have been changes in cost accounting during the late 1980s and early 1990s. Cost accounting in its new and changing form is a necessary adjunct to manufacturing capability and productivity. Not all of these changes have been fully implemented, but the concepts for future cost accounting have now been set. We will develop these concepts in later chapters in this text.

Whether the organization is a manufacturer, merchandiser, or service provider, someone carries the responsibility for accounting and financial activities. The key positions are now presented.

FINANCIAL OFFICERS OF AN ORGANIZATION

The **chief financial officer** is the member of the management team who is primarily responsible for setting financial goals, evaluating alternatives, acquiring capital, managing cash, and establishing financial controls. The title of chief financial officer (CFO) is becoming popular in the larger organizations, but another common title is

vice president of finance. The latter title appears in small- and medium-sized organizations and in divisions of the larger organizations.

The CFO in large organizations is assisted by two other individuals called the **controller** and the **treasurer.** In smaller organizations, the CFO will perform their functions using clerical staff.

Controller

The controller title is somewhat misleading because the controller has authority over only the controller's office and must plan and control the operations of that office. The controller has no authority over other departments or functions. However, a major function of the controller is to assist other departments in planning and controlling their operations. The term *controller* evolved from *comptroller,* based on the French noun *compte,* which means *to account.* Hence, the title *controller* historically relates to accounting, not to controlling. Generally, the controller is responsible for all accounting activities within the organization.

The controller is responsible for a widely diverse set of activities. Although they vary from one organization to another, the duties most frequently assigned to the controller's office include:

1. Designing, installing, and maintaining the accounting system.
2. Preparing financial statements for external users.
3. Coordinating the development of the operating and financial budgets.
4. Accumulating and analyzing cost data.
5. Preparing and analyzing performance reports.
6. Providing information for problem solving and special decisions.
7. Consulting with management about the meaning of accounting information.
8. Planning, administering, and reporting taxes.

In addition to accounting responsibilities, the controller must be familiar with details of all facets of the organization. The controller should have a knowledge of products, services, facilities, pricing, and competitive conditions. A controller has a responsible position within an organization and can observe and often influence both the magnitude and direction of profits.

Treasurer

The treasurer is the financial officer responsible for all money management functions and activities. This individual has the following major areas of responsibility:

1. *Capital.* Identifying the needs for capital, then establishing and executing programs for acquiring it, and maintaining required financial arrangements.
2. *Investor relations.* Establishing and maintaining an adequate market for the organization's securities and maintaining liaison with investment bankers, financial analysts, and shareholders.
3. *Short-term financing.* Maintaining adequate sources for the organization's current borrowing from commercial banks and other lending institutions.
4. *Banking and custody.* Maintaining banking arrangements for receiving, holding, and disbursing the organization's monies and securities, plus having responsibility for the financial aspects of real estate transactions.
5. *Credits and collections.* Establishing procedures for granting credit and following up on the collection of accounts.
6. *Investments.* Investing the organization's funds as required and establishing and coordinating policies to govern investments in pension funds and similar trusts.
7. *Insurance.* Providing coverage as required or recommending and initiating self-insurance plans.

AUTHORITATIVE PROFESSIONAL AND GOVERNMENT ORGANIZATIONS

The accounting profession includes many kinds of accountants—so many that a comprehensive list is difficult to prepare. Some of the more common classifications are auditor, controller, tax accountant, cost analyst, financial planner, and financial manager. Whatever the title, accountants carry a great responsibility and influence many segments of society. Therefore, this section summarizes the major professional and governmental organizations that sway, control, or dominate the way accountants work.

The two organizations with the greatest influence on management accounting in general and cost accounting specifically are the National Association of Accountants and the Cost Accounting Standards Board. These are presented first.

National Association of Accountants (NAA)

NAA has devoted considerable effort to developing management accounting practices. Its membership consists of people who represent a variety of accounting and financial occupations in nearly every type of organization. The common element among the membership is an interest in the use of financial information in managing their organizations. NAA is the largest organization of management accountants in the world.

NAA provides many services to its membership. The important ones include (1) the monthly magazine of technical topics, *Management Accounting,* (2) an aggressive program of research whose results are published in a series of reports, (3) a large variety of continuing education programs at the national and local levels, (4) the certified management accounting program administered by NAA's Institute of Certified Management Accountants, and (5) the Management Accounting Practices Committee pronouncements and technical responses to proposed accounting standards and regulations.

NAA's accounting practice descriptions and research studies help to crystalize management accounting thinking on concepts, standards, and procedures. This work is complemented by that of the Management Accounting Practices Committee. The committee made an important step in codifying management accounting concepts and definitions with its series on management accounting terminology.

Cost Accounting Standards Board (CASB)

The original CASB was established by the U.S. Congress in 1970. The board was charged with the task of developing cost accounting standards to apply to all defense contractors in costing goods and services provided under negotiated defense procurement contracts in excess of $100,000. Congress did not appropriate monies for the CASB's continuation, so the board ceased operations on September 30, 1980. All of the standards, rules, and regulations promulgated by the CASB remain in full force and effect.

In 1984, the Office of the Federal Procurement Policy completed a major effort in simplifying government regulations for contractors of civilian and defense agencies and authorized publication of the Federal Acquisition Regulation (FAR). The FAR extended the cost accounting standards to many contractors of civilian agencies and made certain requirements of cost accounting standards applicable to any contract that meets certain conditions. Consequently, the CASB pronouncements now extend to a broader base of companies doing business with the U.S. government.

A new, independent, five-member Cost Accounting Standards Board has been authorized by Congress and is part of the executive branch of the federal government. The chairman is the administrator of the Office of Federal Procurement Policy. Members of the board are representatives from the Department of Defense, the General

Services Administration, private industry, and the accounting profession. The new board has full authority to amend, delete from, or add to the cost accounting standards promulgated by the original CASB. Any new cost accounting standards will apply to negotiated contracts in excess of $500,000 that are awarded by civilian and defense agencies.

Professional Organizations

A number of other professional organizations have an impact on accounting. Although most seem more concerned with external reporting, their work still interacts with cost accounting. Therefore, several important professional organizations are mentioned here.

American Institute of Certified Public Accountants (AICPA).   The AICPA, founded in 1887, is a national organization of certified public accountants. Besides practicing CPAs, its membership includes many CPAs engaged in industrial, commercial, and governmental accounting and teaching. Although the AICPA's main interest is public accounting, its research and publications include topics of interest to cost and management accountants. Its pronouncements on financial accounting principles began in 1939 and have been instrumental in developing accountants' willingness to adhere to accounting principles and procedures. It publishes a monthly magazine, *The Journal of Accountancy,* and many other helpful guides. *Accounting Trends and Techniques* analyzes the accounting aspects of the financial reports of 600 well-known American industrial companies. The AICPA also prepares, administers, and grades the semiannual CPA examinations. CPA candidates are tested on a wide variety of accounting topics, including cost accounting techniques.

Institute of Internal Auditors.   The Institute of Internal Auditors was organized in 1941 and is composed of people interested in internal auditing. It publishes a bimonthly magazine called the *Internal Auditor.* It also conducts continuing education programs and research studies primarily on internal auditing topics. It sponsors a certified internal auditor (CIA) program that requires candidates to pass a rigorous examination as well as to meet experience and education requirements. Since internal auditing concerns the operations of an organization and the effectiveness and efficiency of their operations, cost accounting is a required background for internal auditors. Although the institute does not have a direct impact on management accounting practices, auditors within individual organizations can dramatically influence how an organization does its work.

Financial Accounting Standards Board (FASB).   The FASB replaced the Accounting Principles Board of the AICPA in 1973. It is a private-sector organization dedicated to establishing standards for financial accounting and reporting. These standards are issued as statements of financial accounting standards. Each statement establishes new standards or amends those previously issued or amends accounting practices approved by the Accounting Principles Board. These standards deal with the many aspects of financial reporting, which includes the problems of measuring costs and identifying those costs with accounting periods; therefore, the standards influence the work of cost accounting.

Financial Executives Institute (FEI).   The FEI has a membership composed of those who perform the controllership, treasurership, and chief financial officer functions. Its monthly magazine, *The Financial Executive,* contains articles of interest to cost and management accountants. FEI has established a separate research organization, known as the Financial Executives Research Foundation, which issues publications in the area of cost and management accounting.

American Accounting Association (AAA).   The AAA is primarily an organization of college and university accounting professors, although it is open to anyone interested in accounting. It is most interested in the overall development of accounting and encourages and sponsors research in accounting education and theory. Topics of interest cover the entire field of accounting, but cost accounting is represented in its publications, committee activities, and annual regional and national conferences. It publishes quarterly a scholarly journal, *The Accounting Review,* and regularly publishes research studies conducted by its members.

The AAA has had several committees on cost concepts and standards. In 1948, it issued a series of articles on the general subject of cost accounting concepts under the title ''Cost Concepts: Special Problems and Definitions.''[3] This was followed by the statement on cost accounting in 1958 and another in 1969. These reports and statements represent important steps toward the development of a conceptual framework for cost accounting useful for planning and control purposes. In 1982, the Management Accounting Section was formed within the AAA to concentrate further on the special needs of cost accounting and the overall area of management accounting.

Government Organizations

Government organizations promulgate rules and regulations with which organizations must comply. These requirements, in many cases, affect the design of the accounting information systems. Those groups that have pervasive impact on organizations are summarized below.

Securities and Exchange Commission (SEC).   The Securities Acts of 1933 and 1934 created the Securities and Exchange Commission and granted it authority to regulate the securities markets in the United States. The SEC requires companies offering securities for public sale, and companies with securities already in public markets, to provide full disclosure of relevant information, financial statements, and supporting schedules, most of which are certified by an independent CPA. Although the SEC has statutory authority to regulate and prescribe the form and content of financial statements, it has worked closely with the FASB and other sections of the accounting profession in developing financial accounting and reporting principles and practices.

Internal Revenue Service (IRS).   The IRS is interested in income determination of which costing of inventories is an important element. As a result, the IRS has issued a number of regulations specifying the costs that must be included in inventory values. It has also issued regulations on asset capitalization criteria, depreciation methods and rates, indirect costs, transfer pricing, and a number of other topics affecting cost accounting. Although a company may keep different sets of accounting records for tax purposes, internal accounting purposes, and financial reporting, companies like to integrate these records as much as possible. Consequently, the IRS influences some of the cost accounting practices used in measuring, assigning, and allocating costs.

Social Security Administration.   The Social Security Administration administers the various medicare programs legislated by the Congress. Medicare legislation in

---

[3] Robert L. Dixon, ''Cost Concepts: Special Problems and Definitions,'' *The Accounting Review* 23 (January 1948), pp. 28–43.

1966 had a significant impact on the cost accounting systems of health care institutions because it required these institutions to submit cost information as the basis for reimbursement. Many health care institutions either did not have cost accounting systems or had inadequate systems for this purpose. Therefore, the years following 1966 were a period when much progress was made in improving the quality of health care cost accounting systems. In 1983, an amendment to the Social Security Act made another change that encourages managers of health care institutions to select techniques that will effectively contain costs and to improve the cost accumulation and reporting processes.

Federal Trade Commission (FTC). The FTC administers the Robinson-Patman Amendment to the Clayton Anti-Trust Act. This amendment forbids quoting different prices (discounts or price concessions) to competing customers unless such discrimination can be justified by differences in costs of manufacturing, sale, or delivery. FTC decisions are based on cost allocations. Since complete cost information for manufacturing, marketing, and distribution is necessary to defend charges under this law, companies have an important motivating force for improving and maintaining cost accounting systems.

Other Organizations. A few other organizations that make an impact on cost are worthy of mention. The Interstate Commerce Commission (ICC) regulates transportation and influences the cost accounting of the entire transportation industry. Banks and savings and loans must meet the requirements of the Federal Deposit Insurance Corporation (FDIC) and of the Comptroller of the Currency. The Government Accounting Standards Board (GASB), successor to the National Council on Governmental Accounting (NCGA), was created in 1984 to establish standards for state and local government entities. These standards influence cost accounting in local governments. And, finally, the U.S. Congress can and has legislated requirements for organizations that dominate accounting and cost incurrence in specific areas. Some of these requirements determine whether businesses will survive or not.

CERTIFIED MANAGEMENT ACCOUNTING

Management accountants have gained increased recognition as a distinct group with its own common body of knowledge and program of certification. In 1972, the National Association of Accountants, acting through its Institute of Certified Management Accountants, established the certified management accountant (CMA) program. A certificate is awarded to aspirants with two years of qualified experience in management accounting who have successfully completed a comprehensive examination. Earning the certificate and becoming a CMA are considered important steps in the professional growth and development of anyone desiring to become an active management accountant or financial manager.

The CMA program was founded on the basis that a management accountant plays an important role in the management process. Consequently, the person seeking the CMA designation must understand and work with the major aspects of business.

The four-part CMA examination covers all of the areas important to a management accountant. The exam concerns economics and business finance with specific areas of enterprise economics, institutional environment of business, national and international economics, working capital management, and long-term finance and capital structure. It covers organization and behavior, including ethical considerations. Its topics are organization theory and decision-making, motivation and perception, communication, behavioral science applications in accounting, and ethics. The exam also deals with public reporting standards, auditing and taxes with the specific areas of reporting requirements, audit protection, and tax accounting. Another important area concerns internal reporting and analysis. The subjects covered include concepts of information, basic financial statements, profit planning and budgetary controls, standard costs, and analysis of accounts and statements. Also covered is decision analysis, including modeling and information systems. Its topics are fundamentals of the decision process, decision analysis, nature and techniques of model building, and information systems and data processing.

SUMMARY

Virtually every participant in economic activity uses accounting information in some form. The needs for accounting information come from managers of internal activities within an organization and the requirements and interests of external parties. From an organization's point of view, management accounting is the framework that supports all accounting information systems. Within that framework, financial accounting is the segment that covers reporting to external parties; cost accounting deals with the information needed for cost determination, planning and decision-making, and control and performance evaluation.

The primary interested parties of internal reporting are top, middle, and lower management. Each level requires different kinds of information. Top management needs information to support its role in strategic planning. Middle managers ensure that resources are obtained and used effectively and efficiently, and they need information for that management control function. Lower management deals with specific tasks on a day-to-day basis. Managers at that level need information for operating control.

Service organizations are gaining in the proportion of productive output within economic activity. The major difference between service organizations and production and merchandising organizations is inventory. Service organizations render services that may be characterized by time and quality, and cannot be inventoried. However, each type of organization still needs cost determination, planning and decision-making, and control and performance measurement, but the needs within these groups have different emphases.

The chief financial officer is the member of the management team who is responsible for setting financial goals, evaluating alternatives, acquiring capital, managing cash, and establishing financial controls. In some companies, the chief financial officer carries the title of vice president of finance. Regardless of the title, the chief financial officer is assisted by the controller and the treasurer. Generally, the controller is responsible for all accounting activities within the organization; the treasurer handles the money management functions and activities.

Many professional and government organizations have a dramatic impact on the accounting profession. The two organizations that have had the greatest influence on management accounting and cost accounting are the National Association of Accountants and the Cost Accounting Standards Board. Other groups are important and have had varying degrees of impact.

Management accountants are gaining increased recognition as a distinct professional group. They have a certification program called the certified management accountant (CMA). That program assumes that a management accountant plays an important role in the management process and that such a person must understand and work with the major areas of business.

KEY TERMS AND CONCEPTS

Management accounting (4)
Financial accounting (5)
Cost accounting (5)
Cost management (6)
Cost determination (6)
Planning (6)
Control (7)
Effectiveness (7)
Efficiency (7)
Performance measurement (7)

Budget (7)
Performance reports (7)
Strategic planning (7)
Management control (8)
Operating control (8)
Chief financial officer (9)
Vice president of finance (10)
Controller (10)
Treasurer (10)

ADDITIONAL READINGS

Ballew, V. B., and R. J. Schlesinger. "Modern Factories and Outdated Cost Systems Do Not Mix." *Production and Inventory Management Journal,* first quarter 1989, pp. 19–23.

Berliner, C., and J. A. Brimson. *Cost Management for Today's Advanced Manufacturing: The CAM-I Conceptual Design.* Boston: Harvard Business School Press, 1989.

Campi, J. P. "Total Cost Management at Parker Hannifin." *Management Accounting,* January 1989, pp. 51–53.

Cooper, R. "You Need a New Cost System When . . . ." *Harvard Business Review,* January–February 1989, pp. 77–82.

Edwards, J. B., and J. A. Heard. "Is Cost Accounting the No. 1 Enemy of Productivity?" *Management Accounting,* June 1984, pp. 44–49.

Foster, G., and C. T. Horngren. "JIT: Cost Accounting and Cost Management Issues." *Management Accounting,* June 1987, pp. 19–25.

Howell, R. A., and S. R. Soucy. "Cost Accounting in the New Manufacturing Environment." *Management Accounting,* August 1987, pp. 42–48.

Johnson, H. T. "Managing Costs: An Outmoded Philosophy." *Manufacturing Engineering,* May 1989, pp.. 42–46.

Johnson, H. T., and R. S. Kaplan. *Relevance Lost: The Rise and Fall of Management Accounting.* Boston: Harvard Business School Press, 1987.

Kaplan, R. S. "The Evolution of Management Accounting." *The Accounting Review,* July 1984, pp. 390–418.

Lammert, T. B., and R. Ehrsam. "The Human Element: The Real Challenge in Modernizing Cost Systems." *Management Accounting,* July 1987, pp. 32–37.

Lander, G. H., and A. Reinstein. "Identifying a Common Body of Knowledge for Management Accounting." *Issues in Accounting Education,* Fall 1987, pp. 264–80.

Mackey, J. T. "11 Key Issues in Manufacturing Accounting." *Management Accounting,* January 1987, pp. 32–37.

Tatikonda, M. V. "Just-in-Time and Modern Manufacturing Environments: Implications for Cost Accounting." *Production and Inventory Management Journal,* First Quarter 1988.

REVIEW QUESTIONS

1. What are the two primary sources of needs for accounting information?
2. Define *management accounting*. Explain how the definition of management accounting includes both financial and cost accounting.
3. What is the primary purpose of financial accounting? Give examples of external parties who require financial accounting information.
4. List ways that cost accounting serves the needs of internal management.
5. Define *cost determination*.
6. Define *planning* and *control*.
7. List five examples of areas that resource decisions affect.
8. Differentiate between effectiveness and efficiency.
9. What is a budget?

10. How do the accounting information needs of lower management differ from the needs of top management?
11. List the types of inventories held by production, merchandising, and service organizations.
12. Explain the difference between public services and internal services.
13. Which two major executives report to the chief financial officer?
14. Differentiate between the general responsibilities of the controller and those of the treasurer.
15. Which two organizations have had the greatest influence on management accounting and cost accounting? Briefly describe each organization.
16. What organizations must meet the standards issued by the Cost Accounting Standards Board?
17. What is a CMA? Identify the parts of the CMA examination.

DISCUSSION QUESTIONS

18. Why might management not want internal accounting information, especially cost information, released to the general public?
19. How are financial accounting and cost accounting interrelated?
20. Can control happen without planning? Can planning occur that does not lead to control? Comment.
21. Would you be willing to fly in the lowest-cost space shuttle that used the least amount of fuel (i.e., is the most efficient)? Comment on the relationship between efficiency and effectiveness in the space program as compared to the efficient and effective manufacture of pencils.
22. Some managers place sole emphasis on maintaining "inventories" of people in the profitability and survival of service organizations. Is this a balanced view? Comment on the relationship between maintaining human capital and maintaining the quality and availability of service by using a law firm and an airline as examples.

CHAPTER

2

Accounting for the Costs of Products and Services

THE PRODUCT COST PROBLEM

The Raider Football Company produces footballs in very large quantities. Raw materials for producing the footballs include synthetic rubber, vinyl in pellet form, vinyl strips, and packaging materials. The rubber is melted in large quantities and pressure extruded to form an interior lining with air intake valve. An exterior cover is formed from vinyl and is trimmed, and lace and valve holes are punched. Then the interior lining is inserted into the cover and the laces are inserted manually. Finally, the completed football is inflated, tested for balance and leaks, and packaged for shipment.

During 19x8, the Raider Football Company purchased $860,000 in direct materials and $16,000 in indirect materials, incurred $518,000 in factory wages ($398,000 for direct workers), and incurred $194,000 in other factory related costs. The inventories for the factory consisted of:

	January 1, 19x8	December 31, 19x1
Materials	$ 60,000	$ 50,000
Work in process	346,000	357,000
Finished goods	70,000	85,000

The company applies overhead to production on the basis of machine hours worked. During the year, $288,000 in overhead was applied to production.

What was the cost of goods manufactured and the cost of goods sold?

**LEARNING
OBJECTIVES**

After studying this chapter, you should be able to:

1. Distinguish among basic cost concepts and give examples of each.
2. Identify and give examples of each of the three cost elements for the production of an item or service.
3. Explain the differences among the income statements for a manufacturing company, a merchandising company, and a service organization.
4. Account for cost elements from the time of incurrence to the sale of the product or service.
5. Prepare a statement of cost of goods manufactured and a combined statement of cost of goods manufactured and sold.

After an initial presentation of cost terms, this chapter discusses the costs that should be allocated to production, traces the flow of costs through production to finished goods inventory, and shows the statements that are prepared to support the income statement.

COST TERMINOLOGY

To begin with, it is essential to have a basic understanding of many concepts and terms that will be used throughout this and later chapters. These terms are presented in the following sections.

Cost is an exchange price, a foregoing, or a sacrifice made to obtain a benefit. For accounting purposes, the National Association of Accountants defined cost as:

> . . . the cash or cash equivalent value required to attain an objective such as acquiring the goods and services used, complying with a contract, performing a function, or producing and distributing a product.[1]

Every product or service purchased has a cost that measures the sacrifices made to acquire it. This cost can be found by adding to the invoice price of the product or service all costs of ordering, shipping, and receiving. Regardless of when we pay, the cost is established. Generally, the monetary measurement is the cash outlay or expenditure, but the exchange may also involve an asset other than cash, such as buildings or equipment.

When a product is manufactured or a service is performed by employees, the cost is more elusive. We cannot find this cost on a price list or an invoice. Instead, we must design, install, and maintain a cost accounting system that is appropriate to specific production methods.

Cost Objective

A **cost objective** is anything for which we want to know the cost. For example, a company might need to know the cost of:

General Objectives	*Specific Objectives*
1. Product	Pair of jeans
2. Service	Hour of surgery
3. Project	Motion picture
4. Process	Galvanizing steel sheets
5. Person	Company president
6. Subdivision	Accounting department

---

[1] National Association of Accountants, *Statements on Management Accounting, Statement Number 2,* "Management Accounting Terminology" (New York: National Association of Accountants, 1983).

Cost Accumulation and Allocation

Costs are accumulated into groups of temporary ledger accounts associated with **cost pools.** These are pools for costs, not for swimming, but the concept is similar. Just as water is accumulated in a swimming pool, costs are accumulated in a cost pool. Thus, the costs of a department such as airline terminal maintenance will be accumulated into temporary accounts for building maintenance. The distribution of accumulated costs to specific cost objectives is called **cost allocation.** A number of terms have been used in cost accounting as synonyms for allocation or to express a subset of allocations. The common verbs used are *assign, charge, apply,* and *distribute.* Although we use these verbs too, the global conceptual term for identifying costs with cost objectives is *allocation.*

Allocations that are the result of measuring the specific usage are called **direct allocations** and result in **direct costs** of the cost objective. If the usage is easy and economical to measure and trace to the cost objective in question, then direct allocation will occur. Allocations based on approximated usage are called **indirect allocations** and result in **indirect costs.** For example, the utility cost of an entire building is measured by the utility companies through meters. Thus, allocation of utility cost to the building is direct because the measurement must occur to generate the utility bill. On the other hand, the utility cost of a specific department or room in the building is inconvenient and expensive to measure. As a consequence, allocations of utility costs to departments or offices are normally indirect and involve selecting a base that represents the usage of the utilities provided. The most frequently used base is the square footage of space occupied.[2]

Product and Period Costs for Financial Reports

In the normal course of operations, an organization will produce many goods and services. **Production costs**[3] include all costs necessary to get a good or service ready for sale. They include the costs of people, materials, equipment, and space. Any production cost may also be called a **product cost.** The costs of units in process or completed units become the basis for recording work in process and finished goods inventories in the financial records. Such costs become expenses when products are sold, and the amounts represent costs of goods sold. Nonproduction costs that have been incurred and are not assets become expenses of the period and are called **period costs.**

When costs can be related to future benefits, they are assets and are called **unexpired costs** (also called **capitalized costs**). All other costs, including the costs of inventory sold, are called **expired costs** and appear in the income statement as **expenses.** Thus, expenses are the sum of cost of goods sold (product costs whose benefits to the company have expired) and period costs (costs incurred during the period that can not be traced to future benefits).

The costs of producing services do not differ in concept from the costs of producing products. For example, providing health care involves the costs of people (doctors, nurses, and other staff), supplies, equipment, and buildings. Producing air transportation includes people (pilots and flight attendants), fuel, food, airport landing and take-off fees, and indirect costs of the aircraft, computers, and other items. Marketing a product consists of sales and advertising staff, supplies, transportation, and other costs. Providing computer service includes the cost of people (machine operators,

---

[2] The subject of interdepartment service allocations is developed further in Appendix 8A.

[3] Factory or manufacturing costs are typical designations. However, they denote manufacturing operations. Because we intend to include services with discussions on products, we are using the broader term *production.*

programmers, and others), supplies of paper and forms, programs, equipment, and space.

The costs of services differ from producing a tangible good in that services cannot be stored (inventoried) and their costs are normally treated as expired costs. There is a presumption that the benefit of services rendered such as marketing, insurance, or banking expires with the receipt of the service. Thus, service costs are normally recorded as expenses for external financial reports. The exception to this general rule is for services rendered in the production of goods or other tangible items. For example, the architectural and engineering service fees related to the construction of a shopping mall are recorded as part of the cost of the mall.

Functional Classifications

Companies usually identify separate functional areas as part of assigning responsibility to managers. The most common functional areas are production, marketing and distribution, and general and administration. In larger companies, these functional areas are further broken down into more specialized departments. In order to evaluate the effectiveness of each functional area and the manager in charge, cost pools must be developed.

Production Costs. **Production costs** include all costs incurred in producing goods or services. We normally think of the production cycle for products beginning with the acquisition of materials, passing through various operations and tasks that transform the materials into products, and ending when the products move to finished goods inventory awaiting sale. The costs include material costs, payroll costs for people working on the product, and the indirect costs of supervision, taxes, utilities, depreciation, janitorial service, and repairs and maintenance of equipment. Similarly, the production cost for services includes the costs of supplies and materials used, service personnel directly providing the service, and the indirect costs of supervision, depreciation, and repairs.

Marketing and Distribution Costs. **Marketing and distribution costs** are the costs of securing customer orders and getting the company's products or services to the customer. They are incurred from the time the production process is complete through delivery to the customer. These costs are period costs and appear as expenses in an income statement. Examples of these costs are advertising, promotional offers, warehousing and shipping products, sales commissions and salaries, and sales travel costs. For an electric utility, the marketing and distribution costs are advertising and promotion of its service, maintenance costs of lines, cables, and meters, and depreciation on the delivery equipment. For an airline, marketing and distribution costs include advertising, promotional materials, travel agent fees, reservations staff salaries, ticket counter staff salaries, and the cost of space and an extensive computer network.

General and Administrative Costs. **General and administrative costs** are the costs of managing the general activities of the company but do not logically fit under either production or marketing and distribution. Examples of these costs include the executive office, personnel, accounting, legal, and similar costs that pertain to the company as a whole. Interest costs are often included.

We will next introduce and compare the operations of three basic types of companies: merchandisers, manufacturers, and service companies.

COMPARISON OF OPERATIONS

The operations of a merchandiser are distinctly different from those of manufacturers, and a service organization is similar in some ways to both. Here we look at the operations to identify similarities and differences.

Merchandisers

Many companies do not manufacture products but facilitate their distribution to consumers by providing facilities for the sale of products. For example, department stores, drugstores, supermarkets, appliance stores, clothing stores, and hobby shops purchase products from manufacturers for resale to consumers. These companies do not incur additional costs to alter the form or nature of the products they acquire; they sell the items purchased in essentially the same condition as received. The company markets the goods and provides a convenient location for consumers to buy them.

Merchandisers incur costs related to the purchase, storage, display, marketing, and sale of goods. The cost of products acquired includes the purchase price plus the costs of transporting the goods and the costs of insuring them during transit. In addition to the cost of goods sold, there are the operating costs: supplies, compensation of sales people, advertising, depreciation on store equipment, rent of space, taxes, and administration.

The income statement for a merchandiser may appear as follows:

Sales		$2,000,000
Cost of goods sold:		
Beginning inventory	$ 250,000	
Add purchases	1,300,000	
Goods available for sale	$1,550,000	
Less ending inventory	350,000	1,200,000
Gross margin (or Gross profit)		$ 800,000
Less operating expenses:		
Marketing and distribution expenses	$ 200,000	
General and administrative expenses	350,000	550,000
Net income		$ 250,000

Manufacturers

The production cost of an item includes materials costs and all of the costs of transforming materials and component parts into a product ready for sale. The company purchases materials, hires workers, and provides the facilities to convert materials to a finished product. For accounting purposes, three categories of production costs receive attention: materials, labor, and production overhead.

Materials.   The primary raw materials, unassembled parts, and subassemblies purchased for use in producing the company's finished products are identified as **direct materials.** The types of materials in this classification depend upon the nature of the operations.

Processing companies often start with natural materials to form their products. Examples include crude oil as direct material to a refinery, bales of cotton in a denim plant, grapes for a wine maker, and cowhide for the manufacture of leather. Other processing plants take this basic output and change it in some way. For example, a plastics company takes some of the output of an oil refinery and processes it further into resins, glues, and plastic pellets. A cola bottler mixes a cola syrup, which is often a processed cocoa bean or citrus derivative, with carbonated water to form the finished cola ready for bottling.

The direct materials for a **fabrication** plant generally include the outputs of basic processing plants. The fabrication plant shapes, treats, or cuts the materials. For example, a ski boot manufacturer combines resins and polyesters to form the ski boot. The direct materials for a steel sheet mill are slabs of steel weighing between 40 and 80 tons, which are the output from a steel plant. The sheet mill rolls the steel into thin sheets by using heat and pressure. The direct materials for a steel stamping plant are steel sheets. The stamping plant changes such materials as thin steel sheets into fenders, roofs, and hoods for automobiles. The stamping mill also presses thick steel sheet into products such as bathtubs or automobile bumpers.

An **assembly** plant presses, welds, bolts, or wires parts together. Assembly plants use as direct materials the outputs of processing and fabrication plants. For example, a computer assembly plant has direct materials including circuit boards, integrated circuit chips, power units, and cabinets. In passenger jet assembly, the direct materials include the fuselage, completed wings, engines, the tail section, the guidance system, passenger seats, and miscellaneous parts.

For service companies, the direct materials are commonly called *materials* or *supplies*. For a transportation company, such as an airline, fuel and food are the major direct materials. For a hospital, the costs of expensive materials, such as antibiotics and surgical setups, are treated as direct materials.

A few industries have little or no direct materials. **Extractive** companies start with mineral rights, labor, and equipment to produce an ore or material product that is normally the input to a processing plant. Supplies are used in the extraction, but the main product comes from nature. Lumber companies produce logs by leasing cutting rights and applying labor and equipment. (Since some lumber companies now grow their own trees, there will be a direct material cost related to cost of growing the trees for 30 years.) Cattle ranches start with a herd, grazing rights, labor, and equipment. The herd produces marketable calves each year. There is no identifiable direct material cost. Instead, there are costs for feed and medicines that relate to the entire herd and can not be traced to specific marketable cattle.

Accounting for materials.   At the time of purchase, the cost of materials and supplies is placed in the Materials Inventory account, which is a control account with subsidiary inventory records. The details of the materials purchased and amounts payable will be kept in computer files variously called *supplier order, completed order, materials received*, and *open invoices*. These files will be used to update the subsidiary files of materials inventory and accounts payable.

As the materials are issued to production, their cost is moved from the Materials Inventory account to the Work in Process Inventory Control account. This account is supported by subsidiary computer files of details on the specific materials and the specific products involved in production.

Materials Inventory may also be called Raw Materials, Direct Materials, or Stores Control. For our purposes, we will use the Materials Inventory account title whether the company has one or many categories of materials.

We will consider the accounting for direct and indirect production material costs more in Chapter 6.

Labor.   The cost of employees who work directly on the product and whose efforts can be economically identified with or specifically traced to a product or service is called **direct labor.** Examples of direct labor include the wages of a printer in a print shop, a sewing machine operator in a jeans factory, or a bricklayer in the construction of a building.

The cost of employees on some products is directly traced to the product, but the cost is not called *direct labor*. For example, the cost of a movie or television cast is recorded as a direct cost of production but is definitely not referred to as direct labor. Instead, various terms such as *the stars, the talent, the troop,* or *the cast* are used.

There are two important accounting journal entries for recording labor. One entry concerns wages payable to show the existence of a liability for the salaries and wages of the workers. The other entry distributes the direct labor cost to the products and the indirect labor to production overhead. These entries will be illustrated later in this chapter, and Chapter 7 will develop the accounting for direct and indirect labor in more detail.

Production overhead. **Production overhead** includes all production costs other than direct materials and direct labor. In a more specific sense, production overhead represents the production costs that cannot be specifically identified with or traced directly to individual units of the finished product. It also includes some costs that might be directly traceable, but it is uneconomical to trace them to the unit. Other terms often used in business are *indirect manufacturing costs, factory overhead,* and an archaic term, *factory burden.* Included in production overhead are such costs as indirect materials, supervision, repairs and maintenance, production depreciation, production scheduling, property taxes, insurance, utilities, janitorial services, security guards, and product inspection.

As overhead costs are incurred, they are recorded in a control account called *Production Overhead* (or *Production Overhead Control*). During production, the overhead is allocated to the products or services. The allocation of overhead to products or services is commonly called *overhead application.* Chapter 8 will discuss primarily the accounting for production overhead costs.

Income Statement. The income statement for a manufacturer may appear as follows:

Sales		$2,500,000
Cost of goods sold:		
Beginning inventory	$ 200,000	
Add cost of goods manufactured	1,400,000	
Goods available for sale	$1,600,000	
Less ending inventory	300,000	1,300,000
Gross margin (or Gross profit)		$1,200,000
Less operating expenses:		
Marketing and distribution expenses	$ 250,000	
General and administrative expenses	500,000	750,000
Net income		$ 450,000

The primary difference between the income statements for a merchandiser and for a manufacturer is that the manufacturer has the entry "cost of goods manufactured" instead of "purchases." Otherwise, the two statements are identical. Supporting the cost of goods manufactured amount will be a schedule of costs of goods manufactured disclosing the materials, labor, and overhead items used to produce the product.

Service Companies

Service companies are similar to manufacturers in that they render services at a cost of materials, labor, and overhead.[4] They are similar to the merchandisers because

---

[4] For an example of the unique costing problems associated with a service company, see D. Wentz, "How We Match Costs and Revenues in a Service Business," *Management Accounting,* October 1985, pp. 36–42.

they distribute the services. Service companies do not hold completed inventories in the normal course of business. They do, however, have supplies and materials inventories. For example, a medical clinic has drugs and surgical supplies. For most service companies, the supplies, labor, and other costs of providing the service are included in the expenses as they occur because services cannot be inventoried.[5]

The income statement for a service organization may look like the following:

Revenues		$1,200,000
Less operating expenses:		
Salaries and wages	$540,000	
Computer services	180,000	
Office rent	60,000	
Promotions	44,400	
Equipment depreciation	38,400	
Telephone	30,000	
Travel	21,000	
Supplies	18,000	
Insurance	18,000	
Miscellaneous	10,200	960,000
Net income		$ 240,000

The statement shows the expenses of the service company grouped by natural classifications, a common approach. Some companies group the costs in functional classifications. When this occurs, the company may include a category for cost of services provided (or rendered) along with the marketing expenses, and general and administrative expenses. The cost of services provided represents the materials, labor, and overhead cost associated with the specific services rendered to customers.

ACCOUNTING FOR THE STAGES OF PRODUCTION

Materials pass through several forms before the finished product is ready for sale. The company has materials stored ready for production but not yet released to the production floor. The costs of these materials are recorded in the **Materials Inventory** account.

The second stage of production is uncompleted work somewhere in the production process, known as work in process. Various names are possible for work in process depending on the type of company: *cases in progress* (law firm), *contracts, in patients* (hospital), *construction in progress, movies in process,* or *real estate development.* As the product passes through the production process, it changes in form and usefulness. Each of these forms of the product may be considered as a stage or phase by the company. For example, consulting firms often divide large engagements into phases or stages and bill clients at the end of each phase.

The accumulated costs for the product are kept in an inventory account called **Work in Process Inventory.** The accumulated costs of services in process are often not kept in general ledger inventory accounts. Instead, these costs are generally kept in subsidiary records that provide the basis for billing clients. In some cases, the company chooses to keep a control account of the unbilled costs of services performed.

The major difference between a manufacturing company and the service company

[5] The exceptions to the general rule of expensing all service costs are (1) when the service is performed for the purpose of supporting the production of a product (see Appendix 8A) and (2) when the service is partially complete as with a contract for research and development, architectural drawings, or legal work.

with respect to the use of an in-process account is providing costs to evaluate profitability. The manufacturing company uses the product costs from work in process to evaluate profitability. The service company often needs to perform special studies as part of its normal pricing and service line evaluations. For example, a study of the profitability of different types of telephone service involves a detailed reconstruction of the past costs of providing each type of service.

The final stage of production is finished goods. As goods are completed, they are moved into a finished goods warehouse. The accumulated allocated cost of the finished goods is recorded in the **Finished Goods Inventory** account. In practice, companies often refer to finished goods by their generic name. For example, a sporting equipment company might refer to its finished goods as Sporting Equipment. A real estate development company might refer to its finished products as Shopping Centers, Commercial Buildings, and Other Developed Real Estate. Although we will use Finished Goods as the general account title, you should be aware that there are many alternative account titles in practice.

From an accounting point of view, each inventory account has a beginning inventory amount (at times, zero), additions or inputs (debits), and outputs (credits). These are summarized as:

Materials Inventory

Beginning balance	
Purchases	Materials used
Ending balance	

Work in Process

Beginning balance	
Materials used	
Direct labor	
Overhead applied	Goods finished
Ending balance	

Finished Goods

Beginning balance	
Goods finished	Goods sold
Ending balance	

Another way to look at the account is to view inventory as similar to the contents of a box at a point in time. For example, in Exhibit 2–1, the contents of the box at any one time are inventory. Units are added to or removed from the box during the period, and whatever is in the box at any time is inventory. A useful algebraic relationship is also present: beginning inventory plus units put into the box equals units taken out of the box plus what is left in the box at the end. This concept will be used later in the chapter.

As a more complete example of the procedures required, the Raider Football

EXHIBIT 2–1   Inventory Box

Account	Inputs	Outputs
Materials	Purchases	Issues to Production
Work in Process	Production Costs — Materials, Labor, and Overhead	Cost of Goods Manufactured
Finished Goods	Cost of Goods Manufactured	Cost of Goods Sold

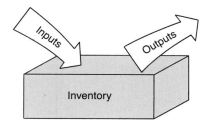

Company produces a single product, not surprisingly, footballs. The activity in each of the three inventory accounts for the current year is illustrated.

Materials Inventory

The company's materials inventory on hand at the beginning and end of the year are $60,000 and $50,000, respectively. During the year, the company had $860,000 in materials purchases and put $870,000 of materials into the production of footballs. A schedule of the direct materials used in production appears as follows:

Beginning inventory, January 1	$ 60,000
Add: Purchases	860,000
Materials available for use	$920,000
Less: Ending inventory, December 31	50,000
Cost of direct materials used in production	$870,000

Every event reflecting either a receipt or an issuance of materials must be recorded in the detail computer files (both the general ledger and subsidiary records). The journal entries that summarize the above activity for the general ledger are:

Materials Inventory	860,000	
Accounts Payable		860,000

To record the purchase of materials for the period.

Work in Process Inventory	870,000	
Materials Inventory		870,000

To record the issuance of materials to work in process during for the period.

Work in Process Inventory

The beginning balance in the Work in Process Inventory account was $346,000 and the ending balance was $357,000. The production costs input during the year include direct materials used of $870,000, direct labor of $398,000, and production overhead applied of $288,000. These events are summarized in the following schedule:

Beginning inventory, January 1		$ 346,000
Add production costs during period:		
Direct materials used	$870,000	
Direct labor	398,000	
Production overhead	288,000	1,556,000
		$1,902,000
Less ending inventory, December 31		357,000
Cost of goods manufactured		$1,545,000

The journal entry to record direct materials used was illustrated in the materials inventory section above. Journal entries for direct labor, overhead application, and cost of goods manufactured are:

Work in Process Inventory	398,000	
Payroll		398,000
To distribute direct labor costs to the work of the period.		
Work in Process Inventory	288,000	
Production Overhead Control		288,000
To apply overhead costs to the work of the period.		
Finished Goods Inventory	1,545,000	
Work in process Inventory		1,545,000
To transfer the costs of goods manufactured during the period to finished goods.		

Finished Goods Inventory

The beginning inventory of finished goods (footballs ready to ship) is $70,000 and the ending inventory is $85,000. Costs transferred in from work in process totaled $1,545,000, as shown above. The cost of goods sold is $1,530,000. A schedule of these costs is:

Beginning inventory, January 1	$ 70,000
Add: Cost of goods manufactured	1,545,000
Goods available for sale	$1,615,000
Less: Ending inventory, December 31	85,000
Cost of goods sold	$1,530,000

The journal entry to record the transfer of the cost of goods manufactured from work in process to finished goods was made in the discussion on work in process inventory above. The entry to reflect the cost of goods sold is:

Costs of Goods Sold	1,530,000	
Finished Goods Inventory		1,530,000
To record the cost of goods sold during the period.		

Production Overhead

Production overhead costs incurred are charged (debited) to the account Production Overhead Control as they are received. Detailed records are also kept for each specific overhead category and the operating departments. In our example, the Raider Football Company incurred overhead of $290,000 during the year, comprised of $35,000 in equipment depreciation, $120,000 in indirect labor and supervision, $41,000 payroll taxes, and $94,000 in utilities, repairs, supplies, insurance, and other costs recorded on account. The Production Overhead Control account includes:

Beginning balance, January 1	$ 0
Plus overhead incurred	290,000
Less overhead applied	(288,000)
Equals: Underapplied overhead	$ 2,000

Overhead Application.   The application of production overhead costs occurs as work is performed and is independent of when the actual production overhead costs are incurred. Companies determine an overhead rate to be applied during the coming time period. This rate is normally calculated by dividing the expected production overhead cost by an expected activity measure, such as direct labor hours, direct labor costs, or machine hours. The overhead rate is computed by dividing the expected overhead cost by the expected activity:

$$\text{Overhead rate} = \text{expected overhead/expected activity}$$

For example, on January 1, 19x8, the Raider Football Company expected overhead cost of $295,000 for the year and expected activity to be 29,500 hours. The overhead rate per hour will then be computed as:

$$\text{Overhead rate} = \$295{,}000/29{,}500 = \$10 \text{ per hour}$$

During 19x8 there were 28,800 hours of actual activity, resulting in overhead applied of:

$$\text{Overhead applied} = \text{overhead rate} \times \text{actual activity}$$
$$\$10 \times 28{,}800 = \underline{\$288{,}000}$$

The application of overhead to production was recorded above in the Work in Process account.[6]

Production overhead incurrence is the result of several events during the year.[7] The entry to summarize these events is:

Production Overhead Control	290,000	
Accumulated Depreciation, Factory		35,000
Payroll		120,000
Payroll Taxes Payable		41,000
Accounts Payable		94,000
To record incurrence of actual production overhead		
costs.		

The ending balance in Production Overhead Control will normally be debited or credited, as appropriate, to Cost of Goods Sold.[8]

Cost of Goods Sold	2,000	
Production Overhead Control		2,000
To close the production overhead accounts and charge		
cost of goods sold with the underapplied amount.		

Cost Flow Through Accounts   Exhibit 2–2 is a diagram of all cost flows affecting production accounts, beginning with Materials Inventory and ending with Costs of Goods Sold.

Materials inventory is increased by purchases and decreased by issuance of materials to production. To this point, we have assumed that materials are direct materials. However, in many companies, direct materials and indirect materials are recorded in

---

[6] Actual overhead will vary from applied overhead for many reasons that are discussed in Chapter 8.

[7] Some production overhead charges may be the result of the allocations among producing departments of service department costs, such as repair or inspection. This topic is covered in Appendix 8A.

[8] If the under- or overapplied overhead is material in amount, it should be allocated among work in process, finished goods, and cost of goods sold. We will develop this concept further in Chapters 8 and 13.

EXHIBIT 2–2   Cost Flow through Manufacturing Accounts

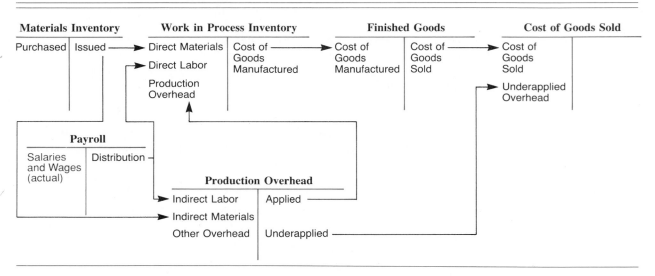

one control account, Materials Inventory or Stores. When this is the case, the cost of indirect materials must be recognized as they are removed from stores and used in production. Direct materials are recorded in Work in Process Inventory, and indirect materials are entered in Production Overhead.

The Payroll account is a clearing account; it should zero out by the end of the period. Debits to the account represent the accrued salaries and wages for each pay period. Credits are the distributions of labor costs to Work in Process and Production Overhead.

Since work on the production line is recorded daily by job or department, a company needs to allocate labor costs on a daily basis, regardless of how often the company accrues its wages payable. Therefore, the Payroll account makes possible the distribution of labor costs independent of the accrual of the liability. The journal entry to accrue wages payable is:

```
Payroll                                        518,000
    Wages Payable                                          518,000
  To accrue the liability for labor costs including direct
  labor, indirect labor, and supervision.
```

Like Materials Inventory, the Payroll account often contains both direct and indirect costs. During the distribution process, direct labor goes to Work in Process Inventory and indirect labor is entered in Production Overhead Control.

The debits to Production Overhead Control are the actual costs incurred during the period. These costs include indirect labor, indirect material, depreciation, insurance, utilities, property taxes, and repairs and maintenance. Credits to Production Overhead Control are the applied amounts of overhead charged to Work in Process during the month.

As work is completed on the various units of product, the cost of those units is transferred from Work in Process Inventory to Finished Goods Inventory. The entry to transfer these costs is a debit to Finished Goods Inventory and a credit to Work in Process Inventory. Total amounts transferred during a period are the cost of goods manufactured for the period. When the finished products are sold, their cost becomes cost of goods sold and they are transferred out of Finished Goods Inventory.

The costs in Exhibit 2–2 are unexpired costs because they flow from one account to the next, and the dollars in inventory accounts represent assets in the balance sheet. Only when the finished products are sold do these costs become expenses to be reflected in the income statement as costs of goods sold.

Cost Flow in Practice.   Exhibit 2–2 presents the usual flow of costs through accounts. Note that there is some variation in practice on the flow of costs. If inventories of work in process and finished goods are small, the accounting may be simplified by charging all production costs directly to a cost of goods sold account; the inventory accounts are not kept. Adjusting entries are required to reconstruct inventory balances.

Similarly, some companies keep only one inventory control account: a work in process account to record all material purchases, labor costs, and production overhead. On a periodic basis, all production costs are charged to cost of goods sold. Adjusting entries may be required at the statement date to reconstruct balances for materials, work in process, and finished goods.[9]

STATEMENT OF COST OF GOODS MANUFACTURED AND SOLD

Companies generate reports as a normal part of the internal accounting activities. A statement of cost of goods manufactured (or a statement of cost of goods manufactured and sold) is a common report from the cost accounting system for the typical manufacturing company. These reports and their uses are the subject of this section.

Statement of Cost of Goods Manufactured

The statement of cost of goods manufactured is a summary of the activity in the production accounts for the period. That is, it shows the specific costs that have gone into the goods worked on during the period and identifies those costs with the units completed and moved to Finished Goods Inventory and the units remaining in the ending Work in Process Inventory.

Exhibit 2–3 gives the cost of goods manufactured statement for the Raider Football Company. The three elements of production cost are presented: direct materials used, direct labor, and production overhead. Notice that the statement details the charges and credits to materials resulting in materials used. The sum of the cost elements is the total cost charged to production during the period. The total production costs are added to the costs held in the beginning work in process inventory to arrive at the total costs in work in process during the period. The ending work in process inventory is then subtracted to arrive at the cost of goods manufactured during the period.

Another way to look at this statement is to return to the box approach for inventory. Exhibit 2–4 shows a box for Materials Inventory, Work in Process Inventory, and Finished Goods Inventory. Remember that the beginning inventory plus current inputs in each box must equal the outputs plus ending inventory. The boxes highlight the flow of costs from one inventory account to the next, and they show that the statement of cost of goods manufactured is a summary of the activity recorded in production accounts for the current period. The boxes reflect all of the numbers needed for the statement of cost of goods manufactured.

By being able to trace costs through the various accounts and knowing the relationships that exist in each account, the accountant has a better understanding of what the numbers mean and how they can be used. Audit tests and the design of

---

[9] This process called *backflushing* has been adopted by some companies to simplify their factory record-keeping. See, for example, G. Foster and C. T. Horngren, ''JIT: Cost Accounting and Cost Management Issues,'' *Management Accounting,* June 1987, pp. 19–25.

EXHIBIT 2–3   Statement of Cost of Goods Manufactured

RAIDER FOOTBALL COMPANY
Statement of Cost of Goods Manufactured
For the Year Ended December 31, 19x8

Direct materials used:			
Beginning inventory, January 1		$ 60,000	
Add purchases		860,000	
Materials available for use		$920,000	
Less ending inventory, December 31		50,000	$ 870,000
Direct labor			398,000
Production overhead applied			288,000
Total production cost			$1,556,000
Add work in process, January 1			346,000
			$1,902,000
Less work in process, December 31			357,000
Cost of goods manufactured			$1,545,000

EXHIBIT 2–4   Manufacturing Cost Flow (inventory box approach)

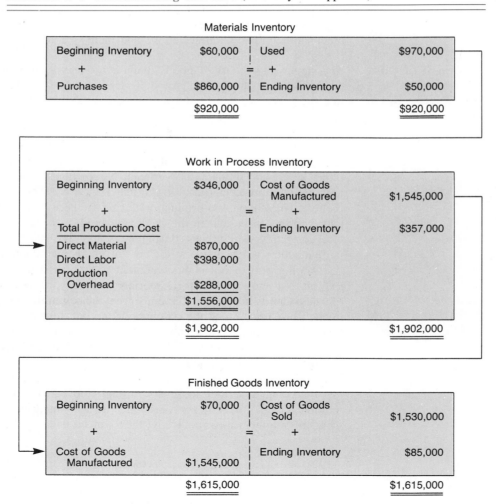

EDP processing controls require that the accountant have the ability to test relationships logically from end results to beginning data. For example, if the amount of direct labor is to be tested, given the other numbers, it is possible to work backward to confirm the direct labor number. In this way, the relationships among the numbers and the system that generates them are tested.

Statement of Cost of Goods Manufactured and Sold

The statement of cost of goods manufactured is a supporting statement to the cost of goods sold number appearing in the income statement. Some companies prefer to combine the statement of cost of goods manufactured and the schedule for cost of goods sold into one statement and use the combined statement to support the line item in the income statement for the cost of goods sold. Exhibit 2–5 is a combined statement for the Raider Football Company. Notice that the schedule for cost of goods sold is merely added to the bottom of the statement for cost of goods manufactured.

EXHIBIT 2–5   Statement of Cost of Goods Manufactured and Sold

RAIDER FOOTBALL COMPANY
Statement of Cost of Goods Manufactured and Sold
For the Year Ended December 31, 19x8

Direct materials used:		
Beginning inventory, January 1	$ 60,000	
Add purchases	860,000	
Materials available for use	$920,000	
Less ending inventory, December 31	50,000	$ 870,000
Direct labor		398,000
Production overhead applied		288,000
Total production cost		$1,556,000
Add work in process, January 1		346,000
		$1,902,000
Less work in process, December 31		357,000
Cost of goods manufactured		$1,545,000
Add finished goods, January 1		70,000
Goods available for sale		$1,615,000
Less finished goods, December 31		85,000
Unadjusted cost of goods sold		$1,530,000
Add underapplied production overhead		2,000
Cost of goods sold		$1,532,000

Statements Using Both Detailed and Applied Overhead

In the previous illustrations with the Raider Football Company, we assumed that the applied production overhead is charged to work in process. Most companies use this approach. However, some companies also disclose the subsidiary actual overhead information along with the overhead applied. Exhibit 2–6 shows one approach to handling this disclosure.

The amount of production overhead charged to work in process during the period is $288,000. But the actual manufacturing overhead costs totaled $290,000. Exhibit 2–6 includes a listing of actual costs less the underapplied amount of $2,000 ($290,000 less $288,000) to arrive at the overhead applied in production costs column. Had there been an overapplied amount, it would have been added to the actual costs to sum to the applied amount. Since the underapplied overhead is closed to Cost of Goods Sold as an addition to that account (overapplied is closed to it as a deduction), an adjustment is necessary at the bottom of the statement to arrive at the adjusted cost of goods sold.

EXHIBIT 2–6   Statement of Cost of Goods Manufactured and Sold Comparing
Actual and Applied Production Overhead

RAIDER FOOTBALL COMPANY
Statement of Cost of Goods Manufactured and Sold
For the Year Ended December 31, 19x8

Direct materials used:		
Beginning inventory, January 1	$ 60,000	
Add purchases	860,000	
Materials available for use	$920,000	
Less ending inventory, December 31	50,000	$ 870,000
Direct labor		398,000
Production overhead:		
Indirect labor	$ 80,000	
Supervisory salaries	40,000	
Payroll taxes	41,000	
Heat, light, and power	36,000	
Depreciation	35,000	
Repairs and maintenance	27,000	
Supplies used	16,000	
Insurance	10,000	
Other overhead costs	5,000	
	$290,000	
Less underapplied overhead	2,000	
Overhead cost applied		288,000
Total production cost		$1,556,000
Add work in process, January 1		346,000
		$1,902,000
Less work in process, December 31		357,000
Cost of goods manufactured		$1,545,000
Add finished goods, January 1		70,000
Goods available for sale		$1,615,000
Less finished goods, December 31		85,000
Unadjusted cost of goods sold		$1,530,000
Add underapplied production overhead		2,000
Cost of goods sold		$1,532,000

Adjustments for Actual Costing

Some companies charge actual overhead costs to production as the overhead costs occur. The entry for actual overhead incurred would be:

Work in Process	290,000	
Accumulated Depreciation, Factory		35,000
Payroll		120,000
Payroll Taxes Payable		41,000
Accounts Payable		94,000
To record the incurrence of overhead.		

There would be no Production Overhead Control account, no entry to apply overhead, and no adjustment required for underapplied overhead.

Exhibit 2–7 is the cost of goods manufactured for the Raider Football Company assuming that **actual costing** is used to account for production costs. Comparing this exhibit with the previous ones, actual costing is simpler in terms of accounting and reporting.

If actual costing is simpler, why do all companies not use it? The answer to this

EXHIBIT 2–7   Statement of Cost of Goods Manufactured and Sold Assuming Actual Production Overhead

RAIDER FOOTBALL COMPANY
Statement of Cost of Goods Manufactured and Sold
For the Year Ended December 31, 19x8

Direct materials used:		
Beginning inventory, January 1	$ 60,000	
Add purchases	860,000	
Materials available for use	$920,000	
Less ending inventory, December 31	50,000	$870,000
Direct labor		398,000
Production Overhead:		
Indirect labor	$ 80,000	
Supervisory salaries	40,000	
Payroll taxes	41,000	
Heat, light, and power	36,000	
Depreciation	35,000	
Repairs and maintenance	27,000	
Supplies used	16,000	
Insurance	10,000	
Other overhead costs	5,000	290,000
Total production cost		$1,558,000
Add work in process, January 1		346,000
		$1,904,000
Less work in process, December 31		357,000
Cost of goods manufactured		$1,547,000
Add finished goods, January 1		70,000
Goods available for sale		$1,617,000
Less finished goods, December 31		85,000
Cost of goods sold		$1,532,000

question is related to the timing of the information and the operations. First, some of the detailed costs of production overhead, especially utility costs, are not known for some time after the month in which goods are produced. Waiting for a month in order to accumulate the actual product costs is not timely for making pricing and product evaluation decisions. Second, some overhead costs occur on a periodic basis. For example, taxes and licensing fees are incurred annually, and maintenance on some equipment occurs quarterly. Overtime and vacations occur more during one time of the year than others. The periodic nature of incurrence will distort the actual cost numbers during both high and low incurrence months. Finally, most organizations are seasonal in nature. For example, hospitals have higher volume in the winter months, the production of ski equipment occurs in the summer and early fall, and merchandisers have high volume in the late fall. As a result of the seasonality, the actual overhead costs per unit appear to decrease during high volume periods and increase during low volume periods.

CLASSIFICATION OF COST SYSTEMS

Identifying the costs of direct material, direct labor, and production overhead, accumulating those costs, and allocating them to units of products or services sounds simpler than is usually the case in practice. A number of cost concepts interact with one another in order to arrive at the cost for finished products or services. In this section, we look at these conceptual groupings: cost accumulation systems, costing methodologies, and cost identification techniques. All three groupings will apply to any situation in which unit costs are necessary.

Cost Accumulation Systems—Job versus Process

Cost accumulation refers to the records, methods, and procedures used to collect costs and allocate them to products. Job order costing and process costing are the two primary cost accumulation systems, but each has some variation. Job order costing collects costs by job or contract and is used for accumulating the costs of constructing a building, producing a movie, or performing a consulting contract. Individual job cost records form the subsidiary ledgers for the Work in Process Inventory account.

Process costing accumulates costs for all items worked on in a process. Process cost systems are common in the production of services, such as banking or insurance, and in the production or assembly of products that are mass produced, such as automobiles, computers, and televisions. Job order costing is assumed throughout this text, unless otherwise stated. The detailed procedures of accumulating material, labor, and production overhead costs using a job order costing system are covered in Chapters 6, 7, and 8. Process costing is the subject of Chapter 9.

Modified or mixed systems utilize an adaptation or combination of job order and process costing for cost accumulation. These are common for companies that continuously produce basic parts and assemblies, but certain operations to finalize production require customer specifications.

Costing Methodology

The methodology for product costs is founded on the concept of absorption costing or variable costing. Basically, the difference between the two is whether fixed production costs are classified as a product cost or as an expense of the period (a period cost). These concepts are important where inventories are present. Thus, they are not important for service companies.

Absorption costing classifies all production costs as product costs; marketing and distribution, and general and administrative costs are period costs. Absorption costing is required for external financial reporting and for tax purposes. Because of these requirements, many companies use absorption costing in their internal record-keeping. Another name for absorption costing is **full costing.** Unless otherwise specified, the early chapters of this text assume absorption costing methodology.

Variable costing, on the other hand, classifies only those production costs that increase or decrease with production as product costs. This means the fixed production costs are treated as period costs. Variable costing may be used to support decision-making, profitability analysis, and performance measurement. Another name for variable costing is **direct costing.** Variable costing is discussed in more detail in Chapter 16.

The methodology selected affects the amount of cost allocated to inventories and the amount of periodic profits. Either methodology can be used with job order costing or process costing.[10] Since the absorption cost of goods includes fixed cost, it is always higher than the variable cost. As a result, different decisions and judgments will be made by management on prices, profitability, and performance, depending upon the method chosen.

---

[10] If variable costing is used for internal record keeping, then the fixed production costs must be allocated among work in process, finished goods, and cost of goods sold for the external financial reports and the income tax return.

Cost Identification Techniques

Accountants use several techniques for identifying costs with products. If the actual costs (that is, costs as they are incurred, or costs known after the fact) of direct material, direct labor, and production overhead are charged to work in process, the cost identification technique is called **actual costing.**

For many reasons, companies can not wait until all of the production overhead costs have been incurred for the period to charge cost to work performed. Therefore, a predetermined rate is used to charge production overhead to work in process inventory. We called this *production overhead application* earlier in the chapter. When we have the combination of actual direct material and direct labor costs together with a predetermined overhead rate, we call the cost identification technique **normal costing.** The term *normal* comes from the concept of normalizing or averaging overhead over time, a subject discussed in more detail in Chapter 8. The value of the technique arises from the fact that actual costs of direct material and direct labor are often easily determinable as work is performed, but production overhead is not so easily assessed. Consequently, estimates of overhead are made by developing predetermined overhead rates. Normal costing is very common in practice. This identification technique is assumed during most of the text.

If predetermined rates are used for direct material, direct labor, and production overhead, the cost identification technique is referred to as **standard costing.** It is common in large, stable production settings. Standard costing is the subject of Chapters 12 and 13.

In summary, there are many possible combinations for cost accumulation systems, cost methodologies, and cost identification techniques. Companies select appropriate combinations based on the nature of the production process and the kinds of information their managers need.

SUMMARY

In this chapter, we discussed the methods of recording and reporting cost flows in merchandising, manufacturing, and service organizations. The business of these organizations is to transform inputs into outputs, whether products or services. Part of the accounting function is to trace the flow of resources and account for their disposition.

The term *cost* can be used in many different ways. We have seen that costs are measured, then assigned to accounting periods, and allocated to cost objectives, if appropriate. This process leads to a distinction between unexpired costs—costs with benefits not yet received—and expired costs—costs whose benefits have been received.

Costs can also be classified as either period costs or product costs. Period costs are expensed (expired) as incurred, but product costs are costs of goods, purchased or produced. In a merchandising company, product costs consist of the purchase price of the merchandise plus the costs of bringing it in (transportation and insurance, for example), and making it ready for sale.

Product costs in a manufacturing company relate to goods manufactured and consist of three categories: direct material, direct labor, and production overhead. These costs flow into work in process inventory while work is underway. As goods are completed, the costs are transferred from work in process to finished goods. As goods are sold, the costs are transferred from finished goods to cost of goods sold in the income statement. The costs of partially completed units and unsold units are carried as assets in the balance sheet.

The costing systems of service organizations are similar to those of manufacturing companies with one important difference—there are no inventories of finished products. Like manufacturing, there are materials, labor, and production overhead costs. Many costing concepts for manufacturing may be applied to service organizations.

One of the important financial statements that supports an income statement for a manufacturing company is the statement of cost of goods manufactured. At times, it will be combined with the cost of goods sold to yield one statement representing the flow of production costs from incurrence to the sale of products.

Various concepts of cost systems interact in the process of cost determination. The conceptual groupings are cost accumulation systems, costing methodologies, and cost identification techniques. Companies must select the combinations appropriate for their specific circumstances.

PROBLEM FOR REVIEW

During 19x1, Rezchek Company purchased materials at a cost of $310,000. Materials inventory at the beginning of the year was $15,000, and $12,000 was left in inventory at the end of the year. Production payrolls for direct labor showed a total of $425,000. Production overhead applied was $459,000. Actual production overhead incurred was $463,000. Beginning work in process inventory was $84,000, with the ending inventory $3,000 less. The finished goods in the warehouse at the beginning of the year cost $100,000. Ninety percent of all finished goods available for the year were sold during the year.

REQUIRED

a. Prepare journal entries for each of the following:
  1. Purchase of materials.
  2. Charging work in process with the cost of materials used.
  3. Charging work in process with the direct labor cost.
  4. Incurrence of actual production overhead cost.
  5. Applying production overhead to work in process for the year.
  6. Transfer the cost of goods manufactured to finished goods inventory.
b. Prepare a statement of cost of goods manufactured and sold showing both the actual and applied production overhead on the same statement.
c. Assuming an actual costing system:
  1. Prepare the journal entry to record incurrence of actual production overhead costs.
  2. Prepare the journal entry to charge work in process for production overhead.
  3. Prepare a statement of cost of goods manufactured and sold.

SOLUTION

a.1. Purchase of materials.

Materials Inventory	310,000	
Accounts Payable		310,000

a.2. Charging work in process with the cost of materials used.

Work in Process Inventory	313,000	
Materials Inventory		313,000

Beginning inventory	$ 15,000
Purchases	310,000
Available	$325,000
Ending inventory	12,000
	$313,000

a.3. Charging work in process with the direct labor cost.

Work in Process Inventory	425,000	
Payroll		425,000

a.4. Recording the incurrence of actual production overhead.

Production Overhead	463,000	
Various Accounts		463,000

a.5. Applying production overhead to work in process.

Work in Process Inventory	459,000	
Production Overhead		459,000

a.6. Transfer the cost of goods manufactured.

Finished Goods Inventory	1,200,000	
Work in Process Inventory		1,200,000

Beginning inventory		$ 84,000
Add production costs:		
Direct materials used	$313,000	
Direct labor	425,000	
Applied production overhead	459,000	1,197,000
		$1,281,000
Less ending inventory ($3,000 less than $84,000)		81,000
Cost of goods manufactured		$1,200,000

b. Statement of cost of goods manufactured and sold.

REZCHEK SUPPLIES COMPANY
Statement of Cost of Goods Manufactured and Sold
For the Year 19x1

Direct materials used:		
Beginning inventory	$ 15,000	
Purchases	310,000	
Available	$325,000	
Ending inventory	12,000	$ 313,000
Direct labor		425,000
Production overhead:		
Actual overhead costs	$463,000	
Less underapplied overhead	4,000	459,000
Total production costs		$1,197,000
Add work in process, beginning		84,000
		$1,281,000
Less work in process, ending		81,000
Cost of goods manufactured		$1,200,000
Add finished goods, beginning		100,000
Goods available for sale		$1,300,000
Less finished goods, ending (10% of $1,300,000)		130,000
Unadjusted cost of goods sold		$1,170,000
Add underapplied production overhead		4,000
Cost of goods sold		$1,174,000

c.1. Recording incurrence of actual production overhead costs.

Production Overhead Control	463,000	
Various Accounts		463,000

c.2. Charging work in process for production overhead.

Work in Process Inventory	463,000	
Production Overhead Control		463,000

c.3. Statement of cost of goods manufactured and sold.

REZCHEK SUPPLIES COMPANY
Statement of Cost of Goods Manufactured and Sold
For the Year 19x1

Direct materials used:		
Beginning inventory	$ 15,000	
Purchases	310,000	
Available	$325,000	
Ending inventory	12,000	$ 313,000
Direct labor		425,000
Production overhead—actual costs		463,000
Total production costs		$1,201,000
Add work in process, beginning		84,000
		$1,285,000
Less work in process, ending		81,000
Cost of goods manufactured		$1,204,000
Add finished goods, beginning		100,000
Goods available for sale		$1,304,000
Less finished goods, ending (10% of $1,304,000)		130,400
Cost of goods sold		$1,173,600

KEY TERMS AND CONCEPTS

Cost (19)
Cost allocation (20)
Cost objective (19)
Cost pool (20)
Direct allocation (20)
Direct costs (20)
Indirect allocation (20)
Indirect costs (20)
Production costs (20)
Product costs (20)
Period costs (20)
Unexpired costs (capitalized costs) (20)
Expired costs (20)
Expenses (20)
Marketing and distribution costs (21)
General and administrative costs (21)
Direct materials (22)

Processing (22)
Fabrication (22)
Assembly (23)
Extractive (23)
Direct labor (23)
Production overhead (24)
Materials inventory (25)
Work in process inventory (25)
Finished goods inventory (26)
Direct costing (36)
Absorption costing (36)
Variable costing (36)
Full costing (36)
Actual costing (34)
Normal costing (37)
Standard costing (37)

ADDITIONAL READINGS

Boros, J. L., and R. E. Thompson. "Distribution Cost Accounting at PPG Industries." *Management Accounting*, January 1983, pp. 54–59.

Chase, R. B., and D. A. Garvin. "The Service Factory." *Harvard Business Review*, July-August 1989, pp. 61–69.

Dividow, W. H., and B. Uttal. "Service Companies: Focus or Falter." *Harvard Business Review*, July-August 1989, pp. 77–87.

Frank, G. B.; S. A. Fisher; and A. R. Wilkie. "Linking Cost to Price and Profit." *Management Accounting*, June 1989, pp. 22–26.

Herzlinger, R. E. "The Failed Revolution in Health Care—The Role of Management." *Harvard Business Review*, March-April 1989, pp. 95–105.

O'Connell, J. F. "How We Simplified Administrative Tasks." *Management Accounting*, December 1984, pp. 40–44.

Rader, F. "Keep on Trucking." *Management Accounting*, April 1989, pp. 43–45.

Robinson, L. A., and L. E. Robinson. "Steering a Boat Maker Through Cost Shoals." *Management Accounting*, January 1983, pp. 60ff.

REVIEW QUESTIONS

1. Distinguish among manufacturing, merchandising, and service organizations.
2. Explain the difference between expired costs and unexpired costs.
3. Explain the difference between a product cost and a period cost.
4. What cost elements are included in production costs?
5. What is included in marketing and distribution costs?
6. What does each of the following four types of operations do: processing, fabrication, assembly, and extractive?
7. Describe how the income statement of a manufacturing company differs from the income statement of a merchandising company and of a service organization.
8. List and describe the uses of the three primary inventory accounts used by a manufacturer.
9. What types of inventories exist in a service organization?
10. Distinguish among the following: direct materials, indirect materials, direct labor, indirect labor, and production overhead.
11. What three time-related differences make the actual costing approach less desirable than the normal costing approach?
12. Describe the flow of materials cost from point of acquisition until the cost becomes cost of goods sold in the income statement.
13. Explain the nature of the statement of costs of goods manufactured and how it relates to the income statement.
14. How do job order and process costing differ?
15. Pallory Company prepares a monthly statement of cost of goods manufactured and sold. How will its income statement differ in format from one prepared using only a statement of cost of goods manufactured?

DISCUSSION QUESTIONS

16. How is it possible for salaries or depreciation to be classified as assets on the balance sheet?
17. What would be the work in process for each of the following: an insurance company, a hospital, and a brewery?
18. Assume that an automated factory with no direct labor and production overhead is fixed per month. Conceptually, what costs will be included in the finished goods inventory for variable costing? for absorption costing?
19. The concept of total quality cost includes all costs necessary to design, manufacture, test, maintain, and repair a product. Taguchi also includes the cost to society in the total quality cost of the product.[11] Describe the total quality costs for an automobile.

EXERCISES

2–1. Production Classification. Beside each of the following companies place one or more of the following letters to indicate the type or types of production performed.

(B. George, Adapted)

[11] See, for example, R. N. Kackar, "Taguchi's Quality Philosophy: Analysis and Commentary," *Quality Process,* April 1986, pp. 18–23.

A Assembly
E Extractive
F Fabrication
P Processing

    _____ 1. Brewery
    _____ 2. Calculator manufacturer
    _____ 3. Wall paper manufacturer
    _____ 4. Coal mining company
    _____ 5. Steel production plant
    _____ 6. Steel sheet mill
    _____ 7. Clothing manufacturer
    _____ 8. Cattle ranch
    _____ 9. Automobile manufacturer
    _____ 10. Pharmaceutical plant

2–2. Cost Classification. Various costs associated with the diversified operations of the Armitage Company are given below.

    _____ a. Production superintendent's salary.
    _____ b. Depreciation on salesperson's automobile.
    _____ c. Wood used in furniture production.
    _____ d. Glue used in furniture production.
    _____ e. Advertising costs.
    _____ f. Plant janitorial salaries.
    _____ g. Wages of workers assembling a product.
    _____ h. Repair and maintenance of production equipment.
    _____ i. Depreciation on executive aircraft.

REQUIRED:
Classify each cost as a product (Pr) or period (Pe) cost. For product costs, classify the cost as direct (D) or indirect (I) to the product.

2–3. Materials Purchase and Usage. The Mann Landscaping Company had beginning inventory of railroad ties of 1,800 valued at $3 each. On September 9, the company purchased 3,000 ties for $9,000. On September 30, it had 1,500 ties left.

REQUIRED:
a. How many railroad ties should be transferred from the account Landscaping Materials to the account Landscaping in Progress? Compute the dollar amount of materials used.
b. Prepare a journal entry to record the purchase of the railroad ties and another entry to summarize the issuance of ties to landscaping projects.

2–4. Cost of Goods Manufactured. The Menger Company had the following balances in its inventory accounts during 19x2 (amounts in $ millions):

	January 1, 19x2	December 31, 19x2
Materials	$ 40	$20
Work in process	120	80

During the year, the company purchased $100 million in materials, charged $50 million in direct labor, and applied $200 million in overhead cost to production.

REQUIRED:
Determine the following amounts:
a. Direct materials used in production.
b. Cost of goods manufactured.

2–5. Adjusted Cost of Goods Sold.   Bystar Jet, Inc., had the following activity during 19x3 (amounts in $ millions):

Purchases of materials	$6,800
Direct labor	2,400
Production overhead incurred	1,800

During the year, $1,850 million in overhead was applied to production. The inventory balances were:

	January 1, 19x3	*December 31, 19x3*
Materials	$ 800	$1,400
Work in process	2,300	2,600
Finished goods	1,400	1,800

REQUIRED:
Calculate each of the following amounts:
a. Direct materials used in production.
b. Cost of goods manufactured.
c. Cost of goods sold (unadjusted).
d. Over- or underapplied overhead.
e. Adjusted cost of goods sold.

2–6. Basic Journal Entries.   The Caliente Plant of Teas Winery had the following activities during 19x4, its first year in operation:
1. Purchased $100,000 in materials on account.
2. Payroll of $150,000 of which $80,000 was direct labor and the remainder was indirect labor.
3. Issued $90,000 in materials to production of which $80,000 was direct materials and the remainder was indirect materials.
4. Incurred $20,000 in plant overhead on account.
5. Depreciation of plant and equipment, $15,000.
6. Applied $110,000 in overhead to production.
7. Completed products costing $260,000.
8. Inventory costing $220,000 was sold for $310,000.

REQUIRED:
a. Prepare journal entries to record the activities for the year. (Journal entry explanations are not required.)
b. Prepare the entry to record the adjustment of cost of goods sold for over- or underapplied overhead. Support your entry with a T account for production overhead control.

2–7. Cost of Production.   Cannon Clothing Mills of Sherwood, Tennessee, produces cotton clothing. It purchases bolts of cotton from a weaving mill, dyes or prints patterns on the cloth, and then cuts the cloth to set patterns. Then the clothing is assembled into finished goods with machines. The clothing is sold primarily through department stores. During the year 19x6, Cannon used materials of $229,700. It had direct labor cost of $86,000 and actual production overhead of $356,200, which consisted of depreciation, supervision, and utilities. The beginning work in process on January 1, 19x6, was $440,000, and the ending work in process was $551,000. The beginning finished goods inventory was $60,000, and the ending finished goods inventory was $77,000.

(J. Lo, Adapted)

REQUIRED:
a. What was the cost of the finished clothing manufactured by the Cannon Clothing Mills during 19x6?
b. What was the cost of clothing sold by the Cannon Clothing Mills during 19x6?

2–8. Cost Flow in a Service Organization.   GETTA & Associates is a business consulting firm consisting of four partners and 10 staff personnel. In November, partners worked 700 hours and the staff worked 1,600 hours. Twenty percent of the partners's time is not billable to clients; 10 percent of the staff time is not billable. Clients are billed at a rate of $100 per hour for all work performed. The partners receive $70 per hour in total compensation, and the staff receive $40 per hour in total compensation. Overhead costs of $30,000 are charged to client work based on billable hours on each job. The cost of nonbillable time is treated as part of overhead costs. Other service-related overhead amounted to $10,000 for the month. The firm also incurred marketing and administration expenses of $7,000. GETTA & Associates close the Overhead Control account at the end of each month to the Cost of Services Provided account.

REQUIRED:
a. Show the flow of costs through T accounts using Payroll, Overhead, Work in Process, and Cost of Services Provided accounts. Over- or underapplied overhead is closed to the Cost of Services Provided account at the end of each month.
b. Prepare an income statement for the month ending November 30, 19x4.

2–9. Overhead Application with Journal Entries.   The Brownfield Construction Company builds single-family dwellings and apartments. Production overhead for the year 19x9 includes depreciation of $500,000 on construction equipment, $262,000 for indirect materials, $616,000 for supervision and inspection, $130,000 for payroll taxes, and $56,000 for utilities, repairs, supplies, insurance, and other costs recorded on account. During the year, $1,600,000 in production overhead was applied to construction in progress.

REQUIRED:
a. Calculate the amount of under- or overapplied overhead for 19x9. (Assume that the under- or overapplied overhead is closed to the Cost of Dwellings Sold account at the end of each year.) Label the amount as under- or overapplied and indicate whether this is a debit or a credit balance.
b. Prepare journal entries to record:
   1. The incurrence of production overhead.
   2. The application of production overhead to Construction in Progress.
   3. The closing of overhead accounts and adjusting of Cost of Dwellings Sold.

2–10. Cost Application.   PKF, Inc., manufactures boats that on average take a month to build. The boats sell for $300,000. On December 31, 19x4, PKF had three boats in finished inventory recorded at $700,000. It also had one boat in progress that has incurred $75,000 of direct materials and $10,000 of direct labor. It applies overhead at a rate of 10 percent of direct materials usage. During 19x4, it incurred $50,000 in indirect labor, $22,000 in indirect materials, and other production overhead of $100,000. During the year, $1,760,000 of direct materials were issued to production.

(M. Kubinski, Adapted)

REQUIRED:
a. Calculate the balance in work in process on December 31, 19x4.
b. Calculate actual production overhead for the year ending December 31, 19x4.
c. Calculate the amount of overhead applied to production during the year.

2–11. Applied and Actual Overhead.   AirFeathers, Inc., manufactures pillows. They are very popular, especially with older customers. Because of the high cost of quality materials, they are sold at a high price.

Materials purchased for the year amounted to $1,532,000, direct labor incurred was $300,000, and production overhead incurred was $108,000. The beginning balance in materials on January 1, 19x2, was $500,000, and the ending balance was $100,000. The beginning balance in work in process was $200,000 and the ending balance on December 31, 19x2, was

$237,000. Finished goods has a beginning balance of $542,000 and an ending balance of $657,000.

(K. Turrichi, Adapted)

REQUIRED:

a. Prepare a statement of the cost of goods manufactured and sold using actual costs.

b. Now assume that the company uses normal costing and applies overhead of $105,000 to production. What will be the amount of over- or underapplied overhead?

PROBLEMS

2–12. Cost of Production with Journal Entries.   Xalipan Productions produces music videos on a contract basis. Each video runs from 6 to 60 minutes with a common video running about 10 minutes. The videos take from three to six weeks to film and have another two to five weeks of editing. The company is working on four or more videos at any one time. On February 1, 19x3, the company had seven contracts in process with an accumulated cost of $382,000. During February, it started six videos, used $122,000 in direct materials, $203,000 in labor directly traceable to videos, and had production overhead of $116,000. Ending inventory consisted of three videos with an accumulated cost of $106,000.

REQUIRED:

a. Prepare a statement of the cost of video contracts completed. (This will follow the format of the cost of goods manufactured.)

b. Prepare journal entries for use of materials, distribution of direct labor, and application of overhead. (Explanations of entries are not required.)

c. Prepare a journal entry for the transfer of completed videos to the expense account Cost of Video Contracts Completed.

2–13. Statement of Cost of Goods Manufactured.   Various cost and sales data for Courteau Manufacturing, Inc., for the year ending December 31, 19x4, have been extracted from the accounting records and presented as follows:

Administrative expenses	$ 59,000
Depreciation on factory	27,000
Direct labor costs	105,000
Finished goods inventory, beginning	34,000
Finished goods inventory, ending	28,000
Indirect labor	34,000
Indirect materials	4,500
Insurance on factory	9,500
Materials inventory, beginning	12,000
Materials inventory, ending	13,000
Purchases of materials	76,000
Repair and maintenance of factory	6,000
Sales	502,000
Selling expenses	92,000
Utilities on factory	29,000
Work in process, beginning	19,000
Work in process, ending	25,000

The company uses actual costs in charging materials, labor, and production overhead costs to work in process inventory.

REQUIRED:

a. Prepare a statement of cost of goods manufactured for the year.

b. Prepare an income statement for the year.

2–14. Cost Flow through the Accounts. The Dement Corporation had inventory balances at the beginning of September 19x4: materials, $2,000; work in process, $6,000; and finished goods, $3,000. The following transactions relating to production were completed during September:

1. Purchased materials costing $18,000 on account.
2. Issued materials to production as follows: direct material, $12,500; indirect material, $3,500.
3. Incurred factory payroll of $21,000 for the month.
4. Distributed $16,000 to direct labor and $5,000 to indirect labor.
5. Depreciation of machinery, $10,500.
6. Production overhead is applied to work in process at a rate of 125 percent of direct labor.
7. The cost of goods manufactured was transferred to finished goods. (The ending work in process balance consisted of $1,200 in direct materials, $1,400 in direct labor, and applied overhead.
8. Eighty percent of the cost of goods available for sale during September was sold.
9. Under- or overapplied overhead was closed to cost of goods sold.

REQUIRED:
a. Prepare the journal entries to record the transactions.
b. Post the journal entries to T accounts for the inventories, overhead, payroll, and cost of goods sold and compute ending balances.
c. Prepare a statement of cost of goods manufactured and sold, including the adjustment for over- or underapplied overhead.

2–15. Cost Concepts and Income Statement. Vector Data Systems (VDS) is a computer design company known as a *value-added reseller*. The company helps a business select computer equipment and software, train employees, install the system, and maintain the system. Using computer equipment purchased from various manufacturers, the company adds value by packaging equipment with customized software and service.

VDS has concentrated on law firms and real estate companies with a minimum of 20 attorneys or agents and a potential for a system costing at least $100,000. These firms need to carefully control documents, customize to meet client needs, and maintain large files. VDS systems also maintain appointment calendars and take phone messages.

VDS has offices in Washington, D.C., Dallas, and Los Angeles. The Dallas office concluded the 19x5 fiscal year on December 31 with revenues of $3.5 million. Expenses included:

Computer equipment	$ 600,000
Software	450,000
Value-added salaries—billed	1,000,000
Value-added salaries—nonbilled	200,000
Value-added employee benefits	180,000
Metro occupancy	200,000
Administrative expenses	240,000
Marketing costs	130,000

Value-added salaries include all consultants, specialists, and programmers who work directly with the design and maintenance of client systems. Metro occupancy relates solely to the space requirements for the value-added personnel. All other personnel and costs are included in the administrative or marketing functions.

At the beginning of 19x5, no jobs were in process. At the end of the year, the Dallas office had one large system in process for Legalese & Associates. The actual expenses incurred during the year for this job were included in the office expenses above. The accumulated costs on the Legalese job included:

Computer equipment purchased	$150,000
Software	80,000
Value-added salaries	220,000
Operating overhead applied (58%)	127,600

The operating overhead is applied at 58 percent of the billable time of those assigned to the job. VDS will price this job to include a markup of 20 percent of total costs in the billing.

REQUIRED:
a. Examine the expenses for the Dallas office and determine which costs are direct (D) to the completion of client systems, which are indirect (I) costs of completion, and which are period (P) costs.
b. Two of the owners of VDS are arguing as to whether the income should be computed as if VDS were a merchandiser with a cost of goods sold based on purchase prices or whether income should be computed as if the firm were a manufacturer producing completed customer systems. They ask you, the accountant, to prepare statements for the Dallas Office with the following assumptions:
  1. Assume that VDS is a merchandiser with product costs based on only the equipment costs and the software costs. Be careful on the treatment of the job held in process (Legalese & Associates).
  2. Assume that VDS is similar to a manufacturer and includes in the product costs both the purchased items and the labor and overhead to complete those items for sale. This will require a statement of cost of jobs completed, which will be similar to a cost of goods manufactured statement. Use VDS's terms for accounts in preparation of this statement.

2–16. Journal Entries and Statement Preparation. The North Company of Washington, D.C., has developed a portable paper shredder for home use. Sales are increasing rapidly and the company is having trouble keeping up with demand. During the current year, the following account balances and activity were noted:

	January 1	December 31
Finished goods	$1,005,000	$ 9,000
Work in process	238,000	405,000
Materials	138,846	139,300

Activities during the year:
1. Administrative and general costs	92,000
2. Advertising	347,000
3. Direct labor costs	493,600
4. Equipment purchased on account	400,000
5. Materials purchased	987,654
6. Issuance of materials to production	?
7. Production overhead applied	987,200
8. Production overhead costs incurred	1,041,700
9. Completion of work in process	?
10. Sales on account	4,538,344
11. Cost of goods sold	?
12. Transportation out	38,000
13. Adjustment for over- or under- applied overhead	?

REQUIRED:
a. Prepare summary journal entries to record the activities during the year.
b. Prepare a statement of cost of goods manufactured and sold.
c. Prepare an income statement.

2–17. Cost of Production with Journal Entries. San Angelo Construction employs about 2,500 people in the construction of apartments and commercial offices. The company is a complete contractor and, except in rare occasions, does not subcontract any of its work.

The inventory of materials on August 1, 19x2, was $3,685,000, and the materials at the end of the month were $368,000. During the year, the company purchased $1,334,000 in materials. A total of $138,000 in indirect materials was used during the month. A total of $6,365,000 was paid out to employees of which $80,000 was administrative, $60,000 was selling, and $1,025,000 was construction supervisors and indirect labor. The company had production-related costs of $342,000 for depreciation, $106,000 for fuel, $242,000 for insurance, and $6,000 for inspection fees.

The construction in progress at the beginning of the month had a balance of $985,000 and the ending balance was $438,650. San Angelo Construction uses a normal costing system and applies overhead at the rate of 35 percent of direct labor.

(W. Smith, adapted)

REQUIRED:

a. Prepare journal entries for:
  1. Purchase of materials on account.
  2. Issuance of materials to production.
  3. Incurrence of the labor cost for the month. Use a temporary account, Payroll.
  4. Distribution of payroll to administration, marketing, work in process, and indirect labor.
  5. Incurrence of the overhead costs for the month other than indirect materials and labor.
  6. Application of production overhead costs to construction in progress.
  7. Completion of construction during the period.
  8. Closing the overhead account to cost of construction sold.
b. Prepare a statement of the cost of construction completed. Include the over- or underapplied overhead in the statement.

2–18. Cost of Goods Manufactured and Income Statement.   The following amounts and accounts were taken from the accounting records of Felic Manufacturing Company for 19x0:

Advertising	$ 125,000
Bad debts expense	36,870
Depreciation—factory machinery	45,000
Depreciation—office equipment	17,000
Direct labor	749,000
Factory rent	244,000
Factory supplies	135,000
Factory utilities	33,250
Finished goods inventory, 1/1/x0	287,000
Finished goods inventory, 12/31/x0	275,000
Indirect labor	176,000
Materials inventory, 1/1/x0	112,000
Materials inventory, 12/31/x0	138,000
Materials purchases	1,319,000
Property taxes—factory machinery	18,500
Property taxes—office equipment	6,970
Repairs and maintenance—factory	47,000
Salaries of administrative personnel	391,000
Sales	3,687,000
Sales and administrative offices	56,000
Sales commissions	108,398
Sales returns and allowances	73,740
Work in process inventory, 1/1/x0	53,000
Work in process inventory, 12/31/x0	66,000

Felic uses an actual costing system for production overhead costs.

REQUIRED:

a. Prepare a statement of cost of goods manufactured for the year ended December 31, 19x0.
b. Prepare an income statement for the year ended December 31, 19x0.

c. The Felic Manufacturing Company is considering changing to a normal costing system for 19x1. Estimate an overhead application rate based on direct labor cost assuming that 19x1 will be very similar to 19x0. Round to nearest whole percentage.

2–19. Overhead Rates, Job Order Costs, and Application. Thompson and Associates manufactures various products using a job order cost system. Information for the current year 19x9 is as follows:

Estimated annual sales	$2,800,000
Estimated total direct labor	470,000
Estimated total production overhead	611,000

Information for the month of July 19x9 is as follows:

Job	27	28	29	30	31	Total
Work in process, 7/1/x9	$14,000	$9,870	$ 3,200	$ 1,900	$1,300	$30,270
Direct material	900	2,300	24,000	17,000	8,500	52,700
Direct labor	2,700	1,800	18,000	12,000	6,500	41,000
Overhead applied	?	?	?	?	?	?
Work in process, 7/31/x9	0	?	0	0	?	?
Units completed	400	0	904	1,236	0	2,540
Units sold	360	0	500	1,100	0	1,960

Actual production overhead costs incurred for July: $58,120

REQUIRED:
a. Calculate a predetermined overhead rate based on direct labor costs.
b. Apply overhead to each job worked on during the period.
c. Compute the total cost for the jobs:
   1. Completed during the period.
   2. In process at the end of the period.
d. Calculate the cost per unit for each of the jobs completed during July.
e. Prepare a statement of cost of goods manufactured.
f. Calculate the over- or underapplied overhead for the month.

2–20. Overhead Journal Entries and Cost of Goods Manufactured. Aromatic, Inc., manufactures a potpourri with peach and apple aromas in a plant in Spokane, Washington. Old petals and leaves are purchased from flower distributors, wood chips and bark from lumber companies and orchards, and, finally, chopped fruit peels and seeds from local fruit processing plants. Aromatic uses its own secret formula to distill the fruit and seeds to a pleasing aroma.

Although some wood products can be kept for a time, most materials are used immediately due to perishability. Beginning direct materials inventory for June 19x4 was $3,600 and ending direct materials inventory for the month was $2,700. The direct materials purchased during the month cost $123,000. Total labor costs were $375,000, of which $13,000 was indirect labor. Production supervisors' salaries totaled $42,000, selling expenses were $29,000, plant insurance was $12,000 for the month, indirect materials were $9,000, and production payroll taxes were $32,300. Aromatic uses normal costing with a rate of 30 percent of direct labor. Work in process on June 1 was $2,300, and June 30 work in process was $57,300.

(K. Craig, Adapted)

REQUIRED:
a. Compute the over- or underapplied overhead for June 19x4.
b. Prepare journal entries for:
   1. Incurrence of the overhead.
   2. Application of the overhead.

3. Close the overhead account with any over- or underapplied amounts adjusting cost of goods sold.

 c. Prepare a statement of the cost of goods manufactured for June 19x4. Use the format that lists all actual overhead costs but then adjust the actuals to the amount of overhead applied.

2–21. Cost of Goods Manufactured and Income Statement.   Davidson Manufacturing, Inc., is a specialty producer of components for laser equipment designed for medical purposes. The Rocky Mountain Division has the following data for the year ending December 31, 19x5:

Accounts receivable	$31,000
Cash	1,800
Cash discounts on direct material purchases	300
Depreciation—factory building	11,500
Direct labor	17,000
Direct materials inventory, 12/31/x5	19,000
Direct materials inventory, 1/1/x5	15,000
Factory insurance	1,900
Factory miscellaneous expense	1,500
Factory repair and maintenance	2,575
Factory supervision	32,250
Factory supplies inventory, 12/31/x5	1,600
Factory supplies inventory, 1/1/x5	2,900
General and administrative expenses	40,000
Indirect labor	9,850
Marketing and distribution expenses	34,100
Purchases of direct materials	34,000
Purchases of factory supplies	2,100
Sales	240,000
Work in process inventory, 12/31/x5	12,000
Work in process inventory, 1/1/x5	21,800

There were 2,500 units completed and transferred to the finished goods warehouse during the year. The finished goods inventory at January 1 was 200 units valued at $45 each. During the year, 2,400 units were sold. The FIFO method is used for costing inventories. Overhead is applied on an actual costing basis.

REQUIRED:

 a. Prepare in good form a statement of cost of goods manufactured and sold for the Rocky Mountain Division.

 b. Prepare in good form an income statement for the Rocky Mountain Division.

EXTENDED APPLICATIONS

2–22. Normal Costing with Journal Entries.   Flowing Springs Sparkling Water started business in 19x0 on a family ranch in central Texas. The company bottles a low sodium, high magnesium mineral water. The mineral water is important to the ranch because the cattle business is very cyclical. A production facility was built over a naturally occurring mineral spring. The facility now ships over 5 million liters of bottled water a year.

Water is pumped from the spring to a production line where liter bottles are filled. Clear bottles are placed on a conveyor, washed and sterilized, and moved to filling stations. After filling, the bottles are capped, labeled, and placed in cardboard cartons of 12 liters per carton. The finished products (called *cases*) are moved to a finished inventory to await shipment to distributors.

Beginning inventories at October 1, 19x2, consisted of:

	Units	Cost	Amount
Materials—bottles	20,000	$0.10	$ 2,000
—cartons	1,000	0.83	830
Work in process—bottles	12,000	0.25	3,000
Finished goods—cases	8,000	3.84	30,720
Total inventory			$36,550

During October 19x2, the following production and sales data appeared in the accounting records:

1. Purchases were made on credit and recorded in a materials inventory account. The month's purchases included:

Bottles	480,000	$0.11	$52,800
Plastic caps	500,000	0.01	5,000
Labels	500,000	0.02	10,000
Cartons	38,000	0.84	31,920
Total purchases			$99,720

2. Materials issued to production during the month were:

Bottles	450,000
Plastic caps	450,000
Labels	450,000
Cartons	37,500

3. Payroll records show $12,240 in direct labor and $3,760 of indirect labor.
4. Additional actual overhead cost include:

Supervision	$3,400
Depreciation	8,000
Utilities	3,500
Insurance	1,460
Fringe benefits	3,600
Repair and maintenance	1,900
Supplies used	2,700
Miscellaneous	4,000

5. Overhead is charged to production at $.07 per bottle issued to production. Underapplied overhead is closed to the Cost of Goods Sold account at the end of each month.
6. Production completed during the month totaled 34,000 cases.
7. The company sold 40,000 cases at $9.60 per case.
8. Over- or underapplied overhead is closed to the Cost of Goods Sold account.

Inventories are maintained on a FIFO basis. The ending work in process consisted of 54,000 bottles valued at $11,830.

REQUIRED:
a. Journalize the activities for the month.
b. Prepare a statement of cost of goods manufactured and sold, including the adjustment for over- or underapplied overhead.

2–23. Cost of Services. Steve Edney wants to start a small business for the summer to earn some money to go to college. His business will be a window cleaning service called Edney Window Cleaning. He expects to work a total of 12 weeks. Steve's brother had a similar business the summer before, and his average revenue per house was $77. The average time to complete one job was five hours. Steve will increase the price by 4 percent due to inflation (round to the nearest dollar). Steve expects to average 12 houses per week, completing 2 houses per day. He will employ his best friend James and compensate him with 30 percent of the revenue.

The supplies needed to run the business for the summer are estimated to be:

	Needed Quantity	Unit Price
Buckets	2	$ 8.00
Hoses	2	18.00
Brushes	2	6.00
Ladders	2	37.00
Cleaning fluid (case)	12	24.50
Squeegees	8	7.50
Truck rental (per month)	3	250.00
Brochures printed (per 1,000 copies)	10	7.00
Insurance (per month)	3	125.00

The buckets, hoses, brushes, and ladders will be used for two summers' employment. They will be stored in Steve's garage until needed next summer. Treat 50 percent of the cost of these items as an expense for this summer.

(C. Cayce, Adapted)

REQUIRED:

a. Estimate the expected revenue for the summer.
b. Calculate the amount for James' expected compensation.
c. Estimate Steve's income for the summer. Use an income statement format. Assume that Steve will make no provision for taxes on this income.

2–24. Cost of Services Provided and Estimated.   You have been elected house manager of the Student Co-op, a small (30 people for the fall and 25 for the spring) student housing cooperative. The cooperative has refurbished an old office building next to campus. Your first job will be to determine room and board payments for the Spring Semester of 19x2. As compensation for your services, your room and board payments are paid for by the other tenants.

The group has decided that the spring price will be based upon actual fall price plus a factor for inflation, which has been set at 5 percent for the spring. This is complicated further by the slightly different number of days in the fall (119 days) and spring (110 days) semesters. The price for the spring is to be adjusted by the relative number of days and the inflation factor.

The cooperative has one part-time employee. A cook is paid to supply dinner for 17 weeks of the semester. The cook works five nights a week for three hours a night at $4 per hour to supply dinner. Otherwise, the students fend for themselves. No employment taxes are paid for the cook.

The following additional expenses were incurred during the Fall 19x1:

Utilities	160	Custodial supplies	50
Depreciation	500	Hospitality expenditure	50
Insurance	50	Building rental	25,000
Telephone	35	Maintenance	500
Food purchases	8,100	Office supplies	60
Repairs	300	Advertisement	50

The beginning inventory of food was $900 and the ending inventory was $500.

(M. Winburn, adapted)

REQUIRED:

a. Prepare a statement of living expenses for the Fall 19x1 Semester using actual costing. For this purpose, use all the expenses of running the cooperative as part of the cost of production. The statement format is similar to a cost of goods manufactured, except that the direct expenses will be the food, the cook, and the building rent. The rest of the expenses will be treated as indirect costs (overhead).

b. Compute an estimate of the member share of expenses for the Spring Semester of 19x2.

2–25. Cost of Production and Service.   Zakball, Inc., produces miniature jet engines used in guided missiles, such as the Cruise Missile. The engines are produced in plants in Michigan (these are primarily development models) and Nevada (main production plant is in Las Vegas). All research is performed on contract with the Department of Defense and recorded in the account Research in Process until reimbursed. The company uses an actual costing system.

The company employs 2,820 people, mostly in the Nevada operation. During a recent year, Zakball rearranged the production facilities in the Nevada plant and purchased and installed robots to handle much of the fabrication. Assembly and inspection are still a manual process. It had beginning materials inventories of $12,988,000 and ending materials of $3,499,000. During the year, it had total payroll of $2,980,000 of which $320,000 related to administration, $390,000 related to research and development, $804,000 related to indirect labor, and the rest related to production. `

Beginning engines in process was $392,000 and ending engines in process was $236,000. Finished engines awaiting shipment at the beginning was $486,000 and at the end was $316,000. Beginning research in process was $68,000, and ending research in process was $92,000.

The company purchased $3,906,000 in materials from suppliers on account of which $104,000 were used indirectly in production and $85,000 were used for research. Depreciation was $300,000 of which $240,000 related to production, $20,000 to administration, and the rest related to research. While on a trip to the Nevada location, the company treasurer lost $58,000 in company funds and was fired. Utilities for the company totaled $96,000 of which $62,000 related to production, $32,000 to research, and the rest to administration.

REQUIRED:

a. Calculate the direct materials used in production of engines.
b. Prepare a statement of the cost of engines manufactured.
c. Prepare a statement of the cost of research completed.

2–26. Cost of Goods Manufactured with Journal Entries.   Cold Creamery produces ice cream for distribution in pint and half-gallon sizes. Cold Creamery uses only premium ingredients and pursues a pricing strategy to reflect the premium product in the market. Since the equipment is completely cleaned after each batch, there is no work in process at the end of each day. The following information is available from the accounting records for the first three months of 19x6:

	January	*February*	*March*	*Total*
Beginning materials inventory	$12,400	$13,800	$ 9,600	$12,400
Ending materials inventory	13,800	9,600	14,100	14,100
Direct labor hours	4,400	4,800	4,700	13,900
1. Direct labor costs	$ 35,200	$ 38,400	$ 37,600	$111,200
2. Direct material purchases	102,555	180,380	140,600	423,535
3. Indirect labor cost	7,200	6,800	4,200	18,200
4. Payroll taxes	3,180	3,390	2,800	9,370
5. Utilities	14,000	9,800	14,000	37,800
6. Depreciation	12,500	12,500	15,000	40,000
7. Repairs and maintenance	11,600	460	480	12,540
8. Supplies used	1,100	1,050	980	3,130
9. Insurance on plant	0	2,700	0	2,700
10. Taxes on plant	3,200	0	0	3,200

The estimated production overhead costs were $485,440 for the year. The estimated annual direct labor hours were 65,600.

(A. Gregory, Adapted)

REQUIRED:

a. Prepare the journal entries to record the January costs incurred and applied assuming actual overhead costing.

b. Prepare the entry for application of overhead and cost of goods transferred to finished goods assuming normal overhead costing. Comment on the difference in amounts between actual and normal costing.

c. Prepare a cost of goods manufactured statement for the first quarter of 19x6 assuming actual costing.

d. Prepare a cost of goods manufactured statement for the first quarter of 19x6 assuming normal costing.

2–27. Manufacturing and Retailing Division Statements.   The Boulanger Shoe Company is well known for its high quality men's shoes. Corporate headquarters and the manufacturing division are located in Ohio. Manufacturing produces the shoes, which are transferred to the retail division at 150 percent of cost. The retail division controls the distribution of shoes to retail outlets throughout the United States. Although many of the stores are owned and operated under the direction of the retail division, shoes are distributed to other stores with a reputation for selling quality men's clothing.

For reporting purposes, the manufacturing division recognizes revenues (150 percent of cost) when shoes are transferred to the retail division. Revenues are recognized by the retail division when shoes are sold through the retail outlets or to other stores. Each division prepares its own financial statements, which will later be consolidated at the corporate level. The tax rate used for computing the division's share of income taxes is 35 percent.

Accounting data extracted from the records for the manufacturing division's operations for 19x3 are summarized below:

Inventories, 1/1/x3:	
Materials	$ 200,000
Work in process	150,000
Finished goods	400,000
Inventories, 12/31/x3:	
Materials	$ 300,000
Work in process	175,000
Finished goods	250,000
Payroll:	
Direct labor	$1,500,000
Indirect labor	300,000
Administrative salaries	500,000
Payroll taxes on production labor	180,000
Payroll taxes on administrative salaries	50,000
Other information:	
Supplies used (factory, $60,000; general office, $20,000)	$ 80,000
Insurance (factory, $15,000; general office, $3,000)	18,000
Depreciation on machinery	150,000
Depreciation on buildings (factory, 80%; general office, 20%)	100,000
Depreciation on office furniture and fixtures	8,000
Purchase of materials	950,000
Factory maintenance and repairs	55,000
Utilities (factory, 80%; general office, 20%)	85,000
Production overhead is applied at the rate of 65 percent per direct labor dollar.	

A search through the accounting records of the retail division reveals the following additional data:

Sales revenue	$7,800,000
Marketing and distribution expenses	1,040,000
Administrative expenses	390,000
Inventories, 1/1/x3	356,500
Inventories, 12/31/x3	231,000

REQUIRED:

a. Prepare, in good form, a statement of cost of goods manufactured and sold, and a net income statement for the manufacturing division for the year 19x3.

b. Prepare, in good form, a net income statement for the retail division for the year 19x3.

2–28. Cost of Goods with Inflation.   The Southeast Lure Company of Jacksonville, Mississippi, makes lures for fishing. The board of directors recently fired the senior managers for failing to earn adequate profits. You have been promoted from assistant controller to controller as a result and have been asked to analyze the situation. While sales have increased in recent years, the profits have declined dramatically. The data for three recent years are:

	19x5	19x6	19x7
Sales	$665,819	$765,692	$857,948
Cost of goods sold	399,793	503,970	677,950
Gross margin	$266,026	$261,722	$179,998

Production costs include:

	19x5	19x6	19x7
Direct materials	$148,770	$187,250	$243,880
Direct labor	178,993	202,230	233,870
Production overhead	72,030	114,490	200,200

(M. Ray, adapted)

In 19x6, the price index for fishing tackle was 107, but this decreased to 91 in 19x7 due to a rapid increase in competition. The price index was 100 for 19x5. For 19x8, the selling price index is expected to be 95. Wages and salaries have increased at a rate of 4 percent per year, and materials have increased in price at a rate of 2 percent per year.

The beginning materials inventory in January 19x8 was $31,000 (including $1,000 in supplies), and the ending inventory was $58,000 (including $3,000 in supplies). The beginning 19x8 work in process was $27,500, and the ending work in process is expected to be $48,000. The beginning 19x8 finished goods was $69,000, and the ending finished goods is expected to be $58,000. During 19x8, the company expects to have the following costs:

Materials purchased	$399,500
Direct labor	287,500
Supervisory salaries	143,750
Other indirect labor	66,125
Supplies purchased	29,000
Machine depreciation	29,000
Plant depreciation	15,000
Insurance	7,000
Utilities	20,000
Property taxes on plant and inventories	7,000

REQUIRED:

Assume that $316,250 in overhead is expected to be applied during 19x8. Prepare a projected statement of cost of goods manufactured and sold that compares actual and applied overheads.

2–29. Cost of Goods Manufactured.   Norton Industries, a manufacturer of cable for the heavy construction industry, closes its books and prepares financial statements at the end of each month. The statement of cost of goods sold for April 19x5 is presented below.

(CMA, adapted)

NORTON INDUSTRIES
Statement of Cost of Goods Sold
For the Month Ended April 30, 19x5
($000 omitted)

Inventory of finished goods, March 31	$ 50
Cost of goods manufactured	790
Cost of goods available for sale	$840
Less inventory of finished goods, April 30	247
Unadjusted cost of goods sold	$593
Underapplied manufacturing overhead	25
Cost of goods sold	$618

Norton employs a periodic inventory system using a first-in, first-out basis. The actual cost of direct materials and direct labor is used to value the inventories. However, manufacturing overhead is applied to production and carried to the inventories at a predetermined rate of $40 per ton of cable manufactured.

The preclosing trial balance as of May 31, 19x5, and additional information follow:

NORTON INDUSTRIES
Preclosing Trial Balance
May 31, 19x5
($000 omitted)

Account	Debit	Credit
Cash and marketable securities	$ 54	
Accounts and notes receivable	210	
Direct materials inventory (4/30/x5)	28	
Work in process inventory (4/30/x5)	150	
Finished goods inventory (4/30/x5)	247	
Property, plant, and equipment (net)	1,140	
Accounts, notes, and taxes payable		$ 70
Bonds payable		600
Paid-in capital		100
Retained earnings		930
Sales		1,488
Sales discounts	20	
Interest revenue		2
Purchases of direct materials	510	
Direct labor	260	
Indirect factory labor	90	
Office salaries	122	
Sales salaries	42	
Utilities	135	
Rent	9	
Property tax	60	
Insurance	20	
Depreciation	54	
Interest expense	6	
Freight-in	15	
Freight-out	18	
	$3,190	$3,190

ADDITIONAL INFORMATION

80 percent of the utilities is related to the manufacturing of cable; the remaining 20 percent is related to the sales and administrative functions in the office building.

All of the rent is for the office building.

The property taxes are assessed on the manufacturing plant.

60 percent of the insurance is related to the manufacturing of cable; the remaining 40 percent is related to the sales and administrative functions in the office building. Depreciation expense includes the following.

Manufacturing plant	$20,000
Manufacturing equipment	30,000
Office equipment	4,000
	$54,000

Norton manufactured 7,825 equivalent tons of cable during May 19x5.

The inventory balances at May 31, 19x5, as determined by physical count, are as follows.

Direct materials	$ 23,000
Work in process	220,000
Finished goods	175,000

REQUIRED:

a. Prepare a statement of cost of goods manufactured for Norton Industries for May 19x5.

b. Norton Industries closes all underapplied or overapplied manufacturing overhead to cost of goods sold.

  1. Identify the conditions under which this treatment of closing underapplied or overapplied manufacturing overhead is valid.

  2. Describe an alternate treatment for closing underapplied or overapplied manufacturing overhead.

2–30. Cost of Services Provided. On July 1, 19x0, Mountain River Sports had 12 trips in process in Northern New Mexico. The company provides canoeing and rafting trips combined with various other activities. During the month of July, 43 trips were scheduled to start, and the owners, Dave and Judy Espar, expected groups to call for another 8 to 10. However, only two more groups called to plan a July trip, and six groups cancelled. The excursions range from one day to two weeks. At the end of July, 17 groups were still out.

Juan Sanchez, the company clerk and a cook's helper, keeps records on the cost of each trip, including meals and supplies issued, time of tour guides, entertainment, transportation, and other costs. About 70 percent (higher for short trips and lower for long) of the cost of a trip is expended before the people leave town. The 12 trips in process at the beginning of the month had an accumulated cost of $23,204. The July 31 trips in process had an accumulated cost of $39,204. The beginning inventory of food was $19,600, and the ending inventory was $7,390. Depreciation of equipment is on a units-of-production basis with a day of use as the basic unit. Insurance is billed according to the number of people per day.

Mr. Sanchez posted the following trip-related activities to the records during July:

Air fares*	$128,200		
Balloon rides*	4,800	Mule and horse rental*	1,290
Depreciation—equipment	7,409	Music groups*	3,600
Emergency medical service	800	Other payroll	4,802
Food purchased*	83,204	Payroll taxes	1,176
Fuel for trips*	8,205	Replace broken equipment	882
Hotels and lodges	3,809	Santa Fe Opera*	17,902
July vehicle insurance	4,500	Telephone	5,890
License fees	1,883	Trip insurance for July	10,609
Limousine services*	1,988	Trip payroll*	24,180
Misc. trip expenses	902	Vehicle maintenance	1,402
		Total	$317,433

* Items recorded directly to trips.

The trip payroll includes daily workers who are directly involved with the conduct of each trip. They are all local people who work whenever there is a trip to run. Otherwise, they hang out around town, mostly at Jesse's Inn down the street. The balloon rides are considered entertainment. The clerk prepares a report titled "The Cost of Trips Completed," which includes the direct cost of food, transportation, entertainment, trip payroll, and other items treated as overhead. The company uses an actual costing system.

REQUIRED:
a. Find the direct cost of transportation, food, entertainment, and trip payroll. Show a subtotal for each direct cost and a total for all direct costs.
b. Prepare a cost of trips completed. This is similar to a cost of goods manufactured report, except that there is a listing for each direct cost (from part a). Instead of direct materials and direct labor, use transportation, food, entertainment, and trip payroll.

CHAPTER

3

Cost Behavior Analysis

■

THE COST ESTIMATION PROBLEM

Michael Formby, plant manager for Mondieu Company, was concerned over the costs of the Pressure Heating and the Laser Etching departments. He would like to bid on a large Illinois state contract that involves both departments, but he is not confident in projecting costs based on current uncertain cost behavior.

The Mondieu Company produces shaped marble counter, table, and desk tops in numerous sizes and forms. Various types of rock are heated up to 8,000 degrees Fahrenheit and formed under pressure into flat and shaped surfaces. The thickness of the final product varies from $\frac{1}{2}$ inch to 2 feet, and the sizes vary from a small 1-foot square to a large 6-foot by 20-foot section weighing 2,200 pounds. There are about 1,800 different products produced in the plant.

Various amounts of hard rock, granite, and marble are purchased from local quarries. The rock is sliced according to thickness specifications in the Diamond Saw Department and then heated and shaped under pressure in the Pressure Heating Department. From there the stone is sent to one of several types of finishing departments. One of the finishing departments, the Laser Etching Department, etches intricate designs into the stone.

Mr. Formby asked Jerrelle Ricardi, plant controller, to study the costs and report back estimated fixed and variable costs for the departments in time to bid on the Illinois state contract.

Decision processes, including bidding on contracts, should be based on how changing activity levels affect total and unit costs. Determining cost behavior is also important for increasing management's understanding of overhead costs, which helps in understanding product costs and in establishing budgets and budgetary controls. This chapter discusses the common cost behavior characteristics and presents approaches to estimating the cost behavior pattern for the various segments of a company.

■

LEARNING OBJECTIVES

After studying this chapter, you should be able to:

1. Identify and explain the differences in the behavior of variable costs, fixed costs, semivariable costs, and step costs.
2. Identify six techniques for separating costs into fixed and variable components.
3. Determine the fixed and variable cost components for a specific situation using scattergraph and visual fit, high-low point method, and simple linear regression.
4. Explain the importance of goodness of fit when statistically determining a formula for cost behavior.

TYPES OF COSTS

The four basic cost behavior patterns are variable, fixed, semivariable (mixed), and step cost. When graphed, activity level is plotted on the horizontal axis, and cost is plotted on the vertical axis.

Variable Cost, Assuming Linearity

A **variable cost** is a cost that changes in total in direct proportion to changes in the activity base, such as sales for a selling function or machine hours for a production function. If the cost is variable, a 20 percent reduction in activity will result in a 20 percent reduction in the cost. Likewise, an increase in activity brings a proportionate increase in total variable cost.

The slope of the total variable cost line represents the variable cost per unit. The greater the amount of variable cost per unit of activity, the steeper the slope of the total variable cost line. However, once the variable cost per unit of activity is established, it is constant per unit throughout a relevant range. Typical variable costs include materials and sales commissions.

As an illustration of variable cost, assume a company manufactures oak computer desks that require 25-board feet of oak at a cost of $2.50 per board foot. In terms of the finished product, each desk would have a wood cost of $62.50. Exhibit 3–1 shows the total variable cost and the variable cost per desk.

Fixed Cost

A **fixed cost** is a cost that remains constant in total as the level of activity changes. For all practical purposes, a fixed cost will not vary with the level of activity on a weekly or monthly basis; hence, it remains constant over a short time frame. Although fixed costs remain constant in total, the cost per unit decreases as volume increases. That is, fixed cost per unit varies inversely with changes in the activity base. Returning to the example of the oak computer desk, suppose that the production process requires one supervisor with the salary of $2,000 per month. Exhibit 3–2 illustrates the fixed

EXHIBIT 3–1   Variable Cost Behavior

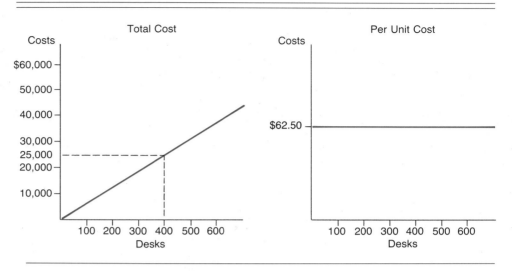

cost pattern for both total cost and cost per unit when activity level changes. The total cost line is a straight line with no slope. The unit cost curve slopes downward with a decreasing slope.

Fixed costs are frequently called **capacity costs** because an organization incurs them in order to provide capacity to render a service or make a product. Capacity costs refer to the people who form the basic organization structure, the equipment to perform operations and processes, and the buildings to house the people and equipment.

Fixed costs can also be divided into committed and discretionary costs. **Committed fixed costs** are those fixed costs arising from the possession of property, plant, and equipment and a basic organization. The level of such costs is primarily affected by management's long-run decisions regarding the desired level of capacity. **Discretionary fixed costs,** also called *managed* or *programmed fixed costs,* arise from

EXHIBIT 3–2   Fixed Cost Behavior

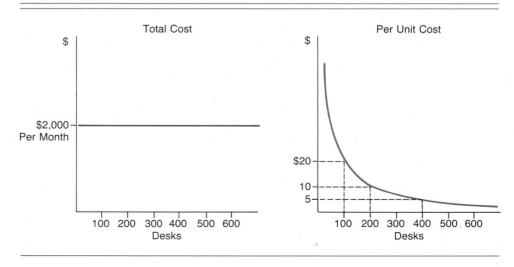

the periodic, usually annual, appropriation decisions that directly reflect management's short-term policies on capacity levels. Management can react quickly to increase or reduce discretionary fixed costs. Impacting the level of committed fixed costs, however, requires a longer period of time.

Semivariable or Mixed Cost

A **semivariable cost,** also called a **mixed cost,** contains both fixed cost and variable cost portions. The fixed cost portion is the minimum cost required if some activity takes place, but as activity increases, total costs increase above this minimum at the proportionate rate. Typical semivariable costs include utilities (gas, electricity, and water) and maintenance of plant and equipment. Exhibit 3–3(a) is a graphical illustration of total cost behavior for a semivariable cost.

Step Cost

A **step cost** is a cost that increases or decreases in lumps of cost with changes in activity. A given amount of cost will sustain some increase in volume without any increase in cost. At some point, however, the cost must go up like a stair step in order to increase volume. A supervisor may be able to supervise any number of employees up to a certain level. Beyond this level, it is necessary to hire an additional supervisor. The cost increases come in indivisible lumps and, therefore, the curve has steps. Exhibit 3–3(b) shows the graph of a step cost.

Other Cost Behavior

Certain costs do not fit the behavior patterns discussed above because these costs are disjointed or otherwise nonlinear in total. As examples, consider the following costs:

1. Commercial water and sewer bill based on the following consumption:

First 100,000 gallons or less	$100 flat fee
Next 1,000 gallons	.002 per gallon
Next 1,000 gallons	.004 per gallon
Next 1,000 gallons	.006 per gallon
And so on	

Exhibit 3–4(a) shows this cost behavior pattern.

EXHIBIT 3–3   Semivariable and Step Cost Behavior

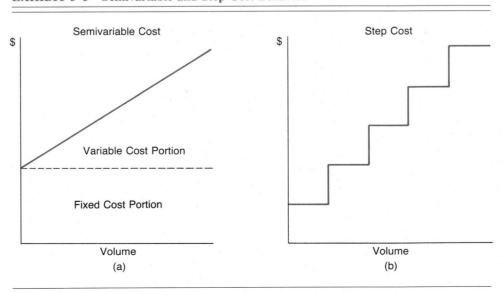

EXHIBIT 3–4   Examples of Cost Behavior

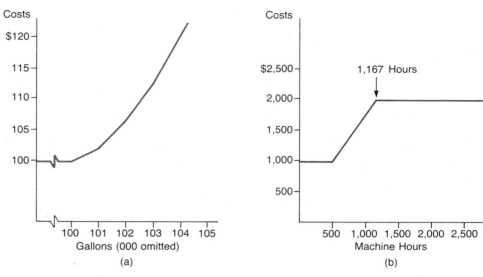

(a)   (b)

2. Monthly lease payments on a machine call for a minimum payment of $1,000 up to 500 machine hours of usage. An additional charge of $1.50 per hour is paid for machine time used above 500 hours. However, the maximum monthly payment will not exceed $2,000.

Exhibit 3–4(b) depicts this cost behavior pattern.

COST ESTIMATION

Many management functions require a knowledge of how costs behave. Therefore, cost estimation becomes an important activity in which accountants are involved. **Cost estimation** is the process of estimating a cost relationship with activity for an individual cost item or grouping of costs. There are six commonly used techniques for estimating a cost to activity relationship:

1. Account analysis.
2. Engineering approach.
3. Scattergraph and visual fit.
4. High-low method.
5. Representative points method.
6. Regression analysis.

In the following sections, we will describe each of these techniques.

Account Analysis   In **account analysis** the accountant estimates the variability of a particular cost directly from information obtained through (1) an inspection of the historical activity of the cost and (2) an interpretation of managerial policies with respect to the cost. Account analysis can be used with a limited amount of data, but it relies heavily on the accountant's professional judgment. The method is the first step any organization should take as it begins a program of cost estimation that involves a number of cost categories. It is a useful approach for new organizations and those that experience a major change in circumstances. The technique is also useful for new products.

When this method is used, the accountant obtains cost and activity data for at least one accounting period. Where the cost data are an aggregate of several cost categories, each category or account is analyzed separately to determine its status as fixed or variable. All cost accounts are classified as either fixed or variable. If a cost account shows semivariable or step cost behavior, either (1) a subjective estimate is made of the variable and fixed portions of the cost or (2) the account is classified as fixed or variable depending on the preponderant cost behavior. Unit variable costs are estimated by dividing total variable costs by the measure of activity.

Interestingly, account analysis is fairly accurate for determining cost behavior in some cases. For example, vendor invoices show that direct materials have a variable cost behavior, and rent on the facilities is fixed. A telephone bill is a semivariable cost; one portion is fixed for the minimum monthly charge, and the remainder may be variable with usage of the telephone. A supervisor's salary is fixed for the accounting period, although it may be increased in the future.

The primary strengths of account analysis are its limited data requirements and its simplicity. Judgment generally comes from experienced managers and accountants who are familiar with the operations and the direction in which costs move as activity levels change. Because operating results of only one period are required, this method is good for new products or situations involving rapid changes in products or technology.

The primary weaknesses of account analysis lie in its lack of range of observations and its subjectivity. Using judgment generates two potential problems: (1) different analysts may develop different cost estimates from the same data and (2) the results of analysis may have significant economic consequences for the analyst, which means the analyst will likely show self-serving estimates. A potential weakness is that data used in the analysis may reflect unusual circumstances or inefficient operations, as is likely with new products; these factors become incorporated in the subsequent cost estimates.

Engineering Approach

The **engineering approach** uses analysis and direct observation of processes to identify the relationship between inputs and an output and then quantifies an expected cost behavior. The basic issue is what amount of direct materials, direct labor, and overhead is required to run a given process.

One way to analyze costs for a unit of output, such as a desk, is to make a list of all materials, labor tasks, and applied overhead costs going into the process. Then the quantity of each item required should be determined, that quantity priced out, and the material cost of the final item determined. However, this does not consider the efficiency with which inputs are converted into outputs. Providing a specific measure for efficiency is what makes the engineering approach valuable.

Direct Materials.   With respect to materials, the engineer will study chemical, physical, and mechanical relationships within the process itself. For example, in a petrochemical plant the chemical reactions necessary to yield a specific type or mix of output are known. A product specification lists materials necessary for production together with quantity and, in many cases, an indication of quality. A metal stamping process or woodcutting operation produces scrap, the cost of which is part of the direct materials used for a completed product. In their role of improving efficiency, engineers will minimize the amount of scrap or waste generated in the production of the product.

At the conclusion of the study of the process, an engineer will provide a list of materials by specific type, quantity, and quality. The purchasing department can price out the materials through catalogs, price lists, and bids. Now material costs can be expressed as a variable cost per unit of the process.

Labor. **A time and motion study** is one technique used to estimate the amount of time required for the tasks to be performed within each process. The purposes of such studies are (1) to identify the most efficient manner to complete a task by eliminating unnecessary motion or waiting and (2) to measure the amount of time needed to complete the task. Individual movements required by each worker at each task are first identified. These movements are timed, allowing for fatigue, breakdowns, and rest breaks. These times are related to job classifications and priced out at expected wage rates. The tasks identified by routings and priced out at the appropriate wage rate make up the labor cost for the process.

Production Overhead. Although the above techniques can be used to some extent for each support activity or process, the engineering approach is usually not applicable to finding how much overhead should be applied to a product. Not only is it difficult to identify relationships, but any cost formulas developed are probably complex. Therefore, engineering approaches are combined with other approaches to identify overhead cost behavior patterns.

Advantages and Disadvantages. A major advantage of the engineering approach is that it details each step required to perform a task. This allows transfer of information to similar tasks in different situations, and it permits an organization to review productivity and identify specific strengths and weaknesses. Another advantage is that it does not require historical accounting data. For this reason, the approach is often used to estimate costs for new products and services.

The major disadvantage is the expensive nature of the approach. Engineering studies require in-depth examinations of tasks and close observation of an individual performing each task. All of this has a cost. An additional disadvantage is that estimates made by the engineering approach are often based on near-optimal working conditions. Since actual working conditions are generally less than optimal, there may be uncontrollable variations in cost performance.

Scattergraph and Visual Fit

Scattergraph and visual fit (also called the *scatter-diagram method*) is an analysis that uses all of the cost observations. The first step is to graph each observation, with cost on the vertical axis and activity on the horizontal axis. The second step is visually and judgmentally to fit a line to the data. Care should be taken to have approximately an equal number of observations on either side of the line. For example, Exhibit 3–5 has the data from the Laser Etching Department and Exhibit 3–6 presents a visual fit.

The third step is to estimate the costs from the plotted line. Fixed costs at the intercept are about $300 (actually, just under $300). The variable costs can be calculated by subtracting the fixed costs from the total costs at some point along the line. For example, at 400 machine hours, the line gives a total cost of approximately $4,000. Compute variable costs per hour as follows:

Total costs at 400 machine hours	$4,000
Less: fixed costs	300
Variable costs	$3,700

EXHIBIT 3–5

LASER ETCHING DEPARTMENT
Department Overhead Cost and Etching Hours
For the 15 Months Ending December 31, 19x4

Month	Departmental Overhead Cost	Etching Hours	
19x3:			
October	$5,350	470	
November	3,400	325	
December	2,300	250	
19x4:			
January	$3,700	365	
February	4,300	435	
March	4,800	460	
April	4,300	490	
May	5,450	525	
June	5,500	600	
July	6,600	630	←Maximum
August	5,400	560	
September	5,000	510	
October	4,600	490	
November	3,500	390	
December	2,300	200	←Minimum

EXHIBIT 3–6   **Laser Etching Department** (scattergraph and visual fit)

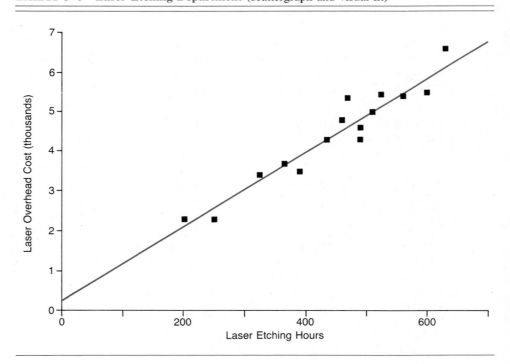

$$\frac{\text{Variable costs: } \$3,700}{\text{Machine hours: } 400} = \$9.25 \text{ per hour}$$

Therefore, the cost formula is Total cost = $300 + $9.25 per hour.

One of the major advantages of the scattergraph and visual fit method is that all observations are considered. This method is frequently used in a preliminary analysis and can be easily applied to many situations. Computer spread sheets can plot data quickly and accurately. Thus, the graphing task is relatively easy to perform.

There are some disadvantages to the technique. When used by itself, the visual fit method is limited by the judgment of the person drawing the line through the data. Reasonable people will disagree on the slope and intercept for a given graph. Interestingly, most of the lines that judgment says could reasonably represent the data will converge near the center of the data. This means that the method may be a useful way to estimate total costs near the center of activity. However, moving away from the central area, the estimates making up total costs will be subject to large errors.

High-Low Point Method

If the relationship between cost and activity level can be described by a straight line, any two observations may be used to estimate fixed and variable costs. Choose observations associated with the highest and the lowest activity levels, not the highest and lowest costs.

Exhibit 3–7 provides a graphical display of the **high-low point method** for the data from the Laser Etching Department. The variable cost is designated as b, the slope of the line connecting the two observations, and is estimated by the following formula:

$$b = \frac{(\text{Cost at highest activity} - \text{Cost at lowest activity})}{(\text{Highest activity} - \text{Lowest activity})}$$

For the data given, this computation is:

	Machine Hours	Overhead Costs
Highest	630	$6,600
Lowest	200	2,300
Difference	430	$4,300

$$b = \frac{\$4,300}{430 \text{ Hours}} = \$10 \text{ per machine hour}$$

The fixed cost (or intercept) is estimated by using the total cost at either the highest or lowest activity level and subtracting the estimated total variable cost for that level, as follows:

$$
\begin{aligned}
\text{Total fixed cost} &= \text{Total cost at highest activity} - (\text{Variable} \\
&\quad \text{cost per unit} \times \text{Highest activity}) \\
&= \text{Total cost at lowest activity} - (\text{Variable} \\
&\quad \text{cost per unit} \times \text{Lowest activity}).
\end{aligned}
$$

If the slope has been calculated correctly, then the fixed cost will be the same at both the high and the low points. Use this technique to check solutions to assignments. For example, consider first the highest point and then the lowest point for the Laser Etching Department:

EXHIBIT 3–7   Graphical Display of High-Low Point Method

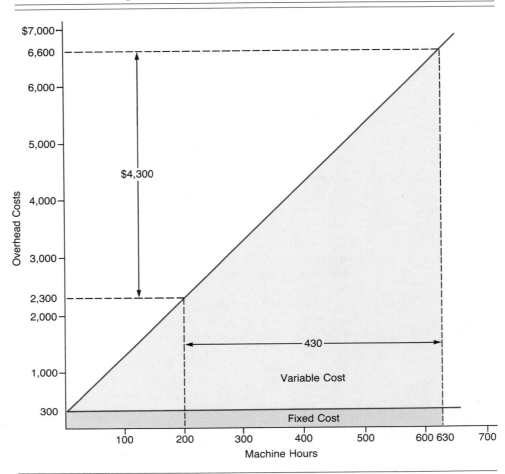

$$\text{Fixed cost} = \$6,600 - (\$10 \times 630) = \$6,600 - \$6,300 = \underline{\$300}$$
$$\text{Fixed cost} = \$2,300 - (\$10 \times 200) = \$2,300 - \$2,000 = \underline{\$300}$$

Thus, the cost formula is $y = \$300 + \$10x$.

What happens if one of the two points is obviously an outlier to the remaining data? The normal procedure is to use the next high or low observation that appears to align better with the data.

The advantage of the high-low method is its simplicity. The primary limitation is that two points usually do not produce reliable estimates of variable and fixed costs unless the high and low points are representative of the points in between. However, in some situations, only two points are available and estimates are needed.

Representative Points Approach

A variation of the high-low method is the **representative points approach.** It is used where actual cost information for anticipated activity levels does not exist. Managers use their knowledge of operations and costs to estimate the costs at two activity levels. These estimates are used in the same manner as the above high-low calculations to obtain an estimated cost formula with variable and fixed cost components.

REGRESSION ANALYSIS

The previous sections discussed methods that either use only some of the data available or are subjective. If enough quality data exist, then regression analysis gives a means to produce an objective description of costs based on all observations.

Regression analysis is included in basic business statistics courses. Thus, the following discussion should not be completely new to you. We will be applying the technique to accounting data and discussing the unique problems with accounting applications. With the existence of computerized spread sheets and statistical packages, regression analysis is more readily available to most practicing accountants. Thus, it will become a more useful tool in the future.

Regression analysis fits a line to the cost and activity data using the least squares method. If you will remember fitting lines with the scattergraph method, judgment was involved in getting an equal number of points above and below the line in order to describe the relationship. The least squares method does the same thing, except that it provides greater precision in a process that minimizes the vertical distance from the points to the line. The technique does this by finding the line that minimizes the sum of the squared distance of the points from the line.

Linear regression is a statistical tool for describing the movement of one variable based on the movement of another variable. For purposes of cost behavior analysis, we usually want to know if a high level of cost tends to be associated with a high level of activity. The **dependent variable** *(y)* is what we want to predict. For cost estimation, the dependent variable is costs. The **independent variable** *(x)* is what we use to predict with. For cost estimation, the independent variable is a measure of activities.

Method of Least Squares

The formula[1] useful for computing the variable cost, the slope of the regression line, is the **method of least squares:**

$$b = \frac{\Sigma(x - \bar{x})(y - \bar{y})}{\Sigma(x - \bar{x})^2}$$

where Σ before a variable indicates the sum over the observations. The $\bar{y}$ and $\bar{x}$ are the average of y and x.

A formula useful for computing an estimate of fixed costs, the intercept, is:

$$a = \bar{y} - b\bar{x}$$

Application to the Example.   The data from Exhibit 3–5 have been expanded in Exhibit 3–8 to give the information needed for solving either of the two formulas.

---

[1] This is derived by finding the a and b that minimize the errors:
$$e = \Sigma(y - y')^2$$
can be expanded by substituting in $y' = a + bx$:
$$e = \Sigma y^2 - 2b\Sigma xy - 2a\Sigma y + 2ab\Sigma x + na^2 + b^2\Sigma x^2$$
Partial differentiating e with respect to a and b:
$$\delta e/\delta a = -2\Sigma y + 2b\Sigma x + 2na$$
$$\delta e/\delta b = -2\Sigma xy + 2a\Sigma x + 2b\Sigma x^2$$
Set these derivatives equal to zero and simplify:
$$\Sigma y = na + b\Sigma x$$
$$\Sigma xy = a\Sigma x + b\Sigma x^2$$
These are called the *normal equations.* We solve these equations simultaneously for the coefficients a and b.

EXHIBIT 3–8   Laser Etching Department (calculations for determining a and b coefficients)

Month	Departmental Overhead Cost (y)	Etching Hours (x)	$(y - \bar{y})(x - \bar{x})$	$(x - \bar{x})^2$
October	$ 5,350	470	$ 21,389	$ 544
November	3,400	325	125,722	14,803
December	2,300	250	419,556	38,678
January	3,700	365	59,889	6,669
February	4,300	435	1,556	136
March	4,800	460	4,889	178
April	4,300	490	(5,778)	1,878
May	5,450	525	79,639	6,136
June	5,500	600	163,556	23,511
July	6,600	630	397,222	33,611
August	5,400	560	109,556	12,844
September	5,000	510	35,889	4,011
October	4,600	490	7,222	1,878
November	3,500	390	52,889	3,211
December	2,300	200	526,222	60,844
Totals	$66,500	6,700	$1,999,417	$208,933

Means $\bar{y} = 4,433.33$ $\bar{x} = 446.67$

1. Variable cost $b = \dfrac{\$1,999,417}{208,933} = \underline{\$9.5696}$

2. Fixed cost $a = \$4,433.33 - (\$9.5696 \times 446.67)$
   $= \underline{\$158.89}$

Regression line: $y' = \$158.89 + \$9.5696x$

The resulting regression equation is at the bottom of Exhibit 3–8: $y' = \$158.89 + \$9.5696x$.

Interpretation of the Regression Line

The method for calculating the **regression line** yields the line that best fits all of the data in a linear relationship. This line has the advantage over the high-low point method because it considers all observations, not just the high and low activity. It has an advantage over the visual fit technique in that the quality of the visual fit line depends on the experience and judgment of the preparer. On the other hand, there is only one regression line for a given set of data.

The value of $158.89 in Exhibit 3–8 is the intercept and is thought of as the fixed cost per month because we used monthly data. However, this does not represent the fixed cost at zero activity. Its value is best interpreted as the fixed cost within the range for which we have observations. If volume actually fell to zero, then management would have to cut costs, and fixed costs might be less than the estimate.

The $9.5696 in Exhibit 3–8 is the slope of the regression line and is interpreted as the variable cost per laser etching hour. Again, the estimate of slope does not apply outside the range for which we have data.

Cost Estimation

For 460 etching hours, the regression equation may be used to estimate costs:

$$y' = \$158.89 + \$9.5696 (460) = \$4,561$$

The estimated cost is the average cost given the specific etching hours. What this means intuitively is that if many actual observations for 460 machine hours are taken, about half of the observations will be above \$4,561 and half below \$4,561. Seldom would an actual cost observation fall exactly on the regression line.

Quality of the Regression

In measuring the functional relationship between a dependent variable (cost) and an independent variable (activity level), we are interested in more than just an equation for estimating cost. We also want to know the *goodness of fit* of the regression line to the cost and activity data and *reliability* of the estimates of cost. Therefore, this section presents some of the measures available for assessing goodness of fit and reliability.

Goodness of Fit.   The **coefficient of determination,** also referred to as goodness of fit or r^2, is the measure of the association identified by the regression line. It can vary from 0 to 1 and represents the proportion of total variation in y that is accounted for (or explained by) the variation in x. Thus, an r^2 close to 0 would indicate that the regression line does not describe the data. That is, the regression line is nearly horizontal and little of the variation in y is explained by the variation in x. If the regression line is very descriptive of the data, then the r^2 would be close to 1.

The error term $e = (y - y')$ is called the residual error,[2] which is the deviation between the actual y values and the estimates from $y' = a + bx$. The sum of the e^2 terms is calculated to estimate the total residual error:

$$\text{Total residual error: } \Sigma e^2 = \Sigma(y - y')^2$$

The mean square error of the actual y values around the average value y (noted as $\bar{y}$) is used as the reference point in judging the quality of the regression line. We calculate the mean square error as:

$$\text{Mean square error: MSE} = \Sigma(y - \bar{y})^2$$

Finally, the coefficient of determination is calculated as follows:

$$r^2 = 1 - \frac{\text{Total residual error}}{\text{Mean square error}} = 1 - \frac{\Sigma(y - y')^2}{\Sigma(y - \bar{y})^2}$$

The $\bar{y}$ is the average and is graphed in Exhibit 3–9 as a horizontal line with a height equal to the average value of all y observations. On the other hand, y' is the conditional mean given an x value and has a slope of b.

Example Analysis.   Exhibit 3–10 gives the data for the $\Sigma(y - y')^2$ and $\Sigma(y - \bar{y})^2$. The calculation at the bottom of the Exhibit shows an r^2 of about .92, which means that about 92 percent of the variation in the cost data can be explained by the regression formula. In other words, less than 8 percent of the change in departmental overhead costs is due to factors other than volume of etching hours.

Sources of Residual Error

The cost estimating equation derived from a set of data is beset with a certain degree of error due to imperfections in the data, data collection, and other processing issues. These imperfections will appear in the total residual error. Because understanding the source of errors is a step toward eliminating or controlling them, this section discusses the common procedures for reducing residual error.

Mechanics of Keying Data and Calculation.   Go over the calculations again. Do you have the right formulae and the correct sums and intermediate calculations? Look

---

[2] An alternative term often found in the statistical literature is *unexplained variation*.

EXHIBIT 3–9   Scatter Diagran and Least Squares

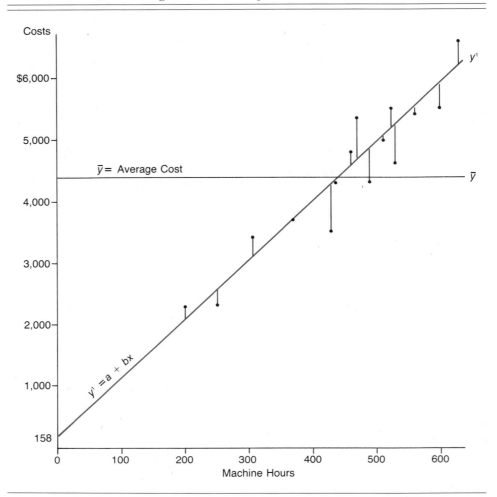

specifically at the errors, $(y - y')$, for outliers, which are large errors. One data keying error can reduce the r^2 substantially and throw off the estimates of both fixed and the variable costs.

There Can Be Material Errors in the Original Data.   Check the cutoff procedures that separate cost transactions into periods, especially for transactions that are outliers. Examine the original data for procedural errors, such as classification of transactions into the wrong accounts.

Selection of Activity Measure.   The r^2 has one other usage important to the accountant in the cost behavior analysis. When multiple activity measures are available, it can be used in determining which of several possible regression equations should be selected. For example, in our departmental overhead case, we could have regression equations using etching hours, direct labor hours, and direct labor costs. Which of the three results, if any, should be used? Conventional wisdom suggests the equation with the highest r^2.

EXHIBIT 3–10   Laser Etching Department (data for sums of squares relating to y)

Month	y Departmental Overhead Cost	x Etching Hours	y'	Residual e $(y - y')$	e^2 $(y - y')^2$	Mean square MSE $(y - \bar{y})^2$
1	$ 5,350	470	$ 4,657	$693	$ 480,801	840,278
2	3,400	325	3,269	131	17,158	1,067,778
3	2,300	250	2,551	(251)	63,147	4,551,111
4	3,700	365	3,652	48	2,324	537,778
5	4,300	435	4,322	(22)	469	17,778
6	4,800	460	4,561	239	57,166	134,444
7	4,300	490	4,848	(548)	300,297	17,778
8	5,450	525	5,183	267	71,326	1,033,611
9	5,500	600	5,901	(401)	160,520	1,137,778
10	6,600	630	6,188	412	169,960	4,694,444
11	5,400	560	5,518	(118)	13,892	934,444
12	5,000	510	5,039	(39)	1,551	321,111
13	4,600	490	4,848	(248)	61,501	27,778
14	3,500	390	3,891	(391)	152,908	871,111
15	2,300	200	2,073	227	51,615	4,551,111
Totals	$66,500	6,700	$66,500	$0	$1,604,637	$20,738,333
Mean	$ 4,433				"Total residual" errors in y	"Mean square" errors in y

$$r^2 = 1 - \frac{1,604,637}{20,738,333} = \underline{\underline{0.92}}$$

Standard Error of the Estimate

Because a regression equation will not result in a perfect fit on the data points, we need a measure of variability in the data with respect to the regression equation. The **standard error of the estimate** (S_e) is a measure of the average deviation between the actual observations of the dependent variable and values predicted by the regression equation. When the regression equation is used to predict future departmental overhead costs in our illustration, S_e gives an estimate of the amount by which the actual outcome might differ from the estimate. The standard error of the estimate is calculated by the following formula:

$$S_e = \sqrt{\frac{\Sigma(y - y')^2}{n - 2}}$$

The numerator is the sum of squares of the residual error. The denominator is referred to as **degrees of freedom,** which is the number of observations (n) reduced by the number of parameters that must be estimated in the regression equation (two parameters for simple linear regression—a and b).

The degrees of freedom is a necessary statistical concept. There must be at least as many observations as parameters. For example, we need at least one observation to estimate an average cost. However, we must have more than one number to estimate the variation in the costs. As another example, a simple regression with only two observations will result in the best-fitting line that passes through both points. Since both points are on the line, $(y - y')^2$ will be zero for both observations. Thus, to have any estimation of the error or goodness of fit of the simple regression line, there must be more than two observations. The number of observations in excess of the number of parameters is called the degrees of freedom.

For our example of departmental overhead and etching hours, the values for $(y - y')^2$ appear in Exhibit 3–10. The following calculation gives the standard error of the estimate:

$$S_e = \sqrt{\frac{1,604,638}{15 - 2}} = \sqrt{123,433.69} = \underline{\underline{351.13}}$$

As a measure of variability, the standard error of the estimate gives us information about where the observations are with respect to the regression line. Looking again at Exhibit 3–10 and the $(y - y')$ column, you would expect to find about two-thirds (or 10 numbers) either less than 351.13 or less negative than (351.13). In other words, there is approximately a 68 percent probability that the actual observation will be within plus or minus 351.13 of the regression line.

Exhibit 3–11 shows graphically how the standard error of the estimate relates to the regression equation for our sample. Here we plot $(y - y')$ as compared to the activity measure.

Error in the Estimate of Cost

In our example, suppose that we wanted an estimate for cost at 600 etching hours. The estimate for 600 hours according to the regression equation is \$5,901 or \$158.89 + (\$9.5696 × 600). How much error might reasonably be expected in the \$5,901? We can build a confidence interval around the \$5,901 to help answer this question. The formula for the upper and lower limits of the interval is presented next.

EXHIBIT 3–11   Laser Etching Department (residuals with volume)

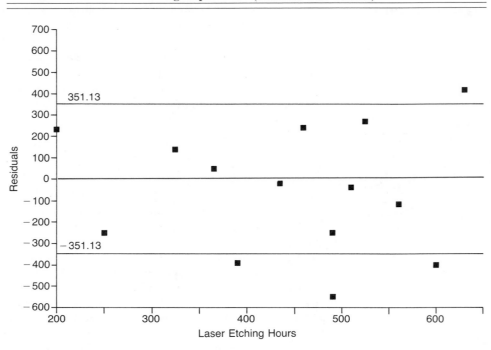

$$\text{Interval} = y' \pm (t_{a/2,n-2})\,(S_e)\sqrt{1 + \frac{1}{n} + \frac{(x_o - \bar{x})^2}{\Sigma(x - \bar{x})^2}}$$

where the *t*-value is taken from the student *t* table at the end of the chapter, x_o is the specific *x* value given, and *n* is the number of observations. The farther away the x_o is from the average *x*, the wider the interval will be. This makes sense because the farther away from the average we are, the fewer observations we have on which to base a prediction.

For our example, assume that we would like a prediction interval of 95 percent (alpha is 5 percent); that is, the probability that an actual observation is outside the prediction interval due to random chance is 5 percent. A *t*-value for alpha/2 with $n - 2$ degrees of freedom means we are looking for a value for .05/2 at $15 - 2$ degrees of freedom. From the *t* table for .025 (which is $1.00 - .025 = .975$ in the table) and 13 degrees of freedom, we get 2.1604.

The computation of the limits is as follows on page 76:

EXHIBIT 3–12 Laser Etching Department (calculations for determining a prediction interval)

Month	*Y* Departmental Overhead Cost	*X* Machine Hours	$(x - \bar{x})$	$(x - \bar{x})^2$
1	$ 5,350	470	23	544
2	3,400	325	(122)	14,803
3	2,300	250	(197)	38,678
4	3,700	365	(82)	6,669
5	4,300	435	(12)	136
6	4,800	460	13	178
7	4,300	490	43	1,878
8	5,450	525	78	6,136
9	5,500	600	153	23,511
10	6,600	630	183	33,611
11	5,400	560	113	12,844
12	5,000	51 J	63	4,011
13	4,600	490	43	1,878
14	3,500	390	(57)	3,211
15	2,300	200	(247)	60,844
Sums	$66,500	6,700	(0)	208,933
Means	$ 4,433	446.67		

Interval calculations for a forecast of cost for 600 hours:

$$t_{a/2,n-2} = t_{.025,13} = 2.1604$$

Standard error of the estimate $= 351.13$

$$\sqrt{1 + \frac{1}{15} + \frac{(600 - 446.67)^2}{208,933.33}} = 1.0859$$

Interval estimate $= (2.1604)(351.13)(1.0859) = \underline{823.75}$

	Lower Limit	Upper Limit
Regression estimate at 600 hours	$5,901.00	$5,901.00
Interval adjustment taken from Exhibit 3–12	(−823.75)	823.75
Prediction interval or control limits	$5,077.25	$6,724.75

If the company chooses a prediction interval of 95 percent, any actual cost for 600 machine hours will fall in the range of $5,077.25 to $6,724.75 about 95 out of 100 times.

Standard Error of the Parameters.   If a and b were perfect predictors of fixed and variable costs, then there would be no residual error in the estimation of costs. We attribute all of the error to the estimate of b, which is thus a conservative measure of the potential error in variable cost. The standard error of the coefficient is the ratio of the residual squared errors in y to the square root of the mean square error of x:

$$\text{Standard error of } b: S_b = \frac{S_e}{\sqrt{\Sigma(x - \bar{x})^2}}$$

For the example data the standard error of the coefficient is equal to:

$$S_b = \frac{351.13}{\sqrt{208,993}} = .768$$

A 95 percent confidence interval on the b coefficient may be calculated as estimate plus and minus the t-value times the standard error (S_b):

	Lower Limit	Upper Limit
Regression coefficient	$5.5696	$5.5696
Interval adjustment (t-value $\times$ S_b)		
(2.1604 $\times$ .786)	(−1.6596)	1.6596
Coefficient confidence interval	$3.9100	$7.2292

ASSUMPTIONS AND LIMITATIONS

We made a number of assumptions in the earlier discussion. Because it is important to understand the assumptions and limitations of the methods that we use, this section discusses the major ones. We need to be aware of the potential problems and correct for them where appropriate.

Relevant Range

The **relevant range** is the range of activity over which the definitions of fixed and variable costs are valid. Because the data used in the cost analysis are taken from a range, extrapolating to activity levels outside this range can lead to misleading results. In our example, the relevant range is 200 to 630 hours. The relationship of costs and activity could well be nonlinear below 200 and above 630 machine hours. Thus, any estimates of fixed and variable cost should not be extended outside the relevant range.

Reasonableness of Relationship

The independent variable should have a **reasonableness of relationship** to the dependent variable. Thus, there should be a reasonable explanation as to why and how the activity causes the cost. For example, there may be a high level of association between the number of new houses built and the price per barrel of oil. Regression analysis shows that they are associated when, in fact, both housing starts and oil

EXHIBIT 3–13   Constant and Nonconstant Variances

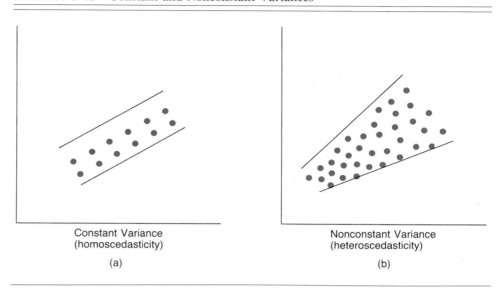

Constant Variance
(homoscedasticity)

(a)

Nonconstant Variance
(heteroscedasticity)

(b)

prices are caused by the general level of economic activity. A **spurious relationship** is one with a high association between two variables that are not related directly.

To ensure that a reasonable relationship exists, the costs and activities must be reviewed for plausibility. Is there some reason why a relationship between the two variables should exist? If a reason cannot be found, any regression results may lead to misunderstandings and inappropriate uses.

Representativeness of Observations

The data are assumed to represent the same population. Use only data that are representative of the period for which cost behavior is to be predicted. We call this **representativeness of observations.** Production processes and organizations change with time. Occasionally, unusual circumstances generate one or more outlier data points. Accountants typically omit outliers from the analysis because they believe that the results will be more representative. Statisticians are not in agreement as to whether this is a sound practice or not.

Constant Variance

We assume the spread of the observations around the regression line is constant throughout the entire range of observations. This means that differences from the line should be randomly and normally distributed throughout the range of activity. Exhibit 3–13(a) indicates constant variance or **homoscedasticity,** while Exhibit 3–13(b) shows a nonconstant variance or **heteroscedasticity.**

In many operations, higher variability in cost data may well occur at higher levels of activity, that is, heteroscedasticity, than at lower levels of activity. Heteroscedasticity biases the estimates toward the effects of the higher activity periods because the regression will place heavier weights on the higher activity values.

Time Independence

We assume that successive observations of the dependent variable are independent of each other. When successive observations of the dependent variable are not independent, the condition is known as **autocorrelation** or *serial correlation*. We can detect it by plotting the residuals across time and looking for patterns. For example, Exhibit 3–14(a) displays the residuals for the Laser Etching Department, and Exhibit

EXHIBIT 3–14   Analysis of Autocorrelation

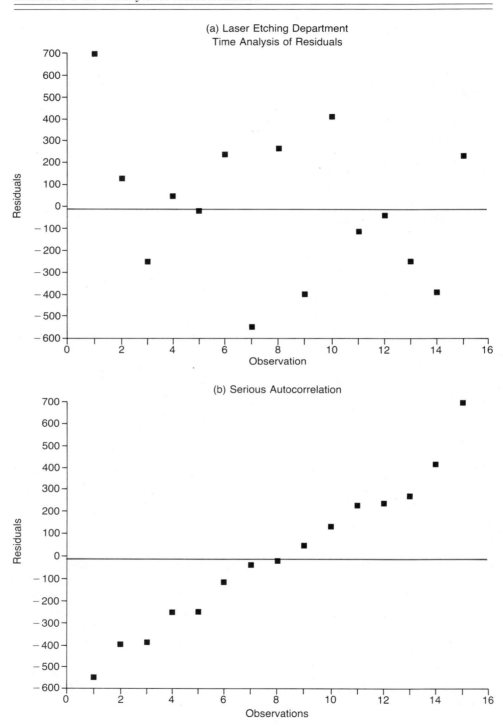

3–14(b) presents a set of residuals with high autocorrelation. With high autocorrelation, the errors are negative in the early periods and positive in the later periods, indicating that the estimates were too high for the early periods and too low for the later periods. The effect of the autocorrelation will be to understate the value of a and overstate the value of b. Thus, the estimate of fixed costs will be too low and the estimate of variable costs will be too high. The techniques to correct for this condition may be found in standard regression texts.[3] If you observe strong autocorrelation, then get the advice of a statistician on correction procedures.

Normality

Another assumption is **normality;** that is the residuals are assumed to be normally distributed. About 68 percent of the residuals should be smaller than the S_e and about 95 percent smaller than about twice the S_e. The normality assumption is necessary if we want to make probability statements using the standard error of the estimate or we want to compute confidence intervals for our cost estimates. Corrections for nonnormality are available, but they require the advice of an expert statistician.

SUMMARY

Cost behavior of individual and groups of costs have a significant impact on how costs are used in planning and control and decision-making activities. The common classifications of cost behavior are variable, fixed, semivariable, and step.

A number of approaches are available for analyzing costs into variable and fixed components. The approaches include account analysis, engineering approach, scattergraph and visual fit, high-low point method, representative points method, and regression analysis.

The regression approach not only yields a best-fitting equation for the cost data but also gives measures for goodness of fit and reliability of the estimates. These measures tell us how useful the regression equation may be and allow development of such helpful aids as confidence intervals.

SUMMARY OF FORMULAS

A number of mathematical and statistical formulas were presented throughout the chapter. This section summarizes those that are key to cost behavior analysis.

Visual Fit Method

1. Fixed costs are where the line crosses the left margin of graph.
2. Variable costs = Total costs − Fixed costs

High-Low Point Method

1. Calculating the variable cost *(b)* in the high-low method:

$$b = \frac{(\text{Cost at highest activity} - \text{Cost at lowest activity})}{(\text{Highest activity} - \text{Lowest activity})}$$

2. Calculating the fixed cost *(a)* in the high-low method:
   a = total cost at highest activity − $b \times$ highest activity
   = total cost at lowest activity − $b \times$ lowest activity

---

[3] For example, see J. Johnston, *Econometric Methods*, 3rd ed. (New York: McGraw-Hill, 1984) for a conceptual presentation, pp. 371–76, or statistical manuals for practical applications.

Regression Analysis

$$a = \bar{y} - b\bar{x}$$

$$b = \frac{\Sigma(x - \bar{x})(y - \bar{y})}{\Sigma(x - \bar{x})^2}$$

The bar above a variable indicates an average. Thus, $\bar{y}$ is the average y and is pronounced "y bar." The Σ indicates a summation across all observations.

Coefficient of determination (goodness of fit):

$$r^2 = 1 - \frac{\Sigma(y - y')^2}{\Sigma(y - \bar{y})^2}$$

Standard error of the estimate:

$$S_e = \sqrt{\frac{\Sigma(y - y')^2}{n - 2}}$$

Formulas for the upper and lower limits of a prediction interval:

$$\text{Interval} = y' \pm (t_{a/2, n-2})(S_e)\sqrt{1 + \frac{1}{n} + \frac{(x_o - \bar{x})^2}{\Sigma(x - \bar{x})^2}}$$

Standard error of the coefficient:

$$S_b = \frac{S_e}{\sqrt{\Sigma(x - \bar{x})^2}}$$

PROBLEM FOR REVIEW

Jerrelle Ricardi found the following costs and activity with respect to the Pressure Heating Department for the 10 months ending December 31, 19x4:

Month	Overhead Cost (y) (in thousands)	Tons of Product (x)	$(y - \bar{y})(x - \bar{x})$	$(x - \bar{x})^2$	$(y - \bar{y})^2$
March	$ 30	227	$ 261	2,830	$ 24
April	27	160	950	14,448	62
May	32	265	44	231	8
June	43	365	687	7,191	66
July	24	120	1,746	25,664	119
August	34	295	(13)	219	1
September	39	320	163	1,584	17
October	60	580	7,525	89,880	630
November	25	170	1,091	12,144	98
December	35	300	2	392	0
Totals	$349	2,802	$12,455	154,584	$1,025
Averages	$ 34.90	280.20			

REQUIRED

a. Using the high-low point method, compute an estimate of the fixed and variable costs.
b. Using the regression analysis, compute:
   1. Variable cost (b)
   2. Fixed cost (a)
   3. Coefficient of determination (r²)

4. Standard error of the estimate of total cost (S_e)

$$\text{(Note: the } \Sigma(y - y')^2 = \$21.352)$$

5. An upper and lower prediction interval of 95 percent for total costs of 500 tons of product
6. Standard error of the coefficient for variable cost (S_b)

SOLUTION

a. High-low point method:

Variable costs:

	October (High)	July (Low)	Division
Costs	$60	$24	$\dfrac{\$36}{460} = \$0.078$
Volume	580	120	

Fixed Costs:
From high point $60 − ($.078 × 580) $\doteq$ $14.7
From low point $24 − ($.078 × 120) $\doteq$ $14.7

b. Regression analysis
1. Variable cost

$$b = \frac{\$12,455}{154,584} = 0.0806$$

2. Fixed cost

$$a = \$34.90 - \$0.0806 \times 280.2 = \$12.316$$

3. Coefficient of determination:

$$r^2 = 1 - \frac{\$21.352}{\$1,024.900} = \underline{97.92\%}$$

4. Standard error of the estimate of total cost:

$$S_e = \sqrt{\frac{21.352}{10 - 2}} = \sqrt{2.66904} = \underline{\$1.634}$$

5. An upper and lower 95 percent prediction interval for total costs of 500 tons of product

$$t_{(.95/2,8)} = 2.306$$
$$y' = \$12.316 + \$.0806 \times 500 = \underline{\$52.602}$$
$$\text{Interval} = \pm\, 2.306 \times \$1.634 \times \sqrt{1 + \frac{1}{10} + \frac{(500 - 280.2)^2}{154,584}}$$
$$= \pm\, \$4.478$$

	Lower	Upper
Estimated	$52.602	$52.602
Interval	(4.478)	4.478
Cost interval	$48.124	$57.080

6. Standard error of the coefficient variable cost:

$$S_b = \frac{\$4.478}{\sqrt{\$154,584}} = \underline{0.0114}$$

KEY TERMS AND CONCEPTS	Variable cost (60)	Independent variable (69)
	Fixed cost (60)	Method of least squares (69)
	Capacity costs (61)	Regression line (70)
	Committed fixed cost (61)	Coefficient of determination (71)
	Discretionary fixed cost (61)	Standard error of the estimate (73)
	Semivariable cost (mixed cost) (62)	Degrees of freedom (73)
	Step cost (62)	Standard error of the estimate for the
	Cost estimation (63)	parameter b (76)
	Account analysis (63)	Relevant range (76)
	Engineering approach (64)	Reasonableness of relationship (76)
	Time and motion studies (65)	Spurious relationship (77)
	High-low point method (67)	Representativeness of observations (77)
	Representative points approach (68)	Homoscedasticity (77)
	Scattergraph and visual fit method (65)	Heteroscedasticity (77)
	Regression analysis (69)	Autocorrelation (77)
	Linear regression (69)	Normality (79)
	Dependent variable (69)	

ADDITIONAL READINGS

Ayers, James B. "Understanding Your Cost Drivers—The Key to Disciplined Planning." *Journal of Cost Management,* Fall 1988, pp. 6–15.

Hakala, Gregory. "Measuring Costs with Machine Hours." *Management Accounting,* October 1985, p. 57.

Johnson, H. Thomas, and Dennis A. Loewe. "How Weyerhaeuser Manages Corporate Overhead Costs." *Management Accounting,* August 1987, pp. 20–26.

Jones, Lou. "Competitive Cost Analysis at Caterpillar." *Management Accounting,* October 1988.

Lesser, Frederic E. "Will the Real Cost Please Stand Up?" *Management Accounting,* November 1986, pp. 29–31.

Mackey, Jim. "11 Key Issues in Manufacturing Accounting." *Management Accounting,* January 1987, pp. 32–37.

Nurnberg, Hugo. "An Unrecognized Ambiguity of the High-Low Method." *Journal of Business Finance and Accounting,* Winter 1977, pp. 427–30.

Shank, John K.; Vijay Govindarajan; and Eric Spiegel. "Strategic Cost Analysis: A Case Study." *Journal of Cost Management,* Fall 1988, pp. 25–32.

Singh, Prem S., and Gordon L. Chapman. "Is Linear Approximation Good Enough?" *Management Accounting,* January 1978, pp. 36–39.

REVIEW QUESTIONS

1. Identify the four basic cost behavior patterns. For each one indicate how total and unit costs change as activity levels change.
2. Explain the difference between committed fixed costs and discretionary fixed costs.
3. Describe the two major steps involved in the account analysis method. Explain under what circumstances this method is useful.
4. Under what conditions would the engineering method be preferred to other cost estimation techniques?
5. What are the purposes of time and motion studies in the engineering method?
6. Why is the engineering method not usually applicable to analyzing production overhead?
7. List the steps for preparing an estimate of fixed and variable costs using the scattergraph method.
8. When using the high-low method, what criteria should be used in selecting the two points?

9. Explain how the high-low method and the representative points approach are similar.
10. Distinguish between a dependent variable and an independent variable in a cost-estimating equation.
11. Why should we be careful in interpreting the intercept as the fixed cost at zero volume?
12. What is the impact of random data input errors on the goodness of fit of the cost equation?
13. The scattergraph and regression methods seem to go hand in hand. Explain.
14. Briefly explain three assumptions of regression analysis.
15. Why is only one observation of cost required to estimate the average total cost, but two observations are required to estimate fixed and variable costs? *Hint:* How do we calculate the degrees of freedom?
16. What is the coefficient of determination and what range of values can it take?
17. What is the correlation coefficient and what range of values can it take?
18. Does a high correlation between x and y prove that a change in x causes a change in y? Explain.
19. What does the standard error of the estimate measure and how can it be used by the accountant?
20. Why is it important that costs be recorded in the proper accounting period? At which points during the accounting period is it most critical to track transactions and ensure that they end up in the proper period?
21. Why should cost data representing periods of unusual circumstances be excluded from the cost behavior analysis?
22. Why should depreciation and applied overhead be generally excluded from cost behavior studies?

DISCUSSION QUESTIONS

23. Describe ways in which complexity can influence the costs of producing a product. Compare a product produced with 2 parts versus one that requires 1,000 parts. How might part numbers be used as a measure of activity?
24. It is common in practice for monthly data to be unadjusted for accruals (wages, interest, and the like). These adjustments occur quarterly. Discuss the potential impact of this on cost behavior analysis.
25. It is common for employee and officer raises to occur annually. What impact will this have on a regression analysis of monthly data that spans several years?
26. Develop a theory for how the number of different materials purchased from different vendors will increase the cost of inspection of incoming materials, the warehousing function, and the purchasing department.
27. Someone has said, "People behave or misbehave, costs only respond." What might the speaker have meant by this? What does this imply we are really doing with cost behavior analysis?
28. Why might a military academy be less costly to administer than a state university of the same size in terms of student body? What does this imply with respect to an analysis of the cost of education with number of students as an activity measure?
29. If fixed costs do not change with respect to volume, why are the fixed costs of a large retailer much higher than those of a small store?
30. Labor costs are very sticky downward because management is reluctant to lay off skilled workers quickly. Why should we adjust the labor cost data (or analysis method) for this fact?
31. For natural resource companies, the costs of mineral rights, permanent equipment placed in a field, and labor to get the field ready for production are included in the cost of the resources to be depleted. Depletion amounts are normally on the units-of-production method. If depletion makes up a large portion of the costs, why will the variable cost estimates be biased for natural resource companies?
32. Why might the estimate of a new product cost developed by a person from marketing

using the representative points approach differ from that developed by an accountant for the same new product?

33. When using historical data to predict the cost behavior pattern, it is possible to have an *a* coefficient that is negative. What can it mean when the estimate of fixed costs is negative?

EXERCISES

3–1. Troublesome Fixed Costs. Heavenly Peace Cemetery provides sequestered burial places and maintains the grounds in an attractive manner. Graves are dug, foundations for monuments are installed, markers and other items are sold, and a crematory with related facilities is operated.

The crematory has been in operation for four years. Costs of operating the crematory are mostly fixed; the major cost is for facilities. Salaried personnel do what little work is required and spend most of their time in other cemetery operations. Other costs are variable but represent less than 3 percent of the total costs. The total costs for the crematory this past year were $50,000, and only 50 cremations were performed.

Ashes Walker, president of Heavenly Peace, believes that the crematory should be dismantled and scrapped. He says that the $1,000 cost per cremation is too high to be profitable; Heavenly Peace cannot charge enough to cover those costs. Dennis Tees, the accountant, says the $1,000 figure is not a good number to use for such a decision.

REQUIRED:
a. Discuss generally the problems created for decision-making when fixed costs are converted to a per unit basis.
b. Explain how you could use a knowledge of cost behavior patterns to help with analyzing the costs of the crematory.

3–2. Account Analysis. The following is a partial list of account titles found in the chart of accounts for Hi-Plains Manufacturing Company:
1. Indirect materials.
2. Depreciation on office equipment (double-declining-balance method).
3. Depreciation on factory equipment (units-of-production method).
4. Direct labor.
5. FICA taxes on direct labor payroll.
6. Rent on finished goods inventory warehouse.
7. Repairs and maintenance of factory equipment.
8. Fringe benefits for office workers (as a percent of salaries).
9. Factory utilities.
10. Insurance expense—Comprehensive on all facilities.

REQUIRED:
a. Classify each of the accounts according to cost behavior: variable, fixed, semivariable, or other.
b. For each variable and semivariable cost, with what would the cost vary?
c. Under what conditions would an account analysis approach be appropriate for identifying cost behavior patterns?

3–3. Account Analysis. You have been drafted into being social chair of the local United Way campaign. Part of this position requires you to arrange for the winter dinner dance for about 220 people. Renting a hall and a kitchen at the convention center will cost $250. The hall will seat up to 300 people. Decorations for the head table, which will seat 16 people, will cost $50. Decorations for each table will cost $10 and each table will seat up to 8 people. You hire for $25 the choir director from one of the local high schools to play piano and sing (softly). The band for the dance costs $250. Typesetting and printing 300 copies of the program costs $75. You expect to use voluntary help—Scouts, Campfire girls, and Explorers—to help set up the meal and serve the dinner. These people are to be given a meal for their trouble. You expect 25 people to help serve. The caterer has offered a full-course meal for $10 per person, but you must guarantee one week in advance. At the time the guarantee was required, you had 205 confirmed people attending for the dinner, including all speakers and dignitaries, but not including helpers. You guarantee for 224 people plus the helpers. Assume that the volunteer servers will eat in the kitchen.

REQUIRED:
a. Estimate the total cost of the winter dinner dance.
b. Estimate the total costs if you had to guarantee for 272 people.

3–4. Account Analysis. Sally Johns is the director of the Kiddo Care preschool and is planning a field trip. The class will visit the Metro Zoo, the Outback Museum, and the Astro Planetarium. All 36 students in the class want to go on the field trip, but 7 students are not allowed to go for various reasons. Three parents have volunteered to drive and help Ms. Johns during the field trip. Vans will be rented at a cost of $50 per day to transport the students and volunteers. Each van will hold 12 people, including the driver. The school will provide canned drinks at a cost of $.37 for everyone. Admission to the zoo is $1.00 for children and $2.50 for adults. The planetarium usually costs $2 per person, but Ms. Johns was able to get a special rate of $30 for the whole group because she made early reservations. The school is paying for the children, the volunteers, and Ms. Johns' expenses.

(B. George)

REQUIRED:
a. What is the total cost for the trip?
b. What would the total cost be if all the children went and four parents volunteered?

3–5. High-Low Method. The Rolling Co. produces tire rims for motorcycles at its plant in Tuna, Texas. One of its costs is a machine that forges the rims. The company would like to estimate the costs associated with using this machine. The costs and number of rims produced for the first seven months of the current year are:

(M. Kubinski)

Month	No. of Rims Produced	Production Cost	Cost per Rim
1	38,400	$5,550	$0.1081
2	36,750	5,400	0.1088
3	40,025	5,700	0.1074
4	35,885	5,300	0.1029
5	36,780	5,450	0.1101
6	39,000	5,650	0.1090
7	39,875	5,575	0.1047

REQUIRED:
a. Estimate the fixed and variable costs using the high-low method.
b. Estimate the total cost of operating the machine for 40,000 rims.

3–6. High-Low Method. Johnny Darling owns and operates Helicopter Ski in Jackson Hole, Wyoming. During winter months, he provides advanced skiers with group trips to the tops of various powder-covered peaks where he lets them out with one of the three paid guides. His business has the reputation in the area of giving locals and visitors alike the most extensive and invigorating powder-skiing adventures in the region. For 10 of the weeks that he was in business last year, Johnny had the following total costs and number of skiers:

(P. McIntosh)

Week	Total Cost	No. of Skiers
1	$ 1,570	162
2	1,640	174
3	1,840	186
4	1,800	178
5	2,060	202
6	2,440	238
7	2,360	230
8	1,910	188
9	1,890	190
10	1,880	186
	$19,390	1,934

REQUIRED:

Using the high-low method, estimate the:

a. Variable and fixed costs.

b. The total costs for 200 skiers.

3–7. High-Low Method.   The following amounts relate to monthly overhead costs and units produced for Skateboard City, Unlimited:

(P. Williams)

Month	Overhead	Units	Unit Cost
January	$9,300	193	$48.19
February	8,000	160	50.00
March	7,200	141	51.06
April	8,700	170	51.18
May	9,100	182	50.00
June	7,800	153	50.98
Average	$8,350	167	$50.15

REQUIRED:

a. Using the high-low method, find variable and fixed costs.

b. What would be the overhead cost for 150 units?

c. What would be the problem with estimating the cost for 500 units?

3–8. High-Low Forecasting.   Mesquite Smoked, Inc., is a meat processing company that specializes in smoking processed meats. Units are expressed in terms of 100 pounds (cwt.). The actual production costs of one smoking process for 13 weeks are given below:

Week	Production in Cwt.	Production Costs
1	210	$2,010
2	200	3,200
3	240	2,990
4	250	2,110
5	230	2,655
6	220	2,360
7	260	1,930
8	300	3,530
9	320	3,425
10	290	2,345
11	310	1,370
12	280	2,485
13	270	2,600

REQUIRED:

a. Develop a cost-estimating formula based on the high-low method.

b. Plot the data on graph paper.

c. If your high-low formula were used, what is the forecasted production cost for 310 cwt.? How does this answer compare with the actual production costs?
d. Would you recommend using the high-low method for the above set of data? Explain.

3–9. High-Low Method. Dr. Giselle A. Zankl is a pediatrician practicing medicine in Angola, Africa. The Zankl Clinic is supported by Bauman Medizin, a West German foundation, and the Barsch Gruppe of Vienna, Austria. Bauman Medizin will pay for the fixed costs of the Zankl Clinic plus 5 percent. The Barsch Gruppe has agreed to reimburse the variable costs of providing the medical care plus 1 mark per patient. At year end Dr. Zankl must report on fixed and variable costs and request reimbursement for the clinic. Dr. Zankl is independently wealthy and covers her own living expenses. The excess of clinic revenues over expenses is used to purchase equipment. During 19x0 the total clinic expenses and patients seen are:

(S. Bradley)

	Total Costs (in West German Marks)	Number of Patients
January	6,500	410
February	5,908	368
March	5,615	310
April	5,090	296
May	4,912	273
June	4,600	291
July	4,450	283
August	4,130	252
September	4,510	301
October	5,215	346
November	5,916	390
December	6,310	380
Total	63,156	3,900
Averages	5,263	325

REQUIRED:
Using the high-low method, estimate the:
a. Variable costs per patient.
b. Amount to be billed to the Barsch Gruppe for the 3,900 patients.
c. Fixed costs per month.
d. Amount to be billed to Bauman Medizin for the 12 months.
e. What amount will be available to purchase medical equipment for the clinic?

3–10. High-Low and Visual Fit. The X-ray lab for the Wagon Mound Metropolitan Hospital has the following costs and number of X rays for the first 10 months of the current year:

Month	X-ray Costs	Number of X rays
1	$ 20,325	768
2	20,580	703
3	19,829	699
4	19,917	790
5	20,035	702
6	16,705	558
7	17,802	641
8	21,359	802
9	18,893	634
10	18,462	565
Total	$193,907	6,862
Averages	$ 19,390.70	686.20

REQUIRED:

a. Using the high-low method:
   1. Estimate the variable and fixed costs.
   2. Estimate the total X-ray cost for 686 X rays.
b. Plot the data and visually fit a line. From this line:
   1. Estimate the variable and fixed costs.
   2. Estimate the total X-ray cost for 686 X rays.

3–11. Describing Regression Results.   As controller of Leafy Tree Top Landscaping, you have been concerned about the cost behavior pattern of overhead costs. You gathered the appropriate data and asked a statistician friend of yours to perform a regression analysis. She has given you the following results:

$$Y = 2,500 + 8.50X$$
$$r^2 = .81$$
$$S_e = 25.75$$

where

$$Y = \text{Overhead cost}$$
$$X = \text{Labor hours}$$

REQUIRED:

a. Explain the meaning of the equation: $Y = 2,500 + 8.50X$.
b. What is the percentage of the variance of overhead cost that is associated with changes in labor hours?
c. The president wants to know what S_e means and how he might use it in evaluating actions. Give him a brief answer.

PROBLEMS

3–12. Simple Regression Analysis.   Cindy Petrie, chief accountant for Mexicale Fabricators, is implementing a budgeting system and needs to know the cost behavior pattern of many production overhead costs. The actual costs to lubricate machines in the grinding department for different levels of machine hour activity are:

Machine Hours	Cost
580	$3,350
590	3,380
650	3,500
670	3,600
710	3,740
720	3,750
750	3,860
800	4,200
820	4,600
840	4,800

Cindy has asked you to perform an analysis of this data and give her a report on the cost behavior pattern.

REQUIRED:

a. Calculate a cost-estimating function using regression analysis.
b. Calculate the coefficient of determination and the standard error of the estimate.
c. Present your reasons as to why this cost-estimating function is or is not a good fit of the data.

d. Compute variable and fixed components of cost using the high-low method and compare with your answer in *(a)* above.

3–13. Analyzing Costs through Account Analysis.   The following is a partial list of account titles appearing in the chart of accounts for the Dalia Agricultural Supply Company:

1. Direct materials
2. Supervisory salaries—Factory
3. Heat, light, and power—Factory
4. Depreciation on the building
5. Depreciation on equipment and machinery (units-of-production method)
6. Janitorial labor
7. Repair maintenance supplies
8. Pension costs (as a percentage of employee wages and salaries)
9. FICA tax expense
10. Insurance on property
11. Sales commissions
12. Travel expenses—Sales
13. Telephone expenses—General and administrative
14. Magazine advertising
15. Bad debt expense
16. Photocopying expense
17. Audit fees
18. Dues and subscriptions
19. Depreciation on furniture and fixtures (double-declining-balance method)
20. Group medical and dental insurance expense

REQUIRED:

a. Discuss each account title in terms of whether the account represents a variable, fixed, or semivariable cost.
   1. If you suggest a variable or semivariable cost, what would the cost vary with?
   2. If you suggest a fixed cost, is it a committed or discretionary cost?
b. Explain the problems associated with using the account analysis approach to establish cost behavior patterns.

3–14. High-Low Forecasting.   Robin's Reliable Office Systems sells and services office copiers. It has a maintenance contract available for businesses desiring that service. With an agreement, a business may call for service at any time and pay only for consumable items, such as toner and developer. Labor and parts are covered by the contract. Robin wants to evaluate her pricing for the maintenance contract to determine a profitable pricing policy for anticipated growth in her business. She asked her accountant, Charlotte Webb, to analyze cost information on service calls. Charlotte has gathered the following data for four weeks in April and four weeks in October:

	Number of Service Calls	Total Service Costs
April:	100	$3,000
	125	3,500
	150	4,000
	175	4,500
October:	225	$5,800
	250	6,300
	275	6,800
	300	7,300

She has come to you with a request to help her determine the cost behavior associated with service calls.

REQUIRED:

a. Plot the data on graph paper.

b. Considering all eight weeks, determine the variable and fixed cost components of service calls using the high-low method.

c. Using the results in *(b)* above, what service costs would you forecast for 250 service calls? Compare this to the actual results in the data for October and note any difference.

d. Is your answer in *(c)* above useful for forecasting? Explain.

e. What recommendations would you make for achieving better results than that produced by the high-low method?

3–15. Basic Linear Regression.   The Crazy Charlie Skydiving School has collected expense and passenger data for the past 10 weeks. The following data have been reported after calculations have been performed:

(M. Ray)

Total costs	$47,055
Total passengers	310
Average cost per week	4,705.50
Average passengers per week	31
Sum $(x - \bar{x})(y - \bar{y})$	1,482,897
Sum $(x - \bar{x})^2$	9,914

REQUIRED: Using the least squares method:

a. Compute the fixed and variable costs for Crazy Charlie's Skydiving School.

b. Estimate the total cost if 43 people decide to "challenge the sky" during a week.

3–16. High-Low Method.   Willie Company produces baseball gloves for major league baseball teams. The company works out of a small shop in Cincinnati, Ohio. It had the following cost and number of gloves for 19x1:

(G. Ochotorena)

Month	Number of Gloves Produced	Production Cost	Cost per Glove
1	1,043	$ 20,100	$19.27
2	1,260	20,650	16.39
3	1,335	21,875	16.39
4	1,501	27,200	18.12
5	1,370	22,300	16.28
6	1,610	28,980	18.00
7	1,480	26,200	17.70
8	1,460	26,700	18.29
9	1,095	19,975	18.24
10	1,063	18,620	17.52
11	915	16,950	18.52
12	940	17,500	18.62
Total	15,072	$267,050	$17.72

REQUIRED:

a. Using the high-low method compute the fixed and variable costs.

b. Estimate the costs for 1000 gloves.

3-17. High-Low and Visual Fit.   The Food Service Department for the Wagon Mound Metropolitan Hospital has the following costs and number of patient days for the first 10 months of the current year:

	Food Cost	Days of Patients
1	$ 67,664	6,753
2	57,675	4,172
3	55,021	4,670
4	66,273	5,810
5	64,346	6,070
6	58,222	4,410
7	68,582	6,312
8	74,792	7,349
9	66,104	5,663
10	69,853	6,257
Total	$648,532	57,466
Averages	$ 64,853.20	5,746.60

REQUIRED:
a. Using the high-low method:
  1. Estimate the variable cost.
  2. Estimate the fixed cost.
  3. Estimate the total food cost for 5,747 patient days.
b. Plot the data and visually fit a line.
  1. Estimate the variable cost.
  2. Estimate the fixed cost.
  3. Estimate the total food cost for 5,747 patient days.

3–18. Choice of Activity Measure.   The company is revising its cost accounting system and wants measures of activity for each department that best relate to incurrence of departmental overhead costs. Your analysis shows that direct labor hours and machine hours are the likely predictors of overhead costs. You have searched through the accounting data and have 15 observations representing weekly periods.

Week	Machine Hours	Direct Labor Hours	Overhead Costs
1	120	200	$4,460
2	150	210	5,225
3	190	205	5,900
4	160	210	5,350
5	200	230	6,125
6	210	235	6,300
7	230	240	6,660
8	220	235	6,450
9	180	205	5,730
10	170	210	5,560
11	140	200	5,050
12	130	195	4,800
13	160	190	5,410
14	180	205	5,760
15	195	210	6,000

REQUIRED:
Choose the measure of activity that is the better predictor of overhead costs. Justify your answer.

3–19. Simple Regression Analysis.   VIDEO EXPERTS has developed a good reputation for repairing and servicing VCRs. The company began only with the intention of renting video tapes. However, many companies selling VCRs had no local servicing; everything was sent away for work. Ross Duncan, one of the partners, enjoyed repair work, so he started tinkering just to help loyal customers. Work was expanding rapidly, and he hired and trained several people to handle repair work. Ross is not certain he is charging a price to cover costs of service and repair. His accountant has developed the following data from the previous 13 four-week periods:

Period	Labor Hours	Costs
1	20	$245
2	26	324
3	29	328
4	31	318
5	34	393
6	38	408
7	41	403
8	43	464
9	46	520
10	50	522
11	53	545
12	55	587
13	60	667

REQUIRED:
a. Calculate a cost-estimating formula using regression analysis.
b. Calculate the coefficient of determination and the standard error of the estimate.
c. Evaluate the results of your review for goodness of fit and usefulness.
d. For this set of data, calculate a prediction interval of 95 percent for 35 labor hours.

3–20. Regression Analysis.   The Flying Tomato Pizza Co. is a chain of Italian restaurants located in a five-state area. One of the most successful locations for the company has been near colleges and universities.

The management of the Flying Tomato would like to obtain an estimate of certain monthly expenditures to provide to new establishments for use in budgeting. One particular estimate that management is interested in is the monthly advertising expenditures of a restaurant near a college or university campus. After considering the nature of advertising to student customers, management decided that advertising could be closely related to two factors: the size of the student population and the number of competitor restaurants near the campus. The following data were obtained from 10 Flying Tomato outlets located near universities:

(S. Whitecotton)

Restaurant	Monthly Advertising	Number of Competitors	Student Population
1	$400	2	3,000
2	470	3	5,000
3	460	4	4,000
4	500	3	6,000
5	700	4	8,000
6	650	5	8,000
7	800	4	16,000
8	795	5	20,000
9	900	6	23,000
10	970	7	27,000

REQUIRED:
a. Prepare two scattergraph plots, showing the relationship between advertising expenditures and competitors and student population. Based on these graphs, which do you think would be a better indicator of advertising?

b. Perform a regression analysis based on each criterion and give the equations for estimating advertising expenditures.

c. How much would you budget for advertising if you were located near a university with 13,000 students? If there were eight nearby competitors?

d. Calculate the coefficient of determination for each set of data. According to this measure, what is a better indicator of advertising, student population or number of competitors?

3–21. High-Low and Regression Methods.   Turrichi, Inc., is based in Savannah, Georgia. The company has 12 exclusive clothing stores located in larger shopping malls throughout the Southeast. In planning new store locations, the company would like to have a good model to predict general and administration (G & A) expenses as a function of sales. They notice that the average total expense as a percentage of sales is 10.1 percent, but the numbers vary from 9.0 to 12.3 percent (see schedule below).

Store	G & A Expense (in millions)	Sales Volume (in millions)	Expense Percentage
1	$1.49	$12.16	12.3
2	1.61	13.10	12.3
3	2.27	23.78	9.5
4	1.47	12.75	11.5
5	1.85	20.00	9.3
6	1.44	15.90	9.1
7	1.63	13.70	11.9
8	2.28	23.64	9.6
9	2.11	20.23	10.4
10	1.84	18.22	10.1
11	2.01	21.48	9.4
12	1.85	20.53	9.0
Averages	$1.82	$17.96	10.1

REQUIRED:

a. Using the high-low method, find the fixed and variable cost for general and administrative expenses per dollar of sales.

b. Using the least squares method, find the fixed and variable costs for general and administrative expenses per dollar of sales.

c. Compare answers and explain the differences.

3–22. Goodness of Fit.   Video Junction is a video rental with five stores located in Idaho. It hopes to expand to cities in Montana. Data have been collected on total costs per month and rentals by store. The following simple linear regression results have been obtained:

(J. Fuller)

Observations	5
Constant	$2,600
X coefficient	$4.99
Average y	57,474
Average x	8,949
Sum $(y - y')^2$	36,754
Sum $(y - \bar{y})^2$	515,515
Sum $(x - \bar{x})^2$	295,559

REQUIRED:

a. Calculate the following:
   1. Coefficient of determination (r^2).
   2. Standard error of the estimate.

b. Calculate an estimate of total cost and a 90 percent confidence interval for the following rentals per month:
1. 2,500
2. 11,555

3–23. Goodness of Fit. You have collected data for total delivery costs and number of deliveries for 30 vehicles in the North Dallas Sales District. To this data you have applied simple linear regression and have the following results:

Observations	30
Constant	$3,499
X coefficient	$6.58
Average X	6,635
Average y	$47,157
Sum $(y - y')^2$	43,652
Sum $(y - \bar{y})^2$	498,002
Sum $(x - \bar{x})^2$	312,312

REQUIRED:
a. Coefficient of determination (r^2).
b. Standard error of the estimate.
c. Calculate an estimate and an upper and lower 95 percent confidence interval for the following deliveries per year:
1. 2,819
2. 6,635
3. 10,215

3–24. Regression Analysis. UROK, Inc., is in the business of servicing the small number of home-owned nuclear reactors in the Chicago region. Because of the nature of the business, it is required that the equipment in each service vehicle be recertified prior to each house call.

The following data on costs and service calls were collected by UROK over the past 12 months.

(P. Hicks)

	Vehicle Equipment Service Cost	Number of Calls
October 19x4	$ 4,600	23
November	3,300	14
December	3,500	17
January 19x5	4,170	21
February	5,420	28
March	7,010	49
April	5,720	32
May	6,780	42
June	3,650	18
July	3,400	16
August	4,650	24
September	5,170	26
Totals	$57,370	310

REQUIRED:
a. Using regression analysis, compute a cost function for vehicle equipment service cost.
b. Compute the coefficient of determination (r^2). Evaluate the adequacy of the fit.
c. Compute the standard error of the estimate.
d. Estimate the costs for 50 service calls. Find a 95 percent confidence interval for the estimate.

3–25. Regression Analysis. Neeves Co. of Paris produces plastic cups using a thermo-form method. The company is a major supplier of disposable containers for the European Economic Community.

The cups are molded from plastic sheets that have been preheated. After molding, the cups are labeled and shipped. The following information is the overhead cost and number of direct labor hours for the past 12 months (in French francs):

(S. Neeves)

	Overhead Costs	Direct Labor Hours
July 19x2	711,000 fr.	600
August	705,000	750
September	756,000	830
October	813,000	880
November	740,000	680
December	830,000	900
January 19x3	845,000	910
February	900,000	1,120
March	867,000	920
April	880,000	970
May	891,000	1,050
June	905,000	1,200
Totals	9,843,000 fr.	10,810

REQUIRED:

a. Calculate the constant and slope using regression analysis.
b. Find the coefficient of determination and the standard error of the estimate.
c. Evaluate the adequacy of the fit.
d. Find a 95 percent confidence interval for estimated overhead cost at 1,080 direct labor hours.

3–26. Regression Analysis. Dr. Brian Cairnes recently purchased Fred's Pest Control of Akron, Ohio. The business specializes in the control of fire ants and termites. Currently, the company has three employees: two exterminators and a receptionist/bookkeeper. Two dogs with very sensitive smell are kept to help locate hives.

The expenses of operation include wages, chemicals, rent, utilities, and dog care. Dr. Cairnes has asked you to study the costs to help determine how the costs of operation vary with volume. The following data have been compiled:

(P. Hutchinson)

Week	Costs	Hours Billed
1	$1,350	84.00
2	1,110	63.75
3	1,522	97.50
4	1,101	65.25
5	1,058	71.25
6	1,253	78.75
7	1,522	92.25
8	1,755	112.50
9	1,221	75.00
10	1,135	66.00
11	1,634	86.25
12	1,025	72.75
Totals	$15,686	965.25

REQUIRED:

a. Calculate the constant and slope using regression analysis.

b. Find the coefficient of determination and the standard error of the estimate.

c. Evaluate the adequacy of the fit.

d. Find a 95 percent confidence interval for estimated overhead cost at 78 billable hours.

3–27. Regression Analysis. Unidraft Company, a consumer product design firm, has just completed its fiscal year ending December 31, 19x3. There appeared to be large variation in the reported costs for the months. This concerned Marla Koepp, the partner in charge.

Ernest Sandoval, an outside consultant, collected the data listed here. It seemed to Mr. Sandoval that there was little cost control by the firm. He believed that budgeting costs by the number of active accounts being worked during a month should be very useful. He now needs the proper analysis to support this conclusion.

(D. Gomez)

	Design Cost	Number of Active Accounts
January 19x3	$ 7,000	600
February	8,000	700
March	7,200	650
April	8,300	800
May	7,600	750
June	8,100	700
July	7,000	750
August	7,800	750
September	10,000	900
October	8,500	850
November	5,500	550
December	7,000	600
Totals	$92,000	8,600

REQUIRED:

a. Calculate the constant and slope using regression analysis.

b. Find the coefficient of determination and the standard error of the estimate.

c. Evaluate the adequacy of the fit.

d. Which month or months should be investigated using the criterion of one standard error of the estimate?

EXTENDED APPLICATIONS

3–28. Cutoff and Clerical Errors. Shirley Jackson was examining the use of surgical supplies at Methodist Hospital. The hospital has six general surgery rooms and four specialized rooms. From the records she has gathered the following data:

	Surgical Supplies	Surgery Hours	Cost per Hour
March 19x7	$10,210	334	$30.57
April	8,033	270	29.75
May	5,962	178	33.49
June	10,475	428	24.47
July	13,986	386	36.23
August	7,034	320	21.98
September	18,854	486	38.79
October	7,437	239	31.12
November	15,176	152	99.84

	Surgical Supplies	Surgery Hours	Cost per Hour
	$5,358	166	$32.28
January 19x8	5,784	207	27.94
February	11,184	354	31.59
March	10,521	346	30.41
April	9,101	288	31.60
May	11,962	370	32.33
June	5,791	247	23.45
July	14,439	247	58.46
August	7,585	430	17.64
September	15,515	328	47.30
October	5,625	211	26.66
November	10,366	368	28.17
Averages	$10,019	303	$33.11

REQUIRED:

a. Prepare a simple linear regression of surgical supplies on the hours of monthly surgical activity. Evaluate and interpret the results.

b. Using the regression in part a., find and list the errors for each of the months. Which months appear likely to have errors in data? (Identify all errors whose absolute value is greater than the standard error.)

c. Ms. Jackson checked the data entry and found the following keying errors:

   November 19x7 hours should be 512, not 152.
   July 19x8 hours should be 427, not 247.

   Correct these errors and rerun the regression. Evaluate and interpret the results.

d. Using the regression in part c., find and list the errors for each of the months. Which months appear likely to have errors in data? (Identify all errors whose absolute value is greater than the standard error.)

e. With some effort Ms. Jackson found that there were some problems with the data for the vacation months during each of the years. She found that for the surgical supplies:

June 19x7 usage recorded in July	$2,520
July 19x7 usage recorded in August	280
August 19x7 usage recorded in September	3,602
December 19x7 usage recorded in January 19x8	408
June 19x8 usage recorded in July	2,608
July 19x8 usage recorded in August	229
August 19x8 usage recorded in September	6,002

   Correct the errors and rerun the regression. Evaluate and interpret the results.

f. What is the effect of keying and cut-off errors on the regression results? Specifically, what is the effect on explained variation, fixed costs, and variable costs?

t — Value Table
(student's t distribution)

					Quantiles					
d.f.	.60	.75	.90	.95	.975	.99	.995	.999	.9995	.9999
1	.3249	1.0000	3.0777	6.3138	12.706	31.821	63.657	318.31	636.62	3183.1
2	.2887	.8165	1.8856	2.9200	4.3027	6.9646	9.9248	22.327	31.599	70.700
3	.2767	.7649	1.6377	2.3534	3.1824	4.5407	5.8409	10.215	12.924	22.204
4	.2707	.7407	1.5332	2.1318	2.7764	3.7469	4.6041	7.1732	8.6103	13.034
5	.2672	.7267	1.4759	2.0150	2.5706	3.3649	4.0321	5.8934	6.8688	9.6776
6	.2648	.7176	1.4398	1.9432	2.4469	3.1427	3.7074	5.2076	5.9588	8.0248
7	.2632	.7111	1.4149	1.8946	2.3646	2.9980	3.4995	4.7853	5.4079	7.0634
8	.2619	.7064	1.3968	1.8595	2.3060	2.8965	3.3554	4.5008	5.0413	6.4420
9	.2610	.7027	1.3830	1.8331	2.2622	2.8214	3.2498	4.2968	4.7809	6.0101
10	.2602	.6998	1.3722	1.8125	2.2281	2.7638	3.1693	4.1437	4.5869	5.6938
11	.2596	.6974	1.3634	1.7959	2.2010	2.7181	3.1058	4.0247	4.4370	5.4528
12	.2590	.6955	1.3562	1.7823	2.1788	2.6810	3.0545	3.9296	4.3178	5.2633
13	.2586	.6938	1.3502	1.7709	2.1604	2.6503	3.0123	3.8520	4.2208	5.1106
14	.2582	.6924	1.3450	1.7613	2.1448	2.6245	2.9768	3.7874	4.1405	4.9850
15	.2579	.6912	1.3406	1.7531	2.1314	2.6025	2.9467	3.7328	4.0728	4.8800
16	.2576	.6901	1.3368	1.7459	2.1199	2.5835	2.9208	3.6862	4.0150	4.7909
17	.2573	.6892	1.3334	1.7396	2.1098	2.5669	2.8982	3.6458	3.9651	4.7144
18	.2571	.6884	1.3304	1.7341	2.1009	2.5524	2.8784	3.6105	3.9216	4.6480
19	.2569	.6876	1.3277	1.7291	2.0930	2.5395	2.8609	3.5794	3.8834	4.5899
20	.2567	.6870	1.3253	1.7247	2.0860	2.5280	2.8453	3.5518	3.8495	4.5385
21	.2566	.6864	1.3232	1.7207	2.0796	2.5176	2.8314	3.5272	3.8193	4.4929
22	.2564	.6858	1.3212	1.7171	2.0739	2.5083	2.8188	3.5050	3.7921	4.4520
23	.2563	.6853	1.3195	1.7139	2.0687	2.4999	2.8073	3.4850	3.7676	4.4152
24	.2562	.6848	1.3178	1.7109	2.0639	2.4922	2.7969	3.4668	3.7454	4.3819
25	.2561	.6844	1.3163	1.7081	2.0595	2.4851	2.7874	3.4502	3.7251	4.3517
26	.2560	.6840	1.3150	1.7056	2.0555	2.4786	2.7787	3.4350	3.7066	4.3240
27	.2559	.6837	1.3137	1.7033	2.0518	2.4727	2.7707	3.4210	3.6896	4.2987
28	.2558	.6834	1.3125	1.7011	2.0484	2.4671	2.7633	3.4082	3.6739	4.2754
29	.2557	.6830	1.3114	1.6991	2.0452	2.4620	2.7564	3.3962	3.6594	4.2539
30	.2556	.6828	1.3104	1.6973	2.0423	2.4573	2.7500	3.3852	3.6460	4.2340
31	.2555	.6825	1.3095	1.6955	2.0395	2.4528	2.7440	3.3749	3.6335	4.2155
32	.2555	.6822	1.3086	1.6939	2.0369	2.4487	2.7385	3.3653	3.6218	4.1983
33	.2554	.6820	1.3077	1.6924	2.0345	2.4448	2.7333	3.3563	3.6109	4.1822
34	.2553	.6818	1.3070	1.6909	2.0322	2.4411	2.7284	3.3479	3.6007	4.1672
35	.2553	.6816	1.3062	1.6896	2.0301	2.4377	2.7238	3.3400	3.5911	4.1531
36	.2552	.6814	1.3055	1.6883	2.0281	2.4345	2.7195	3.3326	3.5821	4.1399
37	.2552	.6812	1.3049	1.6871	2.0262	2.4314	2.7154	3.3256	3.5737	4.1275
38	.2551	.6810	1.3042	1.6860	2.0244	2.4286	2.7116	3.3190	3.5657	4.1158
39	.2551	.6808	1.3036	1.6849	2.0227	2.4258	2.7079	3.3128	3.5581	4.1047
40	.2550	.6807	1.3031	1.6839	2.0211	2.4233	2.7045	3.3069	3.5510	4.0942
41	.2550	.6805	1.3025	1.6829	2.0195	2.4208	2.7012	3.3013	3.5442	4.0843
42	.2550	.6804	1.3020	1.6820	2.0181	2.4185	2.6981	3.2960	3.5377	4.0749
43	.2549	.6802	1.3016	1.6811	2.0167	2.4163	2.6951	3.2909	3.5316	4.0659
44	.2549	.6801	1.3011	1.6802	2.0154	2.4141	2.6923	3.2861	3.5258	4.0574
45	.2549	.6800	1.3006	1.6794	2.0141	2.4121	2.6896	3.2815	3.5203	4.0493

t — Value Table (continued)

d.f.					Quantiles					
	.60	.75	.90	.95	.975	.99	.995	.999	.9995	.9999
46	.2548	.6799	1.3002	1.6787	2.0129	2.4102	2.6870	3.2771	3.5150	4.0416
47	.2548	.6797	1.2998	1.6779	2.0117	2.4083	2.6846	3.2729	3.5099	4.0343
48	.2548	.6796	1.2994	1.6772	2.0106	2.4066	2.6822	3.2689	3.5051	4.0272
49	.2547	.6795	1.2991	1.6766	2.0096	2.4049	2.6800	3.2651	3.5004	4.0205
50	.2547	.6794	1.2987	1.6759	2.0086	2.4033	2.6778	3.2614	3.4960	4.0148
51	.2547	.6793	1.2984	1.6753	2.0076	2.4017	2.6757	3.2579	3.4918	4.0079
52	.2546	.6792	1.2980	1.6747	2.0066	2.4002	2.6737	3.2545	3.4877	4.0020
53	.2546	.6791	1.2977	1.6741	2.0057	2.3988	2.6718	3.2513	3.4838	3.9963
54	.2546	.6791	1.2974	1.6736	2.0049	2.3974	2.6700	3.2481	3.4800	3.9908
55	.2546	.6790	1.2971	1.6730	2.0040	2.3961	2.6682	3.2451	3.4764	3.9856
56	.2546	.6789	1.2969	1.6725	2.0032	2.3948	2.6665	3.2423	3.4729	3.9805
57	.2545	.6788	1.2966	1.6720	2.0025	2.3936	2.6649	3.2395	3.4696	3.9757
58	.2545	.6787	1.2963	1.6716	2.0017	2.3924	2.6633	3.2368	3.4663	3.9710
59	.2545	.6787	1.2961	1.6711	2.0010	2.3912	2.6618	3.2342	3.4632	3.9664
60	.2545	.6786	1.2958	1.6706	2.0003	2.3901	2.6603	3.2317	3.4602	3.9621
61	.2545	.6785	1.2956	1.6702	1.9996	2.3890	2.6589	3.2293	3.4573	3.9579
62	.2544	.6785	1.2954	1.6698	1.9990	2.3880	2.6575	3.2270	3.4545	3.9538
63	.2544	.6784	1.2951	1.6694	1.9983	2.3870	2.6561	3.2247	3.4518	3.9499
64	.2544	.6783	1.2949	1.6690	1.9977	2.3860	2.6549	3.2225	3.4491	3.9461
65	.2544	.6783	1.2947	1.6686	1.9971	2.3851	2.6536	3.2204	3.4466	3.9424
66	.2544	.6782	1.2945	1.6683	1.9966	2.3842	2.6524	3.2184	3.4441	3.9389
67	.2544	.6782	1.2943	1.6679	1.9960	2.3833	2.6512	3.2164	3.4417	3.9354
68	.2543	.6781	1.2941	1.6676	1.9955	2.3824	2.6501	3.2145	3.4394	3.9321
69	.2543	.6781	1.2939	1.6672	1.9949	2.3816	2.6490	3.2126	3.4372	3.9288
70	.2543	.6780	1.2938	1.6669	1.9944	2.3808	2.6479	3.2108	3.4350	3.9257
71	.2543	.6780	1.2936	1.6666	1.9939	2.3800	2.6469	3.2090	3.4329	3.9226
72	.2543	.6779	1.2934	1.6663	1.9935	2.3793	2.6459	3.2073	3.4308	3.9197
73	.2543	.6779	1.2933	1.6660	1.9930	2.3785	2.6449	3.2057	3.4289	3.9168
74	.2543	.6778	1.2931	1.6657	1.9925	2.3778	2.6439	3.2041	3.4269	3.9140
75	.2542	.6778	1.2929	1.6654	1.9921	2.3771	2.6430	3.2025	3.4250	3.9113
76	.2542	.6777	1.2928	1.6652	1.9917	2.3764	2.6421	3.2010	3.4232	3.9086
77	.2542	.6777	1.2926	1.6649	1.9913	2.3758	2.6412	3.1995	3.4214	3.9061
78	.2542	.6776	1.2925	1.6646	1.9908	2.3751	2.6403	3.1980	3.4197	3.9036
79	.2542	.6776	1.2924	1.6644	1.9905	2.3745	2.6395	3.1966	3.4180	3.9011
80	.2542	.6776	1.2922	1.6641	1.9901	2.3739	2.6387	3.1953	3.4163	3.8988
81	.2542	.6775	1.2921	1.6639	1.9897	2.3733	2.6379	3.1939	3.4147	3.8964
82	.2542	.6775	1.2920	1.6636	1.9893	2.3727	2.6371	3.1926	3.4132	3.8942
83	.2542	.6775	1.2918	1.6634	1.9890	2.3721	2.6364	3.1913	3.4116	3.8920
84	.2542	.6774	1.2917	1.6632	1.9886	2.3716	2.6356	3.1901	3.4102	3.8899
85	.2541	.6774	1.2916	1.6630	1.9883	2.3710	2.6349	3.1889	3.4087	3.8878
86	.2541	.6774	1.2915	1.6628	1.9879	2.3705	2.6342	3.1877	3.4073	3.8857
87	.2541	.6773	1.2914	1.6626	1.9876	2.3700	2.6335	3.1866	3.4059	3.8837
88	.2541	.6773	1.2912	1.6624	1.9873	2.3695	2.6329	3.1854	3.4045	3.8818
89	.2541	.6773	1.2911	1.6622	1.9870	2.3690	2.6322	3.1843	3.4032	3.8799
90	.2541	.6772	1.2910	1.6620	1.9867	2.3685	2.6316	3.1833	3.4019	3.8780

t — **Value Table** (*concluded*)

d.f.	.60	.75	.90	.95	.975	.99	.995	.999	.9995	.9999
					Quantiles					
91	.2541	.6772	1.2909	1.6618	1.9864	2.3680	2.6309	3.1822	3.4007	3.8762
92	.2541	.6772	1.2908	1.6616	1.9861	2.3676	2.6303	3.1812	3.3994	3.8745
93	.2541	.6771	1.2907	1.6614	1.9858	2.3671	2.6297	3.1802	3.3982	3.8727
94	.2541	.6771	1.2906	1.6612	1.9855	2.3667	2.6291	3.1792	3.3971	3.8710
95	.2541	.6771	1.2905	1.6611	1.9853	2.3662	2.6286	3.1782	3.3959	3.8694
96	.2541	.6771	1.2904	1.6609	1.9850	2.3658	2.6280	3.1773	3.3948	3.8678
97	.2540	.6770	1.2903	1.6607	1.9847	2.3654	2.6275	3.1764	3.3937	3.8662
98	.2540	.6770	1.2902	1.6606	1.9845	2.3650	2.6269	3.1755	3.3926	3.8646
99	.2540	.6770	1.2902	1.6604	1.9842	2.3646	2.6264	3.1746	3.3915	3.8631
100	.2540	.6770	1.2901	1.6602	1.9840	2.3642	2.6259	3.1737	3.3905	3.8616
∞	.2533	.6745	1.2816	1.6449	1.9600	2.3263	2.5758	3.0902	3.2905	3.7190

APPENDIX 3A Multiple and Nonlinear Regression

Multiple Regression Models

Multiple regression is an extension of simple linear regression and is used in cases in which there is a significant functional relationship between two or more independent variables and the dependent variable. The basic form of the multiple regression model is:

$$y = a + b_1x_1 + b_2x_2 + \cdots + b_mx_m$$

where the x's represent different independent variables and the a's and b's are the coefficients. For example, the costs of a computer center may be a function of the input data lines, computer processing unit time, and the output report pages. This would give three independent variables that establish the costs of computer services.

Dummy Variable

Sometimes a factor affecting the level of cost is not entirely quantitative in nature. For example, the work performed in a hospital radiology department for a medicare patient may be different from that for other patients. The multiple regression models will have one independent variable that will have a value of 1 for a medicare patient and 0 for other patients. These variables are called *dummy variables*. Another application of dummy variables is in correcting for autocorrelation. For instance, assign a value of 1 to periods of rising activity levels and 0 to periods of declining activity levels.

Multicollinearity

A problem to deal with when using a multiple regression model is called **multicollinearity.** It is the existence of very high correlation between two or more independent variables. The variables move together so closely that the technique cannot tell them apart. For example, direct labor hours and direct labor cost would be highly correlated. It is important to recognize this as a correlation between independent variables, not between an independent and a dependent variable.

Multicollinearity is not an issue when the regression equation is used to predict total costs; however, it is when accurate coefficients are needed. For example, the coefficients represent the marginal costs for the independent variables and, without multicollinearity, could be used in pricing decisions and in cost-volume-profit analyses. The existence of multicollinearity makes the accuracy of coefficients suspect, but total cost estimates would not be affected because the errors tend to balance out. When multicollinearity is severe, one or all of the following symptoms will be observed:

1. Negative coefficients when positive are expected.
2. Some coefficients are insignificant, which in theory should be highly significant.
3. Unreasonably high coefficients that do not make economic sense.

When multicollinearity is severe, think through the theory that supports the equation and pull out one of the independent variables (or add the two problem variables together) that is less critical to the setting.

Measure of Multiple Association

Like simple linear regression, the coefficient of determination for multiple regression is still the ratio of the explained variance over the total variance. However, an adjustment must be made because of the number of coefficients that must be estimated as the result of multiple independent variables. The adjusted R^2 is calculated by the formula:

$$R^2 = 1 - \frac{\Sigma(y - y')^2/(\text{Degrees of freedom})}{\Sigma(y - \bar{y})^2/(n - 1)}$$

Standard Error of the Estimate

The standard error of the estimate for multiple regression is an extension of the simple regression measure. The only difference is the degrees of freedom number ($n - $ number of parameters estimated) used in the denominator. If you have two independent variables, the denominator would be ($n - 3$) because we have a, b_1, and b_2 to estimate.

Nonlinear Regression

Multiple regression also permits fitting certain nonlinear functions to cost data. For example, if the scattergraph of the data yields an S-shaped curve, a cubic function is probably appropriate to explain the data. The equation would appear as follows:

$$y = a + b_1x + b_2x^2 + b_3x^3$$

We use regression to find values for the coefficients by squaring and cubing x and including these new variables in a normal multiple regression. For more complex functions, use higher powers of x. However, do not go above powers of 4 for cost data without scaling (dividing by a million or a billion).

   Another nonlinear function found in cost data (see Appendix 6A for a discussion of the learning effect on labor costs) and some financial situations is the exponential function modeled as:

$$y = ax^b$$

In order to use linear regression to find values for the coefficients of the best-fitting equation, it is necessary to transform the equation by taking logs. A linear form results from logs as follows:

$$\log y = \log a + b \log x$$

First, transform the data by taking the log of x and log of y. By including the log of y (instead of y) and the log of x (instead of x) in linear regression, the results are a constant ($\log a$) and a slope, b. Taking the antilog of the constant results in a value for a. Combining this with b, we have the best-fitting equation for $y = ax^b$. The learning curve for labor is a good example of this type of equation.

KEY TERMS AND CONCEPTS

Multiple regression (101)
Multicollinearity (101)

ADDITIONAL READING

Brock, Terry L. ''Multiple Regression on Lotus 1-2-3.'' *Journal of Accountancy*, July 1986, pp. 106–10.

REVIEW QUESTIONS

1. What problems might arise when multiple independent variables are used in cost behavior analysis?

2. What is multicollinearity and how does it pose problems in multiple regression analysis?

3. Explain how a linear regression analysis can be used for an equation of the form $y = ax^b$?

EXERCISES AND PROBLEMS

3A–1. Multiple Regression with Effects of Changing Technology and Inflation.   Malcom Gart, the controller of PZ Industries, is reviewing the effects on overhead costs of an improvement in October of 19x2 in the manufacture of cyclotrons. In reviewing the costs per unit for recent months as compared to a year ago, Mr. Gart was disappointed—they seemed just to go up and down randomly. After some thought, the controller decided to do a high-low analysis before and after the change. He found from this:

Before   Variable costs $= \dfrac{(\$134{,}917 - \$121{,}381)}{(1{,}304 - 443)} = \$15.72$

Fixed costs $= \$134{,}917 - (\$15.7213 \times 1{,}304) = \$114{,}416$

After   Variable $= \dfrac{(\$122{,}022 - \$107{,}386)}{(1{,}312 - 403)} = \$16.10$

Fixed costs $= \$122.022 - (\$16.1012 \times 1{,}312) = \$100{,}897$

These results were not very pleasing. They imply that while fixed costs have decreased by only $14,000, the variable costs have increased by about $.38 per unit. The controller was under the impression that variable overhead costs were closer to $10 than $16 and that about $20,000 per month in fixed costs were saved by the change in production methods.

Then Mr. Gart assigns you, as one of his staff, to study the change in overhead cost. You have gathered the following data for 19x2 and part of 19x3:

	Overhead Cost	Units Produced	Change in Method	Price Index
January 19x2	$116,874	1,015	0	297
February	119,312	715	0	300
March	122,116	778	0	302
April	124,556	580	0	305
May	127,977	851	0	308
June	125,731	1,093	0	309
July	124,032	817	0	311
August	121,381	443	0	313
September	134,917	1,304	0	315
October	98,784	569	1	318
November	110,961	959	1	319
December	107,740	455	1	320
January 19x3	110,944	1,065	1	322
February	112,050	1,271	1	324
March	107,386	403	1	327
April	113,802	1,167	1	329
May	112,786	775	1	332
June	122,022	1,312	1	334
July	109,618	969	1	336
Averages	$116,999	870.58		

REQUIRED:

a. Prepare a simple linear regression of overhead costs on units produced. Evaluate the results.

b. Prepare two simple regressions of overhead cost on units produced. In the first regression, analyze the relationship before the change. In the second regression, analyze the relationship after the change. Evaluate the two regressions.

c. Prepare a multiple regression of overhead cost on both the units produced and the 0–1 (dummy) variable for the change in production methods. Evaluate and interpret the results.

d. Price level adjust the overhead cost data to July 31, 19x3, by dividing by the current index and multiplying by the July 19x3 index. For example, the adjusted value for January 19x2 will be:

$$\left(\frac{\$116,874}{297}\right) \times 336 = \$132,221.09$$

Prepare a multiple regression of the price-level adjusted overhead cost on units produced and the 0–1 (dummy) variable for change. Evaluate and interpret the results. What was the effect of the change on fixed costs? What was the effect of inflation on the estimates and the goodness of fit?

3A–2. Multiple Regression.   The Holloway Supply Company provides construction materials to companies in the St. Louis, Missouri, region. The delivery of materials involves accepting an order, picking materials from the warehouse, packing a truck, driving to a site, and off-loading. Materials movement is a major expense. A part of materials movement cost is the cost for maintenance of forklifts. The company has 18 forklifts with various ages and models for moving pallets of material. Some data on these lifts are included below:

Lift	Cost of Maint.	Hours of Usage	Age	Model Hustle 6A	Cloud 42
1	$ 863	608	1	1	0
2	1,122	1,685	2	1	0
3	1,073	1,237	2	1	0
4	1,045	1,225	2	1	0
5	1,124	909	2	1	0
6	1,336	1,106	3	1	0
7	1,231	1,124	3	1	0
8	1,103	783	3	1	0
9	1,385	1,346	3	1	0
10	620	1,019	2	0	1
11	667	975	2	0	1
12	616	1,397	2	0	1
13	529	549	2	0	1
14	633	942	2	0	1
15	905	1,205	3	0	1
16	848	747	3	0	1
17	953	827	3	0	1
18	1,086	1,170	4	0	1

You have performed a multiple regression on maintenance cost with usage, age, and Hustle 6A as the independent variables. The results are:

First regression output:

Constant	114.379
Std. err. of Y est.	69.822
R^2 squared	0.940
No. of observations	18
Degrees of freedom	14

	Usage	Age	Hustle 6A
X coefficient(s)	0.10	215.48	415.37
Std. err. of coef.	0.06	24.79	34.59
t-Statistic	1.61	8.69	12.01

You have performed another multiple regression on maintenance cost with usage, age, and Cloud 42 as the independent variables. The results are:

Second regression output:

Constant	529.750
Std. err. of Y est.	69.822
R^2 squared	0.940
No. of observations	18
Degrees of freedom	14

	Usage	*Age*	*Cloud 42*
X coefficient(s)	0.10	215.48	−415.37
Std. err. of coef.	0.06	24.79	34.59
t-Statistic	1.61	8.69	−12.01

REQUIRED:
a. Interpret the meaning of the first regression results.
b. Compare the first and second regression results. How would you interpret the −$415.37 coefficient in the second regression? What is the meaning of the $529.75 constant in the second regression?

3A–3. Janis Levinson was asked to study the cost of document processing at the First National Bank of Eagles Nest. The town of Eagles Nest has a population of about 45,000 and an economy based on agriculture and timber. The cost has been rising over the last four years and management would like to plan and control better. The bank has $800 million in assets and about 16,000 checking accounts currently.

The price for checking accounts has been set at $5 plus $.10 per document for personal accounts and $8 plus $.12 for commercial accounts. A competitive bank has been cutting prices and the president is concerned. Senior management would like the total clearing costs analyzed to see the cost per document and the cost per account.

There are two basic types of accounts, personal and commercial. These accounts are somewhat different in terms of handling because federal and state regulations are moderately different. Senior management would like some detailed analysis of the cost of handling these different accounts.

Janis first gathered the data (Exhibit 3A–1) from various computer printouts for total document processing costs, documents, and number of accounts for the last four years. Processing appeared to Janis to be fairly stable during this time period and, based on discussions with various managers, it should be representative of operations next year.

REQUIRED:
a. Plot the cost data against total documents and visually fit a line. Evaluate the line fit and compute the fixed and variable cost from the line. (Use a spread sheet graph function because 48 points are very tedious by hand. If you do not have access to a computer, then plot the last year only.)
b. Plot the cost data against total checking accounts and visually fit a line. Compute the fixed and variable cost from the line. Compare the results with requirement *(a).*
c. Using the high-low method, determine the fixed and variable costs for the following measures of activity:
  1. Total documents.
  2. Total accounts.
  3. Forecast costs for 184,000 documents and 14,000 accounts.
d. Compute a linear regression for each of the measures of activity (include statistics for *a*, *b*, r^2, standard error of the estimate, and standard error of the *b* coefficient.) Use a spread sheet package. (If computing by hand, use just the data for the last 12 months.)
  1. Total documents. Interpret the results and compare them with the high-low method estimates.

EXHIBIT 3A–1

FIRST NATIONAL BANK OF EAGLES NEST
Clearing Operations Cost Study
For the Four Years Ending December 31, 19x9
(in thousands)

	Cost of Clearing	Cleared			Cost of Clearing	Cleared	
		Documents	Accounts			Document	Account
19x6				**19x8**			
Jan.	$83.5	221.0	12.3	Jan.	$ 92.8	191.5	14.0
Feb.	94.2	290.7	12.8	Feb.	100.2	245.8	14.5
March	88.6	253.0	12.9	March	98.8	221.0	14.5
April	91.2	181.4	13.5	April	98.4	229.9	14.7
May	92.3	230.4	13.2	May	91.9	266.4	14.7
June	88.3	167.0	13.4	June	86.8	161.3	14.8
July	96.4	199.9	13.8	July	91.7	214.2	14.9
Aug.	91.8	269.2	14.0	Aug.	92.9	187.8	14.6
Sept.	96.3	313.2	14.1	Sept.	92.7	168.8	14.4
Oct.	91.3	191.6	13.9	Oct.	90.5	227.4	14.6
Nov.	96.4	300.2	14.1	Nov.	95.2	269.5	14.5
Dec.	93.1	245.7	13.8	Dec.	90.4	183.9	14.8
19x7				**19x9**			
Jan.	91.9	225.3	14.2	Jan.	98.9	210.9	15.1
Feb.	90.6	166.6	13.8	Feb.	94.4	176.0	15.4
March	90.9	267.3	13.8	March	102.6	270.4	15.7
April	92.2	220.7	13.5	April	100.0	237.7	16.0
May	91.2	239.1	13.2	May	98.3	245.0	16.0
June	88.7	149.9	13.5	June	103.8	296.6	16.4
July	89.0	188.3	13.8	July	98.4	247.5	16.2
Aug.	96.0	230.4	13.6	Aug.	98.9	247.8	16.0
Sept.	91.9	210.7	13.7	Sept.	100.7	246.2	16.4
Oct.	90.3	220.5	13.4	Oct.	101.6	222.4	16.7
Nov.	87.2	228.9	13.4	Nov.	97.2	152.8	16.4
Dec.	94.1	186.4	13.7	Dec.	98.3	268.2	16.4

    2. Total accounts. Interpret the results and compare them with the high-low method estimates.

    3. Compare the quality of the fit.

  e. From your results (in requirement (*d*)) prepare a forecast of the cost for:

    1. 184 (thousand) documents

    2. 14 (thousand) accounts

    3. Prepare a 95 percent confidence interval for each of your forecasts.

  f. Prepare a multiple regression using both total documents and accounts as independent variables. (If available to you, use Lotus Version 2 spread sheet or a statistical package for this requirement. Do not attempt this without computer software because it will be wasted time and be inaccurate.)

    1. Interpret the results. Evaluate the quality of the fit.

    2. Compare the results with the simple regressions.

    3. Does multicollinearity appear to be a problem?

    4. Prepare a forecast for 184 (thousand) documents and 14 (thousand) accounts.

  g. With the additional data provided in Exhibit 3A–2 prepare a multiple regression with six independent variables: personal documents, commercial documents, individual accounts, commercial accounts, absolute change in personal accounts, and absolute change in commercial accounts.

EXHIBIT 3A–2

FIRST NATIONAL BANK OF EAGLES NEST
Detail of Documents and Accounts
For the Four Years Ending December 31, 19x9
(in thousands)

| | *Cleared* | | | | | *Cleared* | | | |
| | *Documents* | | *Accounts* | | | *Documents* | | *Accounts* | |
	Pers.	*Com.*	*Pers.*	*Com.*		*Pers.*	*Com.*	*Pers.*	*Com.*
19x6					**19x8**				
Jan.	161.5	59.5	8.1	4.2	Jan.	82.9	108.6	8.4	5.6
Feb.	191.3	99.4	8.2	4.6	Feb.	131.3	114.5	8.5	6.0
March	188.1	64.9	8.2	4.7	March	165.6	55.4	8.3	6.2
April	107.2	74.2	8.4	5.1	April	145.6	84.3	8.1	6.6
May	167.6	62.8	8.2	5.0	May	214.7	51.7	8.1	6.6
June	92.9	74.1	8.5	4.9	June	74.7	86.6	8.2	6.6
July	157.3	42.6	8.6	5.2	July	148.2	66.0	8.3	6.6
Aug.	173.3	95.9	8.5	5.5	Aug.	71.2	116.6	8.2	6.4
Sept.	197.5	115.7	8.5	5.6	Sept.	115.7	53.1	8.3	6.1
Oct.	141.2	50.4	8.5	5.4	Oct.	164.3	63.1	8.4	6.2
Nov.	183.2	117.0	8.5	5.6	Nov.	160.0	109.5	8.2	6.3
Dec.	186.3	59.4	8.4	5.4	Dec.	122.5	61.4	8.4	6.4
19x7					**19x9**				
Jan.	127.9	97.4	8.4	5.8	Jan.	124.6	86.3	8.6	6.5
Feb.	111.8	54.8	8.2	5.6	Feb.	96.3	79.7	8.8	6.6
March	186.2	81.1	8.3	5.5	March	161.0	109.4	9.0	6.7
April	167.9	52.8	8.2	5.3	April	134.9	102.8	8.9	7.1
May	139.3	99.8	8.0	5.2	May	140.0	105.0	9.0	7.0
June	71.5	78.4	8.2	5.3	June	181.0	115.6	9.2	7.2
July	133.1	55.2	8.1	5.7	July	108.8	138.7	9.1	7.1
Aug.	166.5	63.9	8.3	5.3	Aug.	154.3	93.5	9.1	6.9
Sept.	109.1	101.6	8.1	5.6	Sept.	135.5	110.7	9.1	7.3
Oct.	180.6	39.9	8.0	5.4	Oct.	177.4	45.0	9.4	7.3
Nov.	149.9	79.0	8.0	5.4	Nov.	77.1	75.7	9.2	7.2
Dec.	112.5	73.9	8.2	5.5	Dec.	186.3	81.9	9.3	7.1

1. Interpret the results. Evaluate the quality of the fit.
2. Compare the results with the regressions in requirements *(e)* and *(f)* above. Do the quality of the fit and the additional information appear to be worth the effort to gather the data, run the regression, and report the results? (Assume that the additional work would take about four hours of Janis's time, worth about $100 per hour.)
3. Does multicollinearity appear to be a problem?

3A–4. Multiple Regression.   Velocite, Inc., manufactures soccer gear in plants in France and Brazil. The gear is marketed under the Velocite brand name in markets throughout the world. The shipments to some countries have not been in line with reported sales revenue. The corporate controller, Rocky Dewbre, was concerned about the potential for theft of inventory by company personnel. While laws and customs vary greatly among cultures, theft is generally considered illegal.

    There are limited resources available for travel for internal auditing of the possible thefts, and the internal auditor has asked you, as a staff auditor, to study the most likely countries where thefts of shipments might be occurring. The company follows a policy to mark up all

EXHIBIT 3A–3

VELOCITE, INC.
Basic Data with Residual Errors
(in millions of French francs)

	Sales	C G S	Resid. Errors	Ending Inventory	Normal Volume	Resid. Errors
1 Albania	0.28	0.28	(0.77)	0.01	0.25	(0.05)
2 Brazil	10.38	8.29	0.78	2.00	8.46	(0.29)
3 China	2.13	2.04	(0.19)	0.47	1.87	(0.03)
4 Cuba	0.68	0.51	(0.80)	0.02	0.54	(0.12)
5 Denmark	5.96	4.74	0.06	1.09	4.79	(0.21)
6 France	7.67	6.57	0.80	1.49	6.28	(0.21)
7 Great Britain	3.00	2.41	(0.38)	0.48	2.47	(0.18)
8 Guyana	1.33	1.07	(0.65)	0.21	0.91	(0.04)
9 India	8.50	8.17	1.87	2.71	8.06	0.52
10 Indonesia	9.63	7.91	0.88	1.78	7.83	(0.34)
11 Japan	5.93	4.92	0.26	1.17	4.96	(0.18)
12 Korea	6.66	5.29	0.16	1.97	5.36	0.52
13 Mexico	9.19	7.21	0.47	1.75	7.40	(0.26)
14 Philippines	3.87	3.06	(0.29)	0.73	3.20	(0.13)
15 Poland	3.38	2.68	(0.35)	0.62	2.76	(0.12)
16 Saudi Arabia	1.59	1.50	(0.38)	0.69	1.36	0.33
17 Spain	6.22	6.92	2.08	2.41	5.83	0.83
18 Sri Lanka	4.01	3.21	(0.22)	0.75	3.30	(0.14)
19 Sweden	3.49	2.68	(0.42)	0.55	2.75	(0.19)
20 Switzerland	5.55	4.39	(0.03)	1.00	4.49	(0.22)
21 Syria	2.33	1.90	(0.46)	0.54	2.06	(0.01)
22 Tanzania	14.11	4.92	(4.98)	2.30	4.85	0.98
23 Turkey	8.00	7.90	1.91	1.66	7.44	(0.36)
24 West Germany	9.01	7.27	0.65	1.87	7.29	(0.11)
Averages	5.54	4.41		1.18	4.35	

Regression analysis for cost of goods sold on sales:

Constant	0.8706 fr.
Std. err. of Y est.	1.3754
R^2 squared	.7384
No. of observations	24
Degrees of freedom	22
Sales	
X coefficient(s)	0.639 fr.
Std. err. of coef.	0.081
t-Statistic	7.880

Regression analysis for inventory on normal volume:

Constant	(0.007)
Std. err. of Y est.	0.370
R^2 squared	.7892
No. of observations	24
Degrees of freedom	22
Normal Volume	
X coefficient(s)	0.272
Std. err. of coef.	0.030
t-Statistic	9.076

shipments at 30 percent above cost for sales to retail stores and soccer teams. Moderate discounts are given for large purchases. Because of currency fluctuation, some variation in markup is expected among countries. The company also follows a policy of constant inventories based on 25 percent of normal annual volume. Thus, the volume of purchases for each subsidiary should approximate the unit volume of sales.

You have gathered data on sales, cost of goods sold, ending inventories, and normal annual volumes. All amounts have been translated into French francs and are stated in millions. Using linear regression, you have regressed the cost of goods sold on sales and computed the residual errors in explaining cost of goods sold. Likewise, you have regressed ending inventory on normal annual volume and computed the residual inventory errors. A summary of your findings is listed in Exhibit 3A–3.

REQUIRED:
a. Review the regression analysis for cost of goods sold on sales. Interpret the meaning of each coefficient.
b. Review the regression analysis for inventory on normal volume. Interpret the meaning of each coefficient.
c. After reviewing the residual errors for cost of goods sold and inventory, which countries seem likely candidates for audits?

3A–5. Nonlinear Multiple Regression.   Christie Haige is the budget analyst assigned to study purchasing cost for CLMC, Inc. The company has 14 divisions, plants, and branches, each with its own purchasing department.

Christie believes that the cost of purchasing materials depends partly on the number of different materials purchased and partly on the number of different suppliers. For example, it is much less work to purchase 100,000 units of the same material from one supplier than to purchase 100,000 different materials from 1,000 suppliers.

The complexity of purchasing may be modeled with the equation:

$$P = a + b \times M + c \times S + e$$

where

$$P = \text{Purchasing department cost}$$
$$M = \text{Number of different materials ordered in a year}$$
$$S = \text{Number of different suppliers}$$
$$e = \text{Error term assumed to be normally distributed}$$

This equation may be estimated using multiple regression. Alternatively, the relationship may be represented as nonlinear with:

$$P = a \times M^b \times S^c \times e$$

If we take the log of both sides, the result is a linear equation:

$$\log(P) = \log(a) + b \times \text{Log}(M) + c \times \text{Log}(S) + \log(e)$$

which can be estimated using multiple linear regression. The purchasing costs and the most recent year's activity for the 14 purchasing departments are:

	P	*M*	*S*
Agricultural Products	$214,198	1,738	1,303
Avionics Division	411,609	2,966	1,503
Barsh Plant	192,120	2,365	713
Burnt Crossing Plant	540,336	3,865	1,142
California Branch	276,524	3,540	890
Cliester Products	111,351	1,444	865
Crystal Products	166,646	2,621	711
Defense Division	232,761	1,861	1,334
Detroit Division	362,069	2,555	1,586
Jacksonville Plant	508,742	3,499	1,398
Little River Division	261,358	2,957	1,117
Newport Division	249,433	2,717	873
Rapid City Plant	222,042	2,444	874
Systel Products	178,662	1,499	973
Averages	$280,561	2,577	1,092

REQUIRED:

a. Perform a linear regression analysis of purchasing costs using the number of materials *(M)* as the independent variable. Evaluate and interpret the results.

b. Perform a linear regression analysis of purchasing costs using the number of suppliers *(S)* as the independent variable. Evaluate and interpret the results.

c. Perform a multiple linear regression analysis of purchasing costs using both the number of different materials *(M)* and the number of suppliers *(S)* as the independent variables. Evaluate and interpret the results in comparison with the simple regressions.

d. Multiply *M* times *S* for the 14 purchasing departments and add this new variable to the multiple regression analysis performed in part *(c)*. The equation for the regression will then be:

$$P = a + b \times M + c \times S + d \times (M \times S) + e$$

Interpret the results.

e. Using the results from parts *(a)* to *(d)*, prepare estimates of the purchase costs for the Agricultural Products and Avionics Divisions.

f. Take the log of *P*, *M*, and *S*. Then perform a multiple regression with the transformed data. Interpret the results.

g. Using the results from part *(f)*, prepare an estimate of the purchase cost for the Agricultural Products and Avionics Divisions.

h. Compare the results of the multiple log regression with the multiple linear regression.

CHAPTER 4

Cost-Volume-Profit Analysis

SALES VOLUME AND REQUIRED RETURNS

Ron Marshall, the owner and manager of Marshall Creations, Inc., is concerned about the future of the company. The operating expenses have recently increased and profits have declined. Marshall Creations, Inc., produces and distributes political and other cartoons for newspapers and magazines. The company produces several cartoon strips for daily distribution, editorial page cartoons primarily for newspapers, and other cartoons, called *floaters* or *fillers*-for magazines. The company employs 12 people in rented office space in Washington, D.C. There are two creative artists, a marketing representative, eight part-time clerical staff, and a full-time owner/manager.

Fixed costs of operations are $18,000 per month. The company distributes the materials on a subscription basis at an average price of $60 per month. The cartoon masters are mailed weekly to each of the publications. Occasionally, a timely cartoon is rushed by wire service to the subscribers. The average variable cost of producing and mailing the masters is $24 per month per subscriber. The owner/manager requires a return of $5,400 per month in order to justify his $162,000 investment in receivables, supplies, and equipment. The company currently has 625 subscribers.

In this chapter we will study techniques useful for analyzing Mr. Marshall's company.

111

**LEARNING
OBJECTIVES**

After studying this chapter, you should be able to:

1. Define the major terms associated with cost-volume-profit analysis.
2. Prepare a basic cost-volume-profit analysis for a product or service.
3. Prepare an analysis that involves profits stated in terms of after-tax income.
4. Solve problems with volume stated in either the dollar volume or composite units.
5. Solve problems when the desired return is either a return on investment or a return on sales.

   Cost-volume-profit analysis (CVP analysis) is the study of the impact of volume changes on revenue, costs, and profits. In this section we will present some representative settings in which CVP analysis is useful.

**New Products and
Services**[1]

The decision to market a new product or a service involves many uncertainties. Without properly assessing the uncertainties and considering a number of other factors, many endeavors fail. An analysis of the potential profitability of new products and services is extremely important to the final decision. In order to evaluate the likelihood of success, management must at a minimum know the level of sales at which the new product or service is expected to break even. As an example, in considering whether to open a new thoracic (primarily heart and lung) surgery unit, the hospital board will want to know the number of patients needed for the new unit to pay for itself. In preparing this analysis, the hospital will study the costs and revenues of similar units across the country. In its decision, the board of directors should consider the likelihood that the volume will exceed the break-even volume after a normal start-up time.

**New Store
Locations**

The analysis of new locations for retail stores is similar to a new product or service decision. There are differences, though. A retail store depends upon the sale of many products and services, not just one. Because of differences in values of units sold, it is common to consider dollars of sales as the volume measure in retail stores. Thus, volume will normally be measured in sales dollars rather than units.

**Employment
Contract
Negotiations**

Employees are the major cost for many service organizations. Employee-related costs will typically comprise 70 percent or more of the total expense. As a part of the wage or salary negotiation with employees, management will consider the impact of each negotiating issue on the profit. For example, airline labor negotiations with pilots and flight crews have included studies of cost, volume, and profit relationships.

COST-VOLUME-PROFIT ANALYSIS

In the following presentation we will make five assumptions:

1. The variable costs per unit are constant throughout the range of normal activity.[2]
2. The selling prices for products sold are constant throughout the range of normal activity.

---

[1] The new product or service decision will be studied in detail in Chapter 22.
[2] This is also called the *cost linearity assumption*.

3. Total fixed costs are constant throughout the range of normal activity.
4. The sales mix is constant throughout the range of normal activity.
5. Inventory levels are constant.

In the latter part of this chapter we will allow some of these assumptions to be relaxed, but for now assume that they hold.

Volume Concepts

There are two volume concepts that are useful in CVP analysis: break-even and required volume. The **break-even volume** refers to the units or sales dollars at which there is no profit or loss; total revenue exactly equals total cost. Of course, profit-seeking companies want to do better than break even, but the break-even volume provides a basis for comparison of alternatives. The **required volume** refers to the units or sales dollars at which the required return is earned. Normally, there is a profit level required for maintaining investment in assets. The required volume is greater than break-even volume.

Contribution Income Statement Analysis

The **contribution margin** is the difference between revenues and variable costs. The **contribution margin per unit** is the selling price minus variable costs per unit.

A **contribution margin format income statement** emphasizes the contribution margin from sales. The format is very useful for analyzing the impact of volume changes on income. In Exhibit 4–1 the contribution margin income statement is illustrated for Marshall Creations, Inc.,[3] which was introduced at the start of this chapter. The company has a selling price of $60 per unit of comics, variable costs of $24 per unit, and fixed costs of $18,000 per month. The required return is $5,400. Two basic questions are:

1. At what volume will the company earn the required return of $5,400?
2. At what volume will Marshall Creations break even?

EXHIBIT 4–1   Contribution Margin Format Income Statements

Format in Concept:

	Totals	Unit Calculations	Formula
Sales	S	Selling price × Quantity sold	SP × Q
Less: Variable costs	(VC)	Variable cost per Unit × Quantity	VCU × Q
Contribution margin	CM	Contribution margin per Unit × Q	CMU × Q
Less: Fixed costs	(FC)		
Income before taxes	IBT		

Format in Application:
MARSHALL CREATIONS, INC.
Income Statement for Expected Volume
For the Month Ended January 31, 19x4
(contribution margin format)

Sales	$ 37,500	$60 × 625 units
Less: Variable costs	(15,000)	$24 × 625 units
Contribution margin	$ 22,500	$36 × 625 units
Less: Fixed costs	(18,000)	
Income before taxes	$ 4,500	

[3] In Chapter 16 on variable costing, the contribution margin statement is elaborated on in much more detail. There is also a comparison and reconciliation with the traditional income statement approach.

Formulas for Required and Break-Even Volumes

The contribution format income statement may be stated in the equation form:

$$S - VC - FC = IBT$$

where

$$
\begin{aligned}
S &= \text{Sales} \\
VC &= \text{Variable costs} \\
FC &= \text{Fixed costs} \\
IBT &= \text{Income before taxes}
\end{aligned}
$$

The total sales and total variable costs may be expressed in terms of quantities:

$$
\begin{aligned}
S &= SP \times Q \\
VC &= VCU \times Q
\end{aligned}
$$

where

$$
\begin{aligned}
SP &= \text{Selling price} \\
VCU &= \text{Variable cost per unit} \\
Q &= \text{Quantity sold}
\end{aligned}
$$

Substituting these relationships into the equation for the income statement will result in:

$$(SP \times Q) - (VCU \times Q) - FC = IBT$$

Adding fixed costs to both sides and collecting the common multipliers of the quantity, Q:

$$(SP - VCU) \times Q = FC + IBT$$

$$Q = \frac{(FC + IBT)}{(SP - VCU)} = \frac{(FC + IBT)}{CMU}$$

When the required return (RR) is earned, the IBT is equal to RR:

Required volume is determined:

$$Q = \frac{(FC + RR)}{CMU}$$

where

$$CMU = SP - VCU$$

The top part of the final formula (FC + RR) is the amount of contribution margin that must be generated to cover fixed costs and provide for the required profits. The bottom part of the formula (CMU) is the amount of the contribution for one unit. The calculation results in the number of units necessary to earn a contribution margin equal to fixed costs plus required return.

For Marshall Creations, the contribution margin per unit is $60 minus $24, or $36. Application of the formula would result in the required subscriptions of:

$$Q = \frac{(\$18,000 + \$5,400)}{\$36} = 650 \text{ subscriptions}$$

In order to find the break-even quantity, the IBT is set equal to zero in the formula

$$Q = \frac{(\$18,000 + \$0)}{\$36} = 500 \text{ subscriptions}$$

EXHIBIT 4–2 Proof of Break-Even and Required Volume Levels

MARSHALL CREATIONS, INC.
Projected Contribution Income Statements
For the Month Ended January 31, 19x4

	Break-Even Volume		Required Volume	
Sales	$60 × 500	$ 30,000	$60 × 650	$ 39,000
Variable costs	$24 × 500	(12,000)	$24 × 650	(15,600)
Contribution margin		$ 18,000		$ 23,400
Fixed costs		(18,000)		(18,000)
Income before taxes		$0		$ 5,400

In order to prove this result, a contribution income statement may be prepared at both the break-even and required volumes as in Exhibit 4–2.

Exhibit 4–3 illustrates these basic CVP relationships in graph form. The graph form of CVP presentation is often very useful for presenting the information to management.[4]

Introduction of Taxes

Taxes, other than those on income, are treated as a part of fixed or variable costs. Thus, taxes on franchises, inventory, real estate, equipment, and some personnel are fixed costs. Taxes on sales, fuel, and some employees are variable costs.

Corporate income taxes are different. Although they may be categorized as expenses for the financial report, they do not arise unless the company is above the break-even volume and shows a profit for tax purposes. In some circumstances involving companies with losses, a loss may be carried back to prior years' tax returns resulting in tax refunds, or the loss may be deductible in future years. Thus, income tax is a positive variable cost above break even and, in some circumstances, an expense reduction below break even.

For Marshall Creations assume that the total of federal, state, and local income taxes is 40 percent of income before tax.[5] Although the actual corporate tax rate increases at low income levels, we will not include this complication in the analysis. The formula for required volume is:

$$Q = \frac{(FC + RR)}{CMU}$$

The RR in this formula is on a before-tax basis. However, the profit is taxable and thus the income taxes must be allowed for in the calculation of required volume. If

---

[4] Another form of this graph, called the *profit volume graph,* shows the amount of loss and profit at each volume level.

[5] Most state and local income taxes are deductible for federal income tax, and many municipal income taxes are deductible for state income tax purposes. Thus, the applicable composite rate of all income taxes must be computed allowing for the deductibility of state and local taxes. When local tax (t_L) is deductible for state tax (t_S) and state tax is deductible for federal income tax (t_F), then the overall tax rate (t_O) is found by:

$$t_O = t_L + t_S \times (1 - t_L) + (1 - t_L) \times (1 - t_S) \times t_F$$

For example, a 5 percent local tax rate, a 15 percent state tax rate, and a 50 percent federal income tax rate result in an overall income tax rate of 57.25 percent:

$$t_O = .05 + .10 \times (1 - .05) + (1 - .05) \times (1 - .10) \times .50 = .5725$$

EXHIBIT 4–3   Marshall Creations, Inc. (basic cost-volume-profit graph)

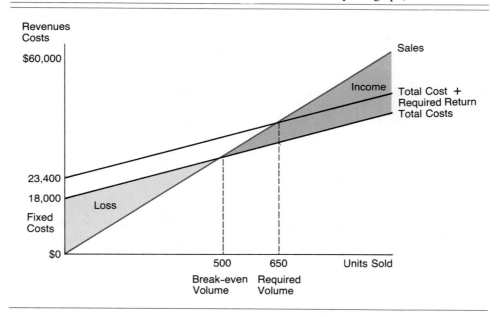

the management requirements are stated in terms of a required net income (RNI), then the RR must be computed:

$$RNI = RR - \text{Income taxes}$$
$$= RR - (RR \times \text{Tax rate})$$
$$= RR \times (1 - \text{Tax rate})$$

Dividing both sides by (1 − Tax rate) and solving for RR:

$$RR = \frac{RNI}{(1 - \text{Tax rate})}$$

With this formula we can solve problems with the required net income stated as an after-tax amount. For example, assume that Ron Marshall had stated that the required net income was $3,240 per month with a tax rate of 40 percent. Income before tax is found by:

$$RR = \frac{\$3,240}{(1 - .4)} = \$5,400$$

The $5,400 is then placed into the formula for the required volume.

Up to this point, we have measured volume in units of product. There are alternatives to this. In certain circumstances, it is more convenient to measure volume in terms of sales dollars or composite units.

ALTERNATIVE VOLUME MEASURES

Volume in Dollars   Volume may be measured in terms of sales dollars rather than in units. This is especially useful for large retail stores with thousands of products. The use of dollars rather than units is useful because the addition of such units as $.40 candy bars with $119 bicycles would not be very meaningful.

For this type of analysis, think of everything in terms of $1 of sales revenue. Thus, variable costs are calculated as the variable cost per dollar of sales, and contribution is stated as a percentage of $1. Further, break-even and required volumes are stated in terms of sales dollars.

The variable cost per dollar of sales (VC percent) for Marshall Creations can be found by:

$$VC\% = \frac{\text{Variable cost per unit}}{\text{Selling price}}$$

$$= \frac{\$24}{\$60} = 40\%$$

In some settings only the total variable costs and total sales are known. For these circumstances, the variable cost rate per dollar is found by:

$$VC\% = \frac{\text{Total variable costs}}{\text{Total sales revenue}}$$

Contribution margin per $1 of sales (also called the *contribution margin ratio*) can be found by:

$$CM\% = (1 - VC\%)$$

The formula for required volume may now be changed to reflect the change in volume measure:

$$S = \frac{(FC + RR)}{CM\%}$$

For Marshall Creations the contribution margin per dollar is [1 − 40 percent] or 60 percent. The required sales are then:

$$S = \frac{(\$18,000 + \$5,400)}{60\%} = \$39,000.$$

The break-even sales level is found by:

$$S = \frac{(\$18,000 + \$0)}{60\%} = \$30,000.$$

Composite Units

A **composite unit** is a combination of the units of individual products in proportion to their normal sales volumes. The composite unit approach is also called the *package unit method, basket unit method,* and *sales mix method* in various industries. First we must present the multiple product detail related to Marshall Creations.

Analysis Setting.   The cartoons that Marshall Creations syndicates are of three types: comic strips, editorial page single items, and floating single items that can appear anywhere. The comic strips and floating items have been adopted by about twice as many publications as the editorials. Thus, a ratio of two comic strips to one editorial to two floaters (2:1:2) would be the appropriate **sales mix** for the composite unit. Notice that the composite unit would contain five individual units. The prices and variable costs for the composite units are given as:

	Revenue		*Variable Cost*	
Comic strips	2 @ $70	$140	2 @ $30	$ 60
Editorials	1 @ $60	60	1 @ $24	24
Floaters	2 @ $50	100	2 @ $18	36
Composite unit		$300		$120

The revenue of $300 and variable costs of $120 per composite unit are then used in the formula. Thus, the previous formula can be used for both single as well as multiproduct firms:

$$Q = \frac{(FC + RR)}{CMU}$$

With composite units, we substitute the contribution margin per composite unit into the formula and solve. For Marshall Creations' composite unit, the CMU is $300 price less $120 variable costs, or $180, and the required volume is:

$$Q = \frac{(\$18,000 + \$5,400)}{\$180} = 130 \text{ Composite units}$$

The break-even volume is:

$$Q = \frac{(\$18,000 + \$0)}{\$180} = 100 \text{ Composite units}$$

The required and break-even volumes will consist of:

	Required	*Break Even*
Subscriptions to comic strips	260	200
Subscriptions to editorials	130	100
Subscriptions to floaters	260	200
Total subscriptions	650	500
Composite units	130	100

Composite units are very useful for summarizing the volume of different products or services. For example, all of the following may be conveniently expressed as composite units:

1. Airline flights to various cities flown by one aircraft.
2. Patients in a hospital.
3. Various priced automobiles coming out of a factory.

Thus, the composite unit concept is useful in many industries.

In addition to the measure of volume that can vary, the desired return may be stated in two alternative ways.

VARIATIONS IN DESIRED INCOME

The desired income may be stated as a return on investment or as a desired return on sales.

Return on Investment

When the required return is stated as a desired rate (DR) on investment, whether assets or owners' equity, we may calculate the amount of the required return:

$$RR = \text{Desired rate} \times \text{Investment}$$

If the required return is stated as an after-tax amount, it must be converted to a pretax amount as discussed previously:

$$\text{Desired rate} = \frac{\text{Desired rate after tax}}{(1 - \text{Tax rate})}$$

For Marshall Creations the investment in assets is $162,000. Now let us assume that the owner desires an after-tax return rate of 2 percent per month on total assets. The desired rate after tax and the required return may be calculated as:

$$DR = \frac{.02}{(1 - .4)} = 3\frac{1}{3}\%$$

$$RR = 3\frac{1}{3}\% \times \$162,000 = \$5,400$$

The RR is then included in the standard formula.

Return on Sales   The desired rate of return may be stated as a return on sales. The desired income before tax will equal the desired income rate before tax times sales:

$$RR = \text{Desired rate before tax} \times \text{Sales} = DR \times S$$

The amount of total sales will equal the selling price times quantity (SP $\times$ Q):

$$RR = DR \times (SP \times Q)$$

We will need to substitute the desired income (with DR as before-tax desired rate) into the general formula and solve for the required volume:

$$Q = \frac{(FC + RR)}{CMU}$$

$$Q = \frac{[FC + (DR \times SP \times Q)]}{CMU}$$

Solving this for Q results in a new computational formula:

$$Q = \frac{FC}{[CMU - (DR \times SP)]}$$

This formula states that, after taking from the contribution margin per unit enough to cover the desired return on each unit sold, the remaining contribution must be enough to cover fixed costs.

Assume that Ron Marshall had a minimum required return on sales of 6 percent after tax. We would find the before-tax rate of return with the tax rate of 40 percent by:

$$DR = \frac{\text{After-tax rate}}{(1 - \text{Tax rate})}$$

$$DR = \frac{6\%}{(1 - 40\%)} = 10\%$$

The quantity of subscriptions required will be given by:

$$Q = \frac{FC}{[CMU - (DR \times SP)]}$$

$$Q = \frac{\$18,000}{[\$36 - (10\% \times \$60)]}$$

$$= \frac{\$18,000}{[\$36 - \$6]} = 600 \text{ subscriptions}$$

At a volume of 600 units, there will be a before-tax profit of $6 per subscription and an after-tax profit of $3.60 per subscription, or 6 percent of revenue. This may be proven with a contribution format income statement and percentages taken on sales:

	Per Unit	Required	Percent
Sales	$60 × 600	$ 36,000	100
Variable costs	$24 × 600	(14,400)	40
Contribution margin		$ 21,600	60
Fixed costs		(18,000)	50
Income before taxes		$ 3,600	10
Income taxes (40%)		1,440	4
Net income		$ 2,160	6

In the next section we will present two useful ratios for the analysis of cost, volume, and profit.

RATIO ANALYSIS

Two concepts related to CVP analysis are the margin of safety and the operating leverage.

Margin of Safety Ratio

The **margin of safety** is the difference between the expected volume and the break-even volume:

$$\text{Margin of safety} = \text{Expected volume} - \text{Break-even volume}$$

For Marshall Creations, the margin of safety is 125 subscriptions, or 625 expected minus 500 break-even subscriptions.

The margin of safety ratio is the margin of safety expressed as a percentage of the expected volume:

$$\text{Margin of safety ratio} = \frac{(\text{Expected volume} - \text{Break-even volume})}{\text{Expected volume}}$$

$$= 1 - \frac{\text{Break-even volume}}{\text{Expected volume}}$$

The volume measures may be either units or dollars. For Marshall Creations, the margin of safety ratio is 20 percent:

$$\text{Margin of safety ratio} = 1 - \left(\frac{500}{625}\right) = 1 - 80\% = 20\%$$

The margin of safety ratio is interpreted as the percentage that sales can drop from the expected volume before the break-even point is reached. A manager may then assess the likelihood of such a drop in sales taking place. A low margin of safety ratio means a relatively small dip in sales demand could result in operating losses. On the other hand, a high margin of safety ratio indicates the company is operating substantially above the break-even point and has more flexibility to deal with the fluctuations in the marketplace and still remain profitable.

Operating Leverage Ratio

The **operating leverage ratio** measures the effect of percentage changes in sales volume on percentage changes in income before taxes. The ratio is also defined by the formula:

$$\text{Operating leverage ratio} = \frac{\text{Contribution margin}}{\text{Income before tax}}$$

Computationally, the operating leverage ratio may be computed by:

$$\text{OLR} = \frac{(SP - VCU) \times Q}{[(SP - VCU) \times Q] - FC}$$

To illustrate, the operating leverage ratio for Marshall Creations based on expected volume is 5 as computed as:

$$\text{Operating leverage} = \frac{(\$60 - \$24) \times 625}{\$22,500 - \$18,000} = \frac{\$22,500}{\$4,500} = 5$$

This means that for every percentage point increase in sales, the increase in profits will be 5 percent. The degree of operating leverage is greatest at expected sales levels near the break-even point and decreases as sales and profits rise.

The operating leverage concept provides managers with a tool so that they can tell quickly the impact of various changes in sales on profits without preparing detailed income statements. The effects of operating leverage can be dramatic near break-even because a small increase in sales can yield a large increase in profits. Or, in the opposite direction, small decreases in sales can result in significant decreases in profit. It should be clear then why managers will often work hard for only a small increase in sales or to avoid a decrease in sales. If the degree of operating leverage is 5, then a 10 percent increase in sales would equate to a 50 percent increase in profits.

The Ratios Are Inversely Related

For any given sales volume, the operating leverage and margin of safety ratios are inversely related[6]:

$$\text{Operating leverage ratio} = \frac{1}{\text{Margin of safety ratio}}$$

Thus, if you are provided with one of the ratios for a given sales level, then the other ratio may be computed as the inverse. For the Marshall Creations example, we can compute the operating leverage ratio from the margin of safety ratio of 20 percent:

---

[6] This can be shown by starting with the inverse of the margin of safety ratio:

$$\frac{1}{\text{Margin of safety ratio}} = \frac{EV}{EV - BV}$$

where

EV = Expected volume and
BV = Break-even volume

Substituting in the formula for break even (FC/CMU):

$$\frac{EV}{EV - FC/CMU}$$

Multiplying through top and bottom by CMU:

$$\frac{1}{\text{Margin of safety ratio}} = \frac{EV \times CMU}{(EV \times CMU) - FC} = \frac{\text{Contribution margin}}{\text{Income before tax}}$$

which is exactly the operating leverage ratio. We can substitute any volume level, except break even, for the expected volume and get the same result.

$$\text{Operating leverage ratio: } 5 = \frac{1}{20\%}$$

Likewise, if we knew that the operating leverage was 5, then the margin of safety could be computed as:

$$\text{Margin of safety ratio: } 20\% = \frac{1}{5}$$

RELAXING THE ASSUMPTIONS

At the beginning of the chapter, we stated the following assumptions for CVP analysis:

1. The variable costs per unit are constant throughout the range of normal activity.
2. The selling prices for products sold are constant throughout the range of normal activity.
3. Total fixed costs are constant throughout the range of normal activity.
4. The sales mix is constant throughout the range of normal activity.
5. Inventory levels are constant.

In this section we will present some practical approaches to solutions when these assumptions cannot be made.

Constant Variable Cost and Selling Price

If the variable cost per unit and selling price may change over the normal volume range, then the required volume function is said to be *nonlinear*. In the general formulation for required volume

$$Q = \frac{(FC + RR)}{CMU}$$

the CMU changes as volume increases.[7] In practical settings, this will require that the approximate required volume be computed in a two-stage process. First, compute the approximate required volume using an average or approximate CMU. Then, in the second stage the CMU is estimated for the approximate required volume and the calculation of required volume performed again. For example, assume for Marshall Creations that the CMU is $36 until 600 units after which it falls to $30. The fixed costs are assumed to remain at $18,000. The break-even volume is still 500 units:

$$Q = \frac{\$18,000}{\$36} = 500 \text{ units}$$

However, the required volume is no longer 650 units, but

$$\text{Stage I: } Q = \frac{(\$18,000 + \$5,400)}{\$36} = 650 \text{ units}$$

$$\text{However, the CMU for 650 units} = \$30$$

$$\text{Stage II: } Q = \frac{(\$18,000 + \$5,400)}{\$30} = 780 \text{ units}$$

---

[7] If we knew the approximate functional form of the change in variable costs with volume, then we could derive the desired volume without iteration. However, the functional form of the variable cost function is often disjointed in practice with changes in materials cost and increases in overtime rates occurring at various intervals.

The Stage I volume is rejected as infeasible because it is 50 units over the volume in which the $36 CMU applies.

Constant Fixed Cost

If fixed costs change over the normal range of operations, then the company is said to have *step costs*. This situation will occur in practice with, for example, supervision and machine rental costs. The practical approach to solving the problems involving step costs is to compute the break-even and required volumes for each fixed cost level up to the point where feasibility is reached. For example, assume that the following fixed costs apply to Marshall Creations:

Volume	Step Fixed Costs
0–399	$16,000
400–599	18,000
600–799	24,000
800–999	26,000

Exhibit 4–4 presents the general approach to the solution for the step cost problem.

EXHIBIT 4–4   Solution to the Step Cost Problem

Volume	FC	Break-even Volume	Required Volume
0–399	$16,000	$16,000/$36 = 445*	($16,000 + $5,400)/$36 = 594*
400–599	18,000	$18,000/$36 = 500†	($18,000 + $5,400)/$36 = 650*
600–799	24,000		($24,000 + $5,400)/$36 = 817*
800–999	26,000		($26,000 + $5,400)/$36 = 873†

* Infeasible solution given the volume restrictions on the cost
† Feasible solution

Constant Sales Mix

If the sales mix changes[8] as volume increases, then there is a nonlinearity with the contribution margin per unit. The solution approach is equivalent to the two-stage process presented for nonlinear prices or variable costs. Thus, first compute the approximate break-even and required volumes using an average or approximate sales mix, then adjust the composite unit to the sales mix at the approximate volumes. Finally, compute the break-even and required volumes with the adjusted composite unit.

Constant Inventory

If inventory of finished goods is expected to change during the time period, then both the break-even and required volumes will be affected by the magnitude of the change in inventories. The detailed solution to this type of problem is the subject of Appendix 16A. Basically, the solution involves allowing for the changes in the fixed costs included in inventory accounts. For example, if the inventory decreases, then more fixed costs will be expensed as cost of goods sold during the current year than are incurred in the plant. Thus, both the break-even and required volumes must be increased to reflect the difference between fixed costs expensed and incurred. Refer to Appendix 16A for a detailed explanation and solution approach.

SUMMARY

Cost-volume-profit analysis is the study of the impact of volume on costs, revenues, and profits. At the break-even volume, there is no profit or loss. The required volume

---

[8] The analysis of sales mix changes will be presented in more detail in Chapter 19.

is that volume necessary to earn the desired profits. The contribution margin is the difference between revenues and variable costs. The contribution margin format income statement was introduced. The assumptions of cost-volume-profit analysis are constant prices, variable costs, fixed costs, sales mix, and inventories.

Formulas were developed for calculating break-even points and the required volume at which the desired income is achieved. Desired income must be restated in before-tax terms. The volume may be in terms of units, sales dollars, or composite units. The desired income may be stated as a return on investment or as a return on sales.

The margin of safety is the extent to which expected sales may fall before break-even volume is reached. The margin of safety may be expressed as units or as a ratio of expected sales. The operating leverage ratio is the effect of a change in volume on income before tax.

As the assumptions of cost-volume-profit analysis are relaxed, the calculation of break-even and required volume must be adjusted.

SUMMARY OF FORMULAS

Required volume in units:

$$Q = \frac{(FC + RR)}{CMU}$$

Break-even volume in units:

$$Q = \frac{FC}{CMU}$$

Income before tax:

$$RR = \frac{RNI}{(1 - \text{Tax rate})}$$

Required volume, sales dollars:

$$S = \frac{(FC + RR)}{CM\%}$$

Return stated on sales:

$$Q = \frac{FC}{[CMU - (DR \times SP)]}$$

Margin of safety:

$$\text{Expected volume} - \text{Break-even volume}$$

Margin of safety ratio:

$$1 - \frac{\text{Break-even volume}}{\text{Expected volume}}$$

Operating leverage ratio:

$$\frac{\text{Contribution margin}}{\text{Income before tax}}$$

PROBLEM FOR REVIEW

The Asphalt Division of Suloe Oil Company uses crude oil sludge and a chemical-heat process to produce paving materials. The asphalt is sold by the 100-gallon lot to paving companies and local government road departments. Sales for next week are expected to be 10,000 lots at a price of $22.50 per lot. Fixed costs are estimated to be $42,000 per week. The total costs for next week are expected to be $177,000. The required income before tax is $50,000 per week to justify the major investment in heat treatment equipment and storage facilities.

REQUIRED

Compute the:
a. Contribution margin and the profit for the week.
b. Contribution margin per unit.
c. Contribution margin rate per sales dollar.
d. Break-even volume in sales dollars.
e. Required volume in sales dollars to earn the desired return.
f. Contribution format income statement to prove the break-even and required volume levels.

g. Margin of safety ratio.
h. Operating leverage ratio.

SOLUTION

a. Contribution margin and the profit for the week:

Sales	10,000 × $22.50	$225,000
Variable costs	$177,000 − $42,000	135,000
Contribution margin		$ 90,000
Fixed costs		42,000
Income before taxes		$ 48,000

b. Contribution margin per unit:

$$\text{Contribution margin/Units} = \frac{\$90,000}{10,000} = \$9.00$$

c. Contribution margin rate per sales dollar:

$$\text{Contribution per dollar} = \frac{\$90,000}{\$225,000} = 40\%$$

d. Break-even volume in dollars: $42,000/40\% = \$105,000$
e. Required volume in dollars to earn the desired return:

$$\frac{(\$42,000 + \$50,000)}{40\%} = \$230,000$$

f. Contribution margin format income statements:

	Per Unit	Break even	Required
Sales	$1	$105,000	$230,000
Variable costs	60%	(63,000)	(138,000)
Contribution margin		$ 42,000	$ 92,000
Fixed costs		(42,000)	(42,000)
Income before taxes		$ 0	$ 50,000

g. Margin of safety ratio:

$$1 - \left(\frac{\$105,000}{\$225,000}\right) = 53.3\%$$

h. Operating leverage ratio:

$$\frac{\$90,000}{\$48,000} = 1.875$$

KEY TERMS AND CONCEPTS

Cost-volume-profit analysis (112)
Break-even volume (113)
Required volume (113)
Contribution margin (113)
Contribution margin per unit (113)

Contribution margin format income statement (113)
Composite unit (117)
Sales mix (117)
Margin of safety (120)
Operating leverage ratio (120)

ADDITIONAL READINGS

Givens, H. R. "An Application of Curvilinear Breakeven Analysis." *The Accounting Review*, January 1966, pp. 141–43.

Martin, H. "Breaking the Breakeven Barriers." *Management Accounting,* May 1985, pp. 31–34.

McGrath, J. "Spreadsheets: Breakeven Analysis." *CFO,* May 1987, pp. 83–89.

Sinclair, K. P., and J. A. Talbott, Jr. "Using Breakeven Analysis when Cost Behavior Is Unknown." *Management Accounting,* July 1986, pp. 52ff.

Suver, J. D., and B. R. Neumann. "Patient Mix and Breakeven Analysis." *Management Accounting,* January 1977.

REVIEW QUESTIONS

1. Cost-volume-profit analysis is the study of interrelationships among several factors. Name the factors involved.
2. To what uses may CVP analysis be put?
3. Define break-even volume and required volume.
4. List the assumptions of CVP analysis.
5. List the elements in a contribution margin format income statement.
6. One volume measure is units. List two other volume measures.
7. What is the formula for required volume? Break-even volume?
8. Why must the desired income be stated on a before-tax basis for CVP analysis?
9. Explain how state and local income taxes are treated in CVP analysis for the following:
   a. Taxes on property and inventory.
   b. Taxes on direct workers and purchase of materials.
   c. Taxes on income.
10. When desired return is stated as a rate after tax on investment, how is it treated for CVP analysis?
11. What is the sales mix? When does this issue arise in CVP analysis?
12. What is the impact of income taxes on the break-even point? What is the impact of income taxes on the sales volume required to obtain a desired profit?
13. Explain what is meant by the margin of safety.
14. Explain the meaning of operating leverage.
15. What is the relationship between the margin of safety ratio and the operating leverage ratio?
16. If the direct labor cost increases at 15,000 units of production because of overtime paid, what effect does this have on the computation of break-even and required volumes?
17. If fixed costs change with volume, then they are said to be *step costs.* How are step costs treated for break-even analysis?

DISCUSSION QUESTIONS

18. A 10 percent increase in the selling price has the same impact on the contribution margin as a 10 percent decrease in the variable costs. Would you agree? Explain.
19. What effect does an increase in facilities to produce and sell have on the break-even point and the profit pattern?
20. Describe how the contribution margin and the operating leverage ratio are related.
21. How does the total contribution margin differ from the gross margin or gross profit that is usually shown on the income statement in published reports?
22. Describe what philosophy management might have if the company had a low margin of safety accompanied by a low contribution margin per unit and high fixed costs.
23. One of the assumptions we make in volume and profit analysis is that variable cost remains constant. What would be the effect on the cost curve if efficiency declines at high volume levels?
24. High Life Insurance Company does considerable direct mail advertising. The work of preparing letters, assembling a packet for mailing, putting materials in and sealing envelopes, and putting postage on the envelopes has always been done manually. The

company has the opportunity to acquire a computerized processing system that will write the letters and do all of the other steps. However, this investment converts a variable cost (labor) to a fixed cost (computer and other components of the system) and raises the break-even point. Is converting variable cost to fixed cost good or bad for the company? Explain.

25. Why is the sum of the break-even points for each of a company's products not necessarily the break-even point for the company as a whole?

26. Explain how a company can have many break-even points and many alternative ways to achieve a desired profit level when it has multiple products.

EXERCISES

4–1. Basic Cost-Volume-Profit Analysis.   Margaret Manufacturing Company manufactures and sells television sets. The selling price is $350, and the variable cost is $200. The fixed cost is $10 million, and the required before-tax income is $500,000.

(J. Lo, adapted)

REQUIRED:
a. What is the break-even volume in units for the firm?
b. What is the volume in units required to generate a before-tax income of $500,000?
c. Prove your results with a contribution margin format income statement for break-even and required volume.

4–2. CVP Analysis with Graph for Service Company.   Ochotorena, Inc., prepares personal income tax returns. There are three part-time tax preparers and one receptionist. Fixed costs are $4,500 per month. Tax returns are prepared at an average price of $20 per return. The average variable costs are $10, primarily labor and some supplies. The desired return to the owner is $3,500 (before tax) per month.

(G. Ochotorena, adapted)

REQUIRED:
a. Calculate break-even volume in units.
b. Calculate required volume in units.
c. Prepare a cost-volume-profit volume graph with break-even and required volume in units.

4–3. Break Even and Ratios.   Rodeo Riders, Inc., produces saddles that are sold on consignment through western wear stores. There are eight workers who make the saddles plus an office staff of two. The fixed costs are $6,075 per month. The saddles sell wholesale for $625, and the variable cost is $400. The expected sales is 36 saddles per month.

(P. Williams, adapted)

REQUIRED:
a. What is the break-even volume in units for this company?
b. Calculate the margin of safety ratio.
c. Calculate the operating leverage ratio.

4–4. Required Return on Investment after Tax.   The Orange Limo Co. would like to earn a 14 percent after-tax rate of return on its $225,000 investment in 10 limousines. The variable cost is $.75 per mile and the fares average $1.50 per mile. The company has total annual fixed costs of $150,000. The income tax rate is 30 percent.

(M. Kubinski, adapted)

REQUIRED:
a. What is the break-even volume in miles for this company?
b. What is the required volume in miles for this company?
c. Prove your results with a contribution income statement for both the break-even and required volumes.

4–5. Cost-Volume-Profit Analysis with Sales Dollars.   The Robin Company has fixed costs of $30,000, and variable costs are 75 percent of sales. Their required return before tax is $40,000.

(L. Leonard, adapted)

REQUIRED:
a. What is the break-even volume in sales dollars for the firm?
b. What is the volume in sales dollars required to generate the desired income before taxes?
c. Prove your results with a contribution margin format income statement for break-even and required volumes.

4–6. Sales Dollars and Returns Measures.   The May West Department Stores have annual volume of $80 million. The cost of goods sold is 60 percent of sales revenue, and the variable selling costs are 12 percent of sales. Fixed costs of operation are $15 million, and income tax rates are 40 percent.

REQUIRED:
a. Compute break-even volume of sales dollars.
b. Compute the required volume of sales dollars to earn a 15 percent *after-tax* return on assets of $30 million.
c. Compute the required volume to earn a *before-tax*, 10 percent return on sales revenues.

4–7. Required Return after Tax.   Drew Hammer is thinking about opening his own full-service car washing business. He has been washing cars for 24 years at Joe's Car Wash and now wants to be his own boss. He believes that he has found an excellent location for his new business. The fixed costs of this car wash are $5,000 per month. He plans on charging a flat rate of $5 per car and expects that the variable costs will be $1 per car. Drew has a secret dream to buy Joe's Car Wash at the end of the first year. He needs $10,000 a month after tax for the year to purchase Joe's Car Wash. Drew's tax rate is 20 percent.

(M. Kubinski, adapted)

REQUIRED:
a. What is the break-even volume in units per month?
b. What is the required volume per month to earn $10,000 a month after tax?

4–8. Break-Even and Operations Changes.   Maria's Mixers is a restaurant catering to the local university crowd. Maria's has been quite profitable until recently when a budget cut at the local university reduced volume. The income statement for February 19x9 is as follows:

New sales		$500,000
Variable costs	250,000	
Fixed costs	400,000	650,000
Operating loss		($150,000)

(M. Joyner, adapted)

REQUIRED:
a. What is the break-even volume in dollars for this restaurant?
b. What amount of sales will result in a before-tax income of $50,000?
c. If fixed costs were cut to $200,000, at what level of sales would a $50,000 before-tax profit be earned?

4–9. Step Costs and Break Even.   Wilhite Computer Company manufactures and sells a personal computer through retail department stores. Deborah Arnold, the product manager, has noticed that the company incurs different fixed costs depending upon its level of operations. Thus, the fixed cost is really a step cost. The selling price for the product is $2,500, and the variable cost is $1,750 per unit. The fixed costs associated with this product are as follows:

	Step Costs
Volume	*(in thousands)*
0	$350
1–300	405
300–600	495
600–2,000	615

(D. Washburn, adapted)

REQUIRED:

a. Compute the break-even volume in units for each level of step costs.
b. At which of the unit volumes in part *(a)* will the company feasibly break even?
c. Prove your answer by preparing a contribution margin format income statement at the break-even volume.

4–10. Composite Units.   Cram, Inc., markets products for the college market. Their three main products are:

	Selling Price	*Variable Cost*
Cram aspirin	$4.00	$1.25
Cram alarm clocks	7.50	4.25
Cram No Sleep	3.25	1.85

Cram sells about three times as many aspirin as alarm clocks or the No Sleep product. Fixed costs are $752,400.

(C. Brown, adapted)

REQUIRED:

Using the composite unit, compute the break-even volume.

PROBLEMS

4–11. CVP and Ratios.   Classie Cuts sells swimwear, sportswear, and accessories to young adults and a few matrons trying to be young again. During June revenue was $450,000 with variable costs of $279,000 and fixed costs of $140,000. Georgia Plunk is a partner with Classie Cuts and manages the store from April to September. (During October to April, she works full-time with a music group called the ClassCuts.) For the six months she is in town she would like the store to earn $50,000 per month before tax.

(M. Joyner, adapted)

REQUIRED:

a. What is the contribution margin ratio?
b. What are the break-even sales dollars?
c. What is the required revenue?
d. What was the margin of safety ratio for June?
e. What was the operating leverage ratio for June?

4–12. CVP Analysis with Changes in Estimates.   Chapton Chemical Co. recently developed a new polymer plastic called Z-211. The product has many commercial applications, and the company is currently studying whether it would be profitable to market. The following costs are associated with Z-211:

	Fixed Costs	*Variable Cost per Pound*
Materials cost		$0.34
Labor cost		0.27
Production overhead cost	$ 800,000	0.21
Selling and administrative	400,000	0.08
Total costs	$1,200,000	$0.90

Z-211 is very similar to a product produced by Charlie Chemical Company, a bitter rival. The Charlie Chemical price is $1.30 per pound with annual sales of about 5 million pounds.

(L. Leonard, adapted)

REQUIRED:
a. Compute the break-even volume for Z-211 assuming a $1.30 price.
b. Prepare a cost-volume-profit graph with a price of $1.30.
c. The plant manager indicates that fixed production overhead costs can be cut to $400,000, but the variable overhead will increase to $.25. The marketing manager guesses that Charlie Chemical will cut its price to $1.10 as a result of the introduction of product Z-211, and, consequently, the price will have to be cut to match. What would the break-even volume be as a result of these changes in estimates?

4–13. Revenue Dollars and Composite Units.   Rocking Delight is a small manufacturing company located in West Texas. It makes various rocking animals including horses, elephants, and giraffes. They are made with high-quality wood and are hand painted. The selling prices for the products are:

Horses	$150
Elephants	175
Giraffes	160

About 500 of the rocking horses are sold each year along with 250 each of the other products. The fixed costs are $30,000, and the variable costs are 60 percent of selling price. The required return is $25,000 before taxes to justify the investment in assets.

(K. Turrichi, adapted)

REQUIRED:
a. Compute break-even and required volume in terms of revenue dollars.
b. Compute break-even and required volume in terms of composite units.
c. Compute the margin of safety ratio.
d. Compute the operating leverage ratio.

4–14. Prices, Required Return on Sales, and Volume.   The president of the Johnson Company believes that the selling price of its product should be set to earn a before-tax return on assets of 20 percent at a sales volume equal to 80 percent of capacity. The company has fixed costs of $220,000, variable costs of $8.50 per unit, and assets of $1,300,000. The annual capacity is 150,000 units.

(L. Leonard, adapted)

REQUIRED:
a. What is the price that meets these requirements?
b. What is the break-even volume for the price set in part (a)?

4–15. Step Costs and Required Returns.   McNally Company produces a high-intensity lamp that it markets through office suppliers and discount stores. Production costs for a normal monthly volume of 10,000 units are:

Direct materials	$59,000
Direct labor	65,000
Variable production overhead	35,000
Fixed production overhead	30,000

At 12,000 units or more, the fixed overhead increases to $40,000. McNally incurs variable selling expenses of $0.05 per unit and fixed selling expenses of $6,500 per month. The lamps currently wholesale for $21.95.

REQUIRED:

a. Calculate the contribution margin per unit and the contribution margin ratio. Round the ratio to the nearest whole percent.

b. Calculate the break-even point in units.

c. Calculate the break even in dollars using the contribution margin ratio from *(a)*.

d. Using a contribution margin format income statement, determine the expected monthly profit at a volume of 10,000 lamps.

e. If the company wants a return of 10 percent on sales, how many lamps per month must it sell?

f. The controller believes the average profit per unit sold should be $3 in order to achieve the profit goal of the board of directors. How many lamps per month must be sold to have a $3 per lamp profit?

g. How many lamps must the company sell to earn a required before-tax return of $33,000 per month?

4–16. Step Costs, Ratios, and Graph. The Gregory Toy Company produces a radio-controlled toy dune buggy that it wholesales for $20 per unit. The variable manufacturing costs are $8 up to 5,000 units and $6 thereafter. The variable marketing costs are $2 per unit. The total fixed costs are $30,000 up to 5,000 units and $36,000 thereafter.

REQUIRED:

a. Compute the break-even point.

b. Starting with 1,000 units over the break-even point up to 8,000 units, compute:
   1. Margin of safety.
   2. Contribution margin.
   3. Income before taxes.
   4. Operating leverage ratio.

c. Prepare a cost-volume-profit graph for the Gregory Toy Company.

4–17. Composite Units. Downhill Racers, Inc., is a small manufacturer of racing skis located in Aspen, Colorado. Bill Mogul, Downhill's founder and president, started the company 10 years ago in his garage. Bill quit his regular job seven years ago to devote full time to making skis. The company now has 30 employees and is considering an expansion of the plant.

Downhill produces three types of skis: the downhill model, which sells to retailers for $105; the slalom model, priced at $97.50; and the cross-country model, priced at $90. The company sells two pairs of downhill skis and three pairs of cross-country skis for every pair of the slalom skis. The company's total sales for 19x7 was 18,000 pairs, but it expects an increase in sales of 30 percent for 19x8.

The fixed costs have been budgeted at $600,000 for 19x8. Variable labor costs were $588,600 for 19x7 with an additional 50 percent in labor-related costs. Variable raw materials cost $377,100 during 19x7. The variable costs for the downhill ski is about 15 percent higher than the average, and the cost for the cross-country ski is 10 percent below average. Mr. Mogul has set an objective of $240,000 in after-tax income for 19x8, and the income tax rate is expected to continue at about 40 percent.

(J. Brown, adapted)

REQUIRED:

a. Compute the break-even volume for 19x8 using the composite unit approach.

b. Compute the required volume for 19x8 using the composite unit approach.

c. Calculate the margin of safety ratio for 19x8.

d. Calculate the operating leverage ratio for 19x8.

e. Draw a cost-volume-profit graph that displays break-even, required, and expected volumes.

4–18. Change in Assumptions for a Service Company. Hicks and Associates provides the many supporting actors needed each month for movie and television productions in process.

The process starts with a list from the production company of the types of supporting actor required and the general nature of the production (for example, western, mystery, romance, and so forth). Each supporting actor or actress must meet face and type requirements for each part. Hicks maintains an extensive computer inventory of supporting actors by type, age, location, availability, and recent work experience. Agents match the production requirements to the computer files. The firm's fee is $250 for each actor found and accepted by a director.

The variable costs average $100 per actor. The fixed operating costs are $7,500 per month. Patricia Hicks, president of the firm, wants to initiate some changes but is concerned about the impact on profitability. The desired income before tax is $5,000 per month.

REQUIRED:
a. How many actors must the firm find each month to reach the break-even volume?
b. What is the required volume to earn the desired income?
c. Calculate the income before tax when 75 actors are found and accepted per month.
d. Hicks believes that advertising needs to be increased, which will add $1,500 per month to the fixed operating expenses. If the additional advertising were undertaken, how many actors must the firm provide to earn the desired income?
e. Independent of (d), Hicks is considering a new computer system that will increase fixed costs by $2,000 per month and decrease variable costs by $20 per actor. Compute the new break-even and required volumes?

4–19. CVP Ratios for a Merchandising Firm.   Shoaib Rug Enterprises is a large importer of the highest quality Asian rugs, carpets, and similar products. The company is divided into 18 segments based on the country of origin of the rugs. The manager for the Indian Rug Group believes that demand for these special rugs is highly flexible, tied closely to the domestic economy and the performance of the U.S. dollar in world markets. However, some customers will purchase the rugs no matter what the price or state of the economy.

Indian rugs are sold by the square foot, currently averaging $50 per square foot. In the fiscal year ending January 31, 19x0, the company sold 1 million square feet of rugs in the Indian Rug Group. The group manager has just received the following statement for the year (in millions):

Sales	$ 50
Variable costs	(30)
Contribution margin	$ 20
Fixed costs	(15)
Income before tax	$ 5

Shoaib has $10 million invested in the Indian Rug Group and thus the $5 million in income before tax represents a 50 percent before-tax rate of return on investment. This is a very good rate of return; however, no one in the company knows how the Indian Rug Group would fare if there were a supply shortage or a downturn in the economy.

REQUIRED:
a. Compute the break-even volume in units and in dollars for the Indian Rug Group for the fiscal year ending January 31, 19x0.
b. Calculate the margin of safety and the operating leverage ratios for the past fiscal year.
c. If sales revenue were 10 percent lower last year, what would be the impact on net income?
d. Is it consistent with the findings in part (b) if sales revenues dropped 40 percent during 19x1 and net income dropped only 50 percent to $2.5 million? Explain.
e. A marketing consultant estimates that sales of the Indian Rug Group could drop to 800,000 square feet this year.
   1. Compute the operating leverage ratio for 800,000 square feet.
   2. Why does the operating leverage ratio for this part differ from part (b)?

4–20. Multiproducts, Changing Mix.   Duffy Furniture, Inc., manufactures three lines of furniture: colonial, western, and continental. Planned sales for July 19x0 are (in thousands):

	Units	Sales	Variable Costs	Contribution
Colonial	125	$20,000	$12,500	$ 7,500
Western	200	32,000	20,800	11,200
Continental	175	28,000	11,200	16,800
Total	500	$80,000	$44,500	$35,500

Fixed costs for the combined sales are $21.3 million per month. During July, selling prices, variable costs per unit, and fixed costs were according to the budget. However, the actual units sold were (in thousands):

Colonial	150
Western	300
Continental	50

REQUIRED:

a. Prepare an income statement (in contribution margin format) for the planned information and for the actual performance.
b. Calculate the break-even volume for the month:
   1. For the planned mix of products.
   2. For the actual performance.
   Use a composite of 500 units sold in the calculation.
c. What was the effect of the change in product mix on the break-even volume?

4–21. Production Locations and Ratios. Joe Momma, owner of Hang Ten, Inc., surf shops, is optimistic about his best selling board, the Woobey. The Woobey is a small, flexible board that is easily transported. The board performs extremely well on small waves, which are from 2 to 5 feet in height. Due to the success of the Woobey, Joe Momma plans to open another production shop. He has narrowed the choices to three locations: Narley Beach, California; Orange Peel, Florida; and Bexar Bottom Beach, Texas. The financial data for the three locations are as follows:

	Narley	Orange Peel	Bexar Bottom
Selling price per unit	$ 200	$ 200	$ 200
Direct labor per unit	80	60	68
Materials per unit	36	27	31
Variable production overhead per unit	20	15	17
Fixed costs	$560,000	$739,900	$378,000

REQUIRED:

a. Compute the expected break-even volume in unit sales for each of the locations.
b. Calculate the margin of safety ratio and the operating leverage ratio for the three locations if the projected sales are as follows:

Narley Beach	12,000 boards
Orange Peel Beach	11,000 boards
Bexar Bottom Beach	10,000 boards

c. Joe Momma realizes that the actual number of boards sold can be 30 percent higher or lower than the projections. Based on your analysis, which location appears to be most promising? What additional data might be helpful in making this decision?

EXTENDED APPLICATIONS

4–22. Step Costs for a Manufacturer. The Lewistown Plant assembles vehicles in a 1.4 million-square-foot plant. The plant may be operated 5, 10, 15, or 20 shifts per week to produce the sedans and pickup trucks in the mid-sized range. Each shift is eight hours long.

There are 80 stations on the line, each requiring from one to eight workers. A full complement of workers for a shift is 500 workers. The full wages plus employee benefits costs per worker average $800 per five-shift week. Whether the line is going slow or fast, the same number of stations and workers is required.

Although there is some variation in the number of work stations required for each model of vehicle, all stations work more or less continuously.

ADDITIONAL INFORMATION

Materials costs	$3,200 per vehicle
Variable marketing costs	$2,100 per vehicle (including $1,000 rebates to buyers and $800 incentives to dealers)
Variable overhead cost	$ 200 per vehicle

Fixed overhead costs:		
	5 shifts per week	$ 60 million
	10 shifts per week	$ 75 million
	15 shifts per week	$ 95 million
	20 shifts per week	$100 million
Fixed administration costs		$ 20 million
Average selling price	$7,500 factory invoice price	

The plant can complete up to 210 vehicles per eight-hour shift. Because of guarantees made to employees, the choice of number of shifts is made for a complete model year each July 1. Thus, the fixed costs are step costs on only one day per model year. Assume 50 weeks of production in your analysis plus 2 weeks for the plant to be closed for model changeover and vacations. The cost of the vacations is included in the employee benefits amounts.

REQUIRED:
a. Compute the break-even volume per year as of July 1. How many shifts are needed for break even?
b. Management desires a 20 percent before-tax return on the investment of $700 million.
   1. Compute the required volume per year.
   2. How many shifts are needed for the required volume?
   3. If this number of shifts were agreed to, what is the break-even volume per year on July 2?
c. Assume that the projected demand is 180,000 vehicles per year:
   1. Select the shifts required to meet the demand.
   2. At the shift level in (c.1), what are the break-even and required volumes to earn $140 million?
   3. Compute the margin of safety ratio and operating leverage ratio at this volume level.

4–23. Step Costs and Required Returns. American Watershed, Inc., has developed a process for biologically changing the nature of grass clippings without lengthy composting. The grass clippings are then used in flower beds to hold more water near the surface for plant roots. The process has a specially active organic powder that is mixed with the clippings and watered. After one day, the clippings may then be added to the soil as the biological process first germinates and then attacks the grass and weed seeds that are in the clippings.

The powder is sold in liter containers at a wholesale price of $20. Recent sales suggest the company has a ready market that can expand quickly. The plan for October 19x3 is to sell 10,000 containers with the following expected results:

Sales revenue		$200,000
Less: Variable production costs	$120,000	
Other variable costs	10,000	130,000
Contribution margin		$ 70,000
Less: Fixed production costs	$ 20,000	
Other fixed costs	8,000	28,000
Income before tax		$ 42,000

In their analysis of this plan, the officers of American Watershed are concerned about a number of assumptions regarding the revenues and costs. At 15,000 units of production, the fixed production costs will jump to $40,000. At 25,000, the fixed production costs will increase to $50,000 until a maximum capacity of 50,000 units is reached.

REQUIRED:
a. If the company wants to double its income before tax to $84,000, how many liters must be sold?
b. The president would like to see a 30 percent return on sales. At what level of revenue would such a return be achieved?
c. The vice president of marketing believes that the profit target should be set at $4 per unit. How many liters must be sold to achieve this target?
d. If the company could sell 30,000 liters without changing the cost structure and selling price, what would be the change in income from the current level?
e. Suppose the variable production costs could be reduced by $1 while fixed manufacturing costs increased by $2,000. How many liters must be sold to achieve a 25 percent return on sales?

4–24. Step Costs for a Service Company.   The Great Bow Winter Park has a small ski slope with three ski lifts and about 12 miles of trails. Skiing is risky business for both the skiers and slope owners. Some years the snow is very good everywhere and there are many new skiers. Other years there is very little snow and the slopes cannot open. The costs of maintaining and operating the slopes and equipment are mostly fixed. The area has to be maintained all year for the ski season that runs from about December 20 through March 31.

The fixed cost of operating the ski slope is $500,000 per year if the slope is in partial operation, which involves maintaining 50 percent of the trails and two of the chair lifts. Partial operation can handle up to 25,000 skiers per season. In full operation the fixed costs are $800,000. In full operation the slope could handle up to 160,000 skiers in a 110-day season, but this is very unlikely because of the competition. In a good snow year, the Great Bow expects about 60,000 skiers. On the other hand, if the snow is adequate for only a partial opening, then the expected volume will be only 20,000 skiers. If the snow is inadequate to open, then fixed costs may be cut back to about $300,000.

The revenue from lift tickets, equipment rentals, lodging, and food averages per skier is $32 per day. The variable cost per skier is $7 per day including food, part-time labor, insurance, and state sales taxes.

The owners, Ben and Julie Bowman and their children, have built the slope up from nothing during the past 27 years. They would like to expand the slope during the coming summer. However, this requires a combination of convincing the bank that it should lend them more money and earning enough income this year to pay for the expansion. They believe that $300,000 is the amount of income before taxes that will allow them to expand next summer.

REQUIRED:
a. Calculate break-even volume in units for:
   1. Partial operation.
   2. Full operation.
b. Calculate required volume in units:
   1. Partial operation.
   2. Full operation.
c. Compute the margin of safety ratio and operating leverage ratio for the 60,000 volume level.
d. Present a cost-volume-profit graph.
e. The likelihood of poor snow is 20 percent, of adequate snow for partial opening is 30 percent, and of good snow for full opening is 50 percent. Compute the expected profit from Great Bow as:

.2 × Loss from not opening due to poor snow
+ .3 × Expected profit from a partial opening
+ .5 × Expected profit from a full opening and good snow.

4–25. Identifying Costs and CVP Analysis   G & G Fulfillment House has contracted with Julie Ann Products to fulfill its latest consumer offer. Julie Ann Products is offering one Mountain Spring T-shirt for three proof of purchase seals from its cocoa butter hand cream plus $4.99. The offer is good for three months, and the highest volume expected is 50,000. Julie Ann Products will provide the 50,000 T-shirts and will retain the $4.99 from its customers. G & G Fulfillment House's costs to complete the contract are expected to be:

Packing and shipping	$ 2.00
Verifying the three proofs of purchase	0.05
Checking for duplication	0.10
Warehousing the 50,000 T-shirts for three months	500.00
Cost per shirt to handle any remaining at the end of the offer period.	.05

(G. Vorhees, adapted)

REQUIRED:
a. What are the fixed and variable costs for G & G?
b. The contract calls for a fee of $3 per shirt sent out plus $.07 for each shirt left by the end of the offer. What is break-even volume for G & G?
c. If 40,000 shirts are sent out, what will G & G's profits be?

4–26. Composite Service Units.   The Meridian Airlines flies among the Pacific islands providing basic passenger service. The management would like you to analyze the volume and profit relationships for Flight 804, which flies from Hawaii to New Zealand to the Philippines and returns to Hawaii. Although the price of tickets varies substantially depending upon dates purchased, packages, and seating, the averages are:

Hawaii to New Zealand	$550
Hawaii to Philippines	625
New Zealand to Philippines	225
Philippines to Hawaii	700

About the same number of passengers fly from Hawaii to New Zealand and from the Philippines to Hawaii as compared with those flying from New Zealand to the Philippines. However, half of the passengers on the New Zealand to Philippines segment board in Hawaii and are continuing on.

The route is flown twice per week, or 104 times per year, and has basic fixed costs of operation of $5 million including basic fuel, depreciation, insurance, crew, landing fees, and miscellaneous costs. Ground support fixed costs are $400,000 per landing location. The aircraft assigned to this route will seat 286 passengers. Variable costs include fuel, food, baggage handling, ticket commissions, insurance, and local boarding and deplaning fees. The variable costs average 30 percent of ticket prices.

Management estimates that the required return is $5 million before taxes in order to justify the investment of $2 million in ground support and $18 million for the aircraft. Management estimates that the plane will be about 80 percent full on average for each leg of the flight, but there will be substantial variation from week to week.

REQUIRED:
a. Compute the break-even volume in terms of revenue dollars.
b. Compute the required volume in terms of revenue dollars.
c. Compute the revenue and variable cost for a composite unit consisting of:

Passengers	Portion of Route
1	Hawaii to New Zealand
1	Hawaii to Philippines
1	New Zealand to Philippines
2	Philippines to Hawaii

d. Compute break-even and required volume for the composite unit developed in part *(c)*. Is the aircraft expected to earn the desired return?

e. Compute the margin of safety ratio at the expected volume.

f. Compute the operating leverage ratio at the expected volume.

4–27. Cost Identification, Foreign Currency, and CVP Analysis. Ms. Joan Crystal, who works at the London Merchandise Exchange, was interested in developing a product that would repel unsavory street types. The product would be sold in a $\frac{1}{5}$-liter spray bottle. The odor is so obnoxious that it stuns the attacker for 5 or 10 minutes. Ms. Crystal approached her acquaintance Johnny Turnipseed to be a partner in the venture to be called Crystal, Turnipseed, & Co. Their plan was to add a secret ingredient, concentrated turnip and cabbage odor, to an inverted alcohol base plus a chemical stabilizer that would increase the shelf life of the product. All production would occur in Madras, India, to take advantage of special incentives provided by the Indian government.

Johnny Turnipseed developed the following estimates for the one liter of output:
Raw materials per liter of repellent:

1.25 liters of inverted alcohol (allowing for
    evaporation
$\frac{1}{2}$ unit of chemical stabilizer
3 dashes of Essence of Turnip and Cabbage
Cost estimates (all costs in rupees):

Materials:	
Inverted alcohol	2.0 per liter
Chemical stabilizer	2.0 per unit
Essence of Turnip and Cabbage	10.0 per dash
Spray bottles	.2 per bottle
Supplies per liter of repellent	1.5 per liter
Direct labor	1.5 per hour
Rental, factory	400.0 per month
Utilities, factory	95.0 per month
Insurance, factory	40.0 per month
Factory supervisor's salary	425.0 per month
Administrative expense	300.0 per month
Warehouse rental and security	225.0 per month

It takes three of the workers 2.5 hours to produce 1 liter of repellent.

The Charm Marketing Company has contracted for the coming year to purchase 2,375 bottles ($\frac{1}{5}$ liter) of the repellent per month at a price of 17.23 rupees per bottle. In addition, the Indian government will give the enterprise a subsidy equal to 15 rupees per liter shipped provided that all materials are purchased locally and only local labor is used. Ms. Crystal and Mr. Turnipseed desire to earn an income before income taxes equal to one fifth of the revenues including the subsidy.

(T. Turnipseed, adapted)

REQUIRED:

a. Identify the variable and fixed costs of Crystal, Turnipseed, & Co.

b. Calculate the contribution margin per bottle for the repellent.

c. Calculate the expected monthly income to the partnership.

d. Calculate the break-even and the required volumes in bottles. What is required volume in sales revenue?

4–28. Composite Units.   Tara Systems, Inc., has developed two devices for handling aggressive animals. Both devices are small, hand-held units that emit both a sonic and an ultrasonic signal. The combination of signals disorients an attacking animal. In tests of the devices, almost all dogs become confused and break off attacks upon hearing the sound. Care must be taken with certain animals, for example a herd of charging elephants, that are not highly sensitive to sound.

One of the products, Scram, is effective to 50 feet and was developed for commercial applications, such as postal and utility workers. Priced at $97, the potential total market for Scram is 2,200,000 with a target penetration of 10 percent for the first year. Currently, variable costs are $74.80, but management believes that these can be reduced to $68.00. The fixed costs associated with producing Scram are expected to be about $3 million.

The other product, Shooboy, is effective to 25 feet and is designed for the consumer market. Available in fashion colors and light-weight cases, the device includes a small stereo tape player with headphones. This should be attractive to joggers, walkers, and bicyclists. Priced at $50.00, the potential market is estimated to be 20 million users. The goal is to attract 1 percent of that market next year. In developing the prototype, variable costs per unit have been $42.35. Management estimates that in full production the variable cost will be $38.50. The fixed costs associated with the Shooboy are expected to be about $2 million.

Seeking to raise venture capital, Tara Systems, Inc., has submitted a business plan to Southern Management Associates of New Orleans. Included in the business plan are the following two analyses (all amounts in thousands):

	Scram	*Shooboy*
Volume	220	200
Revenues	$21,340	$10,000
Costs: Variable	14,960	7,700
Fixed	3,000	2,000
Income	$ 3,380	$ 300

Break-even analysis:

Weights	*Contribution Margins*	*Weighted Contribution*
2.2	Scram ($97 − $68) = $29.00	$63.80
2.0	Shooboy ($50 − $38.50) = $12.50	25.00
		$88.80

Volume needed:

$$\text{Total fixed/Contribution} = \frac{\$5,000}{\$88.8} = 56.306$$

This translates back into break-even volume for:

Scram   56.306 × 2.2 = 124 thousands
Shooboy   56.306 × 2   = 113 thousands

The business plan ends with the comment: "We at Tara Systems feel that the profitability of our venture is evident in the comparison of the product break-even points with the quite reasonable sales projections. We are confident that both the sales projections and the cost reductions can be met."

(D. Matalone & B. Adams, adapted)

REQUIRED:
As the accountant assigned to this proposal by Southern Management Associates of New Orleans, prepare the following study:
a. Determine the break-even points for Scram and Shooboy assuming that fixed costs can be differentiated as indicated in the initial analysis.
b. What are the errors in the break-even analysis as presented in the business plan?

c. What would be the impact on profits if Tara Systems failed to reduce its variable costs as planned?

d. What would be the impact on projected profits if Tara Systems were able to achieve only a 5 percent penetration of the commercial market assuming that all the other objectives were met in the business plan?

4–29. Simple Regression, CVP Analysis.   As an analyst for Leisure Time Equipment Co., you have gathered published quarterly financial report information for one of your major competitors: Crosslane Equipment, Inc. The sales force for Leisure Time has also gathered data on unit sales for each major competitor. Your task is to analyze this competitor's cost, volume, and profit relationships.

Crosslane Equipment sells and services bowling alley pinsetters. The sale of pinsetting equipment is quite sporadic. Another source of revenue is service contracts, which are very stable. Thus, a portion of revenues and costs is quite erratic and another portion is fixed in nature. The quarterly published data (plus volume data) for the five years ending December 31, 19x9 (all dollar amounts in thousands) is as follows:

			Expenses			Pinsetters
Quarter	Sales	CGS	Selling	General	Income	Sold
1	$ 16,370	$ 7,577	$ 4,802	$ 2,745	$ 1,246	1,058
2	12,359	6,612	3,880	2,339	(472)	631
3	24,910	9,784	7,106	3,899	4,121	2,216
4	34,350	12,099	9,419	5,114	7,718	3,440
5	29,303	10,792	8,119	4,392	6,000	2,752
6	18,061	7,968	5,193	2,955	1,945	1,348
7	28,526	10,494	7,786	4,267	5,979	2,616
8	30,613	11,082	8,338	4,506	6,687	2,866
9	27,186	10,206	7,517	4,097	5,366	2,472
10	16,835	7,610	4,903	2,780	1,542	1,150
11	29,866	10,902	8,183	4,483	6,298	2,795
12	24,019	9,451	6,731	3,711	4,126	2,078
13	24,043	9,394	6,787	3,697	4,165	2,074
14	30,406	11,057	8,302	4,507	6,540	2,818
15	13,892	6,895	4,219	2,402	376	780
16	18,765	9,207	5,430	3,086	1,042	1,383
17	29,866	11,854	8,258	4,480	5,274	2,815
18	29,165	11,727	8,230	4,456	4,752	2,714
19	21,540	9,941	6,350	3,346	1,903	1,771
20	27,010	11,236	7,697	4,115	3,962	2,470
Totals	$487,085	$195,888	$137,250	$75,377	$78,570	42,247

The sales amounts include a fixed portion related to service contracts. Purchase prices for materials, labor rates, and rates on service contracts have been fairly stable during the past 20 quarters. The selling price of pinsetting machines has fluctuated in minor amounts.

Crosslane Equipment has total assets of $40 million, and 20 percent before-tax returns per year (5 percent per quarter) are considered adequate for the industry.

REQUIRED:

a. Perform the following regression analyses with pinsetters sold as the independent *(X)* variable:

  1. Revenue.
  2. Cost of goods sold.
  3. Selling expenses.
  4. Administrative expenses.

b. Based on your regression analysis, estimate:
   1. Revenue associated with service contracts.
   2. Selling price per pinsetter sold.
   3. Fixed costs of manufacturing, sales, and administration.
   4. Manufacturing cost, selling cost, and administrative cost per pinsetter sold.
c. Compute break-even volume for an average quarter for Crosslane Equipment.
d. Compute the margin of safety ratio and operating leverage ratio for an average quarter for Crosslane Equipment, Inc.
e. During the next year, variable production costs are projected to increase by 15 percent for the entire industry. Assuming that selling prices will stay the same, what effect will this have on the profitability of Crosslane Equipment?

4–30. Multiple Regression and CVP Analysis.   The Sessnap Systems Group sells graphics software for architectural design. Its two main products are the V12 line for designing office buildings and the XR2 for designing bridges. The software is modified in modest ways to meet the requirements of each customer. However, each customer will often purchase 10 or 15 copies to meet the full office needs. Data from the monthly income statements for the two years ending June 30, 19x0, include the following (all amounts rounded to nearest thousands):

		Expenses				Products	
Month	*Sales*	*Production*	*Marketing*	*General*	*Income*	*V12*	*XR2*
1	$ 3,639	$ 2,075	$ 741	$ 348	$ 475	155	171
2	3,916	2,290	795	350	481	211	162
3	3,884	2,118	732	332	702	166	185
4	4,136	2,313	828	350	645	230	178
5	2,986	2,062	743	311	(130)	179	119
6	4,169	2,300	821	342	706	221	168
7	3,846	2,309	813	332	392	239	137
8	3,058	2,016	758	345	(61)	146	166
9	3,912	2,237	774	346	555	190	170
10	3,686	2,162	778	344	402	179	181
11	3,638	2,072	778	337	451	169	163
12	4,672	2,544	857	358	913	285	173
13	2,822	1,955	745	312	(190)	163	110
14	3,421	2,119	775	336	191	187	134
15	3,262	2,128	739	342	53	184	147
16	4,236	2,481	854	338	563	285	135
17	3,575	2,070	740	340	425	151	170
18	3,555	2,354	798	338	65	251	127
19	3,131	2,045	725	310	51	173	103
20	3,075	1,942	716	325	92	136	152
21	3,707	2,169	786	352	400	193	171
22	3,987	2,340	834	345	468	213	148
23	3,077	1,714	636	319	408	64	166
24	2,699	1,911	688	318	(218)	130	146
Totals	$86,089	$51,726	$18,454	$8,070	$7,839	4,500	3,682

Prices and costs have been fairly stable during the two-year period. The Sessnap Systems Group has a required monthly return of 1.5 percent after tax on investment of $16 million in the development of the software. Sessnap has a 40 percent income tax rate.

REQUIRED:
a. Prepare a multiple regression with V12 and XR2 as the independent variables (X's) for:
   1. Sales.
   2. Cost of goods sold.

    3. Marketing expenses.

    4. Administrative expenses.

b. Prepare an estimate of total fixed costs. Also, estimate the selling prices, total variable costs per unit, and contribution margin per unit.

c. Compute the monthly break-even volume and required volume assuming the average mix of products that prevailed over the 24 months.

d. Compute the margin of safety ratio and the operating leverage ratio for an average month at the average mix.

e. Assume the following data for each of the two products:

	V12	*XR2*
Investment	$10 million	$6 million
Fixed costs	60% of total	40% of total

Compute the break-even volume, required volume, margin of safety ratio, and operating leverage ratio for each of the products.

f. Actual mix of sales between the two products is quite variable. To what extent is the cost-volume-profit analysis based on the average mix a reliable analysis and predictor of future events?

APPENDIX 4A   CVP Sensitivity Analysis

LEARNING OBJECTIVES

After studying this appendix, you should be able to:

1. Define sensitivity analysis and give reasons why the analysis should be performed.
2. Prepare a one-way sensitivity analysis for the estimates made in cost-volume-profit analysis.
3. Prepare a two-way sensitivity analysis on prices and variable costs.

Analytical models, such as cost-volume-profit analysis, are based on uncertain estimates regarding the future. The estimates are necessary to form the data upon which the models rely. An important part of cost-volume-profit analysis is the preparation of a sensitivity analysis related to estimates.

Sensitivity analysis is the study of how important results, such as profit, volume, or rate of return, change with changes in estimates. Sensitivity analysis may be applied to any analytical technique. Because of the uncertainty in the assumptions, sensitivity analysis is appropriate for cost-volume-profit analysis.

The calculation of break-even or required volume is just the initial step in a cost-volume-profit analysis. After the initial estimates of required volume, management will ask "what if" questions, such as "What if our materials costs increase by $2?" The accountant must be able to respond to such questions quickly because management needs a clear understanding of the sensitivity of the results to estimates. Because this understanding by management is so important, some accountants routinely calculate the sensitivity of the results to changes in estimates. Many accountants also prepare sensitivity analyses using electronic spread sheets because changes in assumptions can be made quickly and all results recomputed easily.

Sensitivity to estimates may be displayed either as absolute amounts or as percentage changes from the base estimates or both. Although it is common to change only one estimate at a time, it is possible to change two or more. The results of sensitivity analysis are often presented in tables or graphs.

The steps in performing a sensitivity analysis are to:

1. Compute the break-even or required volume with the basic estimates.
2. List the estimates made.
3. Calculate a break-even or required volume as a result of changing each estimate.
4. Present the results of the analysis.

In the calculation step, each assumption is changed by either a fixed percentage or a fixed amount. With the advent of computer spread sheet programs, sensitivity analysis has become less cumbersome for the accountant. We will illustrate sensitivity analysis using a spread sheet.

Analysis Setting

The manager of Marshall Creations has reviewed the results of the initial cost-volume-profit analysis. He notes that the volume required to earn $5,400 is 650 subscriptions and the break-even volume is 500 subscriptions. However, he is considering several changes over the coming months that may affect the analysis. Postal rates have gone up dramatically, so he is considering a change in the mailing methods, which may cut variable expenses by 10 percent.

Other changes are under consideration. The company may move into larger space, and there should be a pay raise. These changes could increase fixed and variable costs by as much as 20 percent. Mr. Marshall is uncertain whether to increase or decrease the subscription price. Increasing the price would decrease subscriptions. Further, while a required return of $5,400 per month has seemed reasonable in the past, proposed investments in equipment may indicate a higher amount. The manager wants to know how the required number of subscriptions might change as a result of these changes.

Example of Sensitivity Analysis

The manager has requested a sensitivity analysis of the required volume to changes in estimates. Your first step is to compute the required volume with the basic assumptions:

$$\text{Required volume} = \frac{(FC + RR)}{CMU}$$

$$= \frac{(\$18,000 + \$5,400)}{\$36} = 650$$

Now the next step is to list the estimates made:

Selling prices	$ 60
Variable costs per unit	24
Fixed cost	18,000
Required return	5,400

Any one estimate may vary by as much as 20 percent depending upon the choices made by Mr. Marshall.

The next step is to calculate the required volume as a result of changing each of the estimates. Mr. Marshall indicates that increments of 10 percent from −20 percent to +20 percent might be helpful without resulting in an overwhelming amount of detail. Thus, each of the estimates is varied from 80 percent of assumed value up to 120 percent:

	80%	*90%*	*100%*	*110%*	*120%*
Selling prices	$ 48	$ 54	$ 60	$ 66	$ 72
Variable costs per unit	19.2	21.6	24	26.4	28.8
Fixed cost	14,400	16,200	18,000	19,800	21,600
Required return	4,320	4,860	5,400	5,940	6,480

Exhibit 4A-1 presents a spread sheet approach to calculating sensitivity. The top part of the spread sheet is an input area for the selling price, variable cost, fixed costs, and required return. The volume formula is presented next. In the output area is a table of the required volume for each estimate. The upper left corner of the table may be interpreted as "For a 20 percent decrease in selling price, the required volume is 975 subscriptions." This is computed by the values of $48 for the selling price, $24 for the variable cost, $18,000 as the fixed cost, and $5,400 for the required return:

$$\text{Required volume} = \frac{(\$18,000 + \$5,400)}{[(.8 \times \$60) - \$24]} = 975$$

Notice that only one estimate is changed from the original four estimates for each cell in the table.

EXHIBIT 4A–1

MARSHALL CREATIONS, INC.
(sensitivity analysis of volume)

Electronic Spreadsheet

	Per Unit	Input Area Amount
Sales	$60	
Variable cost	24	
Contribution margin	36	
Fixed costs		18,000
Required return		5,400

Volume formula Q = (FC + IBT)/CM = 650

Output Area

*Required volume for each change**

		Selling Price	Variable Cost	Fixed Cost	Required Return
Decrease	−20%	975	574	550	620
	−10%	780	609	600	635
	0%	650	650	650	650
	10%	557	696	700	665
Increase	20%	488	750	750	680

Percentage change in required volume

		Selling Price	Variable Cost	Fixed Cost	Required Return
Decrease	−20	50.0	−11.8	−15.4	−4.6
	−10	20.0	−6.3	−7.7	−2.3
	0	0.0	0.0	0.0	0.0
	10	−14.3	7.1	7.7	2.3
Increase	20	−25.0	15.4	15.4	4.6

* The computations for this table can be performed with an electronic spread sheet tables function. Another approach is to set up a formula for the first column in the following form:

$$(\$FC + \$RR)/(\$SP \times (1 + PER) - \$VC)$$

The $FC is the location of the fixed cost amount. The PER is the location of the −20 percent. Then the formula is copied down the column. The second column is in the form ($FC + $RR)/($SP − $VC × (1 + PER)). The other columns follow similar forms.

Below the required volume table is a table of the percentage changes from 650 as a result of changing each estimate.

In examining the percentage changes for each estimate in the bottom part of Exhibit 4A-1, notice that the changes in required volume are relatively large as a result of changes to the selling price. A decrease in selling price of 20 percent results in an increase in the required volume of 50 percent. On the other hand, a decrease of 20 percent in the required return changes the required volume by only 4.6 percent. The effect of a 20 percent increase in fixed costs (+15.4 percent) is somewhat larger than an increase in variable costs (+11.8 percent).

The manager of Marshall Creations sees that the volume required to earn $5,400 is very sensitive to changes in price and somewhat sensitive to changes in fixed and variable costs. Then he asks a question that is closer to what he is planning: "I think that fixed costs and required return need to be increased by 10 percent. What would happen to required volume if we change both selling price and variable costs at the same time?"

The manager has requested a sensitivity analysis involving the change of two variables: price and variable cost. In order to respond to this more complex request, the spread sheet should be changed to reflect a two-way sensitivity analysis. The manager has asked you to increase the fixed costs and required return by 10 percent. In order to document these changes, you add a "change" column to the input area (see Exhibit 4A–2) and set the last two to 10 percent. The right-hand column, labeled "Result," is then the changed set of basic estimates for analysis.

The increased fixed costs and income before tax result in a required volume of 715 subscriptions:

$$\text{Required volume} = \frac{(\$19{,}800 + \$5{,}940)}{(\$60 - \$24)} = 715$$

The output area now contains a two-way table with variable cost changing across the top and selling price changing down the rows. The upper left corner of the table has the number 894, which is the required volume when both selling price and variable costs are decreased by 20 percent:

$$\text{Required volume} = \frac{(\$19{,}800 + \$5{,}940)}{((.8 \times \$60) - (.8 \times \$24))}$$

$$= \frac{(\$19{,}800 + \$5{,}940)}{(\$48 - \$19.20)} = 893.75, \text{ or } 894$$

The volume appears again to be more sensitive to selling price than to variable cost. Because the manager is familiar with 650 units as the required volume, the percentage changes are all calculated from 650. The changes could also have been compared with 625 (the current volume) or 715 (the required volume with the new estimates for fixed costs and required income).

The manager noted that low prices resulted in very high required volumes. He doubted that any volume over about 800 subscriptions was possible for the coming year, no matter how low the price. Thus, decreasing the price 20 percent was not reasonable. The manager guessed that a price increase to about $63 (a 5 percent increase) would be reasonable given the current inflation rate. The manager estimates that a few newspapers, about 30, might drop the cartoons as a result of this small increase in subscription rate. The decrease in postage and the increase in wages will probably increase the variable cost to about $25. The required volume would be 678 under these circumstances:

$$Q = \frac{(19{,}800 + \$5{,}940)}{(\$63 - \$25)} = 677.37, \text{ or } 678$$

Because the required volume is very high compared to expected volume of 595 (625 current volume less 30 drops), the manager is worried about the potential for inadequate returns. He tentatively decides to keep the current space for the coming year and give only about a 5 percent pay raise. This would result in fixed costs of about $18,600 per month and variable costs of $24.50. With these new numbers, you calculate a required volume of 635:

$$Q = \frac{(\$18{,}600 + \$5{,}940)}{(\$63 - \$24.50)} = 635$$

EXHIBIT 4A–2

MARSHALL CREATIONS INC.
(sensitivity analysis of volume)

Electronic Spreadsheet

Input Area

	Per Unit	Amount	Input Change	Result
Sales	$60		0	$60
Variable cost	24		0	24
Contribution margin	36		0	36
Fixed costs		18,000	0.1	19,800
Income before tax		5,400	0.1	5,940

Note: Fixed costs and required income before tax have been increased by 10%. Thus, the required volume has increased to 715.

Volume formula $Q = (FC + IBT)/CM = 715$

Output Area

Required volume for each change*

		(variable cost change)				
		Decrease			Increase	
		−20%	−10%	0%	10%	20%
Decrease	−20%	894	975	1,073	1,192	1,341
Selling	−10%	740	794	858	933	1,021
Price	0%	631	670	715	766	825
Change	10%	550	580	613	650	692
Increase	20%	488	511	536	564	596

Percentage change in required volume

		(variable cost change)				
		Decrease			Increase	
		−20%	−10%	0%	10%	20%
Decrease	−20%	37.5	50.0	65.0	83.3	106.3
Selling	−10%	13.8	22.2	32.0	43.5	57.1
Price	0%	−2.9	3.1	10.0	17.9	26.9
Change	10%	−15.4	−10.8	−5.7	0.0	6.5
Increase	20%	−25.0	−21.4	−17.5	−13.2	−8.3

Note: Each required volume has been compared with 650 units.

* This table may be computed by a spread sheet two-way table function or by placing a formula in the upper left cell of the following form:

$$(\$FC + \$RR)/((1 + PER1) \times \$PR + (1 + PER2) \times \$VC)$$

where $FC is the location of fixed costs, $RR is the location of the required return, PER1 is the location of the first percentage change for price, and PER2 is the location of the first percentage change for variable costs. The formula is then copied throughout the table.

This result seemed more reasonable to the manager, but he was still concerned about the potential for poor returns and about not expanding the space available for the staff.[1]

---

[1] This example is continued as problem 4A–8.

**KEY TERMS
AND CONCEPTS**

Sensitivity analysis (142)

**REVIEW
QUESTIONS**

1. List the four estimates required for cost-volume-profit analysis.
2. Define sensitivity analysis.
3. In what circumstances is a one-way sensitivity analysis appropriate?
4. In what circumstances is a two-way sensitivity analysis appropriate?
5. Describe the effect of each of the following changes on the break-even point:
   a. Increase in selling prices.
   b. Decrease in selling prices.
   c. Increase in variable cost per unit.
   d. Decrease in variable cost per unit.
   e. Increase in total fixed costs.
   f. Decrease in total fixed costs.
   g. Changes in sales mix to increase the average contribution per unit.

EXERCISES

4A–1. Break-even Sensitivity.   Margaret Manufacturing Company manufactures and sells television sets. The selling price is $350, and the variable cost is $200. The fixed cost is $10 million, and the required before-tax income is $500,000.

(J. Lo, adapted)

REQUIRED:
a. What is the break-even volume in units for the firm?
b. List the estimates used in break-even calculation.
c. Prepare a one-way sensitivity analysis of break-even volume to the estimates made with intervals of 5 percent from − 10 percent to + 10 percent.

4A–2. Required Volume Sensitivity.   Ochotorena, Inc., prepares personal income tax returns. There are three part-time tax preparers and one receptionist. Fixed costs are $4,500 per month. Tax returns are prepared at an average price of $20 per return. The average variable costs are $10, primarily labor and some supplies. The desired return to the owner is $3,500 (before tax) per month.

(G. Ochotorena, adapted)

REQUIRED:
a. Calculate required volume in units.
b. List the estimates made in the required volume calculation.
c. Prepare a one-way sensitivity analysis of required volume to each of the estimates with intervals of 10 percent from − 20 percent to + 20 percent.

4A–3. Break-even Sensitivity.   Rodeo Riders, Inc., produces saddles that are sold on consignment through western wear stores. There are eight workers who make the saddles plus an office staff of two. The fixed costs are $6,075 per month. The saddles sell wholesale for $625, and the variable cost is $400. The expected sales are 36 saddles per month.

(P. Williams, adapted)

REQUIRED:
a. What is the break-even volume in units for this company?
b. Prepare a two-way sensitivity analysis of break-even volume to changes in estimates of price and variable cost with intervals of 10 percent from − 20 percent to + 20 percent on

both price and variable cost. Assume that fixed costs and required return both increase by 10 percent.

4A–4. Break-even and Sensitivity Analysis.   Alternative Air provides air taxi service between Dallas and Fort Worth and local airports. This new company has purchased three helicopters at an annual total fixed cost of $200,000. The variable costs per each 20-minute flight are $80. A passenger helicopter will hold up to 10 passengers who pay a fee of $40 each. It is expected that each flight will have an average of seven passengers.

(M. Kubinski, adapted)

REQUIRED:
a. What is the break-even volume for this company?
b. Prepare a one-way analysis of the sensitivity of break even to changes in price and variable costs from −20 percent to +20 percent in increments of 10 percent.

PROBLEMS

4A–5. Break-even Sensitivity to Changes Proposed.   The Paradee Company produces a single product. Over the past year, sales have fluctuated substantially, some months showing a loss and other months a profit. The income statement for October 19x5 includes:

Sales	$ 360,000
Less: Variable costs	(220,000)
Contribution margin	$ 140,000
Fixed costs	(154,000)
Loss from operations	$ (14,000)

Paradee manufactured and sold 20,000 units during October.

REQUIRED:
a. Compute the contribution per unit and the contribution margin ratio.
b. Calculate the break-even volume in units and in sales dollars.
c. The marketing manager estimates that by increasing monthly advertising by $7,000, sales can be increased by $72,000.
  1. Compute the break-even volume in units if this change is carried out.
  2. Compute the projected profit if this change is carried out.
d. Independent of *(c)*, a marketing research firm suggests that Paradee change the product packaging. The effect of this will increase the variable costs by $0.50 per unit and decrease the fixed costs by $11,000. Compute the break-even volume in units.
e. Prepare a one-way sensitivity analysis of break-even volume in units to changes in selling price, variable costs, and fixed costs. Use intervals of 5 percent from −10 percent to +10 percent on each estimate. Include an analysis of percentage changes from the basic 22,000 units of volume.

4A–6. Composite Units and Sensitivity Analysis.   Joyner Prints, Inc., produces limited edition lithographic prints for various artists in the Seattle, Washington, area. Each artist works on 1 to 10 etching stones, one stone for each color, that are then used to print the work. The flat stones are very valuable because they are quarried in only one centuries-old quarry in northern Germany.

There are between 50 and 200 prints in a run with an average run of 100. Each print is signed by the artist and is legally considered an original work of art. One signed copy of the work is kept as a master proof for later comparison in case there is a question of authenticity. All remaining copies are the property of the artist. Items spoiled in production are destroyed. The artist is present during all printing and drying. Later, the stones are carefully sanded clean of the artist's work.

The artist is charged an average fee of $1,000 per print run. The variable costs average about $600 per print run and include very high quality cloth paper, setup costs, and labor.

Fixed production and administrative costs have been estimated at $443,600. The company requires an after-tax return of $30,000 per year. Its tax rate is 40 percent.

REQUIRED:
Prepare a sensitivity analysis of required volume to changes in price, variable cost, fixed cost, and required return. Use increments of 10 percent from −20 percent to +20 percent for each variable.

4A–7. Sensitivity Analysis.   In the production of IVG Rootbeer, fixed costs of $180,000 and variable costs of $.18 per unit are incurred. IVG is enjoying a surprising growth rate considering that no advertising is used and promotion is limited to the point of purchase. IVG has idle production capacity, and the manager is considering implementing an advertising campaign on the radio that will increase fixed costs by $27,000. She has also received from IVG's container supplier an appealing bottle design, which might enhance IVG's image. The new brown glass "long neck"–style bottle will increase variable costs by 10 percent per unit. Another proposed bottle, the "little giant," will increase variable costs by only 5 percent. The product sells for $.30 per unit to retail stores. The production manager is considering changes in the production process that might decrease variable costs from 5 percent to 10 percent. Selling prices have been held constant since the product was introduced, but the marketing manager is considering changing the price.

(A. Gregory)

REQUIRED:
a. Compute the break-even volume.
b. Consider each of the following situations independently:
   1. If management decides to go with the advertising campaign, what will be the new break-even volume?
   2. If management decides to go with the "long neck" bottle and increase selling prices by 5 percent, what will be the break-even volume?
   3. If management decides to go with the "little giant" bottle and decrease selling prices by 10 percent, what will be the break-even volume?

4A–8. Sensitivity to Proposed Changes.[2]   During late 19x7, Ron Marshall of Marshall Creations, Inc., is considering several changes that will affect the 19x8 revenue and cost relationships. At the time of considering the changes, the following data are projected for 19x8:

	Per Unit	Amount
Selling price	$60.00	
Variable cost per unit	24.50	
Contribution margin	$35.50	
Fixed costs		$18,600
Required return		5,940

The projected volume is 625 units sold. However, with the current situation, the office is too crowded and the return is inadequate. The manager decides to do some investigation. He asks you to consider a proposal that was just presented to him by a syndication service. The service will handle all duplication and distribution of masters, billing of customers, and collection of accounts for a fee of $20 per month per account. After some discussion with the manager, you determine that fixed costs would decline to about $14,400 per month even with a 10 percent pay raise for the remaining staff.

Marshall Creations would still need the marketing person and two clerical staff. The current rented space would be adequate because of the reduction in part-time staff and no longer needing some of the equipment. Other variable costs would be about $2 per subscription.

___
[2] This problem continues the case setting set up in this appendix. Refer to the appendix for discussion of prior decisions.

With this new situation, the manager estimates that a before-tax return of about $3,780 would be adequate.

REQUIRED:

a. Compute the required volume with the costs that would result from the syndication proposal.

b. The manager is concerned about the $20 quoted price from the syndication service because he can get only a six-month contract. He is suspicious that the $20 price is a low price to get the contract but that future contracts will be at higher prices.

   1. Compute the required volume if the syndication service is $22, $24, $26, and $28.

   2. How sensitive is the required volume to the syndication service fee?

c. With the proposed cost structure, compute the required volume assuming selling prices of $55, $57, $59, $61, $63, and $65.

d. Prepare a two-way sensitivity of required volume changing both variable cost ($22, $24, $26, and $28) and selling price ($55, $57, $59, $61, $63, and $65). Present the results in table form.

e. Compute the percentage difference between each of the volume levels in (d) and 650. Present the results in table form.

PART

II

Accounting for Production Costs

CHAPTER

Introduction to Production Cost Systems

PRODUCTION COST SYSTEM PROBLEM

The Barnswick Pump Company manufactures and supplies pumps for various purposes. The company stocks over 12,000 different pumps and has the capacity to manufacture an additional 37,000 different pump and pump-related products. Also, engineers design new pumps to meet customer requirements. With a total annual payroll of $11 million, the company employs 340 people in the production plant of which 89 people are direct workers, 27 people work in sales and distribution, and 48 people work in management and administration. The total sales for 19x5 were $22 million and resulted in a net loss of $2 million. The sales have declined somewhat in recent years because of competitors' pricing policies, foreign competition in the consumer pump market, and declines in the local economy.

Pumps are made for water, oil, gas, gasoline, air, and various other liquid and gaseous products. The pumps vary in size from $\frac{1}{16}$-inch diameter to 10-foot diameter. The pumps may be electric, gas, water, or air driven and made out of plastic, aluminum, brass, or steel. Various levels of pressure may be generated as a result of using the pump.

The market for pumps includes construction companies, water companies, natural gas utilities, chemical processing plants, oil and petroleum product companies, farms, and various retailers. About half of the customer orders are for standard, stocked pumps. The remainder require special production orders. The pumps are manufactured in departments that specialize by the function performed: parts fabrication, assembly, finishing, and quality control. Fabrication, assembly, and finishing require

---

32 percent of the total factory space. There are a large maintenance shop, warehouse, and administrative areas. On average, about 60 percent of the total operating time of the machinery is setup time. Large inventories of materials, work in process, and finished goods have occurred in recent years, and the company currently has $26 million in various inventory accounts. On average 11 percent of the pumps must be serviced or replaced during the standard 12-month warranty period. Customer orders require up to five weeks to fill during busy months, except for rush orders (about 20 percent of total) that are processed in one week. During the slow winter months, a special order can often be completed and delivered in under 24 hours.

Although not large, the Barnswick Pump Company must deal with the same production cost accounting issues as companies with $1 billion in sales. This chapter is the first of four chapters that examine basic production cost systems and the accounting concerns surrounding them.

LEARNING OBJECTIVES

After studying this chapter, you should be able to:

1. Describe the documents and computer files in the production information system for production activities.
2. Explain the general parameters of the information system for accumulating production costs during operations.
3. Distinguish between and cite major advantages and disadvantages of job order costing and process costing.
4. Describe the significant elements of the recent changes in the production environment.

The production of goods and services involves costs of material, labor, and overhead that must be accumulated and assigned to units sold to customers. The method of accumulating costs must be closely related to the approach taken in the management of the production function so that important product-related decisions may be made appropriately. Therefore, production management and the related production cost systems are the subject of this chapter.

PRODUCTION INFORMATION SYSTEM

In this section, we discuss the production information system for a product or service. The objectives of a production information system are twofold:

1. To identify costs with work performed.
2. To provide management with information that assists in controlling costs and in measuring the performance of departments or other activity centers within the operations.

The **production information system** includes the planning and control activities for production and its material inputs. This includes (1) the physical operations and elements of production and (2) the cost elements of production. Even though these two are often treated as separate activities in manual information systems, they are integrated and harder to distinguish in a computerized information system.

Production, also called *operations* or *plant operations,* has the responsibility for production scheduling, materials inventory control, and controlling work in process. It interfaces with the marketing activities of sales order processing and finished goods control and with the accounting activities tied to financial planning, the general ledger, accounts payable, payroll, production overhead, and inventory. These interrelationships are identified as we explain the critical aspects of the production information system for an equipment manufacturer, such as the Barnswick Pump Company.

Customer Order

When a customer places an order for a pump product with the company's sales order group, what happens? If the order is for an off-the-shelf stock pump, a check of finished goods inventory files is made to see if the product is available and in sufficient quantities to meet the customer's order. The finished goods control group should maintain adequate levels of products consistent with approved sales forecasts of standard pumps. If the inventory level for any product runs lower than a reorder point or the quantity of a customer's current order depletes the inventory, an order for the needed quantity is issued to the Production Scheduling Department. Otherwise, the customer order is filled from the inventory of finished pumps on hand.

Should the customer specify product characteristics different from stock items, these specifications go to engineering design for review of product structure and routing (operations) requirements. Once approved, all specifications and appropriate authorizations are sent to the Production Scheduling Department.

Information System Aspects of Production Scheduling

The **production scheduling department** plans for and schedules the physical operations and elements of production and monitors all physical flows through production until the final product is released to finished goods control. That is, it plans what and when work is to be done and provides estimated delivery dates to finished goods control. Exhibit 5–1 presents a computer system flowchart of the information flow for production scheduling.

Production authorization comes to Production Scheduling from two sources: (1) specifications for special orders from engineering design and (2) back orders from sales order processing or finished goods control. Back orders are stock items with completed files on product structure and operations; they are ready for scheduling. Orders coming from engineering design are for special pumps that must be entered into product structure and operations files. The **product structure file** provides the part numbers of the component parts of each manufactured item. The relationships of all parts to each other are organized into a tier of inventory items in a hierarchy rising from simple raw materials to component parts, to subassemblies and complex final products. Bills of materials, which are lists of parts requirements, for any product can be retrieved from this file.

The **operations file** (also known as a *routing file*) specifies the sequence of operations to be performed in shaping, fashioning, and assembling raw materials, component parts, subassemblies, and complex final assemblies required for specific products. It may include the work centers at which the operations are to take place, as well as machine requirements.

Now four files are updated and the system generates the needed production and material reports. The **materials inventory master file** consists of materials records showing receipts, issues, open orders, and on-hand balances of raw materials and purchased parts and subassemblies. The file may also contain purchase or manufacturing lead times and order quantities; it is the subsidiary ledger supporting the

EXHIBIT 5–1   Computer Systems Flowchart for Production Scheduling

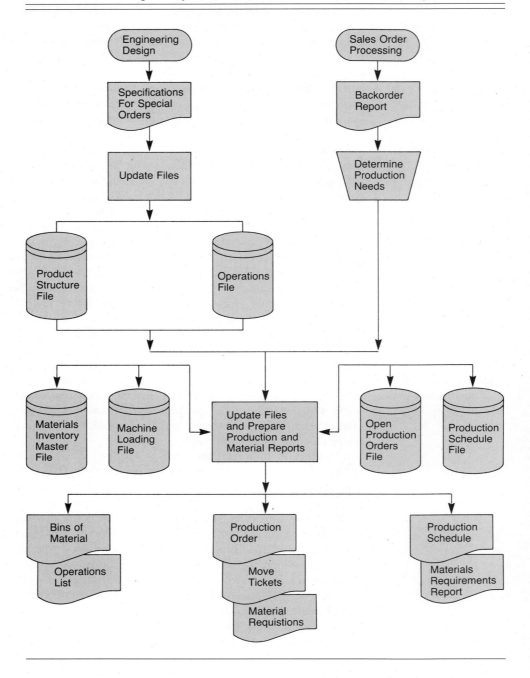

Materials Inventory account in the general ledger. The **machine loading file** contains the status of each machine used in production, including operations completed and operations scheduled on production orders in process. Because the file is organized by work centers, it also reflects the activity status of each work center.

The **open production orders file** contains information on production orders still in process. Each production order has an order number, and space is provided to record the progress of the order through individual production steps in the process. It is therefore a status file for each order. The **production schedule file** contains the assigned priorities for each open production order, the scheduled start date, and the anticipated completion date for each operation.

Several outputs are generated during the scheduling process. Bills of material and listings of operations are produced as needed. Production schedules show the scheduling for a specific period of time. A materials requirement report goes to the storeroom for coordinating the upcoming demand for issues from inventory. The production order authorizes work on a specific order. Move tickets authorize the physical movement of production orders from one work center to another. **Material requisitions** authorize the storeroom to issue specific quantities of materials to the authorized production orders.

Information System Accounting for Operations

As production orders initiate operations, the information system pulls information from the storeroom and the production work centers or departments. Material requisitions show the materials issued by item number, quantity, and production order. Employee time cards, job time tickets, and move tickets come from the work centers and show the amount of labor, labor classifications, and movement of any production order. The **employee time card** gives the time an employee works during a shift, and the **job time tickets** show which jobs received that employee's time.

Two elements of production cost, material and labor, are now in the system. Overhead rates are brought in so that all elements of production cost are available. Exhibit 5–2 is a computer system flowchart showing the flow of information, updating of files, and preparing of reports. We have already mentioned the open production order file, machine loading file, and the materials inventory master file. A new file, work in process inventory file, interfaces with the system at this point. The **work in process inventory file** contains the important data for each open production order identified by product number. It summarizes the cost elements for materials, labor, and overhead costs. This file is the subsidiary ledger supporting the Work in Process general ledger account.

Outputs from the production information system regarding operations are primarily reports on production activity and the cost information necessary to record transactions for work in process in the general ledger accounts. The frequency of generating reports is a function of individual company needs. In larger companies, weekly or even daily runs are appropriate. Monthly reports may be adequate in smaller companies. With complex operations and a diversity of products, report generation may be more frequent.

Completion of Production

Production orders are ultimately completed and the products moved to a warehouse or storage area under the control of those responsible for finished goods. Here the products await customer orders or are shipped on existing customer orders. Open production order and work in process inventory files are updated for the completions, and a record of transfers to the warehouse is made in the finished goods inventory file. This file has a record for each product number that gives important cost data, selling price, manufacturing lead times, reorder points, and normal production quantities.

JOB ORDER COSTING VERSUS PROCESS COSTING

The two most common cost accumulation systems within the production information system are **job order costing** and **process costing.** The production environment (the

EXHIBIT 5–2   Computer System Flowchart of Accounting for Operations

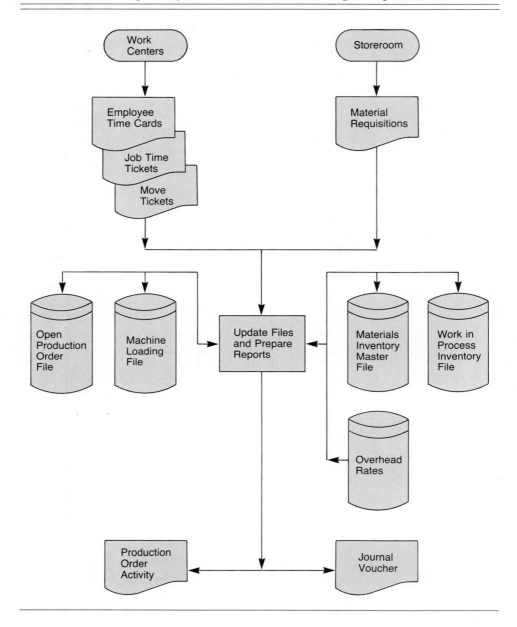

nature of the product and the type and number of processing operations) is the primary determinant of the appropriate system. The following discussion covers job order costing and process costing from the viewpoint of the production environment, the differences in accounting procedures, and the advantages of each system. Exhibit 5–3 summarizes the important characteristics usually cited as differences between job order costing and process costing.

In the next two sections, we will present a general discussion of job order costing and process costing systems.

EXHIBIT 5–3   Significant Differences between Job Order and Process Cost Systems

Job Order Cost System	*Process Cost System*
Production Environment	
Products are unique and are produced individually or in lots or batches.	Products are homogeneous and produced on a continuous basis.
Products receive varying degrees of material, labor, and overhead inputs.	Products receive substantially identical amounts of material, labor, and overhead inputs.
Accounting Procedures	
Costs are accumulated by job and averaged over the units in each job.	Costs are accumulated by process cost center and averaged over units produced during a given time period.
Job order cost sheets for each job form the primary basis for accounting.	Cost of production reports for each department form the basis for accounting.
One Work in Process Inventory account for all jobs in process.	A separate Work in Process Inventory account for each department.

Job Order Cost System

Production Environment.   The environment most suited for job order costing is typically characterized by one-of-a-kind, customized, or special order products. The product or service (whether produced as a unit, lot, or batch) is unique for that specific order. Examples of this kind of product include swimming pools, ships, aircraft, houses, office buildings, custom furniture, and prototypes. Examples of this kind of service include rock concerts, repairs of all types, printing and reproduction, and architectural, engineering, medical, legal, and accounting services.

Customer specifications affect the sequence and type of work to be performed, which in turn usually determines the degree of material, labor, and support required to complete the customer order. Obviously, unit costs can vary markedly from order to order, even when the basic products are similar. Pricing of these orders is often cost-based, tied to the accumulated costs or to specified operations. A need may therefore exist for cost element data accumulated by individual customer order. A company producing under cost-plus agreements or contracts, for example, will generally have a job order cost system.

Job Order Accounting.[1]   A critical part of the job order cost system is the **job cost sheet** (also known as *job cost card, job cost record,* or *job detail file*). The job cost sheet forms the basis for the system of cost accumulation and cost flow. The costs of material, labor, and production overhead associated with each job or batch of units are accumulated on the job cost sheet. These records give a cost summary for the entire production of the job, even if it spans more than one accounting period and many producing departments. Job cost sheets take various forms, including computer disk files. An example of a common version is given in Exhibit 5–4. Whether the job cost sheet is manual or computerized, each job is assigned a number, and the job cost sheet accumulates the information that the system will use to calculate the costs of inventory and provide input for planning, control, and decision-making.

Each time direct material or direct labor is used for a job, the amounts are recorded on the job cost sheet and the amounts are also accumulated for entry in a Work in

---

[1] The detailed accounting procedures for job order costing will be presented in Chapters 6, 7, and 8.

EXHIBIT 5–4   Example of a Job Cost Sheet

JOB COST SHEET

Job Number _____   Date Initiated _____
                                        Date Completed _____

Department _____
Item _____   Units Completed _____
For Stock _____

Materials		Direct Labor			Manufacturing Overhead		
Req. No.	Amount	Ticket	Hours	Amount	Hours	Rate	Amount
	$			$			$

Cost Summary		Units Shipped		
Direct Materials	$	Date	Number	Balance
Direct Labor	$			
Overhead	$			
Total Cost	$			
Unit Cost	$			

Process Inventory account. Production overhead costs are allocated to jobs through a posting to the job cost sheets. Once the entries have been made to the Work in Process Inventory account, the total of the job cost sheets should equal the balance in the Work in Process Inventory account.[2] Unit costs for any particular job can be calculated when the job is completed or at intermediate times if needed by dividing the costs accumulated on the job cost sheet by the units on the job.

A job cost sheet is a ready record that can, when combined with other job cost sheets, serve as a subsidiary ledger for the Work in Process Inventory account. When jobs are completed and units transferred to the warehouse or shipping areas, the

---

[2] For many computerized systems, the posting to the Work in Process Inventory account occurs only once a day to summarize several thousand entries made to job cost sheets during the day.

summarized costs on the job cost sheet represent the cost of goods manufactured and transferred to finished goods inventory.

Advantages/Disadvantages.   Job order cost systems convey an image of accuracy in costing products because costs are accumulated by specific customer orders and averaged over the units on that order. Job cost sheets permit analysis of costs and profits by products when they are completed rather than having to wait until the end of the period. This provides a means to control efficiency of the work in a narrower time span. Finally, job cost sheets provide a basis for pricing and bidding on future jobs that are of a similar nature.

However, these advantages may be offset by more detailed recordkeeping and paperwork. Each job cost sheet must be initiated, the transactions must be entered on a timely basis, and the sheets must be totaled and finally checked for accuracy. Thus, the clerical cost of a job order costing system can be prohibitive. Even fully computerized systems require much clerical effort in maintaining job cost records.

Process Cost System

Production Environment.   Process costing is more suitable for an environment characterized by mass production processing or continuous processing. In other words, each unit of a given product number is identical, or homogeneous, to any other unit of the same number. For example, most processed foods, such as milk, cola, potato chips, chocolate bars, bread, canned goods, and breakfast cereals, are all produced in long production runs. There are three ways to categorize such products: commingled, fabricated, and assembled.

Commingled products are those for which individual units are not distinguishable until contained in some way. A pound of flour in a bin, for instance, cannot be distinguished from any other pound of flour in the bin until the flour is taken out and packaged. Commingled products may be treated by heat, mixture, chemicals, or electronics. Examples of commingled products include soft drinks, flour, ink, soap, ice cream, paper, pharmaceuticals, textiles, sugar, processed meats, rubber, and utilities such as electricity, water, and gas.

Fabricated products are those for which production involves reshaping a material through a cutting, stamping, or molding operation and every unit comes off the line in the same way. Examples include plastic cups, silverware, bicycle tires, phonograph records, bolts, and nuts. These products are characterized as generally having only one part.

Assembled products differ from commingled and fabricated products in that parts and subassemblies are brought together and assembled into a final product and each product passes through the same assembling operations. Examples include motorcycles, television sets, electric irons, kitchen appliances, radios, calculators, typewriters, computer monitors and keyboards, automobiles, and airplanes.

It should be obvious from the foregoing examples that many products are commingled, fabricated, and assembled. Consequently, a process cost system will be a common cost accounting system in companies.

With mass-produced products, customer orders are usually filled from finished goods inventories. Production quality is uniform, which means any given customer order does not affect the production process. Each unit of product is so similar to any other unit that the units cost about the same amount to manufacture.

The main difference between mass-produced services and mass-produced products is that labor and production overhead are the significant cost elements for a service. Material is usually a minor part of the cost. Examples of mass-produced services include check sorting and distribution through the banking system, credit checking for loan applications, sorting of manufacturer coupons accepted by retail stores, baggage handling at an airport, many of the nursing services in a hospital, and insurance application handling.

Process Cost Accounting. Under a process cost accounting system,[3] production costs are accounted for by cost centers over a period of time rather than charging costs to specific products or orders. Costs of direct material, direct labor, and production overhead are accumulated by department, process, or operation on separate cost control sheets or by debits to a Work in Process Inventory account. This information, together with activity for the period, is summarized in a cost of production report for the given accounting period.

The calculation of unit costs is based on a period of time, usually a week or a month, although it could be daily in some cases. Unit costs are computed by dividing total production costs assigned to the department for the given period by the quantities worked on during the period. If a product is routed through several departments, the unit costs from each of the departments are added together to find the finished product unit cost. Although a company may use one Work in Process Inventory account in the general ledger, it is customary to use one inventory account for each cost center.

Advantages/Disadvantages. A process cost system is less expensive and less complicated to operate because detailed recordkeeping is not required for each batch. Labor, for example, is one area in which simplification may exist. Labor is recorded by department rather than by job, which eliminates the need for job time tickets or labor reporting on jobs. Because processes have labor and overhead entering the process at the same time, the distinction between direct labor and indirect labor is not so important as it is when costs are accumulated by job order. Thus, direct and indirect labor may be recorded together as part of each department's conversion cost.

The major disadvantage of a process cost system is its inherent use of broad averages covering a period of time that can generate less accurate product costs for individual units. However, this becomes a problem only if a company does not produce a homogeneous product or the activities accounted for in the production process are not homogeneous. Finally, process costs are often less timely in reporting than are job order costs.

Application to Barnswick Pump Company

The production environment in the Barnswick Pump Company involves elements of both individual job order environment and mass production environment. About 13,000 mass-produced pumps are produced for inventory. These pumps are manufactured with a process of fabricating pump parts and then assembly of pumps. If Barnswick's business were limited to the sale of these mass-produced pumps, its cost accounting system could be based on process costing. However, an additional 37,000 pumps are manufactured only on customer order in addition to pumps that must be designed to meet customer requirements. Because of these unique customer requirements, the cost system for Barnswick will be a job order costing system.[4]

In the next section, we will present recent changes in the production environment that have the potential to change cost accounting dramatically. In later chapters, we will develop the impact of these changes on accounting practice.

---

[3] The detailed accounting procedures for process costing will be presented in Chapter 9.

[4] It is possible to have a hybrid costing system with both process and job order elements. Basically part of the system is process costing, for example the molding of pump parts, and part of the system is job order, for example the final assembly of pumps. These hybrid systems are further described in Chapter 9.

RECENT INNOVATIONS IN PRODUCTION SYSTEMS

Recent innovations in inventory management and production methods have the potential to revolutionize production accounting systems. Many companies are changing to the new production methods because they want to remain competitive and survive in their markets. Proponents of changes herald them as the answer for achieving excellence in world-class manufacturing. This section describes briefly some of the aspects of the new manufacturing environment or Japanese management.[5]

Declining Margins

During the 1980s, the U.S. market for automobiles, electronics, and equipment of all types became much more competitive than in the past. The major competitors were primarily Japanese, Korean, Taiwanese, and German companies. Markups declined and products generally increased in quality. Many U.S. companies went out of business or had large losses because they could not adjust their production processes and marketing efforts quickly enough. Their product quality was lower than the competitors on the world markets.

The drop in markups resulted in the need to reduce drastically the costs per unit for production, marketing, distribution, and administration. At the same time the quality of the product had to increase. In order to survive, a radical change had to happen in production management philosophy. Japanese management or just-in-time management are the terms used in the United States to describe concepts heralded as the solution to the heavy losses of manufacturers. In this section, some of the differences in the approaches are described.

The Basic Concept—Value Added

The basic concept in the new management philosophy is value added. **Value added** occurs only with the actual manufacture (that is, the changing of materials into outputs) of a product desired by customers when they want it and with no defects. Anything less than the highest quality is inadequate because of the potential actions of competitors. No waste adds value. The time required to move, inspect, or store a product is wasted time. All storage space (warehouses), move space (aisles), or inspection space is wasted and adds no value.

Inventory Is Waste

Under old philosophies, inventory was "good." An increase in inventory increased the ratio of current assets to current liabilities. Under traditional cost accounting (as detailed in Chapter 16), the buildup of inventory increases net income through the absorption of fixed production costs into inventory. Inventory is increased during slow periods and sold off during periods of high sales. The theory is that a large inventory increases revenue by allowing immediate delivery of goods to meet orders.

However, large inventories of materials, work in process, and finished goods cause large costs for five reasons:

1. *Storage costs.* Inventories must be safely stored somewhere. Storage space easily costs $10 to $30 per square foot per year. These costs do not add value to the product that will ultimately be sold.
2. *Movement, handling, and administrative costs.* Inventories must be physically moved into storage, moved from storage, and occasionally moved during storage. Heavy or large items must be moved with special equipment through wide aisles. The inventory must be secured from theft. Mis-

---

[5] For a concise and interesting description of these issues applied to a case (Hewlett Packard), see B. R. Neumann and P. R. Jaouen, "Kanban, Zips, and Cost Accounting: A Case Study," *Journal of Accountancy,* August 1986, pp. 132–41.

placed inventory must be searched for. In order to be used, the inventory must be found and on hand. Periodically, someone must physically count the inventory and compare counts with records. The costs incurred for all of these activities do not increase the value of the product.

3. *Deterioration and obsolescence.* Most inventories deteriorate in some way with time. For example, metals corrode, coal oxidizes, grain rots, wood cracks, chemicals oxidize, cloth molds, plastic hardens and cracks, and paper becomes brittle. Finished goods decrease in value through both deterioration and obsolescence. For example, certain crystals (related to the detection and treatment of various types of cancer) are fragile, must be kept at exact temperatures, and have chemical structures that deteriorate within five weeks from production. As another example, retail clothing and accessories become shopworn and go out of style during one season (10 to 26 weeks).

4. *Hiding of management errors.* Many types of errors can be hidden in inventories. For example, errors in scheduling production, new products that will not sell, and promotion efforts that have failed can all be hidden in increased inventories.

5. *Investment.* The purchase or production of inventories requires cash investment. Money has to be borrowed or promising projects have to be deferred in order to increase the inventories.

One of the ways to reduce production overhead and administrative costs substantially is to reduce inventory.

Pull Concept of Product Flow

In order to reduce inventories, a production plant should produce goods to fill customer orders rather than to fill finished goods inventory. The production schedule is "pulled" by customer orders rather than being "pushed" by the receipt of parts and in process inventories. Thus, an order received from a customer should result in a production order that includes fabrication of parts, assembly, and packaging. Purchased parts must be delivered immediately. In order to achieve rapid turnaround of customer orders, the whole production and delivery process must be redesigned to respond quickly.

A **pull production system** indicates the full attainment of the most desirable production system, which will not be possible in all operations. In a pull system, parts are produced only if they are needed by and a signal is received from subsequent operations. If the customer operation is next to the supplier operation, the signal can be verbal or can be indicated by an empty designated area. If the operations are separated, which is less than ideal, the signal can be a *kanban,* which is the Japanese word for *card,* which is essentially an authorization to move or produce parts.

Change in Product Variety—Focus

What causes a higher cost per unit in one plant versus another? High-volume plants tend to have lower unit costs. For high-volume plants, those that produce fewer different products have a lower unit cost than those that have many different products. The more products a plant produces:

1. The larger the inventories of raw materials, work in process, and finished goods.
2. The more complex the production process.
3. The more workers with various skills needed.
4. The larger the factory and the larger the cost.

Focused production is a movement to decrease the variety of products produced in each plant in order to manufacture the products and services that result in the highest contribution margins. Continuing on the concept of focus, some companies have found it useful to reorganize their plants into cells that focus the production of a group of machinery on a product line.[6]

Production plants will often manufacture between 2,000 and 50,000 unique products. Many of these products are produced infrequently or only to special order. Such situations must be carefully analyzed because they require increased capacity (fixed costs). Currently, industrial companies are examining their special order and low demand products to determine which should be dropped and which should have prices increased.

Change in Type of Equipment—Flexible Manufacturing

There is a movement, called **flexible manufacturing,** to increase the variety of products that can be produced on a given machine or group of machines. The purpose of this is to reduce space and cost associated with machinery. By doubling the variety of products that can be manufactured on the same machinery and at the same time halving the total variety of products, the equipment required for production can be cut to about one fourth.

Flexible manufacturing systems (FMS) are automated production systems that produce one or more families of parts in a flexible manner. The system is applicable in low- to mid-volume, mid-variety production situations where numerous related parts are produced in varying quantities. A family of parts consists of several to hundreds of different parts. The production per part often ranges from one piece to more than several thousand pieces a year. The key elements of FMS are the machines and the interconnecting computers. The material handling system is automated and controlled by a computer. The production is done by machine tools that are controlled by computers that are linked together. Finally, robots sometimes perform the tool-changing or parts placement functions.

Simplify Production Setting

It is not enough to set an objective of having less inventory by having fewer products produced in focused factories with flexible machines. In addition, the entire production setting must be redesigned for simplified production.

Product Design—Fewer Parts.   The product must be redesigned to have as small a variety of parts as possible. For example, older office copiers included 16 to 40 different types of screws, bolts, and nuts. Each screw, bolt, or nut must be ordered, stocked, and made available to assemblers. The assemblers had to find the correct screw, bolt, or nut for each place on the copier. In addition, there were up to 150 moving parts. Every moving part is a potential maintenance problem. Assembly and repair required four types of screwdrivers and five to nine wrenches. Now, office copiers have only one or two types of screws and far fewer moving parts.

Redesign Production Process—Reduced Setup Times.   Customer orders come in all sizes. Old production scheduling concepts were based on long setup times and

---

[6] This approach is called **cellular manufacturing** or **group manufacturing.** Similar products are grouped together and manufactured in one area of the plant. The concept may be applied to final products, subassemblies, or groups of parts. The concept works well when the product mix is stable but has some problems when the product mix changes leaving some of the cells idle and others swamped. See U. Wemmerlov and N. L. Hyer, ''Cellular Manufacturing Practices,'' *Manufacturing Engineering*, March 1989, pp. 79–82.

high setup cost. The **setup time** is the time required between jobs to gather the materials, tools, machinery, people, and work space required to perform the next job. The machinery has to be set up, the tools arranged, and the materials made ready.

In order to reduce the need for long production runs, which result in inventory, the setup time between products must be cut substantially. An ideal line would have each item in a sequence of outputs be somewhat different and neither slow down the production line nor increase the unit cost. Reduced setup time is achieved by having computer-driven machinery that can adjust to new requirements quickly and by re-designing the product for easy setup.

Cellular Product Flow.   Older production plants have specialized departments for each production task: parts fabrication, assembly, maintenance, or quality control. This division of labor results in movement and wait time for work in process, a need for a complex scheduling department, and large computer systems. As workers specialize, they lose pride of workmanship, territorial boundaries form, cooperation declines, and inventory and costs increase. There is a need for much paperwork, many managers, and space.

As an alternative, plants are now being reconfigured around the concept of a "cell" that has a receiving area, schedules its own work, produces or orders the parts, assembles, inspects, packages its own products, and has a shipping area. During downtime, it maintains its own equipment. Thus, a *factory cell* is a small factory within a larger factory. Imagine a production cell about the size of a classroom that produces and ships snow skis. This automated line makes 12 different-sized skis starting by receiving the polymer, plastic, and metal edging, then mixing resins, pressure forming, pressing edges, testing and sharpening, and packaging. This line has five workers with the lead worker scheduling and supervising the work.

Worker Involvement and Line Stops.   Part of the change in production design is to have workers involved with the decision process. The involvement of workers tends to result in a better, more reliable product because they care more about the output. The **line stop** technique supports quality control by stopping the entire production cell when a poor-quality product is discovered anywhere in the cell. Then all the workers gather around to discover the cause and fix the problem, if they can. Only if the workers cannot fix their problem are outside engineers or managers brought in. Many companies have discovered that it is less expensive to stop the line and fix the problem immediately than to produce long production runs of poor- or mediocre-quality products.

Direct and Indirect Labor

As production has become more automated, the proportion of direct labor has declined substantially. It is not uncommon for direct labor to be less than 10 percent of total production costs. Many companies have found that it is more effective to consider all labor as a fixed cost rather than as a cost that varies with production.

Indirect labor is also declining as a proportion of total cost. As plants are rearranged to increase volume in a smaller space, whole support departments disappear or are substantially reduced. For example, the maintenance department shifts from maintaining all plant and equipment to maintaining the building and grounds. The quality control and product movement departments disappear. There are fewer supervisors, purchasers, schedulers, and clerical staff.

In some production settings one person operates and maintains four or six continuous operation machines. In other factories one person monitors the production of the entire factory. For example, current technology in the manufacture of plastic pipe allows for a completely automated plant. The lights and ventilation can be shut off and the plant can run all night—computer-driven. Except for emergencies, the maintenance of this plant occurs during the day. Only materials costs and an overhead charge based on machine time are charged to the production because there is no direct labor. Thus, for mass fabrication of metal or plastic parts, there may be no direct labor at all. However, in assembly processes involving many parts, the direct labor cost can still be a significant cost element.

Total Quality Control

Under the old approach, some defective units were considered normal and necessary for efficient operation. Thus, 2 or 3 percent spoilage was accepted, and it was assumed that forcing spoilage lower would increase the total costs. As an alternative, the **total quality control** (TQC) concept assumes that all units produced should be good and no spoilage or defective units are considered acceptable. TQC assumes that total cost per unit will be smaller with no spoilage than when some spoilage is accepted.

The essence of TQC is that everyone throughout the entire company does what he or she is supposed to do to satisfy customer needs and does it right the first time. This includes several elements:

1. Knowing that customer requirements are of primary importance.
2. Anticipating potential defects and complaints.
3. Making all operations fail-safe to the maximum degree; ensuring that things are done right the first time.
4. Inspecting, when necessary, at the source so there is immediate feedback on problems.

Computer-Aided Design and Manufacturing

Many industries, especially automotive and aerospace, have found that computer graphics can drastically reduce the time and cost to design new products. **Computer-aided design** (CAD) is the use of high-quality graphics and software to design new products or change existing products. The software has the capacity to enlarge or reduce the product in size, do cross-sections through the product at various lines, print out part specifications, and print final blueprints for the entire product. As a consequence, CAD reduces the engineering design time.

Computer-aided manufacturing (CAM) occurs when machines or entire production lines are run by computers. The setup time for the machine settings can be reduced from hours to seconds and the settings are accurate. CAM allows one worker to oversee the activities and maintain 3 to 10 production stations. The output and the quality are both increased substantially.

Materials Acquisition

Less Is Better.   The whole process of purchasing materials, receiving, storage, and payment must be simplified as much as possible. Fewer materials, less lead time, less storage space, and simpler payment are required.

Vendor Relationships.   The relationship with vendors needs to be improved from one of competition and antagonism to one of cooperation and partnership. This is achieved by reducing the number of suppliers to one or two for each material, developing personal relationships between those purchasers and the suppliers, and purchasing under long-term contracts.

Suppliers are contacted early in the design of new products to get their input on materials requirements. It also helps to work with suppliers to improve their production process and profitability. Thus, a company is in a stronger competitive position with

50 to 100 suppliers who are concerned about the final product rather than with 1,500 to 2,000 suppliers who do not care.

Quality Deliveries, Just in Time.   Suppliers are expected to deliver 100 percent quality parts just in time for production or assembly. Only a few parts per million are allowed to be deficient. Vendors who cannot deliver this quality on time are eliminated. If vendors can deliver about 100 percent quality just in time to meet needs, then inventories of parts and assemblies need not be kept.

Pragmatic Considerations

These concepts are good and have been successfully applied in some industries: automobile, motorcycle, home appliance, office machinery, and air conditioner. However, many industries are less affected by the new manufacturing environment and the changes that are described in this section. Thus, a manufacturer of concrete and cement is independent of foreign competition because its product is heavy per dollar of sales. Health and processed food products, public utilities, and construction are all protected by law or location.

Labor and Labor Relations.   In Japan, labor is guaranteed a lifetime job at a good wage in exchange for achievement of quality work. Each worker is paid, not by seniority, but by the number of skills that he or she masters. Workers are moved, as needed, throughout the plant. This increases the flexibility of the production. Effort is made to recognize group achievement rather than individuals, in quality and production, thus encouraging team cooperation. Workers are expected to have very strong loyalty to their companies.

   Also in Japan, the distinction between labor and management is minimized with the lead worker providing any supervision required. Bosses with white hats and expensive suits are not allowed. Indeed, the plant managers, engineers, administrative personnel, and workers all dress about the same while in the plant. There are fewer managers in proportion to workers and their compensation is closer to the worker's compensation level.

   The Japanese labor environment cannot be duplicated in American plants for various reasons.[7] There are major differences between Japan and America in culture, attitudes, and history. For example, the old American attitudes of managers ("Workers are lazy and must be pushed.") and workers ("Bosses are the enemy.") fade slowly, but they are fading. Unlike Japan, the United States includes many racial and ethnic groups with diverse languages in a geographically dispersed area.

   In the United States as compared to Japan, workers are laid off and plants are closed. Many people who have spent their lives working for a U.S. company are fired. In Japan, workers are employed for life and are rarely fired. In U.S. companies, many employees have the perception that few promises are made and fewer promises are kept. Alternatively, managers have the perception that too much has been promised and that the cost of U.S. labor is high and the productivity low. Finally, the labor laws in the United States are detailed and often very cumbersome.

Inventory Reduction.   Some production processes will always involve work in process because the process requires time. Thus, processes that involve aging, growth,

---

[7] In a Japanese factory, the working hours are very long, perhaps as many as 75 hours per week, and the working conditions can be very poor. Changes to the Japanese approach can be very unsettling to the workers and their families. See J. A. Klein, "The Human Costs of Manufacturing Reform," *Harvard Business Review*, March–April 1989, pp. 60ff.

or curing will always have a large work in process. Examples include cured or aged food (cheese or meat), wine, distilled beverages, leathers, paper, most lumber, many chemicals, and all agriculture. The pull concept must be adapted with these industries because producing strictly to customer order requires that the customer place the order three months to five years in advance of product completion.

Basic commodities can be sold with forward contracts, which sell future production for delivery on a specific date or dates. The effect will be a "pull" on production. For example, three years' output of a demin plant, which cards, spins, weaves, and dyes cotton, can be forward contracted to Levi Strauss or Sedgefield Jeans. In turn, the denim plant can forward contract three years' output of cotton gins, which separate cotton from seeds.

Small and Labor-Intensive Companies. Small companies do not have enough leverage with suppliers and employees or enough capital to implement the foregoing concepts fully. Thus, if a small manufacturer asks suppliers to deliver "100 percent quality, just in time," the suppliers will naturally be unresponsive. There is not enough volume to justify the supplier's investment in local plant and transportation facilities. Employees are unwilling to cooperate fully with small companies because, realistically, they may have to look for a new job next year because many small companies cease operations each year.

Some production processes are primarily labor intensive. For example, the production of clothing can be somewhat automated, but the basic processes require much hand labor. Thus, success depends on a ready source of inexpensive labor rather than large computer-driven machinery. Service industries are both labor intensive and protected by geographic location. Thus, the health, legal, governmental, and educational organizations do not have to respond to foreign competition to any important degree.

As can be seen, the complete set of the above concepts can be adopted in only a few industries. However, some of the concepts can be applied to most companies because their founding ideals are useful for managing most organizations. That is, 100 percent quality delivery to customers can be the ideal, inventories can be reduced, suppliers can be required to deliver higher quality and faster, production lines can be made more flexible, and workers can be encouraged to learn more skills.

Application to Barnswick Pump Company

Some aspects of the new manufacturing environment philosophy are applicable to the Barnswick Pump Company. As a small company, it is attempting to provide 50,000 different pumps for numerous applications. The plant clearly lacks focus on high-profit pumps for specific markets. The $26 million in total inventories is very high compared to the $22 million sales, which indicates that the company could benefit from a substantial reduction in inventories. The makeup of the work force is heavily oriented toward support staff; thus, a low proportion (89 of 340) of the employees are value-added workers. Of the total employees of the company, only about 28 percent—that is, $(89 + 27)/415$—either produce or sell the product. The other 72 percent are non-value added. Of the total factory space, only 32 percent is value added.

It takes a long time (five weeks) to fill a customer order; even a rush order takes seven days. During the winter months, an order can be completed and delivered in under one day. This indicates that for most of the year, customer orders spend much of the time waiting for available facilities. Thus, there is much wasted time in the plant. Setup time is high (60 percent), indicating that some of the processes could benefit from a reduction in setup times. Finally, why do 11 percent of the pumps fail during the first year? The 11 percent return rate indicates that there is much room for perfection in the quality of the product.

SUMMARY

Manufacturing management plans, controls, and accumulates production costs through a production information system. The central focus of this system is production scheduling because this operation is integrally involved in all aspects of production. It authorizes production orders, schedules machines and tasks, monitors the production process until orders are completed and transferred to finished goods inventory. A production information system with various documents, computer files, and reports will reflect all of the work in production scheduling and accumulate the costs of material, labor, and production overhead for work performed.

Job order costing and process costing are the common cost accumulation systems within the production information system. The nature of the product and the type and number of processing operations are the primary determinants of which system will be used in any situation. Generally, job order costing is used when products are unique because of individual customer specifications; process costing is more appropriate for homogeneous products produced on a continuous basis.

The new manufacturing environment already exists in the automotive, equipment, and related industries. It involves the reduction of inventories, the pull concept, the reduction of product variety, and the simplification of production. All of these promise a drastic reduction in cost per unit. Total quality control, worker involvement, cellular manufacturing, vendor relationships, and just-in-time deliveries are important. The new manufacturing environment does not apply to all companies because some manufacturers are protected, some production requires inventories, small companies cannot implement it, and some processes are primarily labor intensive. However, many of the concepts can be adapted to most companies.

PROBLEM FOR REVIEW

Layle Carriage Shops brings the days of horse-drawn transportation back to life. With sales of $3 million and profits of $400,000, the company has specialized in the manufacture of stagecoaches and wagons based on a similar design. Authentic stagecoaches, wagons, and harnesses are reminiscent of a past century. The coaches and wagons are built $\frac{5}{8}$ the size of those used in the Old West so they can be pulled by Shetland ponies. The primary buyers of the products are amusement parks and zoos where there are many children, and groups frequently participating in parades and similar functions. The owner/manager, William Layle, has had many opportunities to expand the business into period furniture and metalware but has rejected these opportunities with the statement: "We would rather make the best coaches and wagons possible."

A typical coach will weigh 1,400 pounds. The wooden sides are steam-bent, and the tongue and frame are made with blacksmith skills. Everything is as authentic as possible down to the seats, window covers, and kerosene lanterns. Inside and out, the coach can carry as many as nine people, cruising at 4 miles per hour. In a few cases, customers have requested car tires so the coach can be pulled behind a truck on the highway.

Although the basic frame is the same for all products, each coach and wagon are finished to customer specifications. Sales order processing uses a questionnaire to determine exactly what the customer wants. From these details, quotes are developed. Completed orders are shipped immediately, so finished goods inventory is minimal. Each coach is built by a crew of four people in their own workshop. Each workshop is stocked with common carpentry and metalworking tools. The crews are headed by master craftsmen who take great pride in their work and who can perform all of the jobs in building a coach. The crew orders the lumber, metal, paint, and leather from local sources. An experienced crew will have very little leftover material at the end of the production process. There is a total of 14 crew shops. The entire plant consists of the crew shops plus a small administrative office for the company manager, one receptionist/clerk, and one accounting clerk. The sales force consists of agents in various cities working on an 8 percent commission. Each customer order is assigned to the next available shop. There are enough shops so that each customer order can be assigned immediately 90 percent of the time. About 20 percent of the time each shop is idle, during which time the workers maintain the equipment, learn new skills, or take the afternoon off to play in a local softball game. While weather and road hazards can cause problems, only rarely will there be a coach or wagon that has a problem related to manufacture during the 10-year warranty period.

REQUIRED

a. What type of cost accounting system is appropriate for Layle Carriage Shops?

b. Apply the new manufacturing environment concepts to this company. Are any changes indicated?

SOLUTION

a. Type of cost accounting system.

There are elements of both process costing and job order costing production environments described in the problem. The basic design for the coach or wagon is the same for all customers, but each is customized in its finishing. However, the shops are proceeding in a job order fashion by producing each coach from the ground up to meet a specific customer order. Thus, it would be feasible to use job order costing for each order. Alternatively, the company could use process costing to average the costs for all the coaches for each shop. Then, any finishing costs that seem to be unusual could be added to the cost of the units completed.

b. Application of the new manufacturing environment philosophy: Layle Carriage Shops seems to be following the concepts in the Japanese philosophy. They have focused their production rather than branching out into furniture and metalware. There is no or little waste in time or space. Most activities are value added in the description of the production setting. Each of the shops as described is following the cell concept of production. Because all the products start out the same, there should be little setup time. Almost all of the space is producing space, and no inventories are kept. Customer orders are started quickly. Because the full product is produced in one shop, no movement should be required. No storage is required. The supervisors appear to be the master craftsmen; thus, there is no distinction between workers and supervisors. Warranty repairs seem extremely low, especially in light of the long warranty period. This indicates that quality is consistently good. The workers and the owner sound as though they take pride in their quality work. Thus, no changes are indicated.

KEY TERMS AND CONCEPTS

Production information system (154)	Work in process inventory file (157)
Production Scheduling Department (155)	Job order costing (157)
Product structure file (155)	Process costing (157)
Operations file (155)	Job cost sheet (159)
Materials inventory master file (155)	Commingled products (161)
Machine loading file (156)	Fabricated products (161)
Open production orders file (156)	Assembled products (161)
Production schedule file (157)	Value added (163)
Material requisition (157)	Pull production system (164)
Employee time card (157)	Focused production (165)
Job time tickets (157)	Cellular manufacturing (165)

Flexible manufacturing (165)   Total quality control (167)
Setup time (166)   Computer-aided design (167)
Line stop (166)   Computer-aided manufacturing (167)

ADDITIONAL READINGS

Avishai, B. "A CEO's Common Sense of CIM: An Interview with J. Tracy O'Rourke." *Harvard Business Review*, January–February 1989, pp. 110–17.

Ballew, V. B., and R. J. Schlesinger. "Modern Factories and Outdated Cost Systems Do Not Mix." *Production and Inventory Management Journal*, First Quarter 1989, pp. 19–23.

Berliner, C., and J. A. Brimson. "CMS Trends and Issues." In *Cost Management for Today's Advanced Manufacturing: The CAM-I Conceptual Design*. Boston: Harvard Business School Press, 1989.

Brimson, J. A. "How Advanced Manufacturing Technologies Are Reshaping Cost Management." *Management Accounting*, March 1986, pp. 25–29.

Chase, R. B., and D. A. Garvin. "The Service Factory." *Harvard Business Review*, July–August 1989, pp. 61–69.

Dilts, D. M., and G. W. Russell. "Accounting for the Factory of the Future." *Management Accounting*, April 1985, pp. 34–40.

Dividow, W. H., and B. Uttal. "Service Companies: Focus or Falter." *Harvard Business Review*, July–August 1989, pp. 77–87.

Esparrago, R. A. "Kanban." *Production and Inventory Management Journal*, First Quarter 1988, pp. 6–10.

Foster, G., and C. T. Horngren. "JIT: Cost Accounting and Cost Management Issues." *Management Accounting*, June 1987, pp. 19–25.

Gupta, Y. P. "Human Aspects of Flexible Manufacturing Systems." *Production and Inventory Control Journal*, Second Quarter 1989, pp. 30–36.

Howell, R. A., and S. R. Soucy. "Major Trends for Management Accounting." *Management Accounting*, July 1987, pp. 21–27.

Keegan, D. P.; R. G. Eiler; and J. V. Anania. "An Advanced Cost Management System for the Factory of the Future." *Management Accounting*, December 1988, pp. 31–37.

Klein, J. A. "The Human Costs of Manufacturing Reform." *Harvard Business Review*, March–April 1989, pp. 60–70.

Martin, J. M. "Cells Drive Manufacturing Strategy." *Manufacturing Engineering*, January 1989, pp. 49–54.

McIlhattan, R. D. "How Cost Management Systems Can Support the JIT Philosophy." *Management Accounting*, September 1987, pp. 20–26.

Neumann, B. R., and P. R. Jaouen. "Kanban, Zips and Cost Accounting: A Case Study." *Journal of Accountancy*, August 1986, pp. 132–41.

Schrelber, R. R. "The CIM Caper: Motorola's Operation Bandit." *Manufacturing Engineering*, April 1989, pp. 85–89.

Seglund, R., and S. Ibarreche. "Just-in-Time: The Accounting Implications." *Management Accounting*, August 1984, pp. 43–45.

Tatikonda, M. V. "Just-in-Time and Modern Manufacturing Environments: Implications for Cost Accounting." *Production and Inventory Control Journal*, First Quarter 1988, pp. 1–5.

Taussig, R. A., and W. L. Shaw. "Accounting for Productivity: A Practical Approach." *Management Accounting*, May 1985, pp. 48–52.

Wemmerlov, U., and N. L. Hyer. "Cellular Manufacturing Practices." *Manufacturing Engineering*, March 1989, pp. 79–82.

REVIEW QUESTIONS

1. What are the objectives of a production information system?
2. What are the primary functions of the production department?

3. Describe the process a manufacturing company goes through when a customer order is received to determine whether production of the items in the order is required.
4. What is the function of the Production Scheduling Department?
5. Where does the authorization to start a production order come from?
6. What is the basic purpose of each of the following files?
   a. Product structure file.
   b. Operations file.
   c. Materials inventory master file.
   d. Machine loading file.
   e. Open production orders file.
   f. Production schedule file.
   g. Work in process inventory file.
7. What is the purpose of each of the following documents:
   a. Bill of materials.
   b. Materials requisition.
   c. Employee time card.
   d. Employee time ticket.
   e. Move ticket
8. Under what conditions would it be appropriate to use a job order cost system? A process cost system?
9. Costs are accumulated by job in a job order cost system. How are they accumulated in a process cost system?
10. What is the function of a job cost sheet?
11. What are one major advantage and one disadvantage of a job order cost accounting system?
12. What is the difference between fabrication and assembly?
13. Which element of production cost is insignificant in mass-produced services as compared to mass-produced products?
14. What are one major advantage and one major disadvantage of a process cost system?
15. List three characteristics of the new manufacturing environment.
16. What is the basic concept of value added for a manufacturer?
17. List four reasons for large inventories being costly.
18. What is the pull concept of production flow?
19. Why is high product variety costly?
20. What is cellular manufacturing?
21. What is flexible manufacturing trying to accomplish?
22. Why is it important to gain worker involvement? What is the role of line stops in worker involvement?
23. Why is achieving cooperative vendor relationships important to production quality?
24. What is the purpose of (1) computer-aided design and (2) computer-aided manufacturing?
25. Why does the new manufacturing environment not strictly apply to all industries?

DISCUSSION QUESTIONS

26. How does the processing of back orders for a merchandising company differ from a manufacturing company?
27. What would the application of just-in-time purchasing imply for the management of a retail chain with 600 stores?
28. The purposes of colleges and universities are to instruct students and create new knowledge. Apply the value-added concept to the utilization of space at a college or university.

EXERCISES

5–1. Production Accounting Files.   Listed below are computer files related to production accounting systems. Indicate by a letter or letters, the system(s) to which the file relates.

Production Accounting Systems	*Computer Files*
a. Accounting for operations	_____ 1. Machine loading
b. Material purchases	_____ 2. Materials inventory master
c. Material receipts	_____ 3. Open production orders
d. Production scheduling	_____ 4. Open purchase orders
	_____ 5. Operations
	_____ 6. Overhead rates
	_____ 7. Product structure
	_____ 8. Production schedule
	_____ 9. Vendor master
	_____ 10. Work in process inventory

5–2. Matching Production Documents. On your first day on an audit, you have been assigned to the Creoche Defense Plant near San Diego, California. You are assigned to test the work in process inventories. The job is challenging to you because you can not figure out which form does what related to the production of a radar unit that is to be installed in the new F-23 fighter jet.

REQUIRED:

Listed below left are the names of eight forms that are used and on the right are what the forms might do. Match up a number for each letter. *Note:* There is one function that will not match up to a form.

_____ *a.* Materials requisition	1. Lists all materials used in a radar unit
_____ *b.* Move ticket	2. Records employee time in plant
_____ *c.* Employee time card	3. Accumulates costs per radar unit
_____ *d.* Purchase requisition	4. Authorizes the transfer of a radar unit from one area
_____ *e.* Bill of materials	to another
_____ *f.* Production order	5. Records time of employee on specific unit
_____ *g.* Job cost sheet	6. Authorizes the production of a radar unit
_____ *h.* Job time ticket	7. Requests that materials be purchased
	8. Requests authorized suppliers to ship materials
	9. Requests materials be issued from stores to production

5–3. Process and Job Order Costing. Listed below are products and services that require various production processes. Indicate with a J or P whether the process would be most advantageously accounted for with a job order (J) or a process cost (P) system.

(A. Gregory)

_____ *a.* Deluxe brownie mix	_____ *f.* Cut a 26.9 carat diamond valued
_____ *b.* Custom-built house	at $389,000
_____ *c.* Children's winter coats	_____ *g.* Patient visit to a hospital for
_____ *d.* Toothpaste	major surgery
_____ *e.* Engine overhaul for large truck	_____ *h.* Unleaded gasoline

5–4. Job Order and Process Costing. For each of the following companies or plants, indicate P for process costing or J for job order costing as the most likely type of cost accounting system:

(B. George)

_____ *a.* Breakfast cereal company	_____ *e.* Research contractor
_____ *b.* Large ship assembly yard	_____ *f.* Automobile assembly plant
_____ *c.* Construction company	_____ *g.* Bakery specializing in cakes for
_____ *d.* Textile dying company	large weddings
	_____ *h.* Petroleum refinery

5–5. Value-Added Space Costs. The Gately Company prints checks for personal and commercial accounts. Each order is received by an account representative, who sets up and verifies the job. Then the job is sent to the printing room, quality control, binding room, and finally is mailed by the account representative to the customer. The company has leased space in the Houston Industrial Park for the following:

Reception and administration	800
Account representatives	400
Security	300
Quality control	200
Printing room	400
Document storage	1,200
Binding room	100
Currently vacant offices	600
Total leased space	4,000

The lease payments are $5,000 per month, and the utilities average $2,000 per month. The utilities are primarily lighting and air conditioning that relate to all space.

REQUIRED:
Assuming that the value-added employees are the account representatives, printers, and binders:
a. Compute the cost of value-added space on a monthly basis.
b. Compute the cost of non–value-added space on a monthly basis.

5–6. Product Variety and Warehouse Space. The Mission Company fabricates electronic parts and distributes the parts through regional warehouses. Data on the 140,000 parts stocked in the Seattle Warehouse include:

	Per Product Square Feet	Number of Products	Revenues (in millions)
A. High volume	20	10,000	$80
B. Medium volume	10	30,000	20
C. Low volume	5	100,000	10

The square footage is the average amount of floor space allocated to each unique product in the warehouse. The cost of goods sold averages 60 percent of the selling price, and the warehouse space costs $18 per square foot per year. The company can sublease all or any portion of the Seattle Warehouse.

REQUIRED:
a. Compute the total revenues, cost of goods sold, and warehousing cost for the Seattle Warehouse.
b. Compute the total revenues, cost of goods sold, and warehousing cost for each volume level.
c. What portion of the warehouse should be sublet?

5–7. Setup Costs. A web-fed printing machine at Alexander Printing processes very quickly. A 20,000 copy run of a 500-page novel can be printed in about 30 minutes. Unfortunately, the setup time averages 60 minutes. During April 19x7, the following costs were incurred on the #6 Press:

Paper	$380,000
Ink	82,000
Direct labor	87,000
Overhead	148,000
Total press cost	$697,000

Of the overhead, 30 percent is variable and primarily relates to direct labor; 40 percent is variable and relates to machine running time. The press was scheduled to run at maximum capacity throughout the month. The average press run took 30 minutes during the month, and an average setup took 60 minutes.

REQUIRED:

a. Compute the proportion and amount of direct labor that relates to setup time.

b. Compute the proportion and amount of overhead that relates to setup time.

PROBLEMS

5–8. Production Management Systems. In the Byers-Duffy Company production forecasts and profit goals are determined well in advance of actual production. Once production plans have been made and approved, it becomes the responsibility of the production manager to put these plans into effect and control the productive operations in such a way that planned profits will be realized. There are many complex problems of production control, such as determining material requirements, scheduling materials and supplies from vendors, determining which plants to use for the manufacture of which products or components, scheduling production within the plants to avoid bottlenecks, determining labor requirements to manufacture the products, and handling specific assignments to personnel and machines. A computerized production management system makes handling these tasks easier.

Many documents and reports are generated by a computerized production management system. Some of the reports are merely summarizations of the activities of the period or the goods that have been produced. Others specify requirements for scheduling and still others provide status summaries.

REQUIRED:

For each of the following documents or reports, describe which files were probably needed to obtain the data presented in it and why it is important:

a. Production order.

b. Materials requisitions.

c. Production schedule.

d. Operations list.

e. Production order activity.

5–9. Job Order versus Process Cost. Christie Rydell, new controller for Jessie Corcoran Marketing Corporation, has reviewed the company's supermarket coupon processing operations. Supermarkets accepting coupons bundle the coupons received each day (on average 1,600 coupons per bundle) and send them to Jessie Corcoran Marketing for processing and presenting for redemption to the manufacturers. The marketing company pays the supermarket the redemption value less a processing fee. During 19x5, Corcoran sorted and redeemed more than 100 million coupons, earning processing fees of $12,480,000 and an income before tax of $1,434,000.

Each bundle received from a supermarket is given a job number with a job record included in the batch. There are 800 jobs each work day, and there are 312 work days a year. The morning after coupons are received from the supermarkets, they are shipped to plants in Mexico for sorting. The workers use large plastic templates to sort by size, which avoids having to read each coupon. An average job requires three hours to sort. Data are kept on the redemption value by manufacturer for each supermarket bundle. Redemption values are noted on the job records and, at a later time, accounting notes the processing fee charged for that bundle. Labor and overhead are charged to the job based on the redemption value at a rate of 24 percent. At the end of each week, the coupons for each manufacturer are submitted for redemption.

Christie's review of the system suggests that the company is using a job order system because jobs are identified and costs of workers can be traced to the job. Clara Seright, long-time assistant controller, says process costing is really used. The nature of the work of sorting is the same for all batches coming in. The only difference is the size of the batch.

REQUIRED:

a. Choose either job order or process costing for the accounting for the sorting operation and present your arguments for why the sorting operation should be accounted for under the system that you choose.

b. Regardless of your answer in requirement *(a),* explain the function that is currently served by the job record for each supermarket bundle.

5–10. Job Order and Process Cost Systems. Listed below is a set of products and services that are provided by the American economic system.

REQUIRED:
For each item, indicate whether the item is most likely accounted for by a job order costing system (J) or a process costing system (P). For each case, assume that you are concerned with the records of the company that produces the product or service.
a. Crates of 1,000 cartons of paper clips (100 clips per carton).
b. Architectural drawings for a major shopping mall.
c. Aircraft carrier.
d. Rock concert.
e. One thousand cases of cola.
f. A pair of jeans.
g. Passenger flight from New York to Los Angeles (one per day).
h. Restaurant meal (about 2,500 served daily).
i. Construction on major office building in downtown Seattle, Washington.
j. Credit checking for loan applications.
k. Letters moving from New York to Chicago.
l. Lawsuit filed on behalf of the 11,204 retired employees of a bankrupt chemical company.
m. Research contract for a prototype of a portable laser combat unit.
n. Electricity provided to residences in Orono, Maine.

5–11. Production Management Systems. Processing production orders in the Garza Manufacturing Company is performed as follows. Each week production scheduling prepares a list of products, with their respective quantities, that will be produced during the upcoming week. With these data, the operations file, and other appropriate files, the computerized production information system generates production orders for each department and job time tickets for each operation. Copies of production orders and job time tickets are distributed to each department where operations will be performed. Employees will mark on the job time tickets their time of beginning and ending, quantities completed, and any other pertinent information. These time tickets are returned to production scheduling where the data are processed to update the open production order file and to update production schedules for the following day.

REQUIRED:
a. Describe the essential steps necessary to ensure that materials are available at each work station at the time and in quantities needed to perform the operation specified on the daily production schedule.
b. Some operations do not require new material but require some labor or machining operation to be performed on in-process products coming from other departments. Explain what in the information system provides for having the in-process products ready in subsequent departments.
c. When production orders are completed and finished products are moved to the warehouse, what files in the information system must be updated? Which of these interface with the general ledger?

5–12. Inventory Costs. Modern Men's Clothiers in downtown Clairton, Pennsylvania, caters to senior citizens now retired from the Clairton Works, a steel mill. The store specializes in making very large purchases of clothing and holding the clothing until someone wants to buy it. Men's clothing from the 1940s to the present is stocked in sizes from extra small to triple extra large. The goods are stored on shelves and racks that are in floor-to-ceiling glass cases to protect them from dust and mildew. The store is large, approximately 20,000 square feet, and costs $18 per square foot to rent and maintain. The public area for the display of the merchandise has approximately 12,000 square feet, and the fitting rooms and the cash registers have 2,000 square feet. The remaining space is for administrative and private areas. There are five clerks, at a cost of $12,000 per year each, who spend 40 percent of their time keeping clothing neatly stacked and all glass clean. The clerks also help customers find their desired style and size (30 percent of the time), ring up the sale (5 percent of the time), and play checkers or just talk the remainder of the time. About two thirds of the time that the clerk is helping a customer is spent looking through styles and sizes that are incorrect.

It is hard to fit some customers because the stock is low in their size (mostly post-1990 medium and large sizes). A survey of the shirt stock reveals the following data for 19x2:

SALES (in percentages)

	Era of Clothing Sold			
	Pre-1980	1981–90	1990 +	Total
Small and extra small	1	3	6	10
Medium	4	10	20	34
Large	4	12	24	40
Extra large +	1	5	10	16
Totals	10	30	60	100

INVENTORY (in percentages)

	Era of Inventory Stocked			
	Pre-1985	1986–90	1990 +	Total
Small and extra small	14	8	9	31
Medium	3	4	6	13
Large	3	2	7	12
Extra large +	19	11	14	44
Totals	39	25	36	100

ADDITIONAL INFORMATION

Total annual sales	$1.2 million
Total investment in inventory	$2.4 million
Cost of goods sold	50% of sales
Miscellaneous expenses	$40,000 per year
Inventory turnover ratio	.25 per year
Required return on investment	8% per year

REQUIRED:

Assuming that the shirt inventory is representative of the full inventory of the store:

a. Assume that a well-run men's clothing store has an inventory turnover (cost of goods sold/ average inventory) of about 5.0. Comment on why the inventory turnover of Modern Men's Clothiers is low.

b. Compute the annual cost of carrying $1 of inventory in this store. Include in your analysis the cost of space, clerk time, a 4 percent of purchase cost for deterioration and obsolescence, and a return on investment. (Ignore for this purpose the fact that a portion of the inventory is in a deteriorated and obsolete condition.)

c. How much of the clerk's cost is value added? Assume for this analysis that the value-added time of the clerks includes the time to fit and ring up the sale without any waste in the process.

d. Compute an approximate margin after holding costs for various sizes and eras of clothing.

e. Comment on the findings of your analysis.

5–13. Value Added.   On December 31, 19x5, the Lampe Company had 1,247 employees in its departments at the Hartford Manufacturing Plant:

	Direct Workers	Indirect Workers	Supervisors	Total
Purchasing	35	15	9	59
Fabrication	148	142	30	320
Assembly	260	60	40	360
Finishing	102	80	30	212
Quality control	14	5	3	22
Warehousing	65	14	6	85
Maintenance	40	9	6	55
Administration	16	106	12	134
Totals	680	431	136	1,247

The plant manufactures gyroscopes, electric pumps, air conditioners, and small power tools. The annual budget for wages, salaries, and related costs includes:

	Average Salary	Positions	Budget Amount
Supervisors	$55,000	136	$ 7,480,000
Direct workers	18,000	680	12,240,000
Indirect workers	22,000	431	9,482,000
Total personnel		1,247	$29,202,000

REQUIRED:

a. Compute the proportion of the Hartford Manufacturing Plant employees that are value added.

b. Compute the proportion of the total annual budget for wages, salaries, and related costs that is a value-added cost.

c. The plant has not been profitable for the past four years. Comment on why the plant might be unable to compete with imports of products from Japan.

EXTENDED APPLICATIONS

5–14. Product Variety Effects on Unit Cost, Regression.   The Newsport Connection Group manufactures sports-related equipment and clothing. Everett Sutter, production manager, has noticed that the more products produced in a plant, the higher the cost per unit, independent of the volume of production. Thus, the labor and overhead cost per unit is less in a plant that is focused on fewer products. As an example, he collected data on high school football game uniforms from 12 plants and also gathered data on the number of other products produced in the plants for June 19x2:

Plant	Unit Total Cost	Other Products
1	$182	690
2	301	1,022
3	172	515
4	294	1,023
5	333	1,119
6	295	1,100
7	202	691
8	222	590
9	256	861
10	178	628
11	214	704
12	264	749
Averages	$242.75	807.67

Mr. Sutter could not explain why units of the same product cost more in plants that produced more products.

Mr. Sutter has control through plant managers of 48 manufacturing plants in various parts of the country. These plants were acquired as a result of six mergers over the past 10 years. On average, each plant has the capacity to produce 800 different products (and regularly do so), and all of the plants together have the capacity to produce 6,000 different sports-related products. Many products are produced in six or more plants. Thus, there is substantial overlap among the plants.

REQUIRED:

a. Using regression analysis,
   1. Estimate the constant portion of the unit cost and the increase in football uniform cost that results from an additional product produced in the plant.
   2. Project the cost of a football uniform produced in a plant that produces 600 other products.
   3. Project the cost of a football uniform produced in a plant that produces 1,000 other products.
b. The Newsport Connection Group won a contract to produce 115 football uniforms for the Somona High School at a selling price of $300 per complete uniform. In which plant should the uniforms be manufactured? Why?
c. Mr. Sutter is considering focusing the scheduling of production so that each product is produced in only one of the plants. Comment on the advantages and disadvantages of such a change in production plans.

5–15. Job Order, Process Cost, and Management Philosophy.   Medi-Claim Services, Inc., prepares and processes medical and dental claims filed for medicare and insurance purposes. Medi-Claim is housed in spacious quarters (48,000 square feet) on four floors of the Metro Tower. Other tenants of the building include the corporate offices of a Fortune 500 company and several prestigious law firms. The company's advertising touts its ability to save clients the fuss of filing forms plus getting larger reimbursements. Medi-Claim has been successful in attracting clients with fees of $16.2 million and net income from operations of $.8 million. The total compensation (salaries, wages, and commissions) budget is $7.0 million annually for 223 employees. While total fees have increased by 40 percent during the past three years, the profits have declined by 25 percent. The majority of clients are satisfied that claims are filed properly and that reimbursements are higher because the company knows the ins and outs of the coverage of the various plans. The company retains about 82 percent of its accounts from one year to the next. The company has six competitors in the region, and the competition is getting sharper with lower fees prevailing during the past year.

Each client is assigned an account number and a claims processor for all processing. The claims processors are critical employees because they represent 106 of the employees. Fees are charged as 4.5 percent of cash received on claim reimbursements with a minimum charge of $10 per claim filed. Clients with a high dollar volume over the course of a year, which is virtually all clients, are billed only for the percentage; the minimum charge is ignored. Claims Processing Department uses 28,000 square feet of space, but this includes 16,000 square feet of file space for in-process files and 4,800 square feet for the 16 supervisors' offices and 400 square feet for the manager's office. The sales staff includes 11 people who work out of 1,300 square feet. The sales staff is paid a 2 percent commission on fees earned. In addition, there are three marketing managers who occupy 1,200 square feet and a marketing vice president who occupies 800 square feet. The annual space cost of $1.8 million is included in the overhead costs.

The company classifies its work with clients into three categories:

1. *Initial meetings* to determine the client's plan and any special coverage, explain strategies for filing claims to maximize recoveries, and describe claims processing and billing procedures. This averages 12 percent of total claims processor time.
2. *Claims processing* involves preparing forms, copying materials for backup purposes, filing copies, and mailing claims. This represents 47 percent of total claims processor time. The

average claim is for $200 and generates a fee of $9.00. Each account will have from 100 to 500 claims per month with an average of 220.

3. *Follow-up* consists of visits with clients about questionable areas in a claim and telephone calls to medicare and insurance companies to resolve issues. Additional documentation may be required. This represents 32 percent of claims processor time with the remaining time idle.

For internal accounting purposes, the company keeps track of costs incurred for each client as well as the fees earned. The profitability of a client determines whether the company will try to retain that client's business in the future. Employees record time spent on each client for initial meeting, filing claims, and follow-up. A labor cost rate (averages $8 per hour) is applied for each employee based on his or her salary. Additionally, 150 percent of labor cost is charged for overhead costs of the operation. Claims processors are busy 91 percent of the average work day. Also, the cost of the actual number of forms and an estimated amount for telephone and copies is recorded by client. At the end of each month, postage is divided by the number of claims processed and an amount per claim is charged to client's work processed during the month.

The monthly income statement makes no attempt to show the cost of services rendered. Instead, all costs incurred during the month are classified by natural classification (that is, salaries, benefits, taxes, or postage). Therefore, net income is the difference between fees received and the list of expenses incurred during the month. There is an average time lag of 90 days between incurrence of expenses and the receipt of fees.

Perrin Pleton, president of Medi-Claim Services, says the company has a job order cost accounting system because clients are identified and most costs are traced directly or indirectly to the clients who have had work done that month. Deborah Wright, chief accountant, states that the cost system could be viewed as a process cost system because the operations performed are similar for all clients and the costs charged to each client are essentially average costs for a period of time.

REQUIRED:

a. Present the argument that Medi-Claim should use a job order cost system.

b. Present the argument that Medi-Claim should use a process cost system.

c. Discuss the advantages and disadvantages of reporting a cost of services rendered figure in the monthly income statement for management.

d. 1. Compute the average amount of claims in process. Treat the average outstanding period of 90 days as one fourth of a year and use the 4.5 percent fee rate in making the estimate.

    2. Compute the proportion of value-added employees, assuming that claims processors and sales staff are included.

    3. Recompute part (2), without the sales staff.

    4. Compute the value-added costs of claims processing time. Restrict your analysis to just the time to actually file the claims. Use a 2,000-hour work year and an $8 labor rate.

    5. Compute the proportion and cost of value-added space assuming that the sales staff and the claims processors are included. Exclude from this analysis the space for in-process files and supervisors.

    6. Recompute part (5), excluding the sales staff.

e. Apply the concepts from the new manufacturing environment to this service company. Comment on changes that might be made in the activities of Medi-Claim.

6

Materials and Related Costs

■

IDENTIFYING MATERIALS NEEDED AND
SELECTING VENDORS

Cary Braendel, president of Dunsmoor Manufacturing Company, wanted to talk about the restroom-partition company he had started. "Think about it," he said. "Every hotel, restaurant, airport, school, office—every public building, everywhere in the world—has restrooms, and in those rooms are partitions. Somebody has to manufacture those partitions. This is one BIG market."

Cary's products look as if they had emanated from some high-fashion design studio, perhaps for use in a jet-set client's poolside cabana. These high-design cubicles occupy a top-of-the-line niche, selling for $650 or $700 each. Their appeal lies partly in aesthetics (multiple colors and patterns, for example) and partly in their near-indestructibility. These fiberglass or plastic laminated panels can't easily be damaged. Graffiti is easily washed off.

Making the partitions and fashioning them into cubicles isn't as hard as it might seem. You cut the laminated panels to size. You edge them with a custom-designed aluminum extrusion, then fit them into a patented foot, or floor support, obtained from a European company. You add the stylish door latches, complete with red-and-green occupied/vacant indicator.

Because of well-designed parts, Cary's company primarily assembles the materials into completed cubicles and markets the products. Fortunately, Cary has ample suppliers to choose from. He must now decide the quantities to purchase and which suppliers will meet his service requirements.

■

LEARNING OBJECTIVES

After studying this chapter, you should be able to:

1. Explain how a purchase requisition, purchase order, and receiving report are used in the process of acquiring materials.
2. Explain the purpose and role of a materials requisition.
3. Distinguish between periodic and perpetual inventory systems.
4. Define material-related costs and explain alternative treatments for allocating these costs in the accounting system.
5. Prepare a make-or-buy analysis for inputs to a production process.

Manufacturing is a process of converting raw materials into a finished product through the application of labor and facilities and support functions. In this process, materials costs usually represent a significant portion of product costs. Conversion costs (labor, facilities, and support functions) can also be significant cost elements. Labor costs will be a smaller share of total production costs where operations are capital intensive. Service companies will also have materials, but material is not a major cost in the total costs of rendering services.

Accounting for materials is influenced by the acquisition and issuance activities, and the planning and control policies. This chapter covers the accounting for acquisitions and issuances and the major planning and control considerations.

DEFINITIONS OF MATERIALS

Materials can be either direct or indirect. As discussed in Chapter 2, **direct materials** are quantities of material that can be identified with the production of a specific product, that can be easily and economically traced to that product, and whose cost represents a significant part of the total product cost. For example, the molded outer case for a computer console is direct material. **Indirect materials** consist of all other materials and supplies that become part of the product or are consumed otherwise in the production of the product. In other words, they are production materials and supplies that are not classified as direct materials.

Materials is a generic term encompassing many things. No one defines the term directly; instead, examples are used. The reason is that most companies have their own policies about what materials include. Although practices vary, items normally considered as materials are raw materials, purchased parts, and purchased or subcontracted assemblies and subassemblies. Parts and subassemblies often come from other divisions of the same company as interdivisional transfers. This practice does not change the nature of these items as part of materials.

MATERIALS ACQUISITION

The production scheduling process generates a materials requirement report that alerts the storeroom of the need for certain materials to be available at specific work centers on designated dates. Insufficient on-hand quantities of the needed materials mean more must be purchased. In this process, three documents are usually present: a purchase requisition, purchase order, and receiving report.

Document and Systems Flow

Most manufacturing companies have a purchasing department whose function is to order materials and supplies needed for production. The manager of purchasing is responsible for assuring that the items ordered meet quality standards, are obtained at the lowest prices, and are delivered on time. Goods shipped to the company are received at the receiving docks, inspected, and sent to the storeroom. Therefore, we have a purchasing and a receiving function.

Purchasing.   Exhibit 6–1 is a systems flowchart for an integrated computerized system that updates files, generates purchase orders, and interfaces with materials requirement reports. A purchase requisition is not included because it is not needed in such a system. Manual systems and many batch computerized systems use a separate purchase requisition form. Therefore, we include both a purchase requisition and a purchase order in the discussion.

Purchase requisition.   A **purchase requisition** is a written request to the Purchasing Department for the acquisition of materials. Exhibit 6–2 is an example of a purchase requisition form. The storeroom clerk fills out at least two copies of a purchase requisition, one copy for the storeroom files and one for purchasing. Although a purchase requisition is usually preprinted and contains information that varies from company to company, the form should include at a minimum the following infor-

EXHIBIT 6–1   Computer System Flowchart of Material Purchases

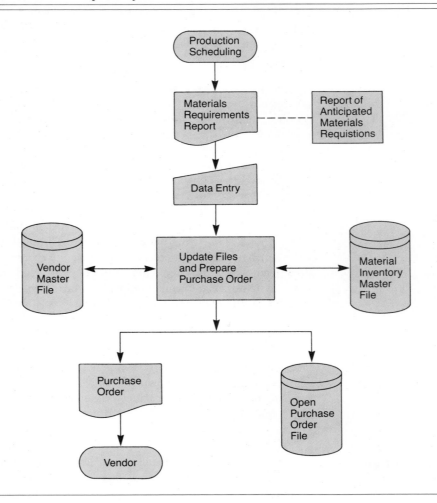

EXHIBIT 6–2 **Purchase Requisition Form**

REQUISITION

Purchase Order No.

Department _____ Date _____

	Quantity	Stock Number	Description	Estimate	
				Unit Price	Total Cost

Proposed Use _____ Confirming?

_____

Required By (Date): _____ Charge To (Acct. No.): _____

Suggested Source

Company _____

Phone _____ Address _____

Requested By.:

Originator	Department Head	Controller

mation: the requisition number, department making the request, quantity requested, stock number and description of item, unit and total price, date delivery is required, and authorized signature. The purchase requisition provides the Purchasing Department with an authorization to act.

Purchase order.   A **purchase order** is a written request to a vendor for specific goods at an agreed-upon price. It usually stipulates terms of delivery and payment, and authorizes the vendor to deliver goods and submit an invoice. At least four copies of a purchase order are prepared. The original goes to the vendor. A copy goes to the Receiving Department as notification of an expected delivery. Another copy goes to accounts payable as preparation for eventual payment. And a copy remains in the Purchasing Department as part of an **open purchase order file;** after materials are received, it becomes part of the vendor's historical file. Exhibit 6–3 is a sample purchase order. The essential information on the form is purchase order number, name and address of vendor, order date, date delivery is requested, delivery and payment terms, quantity of items ordered, catalog number, descriptions, unit and total costs, and an authorized signature.

Receiving.   When the goods that were ordered are received at the receiving dock, the goods are unpacked, counted, and inspected. The count is important to make

EXHIBIT 6–3   Purchase Order Form

PURCHASE ORDER		

DATE		P.O. NUMBER

PLEASE SHOW THIS P.O. NUMBER ON ALL
INVOICES, CORRESPONDENCE, & PACKAGES.

TO:

SHIP TO:

ORDER DATE	SHIP VIA	F.O.B.	TERMS	DATE REQUIRED

ITEM	DESCRIPTION	QTY	UNIT	PRICE	AMOUNT
			SUBTOTAL		
			TAX		
			SHIPPING		

AUTHORIZED SIGNATURE   DATE   TOTAL

certain that all items ordered were received. A good information system will not notify the Receiving Department of quantities expected, thus forcing a count of each receipt. Inspection determines whether goods are damaged and if they meet the specifications of the purchase order. Exhibit 6–4 is a computer system flowchart for material receipts. All receiving information updates the open purchase order file and the material inventory master file. A **receiving report** is generated as physical doc-

EXHIBIT 6-4 Computer System Flowchart of Material Receipts

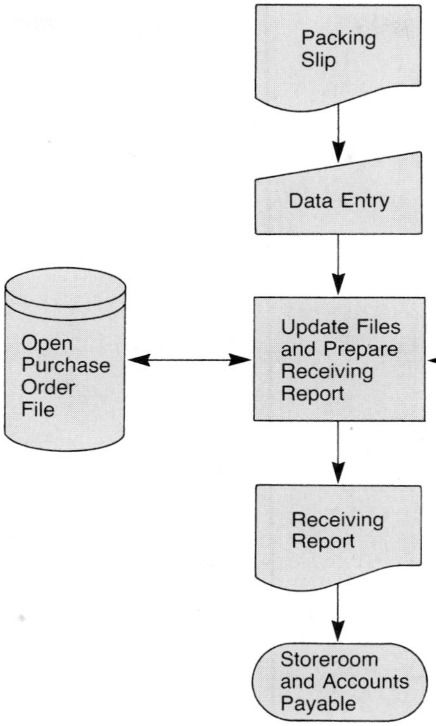

umentation for both the storeroom and accounts payable that the goods were received and the quantities counted.

The receiving report (see Exhibit 6–5 for an example) includes the vendor's name, purchase order number, date delivery was received, quantity received, description of goods, and who counted the items. There should also be space for mentioning discrepancies and comments on damaged goods. Receiving keeps a copy of the report, and other copies are distributed to appropriate departments. For example, the Purchasing Department wants a copy to verify that the order was received. Accounts payable will match a copy of the receiving report with the purchase order and a subsequent invoice to process payment. The storeroom needs to know what was received and where the goods are. A copy goes with the goods as they move from the receiving area to the storeroom. Accounting uses a copy as backup for journal entries recording the purchase and the associated liability.

Materials Costs

In general, the costs companies often associate with materials acquisition include five broad categories:

1. The acquisition cost (purchase price or production cost) of the materials.
2. Transportation charges, including freight, insurance, storage, customs, and duty charges.
3. Credits for trade discounts granted, cash discounts taken, and discounts or allowances granted by vendor.

EXHIBIT 6–5 Receiving Report Form

RECEIVING REPORT			No.
Prepared by	Date	"P.O." number	Vendor

Quantity	Units	Description

Delivered by

Inspected by _____

Remarks:

Shipping weight

4. The costs of functions such as purchasing, receiving, inspection, and storage.
5. Miscellaneous items, such as income from sale or salvage of scrap, obsolescence, and other inventory losses.[1]

Items 1. through 3. are covered in this section. Item 4. is the subject of material-related costs that will be discussed later in this chapter. Item 5. will be covered in Chapter 11.

The National Association of Accountants published a definition of direct materials cost that includes a few explanations for items 1. through 3. above.[2] Besides the purchase price or production cost, materials costs include costs of any outside processing, sales taxes, and the net cost of delivery containers and pallets. If vendors offer cash discounts that are unreasonably high with respect to current interest rates, the excess is a reduction in materials cost. Demurrage charges[3] are not materials costs. Royalty payments and licenses are part of the costs only if they are a function of the quantity to be used in production.

Once a company has identified all cost elements it will use for costing materials, the costs are allocated to the materials by converting all costs to a per unit of material

[1] These miscellaneous items are not really associated with acquisition costs, but many companies use them to adjust materials costs. They are included here to give a complete coverage of those costs that companies track to material processing activities.

[2] "Definition and Measurement of Direct Material Cost," *Statements on Management Accounting, Number 4E,* National Association of Accountants, June 3, 1986, paragraphs 26–30.

[3] *Demurrage* is the detaining of a ship, freight car, or truck beyond the time for loading, unloading, or sailing. Charges assessed for such delays are called *demurrage charges.*

basis. This per unit amount is used to make the accounting entries for materials and to record costs on inventory records.

Journal Entries

As an example of the journal entry to record materials acquisitions, consider the Dunsmoor Manufacturing Company illustration from the beginning of the chapter. Assume the company purchases 500 sheets of laminated plastic panels at $50 each. Shipping costs, taxes, and so forth less cash discounts give a total materials cost of $55 each. In addition, 100 pounds of chrome nuts and bolts, indirect materials, cost $1.80 per pound.

Some companies use one overall inventory account for all materials, and other companies use separate inventory accounts, one for direct material and one for indirect material. We will use one account. For the information above, the journal entry would be:

Materials Inventory			$27,680	
Accounts Payable (or Cash)				$27,680
Panels: 500 at $55.00	= $27,500			
Nuts & bolts: 100 pounds at $1.80	= 180			
	$27,680			

That is a rather simple, straightforward entry. The only question is whether it is made for each purchase or summarized and recorded periodically in total. The individual inventory records should be updated with each purchase transaction. A journal entry to record materials acquisitions in the general ledger may be daily, weekly, or monthly, depending on the needs of management.

MATERIALS ISSUANCE

The storeroom manager is responsible for properly storing, protecting, and issuing materials. Issuance is authorized by a materials requisition form prepared by production scheduling and approved by the individual work center supervisor or department manager. The materials costs identified with each requisition are charged to the appropriate job as direct materials or to production overhead as indirect materials. These amounts also become the basis for journal entries that relieve materials inventory and charge work in process inventory.

Materials Requisition

The **materials requisition** is a form similar to the purchase requisition (see Exhibit 6–2) except that it is issued from production scheduling. The form shows the job number, work center or department requesting the goods, quantity and description, and date needed in production. Unit and total costs, if known by production scheduling, are entered. A storeroom clerk will enter a cost otherwise.

Journal Entries

Costs are taken from the materials requisition forms to record issuance of materials. Returning to the Dunsmoor Manufacturing Company illustration, assume a materials requisition specified 300 panels and 10 pounds of nuts and bolts. The laminated plastic panels represent direct material; the nuts and bolts are indirect materials. The journal entry to record the transfer of materials to work in process is:

Work in Process Inventory (Job #)			$16,500	
Production Overhead (Indirect Material)			18	
Materials Inventory				$16,518
Panels: 300 at $55	= $16,500			
Nuts & bolts: 10 pounds at $1.80	= 18			
	$15,518			

Typically, a company will accumulate materials requisitions for a period—day or week—and make a summary journal entry. A problem arises in a period of changing prices, when the materials are recorded in inventory at different costs. Which costs should be charged to materials requisitions? Which costs should be used to cost out the ending materials inventory? Specific identification, first-in, first-out (FIFO), last-in, first-out (LIFO), weighted average, and moving average are the common inventory costing methods, and management will decide which method is appropriate for each category of material.[4] Also at issue is whether the company uses periodic or perpetual inventory systems. These two systems are presented below.

Inventory Systems

Either the periodic inventory system or the perpetual inventory system may be used to cost materials issued and those remaining in ending inventory. Unless otherwise specified, we assume the perpetual system in the illustrations.

Costing by the Periodic Inventory System.   The **periodic (or physical) inventory system** does not directly determine the costs of materials issued. Instead, any time management needs to know the cost of materials issued, a physical count must be made of materials on hand. The cost of materials issued for the period is determined by subtracting the ending materials inventory from the sum of the beginning inventory and purchases, as follows:

$$
\begin{array}{rl}
& \text{Materials inventory—beginning} \\
+ & \text{Purchases} \\
\hline
= & \text{Materials available for use} \\
- & \text{Materials inventory—ending} \\
\hline
= & \text{Cost of materials issued} \\
\end{array}
$$

The major weakness of this inventory system is the untimely information to management regarding the costs of materials issued and inventory balances on hand. Materials costs flow into work in process and subsequently into finished goods and cost of goods sold. A physical inventory must be taken before any costs can move through the inventory accounts to cost of goods sold and before inventory balances at any point can be determined.

Another disadvantage of the periodic inventory system is loss of control. Because the cost of issues is computed indirectly, we assume that items not in inventory must have been issued. Shortages go undetected, and the cost is hidden in the amount assumed to have been issued to production. Thus, the cost of materials issued is overstated. Recording quantities on hand, received, and issued can overcome this deficiency, but that is not the usual practice with those companies using the periodic inventory system.

The system is more common in operations in which manual accounting systems are used or where physical controls are relied on without the use of accounting controls. Merchandising organizations have been the most frequent users of the periodic inventory system.

Costing by the Perpetual Inventory System.   The **perpetual inventory system** requires an ongoing record of receipts and issuances and associated costs. This means the cost of materials issued to production is charged to the job or department (thus,

---

[4] The inventory costing methods have been covered in courses on the principles of accounting and intermediate accounting. The mechanics of these methods are therefore not repeated here.

CHAPTER 6 MATERIALS AND RELATED COSTS   191

to work in process inventory) at the time materials are issued. Any balance in the Materials Inventory account is the cost of materials still available for use. Consequently, under the perpetual inventory system, both the cost of materials issued and the ending materials inventory can be directly ascertained after each transaction.

Stock record cards, which serve as a subsidiary ledger record, are maintained with a perpetual inventory system. The total of all stock record cards at any time must equal the amount in the Materials Inventory account in the general ledger. Exhibit 6–6 is an example of a stock record card.

The use of the perpetual inventory system also requires a physical inventory count at least once a year in order to check for possible errors or shrinkage due to theft or spoilage. With large inventories, cycle counts will be used where categories of material are counted once a year but inventory counts are occurring throughout the year. If the physical count disagrees with the balances in the Materials Inventory account and stock record cards, adjustments must be made to those records.

Using the perpetual inventory system in a manufacturing company has four major advantages. First, current information is available at all times about the monetary and quantity balance of materials. Every time materials are acquired or issued, the Materials Inventory account is immediately updated. Second, current information is also available on the monetary and quantity balance of work in process inventories. During production steps, materials and conversion costs are recorded and inventory accounts are immediately updated. Costs of each job completed are known at the time work is transferred to finished goods. Consequently, management will have current information throughout the period about the status of work in process inventories. Third, current information will be available on monetary and quantity balances in finished goods inventory. As work is completed, the units and costs are charged to finished goods inventory. As sales occur, the costs of goods sold are removed immediately from finished goods inventory. And fourth, the system gives current information about the monetary and quantity balances of cost of goods sold.

The speed and capability of computers make the perpetual inventory system manageable and effective in providing timely reports to management. Perpetual inventory systems are most frequently used where there are a large number of different material categories and a diversity of products.

MATERIALS RETURNED TO STOREROOM

A number of situations exist in which materials issued to production may later be returned to the storeroom. The three most common categories are excess materials, damaged or defective materials, and materials included in a part or subassembly that will be included in a final product assembly.

Excess Materials

Materials not used for the work requisitioned are returned to the storeroom. Inventory records are adjusted for the return of excessive materials by adding them back to perpetual inventory records and making an adjusting entry in the general ledger for Materials Inventory. Excessive materials occur when too much is requisitioned as a buffer against unexpected losses and the losses are not realized or when efficiencies occur that result in less scrap, spoilage, or defective units.

Damaged or Defective Materials

Some materials arrive on the production floor not meeting the specifications needed for the applicable product or having been damaged in movement from the storeroom to a work center. Either situation requires returning the materials to the storeroom to

EXHIBIT 6–6   Example of Stock Record for a Perpetual Inventory System

						PERPETUAL INVENTORY & STOCK RECORD CARD							
ORDERED			RECEIVED			ISSUED							
DATE	ORDER	QTY	DATE	ORDER	QTY	DATE	ORDER	QTY	BALANCE	DATE	ORDER	QTY	BALANCE

be disposed of according to established procedures. Defective materials may be returned to vendors or may fall under scrap procedures (see Chapter 11).

Parts or Subassemblies

Companies manufacturing products that include many components that will be assembled into the finished product often make the components themselves. If a part or subassembly completes its phase of production and is placed in the storeroom to await another production step or an assembly operation, a record must be generated. These items will have their own stock record just as though they had been purchased as material. In other words, once placed in the storeroom, parts and subassemblies become material for further production efforts.

MATERIAL-RELATED COSTS

Certain costs are closely related to the acquisition and issuance of materials but are considered indirect costs because they cannot be economically and feasibly identified with the materials costs. We call these costs **material-related costs**[5]; they are incurred in the activities from purchasing through the time materials enter production. Such activities include purchasing, receiving, receiving inspection, storeroom costs prior to materials entering production, and issuance and movement of materials to the production area. Storage costs and movement costs subsequent to entering production are more closely tied to production than to acquisition or issuance. Some companies also treat as material-related costs those costs incurred for purchased items in transit, such as insurance and freight.

Material-related costs must be allocated to the departments, jobs, or products requiring materials. A number of alternatives are available to accomplish this task. The actual treatment in practice is a function of convenience, clerical expenses, and perceived benefits. There are four alternatives used:

1. Develop a rate for each identifiable group of activities (such as a department or cost center—purchasing or receiving) and include that rate as an element of material cost as units go into materials inventory.
2. Combine the material-related costs into one cost pool, develop a rate, and apply the rate to materials on the basis of some measure of materials quantity or costs.
3. Combine 1. and 2. above, such as a separate rate for each of insurance costs, freight costs, and Purchasing Department costs, and develop a rate for the cost pool of remaining material-related costs.
4. Include material-related costs, or some portion of them, in production overhead for allocation with overhead costs.

For our purposes, we discuss the first two options because the third is simply a combination of the first two, and the fourth will follow the treatment of production overhead discussed in Chapter 8.

Separate Rates for Material-Related Activities

In the following illustration, we assume the material-related activities are purchasing, receiving, and storing. The question is which measure of activity is appropriate for each department. Here are a few examples:

Department	Measure of Activity
Purchasing	Number of purchase orders, number of items ordered, dollar value of purchases
Receiving	Number of items to be received, dollar value of items received
Storeroom	Number of items, square footage allotted to each category of material, days in the storeroom

[5] A number of other terms for the same costs are found in the business world. The common ones are *material handling, material overhead,* and *material burden,* an archaic term. The accounting literature also suggests the term *material acquisition and handling.*

The Dunsmoor Manufacturing Company has estimated the following items for material-related costs and measures of activity for the year:

Estimated Purchasing Department costs	$ 30,000
Estimated material purchases	500,000
Estimated Receiving Department costs	14,400
Estimated materials receipts	480,000
Estimated storeroom costs	40,500
Estimated materials costs in storage	450,000

Individual rates to apply these costs to materials inventory for the upcoming period can now be calculated. The rate for purchasing is:

$$\frac{\$30,000}{\$500,000} = 6 \text{ percent}$$

For receiving:

$$\frac{\$14,400}{\$480,000} = 3 \text{ percent}$$

For storeroom:

$$\frac{\$40,500}{\$450,000} = 9 \text{ percent}$$

Actual data for the period show the following departmental costs and the dollar amount of materials appropriate for allocating the departmental costs:

Purchasing Department costs	$ 31,500
Receiving Department costs	15,000
Storeroom costs	41,300
Cost of materials ordered (purchased)	550,000
Cost of materials received	510,000
Cost of materials in storeroom	500,000

The journal entry to record the actual costs incurred in each department is:

Purchasing Cost Control	31,500	
Receiving Cost Control	15,000	
Storeroom Cost Control	41,300	
Various Accounts		87,800

Notice that actual costs are debited to the control accounts. When we allocate departmental costs to materials, the control account will be credited.

Allocating the departmental costs is accomplished by a calculation of the actual level for the measure of activity times the rate calculated above. These calculations are:

Purchasing: $550,000 × 6 percent = $33,000
Receiving: $510,000 × 3 percent = 15,300
Storeroom: $500,000 × 9 percent = 45,000

The journal entry to record these amounts is:

Materials Inventory	93,300	
Purchasing Cost Control		33,000
Receiving Cost Control		15,300
Storeroom Cost Control		45,000

Any balance in the control accounts is an under- or overapplied amount. These balances are treated in the same manner as those occurring in production overhead. See Chapter 8 for that treatment. The balances are summarized here as:

	Debits	Credits	Under- or Over-Applied
Purchasing cost control	$31,500	$33,000	($1,500)
Receiving cost control	15,000	15,300	(300)
Storeroom cost control	41,300	45,000	(3,700)
Totals	$87,800	$93,300	($5,500)

Note that materials cost was used in all of the rate calculations above. One might ask why not combine the departments into one rate. As we have seen, the actual materials cost used to allocate the material-related costs differed by department, and that is one reason for keeping the departments separate. The second reason for separation is that each department can have different measures of activity.

Cost Pool for Material-Related Activities

Because separate departmental rates may not be convenient to use or are more complex and expensive than the increased accuracy in allocation is worth, companies will consider a single material-related cost pool. For such a pool, which activity measure is used? The measure representing those costs that dominate the cost pool is generally selected. No department dominates in Dunsmore Manufacturing. We picked the storeroom because we know those goods have been received, inspected, and accepted. We are never certain that the goods ordered will be delivered; it is difficult to match costs incurred with goods not received. The material-related cost rate is $84,900/$450,000 = 18.87 percent.

We have already seen that actual material-related costs total $87,800. The entry for recording actual cost is:

| Material-related Costs | 87,800 | |
| Various Accounts | | 87,800 |

The various accounts will include Cash, Accounts Payable, Accumulated Depreciation, Payroll or Wages Payable, and any other accounts that represent the credit side of specific charges to the material-related accounts.

Allocation of material-related costs is based on the rate times the measure of activity. Here, the allocation is 18.87 percent × $500,000 = $94,350 and it is recorded by the following entry:

| Materials Inventory | 94,350 | |
| Material-related Costs | | 94,350 |

More costs are allocated than incurred by the amount of $6,550. This is an overapplied amount. Treatment of under- or overapplied amounts will be covered in Chapter 8.

Notice the results of separate rates and a combined rate. The difference is modest.

	Debits	Credits	Under- or Over-Applied
Separate rates	$87,800	$93,300	($5,500)
Combined rates	87,800	94,350	(6,550)
Totals	$ –0–	($ 1,050)	($1,050)

MATERIAL SOURCING CONSIDERATIONS

Materials, which include component parts and subassemblies or assemblies, can be produced within an organization or purchased from external sources. That leads to decisions about whether to purchase component parts, subassemblies, or assemblies from the outside or produce them internally. Such a decision is called **the make-or-buy decision.**

Source Selection

The general approach for financial analysis of sourcing alternatives is to identify the differential costs of each alternative for a given time period. That alternative with the least aggregate differential cost is the preferred source from a quantitative point of view. However, adequate consideration must also be given the qualitative factors.

The quantitative part of the analysis will follow the general form presented in Exhibit 6–7. In this example, Dunsmoor Manufacturing Company wants literature printed that will be included with cubicles shipped to customers. Differential costs for these two alternatives represent costs that would not be incurred (costs that can be avoided) if the alternative were not selected. In other words, these costs will be incurred if the alternative is selected.

In some cases, a company will have an alternate use for the manufacturing capacity it does not use if the buy alternative is selected, or certain fixed costs will be saved. Any fixed costs that could be saved are differential costs of the make alternative. The profits or cost savings from the alternate use of the capacity could be listed as opportunity costs of the make alternative or as savings in the buy alternative. For example, ComTele manufactures a small electronic component for a line of telecommunications equipment. It currently produces 50,000 of these components annually, with the following costs:

Direct materials	$ 300,000
Direct labor	250,000
Variable overhead	450,000
Fixed overhead	900,000
Total costs	$1,900,000

EXHIBIT 6–7

DUNSMOOR MANUFACTURING COMPANY
Comparison of Printing Supplier Bids
Fall 19x3

	Dunsmoor Print Shop (make)	Colonial Press (buy)
Typesetting	$ 2,000	$ 6,000
Artwork	12,000	25,000
Paper	40,000	26,000
Printing	15,000	12,000
Binding	3,000	2,000
Labeling	20,000	16,000
	$92,000	$87,000

Comments: Colonial has the lower bid, but it has not done our printing before. However, its samples have high quality. The Colonial staff seem technically competent and seem to really want the job.

The Dunsmoor Print Shop has been late on the last two issues due to equipment problems and personnel turnover. The low-quality artwork and printing have been commented on by the Marketing Department. The Print Shop has to do this type of job on an overtime basis with old equipment.

The cost of distribution will be $39,000 regardless of the supplier.

Another company in the area has offered to make this component for ComTele at $30 per unit. If ComTele accepts the offer, it could eliminate half of the fixed overhead charged to the component, and some of the space could be leased out for storage at $30,000 a year. Should ComTele accept the supplier's offer? The following analysis helps make this decision:

	Alternatives	
	Make	*Buy*
Direct materials	$ 300,000	
Direct labor	250,000	
Variable overhead	450,000	
Fixed overhead (saved)	450,000	
Purchase price		$1,500,000
Lease revenue		(30,000)
Total differential costs	$1,450,000	$1,470,000

The analysis shows that ComTele would be better off to make the component. Its profits would be $20,000 higher per year from this component.

Qualitative Issues

The quality of product, the timeliness of delivery, the stability of the source, and the effects on future sources are some of the important qualitative issues in the sourcing decision. There are circumstance in which the quality merely has to be reasonable for the intended usage. For example, it would not make sense to purchase a component designed to last 40,000 hours for a machine that will only last 10,000 hours in use. There are other circumstances in which superior quality is required. Components for a commercial airliner, for instance, must be superior to meet airline and Federal Aviation Administration requirements.

Although the foregoing issues are important, two areas that require additional comments are supplier financial condition and supplier integrity. Without satisfactory circumstances existing in both cases, it is difficult to deal with suppliers.

Supplier Financial Condition.   Every year many suppliers go under or cease operations. Just look around in your own community and ask how many businesses existing today were there 10 years ago or 5 years ago. How many of the businesses open today will close their doors next year, in two years, or five years? During their last months in operation, such companies provide poor-quality components and service. Because of this, accountants are asked to review the financial condition of current and potential suppliers as part of sourcing decisions.

A large manufacturer will often have more than a thousand important suppliers and another several thousand that are occasionally called upon. A large hospital can easily have 1,500 to 2,000 suppliers. Even smaller hospitals can have 500 to 1,000 suppliers. Because the analysis of supplier financial condition will be a routine task, the accountant should set up a system to handle the details. Specialized computer software and standardized spread sheet templates are available that have a reasonable record in predicting supplier financial problems.

For large manufacturers it is useful to keep several suppliers available for important components. First, competition among suppliers can both improve quality and reduce price. Second, if one goes under, purchases can be shifted to another. Finally, relying on just one supplier may force the others out of existence. Thus, going with a sole supplier (also called a *sole source*) may affect the availability of inputs in future years. Where only one supplier is available and that supplier is having financial difficulty, the company should consider purchasing the supplier from its current owners in order to stabilize it.

Supplier Integrity.   Unscrupulous suppliers can play an interesting game if they get into a position of power. They bid a very low price to get a job but limit quantities or charge large fees for minor changes to the component specifications. They follow the letter rather than the spirit of purchase agreements. With these tricks they are able to increase the price of components substantially. If a purchase is needed in the middle of a large project and is highly dependent on one supplier, there is little the buyer can do. History shows how expensive a project becomes when the supplier's integrity is not at a high level.

SUMMARY

Materials costs represent a significant part of the production costs in a manufacturing company. Proper accounting for materials costs requires recognition of the difference between acquisition activities and issuance activities, and the basic cost of materials and material-related costs. Acquisition activities involve purchase requisitions, purchase orders, and receiving reports to document the flow of information. Issuance activities center on the storeroom and material requisitions. The basic material cost is the purchase price plus freight, insurance, storage in transit, customs, and duty charges less credits for discounts taken or allowances granted. Material-related costs are the cost of purchasing, receiving, receiving inspection, and storeroom activities. These costs are allocated to materials inventory or go into production overhead for allocation to work performed.

Most companies have the option to produce their component parts, subassemblies, or assemblies internally or to purchase them from external sources. The choice between internal and external sources is called the make-or-buy decision. The goal is to select the source with the least aggregate cost for a time period after consideration of qualitative factors.

PROBLEM FOR REVIEW

Denison-Hailey Corporation has the practice to include all material-related costs in the inventoriable costs of materials. It uses the following estimates for applying material-related costs to materials:

Annual estimated Purchasing Department costs	$ 12,675,000
Annual estimated Receiving Department costs	$ 1,890,000
Annual estimated storeroom operating costs	$ 3,500,000
Annual estimated material purchases	$422,500,000
Estimated number of items to be received	700,000

Freight on incoming material is paid by the vendor and included on the invoice. Purchasing is allocated on the basis of dollar value of material purchases. The allocation of receiving and storeroom costs is based on number of items received.

The actual data for the past year, which were recorded in the appropriate accounts, are as follows:

Material purchases	$420,000,000
Purchasing Department costs	$ 12,975,000
Receiving Department costs	$ 1,700,000
Storeroom operating costs	$ 3,510,000
Number of items received	687,500

REQUIRED

a. Develop rates for applying Purchasing Department, Receiving Department, and storeroom costs to materials.

b. Prepare the journal entry(ies) to record the actual cost of purchases and the application of material-related costs for an order of 500 units at a cost of $56,300 with freight of $1,065. (These units are included in the 687,500 units purchased during the year.)

c. Calculate the cost of each unit of material in inventory for the 500 units in (b) above.

d. Prepare the journal entry to close the balances of the material-related costs to cost of goods sold.

SOLUTION

a. Calculation of material-related cost rates.

$$\text{Purchasing: } \frac{\$12,675,000}{\$422,500,000} = 3\%$$

$$\text{Receiving: } \frac{\$1,890,000}{700,000} = \$2.70 \text{ per unit}$$

$$\text{Storeroom: } \frac{\$3,500,000}{700,000} = \$5.00 \text{ per unit}$$

b. Journal entries
Recording the invoice costs of 500 units:

Materials Inventory	$57,365	
Accounts Payable		$57,365

Recording the allocation of material-related costs:

Materials Inventory	$ 5,539	
Purchasing Cost Control		$ 1,689
(3% × $56,300)		
Receiving Cost Control		1,350
($2.70 × 500)		
Storeroom Cost Control		2,500
($5.00 × 500)		

c. Calculation of unit costs in inventory.

$$\text{Purchase cost} \left(\frac{\$56,300}{500}\right) = \$112.60$$

$$\text{Freight} \left(\frac{\$1,065}{500}\right) = 2.13$$

$$\text{Purchasing costs} \left(\frac{\$1,689}{500}\right) = 3.378$$

$$\text{Receiving costs} \left(\frac{\$1,350}{500}\right) = 2.70$$

$$\text{Storeroom costs} \left(\frac{\$2,500}{500}\right) = \underline{5.00}$$

Total cost per unit $125.808

d. Journal entry to close material-related accounts to cost of goods sold.

Support:
Purchasing: $420,000,000 × 3% = $12,600,000
Receiving: 687,500 × $2.70 = $1,856,250
Storeroom: 687,500 × $5.00 = $3,437,500

	Purchasing	Receiving	Storeroom
Actual costs	$12,975,000	$1,700,000	$3,510,000
Applied Costs	12,600,000	1,856,250	3,437,500
	$ 375,000	(156,250)	$ 72,500

Journal entry:

Receiving Cost Control	$156,250	
Cost of Goods Sold	291,250	
Purchasing Cost Control		$375,000
Storeroom Cost Control		72,500

KEY TERMS AND CONCEPTS

Direct materials (183)
Indirect materials (183)
Purchase requisition (184)
Purchase order (185)
Open purchase order file (185)
Materials requisition (189)

Receiving report (186)
Periodic (or physical) inventory system (190)
Perpetual inventory system (190)
Material-related costs (193)
Make-or-buy decision (196)

ADDITIONAL READINGS

Bernard, Paul. "Managing Vendor Performance." *Production and Inventory Management Journal*, First Quarter 1989, p. 1.
Burt, David N. "Managing Suppliers Up to Speed." *Harvard Business Review*, July-August 1989, p. 127.
Deakin, Edward B. "Supplier Management in a Just-In-Time Inventory System." *Journal of Accountancy*, December 1988, pp. 128, 130–33.
Edwards, James Don, and John B. Barrack. "A New Method of Inventory Accounting." *Management Accounting*, November 1987, pp. 49–56.
Meyer, Harry. "Managing Material Handling Resources: A Case Study at Leviton." *Production and Inventory Management Journal*, First Quarter 1989, pp. 19.
Newman, Richard G. "Determining the Fair Price." *Management Accounting*, June 1989, pp. 27–31.
O'Neal, Jason. "The Z-Score: Detecting Financial Distress Early." *CFO*, December 1988, pp. 46–49.
———. "Computing and Graphing Financial Ratios." *CFO*, January 1989, pp. 43–49.
Robinson, Michael A., and John E. Timmerman. "How Vendor Analysis Supports JIT." *Management Accounting*, December 1987, pp. 20–24.
Roth, Harold P. "New Rules for Inventory Costing." *Management Accounting*, March 1987, pp. 32–36, 45.
Towey, John F. "Inventory Shortages." *Management Accounting*, December 1988, pp. 52–53.

REVIEW QUESTIONS

1. Which element of production cost is insignificant in mass-produced services as compared to mass-produced products?
2. Differentiate between direct materials and indirect materials.

3. Although most companies set their own policies for what constitutes a material item, identify those items that are normally considered part of materials.
4. Identify the three forms commonly used in the acquisition of materials. What is usually included on these forms? Where are copies of these forms sent?
5. What are the five broad elements of costs associated with materials acquisition?
6. What document initiates the issuance of materials to production?
7. Discuss the major differences between the periodic and perpetual inventory systems.
8. When using the perpetual inventory system, is it necessary to take a physical inventory? Explain.
9. What categories of materials are returned to the storeroom subsequent to issuance to production? Why are they returned?
10. In what ways can material-related costs be allocated to the work of a manufacturing company?
11. What is the general approach for financial analysis of sourcing alternatives?
12. List four qualitative issues that should be considered in the sourcing decision.
13. Why is the financial condition of suppliers important to the sourcing decision?
14. Why is it useful for a large manufacturer to keep more than one supplier available for important components?
15. Describe the game that an unscrupulous supplier can play to increase the effective price of parts and services.

DISCUSSION QUESTIONS

16. Merick Company includes purchase price and freight-in as costs of materials in inventory. Purchasing Department costs and insurance costs for in-transit items are in general and administrative expenses while all other material-related costs are included in production overhead. Perry Company has materials costs defined as purchase price plus an allocation of all material-related costs. How will product costs differ between the two companies?
17. Refer to question 16. Assume both Merick and Perry have the same kinds of materials. Which company would have the higher unit cost for a unit of material issued to work in process? Explain.
18. Waylen Products combines all material-related costs into one cost pool and applies the rate to material dollars of purchases. Explain the impact of volume (material dollars) changes on the rate Waylen Products develops.
19. Why may two companies in the same industry have different classifications (direct or indirect) for materials costs? Who has the final authority for classifying these costs and determining their relationships to the product?

EXERCISES

6–1. Journal Entries for Materials Costs.   MT Racers, Inc., of Tallahassee runs stock cars on the professional circuit with 6 to 10 races per weekend. Most races are 250 miles, but a few are 500 miles and even fewer are 24-hour races. Materials requisitioned on June 2, 19x3, for the Miami Open that was to take place on June 5, 19x3:

	Units	*Unit Cost*	*Total*
Engine overhaul	1 kit	$ 1,200	$ 1,200
Drive train overhaul	1 kit	70	70
Brake/suspension overhaul	1 kit	360	360
Spare engine	1 engine	19,080	19,080
Racing fuel (J-5)	235 gallons	11	2,585
Racing slicks (Set of 4)	8 sets	640	5,120
Dry ice (Driver cool suits)	100 pounds	2	200
Other materials	1 setup	140	140
Total			$28,755

In addition to the materials listed above, MT Racers paid an entrance fee of $5,000, which it chose to record as a direct material. Car 58 was used to run the race. The company records costs on a job order basis and treats each race as a job. Car 58 placed second in the Miami Open, which resulted in winnings of $120,000.

REQUIRED:
a. Record the requisition of the materials from the storeroom for the Miami Open.
b. The engine and three sets of tires were not needed for the race and were returned to the storeroom on June 7, 19x3. All of the remaining materials were used either during the qualifying run the day before, the rebuild on the night before, or the course of the race. Record the return of the materials to the storeroom.

6–2. Journal Entries for Materials Cost Flow.   The Klinso Plant uses cotton lint as input to the production of cloth. The beginning inventory on October 1, 19x4, of cotton lint is 13,000 units valued at $65,000. Two lots of cotton lint are purchased from the Drejex Delinting Mill with 100,000 units at $6 per unit received on October 10 and 200,000 units at $5.60 received on October 20. The ending cotton lint inventory is 54,000 units. The company has adopted the first-in, first-out cost-flow assumption for all of its inventories.

(B. McDonald)

REQUIRED:
a. Assuming a periodic inventory approach, prepare one journal entry to summarize purchases and another entry to summarize issuances during the month.
b. Assuming a perpetual inventory approach, prepare one journal entry to summarize purchases and another entry to summarize issuances during the month.
c. Compare how the quantity and dollar amount of ending inventory are found for perpetual versus periodic inventory systems.

6–3. Inventory Cost Flow and Inventory Balance.   J. Scott Wayne has just begun a feedlot business outside of Laramie, Wyoming, with the name Nobull Cattle Company. The cattle are fed for three to six months and then are shipped to a local packing plant. The two big costs, besides the range cattle, are cattle feed and bills from the veterinarian. Cattle are kept for two weeks in an observation area (in case of disease or railers) prior to being mingled with the rest of the herd in the main feedlot. Railers, which are cattle that are "thin as a rail" and will not add weight, are sold upon discovery at cost to a packing plant. There are also adjustments for cattle that die in the observation area for one reason or another. Dead cattle cannot be sold and must be buried at a cost of about $50 each. This cost is included in the cost of the live cattle. The transactions for the month of January 19x7 are presented below:

Date	Activity	Head	Cost
1–1	Beginning cattle inventory	0	
1–3	Purchase from Lazy J Ranch	50	$30,000
1–9	Railers shipped (Lazy J Brand)	4	
1–10	Cattle moved from observation (Lazy J)	46	
1–10	Purchase from Wittington Ranch	62	$39,680
1–17	Railers shipped (WR Brand)	7	
1–17	Cattle moved from observation (WR)	55	
1–25	Purchase from Crystal Mountain Ranch	45	$26,100
1–28	Dead cattle in observation (CM Brand)	2	100
1–31	Railers shipped (CM Brand)	8	

The total for the feed cost and bills from the veterinarian for the month is $12,600, of which $1,750 relates to the CM brand cattle in ending inventory.

(V. Mooney)

REQUIRED:
Assuming that the company adopts a FIFO cost-flow assumption for the inventory of cattle in the observation area, what will be the ending balance in the Observation Area account?

6–4. LIFO Inventory Systems.   Chimichanga International Wholesales, Inc., has recently become the national distributor for an electronic check register. The device is a special purpose computer that keeps a running account balance of each of up to 12 checking accounts. A special function allows the entry of cancelled check numbers along with service charges to prepare an account reconciliation. The following activities occurred during January 19x8:

(M. Moreland)

		Units	Unit Price	
1–1	Inventory	1,000	$100	$100,000
1–10	Purchase	2.500	110	275,000
1–11	Sold	1,500		
1–14	Sold	600		
1–18	Purchase	500	90	45,000

REQUIRED:
a. Using the LIFO periodic method, determine the value of ending inventory.
b. Using the LIFO perpetual method, determine the value of ending inventory.

6–5. Material Handling Costs.   The Uwritem Publishing Company provides printing and distribution services to authors of self-help books. The company currently publishes for 12 authors. Its estimated and actual costs for the following material-related items for January 19x0 were:

(C. Lemon)

	Estimated	Actual
Purchasing Department costs	$ 5,000	$ 6,500
Receiving Department costs	3,500	3,000
Warehousing costs	2,500	4,000
Purchases	90,000	100,000
Receipts	90,000	90,000
Materials in storage (average)	90,000	75,000

REQUIRED:
a. Compute the rates for applying purchasing, receiving, and warehousing costs to purchasing materials inventory. Round rates to nearest thousandths.
b. Prepare the journal entry to record the application of material-related costs to the publishing materials inventory.

6–6. Material Handling Costs.   On the Run, Inc., makes athletic clothes and sportswear. It has estimated the following material-related costs and activities:

(P. Williams)

Purchasing Department costs	$ 42,000
Receiving Department costs	21,000
Storeroom costs	48,000
Material purchases	350,000
Material receipts	350,000
Average inventory in storeroom	60,000
Year-end actual data are:	
Purchasing Department costs	$ 40,000
Receiving Department costs	20,000
Storeroom costs	44,000
Material purchases	370,000
Material receipts	320,000
Average inventory in storeroom	70,000

REQUIRED:

a. Develop the rates for applying purchasing, receiving, and storeroom costs to materials inventory.
b. Compute the cost basis for raw materials with an original purchase price of $10,000 that has been in inventory for six months.

6–7. Material-Related Costs. The Iceberg Cooler Company manufactures refrigerators and freezers under the Iceberg brand name. The following estimates and actual costs are available for November 19x3 (in thousands):

(T. McKinney)

	Estimated	Actual
Purchasing Department costs	$ 140.8	$ 172.0
Receiving Department costs	41.3	38.0
Warehousing costs	81.9	94.0
Purchases	3,520.0	3,825.0
Receipts	4,130.0	3,999.0
Materials in storage (average)	910.0	888.0

REQUIRED:

a. Prepare the journal entry to record the application of material-related costs to the publishing materials inventory.
b. Prepare the entry to close the material-related cost accounts to cost of goods sold.

6–8. Materials Costs. The Quita Construction Company was completing a large hotel along the intercoastal waterway of Florida. It ordered 800 tons of polished marble slabs from a firm in Naples, Italy. The invoice price for the marble is $100 per ton with terms of "2/30, net 60; FOB Naples, Italy." (Quita must bear all shipping costs and risks from Naples.) Each slab of marble weighs approximately 1,000 pounds. Shipping insurance was $1,800 for the ocean crossing and $180 for the barge loading, movement, and unloading. The insurance pays only if at least 10 percent of the shipment is lost at sea or is in an unusable condition upon arrival. A shipping fee of $19,403 was paid to Cleianta Shipping, and customs payments of $836 were paid to the customs officials of the Port Authority of Naples. The marble slabs were unloaded at Fort Lauderdale, Florida, moved to a barge, and stored for three weeks until needed at the construction site. It cost $200 per week to rent the barge for four weeks, and the tugboat with operator cost $2,800. The slabs were then shipped by barge up the intercostal waterway. Upon arrival at the construction site, it was found that six of the slabs had been totally damaged in shipment. The cost of purchasing is applied at the rate of 3 percent of purchase price, receiving at a rate of $5 per ton, and inspection at a rate of $1 per ton plus $.50 per item. Quita records purchases at full cost less any discounts.

REQUIRED:
Determine the total cost of the marble slabs.

6–9. Make or Buy. Grissom Products is introducing a new product that consists of many component parts and subassemblies. After reviewing the bill of materials, production schedulers are concerned about whether Part Q–93 should be produced internally or purchased from an outside vendor. Making the part internally would use some available machinery that has been kept on a standby status and is not being used for other purposes. The machinery has no resale value. The space that would be used to make the part has no alternative use at the present time. An outside supplier has quoted $10 per unit if 20,000 units are purchased. An estimate of the costs to make 20,000 units of the part internally appears as follows:

Direct materials	$ 60,000
Direct labor	80,000
Variable production overhead	20,000
Fixed production overhead	100,000
Total costs	$260,000

The fixed production overhead consists of depreciation on the machinery and a share of the costs of the factory (heat, light, building depreciation, taxes, and insurance) based on the floor space occupied.

REQUIRED:
Should the company make or buy Part Q–93? Show an analysis to support your decision.

PROBLEMS

6–10. Materials Transactions. The beginning inventory, purchases, and issuances of materials for the production of MCQ–25 product line for January are presented below:

Jan.	1	Beginning inventory	60 units at $45
	4	Purchases	100 units at $47
	6	Issuances	70 units
	8	Issuances	20 units
	12	Purchases	120 units at $48
	13	Defective units from January 8 issuances returned to storeroom	10 units
	14	Issuances	90 units
	19	Purchases	50 units at $46
	21	Issuances	80 units
	25	Defective units from January 21 issuances returned to storeroom	5 units
	26	Purchases	110 units at $49
	28	Issuances	120 units
	30	Physical inventory count	55 units

The company uses a perpetual inventory system to record purchases and issuances of materials. The cost of defective and damaged material units found in work in process are recorded in a special account called Defective and Damaged Inventory.

REQUIRED:
a. Assuming the company uses a FIFO basis for costing inventories, prepare the journal entries that reflect all transactions (including the adjustment at the end of the month) for the month of January. What is the correct ending inventory balance in dollars?
b. Assuming the company uses a moving average basis for costing inventories, prepare the journal entries that reflect all transactions (including the adjustment at the end of the month) for the month of January. What is the correct ending inventory balance in dollars?
c. Assume the company uses a periodic inventory procedure and the FIFO basis for inventory costing. Calculate the costs in the ending inventory.
d. Assume the company uses a periodic inventory procedure and the weighted average basis for inventory costing. Calculate the costs in the ending inventory.

6–11. Material-Related Cost Pools. The Lehman Company manufactures sophisticated electrical components that become part of missile guidance systems. Instead of including the material-related costs in production overhead, the company separately identifies these costs and applies them to direct materials purchased. Purchasing, Receiving, Inspection, and Storeroom are the departments included in the company's definition of material-related activities.

Information for the budgeted and actual costs and possible allocation bases for the current year are presented below:

	Budgeted	*Actual*
Purchasing Department	$ 3,500,000	$ 3,489,000
Receiving Department	$ 125,000	$ 131,500
Inspection Department	$ 2,700,000	$ 2,693,450
Storeroom	$ 1,225,000	$ 1,305,000
Direct material purchases	$50,000,000	$49,500,000
Number of units received	500,000	505,000

All rate calculations are carried to four decimal places: .xxxx or xx.xx percent.

REQUIRED:

a. Develop rates for the material-related costs applying Purchasing and Inspection departments on the dollar value of direct material purchases and the Receiving Department and storeroom on the number of units received.

b. Prepare the journal entries to record application of the material-related costs and the closing of the departmental accounts at the end of the period.

c. Assume all of the material-related costs are included in one cost pool for allocation purposes. Develop one rate for the cost pool, assuming the dollar value of direct material purchases will be the allocation base.

d. Prepare the journal entries to record application of the material-related costs and the closing of the material-related cost pool at the end of the period.

6–12. Material-Related Costs.   Galdean Enterprises applies material-related costs as individual categories because many of its orders of materials require special care. In developing material-related cost rates, the company has the following annual estimates available:

Estimated receiving and storeroom costs	$ 112,000
Estimated Purchasing Department costs	$ 120,000
Estimated freight-in	$ 140,000
Estimated number of purchase orders processed	15,000
Estimated direct materials purchased	$2,800,000

The actual material-related costs and other pertinent data for August are:

Receiving and storeroom costs	$ 12,500
Purchasing Department costs	$ 11,700
Freight-in costs	$ 13,900
Number of purchase orders processed	1,450
Direct material purchases	$295,000

REQUIRED:

a. Determine individual rates for applying material-related costs assuming freight-in, receiving and storeroom costs are based on direct materials purchases and that Purchasing Department costs are based on number of purchase orders processed.

b. Prepare the journal entries to record actual material-related costs incurred during the month and the applied material-related costs. Close any under- or overapplied amounts to cost of goods sold.

c. Assume that all material-related costs are applied together based on direct material purchases. How much under- or overapplied costs will result in August? Explain why this answer differs from the total under- or overapplied amount from *(b)* above.

6–13. Materials Cost Pools.   The Smart Company makes educational toys for young children. The company has asked you to compare the use of a pool of material handling costs with separate departmental rates for March 19x3. The estimated and actual amounts for the month are:

(C. Cayce)

	Estimated	Actual
Purchasing Department costs	$ 31.5	$ 33.0
Receiving Department costs	18.0	19.5
Warehousing costs	45.0	45.5
Purchases	450.0	500.0
Receipts	450.0	475.0
Materials in storage (average)	450.0	475.0

REQUIRED:

a. Develop the rates for applying material costs using a departmental rate approach.
b. Develop the rate for the pool of materials handling costs. (Assume receipts is the allocation base.)
c. What would be the over- or underapplied amount using the departmental rate approach?
d. What would be the over- or underapplied amount using the cost pool approach?
e. Compare the two approaches to allocation of material-related costs.

6–14. Material Handling Costs.   Turner Electronics supplies parts and subassemblies to manufacturers in the Southwest region. The company stocks about 40,000 different parts and assemblies in a highly automated, million-square-foot warehouse. The electronics parts business is extremely competitive and markups over purchase price average about 18 percent. Company profitability strictly depends upon the efficiency of purchasing, warehousing, and shipping. For 19x3, the company used the following estimates for applying material-related costs to parts and assemblies:

Annual estimated purchasing costs	$ 16,481,700
Annual estimated receiving costs	$ 5,493,900
Annual estimated warehouse costs	$ 19,778,040
Annual estimated order-picking cost	$ 22,014,660
Annual estimated purchases	$549,390,000
Number of items to be received	732,520,000
Number of items to be shipped	733,822,000

Purchasing cost is allocated on the basis of the dollar volume of purchases. Receiving, warehouse, and order-picking costs are allocated on the basis of number of items.
      The actual data for the past year are as follows:

Purchasing Department costs	$ 16,364,124
Receiving Department costs	$ 5,826,460
Warehouse operations costs	$ 19,908,552
Order-picking costs	$ 22,998,193
Purchases	$549,586,000
Number of items received	733,248,000
Number of items shipped	737,388,333

REQUIRED:

a. Develop rates for applying purchasing, receiving, warehouse operations, and order-picking costs to parts and assemblies.
b. Prepare a journal entry to record the purchase of and parts-related costs for $18,000 in parts and assemblies from Jefferson Semiconductors, Inc., of California. There are 22,500 parts and assemblies on this one order.
c. Turner received an order from Johnson Controls for 23,200 parts with a carrying cost of $18,240. The invoice price to Johnson was $21,410. Prepare journal entries to record the sale, cost of goods sold, and the order-picking costs. Treat order-picking costs as an expense.
d. Prepare an entry to close material-related costs to cost of goods sold and picking costs to an expense.

6–15. Inventory Handling Costs, Volume Measures, and Cost Assignment.   As an internal consultant for the Slick Auto Parts Stores, you have noticed that there is a definite relationship between the number of different parts handled by a warehouse and the material handling costs. On the basis of 26 warehouses, you have found that the handling cost per part shipped is $2.40. Further, each unique part added to one warehouse increases its annual fixed costs by $50.00.

   A new line of automobile, the Parable, is being marketed by Irra Motors. If Slick Auto Parts chooses to stock these parts, it would need to stock them in at least 10 of its 26 warehouses. It is estimated that the Parable line will have about 500 unique parts (called *level A: high demand*) and assemblies that will be stocked in each of the 10 warehouses. Further, one of the warehouses will stock an additional 1,000 unique parts (called *level B: low demand*) to be shipped all over the country. Based on sales and service records of Parables, it is expected that each warehouse will have annual average volume of level A parts of 35 per item stocked. Level B volume is expected to be only three parts per item stocked.

REQUIRED:
a. Assume for now that only the 19x5 model year is going to be serviced from the Slick Auto Stores. Prepare an estimate of the increase in material handling costs from accepting the deal with Irra Motors for:
   1. Level A total handling costs.
   2. Level B total handling costs.
b. Auto makers have a history of changing some parts each year. Assume that Irra Motors changes 20 percent of the parts for the 19x6 model year. What effect will this increase in parts variety have on the fixed material handling costs for Slick Auto Parts?

6–16. Journal Entries for Material-Related Costs.   Cajun Oilfield Products has decided to change its accounting system for allocating material-related costs. Dale Streighter, chief accountant, believes material-related costs should be separated from production overhead costs and included in the material costs. Many of the material items require special handling, so Dale suggests using a separate rate for each material-related category. He has generated the following estimates for the next year:

Purchasing Department costs	$ 130,000
Receiving Department costs	$ 72,000
Storeroom costs	$ 120,000
Freight-in	$ 168,000
Dollar value of material purchases	$3,000,000
Number of purchase orders	13,000
Number of items received	24,000

Purchasing Department costs are allocated on number of purchase orders, Receiving Department costs and storeroom costs on dollar value of material purchases, and freight-in on number of items received.

   Actual data for the first quarter are as follows:

Purchasing Department costs	$ 33,225
Receiving Department costs	$ 17,750
Storeroom costs	$ 31,125
Freight-in	$ 48,000
Dollar value of material purchases	$750,000
Number of purchase orders	3,250
Number of items received	7,000

REQUIRED:
a. Determine the appropriate allocation rate for each material-related cost category.

  b. Prepare journal entries to reflect the following transactions:
    1. Actual material-related costs incurred.
    2. Allocation of material-related costs to materials inventory.
    3. Close the balance of each material-related cost account to cost of goods sold.
  c. Calculate an average inventory cost per unit for the material items received during the quarter.

6–17. Make-or-Buy Decision.   The management of Monrovia Fabricators, Inc., faces a dilemma: near full capacity and more work coming in every day. Some of the new work must either be deferred or rejected. The concern is how to expand usable capacity. The production manager suggests that one component presently fabricated internally be purchased from an outside supplier. Pacific Resources has a plant with excess capacity and has tried for some time to get the company's business. Normally, 150,000 units of this component are needed each year. The production cost for these units is as follows:

Direct materials	$1,125,000
Direct labor	655,000
Variable production overhead	425,000
Fixed production overhead that would be saved on this part and available for other production	135,000
Additional fixed production overhead that is allocated to this part but would be incurred even if the capacity were not used	660,000
Total cost	$3,000,000

Pacific Resources is offering to produce the part and sell it for $19.60 per unit. If the space could be made available in the plant by contracting the part to Pacific Resources, Monrovia Fabricators would realize an additional $50,000 in contribution margin from other products manufactured. Pacific Resources has also indicated a willingness to buy some products from the company that would add $35,000 to profits. These purchases are conditional upon receiving the company's order for the 150,000 parts.

REQUIRED:
  a. Prepare an analysis that will show whether Monrovia Fabricators should continue making the part or buy it from Pacific Resources.
  b. From the quantitative analysis, should Monrovia Fabricators buy the part? Explain.
  c. What qualitative factors might be important to this decision? List several.

EXTENDED APPLICATIONS

6–18. Material-Related Costs.   For several years now, the Bellwood Company has included the costs of receiving (and receiving inspection) and storeroom operations with the production overhead costs, which are then allocated to the work on the basis of direct labor cost. A new controller has decided this method of allocating the material-related costs does not accurately reflect the costs of processing the different kinds of materials. He asked the Accounting Department to survey the Receiving Department and storeroom operations to see how materials are processed. The results of this survey showed that material falls into three categories:

Category 1:	Material that is easy and relatively inexpensive to handle.
Category 2:	Material that is twice as expensive to handle as Category 1.
Category 3:	Material that is three times as expensive to handle as Category 1.

The controller has proposed removing the material-related costs from the production overhead, making a separate cost pool, and allocating it on the basis of material cost. The chief accountant suggested a two-step approach: (1) allocate material-related costs to each category, weighted by level of difficulty in handling and (2) develop a material-related overhead rate for each category based on the material cost within the category.

The material, labor, and production overhead for the current period are as follows:

Materials issued to production:		
Category 1: 100,000 units	$750,000	
Category 2: 150,000 units	450,000	
Category 3: 200,000 units	300,000	$1,500,000
Direct labor		754,000
Production overhead:		
Material-related costs	$300,000	
Other	775,000	1,975,000
Total production costs		$3,325,000

Among the many jobs completed during the month is order no. A49002, with direct material and direct labor costs as follows:

Direct material:		
Category 1	$50,000	
Category 2	30,000	
Category 3	20,000	$100,000
Direct labor		60,000

REQUIRED:
a. Develop the rates to allocate material-related costs assuming:
  1. Material-related costs remain in production overhead.
  2. Material-related costs are allocated according to the controller's proposal.
  3. Material-related costs are allocated according to the chief accountant's proposal.
b. Show the amount of material-related costs allocated to order no. A49002 under each of the rates developed in (a).
c. Which method of allocation do you believe is the most appropriate for the Bellwood Company? Explain.

6–19. Material-Related Cost Pools.   Kellee-Rivers Technologies generates about 70 percent of its revenues from contracts with the federal government. The other 30 percent of the revenue comes from commercial business. The company uses common facilities for both government and commercial work. Because the products are similar for both types of customers, there is no attempt to segregate government and commercial work.

The government pressured the company into establishing a number of different cost pools for indirect costs. One of these pools is for material-related costs. The detail on the material-related costs and allocation base for the past year is as follows:

Salaries and wages:		
Indirect labor	$	864,327
Additional compensation		34,392
Overtime premium		5,263
Sick leave		22,018
Holidays		28,100
Suggestion awards		125
Vacations		43,734
Outside services:		
Maintenance	$	192
Other		75
Personnel expenses:		
Compensation insurance	$	4,409
Unemployment insurance		14,871
FICA taxes		19,542
Group insurance		39,847
Travel		36,535
Dues and subscriptions		651
Employee pension funds:		
Salary		16,694
Hourly		10,423
Supplies:		
Operating supplies	$	13,733
Maintenance supplies		423
Stationery, printing, and office supplies		10,162
Utilities:		
Telephone	$	20,322
Heat, light, and power		170,004
Depreciation	$	79,554
Total material-related costs	$	1,435,396
Total direct materials costs		$28,466,900
Material-related rate		5.0%

The activities encompassed in the material-related costs are purchasing, receiving and inspection, and the materials storeroom. Costs incurred represent human resources, facilities, and supplies.

In addition to the material-related cost pool, the company has overhead pools for engineering and production, and a general and administrative (G&A) expense pool for charging costs to government contracts. G&A expenses are not allocated to commercial work.

REQUIRED:
a. Explain under what circumstances a company would combine all indirect costs that it will charge to products in one cost pool rather than in several pools.
b. What are the advantages and disadvantages of using direct material cost as the allocation base for material-related costs?
c. Present arguments in favor of and against more than one material-related cost pool.
d. Assume the material-related costs are combined with production overhead, which is allocated on the basis of direct production labor costs totaling $31,579,271. If a contract calls for $60,000 of direct material cost and $40,000 of direct production labor cost, how much material-related cost is charged to the contract? How much material-related cost would be charged to the contract if a separate material-related cost pool is maintained, as in the original problem? Explain the difference.

APPENDIX 6A Inventory Management and Control

LEARNING OBJECTIVES

After completing this appendix, you should be able to:

1. Identify and explain the characteristics important to inventory management and control.
2. Apply ABC analysis and classification to an inventory setting.
3. Calculate order quantities and reorder points using the EOQ model.
4. Describe the just-in-time (JIT) concept.
5. Explain the basic concepts of a materials requirement planning (MRP) system.

Many companies invest large amounts in materials, parts, subassemblies, and assemblies that are carried in inventories. The proper management and control of those inventories provides an opportunity for considerable cost reduction, cost savings, and cash flow improvement. Whether the business is a manufacturer, merchandiser, or a service organization, inventory is a difficult asset to control and protect. Predictably, businesses have developed a variety of tools and techniques to manage and control their large liquid asset. Complex computer models are often used in this process, but these models are based on the fundamental elements discussed in this appendix. The appendix covers the essentials of a basic inventory management program together with the classical economic order quantity model. Reorder points, stock-outs, and safety stocks are also mentioned. Finally, the appendix introduces recent innovations in just-in-time inventory methods and materials requirement planning (MRP) systems, which are having a considerable impact on inventory management.

Cost Characteristics Related to Inventory Management

Inventory management activities range from stocking replacement parts for a commercial trucking operation to ensuring an adequate selection of different sizes of clothing in the women's department of a retail store to providing a selection of fresh fish and vegetable entries on the menu of a local seafood restaurant. The underlying principles are similar in all three situations. The major objective is to optimize the level of inventory investment by minimizing the total costs of maintaining inventory. Inventories may be too high or too low. If too high, there are unnecessary carrying costs and risks of obsolescence. Low inventory, on the other hand, may disrupt production or may lose sales temporarily or permanently. A balancing act must be performed. As the number of units in inventory increases, the carrying costs increase but the ordering costs (also called *replenishment costs*) decrease. The opposite occurs when the number of units in inventory decreases—the carrying costs decrease while the ordering costs increase.

Purchase or production costs, ordering costs, carrying costs, and stock-out costs are the significant costs composing the total cost of maintaining inventory. The correct quantity to order from vendors or the size of lots submitted to the company's production

212

process involves a search for the minimum total costs resulting from the combined effects of the individual costs. As a rule, purchase or production costs are irrelevant to the decision of an optimal level because we assume that the total annual quantity to be purchased or produced is the same regardless of the tools or techniques used to make the decision. The other three costs are defined in the following sections.

Ordering Costs.   Ordering costs refer to the managerial and clerical costs to prepare the purchase order to a vendor or a production order to a manufacturing operation. The ordering costs related to a purchase order are the incremental costs of identifying and issuing an order to a single vendor, the cost for computing each line item on a single order, the costs to receive and inspect the goods as received, and the cost to process accounts payable and cash payments. Also included in these costs are costs related to the people, facilities and equipment, and supplies needed to maintain an ordering system.

Ordering costs for production orders are called *setup costs*. To make each different product involves obtaining the necessary materials, arranging specific equipment setups, filling out the required papers, appropriately charging time and materials, and moving out the previous stock of material. In addition, other costs may be involved in hiring, training, or laying off workers and in idle time or overtime. If there were no costs or loss of time in changing from the production of one lot or product to another, many small lots would be produced. However, changeover costs usually exist.

The higher the cost per order, the fewer orders will be processed, which results in a higher quantity per order. Fewer orders means higher inventory levels, with the maximum level equaling the order quantity.

Carrying Costs.   **Carrying costs** relate to having quantities of material available. There are two classes of carrying costs: (1) out-of-pocket costs (the costs associated with the physical presence of the inventory) and (2) cost of capital (the opportunity cost of having money tied up in inventory rather than in other income-generating assets). Out-of-pocket costs include such items as insurance on the value of the inventory, inventory taxes, storage facilities, inspections and physical inventory counts, obsolescence, breakage, handling, and pilferage. **Cost of capital** is more than financing costs. It is the weighted average of the cost to obtain funds from the various equities (short-term and long-term debt financing, capital stocks, and retained earnings) of the company. The two classes are usually combined and expressed as either a percentage of the purchase price or production cost or a cost per unit. (See the section on the economic order quantity for an application.)

Obviously, high carrying costs favor keeping inventory levels as low as possible, which suggests frequent replenishment. The more frequent the orders, the smaller the order quantity, and the lower the inventory level. Therefore, we see the need to balance the costs of ordering versus the costs of carrying.

Stock-out Costs.   **Stock-out costs** occur when the demand for an item exceeds the units in inventory or exceeds the ability of the company to meet delivery schedules. A customer order for the item must either wait until the stock is replenished or be canceled. Although the stock-out costs are little more than guesses, a range of such costs usually can be specified. The common measurable costs are the additional administrative effort required to process a back order and the contribution margin lost if the customer goes elsewhere without waiting for the back order. Another important consideration is the loss of goodwill because the customer may not return and may convey dissatisfaction to friends. Because direct measures of stock-out costs are difficult to establish, companies typically do one of two things: (1) establish a safety stock or (2) impute a stock-out cost to customer service levels and select a service level at which to operate. The latter case means the company is willing to accept a certain percentage of customer orders that cannot be filled on demand. Either approach requires increasing inventory levels, which means higher total carrying costs.

ABC Analysis and Classification

Inventory management applies different tools, techniques, and procedures to different classes of inventory. One of the most popular approaches to grouping inventory items is **ABC analysis and classification.** Essentially, the ABC approach breaks down the inventory items into classes A, B, and C in terms of relative value to the business.[1] This value can be expressed in dollar amounts or in terms of how critical the material is to production, or a combination of the two. A is considered most valuable and C is least valuable. After categorizing items into the three classes, management selects appropriate management tools, techniques, and procedures that are cost-effective for each class. This is an understandable, straightforward approach to setting priorities in inventory management.

Typically, class A items are those that, while constituting no more than 20 percent of the total number of items in inventory, make up 80 percent or more of the dollar value of its usage and are the most critical items to the overall production effort. Management efforts should reflect the fact that this class represents a high value of inventory used, not the fact that the class consists of 20 percent or less of the units in inventory. The class A items should be under the tightest control and the responsibility of the most experienced people.

Class B inventory items constitute 40 to 60 percent of the total number of items in inventory, but they may account for 15 percent or less of the dollar value of the inventory usage. Again, the effort and the procedures for management should reflect the economic value of the class, not the total number of items. Economic order quantities tend to play a more important role in this category than in class A inventory because physical control is not as extensive here.

Finally, there are the class C items. These items might be 25 to 40 percent of the total number of items in inventory with a dollar usage no higher than 5 percent of inventory. The management effort will be considerably less than the effort connected with classes A and B. For class C items, economic order quantities or simple physical controls, such as the min-max or the two-bin system with safety stocks, can be used.

The EOQ Model

The two main questions in establishing inventory levels are how much to order at a time and when to order. A key factor is computing the best order size of either a purchase for materials or a production order (work order) for a production run. This best size is called the **economic order quantity** (EOQ) or **economic lot size** and represents the size that minimizes the total annual costs of maintaining an inventory of the item in question. The EOQ model is appropriate for items that are carried for a significant period of time, that tend to have a constant demand rate, and that are related to independent demand items (finished products in inventory demanded by customers; that is, products made for stock).

---

[1] Although the terminology implies three categories (A, B, and C), in practice the concept is expanded to include more than three categories. For example, some companies will have an A, B, C, D, and E classification.

Tabular Solution to the EOQ.   Consider a manufacturing plant that requires 6,000 castings a year for use in assembling motorboat engines. The foundry has a maximum production capacity of 20,000 castings per year. The cost associated with setting up the production run (ordering cost) is $100, and the carrying cost is $20 per unit per year. Which order quantity minimizes total inventory cost?

To identify the appropriate order size, we must first specify the relationships we need for computational purposes. For our purposes, the total cost function for ordering and carrying cost is as follows:

Total cost = (Number of orders × Ordering cost per order) + (Average inventory × The annual cost of carrying one unit of inventory)

In algebraic terms, this formula is:

$$TC = (D/Q)O + (Q/2)C$$

Where:

TC = the total annual costs of ordering and carrying inventory
D = annual demand
Q = quantity to be ordered (the optimum amount is termed *the economic order quantity*)
O = ordering cost per order
C = the annual cost of carrying one unit of inventory

One additional important relationship should also be identified from these symbols: $Q = D/N$, which means the order quantity is the annual demand divided by the number of orders.

Using these symbols, we can construct the following table:

Number of Orders N	Order Quantity Q = D/N	Order Cost N × O	Carrying Cost (Q/2) × C	Total Cost Tc
1	6,000	$ 100	$60,000	$60,100
2	3,000	200	30,000	30,200
3	2,000	300	20,000	20,300
4	1,500	400	15,000	15,400
5	1,200	500	12,000	12,500
6	1,000	600	10,000	10,600
7	858	700	8,580	9,280
8	750	800	7,500	8,250
9	667	900	6,670	7,570
10	600	1,000	6,000	7,000
11	546	1,100	5,460	6,560
12	500	1,200	5,000	6,200
13	462	1,300	4,620	5,920
14	429	1,400	4,290	5,690
15	400	1,500	4,000	5,500
16	375	1,600	3,750	5,350
17	353	1,700	3,530	5,230
18	334	1,800	3,340	5,140
19	316	1,900	3,160	5,060
20	300	2,000	3,000	5,000
21	286	2,100	2,860	4,960
22	273	2,200	2,730	4,930
23	261	2,300	2,610	4,910
24	250	2,400	2,500	4,900

Number of Orders N	Order Quantity Q = D/N	Order Cost N × O	Carrying Cost (Q/2) × C	Total Cost Tc
24.5	245	2,450	2,450	4,900
25	240	2,500	2,400	4,900
26	231	2,600	2,310	4,910
27	223	2,700	2,230	4,930
28	215	2,800	2,150	4,950
29	207	2,900	2,070	4,970
30	200	3,000	2,000	5,000

The table shows that the total relevant costs are minimized at 24 (250 units) and 25 (240 units) orders. Actually, the important point is where the change in ordering costs equals carrying costs; mathematically, that occurs at 24.5 orders, or an order quantity of 245 units. For our purposes, we select 24 orders with a quantity of 250 units. (We could just as easily pick 24 orders with the 240 units because the total relevant costs are the same.) However, to be conservative and to minimize risk, we go with the higher order quantity. Exhibit 6A–1 is a graph of all three costs. The minimum total costs occur at the point ordering costs equal carrying costs.

EOQ Formula.   Tabulating the data for every item in inventory takes considerable time and patience even with a computer. We can easily derive a formula that proves more efficient. We already have a formula for total cost:

$$TC = (D/Q)O + (Q/2)C$$

EXHIBIT 6A–1   EOQ Cost curves

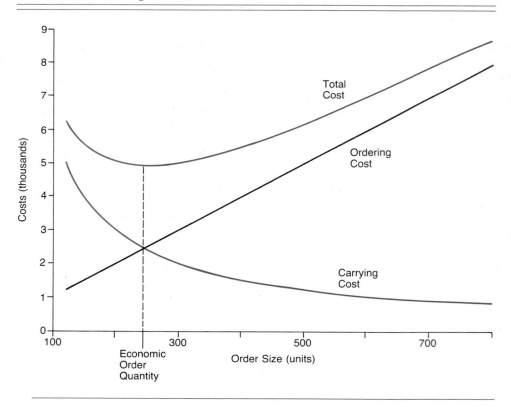

To find the EOQ, we use calculus and differentiate TC with respect to Q, set the result equal to zero, and solve for Q. This results in the following formula:

$$EOQ = Q^* = \sqrt{\frac{2DO}{C}}$$

With this formula, the number of orders can be calculated as:

$$N^* = D/Q^*$$

Applying these formulas to the example, we can find the EOQ and the number of orders. The EOQ is calculated as:

$$Q^* = \sqrt{\frac{2(6,000)100}{20}} = \sqrt{\frac{1,200,000}{20}} = \sqrt{60,000} = 245$$

The number of orders is determined by:

$$N^* = 6,000/245 = 24.5$$

The formula approach gives us 24.5 orders. Because orders are discrete, we would pick either 24 or 25 for the actual orders to place.

Assumptions of the Model.   A number of assumptions have been made in developing and using this model. Here are eight significant assumptions, an understanding of which will help in modifying calculations when the assumptions are relaxed.

1. The unit purchase price or production cost is constant and does not vary with changes in the order size changes.
2. The demand rate is known with certainty and is a constant rate per unit of time. Although the time is normally a year, demand can be stated in other units of time.
3. The ordering cost per order is constant and measured in terms of dollars.
4. Carrying cost is constant over the same time period as that of the demand and is measured in terms of dollars per unit.
5. Stock-out cost is so prohibitively high that inventory is replenished before stock-outs can occur.
6. Order quantity is constant per order.
7. Replenishments of inventory arrive before the inventory level reaches zero or the safety stock level is reached.
8. Lead time for placing and receiving an order is known with certainty and is constant. The time to place an order (reorder point) is when enough inventory remains for the lead time demand.

Any of these assumptions can be relaxed to more appropriately approximate different situations. This will require adjustments in the EOQ formula or additional policies, such as implementing or changing safety stock levels. It is even possible to incorporate probabilities as a means of accommodating uncertainty, although we do not present that material here. For more details on these refinements, see books on inventory and production management.

Lead Time and Reorder Point.   The second major decision that must be made involves the right time to place an order, called the **reorder point.** If instantaneous supply were always available, the reorder point would not be a critical decision. An order for the EOQ would be initiated when the inventory level drops to zero. Because this ideal situation does not exist, establishment of the reorder point is important.

The first significant factor to consider is the lead time. **Lead time** refers to the interval between the time an order is placed and the time the items are received and placed into inventory. The approach to ordering is to combine demand trends with anticipated lead time to establish a reorder point. The reorder point is the quantity level of inventory that triggers the placement of a new order. It is easy to compute when demand and lead time are known with certainty. In many cases, lead time will vary somewhat from order to order. In such situations the average lead time can be used to determine the reorder point. However, if a conservative policy is desired to reduce greatly the possibility of stock-outs, the longest estimated lead time may be used.

Under normal assumptions of the EOQ formula, an order should be placed at the inventory level that permits receipt of the order at precisely the time inventory reaches a zero level (or the safety stock level, if one exists).

To provide an illustration, let R = the reorder point and L = the lead time. The reorder point is equal to the product of annual demand and lead time stated in terms of a fraction of a year. Returning to the example of castings and assuming lead time is 30 days ($\frac{1}{12}$ of a year), we calculate a reorder point as follows:

$$R = D \times L = 6{,}000 \times (\tfrac{1}{12}) = 500 \text{ units.}$$

Therefore, when the inventory level reaches 500 units, an order is placed in the amount of the EOQ.

A problem arises here because the order quantity equals 245 units (or, if we pick 24 orders, we will have 250 units), which also represents the maximum inventory level, and that level is below the reorder point. When the reorder point is higher than the order quantity, the level for comparison with a reorder point is the inventory level plus units on order. We must place one or more orders immediately to get the inventory plus on order to equal a level above the reorder point. For example, we must place two orders to get 500 units on order. Because that equals the reorder point, we place one more order for 250 units. Now we have 750 units in inventory and on order. When the inventory level plus on-order units reaches 500 units, an order for 250 units is placed. The reorder point now becomes 250 units in inventory plus 250 units on order.

Safety Stock and Stock-outs.   When there is uncertainty about the demand or about the timing or amount that suppliers can provide, companies want a buffer. **Safety stock** is the extra inventory carried as a buffer against the possibility of a stock-out. A safety stock will increase the carrying costs and reduce the stock-out costs. The optimum safety stock level is determined by minimizing the carrying costs and the expected stock-out costs. Because we do not have a good measure for the stock-out costs, other approaches are necessary. They are not covered here, but the approaches include mathematical adjustments to the EOQ formula, development of acceptable service levels, and inclusion of expected values from assumptions about probabilities of demand during the lead time.

A simple computation for determining safety stock is to find the difference between a maximum demand during the lead time and the average demand during the same time. For example, if the maximum demand for castings is expected at 550 units during the 30-day lead time and average demand is 500 units (the current reorder point), a safety stock is 50 units (550 units less 500 units). This should take care of most situations if replenishment is timely.

Just-in-Time Inventories

One of the recent developments in inventory management philosophies is known as **just-in-time (JIT) inventory** or a **zero-stock system.** The objective of JIT is to obtain materials just in time for production, move work in process from one department just in time for the needs of the next department, and to provide finished goods just in time for sale. All production facilities are viewed as a pipeline, and all movement of goods between facilities is viewed as a uniform flow of materials, component parts, and subassemblies. This reduces, or potentially eliminates, inventory carrying costs. Advocates of JIT claim it results in (1) reductions in material, work in process, and finished goods inventories; (2) increased equipment utilization; (3) reduced space needs; (4) increased employee productivity; and (5) improved quality of the product.

For JIT to operate efficiently, a company must commit to use only a few suppliers. This means a very open relationship must evolve between buyer and supplier. If all works well, high-quality materials will arrive just in time to enter the appropriate production phases.

It is unlikely that many companies can cut inventories literally to zero, but lowering inventories to immaterial levels has some accounting advantages. First, there is a reduction in the amount of accounting time required to accumulate and transfer costs among inventory accounts. Second, accounting reports can be more responsive to production managers by giving them better, more understandable information in time for their use. A resulting benefit is that accountants have an opportunity to become more a part of the management team.

Material Requirements Planning (MRP)

Many manufacturing operations involve dependent demand, a situation in which component parts and raw materials are produced and/or assembled into finished products according to customer specifications. For example, the Air Force contracts with a major aerospace company for a missile. All of the component parts, raw materials, subassemblies, and assemblies depend on the Air Force's specifications for the missile. Such situations are fertile for the implementation of **material requirements planning (MRP).**

MRP starts with a master production schedule for the final products. On the basis of needs specified by the master production schedule, the requirements for raw materials, component parts, and all subassemblies and assemblies designated for the individual products are determined. MRP identifies when a job needs to be done, and how much and when raw materials need to be purchased or parts and subassemblies acquired from subcontractors. The major advantage of MRP is its capability to coordinate complex and numerous activities efficiently. As a result, a company is able to maintain smaller material inventories and minimize stock-outs.

PROBLEM FOR REVIEW

KCB Enterprises is a distributor of small batteries that power hand-held computers used by business for organizing projects, telephone directories, to-do notes, and appointments. KCB needs 40,000 batteries each year at a cost of $9 per unit. The carrying cost is estimated at $1.44 per unit per year, and the ordering cost is $18 per order. Lead-time demand equals 800 units.

REQUIRED

a. Calculate the EOQ for this situation.
b. How many orders will be placed during a year?
c. Determine the reorder point.

SOLUTION

a. The EOQ is calculated as:

$$Q* = \sqrt{\frac{2(40,000)18}{1.44}} = \sqrt{\frac{1,440,000}{1.44}} = \sqrt{1,000,000} = 1,000$$

b. The number of orders is determined by:

$$N* = 40,000/1,000 = 40 \text{ orders}$$

c. The reorder point is:

$$R = D \times L = 40,000 \times (800/40,000)$$
$$= 40,000 \times (\tfrac{1}{50} \text{ of a year}) = 800 \text{ units.}$$

KEY TERMS AND CONCEPTS

Order costs (213)
Carrying costs (213)
Cost of capital (213)
Stock-out costs (213)
ABC analysis and classification (214)
Economic order quantity (EOQ) or Economic lot size (214)

Lead time (218)
Reorder point (217)
Safety stock (218)
Just-in-time (JIT) inventories or Zero-stock system (219)
Material Requirements Planning (MRP) (219)

ADDITIONAL READINGS

Harhalakis, George; Phani Sharma; and William S. Zachman. "A Dynamic Planning and Control System for Inventories of Raw Materials." *Production and Inventory Management Journal,* Second Quarter 1989, p. 12.

McGrath, Jack. "Calculating Economic Order Quantity." *CFO,* November 1986, pp. 69–73.

Millard, Robert I. "Is MRP Training Aimed in the Right Direction?" *Production and Inventory Management Journal,* Second Quarter 1989, p. 22.

Padgett, Thomas. "Building an Inventory System in Lotus 1-2-3." *Business Software,* August 1988, pp. 28–36.

Rao, Ashok. "Manufacturing Systems—Changing to Support JIT." *Production and Inventory Management Journal,* Second Quarter 1989, p. 18.

Sadhwani, A. T., and M. H. Sarha. "The Impact of Just-in-Time Inventory Systems on Small Businesses." *Journal of Accountancy,* January 1987, pp. 118–33.

———, and Dayal Kiringoda. "Just-in-Time: An Inventory System Whose Time Has Come." *Management Accounting,* December 1985, pp. 36–43.

Sauers, Dale, G. "Analyzing Inventory Systems." *Management Accounting,* May 1986, pp. 30–36.

Sounderpandian, Jayavel. "MRP on Spreadsheets: A Do-It-Yourself Alternative for Small Firms." *Production and Inventory Management Journal,* Second Quarter 1989, p. 6.

REVIEW QUESTIONS

1. Briefly describe the significant costs an organization needs to be aware of when dealing with inventory management and control.
2. Explain the purpose for adopting an ABC classification for inventory management and control.
3. What trade-offs in costs are involved when computing an economic order quantity?

4. Define *safety stock*.
5. What are the consequences of maintaining inadequate inventory levels? What are the difficulties of measuring precisely the costs associated with understocking?
6. Define *lead time*. Explain its relationship to a reorder point.
7. Discuss the purpose of a just-in-time inventory system.
8. What are the basic concepts of an MRP system?

EXERCISES AND PROBLEMS

6A–1. ABC Classification.   An aerospace company is considering stratifying its inventory in one component assembly plant for better inventory control. Inventory usage data for the most recent quarter are presented below:

Part Number	Quarterly Usage	Unit Cost	Total Cost
XP18	8,220	$ 2.50	$ 20,550
XP20	20,400	.25	5,100
XP63	6,840	2.00	13,680
XP88	8,880	3.25	28,860
XP94	30,000	.50	15,000
XQ14	1,000	40.00	40,000
XQ25	2,000	30.00	60,000
XQ42	18,600	1.00	18,600
XQ51	9,980	1.50	14,970
XQ76	4,920	2.00	9,840
XR09	7,560	2.50	18,900
XR11	5,600	10.50	58,800
XR27	24,000	.80	19,200
XR39	28,500	.30	8,550
XR48	500	6.70	3,350
	177,000		$335,400

REQUIRED:
a. Arrange the data in order of the highest total cost to the lowest total cost. Select the ABC classifications from this array of dollars.
b. Explain why you have selected the points for A, B, and C inventories.
c. Construct a graph of the data with cumulative total cost on the vertical axis and cumulative total units on the horizontal axis. Show the ABC break points on the graph.

6A–2. Economic Order Quantity.   Roundtree Hi-Tech Manufacturing has reached its capacity to produce a component part for one of its state-of-the-art robots. Purchasing has found a supplier for the part who can meet the anticipated delivery schedule. The contract calls for a total of 2,000 parts over the next year. Order costs will be $18 per order, and the carrying costs are $5 per unit per year. The purchase price is $25 per part. The lead time is 30 days. No stock-outs are allowed.

REQUIRED:
a. Find the EOQ that minimizes total cost, assuming each of the following approaches:
   1. Use a tabular format.
   2. Use the EOQ formula.
b. Calculate the reorder point.
c. The cost accountant has just informed you that an error was made in calculating the ordering cost per order. The cost should be $32 instead of $18. Explain the effect of this error on the cost of maintaining inventory. Show supporting calculations.

6A–3. Economic Order Quantity.   Clean Water Systems, Inc., has a line of kitchen water faucet filtration systems that the company retails for $240 each. The purchase price from the supplier is $165 per unit. Annual demand runs about 800 units. Freight on incoming shipments averages $8 per unit. Insurance during shipment adds another $2 to the cost. The clerical and other processing costs of placing an order are $25 per order. The company's cost of capital for its various sources of funds is 16 percent. It takes five days from the time an order is released until the units are received. Because the store is in a shopping mall, it is open every day (assume 360 days in a year). The manager currently orders 50 units each time an order is placed.

REQUIRED:
a. Calculate the carrying cost per filtration unit. (*Hint:* determine the cost invested per unit and multiply that amount by 16 percent.)
b. How many units are ordered under economic order quantities? How many orders per year does that result in?
c. What is the reorder point?
d. How much can the company save in costs to maintain its inventory by ordering in economic order quantities?
e. Assume that the demand during lead time fluctuates, although it has never exceeded 20 units. Give a calculation for a safety stock if the company wants no stock-outs. Explain what the safety stock does to the reorder point.

6A–4. Just-in-Time Inventory. The success of the Japanese automotive industry in the world market and particularly in the U.S. market has been attributed to such factors as culture and engineering. Among the causes cited is an inventory control method called "just-in-time" that appears so effective that a number of American manufacturers have adopted it. The phrase, "just-in-time," refers to a method whereby parts required for production arrive from the parts manufacturer just in time to be used. Thus, manufacturers' inventories can be reduced while suppliers will be required to ship more frequently.

In addition, this inventory control method will require other changes in the way managements operate and how businesses are conducted if they are to produce the expected cost savings.

(CMA, adapted)

REQUIRED:
a. For a company that plans to introduce a just-in-time inventory method, discuss the changes, other than inventory investment and receiving schedules, management will need to make with respect to:
   1. Relationships with suppliers.
   2. Management skills.
   3. Management behavior.
b. A company that plans to introduce just-in-time inventory management would want to expedite the transition to the new system. Describe the steps a company could implement to achieve the changes discussed in the paragraph above with respect to the:
   1. Company's suppliers.
   2. Development of management skills and behavior.

6A–5. Inventory Levels. Clyde Peterson, general manager for Adam Desk Company, is exasperated because the company exhausted its finished goods inventory of style 103—modern desk twice during the previous month. This led to customer complaints and disrupted the normal flow of operations.

"We ought to be able to plan better," declared Peterson. "Our annual sales demand is 18,000 units for this model or an average of 75 desks per day based upon our 240-day work year. Unfortunately, the sales pattern is not this uniform. Our daily demand on that model varies considerably. If we do not have the units on hand when a customer places an order, 35 percent of the time we lose the sale, 40 percent of the time we pay an extra charge of $24.00 per unit to expedite shipping when the unit becomes available, and 25 percent of the time the customer will accept a back order at no out-of-pocket cost to us.

"When we run out of units, we cannot convert immediately because we would disrupt the production of our other products and cause cost increases. The setup process for this model results in the destruction of 12 finished desks, leaving no salvageable materials. Once we get the line up, we can produce 200 units per day. I would prefer to have several planned runs of a uniform quantity rather than short unplanned runs often required to meet unfilled customer orders."

The manager of the Cost Accounting Department has suggested that an EOQ model be adopted to determine optimum production runs and then establish a safety stock to guard against stock-outs. The cost data for the modern desk that sells for $110.00 is readily available from the accounting records. The manufacturing costs are as follows.

Direct materials	$30.00
Direct labor (2 DLH at $7.00)	14.00
Manufacturing overhead	
Variable (2 DLH at $3.00)	6.00
Fixed (2 DLH at $5.00)	10.00
Total manufacturing cost	$60.00

Cost accounting estimates that the company's carrying costs are 19.2 percent of the incremental out-of-pocket manufacturing costs. This percentage can be broken down into a 10.8 percent variable rate and an 8.4 percent fixed rate.

The EOQ formula referred to by the cost accounting manager is as follows:

$$EOQ = \sqrt{\frac{2DO}{C}}$$

where:

D = annual demand in units

O = cost of placing an order

C = annual unit cost of carrying inventory.

(CMA, adapted)

REQUIRED:
a. Adam Desk Company can solve part of its production scheduling problems by adapting the EOQ model to determine the optimum production run.
1. Explain what costs the company would be attempting to balance when it adapts the EOQ model to production runs.
2. Calculate the optimum quantity that Adam Desk Company should manufacture in each production run of style 103—modern desk.
3. Calculate the number of production runs of modern desks that Adam Desk Company would schedule during the year based upon the optimum quantity calculated in requirement (a.2)
b. Adam Desk Company should establish a safety stock level to guard against stock-outs.
1. Explain what factors affect the desired size of the safety stock for any inventory item.
2. Calculate the minimum safety stock level that Adam Desk Company could afford to maintain for the style 103—modern desk and not be worse off than if it were unable to fill orders equal to an average day's demand.

CHAPTER

Labor and Related Costs

LABOR COST PROBLEM

International Electronics Enterprises (IEE) has grown from a garage operation with three employees in 1972 to an organization of about 1,200 employees. Russ Duren, founder and president, just recently approved a benefits package for employees that provides a pension plan; compensation for vacations, holidays, and sick leave; and group insurance for life, health, and disability. The approval of the benefits package precipitated a total evaluation of labor rates and salary schedules. Total labor costs were definitely increasing beyond a reasonable level. The company has experienced losses during the past two years, and Mr. Duren is looking for concepts and programs that can make the company more competitive in the specialty electronics market.

With the changes in the total labor package, Mr. Duren realized that the accounting system, which accounted for just the basic wages and salaries, did not adequately trace labor costs to products, nor was he getting information for planning and control purposes. Many labor costs were lumped together and reported as one Employee Benefits account.

Mr. Duren asked Carrie Sessions, controller, to develop recommendations for changing the accounting system. Her recommendations for the way the company ought to account for each component, along with recommendations for controlling labor costs, were due back to the president within the week.

LEARNING OBJECTIVES

After studying this chapter, you should be able to:

1. Differentiate between labor costs and labor-related costs.
2. Account for the flow of payroll costs through the general ledger for distribution, accrual, and payment of payroll.
3. Describe and account for the varieties of labor-related costs.
4. Define value-added labor concepts and compute value-added measures.

Labor is the physical or mental effort expended in manufacturing a product or in rendering a service. **Labor cost** is the price paid to employees in the form of wages and salaries. **Wages** refer to payments based on hours worked or pieces produced and are a variable cost. **Salaries** are characterized by a fixed periodic payment (weekly, biweekly, semimonthly, or monthly); thus, salaries are a fixed cost. The cost elements that make up the total cost of human resources can be divided into labor cost and labor-related cost.

Labor costs and labor-related costs can strongly influence the competitive position of a company. High labor costs will result in a company that cannot compete in its industry. Additionally, the poor use of employees' time will also result in an unprofitable company. Thus, decisions related to labor are critical to the survival of organizations.

LABOR COSTS AND LABOR-RELATED COSTS

Labor costs include the costs of wages and salaries. **Labor-related costs** are any expenditures made by an employer on behalf of employees in addition to the wages and salaries. Labor-related costs may be further divided into:

1. Incentive pay for performance above minimum levels: for example, bonuses, overtime premium, or shift differentials pay.
2. The employer's payroll taxes paid.
3. Fringe benefits, such as insurance or vacations.

While wages and salaries dominate the total costs of many employees, the costs of fringe benefits and payroll taxes will add 25 to 50 percent to the costs of employees. In high-risk employment (for example, chemical plants, petroleum refineries, and explosive manufacture), the wages are high and the benefits often exceed 50 percent of wages.

Direct, Value-Added Direct, and Indirect Labor

The total labor expended for the benefit of the product or service is segregated into direct labor and indirect labor. **Direct labor** is all labor that can be specifically identified with a product or service in an economically feasible manner. **Value-added direct labor**[1] is that portion of direct labor that changes raw material into a finished product or service that is delivered to a customer. For example, value-added direct labor fabricates parts, assembles products, and finishes products. Non–value-added labor moves, inspects, stores, examines, or otherwise handles the products without adding value to the customer. **Indirect labor** is labor that is not readily traced to a product or service. Indirect workers supervise, repair, manage, purchase, inspect,

---
[1] This is a new concept that has been incorporated into accounting during the past decade. Thus, many corporate cost systems do not reflect this concept yet but will in the near future. Some companies are currently redefining direct labor to include only value-added workers.

record, advise, or otherwise support the direct workers. Indirect workers are non-value added in most circumstances.

An improving competitive position involves an improvement in the ratio of value-added workers to total workers:

$$\textbf{Value-added labor ratio} = \frac{\text{Value-added direct labor}}{\text{Total direct and indirect labor}}$$

The ratio may be computed in terms of number of employees or dollars of cost. The number of supervisors, managers, clerical staff, accountants, engineers, inspectors, and all others that are not value-added workers should be reduced. Value-added workers can do their own supervision (by designating a lead worker), train new workers, inspect the product, and maintain equipment. Thus, management should seek to achieve a value-added labor ratio as near as possible to 1.[2] The distinction between value-added and non–value-added labor is critical to the decisions of managers of the company.

For product costing purposes, direct labor has a specific time relationship with products and its cost is charged directly to products on the basis of time expended.[3] Indirect labor cost is first charged to the Production Overhead Control account and from there is allocated to products.

The misclassification of labor results in errors in the amounts of labor costs charged to individual products or projects. If, in addition, the production overhead is allocated on the basis of direct labor,[4] serious errors in overhead allocation will occur as a result of the incorrect hours or costs in the allocation base. This, in turn, will result in errors by managers in decisions to drop or add products and errors in the performance evaluation of production units.

ACCOUNTING FOR LABOR COSTS

Accounting for labor costs has three distinct aspects: (1) distribution of labor cost, (2) accrual of the liabilities, and (3) payment of liabilities.

The labor cost system must provide the information for the appropriate journal entries so that labor costs, liabilities, and payments are properly recorded. Exhibit 7–1 presents the general ledger flow for a labor cost system.

To illustrate the ledger entries, consider the following payroll information for the week ending October 27, 19x4, for the Parts Division of International Electronics Enterprises.

The number of employees and gross payroll:

Production—Direct labor	494	$158,000
Production—Indirect labor	63	40,000
Marketing Department	50	35,000
General & administrative functions	62	56,000
Total	669	$289,000

---

[2] In certain industries, the maximization of the value-added labor ratio is not possible because the production process is totally automated. Thus, petrochemical plants, nuclear power plants, and many fabrication plants do not require any (or less than 2 percent of total cost) direct labor. In these cases the total of all labor cost will often be immaterial to the profitability of the company and thus is not of serious concern to management.

[3] If direct labor cost is small, then it is often effective for product costing to combine it with production overhead and apply all conversion costs together to the product.

[4] Many organizations allocate overhead on the basis of direct labor. As developed further in Chapter 8, this may or may not be appropriate, depending on the circumstances.

EXHIBIT 7–1   Distribution and Accrual of Labor Costs

Withholdings:	
Federal income taxes	$ 18,200
FICA taxes (Employees' share, 7.7%)	22,253
State income taxes	9,675
In addition there are labor-related costs:	
FICA taxes (Employer's share, 7.7%)	$ 22,253
Federal and state unemployment taxes	11,271
Workers' Compensation Insurance	14,450
Health, dental, life, and accident insurance	33,560
County and city occupation taxes	8,726
Compensated absence	23,120
Dependent care	8,000
Total labor-related costs	$121,380

These labor-related costs total 42 percent of the gross salaries of employees. The total cost associated with labor is $410,380 ($289,000 + $121,380). Exhibit 7–2 presents the distribution, accrual, and payment journal entries that summarize the labor-related activity for the week.

Distribution Entry

Distribution of labor costs is the charging of production and expense accounts at or near the time of labor cost incurrence. A labor distribution may be at an earlier time than the accrual of the payroll liability. Time records (time cards, job cards, or computer files) are available at least daily in most operations. Therefore, distributing the costs to appropriate jobs, departments, and projects may be done daily. On the other hand, labor cost liabilities are accrued on a weekly or bimonthly basis.

The Payroll account is a clearing account used for convenience. This account may also be called Labor Control or Employee Costs or may have other similar titles. During the period, the Payroll account is credited for the amounts distributed (debited) to the work in process and various expenses. The amounts distributed are in terms of dollars of total costs,[5] which is found by increasing the gross pay by the rate of employee benefits.

---

[5] Some organizations exclude charges for the labor-related costs in labor distribution entries. Instead, these costs are charged to production overhead.

EXHIBIT 7–2   Summary Journal Entries for Labor Cost

Entry to distribute payroll:		
Work in Process Inventory ($158,000 × 1.42)	$224,360	
Production Overhead Control ($40,000 × 1.42)	56,800	
Marketing Cost Control ($35,000 × 1.42)	49,700	
General & Administrative Cost Control ($56,000 × 1.42)	79,520	
Payroll		$410,380
Entry to accrue the payroll liability:		
Payroll	$289,000	
Wages Payable		$238,872
Federal Income Taxes Payable		18,200
FICA Taxes Payable		22,253
State Income Taxes Payable		9,675
Entry to accrue the liability for labor-related costs:		
Payroll	$121,380	
FICA Taxes Payable (Employer's Share)		$ 22,253
Unemployment Taxes Payable		11,271
Workers' Compensation Insurance Payable		14,450
Employee Insurance Payable		33,560
Accrued Employee Absence		23,120
Occupation Taxes Payable		8,726
Dependent Care Payable		8,000
Entries to pay the liabilities:		
Wages Payable	$238,872	
Cash		$238,872
Pay checks issued to employees.		
Federal Income Tax Payable	$ 18,200	
FICA Taxes Payable	44,506	
State Income Taxes Payable	9,675	
Unemployment Taxes Payable	11,271	
Workers' Compensation Insurance Payable	14,450	
Employee Insurance Payable	33,560	
Occupation Taxes Payable	8,726	
Cash		$140,388
To record various checks issued for employee-		
related and withholding liabilities.		

At the same time as the distribution entry, the subsidiary records are updated in the computer files. Thus, the direct labor amounts are added to job cost files. Indirect labor amounts are assigned to detailed overhead cost pools. Marketing and general and administrative costs are allocated to functions and departments.

Accrual

Accrual of the payroll liability is the recognition of a debt owed the workers. The debit to Payroll is the gross pay for wages and salaries; the credit to Wages Payable is the net pay. Any difference between the debit to Payroll and the credit to Wages Payable is due to withholdings such as federal and state income taxes, FICA taxes (employee share), and voluntary items such as union dues and savings programs. In addition, there is an entry to accrue the labor-related costs.

Payment

This journal entry records the issuance of paychecks to employees. The other entry records the liquidation of liabilities for withholdings and accrued labor-related costs.

This payment must be made on the pay date for most companies.[6] The liabilities for employee absence and dependent care are paid as they are drawn by the employees over the year of employment.

VALUE-ADDED ANALYSIS

The Parts Division of International Electronics Enterprises (IEE) makes electronic parts and components that are shipped to other divisions and to outside customers. The Parts Division has 494 direct workers out of a total of 669 workers for the division. The gross pay of the direct workers is $158,000 out of $289,000. As the controller, Carrie Sessions, examined the job descriptions, she found that all of the direct workers are parts fabricators who turn plastic, computer chips, and metal into electronic parts and components. Thus, all of the direct labor is value added. She computed the value-added labor ratio based on numbers of employees:

$$\text{Value-added labor ratio (Employees)} = \frac{494}{669} = 73.84\%$$

and the ratio based on gross salaries:

$$\text{Value-added labor ratio (Cost)} = \frac{\$158,000}{\$289,000} = 54.67\%$$

Comparable ratios for IEE's major competitors are 82 percent and 75 percent, respectively, which indicates that much can be improved in the labor cost area. In order to improve IEE's competitive position for the Parts Division, more of the workers should be direct workers, and there needs to be less discrepancy between wages paid to direct workers and other employees.

LABOR COST FUNCTIONS

The procedures for controlling labor costs should ensure that (1) persons employed are authorized, (2) persons receiving wages have performed services, and (3) persons employed have worked efficiently. Typically, five functions are involved in a labor system: personnel, timekeeping, production, payroll, and cost accounting. Exhibit 7–3 illustrates a computerized labor accounting system.

The personnel function authorizes additions or deletions of employees, changes to pay rates and payroll deductions, and sends change authorizations to the labor cost system. A **job time ticket file** is maintained by production and includes the time spent by each employee on each job or account. The system reconciles the job time tickets with the total hours worked in the employee time cards file. The costs are then distributed to accounts, based on time worked.

Earnings records are maintained in a **payroll master file,** which contains accumulated earnings to date, plus all of the key information necessary for payroll preparation. Also included are the number of withholding exemptions, any special shift premiums, and wage rates. The output of payroll program includes a payment to each employee (usually a check), a payroll register of each paycheck issued, summary journal entries, and various control and management reports.

---

[6] Very small organizations with only a few employees can pay withholdings and related costs on a monthly or quarterly basis.

EXHIBIT 7–3   System Flowchart for Labor Cost System

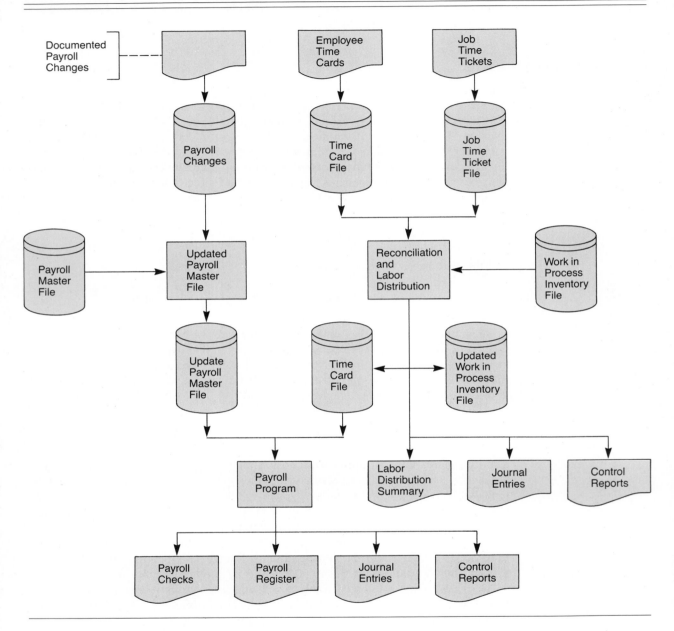

INCENTIVE WAGE PLANS

An **incentive wage plan** is a compensation plan employed by a company as a means to motivate workers. It is an exchange of additional compensation for greater productivity. The plan may apply to individuals, groups, or an entire facility. Successful plans show increases in total payroll accompanied by greater increases in production. In concept, this should result in a lower labor cost per unit completed.

Incentive wage plans vary in format and application. The most common ones relate to piecework. Examples include (1) a higher piece rate or bonus given for production above a set number of units, (2) a bonus rate paid for all pieces after the set number is achieved, and (3) a minimum hourly rate combined with a piecework rate in which the employee receives the hourly rate but can earn more at a piecework rate by producing more.

The following is an example of a minimum amount and a piecework rate as applied to workers who assemble circuit boards. The minimum amount per day is $50, and the piecework rate is $0.80.

Employee	Units Produced	Piece Rate	Piecework Earnings	Amount to Minimum	Total Earnings
C. Angelo	60	$0.80	$ 48.00	$2.00	$ 50.00
R. Caffey	70	0.80	56.00	—	56.00
I. Evans	62	0.80	49.60	.40	50.00
L. Odom	75	0.80	60.00	—	60.00
R. Subia	58	0.80	46.40	3.60	50.00
Totals	325		$260.00	$6.00	$266.00

Three employees did not meet the minimum amount and therefore received the $50 minimum.

Companies may reward employees, especially managers, with bonuses. Bonuses are granted for a number of reasons; the most common is greater productivity. The amount of bonus may be a set figure, a percentage of the profits (a profit-sharing plan), or a percentage of one's salary. More often than not, the bonus is determined at the end of the fiscal year. A bonus given to a production worker should theoretically be included in the cost of production. If so, it is simpler to include the total amount in production overhead.

Cost Management of Employee Incentives

Before adopting an incentive or bonus plan, management must recognize the potential negative effects:

1. Incentive plans require additional recordkeeping, resulting in increased clerical costs.
2. Incentive plans complicate payroll systems greatly.
3. Incentive plans are subject to manipulation by workers or managers and, thus, must be supervised closely.
4. Quantity may become the worker's main consideration rather than the production of quality outputs.
5. In group plans there is the danger that too much competition will arise between individual departments. This threatens cooperation, overall production quality, and, ultimately, the company's profits.

Thus, employee incentive plans have the potential to add significant indirect costs with no value added to products. Because of these negative effects, some companies have decided to eliminate incentive plans in favor of bonuses based on overall division or company profits. This approach tends to support more cooperation and loyalty among workers.

TYPES OF LABOR-RELATED COSTS

Labor-related costs were defined earlier as all expenditures paid by an employer on behalf of employees above the wages and salaries. Although some accountants view them as payroll taxes and employee benefits, we will be more specific in this section.

Employer Payroll Taxes

Federal and state governments levy payroll taxes on employers that are for the benefit of employees. The primary payroll taxes include social security (FICA), federal and state unemployment taxes, and state workers' compensation insurance.

Social Security (FICA) Taxes. The Federal Insurance Contributions Act (FICA) requires employers to match the employees' contribution to social security. To determine the amount of contribution, a fixed percentage is applied to gross earnings up to a maximum limit. The percentage and the maximum limit are determined by current FICA regulations. As the social security rates and maximum limit increase, there are built-in increases in the employer's cost structure. If the employee is paying 7.65 percent of wages or salary up to $51,300 (or $3,924.45) per year, the employer must match that amount as a payment to the social security fund.

Federal Unemployment Taxes. Unlike FICA taxes, federal unemployment taxes are levied on employers only. The funds collected by the federal government are divided among the states to administer their programs. To determine the amount of contribution applicable to federal use, a fixed percentage (0.8 percent) is applied to gross earnings up to a maximum limit ($7,000). The percentage and limit are determined according to current laws. Certain credits are allowed for employers with small numbers of employees collecting unemployment compensation.

State Unemployment Taxes. In most states, this tax is levied on employers only. A few states also require employee contributions, but not necessarily at the same rate as the employer. To determine the amount of contribution, a fixed percentage (5.4 percent) is applied to gross earnings up to a maximum limit ($7,000). Most states have a merit rating plan that allows reduced rates for employers who maintain a low employee turnover rate.

State Workers' Compensation Insurance. **Workers' compensation insurance** compensates workers or their survivors for losses caused by employment-related accidents or occupational diseases. The tax is levied on employers and is based on earnings per employee. The rates also vary according to degree of occupational hazards; the highest rates are paid for jobs having the greatest risk.

Premiums and Allowances

Many companies make additional payments for overtime, work on evening or night shifts, or for geographic assignments. Organizations may provide allowances for travel, entertainment, clothing, meals, education, or dependent care.

Overtime Premium. The Fair Labor Standards Act (1938) requires time-and-a-half pay for hours in excess of 40 hours per week, although employment contracts or other labor-management agreements may increase that amount. Work performed during holidays is customarily paid at double or triple time. For planning and control, and cost determination purposes, earnings are segregated into regular earnings and overtime premium. Accounting for the premium can then be treated separately.

For example, assume that a direct worker earning $8 per hour with time-and-a-half pay for overtime has worked a total of 45 hours in one week. There are five hours of overtime. The earnings are divided as follows:

Regular earnings: 45 hours at $8 per hour	$360
Overtime premium: 5 hours at $4 per hour	20
Total weekly earnings	$380

Overtime premiums paid for hours that result from different causes call for a different accounting treatment. The overtime premium pay should be charged to the job or department if the specific demands or specifications of the job or process result in overtime hours. On the other hand, overtime may be due to a heavier than normal workload and the job or department is by chance placed in an overtime situation. Overtime premium for this case is charged to production overhead because no specific job is the cause of overtime work. In both cases, the jobs are charged with the hours worked times regular rates.

Shift Premiums. Often company policy or employment contract designates a higher wage to employees working evening or night shifts. **Shift premiums** are compensation for working at less desirable times. For example, a company might have the following schedule:

8:00 A.M.–4:00 P.M. shift	$8.00 hourly rate
4:00 P.M.–12:00 A.M. shift	$8.50 hourly rate
12:00 A.M.–8:00 A.M. shift	$9.20 hourly rate

The first shift is considered the regular rate. The additional amount on other shifts is the shift premium or shift differential.

If work in process is charged with regular earnings plus the shift premium, identical goods worked on at different times during a day would carry different unit costs. Because the timing of production makes no difference to the value of the product, the preferable accounting treatment for shift premiums is generally to include them in production overhead.[7]

Cost-of-Living Allowance. Workers may be transferred to off-site locations or facilities at distant geographical locations on temporary assignments. A **cost-of-living allowance** is additional compensation due to the inconvenience of the temporary move or a higher cost of living in the new area. These costs, like overtime and shift premiums, would be charged to overhead costs unless they can be attributed to specific requirements of the work at those locations.

Other Allowances. Employees may work outside a company facility in the normal performance of their duties; examples are auditors, sales staff, construction workers, service personnel, petroleum field workers, and personnel in international operations. Employees receive allowances for travel, hotels, meals, local taxes, and automobile rentals. These types of allowance are commonly charged directly to the job, contract, or function because they relate to being away from home and they vary significantly by location.

Other allowances are made for education or dependent care. These apply to all employees, do not vary by project or job, and are accounted for as production overhead or indirect department expenses.

Cost Management of Premiums and Allowances

Premiums and allowances as a proportion of total labor cost can vary from very low rates (10 percent or less) to very high rates (50 percent or more) depending on how the products, employees, and processes are managed.

---

[7] It may be appropriate at times to directly charge the shift premiums to the job or project. For example, the company notifies the customer on receipt of an order that the schedule is full and the work must be done on the night shift. If the customer wants the work done by a certain deadline and is willing to pay the extra cost, the shift premium is included in the amounts charged to that order.

Overtime Premium.   In most circumstances, overtime premium adds no value to the product or service produced. Therefore, overtime premium is a non–value-added cost or a waste. Overtime premium incurrence is the result of the cumulative effects and faults of the demand, the employees, the product, and the production process. Cost management of overtime premium relates to correcting the faults.

Several products and services involve peak demands on the production process that result in overtime. Thus, food processing, fisheries, livestock, lumber, ski slopes, summer resorts, airlines, and hotels all have peak periods when overtime is prevalent. Product demand can be shifted by increasing the prices charged during high demand periods and decreasing them during the off-peak periods. These industries can also make use of part-time workers who are employed during peak periods at regular or reduced pay rates.

Another part of the overtime is due to employees. When some employees are absent, other employees must work longer hours to make up the work. However, employees who enjoy their work and are committed to the company are rarely absent. Thus, designing jobs to make them interesting and programs that build employee morale is important to limiting overtime related to absenteeism. An inflexible work force with narrow job skills tends to need more workers and more overtime. As product demands peak, some of the inflexible workers will be idle while others are working overtime to get their work completed. With a flexible work force, idle workers will recognize the need and be ready to help others working at beyond their peak capacity. Thus, compensation programs may be established that increase the pay for those who learn more skills and are willing and able to move throughout the plant.

Finally, the product and production process must be designed to facilitate the reduction in overtime. Products that are designed to be easy to understand, assemble, and finish are much easier to produce without error during peak periods. Long setup times and changeover times result in overtime during peak demand periods. By reducing the setup time, the amount of overtime can be reduced. Production processes that flow smoothly with no waiting for parts or supplies also reduce overtime by cutting out idle time. Similarly, equipment that is easy to understand and is very well maintained will break down less and produce higher-quality products. Thus, less overtime will occur due to establishing a production process with fewer breakdowns and product rework.

Shift Differentials.   Employees working in the late evening or at night are costly for the company. Not only is the shift differential costly, but also the personal lives of the employees are disrupted and the quality of production tends to be poorer, especially on the late night shift. Night shift employees tend to be characterized by health problems, social isolation, substance abuse, and absenteeism. More accidents occur late at night, especially with heavy machinery. Therefore, the production schedule should maximize on the day shift production that involves labor and, thus, the number of workers. Flexible work hours (starting earlier or later) can be used to extend the day shift beyond eight hours. Thus, some workers might work 6 A.M. to 2 P.M., while others work from 10 A.M. to 6 P.M., and still others work from 12 noon to 8 P.M. The work force can be filled out with part-time employees on four to six-hour shifts.

The night shift should be minimized in terms of labor. Semiautomated production involving few setups or simple tasks should be reserved for the evening and especially for the night shift. Thus, high demand, perhaps simple products with long production runs should be manufactured on the evening or night shift. Further, products scheduled at night should be those that have few production quality problems—products that are easy to produce well with few employees. Conversely, products with short production runs or that have some complexity should be produced on the day shift.

Other Allowances.   Cost-of-living allowances arise from transporting employees great distances, which is non-value added to the product or service performed. Thus, travel is a non–value-added activity and should be minimized whenever possible. Perhaps travel to new locations for a short stay, especially foreign locations, can be interesting and rewarding to the employee. Such travel is like a vacation, even though employees are working. However, extended or numerous tours of duty that are distant, especially if this involves separation from families with small children and from friends, are stressful and may involve damage to the person or his or her family. For these reasons, the product, the process, and the organizational arrangements should be established to minimize cost-of-living allowances. Specifically, the product should be designed to be simple to service, local labor should be maximized, and agreements should be established with local companies to limit the need for employees to travel.

Allowances for education and dependent care tend to build loyalty and morale. Thus, these allowances tend to reduce turnover and absenteeism of employees, which results in higher-quality production. While these costs should not increase without limit, neither should they be reduced to zero. Instead, a balance should be reached in meeting the needs of employees, allowing for the cost to meet these needs, and producing a high-quality product or service.

Compensated Personal Absence

Most companies permit employees to be absent from work with compensation for various periods of time—**compensated personal absence.** The specific situations are set by company policy or employment contract. Examples are vacations, holidays, sick days, personal leave, jury duty, military training, or civic functions. While employee absence adds no value to a product or service, vacations are necessary for the health and welfare of employees. Thus, compensated personal absence is a necessary employee-related cost.

The expense and related liability for compensated absences are recognized in the year in which it is earned by employees.[8] For example, if new employees receive rights to two weeks' paid vacation at the beginning of their second year of employment, the vacation pay is considered to be earned during the first year of employment. In estimating the liability, a company is permitted to use either current wage rates or anticipated wage rates at time of payment. Most companies will use the current rate because of uncertainties about future rates.

Accruing Compensated Personal Absence.   To illustrate the accrual of these benefits, we will assume that an employee earns $8 per hour and works eight hours per day, and that the employment contract or company policy specifies the employee is to receive 10 working days of vacation and 5 working days of holidays. Benefits are thus estimated as follows:

$$
\begin{array}{ll}
\text{Vacations (10 days} \times \$8 \text{ per hour} \times 8 \text{ hours)} = & \$640 \\
\text{Holidays (5 days} \times \$8 \text{ per hour} \times 8 \text{ hours)} \quad = & \underline{320} \\
& \underline{\underline{\$960}}
\end{array}
$$

---

[8] Financial Accounting Standards Board, *Statement of Financial Accounting Standard No. 43,* "Accounting for Compensated Absences"; and Cost Accounting Standards Board, *Cost Accounting Standard 408,* "Accounting for the Costs of Compensated Personal Absences."

The cost of these employee benefits is spread over the productive labor of each employee. If the employee is paid weekly and each employee has 49 weeks of productive labor (52 weeks less two weeks of vacation less one week for holidays), the amount per week for compensated personal absences is $960/49 weeks = $19.59. The entry to record this is:

Compensated Personal Absence Expense	19.59	
(Production overhead, marketing and distribution, and general and administrative expenses)		
Accrued Compensated Personal Absence		19.59

Payment for Compensated Personal Absence. Withholdings from the employee's gross pay are recorded at the time employees are paid for compensated absences. When the employee above receives payment for one week of vacation, the following entries are made:

Accrued Compensated Personal Absence	320	
(5 days × $8 per hour × 8 hours)		
Federal Income Tax Withheld		23
State Income Tax Withheld		19
FICA Taxes Payable		24
Wages Payable		254

In addition, there will be payroll taxes and benefits that apply to this compensation. The entry for taxes and benefits will be the same as that in Exhibit 7–2.

Administrative and other personnel who receive a fixed salary, regardless of the hours worked, are also entitled to compensated personal absences. The cost of these employee benefits can be treated in the same manner illustrated above for direct labor.

Management of Compensated Absence. Planned employee absence for vacations and holidays builds loyalty and morale without affecting the quantity of production. The production schedule can be adjusted to reflect planned absence. Employees return with better attitudes that should increase quality and quantity of production. This is value added to the product. Unplanned employee absences cause less production, poor-quality production, overtime, and missed opportunities for customer satisfaction and competitive position. Unplanned employee absences result in downtime and waste and, thus, are non-value added to the product.

Unplanned employee absence is caused by illness, low morale, and family problems. Programs that reduce smoking and alcohol and drug abuse also reduce illness and family problems. Personal and family counseling, when needed, also help morale and family problems. Recreation and exercise programs reduce stress and improve loyalty, attitude, and health. The costs of these programs should neither be maximized nor minimized, but rather balanced with the need for quantity and quality of production over a long (five or more years) time horizon. A strong work force with good attitudes builds quality products over many years.

SUMMARY

Labor is the physical or mental effort expended in producing a product, completing a task, or rendering a service. The cost of labor to a company, which can be significant in amount, consists of the price paid for the time unit plus payroll taxes and costs paid to provide benefits. We made a distinction between labor costs and labor-related costs. Labor costs are basic wages and salaries plus the regular pay for overtime.

Labor-related costs are expenditures made by an employer on behalf of employees above the wages and salaries. The labor-related costs are viewed broadly as payroll taxes and benefits, although we discussed many specific examples in each category.

In addition to the distinction between labor and labor-related costs, there is a need to classify production labor properly as direct or indirect labor. Without a clear differentiation, errors can be built into production overhead allocations and measures of labor efficiency can be misstated.

Direct labor is all labor that can be specifically identified with a product or service in an economically feasible manner. Value-added direct labor is that portion of direct labor that changes raw material into finished product or service. Indirect labor is not readily traceable to the product or service. The cost management of labor involves reducing non–value-added workers and shifting them to value-added jobs. In addition, the value-added time of workers may be increased by redesigning the product and production process.

The labor cost system is one of the most important accounting systems. It must provide information for management, proper pay to employees, and journal entries for the general ledger. The entries address distribution, accrual of liability, and payment. Distribution of labor costs to the appropriate accounts can be independent of the liability accrual.

Labor-related costs follow the underlying labor, whether production, marketing and distribution, or general and administrative employees. This is accomplished by including the costs in the unit price of labor or through a broad indirect cost pool (labor-related costs or production overhead) that is allocated to the cost objectives served by labor.

PROBLEM FOR REVIEW

The employees of Turvey Allison Company are paid at the end of each month. November was an extraordinarily heavy month; direct workers had substantial overtime. The overtime is not attributable to any one job. Accounting records show the following data:

	Regular Earnings	Overtime Premium	Total Gross Earnings
Gross pay:			
Direct labor	$21,000	$2,500	$23,500
Indirect labor	8,000	—	8,000
Marketing cost control	5,000	—	5,000
Administrative cost control	3,000	—	3,000
Total	$37,000	$2,500	$39,500
Withholdings:			
Federal income tax			$ 3,550
State income tax			1,185
FICA taxes (Employees' share at 7.65 percent)			3,023
Union dues			500

Other labor-related costs are federal unemployment tax, 0.8 percent; state unemployment tax, 5.4 percent; and compensated personal absences, 3.0 percent. Compensated absence is calculated on all labor costs but the overtime premium.

REQUIRED

a. Prepare the journal entry to record the distribution of labor costs for November. Assume that all labor-related costs follow the labor costs, which means labor-related costs on direct labor are direct labor.

b. Prepare the journal entries to accrue the payroll liability and payment of the payroll.

SOLUTION

a. Distribution of labor costs.

	Regular Earnings	FICA Taxes	Unemployment Taxes		Compensated Personal Absence	Totals
			Federal	State		
Direct labor	$21,000	$1,607	$168	$1,134	$ 630	$24,539
Overtime premium	2,500	191	20	135	0	2,846
Indirect labor	8,000	612	64	432	240	9,348
Marketing	5,000	383	40	270	150	5,843
Administrative	3,000	230	24	162	90	3,506
	$39,500	$3,023	$316	$2,133	$1,110	$46,082

Work in Process Inventory	$24,539	
Production Overhead—Overtime Premium	2,846	
Production Overhead—Indirect Labor	9,348	
Marketing Cost Control	5,843	
Administrative Cost Control	3,506	
Payroll		$46,082

b. Accrual and payment.

Payroll	$46,082	
FICA Taxes Payable—Employee		$3,023
FICA Taxes Payable—Employer		3,023
Federal Unemployment Taxes Payable		316
State Unemployment Taxes		2,133
Accrued Compensated Personal Absence		1,110
Federal Income Taxes Payable		3,550
State Income Taxes Payable		1,185
Union Dues Payable		500
Wages Payable		31,242
Wages Payable	$31,242	
Cash		$31,242

KEY TERMS AND CONCEPTS

Labor (225)
Labor cost (225)
Wages (225)
Salaries (225)
Direct labor (225)
Value-added direct labor (225)
Indirect labor (225)
Labor-related cost (225)
Value-added labor ratio (226)
Distribution of labor costs (227)
Job time ticket file (229)

Payroll master file (229)
Accrual of payroll liability (228)
Incentive wage plan (230)
FICA premiums (232)
Federal unemployment taxes (232)
State unemployment taxes (232)
Workers' compensation insurance (232)
Overtime premium (232)
Shift premium (232)
Cost-of-living allowance (232)
Compensated personal absence (235)

ADDITIONAL READINGS

Berger, W. E. "Compensation Planning for the 1990s for Large Corporations." *Journal of Compensation and Benefits,* January–February 1988, pp. 206–8.

Bhatia, G. "Cash Bonuses: Always a Winner." *CFO*, December 1988, pp. 54–56.

Dietemann, G. J. "Measuring Productivity in a Service Company." *Management Accounting*, February 1988, pp. 48–54.

"First Annual Directory of Human Resources Services, Products, and Suppliers." *Personnel*, January 1988, pp. 65–221.

Givner, B. "Cafeteria Plans Need ERISA Protection." *CPA Journal*, December 1987, pp. 89–91.

Greidanus, J. "Cost of Human Resources: Controlling the Size and Productivity of the Work Force." *Public Utilities Fortnightly*, March 31, 1988, pp. 17–20.

Kazemek, E. A. "Taking a Closer Look at Incentive Compensation." *Healthcare Financial Management*, February 1988, pp. 113–17.

Kilby, L. "Closer Look at the New Flexible Benefits Design." *Compensation & Benefits Management*, Winter 1988, pp. 139–42.

Kohn, A. "Incentives Can Be Bad for Business." *Inc.*, January 1988, pp. 93–94.

Larson, E. R. "Systems Support Cost Accounting and Quality of Care." *Healthcare Financial Management*, March 1988, pp. 38–43.

Lewis, J. "Health Care Monster Rears Its Head Again." *Institutional Investor*, March 1988, pp. 169–72.

McGrath, J. "Using a Spreadsheet for Payroll Calculations." *CFO*, August 1986, pp. 57–62.

Mentzger, R. O., and M. A. Von Glinow. "Off-site Workers: At Home and Abroad." *California Management Review*, Spring 1988, pp. 101–11.

Moscove, S. A. "Labor Reporting Systems Aid in Controlling Costs." *Healthcare Financial Management*, April 1988, pp. 50–56.

O'Neal, J. "The Company Car—Its Value as a Fringe Benefit." *CFO*, September 1988, pp. 50–60.

Riso, G. R., and W. L. Kendig. "Reducing Overtime Costs." *Journal of Accountancy*, December 1987, pp. 127–34.

Rosenfeld, P. *Accounting and Auditing for Employee Benefit Plans*, rev. ed. Boston: Warren, Gorham & Lamont, 1987.

Woods, M. D. "Gainsharing in Industry." *Journal of Accountancy*, June 1989, pp. 143–47.

REVIEW QUESTIONS

1. What expenditures constitute labor costs? How do these expenditures differ from those classified as labor-related costs?

2. Explain the need for properly classifying production labor as direct labor and indirect labor.

3. Explain how the payroll account is used in distributing and accruing labor costs.

4. What is the source document for the distribution of direct labor costs to work in process inventory and indirect labor to production overhead costs?

5. What could cause a difference between the total time reported on an employee's time card and the total of the job time tickets for that employee?

6. Assuming that a manufacturer uses a computerized payroll system, indicate the major items that would probably be stored in the company's payroll master file.

7. List the essential procedures for controlling labor costs.

8. Define value-added direct labor. How does this concept relate to the competitive position of a company?

9. When evaluating an incentive plan, what is the most important factor or factors?

10. List three kinds of labor-related costs that an employer can incur for each worker.

11. Explain under what circumstances overtime premium should be charged to production overhead. To direct labor costs.

12. Why is overtime considered a non–value-added cost?

13. What gives rise to a shift differential? Why are these costs charged to production overhead?

14. What approach might be taken to the cost management of shift differential payments?

15. What accounting treatment is given holiday and vacation pay?

DISCUSSION QUESTIONS

16. Some people believe that labor-related costs on direct labor should be charged to work in process inventory as part of the direct labor cost while others charge these labor-related costs to production overhead. What justifications can you give to support recording labor-related costs as direct labor costs? What justifications for production overhead?

17. Why is it important to an employee for a company to have accurate, understandable methods for calculating payroll?

18. Making a distinction between direct labor and indirect labor is not easy. Cite three examples of situations in which labor costs must be carefully reviewed before classifying the costs.

19. The term *direct labor cost* as used in practice, in literature, and in litigation has a wide variety of meanings. The National Association of Accountants indicates that measurement of labor costs is a function of the quantity of labor effort and unit price. Explore the reasons as to how the two aspects of measurement relate to the diversity of meanings for direct labor cost.

20. A company grants employees sick leave credit based on time worked—one day of sick leave for each month worked. The credit can be accumulated into future years. The credits can only be used for actual illness for a period of three years. Any accumulated credits not used within the three-year limit can then be taken as additional vacation or as additional compensation. How should this plan be accounted for?

EXERCISES

7–1. Direct Labor and Value-Added Labor.   Catlin, Inc., produces air pumps in a small factory in New Orleans, Louisiana. The company employs eight people in its small factory with six direct and two indirect laborers. The following six workers are treated as direct laborers in their accounting system:

_____ 1. *Fabricator:* cuts and grinds metal parts from raw steel, aluminum, and brass.
_____ 2. *Parts inspector:* examines and approves parts produced.
_____ 3. *Warehouse stocker:* keeps parts in inventory and stocks bins used by assembly workers.
_____ 4. *Molder:* molds vinyl seals and plastic fittings by using an injection molder.
_____ 5. *Assembler:* assembles parts into product.
_____ 6. *Product inspector:* inspects the final product.

REQUIRED:
a. Categorize each of the six workers as value added (VA) and non-value added (NVA).
b. Compute the value-added direct labor ratio to total factory workers.

7–2. Value-Added Labor Concept.   For each of the following organizations, identify the value-added direct workers:
a. Major league baseball team
b. Clinic specializing in sports injuries
c. Radio station
d. Airline

7–3. Payroll for One Employee.   Rodney Jones is a violinist for the Houston Symphony. Mr. Jones is employed at the rate of $28 per hour for the first 40 hours worked and $42 per hour for any additional hours. His hours for the week ending November 2, 19x7, totaled 43. Withholdings from his wages include 7.7 percent for FICA, federal withholding tax of $200, insurance of $30, and union dues of $10. The FICA is based on earnings up to a maximum of $45,000. Mr. Jones' cumulative earnings prior to the current week are $44,200. Federal and state unemployment tax limits on this employee have been passed. The Houston Symphony contributes 12 percent of regular earnings (up to 40 hours only) to a pension plan for each employee.

(M. Joyner, adapted)

REQUIRED:
a. Compute the total compensation, including overtime premium, for the week for Mr. Jones.
b. Compute Mr. Jones' net pay.

7–4. Total Compensation.   The Lines Department of Coltown City Power had the following hours worked for the week ending March 12, 19x2:

Employee	Rate	Hours
Bebrett	$18	48
Manchester	15	38
Smith	16	46

It is the policy of Coltown City Power to pay a 50 percent premium for hours worked over 40 per week.

REQUIRED:
Compute the regular wage, the overtime premium, and the total for each employee.

7–5. Payroll Computation.   Velle & Velle Corp. is a family-owned and operated business that produces puppets. All employees are family members paid weekly. The following information is available for the week ending March 24, 19x2:

Employee	Job Title/Hours	Wages
Doug	Administrator	$1,000 per week
Ben	Sales	10% of sales
Jon	Product: direct, 30; indirect, 10	$500 per week
Amy	Product: direct, 20; indirect, 20	$500 per week

FICA taxes are 7.65 percent; federal unemployment taxes, 0.8 percent; and state unemployment taxes, 5.4 percent. Federal and state income taxes on salaries are 10 percent and 4 percent, respectively. During the week puppet sales were $6,000.

(D. Ripple, adapted)

REQUIRED:
a. Determine each employee's gross earnings, withholdings, and net pay for the week.
b. Compute the amount of direct labor cost:
   1. Excluding labor-related costs.
   2. Including labor-related costs.

7–6. Allocations of Labor-Related Costs.   Lemmons Marketing Group has developed a fringe benefit program that will result in labor-related costs of 30 percent. The following gross pay figures come from the payroll data for the week ending November 22, 19x7:

	Hours	Amount
Sales staff	1,000	$ 5,600
Office clerical	600	2,400
Office managers	80	1,200
Warehouse workers	1,900	15,000

REQUIRED:
a. Calculate the labor-related costs by category and total.
b. Compute the labor cost per hour, labor-related costs per hour, and total cost per hour by category.

7–7. Value-Added Labor.   The Makin Plant manufactures specialized electronic parts and has the following employees for the week ending August 24, 19x5

	Workers	Wages/Salaries	Totals
Direct laborers	600	$ 600	$360,000
Indirect laborers	100	800	80,000
Supervisors/Managers	56	1,600	89,600
Clerical/Office	144	800	115,200
Totals	900		$644,800

Of the direct laborers, about 60 percent are considered value added to the product. Assume that the industry leaders in specialized electronic parts have value-added labor of 80 percent of workers and 75 percent of total wages.

REQUIRED:
a. Compute the value-added labor ratio in terms of:
   1. Workers.
   2. Compensation.
b. The Makin Plant has had substantial losses during the past two years. Comment on the potential improvement in competitive position needed with respect to labor cost.

7–8. Value-Added Employees.   WZ90 is an FM radio station with a top-40 format. The station has the following employees and wages paid for the month ending July 31, 19x7:

	Employees	Wages/Salaries	Totals
Lead disk jockeys	8	$1,800	$14,400
Support disk jockeys	8	1,200	9,600
News and weather staff	3	1,600	4,800
Engineering staff	6	2,000	12,000
Supervisors/Managers	5	2,400	12,000
Sales agents	5	500	2,500
Clerical/Office staff	3	800	2,400
Totals	38		$57,700

The sales agents are paid a commission of 5 percent of advertising revenues in addition to their salary. During July, the advertising revenues were $160,000. The station manager considers the lead disk jockeys, news and weather staff, and the sales agents as critical (value added) in changing "dead air" into profitable air time. The other personnel are for support.

REQUIRED:
Compute the ratio of value-added employees to total employees in terms of:
a. Number of workers.
b. Total compensation paid.

PROBLEMS

7–9. Service Hours and Billing.   Carr and Company is a small firm of certified public accountants located in Butte, Montana. Robert and John Carr, brothers as well as partners, require the staff to keep time records of work performed for clients. As the end of October 19x4 approaches, Robert Carr would like to estimate the revenue and labor costs associated with two new clients: Randy Moore, P.C., and Cindy Smith, Inc. The time records and hourly wage rates for the month indicate the following:

(V. Mooney, adapted)

Labor Class	Salary at Hourly Rate	Labor Related	Hours on Job		Billing Rates
			Moore	Smith	
Partner	$40.00	50.00%	4	1	$100.00
Staff accountant	15.00	40.00%	23	15	40.00
Data entry	5.00	30.00%	3	10	20.00
Clerk/trainees	3.15	$0.35	2	10	10.00

REQUIRED:
What amount and rate of profit margin would Carr and Company recognize for each of the accounts?

7–10. Labor-Related Rates.   Redeye Coffee, International, is a roaster and blender of expensive coffees. The company employs master roasters, blenders, and helpers as direct labor. The company is planning to follow a policy of allocating its labor-related costs through the established regular labor rates. For the coming year it has the following estimates:

	Hours	*Rate*	*Wages and Salaries*
Direct labor	40,000	$25	$1,000,000
Indirect labor	30,000	10	300,000
Marketing	4,000	10	40,000
Administration	10,000	5	50,000
Totals	84,000		$1,390,000

The estimated labor-related costs are:

	Cost	*Applies to*
Pension contributions	$111,200	All labor
Overtime premiums	50,000	Direct labor only
Employer payroll taxes	166,800	All labor
Compensated personal absences	55,600	All labor
Medical, dental, and life insurance	41,700	All labor
Idle time	20,000	Direct labor only
Total labor-related cost	$445,300	

Idle time is not included in the 40,000 direct labor hours.

(M. Winburn, adapted)

REQUIRED:
a. Compute the expected total for labor and related costs for each of the four categories of labor.
b. Compute an hourly rate for each of the labor categories that includes both the regular earnings and the labor-related costs.

7–11. Wage Classes, Shift Differentials, and Errors.   Wenzel Groceries, Inc., is a 24-hour grocery store in Phoenix, Arizona. The company has pay rates for regular employees that differ depending on the shift:

Shift	*Time*	*Cashier*	*Stocker*	*Supervisor*
Day	8 A.M.–4 P.M.	$6.50	$5.00	$8.00
Evening	4 P.M.–12 P.M.	6.75	5.25	8.50
Night	12 P.M.–8 A.M.	7.25	5.75	9.25

In addition, there is a 50 percent premium for hours worked over 40. Assume that labor agreements allow each employee to be assigned to only one shift (for example, the evening shift) each week with up to 56 hours allowed in one week.

You are working on the external audit for Wenzel Groceries. Although the company has 106 employees, you have selected 6 for initial testing and have gathered the following data from the employee files for the week ending August 3, 19x2:

(L. Leonard, adapted)

	Position	*Shift*	*Hours*	*Wages on File*
Compton, P	Cashier	Night	39	$282.75
Fletcher, J.	Supervisor	Evening	38	351.50
Howard, D.	Stocker	Evening	56	336.00
Johnson, P.	Cashier	Day	40	266.50
Medely, G.	Stocker	Day	50	325.00
Riley, J.	Supervisor	Night	35	323.75

REQUIRED:

a. Recompute the wages for each employee.

b. You notice that there are some errors in the wages on file. What might be an explanation for each error found?

7–12. Labor Distribution.   The Old Oak Tree Company reproduces antiques in a small shop in Wimberley, Texas. Imogene Jones records the following hours for workers for the week ending February 11, 19x5:

	Job	Hours	Wage Rate	Base Pay
Abe Baker	Rocking chair	40 direct	$20	$ 800
Calvin Duncan	Wardrobes	45 direct	18	810
Elvira Fitz	Dressers	42 direct	20	840
George Hudson	Tables	40 direct	17	680
Imogene Jones	Office	40 admin.	10	400
Karen Lyons	Warehouse	40 overhead	8	320
Michael Newman	Supervisor	46 overhead	15	690
Opal Prewitt	Curios	48 direct	19	912
Totals		341		$5,452

The base pay does not include a 50 percent premium for hours worked over 40 in one week. Labor related costs are:

(K. Turrichi, adapted)

FICA	7.70%
Federal unemployment tax	0.80%
State unemployment tax	2.75%
Compensated personal absence	2.30%
Total	13.55%

REQUIRED:

a. Prepare a journal entry to record the distribution of labor costs for the week. Assume that all labor-related costs follow labor, which means that labor-related costs for direct labor are recorded as direct costs. Remember that both the employer and employee must pay the FICA in equal amounts.

b. Withholdings for this payroll include:

Federal income tax	$563.80
FICA tax	434.12
Life insurance	200.00

Prepare the journal entry to accrue the payroll liabilities.

c. Prepare the journal entry to pay the payroll liabilities assuming that the compensated absence is paid at a later date.

7–13. Labor Distribution.   The Ruff Creek Music Co. makes stringed musical instruments in a small shop in Ruff Creek, Kentucky. It recorded the following hours for workers for the week ending January 18, 19x3:

	Job	Hours	Wage Rate	Base Pay
Board, W.	Supervisor	40 overhead	$12	$ 480
Bones, H. T.	Warehouse	45 overhead	8	360
Drum, B.	Basses	40 direct	10	400
Jugg, L. B.	Office	40 admin.	8	320
Net, Clare A.	Sales	48 selling	10	480
Pickett, L. E.	Fiddles	36 direct	10	360
Saw, I.	Fiddles	45 direct	20	900
Tar, Steel G.	Guitars	50 direct	16	800
Totals		344		$4,100

The base pay does not include a 50 percent premium for hours worked over 40 in one week. Labor-related costs are:

FICA	7.70%
Federal unemployment tax	0.80%
State unemployment tax	2.75%
Compensated personal absence	2.30%
Total	13.55%

REQUIRED:
a. Prepare a journal entry to record the distribution of labor costs for March. Assume that all labor-related costs follow labor, which means that labor-related costs for direct labor are recorded as direct costs. Remember that both the employer and employee must pay the FICA in equal amounts.
b. Withholdings for this payroll include:

Federal income tax	$514.80
FICA tax	330.33
Bank loan payment SGT	150.00

Prepare the journal entry to accrue the payroll liabilities.
c. Prepare the journal entry to pay the payroll liabilities assuming that the compensated absence is paid at a later date.

EXTENDED APPLICATIONS

7–14. Management of Overtime Premium.   Trimble Machine, Inc., has over 200 small plants that manufacture machines and related parts of various types. Selected data for the four plants of the Oil Machine Division for the month ending November 30, 19x9, are:

	Plant No.			
	110	*111*	*112*	*113*
Total hours	118,800	52,800	32,000	128,000
Total wages	$1,454,112	$831,600	$564,000	$798,720
Overtime premiums	28,512	92,400	84,000	30,720
Overtime attributed to:				
Employee absence	95	3,960	336	3,072
Product demand	380	1,320	1,120	1,024
Product quality	475	1,320	3,696	410
Production setup	2,376	3,960	896	819
Machine downtime	950	1,320	4,480	819
Other	475	1,320	672	4,096
Total hours	4,752	13,200	11,200	10,240

The total wages amount includes the overtime premiums. Because overtime premiums add no value to the product, it is company policy to minimize overtime cost.

REQUIRED:
a. For each of the plants, compute the ratio of overtime hours to total hours.
b. Compute the overtime premium per overtime hour for each of the plants.
c. What are the two primary reasons for overtime in each of the plants? Note that plant no. 113 is an assembly plant and that the Other category primarily relates to parts availability.
d. Comment on the actions that might be considered to minimize overtime premium in each of the four plants.
e. As division controller of the Oil Machine Division, where would you concentrate your efforts and the attention of the division manager to reduce overtime for the coming month?

7–15. Value-Added and Quality Costs. The accounting firm of Smith, Jones and Tyler is a regional CPA firm with offices in 16 cities in the northeast and headquarters in New York City. In planning fiscal 19x3, the Executive Committee is considering the following information:

	Professional Accountants at Each Rank			
	Staff	Seniors	Managers	Partners
Employees	550	400	300	320
Hours ratios:				
Chargeable	90%	95%	95%	95%
Billable	80%	82%	60%	40%
Employee turnover	35%	25%	18%	12%
Billing rates	$ 60	$ 100	$ 150	$ 250
Average salary	$30,000	$38,000	$60,000	$120,000
Employee-related				
costs	$18,000	$19,000	$24,000	$ 60,000

The firm works on a 2,080-hour work year with six days per week scheduled during the months January through April. The difference between total time and chargeable time is due to idle or unaccounted for hours. The difference between chargeable time and billable time is the time clients will not pay for.

About 80 percent of the billable time for staff accountants and seniors relates to work performed directly for clients. The other 20 percent relates to review and quality checks. About 50 percent of the billable time for managers relates to actual performance of service for clients; the remainder is divided evenly between managing jobs and review work. The partners' billable time includes 50 percent review and 30 percent managing the largest jobs, and 20 percent of partner billable time is actually performing work for or with clients. The difference between chargeable time and billable time (in percentages) is comprised of:

	Staff	Seniors	Managers	Partners
Training	8	8	5	5
Marketing service		1	13	25
Recruiting	2	2	5	5
Personnel			7	5
Administration		2	5	15
Total	10	13	35	55

The managing partner considers getting jobs (marketing service) plus the actual performance of work for clients as the value-added activities of the firm. Quality costs include the cost of training time and the cost of reviewing work. Clients are becoming increasingly resistant to paying for time for training, managing, and reviewing work. They are increasingly negotiating fees based on outputs (work performed) rather than inputs (hours charged to jobs).

REQUIRED:
a. Compute the amounts billed by employee rank.
b. Compute the total salaries and employee-related costs by employee rank.
c. Compute the margin of billings over the total of labor and labor-related costs for each employee rank.
d. For each employee rank, compute the hours worked per year that relate to:
    1. Work performed for clients.
    2. Marketing of service.
    3. Quality cost time (training plus job review time).
    4. Job management time.
    5. Other overhead time (recruiting, personnel, plus administration).
    6. Idle or unaccounted for time.
e. For each employee rank and for the firm as a whole, compute the ratio of value-added time to total time.

  f. What proportion of the total billings relates to quality review and job management time (non-value added, but billed time)?

  g. The partners are displeased with the overall net profit of the firm, which is $13.8 million. There is general concern that there are too many managers and partners and not enough lower-level employees. Further, clients are increasingly unwilling to pay for review work and job management. The Executive Committee is considering proposed objectives that would over the next five years:

  1. Cut the number of managers to 200 and partners to 160, while at the same time keeping the staff and senior accountants at the current level.
  2. Change the production methods to cut by 75 percent the amount of review time required for each rank.
  3. Change the content of training sessions and job methods to reduce by 60 percent the amount of time that managers and partners require to manage jobs.
  4. Cut the idle and unaccounted for time to 4 percent for staff and 2 percent for each of the other ranks.
  5. Keep the same proportion of time for training, marketing, recruiting, personnel, and administration.
  6. Cut by 40 percent the expenses other than personnel related. Thus, these expenses are to be cut from $100 million to $60 million.

  Assuming that billing rates and wages stay the same as in 19x3, compute the effect of this proposal on:

  (a) Billings for each rank.
  (b) Compensation and employee-related costs for each rank.
  (c) Total margin.
  (d) Projected firm income.

  h. Comment on the changes proposed by the Executive Committee as to effects on:
  1. The firm profit and profit per partner.
  2. The competitive position of the firm.

The Learning Curve and Deferred
Learning Costs

LEARNING OBJECTIVES

After studying this appendix, you should be able to:

1. Describe a learning curve and explain how it can be used in product costing, in planning and control, and in decision-making.
2. Calculate deferred learning costs and explain how they arise.

THE LEARNING CURVE

Familiarity with a task through repetition often results in workers taking less time to complete the task, making fewer mistakes, and increasing units of output. This phenomenon is called a *learning curve (an experience or improvement curve)*. Studies have shown that the time required to complete one unit should decrease at some percentage rate from the first unit until learning stabilizes. Knowledge of a learning curve provides a manager with a tool for projecting future production costs, projecting shop loads, determining manpower requirements, and negotiating the labor cost of contracts. Learning curves are used extensively by federal government contractors, and such curves have been successfully applied where volumes are limited, a variety of products are made, and a job order cost environment exists.

Early development of the learning curve technique assumed improvement was a function of operator learning. Later contributors to the technique have shown that other factors are important too. These factors include management effectiveness, design, production/process engineering skill, tool and equipment selection, the technology level of the product, and quality criteria.

Basic Concepts

The theory of the learning curve is stated as follows: when the total quantity of units produced doubles, the cost per unit declines by a constant percentage.[1] This constant percentage identifies the degree of cost decline or learning experienced. As experience increases, the amount of learning decreases and the average time per unit stabilizes. Thus, a constant stage or steady state is attained when a process becomes routine to the worker, which happens when the life of the process is long or when the production output is large in quantity.

The assumption of the model is that the *incremental unit* cost or time decreases

---

[1] This concept was first formalized in 1936 by T. P. Wright while working in the aircraft industry. The first formulation was with respect to the cumulative average unit cost rather than the incremental unit cost. Wright's method was widely used during the early 1940s and is still preferred for federal government procurement contracts. In the mid-1940s, J. R. Crawford, a statistician with the Stanford Research Institute and Lockheed, developed the incremental unit cost method, which is presented here. The incremental method became widely used in industry during the 1950s and 1960s and is now the preferred method for internal decisions and shop floor management. See D. D. Pattison and C. J. Teplitz, "Are Learning Curves Still Relevant?" *Management Accounting*, February 1989, pp. 37–40.

EXHIBIT 7A–1   Incremental Unit Learning Curve

Number of Units X	Incremental Unit Hours, Y	Cumulative Total	Average Unit
1	100.00	100.00	100.00
2	80.00 (.8 × 100.00)	180.00	90.00
3	70.21	250.21	83.40
4	64.00 (.8 × 80.00)	314.21	78.55
5	59.56	373.77	74.75
6	56.17	429.94	71.66
7	53.45	483.39	69.06
8	51.20 (.8 × 64.00)	534.59	66.82
9	49.29	583.89	64.88
10	47.65	631.54	63.15
11	46.21	677.75	61.61
12	44.93	722.68	60.22
13	43.79	766.47	58.96
14	42.76	809.23	57.80
15	41.82	851.05	56.74
16	40.96 (.8 × 51.20)	892.01	55.75

The hours, Y, for any given unit, X, are found by:

$$Y = aX^b$$

Where a = hours (or cost) of the first unit
b = learning coefficient
X = units produced.
The learning coefficient, b, may be computed as:

$$b = \frac{\log (\text{Learning rate \%})}{\text{Log } (2)}$$

Thus, the b for an 80 percent learning curve is:

$$b = \frac{\text{Log } (80\%)}{\text{Log } (2)} = \frac{-.09691}{.30103} = -.3219$$

by a constant percentage as the cumulative volume doubles.[2] An illustration of an 80 percent incremental unit learning curve is given in Exhibit 7A–1. Note that, as the quantity doubles, the hours per unit are 80 percent of the previous hours. Hours have been used as a basis for this illustration, but costs may be treated in a similar manner.

Exhibit 7A–2 shows the hours per unit on the vertical axis and the cumulative units produced on the horizontal axis. The decline in hours is fairly rapid at first, but as the quantity continues to double, the difference in hours between successive units becomes ever smaller until it ultimately approaches zero. Theoretically, hours would still be declining at infinity, but the difference between the doubling of units would not be feasible to measure. As a practical matter, learning ceases before reaching the

---

[2] This assumption is critical to the application of incremental learning curves. Be aware that this assumption of constant percentage improvement may not apply to specific circumstances and thus the learning curve model is not always appropriate.

EXHIBIT 7A–2   Graph of a Learning Curve

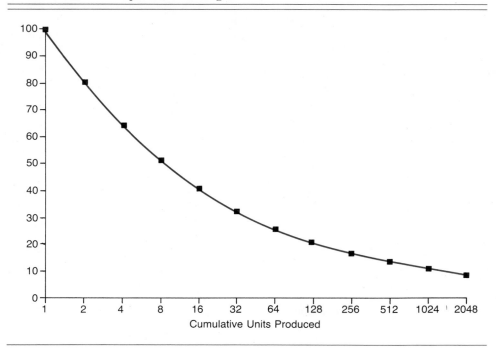

Cumulative Units Produced

large numbers (approaching 5,000 units of output). Even at lower levels, learning may cease if employees are not motivated to improve continuously.

Estimating the Learning Rate

The path of the learning curve (Exhibit 7A–2) represents a geometric series or progression where each point is determined by multiplying the previous point by a constant factor. The plotted curve is a hyperbola with the following formula:

$$Y = aX^b$$

Where Y = time (or cost) for the Xth unit
a = time (or cost) for the first unit
X = cumulative production
b = the exponent related to the rate of learning.

A linear form of the learning curve is derived by converting the above formula to logarithms. This gives a linear[3] equation of:

$$\log Y = \log a + b \,(\log X)$$

One of the problems in analyzing data to determine the presence of a learning effect is that data are not routinely collected in the right form. For example, data are not always available for the time (or cost) to produce each unit or even the cumulative production units to date. It is possible to determine total production of any product within a given accounting period and the total number of hours (or total cost) to produce that quantity. However, it will be necessary to search the records to determine

---

[3] Because most calculators can determine natural logarithms and antilogarithms, we can also use natural logarithms expressed as:

$$ln\ Y = ln\ a + b\,(ln\ X)$$

cumulative output and hours for each unit. Once data are available, the techniques we used in Chapter 3 for determining cost behavior can be used to find the linear curve in logarithms.

From a practical viewpoint, if data are available, a rough approximation of the learning rate that applies to a specific situation can be found by using any two cumulative production levels, where the second level is double the first level. We define the learning rate as:

$$\frac{\text{Time (cost) for the } 2X\text{th unit}}{\text{Time (cost) for the } X\text{th unit}}$$

For example, assume that the first unit required 6,400 hours and that the second unit required 4,736 hours; the learning rate is calculated as:

$$\frac{4{,}736}{6{,}400} = 74\%$$

Factors Influencing Learning

Learning rates are influenced by more than just labor training and effort. For example, learning results are influenced by the degree of preparation by the engineering design staff before production of a new product begins. If a poor engineering job is done, leading to excessive starting costs and production problems, a high degree of learning will result. If a good job of preplanning is done, leading to lower starting costs and fewer production problems, the degree of learning should be low. The low learning rate will have the lowest cost in the long run.

Beyond the planning and design stage, a host of other factors influence learning. Examples of these include:

1. Reductions in production losses, such as scrap and spoilage units.
2. Stabilization of product design resulting in fewer design changes both before and after production begins.
3. Changes in lot sizes.
4. Improvements in special tooling.
5. Implementation of cost-reduction programs.
6. Changing from manual to automatic equipment.
7. Employee turnover.

Limitations of Learning Curves

The learning curve technique can be applied adequately to a new product line or to a product line whose operating process has not reached the end of learning. New products that represent an old product with specific design changes may also benefit from learning theory, but less learning should be expected with an established product.

Products with a long production cycle, such as a year or more, generally are not adaptable to learning curves because (1) learning is lost between units and (2) employee turnover in the interim affects learning. Shipbuilding is a long-term production. However, there are segments of ships, such as bulkheads and panels that are used throughout the ship, which could benefit from learning.

Mass-produced products, such as calculators and clothes washers, should realize a learning curve early in the process. After a few thousand units, however, production methods should be well established and there is little opportunity for improvement.

Applications

Cost savings or increases in profitability can be realized from applications of the learning curve technique:

1. Setting selling prices for future production, such as bidding on jobs.
2. Determining manpower and facilities requirements.

3. Projecting labor loads and other starting costs to bring a new product to production capacity.
4. Control of production labor as a part of budgetary control or a standard cost system.
5. Determining realistic prices for outside work (such as contracting for parts, subassemblies, and assemblies) or for purchased labor.
6. Decision-making such as make or buy, special order, sell or process further, and product combination.

The learning curve technique is useful for progress reports that compare actual results with estimated performance as depicted by the learning curve; it also provides a measure of performance. In addition, it can assist management in establishing various incentive wage systems because bonuses can be tied to work at certain points during or after the learning stage.

Estimating Labor Hours on Intermediate Quantities

Assume a company has just completed the first unit of an eight-unit order in 100 hours and the process is well described by an 80 percent learning curve. The hours required for an additional seven units are the difference between the total hours for eight units and the hours for the first unit:

Total hours for eight units (Exhibit 7A–1)	534.59 hours
Total hours for one unit	100.00 hours
Hours required for seven units after completion of first unit	434.59 hours

Now assume that after completing the first order of eight, the customer requests another order of eight units. How many hours should be budgeted for producing this second order? We calculate these hours as follows:

Total hours for 16 units (Exhibit 7A–1)	892.01 hours
Total hours for first eight units	534.59 hours
Hours required for eight units after completion of eight units	357.42 hours

Once the total hours are known, the material, labor, and production overhead costs can be estimated for the order. Let's assume that each unit has $100 of material cost, a labor rate of $12 per hour, and a production overhead rate of $15 per labor hour. The budgeted production cost of the second order of eight units is as follows:

Material costs: 8 units × $100	$ 800
Labor costs: 357.42 × $12 = $4,289.04	4,289
Overhead costs: 357.42 × $15 = $5,361.30	5,361
Budgeted cost for second eight units	$10,450

DEFERRED LEARNING CURVE COSTS

Marketing managers have difficulty understanding why the cost of identical units are different and, as a result, have difficulty using different costs in cost-based pricing decisions. They find average costs easier to understand, explain, and apply. Therefore, average costs often support bids on jobs or contracts, interdivisional transfer prices, or any case in which forward pricing is part of business decisions. Even for inventory valuation and income determination purposes, accountants use average costs rather than show an increasing trend in profits resulting from the decreasing labor cost per unit. The accountant must handle the difference between the actual costs incurred during work in process and the average costs transferred to finished goods inventory.

For example, assume that a company produces a component part to an infrared sensing device used by municipal police for night-time duty. The company has secured a subcontract to supply a prime contractor with eight of these components. The prototype that won the bid incurred $1,000 of labor cost. The prototype is included with the eight units ordered. Industrial engineering estimates a 90 percent incremental learning curve. Although material and production overhead costs are incurred, this illustration uses only labor costs. The points on the learning curve representing this situation are expressed in dollars as:

	Incremental Unit Cost	*Cumulative Total*	*Average Unit*
1	1,000.00	1,000.00	1,000.00
2	900.00 (.9 × 1,000.00)	1,900.00	950.00
3	846.21	2,746.21	915.40
4	810.00 (.9 × 900.00)	3,556.21	889.05
5	782.99	4,339.19	867.84
6	761.59	5,100.78	850.13
7	743.95	5,844.73	834.96
8	729.00 (.9 × 810.00)	6,573.73	821.72

The average labor cost per unit for these eight component parts is $821.72. Exhibit 7A–3 uses the total costs above to illustrate how deferred learning curve costs are equated to actual costs and average costs.

The journal entry amounts for labor cost may be taken from the exhibit. For the first unit, the entry is:

Finished Goods Inventory	821.72	
Deferred Learning Curve Costs	178.28	
Work in Process Inventory		1,000.00

The entry for the eighth unit is:

Finished Goods Inventory	821.72	
Deferred Learning Curve Costs		92.72
Work in Process Inventory		729.00

While the deferred learning costs are small in this example, they are very large (in the $100 millions) for an order of 50 fighter jets manufactured over six years.

These entries have a smoothing effect on net income, and until a production order

EXHIBIT 7A–3 Deferred Learning Costs

	Unit Cost	*Average Cost*	*DR (CR)*	*Deferred Learning Costs*
1	1,000.00	821.72	178.28	178.28
2	900.00	821.72	78.28	256.57
3	846.21	821.72	24.49	281.06
4	810.00	821.72	(11.72)	269.34
5	782.99	821.72	(38.73)	230.61
6	761.59	821.72	(60.13)	170.48
7	743.96	821.72	(77.76)	92.72
8	729.00	821.72	(92.72)	0.00

is complete, there is an asset on the balance sheet equal to the balance in the deferred learning curve cost account. As goods are transferred from work in process to finished goods inventory, the deferred learning curve cost will gradually decline to zero.

Exhibit 7A–3 can also be used to show the loss attributed to the termination of a production order. Assume in the example above that when four units were completed, the customer cancelled the order. The balance in the deferred learning curve cost account would be $269.34. This $269.34 balance is an additional cost of the job or is written off as a loss in the period the work was cancelled.

PROBLEM FOR REVIEW

Denzer Manufacturing, Inc., has just been awarded a contract for an electronic sensing device that will detect metal and drugs in clothing. The contract calls for furnishing eight devices to the Florida State Prison System. The prototype that won the contract cost $5,000 in material and $9,000 in labor and applied production overhead at 150 percent of labor cost. Materials are not subject to a learning effect. Industrial engineering determined an 82 percent learning rate should be used on the incremental cost.

REQUIRED

a. How much material, labor, and overhead costs should be budgeted for the seven additional devices?
b. If the contract is cancelled after producing a total of four units (the prototype plus three additional units) and the state paid the average cost plus 20 percent, calculate the profit or loss realized by the company on those four units.

SOLUTION

a. Amounts budgeted.

	Incremental Unit	Cumulative Total	Average Unit
1	9,000.00	9,000.00	9,000.00
2	7,380.00 (.82 × 9,000.00)	16,380.00	8,190.00
3	6,571.14	22,951.14	7,650.38
4	6,051.60 (.82 × 7,380.00)	29,002.74	7,250.68
5	5,677.07	34,679.81	6,935.96
6	5,388.33	40,068.15	6,678.02
7	5,155.70	45,223.84	6,460.55
8	4,962.31 (.82 × 6,051.60)	50,186.16	6,273.27

Labor cost for additional seven units:

Labor cost for eight units	$ 50,186.16	
Labor cost for the first unit	(9,000.00)	
Labor cost for seven units		$ 41,186.16
Production overhead applied at 150%		61,779.24
Materials (Seven units at $5,000)		35,000.00
Total budgeted costs		$137,965.40

b. Profit or loss on terminated contract.

	Analysis of Deferred Costs			Deferred
	Actual Unit Cost	Average Cost	DR (CR)	Learning Costs
1	9,000.00	6,273.27	2,726.73	2,726.73
2	7,380.00	6,273.27	1,106.73	3,833.46
3	6,571.14	6,273.27	297.87	4,131.33
4	6,051.60	6,273.27	(221.67)	3,909.66

Deferred labor costs after four units		$ 3,909.66
Overhead charged to deferred labor at 150%		5,864.49
Total labor and overhead deferred		$ 9,774.15
Price charge for four units:		
Materials (4 × $5,000)	$20,000.00	
Labor (4 × $6,263.27)	25,053.08	
Overhead at 150%	37,579.62	
Total average cost	82,632.70	
Markup of 20%	16,526.54	
Total revenues earned		$99,159.24
Costs incurred:		
Average costs from above	$82,632.70	
Deferred labor and overhead cost	9,774.15	
Total actual costs		92,406.85
Profit on terminated contract		$ 6,752.39

ADDITIONAL READINGS

Belkaoui, A. *The Learning Curve: A Management Accounting Tool.* Westport, Conn.: Quorum Books, 1986.

Chen, J., and R. Manes. "Distinguishing the Two Forms of the Constant Percentage Learning Curve Model." *Contemporary Accounting Research*, Spring 1985, pp. 242–52.

Dileepan, P., and L. P. Ettkin. "Learning: The Missing Ingredient in Production Planning Spreadsheet Models." *Production and Inventory Management Journal*, Third Quarter 1988, pp. 32–35.

Johnson, D. L. "The Learning Curve: Which One to Use." *Program Manager*, January–February 1987, pp. 7–10.

Liao, S. S. "The Learning Curve: Wright's Model vs. Crawford's Model." *Issues in Accounting Education*, Fall 1988, pp. 302–15.

McKenzie, P. B. "An Alternative Learning Curve Formula." *Issues in Accounting Education*, Fall 1987, pp. 383–87.

Pattison, D. D., and C. J. Teplitz. "Are Learning Curves Still Relevant?" *Management Accounting*, February 1989, pp. 37–40.

REVIEW QUESTIONS

1. What is the basic theory behind the learning curve?
2. Which denotes the better rate of learning, an 80 percent or a 90 percent learning curve? Explain.
3. Identify three managerial applications of learning curves.
4. Describe how the learning curve might be used (a) budgeting labor costs, and (b) bidding on specific jobs.
5. What issue gives rise to deferred learning costs? Explain.

DISCUSSION QUESTIONS

6. What is the relationship between a learning curve and an incentive wage plan?
7. How would you account for deferred learning curve costs if the quantities in an order did not match the double of quantities in learning curve theory? For example, if seven units

were ordered based on a prototype that was not part of the order, what is the average cost of the seven units?

EXERCISES

7A–1. Learning and Comparisons. J. L. Jaggers, Inc., makes knitting machines. It sells the machines to large sweater manufacturers. Bentley Sweaters, Inc., will buy 100 of the machines if it can be shown that the incremental cost is less than the old knitting machines after the first 10 sweaters.

On a test run, a Bentley worker took one hour to get the knitting machine to knit one sweater. He used $18 in wool to knit the sweater. The wage rate is $7 and the overhead rate is 100 percent of direct labor. The average total cost on the old machine is $25.48. Engineering expects an 80 percent learning curve, and materials are expected to stay at about $18.00 per sweater.

(M. Kubinski, adapted)

REQUIRED:
a. Estimate the labor cost for the 10th sweater. (Apply the formula: $Y = aX^b$.)
b. At what level will the incremental cost of the new machine be less than the old machine?

7A–2. Learning Curve. The Tiger Mechanical Company has developed a new tractor attachment for agricultural use. The attachment may be used for both cultivation and harvesting. It is more efficient than current models because it has less "drag" and requires less fuel and time to process a 1,000-acre field. During regular production of the first unit, the first attachment required 158 hours to manufacture. Direct labor costs $25 per hour, and the industrial engineering staff estimates that a 92 percent learning curve is appropriate. Materials for the attachment cost $3,400, and overhead is applied at a rate of 120 percent of direct labor.

(J. Lo, adapted)

REQUIRED:
a. Estimate the labor cost for the first batch of four.
b. Now assume that the first batch of four is to be sold under contract that allows for full cost plus 30 percent. Compute the total cost and contract price.

7A–3. Estimating Learning Rates. W. Nita Britton is an entrepreneur who has developed a product called Doggie Delite. The direct materials cost per batch is $11.00, direct labor is $3.50 per hour, and overhead is charged at a rate of 75 percent of direct labor dollars. Ms. Britton is predicting the following total hours to produce the first two batches:

(D. Ripple, adapted)

Accumulated Batches	Time To Process (hours)
1	3.00
2	2.10

REQUIRED:
a. Calculate the learning rate for the production of this product based on the two batches.
b. After producing the first two batches in 5.10 hours, Ms. Britton wants you to estimate the total costs for the next two batches.

7A–4. Cost Estimation. Using the formulae, $Y = aX^b$ and $b = \log \text{(learning rate)}/\log(2)$, estimate the following:
a. The incremental labor cost of the 30th unit for an 85 percent learning curve where the first unit takes five hours at a $10 labor rate per hour.
b. The incremental labor cost for the 10th unit for a 92 percent learning curve where the first unit takes 100 hours at a labor rate of $20 per hour.
c. What is the difference in labor cost to make the 50th unit for the following two workers:

1. Rube Clyburn, who takes three hours to complete the first unit, earns $18 per hour, and has a 92 percent learning curve.
2. Clee Rubdown, who takes eight hours to complete the first unit, earns $12 per hour, and has an 80 percent learning curve.

PROBLEMS

7A–5. Learning and Intermediate Quantities. Kelly Earls is a newly hired assistant controller for Kliedenst, Inc., which is a holding company based in Atlanta. He is being trained on many facets of the Kliedenst operations, including the preparation of spread sheet models (called a *spread* by the staff) for potential acquisitions and mergers. Each model contains relevant financial statement information stored in a data base so that potential investments may be compared. Kelly's past experience includes four years of public accounting experience, and this helps him substantially in preparing the first spread for the Kitanning Pipeline Co. It takes him only six hours to develop and enter the data, which is record time. As part of his training, Kelly is expected to prepare 16 spreads over a three-week period in addition to his other tasks. Based on experience with six previous trainees, the controller expects an 80 percent learning curve to apply on the incremental hours.

(M. Winburn, adapted)

REQUIRED:

a. How many total hours should Kelly spend completing the 16 spreadsheets if his performance followed an 80 percent learning curve?

b. Suppose that at the end of four spreads, Kelly has found that he has spent 21.86 hours:

1	6.00
2	5.52
3	5.26
4	5.08

He does not want the controller to think that he is a slow learner, which he is not. After all, he started out much better than the other six people who have completed the training.

1. What learning curve does Kelly appear to be following?
2. Why might Kelly's learning rate be different from the previous six trainees?
3. Using the formula $Y = aX^b$, compute the projected hours for each of the 16 units and the total hours for 16 units.
4. Kelly has the option to complete the spread sheets outside of normal office hours. How much time should he plan to spend on his own in order to meet the controller's expectations?

7A–6. Learning and Pricing. Worley Welding has contracted with Rexett Western Exploration and Production to build 15 sets of $2\frac{3}{8}$-inch tubing weight guards. These guards protect workers from the counterbalance weights of a pumpjack on an oil production location. The workers who fabricate the guards from tubular steel are paid $17 per hour. The tubing costs $1.15 per linear foot. The first set takes 26 hours to build and uses 155 linear feet of tubing. The labor costs are affected by a 90 percent learning curve for this type of product and materials usage. Materials usage is subject to a 95 percent learning curve but cannot fall below 124 linear feet on any unit because of U.S. Department of Labor regulations on weight guard dimensions. Worley estimates overhead at 50 percent of direct labor.

(A. Gregory)

REQUIRED:

a. Determine the total labor cost for 15 units.
b. Determine the total material costs for 15 units.
c. Prepare an estimate of total costs for the first 15 units.

7A–7. Learning, Incentive Pay, and Pricing. Balzer Company constructs wooden pallets for the movement of heavy objects. Lumber is purchased and must be cut to the necessary specifications for each type of pallet design. Laborers construct the pallets, which are then loaded into rail containers for shipment. Balzer recently accepted an order from Kusse Rock Company for 5,000 units of a new pallet design. Materials for the new design are estimated at $2.50 per pallet, and overhead is applied at 125 percent of labor costs. The first unit of the new pallet required 1 hour and the second unit required .90 hour. Learning is expected to occur at this rate for the first 16 units after which learning will cease.

(S. Neves, adapted)

REQUIRED:
a. If the learning implied by the first two units is indicative of the rate for the learning curve:
   1. What is the learning curve rate?
   2. What is the projected labor for the 16th and remaining units?
b. Management has established a training period of the first 16 pallets for any new design during which the employees are paid $5 per hour. After the training period, management desires that the workers receive an average of $6.25 per hour. Workers are to be paid on a piece rate. At what level should the piece rate be set to obtain an average compensation of $6.25 per hour on the remaining units?

7A–8. Deferred Learning Curve Costs.   You and your roommate have noticed that there is very little storage room in most college dormitory rooms. After some thinking and sketching, you have designed a storage device that will fit under most beds or in the back of a closet. With a small tool the device will convert into two suit cases for travel between semesters. All your friends would like to buy this device from you, but the price must be reasonable. However, the first device took $100 in materials and 15 hours of labor. You feel that the materials costs can be cut to $40 with judicious purchasing and design, but you are concerned about labor. With examinations coming up, you do not want this little project to take all of your time. You value your time at $5 per hour but will not consider spending more than 5 hours per week over the next 10 weeks. That will make a total of 100 hours for you and your roommate. Because you are novices at manufacturing this (or any) device, you guess that an 80 percent learning curve is very likely. Because the device can be made in your room with small tools, there is no overhead. You have received down payments of $50 on 16 devices at an agreed price of $100. With this $800 you buy some more materials and start working.

(M. Winburn)

REQUIRED:
a. How many hours will you and your roommate have to work in order to complete the 16 units?
b. What is the expected total cost, including your labor, for the 16 units? What is the average unit cost?
c. How much profit, above your labor cost, do you and your roommate expect to share? Remember that the first unit had a materials cost of $100, but the materials for the rest are expected to cost only $40.
d. You deliver the first unit and receive $50 remaining on the order. This pains you because you remember paying $100 for the materials and working 15 hours to complete this first one.
   1. Prepare a journal entry to record the receipt of the deposits.
   2. Prepare a journal entry for this first sale assuming that an appropriate amount of the $175 cost is to be deferred.

EXTENDED APPLICATIONS Background for Problems 7A–9 and 7A–10

Learning Estimation with Log Regression.   In the formula

$$Y = aX^b, \quad b = \frac{\log \text{(learning rate)}}{\log (2)}$$

Likewise, the learning curve rate, c, may be calculated from b with the formula

$$c = 10^{b \times \log(2)}$$

For example, the learning curve rate for a b of .14 is:

$$c = 10^{-.14 \times .30103} = 90.75\%$$

Given the value of b, the incremental unit cost (Y) for any given cumulative production (X) may be calculated. For example, the incremental unit labor hours for the 19th unit, given a 90 percent learning curve and four hours to complete the initial unit, is:

$$Y = 4 (19)^{-.152} = 2.55676 \text{ hours}$$

The cumulative hours may be approximated[4] for any given X:

$$\text{Cumulative sum} = \frac{aX^{b+1}}{b + 1} - [4.4a(1 - c)]$$

For example, the approximate cumulative hours to make the first 100 units for a 90 percent incremental learning curve when the first unit takes four hours is:

$$\text{Cumulative sum} = \frac{4(100)^{(-.1520 + 1)}}{-.1520 + 1} - 4.4(4)(1 - 90\%) = 232.48$$

Estimation of Coefficients.   If all of the coefficients (a, b, and c) are unknown, then they must be estimated in some manner. One approach divides the average for the $2n$th item by the average for the nth item. Another approach is log regression, which is more accurate because the approach uses all of the available data.

If we take the log of both sides of the cumulative average equation we find:

$$Y = aX^b$$
$$\log(Y) = \log(a) + b * (\log(X))$$

The parameters $\log(a)$ and b may be estimated using linear regression (least squares method) as presented in Chapter 3.

7A–9. Learning Estimates and Total Costs.   The Nishwin Company produces prefabricated houses in San Diego, California. John Nishwin, president and owner, has noticed that the first house for a new design takes longer and requires more materials than later versions. He has gathered the following actual cost data for a recent model, the Sunset Home:

Serial (X)	Actual Cost (Y)	Cumulative Average
1	$46,726	$46,726
2	43,553	45,140
3	40,057	43,445
4	38,017	42,088
5	38,185	41,308
6	36,445	40,497
7	35,707	39,813
8	36,158	39,356
9	34,089	38,771
10	32,914	38,185
11	34,937	37,890
12	33,337	37,510
13	34,347	37,267
14	31,353	36,845
15	32,855	36,579

[4] This approximation is derived from the integral of a continuous function of aX^b, which is:

$$\frac{aX^{b+1}}{b + 1}$$

minus an approximation necessitated because the series is discrete and not continuous. As X becomes large (>150 units) then the approximation converges to near the actual amount. If X is less than 50, then use a spread sheet to compute the actual amounts.

REQUIRED:

a. One approach to estimate the learning rates for a production process is to divide the *n*th item into the 2*n*th item.
   1. Estimate the learning rates using the incremental total cost for the 14th and the 7th house. Round your result to four decimal places.
   2. Compute the value of *b* for the incremental cost equation using your estimate of the learning rate.
   3. Estimate the incremental cost for the 20th house.
b. Another approach to estimate the learning rate in cost numbers is to use log regression on the incremental cost.
   1. Take the log of the serial number and the incremental cost. Then perform a simple linear regression on the logged data.
   2. Compute the learning curve rate that is associated with the *b* found in part (1).
   3. Using your estimates found in part (1), prepare an estimate of the incremental cost for the 20th house.

7A–10. Estimating Labor Time and Service Fee Negotiation.   Marceay Associates, Ltd., is a medical association in Chicago, Illinois, that operates a secondary care, accredited hospital that provides basic dental, eye, and health care to groups at a fixed price per member. Elective procedures may be added as agreed between Marceay and group representatives. The association includes 154 practitioners with various specialties and years of experience. Most of the 8,242 different procedures that are performed on patients are standard; however, every year there are 300 or more new procedures that must be learned.

One new procedure has been nicknamed the "Eagle Eye" by the three ophthalmologists recently trained in the procedure. The technique was developed in the Soviet Union but has just been approved for practice in the United States. For patients in the low-risk group, age 21 to 43 with no chronic health problems, the new procedure is 99.2 percent effective in perfecting vision to 20/20. The procedure is not approved for other than low-risk patients.

The Mid-Western Actors Guild would like to offer the procedure to its members at a "reasonable" price. A search of Marceay's extensive medical records for this regular account indicates that about 600 of the members fit the vision, age, and health pattern to be in the low-risk group. Of these, about 60 percent would be interested in paying for the elective procedure during the current year.

The three ophthalmologists have performed varying numbers of the Eagle Eye procedures since they have been trained. Listed below are the surgical room minutes, as meticulously recorded in the medical records, for the procedures performed by each practitioner:

	Cohn	*Smithton*	*Loninger*
1	168	147	204
2	156	142	173
3	140	146	164
4	143	144	140
5	128	141	139
6	128	132	134
7	123	142	134
8	128	138	128
9	122	135	117
10	117	141	
11	112		
12	118		
13	119		
14	117		

These are the actual minutes of surgery, not an average or a cumulative average. The time starts with setup and goes through patient preparation, surgery, close, and ends when the room is completely ready for the next patient.

REQUIRED: (*Note:* Refer to the presentation before problem 7A–9 for help in answering the following.)

a. One approach to estimate the learning rates for a production process is to divide the cost for the *n*th item into the 2*n*th item.

   1. Compute the learning curve rates as implied by the incremental costs for the eighth and the fourth surgeries for each of the practitioners. Round to the fourth decimal place.

   2. Convert the learning curve rates to *b* coefficients that may be used in estimating incremental minutes for each of the practitioners. Round the result to the fourth decimal place.

   3. Estimate the time in minutes for each practitioner required to perform the 100th Eagle Eye procedure.

b. Using a log regression for each practitioner,

   1. Estimate the coefficients to predict the incremental minutes of surgery.

   2. Convert the *b* coefficients to learning curve rates and compare the results.

   3. Estimate the time in minutes for each practitioner required to perform the 100th procedure.

   4. Cohn and Smithton are somewhat older and have decided to limit their practice to 80 and 50, respectively, of the elective Eagle Eye procedures during the current year. Loninger is younger and is willing to perform whatever procedures are necessary to complete the contract. Compute an estimate of the total time required to complete the contract. Assume that, other than the surgeries already performed, these three ophthalmologists will limit their Eagle Eye practice to the Actors Guild contract.

   5. Marceay Associates, Ltd., desires to set fees to obtain an average of $360 per surgical room hour. Compute an estimate per Eagle Eye procedure that may be used in quoting a fee for the current year for the Mid-Western Actor's Guild contract.

CHAPTER

8

Production Overhead Costs

■

THE PROBLEM OF FAIR
OVERHEAD ALLOCATIONS

Lifeview, Inc., is a manufacturer of medical equipment with revenues of about $250 million per year and net profits of about $15 million. The company has two main product lines: Lifeview Sonagraphs and Lifeview Magnetic Resonating Units (MRU). In addition Lifeview, Inc., provides customer service for the products. The devices provide physicians with the capacity to study visual images and diagnose diseases and conditions without the use of X-rays or surgery. The sonagraph is based on sound, and the magnetic resonating unit is based on the relative density of matter. The MRU is far more accurate, produces a three-dimensional image, and is much more expensive to construct and deliver.

The technology for the devices has developed rapidly since the product concepts were developed in the early 1970s. Sonagraph technical developments have stabilized so that the unit may now be mass produced. Lifeview, Inc., has recently invested $300 million in highly automated equipment to produce the sonagraph. The MRU technology is still changing at a rapid pace. Each MRU has some technical enhancements, and they are somewhat customized to the hospital needs.

In early January 19x3, Kerry Manto, chief executive officer, and Lou Carson, vice president for marketing, were reviewing the gross profits for 19x2 for the product lines and service. The results were (in $ millions):

	Sonagraph	*MRU*	*Service*
Revenues	$120	$90	$40
Cost of goods sold	50	80	20
Gross profit	$ 70	$10	$20

The president and vice president were trying to redefine the corporate strategy. Even though sales have increased rapidly over the past five years, the company's profits have been nearly $15 million each year. The CEO's comments were pointed:

Manto: I think the MRU is a losing game. That $10 million gross profit is not enough to pay the marketing costs and provide adequate profits considering our investment. Should we stop pushing ahead with the MRU or should we consider raising prices?

Carson: Prices are already too high. Our competitors are undercutting us by 20 percent. We have lost MRU market share from about 40 percent down to about 15 percent. As far as costs, I can see no waste in the production of the MRU.

Manto: Well, something has to give. We are selling as many sonagraphs as we can produce, even with our new automated line. We are six weeks behind in our orders and falling back. Still we show little profit. Frankly, the board of directors is losing patience with our performance. I'm tempted to go through and cut budgets 10 percent again.

Carson: Something must be wrong with the numbers. How can we be selling so many of the sonagraphs and be beating the competition on prices? Are they asleep or just playing dead? Sonagraphs have been around for a while now; surely we can't be making that much gross profit on them. Also, we're apparently doing poorly with the MRUs. I know we have a good product and our prices are high. These numbers make no sense at all.

Manto: It might be that these cost figures are throwing us off. I hope that's the problem. I'll have Walt [Walt Johnson, corporate controller] look into it.

LEARNING OBJECTIVES

After studying this chapter, you should be able to:

1. Distinguish between direct costs and indirect costs.
2. Explain the reasons for using predetermined overhead rates.
3. Compute the effects on overhead rates of the concepts of capacity: ideal, practical, normal, and expected actual.
4. Differentiate between the concepts of idle capacity and excess capacity.
5. Consider the relative merits of measures of activity or volume.
6. Compute and apply overhead rates with various measures of activity.
7. Compute and explain the appropriateness of plant-wide and departmental overhead rates.

Production overhead[1] is a large cost for many organizations, such as Lifeview, Inc., in the business problem. Whether the organization is a manufacturer, like Lifeview, or a service establishment, a merchandiser, a governmental agency, or a university, overhead cost and its allocation to products or services is an important

---

[1] *Factory overhead, manufacturing overhead,* and *factory burden* are common terms that connote a manufacturing environment. The concepts of overhead costs also apply to extraction, utilities, construction, publishing, services, and government. Since *production* can imply a broader context than manufacturing, we have chosen the broader term of *production overhead.*

issue. The overhead costs become part of the costs of goods and services produced. The reported costs of goods and services affect many decisions on pricing, product additions and deletions, marketing efforts, budgeting, and personnel retention. These decisions are too important to allow production overhead cost to be allocated without due consideration.

According to the National Association of Accountants, **production overhead cost** is:

> Those costs which cannot, as a practical matter, be assigned to a firm's objectives in a direct fashion; overhead costs are, however, related to the accomplishment of those objectives. Customarily, a consistent method of cost allocation, which seeks to approximate economic sacrifices incurred, is adopted in applying such charges to cost objectives.[2]

Production overhead was not always included in the cost of a product. Prior to heavy mechanization of factories, the primary costs of making a product were direct material and direct labor. Because production overhead cost was originally small, this cost was routinely expensed in the period incurred. With the growth in the number of products, with increased mechanization of production processes, with more levels of people managing operating facilities, and with facilities becoming more expensive, production overhead grew in significance.

The period of the 1920s to the mid-1930s was an era of substantial debate over whether production overhead costs should be allocated to the products manufactured or charged as an expense. By 1936 the battle lines were drawn. One side declared that only the direct material and labor costs were part of product costs. This was originally called **direct costing.** Direct costing was the beginning of what is today called **variable costing,** which includes variable production overhead as a product cost. There were and still are many advocates of direct costing among management accountants, especially members of the National Association of Accountants and of the American Accounting Association.

The American Institute of CPAs (AICPA) and the Internal Revenue Service (IRS) represented the other side by stating that all production costs must be charged to products, which is called **absorption costing.** Because the AICPA at that time directed rule-making for financial reporting, it required attaching production overhead to the products for financial reporting purposes. We will address in more depth the support and criticism of the use of variable and absorption costing in Chapter 16.

This chapter discusses the basic issues associated with distinguishing between the direct and indirect costs. It examines the issues of cost allocation techniques appropriate for products and services. This discussion addresses the purposes for a predetermined overhead rate and the selection of an activity measure that represents the volume. It also looks at the advantages and disadvantages of plant-wide overhead rates versus individual departmental overhead rates.

COST ALLOCATION

The process of identifying[3] an organization's costs with products, services, or other cost objectives is called **cost allocation.** A **cost objective** is a key factor for selecting appropriate allocation methods and techniques. By definition, it represents anything for which we want to measure costs. Cost objectives include products, services,

---

[2] *Management Accounting Terminology* (National Association of Accountants, 1983), p. 74.

[3] Other words that are used to describe this activity include *assigning, apportioning,* and *classifying.*

processes, departments, and many other possible objects. Although this chapter focuses on the cost of products and services, the same concepts apply generally to any situation in which the cost of an object is desired. This section presents a summary of the basic allocation concepts. (See Chapter 25 for a more complete discussion of the concepts.)

To begin with, we find three general classes of relationships that influence the type of allocation methods and techniques used: direct, indirect—demonstrable relationship, and indirect—no demonstrable relationship.

Direct Allocations

In the first class, a specific, identifiable, and immediate relationship exists between the cost and the object to which the cost is allocated. The cost is an integral part of the product or service because we can see, feel, or otherwise sense the resource represented by the cost. For example, a circuit board goes directly into a Lifeview Sonagraph. The circuit board can be identified with the product. A measure is readily available for determining the cost of the circuit board in the sonagraph: the quantity comes off an engineering drawing and the prices can be seen on a purchase invoice. Likewise, an assembly worker inserts and tests the circuit board. The cost of the time it takes for the assembly worker can be measured through the payroll system. We can see the worker insert the circuit board into the sonagraph. These costs are called *direct costs*.

Indirect Cost Allocations

Indirect Allocations—Demonstrable Relationship. In the second class, a demonstrable relationship exists between the cost and the object to which the cost is allocated, but the relationship is not precisely determinable with accuracy and correctness. For example, the electricity and maintenance used by a highly automated production line must be allocated using some reasonable basis. There is a relationship between the electricity and maintenance costs and the production line usage. How much of the electricity and maintenance cost is used up to produce the model 3000 (deluxe) versus the model 2000 (regular) of sonagraph? The nature of the relationship between maintenance cost and line usage requires judgment to select a measure that represents the relationship.

Likewise, the provision of service requires production overhead. The personnel must be hired and trained to provide service to customers. The cost of transportation, salaries, and training for field personnel must be allocated in some reasonable way to determine the costs of specific services provided.

Indirect Allocations—No Demonstrable Relationship. The third class occurs when no demonstrable relationship exists between the costs and the product or service, yet management policy or some external reporting requirement results in the need to allocate these costs to products or services. This is the situation, for example, in trying to charge a plant manager's salary to the products or the services during a specific period. The relationship is remote, and the method of allocating costs takes on a sense of arbitrariness. The degree of arbitrariness increases as the relationship between incurrence of cost and the achievement of the cost objective becomes more remote.

Such allocations have the potential to be used for unscrupulous ends. Thus, one manager or product can be assigned more allocated cost than others depending upon the allocation technique selected. Accountants should try, in as ethical a manner as possible, to avoid allocations that lead to incorrect decisions or result in unfair performance measures of managers. Thus, arbitrariness should be avoided if feasible but should be recognized and disclosed where it cannot be avoided.[4]

Types of Indirect Costs.   Indirect costs are generally grouped into three functional classifications, depending on the nature and purpose of the company: production overhead, marketing and distribution, and general and administrative. The difference among these groups relates primarily to the cause or purpose of the cost.

Production overhead costs are all production costs that cannot be easily and economically identified with (traced to) units of products or services at the time costs are incurred. This lack of traceability is most common when the cost is incurred for numerous units of product or the cost is not susceptible to measurement at the unit level. Because these costs are necessary to produce goods or render services, they are allocated in order to arrive at inventoriable costs for products or to provide production costs for services that become the basis for billing clients.

Examples of production overhead costs in manufacturing include depreciation for machinery, supervision of factory workers, repair and maintenance of factory equipment, supplies, property taxes on a factory, insurance, and utilities. Examples of production overhead in a hospital include malpractice insurance, medical records transcription and filing, billing forms, personnel, custodial, and computer support.

The cost of the salesperson who enters a sales order can be directly identified. Thus, sales commissions and travel often can be directly identified with specific sales orders and thereby to products sold. Other marketing and distribution costs represent a functional area that benefits many products and services, but the relationship is at best indirect. For example, market research often benefits more than one product, as do advertising and promotional efforts. The costs of warehousing and distribution of finished goods often require indirect or arbitrary allocations.

General and administrative costs most often do not benefit any particular product or service. Rather, they support the organization as a whole. Common examples of these costs include corporate accounting and legal and executive-level management.

For external reporting purposes, marketing and distribution costs and general and administrative costs are not allocated to products to arrive at inventory values. Allocation of these costs to products may be appropriate for federal government contracts and certain construction contracts. For internal reporting, these costs are often allocated for decisions related to performance evaluation, planning, facilities management, comparisons of marketing and administrative strategies, and for profitability analysis for product addition and deletion decisions.

ALLOCATING PRODUCTION COSTS TO PRODUCTS AND SERVICES

The Process

The process for allocating production costs to products and services identifies the costs that can be direct costs and those that fall in the realm of indirect costs. This process involves a two-step (stage) approach[5] in which production costs are identified with departments (or cost centers) and then identified with products or services. Although direct costs of products and services can be easily and economically identified

---

[4] For general guidance on ethical conduct in management accounting, see "Standards of Ethical Conduct for Management Accountants," *Statement Number 1C* (New York: National Association of Accountants, 1983). Especially relevant here is the standard on objectivity, which includes: "Disclose fully all relevant information that could reasonably be expected to influence an intended user's understanding of the reports, comments, and recommendations presented." This standard of ethical performance is interpreted to require the full disclosure of methods used in arbitrary allocations that would reasonably influence such judgments as personnel decisions, product marketing, or financial planning.

[5] Robin Cooper, "The Two-Stage Procedure in Cost Accounting: Part One," *Journal of Cost Management in the Manufacturing Industry,* Summer 1987, pp. 43–51, and "Part Two," Fall 1987, pp. 39–45.

with departments, it is not a requirement for costing products because the costs can be easily traced to the products without identifying the department. Departmental classification is, however, important for planning and control purposes and so is incorporated in the allocation process. Thus, materials requisitions and employee time records will clearly indicate the departments to which costs relate.

Production overhead (indirect costs of products and services) must first be allocated to production departments for which they were incurred. Some production overhead (for example, depreciation of department equipment) can be easily allocated to the department. Other production overhead cost (for example, use of computer facilities by the producing department) may require careful analysis. The latter circumstance is called support department allocation and is the subject of Appendix 8A. Finally, a means to allocate production overhead from departments to the final products and services is necessary. This is accomplished through a factory-wide overhead rate or through departmental overhead rates.

Exhibit 8–1 is a graphical illustration of the two-step process. The upper half shows the cost flow with a factory-wide rate, the lower half with departmental rates.

Traceability of Costs

Which costs are direct and which costs are included in the production overhead? A company first identifies all costs associated with production activities. Next, the costs are assigned or allocated to a department. Then, for the department, some of these costs are called *direct material costs* and some *direct labor costs*. What remains in the pool of departmental production costs are called *production overhead costs*. The basis for selecting direct material and labor costs is traceability.

In a practical sense, **traceability** is the idea of seeing, feeling, or sensing. Direct costs can be easily and economically traced to, that is, specifically identified with, a product or service. For example, besides the circuit board in the sonagraph mentioned earlier, the components of the equipment include a cabinet, a television screen, an input monitor, a keyboard, speakers, and various gauges. All of these are integral parts of the product, can be measured, and are easily identified with the sonagraph. As another example, in a hospital, medications that are given to specific patients can be recorded in the patient's medical records. Therefore, the cost of these materials and medications would be *direct material costs*.

Extreme efforts are not made to trace immaterial items to products. For example, screws, bolts, wiring, and solder are all used in the production of the sonagraph. There is generally no attempt made to record these costs for a specific unit because the costs of recording often outweigh the benefits from more precisely knowing the direct materials cost for a given unit. Instead these costs are treated as production overhead costs.

Some labor is performed to produce the sonagraph. The cabinet needs assembly, circuits must be inserted, and the screen, keyboard, and input monitor must be attached. The quality of each step must be checked carefully to assure a high-quality product. Time records show who worked on the sonagraph line and how much time the worker used; payroll records show the appropriate labor costs to producing departments. Because a worker's time can be traced to the sonagraph, this labor cost is *direct labor cost*.

Some production plants are so highly automated or mechanized that there is little, if any, direct labor. For example, large plants that produce matches, cans, nails, screws, pipe, and similar standard products are set up to require little direct labor. The machines do not need the constant attention of an operator. In these plants, all labor is an indirect cost and primarily relates to machine setup, maintenance, and production supervision.

EXHIBIT 8–1   Cost Allocation to Products or Services

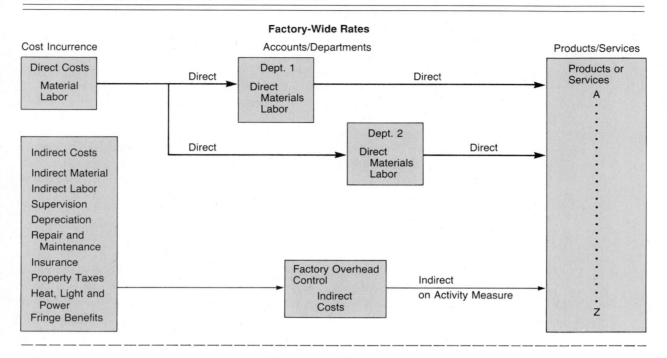

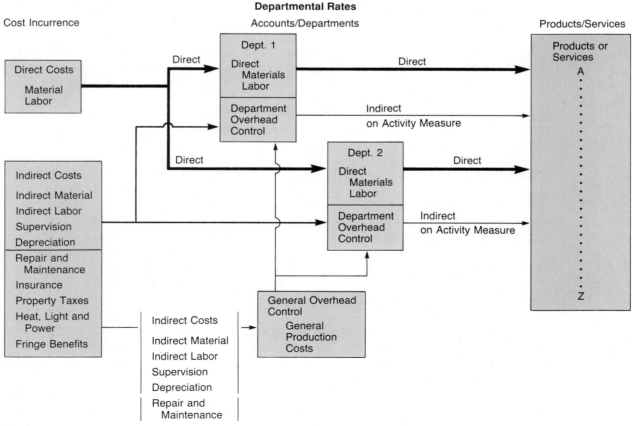

Additionally, many support costs, such as repair and maintenance of the equipment, janitorial services, supervision, power and light, depreciation on the factory building, and some fringe benefits for workers must be accounted for. These costs are part of the production costs but are not readily traceable to or specifically identified with each product. They are, consequently, *indirect costs* and require an indirect allocation technique.

ESTABLISHING A PREDETERMINED OVERHEAD RATE

Total actual overhead costs are not known until the end of an accounting period. However, cost information is frequently needed during the period; for example, pricing and bidding decisions cannot wait until next month. Hospitals bill patients when they are released. Car repair shops want payment when the car is picked up. A janitorial service must have some idea of its anticipated costs when bidding on a contract to clean buildings. Consequently, most companies establish one or many predetermined overhead rates for use in determining prices and in assessing the profitability of goods and services.

Computational Steps

Establishing a predetermined overhead rate can be summarized in four steps.

Step One—Select Measure of Activity. Select a measure or measures of activity that will be used for charging production overhead costs to the products or services in process. This measure should, if possible, represent the productive activity that most nearly explains in a causal or beneficial manner why actual overhead costs are incurred.

Step Two—Estimate Activity Level. Estimate the expected activity level for the measure or measures selected. For example, if normal labor hours is the appropriate measure, then estimate the normal hours of activity during the period.

Step Three—Estimate Total Overhead. Estimate total production overhead costs for the period given the estimate of activity. Where a distinction between variable and fixed production overhead costs is important enough for the company to use individual rates for each type of cost, estimate separately total variable and total fixed overhead costs for the period. The variable cost per unit of activity and the fixed cost for the relevant range can be established through cost behavior analysis, as discussed in Chapter 3. Total variable costs at an estimated level of activity are the product of the variable amount per unit and the estimated activity.

If more than one activity measure is necessary to describe the causes of overhead cost, then estimate the overhead cost associated with each measure of activity. Although this approach may appear more often in service and support functions, it is not commonly used in overhead rates for production departments.

Step Four—Calculate Rate or Rates. Calculate the **predetermined overhead rate** by dividing the estimated overhead costs by the measure of activity. The resulting rate or rates will be used to apply production overhead costs to products or services.

Example Analysis. The managers have agreed that for the Customer Service Department of Lifeview, Inc., the best measure of productive activity for applying production overhead to each maintenance job is hours of activity. Activity includes transportation time to and from the service call plus the hours working on location.

The controller, in cooperation with the managers, estimates that the service workers will attain 600,000 hours. At that level, total service overhead costs are estimated at $6,000,000. The overhead rate for charging service jobs is $10 per hour, calculated as follows:

$$\frac{\text{Estimated total overhead costs}}{\text{Estimated total hours}} = \frac{\$6,000,000}{600,000 \text{ hours}} = \$10 \text{ per hour}$$

To apply overhead to work performed during the period, multiply the actual activity (service hours) for the service job by the overhead rate ($10 per hour) calculated for a unit of that activity measure.

Reasons for a Predetermined Rate

In addition to pricing and bidding issues mentioned earlier, a predetermined overhead rate is preferred over an actual overhead charge for two major reasons. The first is the timing of overhead cost incurrence. For example, the heating and air conditioning costs for the factory building are generally much higher in winter and summer than they are in spring and fall. Should we allocate heating and air conditioning costs more heavily to products produced in winter and summer than to products produced in spring and fall? The facility and workers must be maintained no matter what the weather outside. The facilities and the workers benefit production throughout the year. Therefore, a predetermined overhead rate in effect averages the heating and air conditioning costs over all units of output for the period.

The other major reason for using a predetermined overhead rate is the potential fluctuation in the measure of activity. Most companies do not have a constant level of productive activity each and every month throughout the year; some months are higher or lower than other months. Many companies, for example, schedule employee vacations during months when employees desire to be away with their families. Production may have to be scaled back to accommodate this convenience to employees. These low activity periods are usually used for necessary repair and maintenance work, resulting in higher costs than other periods of peak activity. A predetermined overhead rate averages costs over the units of work regardless of when work is performed. This way no product is penalized in cost because of a low volume month or benefitted by a high volume month.

CONCEPTS OF CAPACITY

When estimating the level of activity to be used in the overhead rate computation, some concept of capacity is assumed. That concept can be a function of management philosophy and policies or an arbitrary decision. Yet, depending on the relevant level of fixed costs in the total overhead amount, the capacity concept used can have a dramatic impact on the overhead rate calculated.

Four Capacity Levels

This section discusses the four generally accepted concepts of capacity for production overhead.

Theoretical or Ideal Capacity.   **Theoretical, ideal, or maximum capacity** is the productive activity under perfect conditions. Here plant, equipment, and people operate at peak efficiency, in an engineering sense. It does not allow for unavoidable but expected interruptions. Neither does it consider short or near-term sales expectancy. This activity level cannot be reached in an actual situation and accordingly does not provide a good basis for allocating production overhead costs to work performed. It does, however, represent a starting point from which departures may be measured in quantifying other concepts of capacity.

Practical Capacity.   **Practical capacity** is theoretical capacity less unavoidable interruptions and delays, such as holidays, vacations, time off for weekends, machine breakdowns, material and labor shortages, and rest breaks. Thus, practical capacity is the level of activity at which a plant can operate if it has all of the production orders to produce at that level. Practical capacity represents the maximum level at which the combination of plant, equipment, and people, given consideration to unavoidable happenings, can efficiently operate.

Normal Capacity.   **Normal capacity** is a long-run concept; it is an average utilization of plant, equipment, and workers over several years to even out the swings in market demand. Three to five years are considered the common period for establishing this average.

Expected Actual Capacity.   **Expected actual capacity** is a short-run concept. It is management's estimate of capacity utilization for the upcoming year, or the productive capacity needed to meet market demand and inventory needs. Many companies prefer this capacity level because each year stands on its own. Management wants the overhead costs incurred in a period allocated to the work of the same period. Because expected actual capacity is a short-term concept, it will be higher in some years and lower in others, as compared to normal capacity.

Effect of Capacity on Overhead Rates

Regardless of the capacity level selected, the variable rate per unit of activity will be the same. Therefore, a selection of the capacity level is important only in determining the fixed production overhead rate. An example of overhead rates in total and by variable and fixed costs at four different capacity levels is given in Exhibit 8–2. The controller for the Cristobal Concrete Company estimated the ideal capacity at 200,000 yards of mixed concrete. He estimated the practical capacity to be 90 percent of ideal, normal capacity to be 80 percent of ideal, and expected capacity for 19x9 to be 70 percent.

Expected actual capacity is not always lower than normal capacity. For any given year these two levels could be reversed. Hence, expected actual capacity could just

EXHIBIT 8–2   Cristobal Concrete Company (effect of capacity concept on overhead rates)

	Levels of Activity			
	Ideal *100%*	*Practical* *90%*	*Normal* *80%*	*Expected Actual* *70%*
Total costs				
Variable cost	$1,604,000	$1,443,600	$1,283,200	$1,122,800
Fixed cost	1,612,800	1,612,800	1,612,800	1,612,800
Total	$3,216,800	$3,056,400	$2,896,000	$2,735,600
Units	200,000	180,000	160,000	140,000
Unit costs				
Variable	$ 8.02	$ 8.02	$ 8.02	$ 8.02
Fixed	8.06	8.96	10.08	11.52
Total overhead rate	$16.08	$16.98	$18.10	$19.54

as easily be at 80 percent as 70 percent, which will result in a much lower overhead rate.

The exhibit illustrates the significant variation in the fixed production overhead rate per direct labor hour as the capacity level increases. Obviously, the higher the capacity level, the lower the fixed overhead rate; the lower the capacity level, the higher the fixed rate. Therefore, if actual production activity differs from the estimated activity, more or less fixed overhead costs will be applied than were anticipated.

IDLE CAPACITY AND EXCESS CAPACITY

Idle capacity is the temporary nonuse of facilities resulting from a decrease in the demand for a company's products or services. It is a short-term condition that can be corrected when the company receives additional customer orders. **Excess capacity,** on the other hand, is due to greater capacity than can normally be used. It will not be corrected in the near future. This excess will normally be identified with specific plant and equipment.

Excess capacity may have occurred because management acquired larger facilities than needed simply because it is more economical in the long run to provide for expected future needs at the time the facilities are available for acquisition. There are also cases in which a company acquires facilities to meet expected demand only to find that the demand does not materialize. For example, a company doing business with the Department of Defense may acquire facilities in anticipation of receiving a major aerospace contract, but the government cancels the program of which this contract is a part, leaving the company with excess facilities. Or a hospital might increase its bed capacity by adding a new wing to the existing building and then find a long-run decrease in patient activity.

Neither internal purposes nor external financial reporting[6] requires any specific capacity concept. The basic treatment that has evolved is that, under circumstances in which significant excess capacity exists, costs related to the excess capacity are written off as a loss during the period. Because idle capacity results from a temporary situation, its costs are generally included in the cost of products and services.

Example Analysis

For purposes of analyzing unused capacity, assume that a plant has a practical capacity of 800,000 units a year. However, only 560,000 units were produced:

Practical capacity	800,000 units
Actual production	560,000 units
Unused capacity	240,000 units

Further analysis shows the following:

Practical capacity	800,000		
		200,000	Excess
Normal or expected capacity	600,000		
		40,000	Idle
Actual production	560,000		

The foregoing example shows 240,000 units of unused capacity consisting of 200,000 in excess and 40,000 in idle capacity. The idle capacity is accounted for as part of product costs. If specific plant or equipment is excess, then all associated costs are expensed.

---

[6] AICPA, "Inventory Cost Basis," *Accounting Research Bulletin 43*, "Restatement and Revision of Accounting Research Bulletins Nos. 1–42" (New York, 1952), Chapter 4, paragraph 5.

If the company produces at the selected capacity level, all of the overhead cost will be charged to products. When actual production falls short of the capacity level selected, some of the overhead will not be applied to production. The underapplied overhead becomes part of the costs charged to inventories and costs of goods sold if the amount is significant. Otherwise, the amount is simply written off to cost of goods sold.

OVERHEAD RATES

Overhead rates are the result of a division:

$$\text{Overhead rate} = \frac{\text{Overhead cost}}{\text{Activity measure}}$$

It is important that there be a logical and reasonable relationship between the numerator (overhead cost) and the denominator (activity). Such a relationship depends on homogeneity and causal or beneficial characteristics.

Homogeneity

The overhead costs gathered together for the rate calculation are said to be a **cost pool.** The amounts charged to a cost pool should be reasonably similar in nature. Vastly dissimilar costs should not be added together in one cost pool; for example, costs such as the fork lift depreciation related to the Baltimore Plant and the overtime for the Los Angeles plant should not be in a cost pool. An allocation that combines depreciation from Baltimore and overtime from Los Angeles will not be homogeneous because there is little likelihood of a common cause for both costs.

Instead, as much as possible, the overhead costs used for an overhead rate should be alike, which is called **homogeneity.** Thus, the variable overhead related to a particular type of machine, such as metal cutters, located in a particular place, such as the Baltimore plant, would be homogeneous with respect to products or services produced with the metal cutter.

Complete homogeneity is an ideal that cannot be achieved in practice, but the concept is useful for selecting meaningful allocation approaches. The determination that a particular cost pool is homogeneous or not relies heavily on the choice of the denominator, the activity measure, used in the overhead rate calculation.

Causal or Beneficial Relationship

A **measure of activity** is needed to represent the work performed by a production department. The best measure is the one that most closely relates to the production overhead cost as the activity increases and decreases. In concept we are asking the question: "What activities or events drive our overhead costs up or down?" Thus, measures of activity are also called **cost drivers** by contemporary writers and accountants. Under this concept, costs do not just happen as a result of activity, but the activity *drives* the costs up or down. Therefore, the accountant's task and contribution to the organization is to find those activities and events that drive overhead cost and to use those activities or events as the basis for allocation.

SELECTING AN ACTIVITY MEASURE

Some reasonable causal or beneficial relationship should exist between the costs accumulated in production overhead accounts to be allocated, the measure of activity selected, and the products or services to which the costs will be allocated. Simply stated, *the activity related to the product or services is the reason overhead costs increase.*

Activity and Departmental Rates

It is easy to say that we are looking for the reasons why overhead costs increase. However, there is an interrelationship between the activity measure identified and the use of factory-wide (plant-wide) or departmental rates. For example, if a company uses direct labor hours as a measure of activity, we would expect overhead costs to consist primarily or exclusively of costs that support direct workers. Such costs may include supervision and provision of work places, as well as travel, training, and fringe benefits of workers. However, the use of plant-wide or departmental rates depends on the diversity of products and services and on the diversity of operations or tasks in the production process of each product. For example, the Sonagraph and MRU are two very different products for Lifeview, Inc. This suggests that a plant-wide rate would result in distorting the overhead allocations to the individual product lines.

Examples of differences that can occur in using plant-wide rates and departmental rates are discussed in connection with individual measures of activity below. Other approaches to developing overhead rates will be mentioned later in the chapter.

Measures of Activity

Although there are many potential measures of activity available for production overhead, we will illustrate the most common ones here:

1. Units of production.
2. Direct labor dollars.
3. Direct labor hours.
4. Machine hours.
5. Product flow time.
6. Transactions.

Other measures of activity that might be used in specific production settings are presented in Exhibit 8–3. Although the list is not exhaustive, it indicates that there are many plausible measures of activity.

Units of Production.   **Units of production** is the total quantity of all products or services produced. It is an easy measure to use because unit data are routinely accumulated within the cost accounting system. It is appropriate if a single product

EXHIBIT 8–3   Other Measures of Activity

Measure	Appropriate for Allocating to
Material costs	Products when most overhead caused by materials cost
Number of products	Plants with varying number of products
Space occuppied	Bulky products
Wait time	Expensive or bulky products
Move time	Heavy or bulky products
Distance traveled	Expensive or bulky products
Setup time	Products that vary on setup time
Number of documents	Products requiring many documents
Number of unique parts	Products requiring many parts
Number of suppliers	Products requiring many suppliers
Number of customers	Products differ in number or nature of customers purchasing
Number of accounts	Products requiring more or less recordkeeping
Engineering changes	Products redesigned frequently

is manufactured, a simple production process is involved, or the products are homogeneous. As long as there is a close causal or beneficial relationship between units produced and the production overhead cost, the activity measure of overhead allocation to production will be adequate.

When the products are significantly different, this measure has the potential for distorting allocations of overhead costs to products. For example, the Lifeview sonagraph and the MRU are very different products requiring very different production support and, thus, they should not be added together for a unit measure of activity.

A units-of-production measure is useful to some service organizations. For example, health-care institutions often use the number of patients staying in the hospital each day (called *a patient day*); marketing companies use the number of sales calls made or the number of sales made; colleges and universities use the number of students enrolled in their programs or the number of credit hours generated.

Direct Labor Costs or Dollars.   One of the oldest and probably most popular measures of volume is a **direct labor dollar.** Direct labor dollars (the terms *cost* and *dollars* are used interchangeably) for a measure of volume assumes that higher-paid workers incur a larger share of overhead costs than the lower-paid workers. This would be true when the more highly paid, better-trained workers operate the expensive, sophisticated machinery and require greater support efforts. A case can also be made for using direct labor dollars when the overhead costs include a significant amount of employee benefits that are based on a percentage of employees' salary or base compensation. The direct labor dollar measure is not appropriate when low-skill workers are using highly automated, expensive equipment and highly paid workers are causing little overhead.

Example analysis.   In the Lifeview, Inc., business problem, the low-paid workers were producing the sonagraphs and using the very expensive automated equipment. The high-paid designers and engineers and skilled workers were involved with the production of the MRU. These workers have less associated overhead cost per dollar of labor cost.

Overhead rates were 300 percent of direct labor dollars as computed by:

$$\frac{\text{Total production overhead}}{\text{Direct labor dollars}} = \frac{\$49,500,000}{\$16,500,000} = 300\%$$

Overhead cost was applied to products on the basis of 300 percent of direct labor costs. The following costs of goods sold occurred for the two product lines:

	Product Line		
	Sonagraph	*MRU*	*Totals*
Materials cost	$40.0	$24.0	$ 64.0
Labor cost	2.5	14.0	16.5
Overhead cost	7.5	42.0	49.5
Total costs of sales	$50.0	$80.0	$130.0

Neither the overhead cost nor the labor dollars are homogeneous for Lifeview, Inc. The causal or beneficial link between total direct labor dollars and total overhead is somewhat tenuous because it depends on the proportions of items produced each period.

After careful analysis of the detailed overhead records, Walt Johnson, the controller at Lifeview, concluded that the departmental overhead associated with the sonagraph line was $32.5 million and with the MRU line of products, $17 million. Thus, the total cost of sales should have been:

	Sonagraph	MRU	Costs of Products
Materials cost	$40.0	$24.0	$ 64.0
Labor cost	2.5	14.0	16.5
Overhead cost	32.5	17.0	49.5
Total costs of sales	$75.0	$55.0	$130.0

Overhead cost of $25 million was incorrectly charged to MRUs when this cost related to sonagraphs.

The approach taken here is called the calculation of *departmental rates* because an overhead rate is calculated for each production department. If overhead rates are computed for an entire plant, as was done by Lifeview, they are called *plant-wide rates*. Departmental rates are superior in concept because departments are more homogeneous in their costs and activities than an entire plant.

If departmental overhead is to be applied on the basis of direct labor cost, then the rates for these two product lines would be:

	Sonagraph	MRU
Overhead cost	$32.5	$17.0
Direct labor cost	$ 2.5	$14.0
Overhead rates	1,300%	121.43%

Both rates are materially different from 300 percent. Consequently, decisions made on the basis of the resulting product cost information are likely to be different.

If we compare product costs, we can see dramatic differences. For example, consider the model 3000 Sonagraph, which requires $2,100 in direct labor:

	Plant-Wide Rates	Departmental Rates
Materials	$16,000	$16,000
Labor	2,100	2,100
Overhead	(300%) 6,300	(1,300%) 27,300
Total	$24,400	$44,662

Similar results, although less dramatic, occur for the model 2000, which has $200 in direct labor costs:

	Plant-Wide Rates	Departmental Rates
Materials	$6,400	$6,400
Labor	200	200
Overhead	(300%) 600	(1,300%) 2,600
Total	$6,800	$9,200

As demonstrated here, care must be taken that each overhead cost pool is homogeneous with respect to the measure of activity. As we will discover shortly, these measures of cost for models 2000 and 3000 are distorted because the direct labor cost is small and causes little of the overhead cost.

The direct labor dollar measure is easy to use, economical, and simple. All requisite data are available from payroll summaries without further recordkeeping. However, there are concerns with this measure. Production overhead costs represent amounts for resources consumed over a period of time and by many types of activities. For example, heat, light, power, insurance, rent, and property taxes usually relate to time periods. Thus, the use of this measure charges more overhead for higher-paid workers when, in fact, much of the overhead results merely from the use of facilities and the handling of activity. Thus, for some settings, overhead cost is not primarily caused by direct labor and therefore overhead charges based on direct labor dollars in these settings distort the allocations.

Direct Labor Hours.   Applying production overhead as a rate per **direct labor hour** assumes that direct labor hours is the primary factor associated with overhead cost increases or decreases. This measure is easy to use and is ideal when the central factor in operations is labor time. Thus, two tasks or operations requiring the same labor time are charged the same amount of overhead, even though the workers themselves may receive different rates of pay. When different pay rates accurately reflect different skills, quality, or speeds of operation, however, a factor other than labor time is generally appropriate.

Total direct labor hours are known from payroll records. In most accounting systems that means the number of hours is already compiled by departments, jobs, and products. Therefore, direct labor hours are available and easy to use.

Machine Hours.   If a plant or a department is highly automated, **machine hours** may be an adequate measure of activity for overhead allocation. Overhead costs in this situation predominantly relate to equipment utilization, such as repairs and maintenance, depreciation, insurance, and property taxes. Also, in any capital-intensive environment, labor and other costs may be significantly different from one machine to another. For example, one operator cares for two or more machines simultaneously, and a single machine elsewhere might require several operators.

Example analysis.   The Sonagraph Department has $32.5 million in overhead costs of which $15 million has been attributed by the engineering staff primarily to the operation of automatic and semiautomatic equipment. The model 2000 requires an average of 16 machine hours per unit, and the normal annual volume is 2,000 units. The model 3000 requires an average 20 hours per unit, and the normal volume is 1,000 units. The normal volume of machine time and the corresponding overhead rate is calculated as:

	Normal Volume	*Machine Hours*	*Totals*
Sonagraph Model 2000	2,000 units	15	300,000
Model 3000	1,000 units	20	200,000
Total activity measure			500,000

$$\text{Overhead rate} = \$15,000,000/500,000 = \underline{\$30.00}$$

The product cost for each of the models would include machine time overhead cost of:

| Model 2000 | 15 hours @ $30 | $4,500 |
| Model 3000 | 20 hours @ 30 | 6,000 |

The same issues of a plant-wide rate versus departmental rates apply here but are not illustrated because the concerns were illustrated in the section on direct labor dollars.

Product Flow Time.   **Product flow time** is the time it takes to convert raw inputs into the final products sold to a customer. Flow time comprises productive time, move time, and wait time. The slower the product flow time, the greater potential for higher inventories in the plant because of move time and wait time. It would be best if the flow time were equal to the productive time.

In some production settings, overhead cost is primarily caused by the handling and movement of heavy, bulky objects, each of which requires much paperwork and attention. In these cases, flow time will be an appropriate measure of activity. For example, the longer products are in the factory, the larger the factory has to be and the more people are required to move, test, count, and keep track of the inventory.

If production overhead is charged on the basis of flow time, then a product that is in the plant 20 days will be charged twice as much overhead cost as a product that is in the plant only 10 days.

Example analysis.   The Sonagraph Department has $32.5 million in overhead costs of which $8 million has been identified by the engineering staff as primarily related to product flow time. The model 2000 requires two days in the plant on average, and the normal volume is 2,000 units. The model 3000 requires six days in the plant, and the normal volume is 1,000 units.

The normal volume of product flow time and overhead rate can then be calculated:

	Normal Volume	*Flow Time*	*Totals*
Sonagraph Model 2000	2,000 units	2 days	4,000 days
Model 3000	1,000 units	6 days	6,000 days
Total activity measure			10,000 days

$$\text{Overhead rate} = \$8,000,000/10,000 = \$800 \text{ per day}$$

The product cost for each of the models would include flow time overhead cost of:

Model 2000	2 days @ $800	$1,600
Model 3000	6 days @ $800	4,800

Transactions.   A **product transaction** occurs every time people must intervene in the process related to the product. The number of transactions relates to the number of products dealt with, the number of parts in each product, the number of times a product must be moved, inspected, packed, unpacked, looked at, repaired, or thought about. The more transactions, the more direct and indirect workers required, the more space, telephones, paper, computer time, and other overhead-related items are needed. Thus, in some production settings, the number of product transactions drives the amount of production overhead cost.

Example analysis.   The Sonagraph Department has $32.5 million in overhead costs of which $9.5 million has been attributed by the engineering staff primarily to transactions and interactions of people related to products. The model 2000 requires an average of 200 transactions, and the normal annual volume is 2,000 units. The model 3000 requires an average 225 transactions, and the normal volume is 1,000 units. The normal volume of transactions and overhead rate is then calculated as:

	Normal Volume	*Transactions*	*Totals*
Sonagraph Model 2000	2,000 units	200	400,000
Model 3000	1,000 units	225	225,000
Total activity measure			625,000

$$\text{Overhead rate} = \$9,500,000/625,000 = \$15.20$$

The product cost for each of the models would include transaction overhead cost of:

Model 2000	200 Transactions @ $15.20	$3,040
Model 3000	225 Transactions @ $15.20	3,420

Summary of overhead allocations by product:

	Model 2000	Model 3000
Using Plant-Wide Labor Rates		
Total overhead costs	$ 600	$ 6,300
Using Department Labor Rates		
Total overhead costs	$2,600	$17,329
Using Multiple Allocation Bases		
Machine usage	$4,500	$ 6,000
Flow time	1,600	4,800
Transactions	3,040	3,420
Total overhead costs	$9,140	$14,220

LEVELS OF OVERHEAD RATES

In the foregoing discussions, we have assumed that the production overhead rates are either plant-wide or departmental. Other approaches may be used for developing overhead rates in varying forms and in greater detail, depending on the particular circumstances of the company and its management philosophy. For example, separate rates have been used for different cost centers within departments, different machines for each product class, categories of costs (material-related, labor-related, or facility-related costs, for example), and cost behavior (variable and fixed). It is not uncommon for companies to allocate some overhead costs on a plant-wide basis, some on a departmental basis, and some on the basis of machine time, flow time, or transaction. The important point is that the company analyze its situation to identify the causal or beneficial relationship and the associated cost drivers. The results can take many forms.

SUMMARY

Over the years, production overhead costs have increased in significance as an element of costs assigned to units of products and services. Production overhead is inherently different from direct material and direct labor costs because it relates to units of output indirectly. As a result, a need arises for differentiating between direct and indirect costs. The major distinction is traceability—seeing, feeling, sensing—of the cost element to individual units of output. Costs that can be traced directly to and specifically identified with a product or service are direct costs. The remaining production costs are overhead costs. Allocations may be direct, indirect, or arbitrary. Arbitrary allocations should be avoided when possible.

Charging of production overhead to work performed is most often accomplished with a predetermined overhead rate based on budgeted costs and a budgeted capacity level. Selection of an appropriate capacity level becomes extremely important as the fixed cost elements in overhead increase in relative proportion to the total overhead costs. The common capacity concepts are ideal, practical, normal, and expected actual capacity. Idle capacity is the temporary nonuse of facilities for lack of demand. Excess capacity is having greater capacity than will reasonably be used in the near future.

An additional consideration in developing a rate is whether a plant-wide or a departmental overhead rate is appropriate for the company's operations.

The activity measure selected should be the primary reason for the increase or decrease in overhead costs. Activity measures may be units produced, direct labor dollars, direct labor hours, machine hours, product flow time, transactions, or numerous other measures.

PROBLEMS FOR REVIEW

PROBLEM A

The Sultra D Corp. manufactures electric motors that vary from 2 horsepower to about 200 horsepower. A large electric motor is expensive because it uses a lot of copper in the motor core and in the electrical magnets that provide the power. The smaller motors are produced on a different line than the larger motors because the equipment required for economic production is very different. The total costs by department are:

	Motor		
	Small	*Large*	*Totals*
Direct materials	$360,000	$320,000	$ 680,000
Direct labor	45,000	155,000	200,000
Production overhead	576,000	100,000	676,000
Total costs	$981,000	$575,000	$1,556,000
Unit volume	1,800	200	2,000

REQUIRED

a. Using the plant-wide rate concept:
  1. And an overhead cost application rate based on direct labor cost, compute:
      (a) Average product unit cost for a small motor.
      (b) Average product unit cost for a large motor.
  2. And an overhead cost application rate based on units of production, compute:
      (a) Average product unit cost for a small motor.
      (b) Average product unit cost for a large motor.
b. Using the departmental rate concept:
  1. And an overhead cost application rate based on direct labor cost, compute:
      (a) Average product unit cost for a small motor.
      (b) Average product unit cost for a large motor.
  2. And an overhead cost application rate based on units of production, compute:
      (a) Average product unit cost for a small motor.
      (b) Average product unit cost for a large motor.
c. For each of the allocation methods in parts a. and b., compute the total overhead assigned to each of the products.

SOLUTION

The direct costs for each of the products will remain the same no matter how the overhead is allocated. These costs can be found by dividing total direct costs for each department by unit volume:

	Small	*Large*
Direct materials	$200	$1,600
Direct labor	25	775
Total direct costs	$225	$2,375

a. Using the plant-wide rate concept:
  1. And an overhead cost application rate based on direct labor cost, compute unit costs:

	Plant-Wide	
Total overhead	$676,000	
Total labor cost	$200,000	
Overhead application rate		338.00%

	(a)	*(b)*
	Small	*Large*
Direct materials	$200.00	$1,600.00
Direct labor	25.00	775.00
Overhead applied 338%	84.50	2,619.50
Total unit cost	$309.50	$4,994.50

2. And an overhead cost application rate based on units of production, compute unit costs:

	Plant-Wide	
Total overhead	$676,000	
Total units produced	2,000	
Overhead application rate	$338.00 per unit	

	(a) Small	(b) Large
Direct materials	$200.00	$1,600.00
Direct labor	25.00	775.00
Overhead applied	338.00	338.00
Total unit cost	$563.00	$2,713.00

b. Using the departmental rate concept:
   1. And an overhead cost application rate based on direct labor cost, compute:

	Small	Large
Total overhead	$576,000	$100,000
Total labor cost	45,000	155,000
Overhead application rate	1,280%	64.52%

		(a) Small		(b) Large
Direct materials		$200.00		$1,600.00
Direct labor		25.00		775.00
Overhead applied	1,280%	320.00	64.52%	500.00
Total unit cost		$545.00		$2,875.00

   2. And an overhead cost application rate based on units of production, compute:

	Small	Large
Total overhead	$576,000	100,000
Units produced	1,800	200
Overhead application rate	$320	$500 per unit

	(a) Small	(b) Large
Direct materials	$200.00	$1,600.00
Direct labor	25.00	775.00
Overhead applied	320.00	500.00
Total unit cost	$545.00	$2,875.00

c. Total overhead assigned to each product by allocation method.

	Small	Large
Units produced	1,800	200
Overhead allocated using:		
Plant-wide rates, direct labor	$152,100	$523,900
Plant-wide rates, production unit	608,400	67,600
Departmental rates, direct labor	576,000	100,000
Departmental rates, production unit	576,000	100,000

PROBLEMS FOR REVIEW PROBLEM B

The Small Motor Department of Sultra D Corp. has $576,000 in overhead that must be distributed to products. The department produces three sizes of motors with the following activities:

Product	Weight (Pounds)	Parts Per Unit	Unit Volume	Flow Time (Hours)	Product Transactions
SM100	120	16	720	5	50
SM200	400	18	360	20	300
SM300	1,200	30	720	25	100

The direct costs of the three products are:

	SM100	SM200	SM300	Total
Direct material	$72,000	$72,000	$216,000	$360,000
Direct labor	11,250	18,000	15,750	45,000
Total direct costs	$83,250	$90,000	$231,750	$405,000

The total overhead of the department has been estimated by the engineering staff and department supervisor to be related to the following activities:

Activities	Percent	Allocate on
Movement of motors	16	Weight
Handling of parts	20	# of parts
Handling units in process	26	Flow time
Handling transactions	30	Transactions
Related to direct labor cost	8	Direct labor
Total	100	

REQUIRED

a. Allocate overhead to each of the three products based on direct labor costs and compute a cost per unit.

b. Allocate overhead to each of the three products based on the activity measures and compute a cost per unit.

SOLUTION

a. Allocate overhead to each of the three products based on direct labor costs and compute a cost per unit.

Overhead Rate

Total overhead cost	$576,000
Total labor cost	45,000
Overhead application rate	1,280%

Total Costs	SM100	SM200	SM300	Total
Direct material	$ 72,000	$ 72,000	$216,000	$360,000
Direct labor	11,250	18,000	15,750	45,000
Overhead applied	144,000	230,400	201,600	576,000
Total costs	$227,250	$320,400	$433,350	$981,000
Units produced	720	360	720	

Unit costs:

	SM100	SM200	SM300
Direct material	$100.00	$200.00	$300.00
Direct labor	15.63	50.00	21.88
Overhead applied	200.00	640.00	280.00
	$315.63	$890.00	$601.88

b. Allocate overhead to each of the three products based on the activity measures and compute a cost per unit.

1. Compute the overhead costs related to activities:

Movement of motors	16%	$ 92,160
Handling of parts	20%	115,200
Capacity to handle units in process	26%	149,760
Capacity to handle transaction	30%	172,800
Related to direct labor cost	8%	46,080
Total overhead	100%	$576,000

2. Start with the raw activity measures per unit:

	SM100	SM200	SM300
Unit volume	720	360	720
Weight	120	400	1,200
Parts	16	18	30
Flow time	5	20	25
Transactions	50	300	100
Direct labor cost	15.63	50.00	21.88

3. Compute the total activity as the product of unit volume and measure:

	SM100	SM200	SM300	Totals
Weight	86,400	144,000	864,000	1,094,400
Parts	11,520	6,480	21,600	39,600
Flow time	3,600	7,200	18,000	28,800
Transactions	36,000	108,000	72,000	216,000
Direct labor (given)	11,250	18,000	15,750	45,000

4. Compute the cost per unit of activity measure:

	Overhead	Activity	OH Rates
Weight	$ 92,160	1,094,400	$0.0842 per pound
Parts	115,200	39,600	$2.9091 per part
Flow time	149,760	28,800	$5.20 per hour
Transactions	172,800	216,000	$0.80 per transaction
Direct labor	46,080	45,000	102.40% direct labor

5. Compute Unit Costs

SM100	Measure	Rate	Unit Cost
Direct materials			$100.000
Direct labor			15.625
Applied overhead based on:			
Weight	120	$0.0842	10.105
Parts	16	$2.9091	46.545
Flow time	5	$5.2000	26.000
Transactions	50	$0.8000	40.000
Direct labor	$15.63	102.40%	16.000
Total unit cost			$254.275

SM200	Measure	Rate	Unit Cost
Direct materials			$200.000
Direct labor			50.000
Applied overhead based on:			
Weight	400	$0.0842	33.684
Parts	18	$2.9091	52.364
Flow time	20	$5.2000	104.000
Transactions	300	$0.8000	240.000
Direct labor	$50.00	102.40%	51.200
Total unit cost			$731.248

SM300	Measure	Rate	Unit Cost
Direct materials			$300.000
Direct labor			21.875
Applied overhead based on:			
Weight	1,200	$0.0842	101.053
Parts	30	$2.9091	87.273
Flow time	25	$5.2000	130.000
Transactions	100	$0.8000	80.000
Direct labor	$21.88	102.40%	22.400
Total unit cost			$742.601

KEY TERMS AND CONCEPTS

Production overhead cost (264)
Direct costing (264)
Variable costing (264)
Absorption costing (264)
Cost allocation (264)
Cost objective (264)
Traceability (267)
Predetermined overhead rate (269)
Theoretical, ideal, or maximum capacity (270)
Practical capacity (271)
Normal capacity (271)
Expected actual capacity (271)

Idle capacity (272)
Excess capacity (272)
Homogeneity (273)
Cost Pool (273)
Measure of activity (273)
Cost drivers (273)
Units of production (274)
Direct labor dollar (275)
Direct labor hours (277)
Machine hours (277)
Product flow time (277)
Product transactions (278)

ADDITIONAL READINGS

Ayers, James B. "Understanding Your Cost Drivers—The Key to Disciplined Planning." *Journal of Cost Management,* Fall 1988, pp. 6–15.
Brimson, James A. "Technology Accounting." *Management Accounting,* March 1989, pp. 47–53.
Carman-Stone, Marie Sandra. "Unabsorbed Overhead: What to Do When Contracts Are Cancelled." *Management Accounting,* April 1987, pp. 55–57.
Fremgen, James M., and Shu S. Liao. *The Allocation of Corporate Indirect Costs.* New York: National Association of Accountants, 1981.
Johnson, H. Thomas. "Managing Costs: An Outmoded Philosophy." *Manufacturing Engineering,* May 1989, pp. 42–46.
Kammlade, John G.; Pravesh Mehra; and Terrence R. Ozan. "A Process Approach to Overhead Management." *Journal of Cost Management,* Fall 1989, pp. 5–10.
McGee, Robert W. "Cost Allocation: The Sound and the Fury." *CFO,* June 1985, pp. 53–54, and 62.
———. "Calculating Inventory Costs after Tax Reform." *CFO,* January 1988, pp. 53–58.
Roth, Harold P., and A. Faye Borthick. "Getting Closer to Real Product Costs." *Management Accounting,* May 1989, pp. 28–33.
Shank, John K., and Vijay Govindarajan. "The Perils of Cost Allocation Based on Production Volumes." *Accounting Horizons,* December 1988, pp. 71–79.
Zimmerman, Jerold L. "The Costs and Benefits of Cost Allocation." *The Accounting Review,* July 1979, pp. 504–521.

REVIEW QUESTIONS

1. What are the criteria for distinguishing between a direct and an indirect cost?
2. What is a direct cost allocation as opposed to an indirect cost allocation?
3. List three types of indirect costs with respect to products.

4. Identify the two levels used to allocate production overhead costs to products.
5. What is the concept of traceability?
6. List the four steps required in establishing a predetermined overhead rate.
7. Give three reasons why overhead rates should be predetermined rather than based on actual overhead.
8. Define the four concepts of capacity and differentiate among them.
9. What is the effect of using an ideal capacity concept rather than a normal capacity concept on the resulting overhead rate?
10. How does idle capacity differ from excess capacity?
11. Why should costs be homogeneous in a cost pool? Why not have very different costs added together?
12. What are the criteria for selecting a measure of activity?
13. When is the units of production measure an appropriate activity measure for establishing overhead rates?
14. When would it be appropriate to use direct labor dollars as a basis for applying production overhead?
15. Why are departmental rates often more justifiable than plant-wide rates?
16. What factors would you consider in determining whether to adopt departmental rates for applying overhead rather than using a single plant-wide overhead rate?
17. What times are included in product flow time? What is the relationship between product flow time and inventory?

DISCUSSION QUESTIONS

18. Explain how an indirect cost to a product or service can also be a direct cost to a department.
19. If a company uses cost-based selling prices in a business that is seasonal or cyclical, which capacity level would be most appropriate?
20. Why should overhead cost be allocated to products and services at all? Why not treat all production overhead as an expense?
21. In highly automated plants, the direct labor cost is insignificant. What is the effect of allocating overhead on the basis of direct labor cost in a highly automated plant?
22. An inherent weakness in using an input such as labor hours, product flow time, or product transactions as a measure of activity is that it incorporates inefficiencies. What might correct this weakness?

EXERCISES

8–1. Terms and Concepts. Match the term or concept with a sentence below.

——— *a.* Excess capacity
——— *b.* Expected capacity
——— *c.* General administrative costs
——— *d.* Idle capacity
——— *e.* Normal capacity
——— *f.* Practical capacity
——— *g.* Production overhead costs
——— *h.* Theoretical capacity

1. Associated with supporting the organization as a whole.
2. Level of activity at which a plant can operate realistically if the company has sufficient orders to operate at that level.
3. Greater capacity than can reasonably be utilized over the coming years.
4. Temporary unutilized facilities due to a decline in demand for the organization's product or service.
5. Average volume over several years.
6. Lacks traceability.

7. Level of productive activity under perfect conditions.
8. Management's estimate of volume for the upcoming period.

(B. George)

8–2. Capacity Costs.   The hospital administrator at Clines Corner General was concerned about the laboratory overhead rates being charged to insurance companies and the state government. She asked the laboratory supervisor and the controller to study the cost and find out why it has been increasing. The supervisor indicates that the laboratory overhead incurred was $416,000, which was well within the budget of $420,000 (of this, $210,000 is considered fixed). The controller indicates that the normal capacity of 70 percent or 280,000 was comparable with similar institutions. The hospital administrator was concerned that the laboratory was not working at planned practical capacity of 360,000 tests per year. After all, "280,000 tests is far less than we built the lab to handle. Maybe we made a mistake in planning it." The laboratory is actually running at a rate of 255,000 tests for the current year.

REQUIRED:
  a. Determine the predetermined variable and fixed overhead rates at 255,000 units, 280,000 units, and 360,000 units assuming that the budget is based on the normal capacity.
  b. The insurance companies are charged the actual overhead rate, which is actual cost divided by actual volume. Explain to the hospital administrator why the actual rate differs from the normal rate.

8–3. Concepts of Capacity.   Beth Lewis, vice president of Pony Enterprises, is upset with a significant increase in the per unit costs of the molding department. She has called in the department supervisor and the controller to find out why the increase occurred and what can be done to reduce costs in the future. The controller said that normal capacity is at 80 percent (30,000 machine hours) with budgeted overhead costs of $240,000 ($150,000 is fixed cost). The vice president expressed concern that the department was not operating at practical capacity of 90 percent. In defense of himself, the molding department supervisor said the department had an actual capacity of 27,000 machine hours with variable and fixed overhead costs in line with the budgeted amounts.

REQUIRED:
  a. Determine the variable and fixed overhead rates at 27,000 hours, 30,000 hours, and at 90 percent capacity.
  b. Explain why the per unit costs would have increased even though actual budgeted overhead costs equaled the budget.

8–4. Production Overhead Bases.   The McCorquedale Products Co. manufactures blenders and mixers used in restaurants. The following data were taken from the budget of the McCorquedale Co.:

Direct materials	$ 900,000
Direct labor (50,000 Hours)	300,000
Marketing manager's salary	40,000
Administrative salaries	60,000
Factory supplies	30,000
Office supplies: Administrative	10,000
Office supplies: Factory	20,000
Office supplies: Sales	15,000
Indirect labor	150,000
Real estate taxes: Factory	30,000
Depreciation: Administration	4,000
Depreciation: Plant	270,000
Depreciation: Sales automobiles	30,000
Depreciation: Plant equipment	400,000
Total	$2,259,000

Machine hours are budgeted at 45,000, product flow hours are expected to be 900,000, and product transactions are expected to be 4,500,000.

REQUIRED:

a. Determine the factory overhead rates on each of the following bases. Round rates to two decimal places.
1. Machine hours.
2. Direct labor dollar.
3. Product flow hours.
4. Product transactions.

b. Calculate the over- or underapplied overhead for each of the bases in (1) above assuming the following actual results: Actual overhead, $890,000; actual machine hours, 46,200; actual direct labor dollars, $270,000; actual product flow hours, 850,000; and actual product transactions, 4,800,000.

8–5. Plant-Wide and Departmental Rates.   The Paint Farm finishes furniture for local manufacturers. The furniture is first sanded and then painted. The following information is available regarding the operations of the Paint Farm during February 19x2:

(R. McCracken)

	Sanding	*Painting*	*Total*
Direct labor	$ 37,000	$ 26,500	$ 63,500
Factory supplies	13,000	8,000	21,000
Direct materials	33,000	45,000	78,000
Depreciation—Office	12,000	16,600	28,600
Supervisory salaries	21,000	18,900	39,900
Depreciation—Factory	28,000	33,000	61,000
Office supplies	3,500	3,500	7,000
	$147,500	$151,500	$299,000

REQUIRED:

a. Rounding to the nearest percent, compute production overhead rates per direct labor dollar for:
1. Each department.
2. Plant wide.

b. Compute the overhead charge on a job requiring $86 of direct labor in sanding and $32 of direct labor in painting using rates for:
1. Each department.
2. Plant wide.

8–6. Measures of Activity.   Jamaica Basketweaving, Inc., has three departments used in making baskets: cutting, coloring, and weaving. Data (monetary amounts in pounds sterling) for the fall season are expected to be:

(K. Craig)

Dept.	*Activity Measure*	*Measure*	*Overhead (Lb. Sterling)*
Cutting	Labor Hours	26,000	13,000
Coloring	Machine hours	16,000	4,000
Weaving	Direct labor sterling	145,000	29,000
Total overhead in pounds sterling			46,000

REQUIRED:

a. Compute overhead rates for each of the departments.

b. Batch #17 is produced for Queen's Market, London. The batch required 4,050 hours of labor to cut, 9,700 hours in the coloring vats, and 19,000 pounds sterling of direct labor in weaving. Determine the amount of overhead, by department, charged to Batch #17.

8–7. Machine Hours, Departmental and Plant-Wide Rates. The Tiny-Tot Hot-Rod Company manufactures small battery-powered cars that young children (up to 80 pounds) can drive around. There are two models. One is shaped like a sleek sports car (the Vetalike) and the other looks like a standard mid-1950s automobile (the '57). Both products sell well. There are three basic departments in the production area: fabrication, assembly, and painting. The following budgets have been estimated for the current year:

	Overhead	Machine Hours
Fabrication	$600,000	20,000
Assembly	200,000	10,000
Painting	32,000	10,000
	$832,000	40,000

The estimated machine hours for a batch of 10 of each of the cars are:

	Vetalike	'57
Fabrication	10	18
Assembly	15	8
Painting	7	4
Totals	32	30

(K. Turicchi)

REQUIRED:
a. Compute production overhead rates:
  1. Plant-wide rate.
  2. Departmental rate for each of the three departments.
b. Compute the estimated overhead cost per batch of each of the two toy cars using:
  1. Plant-wide rate.
  2. Departmental rate for each of the three departments.

8–8. Company and Divisional Rates. The Logan Laboratories does contract research for defense and commercial applications. It has 1,600 employees, many of whom have advanced scientific and engineering degrees. It bills contract research on the basis of direct equipment, direct hours, and an overhead charge. The overhead charge rate has been set at $33.07 per hour to cover the entire laboratory, but some customers and government agencies are questioning this rate as being too high. The lab has six major project areas and support computer and ancillary facilities located in six buildings in the outskirts of Denver, Colorado. The hours and overhead by department are:

	Hours (thousand)	Overhead (thousand)
Air foils	800	$ 13,120
Solar	160	2,112
Laser	496	18,352
Atomic	2,400	120,960
Fluids	400	3,760
Mechanical	1,584	34,848
Totals	5,840	$193,152

REQUIRED:
a. Compute the division overhead rates for the six divisions.
b. Find the estimated overhead charge for the following two projects using the laboratory-wide rate and again using the division rates:
  Project #89004: Four Corners Solar Power Project. Funded by the regional power authority (30 percent) and U.S. Department of Energy (70 percent). During 19x8, this project absorbed 28,200 hours of Solar Division time.
  Project #88097: XR7 Missile Guidance. Funded by the Air Force (100 percent). During

19x8, this project absorbed 47,520 hours of which 23,200 were in the Laser Division and 24,320 were in the Mechanical Division.

PROBLEMS

8–9. Production Overhead Bases.   The Smooth-Finish Company makes hand sanders of various sizes for home use. The following planning or budget data were acquired from the accounting department of Smooth-Finish:

Direct materials	$ 500,000
Direct labor (20,000 hours)	300,000
Supervisor salaries	50,000
Office salaries	30,000
Administrative salaries	70,000
Sales salaries	20,000
Factory supplies	15,000
Office supplies	25,000
Sales supplies	10,000
Indirect labor	100,000
Depreciation: Factory	225,000
Depreciation: Office	135,000
Depreciation: Factory equip.	375,000
Total	$1,855,000

Machine hours are estimated to be 40,000.

(K. Turicchi)

REQUIRED:
a. Determine the amount of the planned factory overhead.
b. Determine factory overhead rates for each of the following bases:
   1. Direct labor hours.
   2. Direct labor dollars.
   3. Machine hours.
   4. Material dollars.
c. With each of the four rates listed in part (b), calculate the over- or underapplied overhead with the following actual cost and hourly amounts:

Factory overhead	$800,000
Machine hours	42,000
Direct labor (20,500 hours)	$320,000
Direct materials	$516,000

8–10. Identification of Idle Capacity.   Salih Ceramics Company manufactures decorated ceramic dishes (plates, saucers, cups, pitchers, and so forth) to customer specifications. Thus, the operations are run under a job order system. Each job is charged the actual costs of direct material and direct labor. Production overhead costs are applied using a predetermined rate. The company uses an expected actual capacity concept for setting the production overhead rate, and the activity measure is direct labor hours.

Salih Ceramics has accumulated the estimated and actual data for 19x8. All work is stated in terms of direct labor hours required for that work:

	Direct Labor Hours
Maximum production capacity	60,000
Practical production capacity	57,000
Normal production capacity	52,000
Expected actual production capacity	53,000
Estimated sales demand for year	51,000
Orders received during the year	44,000

Orders in backlog at beginning of year	5,000
Orders in backlog at end of year	0
Orders produced and delivered during 19x8	46,000
Orders produced during 19x8 but to be delivered in 19x9	3,000

REQUIRED:

a. Determine how many hours represent idle capacity for 19x8.
b. Explain how the costs of idle capacity are handled in the application and analysis of production overhead.

8–11. Company-Wide and Divisional Rates.   Air Tech, Inc., is a manufacturer of automobile air conditioners. It provides units for automobile dealers in Mexico. Because of the flexibility of its design, the units can fit in many makes and models of vehicles. The main products are models Whisper R15 and Vision X15. The Whisper R15 uses some complex fabricated parts, but these have been found to be easy to assemble and test. On the other hand, the Vision X15 uses many standard parts but has a complex assembly and test process.

Air Tech has a number of different processing departments within the manufacturing process. Following are planning data related to four production processes:

	Department Overhead	Machine Hours
Radiator Parts Fabrication	$ 80,000	10,000
Radiator Assembly, Weld, and Test	100,000	20,000
Compressor Parts Fabrication	120,000	10,000
Compressor Assembly and Test	160,000	40,000
	$460,000	80,000

A production batch (10 units of product) has been found to use each of the following hours in these production areas:

(M. Kubinski)

	Whisper R15	Vision X15
Radiator Parts Fabrication	14	8
Radiator Assembly, Weld, and Test	14	34
Compressor Parts Fabrication	16	4
Compressor Assembly and Test	15	33
Total hours per batch	59	79

REQUIRED:

a. Compute production overhead rates:
   1. Plant-wide rate.
   2. Departmental rate for each of the four departments.
b. Compute the estimated overhead cost per batch of each of the two main products using:
   1. Plant-wide rate.
   2. Departmental rate for each of the four departments.

8–12. Plant-Wide and Departmental Rates.   The Stewart Company manufactures the rollers that are included in various types of printing machines. The rollers vary in size from $\frac{1}{4}$ inch to 8 inches in diameter. There are two manufacturing departments: Fabrication and Assembly. The company uses machine hours as the base for allocating production overhead costs to products. The budgeted data for the coming year include the following:

	Fabrication	Assembly	Totals
Machine hours	87,000	33,000	120,000
Overhead	$2,157,600	$277,860	$2,435,460

Consider the machine hours for a batch of 100 of two products:

	Fabrication	*Assembly*	*Totals*
¼″ roller	3	8	11
8″ roller	8	6	14

The prime costs per batch for these two products are:

	¼″ Roller	*8″ Roller*
Materials		
Fabrication	$ 23.70	$ 32.60
Assembly	17.80	22.93
Labor		
Fabrication	47.52	286.72
Assembly	40.96	30.72
Total prime costs	$129.98	$372.97

REQUIRED:

a. Compute the overhead cost per batch of product assuming:
1. Plant-wide production overhead rate.
2. Departmental production overhead rates.
b. Compute the total cost per unit for each of the products assuming:
1. Plant-wide production overhead rate.
2. Departmental production overhead rates.

8–13. Departmental Rates and Overhead Application.   Peterson Laboratories does contract research for pharmaceutical (drug) companies. In the laboratory all of the 16 employees are researchers or research assistants. The laboratory bills contract research on the basis of materials used, labor hours plus an overhead charge, plus a negotiated profit rate. The overhead rate has been set at $27.50 per hour, and some of the contracting agents are questioning this rate as too high. The lab has three research divisions, and the overhead and hours by division are:

(J. Lo)

Division	*Overhead*	*Hours*
Genetic and Biochemical Reactions	$450,000	9,000
Product Testing (FDA Compliance)	240,000	12,000
Product Comparison	300,000	15,000
Totals	$990,000	36,000

REQUIRED:

a. Compute the divisional rates for each of the three divisions.
b. Research contract #251 is for the new pain reliever Serenity. It is estimated that this contract will require 5,000 hours of product testing as is required by the Food and Drug Administration and 3,000 hours of product comparison. Compute the overhead charge for Contract #251 using the laboratory-wide rate of $27.50 and then again using the divisional rates.
c. Research contract #252 is for basic research on splicing genetic material onto the AIDS virus to eventually block the effects of one of the forms of the virus. This contract will occupy one researcher plus an assistant for one year (4,000 hours total). As with all genetic experiments, a complex set of state and federal regulations apply for the safety of the employees and the health and safety of the general public. As a consequence, all work on this contract will be carried out in the Genetic and Biochemical Reactions laboratory, which has very stringent safety and security procedures. Compute the overhead charge for Contract #252 using the laboratory-wide rate of $27.50 and then again using the divisional rates.

8–14. Effect of Overhead Cost on Product Cost.   Fixed production overhead is a significant portion of total cost for Sugeet Precision Tools, Inc. The budgeted overhead costs for the year at several capacity levels are given below.

Machine hours	150,000	200,000	250,000	300,000
Variable overhead	$ 450,000	$ 600,000	$ 750,000	$ 900,000
Fixed overhead	1,500,000	1,500,000	1,500,000	1,500,000
Total overhead	$1,950,000	$2,100,000	$2,250,000	$2,400,000

The plant superintendent is considering two changes that will alter the amount of variable and fixed production overhead costs charged to products. She would like to implement cost-saving technology that would reduce the variable overhead to $2.50 per machine hour. Normal capacity is set at 250,000 machine hours, but the company has operated at 300,000 machine hours for several months. She proposes adjusting production overhead rates to 300,000 machine hours.

The plant superintendent wants to see the effect on product costs and selling prices if the cost-saving technology were implemented and the capacity level were raised to 300,000 machine hours. A representative order that consists of 300 units and requires 70 machine hours will be used to analyze both the present and changed situations. The direct materials and direct labor costs of that order are direct materials, $1,400; direct labor, $500. The company has followed the practice of billing customers at 160 percent of total materials, labor, and production overhead cost.

REQUIRED:
a. Under the present situation, calculate the variable overhead rate and the fixed overhead rate at 250,000 machine hours and 300,000 machine hours.
b. Explain the nature of the cost behavior per unit for variable and fixed production overhead costs in (a) above.
c. Using the representative order, calculate the total cost, unit cost, and unit selling price for each of four alternatives:
   1. Variable overhead cost is $3.00 per machine hour and 250,000 machine hours is the capacity level.
   2. Variable overhead cost is $3.00 per machine hour and 300,000 machine hours is the capacity level.
   3. Variable overhead cost is $2.50 per machine hour and 250,000 machine hours is the capacity level.
   4. Variable overhead cost is $2.50 per machine hour and 300,000 machine hours is the capacity level.

8–15. Idle Capacity. Hayhall-Wertz Metal Products fabricates and machines spare and replacement parts for older, often outdated, equipment based on customer specifications. Overhead is applied to work on the basis of machine hours, and there are 10 machines. The company normally operates five days a week on two 8-hour shifts. Equipment is shut down for 260 hours per year for normal cleaning, maintenance, and repair. Sales demand based on an average over three to five years requires enough work for 34,500 machine hours per year. The expected demand for the current year requires 32,000 machine hours. Budgeted fixed production overhead costs for the year are $1,168,000.

According to the foregoing data, the company has computed four concepts of capacity that could be used in calculating a production overhead rate for the year. These are as follows:

Maximum capacity: 365 days × 16 hours per day × 10 machines		58,400
Practical capacity:		
Maximum capacity		58,400
Less normal downtimes:		
Weekends—104 days × 16 hours × 10 machines	16,640	
Holidays—10 days × 16 hours × 10 machines	1,600	
Cleaning, maintenance, and repairs, etc.	260	18,500
		39,900
Normal capacity:		34,500
Expected actual capacity:		32,000

The choice of capacity base has an effect on how idle capacity is measured and on how the fixed production overhead is applied to the parts produced. Because prices charged customers are cost-based, the concept of capacity selected for allocating fixed overhead costs will also influence the final price charged. Management wants to use a capacity that makes a fair measurement of idle capacity and includes the costs of that capacity in the overhead costs applied to parts.

REQUIRED:

a. Calculate the number of idle machine hours that would exist under each of the four concepts of capacity, assuming the actual capacity utilized is 32,000 machine hours.
b. Calculate the fixed production overhead rate per machine hour for the four capacity levels.
c. Select the concept of capacity that you think should be used for establishing the cost-based prices charged for work performed, and give your reasons for the selection.

8–16. Overhead Rate Revisions.   Upton, Inc., manufactures a line of home furniture. The company's single manufacturing plant consists of the Cutting, Assembly, and Finishing Departments. Upton uses departmental rates for applying manufacturing overhead to production and maintains separate manufacturing overhead control and manufacturing overhead applied accounts for each of the three production departments.

The following predetermined departmental manufacturing overhead rates were calculated for Upton's fiscal year ending May 31, 19x6.

Department	Rate
Cutting	$2.40 per machine hour
Assembly	5.00 per direct labor hour
Finishing	1.60 per direct labor dollar

Information regarding actual operations for Upton's plant for the six months ended November 30, 19x5, is presented below.

	Cutting	Assembly	Finishing
		Department	
Manufacturing overhead costs	$22,600	$56,800	$98,500
Machine hours	10,800	2,100	4,400
Direct labor hours	6,800	12,400	16,500
Direct labor dollars	$40,800	$62,000	$66,000

Based upon this experience and updated projections for the last six months of the fiscal year, Upton revised its operating budget. Projected data regarding manufacturing overhead and operating activity for each department for the six months ending May 31, 19x6, are presented as follows:

	Cutting	Assembly	Finishing
		Department	
Manufacturing overhead costs	$23,400	$57,500	$96,500
Machine hours	9,200	2,000	4,200
Direct labor hours	6,000	13,000	16,000
Direct labor dollars	$36,000	$65,000	$64,000

Diane Potter, Upton's controller, plans to develop revised departmental manufacturing overhead rates that will be more representative of efficient operations for the current fiscal year ending May 31, 19x6. She has decided to combine the actual results for the first six months of the fiscal year with the projections for the next six months to develop the revised departmental application rates. She then plans to adjust the manufacturing overhead-applied accounts for each department through November 19x5 to recognize the revised application rates. The analysis presented below was prepared by Potter from general ledger account balances as of November 30, 19x5.

Account	Direct Material	Direct Labor	Manufacturing Overhead	Account Balance
Work-in-process inventory	$ 53,000	$ 95,000	$ 12,000	$ 160,000
Finished goods	96,000	176,000	48,000	320,000
Cost of goods sold	336,000	604,000	180,000	1,120,000
	$485,000	$875,000	$240,000	$1,600,000

(CMA, adapted)

REQUIRED:

a. Determine the balance of the manufacturing overhead-applied accounts as of November 30, 19x5, before any revision for the:
   1. Cutting Department.
   2. Assembly Department.
   3. Finishing Department.
b. Calculate the revised departmental manufacturing overhead rates that Upton, Inc., should use for the remainder of the fiscal year ending May 31, 19x6.
c. Prepare an analysis that shows how the manufacturing overhead-applied account for each production department of Upton, Inc., should be adjusted as of November 30, 19x5, and prepare the adjusting entry to correct all general ledger accounts that are affected.

8–17. Account Misclassification and Overhead Rates.   The aerospace and defense group of Henninton Corporation designs, engineers, and manufactures ordnance products, aircraft components, precision forgoings, bomb bodies, missile motor casings, arresting gear, wave guides and related components, and electrical motors and generators and related solid-state controls. The electro-hydromechanical division within the group makes actuators and special AC and DC electric motors, primarily for use on airplanes. Actuators are power-driven geared devices for performing various mechanical functions such as opening and closing airplane loading doors, raising and lowering airplane wing-flaps, and opening and closing weapons bay doors. The principal markets for actuators are domestic and foreign aircraft manufacturers.

Airbus Industries requested the electro-hydromechanical division to submit a proposal for 500 SRR-2681 actuators. The following dollar amounts were developed by the marketing office for the proposal:

Direct material (500 units @ $320)	$160,000
Direct engineering labor	31,500
Direct manufacturing labor	140,800
Material-related costs @ 5% of direct material	8,000
Engineering overhead @ 105% of direct engineering labor	33,075
Manufacturing overhead @ 252% of direct manufacturing labor	354,816
	$728,191
General and administrative expenses (G&A) @ 8% of total costs before G&A	58,255
Total costs	$786,446
Profit margin at 15%	117,967
Total price proposed	$904,413
Price per unit	$1,808.83

A subcontract administrator with Airbus Industries said the company was impressed with the quality of the actuators it has purchased from the division in the past. However, she believed the price was high and needed to be reduced in order to obtain the job. She also suggested that the manufacturing overhead rate appeared higher than typical in the industry.

Because similar issues had been raised on other proposals in the past, Jason Duran, assistant controller, was asked to review the accounting system for possible restructuring. He was asked particularly to analyze the manufacturing overhead to see if any changes in accounting were needed there. The budgeted manufacturing overhead for the current year appears below:

Salaries and wages:	
Indirect labor	$1,395,200
Additional compensation	83,900
Overtime premium	112,600
Sick leave	67,700
Holidays	83,600
Suggestion awards	4,200
Vacations	147,800
Personnel expenses:	
Compensation insurance	26,300
Unemployment insurance	52,200
FICA tax	196,400
Group insurance	161,100
Travel expense	127,250
Dues and subscriptions	17,500
Recruiting and relocation—new employees	27,400
Relocation—transferees	35,200
Employee pension funds:	
Hourly	26,300
Salary	65,700
Training, conferences, and technical meetings	25,500
Educational loans and scholarships	9,000
Supplies:	
General operating	428,140
Maintenance	12,180
Stationery, printing, and office supplies	24,150
Material-related costs on supplies	32,590
Repairs	10,870
Rearranging	3,500
Other	2,600
Utilities	189,100
Telephone	53,870
Depreciation	175,640
Equipment rental	10,000
Total manufacturing overhead	$3,607,490
Total direct manufacturing labor	$1,431,540
Manufacturing overhead rate	252%

Duran's review turned up two areas of misclassification. The first related to charging direct and indirect labor. If a direct labor worker performed any indirect labor work, the worker's time was charged direct. If an indirect worker performed direct labor work, the total time was charged indirect. Duran determined that the net effect of these misclassifications would reduce indirect labor costs in manufacturing overhead by $417,400. Direct manufacturing labor should increase by that amount. Duran also found that the company policy is to add the costs of compensation insurance, unemployment insurance, and FICA taxes relating to direct manufacturing labor to the direct labor cost. This policy has not been implemented. The analysis shows that 9.72 percent should be added to direct manufacturing labor with reductions in the following accounts: compensation insurance, 0.94 percent; unemployment insurance, 1.8 percent; and FICA taxes, 6.94 percent.

Duran also recommended the controller give consideration to other policy changes. He suggested that other labor-related costs be separately pooled and allocated over direct/indirect manufacturing labor dollars. The remaining manufacturing overhead costs should be allocated on direct manufacturing labor hours.

REQUIRED:

a. Make the adjustments for the two types of direct/indirect cost misclassification identified by Duran and calculate a revised manufacturing overhead rate.

b. Compute a revised total and unit price proposed for the Airbus Industries order assuming the misclassifications affected the order as follows:

      Net indirect to direct: $41,043

      Additional factor: 9.72%

c. Assume that sick leave, holidays, vacations, group insurance, and pension funds for salary are put in a labor-related cost pool and allocated on the basis of the total direct and indirect manufacturing labor dollars. The remaining manufacturing overhead is allocated on the basis of direct manufacturing labor hours. Make the adjustments and recalculate the total and unit price proposed for the order. The total direct manufacturing labor hours are 120,000. The direct manufacturing labor hours on the proposal total 7,850.

8–18. Transaction Costs, Volume Measures, Multiple Regression. Jonathan Meyers is controller for RLT Enterprises, Inc. The company produces over 15,000 different products in 17 plants spread throughout the United States. Mr. Meyers was concerned about the recent increase in overhead costs at several of the company's plants. He held the concept that overhead per hour should fall as production increased and vice versa. However, in looking at the plant data, he found that a few high-volume plants had high production overhead per direct labor hour. In recent years, RLT Enterprises has tried cutting the support budget in some of the plants, but this resulted in reduction in quality and poor attitudes.

    While attending a conference, Mr. Meyers heard a talk about transaction costs and overhead caused by inventories. The speaker said that it was not strictly the volume of production that caused high overhead, but the amount of "confusion" in the plant. Part of the confusion was caused by the number of different materials, parts, components, and products that people had to look after. Another part of the confusion is caused by high inventory in process or completed.

    Upon returning to the office, Mr. Meyers asked a staff accountant to study the overhead and volume of transactions and see if this reasonably explained the overhead. The following information was gathered by the staff accountant:

Plant	Cost per Hour	Overhead (1,000s)	Direct Labor Hours (1,000s)	Number of Products	Number of Parts	Total Inventory (1,000s)
Aston	$12.81	$31,607	2,467	1,655	4,348	$5,192
Bakersfield	11.91	41,026	3,445	2,888	5,930	6,233
Boston	20.52	37,508	1,828	1,507	6,972	7,177
Christon	13.24	34,895	2,636	2,251	5,981	5,129
Clairton	23.43	27,789	1,186	1,302	3,462	6,261
Clinkerton	15.55	23,160	1,489	1,304	3,118	4,659
Curbyville	8.96	51,184	5,711	2,966	8,418	7,068
Eliria	27.17	34,648	1,275	1,512	5,484	7,369
Georgetown	18.00	46,361	2,576	3,026	7,330	8,808
Grand Rapids	14.03	45,444	3,239	3,151	12,095	6,988
Marytown	12.50	44,213	3,536	2,607	11,423	7,756
Muncie	10.37	31,806	3,068	1,965	7,812	4,244
Phoenix	13.48	30,396	2,255	1,753	5,412	5,155
Smithfield	12.45	35,493	2,850	2,043	6,083	5,500
Spokane	14.69	24,305	1,654	1,168	3,076	4,189
Verta Vera	20.05	20,532	1,024	934	3,634	4,203
Yost	9.82	25,684	2,615	1,485	4,870	2,853
Averages	$13.68	$34,474	2,521	1,972	6,203	$5,811

REQUIRED:

a. Review the data on overhead per hour, direct labor hours, number of products, parts, and inventories. Comment on the two highest and two lowest cost per hour plants. (Comparison with the averages may be helpful.)

b. Using simple linear regression, estimate the fixed and variable overhead costs with direct labor hours as the measure of volume. Interpret the results.

c. Using multiple regression, estimate the relationship between overhead and direct labor hours, number of products, materials, and the amount of inventory. Interpret the results.

d. The Foster alarm clock radio is a low-volume seller. Each radio requires .1 hour of labor and has 48 unique parts. Materials for the radio cost $4.18, and the labor rate is $8 per hour. Inventories of the clock parts and finished product have averaged $24,000 during the past year. Production has been 15,000 units during the past year.

   1. Using the results of the simple regression in part *(b)*, estimate the total and per unit overhead associated with the Foster alarm clock radio.

   2. Using the results of the multiple regression in part *(c)*, estimate the total and per unit overhead associated with the Foster alarm clock radio.

   3. Compare the total cost per unit under each of the approaches to cost estimation.

e. Another product of the company is the Wonder Willy, a children's wooden rocking horse. The company manufactured and sold 150,000 units during the past year. Each unit requires one hour of direct labor and has eight parts that are unique to the rocking horse. Materials for the horse are $3.87 and labor costs $4.50 per hour. The average inventory was $8,000 for parts and finished goods.

   1. Using the results of the simple regression in part *(b)*, estimate the total and per unit overhead associated with Wonder Willy.

   2. Using the results of the multiple regression in part *(c)*, estimate the total and per unit overhead associated with Wonder Willy.

   3. Compare the total cost per unit under each of the approaches to cost estimation.

Support Department Allocations

LEARNING
OBJECTIVES

After studying this appendix, you should be able to:

1. Distinguish among producing, service, and support departments.
2. Allocate support department costs to production departments using the direct, step, and reciprocal methods.

Most companies have several departments involved directly or indirectly in producing goods or rendering services. This situation suggests the development of separate production overhead rates for applying overhead to work performed, as opposed to a single plant-wide rate. The manner in which the rates are developed depends on the interrelationships among the several types of departments.

Production departments represent organizational units most closely tied to the productive effort that results in products or services to customers. On the other hand, **support departments** do not engage directly in a productive effort of outputs. Rather, they provide supporting services that facilitate the activities of the production departments. Support departments include, for example, maintenance, quality control, cafeterias, internal auditing, personnel, accounting, production planning and control, and medical facilities. Although support departments do not have a direct relationship to output, their costs support production and become part of the cost of a finished product or service. A **service department** is a special type of department that produces support services for producing departments and customer service for outside customers. Examples of service departments include engineering consulting, research and development, computer systems design, copying services, and laboratory services.

In Chapter 8, we deemphasized the specifics of allocating the costs of support departments and charging service departments to production departments. In this appendix we look at the procedures for allocating support and service department costs. We will focus on support departments with reciprocal relationships. A reciprocal relationship exists when support departments provide service to each other.

Exhibit 8A–1 illustrates the possible relationships among the producing, support, and service departments. It shows the same two-step process discussed in Chapter 8. Costs are identified with each department. The costs of each support or service center are then allocated to producing departments before production overhead costs are allocated to products and services. The remainder of this appendix discusses the alternatives for allocating costs from support and service centers to the producing departments.

**Steps in
Calculating
Overhead Rates**

When costs are identified with producing, support, and service departments, the calculation of overhead rates follows a similar procedure discussed earlier. However, we must now consider the impact of the individual support and service departments.

Step One: Direct Allocation to Departments. The first step is to identify or assign all possible costs directly with one department or another. For example, depreciation on equipment can be traced to the department in which the equipment is located,

EXHIBIT 8A–1   Relationships among Support, Service, and Producing Departments

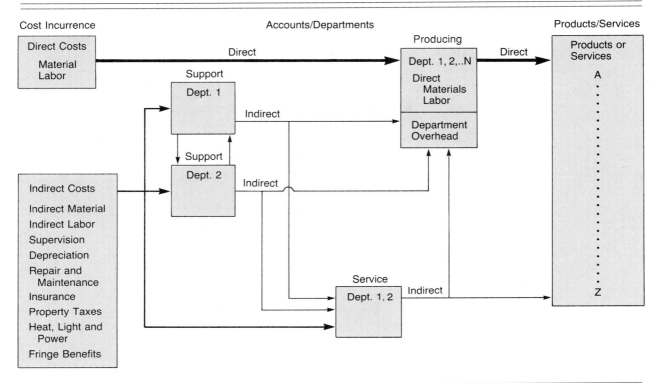

supervisory salaries go to the department in which the supervisor works, and supplies can be identified with the department in which they are used. This will leave some general production costs that apply to the entire facility. These costs are indirect to all departments.

Indirect departmental costs apply to more than one department and are grouped for allocation to the departments involved. Examples are costs of plant superintendence, rent on general facilities, utilities, property insurance, building depreciation, and property taxes. The costs of the building, for instance, are typically grouped into one cost pool with allocations to departments receiving benefits of occupancy, normally on square footage.

Step 2: Select an Allocation Base.   Support department costs are allocated to production departments by means of an allocation rate (sometimes identified as a *charging rate per unit of support activity*). Any number of allocation bases for calculating a rate may be appropriate depending on the nature of the support. Selection of an allocation base is important because once in place, it is reviewed infrequently and then only when inequities are claimed by producing departments.

Examples of allocation bases that could be used are given in Exhibit 8A–2. For support services on government contracts, Cost Accounting Standards give guidance for selecting an allocation base using input activity, output activity, and a surrogate measure. These are briefly discussed in Appendix 25A under Cost Accounting Standards 403 and 418.

EXHIBIT 8A–2   Allocation Bases Used for Support Department Costs

Support Department	*Allocation Bases*
Purchasing	Number of orders; cost of materials; line items ordered
Receiving and inspection	Cost of materials; number of units; number of orders; labor hours
Storerooms	Cost of materials; number of requisitions filled; number of units handled; square or cubic footage occupied
Personnel	Number of employees; periodic analysis of time spent; labor hours
Building occupancy	Floor space occupied
Engineering	Engineering hours: periodic analysis of services rendered
Custodial services	Square footage occupied
Repair and maintenance	Machine hours; labor hours; periodic analysis of services rendered
Factory administration	Total labor hours; number of employees; labor cost
Production planning and control	Labor hours; periodic analysis of services rendered
Cafeteria	Number of employees

Steps 3 and 4: Determine Activity Level and Costs.   If the allocation of support costs is to result in predetermined rates, then determine the expected (or normal) activity level for each of the departments and the expected costs at that level.

Step 5: Calculate Overhead Rates.   Once an allocation base is selected, the calculation of the rate is influenced by whether a support department renders support to other support departments, service or production departments, or only production departments. Thus, there are three general circumstances and three allocation methods appropriate:

1. *Producing departments only.* If all support departments provided service only to production departments, the direct method described below is most appropriate in calculating the rate and charging the costs to departments.
2. *Support departments with no reciprocal relationships.* If some support departments provide service to other support departments, which in turn provide support to production departments, then either the direct method or the step method may be used, but the step method is preferred in concept.
3. *Support departments with a reciprocal relationship among departments.* If support is provided to other support departments, which in turn provide support back, then a reciprocal relationship is said to exist. Either the direct, step, or reciprocal methods may be used, but the reciprocal method is preferred in concept.

Step 6: Apply Overhead to Product or Service.   After overhead rates are computed for the producing departments, the overhead costs are applied to products on the selected activity measures.

Interdepartmental Support

Three approaches are available to allocate the costs of interdepartmental support: direct method, step (sequential) method, and reciprocal (linear algebra) method. In describing the different methods, only support departments with reciprocal services will be illustrated.

A summary of overhead costs in the support, service, and producing departments of Megaron Manufacturing, Inc., is presented in Exhibit 8A–3. The Building and Repair departments are support departments. The Computer Department is a service department because 30 percent of its activity is sold to outside customers. The Machine and Finish departments are both producing departments.

The overhead costs accumulated by support departments plus a share of service department costs must be allocated to the production departments. The production overhead in turn will be allocated to products. The Building Department is allocated on the basis of square footage; the Repair Department, on repair hours; and the Computer Department, on its hours. The Repair Department is responsible for maintaining the building, and Building provides space for the Repair Department. The Computer Department uses part of the Building Department, which is supported by Repair. Data for the allocation bases are at the bottom of Exhibit 8A–3. The Machine Department of Megaron Manufacturing, Inc., is capital intensive, and the Finish Department is labor intensive. Therefore, producing department overhead rates are necessary for reasonable costing of products.

Direct Method. The **direct method** allocations are made from each support or service department to production departments in proportion to activity performed for the producing departments. Thus, the direct method does not assign costs to other support departments for work performed. Allocation of service department costs uses only that operating data pertaining to production departments and allocates to outside service in proportion to work performed.

In Exhibit 8A–4, Building is allocated on the basis of square footage to Machine and Finish. The square footage for Machine (14,400) and Finish (57,600) forms the

EXHIBIT 8A–3

MEGARON MANUFACTURING, INC.
(planned overhead costs and activity measures)

Direct Costs	Building $864,800	Repair $500,000	Computer $300,000	Machine $400,000	Finish $200,000	Total $2,264,800
Budgeted operating data:						
Floor space		9,000	19,000	14,400	57,600	100,000
Repair hours	8,000			22,400	9,600	40,000
Computer hours				16,800	4,200	21,000
Setup hours				5,000		5,000
Machine hours				100,000		100,000
Transactions					400,000	400,000
Product flow time					20,000	20,000

ADDITIONAL INFORMATION

30% of the computer service is provided to outside customers. Thus the total of computer service hours is 30,000, of which 21,000 are internal service.

40% of the mixing costs are to be allocated on setup hours and the remainder on machine hours.

70% of the finish costs are to be allocated on transactions and 30% on product flow time.

Two Jobs Requiring All Activities	#36807	#36808
Setup hours	200	50
Machine hours	100	300
Transactions	200	100
Product flow time	80	900

EXHIBIT 8A–4

MEGARON MANUFACTURING, INC.
(department overhead costs—direct method)

Direct Costs	Building $864,800	Repair $500,000	Computer $300,000	Machine $400,000	Finish $200,000	Total $2,264,800
Building	(864,800)			172,960	691,840	
Repair		(500,000)		350,000	150,000	
Computer			(210,000)	168,000	42,000	
Totals	$ 0	$ 0	$ 90,000	$1,090,960	$1,083,840	$2,264,800

				Unit Costs	
Machine	Allocate	Costs	Units	Machine	Finish
Setup cost	40%	$ 436,384	5,000	$87.2768	
Machine cost	60%	654,576	100,000	$ 6.5458	
		$1,090,960			
Finish					
Transaction costs	70%	$ 758,688	400,000		$ 1.8967
Flow costs	30%	325,152	20,000		$16.2576
		$1,083,840			

allocation base of 72,000 square feet. Building is then prorated over Machine and Finish:

Machine	14,400	20% × $864,800 =	$172,960
Finish	57,600	80% × $864,800 =	691,840
Total	72,000		$864,800

The same approach follows for Repair and Computer. Notice that only 70 percent of Computer is allocated to the production departments with the remainder as a cost of outside services. Once the support and service departments have their costs allocated, producing departmental overhead rates are calculated per unit of activity.

Step (Sequential) Method.   The **step (sequential) method** is an attempt to consider reciprocal services. However, recognition of those services is a one-way process. The support departments are arranged in a sequence and are allocated one after the other. The first department is allocated to all subsequent departments. The second support department is then allocated to departments to the right, but not back to the first department. This process continues until all support and service departments have been included.

Exhibit 8A–5 illustrates the step method for Megaron Manufacturing, Inc. The sequence includes Building, Repair, Computer, and then the producing departments. The costs of Building are allocated to both Repair and Computer and to Machine and Finish on the basis of square footage. For purposes of this allocation, 100,000 square feet is the basis:

Repair	9,000	9% × $864,800 =	$ 77,832
Computer	19,000	19% × $864,800 =	164,312
Machine	14,400	14.4% × $864,800 =	124,531
Finish	57,600	57.6% × $864,800 =	498,125
	100,000		$864,800

EXHIBIT 8A–5

MEGARON MANUFACTURING, INC.
(step or sequential method)

Direct Costs	Building $864,800	Repair $500,000	Computer $300,000	Machine $400,000	Finish $200,000	Total $2,264,800
Building	(864,800)	77,832	164,312	124,531	498,125	
		577,832	464,312			
Repair		(577,832)		404,482	173,350	
Computer			(325,018)	260,015	65,004	
Totals	$0	$0	$ 139,294	$1,189,028	$936,478	$2,264,800

				Unit Costs	
Machine	Allocate	Costs	Units	Machine	Finish
Setup cost	40%	$ 475,611	5,000	$95.1223	
Machine cost	60%	713,417	100,000	$ 7.1342	
		$1,189,028			
Finish					
Transaction costs	70%	$ 655,535	400,000		$ 1.6388
Flow costs	30%	280,943	20,000		$14.0472
		$ 936,478			

The other way to perform this allocation is to divide the overhead cost by the measure and apply the resulting rate to each department. For this example, the rate would be $8.648 per square foot as calculated by $864,800/100,000.

Because Repair does no work for Computer, the Repair cost is allocated between Machine and Finish:

Machine	22,400	70% × $577,832 =	$404,482
Finish	9,600	30% × $577,832 =	173,350
	32,000		$577,832

Finally, 70 percent of the Computer costs are allocated between Machine and Finish leaving $139,294 in cost of services to outside customers. Notice that the cost of services to outside customers ($139,294) is now $49,294 higher than under the direct method ($90,000) because now 30 percent of its share of Building is being charged to those services (30 percent × $164,312). Thus, sale of services will appear less profitable.

How do you arrange the order of support departments? It is determined from a survey of the services rendered by each support department. In some instances, the survey will show that interdepartmental services for some departments are so insignificant they can be ignored. The general rule is to sequence support departments in the order of amount of services provided to other support departments—going from greatest to least. What constitutes "greatest amount of service"? One interpretation is the rendering of service to the greatest number of other support departments. Another is the amount of cost in the service center; the support department with the highest amount of costs goes first. It is not clear which interpretation should be applied. The real issue is to set up a sequence that will provide reasonable and logical allocations.

Reciprocal Method. The **reciprocal (linear algebra) method** uses simultaneous equations to allocate reciprocal services to the appropriate support departments prior to allocating support costs to production departments.

For Megaron Manufacturing, Inc., the simultaneous equations needed for the support departments are as follows:

Let

B = Total departmental overhead costs of Building
  = Direct/indirect Building cost + Allocation from Repair
R = Total departmental overhead costs of repairs
  = Direct/indirect Repair cost + Allocation from Building

We assume that the cost of services received from other support centers with no reciprocal relationship has already been allocated to the Building and Repair departments. Simultaneous equations are then used to determine what the departmental costs will total when reciprocal services are considered. Allocating any costs before consideration of reciprocal services assumes the use of methods already discussed earlier in this appendix and in Chapter 8.

Exhibit 8A–6 shows the allocations of Building and Repair. The simultaneous equations are solved to give us the amounts for Building and Repair that are to be allocated to support and producing departments. The simultaneous equations are given and solved in the bottom half of the exhibit. As can be seen, Building costs that must be allocated to all departments amount to $982,485; Repair costs amount to $588,424.

The results of the simultaneous equations give the costs that must now be allocated to all support, service, and producing departments. Building costs are allocated as follows:

Repair	9,000	9% × $982,485 =	$ 88,424
Computer	19,000	19% × $982,485 =	186,672
Machine	14,400	14.4% × $982,485 =	141,478
Finish	57,600	57.6% × $982,485 =	565,911
	100,000		$982,485

Repair is then allocated to all the departments receiving repair service:

Building	18,000	20% × $588,424 =	$117,685
Machine	22,400	56% × $588,424 =	329,517
Finish	9,600	24% × $588,424 =	141,222
	40,000		$588,424

Notice that allocations go back and forth among the support departments according to the reciprocal services rendered and received. At the same time, producing departments receive their appropriate share of the cost allocations.

Finally, Computer is allocated to Machine and Finish with the remainder as the cost of outside computer services. Notice that the computer services are now more expensive in total. This is due to both Building cost plus the cost of the repair services that have been added to Building cost.

Impact on Product Costs

We have used the direct, step, and reciprocal methods to allocate costs. The unit cost that results from each of these methods is summarized below:

	Direct	*Step*	*Reciprocal*
Machine:			
Setup cost per setup hour	$87.28	$95.12	$91.48
Machine cost per machine hour	6.55	7.13	6.86
Finish:			
Transaction costs per transaction	1.90	1.64	1.71
Flow costs per unit per hour	16.26	14.05	14.63
Computer service to outside customers:			
Computer cost per hour	10.00	15.48	16.22

EXHIBIT 8A–6

MEGARON MANUFACTURING, INC.
(department overhead costs—reciprocal method)

	Building	*Repair*	*Computer*	*Machine*	*Finish*	*Total*
Direct/ind.						
costs	$ 864,800	$ 500,000	$ 300,000	$ 400,000	$200,000	$2,264,800
Building	(982,485)	88,424	186,672	141,478	565,911	
Repair	117,685	(588,424)		329,517	141,222	
Computer			(340,670)	272,536	68,134	
Totals	$(0)	$(0)	$ 146,002	$1,143,531	$975,267	$2,264,800

				Unit Costs	
Machine	*Allocate*	*Costs*	*Units*	*Machine*	*Finish*
Setup cost	40%	$ 457,413	5,000	$91.4825	
Machine cost	60%	686,119	100,000	$ 6.8612	
		$1,143,531			
Finish					
Transaction costs	70%	$ 682,687	400,000		$ 1.7067
Flow costs	30%	292,580	20,000		$14.6290
		$ 975,267			

Solution Method.

We can derive the proportions necessary to complete the equations:

	FROM:	*Building*	*Repair*
TO:	Building	0	8,000/40,000 = 20%
	Repair	9,000/100,000 = 9%	0

Thus, Building uses 20 percent of the Repair service. Repair uses 9 percent of the Building space. This can be placed in equation form:

$$B = \$864{,}800 + (.20 \times R)$$
$$R = \$500{,}000 + (.09 \times B)$$

To solve for B, first substitute the equation for R into B:

$$B = \$864{,}800 + (.2 \times (\$500{,}000 + (.09 \times B)))$$

Multiplying out the right-hand side results in:

$$B = \$864{,}800 + \$100{,}000 + (.018 \times B)$$

Subtracting the $(.018 \times B)$ from both sides and solving for B:

$$.982 B = \$964{,}800$$
$$B = \$964{,}800/.982 = \underline{\$982{,}485}$$

Then, solving for R equals:

$$R = \$500{,}000 + (.09 \times \$982{,}485) = \underline{\$588{,}424}$$

When reciprocal services are present, as they are in the above example, the reciprocal method is the conceptually correct method and provides the best unit costs. Because the direct method ignores reciprocal services and the step method only partially considers the reciprocal services, their results are considered approximations to the appropriate unit costs. The degree of any difference between the conceptually accurate unit costs and the approximations is a bias, the extent of which is a function of the amount and number of reciprocal relationships.

Producing department overhead rate biases for the direct and step methods are unpredictable. Comparing the unit costs for Machine and Finish, we can see that the methods can either be biased on the high side or on the low side. The final overhead rates in practice are often somewhat comparable, thus the amount of the bias is often small. However, in a specific setting, the only way to tell the amount and direction of bias is to solve for unit costs with all of the allocation methods.

The bias in the Service Department costs is known. The direct methods will understate the costs of providing external services. This is because support costs to the Service Department are not included in the cost of the service to outside customers. Thus, Service Department profits on external service will be overstated.

To see the impact of the bias for Megaron Manufacturing, Inc., let's look at the costs allocated to two jobs. The unit costs are those summarized above.

JOB #36807:

	Activity	*Direct*	*Step*	*Reciprocal*
Machine:				
Setup cost	$200	$17,455	$19,024	$18,297
Machine cost	100	655	713	686
Finish:				
Transaction costs	200	379	328	341
Flow costs	80	1,301	1,124	1,170
Overhead charges to job		$19,790	$21,189	$20,494
Bias			(704)	
				695

JOB #36808:

	Activity	*Direct*	*Step*	*Reciprocal*
Machine:				
Setup cost	50	$ 4,364	$ 4,756	$ 4,574
Machine cost	300	1,964	2,140	2,058
Finish:				
Transaction costs	100	190	164	171
Flow costs	900	14,632	12,642	13,166
Overhead charges to job		$21,149	$19,703	$19,969
Bias			1,180	
				(266)

In reviewing these job costs, we see that the direct method costs for job #36807 are biased low and for job #36808 the costs are biased high. The reverse is true for the step method costs. There is no pattern to the direction of the biasing or the size. The step method will often have less bias than the direct method. However, there are no guarantees of this because the step-method bias depends on the relative importance of the Service Department's sales to outside customers.

Behavioral Effects of Service Allocation Methods

Direct Method Effects.   The direct method does not penalize the support departments for the use of services from other support departments. Thus, support from other departments is a "free" good. This can create a problem in that there is no financial control over the use of support services by other support services. Further, the full cost of support services may be understated by the direct and step methods. The managers of producing departments receiving services from support departments may interpret the costs of much reciprocal service as too expensive relative to purchasing the same service from an outside supplier. Thus, there will be circumstances in which producing department managers seek outside service to the detriment of the company as a whole.

Step Method Effects.   For support departments it pays to lobby for having department costs allocated first because little costs will be allocated from the remaining support departments. That means that the earlier a department appears in the allocation steps, the less impact other support departments have on its costs. That means an early department has free use of goods and services provided by other support and service departments and are unaffected by the costs of other support departments. However, the costs allocated to later departments will be higher; thus, the support or service will appear more expensive to the later departments relative to other departments. Managers of the later departments will be unhappy about costs charged to them that they think represent an unfair price for support and services received.

Reciprocal Method Effects.   The reciprocal method is the most theoretically correct of the three presented. However, the method can be difficult to explain to department managers. For whatever reason, the reciprocal method has not gained wide acceptance even in the face of computer software packages that make its application easier. In practical settings with 4 or 5 support and service departments and 10 or more producing departments, the level of confusion and number of journal entries introduced by the reciprocal method may be daunting. On the other hand, a cost accounting system that includes the direct or step method will be less challenging to program and maintain.

KEY TERMS AND CONCEPTS

Production departments (298)
Support departments (298)
Service departments (298)

Direct method (301)
Step (sequential) method (302)
Reciprocal (linear algebra) method (303)

ADDITIONAL READINGS

Cardullo, J. Patrick, and Richard A. Moellenberndt. "The Cost Allocation Problem in a Telecommunications Company." *Management Accounting*, September 1987, pp. 39–44.

Gauntt, James E., and Grover L. Porter. "Allocating MIS Costs." *Management Accounting*, April 1985, pp. 12 and 74.

Hoshower, Leon B., and Robert P. Crum. "Controlling Service Center Costs." *Management Accounting*, November 1987, pp. 44–48.

National Association of Accountants. "Accounting for Indirect Production Costs." *Statement of Management Accounting Number 4G*, June 1, 1987.

————. "Allocation of Service and Administrative Costs." *Statement of Management Accounting Number 4G*, June 13, 1985.

Roth, Harold P. "Guiding Manufacturers through the Inventory Capitalization Maze." *Journal of Accountancy*, July 1988, pp. 60–70.

Schwarzbach, Henry R. "The Impact of Automation on Accounting for Indirect Costs." *Management Accounting*, December 1985, pp. 45–50.

REVIEW QUESTIONS

1. What distinguishes a support department from a service department?
2. What distinguishes a service department (as defined in this chapter) from a producing department?
3. What is the difference between allocating indirect costs to departments and allocating support department costs to production departments?
4. Describe the circumstances in which the three methods for allocating support department costs may be used appropriately.
5. Explain how an indirect cost to a product or service can also be a direct cost to a department.
6. What are interdepartmental support costs? How are such costs allocated to other departments under the step method?

DISCUSSION QUESTIONS

7. Assume a service center produces revenues of some type. How do these revenues enter into the allocation of service center costs to other departments?
8. What guidelines should govern the allocation of variable support department costs to production departments? Fixed support department costs?

EXERCISES

8A–1. Direct and Step Methods.   Cahill-Lively Manufacturing makes several products in a single factory that has three support departments and two operating departments. Barry Matalone, the controller, is currently developing production overhead rates for the operating departments. Budgeted data for the coming year appear as follows:

	Square Feet	Employees	Overhead Costs
Support departments:			
Building Services	100	30	$165,000
Personnel	200	20	90,000
Administration	800	20	330,000
Operating departments:			
Fabrication	1,000	30	265,000
Assembly	2,000	90	420,000

Matalone believes that the correct bases for allocation are Building Services, square footage; Personnel and Administration, employees. In addition, Fabrication will have an overhead rate based on machine hours, and Assembly will use direct labor hours. Budgeted machine hours in fabrication are 50,000; direct labor hours in Assembly are 120,000.

REQUIRED:
a. Allocate the support department costs to operating departments using the direct method. Determine the appropriate overhead rate for each operating department.
b. Allocate the support department costs to operating departments using the step method. The sequence should be Administration, Building Services, and Personnel. Determine the appropriate overhead rate for each operating department.

8A–2. Support Department Costs, Direct Method, and Activity Bases.   The Whilhite Company manufactures computer disks with two support departments and three production departments. The budgeted data for January 19x4 is:

	Overhead Cost	Labor Hours	Machine Hours	Employees
Support departments:				
Plant Administration	$ 50,000	10,000		20
Personnel	35,000	20,000		25
Production departments:				
Cutting	225,000	25,000	200,000	150
Assembly	375,000	35,000	150,000	225
Finishing	400,000	30,000	20,000	175

Whilhite uses the direct method of allocating support department costs. Administrative support costs are to be allocated on the basis of labor hours, and personnel is allocated on the basis of the number of people. The overhead rates in cutting and assembly are based on machine hours. The overhead rate in Finishing is based on labor hours.

(D. Washburn)

REQUIRED:
a. Allocate the support department costs to the producing departments.
b. Compute the overhead rates for each of the producing departments.

8A–3. Support Department Costs, Step Method, and Activity Bases.   Corecote Industries coats new and used oil field pipe with a thick plastic. The harsh environment of the oil field includes both weather and salt water, which results in the rapid rusting of uncoated pipe. All pipe, whether new or old and rusted, goes through a sandblasting and then coating. The plant also has two support departments: Administration and Maintenance. For July 19x8, Corecote has the following budget amounts:

	Administration	Maintenance	Sandblast	Coating
Overhead	$15,000	$8,000	$100,000	$70,000
Employees	25	12	40	30
Labor hours		2,000	6,700	5,000
Machine hours			13,000	11,000

Corecote Industries uses the step method of allocation and allocates administration first on the basis of labor hours and then allocates maintenance on the basis of machine hours. The sandblast overhead rate is based on machine hours, and the coating rate is based on labor hours.

(P. Hicks)

REQUIRED:
a. Allocate the support department costs to the producing departments.
b. Compute the overhead rates for each of the producing departments.

8A–4. Overhead Rate Calculations.   The following budget information is available for Balzer Pallet Company.

	Support		Producing	
	Repair/ Maintenance	Loading/ Shipping	Cutting	Building
Budgeted overhead	$7,200	$19,800	$27,000	$36,000
Labor hours	1,200	2,400	7,200	8,400
Machine hours		7,680	5,760	1,920

Normal capacity is 120,000 pallets, and the above budgeted numbers are based on normal capacity.

(S. Neves)

REQUIRED:
a. Balzer decides a departmental rate is appropriate for the company's operations. Repair/maintenance is allocated on the basis of machine hours, and loading/shipping is allocated next on the basis of labor hours.

1. Using the direct method, prepare departmental overhead allocations. Develop overhead rates for the producing departments. Cutting is based on machine hours, and Building on labor hours.
2. Using the step method, prepare allocations and overhead rates. Assume the same bases as in (1) above.

b. Balzer decides the additional clerical effort necessary for departmental rates is not economical. The company uses an overall overhead rate combining all four departments. Actual overhead costs for the period were $84,000, and 90 percent of normal capacity was reached.

1. Calculate the predetermined overhead rate.
2. Calculate the under- or overapplied overhead for the period.

PROBLEMS

8A–5. Support Department Cost Allocations. Fast Wheels, Inc., manufactures a variety of custom wheels for automobiles. The market for Fast Wheels' products experienced growth in the early 1980s but has now stabilized. The company has three producing departments in its factory in Denver. The Fabrication Department makes all of the parts and components for the 212 different wheel designs. The Assembly Department assembles and spin tests each wheel for balance. Finally, the Packaging Department packages each wheel in cartons for shipment. An Equipment Repair Department is responsible for maintaining all equipment in the plant, and the Building Maintenance Department keeps the building and grounds secure and maintained. Factory Administration includes Personnel, Payroll, Accounting, and General Management. The following budget information is available for the fiscal year ending June 30, 19x0:

	Labor Hours	Square Footage	Overhead Cost
Support departments:			
Administration	20,000	2,000	$225,000
Building Maintenance	10,000	2,000	125,000
Equipment Repair	20,000	3,000	150,000
Producing departments:			
Fabrication	110,000	12,000	400,000
Assembly	190,000	26,000	825,000
Packaging	70,000	7,000	225,000

Fast Wheels, Inc., allocates equipment repair and administration on the basis of labor hours and building maintenance on square footage.

(J. Brown)

REQUIRED:

a. Using the direct method, allocate support department costs to the producing departments and compute an overhead rate per labor hour for each department.
b. Using the step method, allocate support department costs to the producing departments and compute an overhead rate per labor hour for each department. Start with Administration, then Building Maintenance, and finally Equipment Repair.
c. Using the reciprocal method, allocate support department costs to the producing departments and compute an overhead rate per labor hour for each department. Assume that only Equipment Repair and Building Maintenance have a reciprocal relationship. Allocate the two departments using the reciprocal method, then allocate the Factory Administration costs.

8A–6. Overhead Rates. Libby's Clothing Company manufactures skirts to customer order. The budgeted data for the plant for 19x3 are:

	Support		Production	
	Administration	*Maintenance*	*Cutting*	*Sewing*
Overhead	$80,000	$30,000	$500,000	$600,000
Labor hours		10,000	50,000	80,000
Machine hours			100,000	150,000
Square feet	4,500	7,000	50,000	25,000

During the period, job no. 1870 was started and completed for Cleen Jeans. The data for this job include the following direct costs and additional information:

(D. Ripple)

	Cutting		Sewing	
	Hours	*Cost*	*Hours*	*Cost*
Direct materials		$80,000		$ 20,000
Direct labor	8,000	80,000	15,000	144,000
Machine hours	16,000		30,000	

REQUIRED:
(Consider the following requirements independently.)

a. Libby follows a policy of applying overhead for the entire plant on the basis of machine hours.
   1. Calculate a plant-wide overhead rate based on machine hours.
   2. Apply overhead to job no. 1870.

b. Plant administration costs are allocated on direct labor hours; maintenance, on square feet; cutting, on machine hours; and sewing, on direct labor hours. Using the direct method of allocating support department costs:
   1. Allocate support department costs to producing departments.
   2. Calculate departmental overhead rates.
   3. Apply overhead to job no. 1870.

c. Plant administration costs are allocated on direct labor hours; maintenance, on square feet; cutting, on machine hours; and sewing, on direct labor hours. Using the step method of allocating support department costs:
   1. Allocate support department costs to producing departments.
   2. Calculate departmental overhead rates.
   3. Apply overhead to job no. 1870.

d. Compare the results of overhead application with each of the three systems for overhead application.

8A–7. Reciprocal Support Department Costs and Overhead Bases. J-Sports is a manufacturing company specializing in recreational equipment. The factory has three support departments, and the company is currently developing overhead rates for these departments. Budget data are as follows:

Support Departments	*Employees*	*Labor Hours*	*Square Feet*	*Cost*
Cafeteria	5	9,000	900	$ 100,000
Repair and Mainte-nance	15	27,000	200	80,000
Factory Administration	12	21,600	500	250,000

Operating Departments				*Overhead Cost*
Fabrication	40	72,000	2,000	250,000
Assembly	60	108,000	4,500	600,000
Totals	132	237,600	8,100	$1,280,000

It seems reasonable to the controller to allocate the Cafeteria costs on the basis of employees; Repair and Maintenance, on the basis of square footage; and Factory Administration, on the basis of labor hours. The overhead rate for Fabrication will be based on direct labor hours, and Assembly will be based on direct labor dollars. The direct labor budget for assembly shows $540,000 in cost for the 108,000 hours.

(M. Winburn)

REQUIRED:
a. Using the direct method:
    1. Allocate the support department costs to the operating departments.
    2. Compute the overhead rate for each of the operating departments.
b. Using the step method, start with Factory Administration, then Cafeteria, and finally Repair and Maintenance:
    1. Allocate the support department costs to the operating departments.
    2. Compute the overhead rate for each of the operating departments.

8A–8. Support Department Costs.   Trinity Park is a large industrial park that is the home of over 125 different companies. The park encompasses 40 million square feet, which includes 25 percent common areas such as streets, a small river, and other landscaping. Trinity Park has a full-time maintenance staff as well as 24-hour security department.

The tenants (all copartners in a limited partnership) range from very minor business to major corporate offices. A few of the buildings are large warehouse and distribution facilities with very small office space.

The costs are accumulated into four sets of accounts:

General and Maintenance (including security and administration).
Buildings and Grounds (mostly depreciation, but includes all costs related to the physical
    assets of the industrial park).
Common Areas (temporary accounts used for allocation of the common area costs).
Company Accounts (costs traceable and allocated to specific companies).

The direct costs and some additional data related to each of the accounts follow:

(M. Kubinski)

	Direct Costs ($ millions)	Additional Information
General and Maintenance	$15	2 million sq. feet
Buildings and Grounds	45	350,000 G & M hrs.
Common Areas	3	400,000 G & M hrs. and 10 million sq. ft.
Company Accounts	16	250,000 G & M hrs.
		125,000 frontage feet, and 28 million sq. ft.
TOTALS	$79	

REQUIRED:
a. Using the direct method, develop the rates for allocating each of the costs to the Company Accounts for:
    1. Buildings and Grounds (use square footage).
    2. General and Maintenance (use hours).
    3. Common Areas (use frontage feet).
b. Using the step method and the order listed in part (a), develop each of the costs to the Company Accounts.
c. Two of the departments have a reciprocal relationship. Solve for this relationship using the reciprocal method, and develop the rates for applying the costs of these two departments to the others.

8A–9. Allocating Support Department Costs.   The East and West Shopping Center is a shopping mall with about 4 million square feet of space. Of the total space, 60 percent is store leased space, 30 percent is commons areas, and 10 percent is used for maintenance and general administration. The commons areas include fountains, spacious walkways, plantings, and seating for shoppers. The lease space varies from very small ''hole-in-the-wall''–type gift shops to very large department stores. The shopping mall provides these stores with space, maintenance, security, the commons area for walking, and some common advertising.

Costs are accumulated into four cost centers: building and grounds, general and maintenance, commons area, and stores. The Buildings and Grounds account is the basic occupancy costs of building depreciation, interest on indebtedness, parking lots, and building exterior and roof. This account is allocated on the basis of square footage. The General and Maintenance account includes all of the cost of maintenance workers, security, and administration, plus any indirect costs allocated. This account is allocated on the basis of approximate hours worked. The large stores provide most of their own maintenance and security. The Commons Area account includes all costs of having a pleasant pedestrian area between stores. The commons area is allocated to stores on the basis of frontage, which is the number of linear feet on the store front. The Stores account direct costs are traceable directly to each store.

The leases are renegotiated periodically to reflect roughly the costs of providing each store with space and services. Some basic data for 19x1 (costs in millions) are:

	Building and Grounds	General and Maint.	Commons Areas	Stores
Direct costs	$30	$12	$2	$10
Square footage		400,000	1,200,000	2,400,000
Linear feet				20,000
General and mainte- nance hours	200,000		400,000	200,000

REQUIRED:
a. Using the direct method, develop the rates for allocating the costs to stores.
  1. General and Maintenance.
  2. Building and grounds.
  3. Commons Areas.
b. Using the step method, develop the rates for allocating the costs to specific stores. Use the order in part (a).
c. Notice that Buildings and Grounds and General and Maintenance have a reciprocal relationship.
  1. Solve for this reciprocal cost relationship.
  2. Find the rates for Commons and Stores.
  3. Find the rate for the cost of Commons to Stores.
d. Given the following data for two stores, find the total cost for each store with each of the rates developed above:

	Wolforths Dept.	Bigfoot Shoe
Direct costs	$368,400	$12,600
Square footage	200,000	2,500
Linear feet	150	19
General and Mainte- nance hours	200	600

8A–10. Support Department Costs and Allocation Methods. The Dallas Aircraft Company produces luxury small jet aircraft. The company purchases the shell with avionics from an established manufacturer and then customizes the aircraft to customer specifications. There are two producing departments and three support departments with the following budget information (in thousands) for 19x2:

	Administration	Purchasing	Maintenance	Assembly	Finishing
Overhead costs	$1,000	$400	$600	$5,000	$3,000
Labor hours				300	100
Machine hours				200	50
Square footage	100	150	350	1,500	500
Purchase orders	50		50	150	50
Maintenance hours	100	50		300	100

Dallas Aircraft allocates administration on square footage; purchasing, on number of purchase orders; maintenance, on hours spent; assembly, on machine hours; and finishing, on direct labor hours.

(P. Hutchinson)

REQUIRED:

a. Calculate a plant-wide rate based solely on hours of direct labor in the producing departments.

b. Using the direct method, allocate service department costs to the producing departments and compute an overhead rate for each producing department.

c. Using the step method, allocate service department costs to the producing departments and compute an overhead rate for each department. Start with Administration, then Purchasing, and finally Maintenance.

d. Compare the results of the three methods of allocation.

EXTENDED APPLICATIONS

8A–11. Support Department Costs and Direct and Step Methods. Kirwin Legal Services is a large law office organized into three operating departments: Criminal, Civil, and Personal and Family Services (PFS). These departments are supported by a secretarial pool and a research center. At the top of the organization is an administrative function that manages the entire company. Kirwin follows the practice of allocating support activities (secretarial pool and research center) to the three operating departments in order to establish the overhead charge for the various legal services to clients. Costs of the administrative function are simply charged as period costs in the income statement.

Budgeting for the upcoming fiscal year is currently underway. The following direct costs are budgeted.

Direct costs of support departments:

	Secretarial	*Research*
Salaries and wages	$80,000	$120,000
Fringe benefits	5,600	11,200
Depreciation on—		
Equipment, fixtures,		
and furniture	8,000	16,000
Supplies	16,000	3,200

Direct costs of operating departments:

	Criminal	*Civil*	*PFS*
Salaries and wages	$300,000	$400,000	$100,000
Fringe benefits	30,000	40,000	10,000
Depreciation on—			
Equipment, fixtures,			
and furniture	24,000	32,000	8,000
Supplies	4,500	6,000	1,500

The indirect costs that are prorated to administration, support activities, and operating departments are of four varieties: insurance, leasing, utilities, and janitorial services. The following means are used to prorate indirect costs:

1. Insurance costs ($80,000) are for malpractice coverage and for equipment, fixtures, and furniture. The premium ($18,000) representing coverage on equipment, fixtures, and furniture is prorated on the basis of book value. The remainder of the $80,000 is for malpractice. Because malpractice relates to people, the proration is based on the number of people in each department.

2. Leasing costs ($72,000) are incurred for the office space occupied by the firm. Therefore, these costs are prorated based on square footage occupied.
3. Utilities costs ($60,000) are for heat, light, and water. They are prorated on the basis of square footage occupied.
4. Janitorial services ($24,000) to keep the offices clean are contracted out. These costs are prorated on square footage.

In allocating the support activities to the operating departments, the secretarial pool is allocated first; the basis is secretarial time. The Research Center is allocated on the basis of salaries and wages. Overhead rates for the operating departments are determined by using salaries and wages in the criminal and civil departments, and staff time in PFS. The following budgeted data are available for the allocation bases.

	Adminis-tration	Secre-tarial	Research	Criminal	Civil	PFS
Number of people	2	4	6	4	6	2
Book values	$10,000	$70,000	$80,000	$120,000	$160,000	$40,000
Square footage	1,000	2,000	2,000	1,500	2,500	1,000
Staff time	4,000	8,500	12,500	9,000	12,500	5,000
Secretarial time	500	200	2,000	2,000	3,000	1,000

REQUIRED:
a. Using the direct method, develop the overhead rates for each of the operating departments.
b. Using the step method, develop the overhead rates for each of the operating departments.
c. Compare the answers in (a) and (b) and explain why the differences occurred. Which method is preferable? Why?

8A–12. Allocating Service Costs.   The Independent Underwriters Insurance Co. (IUI) established a Systems Department two years ago to implement and operate its own data processing systems. IUI believed that its own system would be more cost effective than the service bureau it had been using.

IUI's three departments—Claims. Records, and Finance—have different requirements with respect to hardware and other capacity-related resources and operating resources. The system was designed to recognize these differing needs. In addition, the system was designed to meet IUI's long-term capacity needs. The excess capacity designed into the system would be sold to outside users until needed by IUI. The estimated resource requirements used to design and implement the system are shown in the following schedule.

	Hardware and Other Capacity-Related Resources	Operating Resources
Records	30%	60%
Claims	50	20
Finance	15	15
Expansion (outside use)	5	5
Total	100%	100%

IUI currently sells the equivalent of its expansion capacity to a few outside clients.

At the time the system became operational, management decided to redistribute total expenses of the Systems Department to the user departments based upon actual computer time used. The actual costs for the first quarter of the current fiscal year were distributed to the user departments as follows:

Department	Percentage Utilization	Amount
Records	60%	$330,000
Claims	20	110,000
Finance	15	82,500
Outside	5	27,500
Total	100%	$550,000

The three user departments have complained about the cost distribution method since the Systems Department was established. The Records Department's monthly costs have been as much as three times the costs experienced with the service bureau. The Finance Department is concerned about the costs distributed to the outside user category because these allocated costs form the basis for the fees billed to the outside clients.

James Dale, IUI's controller, decided to review the distribution method by which the Systems Department's costs have been allocated for the past two years. The additional information he gathered for his review is reported in the three tables presented below.

Systems Department Costs and Activity Levels

	Annual Budget		First Quarter			
			Budget		Actual	
	Hours	Dollars	Hours	Dollars	Hours	Dollars
Hardware and other capacity related costs	—	$ 600,000	—	$150,000	—	$155,000
Software development	18,750	562,500	4,725	141,750	4,250	130,000
Operations:						
Computer related	3,750	750,000	945	189,000	920	187,000
Input/output related	30,000	300,000	7,560	75,600	7,900	78,000
		$2,212,500		$556,350		$550,000

Historical Utilization by Users

	Hardware and Other Capacity Needs	Software Development		Operations			
				Computer		Input/Output	
		Range	Average	Range	Average	Range	Average
Records	30%	0–30%	12%	55–65%	60%	10–30%	20%
Claims	50	15–60	35	10–25	20	60–80	70
Finance	15	25–75	45	10–25	15	3–10	6
Outside	5	0–25	8	3–8	5	3–10	4
	100%		100%		100%		100%

Utilization of Systems Department's Services in Hours (first quarter)

	Software Development	Operations	
		Computer Related	Input/ Output
Records	425	552	1,580
Claims	1,700	184	5,530
Finance	1,700	138	395
Outside	425	46	395
Total	4,250	920	7,900

Dale has concluded that the method of cost distribution should be changed to reflect more directly the actual benefits received by the departments. He believes that the hardware and capacity-related costs should be allocated to the user departments in proportion to the planned, long-term needs. Any difference between actual and budgeted hardware costs would not be allocated to the departments but remain with the Systems Department.

The remaining costs for software development and operations would be charged to the user departments based upon actual hours used. A predetermined hourly rate based upon the annual budget data would be used. The hourly rates that would be used for the current fiscal year are as follows.

Function	Hourly Rate
Software development	$ 30
Operations:	
Computer related	200
Input-output related	10

Dale plans to use first quarter activity and cost data to illustrate his recommendations. The recommendations will be presented to the Systems Department and the user departments for their comments and reactions. He then expects to present his recommendations to management for approval.

(CMA, adapted)

REQUIRED:
a. Calculate the amount of data processing costs that would be included in the Claims Department's first quarter budget according to the method James Dale has recommended.
b. Prepare a schedule to show how the actual first quarter costs of the Systems Department would be charged to the users if James Dale's recommended method was adopted.
c. Explain whether James Dale's recommended system for charging costs to the user departments will:
   1. improve cost control in the Systems Department.
   2. improve planning and cost control in the user departments.
   3. be a more equitable basis for charging costs to user departments.

PART

III

Accounting for Specialized
Production Environments

9

Process Cost Accounting Systems

10

Costs of Joint Production

11

Waste and Scrap, Spoilage and Defective Units

319

CHAPTER

9

Process Cost Accounting Systems

■

THE UNIT COST PROBLEM

Hawks Airjet, Inc., manufactures the X5, a six-passenger jet aircraft. The planes are assembled and finished in a plant in St. Louis and are sold internationally. Each plane is the same except for some finishing detail and paint. That means the same production operations are performed on each and every aircraft manufactured. The current selling price on the plane is $1,200,000, and it is competitive at that price, but the European manufacturers have been cutting their prices recently. Thus, there is pressure to keep the prices and costs low. However, safety and quality of manufacture can not be compromised.

The plant has the capacity to produce about 30 planes per month, and the current capacity has been scheduled for the next two months. Each plane takes a month to manufacture with 20 days in assembly and 10 days in finishing. During September 19x9, the plant completed 30 planes with current plant costs of about $32.3 million. John Riley, company president, was furious over this high cost. In a conference with plant management he made the following statement:

> September was a disaster!
>
> We spent $32.3 million to produce jets that sold for only $36 million. In addition, we had $3 million in selling and $.6 million in general expenses. That only leaves us with $100,000 in profits. We will not survive with that. Since we can't raise our prices, we must cut our costs.

The plant manager and chief engineer were upset. They thought they had kept costs in line. Although materials had gone up in September due to a strike among aluminum workers, everything else seemed reasonable.

How should Hawks Airjet, Inc., determine the cost of planes manufactured and sold? This chapter discusses product costing using a process costing system, which is appropriate for homogeneous products.

■

LEARNING OBJECTIVES

After studying this chapter, you should be able to:

1. Describe the product flow and cost flow through operating departments for which a process costing system is appropriate.
2. Explain how the accumulation of materials, labor, and production overhead costs differs between process costing and job order costing.
3. Identify the differences between the FIFO and the weighted average process costing methods.
4. Compute the equivalent units of production for material, labor, and production overhead for sequential process cost departments using both the FIFO method and the weighted average method.
5. Prepare a cost of production report.
6. Journalize the transactions for cost flow from input costs to costs of goods sold.

A primary goal of any cost accounting system is to determine the product costs that will be attached to the units in ending Materials, Work in Process, and Finished Goods inventories, which in turn determine costs of goods manufactured and costs of goods sold. The method that should be used to accumulate and then allocate costs to units of product depends in large measure upon the production process involved. Continuous product flows and production runs of identical or standard products generally call for a process cost system.

This chapter discusses the procedures companies follow in accumulating input costs, allocating costs to products, and reporting the costs of products manufactured in process departments. Although the concepts presented are those of a manufacturing setting, they also apply to service organizations.

OVERVIEW OF PROCESS COSTING

A **process costing** system identifies production costs with departments[1] for a period of time rather than charging costs to specific product units, jobs, or orders. The costs of direct material, direct labor, and production overhead for each department are accumulated as debits to appropriate inventory accounts. The information on quantity and dollar flow activity is summarized in a departmental cost of production report for the each accounting period.

The calculation of unit costs is based on a period of time, usually a week or a month, although it could be daily in some operations. Unit costs are computed by dividing the production costs assigned to the department for the given period by the equivalent units of production for the period. If a product is routed through several

---

[1] A production department, process, operation, work cell, group, or task is the specific organizational segment. For our purposes, we use the term *department* in a general sense to cover all of these segments.

departments, the costs of all departments are added together to find the product's total cost per unit. The costs per unit for each product are then used to compute cost of goods sold and ending inventories.

FLOW OF PRODUCTS AND COSTS UNDER PROCESS COSTING

The production environment (the nature of the product and the type and number of processing operations) is the primary determinant of whether process costing is appropriate. Once management agrees that process costing will be used, the flow of costs and accounting procedures can be identified.

Environment

Process costing is most appropriate when the flow of product is continuous or each unit of product is processed in a similar manner. In each case, all units of a given product number are identical, or homogeneous, to any other unit of the same number. For example, laundry detergents, cleaning chemicals, cosmetics, perfumes, and vitamins are all produced in long production runs. We typically think a process cost system would be used for products in mass production, whether manufacturing or assembly.

Manufacturing under a mass-production concept is characterized by a stamping or molding operation in which every unit comes off the line in the same way. Examples include plastic cups, silverware, bicycle tires, basketballs, ski boots, records, bolts, and nuts. Assembly under a mass-production concept refers to bringing parts and subassemblies together in an assembly operation to finish the product. Each product passes through the same assembling activities. Examples include motorcycles, television sets, electric irons, kitchen appliances (washing machines and dryers, dishwashers, mixers, toasters, and stoves), radios, calculators, typewriters, computer monitors and keyboards, automobiles, and small airplanes. With mass-produced products, customer orders are usually filled from finished goods inventories. Production quality is uniform, which means that no given customer order significantly affects the production process. Each unit of product is so similar to any other unit that average unit costs may be used for the period.

Physical Flow of Products

An example of the product flow through various production departments for the Tres Rios Plant, maker of denim jeans, is given in Exhibit 9–1. The output of each department is immediately transferred to the next department and becomes a cost input for that new department. Output from the last department in the process represents the completed product, which goes to Finished Goods Inventory to await shipping. Specifically, dyed denim cloth bales are released from the Storeroom (Materials Inventory) and sent to the Cutting Department where the fabric is cut to patterns. The cut pieces are sent in sets to the Stitch and Form Department. There, thread, zippers, and snaps are added to make the completed jean. The jeans move to Inspection and Finishing. Inspection makes certain the jeans meet quality standards; spoiled and defective jeans are removed from the process. After inspection, brand labels are stitched on each pair of jeans. The completed jeans move to the warehouse where they become part of the Finished Goods Inventory.

Now let's look at how the production cost elements are accumulated by department.

Cost Accumulation by Department

There are fewer detailed records and procedures in process costing than in job order costing. The reason is that production costs (direct material, direct labor, and production overhead) are identified with departments rather than with individual jobs.

EXHIBIT 9–1   Tres Rios Plant (physical flow of product)

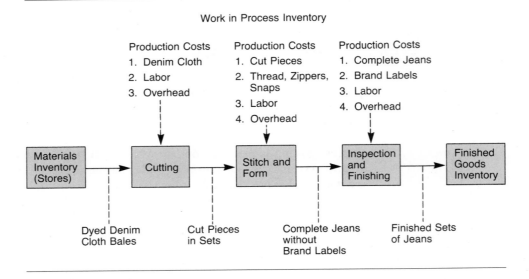

Because costs need to be identified with departments, a process costing system normally includes journal entries to one Work in Process Inventory control account for each production department.

Materials.   In job order costing, the basis for charging direct materials to specific jobs is the materials requisition. Materials requisitions are also used in the process cost system, but the details are considerably reduced because materials are charged to departments rather than jobs, and the number of producing departments using materials is normally much less than the number of jobs. Although a material may be added in any department, it is often issued from the storeroom to the first operating department in the process. As in a job order system, some materials will be indirect and included in the production overhead. For example, the thread, zippers, and snaps in the Stitch and Form Department of Exhibit 9–1 could be treated as indirect materials. However, the distinction between direct and indirect materials is not always as critical in the process cost system.

Direct Labor Costs.   Direct labor costs are identified with and charged to specific departments, thus eliminating the need to accumulate direct labor time and labor costs by jobs. Labor time is recorded into the departmental labor record via daily time tickets or weekly clock cards instead of job time tickets.

Production Overhead Costs.   In both job order costing and process costing, production overhead should be accumulated by category in a **departmental overhead control ledger.** (This overhead subsidiary ledger often consists of detailed computerized files of accounts for each department.) This procedure not only helps identify costs to be attached to products, but also it helps managers plan for and control the overhead in each department. Actual production overhead costs are posted to both a control account and a subsidiary overhead control ledger as the costs are incurred.

Either actual or normal production overhead may be charged to the work in process through departmental overhead rates. If actual costing is used, then the overhead rates are normally computed on a weekly or monthly basis. If normal costing is used, then the rates are commonly set for an entire year.

PROCESS COSTING CONCEPTS

An important purpose of process costing is to determine the production costs that will be allocated to units in ending Work in Process Inventory and to units completed during the period. The accounting system allocates costs to units in the ending inventory of each department and units completed in each department during the period. These allocations are then used to determine the costs of units completing all manufacturing processes during the period (called *costs of goods manufactured*) and units sold during the period *(cost of goods sold).*

Unit Costs

We normally think of a unit cost for a department as the result of a division, as follows:

$$\text{Unit cost} = \frac{\text{Department cost}}{\text{Units}}$$

Determining unit cost under a job order cost system is straightforward: divide the total cost of a job at any point during production by the units in the job. Unless beginning work in process inventories are immaterial or inventory levels are fairly stable, applying the same principle to a process cost system (dividing total costs for a period by units worked on) is complicated by two important factors: the stage of completion and the inputs that enter at different times. Each of these will be discussed in sections below.

It should be understood that there should be a definitive relationship between the departmental costs in the numerator and the units in the denominator. Specifically, if the units had no material added in the department, there would be no material cost in the numerator. If materials were added, however, the material costs should be in the numerator, and the denominator consists of the units receiving materials input in that department. In order to make the relationship between cost and units more explicit in a process cost system, costs are first identified with individual operating departments and by cost element (material, labor, and overhead). Then units are calculated for each cost element in that process cost center.

Stage of Completion

We normally view the goods completed during a period as equal to beginning inventory plus quantity started into production during the period less ending inventory. That works well for a job order cost system because all units in a job are basically at the same level of completion. In a process cost system, the units are at different levels of completion. A production environment consistent with process costing is analagous to a conveyor belt that stops only when there is a breakdown or a new product is set up. At the end of a period, an assessment of work done for the period requires an assessment of the stage of completion of products on the conveyor at the beginning and the end of the period, and the items coming off the conveyor during the period. The stage of completion is the percentage of work completed on a unit of product at any point in time. From this estimate and other known facts, three groupings are defined:

1. Units in beginning inventory completed during the period. The work to complete these units is represented by 100 percent less the stage of completion at the beginning of the period.

2. Units started and completed during the period. These units had 100 percent of the work done during the period.
3. Partially completed units at the end of the period. These units had work done during the period equal to the stage of completion.

Example.   On September 1, 19x9, the finishing Department at Hawks Airjet, Inc., has in process 10 units that are 20 percent complete on finishing effort. During the month of September, the department completed the beginning units in process, started and completed 20 more planes, and had 10 ending units in process that were 70 percent complete. The stage of completion for each group is illustrated in Exhibit 9–2.

Equivalent Units of Production

Equivalent units of production represent the theoretical number of units that could have been produced had the resources been applied only to starting and completing units. The computation of equivalent units works this way:

1. Units in beginning inventory are multiplied by 100 percent less the stage of completion at the beginning of the period to find the equivalent production to complete the beginning inventory.
2. The units started and completed are multiplied by 100 percent because the total work was done during the period.
3. The units in the ending inventory are multiplied by their stage of completion.

The sum of these three computations is called the *current equivalent production for the period*. This is the number of units that could have been produced if all production were started and completed during the period, no beginning or ending inventories.

Example Units Analysis No. 1:   For the Hawks Airjet data, the following equivalent unit analysis would be performed:

To complete beginning units	10 Units × (100% − 20%) =	8
Started and completed	20 Units × 100%	= 20
Ending inventory	10 × 70%	= 7
Equivalent units of production		35

EXHIBIT 9–2   Hawks Airjet, Inc., Finishing (stage of completion)

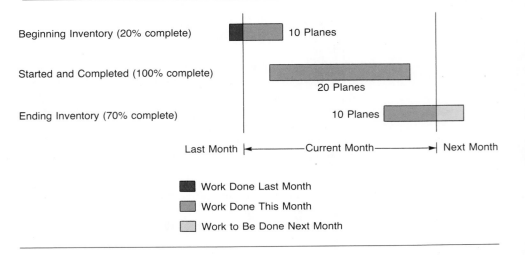

Example Units Analysis No. 2: The Tres Rios Plant makes denim jeans. Its Cutting Department cuts bales of denim pieces. The denim cloth is layered to 3-feet thick (1,000 layers) and the entire pile is cut very carefully to exact specifications for each style and size. The beginning Work in Process Inventory consisted of piles containing material for 10,000 jeans that was 80 percent cut; 100,000 pair were started and completely cut during the period; and 5,000 pair were 40 percent cut at the end of the period. Equivalent production for the period is 104,000, calculated as follows:

To complete beginning inventory	10,000 pair × (100% − 80%) =	2,000
Started and completed	100,000 pair × 100%	= 100,000
Ending inventory	5,000 pair × 40%	= 2,000
Equivalent units of production		104,000

Units Started and Completed. Units started and completed are not generally known but must be calculated. What is known is the number of units started and total units completed, such as for the two examples:

	Hawks Airjet	Tres Rios Plant
Beginning inventory	10	10,000
Started	30	105,000
Available	40	115,000
Less: ending inventory	10	5,000
Completed	30	110,000

Subtracting the beginning inventory units from completed units we find the units started and completed. For the two example analyses:

	Hawks Airjet	Tres Rios Plant
Units completed	30	110,000
Beginning inventory	10	10,000
Units started and completed	20	100,000

Inputs at Different Times

Materials, labor, and production overhead constitute the inputs to manufactured products. These inputs may enter at different points during a process. Material often enters at the beginning of the process and labor and overhead enter continuously throughout the process. Consequently, it is possible for some units in process to have all of their material content but only part of the labor and production overhead. In other manufacturing processes, materials may enter continuously or near the end of the process.

In order to determine unit costs when inputs enter at different points, it is necessary to calculate the equivalent units individually for material, labor, and production overhead. In most operations, labor and overhead are added to the product at the same rate, so we can treat them as one input and call it **conversion cost.**

For example, assume that in the Cutting Department of the Tres Rios Plant the material (denim) enters at the beginning of the process and that the conversion costs (labor and overhead) occur uniformly throughout cutting. The following is a summary of equivalent production for the period:

	Pair	Materials (Percent Complete)	Conversion (Percent Complete)
Beginning inventory	10,000	100	80
Units started and completed	100,000	100	100
Ending inventory	5,000	100	40

	Materials	*Conversion*
To complete beginning inventory		
10,000 × (100% − 100%)	0	
10,000 × (100% − 80%)		2,000
Units started and completed		
100,000 × 100%	100,000	100,000
Ending inventory		
5,000 × 100%	5,000	
5,000 × 40%		2,000
Equivalent units of production	105,000	104,000

Cost Flow Concepts

There are two generally recognized methods for calculating product costs in a process cost system: first-in, first-out (FIFO) and weighted average. The methods use different equivalent units and unit costs in allocations to units completed and ending work in process.

FIFO Equivalent Units. FIFO process costing treats the current period's costs in a department as a batch. Consequently, the **FIFO equivalent units** required for process costing are those related to current production. We have already demonstrated this calculation in previous examples. Specifically, the Cutting Department for the Tres Rios Plant has FIFO equivalent units calculated as:

	Materials	*Conversion*
Equivalent units of production	105,000	104,000

Weighted Average Equivalent Units. The weighted average process costing method averages the costs for the beginning work in process with the current production. Consequently, the **weighted average equivalent units** assumes that the beginning inventory and the started and completed units were all started and completed during the period. This permits an equivalent units calculation consisting of the total units completed plus ending work in process.

Example analysis. Applying the weighted average units concept to the Cutting Department example results in:

	Materials	*Conversion*
Units completed during period	110,000	110,000
Ending work in process		
5,000 units × 100%	5,000	
5,000 units × 40%		2,000
Equivalent units of production	115,000	112,000

FIFO AND WEIGHTED AVERAGE PROCESS COSTING

The computations and results of process costing are commonly displayed in summary report form that is often called the **cost of production report.** Although the report format and name vary substantially among accounting systems, most formats display both units worked on and associated costs. The total and unit costs are determined and summarized either in a cost of production report for each individual department or in a report for a completed product.

Computational Steps

Five important steps generate the information appearing in the cost of production report. We have already discussed and illustrated the first two. The steps are:

1. Determine the physical unit flow.
2. Calculate units of equivalent production.
3. Find total costs to account for.
4. Compute equivalent unit costs.
5. Allocate total costs.

Each of these steps is presented below in the preparation of a cost of production report. The production and cost data for Super Enterprises, Inc., are summarized in Exhibit 9–3. Super Enterprises produces large plastic toys such as jungle gyms. The product is manufactured in two departments: Molding and Finishing. In Molding, plastic pellets are melted and molded into standardized shapes. Then in the Finishing Department units are assembled into sets for a complete product and are packaged for shipment. In the next sections, we will concentrate on the Molding Department. The Finishing Department production will be discussed later in the chapter.

In reviewing the data in Exhibit 9–3, notice that the completion rates are given for both beginning and ending inventories. Further, the transferred-in cost for the Finishing Department is not known until the transferred-out cost has been computed for the Molding Department.

EXHIBIT 9–3

SUPER ENTERPRISES, INC.
Summary of Production Data
For the Month Ending March 31, 19x3

	Departments	
	Molding	*Finishing*
Work in Process, March 1, 19x3:		
Units	1,000	1,800
Stage of completion:		
Transferred in		100%
Materials	100%	100%
Labor and overhead	40%	60%
Costs:		
Transferred in		$21,600
Materials	$ 3,000	1,800
Labor	1,920	1,944
Overhead	1,600	3,456
Beginning inventory total cost	$ 6,520	$28,800
Units started	4,000	4,500
Units completed and transferred out	4,500	4,800
Current period costs for March:		
Transferred-in costs		?
Materials	$14,400	$ 5,130
Labor	17,600	9,840
Overhead	21,120	13,776
Total costs added	$53,120	?
Work in Process, March 31, 19x3:		
Units	500	1,500
Stage of completion:		
Transferred-in		100%
Materials	100%	100%
Conversion	60%	80%

We will now apply the five-step method to the Super Enterprises data for September 19x9.

Step 1: Physical Flow.   Determining the physical flow for a department involves identifying the units in the beginning inventory plus the units started in the department during the period and then tracing the disposition of those units. Some units are completed and transferred to the next department or to Finished Goods Inventory, and the remaining units are in the department's ending inventory.[2] The quantity schedule, a section in the cost of production report, is the vehicle used to show physical flow. This schedule displays whole units, regardless of their stage of completion.

The production data of Super Enterprises show the following physical flow for the super toys in the molding department:

	Molding
Units to account for:	
Beginning Work in Process Inventory	1,000
Units started	4,000
Units to account for	5,000
Units accounted for:	
Units completed and transferred out	4,500
(1,000 units were in beginning inventory	
and 3,500 units were started and completed)	
Ending Work in Process Inventory	500
Units accounted for	5,000

Step 2: Equivalent Units.   The next step in preparing a cost of production report is the calculation of equivalent units, which is necessary to compute the unit cost for material and conversion costs.

	Materials	*Conversion*
FIFO equivalent units:		
To complete Beginning Inventory		
1,000 × (100% − 100%)	0	
1,000 × (100% − 40%)		600
Units started and completed		
3,500 × 100%	3,500	3,500
Ending inventory		
500 × 100%	500	
500 × 60%		300
FIFO equivalent units of production	4,000	4,400
Weighted average equivalent units:		
Units completed		
4,500 × 100%	4,500	4,500
Ending inventory		
500 × 100%	500	
500 × 60%		300
Weighted average equivalent units	5,000	4,800

---

[2] As a technical point, it is possible to have units completed but not transferred at the end of the period. This means there are two types of ending inventory; one is 100 percent complete but the other is at some lesser stage of completion. Unless otherwise specified, we assume that all completed units have been transferred out.

It is also possible to have units spoiled or damaged in the process. This circumstance is treated later in Chapter 11.

Step 3: Find Costs to Account for.   In order to compute unit costs, it is necessary to know the equivalent units and the costs the department is responsible for during the period. There are three sources from which the costs come. First, there may be a beginning inventory of partially completed units. If so, the material, labor, and production overhead costs attached to these units must be accounted for by the department. Second, any prior departments will have costs attached to units transferred into the current department. Transferred-in costs become the responsibility of the current department. And, third, the department incurs material, labor, or production overhead during the current period for its own processing. The total of these costs, which is the total of the debits to Work in Process for the department, must be determined and accounted for. We will defer discussing the transferred-in costs to a later section in which we discuss the effects of prior departments.

There are material cost of $3,000 and conversion cost of $3,520 ($1,920 for direct labor plus $1,600 for production overhead) in the beginning inventory of the Molding Department. The current costs added during the period were materials of $14,400 and conversion cost of $38,720 (direct labor of $17,600 and production overhead of $21,120). The following schedule gives the total costs that must be accounted for in the cost of production report:

	Material	Conversion	Total
Beginning inventory	$ 3,000	$ 3,520	$ 6,520
Current period costs	14,400	38,720	53,120
Total costs to account for	$17,400	$42,240	$59,640

Step 4: Cost Per Equivalent Unit.   Unit costs are necessary to (1) give essential comparative data to managers, (2) provide a basis for transferring costs from one operating department to another or to Finished Goods Inventory, and (3) provide a basis for allocating costs to ending inventories. The unit cost of manufacturing for each cost element—material, labor, and overhead—is calculated by dividing the related cost by the equivalent units of production for that cost element.

FIFO unit costs.   Remember that in unit cost calculations there is supposed to be a relationship between the costs in the numerator and the equivalent units in the denominator. Under the FIFO method, equivalent units represent the units that would have been completed during the period had the inputs been applied only to started and completed units. Therefore, equivalent unit costs are calculated with a division of current costs by equivalent units. The costs in the beginning inventory—those relating to the prior period—are ignored in the unit cost calculations. These costs will be charged directly to the cost of goods completed, as will be seen below in the cost of production report. Because FIFO deals only with current period costs and units, it provides more current information for management in their decision-making.

The unit costs for this example are:

	Material	Conversion	Total
Current period costs	$14,400	$38,720	$53,120
FIFO equivalent production	4,000	4,400	
Unit costs	$3.60	$8.80	$12.40

These FIFO unit costs will be used to allocate costs between the ending work in process of super toys and the units completed during the period.

Weighted average unit costs.   As we stated earlier, in the weighted average method, the beginning inventory is assumed to be included in the units started and completed. Therefore, the costs of the beginning inventory are added to the current costs for purposes of calculating the unit costs. In the weighted average method, divide the weighted average equivalent units into the total costs (beginning inventory plus current period costs) as follows:

	Material	Conversion	Total
Beginning inventory	$ 3,000	$ 3,520	$ 6,520
Current period costs	14,400	38,720	53,120
Total costs to account for	$17,400	$42,240	$59,640
Weighted average equivalent units	5,000	4,800	
Weighted average unit costs	$3.48	$8.80	$12.28

Step 5: Allocation of Costs.   After determining the costs for which the department is responsible, there must be an accounting for the disposition of those costs. Some costs are allocated to the units completed and transferred out, either to another department or to Finished Goods Inventory. Costs are also allocated to the partially completed units remaining in the ending inventory.

FIFO cost allocations.   Under the FIFO method, costs of the current period are allocated to the ending Work in Process Inventory in the department and to the completed units (beginning inventory plus units started and completed). This allocation assumes that materials, labor, and overhead are used in the order in which they enter the process. Therefore, the first costs recorded in a period are incurred to complete units already in process. Subsequent costs are then applied to the new units started in the process during the period. Because FIFO assumes that the ending work in process started the process last, these units are part of those units started during the period.

The calculation of costs for the Super Enterprises, Inc., example is as follows:

Costs of completed units:		
(1) Beginning Work in Process	$6,520	
To complete beginning inventory:		
Materials 1,000 × (100% − 100%) × $3.60	0	
Conversion 1,000 × (100% − 40%) × $8.80	5,280	
Cost of completed beginning inventory		$11,800
(2) Next, allocate costs to units started and completed during		
the period. Use the total cost per unit in this calculation:		
Units started and completed		
3,500 × 100% × $12.40		43,400
Total cost of goods completed and transferred		$55,200
Costs of ending Work in Process:		
Use the equivalent units for ending inventory to allocate		
costs to the ending Work in Process.		
Materials 500 × 100% × $3.60	$1,800	
Conversion 500 × 60% × $8.80	2,640	
Total cost of ending Work in Process		4,440
Total costs accounted for		$59,640

We now have the disposition of the costs accumulated in the department during the period. The ending inventory has a cost allocated to it of $4,440 (material cost, $1,800 and conversion cost, $2,640) and costs allocated to the units completed sum to \$55,200. The cost of production report that reflects the production and cost information plus the above allocation of costs is presented in Exhibit 9–4.

Weighted average allocations.   The weighted average cost method averages the beginning inventory costs with current period production and treats the completed

EXHIBIT 9–4

SUPER ENTERPRISES, INC., MOLDING DEPARTMENT
Cost of Production Report (FIFO Method)
For the Period Ending March 31, 19x3

Quantities

Units to account for:			
Units in process, beginning		1,000	
Units started during month		4,000	
Total units to account for			5,000
Units accounted for:			
Units completed—			
Units in process, beginning	1,000		
Units started and completed	3,500	4,500	
Units in process, ending		500	
Total units accounted for			5,000

Costs

Costs to account for:			
Costs in process, beginning			\$ 6,520
Costs incurred during month			
Materials		\$14,400	
Labor		17,600	
Overhead		21,120	53,120
Total costs to account for			\$59,640
Costs accounted for:			
Units completed—			
Units in process, beginning	\$ 6,520		
Costs to complete	5,280	\$11,800	
Units started and completed		43,400	
Total costs of completed units			\$55,200
Units in process, ending			
Materials		\$ 1,800	
Conversion		2,640	4,440
Total costs accounted for			\$59,640

Additional Calculations

	Molding	
	Materials	*Conversion*
Current period costs	\$14,400	\$38,720
Computation of equivalent units:		
To complete beginning units in process	0	600
Units started and completed	3,500	3,500
Ending inventory	500	300
FIFO equivalent units	4,000	4,400
Equivalent unit costs	\$ 3.60	\$ 8.80

units as if they were all one batch. Thus the allocations are based on units completed and ending work in process:

Units completed	$4,500 \times 100\% \times \$12.28 = \$55,260$

Ending inventory of work in process is computed in the same manner as the FIFO method, except there is a different cost per unit:

Ending work in process	
Materials	$500 \times 100\% \times \$3.48 = \$1,740$
Conversion costs	$500 \times 60\% \times 8.80 = \underline{2,640}$
Total costs of ending Work in Process	$\underline{4,380}$
Total costs accounted for	$\underline{\underline{\$59,640}}$

A cost of production report using the weighted average method is presented in Exhibit 9–5.

Notice that both the FIFO report in Exhibit 9–4 and the weighted average report in Exhibit 9–5 have about the same format with exactly the same amounts down to the "Cost to account for" line. Further, there is little difference in the allocated amounts between the two methods. This similarity in results will generally be true, unless the beginning inventory is relatively large and last period's costs are very different from the current period costs.

Journal Entries

At some time during the period, journal entries will record the dollars shown in the reports. The FIFO and weighted average methods do not influence the physical flow of the product and do not affect the current costs incurred in a department during the period. Therefore, the journal entries to record material usage, labor, and overhead are the same for both methods. Dollar amounts in the following journal entries are taken from the cost of production reports in Exhibits 9–4 and 9–5.

1. Entry to record the requisition of materials from the storeroom and place them into production:

Work in Process—Molding	14,400	
Materials Inventory		14,400

2. Entry to charge labor costs to Molding:

Work in Process—Molding	17,600	
Payroll		17,600

3. Entry to charge production overhead costs to Molding:

Work in Process—Molding	21,120	
Production overhead		21,120

4. Entry to record the transfer of toys from Molding to Finishing:

FIFO method

Work in Process—Finishing	55,200	
Work in Process—Molding		55,200

Weighted average method

Work in Process—Finishing	55,260	
Work in Process—Molding		55,260

Comment on Weighted Average Method

The weighted average method is a much easier and simpler method because it does not require tracking the costs in the beginning inventory separately from those costs added during the current period. The method is justified primarily on its convenience

EXHIBIT 9–5

SUPER ENTERPRISES, INC., MOLDING DEPARTMENT
Cost of Production Report (Weighted Average Method)
For the Period Ending March 31, 19x3

Quantities

Units to account for:		
Units in process, beginning	1,000	
Units started during month	4,000	
Total units to account for		5,000
Units accounted for:		
Units completed	4,500	
Units in process, ending	500	
Total units accounted for		5,000

Costs

Costs to account for:		
Costs in process, beginning		$ 6,520
Costs incurred during month		
Materials	$14,400	
Labor	17,600	
Overhead	21,120	53,120
Total costs to account for		$59,640
Costs accounted for:		
Completed units		$55,260
Units in process, ending		
Materials	$ 1,740	
Conversion	2,640	4,380
Total costs accounted for		$59,640

Additional Calculations

	Molding	
	Materials	*Conversion*
Costs:		
Costs in process, beginning	$ 3,000	$ 3,520
Current period costs	14,400	38,720
Total Costs	$17,400	$42,240
Computation of equivalent units:		
Units completed	4,500	4,500
Ending inventory	500	300
Equivalent production	5,000	4,800
Equivalent unit costs	$ 3.48	$ 8.80

and simplicity. Because the products are homogeneous when process costing is used, each unit should cost about the same regardless of when it is produced. Inflation and labor union agreements are examples of factors affecting the cost elements from one period to the next. By and large, however, one would expect the production costs per unit in one period to approximate the unit cost in the next period. As a result, the weighted average method often gives reasonable results.

SUBSEQUENT DEPARTMENTS

No major complications are introduced into process costing when the output of one department becomes an input to a subsequent one. Simply treat the costs transferred in from the previous department as a current cost incurred at the beginning of the process. It is just like an additional material cost added at the beginning of the process. These costs are called **transferred-in costs** or **prior department costs** and are accounted for separately from any materials added in the subsequent department. With this minor modification, all calculations in subsequent departments are identical to those already illustrated.

One thing to consider is that the output from one department can change its unit of measurement when entering the subsequent department. For example, 2 pounds of a chemical compound produced in one department may go into a 5-pound container produced in a subsequent department. Then the unit of measure becomes a container with 5 pounds of chemical compound instead of individual pounds of the compound.

As an example of a cost of production report for a subsequent department, let's consider the Finishing Department of Super Enterprises. Production data are available in Exhibit 9–3. The cost of production report using the FIFO method appears in Exhibit 9–6; the weighted average method is Exhibit 9–7.

Journal Entries

The journal entries are very similar to those made for Molding. The ending entry for Molding resulted in an increase in the Finishing Work in Process. Remember that there were slightly different amounts depending on the process costing method:

FIFO Method

Work in Process—Finishing	55,200	
Work in Process—Molding		55,200

Weighted Average Method

Work in Process—Finishing	55,260	
Work in Process—Molding		55,260

Additional entries required to account for the activity in the Finishing Department are:

1. Entry to record the requisition of additional materials from the storeroom and place them into production:

Work in Process—Finishing	5,130	
Materials Inventory		5,130

2. Entry to charge labor costs to Finishing:

Work in Process—Finishing	9,840	
Payroll		9,840

3. Entry to charge production overhead costs to Finishing:

Work in Process—Finishing	13,776	
Production Overhead		13,776

4. Entry to record the transfer of completed toys from Finishing to Finished Goods Inventory:

FIFO Method

Finished Goods Inventory	86,876	
Work in Process—Finished		86,876

EXHIBIT 9–6

SUPER ENTERPRISES, INC., FINISHING DEPARTMENT
Cost of Production Report (FIFO Method)
For the Period Ending March 31, 19x3

Quantities

Units to account for:			
Units in process, beginning		1,800	
Units started during month		4,500	
Total units to account for			6,300
Units accounted for:			
Units completed—			
Units in process, beginning	1,800		
Units started and completed	3,000	4,800	
Units in process, ending		1,500	
Total units accounted for			6,300

Costs

Costs to account for:			
Costs in process, beginning			$ 28,800
Costs incurred during month			
Transferred in		$55,200	
Materials		5,130	
Labor		9,840	
Overhead		13,776	83,946
Total costs to account for			$112,746
Costs accounted for:			
Units completed—			
Units in process, beginning	$28,800		
Costs to complete			
(720 units × $4.80)	3,456	$32,256	
Units started and completed			
(3,000 units × $18.207)		54,620	
Total costs of completed units			$ 86,876
Units in process, ending			
Transferred in (1,500 × $12.267)		$18,400	
Materials (1,500 × $1.14)		1,710	
Conversion (1,200 × $4.80)		5,760	25,870
Total costs accounted for			$112,746

Additional Calculations:

	Transferred In	Materials	Conversion
Current periods costs	$55,200	$ 5,130	$ 23,616
Computation of equivalent units:			
To complete beginning inventory	0	0	720
Units started and completed	3,000	3,000	3,000
Ending inventory	1,500	1,500	1,200
FIFO equivalent units	4,500	4,500	4,920
Equivalent unit costs	$12.267	$ 1.140	$ 4.800

EXHIBIT 9–7

SUPER ENTERPRISES, INC., FINISHING DEPARTMENT
Cost of Production Report (Weighted Average Method)
For the Period Ending March 31, 19x3

Quantities

Units to account for:		
Units in process, beginning	1,800	
Units started during month	4,500	
Total units to account for		6,300
Units accounted for:		
Units completed	4,800	
Units in process, ending	1,500	
Total units accounted for		6,300

Costs

Costs to account for:		
Costs in process, beginning		$ 28,800
Costs incurred during month		
Transferred in	$55,260	
Materials	5,130	
Labor	9,840	
Overhead	13,776	
Current period costs		84,006
Total costs to account for		$112,806
Costs accounted for:		
Completed units (4,800 units × $18.136)		$ 87,053
Units in process, ending		
Transferred in (1,500 units × $12.20)	$18,300	
Materials (1,500 units × $1.10)	1,650	
Conversion (1,200 units × $4.836)	5,803	
Total ending work in process		25,753
Total costs accounted for		$112,806

Additional Calculations:

	Transferred In	Materials	Conversion
Costs in process, beginning	$21,600	$ 1,800	$ 5,400
Current period costs	55,260	5,130	23,616
Total costs	$76,860	$ 6,930	$ 29,016
Computation of equivalent units:			
Units completed	4,800	4,800	4,800
Ending inventory	1,500	1,500	1,200
Equivalent production	6,300	6,300	6,000
Equivalent unit costs	$12.200	$ 1.100	$ 4.836

Weighted Average Method		
Finished Goods Inventory	87,053	
Work in Process—Finished		87,053

Again notice that there is only a small difference in the completed unit costs, even after the costs have passed through two departments.

SIMPLIFICATIONS ARISING FROM JIT ENVIRONMENT

Many companies are adopting the just-in-time (JIT) operating philosophy for production and purchasing. In concept, this philosophy means inventories should be reduced to zero. Items are produced to specific orders and shipped immediately upon completion. For example, final departments assemble products just in time to be shipped, and parts, components, and subassemblies are manufactured just in time to meet the assembly needs. Thus each department's production is scheduled to meet the needs of the succeeding department. In fact, quite often there is no distinction among departments. Operations are simply identified along a production line.

The just-in-time philosophy is an approach to eliminate waste and improve quality. Waste is defined as nonproductive activity, viewed as activities that do not add value to the product. For example, inspection, counting, holding, or buffer stocks do not add value to the product. The result is a significant reduction in inventory levels of raw materials, production moving between operations or departments, and finished goods inventories.

JIT, if properly implemented, simplifies accounting for a process cost system. If inventories between operations or departments are immaterial at the close of a reporting period, it is unnecessary to split costs between goods completed and ending Work in Process Inventory. In addition, there is no need to account for the costs transferred from one department to the next. Thus, the costs are accumulated and flow directly into Cost of Goods Sold. Process costs per unit are still calculated, but more on a daily or weekly basis with the costs for each process divided by the units produced.

However, there are two cautions. First, JIT is not always fully implemented and operated properly, thus creating some inventories that must be accounted for. Second, some products involve aging in the production process in which case there will always be significant units in process. Liquors, wines, aged beef, crystal growth (for integrated circuits), certain pharmaceutical products, and many other products require significant time and, thus, work in process inventories. Thus, process costing with equivalent unit calculations will continue to be appropriate for these products.

SUMMARY

The two primary methods used to allocate manufacturing costs to the units produced are job order costing and process costing. Job order costing is used when different products are produced in lots or batches and each lot or batch receives various levels of the cost inputs in each operation or cost center. Process costing is used for homogeneous products manufactured on a continuous basis or mass produced.

The primary reporting document in a process cost system is the cost of production report. Five steps are involved in the preparation of this report:

1. Determine the physical flow of the units during the period.
2. Calculate the equivalent units for each cost input during the period.
3. Find the total costs (costs in the beginning inventory and current period costs) to account for.
4. Compute the unit cost for each input and the total per unit cost for the product or service.
5. Allocate the costs in the department for the period to units completed and transferred out, and to units in the ending inventory.

FIFO and weighted average methods may be used to allocate costs among units completed and ending work in process inventories. The major difference between the two methods is the treatment of the beginning inventory. FIFO treats the beginning Work in Process Inventory as a separate batch while weighted average averages the beginning process inventories with the current production.

As products move from one department to another, the costs of previous departments are treated as if they were material costs added at the beginning of the process. Thus, prior department costs become an additional cost element to consider along with the material, labor, and overhead of the current department.

PROBLEM FOR REVIEW

Hawks Airjet, Inc., has the following information regarding its production for the month ending September 30, 19x9:

	Assembly	*Finishing*	*Total*
Work in process, September 1, 19x9:			
Units	10	10	
Transferred in		100%	
Materials	100%	100%	
Conversion	20%	20%	
Transferred in		$7,000,000	$ 7,000,000
Materials	$ 5,000,000	1,000,000	6,000,000
Labor	100,000	200,000	300,000
Overhead	300,000	200,000	500,000
Total costs in process	$ 5,400,000	$8,400,000	$13,800,000
Units completed	30	30	30
Current period costs			
Materials	$15,360,000	$2,850,000	$18,210,000
Labor	1,800,000	3,430,000	5,230,000
Overhead	5,400,000	3,440,500	8,840,500
Total current period costs	$22,560,000	$9,720,500	$32,280,500
Work in process, September 30, 19x9			
Units	10	10	
Stage of completion:			
Transferred in	0%	100%	
Materials	100%	100%	
Conversion	80%	70%	
Additional data:			
September sales 30 units at $1,200,000			$36,000,000
Selling expenses			3,000,000
Administrative and general expenses			600,000

No inventories of finished goods are kept. All production is to fill orders received.

REQUIRED

a. Using the FIFO method of process costing, prepare a process cost report for the two departments.

b. Using the weighted average method of process costing, prepare a process cost report for the two departments.

c. Assuming a tax rate of 40 percent, prepare an income statement using a cost of goods sold amount based on:
  1. FIFO process costing.
  2. Weighted average process costing.

d. The president has expressed deep concern regarding the profitability of the company. Based on the current period production cost of $32.30 for completed units, he concluded that the company income is only about $100,000, which is inadequate. Prepare a memorandum to Mr. John Riley, corporate president, from Jillel Washington, corporate controller, on why the costs for September appeared to be high relative to a $1,000,000 desired unit cost.

SOLUTION

a. Process cost report using the FIFO process costing method.

HAWKS AIRJET X5
Cost of Production Report
For the Period Ending September 30, 19x9
(FIFO method)

Quantities

	Assembly	Finishing
Units to account for:		
Units in process, beginning	10	10
Units started during month	30	30
Total units to account for	40	40
Units accounted for:		
Units completed	30	30
(10 beginning and 20 started and completed)		
Units in process, ending	10	10
Total units accounted for	40	40

Costs

	Assembly	Finishing
Costs to account for:		
Costs in process, beginning	$ 5,400,000	$ 8,400,000
Costs incurred during month		
Transferred in		21,240,000
Materials	15,360,000	2,850,000
Labor	1,800,000	3,430,000
Overhead	5,400,000	3,440,500
Total costs to account for	$27,960,000	$39,360,500
Costs accounted for:		
Units in process, beginning	$ 5,400,000	$ 8,400,000
Costs to complete	1,600,000	1,570,400
Total costs for beginning	$ 7,000,000	$ 9,970,400
Units started and completed	14,240,000	19,986,000
Total costs of completed units	$21,240,000	$29,956,400
Units in process, ending		
Transferred in		$ 7,080,000
Materials	$ 5,120,000	950,000
Conversion	1,600,000	1,374,100
Total units in process	$ 6,720,000	$ 9,404,100
Total costs accounted for	$27,960,000	$39,360,500

ADDITIONAL CALCULATIONS

	Assembly	
	Materials	Conversion
Current period costs	$15,360,000	$ 7,200,000
Computation of equivalent units:		
To complete beginning inventory		
Materials 10 × (100% − 100%)	0	
Conversion 10 × (100% − 20%)		8
Units started and completed (30 − 10) × 100%	20	20
Ending inventory		
Materials 10 × 100%	10	
Conversion 10 × 80%	—	8
FIFO equivalent units	30	36
Equivalent unit costs	$512,000	$200,000

	Finishing		
	Transferred In	Materials	Conversion
Current period costs	$21,240,000	$2,850,000	$6,870,500
Computation of equivalent units:			
To complete beginning work in process			
Transferred in 10 × (100% − 100%)	0		
Materials 10 × (100% − 100%)		0	
Conversion 10 × (100% − 20%)			8
Units started and completed 20 × 100%	20	20	20
Ending inventory			
Transferred in 10 × 100%	10		
Materials 10 × 100%		10	
Conversion 10 × 70%	—	—	7
FIFO equivalent units	30	30	35
Equivalent unit costs	$708,000	$95,000	$196,300

b. Process cost report using the weighted average process costing method.

HAWKS AIRJET X5
Cost of Production Report
For the Period Ending September 30, 19x9
(weighted average method)

	Quantities	
	Assembly	Finishing
Units to account for:		
Units in process, beginning	10	10
Units started during month	30	30
Total units to account for	40	40
Units accounted for:		
Units completed	30	30
Units in process, ending	10	10
Total units accounted for	40	40

Costs

	Assembly	Finishing
Costs to account for:		
Costs in process, beginning	$ 5,400,000	$ 8,400,000
Costs incurred during month		
Transferred in		21,270,000
Materials	15,360,000	2,850,000
Labor	1,800,000	3,430,000
Overhead	5,400,000	3,440,500
Total costs to account for	$27,960,000	$39,390,500
Costs accounted for:		
Completed units	$21,270,000	$29,985,000
Units in process, ending		
Transferred in		7,067,500
Materials	5,090,000	962,500
Conversion	1,600,000	1,375,500
Total ending work in process	$ 6,690,000	$ 9,405,500
Total costs accounted for	$27,960,000	$39,390,500

ADDITIONAL CALCULATIONS

Assembly

	Materials	Conversion
Costs in process, beginning	$ 5,000,000	$ 400,000
Current period costs	15,360,000	7,200,000
Total costs	$20,360,000	$ 7,600,000
Computation of equivalent units:		
Units completed	30	30
Ending inventory	10	8
Weighted average equivalent production	40	38
Equivalent unit costs	$509,000	$200,000

Finishing

		Transferred In	Materials	Conversion
Costs in process, beginning		$ 7,000,000	$ 1,000,000	$ 400,000
Current period costs		21,270,000	2,850,000	6,870,500
Total costs		$28,270,000	$ 3,850,000	$7,270,500
Computation of equivalent units:				
Units completed	30 × 100%	30	30	30
Ending inventory				
Transferred in	10 × 100%	10		
Materials	10 × 100%		10	
Conversion	10 × 70%			7
Equivalent production		40	40	37
Equivalent unit costs		$706,750	$96,250	$196,500

c. Preparation of income statement using 1. FIFO, 2. Weighted Average
Because no ending finished goods inventories are kept, the cost of goods sold is equal to the cost of goods completed in the Finishing Department. This may be found in the "Cost accounted for" section of the cost of production report for each of the methods.

HAWKS AIRJET, INC.
Income Statement
For the Month Ending September 30, 19x9

	Process Cost Accounting Method	
	1. FIFO	*2. Weighted Average*
Sales	$36,000,000	$36,000,000
Cost of goods sold	29,956,400	29,985,000
Gross margin	$ 6,043,600	$ 6,015,000
Selling expenses	3,000,000	3,000,000
General and administrative	600,000	600,000
Operating income	$ 2,443,600	$ 2,415,000
Income taxes (40%)	977,440	966,000
Net income	$ 1,466,160	$ 1,449,000

d. Memorandum on product cost for the X5. This memo uses very heavily the information found in the FIFO process cost report.

Memorandum

To: John Riley, Corporate President

From: Jillel Washington, Corporate Controller

Regarding: Costs on the X5 for September 19x9

After a careful review of production costs, the following costs per plane were incurred during September:

	Materials	*Conversion*	*Total*
Assembly	$512,000	$200,000	$ 712,000
Finishing	95,000	196,300	291,300
Total costs	$607,000	$396,300	$1,003,300

This cost per plane is quite reasonable when compared with the $1,000,000 target cost.

The reason costs appeared to be so high was because the Assembly Department assembled the equivalent of 36 planes and Finishing performed work that was the equivalent of 35 planes. This occurred because the planes in process in each department at the beginning of the month were only 20 percent assembled and 20 percent finished. The ending inventory was 80 percent assembled and 70 percent finished.

	Assembly	*Finishing*	*Total*
Materials for 30 planes			
30 @ $512,000	$15,360,000		
30 @ $95,000		$2,850,000	$18,210,000
Labor and overhead			
36 @ $200,000	7,200,000		
35 @ $196,300		6,870,500	14,070,500
Totals	$22,560,000	$9,720,500	$32,280,500

Therefore, the September production costs were high because the equivalent of 36 planes was assembled and the equivalent of 35 planes was finished.

KEY TERMS AND CONCEPTS

Process costing (322)
Departmental overhead control ledger (324)
Equivalent units of production (326)
Conversion cost (327)
FIFO equivalent units (328)

Weighted average equivalent units (328)
Cost of production report (328)
Transferred-in costs (336)
Prior department costs (336)

ADDITIONAL READINGS

Bonsack, Robert A. "Cost Accounting in the Factory of the Future." *CIM Review,* Spring 1986, pp. 28–32.

Franke, .Reimund. "Process Model for Costing." *Management Accounting,* January 1975, pp. 45–47.

Howell, Robert A., and Stephen R. Soucy. "Cost Accounting in the New Manufacturing Environment." *Management Accounting,* August 1987, pp. 42–48.

McCollum, James K.; Edward F. Stafford; J. Daniel Sherman; and Carolyn S. Thurman. "Variants of Shift Scheduling for High Tech Continuous Process Manufacturing." *The Southern Business & Economic Journal,* April 1989, pp. 142–51.

REVIEW QUESTIONS

1. What situations are suitable to a process cost system?
2. What accounting record is the backbone of a process cost system?
3. Summarize briefly the five steps to preparing a cost of production report.
4. What are equivalent units and why are they necessary with process costing?
5. What is the distinction between equivalent units under FIFO and equivalent units under the weighted average method?
6. Under what circumstances are identical results obtained under FIFO and weighted average?
7. What purpose does a quantity schedule serve?
8. On the cost of production report, the weighted average method treats all units transferred out in the same way. How does this differ from the FIFO method of handling units transferred out?
9. At what stage of completion are transferred-in units in a subsequent department?
10. Why should we distinguish between transferred-in costs and those associated with materials added in a particular department?

DISCUSSION QUESTIONS

11. What is the effect, this period and next, of overestimating the percentage of completion of ending inventory in a process cost situation?
12. A company wants to use the weighted average method because it is simple to apply. However, the company also wishes to be able to monitor its costs. Is it possible to monitor cost trends using the weighted average method?
13. A company has records of its current activity in Work in Process Inventory and of its ending Work in Process Inventory but has lost records of its beginning inventory. Express in equation form how to compute the needed information about beginning inventory.
14. From the standpoint of cost control, why is the FIFO method superior to the weighted average method?

EXERCISES

9–1. Physical Flow. Find the missing value as indicated by the "?" in each of the following circumstances:

(S. Whitecotton)

	a.	*b.*	*c.*	*d.*	*e.*	*f.*
Beginning inventory	200	500		500	300	?
Started units	600		1,350		?	
Completed units	?	1,600		?	1,750	1,222
Started and completed		?	800	2,000		990
Ending inventory	300	400	?		200	400

9–2. Calculating Equivalent Units.   Calculate the equivalent units for each of the following independent departments. Perform the calculations using *a.* the weighted average method and then *b.* the FIFO method.

	A	B	C	D
Beginning inventory:	0	12,000	6,000	4,000
% Complete—materials	0	100	30	0
% Complete—conversion	0	20	60	70
Units completed	20,000	40,000	80,000	60,000
Ending inventory:	3,000	9,000	6,000	10,000
% Complete—materials	100	100	40	0
% Complete—conversion	80	30	20	10

9–3. Equivalent Units.   Charles and Linda Griffith grow striped bass to stocking size in 10 specially built tanks. Each tank will hold up to 1,000 fish. The average time it takes to grow these bass to a stocking size of 6 inches is three months. At the start of 19x5 they had 8 tanks in which the fish were 50 percent grown. During the year they started and completed 28 tanks. At the end of the year, they had 8 tanks that were 25 percent grown.

(T. Pratt, adapted)

REQUIRED:
Compute the equivalent units of conversion cost using the:
a. FIFO method.
b. Weighted average method.

9–4. Equivalent Units.   Lifeline, Inc., produces a new version of an artificial heart that is successful with patients willing to be confined to a limited space. The machine is portable, but it is heavy and not easily moved outside a residence. The success of the technology is due to the incorporation of a small nuclear reactor in the device along with special coating on the attaching tubes. At the beginning of April 19x7, 10 units were 30 percent complete. During the month 22 devices were completed. At the end of the month five devices were in process with 45 percent completion as to conversion.

(S. Jerden, adapted)

REQUIRED:
Compute the equivalent units of conversion cost using:
a. FIFO method.
b. Weighted average method.

9–5. Equivalent Units Calculations.   The Los Palmas Crystal Unit is a part of the Los Palmas Medical Center. The Crystal Unit grows sets of specific crystals that are used as part of medical tests for specific types of cancer. The crystal sets take about three weeks to grow under normal conditions. At the beginning of October 19x7, there were 1,234 crystals 60 percent complete on growth and 100 percent complete in materials. During the month 4,055 sets were completed. The ending inventory consisted of a batch of 1,500 sets that were 15 percent complete on growth and 100 percent complete on materials.

REQUIRED:
a. Prepare a schedule of units to be accounted for and units accounted for.
b. Compute the equivalent units of production for materials and conversion costs assuming the FIFO method.
c. Compute the equivalent units of production for materials and conversion costs assuming the weighted average method.

9–6. Equivalent Units Calculations.   Fred and Wilma Rodgers run a worm farm in Southern Georgia. They have 40 different beds each consisting of $\frac{1}{4}$ acre of specially prepared soils.

Worm beds are harvested every six months. Each bed is considered 100 percent complete on materials at the time it is started. They started off 19x2 with 10 beds in production that were 40 percent complete. During the year they started 56 beds. At the end of the year they had 15 beds that were 60 percent complete.

(M. Kubinski, adapted)

REQUIRED:
Compute the equivalent units of materials and conversion cost using the:
a. FIFO method.
b. Weighted average method.

9–7. Equivalent Units. Sydney Telex Corp. produces an infused separator that is used to protect workers from voltage surges in power lines. The product is produced in two departments: Molding and Finishing. The data for the month of June 19x3 are:

(S. Whitecotton, adapted)

	Molding	*Finishing*
Beginning inventory units	450	575
Stage of completion:		
Materials	50%	60%
Conversion	40%	40%
Units started during June	1,200	?
Ending inventory units	525	400
Stage of Completion:		
Materials	80%	30%
Conversion	60%	25%

REQUIRED:
a. Present the physical flow for each department.
b. Compute units started and completed for each department.
c. For the Molding Department, complete the equivalent units of materials and conversion cost using the:
   1. FIFO method.
   2. Weighted average method.
d. For the Finishing Department, complete the equivalent units of prior department, material, and conversion costs using the:
   1. FIFO method.
   2. Weighted average method.

9–8. Equivalent Units. Basin Bit, Inc., manufactures and services diamond-tipped, industrial drill bits. The bits are very large, 8 inches to 24 inches in diameter, and somewhat complex. The bits, used mostly to drill through stone, weigh from 500 pounds up to 2,600 pounds. At the beginning of May 19x8, Basin Bit had 8 drill bits that were 62.5 percent complete on conversion and 100 percent complete on materials. During the month of May, 14 drill bits were started. At the end of the month, 10 drill bits were 70 percent complete on conversion and 100 percent complete on materials.

(J. Fuller)

REQUIRED:
a. Prepare a schedule of units to be accounted for and units accounted for.
b. Compute the equivalent units of production for materials and conversion costs using the:
   1. FIFO method.
   2. Weighted average method.

9–9. Weighted Average Unit Costs. On April 1, 19x2, there were 10,000 units in process in the Waxing Department that were 40 percent completed on conversion. The conversion cost of the beginning work in process inventory was $20,000. During April, 150,000 units were started in the process, and costs added were $720,000. At the end of the month, there were 20,000 units in process that were 40 percent complete on conversion.

REQUIRED:

a. Compute the equivalent conversion units using the weighted average method.
b. Determine the weighted average conversion cost per unit.

9–10. Weighted Average Process Costing.   The beginning work in process in the Mixing Department of Talcott Industries on May 1, 19x0, consisted of 40,000 units of product. During the month, 150,000 units were completed and transferred to the bottling department. On May 31, 60,000 units in process in the Mixing Department were 20 percent complete. The unit cost, as computed by the weighted average method, was $6.00. Material, labor, and overhead are added uniformly in mixing process.

REQUIRED:

a. Compute the total cost of work prepared and transferred out.
b. Prepare the journal entry to record the transfer of completed goods.
c. Compute the total costs of work in process on May 31.

9–11. FIFO Process Costing.   There were 5,000 units in process in the Machining Department of Sussman, Inc., on July 1, 19x2. The beginning inventory had a cost of $48,000 and had 60 percent of the machining completed. All materials are added at the beginning of the process. During July, 60,000 units were started and completed. On July 31, 8,000 units in process in Machining were 25 percent machined. The unit costs, as computed by the FIFO method, were $4 for materials and $8 for conversion costs.

REQUIRED:

a. Compute the cost of work completed and transferred to the Finishing Department.
b. Prepare the journal entry for the transfer out of goods.
c. Compute the total cost of work in process on July 31, 19x2.

9–12. Cost of Production Report with FIFO.   Laureen Oil Derivatives, Inc., refines products from residual oils purchased from southwestern refineries. One product is a pavement sealant. The processing steps take place in three sequential departments. The following data pertain to the first department:

1. Beginning inventory includes 12,000 barrels, 100 percent complete for residual oil and 20 percent for conversion costs.
2. Beginning inventory costs consist of $12,960 for residual oil, $288 for labor, and $865 for production overhead.
3. Units started during the period total 20,000 barrels.
4. Costs incurred during the period include $20,000 for residual oil, $3,492 for labor, and $8,730 for production overhead.
5. Ending inventory consists of 2,000 barrels, 100 percent for residual oil and 70 percent for conversion costs.

REQUIRED:

Prepare a cost of production report for this department using the FIFO method.

PROBLEMS   **9–13. Allocating Costs and Journal Entries.**   While working on the Cost of Production Report for the Decarbonizing Unit of the Bay Town Refinery, the clerk is suddenly called away for a family emergency. As he runs out the door, he hands you the partially completed report and, although very distraught, tells you that the journal entries must be keyed into the computer this afternoon. The partially completed report looks like this:

DECARBONIZING UNIT
Cost of Production Report
For the Period Ending April 30, 19x6
(FIFO method)

Units to account for:				
Units in process, beginning		20,000		
Units started during month		80,000		
Total units to account for				100,000
Units accounted for:				
Units completed		60,000		
Units in process, ending		40,000		
Total units accounted for				100,000
Costs to account for:				
Costs in process, beginning		$ 280,000		
Costs incurred during month				
Transferred-in costs		1,600,000		
Labor		192,000		
Overhead		256,000		
Total costs to account for				$2,328,000
Costs accounted for:				
Units in process, beginning	*a.*	________		
Costs to complete	*b.*	________	*c.*	________
Units started and completed			*d.*	________
Total costs of completed units			*e.*	________
Units in process, ending				
Materials	*f.*	________		
Conversion	*g.*	________	*h.*	________
Total costs accounted for			*i.*	________

Additional Calculations

	Materials	***Conversion***
Current period costs	$1,600,000	$ 448,000
Computation of equivalent units:		
Units completed	60,000	60,000
Ending inventory	40,000	20,000
Weighted average units	100,000	80,000
Less: Units in process, beginning	(20,000)	(16,000)
FIFO equivalent units	80,000	64,000
Equivalent unit costs	$20.00	$7.00

REQUIRED:

a. Complete the costs to be accounted for items *a* through *i*.

b. Prepare journal entries to summarize activities in the Work in Process—Decarbonizing Unit account for the month.

9–14. Weighted Average and FIFO Process Cost Report. ALA Film Distributors produces copies of feature length films for distribution on a national basis. The production master is first checked very carefully for quality in the Master Check Unit. Any problems are immediately brought to the attention of the film producer. The film cartridges are copied en mass with up to 900 copies made from each master through a high-speed reproduction process. A feature-length film requires four reels of film for each copy.

The quality of films copied is checked in the Film Review and Control Unit (FREC Unit). Each reel of film is checked to make certain that the sound exactly matches the picture and that the timing mark on the end of the reel is exactly right to start the next reel. Most film producers require that the complete set (average of 900 copies with four reels per copy) be ready before any may be shipped to theaters. The full production process may be represented as:

Master	Reproduction	FREC	Packing and
Check	Unit	Unit	Shipping

On March 1, 19x0, the FREC Unit had 12 sets of film in process, which were 62.5 percent complete. The beginning inventory value of $405,000 consisted of $360,000 in transferred-in costs and $45,000 in direct labor and overhead. The FREC Unit started 36 sets of film and incurred direct labor costs of $120,000 and production overhead of $150,000. The cost of films transferred in from the Reproduction Unit was $1,260,000. Ending inventory consisted of six sets of films that were 50 percent complete.

REQUIRED:
a. Prepare a cost of production report for the FREC unit for March using the FIFO process costing method.
b. Prepare a cost of production report for the FREC unit for March using the weighted average process costing method.

9–15. Process Cost Reports. The KoolAir Company manufactures and distributes after-market air conditioning installation kits for trucks and automobiles. The kit consists of a basic condensor/compressor unit plus installation components that are unique to a make and model of vehicle. The Component Assembly Department receives parts from various fabrication departments and assembles the components that are included in the installation kit. The Final Assembly Department combines the basic condensor/compressor unit with various combinations of installation components to meet the unique requirements of each vehicle. The following data are available for the Component Assembly Department for the month of February 19x4:

Beginning inventory consists of 800 units 60 percent complete with $120,000 in transferred-in costs and $13,000 in conversion costs.
During the month 13,200 units were started, transferred-in costs were $1,980,000, direct labor was $179,000, and overhead was $143,000.
Ending inventory was 1,000 units 40 percent complete.

(J. Brown, adapted)

REQUIRED:
a. Prepare the cost of production report using the weighted average method.
b. Prepare the cost of production report using the FIFO method.

9–16. Cost of Production Report with Weighted Average and FIFO Methods.   Lee Raider Ringers manufactures bells used by fraternities and sororities at pep rallies, football games, and so forth. The manufacturing process is continuous. Materials are added at the beginning of production, and production overhead is applied at 60 percent of direct labor cost. Conversion costs are incurred uniformly throughout the process. The following production data pertain to the year just concluded.

1. Beginning inventory consists of 6,000 bells (40 percent complete for conversion costs) with material costs of $16,800; labor of $4,200, and production overhead of $2,520.
2. Ending inventory includes 4,000 bells (80 percent complete for conversion costs).
3. Units started during the year total 90,000 bells.
4. Costs during the year for materials are $252,000, and labor totals $157,500.
5. Units completed during the year total 92,000 bells.

REQUIRED:

a. Prepare a cost of production report for the year using the weighted average method.
b. Prepare a cost of production report for the year using the FIFO method.

9–17. Cost of Production Report for Two Months.   The Byers Company operates several plants around St. Louis. One plant, the Busch Estates plant, makes a single product that goes through a mixing process followed by a drying process. The data relating to operations of the Mixing Department for June and July are:

	June	July
Beginning inventory in process	0	600
Units started during month	12,400	13,100
Units completed and transferred out	11,800	13,300
Ending inventory in process	600	400
Stage of completion for ending inventory:		
Materials	90%	50%
Conversion costs	60%	30%
Costs:		
Materials put into process	$258,640	$271,760
Conversion costs incurred	526,860	569,770

REQUIRED:

a. Using the FIFO method, prepare a cost of production report for June and one for July. If necessary, carry unit cost calculations to five decimal places. In allocating costs, round total dollar computations to the nearest dollar.
b. Using the weighted average method, prepare a cost of production report for June and one for July. If necessary, carry unit cost calculations to five decimal places. In allocating costs, round total dollar computations to the nearest dollar.
c. Prepare the journal entries for (a) and (b) above that record the transfer of units from the Mixing Department to the Drying Department.

9–18. Missing Data, Journal Entries.   Candles Unique specializes in highly decorative candles. In the Melting Department, waxes are melted, dyed, and formed into various-sized blocks with a wick. Then the blocks go to the Carving Department, where the blocks are shaped into one of 4,206 designs. The company uses the FIFO process costing method. As the internal auditor for the company, you have gathered the following data for the month of August 19x4:

	Melting		Carving	
	Completion	Amounts	Completion	Amounts
Beginning inventory, units		3,000		2,500
Materials	40%	$2,500		$ 0
Transferred in		$ 0	100%	iv
Conversion	30%	$3,700	50%	v
Units started and completed		i		9,000
Costs added during month				
Materials		ii		$ 0
Transferred in		0		vi
Conversion		iii		vii
Ending inventory, units		4,000		3,500
Materials	60%	$2,310		$ 0
Transferred in		$ 0	100%	viii
Conversion	70%	$2,968	70%	$2,940

Notice that beginning and ending inventories are given, except for some of the Carving Department costs. The amount of costs added during the period and the other missing numbers must be found. Costs transferred to Finished Goods Inventory totaled $38,349. As part of your audit tests of the computer system, you will find the missing numbers and later compare them with the amounts appearing in computer printouts and journal entries.

(P. Hicks, adapted)

REQUIRED:

a. Find the missing data as indicated by the lower-case roman numerals, i through viii, in the data given above.
b. Prepare summary journal entries for the two departments.

9–19. FIFO and Weighted Average Process Costing.

Hsiu Seng Bottling Company produces a low-calorie soft drink made from a mixture of domestic and exotic fruit juices. The total production process requires two cost centers: Blending and Canning. Materials (ingredients) enter Blending at the beginning of the process and are mixed according to a recipe. Labor and production overhead are incurred uniformly throughout the mixing operations. The completed mixture moves from Blending to Canning. In Canning, the mixture goes through a cooling process. The cooled mixture moves to a canning line where 12-oz. cans are filled and sealed. The cans represent new material added at the beginning of the Canning cost center process. Production data for April are:

	Blending	*Canning*
Work in process, April 1:		
Units	60,000 gals.	10,000 cans
Stage of completion (labor and overhead)	20%	10%
Costs:		
Transferred in	—	$ 2,770
Materials	$108,600	1,200
Labor	1,280	10
Overhead	8,960	20
Total costs in process	$118,840	$ 4,000
Units started or transferred in	240,000 gals.	2,346,666 cans
Units completed and transferred out	220,000 gals.	2,122,666 cans
Current period costs for April:		
Materials	$432,000	$ 269,900
Labor	27,392	21,940
Overhead	177,408	43,875
	$636,800	$ 335,715
Work in process, April 30:		
Units	80,000 gals.	234,000 cans
Stage of completion (labor and overhead)	60%	30%

Blending uses the FIFO method to account for goods completed and ending inventory, and Canning uses the weighted average method.

REQUIRED:

a. Prepare a cost of production report for the Blending cost center for April. Show supporting calculations.
b. Prepare a cost of production report for the Canning cost center for April. Show supporting calculations.

9–20. Errors in Cost of Production Report.

The internal audit staff of Hoke Wire & Cable Company has completed its periodic audit of the Cable Division. The audit revealed a number of errors in the January cost of production report for the Cutting Department. The January report is below:

HOKE WIRE & CABLE COMPANY
Cable Division—Cutting Department
Cost of Production Report—FIFO Method
For the Month of January

Quantities

Units to account for:

Units in process, January 1 (100% transferred in and materials; 20% conversion costs)	8,000
Units started during month	42,000
Total units to account for	50,000

Units accounted for:

Units completed and transferred out	44,000
Units in process, January 31 (100% transferred in and materials; 50% conversion costs)	6,000
Total units accounted for	50,000

Costs

Costs to account for:

Costs in process, January 1		$ 40,000
Costs incurred during month:		
Transferred in	$81,720	
Material	79,800	
Conversion costs	90,380	251,900
Total costs to account for		$291,900

Costs accounted for:

Cost of goods completed		$262,890
Work in process, January 1:		
Transferred in (6,000 × $1.94)	$11,640	
Material (6,000 × $1.90)	11,400	
Conversion costs (3,000 × $1.99)	5,970	29,010
Total costs accounted for		$291,900

The current accounting policies and procedures manual shows that materials are added at the beginning of the process in the Cutting Department, applied production overhead is at the rate of 100% of direct labor dollars, and the FIFO method is used. The internal audit staff noted the following errors in the preparation of the cost of production report:

1. The stage of completion for conversion costs in the ending inventory was 40 percent instead of 50 percent.
2. The costs transferred in during the period should have been $2,000 higher than the report showed.
3. The material cost for the period was $75,600. That is lower than the cost of production report showed. Material costing $4,200 belongs to February production.
4. Conversion costs should have been $92,000. Payroll and Applied Production Overhead were the accounts affected.
5. The ending Work in Process Inventory was overstated by 2,000 units. These units were completed and in transit to the Polishing Department but were included as in-process units rather than completed units.
6. All unit cost computations were rounded to two decimal places. Company policy requires rounding unit costs to four decimal places and rounding total dollars in ending inventory and goods completed to the nearest dollar.

REQUIRED:
a. Prepare a corrected cost of production report for January for the Cutting Department.
b. Make the necessary adjusting journal entries to correct the amount of costs added during the month and the amount of costs transferred to the Polishing Department.

9–21. Process Operations over Several Months.   Fluvanna Caprock Winery has been in operation for two and one-half years and has been very successful. A new controller with five years of experience with a regional CPA firm has just been hired to oversee the growing need for good accounting policies and procedures. One of his first duties was to evaluate whether the company should use the FIFO method of accounting for the various wine-making activities. It currently uses the weighted average method. The controller gathered production data for the first quarter of the fiscal year, as follows:

	January	*February*	*March*
Gallons charged to Operation 1:			
Work in process, beginning	10,000	20,000	25,000
Started in production	80,000	65,000	70,000
Total units charged	90,000	85,000	95,000
Gallons accounted for:			
Transferred to Operation 2	70,000	60,000	75,000
Work in process, ending	20,000	25,000	20,000
Total units accounted for	90,000	85,000	95,000

The stage of completion for inventories in each month has been identified as:

	Beginning	*Ending*
January	60%	30%
February	30%	70%
March	70%	40%

Cost data for each month are as follows:

	January	*February*	*March*
Work in process, beginning			
Material	$ 10,000	?	?
Conversion costs	20,000	?	?
Costs incurred during month			
Material	$ 80,000	$ 66,000	$ 70,000
Conversion costs	170,000	142,000	156,000

Materials are added at the beginning of Operation 1. Conversion costs flow uniformly throughout the operation.

REQUIRED:

a. Prepare a cost of production report for Operation 1 for all three months using the weighted average method.

b. Prepare a cost of production report for Operation 1 for all three months using the FIFO method.

c. Would you recommend the use of the FIFO or the weighted average method to the controller? Give your reasons.

9–22. Subsequent Departments.   The Lori-Anne Fragrance Company manufactures a full line of cosmetics and women's fragrances. A perfume for juniors uses three sequential departments: Blending, Cooking, and Packaging. Materials are added on a continuous basis in Blending and at the beginning of the Packaging Department. Conversion costs are added uniformly throughout all three departments. A summary of production data appears in the following table:

	Departments		
	Blending	Cooking	Packaging
Beginning inventory:			
Units in gallons	32,000	19,200	27,200
Stage of completion:			
Transferred in	—	100%	100%
Materials	20%	—	100%
Conversion costs	20%	40%	20%
Costs:			
Transferred in	—	$ 79,680	$146,880
Materials	$ 15,360	—	16,320
Conversion costs	11,200	9,600	4,352
Total costs	$ 26,560	$ 89,280	$167,552
Gallons started or transferred in	104,000	?	?
Gallons completed or transferred out	112,000	?	?
Current period costs:			
Materials	$251,520	—	$ 65,280
Conversion costs	183,400	$130,900	99,328
Total current costs	$434,920	$130,900	$164,608
Ending inventory:			
Gallons	24,000	14,400	12,800
Stage of completion:			
Transferred in	—	100%	100%
Materials	30%	—	100%
Conversion costs	30%	25%	60%

The Blending and Cooking departments are accounted for using the weighted average method. Packaging is accounted for with the FIFO method.

REQUIRED:
Prepare a cost of production report for each of the three departments.

9–23. Multiple Departments. Rawlings, Inc., manufactures baseballs in four production departments. The Molding and Leather Wrap departments use FIFO, and the String Wrap and Stitching departments use the weighted average method.
    Information for the month of July 19x1 is as follows:

(A. Gregory, adapted)

	Molding	String Wrap	Leather Wrap	Stitching
Beginning inventories:				
Units	1,800	2,400	2,100	2,200
Stage of completion				
Transferred in	—	100%	100%	100%
Materials	100%	70%	100%	65%
Conversion	45%	70%	45%	40%
Costs:				
Transferred in	—	$1,086	$ 300	$3,141
Materials	$ 780	180	90	42
Conversion	310	580	20	760
Units started	9,000	?	?	?
Units completed	9,600	?	10,000	?
Current costs:				
Transferred in	—	?	?	?
Materials	$3,870	$3,444	$ 6,090	$ 514
Conversion	1,902	8,933	1,993	4,334

	Molding	*String Wrap*	*Leather Wrap*	*Stitching*
Ending inventories:				
Units	?	1,500	?	1,600
Stage of completion				
Transferred in	—	100%	100%	100%
Materials	100%	55%	100%	70%
Conversion	60%	55%	35%	45%

REQUIRED:

a. Prepare a cost of production report for each department.
b. Prepare journal entries to record the transfer of costs from each department to the next department and to Finished Goods.
c. Status Trophy Company has asked Rawlings, Inc., to leather wrap and stitch a special mold provided by Status for use on a line of trophies. If costs remain relatively constant and Status offers to pay Rawlings $3.00 per ball, should Rawlings consider the offer? Why or why not?

9–24. Subsequent Departments.   The Ho Chi Company manufactures boat hulls that are later customized to meet the needs of commercial fishing companies. The boat hulls go through four departments: Molding, Welding, Painting, and Finishing. Materials are added on a continuous basis in Molding and Finishing. Conversion costs are added uniformly throughout all departments. The production data for the month of February 19x2 are as follows:

	Molding	*Welding*	*Painting*	*Finishing*
Beginning inventory:				
Units	300	425	350	400
Stage of completion:				
Transferred in	—	100%	100%	100%
Materials	60%	—	—	80%
Conversion	40%	30%	50%	70%
Costs:				
Transferred in	—	$300,000	$450,000	$525,000
Materials	$120,000	—	—	130,000
Conversion	114,000	125,000	110,000	96,000
Total costs	$234,000	$425,000	$560,000	$751,000
Units started or transferred in	900	?	?	?
Units completed or transferred out	950	?	?	?
Current period costs:				
Materials	$250,000	—	—	$220,000
Conversion costs	225,000	$235,000	$215,000	200,000
	$475,000	$235,000	$215,000	$420,000
Ending inventory:				
Units	250	350	275	300
Stage of completion:				
Transferred in	—	100%	100%	100%
Materials	35%	—	—	65%
Conversion costs	30%	45%	70%	60%

Molding and Welding use the weighted average method for costing and ending inventories. Painting and Finishing use the FIFO method.

(D. Washburn)

REQUIRED:

a. Prepare a cost of production report for each of the four departments.

b. Prepare journal entries to record transfer of costs from one department to the next. Finishing transfers its units to Finished Goods Inventory.

EXTENDED APPLICATIONS

9–25. Errors in Cost of Production Report. Zoth Energitec produces a product that is accounted for under a process cost system in the Assembly and Finishing departments. A new college graduate was hired as a cost accountant in March. His new assignment included preparation of the monthly cost of production reports for the two departments. The basic information for the operations for April is given as:

	Assembly	*Finishing*
Units:		
Beginning inventory	10,000	12,000
Units started	20,000	?
Units completed and transferred out	26,000	?
Ending inventory	4,000	10,000
Costs:		
Material costs added	$22,000	$14,000
Labor costs	8,000	12,000

Beginning work in process in the Assembly Department was one-half complete with respect to conversion costs. Material is added at the start of production. Beginning inventories include $6,000 for material and $2,000 for conversion costs. Production overhead is applied at the rate of 50 percent of labor dollars. Conversion costs are incurred uniformly throughout the process. Ending inventory was two-fifths complete. The FIFO method is used for costing production.

Beginning work in process in the Finishing Department was three-fourths complete with respect to conversion costs. Materials are added at the end of the process. Beginning inventories include $10,000 for transferred costs and $10,000 for conversion costs. Overhead is applied at the rate of 100 percent of labor dollars. Ending inventory was estimated to be one-fourth complete. The weighted average method is used for costing products.

The new accountant prepared the April cost of production report for both departments. Excerpts from his reports are as follows:

Assembly Department

Cost of goods completed (26,000 × $1.2667)		$32,933
Ending inventory:		
Material (4,000 × $.9333)	$ 3,733	
Conversion costs (4,000 × $.3334)	1,334	5,067
		$38,000

ADDITIONAL COMPUTATIONS:

	Material	*Conversion Cost*
Costs in process, April 1	$ 6,000	$ 2,000
Current period costs	22,000	8,000
	$28,000	$10,000
Computation of equivalent units:		
Units completed	26,000	26,000
Ending inventory	4,000	4,000
Equivalent production	30,000	30,000
Unit costs (costs/units)	.9333	$ .3334

Finishing Department

Cost of goods completed		$59,790
Ending inventory:		
Transferred in (10,000 × $1.2667)	$12,667	
Material (10,000 × $.5385)	5,385	
Conversion costs (2,500 × $.4364)	1,091	19,143
		$78,933

REQUIRED:

a. Prepare a corrected cost of production report for the Assembly and Finishing departments.
b. Give the journal entries necessary to correct the costs that are transferred from the Assembly Department to the Finishing Department, and from the Finishing Department to Finished Goods Inventory.

9–26. Subsequent Departments.   The Santini Pizza Company produces Frozen Extravaganza Pizzas, which are sold to several large grocery store chains throughout the Southwest. Their busiest sales period is during football season in the fall.

  The pizzas are processed on a continuous basis through four departments: Mixing, Baking, Packaging, and Freezing. Production of the product begins in the Mixing Department where the pizzas are prepared. Some of the ingredients used include cheeses, pepperonis, olives, onions, tomato sauce, green and bell peppers, beef, sausage, and ham. The pizzas are baked in the Baking Department and then sent to the Packaging Department, where they are placed in cartons and boxes. Finally, the pizzas are frozen in the Freezing Department and transferred to Finished Goods Inventory awaiting shipment. Material costs are incurred at the beginning of the process in Mixing and Packaging. Conversion costs are added uniformily throughout the four departments.

  Guido Santini, the owner, recently terminated the services of his cousin, the company accountant. Mr. Santini has hired you to review the following data and prepare a cost of production report.

(P. Hutchinson, adapted)

	Mixing	*Baking*	*Packaging*	*Freezing*
In process, beginning				
Units	500	200	300	400
Stage of completion:				
Transferred in	—	100%	100%	100%
Materials	100%	0%	100%	0%
Labor	80%	60%	60%	40%
Overhead	10%	20%	30%	40%
Costs:				
Transferred in	$ —	$ 420	$ 530	$ 850
Materials	600	350	280	490
Labor	444	555	333	222
Overhead	123	456	789	321
Total costs	$1,167	$1,781	$1,932	$1,883
Units started/transferred in	5,000	?	?	?
Units completed/transferred out	5,200	?	?	?
Current period costs:				
Materials	$8,000	$ 0	$3,000	$ 0
Labor	750	300	694	282
Overhead	450	800	322	900
Total costs	$9,200	$1,100	$4,016	$1,182

	Mixing	*Baking*	*Packaging*	*Freezing*
In process, ending:				
Units	300	250	180	50
Stage of completion:				
Transferred in	—	100%	100%	100%
Materials	100%	0%	100%	0%
Labor	80%	50%	80%	50%
Overhead	23%	32%	25%	52%

REQUIRED:

a. Prepare a cost of production report for each department using the weighted average method.

b. Prepare a cost of production report for each department using the FIFO method.

c. Compare the transferred-out costs produced by using the weighted average and FIFO methods and comment on the difference.

(Round unit costs to five decimal places and round dollar amounts to the nearest dollar.)

Process Costing: Addition of Materials and Changing Units

After studying this appendix, you should be able to:

1. Compute process costs when the units of production increase due to input of materials and transferred units at the beginning of the process.
2. Compute process costs when the units of production increase due to the input of materials during the process.
3. Compute process costs when the units of production increase due to the input of transferred units during the process.

When materials are added in subsequent departments, the effect on production will either (1) not increase the quantity of items produced, or (2) increase the quantity of the product produced. In the first case, unit cost would be increased. For example, in the production of denim jeans, the thread, zippers, and snaps are added to the cloth in the Stitch and Form Department. There is no increase in the number of jeans, but the unit cost of each pair of jeans increases.

In some situations, adding materials in departments subsequent to the first department increases the quantity produced, thus requiring an adjustment of unit costs. This occurs whenever the product is measured in volume or weight, for example, in the chemical industry where the product is a bulk liquid. After adding the materials, the unit cost of the product transferred into the department must be adjusted to spread the cost over the greater quantity of output than was transferred in. The increase in units from added materials can, in some circumstances, decrease the cost per unit. For example, the addition of water to a concentrate will decrease the cost per gallon of the mixture.

Three general situations with the addition of materials change the units: (1) both material and transferred units are added at the beginning of the process, (2) material units are added during the process, and (3) transferred units are added during the process. In general, *work in process must be expressed in* units of output *in the equivalent unit calculation.* If we do not restate inventories to output units, then the cost per unit of product will be overstated and ending work in process will be understated. In some cases, the effect will be to distort both income and cost per unit amounts materially, which will have an impact on the decisions of managers. We will first consider both material and transferred units added at the beginning of the process.

Material and Transferred Units Added at the Beginning

When both material and transferred units are added at the beginning of the production process, the beginning and ending work in process will have the same measure as the eventual output.

Example Setting A. Neves Creative Paints, Inc., produces and sells paint under private labels. The Mixing Department receives paint pigment from other departments, adds oil paint base at the beginning of the process, and mixes the paint in large vats. The completed paint moves to another department where it is poured into one- and five-gallon containers. At the beginning of the current month, the Mixing Department had 12,600 gallons on hand (30 percent complete for conversion costs). The ending inventory totaled 8,000 gallons (40 percent complete for conversion costs). The 2,610 gallons of paint pigment received from the previous department during the month were mixed with 23,490 gallons of oil paint base. Each gallon of pigment requires 9 gallons of oil paint base to make 10 gallons of paint. The costs are summarized as:

Beginning inventory:		
Transferred-in costs	$37,800	
Oil paint base	12,600	
Conversion costs	7,560	$ 57,960
Current costs incurred:		
Transferred-in costs	$70,200	
Oil paint base added	26,100	
Conversion costs	60,240	156,540
Total costs		$214,500

Computations for Cost of Production Report. We will now make all of the computations necessary to prepare a cost of production report for the month. These computations follow the five steps outlined in Chapter 9.

Step 1: physical flow.

Beginning inventory—gallons	12,600	
Transferred in (gallons started)	2,610	
Oil *added* to transferred-in gallons	23,490	
Gallons to account for		38,700
Completed and transferred out—gallons	30,700	
Ending inventory—gallons	8,000	
Gallons accounted for		38,700

Because the oil paint base is added as paint pigment enters the department's process, all units in process during the period were 100 percent complete for the oil paint base component of cost. That also means the beginning inventory already has oil paint base added to it.

We will first look at the FIFO method for handling this production situation.

FIFO method—Step 2: equivalent units.

	Transferred In	Oil	Conversion Costs
Beginning inventory:			
12,600 gallons × (100% − 100%)	–0–	–0–	
12,600 gallons × (100% − 30%)			8,820
Started and completed × 100%	18,100	18,100	18,100
(30,700 completed − 12,600 beginning)			
Ending inventory:			
8,000 gallons × 100%	8,000	8,000	
8,000 gallons × 40%			3,200
FIFO equivalent units	26,100	26,100	30,120

Step 3: costs to account for. The costs to account for have already been set up in the problem as:

Beginning work in process			
Transferred-in costs	$37,800		
Oil paint base	12,600		
Conversion costs	7,560	$ 57,960	
Current costs incurred:			
Transferred-in costs	$70,200		
Oil paint base added	26,100		
Conversion costs	60,240	156,540	
Total costs to be accounted for		$214,500	

Step 4: computation of unit costs.   The unit cost computation for the FIFO method requires the current period costs divided by the FIFO equivalent units, as follows:

	Transferred In	Oil	Conversion Costs
Current costs	$70,200	$26,100	$60,240
Equivalent units	26,100	26,100	30,120
Equivalent unit costs	$2.68966	$1.00	$2.00
Total cost per unit		$5.68966	

Step 5: allocation of costs.   The purpose of the foregoing steps is to allocate the costs between units completed and units in the ending inventory. For the FIFO method, the allocation is below:

Completed and transferred:			
Units from the beginning inventory:			
Costs in beginning inventory		$57,960	
Costs to complete the beginning inventory:			
Conversion costs:			
12,600 × (100% − 30%) × $2.00		17,640	$ 75,600
Started and completed (18,100 gallons × $5.68966)			102,983
Cost of goods completed and transferred			$178,583
Ending inventory:			
Transferred in (8,000 gallons × $2.68966)		$21,517	
Oil (8,000 gallons × $1.00)		8,000	
Conversion costs (8,000 × 40% × $2.00)		6,400	35,917
Total costs accounted for			$214,500

Let's now turn our attention to the weighted average method. Similar to most situations, the allocations are not significantly different from the FIFO method.

Weighted average method—Step 2: equivalent units.

	Transferred In	Oil	Conversion Costs
Units completed × 100%	30,700	30,700	30,700
Ending inventory:			
8,000 gallons × 100%	8,000	8,000	
8,000 gallons × 40%			3,200
Weighted average equivalent units	38,700	38,700	33,900

Step 3: costs to account for.   This is the same as for the FIFO method.

Step 4: computation of unit costs. The unit cost computation for the weighted average cost method requires an average of the costs in the beginning inventory and the current period costs.

	Transferred In	Oil	Conversion Costs
Beginning inventory	$ 37,800	$12,600	$ 7,560
Current costs	70,200	26,100	60,240
Total costs to be accounted for	$108,000	$38,700	$67,800
Equivalent units	38,700	38,700	33,900
Unit costs	$2.79070	$1.00	$2.00

Total cost per unit $5.79070

Step 5: allocation of costs. The allocation of costs would appear as:

Completed and transferred (30,700 gallons × $5.7907)		$177,774
Ending inventory:		
Transferred in (8,000 × 100% × $2.7907)	$22,326	
Oil (8,000 × 100% × $1.00)	8,000	
Conversion costs (8,000 × 40% × $2.00)	6,400	36,726
Total costs accounted for		$214,500

Material Units Added during the Process

Example Setting B. The engineering staff of the Neves Creative Paints Company has decided to add the oil paint base at 60 percent of completion instead of at the beginning of the process. The plant had 1,260 gallons in process at the beginning of the month (30 percent complete on conversion cost), started 2,610 gallons of pigment, added 27,630 gallons of oil paint base, completed 30,700 gallons, and had 800 gallons (40 percent complete on conversion cost) on hand at the end of the month. The following costs were incurred:

Beginning inventory:		
Transferred-in costs	$37,800	
Oil paint base cost	0	
Conversion costs	7,560	$ 45,360
Current costs incurred:		
Transferred-in costs	$70,200	
Oil paint base added	30,700	
Conversion costs	60,240	161,140
Total costs to account for		$206,500

Because the beginning work in process is at the 30 percent stage of conversion and oil paint base is added at 60 percent of conversion, there is no oil paint base cost in the beginning work in process cost. The cost amounts in the previous example have been adjusted to reflect the increased cost of the pigment in the beginning work in process and the increased usage of oil paint base.

Accounting for the Added Units. When units are added during the process, care must be taken that the beginning and ending work in process inventories are correctly measured in terms of outputs. As we emphasized in Chapter 9, it is critical in the unit cost calculation that there be a definite relationship between the costs in the numerator and the units in the denominator. Equivalent unit calculations in process costing refer to an equivalent unit of output, not a mixture of inputs and outputs. Consequently, all units in the equivalent unit calculation must be in terms of finished output.

Converting Inputs to Outputs. The ingredients for a product are converted into outputs by the efforts of a producing department and the incurrence of conversion costs. The ratio of outputs to inputs is called a **conversion ratio.** For example, each gallon of pigment for Neves Creative Paints has 9 gallons of oil paint base added to result in 10 gallons of paint. Thus, 1 gallon of pigment results in 10 gallons of paint:

$$\text{Conversion ratio} = \frac{10 \text{ gallons of output (paint)}}{1 \text{ gallon of input (pigment)}} = \frac{10}{1} = 10$$

The conversion ratio is used to convert unit measures that are based on inputs into units of output.

Examining Work in Process Inventories. When materials are added during the process, the Work in Process Inventory, either beginning or ending, may or may not be stated in terms of outputs. We must compare the stage of completion of the inventories with the point at which materials are added:

	Stage	Materials Addition	Convert?
Material added	60%		
Beginning process inventories	30%	60%	Yes
Ending process inventories	40%	60%	Yes

Thus, both the beginning and ending work in process must be converted to output measures in the equivalent unit calculations.

Step 1: physical flow. The physical flow calculation occurs in the same manner as before:

Beginning inventory—gallons	1,260	
Transferred in (gallons started)	2,610	
Oil added to transferred-in gallons	27,630	
Gallons to account for		31,500
Completed and transferred out—gallons	30,700	
Ending inventory—gallons	800	
Gallons accounted for		31,500

FIFO method—Step 2: equivalent units. The FIFO equivalent units calculation requires both the beginning and ending work in process be converted from gallons of input (pigment) to gallons of output (paint) by a conversion ratio of 10:

	Transferred In	Oil	Conversion Costs
Beginning inventory:			
1,260 gallons × 10 × (100% − 100%)	–0–		
1,260 gallons × 10 × (100% − 0%)		12,600	
1,260 gallons × 10 × (100% − 30%)			8,820
Started and completed × 100%	18,100	18,100	18,100
(30,700 completed − (1,260 × 10) beginning)			
Ending inventory:			
800 gallons × 10 × 100%	8,000		
800 gallons × 10 × 0%		–0–	
800 gallons × 10 × 40%			3,200
FIFO equivalent units	26,100	30,700	30,120

Step 3: costs to account for.   Based on the problem, the costs to account for are $196,500.

Step 4: cost per unit.

Current costs incurred	$70,200	$30,700	$60,240
FIFO equivalent units	26,100	30,700	30,120
FIFO cost per unit	$2.68966	$1.00	$2.00
Total cost per unit		$5.68966	

Step 5: allocation of costs.

Completed and transferred:		
Units from the beginning inventory:		
Costs in beginning inventory	$45,360	
Costs to complete the beginning inventory:		
Materials: 1,260 × 10 × 100% × $1	12,600	
Conversion costs: 1,260 × 10 × 70% × $2	17,640	$ 75,600
Started and completed (18,100 gallons × $5.68966)		102,983
Cost of goods completed and transferred		$178,583
Ending inventory:		
Transferred in (800 gallons × 10 × $2.68966)	$21,517	
Conversion costs (800 × 10 × 40% × $2.00)	6,400	27,917
Total costs accounted for		$206,500

The weighted average method for this setting is included in problem 9A–5.

Transferred Units Added during the Process

Example Setting C.   The engineering staff of the Neves Creative Paints Company have decided to add the transferred-in pigment at 60 percent of completion and to start with the oil paint base. The plant had 11,340 gallons in process at the beginning of the month (30 percent complete on conversion cost), started 23,490 gallons of oil paint base, added 3,070 gallons of pigment, completed 30,700 gallons, and had 7,200 gallons (40 percent complete on conversion cost) on hand at the end of the month. The following costs were incurred:

Beginning inventory:		
Transferred-in costs	$ 0	
Oil paint base cost	12,600	
Conversion costs	7,560	$ 20,160
Current costs incurred:		
Transferred-in costs added	$82,573	
Oil paint base	26,100	
Conversion costs	60,240	168,913
Total costs to account for		$189,073

Since the beginning work in process is at the 30 percent stage of conversion and pigment is added at 60 percent of conversion, there is no transferred-in cost in the beginning work in process cost. The cost amounts have been adjusted to reflect the cost of the pigment to be added to the beginning work in process and the usage of oil paint base.

Accounting for the Transferred-in Units.   We have now reversed the timing of usage of the materials and the transferred-in units. The production process starts with the materials (oil paint base) and adds the transferred-in units (pigment) at the 60 percent stage of conversion.

Converting Inputs to Outputs.   Nine gallons of oil paint base result in 10 gallons of paint:

$$\text{Conversion Ratio} = \frac{10 \text{ Gallons of Output (Paint)}}{9 \text{ Gallons of Input (Oil Base)}} = {}^{10}\!\!/_{9}\text{ths}$$

Step 1: physical flow.   The physical flow calculation occurs in the same manner as before:

Beginning inventory—gallons	11,340	
Oil paint base started	23,490	
Transferred-in units added to production	3,070	
Gallons to account for		37,900
Completed and transferred out—gallons	30,700	
Ending inventory—gallons	7,200	
Gallons accounted for		37,900

FIFO method—Step 2: equivalent units.   The FIFO equivalent units calculation requires that both the beginning and ending work in process be converted from gallons of input (oil base) to gallons of output (paint) by a conversion ratio of ${}^{10}\!\!/_{9}$ths:

	Transferred In	Oil	Conversion Costs
Beginning inventory:			
$11,340 \times {}^{10}\!/_{9} \times (100\% - 0\%)$	12,600		
$11,340 \times {}^{10}\!/_{9} \times (100\% - 100\%)$		–0–	
$11,340 \times {}^{10}\!/_{9} \times (100\% - 30\%)$			8,820
Started and completed × 100%	18,100	18,100	18,100
(30,700 completed − (11,340 × ${}^{10}\!/_{9}$) beginning)			
Ending inventory:			
$7,200 \times {}^{10}\!/_{9} \times 0\%$	–0–		
$7,200 \times {}^{10}\!/_{9} \times 100\%$		8,000	
$7,200 \times {}^{10}\!/_{9} \times 40$			3,200
FIFO equivalent units	30,700	26,100	30,120

Step 3: costs to account for.   Based on the problem, the costs to account for are $189,073.

Step 4: cost per unit.

Current costs incurred	$82,573	$26,100	$60,240
FIFO equivalent units	30,700	26,100	30,120
FIFO cost per unit	$2.68966	$1.00	$2.00
Total cost per unit		$5.68966	

Step 5: allocation of costs.
Completed and transferred:

Units from the beginning inventory:		
Costs in beginning inventory	$20,160	
Costs to complete the beginning inventory:		
Transferred costs: $11,340 \times {}^{10}/_9 \times \$2.68966$	33,890	
Conversion costs: $11,340 \times {}^{10}/_9 \times 30\% \times \$2$	17,640	$ 71,690
Started and completed (18,100 gallons $\times$ $5.68966)		102,983
Cost of goods completed and transferred		$174,673
Ending inventory:		
Materials ($7,200 \times {}^{10}/_9 \times 100\% \times \$1.00$)	$ 8,000	
Conversion costs ($7,200 \times {}^{10}/_9 \times 40\% \times \$2.00$)	6,400	14,400
Total costs accounted for		$189,073

The weighted average method for this setting is left as problem 9A–6.

**KEY TERMS
AND CONCEPTS**

Conversion Ratio (364)

**REVIEW
QUESTIONS**

1. Why should the inventories of work in process be converted to output measures in the equivalent unit calculations?
2. When both materials and transferred-in units are added at the beginning of the process, will work in process need to be converted to output units?
3. Under what circumstances will work in process need to be converted to output measures when materials are added during the process?
4. Under what circumstances will work in process need to be converted to output measures when transferred-in units are added during the process?

**DISCUSSION
QUESTIONS**

5. What would happen to the calculation of equivalent units if materials are added continuously during processing?
6. What would happen to the calculation of equivalent units if materials were added at the end of processing?
7. What would happen to the calculation of equivalent units if both materials and transferred-in units are added continuously during processing?

EXERCISES

9A–1. Conversion Ratios.   The Clincel Plant produces three types of fertilizer with the following inputs in pounds per unit of output:

	A–402	A–906	B–4382
Transferred in units	10	40	30
Units of materials	40	60	20
Output weight	50	100	50

368 PART III ACCOUNTING FOR SPECIALIZED PRODUCTION ENVIRONMENTS

REQUIRED:
Compute the conversion ratio to convert work in process to outputs assuming that the beginning inventories consist of:
a. Transferred-in units.
b. Materials added during the process.

9A–2. FIFO Equivalent Units. The Trail Mix Department at Walters Company receives shelled and mixed nuts from the Shelling Department and adds a grain mix from the Grain Mixing Department plus honey in the following proportions by weight:

Transferred in	*Weight*
Nut and grain mixes	9 lbs.
Materials, honey	1 lb.
Total	10 lbs.

The nut and grain mixes are placed into process at the beginning and the honey is added at the 40 percent stage of conversion. During the process the nuts and grains are mixed and dried, the honey is added, and the result is baked lightly and dried for 10 hours. Activity for February 19x7 is summarized as:

Beginning work in process	2,000
Nuts and grains	100%
Honey	100%
Conversion	60%
Pounds completed	8,000
Ending work in process	2,250
Nuts and grains	100%
Honey	0%
Conversion	30%

REQUIRED:
Compute the FIFO equivalent units of production for transferred-in costs, materials, and conversion cost.

9A–3. Equivalent Units and Processing Costs. The Clavert Products Company produces an oven cleaner. An acid mix is transferred into the Final Mix Department; 2 parts of inert material are mixed so that the final product can be packaged and safely used by consumers. The equivalent units and costs were computed in the following manner (in gallons):

	Transferred in	*Material*	*Conversion*
Beginning work in process	0	6,000	1,200
Started and completed	40,000	40,000	40,000
Ending work in process	3,000	3,000	1,800
FIFO equivalent units	43,000	49,000	43,000
Cost per unit	$2.10	$0.10	$0.20

REQUIRED:
a. Compute the current period costs for:
   1. Transferred-in costs.
   2. Materials.
   3. Conversion costs.
b. What conversion factor should the company be using to convert from acid mix to units of final product?
c. If the beginning work in process were valued at $12,264, what would be the cost of goods completed during the month?

PROBLEMS

9A–4. Weighted Average Equivalent Units, Two Batches in Ending Work in Process.   The Mixing Department at Siu Quan Tea Company blends dried Yuwong, orange pekoe, and common black teas. The Yuwong tea is allowed to blend in a large sealed container with special spices for 14 days. Then the pekoe is mixed in and the result is placed in another aromatic container for seven more days. The Yuwong is transferred in from another department, and the orange pekoe and common black are purchased as materials by the Mixing Department. At the end of the process, the common black tea is mixed and the result is bagged in aromatic paper and sealed in containers for shipment. The mixture to make 8 ounces of bagged tea: 2 ounces of Yuwong, 3 ounces of Pekoe, and 3 ounces of common black tea.

On July 1, 19x2, the beginning inventory consisted of 18,000 ounces that were seven days into the process. During the month, 64,000 ounces were completed and the ending work in process consisted of two batches:

1. 7,000 ounces that were 3 days into the process.
2. 5,000 ounces that were 18 days into the process.

REQUIRED:
Compute the weighted average equivalent units of production for transferred-in costs, two materials, and conversion cost.

9A–5. Weighted Average Additional Material Units.   For Example Setting B in this appendix, prepare a cost of production report based on the weighted average method.

9A–6. Weighted Average Additional Transferred Units.   For Example Setting C in this appendix, prepare a cost of production report based on the weighted average method.

9A–7. Transferred Units at Beginning and Materials at End.   Premium Gasoline, Inc., is a small Oklahoma refinery processing super and regular unleaded gasoline. Production of gasoline consists of two major processes: refining and blending. Sweet or intermediate crude oil is introduced at the beginning of the refining process. The gasoline portion of the output moves to the Blending Department where is passes through several processing steps. At the end of the blending operations, various petrochemicals are added to improve the octane rating, color, and smell, and eliminate potential vapor lock. Conversion costs in both Refining and Blending departments occur uniformly throughout the process. The completed gasoline goes to a terminal for shipment to distribution centers around the country.

A summary of production data for August appears in the following table:

	Refining	*Blending*
Beginning inventory—August 1:		
Units in barrels	12,500	10,000
Stage of completion:		
Crude oil	100%	—
Transferred-in	—	100%
Processing costs	70%	60%
Costs:		
Crude oil	$ 225,000	—
Transferred in	—	$220,000
Processing costs	35,000	9,000
Total costs in process	$ 260,000	$229,000
Barrels started or transferred in:		
Crude oil	200,000	—
Gasoline	—	204,000
Petrochemicals	—	10,200
Barrels completed and transferred out	204,000	218,200

	Refining	*Blending*
Current period costs for August:		
Crude oil	$3,550,000	—
Petrochemicals	—	$654,600
Processing costs	798,000	325,500
Total period costs	$4,348,000	$980,100
Ending inventory—August 31:		
Units in barrels	8,500	6,000
Stage of completion:		
Crude oil	100%	—
Transferred in	—	100%
Petrochemicals	—	0%
Processing costs	50%	80%

REQUIRED:

a. Prepare the calculations necessary for a cost of production report on each of the two processes, assuming the FIFO method.

b. Prepare the calculations necessary for a cost of production report on each of the two processes, assuming the weighted average method.

9A–8. Increasing Units during a Process.   Dubrof Tank Cleaning Services, Inc., specializes in cleaning tank trailers that are transported over highways. Because of the need to have effective cleaning agents, the company produces its own cleaning compounds and liquids. It developed Agent R, which is effective for cleaning tank trailers hauling milk and other liquid dairy products when the temperature is below freezing.

Agent R is manufactured in a two-stage production cycle in two departments. A number of chemicals are mixed, heated, and cooled in the first department. The mixture moves to the second department (referred to as the Tasting Operation) where another liquid ingredient is added at the beginning of the process. With the additional chemical, the mixture increases in gallons by 10 percent. From this department, Agent R moves to a warehouse to await requisitioning. The company uses the weighted average method to determine costs of goods completed and ending inventories. At the beginning of June, the Tasting Operation had on hand 6,000 gallons of mixture that was 50 percent complete for conversion costs. At the end of June, 8,000 gallons 75 percent complete for conversion costs were on hand. The records show that 42,000 gallons had been completed and transferred to the warehouse during the month. As mixture was transferred in from the previous department, the final liquid ingredient that increased the gallons by 10 percent was added.

An analysis of costs relating to work in process and production activity in the Tasting Operation for June is as follows:

	June 1	*Costs Added*
Transferred-in costs	$12,000	$112,000
New ingredient	2,500	17,500
Labor	400	2,000
Production overhead	1,600	8,000

REQUIRED:

a. Compute the costs of goods completed and the costs in the ending inventory for June.

b. Prepare journal entries to record the input of costs into the operation and to transfer completed product to the warehouse.

9A–9. Change in Units: FIFO Process Costing.   KEVIN & MARILEE is a producer of personal care products created from special formulas with quality ingredients. The variety of products includes family toiletries, fragrances, and cosmetics. The fragrance division has lines for both men and women under the motto "Uncommon Scents for the Uncommon Man and Woman." One of the men's after-shave lines is Conquest, a scent described as light spice against a warm, amber woody background.

Production of Conquest involves three operations: Blending, Cooking, and Bottling. The Blending Operation consists of mixing dry chemicals and spices according to a recipe; the resulting dry powder is transferred to the Cooking Operation. In the Cooking Operation, liquid is added to the powder and the mixture is cooked. The hot after-shave lotion moves to the Bottling Operation where it is cooled and bottled. Production data for May for Blending and Cooking operations are:

	Blending	Cooking
Work in process, May 1:		
Units	8,000 lbs.	5,000 gal.
Costs:		
Transferred in	—	$10,250
Materials	$ 3,600	800
Conversion costs	12,800	2,375
Total costs in process	$ 16,400	$13,425
Units started or transferred in	82,000 lbs.	31,000 gal.
Units completed and transferred out	78,000 lbs.	32,500 gal.
Current period costs for May:		
Materials	$ 38,700	$ 4,992
Conversion costs	124,160	29,906
Total costs added this month	$162,860	$34,898
Work in process, May 30—Units	12,000 lbs.	3,500 gal.

Materials and conversion costs enter the Blending Operation uniformly throughout the process. Beginning inventory was 20 percent complete on May 1; May 31 inventory was 30 percent complete. Materials in the Cooking Operation consist of distilled liquid and the powder from Blending. These are added at the start of the process. May 1 inventory was 50 percent complete, and May 31 inventory was 40 percent complete. FIFO process costing is used for both departments.

REQUIRED:
Prepare the cost of production report for the:
a. Blending Department.
b. Cooking Department.
(Round cost per unit calculations to four decimal places.)

Modified Cost Systems and Flow Sequence

After studying this appendix, you should be able to:

1. Identify and compare modified and hybrid cost accounting systems.
2. Account for costs in a modified or hybrid cost accounting system.
3. Identify the flow sequence of a product through processes.

Modified and Hybrid Systems

A wide variety of industries, products, and processes presents a situation more complex than job order and process cost systems can possibly satisfy. In fact, job order costing and process costing represent the two extremes along a continuum of cost accumulation systems. Therefore, modifications and adaptations are made to meet the needs of specific environments. A **modified cost system** occurs where one or more cost elements use job order and the remaining one or more cost elements use process costing or where some but not all of the cost elements are present. When modified systems are used, products have disparities between them; that is, the products are not completely homogeneous. The variety and degree of differences usually dictate the extent to which the basic methods are modified or adapted. The **hybrid cost system** is one in which one type of costing system (job order or process cost) is used for one segment of a production process, and another system is more appropriate for a subsequent production process.

Modified Cost Systems. An example of a modified cost system is a situation in which the items are essentially alike but have different material and processing requirements. For example, designer jeans are made in different sizes and styles, and with different fabrics. However, the processing operations are essentially the same, differing only in minor ways in the quantity of work expended on each style of jeans. For this situation, jeans are grouped and sized according to a production run. The conversion costs of individual production departments are accounted for using a process cost system. The materials are accounted for using a job order system, and the results are merged at the end of production.

Another modified cost system is used to account for the costs of sorting coupons redeemed in supermarkets and grocery stores. Stores send the coupons collected for a day or week to a processing company that sorts coupons by manufacturer, pays the stores, sends coupons to the manufacturer, and is reimbursed for the coupons plus paid a processing fee. When the processing company receives coupons from a number of stores, it batches them and sends them to a processing site where labor is inexpensive (for example, Mexico). There the workers, using special templates, sort the coupons by manufacturer. Processing costs consist of labor and overhead at the processing site. Because only incidental materials are used in processing, a modified process cost system is used for the labor and overhead.

Hybrid Cost Systems. An example of a hybrid cost system relates to manufacturing products with common processing characteristics but different material requirements. For example, a steel plate mill produces steel plating to customer specifications. The steel grade and characteristics for slabs differ depending on the customer's requirements. The steel is heated in a furnace and then sent through a Hot Roll Department.

Rolling the slabs into steel plating is a function of the length, width, and thickness of the steel plates requested by the customer. The operator sets the thickness by making the necessary number of hot roll passes at the steel. The slab entering the roller mill is under job order costing, but labor and overhead in the rolling mill are accounted for under a process costing system in which the work is measured by the number of roller passes made.

Hybrid systems can follow a number of sequences. One example of such a system is that used by a company manufacturing customized jet aircraft. Some of the materials and component parts are the same for all jets produced and are accounted for under a process cost system. Other materials and component parts are custom made, and the component costs are accumulated using a job order cost system. The assembly operations are essentially the same for all aircraft produced by the company. Therefore, the costs of assembly are accumulated using a process cost system.

Sequence of Production Flow

Products are often the result of a number of production processes. The sequence of production processes—thus, the sequence of departments—depends on the nature of a specific product. Common sequences are sequential, parallel, selective, and joint (split-off of significant products). Normally, a sequential pattern exists in companies producing a single type of product or products all of which receive uniform processing. An illustration of a sequential pattern was given in the demin jeans example in Exhibit 9–1. The joint type of production will be discussed in more detail in Chapter 10 when we cover joint products and by-products. Below are examples of parallel and selective patterns.

Parallel Product Flow. **Parallel product flow** involves processing parts or subassemblies in two or more departments at the same time. The number of possible variations in parallel flow is unlimited. One common pattern is where processes run simultaneously to a merging point, such as final assembly. Another common pattern is where the process begins in the first department and its output is two or more products, each of which follows simultaneous processing steps before the final products emerge in Finished Goods Inventory.

An example of the first type of parallel flow is presented in Exhibit 9B–1. The process is manufacturing sailboats. Hulls are molded using fiberglass and go through a painting and finishing operation. Rigging is cut in one operation but assembled and smoothed in another. Sails are cut and then have the detail painting. Hulls, rigging, and sails are prepared on a parallel basis but come together for assembly of the

EXHIBIT 9B–1   Parellel Product Flows

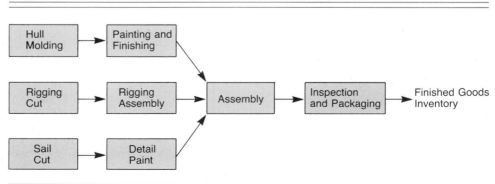

EXHIBIT 9B–2   Selective Product Flows

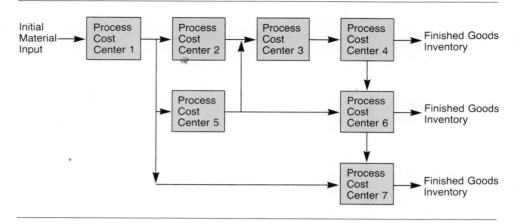

sailboat. Each completed boat then goes through inspection and packaging to await shipping.

The accounting for a parallel product flow system may follow either a job order or process costing approach and is often hybrid in nature with job order costing used for the components that are unique to a product and process costing used for the remainder.

Selective Product Flow.   **Selective product flow** is when the production processes scheduled for a product vary, even in their order, depending on the desired final product. This translates to mixing or combining operations depending on the final product desired. An example in which three products flow from one initial material input but the products go through different departments depending upon the characteristics desired in the product is presented in Exhibit 9B–2.

Accounting for selective product flow often follows a job order costing approach because each product receives a different sequence of processes and treatments and, thus, often requires a different setup in each department. Consequently, the time required for each product batch in each department is very different.

KEY TERMS AND CONCEPTS

Modified cost system (372)   Parallel process flow (373)
Hybrid cost system (372)   Selective process flow (374)

REVIEW QUESTIONS

1. Distinguish between a modified and a hybrid cost system as the terms are used in this appendix.
2. In what circumstances might it be useful to use a job order system to record the fabrication of parts but use a process cost system to record the finishing and assembly of product?
3. Give an example of a product that might require process costing for most of the parts and subassemblies, but require job order costing in the final assembly.
4. Compare and contrast the use of sequential and parallel product flows in the operation of a process cost system.

PROBLEMS

9B–1. Modified Process Costs. The Colitre Company produces seeds for agricultural use. The seeds are grown by specialized farms under contract and then processed in the Colitre Seed Plant in Diluth, Michigan. The seed from each farm has unique results and thus is treated separately in 1-ton units. The seeds must be treated chemically to prevent mold and certain plant diseases and pests. The production is organized into a Treatment Department and a Packaging Department with the seed added at the beginning of the treatment process.

During September 19x2, wheat seed from the Matlich Farm was purchased at a price of $96 per ton for 600 tons. During the month, this seed was treated and packaged for shipment. The Treatment Department had 1,000 tons of various seeds in process at the beginning of the period that were 40 percent complete on conversion and 80 percent complete on chemicals. The department completed 12,000 tons of seed during the month and had 5,000 tons in process that were 30 percent complete on conversion and 60 percent complete on chemicals. The beginning work in process had chemical cost of $8,000 and $4,000 in conversion costs. During the month chemicals costing $56,800 were added to the process and conversion costs of $81,613 were incurred. In the Packaging Department, the wheat seed is placed in 50-pound sealed bags, which cost $.15 each. During the month the Packaging Department processed 480,000 bags of seed with labor costing $48,000 and overhead of $24,000. During October, 20,000 bags of the Matlich Farm Wheat Seed were sold for $68,400.

Colitre uses FIFO cost-flow assumption where appropriate for processes.

REQUIRED:
a. Compute the Treatment Department cost per ton for:
   1. Chemicals.
   2. Treatment.
b. Compute the cost per package and the total cost of treated wheat seed from the Matlich Farm. Include in your analysis the cost of the seed, treatment, and packaging.
c. Compute the gross profit on the sale of the Matlich Farm Wheat Seed for October 19x2.
d. Compute the October 31, 19x2, inventory cost for Matlich Farm Wheat Seed.

9B–2. Modified Service Process Costing. Julian Line Co. is a liquid pipeline transportation company. The line running from New Orleans to Indianapolis is a 30-inch, high-pressure line with a speed that averages 8 miles per hour. A filled line contains 28 million barrels of product that travels an average 192 miles per day. The line speed can be increased safely to about 280 miles per day or slowed almost to a stop. The line can be filled to capacity or be partially empty. Over certain segments, the line moves faster than elsewhere as more product is placed in and taken out. The line carries various products including crude oil of varying weights, home heating oil, and numerous other petroleum products. As a transportation company, the Julian Line does not own the products transported. Instead, it is paid a fee for its services based on moving 10,000 barrels (420,000 gallons) of product mile. The variable cost of running the line is for the 30 pumping stations along the line: the higher the traffic, the higher the fuel cost for pumping.

On July 1, 19x3, the New Orleans to Indianapolis line had 1.44 million units in process (18 million barrels that were to be transported an average of 800 miles), which were 60 percent complete. During the month, the line completed 12 million units of delivered product and had ending units in process of 2 million (20 million barrels to be transported 1,000 miles) that were 40 percent complete. The beginning units in transit had accumulated costs of $8,800,000 of which $2,400,000 were variable costs. During the month, the New Orleans to Indianapolis line had $33,420,800 in variable costs and $81,168,800 in fixed costs. The completed deliveries were billed $134,400,000 for services. Julian Line uses the FIFO method.

REQUIRED:
a. Why should this application be considered a modified process cost system? What is the nature of the costs incurred as to direct materials, direct labor, variable, or fixed production overhead?
b. Compute the equivalent units of production for the New Orleans to Indianapolis line.

c. Determine a cost per unit of output for variable and fixed costs. (Round to four places, if needed.)

d. What were the profits before administrative expenses and taxes made during July 19x3?

c. What were the costs of the units in transit on July 31, 19x3?

9B–3. Job Order and Process Costs. The UniCover Company produces a wide variety of wall covering and flooring from its plant in El Paso, Texas. There are 18,240 identifiable products in the line for spring 19x3. Each covering is unique in the nature of print, materials, and/or the production processes. Most products are kept in the line only one or two seasons and have only one production run. A few products are produced year after year. The Styling and Design Department designs the product. Then the unique materials for the product are prepared and printing occurs in large continuous runs with various types of embossing, printing, and laminating.

Silver Spring, product no. 32402, required designing, preparing the base with a paper and vinyl backing, and printing a pattern in silver ink. The next layer was a thin polymer printed in green and pastel that comes from the Polymer Department. The outer surface was then laminated with a thin hard polymer to make the product easy to clean. The product is embossed with a pattern to create texture. The surface is treated to remove a shiny appearance on the ridges. The final process is rolling, cutting, and packaging the product. The product manager decided that the product would have a total run of 10,000 units. Each unit is a 40-foot roll that is 30 inches wide.

Product no. 32402 had the following costs and processes applied:

1. *Styling and Design Department.* Labor: 29 hours @ $16. Overhead was charged at a rate of 50 percent of styling and design labor.
2. *Base Anneal and Print Department.* This department averages 80 hours of processing per week with labor costs of $24,000 and overhead of $16,000. During the week the department produced 200,000 units of product of which 10,000 units were product no. 32402. Materials for the no. 32402 run are paper, vinyl, and ink costing $25,000.
3. *Polymer Print Department.* This department printed polymer equivalent to 400,000 units during the week; of those units, 10,000 were to be a component of no. 32402. Polymer material cost was $80,000, and conversion cost was $20,000.
4. *Lamination and Emboss Department.* This department averages 80 hours of processing per week and produced 400,000 units of product with materials costs of $30,000 and conversion costs of $40,000. Costs were transferred in from Styling and Design, Base Anneal and Print, and Polymer Print departments for product no. 32402.
5. *Surface Treatment Department.* This department treated 100,000 units of product during the week and had conversion costs of $5,000. Costs were transferred in from the Lamination and Emboss Department related to product no. 32402.
6. *Finishing Department.* This department handled 4 million units of product with costs of $800,000 for packaging materials, $100,000 for labor, and $100,000 for overhead. Costs related to product no. 32402 were transferred in from the Surface Treatment Department.

The company treats transferred-in costs for a product on a job order basis, but the conversion costs for each department are accounted for on a process cost basis. Only the initial materials in the Base Anneal and Print Department are treated on a job order base with other departments' materials treated as a process cost. Thus, materials, except those for the Base Anneal and Print Department, and conversion costs are allocated based on units of production for the department. Only in the Styling and Design Department are product-related hours recorded. The controller believes that this is the only practical, cost-effective method to account for about 20,000 unique products that require similar processing.

REQUIRED:

a. Chart the flow of production processes in a manner similar to Exhibit 9B–1. Does the flow of costs, as described in the cost accounting system, exactly follow the product flow?

b. For each of the six departments determine the:
1. Costs transferred in for product no. 32402.
2. Materials costs allocated to product no. 32402.
3. Conversion Costs allocated to product no. 32402.
4. Costs transferred out for product no. 32402.

c. Determine the cost per unit for a finished product no. 32402.

CHAPTER

10

Costs of Joint Production

■

JOINT COST PROBLEM

Sunnymead Ranch is an egg farm. Its maximum capacity for egg production is 320,000 eggs per day. The hens are housed in long rows of cages in a laying house, with four or five birds to a cage. Food and water are automatically maintained at predetermined levels at each cage. Egg pickers gather the eggs each day and store them in a large refrigerator pending further processing. Eggs come in various sizes—small, medium, large, extra large, and jumbo—depending on the age, condition of the hen, and a host of other environmental factors.

Higher market prices are associated with the large, extra large, and jumbo sizes, but it is difficult to predict how many of each size may be laid on any given day. Regardless of the size egg a hen lays, the bird requires the same amounts of food and water, and the pickers' wages are the same. Processing eggs includes washing them, candling to remove those with cracks or blood spots, sorting by size, and packing them in cartons or on flats.

The medium and larger eggs are accumulated in refrigerated inventory for delivery in orders of 100,000 dozen to grocery chains and distributors. Small eggs are sold at low prices in batches of 100,000 dozen to food processors. The manure is sold for $20 per ton to a local fertilizer plant. Each month the low-producing hens are culled and sold to food processors. How does Sunnymead Ranch determine the cost of products sold and in inventory? This chapter discusses the factors a company considers in determining an appropriate cost accounting system.

■

<table>
<tr><td>LEARNING
OBJECTIVES</td><td>After studying this chapter, you should be able to:</td></tr>
</table>

1. Differentiate between joint products and by-products.
2. Identify joint product costs.
3. Allocate joint product costs using either sales values, net realizable values, or physical measures.
4. Prepare the journal entries for the approaches to account for the costs of by-products.
5. Use accounting data for processing decisions involving joint products and by-products.

One production process can yield many products. For example, at Sunnymead Ranch the products include small, medium, large, extra large, and jumbo eggs along with low-grade eggs, manure, and culled chickens. Any time a resource or input into a process results in two or more outputs with significant value, the multiple products are called **joint products.** The allocation of production costs to joint products is important for inventory costing, income determination, and financial reporting purposes. This chapter explains the accounting for joint products, allocation techniques, and decision-making concerns that involve joint products.

JOINT PRODUCTION ENVIRONMENT

In Chapter 2, we described operations as fabrication, assembly, processing, or extraction. Fabrication and assembly represent a **synthesis production process** in which raw materials and component parts are assembled together to build up the final product. Processing or extractive operations refer to an **analytic production process** in which raw materials are broken down into multiple products with some products more valuable than others.

No special problems arise for multiple products sharing common production facilities if the production of one or more products can proceed without the production of the other products. However, costing problems arise when the production of one product requires the production of another product. Although the conceptual and practical issues inherent in the production of multiple products from common inputs also are applicable to distribution processes and services, this chapter emphasizes manufacturing.

Many manufacturing processes produce multiple products from common inputs. Examples of industries are given in Exhibit 10–1. *Multiple products* is perhaps the broadest term to refer to the output of these industries. Specific terms discussed in the next section include *joint products, by-products, joint costs,* and *separable costs.*

TERMINOLOGY

Joint products, also called **major or main products,** are two or more products so related that one cannot be produced without producing the others, each having relatively substantial value and being produced simultaneously by the same process up to a split-off point.[1] For example, the various-sized eggs are joint products for the

---

[1] *Management Accounting Terminology* (New York: National Association of Accountants, 1983), p. 59.

EXHIBIT 10–1   Multiple Products

Industry	*Products*
Agriculture and food:	
Flour milling	Patent flour, clear flour, middlings, bran, wheat germ, cereals
Meat packing	Meat, hides, fertilizer, shortening, hair, bristles
Cotton ginning	Cotton fiber, cotton seed
Cottonseed processing	Cottonseed oil, meal, hulls, linters
Dairy farming	Cream, skim milk, whole milk, powdered milk, butter, ice cream, cheese
Fishing	Fresh fish, canned fish, fish meal, fish oil, fertilizer
Fruit and vegetable processing	Various grades of fruits and vegetables and juices
Sugar refining	Sugar, molasses, bagasse
Chocolate processing	Chocolate, cocoa, cocoa butter
Paper processing	Paper, paperboard, pulp
Tobacco processing	Cigarettes, cigars, snuff
Extractive:	
Petroleum	Methane, butane, propane, naphtha, gasoline, jet fuels, kerosene, diesel fuel, heating fuels, paraffin, tar, petrochemical feed stocks
Sawmill operations	Various grades and sizes of board, plywood, particle board, feed stock for paper mills
Copper mining	Copper, gold, silver, zinc
Gold mining	Gold, silver, copper
Chemical:	
Soap making	Soap, glycerine
Coke manufacturing	Coke, ammonia, coal tar, gas, benzol
Gas manufacturing	Gas, coke, ammonia, coal tar, sulfur compounds
Cork manufacturing	Cork stoppers, cork shavings, linoleum
Leather tanning	Tanned leather, split leather
Glue manfuacturing	Various grades of glue, grease, tankage stock

Sunnymead Ranch. In the petroleum industry, a gas processing plant takes the natural gas from a gas well and processes it into methane, butane, propane, and other gases. In the entertainment industry, a motion picture project results in a first-run movie to theaters, a second-run movie to theaters, a release (often in various versions) to the world market, a release on video cassette tapes, a release of rights to television, and finally retention or sale of the residual rights.

A **by-product** has relatively minor sales value when compared with joint products. Examples of by-products for Sunnymead Ranch include cracked eggs, manure, and culled chickens. Similarly, residual oils are by-products for some refining processes and gold, zinc, and other metals for copper mining.

An output might be considered a by-product at one point in time and a main product at another time. Such a change in classification could be the result of technological or economic circumstances that changed the value of the product. For example, in the 1890s gasoline was a by-product of the production of heating oil and kerosene (lamp oil). With the widespread use of electric lights and automobiles, gasoline became a joint product and kerosene became a by-product in the 1930s. In the 1960s development of jet aircraft made kerosene, which is a jet fuel ingredient, a joint product again.

Joint costs (also called *joint product costs*) are those material, labor, and production overhead costs incurred during the processing of inputs before the point at which joint products become individually identifiable. In crude oil refining, for example, the costs of crude oil, heating, and other processing costs incurred in operating an ''atmospheric tower'' are joint costs. An atmospheric tower uses combinations of heat and pressure to remove the joint products from the crude oil leaving a residual. The output from the atmospheric tower is the various gases, oils, and the residual. The point at which joint products are individually identifiable is called the **split-off point.** For the Sunnymead egg farm example, the split-off point occurs when the eggs are sorted by quality and size.

Some joint products may go through additional processing after the split-off point before they are marketed. The importance of the split-off point is that the processing costs that are incurred after this point can be directly traced to specific products. The costs after the split-off point are called **separable costs** or *additional costs*. For example, gasoline from the atmospheric tower will have separable costs related to additional processing that purifies and blends the final product.

BASIC CHARACTERISTICS

Exhibit 10–2 is an illustration of potential joint product and by-product processing and cost flows. The accounting for processing and cost flows is discussed later. However, the exhibit gives a starting point for discussing the important basic characteristics of joint production.

Product Categories

The three broad product categories relating to joint products and by-products for a joint process are presented in Exhibit 10–2. The disposition and inventoriable costs are also presented.

For purposes of illustration, joint products are identified with a disposition at the split-off point or after further processing; a by-product will be disposed sometime after split-off. A joint product can be one of two types: (1) Finished Goods Inventory to await sale; or (2) raw material in another process. If the joint product does not require further processing, the inventoriable cost is an allocated share of the joint costs at split-off. Where a joint product is processed further, its inventoriable cost is the allocated joint cost plus the separable costs.

If a joint product becomes a raw material to a further process, the joint product often changes and becomes an integral part of another product. For example, in cotton ginning, the fiber and the seed are separated. Seeds enter into another process, the

EXHIBIT 10–2   Joint Products and Cost Flows

Product Category		*Disposition*	*Inventoriable Cost*
Joint product	Processed further	(1) Finished good (2) Raw material to another product	Allocated joint cost plus separable cost
Joint product	Complete at split-off	(1) Finished good (2) Raw material to another product	Allocated joint cost
By-product	Complete or processed on	By-product inventory	Realizable value or zero value

output of which is cottonseed oil, meal, hulls, and lint. Then the cottonseed meal is mixed with corn, sorghum, and other grains to make cattle and chicken feed. At the time of mixture, the cottonseed meal loses its identity and becomes an integral part of the livestock feed. The cottonseed has lost its identity by being mixed with the other grains.

Joint costs are those incurred up to the split-off point. These costs consist of direct materials, direct labor, and production overhead for the joint process. As a body of costs, joint costs apply to a common process in which separate products are not yet identifiable. Separable costs are incurred for the identifiable products after the split-off point and include the additional direct materials, direct labor, and production overhead necessary to make a joint product salable.

ACCOUNTING FOR JOINT PRODUCTS

Joint costs must be allocated to individual products for external financial reporting and income tax filing purposes. Thus, joint costs are allocated in order to determine the ending Work in Process and Finished Goods inventories, cost of goods manufactured, cost of goods sold, and ultimately net income. However, because joint costs cannot be identified with individual joint products, the basis for allocating joint costs to these products is arbitrary. Consequently, the results of *arbitrary joint cost allocations should not be used for internal decision-making involving the joint products.*[2]

The following two broad categories of methods are commonly used to allocate joint costs:

1. Market value method.
2. Physical measures method.

Although there appear to be only two methods, each of the above categories has many modifications in practice.

Market Value Method

Under the market value method, joint costs are allocated according to some measure related to the market values of the individual joint products. The procedures to be used under this method will depend on whether (1) the market value is known at the split-off point (sales value method); or (2) the market value is not known at the split-off point (net realizable value method).

Sales Value Method. When the sales value is known at the split-off point, the total joint costs are allocated among the joint products on the basis of the ratio an individual sales value bears to the total sales value of all joint products. This ratio is then multiplied by the total joint costs to arrive at the amount allocated to each product. We refer to this as the **sales value method,** but it is also known as the *relative sales value method, sales realization method,* and *gross market value method.*

Example Analysis. Angelo Cotton Gin, Inc., processed 500 bails of raw cotton during November; each bail weighed 500 pounds. The joint products are ginned cotton fiber and cottonseed, both of which are sold at the split-off point. The 500 bails of

---

[2] Although joint costs should not influence internal decisions, in practice the joint costs are reported and appear to managers in the same way as any other inventoriable cost, and thereby joint costs have an influence over decisions such as performance evaluation, pricing, product promotion, and inventory management. This is an example of a weakness in current practice primarily caused by management policy to have internal reports meet external reporting requirements.

raw cotton were processed into 400 bails, also weighing 500 pounds each, of cotton fiber and 100–quarter-ton units of cottonseed. The raw cotton costs $45,000, and conversion costs were $9,000. The current market price for ginned cotton fiber is $146.25 per bail and for cottonseed $65 per quarter-ton unit.

The joint cost of $54,000 (cotton of $45,000 and conversion costs of $9,000) is allocated using the sales value method. First, compute the sales values of the individual products at the split-off point and the ratio of each value to the total sales value:

Product	Units	Unit Sales Value	Total Sales Value	Percent of Total
Fiber	400	$146.25	$58,500	90
Seed	100	65.00	6,500	10
			$65,000	100

Second, we apply the above percentages to determine the amount of joint cost to be allocated to each product:

Product	Percent	Joint Costs	Allocations
Fiber	90	$54,000	$48,600
Seed	10	54,000	5,400
			$54,000

The joint cost allocations are the total inventory values for the products at the split-off point. These products have costs per unit of:

	Allocations	Units	Cost per Unit
Fiber	$48,600	400	$122.50
Seed	4,400	100	54.00
	$54,000	500	

Net Realizable Value Method.   When the sales value is known at the split-off point, it should be used to allocate the joint costs. However, the sales value is not always readily determinable at the split-off point, especially if additional processing is necessary before the product can be sold. When this situation exists, the **net realizable value method (joint products)** is used. This method is also called the *net relative sales value method,* or *the net market value method.* The net realizable value is the estimated selling price less reasonably predictable costs of completion and disposal.[3]

Under the net realizable value method, any estimated separable costs of additional processing and disposal are deducted from the final sales value in order to approximate a hypothetical sales value at the split-off point. Joint costs are allocated to the products by using the ratio of each product's net realizable value to the total net realizable value for all joint products. This ratio is then multiplied by the joint costs to allocate the joint costs to the individual products.

Example analysis.   Denzer Company processes animal products into grease, glue, and tanning stock. During a recent production run, the joint costs were $15,000. Additional information needed for allocating the joint costs are below:

———————
    [3] *Management Accounting Terminology* (New York: National Association of Accountants, 1983), p. 70.

Joint Products	Pounds	Sales Value after Further Processing	Separable Costs
Grease	10,500	$1.40	$7,200
Glue	12,000	2.30	9,600
Tanning	7,500	.75	1,125

Each of the above products must be processed further before it can be sold. Separate production costs incurred beyond the split-off point are easily identified with a particular product. The separable costs are deducted from the sales values after further processing to arrive at net realizable values at the split-off point. Net realizable values then form the basis for joint cost allocation. For the above data, net realizable values are calculated as:

Joint Products	Pounds	Sales Value	Total Sales Value	Separable* Costs	Net Realizable Value	%
Grease	10,500	$1.40	$14,700	$7,200	$ 7,500	25
Glue	12,000	2.30	27,600	9,600	18,000	60
Tanning	7,500	.75	5,625	1,125	4,500	15
					$30,000	

* Technically, the separable costs include both the additional processing costs and the costs of disposal. The disposal costs have been left out to simplify the example.

Now we proceed with the allocation of joint costs as we did with sales values at the split-off point. This allocation is:

Product	Percent	Joint Costs	Allocations
Grease	25	$15,000	$ 3,750
Glue	60	15,000	9,000
Tanning	15	15,000	2,250
			$15,000

The inventory values and the costs per unit for the three products are:

Joint Products	Allocated	Separable Costs	Inventory Cost	Pounds	Cost per Unit
Grease	$3,750	$7,200	$10,950	10,500	$1.043
Glue	9,000	9,600	18,600	12,000	1.550
Tanning	2,250	1,125	3,375	7,500	0.450

Combination of methods.   To this point, we have assumed that all joint products are sold at the split-off point or must be processed further. The sales value at split-off is used in the first case, and the net realizable value applies to the second case. More than likely, there is a combination of sell at the split-off point and process further. What method do we use for this situation? The answer is a mixture of sales value at the split-off point and net realizable value. Taken together they form the total from which percentages are calculated.

Again, the rule is to use a sales value at the split-off point if it is known. If the sales value does not exist, then use a net realizable value. This guidance can be summarized for the different classifications of product as follows:

Product Category	Market Value Used
1. Product is salable only at the split-off point.	Sales value at split-off point

Product Category	*Market Value Used*
2. Product is salable at the split-off point but is processed further.	Sales value at split-off point
3. Product is not salable at the split-off point and must be processed further.	Net realizable value at the split-off point

PHYSICAL MEASURES METHODS

There are various methods to allocate joint costs to joint products according to relative physical characteristics. Each **physical measures method** (also called the *physical volume method*) requires the computation of some average, and the methods differ primarily by whether an average unit or a weighted unit is used. Methods based on physical measures utilize some physical attribute common to all joint products. Weight, volume, surface area, linear measure, atomic weight, heat units, gallons, and cases are examples of the many measures used. Under this procedure, the common attribute is summed, and the joint costs are allocated on the basis of each product's relative portion of it. As a consequence, each product will have the same cost per unit of the measure at the split-off point.

Average Unit Cost   Perhaps the simplest method to allocate joint costs is to count the units of the physical measure of each of the joint products, add these figures together, and divide the total number of units into the total joint cost to obtain an **average unit cost.**

The Denzer Company provides data for an example of physical measures. Denzer has joint costs of $15,000 with additional data of:

Joint Products	*Pounds*	*Sales Value after Further Processing*	*Separable Costs*
Grease	10,500	$1.40	$7,200
Glue	12,000	2.30	9,600
Tanning	7,500	.75	1,125
	30,000		

The joint production cost is $15,000.

The average unit cost is the joint cost divided by the total units:

$$\text{Average unit cost} = \text{Joint cost/Total units}$$
$$= \$15,000/30,000 = \$.50$$

Even though the products must be processed further before a sale is possible, joint costs can be allocated at the split-off point on the basis of pounds.

Product	*Pounds*	*Average Unit Cost*	*Allocations*
Grease	10,500	.50	$ 5,250
Glue	12,000	.50	6,000
Tanning	7,500	.50	3,750
	30,000		$15,000

The products have an inventory cost and a cost per unit of:

Joint Products	*Joint Cost Allocated*	*Separable Costs*	*Inventory Cost*	*Pounds*	*Cost per Pound*
Grease	$5,250	$7,200	$12,450	10,500	$1.186
Glue	6,000	9,600	15,600	12,000	1.300
Tanning	3,750	1,125	4,875	7,500	0.650

Weighted Unit Method

Varying complexities may affect the production of joint products; these include the degree of productive difficulty, the amount of time involved, the quality of labor, the size of the unit, or the amount of space used. Weight factors or points are assigned to each joint product based on these diverse characteristics. These characteristics and their relative weights are combined into a single weight factor. The **weighted unit method** allocates joint costs by multiplying the joint product units by their respective weight factors to arrive at weighted units. Then a cost per weighted unit is computed.

For the Denzer Company example above, assume that management desires to weight the product based on split-off difficulty. Extracting the grease is judged to be about twice as difficult as the tanning stock. Further, assume that extracting the glue base is 75 percent as difficult as the tanning stock. If the weight for the tanning stock is set at 4, then:

$$\text{Grease weight} \quad 200\% \times 4 = 8$$
$$\text{Glue weight} \quad 75\% \times 4 = 3$$

The judgments on the relative difficulty of producing joint products should be made by the production or engineering staff. Applying these weights:

Joint Products	Pounds	Weights	Weighted Pounds
Grease	10,500	8	84,000
Glue	12,000	3	36,000
Tanning	7,500	4	30,000
	30,000		150,000

The cost per weighted unit is $15,000/150,000 = $.10.

Joint costs are allocated using the average cost based on weighted pounds:

Product	Weighted Pounds	Weighted Unit	Allocations
Grease	84,000	$.10	$ 8,400
Glue	36,000	.10	3,600
Tanning	30,000	.10	3,000
	150,000		$15,000

The products have an inventory cost and a cost per unit of:

Joint Products	Allocated	Separable Costs	Inventory Cost	Pounds	Cost per Pound
Grease	$ 8,400	$ 7,200	$15,600	10,500	$1.486
Glue	3,600	9,600	13,200	12,000	1.100
Tanning	3,000	1,125	4,125	7,500	0.550
	$15,000	$17,925	$32,925		

The weighted unit method has many variations used in various industries. In the petroleum industry, for example, one variation is called the *barrel gravity method;* another is called the *gravity-heat method.*

Results of the Allocation Methods

Three methods of joint cost allocation have been applied to the allocation of the Denzer Company joint production costs: net realizable value, average unit cost, and the weighted unit cost. The resulting unit costs for these three methods were:

		Costs		
	Net Realizable	Physical Measures		
	Values	Average Unit	Weighted Units	Selling Prices
Grease	$1.043	$1.186	$1.486	$1.40
Glue	1.550	1.300	1.100	2.30
Tannage	.450	.650	.550	.75

Comments on Market Value Methods. The market value methods may be criticized on practical accounting systems–related issues. Market prices change constantly. Thus, current market prices must be found and the data keyed in. This increases administrative overhead costs.

Market value methods are more complex and costly to program in the computerized accounting systems and, because of the complexity, the lines of programmed code are more with a market value method. Whenever the production process changes, complex computer programs must be updated to reflect the changes.

The allocation of joint cost for a given joint process must wait on estimates of prices, additional processing costs, marketing, and shipping costs. Because the system requires estimates, managers can manipulate net income by changing estimates of selling prices, additional processing costs, and disposal costs. Changes in estimates from week to week and month to month introduce variations into the costs per unit that may be confusing.

Comments on Physical Measure Methods. Under the physical measure approach, there is no relationship between inventoried cost and the value of the product. If costs per unit are computed with the results from the physical measures method, managers are motivated by higher profits to promote those products with high profit margins and to keep in inventory those products with very low gross profit or losses.

Reporting inventory costs based on the physical measures method will encourage managers to increase prices on products with high physical measures (e.g., those that are heavy or big). In turn, an increase in prices will drive down demand for the product and increase inventory. Conversely, low physical measure products will appear less costly, which encourages managers to lower prices on these products. Therefore, prices should not be based on allocations of joint costs, especially allocations using a physical measures method.

In summary, the arguments involving joint cost allocation methods hinge on the relative importance of management motivation issues versus the pragmatic computerized accounting systems issues. In practice, these issues may resolve either way.

In the next section, the accounting for by-products is presented.

ACCOUNTING FOR BY-PRODUCTS

By-products, like major products, are produced from a common raw material or common manufacturing process. The distinction between major products and by-products is largely influenced by the relative revenues of the products involved. Current classifications of joint products and by-products are not permanent. Depending upon sales values and technological changes, products can shift from one classification to another. The two major methods to account for by-products are the (1) **net realizable value method (by-products)** and (2) zero value method.

Net Realizable Value Method

The net realizable value is equal to the estimated sales value less estimated costs of any further processing and disposition. This net realizable value is removed from the joint processing costs. Two important things happen with this approach: (1) a smaller amount of joint processing costs is allocated to joint products, and (2) no revenue is recognized from by-product sales.

Example Analysis. The Washburn Company produces two major products: Pursue and Retreat, which are two bases for an after-shave lotion. A by-product is also produced in the process. During the month, 20,000 gallons of input were processed into 12,000 gallons of Pursue, 7,000 gallons of Retreat, and 1,000 gallons of by-product. The joint costs totaled $76,000. All of the products are sold at the split-off point. The by-product has a net realizable value at split-off of $1.90 per gallon. The journal entry to record the by-product inventory at the split-off point is:

By-Product Inventory		
(1,000 gallons × $1.90)	1,900	
Work in Process Inventory		1,900

The entry at time of sale is:

Cash or Accounts Receivable	1,900	
By-Product Inventory		1,900

The credit to Work in Process Inventory results in the joint costs of the process being reduced by $1,900. Instead of $76,000 of joint costs that are allocated to joint products, we now have $74,100 ($76,000 − $1,900).

Because the by-product is valued at its net realizable value, no gain or loss is recognized if it is sold at the anticipated price. Any differences between actual selling prices and anticipated selling prices used in establishing net realizable values are treated as gains or losses.

If additional processing is needed for the by-products, the separable costs are added as incurred to the inventory cost of the by-product.

Zero Value Methods

Zero value methods are regarded as appropriate when the value of the by-product is uncertain or very small. The by-product inventory is not assigned a value, and all joint costs are allocated to the major products. The method to record the sale of the by-product has several variations: (1) recognize as sales revenue, (2) reduce cost of production, (3) reduce cost of sales, and (4) treat as other income. The four variations for treating the by-product revenues under the zero-value method are illustrated in Exhibit 10–3.

The accounting for joint costs, separable costs, and by-products has been presented.

In the next section, we will consider decisions related to output level, further processing, and pricing.

JOINT COSTS AND MANAGEMENT DECISIONS

Decision-making with respect to joint products generally involves output (quantity and mix) decisions, further processing decisions, and pricing decisions. Joint cost allocations are generally irrelevant for these decisions related to individual products and often prove counterproductive if used. It is important to emphasize that joint cost allocations are made solely for inventory costing, which influences income determination. Such allocations should not influence management in planning and control activities for joint products.

EXHIBIT 10–3   Zero Value Methods of By-Product Revenue

Example Analysis. Assume that the Washburn Company sold all of its production during the current month. The income statement for the major products shows:

Sales of major products:		
Pursue: 12,000 gallons × $7.00		$ 84,000
Retreat: 7,000 gallons × $6.25		43,750
		$127,750
Cost of goods sold:		
Joint production costs		76,000
Gross margin		$ 51,750
Operating expenses		
Marketing and distribution expenses	$11,750	
General and administrative expenses	10,000	21,750
Income from operations on joint products		$ 30,000

The by-product is sold to receive the net realizable value of $1.90 per gallon, which yields revenue of $1,900.

	Sales Revenue	Reduction in Cost of Production	Reduction in Cost of Sales	Other Income
Sales, major products	$127,750	$127,750	$127,750	$127,750
Sales, by-products	1,900			
Total	$129,650	$127,750	$127,750	$127,750
Cost of sales:				
Joint production costs	$ 76,000	$ 76,000	$ 76,000	$ 76,000
Sales, by-products		(1,900)		
Cost of sales (gross)	$ 76,000	$ 74,100	$ 76,000	$ 76,000
Sales, by-products			(1,900)	
Cost of sales (net)	$ 76,000	$ 74,100	$ 74,100	$ 76,000
Gross margin	$ 53,650	$ 53,650	$ 53,650	$ 51,750
Operating expenses	21,750	21,750	21,750	21,750
Income from operations	$ 31,900	$ 31,900	$ 31,900	$ 30,000
Sales, by-products				1,900
Income before taxes*	$ 31,900	$ 31,900	$ 31,900	$ 31,900

* The net income is the same for all four methods because there are no inventories. However, if the situation resulted in ending inventories, then the alternative for reduction in cost of production would include a portion of the reduction in the cost of any ending inventories. Thus, that alternative would yield a net income figure different from the other alternatives.

Output Decisions

An **output decision** for joint products is of two kinds: (1) manufacture a product group and (2) increase or decrease the volume of a product group. The physical characteristics of the joint products in the group require that all products in the group be produced. That means the only decision is all or nothing—produce the product group or not, increase or decrease the volume by a specific amount or not.

When the products are manufactured in fixed proportions, an increase in one quantity of product results in a fixed quantity of the other products in the group. Individual profit for each product is of little significance in this case. Rather, more useful information comes by comparing total revenues and total costs for the entire joint product group.

When the products may be manufactured in varying proportions, the output decision is based on *which mix of joint products generates the highest profit*. For example, in oil refining various proportions of gasoline and home heating oil may be produced depending on how the process is set up. The actual production mix decision depends upon the relationship between the prices of gasoline and home heating oil. Thus, because the price of gasoline is higher in the summer, more gasoline is produced then. Similarly, more home heating oil is produced in the winter because the price is higher then. Thus, mix of outputs from some joint processes may be shifted to meet customer demand and prices.

Further Processing Decisions

In a number of manufacturing situations management must decide whether joint products should be processed beyond the split-off point or simply sold at the split-off point. Petroleum refiners, for example, must decide whether the residual from an atmospheric tower should be sold or processed through one of many other processes to gain a higher yield of gasoline and diesel fuels.

Further processing decisions (also called *sell or process further decisions*) hinge on incremental revenues sufficiently exceeding the incremental costs, *not* on joint cost allocations. Incremental revenue is the difference between revenue after additional processing and revenue at the split-off point. The incremental costs are the additional processing and disposal costs. Joint costs and methods to allocate joint costs to the products provide no useful information and should not influence further processing decision.

Example Analysis. Garrett Gamble Corporation produces three products: Ex, Wy, and Zee. Each product can be sold at the split-off point or processed further. Processing further requires no special facilities, and the additional costs are specifically identifiable with the product involved. Management is now making a decision about which products to sell at split-off and which to process further during the upcoming year. Estimated joint costs are $64,000. Other information needed for the decision are:

Product	Units Produced	Sales Value at Split-off	Separable Costs and Sales Values if Processed Further	
			Sales Values	Added Costs
Ex	8,000	$30,000	$47,000	$8,000
Wy	5,000	46,000	50,000	6,000
Zee	3,000	24,000	33,000	9,000

The incremental revenues are compared with the additional costs of processing to determine which products should be processed further. This analysis is:

	Ex	Wy	Zee
Sales value after processing	$47,000	$50,000	$33,000
Sales value at split-off	30,000	46,000	24,000
Incremental revenues	$17,000	$ 4,000	$ 9,000
Incremental processing costs	8,000	6,000	9,000
Profit (loss) of processing	$ 9,000	$(2,000)	$ —0—

Ex has incremental revenues in excess of additional processing costs and should be further processed before selling. Wy cannot generate sufficient revenue to warrant further processing. Zee presents an interesting situation. Because incremental revenues equal incremental costs, there is no apparent reason to process further. In some cases, management will decide to sell at the split-off point. In trying to maintain a stable work force, or retain highly skilled workers, or any number of other reasons, management may decide to process Zee further knowing that costs will be covered.

Assume management decides to produce Ex and Zee beyond the split-off point and all products are sold during the year. Compare this result with selling all products at the split-off point.

		Sell All Products at Split-Off		Process Ex and Zee Further
Revenues:				
Ex		$ 30,000		$ 47,000
Wy		46,000		46,000
Zee		24,000		33,000
		$100,000		$126,000
Costs:				
Joint costs	$64,000		$64,000	
Processing:				
Ex	–0–		8,000	
Zee	–0–	64,000	9,000	81,000
Profit		$ 36,000		$ 45,000

The difference between the two profit figures is $9,000, which is the profit of processing on Ex that was used earlier in selecting the products to process further. The income statements also show that joint costs are the same no matter which decision is made on further processing. Thus, the joint costs are irrelevant to further processing decisions.

Pricing Decisions

Management assumes all products manufactured will be sold. Thus, pricing individual products is aimed at selling all joint products in the same proportion as they are produced. If the sales value method is used to allocate joint costs, selling prices are used to determine cost allocations. It is circular reasoning then to use the joint cost allocations to set prices. The real issue is that selling prices must be set so that total revenue exceeds total costs—both joint and separable costs. Thus, all products must be sold for as much as possible.

SUMMARY

Many manufacturing operations produce different products simultaneously from common raw materials or a common process (called *joint products*). The costs incurred prior to the split-off point (point where identification of separate products is possible) are joint costs. These consist of the materials, labor, and production overhead costs of the joint process. Separable costs are those incurred by the individual products after the split-off point.

Because product costs are necessary for inventory valuation and income determination, it is necessary to allocate the joint costs to the products resulting from the process. The sales value method and the physical measures method represent two categories of technique to allocate joint costs. A sales value method is preferred in most industries.

Products that contribute only a small amount to the total revenue of the product group are called *by-products*. They may be sold in the same form as originally produced, or they may undergo further processing before sale. Because by-products are generally of secondary importance, cost allocation procedures differ from those of the major products. Methods of costing by-products fall into two categories: (1) net realizable value method, and (2) zero value method.

Current classifications of products as joint products and by-products are not permanent. Depending upon sales values and technological changes, products may be redefined from one classification to another.

Joint cost allocations are made for purposes of inventory valuation and income determination. They are not relevant in output, further processing, or pricing decisions. Output decisions compare the potential total revenues of a product group with the total expected costs. Further processing decisions are made on a comparison of differences in incremental revenues and incremental costs beyond the split-off point. Pricing decisions may look at total costs for the product group as well as a number of market factors.

PROBLEMS FOR REVIEW PROBLEM A

Neves Corporation produces two major products and one by-product from a chemical process. In the Blending Department, Mar emerges as the major product with another liquid that must be processed through the Cooking Department. Mar goes from Blending to Purifying Treatment before it is ready for sale. The yield from the Cooking Department is Cer, which is sold without further processing, and a by-product Resid that can be sold immediately. The company follows the policy not to allocate joint costs to by-products (by-products are valued at zero). Product data for the year just ending and a flow diagram are given below.

Blending processed 115,000 gallons of chemicals at a joint cost of $140,000. The output consisted of 60,000 gallons of Mar that went to the purifying treatment and 55,000 gallons that were transferred to the Cooking Department.

Purifying costs for Mar were $42,000. After processing, Mar was ready for sale. The selling price during the year was $7.90 per gallon. The Cooking Department incurred processing costs of $122,000. Its yield was 50,000 gallons of Cer and 5,000 gallons of Resid. Cer is sold for $5.80 per gallon, and the by-product Resid is sold for $1.15 per gallon. Marketing and administrative expenses to dispose of Resid were $0.10 per gallon.

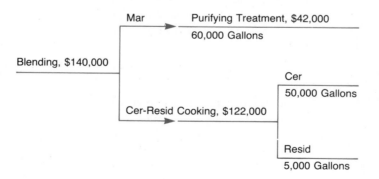

REQUIRED

a. Allocate all joint costs to the major products and show the per gallon inventoriable cost of each product when it is transferred to finished goods inventory. Assume a market value method.

b. Prepare the journal entries that transfer the costs of the joint products from department to department to Finished Goods Inventory.

c. Prepare the journal entries that record all appropriate transactions for the year relating to the by-product. Assume no beginning or ending inventories. The company treats by-products sales as miscellaneous income.

SOLUTION

a. Because the by-product is not allocated a share of joint costs, the only split-off point for allocating joint costs to major products is the Blending Department. Each major product is processed beyond the Blending Department, which means net realizable values are appropriate. The net realizable values and the percentages for allocating joint costs are:

Mar sales value (60,000 gal. × $7.90)	$474,000		
Purifying Treatment	42,000	$432,000	72%
Cer sales value (50,000 gal. × $5.80)	$290,000		
Cooking Department	122,000	168,000	28%
		$600,000	100%

Joint cost allocations begin with the Blending Department. The allocation of the $140,000 joint cost of blending is:

Product	Joint Cost Allocations
Mar	72% × $140,000 = $100,800
Cer	28% × $140,000 = 39,200

To find the total costs of each product, it is necessary to add the separable costs to the joint cost allocations:

Product	Joint Costs	Separable Costs	Total Costs	Inventoriable Cost/Gallon
Mar	$100,800	$ 42,000	$142,800	$2.38
Cer	39,200	122,000	161,200	3.224

b. The journal entries are:

Work in Process—Purifying	100,800	
Work in Process—Cooking	39,200	
Work in Process—Blending		140,000
To record the transfer of costs of Mar and Cer-Resid from Blending.		
Finished Goods Inventory	142,800	
Work in Process—Purifying		142,800
To record the completion of Mar and transfer to finished goods.		
Finished Goods Inventory	161,200	
Work in Process—Cooking		161,200
To record the completion of Cer and transfer to finished goods.		

c. Entries for by-products:

Marketing and Administrative Cost Control	500	
Cash		500
To record the marketing and administrative costs assigned to by-products: 5,000 gal. × $.10 = $500.		
Cash	5,750	
Miscellaneous Income		5,750
To record the sale of 5,000 gallons of Resid at $1.15 per gallon.		

PROBLEMS FOR REVIEW
PROBLEM B

Parker Chemical Supply produces three products from a joint process. Each product may be sold at the split-off point or processed further and then sold. Separable costs of further processing are variable, and no special facilities are required. Joint costs at the split-off point total $90,000. The separable costs and sales values for each product are given below:

Product	Gallons Produced	Sales Value at Split-off	Sales Values	Added Costs
AD–1246	10,000	$35,000	$60,000	$15,000
BC–3784	20,000	70,000	85,000	20,000
EF–2533	5,000	55,000	90,000	30,000

(Separable Costs and Sales Values if Processed Further)

REQUIRED

Which products should be sold at the split-off point, and which should be processed further?

SOLUTION

The incremental revenues are compared with the additional costs of processing to see which product should be processed further. This analysis is:

	AD–1246	BC–3784	EF–2533
Sales value after processing	$60,000	$85,000	$90,000
Sales value at split-off	35,000	70,000	55,000
Incremental revenues	$25,000	$15,000	$35,000
Separable costs	15,000	20,000	30,000
Profit (loss) of processing	$10,000	$ (5,000)	$ 5,000

AD–1246 and EF–2533 have incremental revenues in excess of additional processing costs and should be further processed before selling. BC–3784 does not generate sufficient incremental revenue to warrant further processing.

KEY TERMS AND CONCEPTS

Joint products (379)
Synthesis production process (379)
Analytic production process (379)
Major (or main) products (379)
By-product (380)
Joint costs (381)
Split-off point (381)
Separable costs (381)

Sales value method (382)
Net realizable value method (joint products) (383)
Physical measures method (385)
Average unit cost (385)
Weighted unit method (385)
Net realizable value method (by-products) (387)
Output decisions (389)
Further processing decisions (390)

ADDITIONAL READINGS

Barton, M. F., and J. D. Spiceland. "Joint Cost Allocation as a Principal Cost Control Strategy." *Production and Inventory Management Journal,* Second Quarter, 1987, pp. 117–22.
Cats-Baril, W. L., and J. F. Gatti. "Joint Product Costing in the Semiconductor Industry." *Management Accounting,* February 1986, pp. 28–35.

Fertakis, J. P. "Responsibility Accounting for By-Products and Industrial Wastes." *Journal of Accountancy,* May 1986, pp. 138–47.

Fetterman, A. L. "Update on Not-for-Profit Accounting and Reporting." *CPA Journal,* March 1988, pp. 22ff.

Harrell, H. W., and W. H. Francisco. "Cost Recognition in the Used-Parts Market." *Production and Inventory Management Journal,* First Quarter, 1989, pp. 36–38.

McLaughlin, J. K. "Resolved: Joint Costs Should Be Allocated (Sometimes)." *CPA Journal,* January 1988, pp. 46ff.

Schneider, A. "Simultaneous Determination of Cost Allocations and Cost-Plus Prices for Joint Products." *Journal of Business Finance and Accounting,* Summer 1986, pp. 187–95.

Thomas, A. L. *The Allocation Problem in Financial Accounting Theory–Studies in Accounting Research No. 3.* Sarasota: American Accounting Association, 1969.

REVIEW QUESTIONS

1. Describe the basic characteristics of joint products. What is included in the cost of a finished product that was once a joint product?

2. Are there any similarities or differences between the nature of joint products and by-products? Explain. What is the primary factor that determines whether a product is a joint product or a by-product?

3. Describe the impact that changing market values might have on the classification and accounting for joint products and by-products.

4. Define and contrast joint cost and separable cost and tell at what stage in processing the joint products each typically occurs.

5. Under what condition will the physical measures method of joint cost allocation provide satisfactory results?

6. How does the physical measure method affect the gross margin percentage of the joint products?

7. When weights are used in connection with a physical measure to allocate joint costs, what do these weights represent?

8. What assumption forms the basis of the sales value method of joint cost allocation?

9. What are the reasons cited for using the market value method?

10. What are the criticisms of the market value method?

11. What are the reasons cited for using a physical measures method?

12. What are the criticisms of the physical measures method?

13. Why can the sales value method of joint cost allocation not be used as a basis for price setting?

14. In what way is the sales value method modified if there are separate production costs after the split-off point? Is this modification necessary if the intermediate product has a sales value at the split-off point?

15. Describe how sales prices might be adjusted when they are used as the basis to assign a cost to joint product inventories.

16. Why are allocated joint costs irrelevant in the evaluation of alternative uses of a joint product? Under what circumstances would costing of joint products be useful in determining selling prices?

17. Describe the two general methods to account for by-products. Which method is most closely related to accounting for joint costs?

18. Describe some theoretical and practical considerations in deciding which method of accounting for by-products should be adopted in a particular business situation.

19. List the various income statement presentations that would be made when using a zero value method of accounting for by-products.

20. Describe the method of cost analysis that yields valid results when management needs to decide if a joint product should be processed beyond the split-off point.

21. Show how a physical measures method could allocate costs to products so that the lower of cost or market rule is violated.

22. Throughout the chapter, all allocations assumed that the joint products were to be sold. Some joint products will become raw material or component parts for other processes. If a joint product is not sold but goes to the storeroom to await being issued to another process, explain how you would use the sales value method to allocate the joint costs of the process from which this product comes.

10–1. Distinguishing between Joint Products and By-Products. Listed below are the products produced by Sunnymead Egg Farm along with the volume and revenues generated for the most recent year.

	Product	Unit	Unit Volume	Revenues
_____ a.	Cracked eggs	Dozen	288,000	$ 14,400
_____ b.	Hens to food processor	Hens	180,000	216,000
_____ c.	Eggs with blood spots	Dozen	384,000	19,200
_____ d.	Extra large eggs	Dozen	2,208,000	1,324,800
_____ e.	Jumbo eggs	Dozen	1,536,000	1,075,200
_____ f.	Large eggs	Dozen	2,880,000	1,497,600
_____ g.	Manure	Tons	1,800	36,000
_____ h.	Medium eggs	Dozen	2,112,000	739,200
_____ i.	Small eggs	Dozen	384,000	46,080
	Total Revenues			$4,968,480

The management of Sunnymead Ranch has decided to account for all products that result in less than 5 percent of total revenues as a by-product.

REQUIRED:
For each of the products indicate whether the product is a (1) joint product or (2) by-product.

10–2. Sales Value and Physical Measure Methods. AW, Inc., gins cotton and sells the resulting cotton fiber and seed. No additional processing is required, but substantial ending inventories are involved. During the month ending December 31, 19x4, the company had the following activity:

	Units	Selling Price
Cotton fiber	10,000	$300
Cottonseed	5,000	200

The joint production costs of the cotton gin were $1,875,000.

REQUIRED:
a. Using the sales value method:
    1. Allocate the joint costs to the two products.
    2. Compute the cost per unit for the two products.
b. Using the physical volume method:
    1. Allocate the joint costs to the two products.
    2. Compute the cost per unit for the two products.

10–3. Net Realizable Value and Physical Measure Methods. The Eagle Lumber Processing Mill of Miksawkee, Inc., produces two grades of lumber from debarked pine trees. The lumber is then aged and planed. Miksawkee uses 100 board feet (HBF) as its standard unit of measure. During the month of April 19x4, the mill produced 200,000 HBF of grade A and 300,000 HBF of grade B lumber. The joint production costs for April were $1,500,000 for trees transferred into the unit, $40,000 for direct labor, and $60,000 for production overhead. The additional processing costs for aging and planing were $400,000 for grade A and $300,000 for grade B. Grade A is sold for $14 per HBF after additional processing, and grade B can be sold for only $2 per HBF.

REQUIRED:
Compute the cost for a completed unit using the:
a. Net realizable value method.
b. Physical volume method.

10–4. Net Realizable Value Method.   The Metal Works for Burton County Correction Facility stamps four types of road signs from each sheet of steel. The signs are sold to 95 counties in the region. Because the signs are various shapes, little steel is wasted in the stamping process. After the signs are stamped, they are then painted with reflective paint and wrapped for shipment. During 19x7, the following production occurred:

Type of Sign	Units	Selling Price	Finishing Costs
Stop	2,000	$ 5.00	$2,000
Yield	2,000	4.00	2,550
Speed limit	1,900	5.50	1,900
Road name/no.	3,000	10.00	2,000

The joint costs to produce the signs were $15,000 for the sheet steel, $200 for direct labor (2,000 hours at $.10), and $4,800 for shop overhead. For security purposes, inventories of materials and finished product are never kept at the Metal Works.

(M. Moreland)

REQUIRED:
Using the net realizable value method, determine the costs associated with each type of sign.

10–5. Net Realizable Value and Physical Measure Methods with By-Products.   The Silicon Growth Unit of Trey International, Inc., grows crystal cylinders used in integrated circuit production. The cylinders are sliced into 8-inch diameter wafers called chips, which are later polished. Circuits are then printed and cut into individual chips. Depending on the physical characteristics of the sliced wafers, the chips can be used to print a very high-density and high-speed chip or a medium-speed chip. Each cylinder will produce some of each type of chip. The wafers on the ends of the cylinder are of lower quality and must be used to produce low-speed chips, which are not good for very much and sell for very little per wafer. For October 19x7, the Silicon Growth Unit had the following results:

Wafer Speed	Price	Produced Units	Ending Inventory	Separable Costs
Fast	$60.00	4,000	1,000	$48,000
Medium	20.00	4,000	4,000	40,000
Slow	1.50	2,000	400	2,000
Joint processing costs		$173,878		

There were no beginning inventories, and the ending inventories were complete as to additional processing. The slow chips are treated as a by-product with the net realizable value subtracted from the joint production costs.

REQUIRED:
a. Using the net realizable value method, compute:
   1. Cost per completed unit for each joint and by-product.
   2. Ending inventory cost for each joint and by-product.

b. Using the physical volume method, compute:
  1. Cost per completed unit for each joint and by-product.
  2. Ending inventory cost for each joint and by-product.

10–6. Sales Value and Physical Measure Methods with By-Product.   The Traci Company manufactures three chemical products: Faci, Laci, and Baci (a by-product). The products come from a common process and are processed beyond the split-off point before being sold. The following production and sales information is available for March 19x4:

Product	Units Produced	Selling Price at Split-off	Separable Costs	Units Sold
Faci	8,000	$10	$10,000	7,500
Laci	12,000	5	30,000	9,500
Baci	10,000	0	2,000	6,000

There were no beginning inventories. Baci cannot be sold at split-off but is processed further and sold for $.50 per unit. The company treats the by-product net realizable value as a reduction of joint costs. The joint costs for March are $100,000.

REQUIRED:
a. Based on the sales value method:
  1. Allocate the joint costs to Faci and Laci.
  2. Compute the cost per unit for completed units of Faci, Laci, and Baci.
  3. Compute the cost of ending inventories.
b. Based on the physical measures method:
  1. Allocate the joint costs to Faci and Laci.
  2. Compute the cost per unit for completed units of Faci, Laci, and Baci.
  3. Compute the cost of ending inventories.

10–7. Net Realizable Value, Physical Measures, and By-Products.   The Clenalfree Corporation of Puerto Rico produces three consumer products and a by-product. The products vary in physical properties but result from a common petroleum base. The three products, Clean-it, Alco, and Freedom, separate as the petroleum base is heated and materials are added. Clean-it is ready for sale after split-off, but Alco and Freedom must be further processed. The by-product is a heavy residue in the bottom of the vat. The net realizable value of the by-product is credited against the joint cost of the Heating Department.
  Volume and cost data for February 19x9 are as follows:

	Gallons Produced	Selling Price	Additional Processing
Clean-it	250,000	$1.50	$ 0
Alco	400,000	1.70	30,000
Freedom	300,000	1.80	25,000
By-product	5,000	0.50	0

The Heating Department had $800,000 in costs during the month.

(A. Gregory, Adapted)

REQUIRED:
a. Allocate the Heating Department cost to the three products using the physical volume method.
b. Allocate the Heating Department cost to the three products using the net realizable value method.
c. Calculate the total unit costs for each of the products with the results from the:
  1. Physical volume method.
  2. Net realizable value method.

10–8. Net Realizable Value, Physical Measures, and By-Products. CheeWaw is a partnership located in Arizona that makes pottery of varying quality. The highest quality, N'ka'th (pronounced "Nuh-kay-uth"), is sold for $30 per unit. The medium quality, Ke'ta' (Kee-uh-tah-uh), is sold for $15. The low quality, P'nut (Puh-nut), is cracked and sold for $.75 per unit. The differences among the products are caused by the heat in the kiln and differences in clay quality. After the pottery comes out of the kiln, it is studied carefully for quality, then finished and packaged for sale. Data for May 19x2 include:

	Units Produced	Additional Costs	Units Ending Inventory
N'ka'th	600	$2,000	250
Ke'ta'	1,300	1,250	500
P'nut	3,500	200	1,000

The joint costs of production were $3,500 for clay, $20,000 for labor, and $6,700 for production overhead. CheeWaw treats P'nut as a by-product with the realizable value credited to joint production costs.

(V. Dennis, Adapted)

REQUIRED:
a. Allocate the joint costs to the products using the physical volume method.
b. Allocate the joint costs to the products using the net realizable value method.

10–9. Net Realizable Values and Operating Decisions. A historian is reconstructing the operations of the Kitcane Mine and Smelter that was open from 1860 to 1890 in the Sangre de Christo Mountains of Northern New Mexico.

From old records it was found that the total cost of operations for 1890 was $27,700. Most of this cost was for food and payroll for the 26 men employed by the mine and smelter. During the year, the following production and traceable costs occurred:

	Volume	Price	Separable Costs
Gold	640 ounces	$25.00	$3,000
Silver	4,560 ounces	2.00	2,300
Copper	2,680 pounds	2.00	2,400

The "separable costs" are those that the historian could identify as occurring after the split-off point. For example, some of the costs were for "protection" payments in hauling the metals out of the mountains to safety in Santa Fe.

(K. Graham, Adapted)

REQUIRED:
a. Using the net realizable value method,
   1. Allocate the joint costs of production to the three metals.
   2. Calculate the total cost per unit for producing each of the metals and getting them to safety.
b. Using the results from part *(a):*
   1. If the price of gold dropped to $22.50 per ounce, should production continue? Analyze the total revenues and the total costs.
   2. If the price of gold dropped to $20.00 per ounce, should production continue? Show your analysis.

10–10. Decision to Sell at Split-off or Process Further. The Triton Chemical Plant produces five products from the residue left over from meat packing. The products, volumes, and related costs for July 19x0 are:

| | Production | Prices | | Separable |
Product	Volume	Split-Off	After Processing	Costs
BV83	10,000	$ 4.20	$ 6.80	$ 8,000
DR02	2,000	48.00	60.00	25,000
GK98	60,000	0.30	0.40	1,000
HV80	400	600.00	900.00	14,000
YT04	100,000	.10	5.00	500,000

The management of Triton has decided that a product should be sold at split-off unless the incremental revenues are at least 30 percent above the incremental costs.

REQUIRED:
For each of the products, determine whether the product should be sold at split-off or processed further.

PROBLEMS

10–11. Sales Value Method and Processing Decisions. DRW Chemical of Hong Kong produces five products from oil sludge left over from a local refinery. Each of the products is processed through finishing departments prior to shipment. The products could also be sold in bulk at the split-off point. Operating data for the month of December 19x2 are:

| | Unit | Sales Values at | | Total |
Product	Activity	Split-Off	Final	Allocated Costs
HP3K2	5,000	$ 5	$ 8	$25,000
OXY3	4,500	10	15	50,000
RV2	6,000	7	9	35,000
OXY7	7,500	9	12	55,000
HP5	2,500	4	7	12,500

The costs to operate the joint production process were $100,000 for the month. Allocation of joint costs is performed on the basis of sales value at split-off. The total allocated costs include both the separable costs and the allocated joint costs.

(D. Washburn)

REQUIRED:
a. Calculate the allocated joint cost and the separable costs for each of the products.
b. Analyze each of the products to determine if they should be sold at split-off or processed further.

10–12. Net Realizable Value Method, Physical Volume Method, By-Product. PureKane Co. runs a sugar plant in South Texas. The plant produces two primary products, cane sugar and molasses. Cane pulp, which is used for cattle feed, also results from the production. The cane pulp is treated as a by-product with the net realizable value credited to work in process. The company uses a hundred weight (cwt.) as its unit of measure. The activity and additional processing costs for the month of July 19x3:

	Unit Volume	Price	Separable Costs	Ending Inventory
Cane sugar	150,000	$12.00	$300,000	15,000
Molasses	90,000	6.00	240,000	12,000
Cane pulp	400,000	0.25	2,000	20,000

The costs of purchasing the cane were $900,000, and the production costs prior to split-off were $78,000 for direct labor and $45,000 for overhead. There were no beginning inventories.

(K. Earls)

REQUIRED:

a. Using the net realizable value method, compute:
1. Cost per completed unit for each joint and by-product.
2. Ending inventory cost for each joint and by-product.

b. Using the physical volume method.
1. Cost per completed unit for each joint and by-product.
2. Ending inventory cost for each joint and by-product.

10–13. By-Product Costing and Processing Decisions.   Maui Cooperative Plant purchases 100 percent of the pineapple harvested by three growers on Maui Island. During the 19x2 harvest season the following data related to production:

| | | Sales Value at | | Separable |
	Units	Split-Off	Final	Costs
1. Maui Sliced Pineapple	180,000	$0.64	$0.89	$31,000
2. Maui Pineapple Juice	300,000	0.31	0.45	13,000
3. Gro-Best Pineapple Sets	360,000	0.23	0.23	0
4. Pine-Agro Cattle Feed	140,000	0.00	0.18	4,000

Joint costs for the season totaled $298,000. The plant manager decided to sell products 2 and 3 at split-off and process 1 and 4 further. Thus, the $13,000 in separable juice costs would have been incurred if the manager had decided to can the juice instead of sell it in bulk to another cannery. Product 4 has 12,000 units in ending inventory; otherwise, all of the products were sold by fiscal year end. There were no beginning inventories. General and administrative expenses were $13,100 for the year. Product 4 is treated as a by-product by the cooperative, which has adopted the sales method for allocating joint costs. It is uncertain regarding the treatment and disclosure of the by-product value.

(A. Gregory)

REQUIRED:

a. If the net realizable value of the by-product is treated as a credit to work in process:
1. Allocate the joint costs of production to the main products.
2. Prepare an income statement for the year ending March 31, 19x3.

b. If the by-product is accounted for using the zero value method:
1. Allocate the joint costs of production to the main products.
2. Prepare an income statement for the year ending March 31, 19x3, with four columns showing the plant manager the disclosure options for net revenue from by-product sales.

c. Compute the final prices at which the cooperative should be indifferent as to selling the products at split-off or processing them further.

10–14. Sales Value Method with By-Product.   Cannon Chemical Products makes three chemicals from a single feedstock called TRAX. The Extraction Department is the joint process, and every 16 gallons of TRAX input yields 3 gallons of BREX, 4 gallons of CREX, 6 gallons of DREX, 2 gallons of XREX, and 1 gallon of residue with no market value.

TRAX costs $1.50 per gallon and enters the Extraction Department at the beginning of the process. CREX may be sold at split-off, but it is processed on in the Electrolysis Department. DREX must be processed on the Involution Department before it can be sold. XREX has disposition costs of $.10 per unit. There were no beginning inventories on March 1, 19x2. The following summary of cost prices and other related data are available for March 19x2:

	Extraction	Electrolysis	Involution
Cost of TRAX	$240,000	—	—
Direct labor	15,000	$12,000	$ 6,000
Production overhead	24,000	40,000	42,000

	Products			
	BREX*	**CREX**	**DREX**	**XREX**
Split-off price	$3.48	$2.79	$ .00	$ .00
Price after further processing	—	3.95	3.20	.60
Gallons sold	25,000	30,000	50,000	15,000
March 31 inventory	5,000	10,000	10,000	5,000

* Sold at split-off

Cannon Chemical Products records by-products at net realizable values and the appropriate market value method for allocating joint costs of the Extraction Department.

REQUIRED:
a. Calculate the joint costs to be allocated to BREX, CREX, and DREX.
b. Calculate the unit costs of each product that will be used for inventory purposes.
c. Compute the total dollars of gross profit earned by Cannon Chemical Products earned during March.
d. Compute the total cost of ending inventories.

10–15. Sales Value Method. Multiproduct Corporation is a chemical manufacturer that produces two main products (Pepco–1 and Repke–3) and a by-product (SE–5) from a joint process. If Multiproduct had the proper facilities, it could process SE–5 further into a main product. The ratio of output quantity to input quantity of direct material used in the joint process remains consistent with the processing conditions and activity level.

Multiproduct currently uses the physical measures method of allocating joint costs to the main products. The FIFO (first-in, first-out) inventory method is used to value the main products. The by-product is inventoried at its net realizable value, and the net realizable value of the by-product is used to reduce the joint production costs before the joint costs are allocated to the main products.

Jim Simpson, Multiproduct's controller, wants to implement the relative sales value method of joint cost allocation. He believes that inventoriable costs should be based on each product's ability to contribute to the recovery of joint production costs. The net realizable value of the by-products would be treated in the same manner as with the physical measures method.

Data regarding Multiproduct's operations for November 19x6 are:

	Pepco-1	**Repke-3**	**SE-5**
Finished goods, November 1 (gal.)	20,000	40,000	10,000
November sales (gal.)	800,000	700,000	200,000
November production (gal.)	900,000	720,000	240,000
Sales value at split-off per gallon	$ 2.00	$ 1.50	$ .55*
Additional processing costs	$1,800,000	$720,000	
Final sales value per gallon	$ 5.00	$ 4.00	

* Disposal and selling costs of $.05 per gallon will be incurred in order to sell the by-product.

The joint costs of production amounted to $2,640,000 for November 19x6.

(CMA, Adapted)

REQUIRED:
a. Describe the relative sales value method and explain how it accomplishes Jim Simpson's objective.
b. Assuming Multiproduct Corporation adopts the relative sales value method for internal reporting purposes:
  1. Calculate how the joint production cost for November 19x6 would be allocated.
  2. Determine the dollar values of the finished goods inventories for Pepco–1, Repke–3, and SE–5 as of November 30, 19x6.
c. Multiproduct Corporation plans to expand its production facilities to enable the further processing of SE–5 into a main product. Discuss how the allocation of the joint production

costs under the relative sales value method would change when SE–5 becomes a main product.

10–16. Sales Value Method.   Deer Valley Meat Packers slaughters cattle, cuts carcasses into primary meats, and sells the primary cuts to restaurants and retail stores. Each of three processing operations—Slaughtering, Refrigeration, and Cutting—is treated separately for accounting purposes. The Slaughtering Department is responsible for slaughtering, removing the inedible parts, and cutting the carcass into two sides. The Refrigeration Department chills and ages the sides for about two weeks. The Cutting Department cuts the sides into the primary cuts of chucks, ribs, brisket, tenderloins, sirloins, flanks, and rounds.

The live weight of the cattle averages about 1,000 pounds. The by-products, scrap, and waste resulting from slaughtering leave 680 pounds of side that go to refrigeration. Salable by-products and scrap constitute 250 pounds and can be sold for $120. The two sides lose about 15 pounds as they are aged in the Refrigeration Department. The primary cuts weigh an average of 500 pounds. The difference between the 665 pounds coming out of refrigeration and the 500 pounds of primary cuts represents 75 pounds of fat, and the rest is meat that can be used as hamburger or stew meat. The fat is sold for $0.35 per pound; other meat is sold for $0.75 per pound. The fat and other meat are treated as by-products by Deer Valley with the net realizable value reducing the joint costs.

By-products are recorded at their net realizable value, with joint costs reduced by this amount. Deer Valley uses a sales value method to allocate the joint costs to the various cuts. The distribution among the primary cuts and sales value information are:

Cuts	Pounds	Price per Pound
Chucks	155	$2.00
Ribs	60	1.80
Brisket	25	1.40
Tenderloins	15	7.00
Sirloins	85	3.10
Flanks	30	3.50
Rounds	130	2.90

Processing costs incurred in each of the three operations are based on pounds of input for individual operations. These costs are:

	Material	Direct Labor	Production Overhead
Slaughtering	$.54	$.07	$.07
Refrigeration		.02	.04
Cutting		.12	.24

REQUIRED:
a. Calculate the total joint cost to be allocated to the primary cuts at the end of the cutting operation.
b. Allocate the joint costs to the final primary cuts and determine a cost per pound for each cut of meat.

10–17. Sell or Process Further.   Ricardo Company operates a series of manufacturing processes in its plant. At present, all four products pass through three common processing operations and then pass individually through separate finishing departments. However, the four products could also be sold at the point at which they emerge from the third common processing department. The following data were available for October 19x8:

Product	Units	Prices At Split-Off	Final	Total Costs
KIT	20,000	$ 8	$12	$120,000
LIT	10,000	2	8	40,000
MIT	5,000	10	16	40,000
NIT	5,000	5	6	23,000

The costs of operation for the three joint processing departments were $153,000 for the month. The company allocates the joint costs of the joint processing departments to the products on the basis of the sales value at the split-off point. The total cost column for each product includes the joint cost allocation and the separable costs of finishing the individual products.

REQUIRED:

a. Calculate the separable costs for each of the four products.
b. Prepare an analysis for each product that shows whether the product should be sold at split-off point or should be processed further.

10–18. Physical Volume and Pricing.   The Portle Lumber Mill processes redwood trees into boards of various sizes and grades. During production, bark and sawdust are also created. The bark is packaged for landscaping, and the sawdust is further processed into pressed wood. Although many sizes of lumber are created, there are basically two grades, A and B. The mill uses the physical measures method in allocating costs to production.

The mill recently worked on tree no. 147803 that weighted 5 tons uncut. The tree was purchased for $700 and joint production costs of $350 were applied to milling the tree. The tree produced 2.75 tons of grade A lumber, 1 ton of grade B lumber, and about four times as much bark as sawdust. The grade A lumber was finished at a cost of $200 and sold briskly for $1,089. The grade B lumber was finished at a cost of $100, and half of it sold for $217. The bark was bagged at a cost of $4 into 40 large bags, but only one fourth of it could be sold at the $7.49 per bag price requested. The sawdust was pressed into 20 sheets at a cost of $100 and priced at $10.68 per sheet, but they remain in inventory.

The mill uses the total product cost in setting prices. Each tree is accounted for on a job order basis. The mill desires to keep zero inventories, yet the finished goods inventory is increasing.

(B. McDonald, Adapted)

REQUIRED:

a. Allocate the joint costs to each of the four products using the weight measure.
b. Compute the cost of ending inventory associated with tree no. 147803.
c. Compute the ratio of selling price to total allocated cost for each of the four products. What is the apparent pricing policy for this lumber mill?
d. Why did the grade A lumber from tree no. 147803 sell so quickly and the pressed wood not sell at all? Comment on the pricing policy of this company.
e. What fundamental change would this lumber mill have to make in order to allocate the joint costs on the basis of net realizable values?

10–19. Joint Service Costs.   The Whisper Airlines offers flights to 12 cities along the East Coast. The aircraft has coach seating for 210. Although tickets vary drastically in price, they generally fall into three categories: Regular, Economy, and Super Saver. Although all categories receive the same service while in the air, there are differences in treatment on the ground. Those paying regular fare need not purchase their tickets until flight time, and there is no penalty for failure to board the flight. Economy class travelers must purchase their tickets a week in advance, and there is a 25 percent penalty for failure to board. Super Savers must purchase their tickets a month in advance, but there are no changes or refunds allowed after ticketing. In addition, there are differences due to commission rates paid to travel agents and mileage premiums given to passengers. During the month of June 19x2, there were the following data for the New York to Miami flights:

	Ticketed Passengers	Not Boarding	Average Price	Separable Costs
Regular	8,568	2,399	$450	$560,690
Economy	5,355	589	306	350,183
Super Saver	7,497	375	218	477,656

The joint costs to operate the route were $3,500,000. The airline treats the penalty from not boarding for Economy and Super Saver fares as by-product revenue and accordingly reduces the joint operating costs in the calculation of the cost per unit.

REQUIRED:
a. Using the physical volume method:
   1. Allocate the joint costs to boarding passengers.
   2. Compute the unit cost for each type of boarding passenger.
b. Using the net realizable value method:
   1. Allocate the joint costs to boarding passengers.
   2. Compute the unit cost for each type of boarding passenger.

10–20. By-Product Report.   Haselton Corporation has furnished you with the following data for the current month's operations:

Sales:
Major products	35,000 gallons at $15 per gallon
By-products	6,500 gallons at $1.10 per gallon

Production:
Major products	40,000 gallons
By-products	8,000 gallons

There were no beginning inventories of in-process or completed products.
Costs of further processing the by-product and sale on a per gallon basis:

Materials	$0.05
Labor	0.07
Production overhead	0.04
Marketing and administrative costs applied	0.06
Total production costs of the joint process	$180,000
Total marketing and administrative costs	$ 40,000

The major products are sold at split-off.

REQUIRED:
a. Prepare income statements for the following assumptions:
   1. By-products valued at net realizable value are credited to the joint costs of work in process.
   2. By-products accounted for with a zero-value method. Prepare all four methods of disclosure. (See Exhibit 10–3.)
b. Using the net realizable value method, prepare journal entries to record the costs charged to the by-products.
c. Prepare the journal entry to record the sale of 6,500 gallons of by-products at a higher than anticipated price of $1.30.

10–21. By-Product Report.   Limestone Quarry and Works, Inc., removes limestone-laden rock from a quarry and processes it to get good-quality limestone product. The major customer is a local concrete factory. Operations at the Limestone Quarry consist of Quarrying, Hauling, and several crushing steps: coarse, medium, and fine. After coarse and medium crushing, nonlimestone fragments are screened out. All three crushing steps are performed in the same cost center. The limestone is loaded on train cars and shipped to customers. The nonlimestone fragments form a quality gravel mix for highway construction and railroad bed maintenance. These fragments are currently treated as a by-product because they have not had a high market value.

Statistics for July 19x2 are as follows:

Quarrying and hauling 30,000 tons of rock	$120,000
Crushing operations	$190,000

Variable distribution and administrative for either limestone or fragments	$4 per ton
Fixed distribution and administrative	$24,000
Outputs: 25,000 tons of limestone product sold at $32 per ton	
5,000 tons of non-limestone fragments sold at $8 per ton	

There were no beginning inventories of work in process or finished goods. The company has used the zero value method to account for the by-product production in the past. A recent increase in selling price for the fragments suggests either (1) consideration for the net realizable value method or (2) treating the fragments as a major product.

REQUIRED:

a. Prepare an income statement with four variations for the zero value method of accounting for by-products.

b. Prepare an income statement assuming the by-product is valued using the net realizable value method.

c. Discuss the factors that should be considered in whether a by-product should use the zero value method or the net realizable value method.

d. Allocate joint costs assuming both products are major products and the sales value method is used. Prepare an income statement for this situation.

EXTENDED APPLICATIONS

10–22. Joint Product Cost Allocation with Decision Making.   Stout Creek Manufacturing Company currently produces four joint products without further processing. The marketing and production staffs are looking at the possibility of processing some or all of the products to meet a demand in the marketplace and to increase profits. Neal Wetlock, the controller, has prepared a summary of the cost of further processing and market data for the split-off point and after further processing based on the most recent month data:

			If Processed Further	
	Units Produced	Value at Split-Off	Additional Cost	Market Value
Jag	8,000	$ 60,000	$20,000	$ 82,000
Jet	6,000	84,000	10,000	90,000
Jot	4,000	56,000	8,000	102,000
Jut	2,000	40,000	6,000	46,000
Totals	20,000	$240,000	$44,000	$320,000

Monthly joint costs were $156,000, which meant the profit at the split off point was $84,000 ($240,000 less $156,000).

The marketing manager proposed processing all products further because an additional revenue of $80,000 ($320,000 less $240,000) could be obtained with an additional cost of $44,000. The production manager argued that the decision depends on how the full costs are calculated (assuming joint costs are included). The controller presented the following profit figures per unit based on allocated joint costs at $7.80 per unit:

	Sell at Split-Off	Further Process
Jag	$ (.30)	$ (.05)
Jet	6.20	5.53
Jot	6.20	15.70
Jut	12.20	12.20

In the controller's opinion, Jag is in a loss position and should not be produced at all if there were any way to eliminate its production. Product Jet drops in profit per unit when processed further and thus should be sold at the split-off point. Product Jut has no change in profit per unit and should, therefore, not be processed further. The conclusion is that only product Jot should be processed further.

REQUIRED:
a. In spite of the controller's conclusion, give a reason with numerical analysis as to why the company should process Jag further. Also, determine with an analysis whether Jut should be processed further or not.
b. The production manager believes the decision hinges on how joint costs are allocated.
   1. Allocate the joint costs on the basis of the sales value at the split-off point.
   2. Based on the sales value allocations, would the controller's conclusion change? Explain.
   3. Why should allocated joint costs be excluded from decisions on whether or not to process joint products further?

10–23. Process Costing with Joint Products and Waste.   Lyjewski Organic Chemicals purchases organic feedstock that it refines into organic cleaners for and around food. The products are popular in restaurants frequented by people with environmental concerns. The production is a joint process, the output of which is three grades of cleaner. The feedstock is added at the beginning of the process with labor and overhead incurred uniformly throughout the process. Overhead is applied at a rate of $10 per gallon of equivalent output.
   Production inputs and outputs and costs for January 19x2 are:

Production in gallons:
Beginning inventory (40% complete on conversion) 10,000
Feedstock started into the process 115,000
Output completed:
  Grade 1 ... 15,000
  Grade 2 ... 35,000
  Grade 3 ... 45,000
Ending inventory (60% complete on conversion) 25,000
Costs incurred:
Costs in beginning inventory:
  Feedstock ... $30,000
  Direct labor ... 32,000
  Production overhead ... 40,000 ... $102,000
Feedstock started in process ... 322,000
Direct labor incurred ... 444,000
Production overhead applied ... ?

Waste is identified at the end of the process and is assigned an equivalent cost per unit. However, all waste costs are charged to units completed. The sales values at the split-off point for the three products are:

Grade 1 $31.00 per gallon
Grade 2 $26.00 per gallon
Grade 3 $12.50 per gallon

REQUIRED:
a. Using the FIFO process costing method:
   1. Determine the amount of cost that should be allocated to the joint products in total.
   2. Allocate the total costs for the joint products to the individual grades using the sales value method.
b. Using the weighted average process costing method:
   1. Determine the amount of cost that should be allocated to the joint products in total.
   2. Allocate the total costs for the joint products to the individual grades using the physical measures method.

10–24. Joint Service Costs. The Walker Theatre offers first- and second-run movies on three screens and sells food to patrons. During the month of July 19x4, the Walker Theatre contracted to show two first-run movies for the entire month, and two second-run "B" movies on the third screen. During the month the following activity occurred:

	Additional Costs	Patrons	Ticket Price
Life Spacers	$30,000	7,000	$6
Out of China	18,000	5,000	$6
Second-run movies	2,000	3,000	$1

The movie theatre had $24,000 in costs that were joint to the operations of the theatre. The concession stand had revenues of $45,000 and costs of $15,000. For some reason, the patrons for the first-run movies purchase about half as much at the concession stand as the "B" movie patrons.

REQUIRED:
a. Use the physical volume method to allocate joint costs and the number of patrons as the physical measure. Exclude the concession stand in allocating joint costs.
   1. Allocate the joint cost to each of the movies.
   2. Present an analysis of the profitability of each of the movies and the concession stand.
b. Use the net realizable value method to allocate joint costs. Exclude the concession stand in allocating joint costs.
   1. Allocate the joint cost to each of the movies.
   2. Present an analysis of the profitability of each of the movies and the concession stand.
c. Now include the concession stand in your application of joint costs to the operations of the theater. Using the net realizable value method:
   1. Allocate the joint cost to each of the movies and the concession.
   2. Present an analysis of the profitability of each of the movies and the concession stand.
   3. Allocate the profit from the concession stand to each of the movies in proportion to the concession sales.
d. Compare the results of each allocation method. What are the roles of the second-run movies and the concession stand in the operations of the theater?

Background for 10–25.   The gross margin method for allocating joint costs is a variation of the net relative sales value method that forces every main product to have the same gross profit as a percentage of sales. This variation encourages managers to realize that the products from a joint process are all equally profitable to sell. Although this method has much to recommend it in terms of management incentives, it is only occasionally used in practice.

Assume that there are two products, A and B, resulting from a production process with joint costs of $100,000. Given the following data:

	Price	Units	Revenues	Separable Costs
A	$400	500	$200,000	$ 40,000
B	200	600	120,000	80,000
Total			$320,000	$120,000

With this data the results of using the net realizable value method are:

	Net Realizable Values	Allocated Joint Cost	Total Costs	Cost per Unit	Gross Profit Rates
A	$160,000	$ 80,000	$120,000	$240.00	40.00%
B	40,000	20,000	100,000	$166.67	16.67%
	$200,000	$100,000	$220,000		

The gross profit from product A will appear to be much more profitable than that from product B. This will encourage managers to sell more of product A than product B, which results in the units being left in inventories.

In order to apply the gross profit method, first compute the ratio of total costs to total revenues for all joint products:

$$\frac{\text{Total costs}}{\text{Total revenues}} = \frac{\$220,000}{\$320,000} = 68.75\%$$

Second, apply this ratio to the revenue from each product in order to calculate the total cost assigned to each product. Third, subtract the separable costs to equal the assigned joint costs:

	Revenues	Total Costs	Separable Costs	Joint Costs
A	$200,000	$137,500	$ (40,000)	$ 97,500
B	120,000	82,500	(80,000)	2,500
	$320,000	$220,000	$(120,000)	$100,000

The costs per unit for inventory purposes will be:

	Total Costs	Units Produced	Cost per Unit
A	$137,500	500	$275.00
B	82,500	600	$137.50

10–25. Physical Volume, Net Realizable Value, and Gross Profit Methods.   The Matlock Rendering Plant treats animal by-products from meat packing plants and rends them into usable pet food, oil, fat, and fertilizer. When the rendering plant is finished, nothing is left but usable product. The pet food and fertilizer must be processed after split-off before they can be sold. The fat may be either sold at split-off or processed further into lard. The oil is sold at split-off.

Prices of all of the products and the input vary widely from month to month. The joint cost of production for August 19x2 was $1,100,000 for the animal by-products, $200,000 for direct labor. Overhead is applied at a rate of 100 percent of direct labor. The company uses 1,000 pounds as the basic unit of measure. Operating data for the month are:

	Split-Off Units	Unit Prices At Split	Unit Prices Final	Separable Costs
Pet food	15,000	$ 0	$60	$600,000
Oil	18,000	35	35	0
Fat/lard	10,000	20	25	50,000
Fertilizer	22,000	0	50	88,000
Total input	65,000			$738,000

The weight of pet food and fertilizer increases dramatically during further processing, but the final prices have been restated in terms of the split-off weight. During the month, all of the fat was processed into lard.

(P. Hicks, Adapted)

REQUIRED:
a. Using the physical measures method,
  1. Allocate the joint costs to the production.
  2. Compute a cost per unit for each of the completed products.
  3. Compare the apparent profitability of the products.
b. Using the net realizable value at split-off,
  1. Allocate the joint costs to the production.
  2. Compute a cost per unit for each of the completed products.
  3. Compare the apparent profitability of the products.
c. Using the gross profit method (see background note prior to problem),
  1. Allocate the joint costs to the production.
  2. Compute a cost per unit for each of the completed products.
  3. Compare the apparent profitability of the products.

APPENDIX 10A Costs of Chain Joint Production

LEARNING OBJECTIVES

After studying this appendix, you should be able to:

1. Diagram a chain joint production process, which is a production process with multiple split-off points.
2. Apply the sales value, net realizable value, and physical measure methods of accounting for the costs of chain joint production processes.

In some production situations, the products are produced in chain joint production processes, which have multiple split-off points. **Chain joint production** has at least one output from a joint process that becomes an input for another joint process. To account for the costs of the joint processes it is necessary to apply joint cost allocation methods repetitively.

Accounting for the costs of chain joint processes is simplified by following a three-stage solution approach: (1) diagram the physical flows, (2) for market value methods, find the market values at split-off points, and (3) starting with the first split-off point, work forward allocating the joint costs. In the following sections we will elaborate on these three stages. In this discussion we will use the example in Exhibit 10A–1.

Stage One: Diagram the Physical Flows

The purpose of the diagram is to improve the accountant's understanding of the production setting and the physical flows of products. Start by noting where the split-off points occur and identifying the joint products. Place on a diagram the names of

EXHIBIT 10A–1 Example Chain Joint Process

Hutchison, Inc., produces three chemical compounds in a chain joint process: Rae–2, Kare–16, and Ee–5. For April 19x2, 300,000 gallons of material were started in Department 1. The split-off point for the basic joint process in Department 1 yields 140,000 gallons of Intermediate* Ee, which becomes Ee–5 after additional processing in Department 2, and 160,000 gallons of Intermediate Kare-Rae product that requires an additional joint process in Department 3. In Department 3, the Intermediate Kare-Rae product is input and the output is two products, 70,000 gallons of Kare–16 and 90,000 gallons of Intermediate Rae. Kare–16 is sold without further processing, but Intermediate Rae requires additional processing in Department 4 before it is ready for sale as product Rae–2.

The following production and sales information is available for a typical month:

Product	Gallons	Selling Price
Rae–2	70,000	$ 5
Kare–16	90,000	10
Ee–5	140,000	7

Department	Process	Costs
1	Basic process	$ 460,000
2	Ee process	140,000
3	Kare-Rae process	540,000
4	Rae process	50,000
	Total costs	$1,190,000

* An "intermediate" product is one that is not yet ready for sale, but requires further processing.

departments, the volume of inputs, and the volume of outputs. For Hutchison Company, the split-offs occur in Department 1 and Department 3. Because the revenues of all the products are significant, the three products are joint products and there are no by-products.

The volumes of inputs and outputs as given in the example are:

Department—Process	*Inputs*	*Outputs*
1 Basic process	300,000 of material	160,000 of Kare-Rae
		140,000 of Intermediate Ee
2 Ee process	140,000 of Intermediate Ee	140,000 Finished Ee-5
3 Kare-Rae process	160,000 of Kare-Rae	70,000 of Intermediate Rae
		90,000 Finished Kare-16
4 Rae process	70,000 of Intermediate Rae	70,000 Finished Rae-2

In some problem settings, the connection between input and output will be given as a ratio. For example, the output/input relationship in Department 1 might have been stated as $\frac{8}{15}$ths Kare-Rae and $\frac{7}{15}$ths intermediate Ee. Then the outputs would be computed as:

$$\text{Kare-Rae} \qquad \tfrac{8}{15} \times 300,000 = 160,000$$
$$\text{Intermediate Ee} \qquad \tfrac{7}{15} \times 300,000 = 140,000$$

The next step is to identify in which departments joint costs and separable costs are incurred. Joint costs occur in departments with split-off points. Separable costs occur in subsequent (downstream) departments. The final step is to draw the diagram and fill in the labels and amounts as in Exhibit 10A–2.

Stage Two: Determining Ratios at Split-Off Points

If we are allocating costs using a market value method, then the ratios of market values at split-off must be computed next.

Sales Value Method. In order to allocate joint costs with the sales value method, the sales values at split-off must be known. (Remember that if the sales values at

EXHIBIT 10A–1   Diagram of Physical Flows for a Chain Joint Process

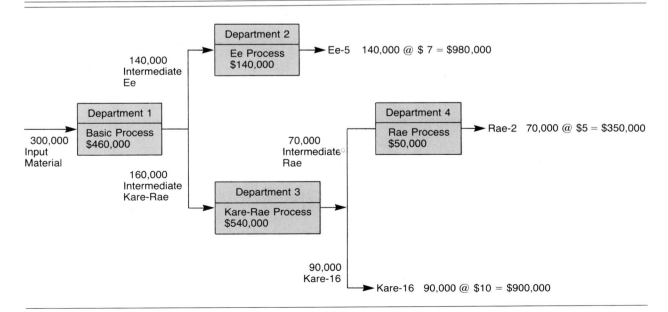

split-off are known, they take precedence over the net realizable values.) For Hutchison, Inc., assume that the market prices at split-off are known to be:

Intermediate Kare-Rae	$ 3.15
Intermediate Ee	4.40
Intermediate Rae	4.06
Kare-16	10.00

Compute the product sales values for each split-off point. Use the units completed for each joint process rather than the units sold during the period. This task may be performed starting with any split-off point, but it is easier to start with the first one and *work forward* to completed products.

The Department 1 ratios at split-off are calculated as follows:

Product	Price at Split-Off	Units	Sales Value	Ratio
Intermediate Kare-Rae	$3.15	160,000	$ 504,000	45%
Intermediate Ee	$4.40	140,000	616,000	55%
Department 1 sales value at split-off			$1,120,000	

The Department 3 ratios at split-off are calculated as follows:

Product	Price at Split-Off	Units	Sales Value	Ratio
Intermediate Rae	$ 4.06	70,000	$ 284,200	24%
Kare-16	10.00	90,000	900,000	76%
Department 3 sales value at split-off			$1,184,200	

Net Realizable Value Method.   This method is appropriate when sales values at split-off points are not known. First, determine the total market values at completion for all final products. In this analysis use the units completed rather than final sales units. For the three products in the example this will be:

Product	Gallons	Sales Price	Market Values
Rae-2	70,000	$ 5	$350,000
Kare-16	90,000	10	900,000
Ee-5	140,000	7	980,000

Now compute net realizable values working from the finished products back to split-off points. Thus, the calculation starts with the ending product and *works backward* to the raw materials. For the Kare-Rae split off in Department 3, the following calculations will be performed:

Product	Market Value	Separable Costs	Net Realizable Value	Ratio
Intermediate Rae	$350,000	$50,000	$ 300,000	25%
Kare-16	900,000	0	900,000	75%
Split-off value of Intermediate Kare-Rae			$1,200,000	

For the split-off in Department 1, the following calculation will be performed:

Product	Values	Separable Costs	Net Realizable Value	Ratio
Intermediate Kare-Rae	$1,200,000	540,000	$ 660,000	44%
Intermediate Ee	980,000	140,000	840,000	56%
Total split-off net realizable values			$1,500,000	

Stage Three: Joint Cost Allocation

Joint cost allocations begin with the basic process and move forward for each of the split-off points until all costs are allocated to products.

Sales Value Method. The joint costs of the basic process and initial separable costs are allocated as follows:

Product	Joint Cost Allocations	+ Separable Costs	= Total Costs
Intermediate Kare-Rae	45% × $460,000 = $207,000	+ $540,000	= $747,000
Ee–5	55% × $460,000 = 253,000	+ 140,000	= 393,000

The total costs for Intermediate Kare-Rae become the joint costs that must be allocated to Kare–16 and Intermediate Rae in the Department 3 joint cost allocation. This allocation is:

Product	Joint Cost Allocations	+ Separable Costs	= Total Costs
Rae–2	24% × $747,000 = $179,280	+ $ 50,000	= $229,280
Kare–16	76% × $747,000 = 567,720	+ –0–	= 567,720

Unit costs for the three products can be determined by dividing the quantities into the total costs. This gives $2.807 for Ee–5; $3.275 for Rae–2; and $6.303 for Kare–16.

Net Realizable Value Method. The joint costs of the basic process and initial separable costs are allocated as follows:

Product	Joint Cost Allocations	+ Separable Costs	= Total Costs
Intermediate Kare-Rae	44% × $460,000 = $202,400	+ $540,000	= $742,400
Ee–5	56% × $460,000 = 257,600	+ 140,000	= 397,600

The total costs for Intermediate Kare-Rae are the joint costs that must be allocated to Kare and Intermediate Rae in the Department 3 joint cost allocation. This allocation is:

Product	Joint Cost Allocations	+ Separable Costs	= Total Costs
Rae–2	25% × $742,400 = $185,600	+ $ 50,000	= $235,600
Kare–16	75% × $742,400 = 556,800	+ –0–	= 556,800

Unit costs for the three products can be determined by dividing the quantities into the total costs. This gives $2.840 for Ee–5, $3.366 for Rae–2, and $6.187 for Kare–16.

Physical Measures Method. Solution using the physical measures method involves computing an average joint cost per unit for each of the departments starting with the first joint process:

$$\text{Average unit cost} = \text{Joint cost/Units produced}$$
$$\$460,000/300,000 = \underline{\$1.533333}$$

The joint costs of the basic process and initial separable costs are allocated as follows:

Product	Gallons	Average Unit Cost	Allocations	Separable Cost	Total
Int. Kare-Rae	160,000	$1.533333	$245,333	$540,000	$ 785,333
Ee–5	140,000	$1.533333	214,667	140,000	354,667
			$460,000		$1,140,000

The total costs for Intermediate Kare-Rae are the joint costs that must be allocated to Kare–16 and Intermediate Rae in the Department 3 joint cost allocation. The Department 3 average joint cost per unit is:

$$\text{Average unit cost} = \$785,333/160,000 = \underline{\$4.908331}$$

This results in an allocation of:

Product	Gallons	Average Unit Cost	Allocations	Separable Cost	Total Cost
Rae–2	70,000	$4.908331	$343,583	$ 50,000	$393,583
Kare–16	90,000	$4.908331	441,750	–0–	441,750
			$785,333	$ 50,000	$835,333

Unit costs for the three products can be determined by dividing the quantities into the total costs. This gives $2.533 for Ee–5, $5.623 for Rae–2, and $4.908 for Kare–16.

The three methods resulted in the following total inventory costs and unit costs for the three completed products:

	Sales Values		Net Realizable Value		Physical Measures	
Ee–5	$ 393,000	$2.81	$ 397,600	$2.84	$ 354,667	$2.53
Rae–2	229,280	3.27	235,600	3.37	393,583	5.62
Kare–16	567,720	6.30	556,800	6.19	441,750	4.91
	$1,190,000		$1,190,000		$1,190,000	

The sales value and net realizable value methods yield similar joint cost allocations. Note that the physical measures approach results in much higher costs for Rae–2 and lower costs for both Ee–5 and Kare–16. Indeed, the $5.62 physical measures full cost for Rae–2 is higher than the selling price of $5.00 and a reduction in profit of $0.62 would appear to occur for each and every unit of Rae-5 sold.

KEY TERMS AND CONCEPTS

Chain joint production (410)

REVIEW QUESTIONS

1. Define a chain joint process.
2. List the three stages of the solution approach to allocate the costs of a chain joint production.
3. Why might an accountant prepare a diagram of physical flows?
4. Should joint costs be allocated among units produced or units sold?
5. In the computation of net realizable values at split-off should the calculation start with inputs and work to finished units or vice versa?
6. In the allocation of joint costs should the calculation start with inputs and proceed to finished unit costs or vice versa?

EXERCISES

10A–1. Diagramming Physical Relationships.   The Extraction Department of Jolton Enterprises removes Altex from a mineral rich clay. Altex is ¼ of the volume and the residual called Betex. The Altex is input in the Centrifuge Department, where it is separated into three joint products: Altrim (50 percent), Beatrim (25 percent), and Craytrim (25 percent). The residual from the Extraction Department is processed in the Diffraction Department in 10 percent bauxite, 5 percent magnesium, 60 percent pure clay, and the residual. The residual from the Diffraction Department is treated as a by-product. During the month of February 19x2, 160,000 tons of mineral-rich clay were processed by the Extraction Department. All of the material was completely processed during the month.

REQUIRED:
a. Compute the inputs and outputs for each department.
b. Diagram the physical flows of product through the Jolton Enterprises plant.

10A–2. Net Realizable Values.   The ThelChem Company produces three solid fuels in a chained joint process: SS–2, VR–7, and YP–3. In the Evaporation Department, fuel materials are started with 70 percent of the input split-off as SS–2 and the residual, VR–YP, is sent to the Electrolysis department. In the Electrolysis Department, the VR–YP is split into 60 percent VR–7 and 40 percent YP–3. All products require additional processing after split-off. There are no by-products. The following data are available for the month of July 19x2:

Product	Separable Costs	Selling Price
SS–2	$576,000	$7.50
VR–7	72,000	5.00
YP–3	96,000	8.00

During the month 400,000 units of product were started into the process and the following joint costs were incurred:

Department	Joint Costs
Evaporation	$400,000
Electrolysis	100,000

The company uses the net realizable value method to account for joint products.

REQUIRED:
a. Compute the physical flow for the products.
b. Compute the net realizable values for each split-off point.
c. Allocate the joint costs on the basis of net realizable values. Be certain to treat some of the cost from the Evaporation Department as transferred in to the Electrolysis Department.
d. Compute the cost per unit for each completed product.

PROBLEMS

10A–3. Joint Cost Allocation and Cost-Volume-Profit Analysis.   ANKO Chemical Products produces two joint products from a single input in the chemical decomposition department: MP1 and MP2. In the process, 1 unit of input yields 3 units of MP1 and 1 unit of MP2. Chemical MP1 must be further processed in the Cooking Department before it can be sold. Chemical MP2 has a ready market, but the company processes it further in a cooling process that yields 2 units of MP3 and 1 unit of MP4 for each unit of MP2 entering the process.

Joint costs are allocated on the basis of sales values. Production costs for August 19x3 are below:

Department	Variable Cost	Fixed Costs
Decomposition	$4 per unit of input	$20,000
Cooking	$2 per unit of MP1	8,000
Cooling	$1 per unit of MP2	15,000

There were 2,000 units of input processed by the Decomposition Department during August 19x3. The purchase price of inputs was $8 per unit. There were no beginning and ending inventories. The sales value information is as follows:

MP1 (After further processing)	$5
MP2	7
MP3	9
MP4	9

REQUIRED:

a. Compute the total costs charged to each product for August.

b. Compute the gross profit percentage of each chemical at the split-off point.

c. Assume the company will consider selling MP2 at the split-off point rather than after it comes from the Cooling Department. How many units of initial input are needed to generate a before tax profit of $108,200? The fixed costs of the Cooling Department can not be eliminated.

d. Under the current processing situation (producing MP3 and MP4), how many units of the initial input are needed to have a before tax profit of $108,200?

10A–4. Net Realizable Values.   The Halifax Wood Products Plant processes large pine trees into various wood products. In the Strip and Trim Department, the log is stripped of all bark and trimmed to an even size. This results in 5 percent (by weight) bark, 10 percent trim, and 85 percent usable log. The stripped bark is then cut into chunks and packaged into 50-pound bags. The trimmings and shavings from the Strip and Trim Department are processed into particle board, which is sold as 4-foot by 8-foot sheets. In the Slicing Department, tons of trimmed logs are sliced with a sharp blade into $\frac{1}{16}$th-inch sheets leaving a 6-inch diameter center called a post, which are sold in 10-foot lengths. The posts are ready for sale, but the $\frac{1}{16}$th-inch sheets are cut, glued, and sanded into 4-foot by 8-foot plywood sheets.

During the month of November 19x6 the following inputs and outputs occurred by department:

Department	Inputs		Outputs	
Strip and Trim	Tree tons	12,000	600	Bark
			1,200	Trimming
			10,200	Trimmed logs
Bark Cut and Bag	Bark	600	24,000	Bags
Particle Board Finish	Trimming	1,200	80,000	Sheets
Slicing	Tons of logs	10,200	9,180	Tons
			81,600	Posts
Plywood Finish	Tons	9,180	459,000	Sheets

For the month the following costs were incurred (in $Canadian):

Department	Materials	Costs Conversion	Total
Strip and Trim	$3,000,000	$ 120,000	$3,120,000
Bark Cut and Bag	15,000	16,000	31,000
Particle Board Finish	16,000	80,000	96,000
Slicing		122,400	122,400
Plywood Finish	120,000	798,000	918,000
	$3,151,000	$1,136,400	$4,287,400

These costs do not include any transferred in costs from prior departments.
The finished products and the selling prices are:

Bags of bark	$ 3.00
Particle board sheets	8.00
Plywood sheets	10.00
Posts	7.00

The costs of disposal (marketing, shipping, and administration) are 10 percent of the selling prices. The company accounts for the bark as a by-product and uses the net realizable value method in allocation of joint production costs.

REQUIRED:

a. Diagram the physical flows for the joint production processes.
b. Compute the net realizable values at each split-off point.
c. Allocate the joint production costs to the products. Round proportions of net realizable values to 5 places.
d. Compute the cost per unit for each completed product.

10A–5. Market Value Method. Talor Chemical Company is a highly diversified chemical processing company. The company manufactures swimming pool chemicals, chemicals for metal processing companies, specialized chemical compounds for other companies, and a full line of pesticides and insecticides.

Currently, the Noorwood plant is producing two derivatives, RNA–1 and RNA–2, from the chemical compound VDB developed by Talor's research labs. Each week 1,200,000 pounds of VDB are processed at a cost of $246,000 into 800,000 pounds of RNA–1 and 400,000 pounds of RNA–2. The proportion of these two outputs is fixed. RNA–1 has no market value until it is converted into a product with a trade name Fastkil. The cost to process RNA–1 into Faskil is $240,000. Fastkil wholesales at $50 per 100 pounds.

RNA–2 is sold as is for $80 per hundred pounds. However, Talor has discovered that RNA–2 can be converted into two new products through further processing. The further processing would require the addition of 400,000 pounds of compound LST to the 400,000 pounds of RNA–2. The joint process would yield 400,000 pounds each of DMZ–3 and Pestrol, the two new products. The additional raw materials and related processing of this joint process would cost $120,000. DMZ–3 and Pestrol would each be sold for $57.50 per 100 pounds. Talor management has decided not to process RNA–2 further based on the analysis presented below:

| | RNA–2 | Process Further | | |
		DMZ–3	Pestrol	Total
Production in pounds	400,000	400,000	400,000	
Revenues	$320,000	$230,000	$230,000	$460,000
Costs:				
VDB	$ 82,000	$ 61,500	$ 61,500	$123,000
Additional raw material (LST) and processing of RNA–2		60,000	60,000	120,000
Weekly gross profit	$238,000	$108,500	$108,500	$217,000

Talor uses the physical measures method to allocate the common costs arising from joint processing.

A new staff accountant who was to review the analysis above commented that it should be revised and stated, "Product costing of products such as these should be done with the net relative sales value basis, not a physical volume basis."

(CMA, Adapted)

REQUIRED:

a. Discuss whether the use of the net relative sales value method would provide data more relevant for the decision to market DMZ–3 and Pestrol.
b. Critique the Talor Company's analysis and make any revisions that are necessary. Your critique and analysis should indicate:
   1. Whether Talor Chemical Company made the correct decision.
   2. The gross savings (loss) per week of Talor's decision not to process RNA–2 further, if different from the company prepared analysis.

**EXTENDED
APPLICATIONS**

10A–6. Multiple Split-off Points.   Seeluft is a demonstration project on the West German Coast that produces power and bottled oxygen, hydrogen, salt, and trace minerals from ocean water. Liquid hydrogen is extremely cold and used primarily in the development of super conductors and in physics laboratories. The plant uses tidal action to generate electricity of which part is sold commercially and part is used to run the plant. The remaining production process starts with salt water that is purified by a filtration and distillation process to remove the mineral salts, which average 3.5 percent of the volume. The pure water is then separated into gasses by placing the water in a strong magnetic field and electric current. The oxygen stays near the magnet, and the hydrogen expands away to the sides and is drawn off. Oxygen is relatively easy to bottle and ship. On the other hand, hydrogen is difficult to process and must be bottled at extreme pressure and in a liquid state, which requires cooling to 5 degrees Kelvin. The mineral salt is purified and the residual is sold. The pure salt (85 percent of the mineral salt) is sold in bulk for 5 deutsche marks per unit. The mineral residual is sold in bulk for 2 marks per unit. There are 20 units in a metric ton of salt.

The oxygen is sold for 3 marks per mml. (million liters), and the hydrogen is sold for 7 marks per mml. The costs and volume for the production departments for June 19x2:

	Conversion Cost	Input Volume	Power Usage
Power Plant	2,304,000 DM		
Filter and Distill	90,909	113.64 mml.	6
Electronic Separator	197,386	109.66 mml.	180
Salt Purification	38,182	3,818 metric tons	4
Oxygen Bottling	93,068	132,954 mml.	10
Hydrogen Bottling	279,203	265,907 mml.	50
Total costs	3,002,748 DM		250

Power output was 1,440 units of mega-watt days, which are based on a million watts for 24 hours. Remaining power is sold for 1,800 DM per unit. Seeluft treats the residual minerals as a by-product of salt purification and credits the salt purification department for the net realizable values. Inventories were immaterial at the beginning and ending of the month.

REQUIRED:
a. Starting with the production of electricity, draw a diagram of the production process including the following parts:
    1. Production departments.
    2. Joint costs.
    3. Additional processing costs.
    4. Selling prices.
    5. Unit volumes.
b. Allocate the power costs to the other producing departments and commercial sales on the physical volume measure.
c. Compute the net realizable values of the:
    1. Residual Minerals.   4. Oxygen.
    2. Salt.   5. Hydrogen.
    3. Mineral Salts.   6. Purified Water.

d. Using the net realizable value method, allocate the joint costs of filtration and distillation to:
    1. Mineral Salts.   2. Purified Water.

e. Using the net realizable value method, allocate the electronic separator costs to oxygen and hydrogen.
f. Compute the cost per unit for each completed product.

10A–7. Multiple Split-Off Points.   The Bearville Extraction Plant processes 100-pound blocks of ore purchased from a quarry that is next to the plant. The ore is very rich in certain rare metals, crystals, and bases. The production plant includes the following departments and product data:

Crush and Centrifuge Unit (CCU):

Inputs:	100-pound blocks of Ore at $10 per block
Process:	Ore is crushed to powder, mixed with water, and spun until the contents are sorted by density.
Outputs:	10 pounds of light powder
	80 pounds of medium powder
	10 pounds of heavy powder, mostly magnesium compounds, is sold for $2 per 10-pound unit

Light Processing Unit (LPU):

Inputs:	10-pound units of light powder
	40-pound units of organic fiber, $.20 per unit
	50 empty boxes at $.05 each
Process:	The powder, which is rich in calcium, is purified and then the fiber is mixed. The mixture is pureed and dried into crunchy wafers and boxed.
Outputs:	50 boxes of Ocean Crunchies sold for $.50 per box

Medium Processing Unit (MPU):

Inputs:	80-pound units of medium powder.
	16 moles of hydrochloric acid at $.20 per mole
Process:	The medium powder is mixed with the acid, heated to 1200 degrees Fahrenheit for 4 hours, and berridyte salt forms in the surface foam. The berridyte salt is skimmed off the surface and then the mixture is heated to 2800 degrees for 18 hours and subsequently cooled for 6 hours. During the cooling Sagium crystals are formed.
Outputs:	2-pound container of Berridyte Salt
	1-pound of Sagium crystals, which are packaged for $.20 and sold for $6.20 per pound.
	77-pound vat of medium residual.

Berridium Desalting Unit (BDU):

Inputs:	2-pound container of Berridyte Salt.
Process:	The Berridyte Salt is mixed with water and the pure Berridyte is removed with an electronic process.
Outputs:	1 ounce of Berridyte, sold for $10 per ounce.
	31 ounces of a residual salt that is sold to highway departments for $.02 per pound.

Medium Residual Unit (MRU):

Inputs:	77-pound vat of medium residual.
Process:	The medium residual is heated quickly to 4000 degrees and allowed to cool slowly. As it cools, a crust forms that is rich in Seiritium. On the bottom of the vat is a thin layer of a rare metal, Cyclotium.
Outputs:	7.5 ounces of Seiritium, sold for $2 per ounce
	.5 ounces of Cyclotium, sold for $68 per ounce
	76.5 pounds of slag, which is returned to the quarry as a solid block

The costs recorded for the month of June 19x1:

Dept.	Direct Materials	Transferred In	Direct Labor	Overhead
CCU	$50,000		$20,000	$50,000
LPU	11,475	?	1,500	2,000
MPU	13,680	?	4,800	13,200
BDU	0	?	2,355	4,200
MRU	0	?	3,900	11,900
TOTALS	$75,155		$32,555	$81,300

Assume that there are no beginning inventories and that work in process is immaterial. The June production and ending inventories include the following units:

	Unit Size	Unit Cost	Purchased/ Produced	Units of Inventory
Raw materials:				
Ore	100 pound	$10.00	5,600	600
Organic fiber	40 pounds	0.20	4,650	400
Empty boxes	1 each	0.05	213,000	500
Hydrochloric acid	1 mole	0.20	64,200	200
Intermediate products:				
Light powder	10 pounds	?	5,000	750
Medium powder	80 pounds	?	5,000	600
Berridyte Salt	2 pounds	?	4,400	400
Medium residual	77 pounds	?	4,400	400

	Unit Size	Price	Produced	Inventory
Final products:				
Heavy powder	10 pounds	$ 2.00	5,000	300
Ocean Crunchies	1 box	0.50	212,500	12,500
Sagium crystals	1 pound	6.20	4,400	600
Berridyte	1 ounce	10.00	4,000	600
Residual Salt	1 pound	0.02	7,750	800
Seiritium	1 ounce	2.00	30,000	600
Cyclotium	1 ounce	68.00	2,000	300

The Residual Salt is treated as a by-product with the realizable value credited to Work in Process—BDU. There are separate Work in Process accounts for each producing department in the plant.

REQUIRED:

a. Using the physical units method:
   1. Allocate the costs of production to intermediate and final products.
   2. Compute the cost to be assigned to ending inventories.
b. For each final product, compute the realizable value at selling point and net realizable value at split-off point. Use the total units produced in your calculations.
c. Compute the net realizable value for:
   1. Berridyte Salt.
   2. Medium residual.
   3. Medium powder. (Use the results from parts 1 and 2.)
   4. Light powder.
d. Using the net realizable value method:
   1. Allocate the costs of production to intermediate and final products starting with the CCU.
   2. Compute the cost to be assigned to ending inventories.
e. Compare the results from parts (a) and (d). Comment on the following:
   1. Difficulty in calculation.
   2. Ease with which the method could be accurately and reliably computerized.
   3. Materiality of the differences.

CHAPTER

11

Waste and Scrap, Spoilage and Defective Units

■

BUSINESS PROBLEM

HomeTech Manufacturing, Inc., specializes in making home products that represent the latest materials and technologies available. The company has a reputation for excellent quality and for entering the market with the best products at reasonable prices.

The Cookware Division has two product lines: Chef's Delight, a 9-piece set, and Gourmet Ease, a 20-piece set. Chef's Delight is top-quality featuring anodized solid-spun aluminum for fast, even heat conductivity and satin finish for easy cleaning. It has bright stainless steel lids and nickel-plated cast iron handles. Stamping operations are needed for the pots, frying pans, and lids. Handles attached to all pots and pans require a molding operation. The handles for each lid are made from stainless steel rods that are bent to shape and flattened where attached to lids. Holes are drilled into each pot, pan, and lid so handles can be attached with screws. The pieces are polished and assembled and placed in the finished goods warehouse.

The production costs for the set of Chef's Delight are as follows:

	Total 9 Pieces	Average per Piece
Material	$ 92.70	$10.30
Stamping and Molding:		
Direct labor	10.80	1.20
Production overhead	32.40	3.60
Drilling and Assembly:		
Direct labor	18.00	2.00
Production overhead	27.00	3.00
	$180.90	$20.10

Inspection takes place at the end of each major operation. The outlines and trimmings resulting from stamping, molding, and drilling are scrap, which is sold for the value of the materials. Work from the drilling operation through final assembly that does not meet quality standards is either spoilage or defective work, depending on the inspector's decision.

Over the past three years the Cookware Division has substantially reduced the number of rejected units as a result of improved training and maintenance. The division has worked with the employees, especially those in Stamping and Molding, to build a keen awareness and pride in the quality of the pots produced. The ultimate goal is to achieve zero defects.

LEARNING OBJECTIVES

After studying this chapter, you should be able to:

1. Distinguish among waste, scrap, spoilage, and defective units.
2. Apply the appropriate accounting treatment for scrap given a particular business situation.
3. Explain the appropriate accounting treatment for normal spoilage and abnormal spoilage.
4. Apply the appropriate accounting treatment for spoilage using both a job order cost system and a process cost system.
5. Apply the appropriate accounting treatment for defective units, with an emphasis on a job order cost system.

Value-added costs include only those costs involved with the production of the good outputs desired by customers. Although waste, scrap, spoilage, and defective units come from a production process along with the good units, these are not desired by customers and thus result in non-value-added costs. Management should set continuous improvement as an important objective for production processes to eliminate waste, scrap, spoilage, and defective units.

This chapter presents the issues related to waste and scrap, as well as appropriate definitions. It also illustrates the accounting and reporting for losses and output reductions primarily due to scrap, spoilage, and defective units.

TERMINOLOGY

Although waste, scrap, spoilage, and defective units have similarities, they are different. Waste and scrap are associated with inputs. Spoilage and defective units are outputs, albeit bad outputs. The differences are explored below.

Waste and Scrap

Waste and scrap represent material inputs that do not become part of production outputs. The costs of waste and scrap typically are included in the costs of the good output for external financial reporting.

Waste is material that is lost, evaporates, or shrinks during a production process or is a residue. Examples of waste include gases, dust, smoke, toxic residues, evaporation, and losses due to temperature variations and chemical reactions. Waste has either no recovery value or recovery value that is not worth measuring. Disposing of waste can be costly. For example, disposal of chemical or radioactive waste requires additional treatment costs in order to meet state and federal government environmental standards.

Scrap is a material input residual that has a recovery value significant enough to measure. It may be sold in some outside market or reused in a production process. Examples of scrap include shavings and short lengths from a woodworking operation, flash from a casting operation in a foundry, remnants from the manufacturing of clothing, outlined metal from a metal stamping operation, or filings, turnings, borings, and dust. Scrap metals, especially aluminum, copper, gold, and silver, are reprocessed.

Production companies accept certain levels of waste and scrap because the costs of reduction exceed the benefits. Thus, some minimum level of waste and scrap is included in the specifications for the material needed to produce each unit of output. For example, if a 5 percent waste and scrap level is considered minimal, then raw materials requisitions will have 5 percent extra materials as compared to the finished product.

Periodically, the minimal level of waste and scrap should be reevaluated to determine if the level is still minimal with respect to current technology and is acceptable in comparison with the actions of competitors. Actual waste and scrap level that is above the minimal should be considered abnormal and should be highlighted in reports to those managing the production process.

Common causes for waste and scrap include:

1. Variation in the purity or quality of the material.
2. Variation in the size or shape of materials.
3. Improper scheduling that wastes materials in feed lines or on the production line itself, such as paint or chemicals that must be flushed out of the lines before a new job.
4. Production processes that leave a liquid or solid residue.
5. Improperly maintained or adjusted machinery.
6. Poorly trained workers.

Management should develop strategies that prevent these causes of waste and scrap. For example, purchasing materials, scheduling jobs, and managing production must all be carefully examined to minimize waste and scrap.

Spoilage

Spoilage represents units of output that do not meet quality standards. The units may be partially or fully completed, depending on where in the process the spoilage is identified. No amount of rework can make these units salable as ''firsts'' or ''seconds.'' Therefore, spoiled units are sold in another type of market, often at a price that represents only the value of material content. Examples of spoilage include products manufactured with design flaws, cracked or scratched ceramic tile, books with ink blots, off-quality paint, bruised produce, and improperly ground eyeglass lenses.

Because spoiled units have passed through at least part of a production process, they bear the material, labor, and production overhead costs charged for work done. Thus, a spoiled unit, once identified, can be assigned a cost. However, these costs are usually included in the cost of good outputs. This cost is net spoilage cost, which is calculated as:

1. The sum of costs accumulated to the point in the process where spoilage is detected.
2. Plus the costs to dispose of the spoiled units.
3. Less the disposal value.

Defective Units

Defective units are outputs that do not meet quality standards and can be sold as second-quality goods ''as is'' or can be reworked and sold as first- or second-quality goods. Quite often the company has a choice of using regular channels or alternate channels for marketing ''as is'' or reworked units.

Any unit identified as defective is still treated as a good unit but must be tagged for a decision about whether to rework it. The costs to rework the units should be accumulated and allocated by a systematic method.

Neither spoiled nor defective units meet quality standards. The difference between them is that spoiled units cannot be reworked and sold as regular products, whether first or seconds. Defective units can be reworked and sold as a first- or a second-quality product. Consequently, the relative sales value of defective units is significantly higher than the relative sales value of spoiled units.

The production of spoiled or defective units is a non-value-added activity. The causes of spoiled and defective units are similar to the causes for waste and scrap, for example, the quality of materials, process controls, machine maintenance, and employee training. The rate of spoiled and defective units should be minimized. Thus, zero defects and total quality control programs should be initiated to sensitize employees to the need to eliminate spoilage and defective units. Their cost should be reported to management for action.

METHODS TO ACCOUNT FOR THE SALES VALUE OF SCRAP

The financial reporting of scrap has many alternatives. The proceeds from the sale of scrap are accounted for by either reducing production costs or increasing other income. The procedure to accomplish this depends on the specific company policies. Scrap is most often treated as equivalent to a by-product of the production process and follows by-product accounting as in Chapter 10. Thus, scrap is either recorded with (1) the net realizable value method, which assigns a value at the time of incurrence, or (2) the zero-value method, which records nothing until the time of sale.

Another factor to consider in accounting for scrap is whether scrap is (1) linked to particular jobs or products, (2) treated as part of production overhead, or (3) considered a source of income. One approach is to trace the sale of scrap to the specific jobs or products that generate it, which is appropriate in two cases. First, significant amounts of scrap occur because of tight customer or product specifications. Second, the customer, in agreeing to prices, has negotiated for credits resulting from scrap sales.

If an amount of scrap results from operations regardless of which jobs or products are being produced, then the sale of scrap may be credited to production overhead. In this manner, all jobs and products share in scrap proceeds through the allocation of a reduced production overhead. This is the most common approach used by manufacturing companies.

Some companies treat the sale of scrap as a source of income. This approach is justified when the amount of scrap sales is insignificant. This method cannot be justified when the realizable value from scrap sales has a material impact on income or assets.

Regardless of the accounting for the value of scrap sold, the quantity of waste and scrap should be monitored by those managing the production process. Because waste and scrap are inputs that do not turn into outputs, any occurrence above a minimal rate represents a reduction in the quantity of outputs. This is a non-value-added activity that must be monitored and corrected, where necessary, to maintain the competitive position of the company.

An Example

HomeTech Manufacturing, Inc., has 2,200 pounds of scrap for the week of September 7–12. The sales value is $3.80 per pound, and the total proceeds are $8,360 (2,200 pounds $\times$ $3.80). The journal entries for the six possible ways to account for scrap appear in Exhibit 11–1.

Difference between Actual and Estimated Sales Value

If the actual sales price differs from the estimated sales price, a difference will result in the necessity for an adjusting entry. The account adjusted will be Work in Process Inventory, Production Overhead, or Income from Sale of Scrap, consistent with the account credited when scrap was initially recorded. If the job has been completed or sold, or the accounts have been closed at the end of the period, the adjustment will probably be to Other Income.

Recycled or Reused Scrap

Scrap is sometimes recycled or reused as direct material rather than sold as scrap. For example, aluminum outlines from a stamping process may go back to the company's foundry for melting into new ingots for use in a rolling mill. Or scrap wood from a cutting operation goes to a particle board process. In both of these cases, even though the scrap is not sold, it has a value in use. The accounting treatment in practice is to record this scrap as a category of raw material carried at an estimated sales value.

ACCOUNTING PROCEDURES FOR SPOILAGE

The cost accounting system for spoilage should do several things:

1. Capture and record the costs of spoilage.
2. Provide managers information for decisions regarding the level and causes of spoilage.
3. Provide measures of the production performance and information for corrective action.

The accounting system should also support the security of the physical units.

Normal and Abnormal Spoilage

Normal spoilage is expected to occur under efficient operations, within the economical production methods, procedures, and processes established. Therefore, normal spoilage is the planned minimal level and is an inherent result of the process. As such,

EXHIBIT 11–1 Methods of Accounting for Scrap—Journal Entries

Costing Treatment	Value Assigned When Scrap Sold		Value Assigned When Scrap Occurs	
1. Scrap is directly associated with job	Scrap returned to storeroom:		Scrap returned to storeroom:	
	No entry (memo)		Scrap Inventory (NRV)	8,360
			Work in Process Inventory (NRV)	8,360
	Scrap is sold:		Scrap is sold:	
	Cash or Accounts Receivable	8,360	Cash or Accounts Receivable	8,360
	Work in Process Inventory	8,360	Scrap Inventory	8,360
2. Scrap is associated with general production operations.	Scrap returned to storeroom:		Scrap returned to storeroom:	
	No entry (memo)		Scrap Inventory (NRV)	8,360
			Production overhead (NRV)	8,360
	Scrap is sold:		Scrap is sold:	
	Cash or Accounts Receivable	8,360	Cash or Accounts Receivable	8,360
	Production Overhead	8,360	Scrap Inventory	8,360
3. Scrap is source of other income.	Scrap returned to storeroom:		Scrap returned to storeroom:	
	No entry (memo)		Scrap Inventory (NRV)	8,360
			Income from Sale of Scrap	8,360
	Scrap is sold:		Scrap is sold:	
	Cash or Accounts Receivable	8,360	Cash or Accounts Receivable	8,360
	Income from Sale of Scrap	8,360	Scrap Inventory	8,360

it is not controllable in the short run. Costs of normal spoilage are typically included in the costs of good units produced under the theory that attaining any lower level of spoilage would involve even higher costs.

Abnormal spoilage is any spoilage in excess of normal spoilage. Causes of abnormal spoilage include improperly adjusted machinery, machinery breakdowns, accidents, poorly trained workers, and inferior or defective materials. Abnormal spoilage is not a cost of obtaining good output. It is considered a loss of the period.[1]

Management's attention to preventive maintenance, proper materials, training employees, and similar aspects of production can reduce losses from abnormal spoilage. Consequently, it is important to (1) measure and report spoilage occurring during a period and (2) identify and segregate the costs of normal and abnormal spoilage.

Applying Normal Spoilage Ratios

Normal spoilage should be calculated from good output. For example, assume that HomeTech Manufacturing, Inc., establishes a normal spoilage rate of 5 percent of good output. If 40,000 good units were produced from the 48,000 units input, then the normal spoilage is 2,000 units (5 percent × 40,000). The abnormal spoilage units will be 8,000 total spoilage (48,000 input less 40,000 output) minus the normal spoilage of 2,000 units, or 6,000 units.[2]

Using input as the basis for the computation distorts the results when there is a significant amount of abnormal spoilage. For example, if the rate of normal spoilage for cookware in the HomeTech Manufacturing, Inc., situation were 4.76 percent of input, an input of 48,000 units is expected to produce 2,285 (4.76 percent × 48,000) spoiled units. However, suppose that the 48,000 units are input and all the units are spoiled because of poor machine maintenance. In this circumstance, all of the spoilage should be treated as abnormal (a loss) and no part of the spoilage should be treated as production overhead to be allocated to products.

Importance of Timing of the Inspection Point

Spoiled units are discovered at the time of inspection. Materials and conversion costs have been added to them, as to the good units, up to the time of inspection. Because spoilage remains unknown until the time of inspection, the costs of the spoiled units are tied to the location in the production process of the inspection points. The later the inspection point, the higher the total costs of spoiled units. Thus, the costs of spoilage are minimized by having the inspection as early as possible. However, inspection points that are too early in the process will miss units that are spoiled later. Hence, the timing of the inspection point(s) is key to controlling both the level and cost of spoilage.

---

[1] Some companies record abnormal spoilage as part of overhead but do not include the abnormal spoilage in overhead rates. Thus, the abnormal spoilage results in underapplied overhead, which is then charged as an adjustment to cost of goods sold. This has the same impact on income as recording the abnormal spoilage in a loss account.

[2] Rates based on input are appropriately reduced to reflect normal spoilage in input. Thus, a 5 percent rate of good output is equivalent to a 4.76 percent rate on inputs:

$$5\%/(100\% + 5\%) = 4.76\% \text{ (rounded)}$$

Applying the input rate to the inputs in the example:

$$4.76\% \times 48,000 = 2,285$$

which overstates normal spoilage by 285 units (2,285 − 2,000). The amount of the overstatement will be exactly equal to the input rate times the true abnormal spoilage:

$$4.76\% \times 6,000 \text{ units} = 285$$

with any differences due to rounding the rates.

Quality assurance programs vary. For example, in some programs, the units are pulled off the line only when workers notice that they are bad. Some quality assurance programs inspect every unit, others take a sample hourly, and still others inspect in detail only when there is a signal that something is wrong with the production process.

When quality testing requires a destructive test (as in tests for taste, strength, durability, disease, or chemical content), inspections have to occur periodically rather than for every unit. Otherwise, all units are consumed in the quality tests. Nondestructive tests (as in checking dimensions, weight, color, or appearance) can be made continuously by either the production workers or quality control inspectors using various gauges and instruments.

For example, every commercial aircraft is thoroughly tested at every stage of production. Hundreds of X rays, sonagrams, metal stress tests, circuit tests, and systems checks are performed on each aircraft. Additionally, each airliner receives periodic safety tests, and extensive tests must be performed if cracks appear on a flying (exterior) surface. On the other hand, beverage cans, which are a less critical product than airliners, are tested periodically, for example, every 1,000th can.

Accounting Issues

In practice there are two basic approaches to treating the cost of spoilage: (1) ignore spoilage entirely and average the total cost of production (which includes spoilage) over the good units inspected and units not inspected during the period and (2) separately identify spoiled units and the related costs and make specific adjustments to costs of good units.

The first approach (ignoring spoilage) is easy to implement but is not conceptually correct. The approach leaves spoiled units out of the denominator but leaves spoilage costs in the numerator. The costs of all spoilage, both normal and abnormal, are charged to both completed units and ending Work in Process Inventory, including units that have not reached the inspection point. Units in work in process inventories will be charged twice for spoilage, once in the period started and once in the period completed. Thus, costs per unit can vary dramatically from period to period.

When spoilage costs are accounted for separately, the spoiled units are identified and included in the unit cost computations. The costs of normal spoilage are charged to good units passing inspection, and the costs of abnormal spoilage are treated as a loss and are brought to the attention of management.

Normal spoilage is specifically charged to good units that have been inspected during the current period. Thus, normal spoilage becomes part of the finished goods cost and thereby the cost of goods sold. In order to determine which units should be charged for the normal spoilage, the accountant must know which good units have been inspected *this month*. To find the answer, the accountant will divide production into three parts:

Beginning Work in Process	Production Started and Completed	Ending Work in Process

Note that the units started and completed must have been inspected during the current period and receive a share of the cost of normal spoilage.

Beginning Work in Process.   The accountant will first examine beginning inventories. Were they inspected last month or this month? If the beginning units were inspected last month, then they were already charged for spoilage last month and will not be charged again. If the beginning units were inspected this month, they will be charged for a share of this month's normal spoilage.

Ending Work in Process.   The accountant reviews ending inventories. Have they been inspected yet? If they have, then the accountant will include ending inventories in the calculation and allocate a portion of the normal spoilage to outputs.

We will now apply these general concepts with the procedures appropriate for a job order costing system.

JOB ORDER COSTING SPOILAGE

There are three types of spoilage found in a job shop:

1. Normal spoilage that is related to the production process in general. This spoilage is charged to production overhead.
2. Normal spoilage that is caused by the unusually strict requirements of a particular job. This spoilage is charged to the particular job.
3. Abnormal spoilage that is caused by a production process that is out of control. This spoilage is charged as a loss for the period.

If normal spoilage results when machines and labor are operating at desired levels of precision, these costs should be charged[3] to all production. The mechanism for doing this is to include an estimated amount in the predetermined production overhead rate. On the other hand, if spoilage is caused by exacting job specifications, difficult processing, or unusual or unexpected conditions, this is normal spoilage that should be charged directly to the particular job.

Job Order Example

HomeTech Manufacturing, Inc., may account for the cost of normal spoilage by charging either overhead or a particular job, depending on the nature of the job requirements. Assume production of 50,110 pots and pans on September 8, and the inspectors found 2,500 of them spoiled. Each unit had an average cost of:

Direct material	$10.30
Direct labor	3.20
Production overhead	6.60
Total per unit	$20.10

The production overhead rate includes $.66 for normal spoilage. Assume that the sales value is $4.50 per spoiled unit less disposal costs of $.30 per unit to give a net realizable value of $4.20 per unit.

Spoiled Units Charged to Production Overhead

The summary entry to record the costs incurred during the day for the 50,110 units at a cost of $20.10 is:

Work in Process Inventory	1,007,211	
Materials Inventory ($10.30 × 50,110)		516,133
Payroll ($3.20 × 50,110)		160,352
Applied Production Overhead ($6.60 × 50,110)		330,726

At the end of the day, there are 2,500 total spoiled units. Notice that both spoiled and good units have been charged $.66 normal spoilage through the overhead charge. The spoiled units should not be charged with an allowance for normal spoilage. Thus, we need to adjust the overhead applied to remove the normal spoilage charged to the spoiled units:

---

[3] The cost of spoilage is recorded as the net of the costs incurred to the inspection point and costs of disposal less any disposal value. We typically combine disposal costs with disposal value to arrive at the anticipated net realizable value and subtract this from costs incurred to the inspection point.

Production Overhead Control ($.66 × 2,500)	1,650	
Work in Process		1,650

We have now reduced the cost of spoiled units to $19.44 ($20.10 less $.66).

In order to distinguish the cost of the spoiled units and to recognize the net realizable value of each unit, the entry is:

Spoiled Goods Inventory ($4.20 × 2,500)	10,500	
Production Overhead Control—Spoiled Goods		
($19.44 − $4.20) × 2,500	38,100	
Work in Process Inventory ($19.44 × 2,500)		48,600

This entry establishes an inventory amount of $10,500 for the spoiled units awaiting disposition. It also transfers the costs of materials, labor, and overhead on spoiled units from work in process inventory to production overhead.

The 47,610 good units for the day are transferred to Finished Goods Inventory at a cost of $20.10 per unit:

Finished Goods Inventory	956,961	
Work in Process Inventory		956,961

The $956,961 includes a charge of $31,422.60 ($.66 × 47,610) for normal spoilage.

When the spoiled units are sold, there may be a difference between the net disposal value realized and the net realizable value recorded as spoiled goods inventory. Any difference becomes an adjustment to Production Overhead—Spoiled Units.

If the net realizable value of spoiled units cannot be estimated at the time spoilage is identified, no amount can be recorded for the inventory. Instead, the full unit cost of spoilage is charged to production overhead. When the spoiled units are subsequently sold, the proceeds of the sale are credited to production overhead.

Abnormal Spoilage Charged to Loss Account

We will now assume that the normal spoilage rate is established at 3.86 percent of the good units produced. Further, we will assume that the company continues to record normal spoilage as part of overhead and records abnormal spoilage in a separate loss account.

The net cost for a spoiled unit is $15.24 ($20.10 − $.66 − $4.20). The normal spoilage units may be found by taking the rate of 3.86 percent of the 46,710 units and finding 1,803 as normal spoilage. The abnormal spoilage would be 697 units (2,500 less 1,803). The entry would be:

Spoiled Goods Inventory	($4.20 × 2,500)	10,500
Production Overhead Control—Spoiled		
Goods	($15.24 × 1,803)	27,478
Loss on Spoiled Goods	($15.24 × 697)	10,622
Work in Process Inventory		48,600

Spoilage Charged to Specific Job

There are cases in which a job has such demanding specifications that spoilage cannot be avoided. Because the spoilage is directly attributable to specific work, there is ample justification to charge the job.

We will change the assumptions of the HomeTech example and now assume that there is no normal spoilage. Further, assume that all 2,500 spoiled units are traceable to the unusual specifications of one particular job: the day's production is for an upscale chain of gourmet stores that has exacting requirements on size, weight, and appearance.

Because all the spoilage is traceable to jobs, the production overhead rate will not include an allowance for normal spoilage. Thus, the production overhead per unit would be applied at $5.94 instead of $6.60, and the total cost per unit would be $19.44 instead of $20.10. The entry to record charges to Work in Process Inventory for the day's effort would be:

Work in Process Inventory ($19.44 × 50,110)	974,138	
Materials Inventory ($10.30 × 50,110)		516,133
Payroll ($3.20 × 50,110)		160,352
Applied Production Overhead ($5.94 × 50,110)		297,653

Now, we credit Work in Process Inventory for the net realizable value of the spoiled units:

Spoiled Goods Inventory	10,500	
Work in Process Inventory		10,500

This forces the good units in the job to bear the net spoilage costs of $38,100, which is $15.24 for 2,500 units ($19.44 per unit less $4.20 net realizable value). The 47,610 good units for the day are transferred to finished goods inventory and the entry is:

Finished Goods Inventory	963,638	
Work in Process Inventory		963,638

The cost of $963,638 results in a cost per unit of $20.24 ($963,638 divided by 47,610 units). The cost per unit includes $.80 in spoilage ($38,100 spoilage divided by 47,610 units).

We have considered the effects of spoilage on job order costing. In Chapter 9 we covered process costing systems in detail. In the next section we will illustrate the effects of spoilage on process costing.

SPOILAGE IN PROCESS COSTING SYSTEMS

A process cost system accumulates costs in departments and allocates the costs from the departments to units. Each unit passing through a department is assumed to be like any other in terms of cost. This simplifies recordkeeping immensely because cost records on specific batches are not kept.

Example, Process Costing Setting

Weiberg, Inc., produces musical instruments and uses a process cost system. In its acoustical guitar line, all materials are cut, dried, and shaped separately and placed in a temporary storage area. Pickers select the parts needed for each guitar, pack them as kits, and send the kits to the assembly area. Finishing a guitar takes up to 12 days, depending on the specific graining of the wood. Finishing involves laminating, gluing, lacquering, final drying, and stringing. Inspection and testing occur at the end of assembly (i.e., the ending work in process inventory has no spoilage detected). Normal spoilage consists of 4 percent of good guitars. These units will not tune properly, have misplaced frets, or have a sounding box that lacks adequate resonance due to uneven wood density.

During June, 5,500 kits containing $90,000 of materials were started in process and $155,000 of conversion costs were incurred. Of the 5,500 guitars started, 3,400 were transferred to finished goods and 1,300 guitars were still in process. Spoilage included 136 (.04 × 3,400) units normal spoilage and 664 units abnormal spoilage. The ending work in process units were 100 percent complete for component parts and 60 percent complete for conversion costs.

Exhibit 11–2 is the cost of production report for Weiberg, Inc. Because there are no beginning inventories, the results will be the same whether we use the weighted

EXHIBIT 11–2

WEIBERG, INC.—ASSEMBLY DEPARTMENT
Cost of Production Report
For the Month Ended June 30, 19x8

Quantities

Units to account for:		
Units in process, June 1		–0–
Units started during month		5,500
Total units to account for		5,500
Units accounted for:		
Units transferred to finished goods		3,400
Units of normal spoilage (100% complete)		136
Units of abnormal spoilage (100% complete)		664
Units in process, June 30 (100% materials; 60% conversion)		1,300
Total units accounted for		5,500

Costs

Costs to account for:			
Costs in process, June 1			$ –0–
Costs incurred during month:			
Components		$ 90,000	
Conversion costs		155,000	245,000
Total costs to account for			$245,000

	Units	Costs	Totals	
Costs accounted for:				
Finished goods	3,400	$47.488	$161,460	
Plus normal spoilage	136	$47.488	6,458	$167,918
Abnormal spoilage	664	$47.488		31,532
Work in process, June 30:				
Components	1,300	$16.364	$ 21,273	
Conversion costs	780	$31.124	24,277	45,550
Total costs accounted for				$245,000

Additional Calculations

	Components	Conversion Costs	Total
Costs in process, June 1	$ –0–	$ –0–	$ –0–
Current period costs	90,000	155,000	245,000
Total costs	$90,000	$155,000	$245,000
Computation of equivalent units:			
Units completed	3,400	3,400	
Normal spoilage	136	136	
Abnormal spoilage	664	664	
Equivalent units in ending inventory	1,300	780	
Equivalent production	5,500	4,980	
Unit costs (Costs divided by units)	$16.364	$31.124	$47.488

average or FIFO method. Note the inclusion of spoiled units in the equivalent unit calculation at the bottom of the cost of production report. Thus, the cost per equivalent unit applies to spoiled units. Also note the treatment of spoilage costs in the "Costs accounted for" section.

The cost of normal spoilage is included in the cost of guitars passing inspection. Abnormal spoilage is separately identified in the report, and its costs are shown. The journal entry to record the month-end transfer of units and recognize abnormal spoilage is:

Finished Goods Inventory	167,918	
Loss on Abnormal Spoilage	31,532	
Work in Process: Assembly		209,440

Normal Spoilage and Work in Process Inventories

If the ending work in process inventory has been inspected, then a portion of the normal spoilage must be allocated to ending work in process. For example, assume that for Weiberg, Inc., the inspection point occurs at 50 percent of completion. Materials and conversion costs are assumed to be the same on a per unit basis as in the original example.[4] The cost for each spoiled unit will be:

Materials	$16.364 × 100% =	$16.364
Conversion	$31.124 × 50% =	15.562
Total spoiled unit cost		$31.926

For this example, the normal spoilage will be 188 units with 136 (4% × 3,400 completed units) related to completed units and 52 units (4% × 1,300 ending work in process) related to ending work in process. The cost of goods completed will be:

Finished goods	3,400 units × $47.488	$161,460
Plus: Normal spoilage	136 units × $31.926	4,342
Total cost of completed goods		$165,802

The cost of ending work in process will be:

Components	1,300 units × $16.364	$21,273
Conversion costs	780 units × $31.124	24,277
Normal spoilage	52 units × $31.926	1,660
Total cost of ending work in process		$47,210

The loss from abnormal spoilage will be based on 612 units (800 total less 136 completed units less 52 ending work in process):

Abnormal spoilage loss	612 units × $31.926	$19,539

If the beginning work in process inventories were inspected last period, then the inventory amount includes spoilage costs from the prior period. Therefore, in this circumstance beginning work in process inventories should be excluded both in the calculations of normal spoilage and in allocations of the normal spoilage to good units inspected during the current period.

ACCOUNTING PROCEDURES FOR DEFECTIVE UNITS

A defective unit contains imperfections that can be reworked so the unit becomes a standard salable product as a "first" or "second," depending on the extent of the defects. Accounting for defective units parallels accounting for spoiled units presented in the previous section.

---

[4] This assumption implies that there will be $12,450 (800 spoiled units × 50% × $31.124) less conversion costs incurred during the period because the spoiled units are discovered earlier and not processed to completion. Thus, the current period conversion costs would have been $142,550 ($155,000 − $12,450) under this assumption.

If defective units are a random occurrence during normal operations, the additional reworking costs required to correct defects are charged to overhead and allocated to all units produced. To accomplish this, an estimate of rework costs is made at the beginning of the period and is included as part of the predetermined overhead rate. However, if defective units are the result of unusual specifications or job-related requirements, the cost of reworking defective units is charged directly to that job.

Although the following discussion assumes a manufacturing setting, defective work can also occur in service organizations. For example, a financial planner completes a spread sheet analysis of a client's cash flow needs for her children's college education. When reviewing the analysis with the client, the financial planner realizes he used a few incorrect numbers. He must now rework the analysis with correct data, which means incurring rework labor and overhead costs.

To illustrate the accounting for defective units, return to the HomeTech Manufacturing example. HomeTech Manufacturing, Inc., uses a job order cost system. Assume that 1,075 defective, but fixable, units are found after assembly. Six hundred units require a new handle and touch-up work. The handle material cost is $2.15 per unit; labor is $1.00 per unit; overhead is applied to rework at 150 percent of labor. The remaining 475 units must be polished and refinished, which requires reworking labor of $0.80 per unit, and overhead is applied to the rework at 150 percent of labor. Note that the overhead rate for rework is lower because it occurs off the main line with small hand tools rather than with the heavier main assembly and finishing equipment. The rework costs are summarized as follows:

	600 Units	475 Units	Total Costs
Materials	$1,290	$ —	$1,290
Direct labor	600	380	980
Overhead @ 150%	900	570	1,470
	$2,790	$950	$3,740
Unit costs	$4.65	$2.00	

Costs Charged to Production Overhead

If defective work is experienced during regular operations, any rework cost is charged to production overhead. The difference between estimated rework costs (included in computing a predetermined overhead rate) and the actual reworked costs charged to overhead becomes part of an overhead variance that will be closed to Cost of Goods Sold. The entry to record the rework costs shown in the earlier table is:

Production Overhead Control—Rework	3,740	
Materials		1,290
Payroll		980
Applied Production Overhead		1,470

These are minor amounts, as they should be with a controlled production process.

Why apply production overhead to rework at all, given that the costs of rework are to be charged to overhead? After all, the effect is offset in the Overhead Control account. The full cost of the rework must be found and reported to management. Because labor is the basis for allocating overhead, we assume that overhead costs must be incurred to support that labor. When labor is in place, whether for good units or defective units, support costs must also be incurred. Therefore, additional overhead must be incurred to support the cost of the rework.

Costs Charged to Particular Job

Now suppose the company received a contract for 5,000 units with a provision that any rework costs for defective units would be charged to the contract. Assume that

200 of the defective units requiring materials occurred on this job. These cost $4.65 per unit for rework (material is $2.15 per unit, labor is $1.00 per unit, and overhead is at a rate of 150 percent). Because the rework costs are charged to jobs, the overhead rate would not include a rework estimate. Assume that the rework estimate is $.05 per good unit. Thus, the adjusted costs per completed unit without rework are:

Materials	$10.30
Direct labor	3.20
Production overhead	6.55 (instead of $6.60)
	$20.05

The entries for this situation are:

(1) To record the original costs of 5,000 units.

Work in Process	100,250	
Materials ($10.30 × 5,000)		51,500
Payroll ($3.20 × 5,000)		16,000
Applied Production Overhead ($6.55 × 5,000)		32,750

(2) To record the costs of reworking defective units.

Work in Process	930	
Materials ($2.15 × 200)		430
Payroll ($1.00 × 200)		200
Applied Production Overhead ($200 × 150%)		300

(3) To transfer costs of completed units to finished goods

Finished Goods	101,180	
Work in Process		101,180

The unit cost of production is $20.236 ($101,180 divided by 5,000 units) instead of the $20.05 original cost. The rework added $.186 to the cost of units on this job.

Defective Units in a Process Cost System

The basic approach for defective units under a process cost system is similar to the treatment for spoiled units in process costing. Thus, defective units are identified as normal and abnormal. Normal rework costs are assigned to units inspected during the period. Abnormal rework costs should be charged to the period as a loss.

SUMMARY

Waste is input that does not end up in the final product and has no significant value. However, there may be a cost to dispose of it. Scrap is similar to waste, except that it has a measurable selling value. Spoilage is output that does not meet quality standards and cannot be reworked for normal sale. Defective units do not meet quality standards but may be reworked and sold as a "first" or a "second."

Waste and scrap are normal costs of production, but they are controllable to some extent and should be kept to a minimum consistent with current technology. Because scrap has a value, it should be physically controlled like other inventories. The scrap value may be recorded at net realizable value or may not be recorded until sale. Scrap sales may be accounted for as specific job related, credited to an overhead account, or accounted for as other income. Recycled scrap should be recorded at an estimated net realizable value.

Normal spoilage is expected to occur under efficient operations within the established procedures. Normal spoilage is a cost of producing good units. Abnormal spoilage is above the normal limits and is treated as a loss of the period. In computing normal spoilage, it is important to base the calculation on good outputs rather than units input.

Spoilage is discovered at an inspection point, and it has a production cost at that point. Consequently, placement of an inspection point influences spoilage cost. Normal spoilage should be charged to all units passing inspection this month. Spoilage that is traceable to job requirements should be charged to the job.

Accounting for defective units is similar to spoilage, except that the defective units have a significant realizable value. The costs of normal rework should be included in overhead rates. Rework traceable to specific jobs should be assigned to the job.

PROBLEM FOR REVIEW

Joe Dale Manufacturing produces a single product through one department. Spoilage occurs during the process but is detected only when units are completed because inspection occurs only at the end of the process. The company uses the FIFO method for costing inventories. Production data for June 19x2 appear below:

Work in process, June 1:	
Units	1,000
Stage of completion:	
Materials	100%
Conversion costs	80%
Costs:	
Materials	$ 2,750
Conversion costs	3,280
Total costs in process	$ 6,030
Units started	9,000
Units completed	6,200
Spoilage:	
Normal	1,200
Abnormal	100
Current period costs for June:	
Materials	$22,500
Conversion costs	30,800
Total current period costs	$53,300
Work in process, June 30:	
Units	2,500
Stage of completion:	
Materials	100%
Conversion costs	40%

REQUIRED

Assuming the company separately identifies the cost of spoilage, prepare the following calculations that are necessary for a cost of production report:

a. Physical flow of units.
b. Equivalent units.
c. Costs per equivalent unit.
d. Allocation of costs to goods completed, ending inventory, and abnormal spoilage.

SOLUTION

a. Physical flow of units.

Beginning inventory	1,000
Units started	9,000
	10,000

Units completed	6,200	
Normal spoilage	1,200	
Abnormal spoilage	100	7,500
Ending inventory		2,500
Units completed		6,200
Less: Beginning inventory		1,000
Started and completed		5,200
Units started		9,000
Less: Ending inventory	2,500	
Normal spoilage	1,200	
Abnormal spoilage	100	3,800
Started and completed		5,200

b. Equivalent units.

Because spoilage is identified at the end of the process, only those units completed will share in the cost of normal spoilage. Ending inventory will have no spoilage cost assigned it.

	Materials	Conversion Costs
Units completed × 100%	6,200	6,200
Normal spoilage × 100%	1,200	1,200
Abnormal spoilage × 100%	100	100
Ending inventory:		
Materials 2,500 × 100%	2,500	
Conversion costs 2,500 × 40%		1,000
	10,000	8,500
Beginning inventory:		
Materials 1,000 × 100%	1,000	
Conversion costs 1,000 × 80%		800
Equivalent units	9,000	7,700

Another approach to the computation is as follows:

	Materials	Conversion Costs
Beginning inventory:		
Materials 1,000 × 0%	0	
Conversion costs 1,000 × 20%		200
Started and completed	5,200	5,200
Normal spoilage	1,200	1,200
Abnormal spoilage	100	100
Ending inventory:		
Materials 2,500 × 100%	2,500	
Conversion costs 2,500 × 40%		1,000
Equivalent units	9,000	7,700

c. Costs per equivalent unit.

	Materials	Conversion Costs
Current costs	$22,500	$30,800
Equivalent units (FIFO)	9,000	7,700
Unit costs (FIFO)	$2.50	$4.00

$6.50

d. Allocation of costs.

Cost of goods completed:		
Beginning inventory		
Costs in process	$ 6,030	
Costs to complete:		
Conversion costs (200 × $4.00)	800	$ 6,830
Started and completed (5,200 × $6.50)		33,800
Normal spoilage (1,200 × $6.50)		7,800
		$48,430
Abnormal spoilage (100 × $6.50)		650
Ending inventory		
Materials (2,500 × $2.50)	$ 6,250	
Conversion costs (1,000 × $4.00)	4,000	10,250
Total costs accounted for		$59,330

KEY TERMS AND CONCEPTS

Value-added costs (422)
Waste (423)
Scrap (423)
Spoilage (423)

Defective units (424)
Normal spoilage (425)
Abnormal spoilage (427)

ADDITIONAL READINGS

Chung, C. "Quality Control Sampling Plans under Zero Inventories." *Production and Inventory Management,* Second quarter, 1987, pp. 37–41.

Clark, R. L., and J. B. McLaughlin. "Controlling the Cost of Product Defects." *Management Accounting,* August, 1986.

Clemmensen, J. M. "Electric Utility Options in Power Quality Assurance." *Public Utilities Fortnightly,* June 11, 1987, pp. 26–35.

Edmonds, T. P.; B. Tsay; and W. Lin. "Analyzing Quality Costs." *Management Accounting,* November, 1989, pp. 25–29.

Godfrey, J. T., and W. R. Pasework. "Controlling Quality Costs." *Management Accounting,* March, 1988, pp. 48–51.

Labovitz, G. H., and Y. S. Chang. "Tough Questions Senior Managers Should Ask about Quality." *Corporate Accounting,* Spring, 1987, pp. 73–76.

Loewe, D. A. "Quality Management at Weyerhaeuser." *Management Accounting,* August, 1989, pp. 36–41.

Mensah, Y. M., and G. S. Chatwal. "Accounting for Shrinkage in Continuous Flow Industries: An Expository Note." *Abacus,* March, 1987, pp. 31–42.

Morse, W. J., and K. M. Poston. "Accounting for Quality Costs in CIM." *Journal of Cost Management for the Manufacturing Industry,* Fall, 1987, pp. 5–11.

Rogoff, D. L. "Scrap into Profits: How to Fully Exploit Scrap as a Revenue Source." *Journal of Accountancy,* February, 1987, pp. 106ff.

Sherden, W. A. "Erosion in Service Quality." *Best's Review* (Property & Casualty), September, 1987, pp. 51–55.

Shetty, Y. K. "Product Quality and Competitive Strategy." *Business Horizons,* May–June, 1987, pp. 46–52.

Simpson, J. B. "Quality Costs: Facilitating the Quality Initiative." *Journal of Cost Management for the Manufacturing Industry,* Spring, 1987, pp. 25–34.

REVIEW QUESTIONS

1. How are waste and scrap similar? How are they different?

2. How does the anticipated level of scrap determine the quantity of material that is needed for operations?

3. Because there is no separate identity of cost with scrap, explain how costs of scrap are charged to the production of a period.

4. Under what conditions is it appropriate to record a value for scrap at the time scrap occurs?

5. Discuss the justification for crediting production overhead for the proceeds recovered from the sale of scrap.

6. How do you account for the difference between actual and estimated sales value on scrap for job Z3R41, if the job is complete and the units are in finished goods inventory?

7. What is the major difference between a spoiled unit and a defective unit?

8. Explain the difference between normal and abnormal spoilage.

9. Assume a company has a 3 percent spoilage rate, has input 20,000 units, and has good units of output totaling 18,430. Explain why the difference between the input and output does not comprise 600 units of normal spoilage and 970 units of abnormal spoilage.

10. Which units are charged with cost of spoilage if inspection occurs at the 60 percent stage of completion?

11. When would a company select to charge the cost of spoiled units to production overhead? To a particular job?

12. Suppose the actual net disposal value of spoiled units was different from the estimated net realizable value. How would you account for this difference, assuming the sale occurred during the same period the spoilage was detected?

13. In some situations, labor and materials costs incurred in reworking defective work are treated as production overhead. In other cases, those costs are charged directly to the job. Explain the appropriate use of each accounting treatment.

DISCUSSION QUESTIONS

14. Waste and scrap usually relate to materials put into a production process, and spoilage and defective units are products—outputs of the process. How does the distinction of inputs versus outputs affect the accounting procedures for waste and scrap, and for spoilage and defective units?

15. Under what conditions would the unit cost of normal spoilage differ from the unit cost of abnormal spoilage?

16. Ignoring spoilage costs in a process cost system supposedly spreads spoilage cost to the units in a convenient manner. Explain why ignoring spoilage costs is not a conceptually correct approach.

17. In the control of materials cost, why is the knowledge that there is excessive scrap likely to be of greater importance to managers than the income derived from the sale of scrap?

18. Inca Sheet Metal Fabricators threw away all scrap metal from its operations. The company's external auditor suggested Inca could sell the scrap and thereby reduce costs. So the company began selling the scrap at the end of each week. A scrap report for the first month showed a steady increase in scrap levels even though production volume remained relatively stable. In fact, scrap levels had never been this high before. How might the change in the scrap policy affect a worker's attitude toward scrap?

19. Carrizo Refining, Inc., is a small operation that refines a light grade of crude oil into liquified petroleum gases, gasoline, jet fuel, and diesel fuel. Methane gas emerges from the refining process and is treated as a by-product because it is in the crude oil (material) but is not a final product. The methane is mixed 50–50 with natural gas from a local utility company, and it is the fuel for the furnaces that generate heat for the refining process. Carrizo values methane at its net realizable value. How would you determine a net realizable value? What impact would this value have on refining costs?

20. Minyard Companies makes plastic cups and cereal bowls. Spoiled units are accumulated and eventually sold to stores specializing in railroad salvage or deep discounted product stores. The net realizable value of spoiled units is not known at the time the units are identified, and sales occur at infrequent intervals. How would you account for the sale of spoiled units if the sale were after the year end and the books have been closed?

21. Show that if normal spoilage is based on total inputs, then the misstatement rate in the loss from abnormal spoilage will exactly equal the normal spoilage rate.

22. Compare the problems in controlling diamond dust, a valuable scrap, with sawdust, which is much less valuable.

23. Explain the possible ways to account for the cost of defective units and rework costs when a process cost system is in use.

EXERCISES

11–1. Concepts.   For each of the following statements, choose the number that best matches the description from the chapter reading.

(B. George, adapted)

1. Scrap   3. Defective units
2. Spoilage   4. Waste

_____ a. Gases and evaporation.
_____ b. Gold shavings.
_____ c. No recovery value.
_____ d. May be sold as "firsts" or "seconds."
_____ e. Usually sold only for the value of the material.
_____ f. May be reused in the production process.
_____ g. May be reworked.
_____ h. Apply material and labor costs for partial work.

11–2. Spoilage in Services.   The Haught Airline allows normal luggage damage and misplacement allowance of $900 per 1,000 passenger boardings. The liability on each piece of luggage is limited to $500.

On Flight 552 from Chicago to Hawaii with 280 passengers on board, the water supply leaked to the forward lavatory. The water damage was noticed upon arrival at Honolulu International. The leak caused complete damage to 82 pieces of luggage and partial damage to 12 other pieces.

Each of the 47 people with totally damaged luggage was given $500 in cash per item plus $760 in ticket allowances for anywhere the airline flies. The $760 is the average price paid for round-trip tickets on the flight. Fulfilling the ticket allowance requirements is estimated as a 60 percent cost. Those people with the 12 partially damaged items were given an average of $300 each to purchase new luggage.

REQUIRED:
a. Estimate the total cost of the service spoilage.
b. Should the airline treat this spoilage as normal or abnormal spoilage? Why?

11–3. Scrap Losses.   The Karen Jean Company makes a number of products from copper sheet metal. The scrap currently sells for $.70 per pound. During November 19x3, the company generated 10,080 pounds of scrap. Also in that month, the company paid $2.62 per pound for copper sheet metal for the production process.

Karen Jean Company records scrap at its realizable value and recognizes no revenues at the time of scrap sales.

REQUIRED:
Prepare the journal entries to record:
a. Transfer of scrap from production to storeroom.
b. Sale of the scrap at $.70.

11–4. Defective Units.   Subia Company incurred the following costs during October 19x7 on job 1818, which consisted of 300 electrical block boxes:

Direct materials	$1,020
Direct labor	1,200
Production overhead	1,920

During the final inspection, 15 boxes were determined to be defective. The exacting specifications of the job suggested the full rework costs should be charged to the job. Direct work costs for the 15 units were:

Direct materials	$175
Direct labor	225

Subia Company uses a production overhead rate of 160 percent for rework costs.

REQUIRED:
Calculate the completed cost per unit for the 300 block boxes.

11–5. Journal Entries for Defects.   Geri Bunker Company produces the Bunker digital clock radio. The cost per unit includes materials of $20, direct labor of $15, and production overhead of $25. During August 19x5, inspection identified 150 clock radios that failed to meet quality standards. Each defective unit can be sold for about one third of the production cost. Defective units are moved from the production area to a storeroom to await disposition. The accounting for the defective units might result in one of the following entries:

a. Defective Goods Inventory	3,000	
Production Overhead—Defective Units	6,000	
Work in Process Inventory		9,000
b. Defective Goods Inventory	3,000	
Work in Process Inventory		3,000
c. Defective Goods Inventory	3,000	
Loss on Defective Units	6,000	
Work in Process Inventory		9,000
d. Defective Goods Inventory	9,000	
Work in Process Inventory		9,000

REQUIRED:
Explain under what circumstances each of the above entries is appropriate. Should an entry not be appropriate, indicate why.

11–6. Job Order Spoilage.   Edwin Manufacturing produces high-quality sportswear. During September 19x6, the company manufactured 3,300 ski parkas in job order JCP–X610 with the resulting costs per unit on the order:

Direct materials	$10
Direct labor	5
Production overhead	6

The production overhead includes an allowance of $1 for spoiled work. During final inspection of job JCP–X610, inspectors determined that 300 parkas were spoiled and could not be reworked. They were sold to a salvage dealer for $2,400. Edwin Manufacturing removes from the cost of spoiled units that portion of production overhead related to the allowance for spoilage.

REQUIRED:

a. Assume that all the spoilage is considered normal and is charged to production overhead. What unit cost would be used for the good parkas on job JCP–X610?

b. Assume that 30 percent of the spoilage is considered normal and is charged to production overhead, and the remainder is due to the exacting requirements for the ski parka. What unit cost would be used for the good parkas on job JCP–X610?

11–7. Inspection Points and Inventories.   Janet Bruns, the controller at the Vugh Company, is considering various inspection points and their prospective impact on the accounting system. She is considering inspection at 50, 75, 90, and 100 percent of completion in terms of conversion costs. The company is currently inspecting at the end of the production process. Ending inventory data for recent months in 19x2 are:

Inventory Date	Completion Proportion:
January 31	72%
February 28	82%
March 31	48%
April 30	78%

REQUIRED:

a. For each inventory date, indicate the *month* in which the units were inspected if the inspection point is
   1. 50 percent of completion.
   2. 75 percent of completion.
   3. 90 percent of completion.
b. What are the advantages and disadvantages of inspecting the units at the 50 percent point?

11–8. Journal Entries for Spoiled Units.   The Austin Plant manufactures radar units with a cost per unit of $25 for materials, $10 for labor, and $7 for overhead. Spoilage for June was 200 units. Inspection is at the completion of production. Spoilage may be sold for 25 percent of cost.

(D. Washburn, Adapted)

REQUIRED:

Prepare the journal entry to record the spoilage, if:

a. All spoilage is normal and is charged to production overhead.
b. All spoilage is abnormal.
c. All spoilage is normal and relates to a specific job.
d. Half of spoilage is normal and the other half is abnormal. Normal spoilage is charged to production overhead.

11–9. Job Order Rework and Spoilage.   The following transactions related to job order 379B of Roush Manufacturing took place during July 19x9:

1. Job order 379B with 900 units required rework of 30 units. Rework costs per unit were rework materials, $7; rework labor, $4; production overhead, applied at 125 percent of rework labor.
2. Upon inspection in the final department of the assembly process, 100 units of job order 379B were deemed spoiled. The per unit costs accumulated on the spoiled units were $12.00 of direct materials, $9.00 of direct labor, and $4.50 of production overhead. The disposal value of the spoiled units is $8 per unit.

REQUIRED:

a. Record the events assuming that the company records rework and spoilage costs as a charge to job order 379B.

b. Record the events assuming that the rework and spoilage costs are to be charged to all production.

11–10. Rework Costs. Eaton Company produces picnic tables that consist of 2-foot by 6-foot pine planks for the table tops and seats and 2-foot square steel tubing for the base. At the end of the production line, the tables are inspected. A table is defective when a plank is severely warped or cracked during production. Defective units are reworked to replace the planks, refinish the surface, and disassemble for shipping. The costs to produce the table are $18.75 for materials, $7.25 for labor, and production overhead of $11.50. Rework costs average $2.25 for materials and $1.80 for labor, and overhead is applied at 150 percent of rework labor.

During July 19x2, the company produced 2,800 tables with 85 found to be defective.

(T. Pratt, Adapted)

REQUIRED:
Prepare the journal entry for:
a. Production of the 2,800 units.
b. Rework of the 85 defective units.

11–11. Journal Entries for Scrap. Shamrock Shirts manufactures children's shirts. During a month's production, the scrap accumulates in the storeroom and is sold for about $0.50 per yard toward the end of the month. The sale of scrap material is treated as other income.

During the month of April 19x2, Shamrock Shirts had 970 yards of scrap material. The scrap was sold for $490.

(M. Nave, Adapted)

REQUIRED:
Prepare the journal entries to record the return of scrap to the storeroom and subsequent sale assuming:
a. The scrap is assigned a value at the time of occurrence.
b. The scrap is assigned a value at the time of sale.

PROBLEMS

11–12. Defective Products. The HPZ Chemical Plant produces many products associated with the by-products of other plants. For example, Duro-Gro is a fertilizer manufactured from petroleum by-products. Another product is Rat-Zap, which is a rodent poison based on petroleum and wood by-products. Both products are packaged in 100-pound paper sacks with plastic linings. Both products are chemically very similar except for the addition of a scent and sawdust to the rodent poison. The scent and the sawdust make the product irresistable to rats. Both products are sold for farm and ranch usage, and both cost $8.75 to produce and are sold for $13 per bag. Buyers pay shipping costs of $0.75 per bag.

On a long packaging run in early July 19x3, the plates to print labels for the two products onto the paper sacks were accidentally switched. During the day, 24,000 bags of the fertilizer and an equal amount of rodent killer were packaged and shipped with the wrong labels. On July 22, the error was discovered by a feed store in Dodge City, Kansas. The feed store owner called to complain that the "Rat killer isn't worth anything. The rats just ignore it." Upon investigation, the nature of the labling error was discovered, and the product was immediately recalled. At this point, 16,000 bags of fertilizer and 20,000 bags of the rodent killer were still in the stores. Repackaging each unit cost $0.10 for materials, $0.19 each for labor, and $0.23 for overhead plus $0.40 for shipping and handling.

(K. Craig, Adapted)

REQUIRED:
Prepare the journal entries for the return of the product and repackaging assuming:
a. None of the farmers noticed the error, all of the products were returned by retailers, and the loss from repackaging is charged to production overhead.

b. The same as part *(a),* except that all of the farmers noticed the switch and claimed in a class action suit that their land was poisoned by the error. Settlement resulted in $625 paid per bag of poison sold as fertilizer. The settlement is considered abnormal and is charged to a loss account.

11–13. Job Order Spoilage and Defects. The Wahoo Woodworking Shop produces wooden game boards by special order. Wahoo uses a job order system with normal spoilage charged to an overhead account. Normal spoilage is 2 percent of good units.

The following two orders were produced on May 13, 19x2:

Order 051301: Nick, Inc., ordered 100 game boards with very exacting specifications. The resulting costs per unit were $1.00 for materials, $2.50 for labor, and $3.13 for overhead, which includes a $0.13 allowance for spoiled boards. On final inspection, it was found that 15 of the boards did not meet specifications and had to be scrapped. To complete the order, 15 more boards were produced. Assume that the spoilage above normal was considered entirely due to the job specifications.

Order 051302: Czevrcheaist, Inc., ordered 100 game boards. The cost of production was $1 for materials, $2.50 for labor, and $3.13 for overhead applied. Production was 102 units with 2 units considered spoiled. Unfortunately, the customer's name was spelled wrong on the boards, and this had to be corrected at a unit cost of $1.25 for labor and 60 percent for applied overhead.

(S. Neves, Adapted)

REQUIRED:
a. For order 051301:
  1. Prepare journal entries for the costs associated with completing the order. Apply overhead at a lower rate on the spoiled units.
  2. Compute the unit cost for the completed boards.
b. For order 051302:
  1. Prepare journal entries for the costs associated with completing the order. Apply overhead at a lower rate on the spoiled units.
  2. Compute the unit cost for the completed boards.

11–14. Job Order Defects and Realizable Values. Linduzi is an offshore electronics company with a contract to supply the United States Navy with 24,000 units of the CR102 sonar device for $400 each. Linduzi has a highly automated plant that normally incurs zero defective units; however, the first 1,000 units produced had a slight design flaw so that they would not meet U.S. Navy performance tests. Because of the nature of the flaw, Linduzi, Ltd., chose to sell the defective units through alternative channels rather than rework them. Much to the displeasure of the U.S. Navy and contrary to U.S. Department of Defense policy, Linduzi sold the defective units to a third party for $198,000.

Twenty-four thousand devices were produced and shipped without flaw. Upon receipt, the Navy impounded the devices and cancelled the CR102 contract. Linduzi filed suit for payment of the CR102 contract and deferred an avionics contract for the U.S. Air Force on which $8.2 million had been advanced. Costs associated with producing the 25,000 sonar units were $2.3 million for materials, $1.0 million for labor, and $3.8 million for overhead.

Linduzi follows the policy of reducing the production cost by the net realizable value of the defective units. Linduzi has been advised by its U.S. attorneys that the sale to the third party is likely to be found technically legal because the technology is well developed and not secret. However, the sale was very displeasing to the U.S. government. Further, the attorneys advised that the deferral of the avionics contract may cause a future problem and subjects the contract to automatic cancellation. Therefore, Linduzi should continue work on the avionics contract and allow the courts to settle the sonar contract.

(C. Blanton, Adapted)

REQUIRED:

Record the journal entries for:

a. Assignment of the production costs to Work in Process.
b. Sale of the defective units to the third party.
c. Delivery of the CR102 units to the U.S. Navy.

11–15. Spoilage and Defective Units.   The Arriba Picante Sauce Plant had a mix-up with its production of mild and hot picante sauce during August 19x7. The production orders were reversed as an oversight. As a result, the labels were reversed on a week's production or 30,000 cases of twelve 24-ounce jars. The production costs of each case were:

Raw materials	$4.80
Packaging materials	1.00
Labor	0.40
Overhead	0.80
Total production cost	$7.00

During early September, 20,000 of the cases were shipped to distributors in the southwestern region at a cost of $.50 per case. These sales generated revenue of $10.20 per case. The remaining 10,000 were in the production warehouse. On September 11, the first retail sales and complaints started. Both the purchasers of mild (which was very hot) and the hot (which was very bland) were upset. The company immediately recalled the product from store shelves. It reimbursed the stores at a rate of $12.50 per case and paid the stores $.50 per case to dispose of the product. Most of the 8,000 cases were donated to charitable institutions such as children's homes and regional food banks for the poor. The final disposition of the 30,000 cases included the following:

	Quantity	*Disposition*	*Per Case*
In production warehouse	10,000	Relabeled	$ 1.50
In distributor's warehouse	8,000	Returned and relabeled	2.35
On retail shelves	8,000	Disposed of	13.00
Sold to consumer or unaccounted for	4,000	Unknown	
Total cases	30,000		

The Arriba company uses process costing with no material difference in the cost to produce mild and hot picante sauce. Work in process at the end of the day is negligible. Management decides that the costs associated with the mislabeling should be recorded as a loss.

REQUIRED:

a. Prepare a journal entry to summarize the incurrence of the production costs for the 30,000 cases and the transfer to the finished goods warehouse.
b. Prepare a journal entry to summarize the sale and shipment of the 20,000 cases to distributors.
c. Record the loss related to relabeling for the 10,000 cases in the production warehouse. Record this as "Loss from mislabeling." Included in the $1.50 are:

Packaging materials	$0.80
Labor	0.40
Overhead	0.30

d. Record the return of the 8,000 cases by the distributors. Shipping costs for the return were $.50 per case, and distributors received $10.20 per case refund plus $.35 per case handling charge. Thus, each distributor had $10.55 per case credited to his or her account. The cost of relabeling and repackaging was $1.50 as in requirement *(c)* above.

e. Record the loss related to retail stores. Treat $10.20 per case as a reduction in revenue. Credit cash for $13 per case issued to each store.

f. Prepare a report summarizing the loss due to the error in the production order.

11–16. Breakage and Defective Service. The Drasett Trucking Co. is licensed to haul goods on an interstate basis. Goods shipped with Drasett Trucking are guaranteed arrival at the designated place within an agreed two-hour period. Penalty for late arrival is 10 percent off the shipping rate. Each day late is 20 percent off shipping rates.

Breakage of shipped goods results in additional cost related to replacing the goods, reshipping them to their destination, and the disruption of the customer's business. Drasett follows the policy of paying replacement costs on all broken goods, refunding shipping charges on damaged shipments, and paying a 30 percent surcharge on the replacement cost for business interruption.

The following proportion of shipments will arrive late:

More than 2 hours but less than 1 day late	3%
1 day late	2%
2 days late	1%

In addition, approximately 1 percent of the goods shipped (in dollar value) will be damaged in shipment.

During October 19x2, Drasett Trucking expects to make 6,400 shipments with total revenues (before spoilage and defective service) of $5,120,000. The average shipment is expected to have a replacement cost of $8,000. The variable costs of shipment are equal to 70 percent of the billed shipping rate. Fixed costs are $900,000 per month.

REQUIRED:

a. Prepare an estimate of the penalties, or revenue lost, from late shipments during October 19x2.

b. Prepare an estimate of the cost of shipments with breakage.

11–17. FIFO Cost of Production Report. You are given the following partially completed cost of production report for the Drandon Company. Find the missing amounts as indicated by the letters *a.* through *l.*

DRANDON COMPANY
Cost of Production Report
For the Period Ending March 31, 19x2

Units to account for:		
Units in process, beginning	2,000	
Units started	*a.*	
Total units to account for		*b.*
Units accounted for:		
Good units completed	2,520	
Normal spoilage	252	
Abnormal spoilage	128	
Units in process, ending	*c.*	
Total units accounted for		3,500
Costs to account for:		
Costs in process, beginning	$26,400	
Costs incurred during month:		
Materials	7,500	
Labor	2,583	
Overhead	12,054	
Total costs to account for		$48,537

DRANDON COMPANY (*cont.*)

Costs Accounted for:
Units in process, beginning	d.	
Costs to complete beginning	e.	
Started and completed	f.	
Normal spoilage	g.	
Total cost of goods completed		$43,408
Abnormal spoilage		h.
Units in process, ending		
Materials	i.	
Conversion	j.	
Total costs accounted for		k.

Additional Calculations:

	Materials	Conversion
Current period costs	$ 7,500	l.
Computation of equivalent units:		
Units completed	2,520	2,520
Normal spoilage	252	227
Abnormal spoilage	128	115
Ending inventory	600	60
Weighted average units	3,500	2,922
Less: Units in process, beginning	(2,000)	(1,200)
FIFO equivalent units	1,500	1,722
Equivalent unit costs	$5.00	$8.50

11–18. Weighted Average Process Costing Spoilage.   The Chisom Plant has the following data for the production of electric motors during July 19x3:

Beginning inventory	
Units	1,500
Completion	40%
Units started	12,000
Good units completed	11,000
Ending inventory	
Units	2,200
Completion	70%
Cost per unit (weighted average method):	
Materials	$6
Conversion	$4
Normal spoilage	1% of units completed
Inspection Point	80%

Materials are added at the beginning of the process.

REQUIRED:
Compute the amount of the following:
a. Normal spoilage in units.
b. Abnormal spoilage in units.
c. Cost of finished motors.
d. Loss from abnormal spoilage.

11–19. FIFO Process Costing Spoilage.   The Dryden Gulch Company has the following data on the processing of wine during the month of October 19x4:

Work in process inventory, October 1		300,000 units
Materials (100% complete)	$ 600,000	
Conversion (40% complete)	72,000	

Completed during the month		670,000 units
Material added	$1,500,000	
Labor added	248,000	
Production overhead	496,000	
Work in Process Inventory, October 31		150,000 units
Materials (100% complete)		
Conversion (20% complete)		

Inspection occurred at the midpoint in the production process and 80,000 units failed to pass inspection. Normal spoilage is 2 percent of good units passing inspection.

REQUIRED:
Prepare a FIFO cost of production report.

11–20. FIFO Process Costing Spoilage.   The Taos Pottery Co. manufactures "greenware" pots that are to be painted and baked by local artists. Although each type of pot is different in some respect, the production process has been standardized for the majority of the work. The company has experienced managed growth and has a reputation for high-quality pots. Normal spoilage is 2 percent of good units, and the inspection point is at 70 percent of completion. You have the following information available for July 19x8:

Beginning inventory:		
Units (30% complete)		12,000
Costs of $36,000 for materials,		
$25,000 for conversion.		
July data:		
Completed		178,000 units
Spoiled		7,500 units
Costs added: Materials	$534,000	
Labor	$756,000	
Overhead	$490,000	
Ending inventory:		
Units (40% complete)		15,000

All materials are added at the beginning of the process.

(J. Brown, Adapted)

REQUIRED:
Prepare a cost of production report for the month using the FIFO method.

11–21. Spoilage in FIFO Process Costing.   Ronnie Beth Company had the following cost and production results for one of its processes during July 19x8:

Work in process inventory, July 1		1,000 units
Materials (100% complete)	$ 40,000	
Conversion costs (40% complete)	22,000	
Units started into the process		47,600 units
Materials added	$154,400	
Conversion costs added	210,650	
Work in process inventory, July 31		8,000 units
Materials (100% complete)		
Conversion cost (25% complete)		
Normal spoilage during the month		350 units
Units completed and transferred out		40,000 units

Materials are added at the beginning of the process, and conversion costs occur uniformly throughout the process. The inspection is at the midpoint of the process. The costs for both abnormal and normal spoilage are separately identified in the cost reporting. The FIFO cost method is used.

REQUIRED:

a. Determine the number of abnormal spoiled units.
b. Calculate the equivalent units and unit costs for material and conversion costs.
c. Prepare the section of the cost of production report that shows the allocation of costs to units completed, units spoiled, and ending work in process.

11–22. Weighted Average Process Costing with Spoilage.   The Crystal Processing Unit has the following data for the month of January 19x9:

Work in process inventory, January 1		120,000
Materials (100% complete)	$ 240,000	
Conversion costs (50% complete)	1,620,000	
Good units completed during the month		131,500
Materials added	$ 420,000	
Labor cost added	1,478,700	
Production overhead added	4,929,000	
Units spoiled		28,500
Work in process inventory, January 31		100,000
Materials (100% complete)		
Conversion (70% complete)		

Materials are added at the beginning of the process. Normal spoilage is 5 percent of units passing inspection, which occurs at the 80 percent completion point. The company uses the weighted average method of process costing.

REQUIRED:
Prepare a cost of production report.

11–23. FIFO Process Cost Report.   The Kansas City Meat Company ages beef in large meat lockers. On March 1, 19x3, the company had a work in process inventory of 10,000 units that was 30 percent complete on aging and had costs of $1,100,000 for materials and $90,000 for conversion. The company completed 35,000 units during the month, but 5,000 were spoiled because they could not pass inspection. Normal spoilage is 10 percent of good units inspected. During the month $4,200,000 in materials and $1,750,000 in conversion costs were added. The inspection point is at 70 percent of completion. The ending inventory consists of 5,000 units that were 90 percent complete on aging.

REQUIRED:
Prepare a FIFO cost of production report.

11–24. Weighted Average Process Costing, and Defective and Spoiled Units.   Myint, Inc., manufactures hydraulic lifts on a continuous basis in two departments: Fabrication and Assembly. Production is started in Fabrication where all materials enter the process. The parts for each lift are placed in large plastic buckets as they leave Fabrication and are transferred to Assembly. Inspection occurs at the end of the process in Assembly.

The company uses the weighted average process costing method for all work in process. Production overhead is applied at a rate of $15 per machine hour in Fabrication and 120 percent of direct labor cost in the Assembly Department. The costs of normal spoilage and rework are not included in production overhead accounts, but these costs are identified separately and are charged to good units completed. The costs of abnormal spoilage are charged as a loss of the period. During October 19x1, the following data are available for the Assembly Department:

Work in process inventory, October 1		1,000 units
Transferred-in costs (100% complete)	$ 20,000	
Conversion costs (50% complete)	10,000	

Units transferred in		8,000
Transferred-in costs	$160,000	
Conversion costs applied	70,400	
Units spoiled (50 units normal; 20 units abnormal)		70
Defective units reworked		30
Rework materials	$ 150	
Rework labor	200	
Work in process inventory, October 31		1,500 units
Transferred in (100% complete)		
Conversion costs (30% complete)		

Production overhead is applied to assembly rework at a rate of 120 percent. The actual Assembly Department production overhead amounted to $39,500.

REQUIRED:
a. Prepare the Assembly Department cost of production report.
b. Make all journal entries for the costs to account for and the costs accounted for as they affect Work in Process—Assembly and Production Overhead Control—Assembly.

11–25. FIFO Process Costing, Normal Shrinkage, Two Months. Global Coatings, Inc., is a supplier of factory-applied coatings for wood, metal, plastic, and paper products. Additionally, the company manufactures high-performance corrosion-control coatings and specialty polymers. One of its products is a coil coating for prepainted appliance manufacturing. By coating coiled steel prior to bending and shaping, appliance producers can reduce production costs.

The ingredients for coil coating are mixed in two departments: Basic Mixture Department and Specialty Mixture Department. The two mixtures are then transferred to the Cooking Department where they are mixed (in a ratio of 4 basic units to 1 specialty unit), cooked, and cured. Because of evaporation in heating, the final coating is normally about 20 percent less than the number of gallons placed in the process. The amount of evaporation is measured before curing, which starts at 70 percent of completion point.

Production and cost data for November and December of 19x4 are as follows:

	November	December
Work in process inventory, Beginning (Units)	16,000	11,000
Transferred in—Basic (100% complete)	$ 153,600	?
Transferred in—Specialty (100% complete)	$ 115,900	?
Conversion costs (50% complete November 1)	$ 68,200	?
Units started during the period		
Transferred in—Basic units	100,000	90,000
Transferred in—Specialty units	25,000	22,500
Transferred in costs—Basic	$2,200,000	$2,781,470
Transferred in costs—Specialty	$ 985,000	$ 900,000
Conversion costs	$1,894,100	$1,635,776
Units completed—Transferred out	104,000	92,000
Work in process, ending (Units)	11,000	12,500
Transferred in—Basic (100% complete)		
Transferred in—Specialty (100% complete)		
Conversion costs (70%, November 30; 40%, December 31)		

Global Coatings uses the FIFO method of process costing.

REQUIRED:
a. Compute the cost of goods completed and ending work in process inventories for November and December.
b. Explain how shrinkage costs in ending inventories affect the process cost computations in the following month.

11–26. FIFO Process Costing, Spoilage, and Varying Inspection Points.   Texas Electric manufactures hand-held solar calculators. Plastic bags, each containing the complete materials for one unit, come from the Fabrication Department at the beginning of the assembly process. The assembly phase of production is accounted for using a FIFO process cost method. All spoilage occurring during assembly is treated as normal spoilage, and the costs of normal spoilage are charged to the calculators clearing the inspection point.

The work in process at the start of the week beginning April 7, 19x8, consisted of 1,500 calculators 60 percent complete in assembly conversion costs. The beginning Work in Process account included $4,500 for transferred-in costs and $2,700 for conversion costs. During the week, 10,000 calculators were started in assembly. Also during the week, $31,000 in costs were transferred in and $27,600 of conversion costs were incurred.

The work in process at the end of the week consisted of 2,000 calculators 40 percent complete in assembly conversion costs. Product transfer records indicated that 9,300 calculators were completed and transferred to finished goods.

REQUIRED:
Calculate the cost of goods completed and the cost of ending inventory for each of the following independent situations (where necessary, round unit costs to four decimal places):
a. Inspection for spoilage takes place at the 30 percent point in the assembly. Assume that the spoilage charge related to beginning inventory amounts to $468.
b. Inspection for spoilage takes place at the 50 percent point in the assembly. Assume that the spoilage charge related to beginning inventory amounts to $540.
c. Inspection for spoilage takes place at the end of the assembly.

EXTENDED APPLICATIONS

11–27. Hybrid System, Service Spoilage.   The Goliath Moving and Storage Company provides commercial and residential moving of furniture, goods, and equipment. The unit of measure for movement is in ton-miles (the tonnage times the miles moved); the measure for packing and unpacking is in tons. For example, it is 641 miles from Indianapolis, Indiana, to Richmond, Virginia. The movement of 2 tons this distance is 2 times 641 miles or 1,282 ton-miles. Because of the size of the trucks, each one carries several shipments with wooden partitions placed between each shipment. Customers are given an approximation of the time for pickup and delivery of the goods. Goliath prices its moves to average $1 per ton-mile plus $60 per ton to pack and unpack. Goliath gives each customer a guaranteed date for delivery after which a reduction in price of $20 per ton per day late is given. The expected costs for providing these services are:

| | Per Ton | | Per Ton-Mile |
	Packing	Unpacking	Transit
Materials	$12.00	$ 0.00	$0.03
Labor	10.00	10.00	0.05
Overhead	5.00	5.00	0.12
	$27.00	$15.00	$0.20

The drivers average 50 miles per hour with a 12-ton load or 600 ton-miles per hour. The transit overhead is applied at a rate of $0.12 per actual ton-miles driven. The overhead charges include a $3 per ton and a $0.02 per ton-mile normal breakage allowance. Most damaged goods are discovered upon unpacking. Actual costs above the allowance amount are charged to a loss account.

Goliath Moving uses a hybrid system with the packing and unpacking treated as a job and transit costs accounted for with a process costing system. The transit costs are averaged among all jobs. For packing, the actual cost of materials and labor is used. For unpacking, the actual cost of labor is used. For both packing and unpacking, overhead is applied at a 50 percent rate. The actual materials and labor for transit, along with applied overhead, are averaged for the month and applied to individual contracts.

On August 1, 19x8, 1,600 tons related to 600 contracts were in transit with accumulated packing materials of $19,360 and labor of $16,400, accumulated transit costs of $194,880, and accumulated ton-miles of 960,000.

During August, 804 contracts were started with 2,610 tons. A total of 2,920,400 ton-miles was driven on contracts completed during the month. The following costs were incurred during the month:

	Packing	Transit	Unpacking
Materials (Actual)	$31,581	$ 63,986	
Labor (Actual)	26,361	125,686	$37,279
Overhead (Applied)	13,181	274,224	18,640
Total	$71,123	$463,896	$55,919

During the month, a total of 46,000 pounds of goods was damaged and replaced for customers at a cost of $98,802. Also, 140 tons were delivered an average of three days late. The ending contracts in transit included 406 tons on 160 contracts with a total of 324,800 ton-miles completed. The accumulated packing costs for the ending goods in transit were $11,064.

REQUIRED:
a. Compute an estimate of the total revenue earned during August 19x8 operations. Prorate the $60 revenue per ton packing/unpacking as 65 percent packing and 35 percent unpacking. Account for the late penalty.
b. Compute the amount of the normal and abnormal spoilage. Base your estimate on contracts completed.
c. What was the average transit cost per actual ton-mile driven?
d. What was the total cost of service for goods in transit at the end of August?
e. Compute the following costs for all completed contracts for the month:
   1. Packing   2. Transit   3. Unpacking

11–28. Job Order Spoilage and Defective Units. The Andover Glass Products Company produces seasonal ornaments and gift items. Because each product is different, a job order costing system is used. One product is a selection of glass ornaments for the holiday season. The cost per carton (12 boxes of 12 each) includes direct materials of $2.00, direct labor of $1.50, and overhead of $3.50. The overhead includes $0.25 for normal spoilage. At the end of the production process, each bulb is carefully inspected for poor shape or cracks. The bulbs are thin glass, and 4 percent spoilage is expected with normal spoilage charged to overhead and abnormal spoilage charged to a loss account. The bulbs may be customized for various companies to give to their valued customers. The cost of customizing a carton of bulbs is $0.50 for materials, $3 for labor, and $1 for overhead. Customizing is very labor intensive, and 5 percent breakage is expected. The overhead charge includes $0.40 for normal spoilage. Both customized and regular spoiled cartons are salvaged at a cost of $0.35 with $1.00 in usable materials received.

During the month of July 19x4 the company had a total output of 50,000 cartons of ornamental bulbs. The spoilage for the month totaled 4,000 cartons of ornaments. Customers requested customizing on 4,600 cartons of which 300 were spoiled. In addition, one order for 200 cartons from Bullock's Department Store had a major error: the store's name was mis-spelled. The cost per carton to correct the defect was $1 for labor and $1 for overhead to acid wash all the paint off all the bulbs, which were then customized and shipped.

(B. McDonald, Adapted)

REQUIRED:
Prepare journal entries for the following:
a. Production costs for the 50,000 cartons of regular production and discovery of the 4,000 cartons of spoilage.
b. Transfer of 41,400 cartons to finished goods, 4,600 cartons to customizing.
c. Transfer of an additional 300 cartons from finished goods to customizing to cover the spoiled units.

d. Customizing costs for 4,600 cartons.
    e. Transfer of 4,400 cartons from customizing to finished goods.
    f. Incurrence of rework costs on the Bullock order.
    g. Incurrence of the recustomizing costs on the Bullock order and transfer of the order to finished goods.

11–29. Accounting for Missing Scrap and Spoilage. The Carolina Cola Plant cans store-named sodas and colas for regional grocery chains. The soda is in aluminum cans, which are printed on sheet aluminum, cut, molded, filled, capped, and sealed under pressure. The cutting and capping processes generate scrap aluminum that should average 4 percent of the input sheet. Aluminum sheet comes in a 10,560-foot roll that weighs 17,952 pounds. The roll is fed continuously into the canning line. Scrap aluminum can be sold for an average of $.36 per pound, but the price varies from week to week. The output unit of measure is a case of canned cola with twenty-four 12-ounce cans. Each case requires the following estimated costs:

Materials:	*Input*	*Cost*
Aluminum, linear feet	0.9	$1.22403
Cola, fluid ounces	292	0.87600
Labor hours	0.03	0.13500
Overhead (applied on materials cost)		0.21000
Total production costs		$2.44503

On a normal basis, 2 percent of the cans of cola are spoiled because the can is misprinted, misshapen, or fails to seal properly. These spoiled cans are emptied and the aluminum is salvaged. The overhead applied contains a $0.05 charge for normal spoilage. Carolina Canning charges all spoilage to overhead. Revenue from the sale of scrap aluminum is recorded at the time of sale as a credit to Other Income. The cola is priced to sell at $2.90 per case.

    John Crawford, the plant manager, is concerned about the recent cost per case of good output. The total of actual prime cost and applied overhead is divided by good units produced. Mr. Crawford suspects that some of the scrap is stolen. Further, he suspects that some of the coils of aluminum are stopped short and the remaining portion is unaccounted for. Further, because the pounds of scrap are recorded manually at the end of each shift, some of the scrap may not be recorded.

    As the new internal auditor, you have been asked to review the plant's operating data for discrepancies. For the five weeks ending July 7, 19x9, you collect the following operating data from the computer files:

Week	1	2	3	4	5
Good cases	457,092	380,478	523,670	50,294	374,567
Cost per case	$2.62211	$2.74776	$2.84302	$2.92236	$2.87697
Alum. coils used	44.4	37.9	52.5	5.1	36.7
Coil price	$13,952	$14,362	$15,183	$15,593	$16,003
Cola (1,000 oz.)	136,907	117,933	162,364	15,808	114,397
Cola cost per 1,000 oz.	$3.02	$3.01	$2.99	$3.00	$3.01
Spoiled cases	11,389	19,988	31,236	3,168	13,293
Scrap, pounds	45,779	54,235	79,870	7,958	43,759
Scrap revenues	$2,268	$18,704	$1,699	$819	$10,201
Scrap price	$0.34	$0.35	$0.37	$0.38	$0.39

The beginning inventory of scrap was 18,200 pounds, and the ending inventory was 11,640 pounds.

REQUIRED:
    a. Estimate the pounds of recorded scrap that are unaccounted for by the sales and change in inventory. What is the value of the missing scrap in terms of the most recent price?
    b. While in the cafeteria, you overhear one of the lift operators talking about his younger brother's concern regarding the night shift canning supervisor. The supervisor will declare

spoiled almost any case of cola and yell at the workers for messing them up. The brother can see no difference between the good cases and the cases supposedly spoiled. Estimate the amount of spoilage above the normal level for each week. At the "expected" cost, what is the total cost of the abnormal spoilage?

c. While examining the data, you notice that the use of cola fluid seems high given the good output and spoiled units. Because liquid cola without a container is worthless, you develop a theory that either some of the "good" production is unaccounted for or some of the spoilage is not recorded. There is no evidence that any unusual spillage of liquid has occurred.

1. Using the output and the fluid usage, estimate the amount of unrecorded output for each week.

2. Assuming that all of the unrecorded output is spoilage, compute the total value of the scrap aluminum missing using the most recent price.

3. Assuming that all of the unrecorded output is good output, compute the total value of the lost revenues.

d. You find that there is currently one security guard at the plant. The guard works an unusual shift (8 P.M. to 4 A.M.) because this is the time during which young hooligans have vandalized company trucks in the past. A security firm estimates that it will take surveillance cameras plus three guards around the clock to secure the plant against the theft discovered in parts (a) through (c). It will cost an estimated $7,000 per week to lease equipment and guards. Recommended changes in scheduling, warehouse personnel, and procedures will cost Carolina Cola $2,200 per week in additional overhead. The security company estimates that 90 percent of the theft will be deterred by this program. The existing guard, who costs $300 per week, would be hired by the security company but placed at a different plant. Compute the average value per week of this proposed program.

11–30. Errors in Normal Spoilage in Two Departments, Weighted Average Method.   Resler Division is a segment of RYCR, Inc. The division prides itself on being a low-cost, high-quality specialized producer in the defense contracting business. Its products fall generally into four basic categories: military night vision, weapons delivery, military power systems, and applied optics. One product line within the applied optics category is precision metal mirrors that range in size from $\frac{1}{4}$ inch to 40 inches in diameter. The primary market for this product is target/fire control systems for tanks and missiles. (Precision metal is used rather than glass or plastic because glass mirrors shatter and plastic warps too easily in combat.)

The company has a contract to produce 10,000 units of a small metal mirror over a three-month period. The production process involves the Machining Department, where the metal is cut and shaped to specifications, and the Grinding Department, where the mirror surface is prepared and polished. Materials are added at the beginning of the Machining Department. Grinding compounds are added in the Grinding Department, but their costs are included in production overhead. Inspection occurs at the end of each department and at that time normal and abnormal spoilage is determined. The costs of normal spoilage are charged to good units completed in that department and are thus a reimbursable cost under the contract. Abnormal spoilage is a loss of the period. Resler uses the weighted average method of process costing for the metal mirrors.

The division records indicate the following information for May 19x2:

	Machining	Grinding
Work in process, May 1	1,000	800
Materials (100% complete)	$40,000	—
Transferred in (100% complete)	—	$44,000
Conversion costs	7,500	7,000
Conversion is 50% complete for Machining and 25% complete for Grinding		
Units started during the period	8,000	6,660
Materials costs added	$320,000	—

	Machining	*Grinding*
Direct labor added	$79,000	$ 33,900
Production overhead added	$39,500	$203,400
Units transferred out during the period	6,660	5,990
Spoilage: Normal	240	200
Abnormal	100	70
Work in process, May 31	2,000	1,200
Materials	100% complete	
Transferred in costs		100% complete
Conversion	70% complete	60% complete

After the May cost of production report was prepared, the internal auditors reviewed the inspection data for each department. They determined that normal spoilage should have been 210 units in the Machining Department. The Defense Contract Audit Agency (DCAA) performed an overhead audit during the same month. DCAA agreed with the internal audit finding and further questioned how inspectors distinguished between normal and abnormal spoilage in the Grinding Department. DCAA's audit report stated that normal spoilage for the Grinding Department should be only 160 units with the difference as additional abnormal spoilage.

REQUIRED:

a. Prepare the cost of production report for the two departments for May 19x2 before any adjustments have been made.

b. Prepare the journal entries for the two departments that:
1. Record the cost of units transferred out during the month.
2. Record the abnormal spoilage.

c. Prepare a corrected cost of production report that reflects the changes required by the internal audit and by DCAA.

d. Prepare an adjusting entry or entries that reflect the changes required by the internal audit and by DCAA.

Planning and Control
of Activities

CHAPTER

12

Standard Costs for Materials and Labor

◼

THE STANDARD COST OPTION

Dress Shirts Unlimited is a specialty manufacturer of an unlabeled quality long-sleeve dress shirt. An individual store can order according to its own specifications in lots of a dozen each, with its own label attached to each shirt. The company advertises under the motto "Go custom on your shirts." For Dress Shirts Unlimited, custom-made means that a pre-existing pattern is altered to fit the specifications of the order. The shirts are well known for their special features and flattering fit.

The basic selling point for the shirts is fit. If the size that's right for a man's frame is aways a tad tight in the neck, he will appreciate a collar being cut to the quarter-inch. Left cuffs (or, if ordered, right cuffs) are slightly wider to accommodate a wristwatch. Sleeve length is cut to the half-inch. Because they fit better, the shirts often last longer. Friction that wears out the collar or splits the underarm has been eliminated.

There are also cosmetic pluses: a higher collar front can hide neck wrinkles, and a medium-tapered waist flatters a skinny shape. Options that come as standard, if ordered, are such things as pocketless shirts or French cuffs. Also, there is a wide selection of fabric.

Dress Shirts Unlimited uses a standard cost system. Standards exist for each option in each of the sizes. When an order arrives, its specifics are entered into the computer and a standard cost sheet is generated for that lot. Actual quantities and time can be tracked as the order is processed.

◼

LEARNING OBJECTIVES

After studying this chapter, you should be able to:

1. Describe the characteristics of a standard cost system.
2. Explain the importance of a standard cost sheet to accounting procedures of a standard cost system.
3. Calculate material price and quantity variances for individual categories of material.
4. Prepare journal entries for purchasing and issuing materials using a standard cost system.
5. Calculate labor rate and efficiency variances.
6. Prepare journal entries that distribute direct labor costs to work in process under a standard cost system.
7. Explain the interrelationships that exist among material and labor variances.

STANDARD COST SYSTEMS

Standard cost systems are appropriate in production environments that have standardized products, services, or operations. Within this context, we define a standard cost, identify the types of standard, and show advantages.

Terms Defined

A **standard cost** for a product consists of a **price standard** (price for materials, rate for labor) and a **quantity standard** (quantity for materials, time for labor). Quantity identifies a material or task or activity, and price represents how much it should cost. The level of price and quantity standards is influenced by the type of management, corporate philosophy, size and structure of the organization, and actual or desired state of efficiency. In smaller organizations, the personal opinions of individual managers can significantly affect the standards set. The production environment in any size organization also has an impact. Exhibit 12–1 shows the important factors of the production environment.

In a general sense, a standard is a target that shows what is planned or expected (some would call it a *should cost*.) Setting (and later revising) standards requires knowledge of (1) the bases and criteria (engineering studies, past performance, etc.) for setting a standard, (2) the period for which the standard will remain in effect, (3) the levels of performance, and (4) the conditions reflected by the standard. The definition of acceptable efficiency is important to all of these considerations so that actual performance can be evaluated in terms of the standards.

Conditions Requisite for Standard Costs

Standard costs can be used with both job order and process cost systems. However, a cost-effective and efficient system requires a level of activity, standardization, and controllability. A sufficiently high level of activity is needed to make the cost of implementing standard costs and maintaining and updating standards worthwhile.

Standardization is essential. Either the products or each operation must be standardized regardless of the products passing through the operation.[1] Standard products are those that are essentially similar. Small differences, such as color or labeling, can exist, but the products are basically the same. Although a standard product is made using standardized operations, many nonstandard products are produced by standardized operations. For example, a print shop has standard operations, but each customer requests the operations needed for the job. Steel plates are made by stan-

---

[1] Stanley B. Henrici, *Standard Costs of Manufacturing* (New York: McGraw-Hill, 1947), p. 47.

EXHIBIT 12–1   Production Environment Factors Important to Setting Price and Quantity Standards

Product design	Materials (identified on bill of materials)
	Batch size
	Yield factors
	Container size or packaging
	Handling care
	Use of product
Production process	Required operations
	Sequence of operations
	Machines and tools
	Locations
Work methods	How operations are to be performed
	Workspace required
	Flow of operations
	Skills required
	Times required
	Mechanical activity
	Operator activity
Tools and equipment	List of tools and equipment used in each operation
Plant layout	Locations of tools and equipment
	Locations of materials and supplies
	Material-handling equipment
	Location of services (utilities)
	Man-machine relationships
Human factors	Personal time requirements
	Fatigue factors
	Idle time

dardized operations. The ingot is prepared according to the customer's metallurgical specifications. The rolling mill shapes the ingot into the size and thickness required. Each pass through the rollers reduces the thickness by a given amount. Customer specifications for the final product determine how many passes through the rollers an operator will make. Manufacture of a prefabricated home is another example of standardized operations. Modular construction permits a different configuration for each home, but the building components are standardized modules.

Controllability is also important. Management must control either a significant number of the cost elements or quantity factors that would comprise the standard cost. Controllability implies the assignment of responsibility for variances to specific managers and that the impact on costs from changes in performance variables can be isolated. Without controllability, a standard cost system is meaningless.

Types of Standards

Standard costs for material and labor are related to both time and level of performance.

Time Period.   When referring to time period, standards should be current, that is, represent current operations. These standards are based on prices, quantities, and efficient operations expected during the forthcoming period. Only significant changes in prices or operations result in revisions to the standards before year end. Variances identify current inefficiencies. Current standards should be reviewed at regular intervals, at least annually, and revised as necessary.

Level of Performance.   Ideal, currently attainable, and loose or lax are the three standards that companies have used for level of performance. The level selected influences workers' motivations because it reflects management's attitudes toward standards and the expectations as to what standard costs should do.

Performance lies on a continuum, ideal toward one extreme and loose or lax toward the other. Currently attainable is not ideal but is somewhat to the left of midpoint. This is graphically portrayed as:

Ideal   Currently   Loose or Lax
          Attainable

Ideal standard.   An **ideal standard** also goes by other names: *perfection, maximum,* or *theoretical standard*. It allows for no work interruptions (machine breakdowns, for example) and calls for a level of effort that is achieved only by the most skilled and experienced workers operating at peak efficiency 100 percent of the time. Besides motivation, cost reduction is one goal sought by managers favoring this kind of standard.

Because an ideal standard is attained only under the best circumstances, it is considered unattainable and therefore unrealistic. Motivation is based on both challenges and rewards for achievement. Although the ideal standard represents a challenge, the variances are always highly unfavorable, which will ultimately result in a negative work environment. Workers who never reach the goal become demoralized and unmotivated.

From an informational point of view, variances from an ideal standard have little meaning because they contain both controllable and uncontrollable inefficiencies. As a result, isolating cause and responsibility for variances is difficult, if not impossible. This, coupled with traditionally large variances, leads to ineffective control.

Currently attainable standard.   **Currently attainable standards** are sometimes called *practical standards*. They represent the cost that should be incurred under forthcoming efficient operating conditions. Such standards do not include allowances for unacceptable inefficiency (excessive waste, spoilage, and downtime, for instance). Acceptable inefficiencies are those that management considers impractical to eliminate at the present time. Although the cost and quantity standards include an allowance for acceptable inefficiency, they aim for a high level of efficiency that the majority of the workers are capable of accomplishing. The best motivated workers like to have clear-cut objectives before them, but those objectives must be attainable.

Variances from the standard costs are deviations that fall outside the acceptable inefficiencies and signal the need for management attention. Both favorable and unfavorable variances can occur, something not possible with ideal standards. Workers can achieve a goal and feel a sense of accomplishment. Psychologically, managers and workers like these standards better than ideal standards. Consequently, cost control is more effective.

Currently attainable standards can serve multiple purposes. They are useful for cash planning, inventory and production planning, inventory valuation, and a number of decisions faced by managers. The reasons the standards are useful are that (1) *currently* means a time-period standard recognizing current operations and (2) *attainable* refers to the ability of most workers to meet or better the standard. We assume currently attainable standards in this text.

Loose or lax standard.   A **loose or lax standard** (also called *past performance standard*) generally refers to an average of previous actual costs. It does not establish what should be. These standards contain all of the inefficiencies of the past and, therefore, do not represent reasonable targets or benchmarks. Variances will be favorable because these standards are easy to achieve. Because loose or lax really are not standards at all, they have little value for an ongoing standard cost system.

Advantages of Standard Costs

Standard costs have many advantages, depending on the sophistication of the system and on how well individual managers accept them. Early interest in standard costs centered only on cost control. Although that continues as the main purpose, additional benefits have been realized. This section covers five major advantages of standard costs.

Cost Control.   **Cost control** is achieved by comparing actual performance with the standard performance, analyzing variances to identify controllable causes, and taking action to eliminate inefficient performance in the future. Costs can change for at least four reasons: changes (1) in price levels, (2) in efficiency, (3) in volume, and (4) in mix. A good standard cost system will separate these causes of change and identify responsibility and indicate magnitude for each.

The use of standard costs makes **management by exception** possible. This simplification means less bulk for managers to study and less clutter on which to make decisions about corrective action. In other words, if costs remain within an acceptable range of standard, no management attention is needed. If costs fall outside this range, the matter is highlighted as an exception. By establishing a standard cost system and focusing only on situations that need investigation, management has an effective tool for controlling activities.

Recordkeeping Costs.   Standard costs can result in a significant savings in record-keeping costs. For example, with an actual cost system, each item issued from stores or each product transferred from work in process to finished goods must be costed using specific identification, FIFO, LIFO, or some average cost method. With thousands of different materials and even a tenth of that number in final products, this can be an enormous task. With a standard cost system, only quantities need be recorded because costs are determined by multiplying quantities by standard costs.

The savings in recordkeeping costs are partially offset by the added cost of tablishing and revising standards. In the long run, however, the savings in record-keeping costs are usually much greater than any increased costs. Therefore, the primary benefit is that material inventories are always stated at standard regardless of actual costs and quantities.

Cost Reduction.   **Cost reduction** is as simple as decreasing the costs of operations through improved methods and procedures, better selection of resources (people and materials), or capital investments. A standard cost system aids in reducing costs in several ways. When a system is first established, a thorough analysis of operations is made to uncover inefficiencies that can be eliminated. Examples of such inefficiencies include material waste and scrap, spoilage and defective units, lost machine time, and idle worker time. When variances focus on out-of-control situations, an organization can institute changes that reduce costs. A standard cost system also creates an environment of cost reduction. It administers a psychological injection that makes people cost conscious, always looking for ways to improve operations and products.

Inventory Valuation. Standard costs improve inventory valuation by providing more rational costs. A standard cost system records the same costs for physically identical units of materials and products; an actual cost system can record different costs for physically identical units. Differences between the two costs are inefficiencies that are conceptually period costs when incurred. They should not be capitalized and deferred in inventory values.

Decision-Making. Standard costs are useful in decision-making if material and labor costs are currently attainable. Examples of decisions for which standard costs can be used are regular and special order pricing; make or buy, sell or process further decisions; setting transfer prices; cash planning; and inventory and production control.

STANDARD COST SHEET AND INVENTORIES

Once standards have been set for the various categories of direct materials used, the direct labor operations employed, and the departmental production overhead costs to support operations identified, the costs are compiled on a **standard cost sheet** (also called a *standard cost card*). In practice, a standard cost sheet for an individual product can be a lengthy form containing considerable detail. Stripped to its barest essentials, a standard cost sheet for Dress Shirts Unlimited shows standard quantities and standard prices needed to produce one dozen shirts categorized by the product number MFHP3400.

Standard Cost Sheet

Direct materials:		
Fabric—25 yards at $3.10	$77.50	
Buttons—120 at $0.30	36.00	$113.50
Direct labor—3.5 hours at $4.80		16.80
Production overhead—3.5 hours at $4.40		15.40
Standard cost per dozen		$145.70

Perfection is not expected because only 24 yards of fabric and 108 buttons are needed for one dozen shirts. The extra amounts are allowances made to cover anticipated waste, scrap, and spoilage. Similar allowances are also made for overtime, rework, and similar things in establishing direct labor costs.

Preparation of a standard cost sheet for a product greatly facilitates the accounting for costs as products flow from Work in Process Inventory to Finished Goods and later to Cost of Goods Sold. Exhibit 12–2 is a Work in Process Inventory account in T-account form with all of the inflows and outflows of costs stated in terms of standard costs. The beginning inventory will be the standard cost associated with the stage of completion of the beginning inventory. Current production costs consist of direct materials, direct labor, and the applied production overhead, all based on the standard cost sheets. During the period, the standard costs of units completed are transferred to Finished Goods Inventory, leaving an ending balance that represents the standard cost associated with the stage of completion for those units in the ending inventory.

The standard cost sheet gives the total unit cost that will be attached to any completed unit of a given product. This unit cost is transferred to Finished Goods Inventory as the cost of goods manufactured and later to Cost of Goods Sold as the unit cost of products sold.

In the Dress Shirts Unlimited case, assume that the company had beginning work in process inventory of 90 dozen shirts number MFHP3400, with all their material content and 20 percent of the labor and overhead content. Another 1,200 dozen were

EXHIBIT 12–2   **Work in Process Inventory Account In a Standard Cost System**

Work in Process Inventory

Beginning balance: Standard costs of units in process at given stage of completion	Cost of goods manufactured for the period: Units completed multiplied by standard cost per unit of each product
Current production costs:	
Direct materials—Standard quantities allowed for production multiplied by the standard price	
Direct labor—Standard hours allowed for production multiplied by the standard labor rates	
Applied production overhead—Standard volume allowed (direct labor hours or machine hours, for example) multiplied by appropriate standard overhead rate	
Ending balance: Standard costs of units in process at given stage of completion	

started in production during the month. Ending inventory consisted of 100 dozen partially completed shirts that had the material but were only 50 percent complete for labor and overhead. In summary, the flow of dollars for work in process inventory is:

```
Beginning inventory:
   Direct material—90 dozen × 100% × $113.50  = $ 10,215.00
   Direct labor—90 dozen × 20% × $16.80       =        302.40
   Overhead—90 dozen × 20% × $15.40           =        277.20
                                                 $ 10,794.60

Current production costs:
   Direct material—1,200 dozen × $113.50              = $136,200.00
   Direct labor—1,222* equivalent dozen × $16.80  =   20,529.60
   Overhead—1,222 equivalent dozen × $15.40       =   18,818.80
                                                        $175,548.40
Total costs in process during the month                 $186,343.00

Less: Ending inventory
   Direct material—100 dozen × $113.50        = $ 11,350.00
   Direct labor—100 dozen × 50% × $16.80     =       840.00
   Overhead—100 dozen × 50% × $15.40         =       770.00
                                                 $ 12,960.00

Equals: cost of goods manufactured
   (1,190 units × $145.70)                    = $173,383.00
```

> * Completed 1,190 units plus ending inventory of 100 × 50% less beginning inventory of 90 × 20% = 18, or a total of 1,222.

All of this information is known without any details of the actual quantities used, the actual hours worked, and the actual dollars paid for material and labor. Only the standard cost sheet, the quantities worked on, and the stage of completion are needed.

STANDARDS FOR MATERIALS

Variances are calculated for both price and quantity factors by comparing actual performance with the standards established for price and quantity. These variances are called *material price variance* and *material quantity variance*.

**Material Price
Variance**

Setting the Price Standard.   The purchase price is usually the largest cost consideration in the price standard, but even that is influenced by the quantity purchased. Therefore, the standard price will be a function of a normal purchase quantity (i.e., economic order quantity or minimum buys) adjusted for quantity and trade discounts.

In addition to purchase price, other factors to consider include cash discounts, the cost of transportation in, and the cost of insurance for materials in transit. Some companies will also include a material-related cost factor in the total unit cost.

Why be concerned about identifying the various components that could affect standard price? When variances occur, we look to the changes in the components to identify the causes of the variations.

Once a determination is made as to which costs to include in the standard price, the next step is to establish amounts. Several approaches are used, including the use of (1) statistical forecasting, (2) prices agreed upon in long-term contracts or purchase commitments, (3) a weighted average of purchase prices on the most recent purchases, or (4) estimates based upon knowledge and experience in the particular type of business.

Calculating a Price Variance.   Calculating a material price variance requires holding the quantity factor constant while varying the price factor. We use the actual price paid for the actual quantity purchased and then the standard price for the same quantity. Therefore, the price variance is a difference calculated as:

$$
\begin{array}{ll}
 & \text{Actual price} \times \text{Actual quantity purchased} \\
- & \text{Standard price} \times \text{Actual quantity purchased} \\
\hline
= & \text{Material price variance}
\end{array}
$$

Algebraically, this can be reduced to (Actual price − Standard price) × Actual quantity purchased. The following symbols will be used in our discussion in lieu of writing the words:

$$
\begin{array}{rl}
AP &= \text{Actual price} \\
SP &= \text{Standard price} \\
AQP &= \text{Actual quantity purchased} \\
MPV &= \text{Material price variance}
\end{array}
$$

The typical journal entry for recording material purchases debits Material Inventory and credits Accounts Payable. The debit is the standard price times the actual quantity purchased. That is, all quantities in materials inventory are carried at standard prices. Accounts Payable is credited for the actual price paid times the actual quantity purchased. Any difference between the actual price and standard price results in a material price variance. All favorable variances are recorded as credits to variance accounts (because favorable variances reflect positive operating activities similar to earning of income), and all unfavorable variances are recorded as debits to variance accounts (because unfavorable variances represent negative activities similar to incurring expenses).

Dress Shirts Unlimited purchased during the current month 32,500 yards of fabric at $3.12 per yard (or $101,400) and 156,000 buttons at $0.28 each (or $43,680). If the materials had been purchased at standard prices, the costs would be:

Fabric:	$3.10 × 32,500 yards =	$100,750
Buttons:	$0.30 × 156,000 =	46,800

The data necessary to record this transaction are summarized as:

Material	AP × AQP	SP × AQP	(AP − SP) × AQP	
Fabric	$101,400	$100,750	$ 650	Unfavorable
Buttons	43,680	46,800	3,120	Favorable
	$145,080	$147,550	$2,470	Favorable

The actual journal entry to record the purchases is:

Materials Inventory	$147,550	
Material Price Variance		$ 2,470
Accounts Payable		145,080

The cost flow of actual and standard costs through the accounts would appear as follows:

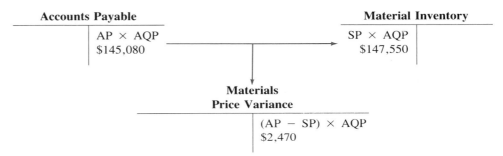

Reasons for Price Variances.   There are innumerable possibilities to explain why a variance occurs. Exhibit 12–3 summarizes the common sources of the material price variance. Notice that the examples listed pertain primarily to those items making up purchase prices, cash discounts, insurance, and transportation in. Outdated standards (those not adequately reviewed and revised as circumstances dictate) are also a source of variances.

EXHIBIT 12–3   Some Causes of Material Price Variances

Unfavorable	*Favorable*
Random fluctuations in market prices	Random fluctuations in market prices
Unexpected price inflation	Fortunate buy
Material substitutions	Material substitutions
Market shortages of materials resulting in premium prices	Excess materials on market resulting in price decreases
Purchasing from suppliers other than those offering the terms used in the standard	Purchasing from suppliers other than those offering the terms used in the standard
Changes in production schedule that result in rush orders or additional materials	Purchasing lower-quality materials at a lower price
Purchasing higher-quality materials at a higher price	Unusual discount due to quantity purchased
Purchasing in nonstandard or uneconomical quantities	Changes in mode of transportation
Failure to take cash discounts	Changing suppliers located at shorter distances that have lower costs for transportation
Changes in mode of transportation	
Changing suppliers located at greater distances that have higher costs for transportation	

Some accountants suggest that price variances are probably more a measure of forecasting ability than a failure to buy at predetermined prices. When this is true, the emphasis on variance analysis may be directed toward quantities rather than price.

Responsibility for Price Variances.   The purchasing department is usually charged with the responsibility for price variances. Once the standard price is set, purchasing must place orders with vendors consistent with the standard prices. Differences between actual and standard are then assumed to be controllable by purchasing. That point is arguable, but we will not pursue it here.

There are at least two situations in which production departments should be charged with the responsibility for price variances: (1) if production has requested a specific brand name for a material rather than identifying specifications and having purchasing buy by specification and (2) if a rush order is necessary due to production activities. An example of the latter case is a change in production scheduling that results in products coming on line immediately but the necessary materials are not available in the storeroom. Another example involves machinery that is improperly adjusted and causes excessive material waste and scrap, necessitating a rush order for more materials to meet production schedules.

Material Quantity Variance

Setting the Quantity Standard.   The quantity portion of a material standard cost is based primarily on engineering specifications, blueprints, and bills of material that designate the quality, size, thickness, weight, and any other significant factors necessary for a good unit of final product. Included also is an allowance for normal acceptable waste, scrap, shrinkage, and spoilage that can occur during production. The factors used in determining the quantity standard are those that will be examined when variances are investigated.

Calculating a Quantity Variance.   Calculating a material quantity variance requires holding the price factor constant while varying the quantities. Remember, the materials were entered into inventory at the standard price, and that price is used in calculating the material quantity variance. The quantities of concern are actual quantities used and standard quantities allowed. The calculation of a material quantity variance is the following difference:

$$
\begin{array}{rl}
 & \text{Standard price} \times \text{Actual quantity used} \\
- & \underline{\text{Standard price} \times \text{Standard quantity allowed}} \\
= & \text{Material quantity variance}
\end{array}
$$

A short-cut formula for a material quantity variance is:

Standard price × (Actual quantity used − Standard quantity allowed)

The term *standard quantity allowed* is really part of a longer expression: *the standard quantity allowed for actual units produced*. The standard quantity allowed is found by identifying the units completed during the period and the stage of completion for partially completed units and multiplying these units by the material quantity specified in the standard cost sheet for the completed product or for that stage of completion.

At this point, three additional symbols are added to the presentation:

$$
\begin{array}{rl}
\text{AQU} = & \text{Actual quantity used} \\
\text{SQ} = & \text{Standard quantity allowed} \\
\text{MQV} = & \text{Material quantity variance}
\end{array}
$$

Other names are also used for material quality variance. The common ones are *material usage* (or *use*) *variance* and *material efficiency variance*. We will use the term *material quantity variance*.

We withdraw materials from Material Inventory at the standard price (because that is how the materials were originally recorded in Material Inventory) times the actual quantity used (issued). The debit to Work in Process Inventory is the standard price times the standard quantity allowed. Any difference between the actual quantity issued and the standard quantity allowed becomes a quantity variance. An unfavorable variance is a debit, and a favorable variance is a credit.

As a means to control material costs, a standard bill of materials (sometimes called a *master requisition*) listing the various kinds and standard quantities for materials that should be used to complete the finished product is prepared by a production scheduling and control department before the process starts. The bill of materials and a production schedule authorize storeroom personnel to issue the standard quantities required for the planned production. In the event that an operation runs short of material because of waste, scrap, or spoilage in excess of standard allowances, the production department manager must requisition excess material.

In recording material issues, the standard quantities called for by the bill of materials priced at the standard cost are debited to the Work in Process account. Excess requisitions for materials are debited to the Material Quantity Variance account. Waste, scrap, or spoilage will occasionally run below standard allowances, and the unused material must be returned to the storeroom. The return of materials is credited to the Material Quantity Variance account as a savings in material cost.

Dress Shirts Unlimited, in an earlier illustration, had the following production statistics:

	Physical Dozens	Equivalent Dozens
Beginning inventory	90	–0–
Started in process and completed	1,100	1,100
Ending inventory	100	100
Production for materials		1,200

The standard quantity allowed is calculated as:

Fabric:	1,200 dozen × 25 yards =	30,000
Buttons:	1,200 dozen × 120	= 144,000

At standard prices, these amounts equate to 30,000 yards × $3.10 = $93,000 for fabric and 144,000 × $0.30 = $43,200 for buttons. If the actual quantities used for the month were 29,850 yards of fabric and 144,100 buttons, we have costs of 29,850 yards × $3.10 = $92,535 for fabric and 144,100 × $0.30 = $43,230 for buttons. Data for journal entries and calculation of variances are summarized below:

Material	SP × AQU	SP × SQ	SP × (AQU − SQ)	
Fabric	$ 92,535	$ 93,000	$465	Favorable
Buttons	43,230	43,200	30	Unfavorable
	$135,765	$136,200	$435	Favorable

The summary journal entry to record charges to Work in Process Inventory and relieve Materials Inventory is:

Work in Process Inventory	136,200	
Material Quantity Variance		435
Materials Inventory		135,765

In T-account form, the flow of costs associated with a material quantity variance appears as:

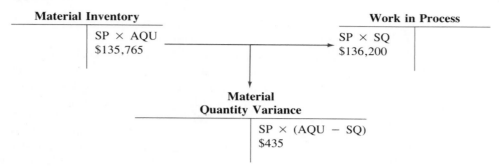

Reasons for Quantity Variances.   Why will quantity variances occur? The more common reasons are summarized in Exhibit 12–4.

Explanations of why variances occur need not wait until the end of the month or accounting period. For example, quantities that exceed the standard quantity allowed are usually drawn by a special requisition, which signals management that material use is unfavorable. If the cause of a variance can be eliminated, steps should be taken immediately to prevent further losses.

Responsibility for Quantity Variance.   The quantity variance is the responsibility of production departments in which those variances are generated because control is centered there. There are situations in which purchasing should have responsibility for a quantity variance, as when nonstandard materials are purchased at lower prices but create higher levels of waste or spoilage. As a practical matter, quantity variances are seldom charged to purchasing.

Interrelationship of Price and Quantity Variances.   The emphasis in variance analysis is to isolate and analyze individual variances. In many cases, the event that causes one variance also causes one or more other variances. For example, as shown above, purchasing buys nonstandard material at an excellent discount—a favorable material price variance. However, the nonstandard material results in higher waste in production, thereby generating an unfavorable material quantity variance. Analyzing the two variances in isolation gives credit to the purchasing department while the

EXHIBIT 12–4   Some Causes of Material Quantity Variances

Unfavorable	*Favorable*
Changes in product specifications	Changes in product specifications
Modifications of quality control standards	Modification of quality control standards
Material substitutions	Material substitutions
Lower-quality material	Higher-quality material
Improper handling or sloppy workmanship (carelessness)	Extra care by workers
	Improvements in production process
Use of lower-skilled workers	Use of more highly skilled workers
Improperly adjusted machines	Better-quality machines
Standard but defective materials	
Hoarding for use at other times	
Pilferage	

production manager realizes a poor performance evaluation. An opposite case also exists. A higher-quality material may be purchased at a higher price because it is the only material the purchasing agent could acquire in time to meet production schedules. This higher-quality material realizes lower waste, scrap, and spoilage during production.

The foregoing situation is a good example of the possible misjudgment people can make of favorable and unfavorable variances. A natural tendency is to view favorable variances as good and unfavorable variances as bad. Until we know the cause of the variance, judging it as good or bad is difficult. We can say, however, that both situations are deviations from the standard.

Production activity can also impact the material price variance. For example, improperly adjusted machines incur higher than usual waste. Excessive waste means more materials must be requisitioned from inventory in order to complete the required good units of finished product. However, when inventory does not have the needed materials, purchasing must submit additional orders for materials. To do so often leads to rush orders or purchases in uneconomical quantities, both of which give higher priced materials.

Alternatives for Isolating Price and Quantity Variances

We have isolated the material price variance at time of purchase and the material quantity variance at time of issue. We did that under the philosophy that good cost control requires isolating the variances as soon as possible. Another alternative measures the material price variance at the time materials are issued to production. Under this approach, Materials Inventory is recorded at the actual price times actual quantity: no material price variance is recognized at this point. As materials are issued to production, a price variance is calculated as $(AP - SP) \times AQU$. The materials quantity variance would still be calculated as $SP \times (AQU - SQ)$. This approach has at least two disadvantages. First, control over the price variance is lost because a piece of that variance is hidden in the Materials Inventory account until the material is used. Second, a company loses one recordkeeping advantage of standard costs; a cost-flow assumption is needed when goods are issued to production. Specific identification, FIFO, LIFO, or an average method involves more book work than a standard cost system.

STANDARDS FOR LABOR

Setting Rate Standards

The price factor for labor is called a *rate*. Two fundamental questions are pertinent to setting labor rate standards: What labor skills are needed to perform the operations? What rate should be paid for these skills? Management will then decide which, if any, of the various labor-related costs should be added to the basic labor rate to arrive at the standard labor rate.

Basic Labor Rate. As a rule, each skill level is a different labor classification with its own standard rate. The available labor skills and the rates paid each skill level are frequently established in contract negotiations. In other cases, the rates may be determined by the prevailing rates in the location where the work is performed. Whatever the conditions under which the rates are set, job classifications must be carefully established, and the rate for each classification should fairly represent the qualifications needed to perform the activity. The classification should provide for a definite set of specifications, covering level of skill, training, education, experience, special physical abilities, and any other important factors.

The wage payment plan currently used also has a bearing on the labor rate standard because different wage plans can result in different labor costs for a unit of work. Examples of wage plans commonly encountered are daily or hourly wage, piece-rate wage, and crew- or gang-rate.

Labor-Related Costs.   In addition to the type of wage plan, a company must decide whether the standard rate will include any of the many labor-related costs. (See Chapter 7 for more detail on labor-related costs.) The most common ones considered are overtime premiums, shift premiums, bonuses, payroll taxes, and fringe benefits. Whether management includes any of the labor-related costs in the standard rate will be a management policy. There is nothing right or wrong about having labor-related costs in a standard rate.

Setting Time Standards

Time standards are more difficult to establish than quantity standards for material because time standards are based on people whose productivity from one period to another varies to a greater degree than the materials employed in making a product. Setting time standards involves answering two questions: What operations are performed? How much time should be spent in each operation for the product made or the service rendered? The answer to the first question is determined by studying past and anticipated procedures, process charts, and standard operation and routing lists. The answer to the second may be determined from:

1. Time and motion studies conducted by industrial engineers.
2. Dividing each operation into elementary body movements (such as reaching, pushing, turning over, and so forth). Published tables of standard times for such movements are available. These standard times can be applied to the individual movements and then added together to determine the total standard time allowed per operation.
3. Averages of past performance, adjusted for anticipated changes.
4. Test runs through a production process.

Calculating Rate and Efficiency Variances

Because labor is purchased as used, rate and efficiency variances can be measured and reported simultaneously with no loss of control. Therefore, the variances will be discussed together in this section. For purposes of discussion, the following symbols will be used:

AR = Actual rate
SR = Standard rate
AH = Actual hours worked
SH = Standard hours allowed
LRV = Labor rate variance
LEV = Labor efficiency variance

Dress Shirts Unlimited has a standard labor cost per dozen of shirt MFHP3400 of $16.80 (3.5 hours × $4.80 per hour). Production statistics for the current month, as shown earlier in the chapter, are:

Beginning inventory—90 dozen, 20 percent completed for labor.
Started into production—1,200 dozen.
Ending inventory—100 dozen, 50 percent completed for labor.
Completed—1,190 dozen.

All of this information reduces to 1,222 equivalent dozen produced during the month:

Beginning inventory: 90 × (100% − 20%)   =   72
Started and completed: (1,190 − 90) × 100% =   1,100
Ending inventory: 100 × 50%   50
                                                                              1,222

The standard labor cost for these units is $20,529.60 (1,222 equivalent dozen times $16.80 per dozen). Payroll records show 4,240 hours worked at $4.85 per hour.

Rate Variance.   The **labor rate variance,** also called a *labor price variance,* results whenever the actual rate paid a worker differs from the standard rate. Calculating a labor rate variance requires holding the hours constant while varying the rate. The calculation is:

$$
\begin{array}{lll}
& AR \times AH & \$4.85 \times 4,240 = \$20,564 \\
- & SR \times AH & \$4.80 \times 4,240 = 20,352 \\
\hline
= & LRV & \$212 \text{ Unfavorable}
\end{array}
$$

LRV is (AR − SR) × AH. For the illustration, this computation is ($4.85 − $4.80) × 4,240 = $212, unfavorable because the actual rate exceeds the standard rate.

Efficiency Variance.   The **labor efficiency variance,** also referred to as *labor usage variance* or *labor time variance,* results from how the worker's time is used. Calculating a labor efficiency variance requires holding the rate constant while varying the hours. In this case, the constant rate is the standard rate because we assume the rate variance has already been removed. The hours are actual hours worked and standard hours allowed for the actual output. The calculation is the following difference:

$$
\begin{array}{lll}
& SR \times AH & \$4.80 \times 4,240 = \$20,352 \\
- & SR \times SH^2 & \$4.80 \times 4,277 = 20,529.60 \\
\hline
= & LEV & \$177.60 \text{ Favorable}
\end{array}
$$

LEV is SR × (AH − SH), or $4.80 × (4,240 − 4,277) = $177.60 favorable for Dress Shirts Unlimited. A favorable variance occurs any time the actual hours worked are less than the standard hours allowed, a savings in time expended. The opposite is of course true for an unfavorable variance.

Simultaneous Calculations.   Because the hours purchased and used happen at the same time, rate and efficiency variances can be calculated together. The following format is useful:

AR × AH	*SR × AH*	*SR × SH*
$4.85 ×	$4.80 ×	$4.80 ×
4,240	4,240	4,277
$20,564	$20,352	$20,529.60
Rate Variance	Efficiency Variance	
$212 Unfavorable	$177.60 Favorable	

[2] The standard hours represent the standard hours allowed for the equivalent units produced. In this case, the standard hours allowed can be determined by multiplying the standard hours allowed per unit (3.5) by the equivalent units: 3.5 × 1,222 = 4,277.

The journal entry to record this information in a standard cost system is:

Work in Process Inventory	20,529.60	
Labor Rate Variance	212.00	
Labor Efficiency Variance		177.60
Payroll		20,564.00

Note that we are using the Payroll account independent of the Wages Payable account to make a distinction between distributing labor costs to work of the period and accruing the liability for the labor. Companies not making this separation would credit Wages Payable in the entry above.

Reasons for Rate Variances

It is common for labor rates to be set by contract, negotiations, or by other means such as the federal minimum wage laws. Consequently, accountants may wonder why a labor rate variance would occur at all. The standard labor rate may include labor-related costs above the basic labor rate, and any changes in these during the period are reflected in a rate variance. Additionally, the standard labor rate is frequently an average for a task, operation, or department. If a supervisor shifts workers around because of a shortage of personnel, substituting higher- or lower-paid workers, the average changes and results in a rate variance. Exhibit 12–5 contains the common sources for favorable and unfavorable labor rate variances.

Reasons for Efficiency Variances

Innumerable possibilities exist as to why a labor efficiency variance appears. Exhibit 12–6 gives many of the common sources for favorable and unfavorable variances. In each case, actual hours worked differ in some way from the hours established as the standard.

Responsibility for Variances

Labor variances are the responsibility of the production departments. Charging the rate variance to a production supervisor is justified on the basis of controllability. The supervisor determines who is working and where, and those decisions impact the labor cost per unit of work and the cost per hour. Supervisors are responsible for seeing that employees achieve the standard hours, so supervisors are charged with the responsibility for labor efficiency variances too. Admittedly, this assumption of controllability is not always valid. Most supervisors do not control the wage rates, and some supervisors may not schedule or oversee the workers.

Interrelationship of Variances

The event that causes one variance can also cause one or more other variances. Below we look first at the interrelationship of labor rate and labor efficiency variances, then

EXHIBIT 12–5   Some Causes of Labor Rate Variances

Unfavorable	*Favorable*
Inaccurate standards	Inaccurate standards
Use of highly skilled (higher-paid) workers	Use of more lower-skilled (lower-paid) workers
Change in mix of workers	Change in mix of workers
Change in payment method	Change in payment method
Change in labor-related costs	Change in labor-related costs
Change in union scale or basic rate	
Increased overtime	
Changes in average shift premium	

EXHIBIT 12–6   Some Causes of Labor Efficiency Variances

Unfavorable	*Favorable*
Use of lower-skilled workers	Use of more highly skilled workers
Inaccurate standards	Inaccurate standards
Effects of learning curve	Effects of learning curve
Lower-quality materials	Higher-quality materials
Change in production methods	Change in production methods
Changes in production scheduling	Changes in production scheduling
Poorly maintained equipment	New equipment
Machine malfunctions	
Use of wrong equipment for operations being performed	
Delays in routing work, materials, tools, and instructions	
Work interruptions	
Insufficient training, incorrect instructions, or worker dissatisfaction	

at labor and material variances. Cost control can be improved when these interrelationships are identified and used in planning and control.

Rate to Efficiency.   There are many examples of how labor rate and efficiency variances are related. A few examples are presented here. Due to illness, several employees are unable to work on a particular day. Temporary employees are hired through an outside service. The rate of pay differs for temporaries, and their levels of efficiency will be less than those of regular workers. Depending on the pay rates, an unfavorable or favorable rate variance could occur. Now assume that the supervisor opts not to hire temporaries. Instead, the supervisor shifts workers around and ends up with a higher-paid and more skilled worker in a particular operation. Certainly, the rate variance is unfavorable, but if the more skilled worker is also more efficient, the efficiency variance is favorable.

As another example, an improperly adjusted machine causes a worker to spend more time than normal. The supervisor may put a more skilled worker on that machine to keep things on schedule. Doing so could reduce an unfavorable efficiency variance but could generate an unfavorable rate variance.

Material to Labor.   Material and labor variances can also be caused by the same source. Assume, for instance, that the purchasing agent buys nonstandard materials at a substantial discount—a favorable price variance. When the materials are worked on in production, they crumble and more materials are needed—unfavorable quantity variance. The time wasted on bad materials means that more labor time is used—unfavorable efficiency variance. A supervisor, concerned about the scrap and excessive labor time, substitutes workers, and this affects both rate and efficiency variances.

Another situation occurs when temporaries hired to replace sick workers scrap a higher incidence of materials than usual. The effort expended on scrap is inefficient labor. The higher scrap means that more material is needed, which may require a rush order (higher material costs) to get enough material in time to meet production schedules.

Alternatives for Isolating Rate and Time Variances

We have assumed that both rate and efficiency are isolated prior to, or at least no later than, charging Work in Process Inventory for the standard labor cost. (No variances appear in Work in Process Inventory.) Some companies will charge Work in Process Inventory with only the rate variance removed. Then, after all of the production data are available for a period of time, the efficiency variance is identified and removed from the Work in Process Inventory.

SUMMARY

Standard cost systems operate effectively where there are standardized products or standardized operations. Although the primary emphasis is on cost control, a number of other advantages can be realized: savings in recordkeeping costs, cost reduction, better values for inventories, and decision-making aids. Success of the system is highly dependent on management's support and on the employees' capability to operate the system.

A standard cost for a product or service consists of a price factor and a quantity factor that become the basis for computing and analyzing variances. Standard costs for material and labor should represent the current operations with an appropriate level of performance. Levels of performance are expressed as ideal, currently attainable, or loose or lax. The preferred standard for all purposes is current and attainable.

One of the important keys in establishing a standard cost system is preparing a standard cost sheet for each product or service. Here the standard quantities and prices are stated for direct material, direct labor, and production overhead. The standard cost sheet gives the total unit cost that will be attached to any completed unit of a given product. It therefore facilitates the accounting for costs as they flow from Work in Process Inventory to Finished Goods and to Cost of Goods Sold.

Material standards are set after giving consideration to purchase price and other dollar amounts that should be included and to quantities needed for the intended operations. A material price variance occurs any time the actual price differs from the standard price. The dollar amount of variance is calculated as (actual price less standard price) times actual quantity purchased. A material quantity variance is caused by using more or less material than the standard calls for. The variance is calculated as standard price times (actual quantity used less standard quantity allowed). Price variances are usually the responsibility of the purchasing department; quantity variances, the responsibility of production supervisors.

In establishing labor standards, consideration is given to what operations are performed, how much time should be spent in each operation, what labor skills should perform the operations, and what rate should be paid. A labor rate is the rate based on a payment plan plus any of the labor-related costs management chooses to include. A rate variance is computed as (actual rate less the standard rate) times the actual hours worked. The labor efficiency variance is standard rate times (actual hours worked less standard hours allowed). Both variances generally fall under the responsibility of production supervisors.

PROBLEM FOR REVIEW

Odom Corporation has a standard cost system. For one of its products, the company has the following standard cost sheet:

Direct material—3 pieces at $2.20	$ 6.60
Direct labor—5 hours at $6.00	30.00
Production overhead:	
Variable—$3.50 per direct labor hour	17.50
Fixed—$1.50 per direct labor hour	7.50
Total cost per unit	$61.60

During the month, 500 units were completed. The accounting records show the following actual costs and other production data for the month:

Direct materials purchased—1,700 pieces at $2.10 =	$ 3,570
Direct materials used—1,550 pieces	
Direct labor payroll—2,450 hours at $6.20 =	$15,190

REQUIRED

a. Calculate the following material and labor variances:
1. Material price variance.
2. Material quantity variance.
3. Labor rate variance.
4. Labor efficiency variance.
b. Prepare the journal entries that record the actual costs, standard costs, and variances. Assume that materials inventory is carried at standard cost.

SOLUTION

a. Variances calculated.
1. Material price variance:

Actual price × Actual quantity purchased	
$2.10 × 1,700 pieces =	$ 3,570
Standard price × Actual quantity purchased	
$2.20 × 1,700 pieces =	3,740
(Actual price − Standard price) × Actual quantity	
($2.10 − $2.20) × 1,700 =	$(170) F

2. Material quantity variance:

Standard price × Actual quantity used	
$2.20 × 1,550 pieces =	$ 3,410
Standard price × Standard quantity allowed	
$2.20 × (3 × 500) =	3,300
Standard price × (Actual quantity used − Standard quantity allowed)	
$2.20 × (1,550 − 1,500) =	$ 110 U

3. Labor rate variance:

Actual rate × Actual hours	
$6.20 × 2,450 hours =	$ 15,190
Standard rate × Actual hours	
$6.00 × 2,450 hours =	14,700
(Actual rate − Standard rate) × Actual hours	
($6.20 − $6.00) × 2,450 =	$ 490 U

4. Labor efficiency variance:

Standard rate × Actual hours
$6.00 × 2,450 hours = $14,700
Standard rate × Standard hours allowed
$6.00 × (5 × 500) =   15,000
Standard rate × (Actual hours − Standard hours allowed)
$6.00 × (2,450 − 2,500) = $(300) F

b. Journal entries.
   1. Material price variance:

Materials Inventory	3,740	
Material Price Variance		170
Accounts Payable		3,570

   2. Material quantity variance:

Work in Process Inventory	3,300	
Material Quantity Variance	110	
Material Inventory		3,410

   3. Labor variances:

Work in Process Inventory	15,000	
Labor Rate Variance	490	
Labor Efficiency Variance		300
Payroll		15,190

KEY TERMS AND CONCEPTS

Standard cost (460)   Management by exception (463)
Price standard (460)   Cost reduction (463)
Quantity standard (460)   Standard cost sheet (464)
Ideal standard (462)   Material price variance (466)
Currently attainable standard (462)   Material quantity variance (468)
Loose or lax standard (463)   Labor rate variance (473)
Cost control (463)   Labor efficiency (473)

ADDITIONAL READINGS

Balakrishnan, Ramji. "On the Decomposition of Direct Material Variances." *Issues in Accounting Education,* Spring, 1989, pp. 193–202.

Barnes, John L. "How to Tell if Standard Costs Are Really Standard." *Management Accounting,* June, 1983, pp. 50–54.

Calvasina, Richard V., and Eugene J. Calvasina. "Standard Costing Games that Managers Play." *Management Accounting,* March, 1984, pp. 49–51, 77.

Caricofe, Ronald L. "Establishing Standard Costs in the Concrete Pipe Industry." *Management Accounting,* February, 1982, pp. 45–49.

Clark, John. "The Labor Mystique." *Management Accounting,* December, 1982, pp. 36–39.

Fasci, Martha A.; Timothy J. Weiss; and Robert L. Worrall. "Everyone Can Use This Cost/Benefit Analysis System." *Management Accounting,* January, 1987, pp. 44–47.

Marcinko, David, and Enrico Petri. "Use of the Production Function in Calculation of Standard Cost Variances—An Extension." *The Accounting Review,* July, 1984, pp. 488–95.

Martin, James R., and Eugene J. Laughlin. "A Graphic Approach to Variance Analysis Emphasizes Concepts Rather Than Mechanics." *Issues in Accounting Education,* Fall, 1988, pp. 351–64.

Peterson, Raymond H., and Alyce Zahorsky. ''Telephone Industry Develops New Cost Standards.'' *Management Accounting*, December, 1988, pp. 47–49.

Schaeberle, F. W., and Max Laudeman. ''The Cost Accounting Practices of Firms Using Standard Costs.'' *Cost and Management*, July–August, 1983, pp. 21–25.

Truitt, Jack. ''Does the Joint Variance Make Economic Sense?'' *Cost and Management*, May–June, 1987, pp. 30–33.

Zannetos, Zenon S. ''On the Mathematics of Variance Analysis.'' *The Accounting Review*, July, 1963, pp. 528–39.

REVIEW QUESTIONS

1. What is a quantity standard? What is a price standard?
2. What circumstances must exist for a standard cost system to have a chance to be successful?
3. Why is it imperative that the standard cost system have the support of top management before its initiation?
4. Distinguish between an ideal and a currently attainable standard.
5. If employees are unable to meet a standard, what effect would you expect this to have on their productivity?
6. Why must a standard for the future be more than simply a projection of the past?
7. What factors should a company consider in deciding how tight standards should be?
8. Discuss the advantages of a standard cost system.
9. What is meant by the term *management by exception?*
10. Why is a standard cost sheet important to a standard cost system and the way in which inventories are accounted?
11. Why are variances generally segregated in terms of a price variance and a quantity variance?
12. Explain the procedures that can be used to establish material price variances.
13. Who is generally responsible for the materials price variance? The materials quantity variance?
14. Under which circumstances would a production department supervisor be responsible for a materials price variance?
15. Explain why favorable variances may be bad for a company.
16. Who is generally responsible for the labor rate variance? The labor efficiency variance?
17. What effect, if any, would you expect poor-quality materials to have on direct labor variances?
18. What labor cost is debited to Work in Process Inventory if a standard cost system is in operation? How is this amount determined?
19. Explain how a labor efficiency variance and a material price variance are interrelated.

DISCUSSION QUESTIONS

20. The principle of management by exception is considered desirable because it calls attention to weak areas that require control and saves management the task of reviewing results that require no attention. When applied to people, might this principle result in causing a negative attitude among workers? Discuss the drawbacks of management by exception when the human factor is considered.
21. The chapter material assumes that standards are established for material, labor, and production overhead. A number of other options exist. For example, some companies set quantity standards for material and labor but do not set price and rate standards and ignore production overhead altogether. Explain why a company would not have price factors established for material, labor, and production overhead.
22. The valuation of inventories at year end and the beginning of the next year raises an issue. Although these two dates are consecutive, the new year generally means revised standard costs. Should closing inventories be valued at standard costs applying at year end, at the start of the new year, or at a compromise figure adjusted in some way by variances? Not

adjusting to revised standards means items in inventory are not valued at current standard costs—back to cost-flow assumptions like FIFO.

EXERCISES

12–1. Materials Price Variance. The VisiTel Corporation has developed a product that has started to sell well. The VisiTel is a picture telephone that can send photographic images of anything to a distant location. This expensive device looks like a television with a 4-inch screen, and it has a camera lens and a cord that plugs into a telephone jack. The side panel of the device is made of molded plastic with an inset chrome-plated handle. The side panel is purchased from various suppliers. The standard price for the side panel is $1.50. On March 10, 19x3, 1,200,000 of the side panels were purchased for $1,788,000.

(A. Gregory, adapted)

REQUIRED:
a. Calculate the materials price variance.
b. Prepare a journal entry to record the purchase assuming:
   1. Materials inventory is maintained at standard cost.
   2. Materials inventory is maintained at actual cost.

12–2. Explaining Materials Variances. Engine, Inc., holds almost half of the U.S. market for large diesel truck engines. Recently, top management has discovered that a competitor was offering prices that were 40 percent lower. Senior management knows that costs must be cut. Staff accountants have noted substantial unfavorable materials price and quantity variances.

(A. Gregory, adapted)

REQUIRED:
a. Explain what materials price variances and materials quantity variances are.
b. List six possible reasons or causes for each unfavorable variance.
c. Do any of the reasons or causes cited above for the material price variance also relate to the material quantity variance? If so, explain how.

12–3. Materials Price Variances. The Legend Company manufactures jeans and jackets under the Legend brand name. The El Paso plant purchases the output from various denim plants on a going-price basis. The El Paso plant has a standard cost system with a standard price for denim of $1.10 per yard. Recent acquisitions of denim are:

Date	Vendor	Quantity	Invoice
March 3	Brownfield Mill	21,400	$ 24,610
7	Jose Cotton	46,000	48,760
12	Lists Dist.	32,600	38,794
22	Jose Cotton	48,000	51,360
30	Brownfield Mill	24,000	27,840
	Total for March	172,000	$191,364

REQUIRED:
a. Compute the materials price variance for each purchase and the total for the month.
b. Prepare a journal entry to summarize the purchasing activity for the month. The El Paso plant records inventory at standard price.

12–4. Material Variances. Stacy Lee Company had the following material costs during May for the manufacturing of its new product line:

Actual purchase price	$7.50
Actual quantity purchased	5,200 pounds
Actual quantity used in production	5,100 pounds
Standard price	$7.60

Standard quantity allowed for actual production	5,150 pounds

REQUIRED:

a. Calculate the material price variance and the material quantity variance. (Assume that the price variance is isolated at time of purchase.)

b. Make the journal entries to record the purchase of materials and the issuance of materials to production.

c. Explain which department is primarily responsible for the price variance.

d. Which department is primarily responsible for the quantity variance?

12–5. Material Price and Quantity Variances.   The Elderhard plant produces rocket hulls from specially hardened aluminum. The hulls are cast in two pieces and the seams are welded together. The company uses a standard cost system for the materials for two sizes of rocket:

	Standard	
	Quantity	*Cost*
80-ft.-class hyper rocket	17,600	$14,080
120-ft.-class switch rocket	38,400	30,720

During November 19x2, the Elderhard plant ordered 820,000 pounds of aluminum from suppliers and was invoiced for $639,600. The following materials were issued for production:

	Materials	*Units Produced*
80-ft.-class hyper rocket	284,405	16
120-ft.-class switch rocket	522,170	14

REQUIRED:

a. Compute the aluminum price variance for the month of November.

b. Record the purchase of aluminum assuming that inventories are kept at standard price.

c. Compute the materials quantity variance for each class of rocket.

d. Record the issuance of materials to Work in Process.

12–6. Isolating the Material Variances.   Consider the data compiled by Ross Manufacturing for 10,000 units of finished product:

Actual material purchases (1,500 units at $3)	$4,500
Materials issued to production	700 units
Standard material cost per unit purchased	$2.50
Standard quantity allowed for actual production	800 units

REQUIRED:

a. Prepare journal entries for materials that recognize price variances at the time of purchase and quantity variances at time of issuance.

b. Prepare journal entries for materials that recognize price and quantity variances at the time of issuance.

12–7. Material Variances, Journal Entries.   The Foster Company has the following data for the month of August 19x9:

Units produced	17,000
Materials purchased, 2,600 pounds	$8,580
Materials used in production	1,320 pounds
Materials quantity variance	$384 Unfavorable

The standard price per pound is $3.20.

(D. Ripple)

REQUIRED:

a. Using the amounts for the quantity variance and the materials used, find the standard quantity allowed for actual production.

b. Prepare the following assuming that the price variance is isolated at the time of purchase:
1. Journal entry for the purchase.
2. Journal entry for issuance to production with quantity variance.

c. Prepare the following assuming that the price variance is isolated at the time of issuance to production:
1. Journal entry for the purchase.
2. Journal entry for issuance to production with quantity variance.

12–8. Labor Rate Variances. The Holmberg Company has four classes of labor in one of its operations but uses an overall labor rate for its standard cost system. The labor rate standard is calculated as follows:

Class 1	2 hours at $ 6.25	$12.50
Class 2	3 hours at $ 8.90	26.70
Class 3	1.5 hours at $11.00	16.50
Class 4	1.5 hours at $12.20	18.30
	8.0 hours	$74.00

Standard rate = $74.00/8 hours = $9.25

During February, 8,500 units of product were manufactured. The payroll records show the following labor costs:

Class 1	17,100 hours at $ 6.40	$109,440
Class 2	25,300 hours at $ 8.80	222,640
Class 3	12,750 hours at $11.50	146,625
Class 4	12,850 hours at $12.30	158,055
	68,000 hours	$636,760

REQUIRED:
Calculate the labor rate variance for each class and in total for February.

12–9. Labor Variances. The Boom Breakfast Cereal Company has the following labor standards for the production of 10,000 boxes of Boom cereal:

	Rate	Hours	Standard Cost
Crushing	$10	100	$1,000
Mixing	8	20	160
Baking	6	40	240
Packaging	6	40	240
Total labor cost		200	$1,640
Labor cost per box			$0.1640
Labor rate per hour			$8.20

During April 19x9, the company produced 830,000 boxes and had the following results:

	Cost	Hours Worked
Crushing	$ 79,679	8,400
Mixing	14,586	1,410
Baking	26,376	3,820
Packaging	14,684	2,653
Total	$135,325	16,283

REQUIRED:

a. Compute the labor rate variance for each department.

b. Compute the labor efficiency variance for each department.

c. Prepare a journal entry summarizing the incurrence of the labor cost for the month of April. The company uses only one general ledger Work in Process account but uses separate accounts to keep track of rate and efficiency variances for each department.

12–10. Material and Labor Variances.   Tidings, Inc., produces festive banners made of thin metallic or plastic strips. The product is made by cutting a 36-inch-wide sheet into six strips. Both sides of the strips are shredded leaving a 1-inch-wide middle. The strips are then twisted resulting in a strong core surrounded by tinsel. The product, which comes in different colors and combinations, sells for $1.50 per banner. A case of 100 of the packaged banners has the following standard cost:

	Standards		
	Input	*Price*	*Cost*
Materials, square yards	100	$0.365	$36.50
Direct labor, hours	5	6.000	30.00
Overhead (machine hours)	5	1.500	7.50
Total standard cost			$74.00

During September 19x5, the company purchased 100,000 square yards of materials at a cost of $35,000 with 60,000 yards of this material issued to production. The actual labor hours worked were 3,000, costing $18,600 in the production of 550 cases of product.

(B. McDonald, adapted)

REQUIRED:

a. Calculate the materials price and quantity variances.

b. Calculate the labor rate and efficiency variances.

c. The beginning inventory was 39 cases, and the ending inventory was 80 cases. What inventory value would appear on the September 30, 19x5, balance sheet?

12–11. Materials and Labor Variances.   The P. D. Teagarden Company has the following information on a standard cost card for one of its products:

Direct material, 2 pounds at $5.70	$11.40
Direct labor, 1.5 hours at $11.50	17.25
	$28.65

Production data for January showed that 6,000 units of finished products were produced. Direct material purchases were 13,000 pounds at a cost of $74,620. The amount of material used in production totaled 12,125 pounds. Direct labor payroll showed 8,980 hours at $102,372 of regular pay and 80 hours at $1,380 of overtime (regular pay and overtime premium).

REQUIRED:

a. Calculate the material price variance and the material quantity variance. (Assume the price variance is isolated at time of purchase.)

b. Calculate the labor rate variance and the labor efficiency variance.

c. Explain which department is primarily responsible for the rate variance and the efficiency variance and why.

12–12. Material and Labor Variances.   Boytt, Inc., produces luggage called the Walk-In Closet. The Walk-In Closet fits in an airplane overhead rack for flights but unzips to contain very large, clear plastic pockets for clothing and accessories. The bottom of the luggage has wheels for easy movement in airports. The luggage is made by cutting vinyl into various shapes, sewing in zippers and seams, and attaching the wheels, handle, and carrying strap. The standard cost per unit includes:

	Standards		
	Input	*Price*	*Cost*
Direct materials, yards	5	$ 0.45	$2.25
Direct labor, hours	0.2	12.00	2.40
Production overhead	0.2	20.00	4.00

The attachments have a minor cost and are included in indirect materials, which is part of overhead.

During November 19x3, the company purchased 30,000 yards of vinyl for $14,000; 26,000 yards were issued to production. There were 1,050 direct labor hours worked at an actual cost of $12,810. The output was 5,000 pieces of luggage.

(A. Gregory, adapted)

REQUIRED:
a. Calculate the materials price and quantity variances.
b. Calculate the labor rate and efficiency variances.

12–13. Standard Cost Sheet.   Allmake Furniture, Inc., produces a number of different styles of office furniture. It is currently trying to set up a standard cost system to help with product costing as well as provide for more efficient cost control. One of the products is the Executive Workstation. The Engineering Department and the Accounting Department have studied the production process and analyzed the costs. The process involves four departments: Cutting, Assembly, Staining, and Finishing. Costs incurred within a department are accumulated in the accounting records by that department. The information that has been gathered is now ready to be formalized into a standard cost sheet.

Raw materials include lumber, stain, drawer handles and fixtures, screws, dowels, and glue. Each workstation requires 78 feet of lumber at $1.50 per foot. Drawer handles and other drawer fixtures are $18.90 per desk. Stain is .90 gallons at $15.70 per gallon. Screws, dowels, and glue are not identified with each workstation; their costs are included in the production overhead of the Assembly Department. Lumber enters the process in the Cutting Department; drawer handles and other drawer fixtures in the Assembly Department; and stain in the Staining Department.

Direct labor occurs in Cutting, Assembly, and Finishing. Staining is an automated department. Cutting requires 20 minutes per workstation with labor at $10.50 per hour. Assembly requires two hours per workstation with a labor cost of $12.60 per hour. Finishing requires 30 minutes with a labor cost of $8.40 per hour.

Production overhead is applied to Work in Process on the basis of direct labor hours in Cutting, Assembly, and Finishing. The Staining Department overhead is applied on the basis of machine time. Cutting is $15.00 per hour; Assembly is $11.20; and Finishing is $10 per hour. The Staining Department has an overhead rate of $20 per machine hour, and each workstation requires 15 minutes of machine time.

REQUIRED:
a. Prepare a standard cost sheet showing the standard cost of a completed workstation.
b. Prepare a standard cost sheet showing the standard cost of a workstation at the end of each department.

PROBLEMS

12–14. Material and Labor Variances.   The Fruit-Sun Corporation produces an all-natural fruit drink, which is distributed throughout the Southwest. The standard costs for a case of Fruit-Sun have been set as follows:

	Standard Cost
Fruit (24 pounds at $0.20/pound)	$4.80
Direct labor (0.3 hours at $4.50/hour)	1.35
Overhead ($3 per labor hour)	0.90
Total cost per case	$7.05

The cost of the paper containers is recorded as indirect materials, which is part of overhead. Fruit-Sun keeps all inventories at standard cost.

During May 19x0, the company produced 15,300 cases of Fruit-Sun. It purchased 380,000 pounds of fruit at a cost of $70,300. There were 360,000 pounds of fruit issued to production. Direct labor hours worked were 4,130 at a cost of $19,204.50.

(S. Whitecotton, adapted)

REQUIRED:
a. For the materials:
   1. Calculate the fruit price variance.
   2. Record the purchase of the fruit.
   3. Calculate the fruit quantity variance.
   4. Record the issuance of fruit to production and the quantity variance.
b. For the direct labor:
   1. Calculate the labor rate variance.
   2. Calculate the labor efficiency variance.
   3. Prepare the journal entry for the application of direct labor to Work in Process.

12–15. Entries and Variances for Material and Labor.   The K & R Corporation produces a single product. The standard cost per unit is set by the Cost Accounting Department and is as follows:

Direct materials (3 pints at $1.75/pint)	$ 5.25
Direct labor (5 hours at $3.50/hour)	17.50
Production overhead ($2.00/hour)	10.00
Total cost per unit	$32.75

The standard production for April is 3,250 units. The company actually produced 3,350 units. It purchased 12,000 pints at a cost of $19,920. Production requisitioned 11,000 pints for work in process. The actual direct labor hours worked were 15,075 at a rate of $3.70.

REQUIRED:
a. Calculate the following variances:
   1. Direct materials price variance.
   2. Direct materials quantity variance.
   3. Direct labor rate variance.
   4. Direct labor efficiency variance.
b. Prepare journal entries for direct materials assuming that:
   1. Materials inventory is maintained at standard cost.
   2. Materials inventory is maintained at actual cost.
c. Prepare journal entries for direct labor to record the distribution of the payroll and identify the labor variances. Ignore payroll taxes.

12–16. Material and Labor Variances.   The Whimpy Works produces pressed frozen hamburgers for sale to Whimpy franchises throughout the Northwest. The company has established the following standards for a box of 10 burgers:

	Rate	Quantity	Standard
Meat	$0.80	2.50	$2.00
Packaging	0.10	1.00	0.10
Labor	4.00	0.20	0.80
Total			$2.90

During the month of November 19x7, the company had the following production data and cost:

Burgers produced	400,000 boxes
Labor cost	$321,111
Labor hours	80,617
Meat cost	$801,000
Meat quantity	1,002,500 pounds*
Packaging cost	$39,889
Packaging quantity	400,120*

* Quantities equal purchased and used

REQUIRED:

a. Compute the materials price variances.

b. Record the purchase of materials and the price variances.

c. Compute the materials quantity variances.

d. Record the materials quantity variances.

e. Compute the labor rate and efficiency variances.

f. Record the incurrence of the labor cost with both the labor variances in one entry.

12–17. Reconstructing Actual Costs from Outputs. Mason McGee Corporation manufactures a number of different products. Its most profitable product comes from the Leeming Division, which has the following standard cost sheet:

Materials (2 pounds at $8.50 per pound)	$17
Labor (½ hour at $12 per hour)	6
Overhead ($18 per direct labor hour)	9
Total product cost	$32

Income statements are prepared for each product line on a monthly basis. At the end of a recent month, the following income statement information was available for the product listed above:

Sales ($45 × 92,000 units)		$4,140,000
Cost of goods sold at standard		
($32 × 92,000 units)		2,944,000
Gross profit at standard		$1,196,000
Production cost variances:		
Material price	$ 7,500 F	
Material quantity	8,500 U	
Labor rate	5,900 U	
Labor efficiency	12,000 F	5,100
Adjusted gross profit		$1,201,100

Material purchases for the month were 300,000 pounds. Production was 120,000 units, with no work in process at the beginning or ending of the month. All variances are closed to the Cost of Goods Sold account at the end of each month.

REQUIRED:

a. Calculate each of the following items for the month:

1. Actual material price per pound on purchases.

2. Actual pounds of material used during the month.

3. Actual labor hours worked.

b. Prepare the journal entries that could have been used to record the transactions that resulted in the listed variances (prior to closing to Cost of Goods Sold). Assume that variances are isolated as early as possible in the system.

12–18. Materials and Labor Variances.   Sargent Plastics, Inc., makes plastic cups and dishes for home use. The production process consists of combining the powdered plastic base with a color additive, putting the mix in a press with a mold for the product, and pressing the mixture in the mold. The mixture melts under heat and pressure to form the product according to the shape of the mold.

The cereal dish is one of the more popular products because of its versatility. Each one requires 29 grams of plastic powder at a standard cost of $0.003 per gram and 5 grams of additive at a standard cost of $0.004 per gram. Labor consists of four activities: mixing, molding, trimming, and packing. Labor is measured in terms of 1,000 dishes per lot. Standard times per lot and rates are mixing, .25 hours at $5 per hour; molding, .5 hours at $12 per hour; trimming, .6 hours at $9 per hour; and packing, .3 hours at $6 per hour.

During 19x9, Sargent Plastics produced 5,000,000 cereal dishes. Actual costs and quantities are shown below:

Materials:
  Plastic purchases—150,000,000 grams at $0.0035 per gram
  Plastic used—148,750,000 grams
  Additive purchases—27,000,000 grams at $0.00375 per gram
  Additive used—24,950,000
Labor:
  Mixing—1,300 hours at $5.25 per hour
  Molding—2,490 hours at $12.25 per hour
  Trimming—3,000 hours at $8.50 per hour
  Packing—1,600 hours at $6 per hour

REQUIRED:
a. Calculate the standard material and labor cost per 1,000 dishes.
b. Compute each of the following variances for 19x9:
  1. Materials price (at time of purchase).
  2. Materials quantity.
  3. Labor rate.
  4. Labor efficiency.
c. Prepare all journal entries for the year, based on the data provided. All variance accounts are closed to Cost of Goods Sold at year end.

12–19. Setting Material Standards.   Ogwood Company is a small manufacturer of wooden household items. Al Rivkin, corporate controller, plans to implement a standard cost system for Ogwood. Rivkin has information from several co-workers who will assist him in developing standards for Ogwood's products.

One of Ogwood's products is a wooden cutting board. Each cutting board requires 1.25-board feet of lumber and 12 minutes of direct labor time to prepare and cut the lumber. The cutting boards are inspected after they are cut. Because the cutting boards are made of a natural material that has imperfections, one board is normally rejected for each five that are accepted. Four rubber foot pads are attached to each good cutting board. A total of 15 minutes of direct labor time is required to attach all four foot pads and finish each cutting board. The lumber for the cutting boards costs $3.00 per board foot, and each foot pad costs $.05. Direct labor is paid at the rate of $8.00 per hour.

(CMA, adapted)

REQUIRED:
a. Develop the standard cost for the direct cost components of the cutting board. The standard cost should identify for each direct cost component of the cutting board the following:
  1. Standard quantity.
  2. Standard rate.
  3. Standard cost per unit.
b. Identify the advantages of implementing a standard cost system.

c. Explain the role of each of the following persons in developing standards.
1. Purchasing manager.
2. Industrial engineer.
3. Cost accountant.

12–20. Effects of Changes in Material and Labor Contracts. NuLathe Co. produces a turbo engine component for jet aircraft manufacturers. A standard cost system has been used for years with good results.

Unfortunately, NuLathe has recently experienced production problems. The source for its direct material went out of business. The new source produces a similar but higher-quality material. The price per pound from the original source has averaged $7.00 while the price from the new source is $7.77. The use of the new material results in a reduction in scrap. This scrap reduction reduces the actual consumption of direct material from 1.25 to 1.00 pounds per unit. In addition, the direct labor is reduced from 24 to 22 minutes per unit because there is less scrap labor and machine setup time.

The direct material problem was occurring at the same time that labor negotiations resulted in an increase of over 14 percent in hourly direct labor costs. The average rate rose from $12.60 per hour to $14.40 per hour. Production of the main product requires a high level of labor skill. Because of a continuing shortage in that skill area, an interim wage agreement had to be signed.

NuLathe started using the new direct material on April 1, the same date that the new labor agreement went into effect. NuLathe has been using standards that were set at the beginning of the calendar year. The direct material and direct labor standards for the turbo engine component are as follows.

Direct material	1.2 lbs. at $6.80/lb.	$ 8.16
Direct labor	20 min. at $12.30/DLH	4.10
Standard prime cost per unit		$12.26

Howard Foster, cost accounting supervisor, had been examining the performance report shown below that he had prepared at the close of business on April 30. Jane Keene, assistant controller, came into Foster's office, and Foster said, "Jane, look at this performance report. Direct material price increased 11 percent and the labor rate increased over 14 percent during April. I expected greater variances, yet prime costs decreased over 5 percent from the $13.79 we experienced during the first quarter of this year. The proper message just isn't coming through."

"This has been an unusual period," said Keene. "With all the unforeseen changes, perhaps we should revise our standards based on current conditions and start over."

Foster replied, "I think we can retain the current standards but expand the variance analysis. We could calculate variances for the specific changes that have occurred to direct material and direct labor before we calculate the normal price and quantity variances. What I really think would be useful to management right now is to determine the impact the changes in direct material and direct labor had in reducing our prime costs per unit from $13.79 in the first quarter to $13.05 in April—a reduction of $.74."

(CMA, adapted)

REQUIRED:
a. Discuss the advantages of:
1. Immediately revising the standards.
2. Retaining the current standards and expanding the analysis of variances.
b. Prepare an analysis that reflects the impact the new direct material and new labor contract had on reducing NuLathe Co.'s prime costs per unit from $13.79 in the first quarter to $13.05 in April. The analysis should show the changes in prime costs per unit that are due to the:
1. Use of new direct material.
2. New labor contract.

This analysis should be in sufficient detail to identify the changes due to:
- Direct material price.
- Direct labor rate.
- The effect of direct material quality on direct material usage.
- The effect of direct material quality on direct labor usage.

NuLathe Co.—Analysis of Prime Costs

Standard Cost Variance Analysis for April 19x5

	Standard	Price Variance		Quantity Variance		Actual
Direct materials	$ 8.16	($.97 × 1.0)	= $.97 U	($6.80 × .2)	= $1.36 F	$ 7.77
Direct labor	4.10	$\left(\$2.10 \times \dfrac{22}{60}\right)$ =	.77 U	$\left(\$12.30 \times \dfrac{2}{60}\right)$ =	.41 U	5.28
	$12.26					$13.05

Comparison of 19x5 Actual Costs

	First Quarter Costs	April Costs	Percentage Increase (Decrease)
Direct materials	$ 8.75	$ 7.77	(11.2)
Direct labor	5.04	5.28	4.8
	$13.79	$13.05	(5.4)

12–21. Variances and Reconstructuring Actuals.   STQ Woodworking, Inc., produces several thousand different wood products. One product is the 401 dog house kit made of plywood. The kits are marketed through hardware stores at a wholesale price of $12. A production run for the 401 dog house consists of 250 units. Each run has a standard cost for materials of $1,000 (250 sheets at $4) and for labor of $625 (50 hours at $12.50). As part of the implementation of a standard cost reporting system, you are seeking to verify the programmed calculations.

(S. Neves, adapted)

REQUIRED:

Consider the following three cases and compute the required amounts:

a. Six production runs (1,500 units) were completed during the week ending November 3, 19x2. There were 2,000 sheets of plywood purchased at a cost of $7,925. Production requisitioned 1,700 sheets of plywood during the week and returned 100 of them at the end of the week. Payroll records showed 280 hours worked at regular pay and another 40 hours worked at a 50 percent overtime premium.
   1. Compute the plywood price and quantity variances for comparison with computer reports.
   2. Compute the labor rate and quantity variances for comparison with computer reports.

b. For the week ending November 10, 19x2, the company purchased 2,500 sheets of plywood at a discount. The printout shows that a $625 favorable price variance and a $1,000 unfavorable quantity variance resulted when 2,300 sheets were issued to production and 50 were returned at the end of the week.
   1. Calculate the actual price per sheet of plywood for later comparison with the invoiced price.
   2. Calculate the number of units produced for comparison with the finished goods warehouse receipt report.

c. For the week ending November 17, 19x2, the production report showed a favorable labor rate variance of $125 for the production of 1,250 units. Payroll records show the actual labor cost was $2,750.
   1. Calculate the actual hours worked for verification with payroll records.
   2. Calculate the labor efficiency variance for comparison with the production report.

12–22. Impact of Labor Standards. The Hagee Train Shop sells toys and accessories associated with railroads. The shop is located in Durango, Colorado, near the Durango & Silverton Railroad. Some of the business is from tourists riding the train, and additional sales are by mail order to hobbyists and hobby shops. Much of the tourist business occurs in July and August. Much of the mail order business occurs during October and November for the holiday season. One product is a scale-model, working replica of a steam-powered train. Three craftsmen are employed to produce and test the trains and scaled narrow-gauge track. The shop is tight for space with room for only three workers and their tools. Labor cost per month is $2.640 craftsman, which is $15 per labor hour. Materials for the train average $20, including $1 in scrap losses. There is a significant backlog of orders for the trains, and each train produced can be sold at the long-established price of $100. Overhead costs average $10 per train.

Mike Hagee recently set a new standard for the craftsmen. He now expects 100 trains per month from each employee. Mike noted that each of the three craftsmen had averaged 60 trains per month with no defective units prior to setting the new standard. After the new standard was established, the craftsmen together have averaged 264 trains per month. However, materials scrap cost increased by $600 over the expected monthly level, and 48 trains per month are defective and have to be reworked, requiring an average of 1.5 hours of labor. One of the workers is paid overtime ($22.50 per hour) to rework the defective trains. Material prices have been very stable.

Mr. Hagee is very upset by the failure to meet the standard, the increase in scrap, and the defective units. He is seriously considering whether he should drop the concept of the standard for production.

(K. Agee, adapted)

REQUIRED:
a. What was the actual labor cost per unit before the new standard was established?
b. What would the labor cost per unit have been if production had occurred at standard, assuming no defective units?
c. What would the labor cost per unit have been if 264 trains were produced, assuming no defective units?
d. What was the actual labor cost per unit when 264 units were made with 48 defective trains, which were reworked at overtime?
e. What was the revenue from the sale of trains before and after the new standard was established?
f. Prepare a partial income statement for before and after the new standard was established.
g. Comment on the effect of establishing the new labor standard on the operations of the Hagee Train Shop.

12–23. Identifying Causes of Variances. Benton Research is an engineering company that makes prototypes under contract to large aerospace companies. If the prototype turns out to be practical and an efficient process is identified, the aerospace company will either contract with someone else for production or will produce the item itself.

A new product was under consideration that required 10 units for initial testing. Benton was asked to make the 10 containers needed to house the internal electrical control center of this new product. Benton has done work similar to this before and had standard costs available for this project. The contract finally accepted by Benton was fixed price. Therefore, cost overruns would only reduce Benton's profits for the work.

The standard cost sheet developed for one container shows the following material and labor:

Direct material (8 pieces at $5.00)	$40
Direct labor (5 hours at $12.60 per hour)	63

All 10 units were completed. Purchasing and inventory records show that the 90 pieces of material were purchased for $450. Another 10 pieces were purchased for $6.50 each. The purchasing agent said that a rush order for 10 pieces came from the storeroom and she had to pay overnight shipping costs in order to get the materials by the next day. The storeroom reports that all 100 pieces received were requisitioned from production, released to production, and no excess was returned to the storeroom. The supervisor on the job indicated that an improperly adjusted machine ruined several pieces of material. When he requisitioned more from the storeroom, none was in stock.

Payroll records show 55 hours on this job at an average cost of $12.70 per hour. The production supervisor said several people had been ill for several days and temporary people were hired at a wage higher than that for the workers who were ill. The improperly adjusted machine was operated by one of these temporary workers until the supervisor put a more experienced worker on it.

REQUIRED:
a. Calculate all appropriate variances for direct material and direct labor, indicating which are favorable and which are unfavorable.
b. Identify and explain the potential cause of each variance.

12–24. Multiple Material and Labor Inputs.   Choc-O-Chip Cookie Company is a regional producer of a popular chocolate chip cookie. Each package of cookies coming off the production line contains one dozen cookies. The company has established a standard cost system for its production process. Standards are measured in terms of 1,000 dozens, as follows:

Direct materials		
Ingredients:		
Flour	320 pounds at $0.18 per pound	$ 57.60
Chocolate chips	30 pounds at $0.78 per pound	23.40
Sugar	90 pounds at $0.27 per pound	24.30
Eggs	140 dozen at $0.51 per dozen	71.40
Packaging	1,000 packages at $0.11 per package	110.00
		$ 286.70
Direct labor		
Semi-skilled	150 hours at $4.25 per hour	$ 637.50
Skilled	50 hours at $6.70 per hour	335.00
		$ 972.50
Total material and labor costs		$1,259.20

November is one of the biggest production months of the year because of Thanksgiving, Christmas, and New Years all within a six-week period. During November, the company produced and shipped 80,000 dozen cookies. There was no work in process inventory of cookies at the beginning or end of the month. Actual inventory, purchase, and payroll data are as follows:

Materials inventories (stated at standard cost):

	Beginning	*Ending*
Flour	2,600 pounds	3,000 pounds
Chocolate chips	240 pounds	200 pounds
Sugar	800 pounds	600 pounds
Eggs	1,000 dozen	400 dozen
Packages	5,000	6,000

Direct material purchases:

Flour	26,600 pounds for $4,522
Chocolate chips	2,460 pounds for $1,968
Sugar	6,900 pounds for $1,863
Eggs	11,200 dozen for $6,048
Packages	85,000 for $8,500

None of the materials issued to production were returned to the storeroom during the month, and there was no materials inventory in the production area at the end of the month.

Payroll:
Semi-skilled   12,100 hours at a cost of $50,820
Skilled   3,890 hours at a cost of $26,841

REQUIRED:
a. Calculate a price and quantity variance for each of the five individual materials.
b. Calculate a rate and efficiency variance for each of the two categories of labor.
c. Prepare the journal entry to transfer the completed cookies from Work in Process Inventory to Finished Goods. (Ignore production overhead.)
d. Prepare a journal entry that closes all variance accounts to Cost of Goods Sold. Assume that the company has only four variance accounts: Material Price Variance, Material Quantity Variance, Labor Rate Variance, and Labor Efficiency Variance.

12–25. Standard Costs in a Service Organization.   Girton & Gresham, MIS Consultants, designs and installs all types of manufacturing cost and control systems and other information systems. The firm's costs for each job are primarily labor and overhead. These costs are accounted for under a standard cost system. Standards for labor are set by category. Therefore, an average rate is used when in fact a range of actual rates exists within each category. These rates are partner, $80 per hour; senior manager, $50 per hour; manager, $30 per hour; senior consultant, $22 per hour; and consultant, $16 per hour. Hardware and purchased software are specific to individual jobs and are charged at actual costs. Any of the firm's materials, basically supplies, are included in overhead.

The firm has won a contract to design and implement a material requirements planning system. The proposal established a fixed fee for the whole project. Supporting documents for the proposal in the work file show a projected manpower utilization for three phases as follows:

Planning Phase

	Number	Hours	Total Cost
Partner	1	10	$ 800
Senior manager	1	20	1,000
Manager	1	40	1,200
Senior consultant	2	160	3,520
Consultant	2	160	2,560
			$9,080

Installation Phase

	Number	Hours	Total Cost
Partner	1	8	$ 640
Senior manager	1	15	750
Manager	1	20	600
Senior consultant	2	160	3,520
Consultant	2	320	5,120
			$10,630

Training Phase

	Number	Hours	Total Cost
Partner	1	4	$ 320
Senior manager	1	8	400
Manager	1	16	480
Senior consultant	1	16	352
			$1,552

The actual results for this job differ from the planned utilization both in time worked and in the individuals actually assigned to the job. The summary of actual hours and costs are as follows:

	Planning		*Installation*		*Training*	
	Hours	*Cost*	*Hours*	*Cost*	*Hours*	*Cost*
Partner	8	$ 640	8	$ 640	4	$320
Senior manager	24	1,152	20	1,040	4	200
Manager	56	1,736	24	696	8	240
Senior consultant	176	4,224	120	2,640	24	768
Consultant	96	1,536	360	1,344	—	—

REQUIRED:

a. Summarize the total actual and standard cost and total variance for each phase and by category within the phase.

b. Summarize the rate and efficiency variances for each category within each phase.

12–26. Outdated Standards.   Cogdill Powder is a high-quality producer of commercial and industrial explosives. The company manufactures and distributes explosives for mining, quarrying, construction, and seismic exploration companies. Products include nitroglycerine-based explosives, emulsions, electronic and nonelectric detonators, other blasting supplies, ammonium nitrate, and urea.

Cogdill Powder established a standard cost system for its nitroglycerine-based explosives. The standards were set five years ago and have not been revised since. The controller says the standards are used primarily as an index to show how costs change over time. He admits the standards are also used in bidding on commercial contracts. A 12 percent cost adjustment factor is added to the bids to compensate for changes since the standards were set.

On a recent bid for 5,000 pounds of explosive, the projected costs appeared as follows:

Direct materials	$ 2,500
Direct labor	5,000
Production overhead	10,000
	$17,500
Cost adjustment at 12%	2,100
Costs before profit factor	$19,600

Materials consist of five ingredients and labor is in three categories. A comparison of the standards per 100 pounds with current operations gives the following changes for this explosive:

	Standard		*Current Operations*	
	Quantity	*Cost per Cwt.*	*Quantity*	*Cost per Cwt.*
Materials 1	30 pounds	$14.00	28 pounds	$16.00
2	25 pounds	12.50	26 pounds	14.00
3	18 pounds	9.50	18 pounds	11.00
4	13 pounds	4.00	13 pounds	3.80
5	14 pounds	10.00	15 pounds	9.20
	100 pounds	$50.00	100 pounds	$54.00

	Hours per Cwt.	*Cost per Hour*	*Hours per Cwt.*	*Cost per Hour*
Labor 1	5 hours	$ 6.00	4 hours	$ 6.50
2	5 hours	8.00	3 hours	9.00
3	3 hours	10.00	1 hour	12.00

REQUIRED:

a. Explain the difference between a basic standard and a currently attainable standard.

b. Recompute the supporting costs for the bid assuming that the standards are revised to current operations and that production overhead is applied at 200 percent of direct labor cost.

c. Explain how you would adjust any materials in inventory priced at the old standard to revised standard.

12–27. Information Processing Costs, Standard versus Actual.   The Estex Products Company manufactures electronic parts associated with telephones and communications and is considering implementing a standard cost system in place of its normal cost system. You are to prepare cost estimates associated with a proposal for the new standard cost system. Part of the value of a standard cost system is the reduction in data processing costs from keeping inventories at standard instead of actual prime cost plus applied overhead. The current system accounts for the actual costs of 18,204 different materials, parts, and components along with the time for 2,640 employees in 410 labor categories as they apply to the company's 1,206 products.

The current system is a FIFO job order costing system for most departments and products. The system was designed and installed between the years 1976 to 1978. At the time of installation, it was designed to grow with the plant for 8 to 12 years, after which new concepts or technology might be available. The costing system has 103 programs running in 16 different program streams. On-line access is allowed to most inventory files from each terminal. (Certain of the inventories are heavily secured because they relate to defense contracts.) The information and reports generated by the system are considered by most production managers to be reasonably reliable and accurate. On occasion, the system response time is slow, and the reports are late due to running priorities and keying bottlenecks.

The only problem with the existing system is that it is just too expensive to operate. The current cost per year to operate the computer system is $14,120,000, which includes 14 other applications in addition to the costing system. The plant manager complains that the system swallows mountains of paper and an army of people (actually only 237). The current budget for the computerized accounting system is presented at the top of the next page.

The current system prints out an inventory status report for raw materials and finished goods on a weekly basis. The materials status report is printed in three versions. The materials are sorted by location, by supplier, and by production department. Then the three versions are separated into segments and distributed. The finished goods status report is printed by product line and warehouse location.

The laser printers can work reliably at speeds of 60 pages per minute. The paper handlers tend to fail at higher continuous speeds. A box of paper has 2,600 pages, and a container of dry ink lasts for 15,000 pages. The printers require an overhaul (at a cost of $150) every 100,000 pages. The current system requires six lines per average material or product to print the FIFO cost information. The new system will require only one line per material or product. Each printed report page has 60 lines available for detail lines.

In the current system, the line workers must clock in and out on each job. On average, each person will work on four different jobs in one shift. At one time, a computerized system kept track of actual hours. A worker would key in the job number at the completion of the job and then insert his or her badge into a magnetic strip reader. The shift workers made so many mistakes in keying the 14-digit job number (32 percent errors) that the system was abandoned in 1980. Now each worker stamps a preprinted job ticket with the time clock and uses a simple rubber stamp that identifies the worker to indicate completion.

A given job requires the attention of an average of eight workers in each department and must pass through an average of six factory departments. This approach has reduced error to about 4 percent but requires that each of the job ticket lines be keyed in. The new system will not require workers to key in jobs or handle the job tickets. Instead, the job will be clocked into and out of the department resulting in one keying line per job per department. An average of 220 jobs is completed each production day. The new system is expected to have a 1 percent error rate or better in completion of the job tickets. About 75 percent of the errors are insignificant and are never corrected. The remainder are corrected, which takes one hour of clerical time for each error.

ESTEX PRODUCTS COMPANY
System Operating Budget
For the Year Ending July 31, 19x8

	Units	Unit Cost ($ thousands)	Budget ($ thousands)
Materials			
Paper forms, cartons	93,600	$ 0.028	$ 2,621
Output reports, boxes	112,320	0.022	2,471
Printer dry ink, package	6,240	0.030	187
Labor			
Keying	170	$ 11.6	1,780
System operators	24	15.6	374
Programmers and analysts	17	26.8	456
Equipment maintenance	5	15.2	76
Supervisors	19	32.5	618
System manager	1	68	68
Labor-Related Costs			
Employment taxes		9.20%	329
Pension expenses		15.50%	554
Insurance, per employee		$1,640	378
Other		4.40%	157
Hardware—Leases			
CPU	1	$846.67	847
Disks	16	32.00	512
Tape drives	4	6.00	24
Printers, impact	460	0.30	138
Printers, laser	10	7.80	78
Lines	387	0.30	116
Terminals	780	0.80	624
Software—Annual leases			
Operating systems	5	10	50
Application packages	12	25	300
Other			
Space costs, 1,000 sq. feet	18	42	756
Air handling	1	200	200
Training and conferences			116
Personnel			92
Total budgeted expenditures			$14,120

The keying of job tickets requires one hour per 100 lines. There is a 2 percent error rate in keying. The current system catches about 80 percent of the keying errors during entry. Half of the remaining errors are immaterial and are rarely found. The remaining errors require half an hour each of clerical time to find and correct. (Clerks are paid $5.60 per hour.) The new system is expected to have about the same error rates. Three of the programmers spend all of their time keeping the old actual cost system in good working order. The new system, which promises to be far simpler, should require the attention of only one full-time programmer. The current system requires all four disk drives for on-line support and backup. The new system will require only two drives.

REQUIRED:

a. For the current normal cost system, estimate the annual paper and printer costs for preparing the following weekly reports:
   1. Raw Materials Inventory Status Report.
   2. Finished Goods Inventory Status Report.

b. For the proposed standard cost system, estimate the annual paper and printer costs for preparing the following weekly reports:
   1. Raw Materials Inventory Status Report.
   2. Finished Goods Inventory Status Report.
c. Using a 2,080 hour work year, estimate the annual cost to key the job ticket lines under:
   1. The current system.
   2. The proposed system.
d. Estimate the cost of correcting keying errors on job tickets under:
   1. The current system.
   2. The proposed system.
e. Estimate the cost of finding and correcting errors made in the completion of the job tickets (as opposed to the keying) under:
   1. The current system.
   2. The proposed system.
f. Estimate the annual cost of programmer time and disk space under:
   1. The current system.
   2. The proposed system.

12–28. Process Costing, Error Correction.   The Charleston Division of UA Steel Industries, Inc., performs the final assembly for shipping containers. The containers are used for rail and ship transportation of heavy goods such as steam generators. The containers are made primarily of steel sheets that are bolted onto an I-beam frame. The frame is first bolted together and then the side, top, and bottom sheets are bolted on, door hinges are bolted on, and finally the front and rear doors are assembled and mounted. The units are tested by a load of 140 tons that is lifted, moved, and lowered. The maximum use rate is 100 tons, and the breaking load (a theoretical maximum that should never be reached) is 240 tons. If the structure shows any X ray stress cracks after the 140-ton test, the entire unit must be scrapped under current insurance agreements. The I-beams and steel sheets are produced by other divisions and transferred in at standard cost. The bolts and hinges are purchased locally. The standard costs for one container are:

	Units	Cost	Total
Transferred-in costs	30	$19.00	$570
Bolts	100	$ 1.80	180
Hinges	4	$ 4.00	16
Labor	12	$ 9.00	108
Overhead	12	$ 6.30	76
Total			$950

The containers are sold for $1,400 each. During the past three weeks, the following activity was recorded:

Week Ending	March 6	March 13	March 20
Beginning inventory	540	636	510
Units started	800	680	720
Units completed	700	800	980
Units spoiled	4	6	2
Ending inventory	636	510	248
Bolts completion	50%	40%	30%
Assembly completion	25%	70%	60%

The beginning inventory was 60 percent complete on bolts and 45 percent complete on assembly. The costs of the spoiled units are charged to overhead at a standard rate of $950 per unit. The summarization of variances recorded for the three weeks is:

Week Ending	March 6	March 13	March 20
Transferred-in usage variance	330	–0–	1,170
Bolt price variance	(65)	313	352
Bolt usage variance	449	27,600	(14,058)
Hinge price variance	1,106	141	642
Hinge usage variance	422	726	166
Labor rate variance	1	–0–	(8)
Labor efficiency variance	(627)	(16,284)	8,549

The assembly division manager is furious about the bolt usage and labor efficiency variances in the reports of March 13 and 20. (The rate and price variances are accurate.) Upon investigation, you discover that the ending inventory completion rates have been input wrong for the past two weeks. A new clerk has reversed the percentages of completion for bolts and assembly on the input form resulting in:

	Data Entered		Correct Data	
	March 13	March 20	March 13	March 20
Bolts completion	40%	30%	70%	60%
Assembly completion	70%	60%	40%	30%

Although this error seems like a small thing, the division manager is upset because the bolt usage variance and the labor efficiency variance make him look like he has lost control of operations.

REQUIRED:

a. Compute the equivalent units for bolts and assembly for the weeks ending March 13 and 20.

b. Compute the bolts, labor, and overhead that should have been applied to work in process for weeks ending March 13 and 20.

c. Recompute the bolt usage and labor efficiency variances for the weeks ending March 13 and 20. Amounts in brackets indicate a favorable variance.

d. Prepare a correcting entry for each week for the:
   1. Bolt usage variance and work in process.
   2. Labor efficiency variance and work in process.
   3. Overhead applied to work in process.

e. Compute the amount of ending work in process for March 20.

Mix and Yield Variances

After studying this appendix, you should be able to:

1. Calculate mix and yield variances for both materials and labor.
2. Describe the conditions under which mix and yield variances would be part of variance analysis.

In many production operations, a recipe or formula is used to indicate the specifications for each category of material or class of labor. If these multiple materials (or labor) are to some extent interchangeable or if the mix can be altered to improve a yield, a new set of variances is necessary to isolate the effects of mix and yield. In effect, we replace the materials quantity variance and labor efficiency variance with mix and yield variances. Material price and labor rate variances are calculated as before for individual material categories and labor classes.

The variances previously calculated for material and labor were based on changes in a price factor and a quantity factor. Mix and yield variances add a third factor for consideration: the recipe or formula mix. This is illustrated below.

Illustration Data

Because mix and yield variances are calculated in exactly the same way for both material and labor, the illustration will cover material only. Direct material standard costs for one gallon of finished product is:

$\frac{3}{4}$ gallon chemical feedstock at $2 per gallon	$1.50
$\frac{1}{4}$ gallon additive at $4 per gallon	1.00
$\frac{1}{4}$ gallon color base at $3.00 per gallon	.75
Standard material cost per gallon	$3.25

It takes $1\frac{1}{4}$ gallons of input materials to complete one gallon of finished product. The proportions of input are 60 percent ($\frac{3}{4}$ divided by $1\frac{1}{4}$ gallons) feedstock, 20 percent additive, and 20 percent color base.

Because price variances have already been eliminated in recording materials in inventory, we need be concerned only about the standard price (SP), actual quantities (AQ), actual mix (AM), standard quantities (SQ), and standard mix (SM) for computing material mix and yield variances.

The current month shows 90,000 gallons of completed product using actual materials totaling 125,000 gallons. The quantities, extended at standard prices, result in the following amounts:

Feedstock	82,500 gallons × $2.00 =	$165,000
Additive	5,000 gallons × $4.00 =	20,000
Color base	37,500 gallons × $3.00 =	112,500
	125,000 gallons		$297,500

Mix Variances

Mix variances show the cost changes that result from combining quantities of material and labor in a ratio that differs from standard specifications. Material mix variances come from changing the recipe or formula. They are common in industries such as chemicals, food processing, textiles, and rubber. Labor mix variances occur when operations are performed by teams consisting of workers earning different rates.

The material mix variance is caused by a difference between the actual mix of materials used in production and the standard materials that should have been used. The actual quantities and mix are already given. Next, convert the total actual materials (125,000 gallons) to the standard proportions of 60:20:20 as follows:

Feedstock	0.60 × 125,000 gallons =	75,000
Additive	0.20 × 125,000 gallons =	25,000
Color base	0.20 × 125,000 gallons =	25,000
		125,000

The variance computation is:

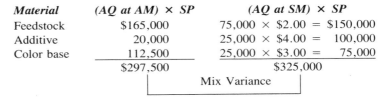

Material	(AQ at AM) × SP	(AQ at SM) × SP
Feedstock	$165,000	75,000 × $2.00 = $150,000
Additive	20,000	25,000 × $4.00 = 100,000
Color base	112,500	25,000 × $3.00 = 75,000
	$297,500	$325,000

Mix Variance

$27,500 Favorable

In this example, there was a shift in the proportions that resulted in a lower cost to the company. Feedstock was 82,500 gallons when it should have been 75,000 gallons; additive was 5,000 gallons but should have been 25,000 gallons; and color base was 37,500 gallons but should have been 25,000 gallons. That was a switch from the more expensive additive to lower-priced materials. The net effect saved the company $27,500.

A mix variance for individual materials using the computations here is meaningless. To bring meaning to such variances requires a different computation, as presented in Chapter 19.

Yield Variances

Yield variances show the cost changes that result from an actual yield of finished product that is different from the standard quantity of product established for a given input of materials and labor. They are typical when losses are inherent in the production process and can produce actual yields that differ from standard yields for the inputs of materials and labor.

Yield variances cause changes in the average costs for both materials and labor. A substandard yield means that fewer units of finished products are available for the materials and labor input to production. This means the costs of material and labor to produce one unit of good output increase.

A material yield variance occurs when the output from production, given a specific amount of material input, differs from the output established as the standard yield. The computation of the variance is the difference between the actual quantities of material used in production and the standard quantities allowed for the completed product. In the above example, the actual quantities totaled 125,000 gallons, and the actual output was 90,000 gallons. The standard quantity at the standard mix for 90,000 gallons of product is:

Feedstock	¾ gallon × 90,000 =	67,500 gallons
Additive	¼ gallon × 90,000 =	22,500 gallons
Color base	1.4 gallon × 90,000 =	22,500 gallons
		112,500 gallons

One approach to the calculation is below:

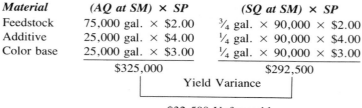

Material	(AQ at SM) × SP	(SQ at SM) × SP
Feedstock	75,000 gal. × $2.00	¾ gal. × 90,000 × $2.00
Additive	25,000 gal. × $4.00	¼ gal. × 90,000 × $4.00
Color base	25,000 gal. × $3.00	¼ gal. × 90,000 × $3.00
	$325,000	$292,500

Yield Variance

$32,500 Unfavorable

Individually, the yield variances would appear as:

The column labeled (AQ at SM) × SP is the same column used previously in computing a mix variance. The last column represents the quantities that should have been used to produce 90,000 gallons of product.

Similar to the mix variance, yield variances for individual materials require a special calculation. It is the same adjustment illustrated for a quantity variance in Chapter 19.

Another approach to computing the yield variance is to compare what the actual input should have yielded with the actual yield:

Standard yield of actual input (125,000 gallons/1.25 gallons)	100,000 gallons
Actual yield	90,000 gallons
Difference in yield	10,000 gallons
Standard material cost per gallon	$3.25
Unfavorable yield variance	$32,500

Interaction of Mix and Yield

In the situation just described, the company shifted to a mix of the less costly materials and saved $27,500. However, the change in recipe or formula required more quantities to achieve the same output. This is shown in an unfavorable yield variance of $32,500. Whoever made the decision to change inputs caused an increase in production costs of $5,000.

SUMMARY

When a production process is based on a recipe or formula for inputs of various categories of material and classes of labor and the materials and labor are somewhat interchangeable, a new set of variances occurs. Mix and yield variances replace the materials quantity variance and labor efficiency variance. Mix variances show the cost changes that result from combining quantities of material and labor in a ratio that differs from standard specifications. Yield variances show the cost changes that result from an actual yield of finished product that is different from the standard yield for given input of materials and labor.

KEY TERMS AND CONCEPTS

Mix variances (498)
Yield variances (499)

ADDITIONAL
READINGS

Becker, Edward A., and K. J. Kim. "Direct Material Variances: Review of Mix and Yield Variances." *Issues in Accounting Education,* Spring, 1988, pp. 1–16.

Peles, Yoram C. "A Note on Yield Variance and Mix Variance." *The Accounting Review,* April 1986, pp. 325–29.

REVIEW
QUESTIONS

1. For what types of operations would mix and yield variances be appropriate?
2. Discuss the significance of a mix variance.
3. Discuss the significance of a yield variance.
4. Distinguish between mix and yield.
5. What variance do mix and yield variances replace for material? For labor? Explain.

DISCUSSION
QUESTIONS

6. If normal loss is built into the standards, should there be a yield variance?
7. Should mix and yield variances for materials and labor be routinely calculated for all companies that use a standard cost system?
8. Should labor mix and yield variances be calculated and reported when a production department supervisor has no control over the number of workers of each labor category? Explain.

PROBLEMS

12A–1. Materials Price, Mix, and Yield Variances.   The Concho Valley Winery makes chablis from a mixture of grapes. The mixture includes some high-quality grapes (to add taste and smoothness) and some low-quality grapes (to add volume). Higher-quality grapes have more liquid per pound as well as more flavor. The batch size is 500 gallons and has the following standard materials mix and cost for the pressing unit:

Grape Quality	Price	Pounds	Standard Cost
Bulk grade	$0.20	2,500	$ 500
Medium white	0.30	2,000	600
Medium red	0.60	1,000	600
Premium white	0.80	500	400
Totals		6,000	$2,100
Standard per output gallon			$4.20
Standard per input pound			$0.35

During the month of October 19x3, the company had the following results from the Pressing Unit for producing 24 batches of chablis:

Grape Quality	Cost	Pounds Used
Bulk grade	$11,278	62,000
Medium white	12,917	50,500
Medium red	13,923	23,000
Premium white	8,234	10,000
Total	$46,352	145,500

REQUIRED:
a. Compute the grape price variance for each grade and the total.
b. Compute a materials quantity variance for each grade and the total.
c. Compute the materials mix and yield variances. Note that the total of the mix and yield variances must equal the total quantity variance.
d. Prepare one journal entry to summarize materials for the pressing unit for October. The company maintains a separate Work in Process account for each producing unit. Only the total for each type of variance is recorded. Because grapes are pressed as soon as they arrive, there are no raw materials accounts. (Record the mix and yield variances but not the materials quantity variance.)

12A–2. Labor Variances.   Smith, Hampton, Jonessa & Co. is a CPA firm based in London with offices worldwide. The firm uses a standard mix input per 100 billed hours of audit work:

	Cost	Hours	Standard Cost
Partners	$70	4	$ 280
Managers	34	21	714
Seniors	25	40	1,000
Staffs	18	60	1,080
Totals		125	$ 3,074
Cost per hour billed			$30.740
Cost per input hour			$24.592

Note that the firm expects that on average 80 percent of audit input hours will be billable to specific clients.

During the month of March 19x9, the firm had the following results for the New York City audit practice:

Billed to clients for audit   20,520 hours

	Cost	Time Sheet Hours
Partner	$ 63,056	901
Manager	141,700	4,109
Senior	216,621	9,208
Staff	248,096	12,412
Total	$669,473	26,630

REQUIRED:
a. Compute the audit labor rate variance for each level and the total.
b. Compute an audit efficiency variance for each level.
c. Compute the mix and yield variances.
d. Prepare a report by audit level of the costs and variances for the audit partner in charge.

12A–3. Material and Labor Variances.   The LeTrose is an exclusive dinner club established in Atlanta, Georgia. The club is open Tuesday through Sunday from 6 P.M. until 1 A.M. for dinner and cocktails for members and their guests. The meals are served at a leisurely pace in private gardens and dining areas. Live entertainment is available in the piano bar. Other amenities are available to regular members, and every employee is extremely discrete. There are no prices on the menus, nor is tipping allowed. Members' bank accounts are billed directly on a monthly basis. The price is $100 per person per evening, which covers all food, beverage, and entertainment. Most employees work on an hourly basis with an average standard cost of $11.41732 per hour. The club director has recently established the following standards for labor for an average day:

	People	*Hours*	*Standard Hours*	*Rate*	*Standard Cost*
Waiters	4	7	28	$ 9	$ 252
Matre'de	1	6	6	12	72
Bartender	1	7	7	7	49
Water and cleanup	1	6	6	4	24
Bar back	1	6	6	4	24
Chefs	3	8	24	15	360
Wine master	1	8	8	15	120
Clerk/Cashier	1	6	6	8	48
Dishwasher	1	7	7	4	28
Entertainers	2	5	10	25	250
Dietician	1	5	5	25	125
Security	2	7	14	7	98
			127	$11.41732	$1,450

The cost of food and beverage is expected to average $35 per person. The expected average volume is 30 members and guests per evening. A volume of about 40 persons is expected on Wednesday, Friday, and Saturday evenings and about 20 on other evenings. During the four weeks ending January 28, 19x2, the club director noticed the following data:

Billings	$75,600
Food and beverages used	$30,561
Labor hours for the month	3,251
Total payments to employees	$37,507

The club director noted that food and beverage consumption was about 10 percent above expected and prices were up by 5 percent.

The following payroll data were available for January:

	Actual Hours	*Actual Cost*	*Actual Hours at Standard*
Waiters	725	$ 6,636	$ 6,525
Matre'de	148	1,877	1,776
Bartender	178	1,256	1,246
Water and cleanup	156	846	624
Bar back	158	652	632
Chefs	601	9,217	9,015
Wine master	202	3,132	3,030
Clerk/Cashier	159	1,312	1,272
Dishwasher	183	762	732
Entertainers	259	6,253	6,475
Dietician	134	3,148	3,350
Security	348	2,416	2,436
	3,251	$37,507	$37,113

REQUIRED:

a. Calculate the materials price and quantity variances.

b. Calculate the labor rate and efficiency variances.

c. Calculate the labor mix and yield variances.

d. Comment on the usefulness of each of the variances to the club director in the management of club operations.

12A–4. Material and Labor Mix Variances.   AGRI-NUTRITION was founded two years ago. At that time, farmers planted more acreage to compensate for bad harvests. That year was a financial success for the fertilizer business—fertilizer ended up smelling like roses. CEO

Chester Tutor founded the company when he bought a closed Idaho plant that produced high phosphorous fertilizer used on wheat and corn crops. He renovated the plant and added specialty fertilizers for fruits and vegetables. With the standardized procedures for each product line, the company implemented a standard cost system.

In January of this year, the company introduced a fertilizer for the home gardener. Packages were produced in 20-pound units. Standard direct material and direct labor costs for one 20-pound package are as follows:

Material:		
Ingredient N–84—5 lbs. at $2.10	$10.50	
Ingredient P–99—14 lbs. at $1.40	19.60	
Ingredient Z–07—1 lb. at $0.90	.90	$31.00
Direct labor:		
Unskilled—2 hours at $4.25	$ 8.50	
Skilled—1 hour at $7.10	7.10	$15.60

During April, problems of different kinds converged to make production an off-standard month. The supplier for ingredient P–99 had a strike, making it difficult to procure sufficient quantities. The company altered the recipe so more of the other ingredients were used in the mix. A flu virus had an unusual success rate on the skilled workers, which resulted in higher than normal absenteeism. The unskilled workers were asked to work at skilled jobs, and additional unskilled workers were hired on a temporary basis. Material and labor costs recorded in completing 9,000 20-pound bags of fertilizer were as follows:

Material:	
Ingredient N–84—73,000 lbs. at $2.00	$146,000
Ingredient P–99—90,000 lbs. at $1.70	153,000
Ingredient Z–07—27,000 lbs. at $0.85	22,950
Direct labor:	
Unskilled—27,000 hours at $4.75	$128,250
Skilled—6,750 hours at $7.00	47,250

REQUIRED:

a. Compute the following variances for material: price, mix, and yield.

b. Computer the following variances for direct labor: rate, mix, and yield.

12A–5. Material and Labor Yield Variances.   Snyder Cottonseed Oil Company, a division of Puritan, Inc., processes cottonseed to obtain cottonseed oil (considered a vegetable oil) that will be sold to another division for use in making margarine. The standard yield for 1 ton of cottonseed is 60 percent oil and 40 percent waste (currently disposed for the cost of that disposition).

The company uses a standard cost system. Standard costs for cottonseed and direct labor are set as follows:

Cottonseed—$65 per ton
Direct labor—2 hours per ton of cottonseed at $5.50 per hour

During November, 4,000 tons of cottonseed were put into the process. This year's cotton crop was one of the best in many years, and the oil content of the seeds was higher than standard. The actual yield of oil was 71 percent. The actual costs incurred during November are as follows:

Cottonseed—4,000 tons at $68	$272,000
Direct labor—8,200 hours at $5.80	47,560

REQUIRED:

a. Compute the material price and material yield variances.

b. Compute the labor rate, labor efficiency, and labor yield variances.

c. Explain the difference between a material mix variance and a material yield variance.

12A–6. Materials Variances.   Maidwell Company manufactures washers and dryers on a single assembly line in its main factory. The market has deteriorated over the last five years and competition has made cost control very important. Management has been concerned about the materials cost of both washers and dryers. There have been no model changes in the past two years and economic conditions have allowed the company to negotiate price reductions in many key parts.

Maidwell uses a standard cost system in accounting for materials. Purchases are charged to inventory at a standard price with purchase discounts considered an administrative cost reduction. Production is charged at the standard price of the materials used. Thus, the price variance is isolated at time of purchase as the difference between gross contract price and standard price multiplied by the quantity purchased. When a substitute part is used in production rather than the regular part, a price variance equal to the difference in the standard prices of the materials is recognized at the time of substitution in the production process. The quantity variance is the actual quantity used compared to the standard quantity allowed with the difference multiplied by the standard price.

The materials variances for several of the parts Maidwell uses are unfavorable. Part no. 4121 is one of the items that has an unfavorable variance. Maidwell knows that some of these parts will be defective and fail. The failure is discovered during production. The normal defective rate is 5 percent of normal input. The original contract price of this part was $.285 per unit; thus, Maidwell set the standard unit price at $.285. The unit contract purchase price of part no. 4121 was increased $.04 to $.325 from the original $.285 due to a parts specification change. Maidwell chose not to change the standard, but to treat the increase in price as a price variance. In addition, the contract terms were changed from n/30 to 4/10, n/30 as a consequence of negotiations resulting from changes in the economy.

Data regarding the usage of Part No. 4121 during December are as follows.

• Purchases of part no. 4121	150,000 units
• Unit price paid for purchases of part no. 4121	$.325
• Requisitions of part no. 4121 from stores for use in products	134,000 units
• Substitution of part no. 5125 for part no. 4121 to use obsolete stock (standard unit price of part no. 5125 is $.35)	24,000 units
• Units of part no. 4121 and its substitute (part no. 5125) identified as being defective	9,665 units
• Standard allowed usage (including normal defective units) of part no. 4121 and its substitute based upon output for the month	153,300 units

Maidwell's material variances related to part no. 4121 for December were reported as follows.

Price variance	$7,560.00 U
Quantity variance	1,339.50 U
Total material variances for Part No. 4121	$8,899.50 U

Bob Speck, the purchasing director, claims the unfavorable price variance is misleading. Speck says that his department has worked hard to obtain price concessions and purchase discounts from suppliers. In addition, Speck has indicated that engineering changes have been made in several parts increasing their price even though the part identification has not changed. These price increases are not his department's responsibility. Speck declares that price variances simply no longer measure the Purchasing Department's performance.

Jim Buddle, the manufacturing manager, thinks that responsibility for the quantity variance should be shared. Buddle states that manufacturing cannot control quality arising from less expensive parts, substitutions of material to use up otherwise obsolete stock, or engineering changes that increased the quantity of materials used.

The accounting manager, Mike Kohl, has suggested that the computation of variances be changed to identify variations from standard with the causes and functional areas responsible for the variances. The following system of materials variances and the method of computation for each was recommended by Kohl.

Variance	Method of Calculation
Economics variance	Quantity purchased times the changes made after setting standards that were the result of negotiations based on changes in the general economy.
Engineering change variance	Quantity purchased times change in price due to part specifications changes.
Purchase price variance	Quantity purchased times change in contract price due to changes other than parts specifications or the general economy.
Substitutions variance	Quantity substituted times the difference in standard price between parts substituted.
Excess usage variance	Standard price times the difference between the standard quantity allowed for production minus actual parts used (reduced for abnormal scrap).
Abnormal failure rate variance	Abnormal scrap times standard price.

(CMA, adapted)

REQUIRED:

a. Discuss the appropriateness of Maidwell Company's current method of variance analysis for materials and indicate whether the claims of Bob Speck and Jim Buddle are valid.

b. Compute the materials variances for part no. 4121 for December using the system recommended by Mike Kohl.

c. Indicate who would be responsible for each of the variances in Mike Kohl's system of variance analysis for materials.

CHAPTER

13

Standard Costs for Production Overhead

THE PROBLEM OF ANALYZING OVERHEAD

Jason-Court Products, Inc., manufactures special measuring and monitoring products for the outpatient health care market. The company employs a standard cost system with separate standard cost sheets prepared for each product.

One of its newest and fastest growing products is a glucometer for diabetics to monitor their blood sugar levels without going to a laboratory. Components are produced in several departments and are then routed to the Assembly Department. There each glucometer is assembled, inspected, packaged, and sent to the finished goods warehouse.

Direct labor hours is the measure of activity in the Assembly Department and is the basis for a flexible budget used to plan and control assembly overhead costs. Standards are reviewed for possible revision at the beginning of each year. Standard overhead costs for the Assembly Department's work on the glucometer are:

Variable overhead:	
$\frac{1}{2}$ hour at $11.20 per direct labor hour	$5.600
Fixed overhead:	
$\frac{1}{2}$ hour at $2.25 per direct labor hour	1.125
Total assembly overhead per unit	$6.725

These overhead rates are based on a normal capacity of 4,000 direct labor hours per month. However, the company has a practical productive capacity of 5,000 direct labor hours per month.

During March, 8,200 glucometers were produced with 4,150 actual direct labor hours. The actual overhead costs for the Assembly Department were variable, $49,275 and fixed, $8,850.

The company needs a framework with which to analyze the variances from standard overhead costs. Shelley Beckman, controller, knows she can use two-way, three-way, or four-way analyses to analyze an underapplied or overapplied overhead.

■

LEARNING OBJECTIVES

After studying this chapter, you should be able to:

1. Explain the major considerations in establishing standard costs for production overhead.
2. Identify the uses of flexible budgeting in production overhead planning and control.
3. Compute production overhead variances using two-way, three-way, and four-way approaches.
4. Discuss the meaning of each of the following variances:
   (a) Budget variance.
   (b) Spending variance.
   (c) Efficiency variance.
   (d) Volume variance.
5. Account for the disposition of production overhead variances.
6. Describe how standard costs can be used in a process cost system.

STANDARDS FOR PRODUCTION OVERHEAD

As defined in earlier chapters, **production overhead** consists of those costs incurred in a production operation other than direct materials and direct labor. Traceability determines which costs are direct. Most production overhead costs cannot be traced to specific units of product or service; therefore, they are indirect costs and must be allocated to arrive at a product cost. The allocation mechanism is a predetermined overhead rate (a standard overhead rate for a standard cost system).

Standard costs for production overhead are expressed as the per unit amount expected to be incurred under normal efficient operating conditions. Although standard costs are appropriate for many purposes, they are primarily used in allocating costs to products and services and in planning and controlling activities.

An essential first step is understanding which costs go into the overhead and how the rates are developed.

Development of Overhead Rates

Production overhead, like standard costs for direct material and labor, has price and quantity factors. Price is reflected in one or more overhead rates; quantity is the measure of activity. Because price and quantity are integrally tied together for overhead, the major considerations for implementing standard costs are discussed together.

The beginning point is selecting which cost elements should be included in production overhead. Otherwise, an effective cost control program is difficult to implement. A few of the specific cost categories are indirect materials, indirect labor, supervision, property taxes, depreciation, payroll taxes, insurance, fringe benefits, security, utilities, and occupancy. The significance of identifying these categories is that when a spending variance occurs, these categories will be examined for the specific causes of variations.

Selection of the **measure of activity** is the next consideration. A measure of activity represents the factor that best expresses how costs change as volume increases or decreases. We have seen in earlier chapters that many factors can influence costs. However, we select, as a rule, the dominant factor in developing an overhead rate. The most common activity measures used are direct labor hours or costs and machine hours. Units of production can be used, but, as we will see in this chapter, that measure is usually converted to an activity allowed. Material dollars are appropriate only if the overhead costs for which a rate is established are dominated by material-related costs (see Chapter 6). Overhead variance analysis has meaning only if the right measure of activity is selected. An inappropriate measure leaves us with essentially useless variance information.

Closely related to the measure of activity is the concept of capacity and its anticipated level. We discussed four concepts of capacity for production overhead in Chapter 8: theoretical (or ideal or maximum), practical, normal, and expected actual. The capacity concept selected for the period significantly affects the amount set for the fixed overhead rate.

Another consideration is cost behavior. The behavior of each cost category is important because management plans for and controls variable costs differently than it plans for and controls fixed costs. (See Chapter 3 for a discussion of this subject.) Therefore, in analyzing overhead variances by cause and responsibility, variable and fixed cost distinctions are vital determinants. It is common in a standard cost system to establish separate overhead rates for variance overhead and for fixed overhead.

Finally, there is the consideration of setting standard overhead rates as plantwide rates or as departmental rates or on the basis of some other structure. Departmental rates are preferred over plantwide variable and fixed rates because they are more effective for implementing control. However, such rates create more complexity in the cost accounting system. A key to determining whether plantwide rates are useful is the measure of activity in combination with the type of products or services worked on in the departments. For example, homogeneous products with machine hours in all departments can easily use a plantwide rate. Different products or departments requiring different measures of activity should use departmental rates or, in some cases, look for another rate structure.

Applied Overhead   As the product (or service) goes through the production process, overhead is applied at the standard cost. Because a standard cost system uses labor hours, dollars, or machine hours as the measure of activity, standard overhead rates can be stated either as rates per unit of activity allowed or as rates per unit of actual output. For example, Jason-Court Products, Inc., produced 8,200 glucometers during March. The standard cost calls for one-half direct labor hour in assembly, which means the direct labor hours allowed for actual production are 4,100 ($\frac{1}{2}$ direct labor hours × 8,200 glucometers). The overhead accounts with actual and applied costs for variable and fixed production overhead are given in Exhibit 13–1. The applied costs are shown on the basis of both actual units of output and the activity allowed for the output.

FLEXIBLE OVERHEAD BUDGETS

In this section, we look at the importance and uses of a flexible budget. The discussion centers on production, but the concepts discussed here are appropriate for marketing

EXHIBIT 13–1   Production Overhead Accounts—Jason-Court Products, Inc.

ONE-ACCOUNT APPROACH

Production Overhead

Actual		*Applied*	
← Variable	$49,275	Variable	$45,920 →
		(8,200 units at $5.60 or	
		4,100 hours at $11.20)	
← Fixed	8,850	Fixed	9,225 →
		(8,200 units at $1.125 or	
		4,100 hours at $2.25)	
← Total	$58,125		$55,145 →
		(8,200 units at $6.725 or	
		4,100 hours at $13.45)	
Underapplied	$ 2,980		

TWO-ACCOUNT APPROACH

Production Overhead Control		*Applied Production Overhead*	
→ Variable	$49,275	Variable	$45,920
→ Fixed	8,850	Fixed	9,225 ←
→ Total	$58,125		$55,145 ←

Underapplied $ 2,980

and distribution activities and for general and administrative costs. Flexible budgeting can be used for any activity for which the costs can be separated into variable and fixed components.

A **flexible overhead budget** is based on a formula that expresses the budgeted production overhead at any point within the relevant range of activity. The cost of some components of production overhead, such as supervision salaries and depreciation, are not expected to change as volume moves up and down because they are fixed costs. The cost of other production overhead components, such as indirect materials and indirect workers who earn hourly wages, are variable costs and are expected to change in the same direction as volume increases and decreases.

The flexible budget in Exhibit 13–2 is for the Assembly Department of Jason-Court Products, Inc., and includes each item of production overhead for the department.

Management has estimated the variable and fixed component for each cost item. For example, the supervision cost is estimated at a fixed cost of $47,000 for the year, and the indirect labor cost is estimated at a variable cost of $2.40 per direct labor hour. Repair and maintenance has both a fixed and a variable cost component. At the bottom of the exhibit, the individual cost items in the flexible budget are converted into a formula called *the flexible budget formula*. In this case, formulas for both an annual and a monthly budget are shown. (A monthly flexible budget formula is derived

EXHIBIT 13–2

JASON-COURT PRODUCTS, INC.
Overhead Flexible Budget Formula
Assembly Department
For the Year Ended 19x5

Cost Item	Fixed Cost	Variable Cost per Direct Labor Hour
Indirect materials	—	$ 3.60 per hour
Indirect labor (hourly)	—	2.40 per hour
Miscellaneous supplies	—	1.20 per hour
Repair and maintenance	$ 8,000	2.10 per hour
Utilities and occupancy	23,000	1.90 per hour
Supervision	47,000	—
Depreciation	30,000	—
	$108,000	$11.20 per hour

Annual formula = $108,000 + ($11.20 × hours)
Monthly formula = $9,000 + ($11.20 × hours)

from the annual formula by dividing fixed costs into 12 equal parts. The variable costs per unit of activity remain the same.)

Uses of Flexible Overhead Budgets

Flexible budgets can be used in a variety of businesses to estimate and control costs. Although they were developed within a manufacturing environment, they are useful for any organization. The factor that makes them useful is the ability to identify variable and fixed cost behaviors and to generate a budget formula. With that information, a flexible budget can be used in two ways. First, it becomes the vehicle to estimate overhead costs at a predicted level of operations. Second, it can be used after performance to identify the amount of cost that should have been incurred at the actual level of activity achieved. The first use sets the direction operations will take, and the latter use facilitates a comparison of actual performance with the flexible budget for that level. This is where budgetary control enters in.

We have already used the concept of a flexible budget in developing the predetermined overhead rate in Chapter 8. As suggested above, we estimate the amount of production overhead cost that *should* be incurred at each anticipated level of production. At the end of a period, the actual overhead costs incurred are easily compared with the overhead costs that should have been incurred given the actual production level. This after-the-fact comparison aids management in evaluating to what extent production overhead costs were controlled during the period.

Departmental Flexible Budgets

Flexible budgets are usually developed for each department in a production facility for two reasons. First, the activity measure used for allocating production overhead to the product may be different for each department. For example, a metal stamping department or a robotics operation can use machine hours as its activity measure, and an assembly department will probably use direct labor hours. Second, the responsibility for controlling production overhead costs rests with departmental managers, and any variances should be brought quickly to their attention, analyzed, and remedied. As will be seen in the following sections, the flexible budget becomes an essential element in analyzing variances to identify potential sources for the causes.

FRAMEWORK FOR OVERHEAD VARIANCE ANALYSIS

Because different factors give rise to over/underapplied overhead (sometimes called *total* or *net overhead variance*), we need a framework in which to identify the areas of potential causes of variation. Therefore, the under/overapplied amount is decomposed into two or more variances, each one calculated to highlight specific areas for which causes of variations can be identified quickly.

Depending on the level of detail desired, under/overapplied overhead can be analyzed by three general approaches. Each approach requires a decomposition of the total overhead variance into greater detail. The more detailed the analysis, the more potential for fine-tuning the operations. Exhibit 13–3 shows the relationship of the three approaches we call *two-way, three-way,* and *four-way analyses.*

Two-Way Analysis

The **two-way analysis** decomposes the under/overapplied overhead into a budget variance and a volume variance. We use the tabular approach to perform the analysis because the table can easily be expanded to incorporate the three-way and four-way analyses. Later, we summarize computations for individual variances.

Mechanics of Variance Analysis.   A tabular approach to calculate a budget and a volume variance is displayed in Exhibit 13–4. The data are those for the Jason-Court Products, Inc., example.

The column Actual Overhead Incurred is the debit side of the Production Overhead or Production Overhead Control account. It contains the actual variable and fixed overhead costs for the period under consideration. The other extreme, the column Applied (Charged to Production), is the credit side of the Production Overhead or Applied Production Overhead account and represents the standard overhead costs charged to the work in process during the period. (Exhibit 13–1 shows how the applied amounts are calculated.)

The heading Flexible Budget for 8,200 is the budget we would have prepared from the flexible budget formula had we known in advance that production activity

EXHIBIT 13–3   General Framework for Overhead Variance Analysis

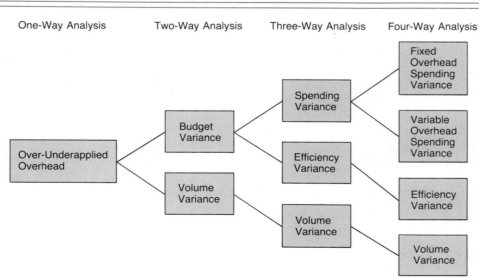

EXHIBIT 13–4 Budget and Volume Variances—Two-Way Analysis

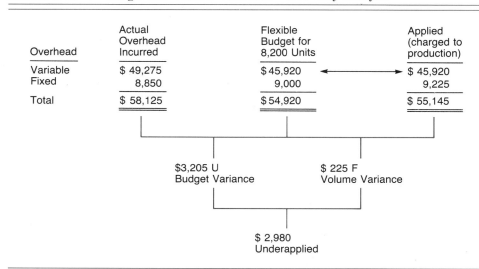

would lead to 8,200 glucometers. Our monthly budget formula is $9,000 plus $11.20 times the number of direct labor hours or, in terms of standards per unit, is $9,000 plus $5.60 times the number of units produced. Therefore, the variable costs are $45,920 ($5.60 × 8,200 units). Alternatively, the variable costs could have been calculated by using the standard hours allowed. If 8,200 units are produced, each requiring one-half hour, the standard hours allowed are 4,100 (8,200 × ½ hour). The budget amount is figured as $11.20 per hour times 4,100 standard hours allowed. The fixed costs are taken from the budget formula.

An arrow indicates that variable overhead costs in the flexible budget are the same as those applied. This should always be the case because the amounts are based on the same standard cost and same activity level.

Budget Variance. A **budget variance** is the difference between actual overhead costs incurred and the flexible budget for actual units produced. (*Controllable variance* is another title given the budget variance.) This variance in Exhibit 13–4 is unfavorable, which means that more dollars were spent than were budgeted for 8,200 units. It indicates there may be ways to improve the efficiency and effectiveness of some overhead cost components. A more detailed examination of the variance is needed to identify areas in which corrective action is necessary. One could perform three-way or four-way analyses at this point, as suggested in Exhibit 13–3, or investigate the identifiable underlying causes for variation.

A number of causes may exist for a favorable or unfavorable budget variance, all of which are assumed to be under the responsibility of the department or line supervisor. The common causes are changes in the terms for buying supplies and services, waste or savings in indirect material usage, avoidable machine breakdowns, different grades of indirect material or skill for indirect labor, and less efficient or more efficient scheduling of indirect labor. Because a flexible budget is involved in determining the budget variance, forecasting errors can also cause variances. Such errors come in two varieties: (1) the inaccuracies in predicting what will occur in the future, and (2) the reliability of approximations made in separating the overhead costs into variable and fixed categories.

The budget variance is controlled by the operating departments. Consequently, the two-way analysis identifies one variance traceable to the Assembly Department supervisor. The volume variance is usually treated as controllable by someone higher on the organizational ladder.

Volume Variance.   A **volume variance** is the difference between the flexible budget for the actual units produced (or the standard hours allowed for the actual production) and the amounts applied to work in process. Because the variable overhead costs are the same in each column, the volume variance is the difference between the budgeted fixed overhead and the applied fixed overhead. Therefore, the volume variance is the amount of budgeted fixed overhead not applied (unfavorable) or the amount applied in excess of the budget (favorable). It represents the component of the total overhead variance that results when actual production differs from the capacity level used to calculate the standard fixed overhead rate.

Normal capacity (or any other concept of capacity discussed earlier) and standard hours allowed sometimes create confusion for those trying to understand the computations. The selected capacity level is used to determine the production overhead rate for fixed costs. That rate is used with the variable rate to apply overhead to work in process. After the fact, we ask, ''How many units of product were produced in this department or operation?'' Once we know the units of output, we convert them to the number of units of that activity measure allowed for that output. When direct labor hours is the activity measure, the results are standard hours allowed. The difference between normal capacity and standard hours allowed gives rise to the volume variance that is illustrated in the following example.

For Jason-Court Products, Inc., the volume variance is $225 favorable. That means more fixed overhead cost was charged to production than the total budgeted fixed cost. It should be obvious the company planned for 8,000 units per month because normal capacity is 4,000 direct labor hours with one-half hour allowed per completed glucometer. The fixed overhead rate of $2.25 per hour or $1.125 per unit was set at normal capacity. Because more units were produced than the capacity level selected, we used, in effect, an incorrect fixed overhead rate.

Generally speaking, the volume variance is treated as uncontrollable by the departmental managers because volume considerations are determined by some other part of the organization. However, departmental managers control factors that can influence how much capacity is available. For example, inefficient use of labor time or machine time limits the amount of capacity that can be used to produce units or provide a service. When such factors are identified, the variance is controllable by the departmental manager and should be charged to that department.

Why does actual production differ from planned production? Many causes can be responsible. Common ones include decrease or increase in customer demand, less or more efficient production scheduling, unusual machine breakdowns, natural disasters, strikes or work slowdowns, and fluctuations over time (if a normal capacity concept is used rather than expected actual capacity). In some cases, overhead rates are not adjusted for anticipated idle capacity because this is a temporary condition.

The foregoing material discussion presents the basic concepts of volume variance, but further explanation will help you to understand this variance. Also, an alternate method for computation will be presented.

A volume variance is a result of the way we account for fixed production overhead. In our example, the budgeted fixed overhead costs are expected to remain constant at $9,000 for a month independent of the activity level. However, when we apply fixed overhead costs to products, we multiply the fixed component of the standard overhead rate times the standard direct labor hours allowed. This means the applied fixed overhead cost behaves as though it were a variable cost. For Jason-Court Products, Inc., the fixed overhead rate per hour is $2.25 (or $1.125 per unit). The volume variance is the difference between the budgeted and the applied fixed overhead costs. A zero-volume variance occurs only when the budgeted capacity (whether practical, normal, or expected actual) equals the standard hours allowed for the actual units produced. Normal capacity for Jason-Court Products, Inc., is 4,000 direct labor hours per month. If 8,000 units (4,000 standard direct labor hours allowed) are produced, the volume variance would be zero. If volume runs less than normal capacity, the variance is unfavorable because insufficient fixed standard costs are charged to products. On the other hand, volume higher than normal capacity yields a favorable variance. Consequently, the volume variance does not provide management with a measure to evaluate performance or monitor cost control. Rather, it simply measures whether actual production volume was above or below that expected.

Because the volume variance is a function of the difference between normal capacity and the standard capacity allowed for actual production, we have an alternate approach to calculating the volume variance. It is the fixed overhead rate per hour times the difference between normal capacity and the standard hours allowed for actual production units. Numerically, this works out to $2.25 × (4,000 hours for normal capacity − 4,100 standard hours allowed for 8,200 units) = $225 favorable.

Three-Way Variance	A **three-way analysis** of overhead variances provides more detail on the budget variance by separating it into a spending variance and an efficiency variance. The volume variance is identical to the two-way analysis.

Mechanics of Variance Analysis.   Continuing with a tabular approach, Exhibit 13–5 shows the computation of three variances: spending, efficiency, and volume.

Two things differ in Exhibit 13–5 from the two-way analysis. A minor difference is the addition of standard hours allowed to the heading of flexible budget for actual units. The reason for this becomes apparent in the discussion below. A major difference is the insertion of a flexible budget for the actual direct labor hours worked. Its presence permits dividing the budget variance into two parts.

The heading Flexible Budget for 4,150 Hours Worked represents variable and fixed overhead costs that would have been budgeted if 4,150 hours were the planned level. The variable overhead costs are calculated as 4,150 hours × $11.20 per direct labor hour = $46,480. Budgeted fixed overhead costs are $9,000, which is the amount from the monthly budget formula. The amount of the budgeted total fixed overhead is the same whether units of output or hours allowed is used.

Spending Variance.   A **spending variance** is the difference between actual overhead costs and the flexible budget for actual hours worked, and this variance includes both variable and fixed costs. In other words, the actual overhead is what was spent to work 4,150 direct labor hours, and this amount is compared with the budget for those hours. The variance assumes that the best measure of how much should be spent on overhead is the actual number of direct labor hours (or other activity measure if direct labor hours is not selected) rather than the standard allowed. For Jason-Court Products, Inc., the spending variance is $2,645 unfavorable. Like other variances, more detail about causes is needed before managers can institute corrective action.

Some causes of variation discussed for the budget variance in a two-way analysis also occur in the spending variance. However, the three most common areas that are investigated when variances occur are (1) changes in prices of individual overhead

EXHIBIT 13–5   Spending, Efficiency, and Volume Variances—Three-Way Analysis

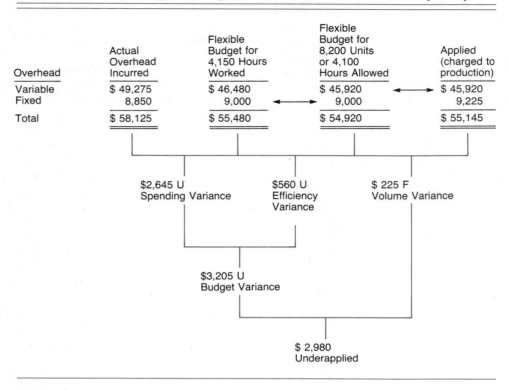

cost components, (2) efficient or inefficient use of individual overhead items, and (3) reasonableness of approximations used to separate overhead costs into variable and fixed categories.

Efficiency Variance.   The **efficiency variance** is the difference between the flexible budget for actual hours worked and the flexible budget for standard hours allowed. Because fixed overhead costs are identical in both budgets, the efficiency variance consists only of differences in variable overhead costs.

In some sense, the term *efficiency* is a misnomer because it does not measure the efficient or inefficient use of individual overhead items. These are included in the spending variance. As used here, *efficiency* comes from an engineering concept for comparing input with output. The flexible budget for actual hours worked is input for the output achieved, and the flexible budget for standard hours allowed is for the output achieved. The variance measures the additional overhead costs incurred or saved as a result of the inefficient or efficient use of the activity upon which overhead is based. In other words, overhead must be incurred to support activity. If the activity is inefficient, overhead costs are incurred to support that inefficiency. If management was efficient in using the activity and beat the standard, overhead costs are saved. For example, when the activity base is machine hours, the efficiency variance measures the additional overhead costs incurred or saved because of inefficient or efficient use of machine time. If direct labor hours is the activity base, the variance represents overhead costs incurred or saved with the usage of labor time.

When direct labor hours are the activity base, a relationship exists between the labor efficiency variance and the overhead efficiency variance—they move in the same direction. If labor hours are inefficiently used, the labor efficiency variance measures the labor costs of that inefficiency, and the overhead efficiency variance is the additional overhead incurred to support that inefficient labor. A favorable labor efficiency variance means the overhead efficiency variance must be favorable also. Consequently, to find the causes of an overhead efficiency variance for an activity base of direct labor, look to the causes of efficient or inefficient use of labor. The same applies when direct labor dollars are used as the measure of activity.

Jason-Court Products, Inc., has a $560 unfavorable efficiency variance. If direct labor hours are an appropriate activity base, the variance is the additional overhead costs incurred to support an inefficient use of direct labor in the Assembly Department.

With the overhead efficiency variance consisting only of variable costs, we have an alternate means to calculate the variance. The formula is similar to that used for material quantity and labor efficiency variances: standard variable overhead rate per hour × (actual hours worked − standard hours allowed). For our example, this is $11.20 × (4,150 hours worked − 4,100 standard hours allowed) or $11.20 × 50 = $560 unfavorable. It is unfavorable because the actual hours exceeded those allowed.

Four-Way Analysis

The **four-way analysis** of overhead variances produces yet another level of detail and understanding by separating the spending variance into its variable and fixed components. (This assumes that actual costs can in fact be separated into variable and fixed components. This may not be possible with some mixed or semivariable costs.) Efficiency and volume variances remain the same as in the three-way approach. Now we have two variances with variable costs—variable overhead spending variance and overhead efficiency variance—and two variances for fixed costs—fixed overhead spending variance and volume variance.

Because the information for the three-way approach has been presented in Exhibit 13–5, only the pertinent columns for the spending variances are reconstructed as follows:

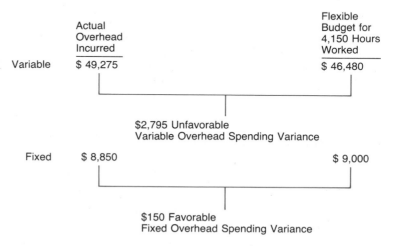

The **variable overhead spending variance** can also be calculated as the difference between actual variable overhead costs incurred and the variable overhead rate per hour times the actual hours worked. For our illustration, that equates to $49,275 − ($11.20 per hour × 4,150 actual hours worked) = $2,795 unfavorable. The company spent more on overhead items than the budget called for at the hours worked.

The **fixed overhead spending variance** (sometimes called the *fixed budget variance*) is the difference between actual fixed costs incurred and budgeted fixed costs. For Jason-Court Products, Inc., the difference is $150 favorable. That is, the company did not spend as much as budgeted. Remember that fixed costs may change even though they are expected to remain the same within the relevant range of activity. However, changes in production volume do not change the level of fixed costs; other factors do that.

Summary of Overhead Variance Computations

As we progressed from under/overapplied overhead to four-way analysis, we introduced alternate ways to calculate the four possible variances. These are summarized here for convenience.

Variable overhead spending variance = Actual variable overhead − (Standard variable rate per hour × Actual hours)

Variable overhead efficiency variance = Standard variable rate per hour × (Actual hours − Standard hours allowed)

Fixed overhead spending variance = Actual fixed overhead − Budgeted fixed overhead

Fixed volume variance = Standard fixed rate per hour × (Normal capacity[1] in hours − The standard hours allowed for actual units produced).

If you choose to do a three-way analysis, combine the computations for variable and fixed overhead spending variances. The two-way analysis can be approached in one of two ways: (1) by combining the spending variances and efficiency variance calculations or (2) by subtracting the volume variance from the under/overapplied amount.

DISPOSITION OF VARIANCES

In our discussion of material and labor variances, we established variance accounts for material price, material quantity, labor rate, and labor efficiency variances. To a large extent, the variances were isolated as a normal part of journalizing transactions. Overhead variances are not isolated in a similar way. The under/overapplied amount is analyzed into those variances management finds meaningful. This can be done on worksheets with the results never entering the accounting records, or separate variance accounts can be established. Most companies prefer the worksheet approach because they do not have constantly to enter and close variance accounts. The only entry necessary when separate variances are not recorded is the closing of the under/overapplied amount.

Separate Overhead Variance Accounts

If a company records separate variances for standard costs, debit balances represent unfavorable variances and credit balances favorable variances. An entry to create separate variance accounts for Jason-Court Products, Inc., assuming the four-way variance analysis, is:

Variable Overhead Spending Variance	2,795	
Variable Efficiency Variance	560	
Fixed Overhead Spending Variance		150
Fixed Volume Variance		225
Production Overhead		2,980

[1] We are using normal capacity here, but any of the capacity concepts we have discussed, if used, are appropriate. In the formula, we want the level of capacity used for determining the standard fixed overhead rate.

If the company uses two production overhead accounts rather than one, the entry is:

Applied Production Overhead	55,145	
Variable Overhead Spending Variance	2,795	
Variable Efficiency Variance	560	
Fixed Overhead Spending Variance		150
Fixed Volume Variance		225
Production Overhead		58,125

The under/overapplied amount or the separate variance accounts must be closed at the end of the period and the amounts disposed of in an appropriate manner. These procedures will be discussed below as a part of the period cost/product cost consideration.

Variances as Period or Product Costs

Another decision management must make with respect to variances is whether they are period costs or product costs. The results determine how variances are handled when recording their effects in the accounting records.

Two basic procedures are used for the disposition of all standard cost variances: (1) close entirely to Cost of Goods Sold or Income Summary as a period cost, or (2) allocate to inventories and Cost of Goods Sold. As an illustration, we use the production data from Decolor Manufacturing:

	Unfavorable (Debit)	Favorable (Credit)
Material price variance	$ 800	—
Material quantity variance	—	$600
Labor rate variance	—	700
Labor efficiency variance	1,000	—
Underapplied overhead	1,800	—

	Cost Components at Standard		
Inventories/Cost of Goods Sold	Materials	Labor	Overhead
Materials inventory	$ 20,000	—	—
Work in process inventory	15,000	$ 10,500	$ 14,700
Finished goods inventory	30,000	21,000	29,400
Cost of goods sold	115,000	80,500	112,700
Totals	$180,000	$112,000	$156,800

Variances Treated as Period Costs. Standards are set with an assumed level of efficiency. If this level is not met during production, the cost incurred is for inefficiency or waste and should be controllable by someone in the organization. One viewpoint is that these costs should not be charged to products but to the period in which the inefficiency or waste occurred. That is, variances from the standard are period costs rather than product costs. Variances are therefore closed either to Cost of Goods Sold or Income Summary. If variances are considered the responsibility of production personnel, Cost of Goods Sold is the appropriate account. Otherwise, the Income Summary should be used. Cost of Goods Sold is the more common account in practice.

Insignificant variances, whether unfavorable or favorable, are usually treated as period costs because of the simplicity of this method of accounting. In this case, the account charged or credited for income statement purposes is irrelevant, although Cost of Goods Sold is the frequently used account.

The entry to close the variance accounts of Decolor Manufacturing treating variances as period costs is:

Materials Quantity Variance	600	
Labor Rate Variance	700	
Cost of Goods Sold	2,300	
Materials Price Variance		800
Labor Efficiency Variance		1,000
Production Overhead		1,800

Variances Treated as Product Costs.   The other procedure is to treat variances as a cost of the product and allocate them to appropriate inventories and Cost of Goods Sold. The purpose of allocating variances is to adjust the standard cost to actual cost. This approach is used when variances are significant and the standard costs do not represent the reasonable cost of production and cost of goods sold.

A variety of methods can be used to allocate the variances. The less-detailed approach allocates variances in proportion to the ending balances in the inventories and Cost of Goods Sold accounts. These allocations are summarized in Exhibit 13–6. The entry that closes variance accounts under this approach is:

Material Quantity Variance	600	
Labor Rate Variance	700	
Material Inventory	35	
Work in Process Inventory	213	
Finished Goods Inventory	424	
Cost of Goods Sold	1,628	
Material Price Variance		800
Labor Efficiency Variance		1,000
Production Overhead		1,800

A more elaborate and most detailed approach allocates variances on the basis of cost components in each inventory account and Cost of Goods Sold. Under this method, the materials price variance is allocated to the Materials Inventory, Material Quantity Variance, Work in Process Inventory, Finished Goods Inventory, and Cost

EXHIBIT 13–6   Percentages of Costs in Inventories and Cost of Goods Sold and Allocation of Variances

	Percentages of Costs in Inventories and Cost of Goods Sold				
Standard Costs	*Material Inventory*	*Work in Process*	*Finished Goods*	*Cost of Goods Sold*	*Total*
For material price	$20,000	$40,200	$80,400	$308,200	$448,800
—percent	4.4%	9.0%	17.9%	68.7%	100.0%
Other variances		$40,200	$80,400	$308,200	$428,800
—percent		9.4%	18.7%	71.9%	100.0%

			Variance Allocation				
Accounts	*Standard Cost Balances*	*Material Price*	*Material Quantity*	*Labor Rate*	*Labor Efficiency*	*Under-applied*	*Ending Balances*
Materials inventory	$ 20,000	$ 35	–0–	–0–	–0–	–0–	$ 20,035
Work in process	40,200	72	($ 56)	($ 66)	$ 94	$ 169	40,413
Finished goods	80,400	143	(113)	(131)	187	337	80,824
Cost of goods sold	308,200	550	(431)	(503)	719	1,294	309,828
	$448,800	$800	($600)	($700)	$1,000	$1,800	$451,100

of Goods Sold in proportion to the amount of standard materials cost in each account. The materials price variance is allocated to Material Quantity Variance because the quantity issued has a price variance associated with it that was removed when the original entry to Material Inventory was recorded at standard cost. Therefore, the Material Quantity Variance should be adjusted for a piece of a material price variance just like the other accounts. After this adjustment, the Material Quantity Variance with its portion of Material Price Variance is allocated to Work in Process, Finished Goods, and Cost of Goods Sold in proportion to the amount of standard material cost in these accounts. The rationale for not allocating any material quantity variance to Material Inventory is that the quantity relates to usage of materials, not to the acquisition of materials.

The same allocation procedure is used for conversion costs. Labor and overhead variances are allocated in proportion to the amount of the respective labor and overhead standard costs in these accounts.

Exhibit 13–7 presents the percentages and allocations. With these data, the journal entry to close variance accounts is:

Material Quantity Variance	600	
Labor Rate Variance	700	
Material Inventory	89	
Work in Process Inventory	207	
Finished Goods Inventory	414	
Cost of Goods Sold	1,590	
Material Price Variance		800
Labor Efficiency Variance		1,000
Production Overhead		1,800

EXHIBIT 13–7   Percentages of Costs in Inventories and Cost of Goods Sold and Allocation of Variances

Percentages of Costs in Inventories and Cost of Goods Sold

Standard Costs	Material Inventory	Material Quantity Variance	Work in Process	Finished Goods	Cost of Goods Sold	Total
Material—dollars	$20,000	$600	$15,000	$30,000	$115,000	$180,600
—percent	11.1%	0.3%	8.3%	16.6%	63.7%	100.0%
Material—dollars			$15,000	$30,000	$115,000	$160,000
—percent			9.4%	18.7%	71.9%	100.0%
Labor—dollars			$10,500	$21,000	$80,500	$112,000
—percent			9.4%	18.7%	71.9%	100.0%
Overhead—dollars			$14,700	$29,400	$112,700	$156,800
—percent			9.4%	18.7%	71.9%	100.0%

Variance Allocation

Accounts	Standard Cost Balances	Material Price	Material Quantity	Labor Rate	Labor Efficiency	Under-applied	Ending Balances
Materials inventory	$ 20,000	$ 89	–0–	–0–	–0–	–0–	$ 20,089
Material quantity	(600)	2	–0–	–0–	–0–	–0–	(598)
Work in process	40,200	66	($ 56)	($ 66)	$ 94	$ 169	40,407
Finished goods	80,400	133	(112)	(131)	187	337	80,814
Cost of goods sold	308,200	510	(430)	(503)	719	1,294	309,790
	$448,200	$800	($598)	($700)	$1,000	$1,800	$450,502

REVIEW OF STANDARDS FOR REVISION

Standard costs should be reviewed periodically to see if revisions are necessary. Customary practice is to review standards once each year, thus holding down the administrative costs and inconvenience of review and revision. Exceptions exist, however. In cases in which trade, for example, is seasonal or cyclical, a shorter or longer period may be more appropriate.

The typical kinds of changes that outdate standards are:

1. Change in the general price level of basic materials.
2. New wage schedule negotiated or payment plan changed.
3. Products added or modified.
4. Material type or specification changed.
5. New equipment added and old equipment retired.
6. Operations or procedures modified.
7. Change in management policy that affects the way costs are accumulated and charged to work.

Examples of changes in management policy that influence standard costs are a redefinition of the desired level of capacity, depreciation methods, and capitalization/ expense policies. A redefinition of capacity can be due to increasing or decreasing hours of operation, or decreasing demand. Depreciation methods may change for new equipment, or the company may institute a policy of changing from a declining balance method for existing equipment to a straight-line method at about the midlife point of the asset life. Any change in criteria for the capitalization/expense decision alters the amount of costs in depreciation and other cost categories.

Some companies have a department that spends full time reviewing standards. Any standards that need revision will be changed during the period rather than waiting until the end of the period. When this occurs, we have accumulated variances that are a mixture of the old and new standards. Accountants will, for reporting purposes, separate that part of the variance due to using an outdated standard. For example, if labor rates change, any accumulated rate variances will be divided into the amounts related to the old rates and any variances tied to the new standard rates.

STANDARD COSTS IN A PROCESS COST SYSTEM

Although our discussions have assumed a job order cost system, any company that uses a process cost system usually meets the conditions for a standard cost system. For example, homogeneous products or services, continuous and repetitive operations, and a predetermined production sequence are characteristics of a process cost system that meet the requirements for a standard cost system. Standard cost variances are calculated in a process cost system on the basis of FIFO equivalent units of production. Equivalent units may be different for materials, labor, and overhead, but the variances are computed and analyzed in the same way we have discussed in the last two chapters.

An illustration of the process cost situation should be helpful. Consider first the following data. The Solomon Company places material in production at the beginning of operations. In September, costs of materials issued to production totaled $73,692, direct labor cost, $15,511, and overhead costs, $46,533. The beginning inventory for the month was 16,400 units (100 percent complete for material, 25 percent complete for conversion costs). The standard costs of the September 1 Work in Process Inventory were $11,808, separated as $9,840 for materials, $492 for direct labor, and $1,476 for overhead. During the month, 120,000 units were started, and 130,900 units were completed and transferred out. Of those units completed, 114,500 were started and completed (130,900 completed units less 16,400 units in the beginning inventory; or 120,000 units started less 5,500 units in the ending inventory). The ending inventory of 5,500 units had all of its material content but was 40 percent complete for conversion costs. The standard costs have been set at:

Materials	$0.60
Direct labor	0.12
Overhead	0.36
Total	$1.08

In Chapter 9 we presented the first-in, first-out (FIFO) and weighted average methods for calculating equivalent units. Because standard costs represent current production, we do not want to mix work done in a prior period with that of the current period. Therefore, the FIFO method is used to calculate equivalent units in a standard cost system. For the Solomon Company, the equivalent units are:

	Material	*Conversion*
Work in process September 1:		
16,400 × (100% − 100%)	–0–	
16,400 × (100% − 25%)		12,300
Started and completed	114,500	114,500
Work in process, September 30:		
5,500 units × 100%	5,500	
5,500 units × 40%		2,200
Equivalent units of production	120,000	129,000

The standard costs charged to the Work in Process Inventory account for September are calculated by using the appropriate equivalent unit number times the standard cost per unit, as follows:

Materials:	120,000 units × $.60 =	$ 72,000	
Direct labor:	129,000 units × $.12 =	15,480	
Overhead:	129,000 units × $.36 =	46,440	
		$133,920	

Add to this amount the standard costs in the beginning inventory of $11,808 and you arrive at costs of $145,728 that will be allocated to goods completed and ending inventory.

Allocation of costs to goods completed and to Work in Process Inventory at September 30 is straightforward:

Units completed:	130,900 units × $1.08 =	$141,372
Work in process inventory, September 30:		
Materials:	5,500 units × $0.60 =	$ 3,300
Direct labor:	2,200 units × $0.12 =	264
Overhead:	2,200 units × $0.36 =	792
		$ 4,356
Total costs accounted for		$145,728

Variances can be calculated by comparing actual costs with standard costs. For materials, the price variance was isolated when the goods went into inventory. So the cost of materials issued is the standard cost of material times actual quantity issued. We have that amount as $73,692. The standard cost charged to Work in Process from above is $72,000. The materials quantity variance is $1,692 unfavorable.

Actual direct labor cost incurred totaled $15,511, and the standard cost charged work in process was $15,480. The difference of $31 unfavorable is a composite of both labor rate and labor efficiency variances. Given the hours worked and labor rates involved, these variances can be computed.

The overhead amounts give an underapplied amount of $93 ($46,533 actual − $46,440 applied). To calculate two-way, three-way, or four-way variances, we need the overhead flexible budget formula and information on actual and standard hours.

Variance analysis in a process cost system does not differ from the approaches taken in a job order cost system. The key ingredient for variance analysis with a process cost system is the computation of equivalent units based on a FIFO method.

SUMMARY

A standard cost for production overhead has price and quantity factors similar to those of direct materials and direct labor. The price is reflected in one or more overhead rates, and the quantity is the measure of activity. In establishing the appropriate overhead rates, management should consider five major areas: (1) the cost elements to include in production overhead, (2) the activity measure that best relates overhead costs to work performed, (3) the capacity concept for the selected activity measure, (4) the cost behavior of each overhead cost, and (5) the overhead rate structure—plantwide rate, departmental rates, or some other structure.

A flexible budget is a formula expressing the expected overhead cost for a period in terms of the activity measure. It is designed to cover a range of activity and can be used to develop budgets at any point within the range. Flexible budgets are used to estimate overhead costs at a predicted level of operations and to identify the amount of cost that should have been incurred at the actual level of operations. The goal is to facilitate cost control and performance evaluation.

During any period, the actual overhead costs incurred can differ from those applied. In order to understand the significance of the under/overapplied amount, we calculate variances that highlight areas in which causes of variations can be easily identified. This variance analysis will follow either a two-way, three-way, or four-way approach. A two-way approach calculates a budget variance and a volume variance. A three-way approach decomposes the budget variance into spending and efficiency variances; the volume variance remains the same. A four-way approach decomposes the spending variance into a variable overhead spending variance and a fixed overhead spending variance; efficiency and volume variances are the same as those in a three-way approach.

A budget variance is the difference between actual overhead costs incurred and the flexible budget for actual units produced. It represents those overhead elements over which the departmental manager has control.

A spending variance is the difference between actual overhead costs and the flexible budget for actual hours worked. The most common causes of this variance are changes in prices of overhead cost elements, efficient or inefficient use of the overhead cost items, and errors in the approximations used to separate overhead costs into variable and fixed categories. In the three-way approach, the spending variance comprises both variable and fixed overhead costs. The four-way approach separates the cost behavior and has a spending variance for variable overhead and another for fixed overhead.

An efficiency variance is the difference between the flexible budget for actual hours worked and the flexible budget for standard hours allowed. It is made up of only variable costs. This variance does not mean that overhead items are efficiently or inefficiently used. Instead, it is the added overhead cost to support inefficient use of the activity measure or the overhead cost saved with efficient use of the activity measure.

The volume variance is the difference between the flexible budget for actual units produced and the amounts applied to Work in Process. It is made up of only fixed overhead costs and represents the amount by which actual production differs from planned capacity used to calculate the standard fixed overhead rate.

Two basic procedures are available to dispose of variances at the end of a period: close entirely to Cost of Goods Sold or Income Summary, or allocate to inventories and Cost of Goods Sold. The first method is appropriate for insignificant variances and in cases in which variances are costs of inefficiency. The other method is used when variances are significant or when inventories and cost of goods sold should be converted to actual costs.

Standard costs can also be used in a process cost system. We set standards for material, labor, and overhead for a process cost system in the same manner as for a job order cost system. Because a process cost system relies on equivalent units of production for determining costs of production and inventories, equivalent units are also relied on for implementing standard costs. Caution must be exercised to note that different equivalent units can exist for material, labor, and overhead. Equivalent units must be calculated with the FIFO method.

PROBLEM FOR REVIEW

Sheree Bunch, Inc., is a manufacturer of specialized components used in industrial power systems. The following production data appear in the company's records for the current year:

1. Standard costs are $3 per unit of material and $9 per hour of direct labor. The overhead flexible budget for the year is $90,000 + $3.00 per direct labor hour, and normal capacity is 90,000 direct labor hours.
2. Materials purchased for the year totaled 95,000 units at an actual cost of $3.10 per unit. Only 83,000 units were issued to work in process. The standard material allowed for the units produced was 80,000 units.
3. The company operated at 78,000 direct labor hours but produced the quantity of product that had 80,000 direct labor hours allowed. The actual labor rate paid was $9.80.
4. The actual overhead costs incurred were variable, $233,000 and fixed $88,500.

REQUIRED

Compute the following standard cost variances:
a. Material price and material quantity variances.
b. Labor rate and efficiency variances.
c. Overhead variances using:
  1. Two-way analysis.
  2. Three-way analysis.
  3. Four-way analysis.

SOLUTION

a. Material price variance:

$3.10 × 95,000 units purchased = $294,500
$3.00 × 95,000 units purchased = 285,000
($3.10 − $3.00) × 95,000 units = $ 9,500 U

Material quantity variance:

$3.00 × 83,000 units =	$249,000	
$3.00 × 80,000 units =	240,000	
$3.00 × (83,000 − 80,000) =	$ 9,000	U

b. Labor rate variance:

$9.80 × 78,000 hours worked =	$764,400	
$9.00 × 78,000 hours worked =	702,000	
($9.80 − $9.00) × 78,000 hours =	$ 62,400	U

Labor efficiency variance:

$9.00 × 78,000 hours worked =	$702,000	
$9.00 × 80,000 hours allowed =	720,000	
$9.00 × (78,000 − 80,000) =	$ 18,000	F

c. 1. Two-way analysis:

Budget variance:

Actual overhead incurred		
Variable	$233,000	
Fixed	88,500	$321,500
Flexible budget for 80,000 hours allowed		
Variable ($3.00 × 80,000 hours)	$240,000	
Fixed (Budget at normal)	90,000	330,000
		$ 8,500 F

Volume variance:

Flexible budget for 80,000 hours allowed		
Variable ($3.00 × 80,000 hours)	$240,000	
Fixed (Budget at normal)	90,000	$330,000
Applied (Charged to production)		
Variable ($3.00 × 80,000 hours)	$240,000	
Fixed ($1.00 × 80,000 hours)	80,000	320,000
$1.00 × (90,000 − 80,000)		$ 10,000 U

c. 2. Three-way analysis:

Note: Because the volume variance is the same as in the two-way analysis, we will only decompose the budget variance into spending and efficiency variances.

Spending variance:

Actual overhead incurred		
Variable	$233,000	
Fixed	88,500	$321,500
Flexible budget for 78,000 hours worked		
Variable ($3.00 × 78,000)	$234,000	
Fixed (Budget at normal)	90,000	324,000
		$ 2,500 F

Efficiency variance:

Flexible budget for 78,000 hours worked		
Variable ($3.00 × 78,000 hours)	$234,000	
Fixed (Budget at normal)	90,000	$324,000
Flexible budget for 80,000 hours allowed		
Variable ($3.00 × 80,000 hours)	$240,000	
Fixed (Budget at normal)	90,000	330,000
$3.00 × (78,000 − 80,000)		$ 6,000 F

c. 3. Four-way analysis:

Note: We calculate only the two spending variances because efficiency and volume variances are the same as those in the three-way analysis.

Variable overhead spending variance:

Actual variable overhead	$233,000
Variable costs at 78,000 hours	
($3.00 × 78,000 hours)	234,000
	$ 1,000 F

Fixed overhead spending variance:

Actual fixed overhead	$ 88,500
Fixed costs at normal capacity	90,000
	$ 1,500 F

KEY TERMS AND CONCEPTS

Production overhead (508)	Three-way analysis (515)
Measure of activity (509)	Spending variance (515)
Flexible overhead budget (510)	Efficiency variance (516)
Two-way analysis (510)	Four-way analysis (517)
Budget variance (513)	Variable overhead spending variance (517)
Volume variance (514)	Fixed overhead spending variance (518)

ADDITIONAL READINGS

Brown, Clifton. "Effects of Dynamic Task Environment on the Learning of Standard Cost Variance Significance." *Journal of Accounting Research,* Autumn, 1983, pp. 413–31.

Cheatham, Carole. "Reporting the Effects of Excess Inventories." *Journal of Accountancy,* November, 1989, pp. 131–40.

Chow, Chee W. "The Effects of Job Standard Tightness and Compensation Scheme on Performance: An Exploration of Linkages." *Accounting Review,* October, 1983, pp. 667–85.

Jaouen, Pauline R., and Bruce R. Neumann. "Variance Analysis, Kanban and JIT: A Further Study." *Journal of Accountancy,* June, 1987, pp. 164–73.

Marcinko, David, and Enrico Petri. "Use of the Production Function in Calculation of Standard Cost Variances—An Extension." *Accounting Review,* July, 1984, pp. 488–95.

Wolf, Warren G. "Developing a Cost System for Today's Decision Making." *Management Accounting,* December, 1982, pp. 19–23.

REVIEW QUESTIONS

1. Discuss the major considerations for implementing standard costs for production overhead.
2. In applying production overhead to work in process, is the basis the units produced or the activity allowed? Explain.
3. What is a flexible budget?
4. How do you convert an annual flexible budget to a monthly flexible budget? How do you convert a monthly flexible budget to an annual flexible budget?
5. Why should flexible budgets be developed on a departmental basis rather than on the basis of one budget for the entire production facility?
6. Give the framework and related formulas for analyzing the under/overapplied overhead using (a) a two-way analysis, (b) a three-way analysis, and (c) a four-way analysis.
7. What are the primary causes of the budget variance?
8. What are the primary causes of the overhead spending variance? Of the overhead efficiency variance?

9. What information does an overhead efficiency variance offer management?
10. Why is the term *overhead efficiency variance* a misnomer?
11. Explain how an overhead efficiency variance might relate to the labor efficiency variance.
12. What information does the volume variance offer management?
13. What is the meaning of a favorable volume variance and an unfavorable volume variance?
14. Fixed and variable overhead costs are applied to work in process as though all overhead costs are variable. What are the consequences of applying fixed overhead as though it were a variable cost?
15. How does the variable spending variance differ from a materials price variance or a labor rate variance?
16. If the production overhead is underapplied for the month of June, would you expect the total of all overhead variances for June to be favorable or unfavorable? Why?
17. Explain two methods to account for standard cost variances at the end of an accounting period. Discuss under what circumstances each method would be used.
18. Why should standards be reviewed periodically and consideration given for revisions?
19. What are the typical kinds of changes that outdate standards?
20. What are the primary differences between using standard costs in a job order cost system and a process cost system?

DISCUSSION QUESTIONS

21. For allocating production overhead to products and services, a measure of output is preferred to a measure of input. For example, actual direct labor hours worked is an input measure and standard direct labor hours allowed is an output. Units of production is an output measure. For each of the following measures of volume, explain why an output measure is preferred to an input measure, and identify both an input measure and an output measure: (1) direct labor cost or dollars, (2) machine hours, and (3) material costs.
22. An overhead volume variance is treated as uncontrollable at the departmental manager level. However, there may be circumstances under which this variance is controllable. Identify and explain those circumstances.
23. We have suggested that variance analyses extend to causes and responsibility. In most of the illustrations, variances have been departmentalized (particularly with respect to overhead). Some accountants suggest that all variances be identified with products or product lines. Discuss the advantages and disadvantages of variances by product.
24. Using actual costs, the budget formula, and applied costs, prepare a graphical analysis of the three-way approach that shows spending, efficiency, and volume variances on one graph.

EXERCISES

13–1. Production Overhead Analysis, Two-Way Method. Image, Inc., manufactures various products including a line of wrist watches. The Customizing Department will imprint a company logo on the watch face before assembly. The production process is highly automated, and machine hours are used to measure production activity in a standard cost system. The standard cost sheet shows machine time of one hour per batch of 200 watch faces at a standard overhead cost of $40 per hour with a $10 variable cost and $30 fixed cost. Normal capacity used to set the standard is 1,000 machine hours per month.

During June 19x0, 950 machine hours were used to customize 186,000 watch faces. The Customizing Department overhead costs were $9,000 variable cost and $26,900 fixed cost.

(A. Gregory, adapted)

REQUIRED:
a. Calculate the over- or underapplied overhead.
b. Calculate the following variances and show whether they are favorable or unfavorable:
   1. Controllable variance.
   2. Overhead Volume Variance

13–2. Service Overhead Analysis, Three-Way Method.   Schrade Studio produces episodes of detective and murder mysteries for television. It has sound stages and mobile units for on-site production. The monthly flexible budget for the studio is as follows:

Fixed production costs	$900,000
Variable production costs	$500 per hour
Normal activity in hours	1,250 per month

During May 19x4, the studio had the following actual data:

Fixed production costs	$890,000	(W. Smith, adapted)
Variable production costs	$950,000	
Hours billable to networks	1,300	
Hours in operation	1,350	

REQUIRED:
Calculate the following variances:
a. Overhead spending.
b. Overhead efficiency.
c. Overhead volume.

13–3. Production Overhead Analysis, Four-Way Method.   The Consumer Products Division of UT Industries, Inc., has standard costs for a batch of 100 electric curlers produced by the Curler Assembly Unit:

	Units	*Unit Cost*	*Standard*
Materials, component sets	100	$1.20	$120
Direct labor	3	6.00	18
Variable overhead	3	3.00	9
Fixed overhead	3	4.00	12
Total standard per batch			$159

Overhead for the unit is applied on the basis of labor hours. In a normal month, volume is 600 hours.

During September 19x9, the Curler Assembly Unit produced 170 batches of output with actual variable overhead costs of $1,615 and actual fixed overhead costs of $2,142. Actual hours worked totaled 540.

(D. Ripple, adapted)

REQUIRED:
a. Calculate the following variances:
   1. Variable overhead spending.
   2. Variable overhead efficiency.
   3. Fixed overhead spending.
   4. Overhead volume.
b. Explain the meaning of each of the variances in part (a).

13–4. Service Overhead Analysis, Three- and Four-Way Methods.   Advanced Installation, Inc., installs overhead doors for suppliers. The majority of its market is new residences. The flexible budget for Advanced Installation is:

Fixed production costs	$15,000
Variable production costs	$25 per hour
Normal activity in hours	160 per month

During May 19x8, the company had the following activity:

Fixed production costs	$14,500
Variable production costs	$ 4,750

Hours billable to suppliers	148
Hours in operation	165

The suppliers of doors are billed on the basis of the standard hours allowed to install each type of door.

REQUIRED:
a. Prepare a three-way analysis of overhead.
b. Prepare a four-way analysis of overhead.

13–5. Service Overhead Analysis, Two- and Three-Way Methods.   Jonus Presbyterian Hospital has a helicopter rescue team for aiding victims of accidents and emergencies distant from the hospital. The monthly flexible budget for the two helicopters is:

Fixed service costs	$37,800
Variable service costs	$75 per hour
Normal activity in hours	200 per month

During April 19x9, the helicopters had the following activity:

Fixed service costs	$38,000
Variable service costs	$17,300
Hours billable to patients	180
Hours in operation	210

The Hours billable to patients item is a standard allowed for miles flown and has been allowed by insurance companies.

REQUIRED:
a. Prepare a two-way analysis of the helicopter service overhead.
b. Prepare a three-way analysis of the helicopter service overhead.

13–6. Overhead Analysis, Four-Way Method with Journal Entries.   Union Co-op Gin produces cotton lint, cottonseed, and unopened bolls from harvested cotton. The cotton is purchased from local farmers. The cotton lint and cottonseed are sold as main products, and the unopened bolls are chopped for cattle feed as a by-product. As a cooperative, the profits are shared by members.
   The overhead budget for the cooperative is set on an annual basis:

Fixed production costs	$75,000 per year
Variable production costs	$200 per hour
Normal activity in hours	2,480 per year

A bale of cotton weighs 500 pounds and is ginned in six minutes. Overhead is applied on the basis of ginning hours allowed. There was a large crop in 19x7, and the Union Co-op had the following results:

(G. Heinrich)

Fixed production costs	$ 85,000
Variable production costs	$488,800
Bales of cotton ginned	50,000
Actual ginning hours	3,200

REQUIRED:
a. Prepare an analysis of overhead variances using the four-way method.
b. Prepare journal entries for overhead for the year.

13–7. Overhead Variances.   Bay City Hospital has a magnetic resonating unit (MRU) that can generate three-dimensional images of patients. The images are computer enhanced and can be enlarged up to 100 times original size. The monthly flexible budget for the MRU operation is:

Fixed costs	$24,000
Variable costs	$50 per hour
Normal activity	160 hours

During November 19x2, the MRU had the following actual data:

Fixed costs	$25,200
Variable costs	$11,900
Hours billable to patients	150
Hours in operation	170

Treat the hours billable to patients as the standard hours allowed for good output. Treat the hours in operation as the actual hours worked.

REQUIRED:
a. Prepare an analysis of the MRU costs using a two-way variance method. Use the billable hours in computing the flexible budget amount.
b. Prepare an analysis of the MRU costs using a four-way variance method.

13–8. Overhead Variances.   The De-Sulfuring Unit (DSU) removes sulfur during the processing of heavy crude oil residuals. The unit has the following costs planned on an annual basis:

Fixed costs	$46,398
Variable costs	$0.20 per barrel
Barrels per hour	150
Variable costs	$30.00 per hour
Normal activity	3,800 hours and 570,000 barrels

During 19x5, the following actual results were achieved:

Fixed costs	$42,819
Variable costs	$112,320
Barrels of oil de-sulfured	555,000 barrels
Hours in operation	3,900 hours

You will need to compute the hours allowed for oil de-sulfured. This will be the hours allowed for good output. Treat the hours in operation as the actual hours worked.

REQUIRED:
a. Prepare an analysis of the DSU costs using a three-way variance method.
b. Prepare an analysis of the DSU costs using a four-way variance method.

13–9. Preparation of Flexible Budgets and Overhead Rates.   Woods Brothers, Inc., is a manufacturer of racing slicks for stock race cars. The production of racing slicks involves tire resin and tire black mix, steel form set, hot pressure intrusion of steel with the resin and tire black, and final trimming and testing. The production is highly automated and has the following overhead costs per hour:

	Overhead Costs
Indirect labor	$24.00
Power	28.00
Employee benefits	25.00
Indirect materials	8.50
Purchasing	2.90
Product movement	9.50

The following fixed costs per month were planned:

Depreciation	$30,000
Insurance	18,000
Plant taxes	14,500
Supervision	6,000
Other	4,000

The normal activity expected per month is 200 operating hours with 80 tires produced per hour.

REQUIRED:

a. Compute the flexible overhead budget amounts for 80 percent and 100 percent of normal activity.

b. Compute the following standard overhead rates per hour of production:
   1. Variable overhead rate.
   2. Fixed overhead rate.

c. Compute the standard overhead cost for each tire.

13–10. Disposition of Overhead Variances.   Woody's, Inc., manufactures desks under the brand name Woody. The desks are manufactured from sawdust and have metal attachments. The sawdust is obtained at a price of $2 per ton from local sawmills. The sawdust is first mixed with glue and pressed into pieces that exactly fit to form the desk. Then an oak or walnut veneer is glued to the top, front, side, back, and drawer frontal pieces. The pieces are assembled with wood screws, metal slides, and locks. The standard overhead applied per unit is $6.00. Woody's, Inc., follows the policy of keeping all internal inventories at standard cost and approximating actual costs for tax purposes by allocating the variances. The company records overhead variances in separate accounts.

During 19x2, the following production overhead variances were recorded:

Variable overhead spending	9,620 Unfav.
Variable overhead efficiency	3,020 Unfav.
Fixed overhead spending	200 Fav.
Fixed overhead volume variance	8,860 Unfav.

Beginning inventories were negligible. The plant and sales accounts have the following ending balances:

	Materials	*Labor*	*Overhead*	*Account Balance*
Raw materials	$15,000			$15,000
Work in process	16,000	$4,000	$12,000	32,000
Finished desks	16,000	8,000	24,000	48,000
Cost of desks sold	114,000	57,000	114,000	285,000

REQUIRED:

a. Prepare a journal entry to summarize the overhead application and variances.

b. Prorate the overhead variances among the accounts and compute the adjusted ending balances.

13–11. Establishing and Revising Overhead Standards.   The Lazy Phone Co. manufactures two types of cordless phone: the Walker and the Deluxe. The Walker has a 250-foot range and the Deluxe has a 500-foot range. During 19x6, the planning data included:

Fixed overhead costs	$4,250 per month
Variable overhead costs	$30 per hour
Normal activity in hours	170 per month

The Walker requires 15 production minutes, and the Deluxe requires 30 production minutes. During 19x6, the company was unable to produce enough of the units to meet demand, and competitors were starting to offer a similar product at lower prices.

For 19x7, the plant manager decided to increase normal production to two shifts per day resulting in 340 hours of production per month. The fixed overhead is expected to increase to $20,400, and the variable overhead costs will decrease to $5.50 per hour. The products have been simplified, and the production process has been improved so that the Walker phone should now require 10 minutes to produce and the Deluxe should require 20 minutes.

(J. Lawlis, adapted)

REQUIRED:
a. Compute the standard overhead cost for each product for 19x6.
b. Compute the revised overhead standard for 19x7.

13–12. Overhead Variances.   Nolton Products developed its overhead application rate from the current annual budget. The budget is based on an expected actual output of 720,000 units requiring 3,600,000 direct labor hours (DLH). The company is able to schedule production uniformly throughout the year.

A total of 66,000 units requiring 315,000 DLH was produced during May. Actual overhead costs for May amounted to $375,000. The actual cost as compared to the annual budget and $\frac{1}{12}$th of the annual budget are shown below.

(CMA, adapted)

	Annual Budget				**Actual**
	Total Amount	*Per Unit*	*Per DLH*	*Monthly Budget*	*Costs for May 19x3*
Variable					
Indirect labor	$ 900,000	$1.25	$ .25	$ 75,000	$ 75,000
Supplies	1,224,000	1.70	.34	102,000	111,000
Fixed					
Supervision	648,000	.90	.18	54,000	51,000
Utilities	540,000	.75	.15	45,000	54,000
Depreciation	1,008,000	1.40	.28	84,000	84,000
Total	$4,320,000	$6.00	$1.20	$360,000	$375,000

REQUIRED:
Calculate the following amounts for Nolton Products for May 19x3. Be sure to identify each variance as favorable (F) or unfavorable (U).
a. Absorbed overhead costs.
b. Variable overhead spending variance.
c. Fixed overhead spending variance.
d. Variable overhead efficiency variance.
e. Volume variance.

13–13. Overhead Variances with Process Costs.   The House of Scents produces a woman's fragrance, Seductive. The company plans for 750 batches of the fragrance per month, with fixed production overhead of $90,000. Because of the repetitive nature of the process, a standard cost system is used to accumulate costs of production and determine cost of goods sold. The standard costs per batch are as follows:

Direct material (160 gallons)	$ 64
Direct labor (45 hours)	243
Total production overhead (30 machine hours)	378
	$685

During July, 700 batches were completed with an additional 108 batches 100 percent completed for material, 80 percent for direct labor, and 50 percent for production overhead. There was no work in process inventory at the beginning of July. The following actual production data regarding production overhead are available for July:

Actual variable production overhead	$195,680
Actual fixed production overhead	$ 90,890
Actual machine hours	23,500

REQUIRED:

a. Analyze the production overhead using the two-variance method.
b. Analyze the production overhead using the three-variance method.
c. Convert the spending variance in the three-variance method to a variable overhead spending variance and a fixed overhead spending variance.

PROBLEMS

13–14. Materials, Labor, and Three-Way Overhead. DW Print, Inc., prints college text pages for established publishers. (The text pages are then collated, trimmed, and bound by TR Binders, Inc.) DW Print has a flexible budget of $42,000 plus $70 per machine hour. The standard cost for a print run of 10,000 texts of 800 pages is:

Paper, rolls	2 rolls	$10,000	$20,000
Labor	24 hours	$ 18.50	444
Variable overhead	6 hours	$ 70.00	420
Fixed Overhead	6 hours	$100.00	600
			$21,464

The ink is included as indirect materials. The normal production is 420 printing hours a month. Overhead is applied on the basis of printer hours.

During the month of July 19x9, DW Industries completed 75 print runs:

(D. Washburn, adapted)

	Usage	*Cost*
	*Actual*	
Paper, rolls	153	$1,540,000
Labor hours	1,780	32,730
Variable overhead, machinery	470	39,700
Fixed overhead		43,000
Total actual costs		$1,655,430

REQUIRED:

a. Calculate the paper price and quantity variances.
b. Calculate the labor rate and efficiency variances.
c. Perform an overhead variance analysis using the three-way method.

13–15. Reconstructing Actuals, Three-way Method. Jill's Bikes, Inc., is a small company founded by Jill Jacob in Waynesburg, Pennsylvania. The company manufactures off-road bicycles and motorcycles. One of the production units fabricates and assembles pedals for 15-speed mountain bicycles.

Overhead for the pedal unit is applied on the basis of machine hours at rate of $10 per hour with $6 of variable overhead and $4 of fixed overhead. A batch of 25 pedals requires one hour of standard machine time. Normal capacity is 200 machine hours per month. The fixed overhead costs are expected to be $800 per month.

For the month of July 19x2, the underapplied overhead was $500, which included an unfavorable overhead spending variance of $300, an unfavorable efficiency variance of $120, and a volume variance.

(B. McDonald, adapted)

REQUIRED:

a. What was the overhead volume variance?
b. How many batches were produced? (*Hint:* The overhead volume variance is equal to $4 times the number of hours below normal volume.)

c. What was the total overhead applied to production?
d. What was the actual total overhead cost?
e. How many machine hours were used? (*Hint:* The overhead efficiency variance is equal to $6 variable cost per hour times the difference between actual machine hours and hours allowed for good output.)

13–16. Overhead Variances, Journal Entries.   Tribo-Martin is a major provider of natural spring mineral water in the Southwest. The company has three major products: (1) a liter bottle of mineral water ideal for social gatherings, (2) a gallon container of mineral water for general home use, and (3) a coin-operated machine to refill gallon containers. The machines are especially popular in apartment complexes. The company manufactures the machines and leases space for them in apartment complexes. If an investment group wants to buy the machines and a service and maintenance agreement, such an arrangement is also available.

Tribo-Martin Mineral Waters uses a standard cost system for all of its operations. The data on production overhead for the operations of the coin-operated machine division for the month are as follows:

Actual machines produced	1,100
Standard hours allowed for actual production	3,300
Normal capacity in hours	3,000
Actual variable overhead costs	$26,140
Actual fixed overhead costs	$31,560
Actual hours worked	3,150
Standard variable overhead per unit (3 hours at $8 per hour)	$24
Standard fixed overhead per unit (3 hours at $10 per hour)	$30

REQUIRED:
a. Calculate the under- or overapplied production overhead for the month.
b. Compute the production overhead variances for the month, indicating whether they are favorable or unfavorable, using the:
   1. Two-variance method.
   2. Three-variance method.
   3. Four-variance method.
c. Prepare the journal entries to record the variances in the accounts for the month and then close the accounts to Cost of Goods Sold. Assume the three-variance method.

13–17. Factory Overhead Variances.   Carlile Software Corporation has a project management and control software package. For the upcoming month, Stacy Whipple, controller, has prepared the following estimates for overhead costs relating to the production of the software packages:

$$\text{Budgeted overhead} = \$4,000 + \$4 \text{ per machine hour}$$
$$\text{Normal capacity} = 1,000 \text{ packages} \times 2 \text{ machine hours}$$
$$= 2,000 \text{ machine hours}$$

Actual data for the month are:

Variable overhead	=	$11,000
Fixed overhead	=	4,750
Units produced	=	1,200
Machine hours	=	2,500

REQUIRED:
a. Calculate the under- or overapplied overhead.
b. Perform a variance analysis under each of the following approaches:
   1. Three-way approach.
   2. Four-way approach.
c. Calculate the overhead efficiency variance using the standard rate and differences in actual and standard hours.

d. Calculate the volume variance using a comparison of normal capacity with capacity achieved.

13–18. Overhead Variances, Journal Entries.   Hammond-Cole Health Foods manufactures a wide variety of weight control products, speciality food supplements, and vitamin and mineral products. One of the company's divisions makes a food bar with flavors in peanut butter and cocoa walnut. Advertising claims a single food bar combined with a glass of 2 percent lowfat milk provides a complete meal containing one third of the U.S. required daily allowance of all essential vitamins, minerals, and protein, significant quantities of four valuable trace minerals, and two grams of dietary fiber.

The manufacturing process for the food bar is automated; consequently, machine hours are used as the measure of productive activity. Because of the repetitive nature of the process, a standard cost system is used to cost each dozen food bars. The standard cost sheet shows a machine time of 30 minutes per dozen at a standard overhead cost of $6 per hour ($2 dollars is variable; the remaining $4 is fixed). Normal capacity for a month is 60,000 machine hours.

During May, the company worked 55,000 machine hours and manufactured 117,000 dozen food bars. Actual overhead costs were $105,000 variable and $243,000 fixed.

REQUIRED:
a. Compute the production overhead variances for the month using the three-way method. Indicate whether the variances are favorable or unfavorable.
b. Prepare the journal entries to record the variances in the accounts for the month and then close the accounts to Cost of Goods Sold.
c. Explain the relationship between the two-variance method and the three-variance method. Show how to arrive at the variances for a two-variance method using only the variances from the three-variance method.
d. Explain the relationship between the four-variance method and the three-variance method.

13–19. Variances, Journal Entries, and Proration.   Vision-Clear, Inc., manufactures and sells a variety of eye care products such as corrective lenses, lens cleaners, disinfecting units, and sterile solutions. The Midwest division is responsible for manufacturing two types of saline solution. One type is thimerosal-free for sensitive eyes, and the other is plain sterile saline. The production process is basically the same for both types of solution.

Because the production process of saline solution is highly automated, machine hours are used as the measure of productive activity. All production labor is treated as indirect cost. The standards for a case (12 bottles) of solution include machine time of one hour. The standard overhead rate is $12 per machine hour with $4 considered variable. Normal activity is 54,000 machine hours. A case of thimerosal-free sells for $25 and of the sterile saline for $20.

During May 19x0, 16,000 cases of the thimerosal-free and 10,000 cases of the sterile saline were sold. There were 50,000 equivalent cases of solution produced using 53,000 machine hours. The production overhead costs were $230,000 variable and $418,000 fixed. The ending inventories and cost of goods sold consisted of:

	Cases	*Cost*
Work in process, equivalent units	2,000	$ 30,000
Thimerosal-free	6,000	90,000
Sterile saline	16,000	240,000
Cost of cases sold	26,000	390,000

Included in the cost is $3 standard cost per case for materials. There were no beginning inventories or ending materials inventories. The unfavorable materials price variance was $5,000, and there was no materials quantity variance.

(S. Whitecotton)

REQUIRED:
a. Prepare an overhead analysis using the two-variance approach.
b. Prepare an overhead analysis using the three-variance approach.
c. Prepare an overhead analysis using the four-variance approach.
d. Prepare journal entries for:

1. Purchase and use of materials.
2. Application of overhead to production and recording of the four variances.
e. When the Midwest division reports performance to Vision-Clear, Inc., it must convert the standard costs into actual costs.
   1. Prorate the May 19x0 materials and overhead variances among the inventories and Cost of Goods Sold.
   2. Compute the actual costs of inventory and goods sold for May 19x0.

13–20 Overhead Analysis.   Borg Enterprises operates with a standard cost system and produces a single product. Selected information from the accounting records for the current year are:

Budgeted variable overhead	$27,200
Budgeted fixed overhead	$56,000
Normal capacity in direct labor hours	16,000

During the year, the following operating data resulted:

Actual variable overhead	$24,470
Actual fixed overhead	$55,800
Actual direct labor hours	14,100
Standard direct labor hours allowed for actual production	15,200

The company applies both variable and fixed production overhead on the basis of direct labor hours. The Production Overhead account for the year is summarized as:

Production Overhead

Actual	80,270	Applied	79,040
Balance	1,230		

REQUIRED:
a. Calculate the predetermined overhead rates for variable and fixed production overhead that were used during the year.
b. Calculate the following variances that explain the underapplied amount:
   1. Variable spending variance.
   2. Variable efficiency variance.
   3. Fixed spending variance.
   4. Fixed volume variance.
c. Explain the meaning of each of the four variances calculated above.

13–21. Materials, Labor, Flexible Budget, and Journal Entries.   The Well-Chem Division analyzes the chemical and bacterial composition of well water under a contract with the California Department of Health. The contract price is $25.20 per test performed. The normal volume is 10,000 tests per month. Each test requires two testing setups, which are $3.80 each at standard price. Direct labor to perform the test is 10 minutes at $22.80 per hour. At the normal volume, the overhead costs are:

Variable costs:	Indirect Labor	$ 18,000
	Utilities	4,000
	Labor related costs	15,000
	Laboratory maintenance	11,000
Fixed costs:	Supervisor	30,000
	Depreciation	28,000
	Base utilities	9,000
	Insurance	2,000
	Total overhead	$117,000

During the month of November 19x6, 9,000 tests were performed. The accounting records show the following actual costs and production data:

		Activity	Actual Cost
Material setups purchased		19,000	$70,300
Material setups used		18,500	
Direct payroll		1,623	37,646
Production overhead	Variable		45,200
	Fixed		68,500

No ending tests were in process, and test setups are kept in inventory at standard cost. The division does not keep a work in process account, but instead uses the account Cost of Tests Performed.

(A. Gregory, adapted)

REQUIRED:
a. Prepare a flexible budget for the month based on 80 percent and 90 percent of normal volume.
b. Prepare a standard cost sheet for a water test.
c. Calculate the prime cost variances:
   1. Materials price and quantity variances.
   2. Labor rate and efficiency variances.
d. Calculate the laboratory overhead variances for the month indicating whether they are favorable or unfavorable using the four-variance method.
e. Prepare journal entries to record the actual costs, standard costs, and variances.
f. What was the actual cost for each test performed during the month?

13–22. Variances, Missing Data. You are reviewing the records of the MSW Smelter, which produces copper ingots for the production of wire. During the month of December 19x0, the plant had the following variances:

Materials price	9,200 U
Materials quantity	1,792 U
Labor rate	604 U
Labor efficiency	1,500 U
Variable overhead efficiency	?
Fixed overhead budget	(2,040)F
Variable overhead spending	?
Volume variance	1,800 U

The standard cost sheet for twenty 50-pound ingots:

	Per Input	Total
Materials, 8% ore per ton	$56.00	$350
Labor (6 hours)	$15.00	90
Variable overhead	$12.00	72
Fixed overhead	$ 7.50	45
Total		$557

The debit to the Production Overhead Control account for actual overhead was $66,514. The standard rates are based on 600 batches of ingots. MSW applies overhead on the basis of labor hours.

REQUIRED:
a. How many units were produced?
b. What should be the amount debited to Work in Process assuming that the company records all inventories at standard cost?
c. How many tons of raw materials were used?

d. What is the amount of the variable overhead efficiency variance?
e. What is the amount of the variable overhead spending variance?

13–23. Full Standard Costs. As part of an internal audit of the Machine Tool Unit, you are reviewing the records for the month of March 19x7. You find the following standards for the unit:

	Input Units	Per Input	Total
Materials	7	$36.00	$252
Labor (6 hours)	6	$12.00	72
Variable overhead	4	$12.00	48
Fixed overhead	4	$28.00	112
Total			$484

Overhead is applied on the basis of machine hours. During the month the department had the following summarized journal entries.

Materials	57,600	
Materials Price Variance	1,010	
Accounts Payable		58,610
Work in Process	50,400	
Materials Quantity Variance		3,168
Materials		47,232
Work in Process	14,400	
Labor Rate Variance	106	
Labor Efficiency Variance		1,320
Factory Payroll		13,186
Variable Factory Overhead Control	10,722	
Fixed Factory Overhead Control	29,113	
Accounts Payable		18,907
Accumulated Depreciation		8,004
Factory Payroll		12,924

From a variance report you find that the variable overhead efficiency variance is $1,620 favorable; overhead volume variance is $4,480 unfavorable.

REQUIRED:
a. How many units were apparently produced?
b. How many units of materials were used?
c. How many direct labor hours were apparently worked?
d. What should be the variable overhead spending variance?
e. How many machine hours should be recorded for the unit?
f. What is the amount of the fixed overhead budget?
g. What is the number of machine hours of normal activity used to calculate the standard costs?

13–24. Material, Labor, and Overhead Analysis with Variance Proration. Wee Shu Company is a manufacturer of electrical equipment. Its transformer division produces a well-known and popular industrial transformer in a labor-intensive process. Division management has installed a standard cost system and requests an extensive analysis of all variances each month. Performance reporting is based on a flexible budget. A summary internal income statement for transformer activity during May is as follows:

	Budget	Actual
Sales (700 transformers at $120)	$84,000	$84,000
Less: Cost of goods sold at standard		
(700 transformers at $70.50)	49,350	49,350
Gross margin at standard	$34,650	$34,650

	Budget	*Actual*
Variances from standard:		
Direct material variances		$ 1,734
Direct labor variances		(443)
Production overhead variances	—	1,142
	—	$ 2,433
Gross margin at actual	$34,650	$32,217
Less: Selling and administrative	25,000	25,000
Net income	$ 9,650	$ 7,217

The standard costs for each transformer are presented as:

Direct materials:		
5 sheets, soft iron at $1.63 each		$ 8.15
2 spools, copper wire at $3.41 each		6.82
Direct labor: 4.5 hours at $6.50 per hour		29.25
Production overhead:		
Variable—4.5 hours at $3.50 per hour	$15.75	
Fixed—4.5 hours at $2.34 per hour	10.53	26.28
Standard cost per unit		$70.50

Additional information available:

1. There were no beginning inventories at May 1 for materials, work in process, and finished goods.
2. The division purchased 6,000 sheets of soft iron at $1.68 per sheet and 2,300 spools of copper at $3.75 each. Materials used in production during the month were 4,900 sheets of soft iron and 1,800 spools of copper.
3. The division worked 3,700 actual direct labor hours at an average cost of $6.60 per hour.
4. Production overhead rates are based on a normal capacity of 1,000 transformers per month, which equals 4,500 direct labor hours allowed. Actual variable production overhead for the month was $12,980; fixed production overhead, $10,500.
5. Material enters at the beginning of the process, and conversion costs are incurred uniformily throughout the process.
6. Of the 900 units started during the month, 800 units were completed and placed in finished goods inventory. The remaining in-process units were 50 percent complete for labor and production overhead.

REQUIRED:

a. Calculate material price and quantity variances.
b. Calculate labor rate and efficiency variances.
c. Analyze production overhead using the three-variance method.
d. Assume all variances are significant. Prorate the variances to the appropriate accounts. Material variances are prorated on direct material content (including material quantity variance); labor and overhead are prorated on conversion cost content.

13–25. Multiple Products and Overhead Analysis.   Utah Electronics, Inc., manufactures three product lines: electronic support devices (ESD), electronic counter measure devices (ECMD), and electronic counter counter-measure devices (ECCD). The company has one large production facility in Salt Lake City. Most of the components are manufactured internally, although a few are purchased from outside vendors. Design and development are segregated by product line, but all product lines use the same production areas. The Assembly Department is responsible for the final assembly of all three product lines.

Assembly operations are rather uniform and easily adaptable to a standard cost system. The operations are labor intensive; Assembly overhead costs are allocated to products on direct labor hours. The standard overhead charges for Assembly on each of the three product lines are as follows:

	Hours	*Variable*	*Fixed*	*Total*	*Per Unit*
ESD	3.0	$10.00	$7.50	$17.50	$52.50
ECMD	4.0	10.00	$7.50	17.50	70.00
ECCD	5.0	10.00	7.50	17.50	87.50

Normal capacity for Assembly is 36,000 direct labor hours per month.

During October, the Assembly Department records showed the following hours worked for each product line:

	Units	*Hours Worked*
ESD	3,700	10,400
ECMD	2,400	10,100
ECCD	2,100	11,500

Actual variable production overhead amounted to $305,260 for the month. Actual fixed production overhead totaled $271,000. There were no in-process inventories at the beginning and ending of the month.

REQUIRED:

a. Compute the standard direct labor hours allowed for the month.

b. Calculate the under- or overapplied Assembly Department overhead for the month.

c. Analyze the under- or overapplied Assembly Department overhead using the four-variance approach.

13–26. Variance Analysis with Process Costing. Ultimate Rice, Inc., was founded to take advantage of the demand for rice dishes. Up to 50 percent of the rice crop is lost in the milling process that removes the grain's husk. The ''broken rice'' has traditionally been sold as animal feed. If broken rice were cooked, it would become an unpalatable goo. Ultimate Rice, Inc., developed a process to make that waste tasty. It adds alginate, a gelatin derived from seaweed, to bind the broken bits of rice back together again. The paste is pushed through an extruder to produce grain-like bits that look similar to the pasta called *orzo*. The reconstituted rice tastes just like the real thing but is ready to eat just seconds after water is added. The nutritional value of the product can be boosted by adding Vitamin A, iron, and various proteins during production.

Overhead for the company is applied on standard productive machine hours using a standard capacity of 60,000 machine hours per month. Fixed overhead is budgeted at $180,000 per month. The standard cost per pound has been set as follows:

Materials:		
Broken rice: 0.7 pounds at $0.06 per pound		$0.042
Alginate: 0.2 pounds at $0.04 per pound		0.008
Nutrients: 0.1 pounds at $0.20 per pound		0.020
		$0.070
Direct labor: 0.5 minutes at $3.60 per hour		0.030
Production overhead:		
Variable: 0.5 minutes at $1.80 per hour	$0.015	
Fixed: 0.5 minutes at $3.00 per hour	0.025	0.040
		$0.140

Materials are added at the beginning of the process. Direct labor and overhead costs are incurred uniformly throughout the process.

The company produced 7,200,000 pounds of Ultimate rice during June. This required 61,000 machine hours. The production and cost data for the month appeared as follows:

Quantities:	
In process, June 1: 40% complete for labor	
and overhead	100,000 lbs.
Started in process	7,600,000 lbs.

Units completed	7,200,000 lbs.
In process, June 30: 60% complete for labor and overhead	500,000 lbs.

Costs incurred:
  Broken rice issued—5,300,000 pounds (actual cost $0.055 per lb.)
  Alginate issued—1,550,000 pounds (actual cost $0.038 per lb.)
  Nutrients issued—760,000 pounds (actual cost $0.195 per lb.)
  Direct labor—58,000 hours for a cost of $232,000
  Variable production overhead—$105,400
  Fixed production overhead—$176,000

REQUIRED:
a. Calculate the equivalent units for material and conversion costs for June. (The FIFO method is used for standard costs.)
b. Determine the following amounts:
  1. The costs in the beginning Work in Process Inventory.
  2. The costs charged to Work in Process during the month.
  3. The costs charged to the Cost of Goods Completed.
  4. The costs charged to the Ending Work in Process Inventory.
c. Compute the material quantity variance for each of the three materials.
d. Determine the labor efficiency variance on direct labor.
e. Analyze the production overhead using the three-variance approach.

13–27. Proration of Overhead Variances.   C. C. McDonnough, Inc., makes a single product. The standard cost sheet for the product shows the following unit costs for material, labor, and production overhead:

Material: 3 lbs. at $1.70 per pound		$ 5.10
Labor: 1.5 hours at $5.00 per hour		7.50
Production overhead:		
Variable: 1 machine hour at $4.00 per hour	$4.00	
Fixed: 1 machine hour at $2.00 per hour	2.00	6.00
		$18.60

Normal capacity for production overhead rates is 10,000 machine hours per month.
    Accounting policies say that all inventory accounts are recorded at standard. Data for September show the following transactions:
1. Materials purchased during September totaled 29,000 pounds at $43,500. The Beginning Materials Inventory balance was 5,000 pounds at standard cost.
2. Beginning Work in Process was 1,000 units in process, 100 percent complete for materials and 80 percent complete for labor and production overhead.
3. Production inputs for the month were as follows:
   Materials issued and consumed—31,000 pounds.
   Direct labor hours worked—12,800 hours.
   Direct labor payroll—$69,120.
   Actual production overhead incurred—$56,800.
   Actual machine hours—8,500 hours.
4. Ending Work in Process consisted of 2,000 units, 100 percent complete for material and 30 percent complete for labor and production overhead.
5. Of the 8,000 units completed, 7,000 units were sold. There was no balance on hand for Finished Goods Inventory at the beginning of the month.

REQUIRED:
a. Calculate the September 30 balances in Materials Inventory, Work in Process Inventory, Finished Goods Inventory, and Cost of Goods Sold. All inventory accounts are stated at standard.

b. Determine the following variances:
   1. Material price and material quantity.
   2. Labor rate and labor efficiency.
   3. Overhead spending, efficiency, and volume.
c. Prorate variances on the basis of ending inventory balances and cost of goods sold. (Round final numbers to nearest dollar.)
d. Prorate variances on the basis of cost element (material variance on material content, labor variances on labor content, etc.) in ending inventory balances and cost of goods sold. (Round final numbers to nearest dollar.)

13–28. Establishing Standard Costs. Turfland Corporation provides commercial landscaping services. Linda Dake, the firm's owner, wants to develop standard cost estimates that she can use to prepare bids on jobs. After analyzing her costs, Dake has developed the following preliminary cost standards for each 1,000 square feet of landscaping.

Direct materials	$400
Direct labor (5 DLH at $10/DLH)	50
Overhead (5 DLH at $18/DLH)	90
Total cost per 1,000 square feet	$540

Dake is quite certain about the estimates for direct materials and direct labor. However, she is not so comfortable with the overhead estimate. The estimate for overhead is based on the overhead costs that were incurred during the past 12 months as presented in the following schedule. The estimate of $18 per direct labor hour (DLH) was determined by dividing the total overhead costs for the 12-month period ($648,000) by the total direct labor hours (36,000).

	Total Overhead	Regular Direct Labor Hours	Overtime Direct Labor Hours	Total Direct Labor Hours
January	$ 47,000	2,380	20	2,400
February	48,000	2,210	40	2,250
March	56,000	2,590	210	2,800
April	54,000	2,560	240	2,800
May	57,000	3,030	470	3,500
June	65,000	3,240	760	4,000
July	64,000	3,380	620	4,000
August	56,000	3,050	350	3,400
September	54,000	2,910	190	3,100
October	53,000	2,760	40	2,800
November	47,000	2,770	30	2,800
December	47,000	2,120	30	2,150
Total	$648,000	33,000	3,000	36,000

Dake believes that the overhead is affected by the total monthly direct labor hours. The overtime premium, 50 percent of the direct labor rate, is not included in the total overhead. Instead, the overtime is regarded as a special item associated with each project and considered a rate variance. Dake decided to perform a least-squares regression of overhead (OH) on total direct labor hours (TDLH). The following regression formula and statistics were obtained from the regression.

(CMA, adapted)

$$OH = 26,200 + 9.25 \text{ TDLH}$$
$$r = 0.92718$$
$$S_e = 2,434$$

REQUIRED:

a. The overhead rate developed from the least-squares regression is different from Linda Dake's preliminary estimate of $18 per direct labor hour. Explain the difference in the two overhead rates.

b. Using the overhead formula that was derived from the least-squares regression, determine a standard cost estimate for each 1,000 square feet of landscaping.

c. Linda Dake has been asked to submit a bid on a landscaping project consisting of 50,000 square feet. Dake estimates that 40 percent of the direct labor hours required for the project will be on overtime. Calculate the minimum bid that Dake should submit on this project if she uses the overhead formula that was derived from the least-squares regression.

d. Should Turfland Corporation rely on the overhead formula derived from the least-squares regression as the basis for the overhead component of its cost standard? Explain your answer.

EXTENDED APPLICATIONS

13–29. Standard Costs and Cost Reduction. Paste Products manufactures paste for commercial customers that is marketed in 10-gallon metal containers. Always cost conscious, the firm uses a standard cost system that is revised annually on November 1, the start of the company's fiscal year. Paste Products uses the standard costs to evaluate performance and prepares monthly variance reports for this purpose. The following revised standard cost card has been developed for commercial paste for the 19x6–x7 fiscal year.

Standard Cost for Commercial Paste
One 10-Gallon Container

Description	Standard Cost		Unit Cost
Direct materials			
2 lbs. monocloro	$ 6.00/lb.	$12.00	
1 lb. oxotone	0.80/lb.	0.80	
4 gals. distilled water	0.30/gal.	1.20	$14.00
Direct labor			
0.2 hours	11.00/hr.		2.20
Variable overhead			
0.2 hours maintenance	15.00/hr.	$ 3.00	
0.2 hours supplies	1.00/hr.	0.20	
0.2 hours indirect labor	18.00/hr.	3.60	6.80
Fixed overhead			
0.2 hours	2.00/hr.		0.40
Total standard cost			$23.40

The composition of Paste Products' fixed factory overhead and the annual budget for the current fiscal year is as follows.

Factory supervision	$130,000
Contract maintenance	40,000
Utilities	120,000
Property taxes	70,000
Factory depreciation	550,000
Miscellaneous	50,000
Total annual fixed factory overhead	$960,000

PASTE PRODUCTS
Analysis of Production Cost Variances
For the Six Months Ended April 30, 19x7

Actual production in units: 1,600,000

	Standard Usage at Standard Rates	Actual Usage at Standard Rates	Actual Costs	Quantity (Efficiency) Variance	Price (Rate) Variance	Total Variance
Direct Materials						
Monocloro	$19,200,000	$19,323,096	$19,387,506	$123,096U	$ 64,410U	$187,506U
Oxotone	1,280,000	1,278,400	1,246,440	1,600F	31,960F	33,560F
Distilled water	1,920,000	1,921,200	1,857,160	1,200U	64,040F	62,840F
Direct labor	3,520,000	3,564,000	4,043,400	44,000U	479,400U	523,400U
Variable overhead						
Maintenance	4,800,000	4,860,000	4,310,050	60,000U	549,950F	489,950F
Supplies	320,000	324,000	335,400	4,000U	11,400U	15,400U
Indirect labor	5,760,000	5,832,000	5,978,000	72,000U	146,000U	218,000U
Total variable cost variances				$302,696U	$ 55,260U	$357,956U
	Applied Fixed Overhead	Budgeted Fixed Overhead	Actual Fixed Overhead	Volume Variance	Spending Budget Variance	
Fixed overhead	$640,000	$480,000	$480,000	$160,000F	-0-	160,000F
Total variance						$197,956U

All direct materials and indirect supplies are purchased from outside vendors on a two-week production lead time basis. The variable maintenance cost is for maintenance performed by Paste Products' employees; contract maintenance is under annual contract with the manufacturers of specific equipment. Depreciation is calculated on the straight-line basis. Miscellaneous fixed overhead includes factory insurance and other sundry items.

Variable manufacturing overhead is considered to vary with direct labor hours. Therefore, Paste Products applies both variable and fixed overhead to production on the basis of direct labor hours. Manufacturing activities and the incurrence of production costs are expected to occur uniformly throughout the fiscal year.

In January 19x7, the company was forced to reduce its sales price from $79.95 per 10-gallon container to $49.95 due to aggressive foreign competition. Although the price reduction resulted in increased sales, the income statement for the first six months revealed dwindling profits. Management immediately mandated a product cost reduction program and called upon Jill O'Connor, cost accountant, to prepare a report specifying target areas for such a program. O'Connor prepared the analysis of production costs on page 545 to determine if any costs were above standard.

After completing her analysis, O'Connor observed that the net production variances were unfavorable to budget; however, the fixed overhead volume variance partially offset the variable manufacturing variances. She also observed that the direct labor variances exceeded standard by almost 15 percent. Investigating further, she learned that the manufacturing plant had been working 10 hours per day, six days per week since late January. Workers are paid time-and-one-half for overtime. While she knew that the plant had scheduled overtime, she was not aware of the magnitude. A closer examination of production records revealed the following facts.

	Regular Production	Overtime Production	Total
Direct labor hours	268,800	55,200	324,000
Direct labor cost	$3,091,200	$952,200	$4,043,400
Units produced	1,350,000	250,000	1,600,000

O'Connor plans to use her analysis of production variance as well as the additional data she has accumulated as the basis for her recommendations.

(CMA, adapted)

REQUIRED:
a. In order to analyze the situation and advise management on the product cost reduction program, Jill O'Connor should determine the number of units Paste Products had planned to produce annually. Calculate the number of units that Paste Products had planned to produce during its fiscal year beginning November 1, 19x6.
b. Jill O'Connor has decided to revise the variance analysis to reflect the impact that overtime had on direct labor production costs.
  1. Expand the direct labor variance analysis to reveal as much detail about the direct labor costs as possible from the information provided. This would entail a separate calculation of regular time and overtime variances.
  2. Based on your analysis in (b.1)., comment on the impact that overtime had on Paste Products direct labor production costs.
c. Jill O'Connor observed that the fixed overhead volume variance partially offset the variable production variances. She wondered if there would be an advantage to Paste Products of shifting variable costs to fixed costs.
  1. Explain the nature of the fixed overhead volume variance.
  2. Discuss the advantages and disadvantages of shifting variable costs to fixed costs.
d. Discuss the overall impact that Paste Products' recent change in pricing strategy has had on the company.

13–30. Process Costing.   Webb & Company is engaged in the preparation of income tax returns for individuals. Webb uses the weighted average method and actual costs for financial reporting purposes. However, for internal reporting, Webb uses a standard cost system. The standards, based on equivalent performance, have been established as follows:

Labor per return	5 hrs. at $20 per hr.
Overhead per return	5 hrs. at $10 per hr.

For March 19x7 performance, budgeted overhead is $49,000 for the standard labor hours allowed. The following additional information pertains to the month of March 19x7:

(CPA, adapted)

Inventory data

Returns in process, March 1 (25% complete)	200
Returns started in March	825
Returns in process, March 31 (80% complete)	125

Actual cost data

Returns in process March 1:

Labor	$ 6,000
Overhead	2,500
Labor, March 1 to 31	
4,000 hours	89,000
Overhead, March 1 to 31	45,000

REQUIRED:

a. Using the weighted average method, compute the following for each cost element:
   1. Equivalent units of performance.
   2. Actual cost per equivalent unit.
b. Compute the actual cost of returns in process at March 31.
c. Compute the standard cost per return.
d. Prepare a schedule for internal reporting analyzing March performance, using the following variances, and indicating whether these variances are favorable or unfavorable:
   1. Total labor.
   2. Labor rate.
   3. Labor efficiency.
   4. Total overhead.
   5. Overhead volume.
   6. Overhead budget.

13–31. Developing New Standards, Changing Measures of Activity.   Quintar, Inc., produces three sizes of computer disk drives for personal computers: 360K flexible (floppy), 1,000K rigid, and the 20,000K fixed disk. Each of the disks has about the same internal working mechanisms, though the higher the storage capacity the finer the machining and electronics required. For 19x2, Quintar used the following standard costs:

	360K	1,000K	20,000K
Materials	$35.80	$38.60	$ 58.90
Direct labor	8.20	12.30	16.40
Overhead	24.60	32.80	32.80
Total standard costs	$68.60	$83.70	$108.10

Overhead is applied at a rate of $24.60 per machine hour with normal volume as 17,000 machine hours per month. The standard direct labor rate is $16.40 per hour. There are 23 different types of machines used to produce, calibrate, and test each drive. The machines are used in different sequences, and a few of the machines are unique to each product. Quality control is a major issue, and spoilage and defective units vary substantially among the three products.

During 19x2, several of the product engineers questioned whether the overhead allocations were fair and reasonable. The 360K product is very simple in concept and has a very low spoilage and defective unit rate. The 1,000K is somewhat complex in parts and assembly. Finally, the 20,000K disk is very complex to set up and keep the production going. In terms of additional resources, the 20,000K requires far more people to keep production going. The engineers have proposed a "complexity index" with the following weights: 1 for the 360K, 3 for the 1,000K, and 6 for the 20,000K. Further, they propose that 60 percent of the overhead be allocated on the complexity factor and only 40 percent be allocated on machine hours. The 19x3 monthly budgeted overhead costs will increase by 10 percent. Production volume is expected to be about the same as in 19x2 with monthly unit volumes of:

	360K	*1,000K*	*20,000K*
Projected monthly volume	6,000	6,000	2,250

Materials costs have decreased by 10 percent, and wage rates have increased by 5 percent.

REQUIRED:
a. Compute the 19x3 budget monthly overhead for the plant.
b. Apportion the overhead into the parts due to:
    1. Machine hours.
    2. Complexity.
c. Compute 19x3 overhead rates (to four places) for each:
    1. Machine hour.
    2. Complexity.
d. Prepare the 19x3 standard costs for each product with the inclusion of the proposed complexity index overhead allocation base.

Overhead Analysis for a Normal Cost System

After studying this appendix, you should be able to:

1. Calculate spending and volume variances for production overhead in a normal cost system.
2. Explain the primary reasons that spending and volume variances occur.

A normal cost system uses actual costs for direct materials and direct labor but a predetermined overhead rate to apply production overhead costs to work in process. The basis for applying overhead using the predetermined rate is a measure of the actual activity. Common measures of activity for production overhead, as we have already seen, included direct labor hours or costs, machine hours, and units of production.

Although a predetermined overhead rate in a normal cost system can be identical to a standard overhead rate in a standard cost system, the two systems are different in concept and procedure. A standard cost system applies overhead on the basis of actual output.[1] The normal cost system applies overhead to the actual direct labor hours or cost, actual machine hours, or units produced. The measure selected depends on a company's individual circumstances. Only in the case in which the normal cost system uses units of production will both the normal and standard cost systems yield the same production overhead applied to work in process.

Because we deal only with actual activity, not actual and standard activity, the under/overapplied amount is decomposed into two variances: spending variance (also known as a *budget variance* or a *controllable variance*) and volume variance (also called a *capacity variance*). The names of the variance are similar to those in standard costs, but composition of the variances is not always similar.

To illustrate the decomposition of under/overapplied overhead into spending and volume variances, consider the data from the Herlinda Company. It has a normal capacity of 80,000 machine hours per year for its operations. Fixed costs at this level are estimated at $280,000 with variable costs at $2.50 per machine hour. Factory and accounting records show that 82,000 actual machine hours were used during the year at total actual production overhead costs of $489,100. The overhead rate per machine hour for applying overhead is made up of two rates:

Variable overhead rate	$2.50
Fixed overhead rate ($280,000/80,000 machine hours)	3.50
Total overhead rate	$6.00

The overapplied overhead for the year is calculated as follows:

Actual overhead incurred		$489,100
Applied overhead:		
Variable ($2.50 × 82,000)	$205,000	
Fixed ($3.50 × 82,000)	287,000	
Total ($6.00 × 82,000)		492,000
Overapplied overhead		$ 2,900

---

[1] Actual output is often converted to standard activity allowed, and a standard rate is applied to the activity allowed. Because the two are equivalent, we know that overhead in a standard cost system is always applied on the basis of units produced.

EXHIBIT 13A–1   Spending and Volume Variances—Normal Cost System

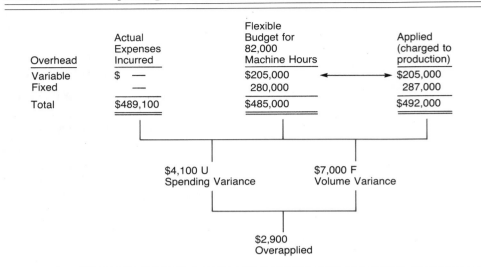

Exhibit 13A–1 is a calculation of spending and volume variances. It shows an unfavorable spending variance of $4,100 and a favorable volume variance of $7,000.

The actual overhead costs are given, and the applied amounts were calculated above. Amounts for the flexible budget must be computed. The variable cost is $2.50 per hour × 82,000 actual machine hours = $205,000. Fixed costs are those budgeted at normal capacity and are given at $280,000.

The format for variance computations is similar to the two-way approach in standard cost. Let actual overhead costs and the applied costs be the extreme points. Place between those extremes a flexible budget based on the actual capacity used. The dollar amounts for actual capacity used are the budgeted variable and fixed costs for that level. Had we known at the beginning of the period which capacity level we would have achieved, these costs would have been budgeted. Segregating actual and applied costs into variable and fixed components is nice and gives additional information, but we can still do the analysis without them. The budget for actual capacity used, on the other hand, must identify variable and fixed costs.

Notice that the budgeted variable cost always equals the variable cost applied to production. The reason is that both the budget and the applied have the same variable overhead rate applied to the same actual machine hours.

The spending variance is the difference between the actual overhead costs and the budget for the actual capacity used. Whenever the actual overhead costs exceed the budget for actual capacity used, the spending variance is unfavorable. It means you spent more than you budgeted for that level. The opposite would be true for a favorable variance. The volume variance is the difference between the budget for the actual capacity used and the applied (charged to production). If the budget for the actual capacity used exceeds what was charged to production, insufficient overhead costs are charged to production. This is an unfavorable volume variance. The opposite is a favorable volume variance.

Many reasons exist to explain why these variances occur. Let's look at a few of them. The spending variance is made up of four major factors if the measure of volume is units of production. These are:

1. Price changes in the individual cost components making up overhead costs.
2. Quantity changes in individual items within overhead cost components.
3. Estimation errors in segregating variable and fixed costs.
4. Any overhead costs that are incurred or saved because of inefficient or efficient use of labor or machinery that the overhead supports.

The volume variance is the difference between the fixed overhead costs budgeted and those charged to production: the monetary amount associated with the difference between actual capacity used and the original capacity planned. Reasons for the difference include sales demand that changed, which affected production schedules, plans for buildup or liquidation of inventories that changed, or equipment breakdowns that exceeded expectations.

The only time the normal cost spending and volume variances would be identical to those of the two-way approach in standard costs is when units of production is the measure of activity for applying overhead costs. Generally, the normal cost spending variance is the same number as the spending variance in the three-way approach in standard costs.

REVIEW QUESTIONS

1. What is the primary difference between a normal cost system and a standard cost system for applying production overhead costs to work in process inventory?
2. Why is the variable overhead cost budgeted for the actual capacity used equal to the variable overhead cost applied?
3. Explain why variable and fixed costs must be known for the flexible budget used in overhead cost analysis but is not essential for the actual costs.
4. The spending variance is unfavorable when actual costs exceed the applied costs. Comment.
5. Identify the four major reasons that spending variances occur.
6. What reasons explain volume variances?
7. If units of production is the measure of capacity, the spending and volume variances will be different from those variances when machine hours measure capacity. Explain.

EXERCISES

13A–1. Under/Overapplied Overhead, Spending, and Volume Variances. Production overhead for Kingsland Company is estimated using a budget formula of $4 per direct labor hour for variable overhead costs and $75,000 for fixed overhead costs. Capacity for the month is set at 15,000 direct labor hours. Production for the month reached 90 percent of budgeted capacity. Actual production overhead incurred was $127,480.

REQUIRED:
a. Determine the amount of under/overapplied production overhead.
b. Calculate the spending and volume variances.

13A–2. Spending and Volume Variances. Jackson Manufacturing has a production overhead formula of $87,000 fixed overhead plus $3 per machine hour, yielding a total overhead rate of $6 per machine hour worked. The actual machine hours for the month were 31,200. Actual production overhead totaled $180,600.

REQUIRED:
Calculate the spending and volume variances.

13A–3. Overhead Analysis under Normal Costing. Hardcastle Graphics Corporation derives its revenues from the production and sale of printing presses, collators, and auxiliary equipment and parts. It also provides maintenance contracts for customers seeking that type of service. Its production facilities are in 19 states, and its distribution centers are in every major city in the United States.

The El Paso assembly plant budgeted production overhead for the current year at $1,992,000, of which 75 percent is variable cost. Production overhead is applied to Work in Process on the basis of direct labor hours, which were budgeted at 120,000 hours for the current year. Actual overhead costs totaled $1,870,000 for 110,000 direct labor hours worked.

REQUIRED:
a. Calculate the production overhead rate for variable cost, fixed cost, and total overhead cost.
b. Analyze the production overhead, assuming a normal cost system, into a spending variance and a volume variance.
c. Prepare the journal entry that closes the under- or overapplied overhead to Cost of Goods Sold.

13A–4. Overhead Analysis under Normal Costing.   LETO Containers Produces dumpsters that are used to collect garbage and trash at residential, commercial, and industrial sites. The production process is totally automated, and overhead is charged on the basis of machine hours.

The company has a normal capacity of 87,600 machine hours per year. At this level, the budgeted variable overhead costs are $262,800, and the fixed overhead costs are $1,752,000. The company incurred $2,136,000 of production overhead costs during the current year and worked 89,000 machine hours.

REQUIRED:
a. Compute the amount of under- or overapplied overhead.
b. Analyze the under- or overapplied overhead into spending and volume variances.
c. Identify three reasons that a spending variance occurs and two reasons that a volume variance occurs.

CHAPTER

14

Planning of Operations

∎

PLANNING PROBLEM

Rapid Robotics was formed in 1973 by three engineers who wanted to design and market a practical robot for production tasks such as painting automobiles. After several trying years, the engineers established themselves with a product and a market. The company has expanded very quickly, and recent sales growth has been especially satisfying. The founders still work with the company in the research and development laboratory and hold about 12 percent of the outstanding common shares.

There are three basic types of robots: fixed position, pattern moving, and free moving. The fixed-position type can be fitted with different attachments. This robot type is primarily used in parts fabrication or on assembly lines performing such functions as welding, checking quality control, or painting. The pattern-moving robot follows a specific pattern set on the floor or within its program. For example, one model of pattern-moving robot is used to travel the interior of pipelines or large tanks, freeing impediments and checking for surface cracks. The final type of robot, free moving, is still experimental, but it is intended to perform such tasks as moving on the ocean bottom to search for mineral outcroppings or to perform risky functions on contaminated battle fields or in space. Although this type of robot is featured in popular movies as almost human, current versions are limited in capability.

Rapid Robotics divides the sales staff into 28 sales teams that specialize in different types of robots for specific industries. The method of selling involves personal and team presentations. The company also advertises in trade journals and demonstrates its products at industrial trade shows.

A sales contract is a major event because the robots are expensive, and the usual contract covers many units over multiple years. Revenues have increased over the past five years from $280 million to over $2 billion.

The standard parts (cabinet, computers, input devices, power sources, motors, and wiring) of a robot are only a small part of the total cost of contract completion. A large cost of completing most sales orders is tailoring computer programs and engineering the specialized attachments to meet customer specifications.

One of the assistant controllers was appointed as the budget director in early 19x8 to assist in the planning process for fiscal 19x9. The immediate task of the new budget director is to design and implement a budget system.

■

LEARNING OBJECTIVES

After studying this chapter, you should be able to:

1. List and explain the steps required to administer the budget process.
2. Describe the types of computer support available for the planning function.
3. Explain the types of budget a budget director has available for use.
4. Prepare budgets for sales, materials purchases, labor, production overhead, and general and administration expenses.
5. State and give examples of the benefits of budgeting.
6. State and give examples of the challenges of budgeting.

If the planning and budgeting program is set up effectively, communication, coordination, and performance evaluation can be enhanced. On the other hand, if the planning approach is inflexible and heavily bureaucratic, the results can be very unproductive. In this chapter, we will study the planning and budgeting procedures required for companies like Rapid Robotics.

Operations refers to the detailed activities of an organization. The operations for a manufacturing company include marketing, production, distribution, research and development, and administration. The operations of a professional baseball team include contracting with players, training camp, scouting, coaching, purchasing and maintaining equipment, scheduling games, transportation, practice, ticket sales and promotion, concessions, security, public relations, and administration.

A **plan of operations** is a description of desired activities. A flexible plan is one that can be changed as opportunities arise. A **budget** of operations is a plan expressed in monetary terms.

We will consider the organization of the budget process and the detailed planning required for the operations of a manufacturer. Then we will present the benefits and challenges associated with budgeting.

BUDGET ORGANIZATION

The **budget director** is the person who organizes the planning function for a company. The title for the budget director may also be planning director, planning officer, or vice president for planning. This person hires the planning staff, sets up the planning schedule, coordinates planning efforts, and presents results to other managers.

The output of the planning function is the **master budget.** It consists of a planned income statement, a statement of cash flow, and a balance sheet. The document is supported by schedules that reflect the estimates of each manager in the organization.

Computer Support

The planning function for a large organization will need substantial computer support. Each part of the operations plan must be consistent with the details that are present in other parts. As estimates and relationships change, the plans should be adjusted. For example, if a new product is planned, the budgets for purchasing materials and production should be changed. Further, it is common for a plan to go through many changes prior to approval. Even after approval, there will be changes to the budget to reflect changed conditions. Thus, the budget process must be set up to handle many changes in estimates. A computerized approach to budget preparation makes it possible to reflect quickly the effects of changes on projected financial results.

Various software packages are available to companies to support the planning function. These include special-purpose programs, financial planning packages, and computer spread sheet programs.

Many large companies have developed their own software to support the planning function. These programs can be made highly specific to the needs of the particular company and are called **special-purpose software.** In general, specialized planning systems meet specific needs and are well integrated into the accounting system of the company. Thus, the systems take full advantage of existing data files and equipment that are part of the regular accounting system. However, these systems require expert programmers and are expensive to maintain over long time periods. Further, the budget system is difficult to change once implemented.

A second approach to computerization of budgets involves general **financial planning packages** that are sold commercially. More than 50 of these are currently available. For example, the Interactive Financial Planning System (IFPS) is one commonly used package. These planning models are self-documenting, are easier to audit than special-purpose programs or electronic spread sheets, and are more reliable. These systems are structured to handle large budgets involving hundreds of department-level budgets. The two drawbacks to such packages are that they require expert programmers and that they are moderately expensive ($10,000 to $100,000 lease cost per year).

Another approach to supporting the planning function is referred to as the **electronic spread sheet.** This approach is commonly implemented on a personal computer or a minicomputer. These programs are easier to learn than the large financial planning systems, and they are less expensive per copy ($50 to $300). Many users consider computer spread sheets very flexible and productive: budgets can be prepared quickly and with less effort than with financial planning packages. Expert programmers are not required, and budget revisions can be made quickly. Examples of spread sheet programs are Excel, Lotus 1–2–3, and Supercalc.

Computer spread sheet use in planning requires careful supervision because the spread sheet budget models, called *templates,* are often not well documented. Because the models are relatively easy to change, errors can occur because of undocumented changes to the models. In large or complex planning models, the errors are often untraceable. Thus, some budget directors consider electronic spread sheets to be unreliable for budget systems involving hundreds of departments and thousands of accounts.

Administering the Plan

The budget director has to work with many people and develop a budget system that satisfies a multitude of needs. A major management area for the budget director is working with a steering committee and setting up a budget preparation timetable. In addition, the budget director must decide which of the many types of budgets are to be administered under the budget system.

Budget Steering Committee.   A useful control over the planning process is the existence of a budget steering committee. This group should include representatives from each major department or division. The committee's task is to provide input, to review and approve the work of the budget director, and to communicate information to the departments. This committee can add substantial quality to the budget process.

Setting up the Timetable.   A plan for a large company cannot be completed quickly. Each manager in the company submits estimates that must be made consistent with other parts of the organization. For example, the plan for production should follow the sales plan, and the purchasing plan should follow the production plan. Organizations will have a normal order in which plans are prepared. For example, the following order is normal for many manufacturing organizations:

1. Revenue budget.
2. Production budget.
3. Purchasing budget.
4. Labor budget.
5. Overhead budget.
6. Capital projects and research and development.
7. Marketing, general and administrative expense budgets.
8. Cash budget.
9. Budgeted income statement and balance sheet.

Exhibit 14–1 presents the normal relationships among budget steps. What is not disclosed in the flowchart is that there will be several iterations of these plans before the final ones are accepted by top management. Further, there is a time lag between the first estimates and the final plan. Consequently, it is common to start the planning process three months to a year prior to the beginning of the fiscal year.

TYPES OF BUDGETS

The budget director has several options in selecting types of budget program for implementation.

Annual Budgets and Rolling Budgets

When planning occurs only once per year, the budget is referred to as the **annual budget.** It is also possible to plan for an entire year by quarter or month. Then each quarter or month, a new period is added and the others are changed to reflect new information. This type of budget process is called a **rolling** or **continuous budget.** Rolling budgets are useful when significant changes that require reaction by the company occur throughout the year. Rolling budget approaches require a more co-ordinated effort by the budget director. Annual budgets are simpler but less flexible in application. Most companies that have formal plans will start with an annual budget, then shift to rolling budgets if they prove necessary.

Fixed and Flexible Budgets

The plan can be fixed at the beginning of the year with no changes in financial amounts depending upon activity levels. This is referred to as a **fixed (or static) budget** and is common for administrative expenses and governmental expenditures. The alternative is a **flexible budget** in which the financial budgets are adjusted for the amount of the

EXHIBIT 14–1 Normal Relationships among Budget Steps

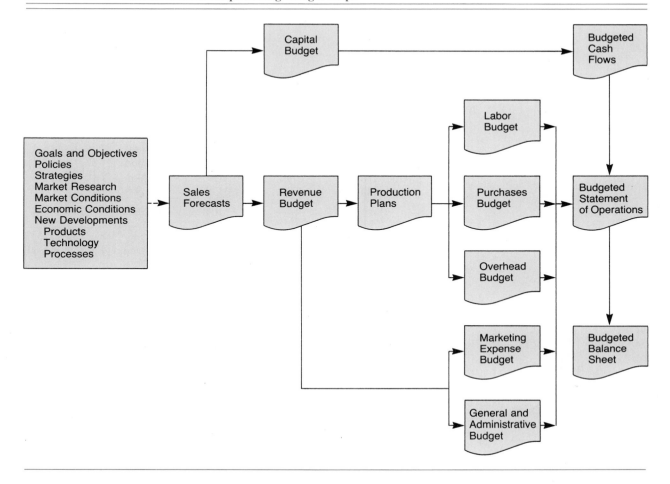

activity that occurs. For example, it is common for the budget for equipment maintenance to be adjusted depending upon the hours of machine activity in the factory.

Even a fixed budget should allow for change due to unforeseen circumstances.
Each change should be justified, however, to the manager's superior.

**Incremental and
Zero-Based
Budgets**

There are two basic approaches to planning the changes from last year's budget
amounts for expenses: incremental and zero based. The **incremental budgeting**
approach is most common in practice. Each year the budget is adjusted by an amount
to reflect the expected change in the operations plus a percentage for inflation. Thus,
the budget for production overhead might be increased by $500,000 to reflect a change
in employee benefits filed plus 5 percent for projected increase in activity.

The **zero-based budget** (also called a *sunset review*) requires that all of the
expenditure for a function be justified. This approach is advocated in government
and is found in some companies. When this approach is adopted, every function is
reviewed on a standard cycle, say every five years. Outside the review year, the
department operations are budgeted on an incremental basis.

A zero-based approach is annoying to segments that are going through a sunset
review. No one likes to see his or her department threatened with termination. The

EXHIBIT 14–2

TREASURER'S OFFICE
Account-Item Budget
For the Year Ending September 30, 19x9

Account	Description	Budget
06–8307–801	Salaries	$ 780,000
06–8307–802	Employee benefits	300,000
06–8307–803	Hourly wages	80,000
06–8307–810	Supplies	50,000
06–8307–812	Education	6,000
06–8307–820	Equipment	20,000
06–8307–830	Computer charges	25,000
06–8307–890	Other	29,000
Total		$1,280,000

shock is like pulling up a tree by its roots to see if the roots are any good. If this is done very often, the tree dies. On the other hand, organizations must be efficient in order to survive, and if the incremental budget approach is used strictly, then some activities will be continued far longer than needed. Thus, a zero-base review every five years can be very useful for organizational efficiency.

Account Level, Function, and Program Budgets

Account-level budgets list the expected amounts in specific accounts. These budgets are very detailed and provide basic information to form the other types of budget. These budgets are also called departmental budgets and **line-item budgets.** For example, the account-level budget for the treasurer's office might look like the budget in Exhibit 14–2.

A **functional budget** (also called an *activity budget*) combines account-level budget totals for functional departments such as the departments that report to one vice president or manager. Each department is summarized as one line. For example, the budget for the vice president of finance and administration might look like the budget in Exhibit 14–3. Notice that the functional budget approach emphasizes the function that is served by spending the money. Rather than focusing top managers' attention on which departments are spending what money, the approach focuses on the activities that the company is spending money for. Each line will generally represent a department, but not always. For example, interest on indebtedness is an important line in a functional budget, but it is not a separate department.

EXHIBIT 14–3

FINANCE AND ACCOUNTING
Functional Budget
For the Year Ending September 30, 19x9

Accounting	$ 3,900,000
Planning	225,000
Internal audit	2,800,000
Treasury	1,280,000
Information systems	4,300,000
Purchasing	2,400,000
Interest on indebtedness	57,600,000
Total	$72,505,000

EXHIBIT 14–4

ACCOUNTING SYSTEMS PROJECT
For the Year Ending September 30, 19x9

	(In thousands)
Accounting	$120
Internal audit	240
Treasury	60
Information systems	360
Software acquisitions	180
Total	$960

Project budgets are related in concept to functional budgets. A project may involve the efforts of several functional departments to achieve a common objective. However, managers of functional departments are very competitive people. Getting managers to give up a share of their budget for the common good is like asking several city street gang leaders to give up a share of their turf. Department managers are more civilized than street gang leaders, but the principle of turf is the same. In order to encourage cooperation among departments, top management uses the concept of a funded project in which the departments participate.

A **project budget** provides the funding for a project that may or may not encompass portions of different functional areas. For example, assume that a new accounting system is being developed and that the current year's activities are provided for in a special budget that involves the accounting, internal audit, treasury, and information systems departments. The accounting system's project budget might look like the one in Exhibit 14–4.

The flexibility to prepare budgets of this type can add much to getting the work done in organizations. Project-oriented companies such as defense and construction contractors find this budgeting technique essential for effective planning.

The technique of project budgeting is also called **program budgeting** in governmental planning. For example, a drug prevention program in a city may involve schools, police, hospitals, correctional facilities, and other functional departments.

We will now present the detailed operations planning for a hypothetical company, Rapid Robotics, Inc. The example illustrates the typical first-year planning experiences of a manufacturing company that has a significant service component. The company does most things right and a few things wrong, but generally it makes an adequate first-year effort.

OPERATIONS PLANNING

Staffing and Computer Support

In staffing the budget office, the new director requisitioned the time of four people: two analysts and two clerical staff. The two analysts had general experience in accounting and internal auditing. The budget director requisitioned a minicomputer with five terminals, 10 million characters of core memory, 100 million characters of hard disk storage capacity, and a high-quality laser printer. The computer came with a spread sheet program for preparing plans, a communications package to interact with the main computer files, a word processor for generating budget reports, and a statistical package for the analysis of costs and revenues. The director decided that for the first year no format would be required for the plan inputs, but instead each manager would submit estimates and requests in the most convenient form.

Top management (president and three senior vice presidents) estimated that sales growth of 20 percent and profit growth of 15 percent were necessary to maintain their position in the industry. The planning director immediately assigned one of the budget analysts to work with the marketing staff and the other to work on the production plans.

Budget Steering Committee

Top management wanted the budget process to be generally participative. Therefore, the budget director consulted with the vice presidents and had each designate an assistant vice president for the Budget Steering Committee. The budget director's office was to act as the staff support for this committee.

Budget Revision Approach

Budget revisions were to be submitted on a monthly basis with changes to be effective immediately upon approval and communication. Again, the managers could submit the changes in a convenient format. The immediate supervisor was designated to review and approve plan change requests.

Planning Schedule

On February 14, the budget director suggested a budget schedule to the Budget Steering Committee. After revising some dates and changing some steps, the budget schedule presented in Exhibit 14–5 was approved by the committee.

We have sketched the budget director's initial design of the budget system. We will now review the significant events that occurred during the first budget cycle. In this presentation, we will focus on the budgets surrounding the sale, production, and

EXHIBIT 14–5   Budget Schedule

RAPID ROBOTICS, INC.	**DATE: February 14, 19x8**

Schedule for Budget Preparation
For Fiscal Year 19x9

April 1	Economic forecasts sent to sales team managers
April 21	New contract sales estimates due
	Parts estimates on existing contracts
	Service estimates due on existing contracts
June 1	Production plans due
	General materials plans
June 15	Initial concepts due for capital projects
July 1	Personnel requirements due
	Marketing, production, software, engineering, research, administrative plans due
August 1	Major revisions to prior plans due
	Market revisions
	Production revisions
	Final capital project requests
August 7	Intermediate approval and revisions by vice presidents
August 15	Consolidation of estimates into total plan
	Final revisions by functions
August 25	Financing plans due
September 1	Completed plan to president
September 15	Final revisions
	Final financing plans
September 22	Presentation of the completed plan to the board of directors

EXHIBIT 14–6

RAPID ROBOTICS, INC.			**DATE: April 1, 19x8**

RAPID ROBOTICS, INC.　　　　　　DATE: April 1, 19x8
Robotics Economic Data
For the Year Ending September 30
(In millions)

	19x8	19x9	Growth
Vehicle production	$13,810	$15,643	13%
Petroleum and minerals	8,794	11,572	32%
Other industry	5,778	8,800	52%
Research contracts	857	3,457	303%
Totals	$29,239	$39,472	35%

servicing of the product. In Chapter 15, we will examine the cash planning aspects of operations for Rapid Robotics.

SALES PLANS

On April 1, the industry projections reported in Exhibit 14–6 were sent to each of the 28 sales team managers. The 19x8 sales for the current year were estimated based on projected total industry sales. The 19x9 projections are for a very good year in robotics with expected growth at 35 percent with the fastest growth expected in research contracts.

Initial Sales Estimates

During April, the sales plans were received from 26 of the 28 sales team managers. The budget director telephoned the other two managers, who sent their plans in later. The budget analysts had to call half of the sales team managers because their projections were difficult to read or interpret. The 28 estimates were then consolidated into an overall schedule by the budget staff. The plan in Exhibit 14–7 was then presented to the Budget Steering Committee.

It was immediately obvious to the Budget Steering Committee that some revision was required because the total projected revenue was 2 percent lower than the current year's sales. Because this would be unacceptable to top management, the committee reviewed the numbers very closely. There were declines projected in all areas except for service contracts.

EXHIBIT 14–7

RAPID ROBOTICS, INC.　　　　　　DATE: April 28, 19x8
Projected Revenues
For the Year Ending September 30
(in millions)

Robot Types	19x8	19x9	Change
Fixed position	$ 542	$ 530	−2%
Pattern movement	650	628	−3%
Free movement	246	119	−52%
Service contracts	626	749	20%
Total	$2,064	$2,026	−2%

The decline projected for free-moving robots was dramatic. This was unusual because a portion of the revenue from free-moving robots is related to research contracts, which were projected to have a dramatic increase on an industry-wide basis.

As a result of the unexpected and dismaying forecasts, the committee decided to investigate further. The committee members knew that if they allowed these estimates to be sent to top management, their own judgment would be called into question.

Committee Investigation

Over the next two days, the marketing assistant vice president talked with each of the sales team managers. Several of the managers openly commented that because the estimates were going to be used for their performance evaluation, they wanted their performance to look good. In addition, several of the managers had made errors partly because their estimates were based on old information on the current year's sales. Finally, three of the managers were inexperienced and had overestimated the amounts.

The Budget Steering Committee concluded that in the future the managers should be provided with more historical and current data. Further, the estimates would be submitted through the four assistant marketing vice presidents with a negotiation occurring between the managers and their assistant vice president. *In general, budgets set by managers without a negotiation with immediate supervisors are generally too easy to achieve and do not represent a challenge.*

Committee Projection

After some heated discussions, the Budget Steering Committee developed its own projections. They were a combination of the original estimates and rough projections from historical data. With these projections, the committee drafted the proposal for the revenue estimate in Exhibit 14–8 to be presented to top management.

Underlying the revenue budget is the number of sales contracts to be signed for each type of product. For the final 19x9 fiscal year, the following contracts were planned:

Product	Contracts
Fixed position	261
Pattern movement	118
Free movement	82
Service contracts	3,900

Top Management Reactions

Top management found that the overall revenue plan was acceptable but expressed concern. In its discussion, two areas for improvement were developed. First, a more

EXHIBIT 14–8

RAPID ROBOTICS, INC.   DATE: May 13, 19x8
Projected Revenues (Revised)
For the Year Ending September 30
(in millions)

Product	19x8	19x9	Change
Fixed position	$ 542	$ 673	24%
Pattern movement	650	764	18%
Free movement	246	258	5%
Service contracts	626	780	25%
Total	$2,064	$2,475	20%

aggressive approach should be taken to get outside research contracts, which primarily related to free-moving robots. Second, marketing of free-moving robots should be more aggressive. As a result, new marketing teams were to be formed over the next two years. Management also decided that additional resources were to be made available to the research group for the development of free-moving robots.

Production Plans

The production of robots is divided into six areas: engineering, software development, parts fabrication, attachment assembly, final assembly, and testing. Engineering and software development work closely on the design to meet customer requirements. This is the most time-consuming part of the contract completion. The fabrication, assembly, and testing of the units are then scheduled.

The production process at Rapid Robotics has been designed around the "pull" concept of production planning. Thus, all production is scheduled around contracts received rather than producing inventory for future sales. The plan assumes therefore that units produced will coincide with the number of robots necessary to complete the contracts expected to be signed during 19x9.

Materials Purchases Budget

The materials required for a robot include special-purpose computers, motors, power sources, cabinets, wiring, attachments, and parts sets. Although the detailed designs and programs vary, the types of material components in a given type of robot are standard. For example, each fixed-position robot requires two computers, one for vision and one for movement of attachments. A fixed-position contract averages 50 robots. Thus, completing a fixed-position contract requires 100 (2 × 50) special-purpose computers. Because 261 fixed-position contracts are planned for 19x9, the number of computers required for production is 26,100 (100 × 261). Similarly, the computers required for pattern-movement, free-movement, and service contracts may be computed as in Exhibit 14–9.

EXHIBIT 14–9

	RAPID ROBOTICS, INC.		DATE: June 1, 19x8
	Computer Usage Plan		
	For the Year Ending September 30, 19x9		
Product	*Contracts*	*Per Contract*	*Usage by Product*
Fixed position	261	100	26,100
Pattern movement	118	60	7,080
Free movement	82	25	2,050
Service contracts	3,900	50	195,000
Total computer usage			230,230

Exhibit 14–10 presents computations of computer purchases by adding desired ending inventory to computer usage and subtracting the beginning inventory. Notice that the desired inventory is about 20 percent less than the beginning inventory. Rapid Robotics has cut materials inventories by 20 percent per year for the past three years.

In Exhibit 14–11, the materials purchases budget is presented. This budget of $313,293,000 gives the director of purchasing the authority to set up a purchasing system capable of handling approximately that volume. The decisions on specific purchases of which computers and which motors will come later as the details of contract requirements become known. The materials purchases budget is to be adjusted as sales occur throughout the year.

EXHIBIT 14–10

RAPID ROBOTICS, INC.	DATE: June 1, 19x8

Computer Purchases Budget
For the Year Ending September 30, 19x9

Computer usage (Exhibit 14–9)	230,230
Plus: Desired ending inventory	16,805
Less: Beginning inventory	(21,005)
Computer purchases	226,030
Times: Standard price per input	$400
Computer purchases budget	$90,412,000

EXHIBIT 14–11

RAPID ROBOTICS, INC.	DATE: June 1, 19x8

Materials Purchases Budget
For the Year Ending September 30, 19x9
(in thousands)

Computers	$ 90,412
Motors	61,190
Power sources	36,897
Cabinets	943
Wiring/Cables	23,157
Attachment sets	62,873
Other setups	37,821
Total	$313,293

Hours Worked and the Production Labor Budget

The production of robots requires engineers, programmers, and laborers of various types. The engineering time required to complete a contract is substantial. For example, to complete a fixed-position contract requires 4,200 hours at standard. Because 261 contracts are projected, the number of required engineering hours for this type of contract is 1,096,200 (261 contracts × 4,200 hours). Similarly, the number of engineering hours required for each type of contract is estimated and presented in Exhibit 14–12.

Note that no enginering hours are required to complete service contracts.

The hours required for programming, field service, fabrication, attachment, assembly, and testing are all planned in a manner similar to that for engineering.

EXHIBIT 14–12

RAPID ROBOTICS, INC.	DATE: May 20, 19x8

Engineering Hours Planned
For the Year Ending September 30, 19x9

Product	*Contracts*	*Per Contract*	*Usage by Product*
Fixed position	261	4,200	1,096,200
Pattern movement	118	9,600	1,132,800
Free movement	82	30,000	2,460,000
Total engineering hours			4,689,000

EXHIBIT 14–13

RAPID ROBOTICS, INC.   DATE: May 20, 19x8
Production Labor Budget
For the Year Ending September 30, 19x9

	Labor Hours (thousands)	Hourly Rates	Labor Cost (thousands)
Engineering	4,689	$21	$ 98,469
Programming	5,740	17	97,580
Field service	23,400	14	327,600
Fabrication	2,697	12	32,364
Attachments	2,042	7	14,294
Assembly	4,038	6	24,228
Testing	1,456	8	11,648
Total production labor budget			$606,183

Converting from total hours to the production labor budget is accomplished by multiplying the hours for each function by the average labor rate per function. This is illustrated in Exhibit 14–13.

Production Overhead Budget

The fabrication and assembly of the robots are accomplished in plants located in Michigan, Georgia, and California. Engineering and programming are located in large offices and development laboratories in Los Angeles, Boston, and Dallas. Field service is located in offices throughout the world. Each of the functions has overhead. The engineering overhead budget is presented in Exhibit 14–14.

The production overhead related to all of the functional areas is presented in summary form as in Exhibit 14–15.

There are additional detailed overhead budgets for each location and function. Please note that production department overhead budgets should be flexible budgets

EXHIBIT 14–14

RAPID ROBOTICS, INC.
Engineering Overhead Budget
For the Year Ending September 30, 19x9
(in thousands)

*Travel	$ 5,532
*Employee benefits	55,200
*Conferences	3,425
*Indirect labor	23,050
*Indirect materials	23,119
*Maintenance—Outside	2,610
Supervision	3,920
Depreciation	5,600
Other	2,000
Totals	$124,456

* Flexible (variable) items depending upon contract volume.

EXHIBIT 14–15

RAPID ROBOTICS, INC.		DATE: May 20, 19x8
Production Overhead Budget		
For the Year Ending September 30, 19x9		
Engineering	(Exhibit 14–14)	$124,456
Programming		98,413
Field service		303,024
Fabrication		50,729
Attachments		25,986
Assembly		26,666
Testing		10,181
Total production overhead budget		$639,455

with a fixed amount and a variable portion based on activity. Exhibit 14–16 presents the flexible overhead budget for an assembly department in one of the Georgia plants. This budget was based on last year's actual data and allowed 8 percent for inflation over two years and 10 percent for increased activity. No input was requested directly from the department supervisor. The Budget Steering Committee took the expedient approach on overhead estimates, but members agreed that they will seek input from the department supervisor next year. They simply ran out of time on the overhead estimates.

MARKETING BUDGET

The accomplishment of the sales plan will require both marketing effort and expense. The sales teams will visit hundreds of client locations for demonstrations, attend the trade shows of over 300 industry groups, and advertise in over 800 trade journals all over the world. The teams will submit about 2,500 proposals in response to client requests for proposals.

As part of the sales plan, the vice president for marketing submitted a budget of $78 million for marketing and distribution (Exhibit 14–17). The budget was approved by top management with minor revisions.

EXHIBIT 14–16

FIXED ROBOT ASSEMBLY DEPARTMENT	
Atlanta Plant	
Production Overhead Budget	
For the Year Ending September 30, 19x9	
(in thousands)	
*Employee benefits	$ 5,200
*Indirect labor	3,050
*Indirect materials	3,119
*Maintenance—Outside	610
Supervision	920
Depreciation	600
Other	200
Totals	$13,699

* Flexible (variable) items depending upon contract volume.

EXHIBIT 14–17

RAPID ROBOTICS, INC.			**DATE: May 13, 19x8**
Marketing and Distribution Budget			
For the Year Ending September 30, 19x9			
(in thousands)			
Marketing			
Commissions (1.5%)		$37,125	
Salaries		5,000	
Team support		1,449	
Travel		13,222	
Trade shows		10,080	
Advertising		5,880	
Administration		976	
Lease expense		529	
Supplies		1,008	
Total marketing			$75,269
Distribution			
Packing		$ 230	
Shipping		600	
Installation		2,286	
Total distribution			3,116
Total marketing and distribution			$78,385

ADMINISTRATIVE AND GENERAL BUDGETS

The administrative and general area contains many specific functions such as research, legal, accounting, and corporate headquarters activities. The budgets allowing for these functions are often set at the discretion of top management. As an example, we will consider the research budget and then review the entire administrative and general budget.

Research Budget

Exhibit 14–18 presents the research budget for 19x9. Top management believes in a program of basic research in robotics. This includes studies for improving robot heuristic learning, speech, verbal comprehension, circuit design, optics, strength, dexterity, movement, and power sources. Recent research on life-support systems has particularly interested the chairman of Rapid Robotics. About a third of the research is contracted out to various universities.

Note that each research project is summarized as one line. There would also be a project-level budget to indicate funding by department or organization. Also notice that the projects involve several years and many different organizations.

General and Administrative Budget

Exhibit 14–19 presents the general and administrative budget by function. Research is the first line of the general expenses. The amounts for the other functions, such as executive office, would be further detailed by specific expense items in department budgets. This initial budget was approved by top management with some discussion on both the personnel and the research plans. Notice that the general and administrative budget is a mixture of functions, department names, and a few specific accounts. The budget director used a convenient mixture that helped him portray the company's

EXHIBIT 14–18

RAPID ROBOTICS, INC.				**DATE: June 1, 19x9**
Research Budget				
For the Year Ending September 30, 19x9				

Research Projects	*Location*	*Year of Study*	*Study Length*	*Current Funding*
Optics	Rutgers University	2	2	$12,000
Vebal comprehension	Stanford University	2	3	8,900
Life support	Kettering Institute	1	10	8,200
Heuristic learning	Leads University	3	5	6,800
Free movement	RR Labs	1	3	3,908
Speech synthesis	RR Labs	3	4	3,020
Power sources	MRC, INC.	3	3	2,500
R2D1	RR Labs	4	5	2,410
Project reserves				4,780
Total project research funds				$52,518
Research facility				2,000
Research administration				3,000
Total research budget				$57,518

EXHIBIT 14–19

RAPID ROBOTICS, INC.		**DATE: June 30, 19x8**
General and Administrative Budget		
For the Year Ending September 30, 19x9		

Administrative expenses		
Personnel	$99,201	
Finance and accounting	72,505	
Executive office	13,010	
Legal and contracts	3,600	
Public relations	5,200	$193,516
General expenses		
Research	$57,518	
Patent amortization	16,700	
Goodwill amortization	6,002	
Depreciation—Home office	66,000	
Other	1,370	147,590
Total general and administrative		$341,106

plans. Because this is his first time preparing a budget for this company, he did not feel constrained by custom or accounting textbooks. Furthermore, once the system is set up, he intends to modify it to meet the company's needs.

The budget director then summarized the Rapid Robotics operations plan with a budgeted statement of operations (Exhibit 14–20). Notice that the budget director needs additional information to prepare this statement:

1. Estimated sales discounts and allowances are $52.5 million.
2. Estimated purchase discount rates of 1.3 percent.

EXHIBIT 14–20

RAPID ROBOTICS, INC.			DATE: June 30, 19x8
Budgeted Income Statement			
For the Year Ending September 30, 19x9			
(in millions)			
Sales			$ 2,475.0
Less: Sales discounts and allowances			(52.5)
Net sales			$ 2,422.5
Production costs			
Materials	$ 317.9		
Less discounts	(4.1)		
Labor	606.2		
Overhead	639.4	$1,559.4	
Plus beginning work in process		151.9	
Less: Ending work in process		(135.9)	
Cost of goods sold			(1,575.4)
Gross margin			$ 847.1
Sales and distribution		$ 78.4	
General and administrative		341.1	(419.5)
Income from operations			$ 427.6
Other income			2.0
Income before tax			$ 429.6
Income tax (Estimated at 52%)			(223.4)
Net income			$ 206.2

3. Beginning and ending work in process of $151.9 million and $135.9[1] million, respectively.
4. Estimate of other income of $2 million.
5. Estimate of the income tax rate of 52 percent, including federal, state, and local taxes.

The budgeted income statement helps top management to place the operations in perspective and proportion. As a result of seeing this "big picture," management decided that marketing should more aggressively pursue the development of new marketing teams, a few more proposed research projects would be undertaken, and production costs—especially overhead—should be studied over the coming year.

We have completed the description of the initial planning of operations at Rapid Robotics. They have now organized the process. The planning office has aided in the preparation of account-level plans for all departments, teams, projects, and functions in the organization. These detailed plans were consolidated into plans for plants, regions, divisions, product lines, vice presidents, and laboratories. The consolidated operating plans were summarized in a budgeted statement of operations. The budget office still has much work to do before the pro forma financials, the master budget, are approved by the board of directors at its September meeting. The budget office must:

1. Review capital project proposals.
2. Gather details on proposed corporate financing.

---

[1] The ending inventory of work in process reflects senior management's desire to reduce inventories of all types by 10 to 11 percent per year in order to reduce production space required for work in process and to reduce investment in inventories.

3. Complete projections of cash receipts and disbursements.
4. Prepare pro forma financial statements.

In July and August, numerous changes and corrections will be made. Perhaps as many as 100 to 800 changes will occur to the detailed operating plans. These changes must be handled accurately and efficiently.

During the fiscal year, the planning staff will be involved with changes and corrections to the plans. Through these numerous changes, the plans will be adjusted to opportunities and unforeseen circumstances. Thus, the plans are made to be flexible and responsive to changing conditions.

The planning office will also start its preparations for the next budget cycle. The planning schedule will be examined very closely because some problems were encountered during May and June of the current year. Input forms and the input process for the various estimates required must be designed. Communication lines with regional headquarters and plants need to be set through the main corporate computer network so that changes can be entered more quickly by various departments and approvals can be quickly verified.

As the Rapid Robotics circumstances have demonstrated, certain benefits and challenges are associated with the budget process. We will now present these in more general terms.

BENEFITS AND CHALLENGES OF BUDGETING

Benefits of Budgeting

A good budget system provides decision support for managers in their planning and controlling activities. There are many benefits to budgeting. For this discussion, we classify the benefits into six convenient groups: (1) performance measurement, (2) communication of goals and objectives, (3) coordination of activities, (4) effective and efficient spending, (5) authorization of operations, and (6) the discouragement of fraud.

Performance Measurement.   The budget provides part of the basis for evaluating managers. Reports that compare the actual performance with planned performance for each manager are prepared. Thus, the budget becomes the standard against which a manager's performance is evaluated. Over several time periods, these comparisons allow managers to build a performance history that can be used as part of the information for salary adjustments and promotions. Consequently, the budget process should result in focusing and motivating managers toward specific objectives.

Communication of Goals and Objectives.   The process of preparing a budget communicates to managers the goals and objectives of top management. This communication is very important. It tells the managers what level of performance is expected and will be rewarded. Further, the communication gives top managers a convenient way to move the organization in directions that they desire.

Participation is said to occur when lower level managers are encouraged to suggest changes to top managers' objectives and the direction of the organization. If participation in the budget process is consistent with the overall approach, often referred to as the *management style,* of top management, then the results of the participation will generally be higher motivation for performance by managers. Of course, managers are human and some respond much better to participation than others.

Coordination of Activities.   The specialized parts of an organization should seek the common goals and objectives of senior management. This requires coordinating the timing of the activities of those parts. For example, the purchasing department should carefully coordinate with the production plant so that raw materials inventories are kept at a minimum, required quality is maintained, production flows smoothly, and costs are kept down. The budget (and changes to it) provides an instrument for coordinating these specialized activities.

Effective and Efficient Spending.   Spending money without careful thought is seldom an effective solution to a problem. For example, a manager of a production plant was having a problem with the late delivery of parts from suppliers. Further, a high number of parts were rejects. The plant manager hastily ordered purchasing to shift purchases to higher-quality suppliers that guaranteed fast delivery. Unfortunately, the problem did not go away. It turns out that purchasing and production were not coordinating their activities. Production supervisors would demand materials at the last minute, and purchasing would scramble for them. The continuous panic demands over the telephone from purchasing came across to suppliers' clerks as very rude. The supplier's clerks tired of this behavior and "got even" by placing a low priority on the orders or shipping lower-quality materials. Switching to a new, more expensive supplier gave the plant a few months' grace period, but then the same old problems started to occur again. Therefore, the allocation of additional money was an ineffective solution.

   The budgeting process encourages managers to think through problems and solutions before resources are committed. Without a budget, some managers are tempted to take the easy way out and throw money at a problem rather than think their way to a solution. Spending money is never a substitute for careful thinking.

Authorization of Operations.   Internal controls are important in the design of accounting systems. One important control is that all transactions should be authorized by responsible management before incurrence. A budget provides the general authorization for the departmental expenditure of money, time, people, supplies, equipment, and space. Expenditures made within the budget have been authorized by top management.

Discouragement of Fraud.   Because budgets should be based on careful estimates, the comparison of actual events with the estimates makes hiding fraudulent activities more difficult. The budget process encourages managers to look carefully at each phase of their activities. For example, an annual review of the budget for advertising led marketing management to question the amount of advertising directed toward several small television stations. A close inspection found that the company's advertising manager received a "fee" from the stations, which was contrary to company policy. The process of budgeting brought out the fraud that might otherwise have gone unnoticed.

The Challenges of Budgeting

Like any human process, there are challenges with budgeting and planning in organizations. The budget system becomes the vehicle for both creating and resolving the frictions in human behavior. Some accountants call these the disadvantages of budgeting. We believe they are challenges, the resolution of which demonstrates the dynamic nature of the process and the caution managers must exercise.

Budgetary Slack or Padding.   **Budgetary slack** (also called *padding*) is the excess in a budget above the minimum necessary to run an efficient operation. This excess is expressed in higher estimates for expenditures or lower estimates for revenues.

Some top managers treat any budgetary slack as if it were a disease to be cured by budget directors or internal auditors. However, the future demands on operations are uncertain, and budgetary slack does provide the flexibility to absorb sudden changes in demand. Thus, some slack is necessary for an effective operation. A higher uncertainty about demands should result in more budgetary slack.

Counter-Productive Budget Cuts.   Care should be taken that the review of efficiency and effectiveness does not become shortsighted. There is a tendency to reduce expenditures in the less-visible areas of maintaining employees, fixed assets, new product research, and advertising. These are called *short-run budget cuts*. They can occur during economic downturns or whenever managers are pressured to show better performance than is reasonable under the circumstances. Top managers should guard against these short-run cuts by considering both the income earned and the way in which it was earned.

A variation on counterproductive cuts is called the **ratchet effect.** Like a ratchet wrench, top management tightens a department's expense budgets (or increases the return or revenue requirements) each year. Thus, the more efficient and effective the department, the more difficult its budget becomes. Eventually, the operations of the department lose effectiveness and falter like a bolt breaking from being tightened too much by a wrench. Top management should avoid the temptation to use the budget as a vehicle for cutting departments too much. The effects can be seriously damaging over several years.

Arbitrary and Capricious Allocations.   Surprising or disturbing events can occur during the allocation process. The results are often caused by a lack of competence, sensitivity, or knowledge by those allocating the resources. For example, the budget director for a city was in a late-night planning session with the city council and was alarmed to find that the council was eliminating his own position from the city budget. He was devastated. He called his wife at 2:00 A.M. to tell her that his position was gone. By the time he arrived home at 7:00 A.M., his position had been restored. However, the budget director was not amused by the insensitivity of the city council and immediately sought employment elsewhere. Top managers should guard against being arbitrary and capricious in their budget allocations. This behavior is interpreted by lower-level employees as either insensitive or incompetent. This in turn can result in lowered confidence, motivation, and initiative.

Rigid Budgets and Performance Goals.   **Bureaucratic behavior** is the strict following of rules and standardized operating procedures. The environment is one in which rules become more important than economic substance, and standard procedures replace rational thought. Creativity is stifled and opportunities are lost. Rigid budgets and performance goals are a symptom of bureaucratic behavior.

A highly bureaucratic budget and performance evaluation process encourages excessive budget slack. As managers pad parts of their budget for future contingencies, they create reserves that must be spent by the end of the year. Thus, expenditures are made for unnecessary people, equipment, and supplies so that the budget is spent during the period. Further, because most companies have internal auditors, the expenditure of excessive slack must be carefully disguised. All this activity requires significant energy and creativity on the part of managers that could be better spent elsewhere.

Inflexibility in budgets is partly an information system problem and partly caused by the performance evaluation criteria of top management. The budget system can be made more flexible by allowing for frequent, rapid budget revisions as a software design requirement. Top management can guard against inflexibility by rewarding creativity and flexible response to opportunities rather than strict conformity to budget amounts.

Pseudoparticipation.   **Pseudoparticipation** is top management seeking the input of lower management in the budget process, but ignoring the input when it is given. Top management wants lower management to feel that it is important and wants lower-level managers to be motivated to work toward budget objectives. Lower managers talk and recommend, but top managers do not respond. Managers are intelligent; consequently, they become aware that psuedoparticipation is a form of manipulation by top management, and they become disenchanted with both top management and the budget process.

You should now be aware that budgeting for operations is beneficial and important but that it also has the potential for creating serious problems.

SUMMARY

Operations are the detailed activities of an organization. A budget is a plan of operations expressed in monetary terms.

The budget director organizes the budget process. This person suggests basic approaches, sets a timetable, provides computer support, and interacts with managers. The result of the budget director's efforts is a master budget, which is the planned income statement and balance sheet. There are various approaches to budgeting including annual, rolling, fixed, flexible, incremental, and zero based. Budgets occur in levels of summarization including account level, functional, project or program, and total operations. The normal order of preparation of operations budgets for a manufacturer is (1) sales; (2) production; (3) purchases, labor, and overhead; (4) general and administrative expenses; and (5) statement of operations.

The process of developing a budget helps communicate goals and objectives from top management to lower levels. If lower levels of management are expected to communicate back to top management, there is participation in the process.

The budget provides part of the basis for performance evaluation. Budgeting often results in operations that are better coordinated, more efficient, and more effective.

There are challenges associated with budgeting. Although some budgetary slack (padding) is useful for responding to changes in demands, excessive slack is sometimes a symptom of rigid and bureaucratic budget approaches. During lean times, top managers tend to make counterproductive budget cuts. They reduce budgets for departments in spite of needs, which is called the *ratchet effect*. Sometimes, top managers are arbitrary or capricious in their allocations, which results in a lack of confidence by lower-level managers. Budgets should not be rigid or fixed. Participation should not be faked or it might result in poor attitudes by managers.

PROBLEM FOR REVIEW

Sales and Production Planning with Budget Revisions. LLB, Inc., produces rubber fishing boots in a small plant in Bellefonte, Pennsylvania. The company expects to sell 9,000 units in the Eastern region and 4,000 units in the Western region during 19x9. The product is marketed at a price of $37 through outdoors catalogs. LLB, Inc., has a beginning inventory of 3,500 pairs and would like to reduce this to 1,600 pairs during 19x9. Each pair of boots requires 3 pounds of specially conditioned latex at a cost of $4 per pound. Beginning and desired ending inventories of latex are 6,000 and 2,300 pounds, respectively. Each pair of boots requires 1.5 hours of labor at a cost of $8 per hour. Fixed overhead for the line is expected to be $28,000, and the variable overhead is $2 per hour plus $0.70 per pair. Costs and production are spread evenly throughout the year.

REQUIRED

Compute the following given the current projected sales:
a. Sales revenue budget.
b. Production-unit plan.
c. Materials purchases budget.
d. Production labor budget.
e. Production overhead budget.

SOLUTION

a.
LLB, INC.
Sales Revenue Budget
For the Year Ending December 31, 19x9

Eastern region	9,000 at $37	$333,000
Western region	4,000 at $37	148,000
Totals	13,000	$481,000

b.
LLB, INC.
Production Unit Plan
For the Year Ending December 31, 19x9

Sales units	13,000
Plus: Desired ending inventory	1,600
Less: Beginning inventory	(3,500)
Production units planned	11,100

c.
LLB, INC.
Materials Purchases Budget
For the Year Ending December 31, 19x9

	Units	Pounds/Unit	Materials
Production units planned	11,100	3	33,300
Plus: Desired ending inventory			2,300
Less: Beginning inventory			(6,000)
Purchased units needed			29,600
Purchase price			× $4
Materials purchases budget			$118,400

d.
LLB, INC.
Production Labor Budget
For the Year Ending December 31, 19x9

	Units	Hours/Unit	Total Hours
Production planned	11,100	1.5	16,650
Labor rate			× $8
Labor budget			$133,200

e.

LLB, INC.
Production Overhead Budget
For the Year Ending December 31, 19x9

	Units	Rates	Overhead
Unit variable costs	11,100	$0.70	$ 7,770
Hourly variable costs	16,500	$2.00	33,000
Fixed overhead costs			28,000
Total budgeted overhead cost			$68,770

KEY TERMS AND CONCEPTS

Operations (554)
Plan of operations (554)
Budget (554)
Budget director (554)
Master budget (554)
Special-purpose software (555)
Financial planning packages (555)
Electronic spread sheets (555)
Annual budget (556)
Rolling or continuous budget (556)
Fixed budget (556)
Flexible budget (556)

Incremental budget (557)
Zero-based budget (557)
Account-level budget (558)
Line-item budget (558)
Functional budget (558)
Project budget (559)
Program budgeting (559)
Participation (570)
Ratchet effect (572)
Budgetary slack (572)
Bureaucratic behavior (572)
Pseudoparticipation (573)

ADDITIONAL READINGS

Bernstein, G. L. "The Art of Using Forecasting Effectively." *L&H Perspective,* No. 1, 1984, pp. 8–10.

Bothwell, C. "How to Improve Financial Planning with a Budget Manual." *Management Accounting,* December, 1984, pp. 34–38, ff.

Carruth, P. J., and T. O. McClendon. "How Supervisors React to 'Meeting the Budget' Pressure." *Management Accounting,* November, 1984, pp. 50–54.

Dillon, G. J. "Getting the Most from Your Forecasting System." *Management Accounting,* April, 1984, pp. 28–32.

Hayen, R. L., and R. M. Peters. "How to Ensure Spreadsheet Integrity." *Management Accounting,* April, 1989, pp. 30–33.

McGrath, J. "Basic Budgeting: Keeping the Variables Visible." *CFO,* August, 1987, pp. 43–51.

———. "Setting Corporate Financial Goals." *CFO,* February, 1987, 65–69.

Miller, T. C., and M. J. Liberatore. "Production and Distribution Planning in a Processing Firm." *Production and Inventory Management Journal,* First quarter, 1989, pp. 44–48.

Ntuen, C. A. "Forecasting Maintenance Crew Size Requirements Based on Periodic Maintenance Records." *Production and Inventory Management Journal,* Second quarter, 1989, pp. 41–43.

Ranck, J. H. "Avoiding the Pitfalls in Sales Forecasting." *Management Accounting,* September, 1986, pp. 51–55.

Searfoss, D. G. "Some Behavioral Aspects of Budgeting for Control: An Empirical Study." *Accounting, Organizations, and Society,* November, 1976, pp. 375–385.

Shelton, F. A., and J. C. Bailes. "How to Create an Electronic Spreadsheet Budget." *Management Accounting,* July, 1986, pp. 40–47.

REVIEW QUESTIONS

1. List the normal operations for a manufacturing company.
2. What is a budget and how does it differ from a plan?
3. What is the job of the budget director?
4. List three types of computer support available for the budgeting function. What are the advantages and disadvantages of each approach?
5. What is the role of the Budget Steering Committee?
6. Why is a budget timetable important?
7. Who gives approval to a budget?
8. List the normal steps for preparing a budget in many organizations.
9. What is the difference between an annual budget and a rolling budget?
10. What is a sunset review?
11. Why should a zero-based budget approach not be adopted for every organization unit every year?
12. How does an account-level budget differ from a functional budget?
13. Why is a project budget a useful device for getting cooperation among departments? What problem does it try to solve?
14. What is the formula for converting material usage to material purchases?
15. What is management participation?
16. List and briefly describe the major benefits of budgeting.
17. List and briefly describe the major challenges of budgeting.
18. Why does an unplanned operation tend to encourage fraud?
19. What is the ratchet effect and what are its eventual results?
20. What is the effect of arbitrary allocations by top managers on the attitudes of managers?
21. What is pseudoparticipation? What effect does it tend to have on attitudes?
22. Why is some budgetary slack useful?

DISCUSSION QUESTIONS

23. If there is a budget steering committee, why should the budget director endeavor to involve it in important decisions and judgments?
24. Why might a rolling budget tend to be less rigid than an annual budget?
25. Why would a flexible budget approach be more useful than a fixed budget for performance evaluation?
26. Why might organizations find industry estimates and extrapolations from historical data useful in estimating sales? Why not just go with the sales estimates of regional sales managers? Or even better, the estimates of individual sales staff members?
27. Would having a standardized input form for sales estimates encourage estimators both to be more punctual in supplying their estimates and to be more careful? Why might the form make the planning system less flexible?
28. Why would a budget steering committee want to work on the budget to get it as close as possible to the desires of top management? Why not just combine the input estimates and pass them on and let the top managers kick the budget back if they are displeased? (*Hint:* Think through why a budget steering committee was appointed in the first place. What is its function and whom does it represent?)
29. Why would top managers tend to react with strategic decisions as a result of reviewing the annual budget?
30. Some people believe that they are in control of the future (internal locus of control). Other people believe that something or someone other than themselves controls what happens (external locus of control). Why would a person with a strong internal locus of control react better to and be more motivated by a participative budget-setting process than a person with a strong external locus of control?
31. How does the budget process facilitate the communication of top management goals and

objectives? Why does it encourage top managers to make definite their goals and objectives (or occasionally to change them)?

32. In what ways would the job of the budget director differ with an authoritative, top-management style versus a participative style?

33. Why would a manager's performance differ between being allowed to participate in the budget process and being given a budget by top management?

34. In which of the following budgetary situations would you expect more budgetary slack (padding) as a percentage of total budget? Why?

  a. A budget for an electric utility or a budget for a war with the Soviet Union.

  b. A budget in which absolutely no change is allowed after adoption or one that can be changed easily.

  c. An overhead budget for the assembly department set by the department supervisor or one set in negotiation with the plant manager.

EXERCISES

14–1. Terms.

REQUIRED:
Match the following terms with the best-fitting numbered phrase.

(B. George, adapted)

_____ *a.* Sunset review.	1. Adjusted for activity.
_____ *b.* Account-level budget.	2. Entity must justify existence.
_____ *c.* Ratchet effect.	3. Also called *program budgeting*.
_____ *d.* Psuedoparticipation.	4. Input of lower managers is ignored.
_____ *e.* Functional budget.	5. Adjusted from last year.
_____ *f.* Budget steering committee.	6. Reviews and approves budget.
_____ *g.* Flexible budget.	7. Tightening of budget.
_____ *h.* Budget slack.	8. Provides flexibility to meet sudden changes in demand.
_____ *i.* Incremental budget.	9. Lists amounts by general ledger account.
_____ *j.* Project budget.	10. Also called an *activity budget*.

14–2. Revenue Budget.   Creations, Inc., sells chairs that resemble different common zoo mammals through a store in a local mall and through mail-order catalogs. Its 19x3 sales were as follows:

	Store Sales	*Mail Order*	*Total*
Elephants	175	400	575
Giraffes	125	350	475
Hyenas	200	400	600
Lions	150	350	500
Zebras	225	600	825

All chairs were sold for $125 during 19x3.

In 19x4, sales are expected to increase by 4 percent in the store and 12 percent for mail orders. The price for the chairs will be increased by 8 percent.

(M. Nave, adapted)

REQUIRED:
Prepare a revenue budget by product for 19x4.

14–3. Projected Revenue Budget.   The Boucke Company sells and services communication products, mostly telephone systems. The 19x8 sales numbers are:

	Eastern	Central	Western	Total
Switching	$300	$ 250	$200	$ 750
Office	400	500	100	1,000
Cellular	100	200	300	600
Service	50	100	100	250
Total	$850	$1,050	$700	$2,600

Sales are projected to increase by 10 percent in the Eastern district, 8 percent in the Central district, and 12 percent in the Western district.

REQUIRED:
Prepare a projected revenue budget for 19x9.

14–4. Production-Unit Plans.   Kentucky Killer Company produces three types of ball bats: two for baseball and one for softball. The company has developed a new policy of ending inventories equal to 20 percent of current monthly sales. Data for June 19x6 are as follows:

(J. Fuller, adapted)

Brand Names	Beginning Inventories	Projected Sales
Pro Killer	17,840	31,360
College Killer	12,960	64,800
Soft Killer	49,405	148,215

REQUIRED:
Prepare a production-unit plan for the three products for June 19x6.

14–5. Production-Unit Plans.   The ProDriver Golf Company produces three golf clubs in its Birmingham plant. Unit information for beginning inventories and projected sales is included below for April 19x0:

	Beginning Inventories	Projected Sales
Wood	4,200	13,400
Iron	1,600	12,800
Wedge	100	2,600

The desired ending inventory is 10 percent of current projected sales.

REQUIRED:
Prepare a production-unit plan for each of the products for April 19x0.

14–6. Materials Purchases.   The Hetzel Company produces ring binders with the following standards for materials:

	Standards	Cost	Cost	Units in Inventory
Metal rings	3.0 each	$0.060	$0.18000	27,000
Metal center	1.0 each	$0.140	0.14000	6,000
Plastic	2.5 feet	$0.025	0.06250	18,000
Cardboard	1.3 feet	$0.008	0.01040	10,000
Total standard cost			$0.39290	

The company projects production of 12,000 binders for May 19x8. The production manager would like to have about a third of a month's materials in inventory.

(K. Earls, adapted)

REQUIRED:
Prepare a materials purchase budget for May 19x8.

14–7. Materials Purchases.   The Settee Plant uses four materials to manufacture chairs:

	Standards		
Item	*Description*	*Per Unit*	*Beginning Inventories*
Framing	100 board feet	$ 0.11	65,000 board ft.
Cloth	6 square yards	$ 3.00	20,000 yards
Stuffing	10 cubic feet	$ 0.05	10,000 cubic feet
Packaging	1 set	$15.00	42 sets

The plant has projected production of 1,350 chairs for the month of January 19x3. The plant manager would like to set materials inventories to about 10 days' worth (about a third of a month).

REQUIRED:
Prepare a materials purchases budget in units and dollars for January 19x3.

14–8. Labor Force Budget.   The Maucet Parts Company produces electronic parts for various manufacturers. In the past, the warehousing manager has had one supply stocker to handle each 1,000 different parts plus picker/shippers to handle each 120,000 items shipped per year. Last year the warehouse handled 40,000 different parts with a total volume of 1.2 million shipped. There is currently one supervisor for each eight workers.

During coming year, the manager expects to organize the work force into one supply stocker for each 1,200 parts and have one picker/shipper handle 80,000 items shipped per year. The management has decided to cut the number of different parts by 20 percent, which will decrease shipments by only about 2 percent.

Workers are currently paid $8,000 per year, and supervisors are paid $14,000 per year. The expected wage rate will be 20 percent higher for workers and 10 percent higher for supervisors during the coming year. Normal turnover is 20 percent for workers and 10 percent for supervisors. Using a new management concept, the warehouse manager expects to need only one supervisor for each 12 workers. Labor-related costs are 25 percent of base salary.

REQUIRED:
a. Determine the number of workers in each category required to handle the current parts and volumes. (A partial person is achievable with part-time employees.)
b. Compute the budget for the warehouse staff for the past year.
c. Prepare a warehouse labor budget for the coming year using the manager's projections and proposed policies.
d. Determine whether the warehouse manager can use normal turnover during the next six months to result in the reduction of required personnel.

14–9. Labor Budget.   Clandiss Seating Company produces various types of wooden chairs, couches, and benches. One of its products is a church pew that comes in three sizes: a long size for large churches, a short size that is used for small chapels, and a midsize that is very heavy and is used primarily in funeral homes. The short pew requires 5 labor hours, the midsize, 5.5 hours, and the long size requires 6 hours. Each worker works 170 hours per month and is paid $14.25 per hour.

For January 19x8, the unit production plans are:

Pews Produced	
Short	100
Midsize	60
Long	125

REQUIRED:
Assuming that each worker is employed full-time for a full month, prepare a labor budget in terms of hours, people, and monetary amounts. Include in the budget an estimate of the cost of idle time.

14–10. Labor Force Planning.   The Cincinnati Defense Plant has 2,288 engineers on January 1, 19x2. It recently lost bids on contracts for the B-2 tactical bomber and all proposed fighters. As a consequence, it must reduce the engineering staff to 1,250 by July 1, 19x4. Normal annual attrition is 18 percent of the beginning engineers. The average salary for the engineering staff is $36,000 with 25 percent allowed for fringe benefits. The plant manager plans to give a severance bonus of $12,000 to all engineers who must be terminated on July 1, 19x4. Assume constant attrition, which occurs on average halfway through each time period.

(K. Craig, adapted)

REQUIRED:

Prepare an engineering labor budget for each of the following:

a. Year ending December 31, 19x2.
b. Year ending December 31, 19x3.
c. Six months ending July 1, 19x4. Include the required severance pay.

PROBLEMS

14–11. Marketing Budget.   The Richardson Motors Company sells new and used cars and provides service for them. The marketing budget for the fiscal year ending August 31, 19x3, was:

	19x3 Budget
Sales commissions (5% of sales)	$3,000,000
Advertising and promotion	600,000
Employee benefits (22% of compensation)	715,000
Sales managers	250,000
Other selling expenses	320,000
Total marketing budget	$4,885,000

All sales and marketing staff are on commission, and all managers are on salary. Employee benefits are paid for all personnel.

During fiscal 19x4, Shiela Jones, vice president of marketing, plans to increase the sales commission to 5.25 percent, increase advertising by 12 percent, and increase sales managers' salaries by 20 percent. The employee benefits are being changed so that the rate will be only 18 percent of total compensation. Sales are expected to increase to $75 million, and other expenses will not be changed.

REQUIRED:

Prepare a marketing budget for fiscal 19x4.

14–12. Overhead Budget.   The Josten Pipe Works has plant overhead that is a function of transactions as follows for 19x6:

	Overhead Cost per Event
Purchase	$ 50
Production setup	150
Engineering change	400
Production order	100

In addition, there is $20,000 in production administration. Production for 19x6 calls for many different varieties of pipe to be produced with the following results in expected events:

Purchases	450
Production setups	2,600
Engineering changes	1,500
Production orders	2,080

For 19x7 a new computer-controlled machine that decreases setup overhead to $50 will be installed. An increase of 25 percent is projected for pipe production for the coming year; this increase is expected to result in 10 percent more transactions. In addition, dramatic changes in the competition are expected to require a 30 percent increase in engineering changes to products.

REQUIRED:
a. Prepare an estimate of plant overhead for 19x6.
b. Prepare a budget of projected plant overhead for 19x7 using the functional budget approach.

14–13. Departmental Budgeting. Marshall Electronics, a subsidiary of Kramer Industries, manufactures microchips for a wide variety of applications. Four months ago, Kramer sent a team from its Internal Audit Department to Marshall Electronics to perform a routine review of operations. A portion of the audit report presented to Kramer on the operations of Marshall Electronics is presented below.

Prior to making the preliminary management response presented in the audit report below, the president and the controller of Marshall Electronics announced to the departmental managers that the company was planning to accept the audit recommendations to implement a departmental budgeting system. The managers were asked for suggestions on implementation procedures and were encouraged to raise any questions they might have about the budget system.

Internal Audit Report

Observation. Departmental budgets are not being utilized at Marshall Electronics. Currently, the division does not have the automated systems capability to produce budget analyses at the departmental level. Traditionally, the plant's costs have been controlled through a total plant concept rather than a departmental approach to cost control. Given present business conditions, this approach may no longer be the optimum control process. Increased competition in the marketplace, declining profits, deteriorating margins, and increased costs have combined to necessitate an aggressive approach to cost reduction. Based on experience at other Kramer plants, we believe Marshall Electronics would benefit from the development and use of departmental budgets for all functions.

Recommendations. We recommend that Marshall Electronics establish a management objective to develop and utilize flexible departmental expense budgets for all departments. Resources and systems development efforts should be devoted to this objective as they become available. We suggest, as an interim step, that operating budgets be employed on a monthly basis. Operating targets for both direct labor and indirect labor expense should be established for each manufacturing department monthly. Departmental managers should track performance and explain deviations from targets as part of the regular agenda at the weekly production meetings.

Preliminary Management Response. The Marshall Electronics plant will develop and utilize a flexible departmental budget system. In the interim, work has begun to establish daily, month-to-date, and annual targets for direct and indirect labor for the manufacturing departments. These targets include efficiency objectives, overtime objectives, and indirect labor-staffing objectives based on volume and product mix.

(CMA, adapted)

REQUIRED:
a. Describe the benefits, other than better cost control, that are likely to accrue to Marshall Electronics from the implementation of departmental budgeting.
b. Discuss the behavioral impact the introduction of departmental budgeting is likely to have on the following at Marshall:
   1. Departmental managers.
   2. Production workers.
c. Discuss the managerial mistakes that Marshall Electronics must avoid in order to gain acceptance of this change in operating procedure.

14–14. Overhead Budget.   Met Airlines provides feeder service to Denver, Albuquerque, and Phoenix. The small airline has three 12-passenger and one 28-passenger plane. All planes must receive maintenance after each 100 hours of flying and a complete overhaul after every 1,000 flying hours. Maintenance and overhauls must be performed by mechanics who have been licensed by the Federal Aviation Administration. Airplane mechanics charge $30 per hour for their time plus parts. Regular maintenance on the smaller plane requires 6 hours for the mechanic plus $120 for parts and oil. The larger plane requires 9 hours of maintenance plus $200 for parts and oil. Each plane must have a check-out flight after regular maintenance at a cost of $60. A complete overhaul requires 30 hours of time plus $6,000 in parts for the smaller plane and 40 hours plus $12,000 in parts for the larger. The check-out for either plane after a complete overhaul costs $300. Data on the four planes for 19x4 are as follows:

Call ID	Passengers	Hours Since Last Overhaul	19x4 Projected Hours
XAA42	12	308	1,120
YAZ21	12	614	843
YBT33	12	901	750
AVT10	28	604	1,560

REQUIRED:
Prepare a maintenance budget for 19x4 detailing amounts for parts, mechanic labor, and check-out flights.

14–15. Administration Budgets.   On February 15, 19x2, William T. Clanton, the superintendent of the Worthington Independent School District, requested the following administrative budget for the school year starting September 1, 19x2:

Line	Purpose	Request
100	Administration:	
100–110	District Office	$ 88,000
100–111	Personnel Center	48,000
100–112	Computer Center	85,000
100–113	Copy Center	150,000
100–114	Service Center	45,000
100–199	Development	162,000
100–200	High school	192,000
100–300	Junior high school	144,000
100–400	Elementary school	320,000
	Total administration	$1,234,000

This function budget was supported by an account-level budget for each of the administrative functions. Mr. Clanton was very well aware that the school board would not allow the total administrative budget. In the past, the board has haggled over amounts. Some "extra" is necessary in each of the administrative budgets to make each function run smoothly. Thus, Mr. Clanton has learned from 32 years of experience to allow some extra money in the budget.

As expected, the school board objected to the size of the administrative budget. However, instead of haggling over the budget during the meeting, the board requested Mr. Clanton to come back in two weeks with a revised budget that totaled $1,080,000. Mr. Clanton is secretly very pleased because he has placed about 22 percent slack in each of the school budgets, 35 percent in the center budgets, and 50 percent in the development budget. Based on prior experience, Mr. Clanton estimates that each of the schools could get along adequately with 15 percent slack, and the centers need about 20 percent slack. The district office budget cannot be cut, but all the slack can be cut out of development.

REQUIRED:
Prepare the revised administrative budget that Mr. Clanton will present to the school board on March 1.

14–16. Operations Planning. WestWood Corporation is a wood stove manufacturer located in southern Oregon. WestWood manufactures three models: small stoves for heating a single room, medium-sized stoves for use in mobile homes and as a supplement to central heating systems, and large stoves with the capacity to provide central heating.

The manufacturing process consists of shearing and shaping steel and fabricating, welding, painting, and finishing it. Molded doors are custom built at an outside foundry in the state, brass plated by a plater, and fitted with custom-etched glass during assembly at WestWood's plant. The finished stoves are delivered to dealers either directly or through regional warehouses located in the western United States. WestWood owns the three tractor trailers and one large truck used to ship stoves to dealers and warehouses.

The budget for the year ending February 28, 19x6, was finalized in January 19x5 and was based upon the assumption of the continuation of the 10 percent annual growth rate that WestWood had experienced since 19x0.

Stoves are seasonal products, and the first quarter of WestWood's fiscal year is usually a slack period. As a consequence, inventory levels were down at the start of the current fiscal year on March 1, 19x5. WestWood's sales orders for the first quarter ended May 31, 19x5 were up 54 percent over the same period last year and 40 percent above the first quarter budget. Unfortunately, not all the sales orders could be filled due to the reduced inventory levels at the beginning of the quarter. WestWood's plant was able to increase production over budgeted levels but not in sufficient quantity to compensate for the large increase in orders. Therefore, there is a large backlog of orders. Furthermore, preliminary orders for the busy fall season are 60 percent above budget, and the projections for the winter of 19x5–x6 indicate no decrease in demand. WestWood's president attributes the increase to effective advertising, the products' good reputation, the increased number of installations of wood stoves in new houses, and the bankruptcy of WestWood's principal competitor.

(CMA, adapted)

REQUIRED:
a. WestWood Corporation's sales for the remainder of the 19x5–x6 fiscal year will be much greater than were predicted five months ago. Explain the effect this increase will have on the operations in the following functional areas of WestWood:
1. Production.
2. Finance and accounting.
3. Marketing.
4. Personnel.
b. Some companies follow the practice of preparing a continuous budget.
1. Explain what a continuous budget is.
2. Explain how WestWood Corporation could benefit by the preparation of a continuous budget.

14–17. Revenue and Cost of Goods Sold Planning. Molid Company was founded in 19x3 by Mark Dalid. The company produces a modulation-demodulation unit (modem) for use with minicomputers and microcomputers. Business has expanded rapidly since the company's inception.

Bob Wells, the company's general accountant, prepared a budget for the fiscal year ending August 31, 19x6. The budget was based on the prior year's sales and production activity because Dalid believed that the sales growth experienced during the prior year would not continue at the same pace. The pro forma income and cost of goods sold that were prepared as part of the budget process are presented below (in thousands):

Net sales		$31,248
Cost of goods sold		20,765
Gross margin		$10,483
Operating expenses:		
Marketing	$ 3,200	
General and administrative	2,200	5,400
Income from operations before taxes		$ 5,083

Cost of Goods Sold

Direct materials inventory, 9/1/x5	$ 1,360	
Materials purchases	14,476	
Materials available for use	$15,836	
Direct materials inventory, 8/31/x6	1,628	$14,208
Direct labor		1,134
Factory overhead:		
Indirect materials	$ 1,421	
General factory overhead	3,240	4,661
Cost of goods manufactured		$20,003
Finished goods inventory, 9/1/x5		1,169
Goods available for sale		$21,172
Finished goods inventory, 8/31/x6		407
Cost of goods sold		$20,765

On December 10, 19x5, Dalid and Wells met to discuss the first quarter operating results (i.e., results for the period September 1 to November 30, 19x5). Wells believed that several changes should be made to the original budget assumptions that had been used to prepare the pro forma statements. Wells prepared the following notes that summarized the changes that would not become known until the first quarter results had been compiled. The following data were submitted to Dalid:

1. The estimated production in units for the fiscal year should be revised upward from 162,000 units to 170,000 units with the balance of production being scheduled in equal segments over the last nine months of the fiscal year. Actual first-quarter production was 35,000 units.
2. The planned ending inventory for finished goods of 3,300 units at the end of the fiscal year remains unchanged. The finished goods inventory of 9,300 units as of September 1, 19x5, had dropped to 9,000 units by November 30, 19x5. The finished goods inventory at the end of the fiscal year will be valued at the average manufacturing cost for the year.
3. The direct labor rate will increase 8 percent as of June 1, 19x6, as a consequence of a new labor agreement that was signed during the first quarter. When the original pro forma statements were prepared, the expected effective date for this new labor agreement had been September 1, 19x6.
4. Direct materials sufficient to produce 16,000 units were on hand at the beginning of the fiscal year. The plans for direct materials inventory to have the equivalent of 18,500 units of production at the end of the fiscal year remained unchanged. Direct materials inventory is valued on a FIFO basis. Direct materials equivalent to 37,500 units of output were purchased for $3,300,000 during the first quarter of the fiscal year. Molid's suppliers have informed the company that direct materials prices will increase 5 percent on March 1, 19x6. Direct materials needed for the rest of the fiscal year will be purchased evenly through the last nine months.
5. On the basis of historical data, indirect material cost is projected at 10 percent of the cost of direct materials consumed.
6. One-half of general factory overhead and all of marketing and general and administrative expenses are considered fixed.

After an extended discussion, Dalid asked for a new estimate of sales and a pro forma statement cost of goods sold for the fiscal year ending August 31, 19x6.

(CMA, adapted)

REQUIRED:
a. Based on the revised data presented by Bob Wells, calculate Molid Company's projected sales for the year ending August 31, 19x6, in:

1. Number of units to be sold.
2. Dollar volume of net sales.

b. Prepare the pro forma statement of cost of goods sold for the year ending August 31, 19x6, which Dalid has requested.

14–18. Plant Overhead Functional Budget. The Halifax Tool Plant manufactures sets of hand tools used for automotive repair. Sales have fallen during the past two years, and the plant manager, John Murdock, has been told to cut costs and prepare for the worst. The Korean manufacturers have been producing a superior product and are able to sell at a price (even with import duties) that is 15 percent less than the Halifax total cost per unit. The standard current cost for a tool set is as follows:

Materials	$ 5.00
Labor	3.00
Overhead	4.50
Total standard cost	$12.50

During the past three years, the manager has focused on direct materials and labor and has been able to reduce costs by about 40 percent. However, during this time, overhead has increased from $2.80 to $4.50 per unit, partly due to the decline in volume.

The plant overhead budget for 19x4, presented in a functional format, is as follows:

	Variable	*Fixed*	*Totals*
Materials storage and handling	$320,000	$ 480,000	$ 800,000
Engineering	–0–	710,000	710,000
Maintenance	192,000	448,000	640,000
Quality control	58,000	232,000	290,000
Plant administration	–0–	260,000	260,000
Total plant overhead costs	$570,000	$2,130,000	$2,700,000
Unit volume	600,000	600,000	
Standard overhead cost per unit	$0.95	$3.55	$4.50

Mr. Murdock has decided to adopt a ''new'' approach to overhead. The approach involves cutting inventories to a minimum, having production workers perform all quality control and much of the maintenance, and simplifying the production process to minimize the movement of materials and paper requirements. As a consequence, the fixed portion of materials storage and handling will be cut in half—as will the variable portion. The Engineering Department, which has not been very productive of late, will be cut from the current level to $400,000. The fixed portion of Maintenance will be cut to $200,000, and the variable portion will be cut to $0.20 per unit. The Quality Control Department will be eliminated. Plant Administration will be cut to $220,000. Even with price reductions, the unit volume is expected to fall to 500,000. Given the dire shape of the company, Mr. Murdock has decided that all wage rates and other costs will be held constant. The impact of these changes on direct materials and labor is expected to be immaterial.

REQUIRED:
a. Prepare a functional overhead budget with the changes as proposed by Mr. Murdock.
b. Compute the new overhead standard cost per unit.

14–19. Production Overhead Budgets. ZZT Company manufactures 2,100 small appliances and power tools. The Maintenance Department tests and maintains all plant equipment. During 19x8, the monthly account-level budget for the Maintenance Department was:

Account Title	Positions	Rates	Budget
Maintenance workers	7	$1,400	$ 9,800
Clerical	2	820	1,640
Departmental supervisor	1		3,200
Employee benefits		25%	3,660
Equipment depreciation			1,400
Maintenance parts and supplies			4,000
Training and conferences			1,400
Other expenses			600
Total maintenance costs			$ 25,700
Production unit volume			200,000
Maintenance cost per unit of output			$0.12850

For 19x9, the plant manager plans to stop producing 900 of the least profitable products. Although this seems drastic, these products make up only 8 percent of total unit volume and 4 percent of total revenue. The volume of the other products is expected to stay about the same. The variety of equipment will be reduced slightly, and equipment changes will be cut drastically. The effect on maintenance will be that three of the workers and one clerical staff can be shifted out of the department and into production positions. The departmental supervisor is going to be shifted into an assistant plant manager's position. One of the remaining workers will be elected as the team leader. The maintenance workers' monthly pay will increase to $1,700 with the elected team leader being paid $1,900. Clerical wages will be increased by 5 percent. Because of increases in medical costs, the benefits rate needs to increase to 36 percent.

The training and conference amounts will be $250 per worker. The parts and supplies cost will remain the same at $0.02 per unit produced. Finally, depreciation and other costs will not be changed for next year.

REQUIRED:

a. Prepare a monthly account-level budget for the maintenance team for 19x9.

b. What effect are these changes expected to have on the maintenance cost per unit of output?

14–20. Production Plans.   Relmond Petrochemical Products manufactures and sells a cleaning solvent. Although the company accounts for production by the gallon, it sells the product in 42-gallon barrels at a selling price of $95 per barrel. The company expects to sell 100,000 barrels during April 19x0. The finished goods inventory at April 1 is 15,000 barrels at a cost of $855,000. The April 30 finished goods inventory is expected to be 18,500 barrels. The company uses the FIFO method to account for all inventories.

The production process consists of refining a petroleum feedstock and then blending it with two other chemicals. Each barrel of final product requires 34 gallons of refined feed stock, 6 gallons of blending agent MZ–44, and 2 gallons of blending agent RD–63. Materials inventory information is:

	April 1, 19x0		April 30, 19x0	
	Gallons	Cost	Gallons	Cost
Feedstock	50,000	$0.60	60,000	$0.65
MZ–44	20,000	0.24	18,000	0.25
RD–63	5,000	0.09	9,000	0.10

Unit costs in the ending inventory are anticipated costs for materials purchased during April.

Direct labor workers are paid $10 per hour. One-half hour is needed to produce one barrel of solvent. Variable production overhead is expected to be $18 per direct labor hour, and fixed production overhead is expected to be $1,200,600 for the month. Production overhead is applied to production on the basis of direct labor hours.

REQUIRED:
Prepare the following plans and budgets:
a. Production-unit plan.
b. Materials purchase unit plan and budget.
c. Schedule of production unit costs.
d. Cost of goods sold budget.

14–21. Production-Unit and Direct Labor Planning.   Roletter Company makes and sells artistic frames for pictures of weddings, graduations, christenings, and other special events. Bob Anderson, controller, is responsible for preparing Roletter's master budget and has accumulated the information below for 19x5:

	January	February	March	April	May
Sales units	10,000	12,000	8,000	9,000	9,000
Selling price	$50.00	$47.50	$47.50	$47.50	$47.50
Unit labor hours	2.0	2.0	1.5	1.5	1.5
Wages per hour	$8.00	$8.00	$8.00	$9.00	$9.00

Labor-related costs include pension contributions of $0.25 per hour, workers' compensation insurance of $0.10 per hour, employee medical insurance of $0.40 per hour, and social security taxes. Assume that as of January 1, 19x5, the base figure for computing social security taxes is $45,000 and that the rates are 7 percent for employers and 7 percent for employees. The cost of employee benefits paid by Roletter is treated as a direct labor cost.

Roletter has a labor contract that calls for wages to increase to $9.00 per hour on April 1, 19x5. New labor-saving machinery has been installed and will be fully operational by March 1, 19x5.

Roletter expects to have 16,000 frames on hand at December 31, 19x4, and has the policy of carrying an end-of-month inventory of 100 percent of the following month's sales plus 50 percent of the second following month's sales.

(CMA, adapted)

REQUIRED:
Prepare a production budget and a direct labor budget for Roletter Company by month and for the first quarter of 19x5. The direct labor budget should include direct labor hours and show the detail for each direct labor cost category.

14–22. Production-Unit and Materials Planning.   The Joyce Division of Betasso Corporation manufactures an intricate subassembly for an infrared disposal unit produced by the Plainview Division. This disposal unit was developed primarily for disposal of toxic chemicals and waste. The unit uses an infrared beam to break down complex chemical compounds into simpler, commercially useful compounds.

The division manager, Arlo Mylander, has requested that the division controller, Telford Ralls, start preparing a budget for the fourth quarter of the current fiscal year. Mr. Ralls has gathered the data presented below.

Sales of subassemblies through September 30 are 36,000 units, and the division expects to sell an additional 18,000 units by year end. Actual and projected sales are listed below:

Recent Months' Sales		Projected Sales	
August	4,000	October	7,000
September	5,000	November	6,000
		December	5,000

The sales are projected to be 5,000 units for both January and February of next year.
The direct materials for the subassembly consist of four raw materials:

Material	Units Needed for Final Subassembly	Purchase Price
AD–2418	4	$12.00
CF–6531	3	$14.00
PF–4235	2	$16.00
MO–5902	1	$18.00

The division keeps a materials inventory equal to 80 percent of the following month's expected production needs.

The production process consists of fabrication, assembly, and finishing. Each subassembly requires one-half hour of fabrication at $15 per hour, one hour of assembly at $12 per hour, and one-quarter hour of finishing at $8 per hour. Overhead is divided into variable and fixed portions with variable cost budgeted at $5.50 per unit and fixed costs of $240,000 per year occurring evenly throughout the year. Fixed overhead is applied on the basis of the planned production for each month.

At the end of each month, 10 percent of next month's sales units is in finishing awaiting transfer to the finished goods warehouse, and 60 percent of next month's sales is already in finished goods.

The projected inventory balances for September 30, 19x3 are:

Material/Product	Units	Cost	Amount
AD–2418	22,000	$12.00	$264,000
CF–6531	16,000	$14.00	224,000
PF–4235	11,000	$16.00	176,000
MO–5902	5,000	$18.00	90,000
Work in process—Finishing	700	?	?
Finished goods	4,200	?	?

REQUIRED:

Prepare the following plans and budgets for each month during the final quarter of the fiscal year.

a. Production-unit plan.
b. Materials purchase unit plan and budget.
c. Cost of goods sold budget (FIFO method).

 14–23. Comprehensive Budgeting with FIFO Costs.   The budget director for NeuTech Enterprises, Inc., has gathered the following data. Based on this initial information, the director will present a series of prospective budgets for negotiating a final master budget. The FIFO method is used for all inventory costing.

The company makes three versions of an insecticide used in wheat farming. The beginning inventories and projected sales for 19x9 are:

Product	Beginning Inventory Units	Beginning Inventory Cost	Projected Sales Units	Projected Sales Price	Desired Ending
Alitane	15,000	$24	75,000	$64	14,000
Slissocide	10,000	18	60,000	80	11,000
Borretane	2,000	9	10,000	28	1,000

The January 1, 19x9, inventories of raw materials and desired ending units required are expected to be:

Raw Material	Beginning Inventory Units	Beginning Inventory Cost	Desired Ending Units	Expected 19x9 Prices
RW03	3,000	$0.60	4,000	$1.60
RX01	18,000	$0.75	21,000	$0.80
SY07	40,000	$0.35	40,000	$0.32
SZ43	9,000	$1.05	10,000	$1.10

There are no beginning inventories of work in process and none is planned for the ending inventory. The production of each of the insecticides requires various units of material:

	Requirements for Each Product		
Material	Alitane	Slissocide	Borretane
RW03	½	0	0
RX01	0	2	1
SY07	7	11	5
SZ43	1	0	4

The production process for Alitane and Slissocide requires mixing and then packaging; Borretane is sold in bulk and requires no packing. Given the dangerous nature of the products, special care must be taken in both mixing and packaging. The estimated labor hours per unit of output are:

		Requirements for Each Product		
Material	Labor Rate	Alitane	Slissocide	Borretane
Mixing	$10	2	1	4
Packaging	$18	1	½	–0–

Estimated factory overhead costs for 19x9 are:

Indirect factory labor	$280,000
Depreciation	265,000
Supervision	290,000
Utilities	170,000
Indirect materials	85,000
Maintenance	72,000
Property taxes and insurance	68,000

Factory overhead is allocated on the basis of direct labor hours. The estimated selling expenses are $420,000, and general expenses are $175,000. The estimated income tax rate is projected to be 30 percent.

(A. Gregory, adapted)

REQUIRED:
a. Prepare the following schedules:
   1. Sales revenue.
   2. Production units.
   3. Direct materials purchases units and dollars.
   4. Direct labor hours and dollars.
   5. Overhead schedule and rate per hour.
b. Prepare a cost of goods sold budget for 19x9.
c. Prepare a budgeted income statement for 19x9.

EXTENDED APPLICATIONS

14–24. Comprehensive Operations Budget. Allan Watership, Inc., produces a special-purpose microcomputer that is used to design integrated circuits. The product goes by the brand name Circuit Judge. The computer has an input device that can read the contents of a circuit board and translate it into pictures. The designer works with the circuits on a high-quality screen, tests the new circuits with a simulator, and then outputs high-quality circuit plots. The plots are then etched onto circuit boards or integrated circuit chips.

There are two varieties of the product: Honest and Supreme. The products differ according to the programs stored permanently on chips inside the computer. The selling price of Honest is $30,000, and Supreme is sold for $60,000. The standard cost of production includes:

			Honest	*Supreme*
Materials				
Chip set (Includes royalty)			$10,000	$20,000
Computer			3,000	3,000
Input/Output setup			4,100	4,100
Packaging materials			100	100
	Hours	*Rates*		
Assembly				
Labor	15	$11.00	165	165
Overhead		$30.00	450	450
Packaging				
Labor	5	$14.00	70	70
Overhead		$23.00	115	115
Total standard costs			$18,000	$28,000

The estimated sales for 19x3 are 600 Honest Circuit Judges and 300 Supreme Circuit Judges. The beginning inventories are projected as follows:

	Units	*Price*	*Amount*
Honest Circuit Judge	48	$18,000	$ 864,000
Supreme Circuit Judge	2	28,000	56,000
Honest chip set	50	10,000	500,000
Supreme chip set	40	20,000	800,000
Computer	50	3,000	150,000
Input/Output setup	40	4,100	164,000
Packaging material	400	100	40,000
Total inventories			$2,574,000

Top management would like ending inventories for 19x3 to be about 20 percent of the annual sales units. The selling and general budget is to be set at $5,000,000 plus 8 percent of sales revenue.

REQUIRED:

a. Prepare a projected revenue budget.

b. Prepare a production units plan for the two products with the following columns:

Sales Units	*Desired Ending Units*	*Beginning Units*	*Planned Production*

c. Prepare a schedule of hours for production by product and function.

d. Prepare a production labor budget by function.

e. Prepare a materials usage plan by material and product.

f. Prepare a materials purchases budget in dollars.

g. Prepare an overhead budget by department. Assume the following variable and fixed costs by department:

	Assembly	*Packaging*
Variable per hour:		
Employee benefits	$6	$5
Indirect labor	3	2
Supplies	1	3
Maintenance	2	1
Fixed charges:		
Supervision	$ 49,100	$25,800
Depreciation	160,000	31,000
Other	69,000	5,000
Total fixed	$278,100	$61,800

h. Compute the amount of the selling and administrative budget.

i. Prepare a budget statement of operations.

14–25. Merchandising Plans. Elwood Cleaver, 26, is the new manager of the sporting goods section of Cray-Mart Stores in Philadelphia. Sporting goods has been given a varying number of merchandise aisles, including one with a restricted cabinet area. The restricted cabinet contains mostly guns, ammunition, and other expensive items. The five seasons for selling sporting goods follow local weather patterns and school calendars to a certain degree. By far the highest traffic and sales occur in the summer months. Mr. Cleaver uses the following periods in planning his promotion and buying.

Period	Dates	Weeks	Major Promotions	Aisles
A	4/10 to 6/19	10	Fishing/Camping/Picnic	7
B	6/20 to 9/4	11	Organized sports/Camping	9
C	9/5 to 11/13	10	Hunting	5
D	11/13 to 1/29	11	Winter sports equipment	4
E	1/29 to 4/9	10	Slow period	4

Mr. Cleaver must order specific merchandise from the national buying office 12 weeks prior to the time each item is needed on the shelf. This lead time is sufficient for manufacturing and shipping. The merchandise is delivered during a one-week period surrounding the date requested. Mr. Cleaver can select from up to 12,600 different items, any one of which can be a promotional item, but those in the $5 to $15 range work best. He knows that his success or failure depends mostly upon which items he picks and when he places the orders.

In this type of store, every section must contribute to drawing in shoppers, which is called *generating traffic*. During certain times of the year, some sections draw more than others. The sole purpose of promotional items is to generate traffic; items are priced very low and are highly promoted for about two weeks. For example, a promotional item might be a 50-gallon, name-brand freezer chest priced at $12.95 that is offered the two weeks before the fourth of July. The basic traffic for any one section is partially due to the promotional efforts of the other sections. Each promotion draws an average of 200 people. Listed below are some basic traffic data by period for sporting goods:

Period	Weekly Traffic Basic	Weekly Traffic Needed	Percent Purchases	Average Purchase	Inventory Allowed
A	600	1,000	60	$22	$ 66,000
B	800	2,000	75	34	255,000
C	500	900	60	40	108,000
D	300	700	50	26	45,500
E	100	300	30	11	25,000

The traffic needed is a quota that has been set by the store manager based on space allocations and a standard formula. The proportion of traffic actually buying something varies dramatically by season, as does the amount of the average purchase. The proportion and average sales presented here exclude the promoted items. The inventory allowed is set by the store manager and is also formula driven. The inventory allowed does not include those items designated as promotional.

The advertising for each promotional item costs $400. The gross margin on promoted items averages 10 percent above purchase price with an average promoted price of $11. Of the customers who are drawn by the promoted item, 60 percent actually purchase it; these customers account for 80 percent of the sales of the promoted item. The gross margin on regular stock is 40 percent of the revenue. Variable selling and general costs are 5 percent of total revenues. The Sporting Goods Department has to pay rent to the store of $100 per aisle per week plus 6 percent of total sales. Mr. Cleaver's salary is $200 per week plus a bonus of 15 percent of departmental profits before the bonus. Seasonal, part-time workers are directly employed by the department for the B season only at a cost of $160 per week.

On March 10, Mr. Cleaver must file his plans with the store manager for the B time period, and he has asked for your help.

REQUIRED:

a. How many promotional items are needed during the 11 weeks of period B to attain the required number of customers?

b. For the promotional items computed in part *(a)* prepare the following plans and schedules:
  1. Revenue from sales of promoted items.
  2. Cost of goods sold of promoted items.
  3. Variable store rental charges for promoted items.
  4. Variable selling and general costs for promoted items.

c. Assuming that the needed traffic is generated from the promotion items, prepare the following plans and schedules:
  1. Revenue from sales of regular stock.
  2. Cost of goods sold of regular stock.
  3. Variable store rental charges for regular stock.
  4. Variable selling and general costs for regular stock.
  5. Fixed store rental charge.
  6. Departmental fixed salaries and wages.

d. The beginning inventory is projected to be $66,000, and the desired ending inventory is $108,000. Prepare a weekly and a total Period B purchasing budget for sporting goods with columns for regular stock and promotional items. Assume the inventory at the end of week 1 will be $255,000. Thereafter, the weekly inventory, excluding promotions, should decrease uniformly to $108,000.

e. Prepare a budgeted departmental profit and loss statement for period B with columns for regular sales, promotional sales, and a total. Use the total column to calculate the estimated amount of Mr. Cleaver's bonus and the departmental operating income.

f. Mr. Cleaver could plan to go above the required number of promotional items, but additional promotions become less effective. For example, if he chose to go over seven promotions a week, they would be likely to draw only about 150 customers for two items and then fall to about 100 customers for the remainder.
  1. Would a promotion that draws in only 150 people be worth doing?
  2. Would a promotion that draws in only 100 people be worth doing?
  3. How many customers must a promotion draw before Mr. Cleaver breaks even on offering the promotional item?

14–26. Service Capacity Planning with Constraints.   Christa Jefferson is the new unit supervisor for the East Wing Intensive Care unit of Portland County Hospital. She is attempting to prepare the unit budget for 19x4. The hospital has just been through a Medicare review because of complaints by several indigent patients to the Social Security Administration. Further, several previous employees, now in jail, had been forging doctors' signatures on prescriptions. Although the hospital passed the Medicare review, the review report found fault with the adequacy of emergency room documentation, procedures in the postoperative care unit, and certain irregularities in the East Wing Intensive Care Unit. Failure on the Medicare review would result in the withdrawal of all Medicare funding, which has averaged about $6.2 million per month. The Medicare reviewers will be back again in 12 months to check on the hospital's progress toward compliance.

In preparing a 19x4 budget, Ms. Jefferson increased the current year's numbers by 10 percent and submitted them to the hospital administration:

EAST WING INTENSIVE CARE UNIT
Unit Operating Budget
For the Year Ending October 31, 19x4

	Units	*Cost*	*Budget*
Registered nurses	12	$30,000	$ 360,000
Licensed practicing nurses	29	$18,000	522,000
Nurse's aids	12	$11,000	132,000
Employee benefits (Rate)		28%	295,680
Part-time RN hours	3,000	$20.00	60,000
Part-Time LPN hours	6,000	$12.00	72,000
Part-time nurse's aid hours	3,000	$7.00	21,000
Overtime hours	8,000	$24.00	192,000
Supplies			200,000
Training			50,000
Occupancy charge	40	$5,000	200,000
Unit supervisor			42,000
Total care cost			$2,146,680
Planned patient days (Average of 24 per day)			8,760
Cost per patient day			$245.05

The administration returned the budget with a memorandum requesting that Supervisor Jefferson prepare a budget that is about $220 per day and shows about 70 percent utilization of facilities. She was told informally that there should be no problem in meeting these requirements.

The state hospital licensing requirements for intensive care units prescribe one RN plus a nurse's aid for each five patients, or one LPN for each three patients. Insurance companies require at least one RN on duty at all times. Regional peer review standards for intensive care units recommend that at least 40 percent of the total nursing staff be RNs. There are 40 beds in the East Wing Intensive Care Unit. Supervisor Jefferson is expected to plan for an average bed utilization of 70 percent during the coming year. During 19x3, the average census has been 22.4 patients, or 56 percent utilization. The average for 19x4 is expected to be about 24 patients per day. Nurses are entitled to 15 days of personal leave, and they are given five national holidays off. The five holidays are covered by paying overtime rates to part-time staff. Because Ms. Jefferson is new at the budget game and has already had her first budget proposal returned by the administration, she has come to you for help in preparing her 19x4 budget.

REQUIRED:
a. Assuming an average load of 24 patients and that the 21st shift each week plus all vacations will be covered with part-time nurses, compute the following:
   1. The number of full-time RN/nurse's aids and part-time hours required to meet the state standards assuming no LPNs are used.
   2. Expected total cost for the option in part (a.1).
   3. The number of full-time LPN units and part-time hours required to meet the state standards assuming that only one RN and one nurse's aid are scheduled per shift.
   4. Expected total cost for the option in part (a.3).
   5. The number of RNs, nurse's aids, and LPNs required to meet the 40 percent minimum of the regional peer review standards.
   6. Expected total cost for the option in part (a.5).
b. Ms. Jefferson would like to shift some of the rooms to the East Wing Acute Care Unit. She knows that it is desperately short of rooms because she is also supervising that unit on an acting basis. Because the units adjoin, the transfer would require only the movement of one set of double doors at a nominal cost.

1. How many rooms would you recommend moving to the Acute Care Unit?
2. Compute the impact on cost per intensive care day to shift the rooms in part (*b*.1). to Acute Care.

c. If Ms. Jefferson chose to meet all requirements and recommendations and reduce the number of assigned beds, estimate the cost per patient day. How much slack would there be in a budget that results in $220 per patient day?

d. Discuss the relationship between the prospect of another intensive Medicare review next year and the need for slack in Ms. Jefferson's 19x4 budget.

14–27. Comprehensive Operations Plan, Multiple Products, and Materials.   Battleship Rock, Inc., produces sofa chairs at the Hueco Tanks Division. There are two varieties of the product: Regular and Super. The products differ dramatically by the quality of the materials used. The selling price of the Regular is $120, and the Super is sold for $300. The standard cost of production is:

Materials		Hourly Rate	Regular	Super
Wood set			$20.00	$ 20.00
Hardware set			20.00	40.00
Cloth bundle			14.00	30.00
Shipping carton			9.00	9.00
Assembly	Labor	$6.00	6.00	18.00
	Overhead	$7.00	7.00	21.00
Packaging	Labor	$4.50	4.50	4.50
	Overhead	$3.00	3.00	3.00
Total standard costs			$83.50	$145.50

The estimated sales for 19x4 are 6,400 Regular chairs and 3,200 Super chairs. The beginning inventories are projected as follows:

	Units	Price	Amount
Regular chair	500	$ 83.50	$41,750
Super chair	300	145.50	43,650
Wood sets	200	20	4,000
Regular hardware set	100	20	2,000
Super hardware set	180	40	7,200
Regular cloth bundle	60	14	840
Super cloth bundle	200	30	6,000
Shipping carton	400	9	3,600

Senior management would like ending inventories for 19x4 to be about 10 percent of the annual sales units. The selling and general budget is to be set at $500,000 plus 6 percent of sales revenue.

REQUIRED:
a. Prepare a projected revenue budget.
b. Prepare a production-unit plan for the two products.
c. Prepare a schedule of hours for production by product and function.
d. Prepare a production labor budget by function.
e. Prepare a materials usage plan by material and product.
f. Prepare a materials purchases budget in dollars.
g. Prepare an overhead budget by department. Assume the following variable and fixed costs by department:

		Assembly	Packaging
Variable charges	Employee benefits	$1.50	$1.00
per hour	Indirect labor	0.50	0.50
	Supplies	0.75	0.25
	Maintenance	0.25	0.25

		Assembly	Packaging
Fixed charges	Supervision	$20,000	$22,000
	Depreciation	10,000	4,000
	Other	5,000	6,000

h. Compute the amount of the selling and administrative budget.

i. Prepare a budget income statement assuming a tax rate of 40 percent.

14–28. Direct Labor Capacity Planning.   One product line of Song-Sung, Ltd., is automobile oil pumps. Its three oil pumps differ slightly in the nature of the machining of the purchased components and in the indirect materials required. Specifically, the inflow and outflow plates have to be machined to fit recent models of the SS404 stock engine. The oil pumps are delivered on a daily basis to a nearby motor assembly plant. The contract requires that the pumps be delivered on time with 100 percent quality. If any oil pump fails during the first 60,000 miles of engine use, then Song-Sung must pay the engine manufacturer $3,500. The current failure rate has been running at 2.2 per 100,000 pumps delivered.

During fiscal 19x3, 70 machinists and 140 assemblers have been assigned to manufacture oil pumps. Every employee works an 8-hour shift with a 40-hour week. Company policy strongly discourages overtime. The 210 workers have been organized into 35 work groups, each of which consists of two machinists and four assemblers. Each machinist needs three hours per week for normal cleaning, oiling, and computer testing plus three hours for training and quality control meetings. Assemblers need four hours per week for training and quality control meetings. Workers have been cross-trained for the different oil pumps and can move where needed. Assemblers are paid an average of $17,680 per year, and machinists are paid an average of $21,840 per year. All employees receive two weeks of vacation per year plus five paid national holidays. Employees are guaranteed full employment; normal turnover is 4 percent per year. Quality and output bonuses at current group output levels are 15 percent of base, and employee benefits are an additional 22 percent of base compensation. Direct labor for the oil pump is treated as a short-term fixed cost for decision-making and planning. Work groups are formed and are separated only upon death, retirement, or at the request of group members. Some of the best performing groups have been together many years. The standard hours required for each of the three pumps are:

Oil Pump	Machining	Assembly
A7–404A	0.10	0.20
A7–404B	0.15	0.30
A7–404C	0.20	0.40

It is the policy of Song-Sung to reduce costs as much as possible within the constraint of high quality. The inventories of products have proven unnecessary given the steady pace of engine production. Thus, the plant manager would like to cut inventory from the current levels. The plant manager feels comfortable with cutting current inventory to about three days' sales units in inventory. The projected data for the year ending August 31, 19x4 are:

	Inventories		
Oil Pump	(Projected) 8/31/x3	(Desired) 8/31/x4	Contracted Sales
A7–404A	15,000	986	120,000
A7–404B	18,900	1,397	170,000
A7–404C	12,500	2,055	250,000

The oil pump line has been less profitable than desired partly due to underutilization of labor and overstocking of finished goods inventories. The plant manager would like to plan for labor utilization of close to 76 percent of total hours and close to, but no more than, 90 percent of productive hours available. The 10 percentage "extra" will allow for variations in pump demand. If average utilization is above 90 percent, quality declines during peak periods. Any work groups not needed in the oil pump production area are needed in other departments in the plant. If a work group is near the desired utilization level, the quality and quantity bonus increases to 30 percent of the base pay.

(J. Mawanda-Kibuule, adapted)

REQUIRED:

a. Prepare a production-unit plan for the year ending August 31, 19x4.

b. Assuming that the standard year has 2,080 hours (52 weeks with 40 hours), compute for the 35 work groups:
1. Projected utilization rates based on total hours for oil pump component machinists and oil pump assemblers.
2. Projected utilization rates based on productive hours available for oil pump component machinists and oil pump assemblers.

c. How many work groups are needed to get as close as possible to the plant manager's capacity utilization (load) requirements without going over them? (Remember that the work groups are kept intact on a move.)

d. The base pay for all machinists and assemblers is scheduled to increase by 6 percent for 19x4. Bonuses and fringe benefit allowances will continue to be computed in terms of percentages of base pay. Prepare a production labor budget for fiscal 19x4 assuming that:
1. The current 35 work groups are kept.
2. The number of work groups is changed as computed in (c).

e. What would be the cost savings in allowing the average utilization of available productive hours to increase from 90 percent to 96 percent? Assume in your analysis that the oil pump failure rate will increase from 2.2 to 6.0 per 100,000 pumps delivered.

14–29. Multiple Product, Multiple Periods. Kiwi, Inc., is a supplier of propellers for small aircraft. The product is made from either aluminum, polymer, or steel and comes in three sizes: 3.5, 4.25, and 5 feet. The propeller blades are manufactured on the day that orders are received. Each blade is balanced precisely and is then performance tested by a person trained by the Federal Aviation Administration. Sidney Perth, the company's owner and manager, needs help in preparing a quarterly production capacity and purchasing schedule for the year ending December 31, 19x0.

The product sizes have been given names that relate to the type of aircraft on which they are mounted. The standard materials for each of the products are as follows:

Product	Size (Feet)	Aluminum Spun (Pounds)	Polymer and Graphite (Gallons)	Steel Stainless (Pounds)
General aviation	3.50	9.6	4.5	18.0
Commercial	4.25	12.2	5.7	22.7
Cargo	5.00	15.0	6.9	27.6
Price per input unit		$3.00	$2.12	$0.40
Materials inventory,				
Beginning units		1,812	1,620	804
Desired ending units		420	500	400

Mr. Perth would like to decrease the materials inventories evenly to the lower balances. Late in the year he would like to expand the size of the testing area because that is currently a production bottleneck.

The expected sales for each of the blades is:

	Total Units	Aluminum	Polymer	Steel
General aviation	1,600	20%	30%	50%
Commercial	2,400	40%	20%	40%
Cargo	1,800	10%	10%	80%

In the past, sales by quarter have been fairly stable with more sales in the late spring than in other quarters: 1st, 20 percent; 2nd, 30 percent; 3rd, 27 percent; and 4th, 23 percent. The selling price for the blades depends on the size and materials:

(B. Lemmons, adapted)

	Aluminum	*Polymer*	*Steel*
General aviation	$200	$300	$120
Commercial	250	375	150
Cargo	300	450	180

REQUIRED:
a. Sales unit schedule by quarter.
b. Quarterly revenue budget.
c. Quarterly production materials/units schedule.
d. Quarterly purchases budget.

CHAPTER

15

Cash Budgeting

■

CASH FLOW PROBLEM

Memorandum

To: George Morrison, Budget Analyst   Date: July 10, 19x8
From: Walter Harragan, Budget Director
Subject: Cash Projections for the Quarter Ending December 31, 19x8

We now need to concentrate on the cash flow estimates for the coming fiscal year. Let's start working on the first quarter. The sales and materials purchase estimates are (in millions):

	Sales	*Purchases*
October	$174	$25
November	193	21
December	172	24

The production labor cost is estimated at about $909 million for the year. Payments for various operating expenses are expected to be about $465 million per year. Interest payments are about $68 million per year, and our estimated tax payments are going to be about $220 million per year. Don't forget that we have purchases and sales of equipment to plan for and also some debt and dividend payments. Look these up in the board minutes.

Finally, top management wants a cash flow format that is consistent with external financial reports.

■

LEARNING OBJECTIVES

After completing this chapter, you should be able to:

1. Estimate and apply a pattern for cash receipts.
2. Estimate and apply a pattern for cash disbursements to vendors.
3. Determine the effects of labor, overhead, selling, and general expenses on cash disbursements.
4. Prepare a cash flow budget.

The success of a company depends upon its ability both to earn income and to stay liquid. **Liquidity** is the ability to pay bills as they are due and is especially important for retailers, equipment manufacturers, construction companies, the tourist industry, and service companies that have definite "seasons." On an annual basis, many companies plan their expected cash receipts and cash disbursement needs. The objective for cash planning is to provide for liquidity throughout the fiscal year.

We do *not* need exact receipts and disbursements to predict cash-poor and cash-rich time periods. Exact numbers are time consuming and expensive to produce and will be subject to error no matter how accurate we try to be. Instead, we need reasonable estimates of the flow of cash receipts and disbursements throughout the year.

ESTIMATING CASH FLOW FROM OPERATIONS

In this section, we will study techniques related to estimating cash flow from operations.[1] We will begin with estimating the cash receipts from operations.

Estimating Cash Collections from Customers

We will present two approaches to estimating cash collection patterns:

1. Judgment.
2. Customer account analysis.

Appendix A illustrates an approach to estimating cash collection patterns based on regression analysis.

Judgment. One approach to estimating the pattern of cash collections is to ask someone with considerable experience with collections on account. For example the credit manager might be asked what collections pattern can be expected during the budget period. Generally, the answers received are rough approximations. Unless the manager has recently studied cash flows in detail, the response will be something like: "Collections are about half during the month of sale, 40 percent the next month, and 10 percent the following month." Judgments will be biased to some extent by memorable events (for example, the bankruptcy of a large customer), representativeness (stereotyping of customers), and recent payment patterns. Thus, do not rely heavily on judgment without further substantiation.

The following open-ended questions will draw out useful information:

What types of customers pay faster (or slower) than others?
In what months are customers more likely to pay faster (or slower)?
How has the payment pattern improved or declined during the past year?
How do you expect the payment pattern to differ over the coming year from past years?

---

[1] The definitions of operations, investing, and financing activities in this chapter have been adapted from the *Statement of Financial Accounting Standards No. 95*, "Statement of Cash Flows" (Stamford, Conn.: Financial Accounting Standards Board, 1988).

EXHIBIT 15–1

WASHBURN COMPANY
(Account W3–160–406)
Account Analysis
For the Year Ending December 31, 19x9

Invoice Date	Payment Date	Invoice Number	Invoice Amount	Payment Amount	Paid during Month		
					Current	Next	Following
01/29	02/12	128676	$11,200	$10,976	–0–	$10,976	–0–
03/03	03/22	130089	4,689	4,689	$ 4,689	–0–	–0–
06/12	06/15	134257	1,000	980	980	–0–	–0–
08/09	08/23	142726	2,600	2,600	2,600	–0–	–0–
09/12	09/25	144793	10,000	9,800	9,800	–0–	–0–
10/29	11/20	148702	5,200	5,200	–0–	5,200	–0–
	Totals		$34,689	$34,245	$18,069	$16,176	$0
					52.1%	46.6%	

These questions do not lead to a "yes" or "no" response but require the manager to recall specific cases that are important for cash flow projections. An additional analysis that may be performed is a customer account analysis on a sample of customer accounts.

Customer Account Analysis. In order to prepare a **customer account analysis,** the collection pattern is first established for a sample of customers' accounts. For each customer, list the invoice and payment amounts and categorize the payments into months by date. Then total the payments by month. Some customers will have only a few invoices, and others will have several hundreds or thousands. As an example of account analysis, consider Exhibit 15–1 for the Washburn Company. The credit terms allow for a 2 percent discount for payment within 15 days of invoice date.

Exhibit 15–2 presents an estimate of the collection rates based on a sample of five accounts. The payment amounts have been computed for each of the accounts as for the Washburn account. The amounts are then totaled, and the collection rates for each month are computed.

EXHIBIT 15–2   Estimates of Collection Rates (for the 12 months ending August 31, 19x8)

Account Number	Company	Annual Sales	Paid during Month		
			Current	Next	Following
B1–002–001	Bateson Tooling	$ 29,882	$16,734	$ 148	$12,402
C2–899–030	Crystal SYS	20,121	8,048	9,054	2,616
S4–662–088	Streich, Inc.	49,998	22,499	22,499	4,000
T1–003–882	Trobe, Inc.	30,411	18,247	10,644	912
W3–160–406	Washburn Co.	34,689	18,069	16,176	–0–
	Sample total	$165,101	$83,597	$58,521	$19,930
Average collections rates			50.6%	35.4%	12.1%

In practice, more than five accounts should be used to represent the purchasing and payment habits of customers. Perhaps 50 to 100 accounts will be necessary for an adequate sample. As long as the sample taken is representative of future customer payment patterns, the results of an account analysis will be reasonably accurate. If the sample is taken at year end, be certain to include a representative number of accounts that have been written off as uncollectible accounts.

Although large samples will be more accurate than small ones, they require more computer time for processing. An analysis of every invoice and account generally will be impractical because companies often have 20,000 or more accounts containing 100,000 or more invoices. Large retail department stores will have millions of accounts. The results from an analysis of every account would be only marginally better than a random sample of 1,000 accounts.

If economic conditions are expected to change from the past year, care should be taken to adjust the collection rates. For example, if interest rates have risen dramatically from last year, collections will be somewhat slower. Likewise, if the economy has slowed somewhat, collection of accounts receivable will be slower. If the collection pattern is observed to be seasonal, it is necessary to prepare the estimate of collection rates for each season of the year.

Unusual Collection Patterns.   Governmental units (especially counties, cities, and school districts) will often have seasonal collection patterns. Their revenues include taxes assessed on an annual basis with payments due on specific days. Thus, the majority of revenues may occur near one day per year for personal property and real estate taxes. Sales and use taxes (theaters, motels, and restaurants) are often collected by the state government and then paid back to the local government on one day in the following month, say the 20th of the following month.

Federal and state governments have been able to even out the receipt patterns with various devices, but seasonality still exists. Most federal receipts come from personal income taxes that are paid evenly throughout the year. State governments' receipts are from sales, personal income, property, and vehicle taxes, and from numerous user fees. Collections for employment taxes are higher early in the year, and estimated income tax payments are higher later in the year to even out the pattern. Receipts peak around April 15 and near the estimated payment dates. Collections of sales taxes tend to be higher in November and especially December.

Agencies of the various governments have stable receipt patterns. Receipts are a function of appropriations that are set a year in advance. Each agency will know the exact amounts allotted and the day on which payments are due. Most governmental agencies do not receive cash; instead, they receive permission to issue checks or warrants on a central treasury.

Health-care organizations' receipts come mostly from governmental agencies, health insurance companies, and cooperative health plans. There will be relatively few payers, say 10 to 20, for any given hospital or nursing home making up the majority (85 percent or more) of the receipts. Payment for health care is slow with delays of 90 days and longer, and insurance companies and other health plans generally disallow some amount of total billings. Therefore, estimating cash receipts for health-care organizations involves an account analysis of the 10 or 20 major payers.

Estimating Cash Receipts from Sales

Once a collection pattern has been established, a projection of cash receipts may be calculated. As an example, assume that an analysis of a sample of 100 accounts indicates the following collection pattern:

EXHIBIT 15–3   **Projected Cash Receipts from Sales** (for the quarter ending December 31, 19x8)

		(millions) Collections from Sales			
Projected	*Sales*	*Current*	*Last*	*Before Last*	*Cash Receipts*
October 19x8	$174	$ 87.174	$67.743	$21.844	$176.761
November	148	74.148	61.074	24.511	159.733
December	215	107.715	51.948	22.098	181.761
Total for quarter	$537				$518.255

> 50.1 percent of the *current* month's sales
> 35.1 percent of *last* month's sales
> 12.7 percent of sales from the month *before last*
> 97.9 percent

The percentages add up to 97.9 because of a 2.1 percent allowance for doubtful accounts and cash discounts. Assume further that the projected sales for August, September, and October are $172, $193, and $174 million, respectively.

The projected cash receipts for the month of October 19x8 are found by calculating the following:

	(Millions)
50.1% of October sales of $174 =	$ 87.174
35.1% of September sales of $193 =	67.743
12.7% of August sales of $172 =	21.844
October 19x8 Cash Receipts	$176.761

If we are given projected monthly sales for November and December, cash receipts may be estimated for the first quarter of the fiscal year as presented in Exhibit 15–3.

CASH DISBURSEMENTS FOR OPERATIONS

The estimation of cash disbursements for operations is somewhat involved. The operations plan will have several thousand cost and expense accounts. Fortunately, costs and expenses have common payment patterns. For purposes of presentation, cash disbursements will be divided into four types:

1. Materials, merchandise, and services purchased.
2. Labor and related costs.
3. Rents and lease payments.
4. Interest payments.

Payments for Materials, Merchandise, and Service

A large organization will have several thousand suppliers. For a manufacturer or construction contractor, payments for materials will represent 40 to 60 percent of total expenditures. For a retailer, payments for merchandise will be 50 to 75 percent of total expenditures. For institutions, governments, and service organizations, payment for materials and outside services will be 10 to 30 percent of total costs.

Estimating the payment pattern for the purchase of materials and merchandise will involve a conglomeration of payment policies from many suppliers. Some suppliers will give cash discounts; others will not. Some will require cash on delivery; others will take payment over an extended period. The clerical staff in the accounts payable department will pick the most advantageous date for paying each invoice. The most advantageous date will involve payment on the last day to get a discount or on the due date for those suppliers not offering discounts.

We will begin with the judgment approach to estimating payment patterns.

Judgment.   One approach to estimating a payments pattern is to seek the assistance of knowledgeable people. For example, the supervisor of accounts payable might be able to give reasonable estimates of the lag between purchases and payments. This is especially true for small organizations in which one or two people handle all of the transactions, and the details of payments can be easily reviewed.

For a large accounts payable system, for example one handling more than 50,000 purchases per year, the system prepares a daily payment schedule that indicates which vouchers should be paid each day, along with the payment terms. In these systems, a check is automatically produced and mailed on the required day when the purchase order, the vendor invoice, and the receiving report match up. The clerical and supervisory staff intervene only when there is a problem with a transaction. The system contains thousands or millions of details on transactions, which is too much detail for the supervisor to be able to give a reasonable estimate of the payment pattern. Thus, without special analysis, the staff does not know the profile of times between purchases and final payment. The staff can project payments for the coming month based on invoices already received or purchase orders placed.

Supplier Account Analysis.   Supplier account analysis is performed in exactly the same manner as customer account analysis. First, take a sample of supplier accounts and gather the details on purchase dates, amounts, and payment dates. Then prepare the analysis in the same manner as the one used in Exhibits 15–1 and 15–2. As long as the sample is representative, the resulting payment pattern should be adequate for projecting payments for the budget year.

This technique will be somewhat cumbersome in practice because there are often thousands of purchases from a few main suppliers.

Credit Terms Analysis.   If we can make some assumptions regarding the purchasing and payment behavior of a company, a variation of account analysis that requires less effort can be performed. The assumptions required are:

1. Purchases occur evenly throughout a month.
2. All discounts offered are taken.
3. Payment is made on the last date allowed.
4. Cutoff dates occur evenly throughout the month.
5. The average month has 30 days.

In concept, credit terms analysis weights the payment pattern for each credit term by the amount of purchases made under it. Thus, this technique does not require the analysis of the detailed invoice data for the sample.

Common credit terms are listed in Exhibit 15–4. Notice the three basic types of terms: cash on delivery, invoice billing, and statement billing. **Invoice billing** requires payment for each invoice submitted by creditors; the timing of payment is determined by the invoice date. A monthly statement may be sent for information about purchase and payment activity. With **statement billing,** also called **cycle billing,** the statement is the bill with the timing of payment determined by a monthly statement cutoff date.

EXHIBIT 15–4   Common Credit Terms and Payment Patterns (in percentages)

Credit Terms	Estimated Payment Month		
	Current	Next	After Next
Cash on delivery	100.0		
Invoice billing:			
End of month	100.0		
Net 10	66.7	33.3	
Net 30		100.0	
1/10, Net 30	66.0	33.0	
2/10, Net 30	65.3	32.7	
3/10, Net 30	64.7	32.3	
Net 45		50.0	50.0
1/10, Net 45	66.0	33.0	
2/10, Net 45	65.3	32.7	
Statement (cycle) billing:			
Net cutoff		50.0	50.0
1/10, Net cutoff	22.0	71.5	5.5
2/10, Net cutoff	21.8	70.8	5.4
3/10, Net cutoff	21.6	70.1	5.4

Purchases that occur after the cutoff date appear in next month's statement. Vendors' statements list items purchased, payments received, and a balance due. For example, "2/10, net cutoff" indicates that a 2 percent discount is given for payments within 10 days from the statement date or the full amount is due by the next statement cutoff date.

The credit term *2/10, net 30* means that a 2 percent discount is offered for payment within 10 days of the invoice date and full payment is due in 30 days. Because the company takes all discounts, every payment will be made to arrive on the 10th day after invoice date. The purchases during the first 20 days of each month will have to be paid for that month, which results in a payment of $\{20/30 \text{ days} \times (100\% - 2\%)\} = 65.3\%$. The purchases during the 21st to the 30th day must be paid early next month $\{10/30 \text{ days} \times (100\% - 2\%)\} = 32.7\%$.

If purchases, invoices, and statements occur evenly throughout the month, we can estimate the other payment patterns as in Exhibit 15–5 for a small sample of five suppliers. The expected payment months for each credit term (as compared with the purchase month) are detailed into a *current* payment (must be paid in month of purchase), *next* (paid next month), and *after* (paid month after next). Those terms offering discounts have been adjusted downward to reflect the discount.

In practice, use a sample larger than five vendors. Sample enough creditors, perhaps 100, so that the sample is representative of the payment process. For example, assume that the pattern that results from a sample of 100 suppliers is 36.2, 52.4, and 10.1 percent. These add up to 98.7 percent, with an average discount taken of 1.3 percent.

Although credit terms analysis will be reasonably accurate, the assumptions required may limit the technique's applicability for certain companies. Thus, if there are problems with the accounts payable system so that payments are made sporadically or purchases are made only on certain days of the month, the credit terms technique will be inaccurate. Appendix A presents an estimation approach based on regression analysis that is likely to be more accurate than credit terms analysis.

EXHIBIT 15–5   Estimates of Collection Rates (for the 12 months ending August 31, 19x8)

(in thousands)

| | | | | Paid during Month | | |
Account	Company	Terms	Annual Purchases	Current	Next	After Next
A002	ARV Cabinet	Net 30	$ 5,600	–0–	$ 5,600	–0–
C620	Contile Interiors	2/10,NCO	5,700	$1,243	4,036	$ 308
F430	Frick Motors	2/10,N45	3,200	2,090	1,046	–0–
M403	Merchants, Inc.	COD	3,200	3,200	–0–	–0–
S400	Stylistic, Inc.	Net 45	2,100	–0–	–0–	2,100
Sample total			$19,800	$6,532	$10,682	$2,408
Average payment pattern			99.1%	33.0%	53.9%	12.2%

Disbursements Estimates

The next step is to multiply the payment pattern times expected monthly purchases. The purchases for the last two months of the previous year will result in payments during the first few months of the projected fiscal year. Assume that the purchases of materials are projected to be $20, $21, and $25 million for August, September, and October, respectively. Thus, the expected payments for October 19x8 are found by:

October purchases	36.2% × $25 =	$ 9.050
September purchases	52.4% × $21 =	11.004
August purchases	10.1% × $20 =	2.020
Total October payments		$22.074

Exhibit 15–6 presents a standard format for this analysis for the first quarter of the fiscal year.

We have now completed our illustration for cash payments related to manufacturing materials. In addition to manufacturing materials, the budget analyst will prepare estimates of disbursements for:

1. Materials and supplies.
   a. For marketing and distribution.
   b. For administrative and general uses.

EXHIBIT 15–6   Purchases Disbursements Estimates (for the quarter ending December 31, 19x8)

(in millions)

| | Projected Purchases | Payments for Purchases During | | | Total Payments |
		Current	Last	Before Last	
19x8 October	$25	$9.050	$11.004	$2.020	$22.074
November	21	7.602	13.100	2.121	22.823
December	24	8.688	11.004	2.525	22.217
Totals	$70				$67.114

2. Outside services used.
   a. Manufacturing.
   b. Marketing and distribution.
   c. Administration and general.
3. Regulated utilities: Gas, water, electric, and telephone.
4. Local and state taxes on real property, inventories, vehicles, and franchises.

The estimates for these items will tend to be smaller than for manufacturing materials but are still necessary for the cash disbursements estimates.

Payments for Salaries, Wages, and Bonuses and Related Costs

Payments to employees and for employee-related costs will range from a low of 20 to 25 percent for some manufacturers to a high of 70 percent of total expenditures for a service company. Payments will be for salaries (a monthly or annual amount), wages (an hourly amount), bonuses, various incentives for performance, plus all of the employee-related costs that we studied in Chapter 7.

Salaries.   Payments for salaries are made regularly throughout the year. Some salaries are paid twice a month and others are paid once a month. Thus, the cash outflow for salaries is relatively fixed throughout the year.

Wages and Bonuses.   The paychecks for employees paid hourly wages, piece rates, sales commissions, and performance bonuses will generally lag two weeks to one month behind performance. This allows time for the careful calculation of wage and bonus amounts by the payroll department. Employees paid on an hourly wage or performance basis are often paid every two weeks. Thus, payments for wages, commissions, and bonuses will lag behind the expense by about half a month.

Employment-Related Disbursements.   Employee-related disbursements will be 25 to 40 percent of base salaries and wages. The timing for payments varies with the type of benefit. Most employment taxes are deposited on the pay date. Payments for FICA, unemployment taxes, and workers' compensation are somewhat larger early in the year because of limits on the payment amounts. Increased cash outflows are often experienced in the summer when many employees take vacations and are replaced with temporary staff.

Payments for insurance are due in advance. Life insurance is often paid semiannually or annually, although monthly payments for a large group are not uncommon. Health insurance is normally paid on a monthly basis. Payments to pension and profit-sharing plans may occur monthly, quarterly, or annually.

Other costs related to employees include training, travel, and special employee programs. Payments for training programs involve advance payments for registration with travel, lodging, and meals often being paid on a reimbursement basis—the employee pays for travel costs and is reimbursed later. Sales staff and managers who engage in considerable travel often have their travel costs billed directly to the employer through travel agencies and credit cards.

Many organizations provide programs to improve the health, education, or attitudes of their employees. These programs might provide memberships in recreational clubs, university tuition payment, scholarship programs for children of employees, memberships in organizations, and subscriptions for journals and books. The cash disbursement requirements for each program vary but generally involve payment in advance. Special programs may be funded through an affiliated foundation rather than directly from company accounts. The funding of foundations is most often on an annual basis near the end of the fiscal year.

EXHIBIT 15–7 **Projected Cash Outflow for Production Labor Costs** (for the quarter ending December 31, 19x8)

	(in millions)		
	Fixed Costs	*Variable Costs*	*Total Cash Outflow*
October	$ 45.465	$25.602	$ 71.067
November	45.465	21.776	67.241
December	45.465	31.634	77.099
Totals	$136.395	$79.012	$215.407

The payment pattern for salaries and wages follows transaction levels. Sales and distribution are associated with sales activity, production labor relates to production activity, and administrative costs relate to total transaction levels.

As an example, assume that 40 percent of the production labor and related costs is variable with respect to production. These costs primarily related to performance bonuses, overtime, and part-time workers. Further, assume that the total projected annual labor and related costs are $909.3 million. Thus, the estimated variable and fixed labor cost on an annual and on an average monthly basis are:

		Annual	*Monthly*
Variable cost	40% × $909.3 =	$363.72/12 =	$30.310
Fixed cost	60% × $909.3 =	545.58/12 =	45.465
	Total production labor cost =	$909.30	$75.775

If we have a projection of monthly activity, we can project the monthly cash outflow related to production labor. For example, assume that we project activity of $174, $148, and $215 (in millions) for October, November, and December, respectively, and that the average activity if $206 million. We estimate the cash outflow for each month's production labor and related costs as shown in Exhibit 15–7. For October, the calculation for variable cost is:

$$\$30.31 \text{ million} \times \$174/\$206 = \$25.602 \text{ million}$$

A similar analysis is performed for marketing and general administrative labor. In Exhibit 15–8, all labor and related costs are summarized.

Rents and Leases   Rentals and lease payments are generally paid *in advance* on a monthly basis. Retail store leases often include an additional payment based on a percentage of revenue—for example, 4 percent of net sales revenue—that is due and payable at the *end* of each month or quarter. Natural resource leases (minerals, drilling, grazing, timber,

EXHIBIT 15–8 **Cash Flow for Labor Cost** (for the quarter ending December 31, 19x8)

	Labor and Labor Related Costs		
	Production	*Marketing*	*General Administrative*
October	$ 71.067	$ 4.270	$10.980
November	67.241	4.020	10.668
December	77.099	4.650	11.465
Totals	$215.407	$12.940	$33.113

EXHIBIT 15–9   Projected Payments on Rentals and Leases (for the quarter ending December 31, 19x8)

(in thousands)	*October*	*November*	*December*
Rentals			
Training center	$1,067	$1,067	$1,067
RR laboratory	139		
Denver warehouse	40	40	40
California regional office		39	
European administrative office	13	13	13
Total rental payments	$1,259	$1,159	$1,120
Leases			
Executive jet	$ 340	$ 340	$ 340
IBM 39000	468	468	468
Office equipment	208	208	400
Total lease payments	$1,016	$1,016	$1,208

or water) are often paid annually with some proportion affected by the volume or usage. Rental and lease payments are computed exactly from the wording of the contracts.[2] Exhibit 15–9 presents the projected payments for five rentals and three leases for the first fiscal quarter.

Short-Term Interest Payments

Payments for short-term loans should be divided into the portion related to interest and that related to principal payments. The interest payments are included in operating cash flow, and the principal payments are included with financing activities.

The amount and timing of loan payments are a function of the loan agreement, which often contains loan payment schedules. Many loan agreements, often called *installment loans,* require a fixed monthly payment, for example, $277,000 per month in principal and interest. Fixed payments are common for bank loans and equipment loans. **Serial loans** require that a constant amount of principal, say $10,000, be paid monthly in addition to the interest for the month. Finally, with some loans, often called **credit line accounts,** only interest must be paid during any particular month; the principal may be paid at any time. Exhibit 15–10 illustrates the cash payments related to short-term debt. The monthly interest payment is approximated by taking the annual interest rate times the balance and dividing by 12.[3] For example, the first loan is for Beneficial Commerical Credit #189807403 for $4,899, which has a 9 percent rate:

$$\$4,899 \times .09/12 = \$37 \text{ per month (rounded)}$$

The total interest cash outflow is estimated at $717 per month, which is subtracted from loan payments for each month to result in the approximate cash outflow for principal payments.

---

[2] The rentals and leases discussed here are assumed to be operating leases. The treatment of capitalized lease payments would be similar to that of a long-term installment loan with an apportionment of the monthly payment into interest and principal components. Because the lease payments are generally known with certainty, the only issue is the extent to which they are reported as an operating or a financing activity.

[3] The exact interest payments may be computed by taking the effective monthly interest rate times the declining monthly balance for each loan. However, this precision is not normally justified for cash planning purposes because the total monthly payment will be known and all the calculation does is allocate the known payment into interest and principal portions.

EXHIBIT 15–10   Projected Payments on Short-Term Debt (for the quarter ending December 31, 19x8)

(in thousands)

	Balances	Rate	Monthly Interest	Scheduled Payments		
				January	February	March
Beneficial Credit						
#189807403	$ 4,899	9.0%	$ 37	$ 467	$ 463	$ 459
#189117001	1,377	9.9%	11	470	465	460
#189117023	4,189	8.0%	28	399	396	393
First National Bank						
#483	400	10.0%	3	108	108	108
#486	3,200	11.0%	29	277	277	277
#492	1,280	10.8%	12	117	117	117
ITT Commercial Credit						
#004–983 $100 MM	10,916	10.0%	91	1,015	1,000	985
#004–002 $300 MM	43,919	11.8%	432	4,088	4,040	3,992
#004–067 $ 50 MM	9,820	9.0%	74	2,300		
	$80,000					
Total short-term payments made			$717	$9,241	$6,866	$6,791
Total interest payments				(717)	(717)	(717)
Total principal payments				$8,524	$6,149	$6,074

Long-Term Debt Interest Payments

Bonds are long-term loans from investors that require periodic (quarterly or semi-annual) interest and principal payments. Bond principal payments may be at the end of the term, annually (serial bonds), or at the discretion of management (callable bonds). Computing the cash disbursement requirements for bonds requires the examination of each bond contract. In many cases, we can follow the previous year's payments.

Quarterly Estimated Tax Payments

Estimated income tax is due quarterly and is based on projected income for the taxable year. The current year's taxable income is expected to be $384.6 million with an expected 52 percent effective federal and state tax rate for a total estimated tax of about $200 million of which the last fourth ($50) is due October 15. Assuming that the projected taxable income for fiscal 19x9 is $429.6, the total estimated income tax is $223.4 million, of which $55.8 million is due each subsequent quarter.

CASH FLOW FROM INVESTMENT ACTIVITIES

Investment activities include all activity related to the purchase or sale of long-term assets. Thus, the purchase or sale of plant, equipment, stocks and bonds of other companies, and intangible assets is an investment activity.

Cash Receipts from Sale of Noncurrent Assets

The sale of assets other than inventory results in cash. Any asset or security can be sold quickly for a price. However, in order to get a reasonable price, some time may be required. For example, a $1 million production plant may require several years to sell but could be sold much faster with a $250,000 asking price. On the other extreme, equity securities may be sold immediately with little or no loss.

The sale of equipment and real estate requires the approval of the board of directors. Thus, which real estate is to be sold and which equipment is to be disposed of will generally be known. Proceeds from the sale of surplus equipment and intangible assets must be estimated on the basis of account balances and experience. For example, assume that there is $20 million of book value in surplus machinery, and about half of the surplus is culled and disposed of evenly during the year. Further assume that a 20 percent gain after tax is expected. This will result in:

(in millions)

Book value of items sold (0.5 × $20)	$10
Expected after-tax gain (0.2 × $10)	2
Proceeds expected	$12
Cash receipts per month ($12/12)	$ 1

The $1 million per month will then be included in the cash receipts from investment activities, which will appear right after the net cash from operations. The sale of investments in bonds and stock of other companies would receive similar treatment.

Plant and Equipment Purchases

Payment for most equipment purchases will be equivalent to materials purchased on account. Thus, there will be an invoice and a payment due date for each piece of equipment. The amount of equipment purchased will generally be set in advance as a part of the budget process. Large or special-purpose equipment, for example an electric power generator, may require partial payment in advance and then months of installation and testing before the final payment is due.

Payment for most construction will occur on a percentage-of-completion basis with a small portion (for example, 10 percent) held for final approval of the construction. The payments occur on a monthly basis as the result of billings by the contractors. A large plant requires 9 to 24 months for site preparation, construction, and inspection. As an example, an automobile assembly plant requires an investment of about $250 million over a 24-month period.

We must examine each capital project to determine the required cash outflow for a month. Some rough estimates are required of the percentage of completion for construction. The cash flow for long-term asset purchases is necessarily a rough estimate early in the budget preparation process because most capital projects have not yet been approved by the board of directors.

CASH FLOW FROM FINANCING ACTIVITIES

Financing activities include all issuances and repayments of loans, issuances or repurchases of bonds or stocks, and payments of dividends to owners. All such activities

EXHIBIT 15–11   Projected Payments for Dividends (for the quarter ending December 31, 19x8)

	S1	S2	S3	S4	Total
	(in thousands)				
October			$13,251	$3,329	$16,579
November					–0–
December	$1,500	$3,000			4,500
Total payments					$21,079

	Quarterly Dividends	
Stock Issued	**Per Share**	**Total**
S1 $6 preferred 1,000,000 shares	$1.50	$ 1,500,000
S2 $8 preferred 1,500,000 shares	2.00	3,000,000
S3 Common, Class A 26,501,200 Shares	0.50	13,250,600
S4 Common, Class B 8,322,228 Shares	0.40	3,328,891

normally require the prior approval of the board of directors and, thus, the timing and amounts are generally known in advance.

Dividend payments for preferred and common stock are typically made on a quarterly basis with a payment date set by the board of directors. Both common and preferred dividends typically have a specified amount paid for each quarter, say $2 per share for 8 percent $100 par preferred and $0.50 per share for common stock. An extra dividend that reflects the board of directors' reactions to current and expected earnings may be declared once a year for common stock. Exhibit 15–11 provides an example of estimates for dividend payments.

CASH FLOW BUDGET

The cash flow budget is prepared after the details of operating, investing, and financing activities have been estimated. The cash flow budget is a working plan of operating cash flow, investment, and financing for the coming year. Many companies revise the cash budget monthly as new information becomes available about sales, collec-

EXHIBIT 15–12   Cash Budget (for the quarter ending December 31, 19x8)

	(in millions)			
	October	*November*	*December*	*Totals**
Operating activities:				
Receipts from customers	$176.76	$159.73	$181.76	$518.25
Less disbursements for:				
Production				
Materials	22.07	22.82	22.22	67.11
Labor and related	71.07	67.24	77.10	215.41
Other overhead	15.97	15.97	15.97	47.91
Marketing labor costs	4.27	4.02	4.65	12.94
Other marketing	1.96	1.96	1.96	5.88
Administrative labor costs	10.98	10.67	11.47	33.12
Rents and leases	2.28	2.18	2.33	6.79
Other administrative costs	2.70	2.70	2.70	8.10
Short-term interest	0.72	0.72	0.72	2.16
Long-term debt interest			14.00	14.00
Estimated income tax	50.00			50.00
Total disbursements	$182.02	$128.28	$153.12	$463.42
Operations cash flow	$ (5.26)	$ 31.45	$ 28.64	$ 54.83
Investment activities:				
Long-term asset purchases	(9.50)	(10.30)	(10.80)	(30.60)
Sale of equipment	1.00	1.00	1.00	3.00
Net investment flow	$ (8.50)	$ (9.30)	$ (9.80)	$ (27.60)
Financing activities:				
Short-term loan payments	$ (8.56)	$ (6.24)	$ (6.22)	$ (21.02)
Dividends	(16.58)	0.00	(4.50)	(21.08)
Net financing flow	$ (25.14)	$ (6.24)	$ (10.72)	$ (42.10)
Net cash flow	$(38.90)	$ 15.91	$ 8.12	$(14.87)
Plus beginning cash	72.00	33.10	49.01	72.00
Ending cash balance	$ 33.10	$ 49.01	$ 57.13	$ 57.13

* Numbers are rounded.

EXHIBIT 15–13   Cash Budget (for the year ending September 30, 19x9)

	1st October/December	2nd January/March	3rd April/June	4th July/September	Total*
	(in millions)				
Operating activities:					
Receipts from customers	$518.25	$690.94	$600.12	$590.04	$2,399.35
Less: Disbursements					
Production					
Materials	$ 67.11	$ 81.69	$ 83.59	$ 73.31	$ 305.70
Labor and related	215.41	245.72	221.44	226.74	909.31
Other overhead	47.90	47.90	47.90	47.90	191.60
Marketing labor costs	12.95	14.94	13.34	13.68	54.91
Other marketing	5.88	5.88	5.88	5.88	23.52
Administrative labor costs	33.13	35.66	33.62	34.06	136.47
Rents and leases	6.78	6.78	6.78	5.76	26.10
Other administrative costs	8.10	8.10	8.10	8.10	32.40
Short-term interest	2.15	2.15	2.15	2.15	8.60
Long-term debt interest	14.00	10.50	13.17	10.50	48.17
Estimated income tax	50.00	55.85	55.85	55.85	217.55
Total disbursements	$463.41	$515.17	$491.82	$483.93	$1,954.33
Operations cash flow	$ 54.85	$175.77	$108.30	$106.11	$ 445.02
Investment activities:					
Long-term asset purchases	$ (30.60)	$ (33.98)	$(839.61)	$(131.60)	$(1,035.79)
Sale of equipment	3.00	3.00	3.00	3.00	12.00
Investment cash flow	$ (27.60)	$ (30.98)	$(836.61)	$(128.60)	$(1,023.79)
Financing Activities:					
Short-term loan payments	(21.03)	(19.15)	(18.89)	(16.46)	(75.53)
Issue 12% 20-year debenture				50.00	50.00
Retire long-term debt			(10.00)		(10.00)
Issue 20 million shares Common A			800.00		800.00
Dividends	(21.08)	(21.08)	(21.08)	(31.08)	(94.32)
Financing cash flow	$(42.11)	$(40.23)	$750.03	$ 2.46	$ 670.15
Net cash flow	$(14.87)	$104.56	$ 21.72	$ (20.03)	$ 91.38
Plus beginning cash	72.00	57.13	161.69	183.41	72.00
Ending cash balance	$ 57.13	$161.69	$183.41	$163.38	$ 163.38

* Numbers are rounded.

tions, and cash commitments. A few organizations revise estimates of collections and disbursements on a daily basis. Computer software is available to support the management of daily receipts and disbursements among numerous bank accounts.

Exhibit 15–12 illustrates a complete cash flow budget presented for one quarter of the year. Notice that the statement includes all transactions involving cash: operations, investments, and financing. Exhibit 15–13 presents the cash flow budget for the four quarters of the fiscal year. In Exhibit 15–13 notice in the financing activities the issuance of a $50 million debt in the fourth quarter and of $800 million in stock in the third quarter.

FINAL NOTE

Depreciation, Amortization, and Depletion

Remember that there is *no cash flow* for the depreciation of buildings and equipment, the amortization of intangible assets, or the depletion of natural resources. Depreciation expense is the allocation of a prior expenditure to a time period for external financial reporting purposes. The cash flow occurs with the purchase or construction, not with the later allocation. Thus, amounts in overhead or administrative costs that relate to depreciation must be eliminated before cash flows are estimated.

SUMMARY

The objective of cash flow budgeting is to provide for liquidity, which is the ability to pay bills when due. Cash receipts and disbursements from operations, investment, and financing must be estimated before the cash flow budget can be prepared.

Cash receipts may be estimated by using collection rates from either judgment or customer account analysis. Judgment from the credit manager may be useful. A customer account analysis, a weighted average of the payments made by individual accounts, may also be helpful. A sample of customer accounts may be useful to reduce computational effort.

Cash disbursements involve estimates for materials, labor and related costs, and other costs. Estimating payments for materials involves the application of a payment pattern to projections of purchases. The payment pattern may come from judgment, supplier account analysis, or credit terms analysis. For small accounts payable systems, the judgment of the accounts payable supervisor can be accurate. For larger systems, the supervisor may have only a general concept of payment timing. Credit terms analysis is performed by analyzing the payment requirements for each credit term and weighting it by purchases expected.

Disbursements for labor relate to the activity levels. Most companies have moderately stable cash requirements for production, sales, and administrative labor. Companies in a highly seasonal business have highly variable labor expenditures.

Cash receipts from the sale of fixed assets or securities are stable and reflect the policies of the board of directors. Disbursements for fixed assets are determined by the long-range plans of the organization. The disposal of fixed assets requires the approval of the board of directors and, as a consequence, tends to be predictable as to amount and timing. Payments for fixed assets follow acquisition in a pattern somewhat like the purchase of materials.

Financing cash flow is generally determined by the precise wording of contracts or actions of the board of directors. Financing includes loans, bonds, and stocks. The amounts and timing of payments can be calculated months or years in advance and seldom create an obstacle in the preparation of the cash flow budget.

PROBLEM FOR REVIEW

The Medical Products Division is the manufacturing division of a multinational company that produces extremely reliable surgical gloves. Macy Wildon, division general manager, has requested a cash budget for the first quarter of 19x3. The balance sheet for December 31, 19x2, contains the following balances: Cash, $250,000; Marketable Securities, $600,000; Accounts Receivable, $531,300; and Accounts Payable, $56,280.

The gloves are sold in lots of 100 with a selling price of $280. The projected monthly sales lots for the first quarter of 19x3 are as follows:

January	3,900
February	4,050
March	4,200

All sales are on credit with 60 percent paid during the month of sale, 35 percent paid the following month, and 5 percent collected the second month following sale. The sales for November 19x2 were 4,150 lots and for December 19x2 were 4,225 lots.

The process is highly automated with virtually all of the variable costs in materials. The materials, primarily latex, are purchased at the beginning of each calendar quarter, which results in a substantial discount. Materials costs, net of the discount, are 75 percent of the selling price. Payment for purchases occurs during the month of purchase. Depreciation on the plant and equipment is $17,355 per month. Payments for other manufacturing costs are fixed at $60,700 per month. Payments for the selling and administrative costs are fixed at $80,000 per month.

The Medical Products Division requires a minimum cash balance of $250,000 with all excess cash used to purchase marketable securities. Marketable securities may be sold, and a line of credit is available at the home office with $750,000 available. Any balance in Marketable Securities in excess of $800,000 is to be sent to the home office. Assume that interest income and expenses are immaterial. During January, equipment with a book value of $400,000 will be sold for cash at no gain or loss. During February, equipment costing $300,000 will be delivered and will be paid for during March.

REQUIRED

For the first calendar quarter of 19x3:
a. Estimate the cash receipts from operations for each month.
b. Estimate the cash payments from operations for each month.
c. Prepare a cash budget by month.

SOLUTION

a. Estimate the cash receipts from operations for each month.

	Unit Sales	Revenues	Collections from Current	Collections from Last	Collections from Before Last	Total Receipts
January	3,900	$1,092,000	$655,200	$414,050	$58,100	$1,127,350
February	4,050	1,134,000	680,400	382,200	59,150	1,121,750
March	4,200	1,176,000	705,600	396,900	54,600	1,157,100

b. Estimate the cash payments from operations each month.

	Unit Sales	Revenues	Purchases
January	3,900	$1,092,000	
February	4,050	1,134,000	
March	4,200	1,176,000	
		$3,402,000 × 75% =	$2,551,500

Payments during each month

	January	February	March
Purchases	$2,551,500	–0–	–0–
Other manufacturing	60,700	60,700	60,700
Selling and administrative	80,000	80,000	80,000
	$2,692,200	$140,700	$140,700

c. Cash budget by month.

MEDICAL PRODUCTS DIVISION
Monthly Cash Flow Budget
For the Three Months Ending March 31, 19x3

	January	*February*	*March*
Operations:			
Cash receipts	$1,127,350	$1,121,750	$1,157,100
Cash payments:			
Purchases	2,551,500	–0–	–0–
Other manufacturing	60,700	60,700	60,700
Selling and administrative costs	80,000	80,000	80,000
Total cash payments	$2,692,200	$ 140,700	$ 140,700
Operations cash flow	$(1,564,850)	$ 981,050	$1,016,400
Investing activities:			
Purchases of equipment	–0–	–0–	$ (300,000)
Sale of fixed assets	$ 400,000	–0–	–0–
Investment cash flow	$ 400,000	–0–	$ (300,000)
Financing activities:			
Debt payments	–0–	$ (564,850)	–0–
Loans	$ 564,850*	–0–	–0–
Excess sent to headquarters	–0–	–0–	$ (332,600)†
Financing cash flow	$ 564,850	$ (564,850)	$ (332,600)
Net cash flow	$ (600,000)	$ 416,200	$ 383,800
Plus:			
Cash balance	250,000	250,000	250,000
Marketable securities sold	600,000		
Marketable securities purchased		(416,200)	(383,800)‡
Ending cash balance	$ 250,000§	$ 250,000	$ 250,000

* This amount must be borrowed during January in order to keep the cash balance of $250,000.

† The cash sent to headquarters is computed as cash above that required to bring marketable securities up to an $800,000 balance.

‡ This amount will bring the balance in marketable securities up to $800,000.

§ The ending cash balance must be forced to equal $250,000 each month in order to meet the problem requirements.

<table>
<tr><td>**KEY TERMS AND CONCEPT**</td><td>Liquidity (599)
Customer Account Analysis (600)
Invoice billing (603)
Statement billing (603)</td><td>Cycle billing (603)
Serial loans (608)
Credit line accounts (608)</td></tr>
</table>

ADDITIONAL READINGS

Gleason, S. "Finding the Hidden Cash in Your Company's Operation." *Journal of Accountancy,* May 1989, pp. 137–40.

Kastanin, J. T., and R. A. Alexander. "Remaining Liquid." *Journal of Accountancy,* January 1989, pp. 120–23.

Loeser, D. "Improving Accounts Receivable Management." *Journal of Accountancy,* November 1988, pp. 116–18.

Mahoney, J. J.; M. V. Sever; and J. A. Theis. "Cash Flow: FASB Opens the Floodgates." *Journal of Accountancy,* May 1988, pp. 25–38.

Mazhin, R. "A Spreadsheet Template for the Statement of Cash Flows." *Journal of Accountancy,* March 1989, pp. 110–13.

McGrath, J. "The True Cost of Borrowing." *CFO,* June 1986, pp. 57–60.

———. "Calculating Cash Flow from Credit Sales Patterns." *CFO,* July 1986, pp. 57–60.

———. "Forecasting Cash Flow: A Model for Managers." *CFO,* March 1987, pp. 57–62.

———. "Cash Flow Statements According to *FASB 95.*" *CFO,* April 1988, pp. 43–52.

Post, D. B., and S. I. Hockberg. "Improving Collection Practices at a Troubled Company." *Journal of Accountancy,* September 1989, pp. 133–38.

Shafer, D. L. "Cash Management: A Cost Effective Approach." *Journal of Accountancy,* March 1987, pp. 114–17.

REVIEW QUESTIONS

1. What is the concept of liquidity?
2. Why do we not attempt to achieve an exact projection of cash receipts and disbursements?
3. List three types of biases in the judgments of managers as related to cash collections from sales.
4. Give two examples of open-ended questions that might be useful in drawing out collections expectations.
5. How is a customer account analysis for receipts pattern performed?
6. What is the major disadvantage of the account analysis method for estimating payment patterns?
7. Why are wages and bonuses generally paid two to four weeks after they are earned?
8. Why is the amount of plant and equipment purchases fixed at the beginning of the fiscal year?
9. List four examples of disbursements that may be categorized as financial rather than operating.
10. What supporting analyses need to be performed before the cash budget can be prepared?
11. How are depreciation, depletion, and amortization expenses treated in the cash budget?

DISCUSSION QUESTIONS

12. Discuss the relationship between good versus poor liquidity and credit ratings.
13. Discuss the relationship between poor liquidity and employee attitudes.
14. Why is the judgment of managers about collection rates a rough approximation, especially for very large accounting systems?
15. Why do the biases of credit managers make their estimates unreliable unless they have recently completed a special study?
16. Why is a portion of the payment for construction held for final approval of the work?
17. Why might an organization wish to prepare cash projections on a daily basis?
18. Why would a corporation have more than one checking account? Why might it have one for each division or branch?
19. Why would a company have zero-balance checking accounts for all of its subsidiaries, divisions, and branches?
20. Find the reporting options for handling sales and purchase discounts from an intermediate financial text. List the options for each discount. Why does taking one reporting option or another make little difference to cash flow projections?
21. Why should a company follow the practice of taking all purchase discounts?

EXERCISES

15–1. Estimating Cash Receipts. The Crinton Broadcasting credit manager estimates that about 50 percent of the sales are collected during the month of the sale, 45 percent the following month, and 4 percent the second month. The actual and estimated sales for the following months were found:

November	$200,000	Actual
December	300,000	Estimated
January 19x9	120,000	Estimated

REQUIRED:
Estimate the cash receipts for the month ending January 31, 19x9.

15–2. Computing Past Cash Received on Account. The Las Vegas Clinic had the following balance in patient accounts receivable:

March 1, 19x2	$2,302,240
March 31, 19x2	2,907,780

During the month there were charges to patient accounts of $780,400. There were noncash credits to the following accounts:

Professional discounts	$ 3,408
Welfare write-offs	12,420
Insurance adjustments	13,406
Uncollectible accounts	37,400

REQUIRED:
Compute the cash receipts for the month of March 19x2.

15–3. Bank Statement Receipts. The Charleston Department Store had the following information related to its First National account 102–9–292:

December 1, 19x2	$ 82,402
Plus: Credits	1,003,021
Less: Charges	(604,002)
December 31, 19x2	$ 481,421

This account is used to receive all money from customers. Cash is deposited three times daily during December. Included in the credits to the account are $4,200 in interest income on the account balance and $49,400 in notes receivable collections. Included in the charges are $1,400 in checks that were returned for nonsufficient funds (NSF).

REQUIRED:
Compute the cash receipts from sales for the month of December 19x2.

15–4. Cash Payments for Materials. The Loestar Brewery estimates payments for materials on the following basis:

Current purchases	45%
Last month's purchases	40%
Prior month's purchases	14%

The actual and estimated purchases of materials are:

May 19x2	$406,000 Actual
June	608,000 Actual
July	772,000 Estimated

REQUIRED:
a. Estimate the cash payments for purchases for the month ending July 31, 19x2.
b. Estimate the amount of the purchase discounts for July 19x2.

15–5. Cash Payments for Labor. The Svenville Plant pays all labor a fixed base pay. Production labor can also earn incentive pay, which is based on the quantity and quality of output. The base pay is disbursed during the month earned. The incentive pay is disbursed the following month. Labor-related costs are 40 percent of base pay and 20 percent of incentive pay. All amounts withheld from base and incentive pay are paid immediately. Of the labor-related costs on base pay, 50 percent are paid on the pay date, 30 percent are paid the following month, and 20 percent are paid at the end of the calendar quarter. The labor-related costs on incentive pay are paid in the month of incentive payment. Base and incentive payments estimates are:

	Base Pay	*Incentive Pay*
December 19x2	$400,000	$200,000
January 19x3	420,000	120,000

The increase in base pay for January 19x3 represents a 5 percent base pay raise. The base pay is expected to stay at $420,000 for February and March 19x3.

REQUIRED:
Estimate the cash payment for labor and labor-related costs for the month of January 19x3.

15–6. Cash Receipts from Sale of Assets.   The Catfish Station Company has excess equipment, supplies, and furniture with an original cost of $36 million and accumulated depreciation of $18 million. Of the excess assets, 60 percent are expected to be sold during the first quarter of 19x2 at about 120 percent of net book value. The tax rate is 40 percent, and the gains are taxable at this rate. Estimated tax payments are due 15 days before the end of each calendar quarter. All sales of excess equipment are on a cash basis.

REQUIRED:
Estimate the amount of net cash expected from the sale of excess assets during the quarter ending March 31, 19x2.

15–7. Customer Account Analysis.   The Pepperidge Company invoices customers on the date of shipment of products. Payment terms are 2/10, Net 30 from shipping date. The Los Frios Company, account 14–006–10, has the following invoice amounts and payments for the year ending December 31, 19x2:

Invoice	Date	Amount	Payment Date	Payment
12883	1/12/x2	$ 32,000	1/22/x2	$ 31,360
14102	4/02/x2	62,000	4/08/x2	60,760
14205	4/28/x2	74,000	5/28/x2	74,000
16223	9/26/x2	88,000	10/29/x2	88,000
18002	10/14/x2	104,000	12/06/x2	104,000
		$360,000		$358,120

REQUIRED:
a. Estimate a receipt pattern for Los Frios for the current month, next month, and the following month.
b. Comment on the trend in sales and collections for the Los Frios account.
c. Based on your comments in (b), comment on the reliability of the estimate for future cash receipts on accounts like the one for Los Frios.

15–8. Receipts Pattern.   The following sample of sales and payment patterns was taken from the accounts of the Carlsbad Garage. The accounts are considered representative in terms of sales amounts and payment patterns.

Account	Sales	Payment Patterns Current	Next	Following
C & A Flower Shop	$ 6,311	10%	80%	10%
Jacobi Printing	4,253	30%	40%	30%
Martha's Crystal	1,372	80%	20%	
Robert W. Salin	1,784	90%	10%	
Total	$13,720			

REQUIRED:
Estimate the average receipts pattern for this sample of customers.

15–9. Vendor Credit Terms Analysis.   In reviewing the accounts for Lockley Welding and Supplies, you find that four credit terms are applied predominantly by vendors during 19x0:

	Percentage of Purchases
Cash on delivery	10
Invoice billing:	
Net 30	30
2/10, Net 30	20
Statement billing:	
2/10, Net cutoff	40

REQUIRED:

Using the payment percentages in Exhibit 15–4, estimate the disbursement pattern for Lockley Welding and Supplies.

15–10. Production Overhead and Cash Disbursements. The plant overhead budget for the Johnson Bay Refinery includes the following amounts for 19x1:

Indirect labor	$2,400,000
Employee benefits	3,600,000
Supplies	300,000
Refinery: Depreciation	2,000,000
Trucks: Depreciation	200,000
Total overhead	$8,500,000

The costs are spread evenly throughout the year. It is the policy of the plant manager to pay all bills when due. The following balances are estimated:

	1/1/x1	*12/31/x1*
Accrued indirect labor	$100,000	$200,000
Accrued employee benefits	200,000	250,000
Supplies inventory	50,000	40,000
Supplies payable	30,000	40,000

REQUIRED:

Compute the total cash payments required for production overhead for 19x1.

PROBLEMS

15–11. Estimated Cash Receipts and Disbursements. Debbie Dolls, Inc., wants to expand its facilities over the next several years. Deborah Johanne, president and major stockholder, resists debt financing. She prefers to let operations generate the cash needed. As a result, she watches cash flow carefully and estimates cash inflows and outflows for each month.

Selected estimates for February 19x1 are as follows:

Sales	$700,000
Gross profit rate	40%
Increase in accounts receivable	
during the month	$ 30,000
Increase in inventories	$ 10,000
Decrease in accounts payable	$ 4,000

Total marketing and administrative expenses are $55,000 per month plus 14 percent of sales revenues. These expenses include a charge of 1 percent of sales for doubtful accounts and $16,000 for depreciation. Cash flow items of marketing and administrative expenses are paid in the month incurred.

REQUIRED:

a. Determine the projected cash receipts for February 19x1.
b. Determine the projected cash disbursements for February 19x1.

15–12. Seasonal Revenue and Receipt Patterns.   The Slocum Air Products Company supplies construction and mechanical companies with compressed gas and compression machines. The gas and compression machines are used for field welding, painting, truck mechanics, and similar activities. Mason Winn, controller, has noticed that customers pay later during the months April through September than during other months. Based on five years of payment data, Mr. Winn has estimated the following payment patterns:

	(in percentages)	
Collections	*October to March*	*April to September*
Current	23	21
Next	60	38
Discounts Taken	2	1
Second month	12	24
Third month	2	13
Written off	1	3
Total	100	100

Slocum Air offers credit terms of 3/15, Net 45 on customer billings. The discounts taken and account write-offs in the fourth month after sale are disclosed as a reduction of net revenue.

As part of the current budget preparation, Mason Winn has the following actual and estimated customer billings during the end of 19x2 and the months of 19x3:

October 19x2	$62,224	June 19x3	$105,000
November	22,114	July	260,000
December	20,230	August	350,000
January 19x3	20,000	September	202,000
February	21,000	October	88,000
March	22,000	November	30,000
April	42,000	December	22,000
May	62,000		

The data for October through December 19x2 are actual charges. The amounts for 19x3 are all budgeted amounts. Projected write-offs for January are $1,584.

REQUIRED:

a. For the quarter ending March 31, 19x3, estimate:
  1. Net revenue.
  2. Cash receipts.
b. For the quarter ending September 30, 19x3, estimate:
  1. Net revenue.
  2. Cash receipts.

15–13. Estimates of Receipts, Group Judgments.   Kimberly Sidwell, controller for Krebs Clothiers, Inc., was developing the collection estimates for sales in the Midwest region. The Midwest region has seven sales districts, each with a sales manager and a credit manager. The credit managers prepared estimates of collection as a proportion of billings for the coming fiscal 19x1:

	(in percentages)			
	Current	*Next*	*Following*	*Totals*
Columbus	40	48	10	98
Chicago	40	40	20	100
Detroit	38	40	21	99
Indianapolis	36	42	15	93
Minneapolis	41	42	16	99
Lexington	39	47	14	100
St. Louis	38	37	21	96
Averages	38.86	42.29	16.71	97.86

Estimated customer billings for the Midwest region for the first two quarters of 19x1 (in thousands) are:

January	$1,800	April	$3,800
February	2,600	May	4,200
March	3,900	June	5,400

After reviewing the collection estimates, Ms. Sidwell decided that several of the estimates must be biased upward because less than 97.86 percent of billings was collected. For fiscal 19x0, the following amounts were found in the accounts for the Midwest region (amounts in thousands):

Customer billings		$40,000
Sales returns and allowances		480
Sales discounts		395
Doubtful accounts expense		878
	1/1/x0	*12/31/x0*
Accounts receivable	$2,200	$2,220
Allowance for doubtful accounts	220	280

The sales for 19x0 were about the same as the previous year.

REQUIRED:
a. Apply the average proportions from the district managers to estimate the cash flows for the second quarter of 19x1.
b. Based on the account data for 19x0, compute the amount of:
   1. Accounts written off.
   2. Cash collected on account.
c. Estimate the percentage of customer billings that will be collected in 19x1 based on 19x0 account data.
d. Revise the collection estimates from the Midwest region managers to reflect the estimate in part (c). (In this revision, each of the individual estimates should total to the part (c) estimate.) Carry the percentage estimates to the nearest $1/100$th of a percent.
e. Apply the revised collection proportions from part (d) to the customer billings and estimate collections for the second quarter of 19x1.

15–14. Cash from Operations.   Lutztown Co. wholesales safety supplies to industrial plants. The supplies include fire extinguishers, first-aid kits, gloves, goggles, and warning signs. Lutztown relies on volume sales at low prices, and cash management is very important to maintaining company liquidity.

The company has asked your help in preparing a schedule of purchase requirements and a cash plan for the three months ending December 31, 19x7. The September 30, 19x7, balance sheet showed the following account balances:

Cash	$ 20,100
Accounts receivable	995,816
Inventories	660,000
Accounts payable	289,000

All sales are on credit, and billings occur on the last day of each month. Credit terms allow a 3 percent discount if payments are made within 10 days after the billing date. The collection pattern includes 60 percent within the discount period, 25 percent during the rest of the month following billing, 9 percent in the second month after billing, and 6 percent uncollectible.

Cash payments for materials purchases, selling, and general expenses are paid 54 percent during the month and 46 percent the following month. Each month's ending inventory is 120 percent of next month's expected sales. Cost of goods sold is $5 per average unit. Marketing and administrative expenses, including the bad debts expense and $3,500 in depreciation, are about 16 percent of the current month's sales.

Sales attained and expected are:

	Billings	**Units Sold**
August 19x7	$750,000	100,000
September	787,500	105,000
October	836,000	110,000
November	851,200	112,000
December	874,300	115,000
January 19x8	896,800	118,000

Equipment costing $200,000 is to be paid for in November, and dividends of $40,000 are to be paid in December.

(C. Seely; A. Evans; and P. Anne, adapted)

REQUIRED:

a. Prepare a schedule of purchase requirements for each month of the last quarter of 19x7.
b. Prepare a schedule of cash from operations by month for the last quarter of 19x7.

15–15. Cash Budget with Seasonality.   Good, Inc., manufactures two-cylinder engines for motor scooters. The planned revenues from June 19x8 to January 19x9 are as follows:

June	$400,000	October	$550,000
July	450,000	November	400,000
August	600,000	December	300,000
September	500,000	January	325,000

Accounts are billed on the first day of each month. The collection pattern varies by season (in percentages):

	June, July, August	**September to May**
Month billed	50	40
Following month	45	30
Second month	5	20

The month of sale determines the collection pattern that applies. The selling and general expenses include cash costs of $50,000 per month plus 5 percent of sales. The production plan calls for a fixed level of production with cash production costs of $350,000 per month.

Quarterly cash dividends of $1,000 are paid beginning on June 15. The company has the policy to keep $25,000 in the cash account and to invest in marketable securities with any excess cash. Cash shortages may be made up using a $500,000 line of credit.

The cash balance on August 1, 19x8, was $25,000, no marketable securities were on hand, short-term loans nor were any outstanding.

(V. Stauber and D. Carrell, adapted)

REQUIRED:

a. Estimate cash receipts for each of the six months ending January 31, 19x9.
b. Assuming that interest expense and income are immaterial, prepare a monthly cash plan for the six months ending January 31, 19x9.

15–16. Cash Receipts from Sale of Assets.   SLC Minerals, Inc., has plant and equipment at its San Cristobal potash mine that it plans to liquidate over the quarter ending September 30, 19x9. The following balances are found in the accounts on July 1, 19x9 (in millions):

	Cost	**Accumulated Depreciation/Depletion**
Mineral leaseholds	$24.20	$21.40
Buildings	2.00	1.80
Equipment	8.00	6.40
Vehicles	1.20	1.00
Tools	0.40	0.40
Total	$35.80	$31.00

The vehicles and tools will be salvaged during July at an expected before-tax gain of $300,000. During August, the equipment will be auctioned off at the mine site for an estimated $2.5 million in cash. The buildings will be salvaged during September and are expected to yield $100,000 in scrap iron, steel, and lumber. The building salvage company will be paid a fee of $40,000. The leasehold has no value, and any loss on it will reduce estimated income taxes. SLC Minerals pays income tax at a rate of 40 percent. The next estimated tax payment is due on September 15, 19x9.

REQUIRED:
a. Compute the expected cash effects of the liquidation during:
   1. July 19x9.
   2. August 19x9.
   3. September 19x9.
b. Compute the total effect of the liquidation on:
   1. After-tax income for the three months.
   2. Cash flows for the three months.

15–17. Cash Receipts.   RANCO is a small manufacturing firm that sells only to distributors. All sales are made on credit with terms of n/15. Dave Leemon, the controller, has asked Barbara Tracey, the credit manager, to design a cash receipts projection model. He wants to know whether cash collections can be projected accurately by week and from current Accounts Receivable. Tracey is to consider only credit sales already made.

Tracey asked Jim Hurd, the supervisor of Data Processing, to analyze Accounts Receivable for the last six months and determine the average days that elapse between the invoice date and the date payment is received. Hurd gave her the following report.

Customer	*Average Days from Invoice to Payment*
Morse Chemical	42
Farrel Industries	35
Rhodes Discount	33
Yale Union	31
TechCo	25
All other customers	17
Average for all customers	34

Hurd indicated that the Accounts Receivable records show that over 90 percent of all credit sales are with the five companies detailed and that the other 20 distributors account for the remainder. He also indicated that the only uncollectible accounts occurred in the All other customers category and averaged 2 percent of billings. Hurd gave Tracey the following age analysis of the Accounts Receivable file as of November 30, 19x4:

(CMA, adapted)

	1	*2*	*3*	*4*	*5*	*6*	*Total*
			Week				
Morse Chemical	$ 13,000	$40,000	$ 90,000	$ 22,000	$25,000	$30,000	$220,000
Farrel Industries	5,000	10,000	5,500	12,000	20,000	7,500	60,000
Rhodes Discount	235,000	15,000	20,000	25,000	15,000	–0–	310,000
Yale Union	27,500	1,000	–0–	35,000	16,500	–0–	80,000
TechCo	2,500	4,000	18,500	15,000	–0–	7,000	47,000
All others	18,000	13,000	17,000	3,000	1,500	500	53,000
Totals	$301,000	$83,000	$151,000	$112,000	$78,000	$45,000	$770,000

REQUIRED:
a. Prepare a projection of cash collections by customer by week for the first three weeks of December 19x4 using the age analysis of the Accounts Receivable file that is presented and the average collection period of each individual customer.

b. Explain why Barbara Tracey should use the average collection period of each individual customer rather than using the overall collection period of 34 days.

c. The projection of cash collections by week was prepared for a three-week period only.

    1. Identify the maximum period of weeks for which the projection can be prepared before it becomes inaccurate.

    2. Explain why the projection becomes inaccurate if it is extended beyond this period.

d. Barbara Tracey would like to develop a computer model to generate this projection of cash collections by week. Describe a computer model that would produce a projection of cash collections.

e. Can the data Jim Hurd produced be used by RANCO for any purposes other than cash management? Explain your answer.

15–18. Cash Budget. Bickmoore Company is in the process of preparing its cash budget for the second quarter of 19x8. Information about revenues and expenditures for each month of the second quarter is summarized below. The dollar sales are expected to be $60,000 for April, $70,000 for May, and $80,000 for June. Sales are collected 60 percent in the month of sale; 30 percent the following month; 8 percent the second month following sale; 2 percent will not be collectible. The Accounts Receivable net of Allowance for Doubtful Accounts as of March 31 is $13,800. Sales were $30,000 each for February and March.

Expenditures are made up of manufacturing costs plus the operating expenses of selling, general, and administration. Material costs are paid 70 percent in the month of purchase and 30 percent the month after. Other costs are paid in the month of incurrence. The budgeted expenditures for each month are:

	Material	Labor	Overhead	Operating
April	$20,000	$16,000	$20,000	$14,000
May	25,000	18,000	22,000	16,000
June	28,000	20,000	25,000	17,000

Overhead and operating expenses include monthly depreciation of $4,000 and $2,000, respectively. The Accounts Payable balance for material purchases is $5,000 at March 31.

The cash balance at March 31 is $10,000. The company would like to maintain that balance at the end of each month. Cash in excess of this balance is put into temporary investments that yield income of 1 percent per month. If additional cash is needed, the company will first dispose of the temporary investments and then turn to a line of credit with its bank. The bank charges 1 percent interest per month on the outstanding balance and requires the company to use excess cash balances to reduce the debt. Bickmoore had no outstanding balance in the line of credit at March 31, but it had $2,000 in temporary investments.

REQUIRED:
Prepare a cash budget for each month and for the quarter in total for the Bickmoore Company.

15–19. Cash Budget. Voorhees Hospital provides a wide range of health services in its community. Voorhees' board of directors has authorized the following capital expenditures:

Interaortic balloon pump	$1,100,000
CT scanner	700,000
X ray equipment	600,000
Laboratory equipment	1,400,000
	$3,800,000

The expenditures are planned for October 1, 19x4, and the board wishes to know the amount of borrowing, if any, necessary on that date. Marc Kelly, hospital controller, has gathered the following information to be used in preparing an analysis of future cash flows.

    1. Billings made in the month of service for the first six months of 19x4 were:

January	$4,400,000
February	4,400,000
March	4,500,000

April	$4,500,000
May	5,000,000
June	5,000,000

Of Voorhees' billings, 90 percent are made to third parties such as Blue Cross, federal or state governments, and private insurance companies. The remaining 10 percent of the billings are made directly to patients. Historical patterns of billings collections are (in percentages):

	Third Parties	*Direct Patient*
Month of service	20	10
Month following service	50	40
Second month following service	20	40
Uncollectible	10	10

2. Estimated billings for the last six months of 19x4 are:

July	$4,500,000
August	5,000,000
September	5,500,000
October	5,700,000
November	5,800,000
December	5,700,000

The same billing and collection patterns that have been experienced during the first six months of 19x4 are expected to continue during the last six months of the year.

3. The purchases that have been made during the past three months and the planned purchases for the last six months of 19x4 are presented in the following schedule.

April	$1,100,000
May	1,200,000
June	1,200,000
July	1,250,000
August	1,500,000
September	1,850,000
October	1,950,000
November	2,250,000
December	1,750,000

All purchases are made on account, and Accounts Payable is remitted in the month following the purchase.

4. Salaries for each month during the remainder of 19x4 are expected to be $1,500,000 per month plus 20 percent of that month's billings. Salaries are paid in the month of service.

5. Voorhees' monthly depreciation charges are $125,000.

6. Voorhees incurs interest expense of $150,000 per month and makes interest payments of $450,000 on the last day of each calendar quarter.

7. Endowment fund income is expected to continue to total $175,000 per month.

8. Voorhees has a cash balance of $300,000 on July 1, 19x4, and has the policy to maintain a minimum end-of-month cash balance of 10 percent of the current month's purchases.

9. Voorhees Hospital employs a calendar year reporting period.

                                                                    (CMA, adapted)

REQUIRED:

a. Prepare a schedule of cash receipts by month for the third quarter of 19x4.

b. Prepare a schedule of cash disbursements by month for the third quarter of 19x4.

c. Determine the amount of borrowing, if any, necessary on October 1, 19x4, to acquire the capital items totaling $3,800,000.

**EXTENDED
APPLICATION**

15–20. Cash Budget. Paul Jans is controller for Rendell Rest, Inc., an employee-owned, job-order printer of religious materials with annual sales of $45 million. Mr. Jans is in the process of preparing the cash plan for the first quarter of 19x3. The January 1, 19x3 and the March 31, 19x3 desired ending balances are projected to be:

	1/1/x3	3/31/x3 (Desired)
Cash	$ 148,000 Dr.	$200,000 Dr.
Accounts receivable	4,240,000 Dr.	?　Dr.
Allowance for bad debts	79,000 Cr.	?　Cr.
Materials	180,000 Dr.	180,000 Dr.
Work in process	500,000 Dr.	500,000 Dr.
Accounts payable	1,425,000 Cr.	?　Cr.
Accrued liabilities	870,000 Cr.	?　Cr.

The projected income statement for the quarter ending March 3, 19x3, is:

	Planned	Common $	Fixed Costs
Customer billings	$12,000,000	100.0%	
Cost of goods sold	9,000,000	75.0%	$4,500,000
Gross margin	$ 3,000,000	25.0%	
Selling expenses	720,000	6.0%	240,000
Administrative expenses	600,000	5.0%	180,000
Income from operations	$ 1,680,000	14.0%	
Income tax (40%)	672,000	5.6%	
Net income	$ 1,008,000	8.4%	

Included in the income statement amounts are depreciation of:

Printing plant	$450,000 in cost of goods sold
Sales facilities	$ 90,000 in selling expenses
Office and equipment	$ 60,000 in administrative expenses

The sales expenses include a doubtful accounts expense of 1 percent of billings. The expected customer billings are:

November	$4,100,000
December	3,800,000
January	3,500,000
February	4,000,000
March	4,500,000

Credit terms are Net 30 with some customers allowed extended payment. The average payment pattern experienced is 10 percent during month of sale, 70 percent the following month, and 19 percent two months later.

The company keeps no finished goods inventories and pays for all purchases in the month following purchase. Labor and all other expenses are paid 50 percent during the month and 50 percent the following month. The cost of goods sold includes 50 percent materials, 25 percent labor, and 25 percent overhead. The direct labor and overhead are considered fixed costs and total $1,500,000 per month. Estimated income taxes are paid the last month of each quarter. A new printing press with a cost of $800,000 will be delivered and paid for in March. Equipment costing $600,000 will be sold at a loss of $200,000, which will be deductible from ordinary income. The company follows the policy of debt-free purchase of all plant and equipment. Thus, payment for the equipment must come from current operating flows. Dividends totaling $100,000 will be paid during March.

REQUIRED:

a. Compute the cash receipts from operations during the first three months of 19x3.

b. Compute the cash payments for operations by month for the first three months of 19x3 for:

1. Materials.
2. Direct labor.
3. Production overhead.
4. Selling expenses.
5. Administrative expenses.

c. Prepare a cash plan by month for the quarter ending March 31, 19x3.

APPENDIX 15A   Regression Analysis of Cash Flows

LEARNING OBJECTIVE

After completing this appendix, you should be able to:

1. Interpret the results of multiple regression models as they are applied to the estimation of cash receipts and disbursements.

In Chapter 3, we studied six estimation techniques, one of which was regression (least squares) analysis. In Appendix 3A, we introduced multiple regression. We will apply multiple regression analysis to cash flow estimation.

In preparing the regression model, we recognize that the cash receipts for any month are the result of sales of the current and previous months:

$$CR_t = a + b_1 \cdot S_t + b_2 \cdot S_{t-1} + b_3 \cdot S_{t-2} + e_t$$

where

$$
\begin{aligned}
CR_t &= \text{The cash receipts for the current month} \\
a &= \text{Constant collections on accounts receivable}[1] \\
b_i &= \text{The collection rates for each month} \\
S_t &= \text{The sales for the current month} \\
S_{t-1} &= \text{The sales for the past month} \\
S_{t-2} &= \text{The sales for the month before last} \\
e_t &= \text{Error term.}
\end{aligned}
$$

For example, the cash receipts for March are a function of the sales for March, the sales for February, and the sales for January. Three months' sales should be adequate for the regression models that you will be working with. In southern Europe or Latin America, where 90-day credit terms are common, four or five months may be required in the analysis.

Amounts for total sales and cash collections on account for 18 months (or longer) are desirable. The analysis can be performed with as few as four months' data, but the error rate will be very high. The sales data should be readily available from the monthly income statements. Cash receipts can be found as summary debits to the Cash accounts in the general ledger or as summary credits to the Accounts Receivable Control account. When working with branch offices and locations, this may require consolidation of Cash and Accounts Receivable accounts. Do not assume that all debits to Cash are sales receipts because the debits also include loan proceeds, asset liquidations, stock issuances, note collections, and account transfers. Likewise, not all credits to Accounts Receivable represent sales receipts but include sales returns and allowances, shipping adjustments, special sales promotions, and accounts written off. Therefore, work carefully with the cash receipts data for possible receipts that are not based on sales.

For some companies, the easiest way to find past monthly cash receipts is to reconstruct them based on financial statements. From these statements, we obtain the beginning and ending balances for Accounts Receivable, Sales, and Accounts Re-

---

[1] The regression constant generally should be zero or immaterial because cash receipts from operations are strictly a function of current and past sales. Thus, for most estimations, the constant should be forced to equal zero. However, if the Accounts Receivable account increases or decreases noticeably over the time period, then allow for a constant in the estimation.

ceivable adjustments. Then we calculate the cash receipts by adding sales to the beginning balance and subtracting both the adjustments and the ending balance. For example, assume that we have found that the beginning Accounts Receivable was $140.46 million, Sales was $150.24 million, the ending Accounts Receivable was $109.21 million, and $3.47 million included amounts allowed as discounts or written off as bad debts. We would estimate cash receipts on account as:

Beginning accounts receivable	$140.46 million
Plus: Sales	150.24
Less: Adjustments	(3.47)
Ending accounts receivable	(109.21)
Cash receipts for month	$178.02 million

This technique will work for calculating *past cash receipts* because all data are available. However, it will not work for projections of future cash receipts because beginning and ending Accounts Receivable balances are not known.

Exhibit 15A–1 presents an example of a regression analysis performed on data

EXHIBIT 15A–1   Regression Estimate of Collection Rates (sales and collections for past 18 months)

(Amounts in millions)

		Collections	Sales Amounts during Months		
			Current	*Last*	*Before Last*
19x7	March	$ 178.02	$ 150.24	$ 227.72	$ 178.31
	April	135.10	105.26	150.24	227.72
	May	160.06	197.95	105.26	150.24
	June	167.40	179.22	197.95	105.26
	July	144.33	115.73	179.22	197.95
	August	139.07	162.76	115.73	179.22
	September	163.82	192.80	162.76	115.73
	October	159.94	144.98	192.80	162.76
	November	135.66	123.17	144.98	192.80
	December	156.65	178.96	123.17	144.98
19x8	January	147.65	133.63	178.96	123.17
	February	213.32	285.04	133.63	178.96
	March	223.11	204.38	285.04	133.63
	April	173.96	123.61	204.38	285.04
	May	162.94	188.98	123.61	204.38
	June	168.46	169.14	188.98	123.61
	July	151.27	147.62	169.14	188.98
	August	159.73	171.70	147.62	169.14
	Totals	$2,940.47	$2,975.16	$3,031.18	$3,061.87

Regression Output:

Standard error of Y estimated	3.81740	
R^2	0.97681	
Number of observations	18	
Degrees of freedom	15	

	Current	*Last*	*Before Last*
X coefficients	50.09%	35.06%	12.71%
Standard error of coefficient	0.0157	0.0167	0.0152
t-statistics	32.00	20.95	8.36

collected for 18 months. The regression results obtained are very good with an R^2 of 97.681 percent, which indicates a very close relationship between sales and cash collections on account. This is an indication of a stable relationship throughout the year with few errors in the sales and collections data.

The equation to be used for estimation is:

$$CR_t = (0.5009 \times S_t) + (0.3506 \times S_{t-1}) + (0.1271 \times S_{t-2})$$

The estimate of the combined discounts taken and accounts written off may be found by totaling the monthly rates and subtracting from 100 percent:

Total sales		100.00%
Current collections	50.09	
Last month's sales	35.06	
Before last month's sales	12.71	97.86%
Estimate of discounts and write offs		2.14%

Disbursements Regression Analysis

The approach taken to estimate the cash receipts pattern in Exhibit 15A–2 is the same as for the cash payments pattern. The dependent variable is cash payments, and the independent variables are the current and past purchases. The regression model takes the form:

$$CP_t = a + b_1 \cdot P_t + b_2 \cdot P_{t-1} + b_3 \cdot P_{t-2} + e_t$$

where

$$\begin{aligned} CP_t &= \text{Cash payments during the current month} \\ a &= \text{Constant cash payments on accounts payable}^2 \\ b_i &= \text{Payment rate for purchases made during month i} \\ P_t &= \text{Purchases during the current month} \\ P_{t-1} &= \text{Purchases during the past month} \\ P_{t-2} &= \text{Purchases of two months ago} \\ e_t &= \text{Error term.} \end{aligned}$$

The equation to project cash payments (CP_t) for materials is:

$$CP_t = (0.3615 \times P_t) + (0.5247 \times P_{t-1}) + (0.1007 \times P_{t-2})$$

The interpretation of this equation is that the estimated cash payments for this month are 36.15 percent of current purchases (P_t) plus 52.48 percent of last month's purchases (P_{t-1}) plus 10.07 percent of purchases for two months ago (P_{t-2}). An estimate of the discounts taken may be found by totaling the payment rates and subtracting from 100 percent:

Total purchases		100.00%
Current purchases	36.15	
Last month's purchases	52.47	
Before last month's purchases	10.07	98.69%
Estimate of discounts taken		1.31%

Technical Notes on Gathering Data

In large accounts payable systems, thousands of purchases are accounted for each day with summary debits made to materials control accounts and credits to Accounts Payable. The debits to materials should be accumulated by month to provide the purchases input to the regression. A daily ledger entry for all checks issued is also

---

[2] This constant is most often forced to zero unless there is a noticeable increase or decrease in the balance of Accounts Payable from the beginning to end of the data.

EXHIBIT 15A–2   **Materials Purchases and Payments** (estimate of monthly payments pattern)

				Purchases for Month	
		Payments	*Current*	*Last*	*Before Last*
19x7	March	$ 21.71	$ 23.63	$ 22.60	$ 15.64
	April	20.46	18.43	23.63	22.60
	May	19.03	17.26	18.43	23.63
	June	16.94	17.84	17.26	18.43
	July	17.67	16.02	17.84	17.26
	August	17.29	16.92	16.02	17.84
	September	17.54	17.35	16.92	16.02
	October	18.10	20.17	17.35	16.92
	November	18.53	17.11	20.17	17.35
	December	18.21	19.75	17.11	20.17
19x8	January	19.34	18.62	19.75	17.11
	February	20.84	26.90	18.62	19.75
	March	26.57	28.13	26.90	18.62
	April	25.13	21.94	28.13	26.90
	May	21.62	20.55	21.94	28.13
	June	20.36	21.24	20.55	21.94
	July	19.64	19.08	21.24	20.55
	August	19.13	20.14	19.08	21.24
	Totals	$358.11	$361.09	$363.54	$360.10

Regression Output

Standard error of Y estimated			0.58104
R^2			0.95602
Number of observations			18
Degrees of freedom			15
	Current	*Last*	*Before Last*
X coefficient(s)	36.15%	52.47%	10.07%
Standard error of coefficient	0.0442	0.0563	0.0393
t-statistics	8.97	9.53	2.18

made. These entries are not exactly the cash disbursements data we want because the entry will include all payments—not just those related to materials. In order to get around this systems limitation, accumulate the payment (debit) entries in the detailed vendor files. All (or a sample of) vendor accounts will have to be processed, but this is much easier than summarizing the paid invoice file.

It might be useful to separate the purchases and payments into types of materials purchased in order to get more accurate estimates. For example, a budget analyst might separately analyze purchases of computers, motors, power sources, cabinets, wiring, and attachments. This will require detailed analysis of purchase orders and cash payments, which would result in heavy computer usage.

Seasonal Patterns

There may be a seasonal pattern to the collections with more rapid collections occurring during one part of the year as compared to another. If a seasonal pattern is suspected, estimate two regression models: one for the faster collection months and another for the slower collection months.

1. What is the problem with using only six months' data to estimate a materials payment using regression analysis?
2. In preparing a regression analysis of payments, what is the dependent variable and what are the independent variables?

15A–1. Interpreting Receipts Regression Results.   The controller for the Alpine Ski Co. has performed the following regression analysis on cash receipts and sales for the year ending September 30, 19x6:

Regression output:
Standard error of Y estimated	$293
R^2	0.87722
Number of observations	12
Degrees of freedom	9

	Current	Last	Before Last
X coefficients	51.2%	30.8%	16.5%
Standard error of coefficient	5.5%	5.0%	5.6%

The estimated sales for the quarter ending December 31, 19x6 are:

October 19x6	$ 400,000
November	600,000
December	1,400,000

REQUIRED:
a. Interpret the meaning of the regression analysis.
b. Estimate the allowance for doubtful accounts.
c. Estimate the cash receipts for December 19x6.

15A–2. Interpreting Disbursements Regression Results.   MacElwaney, Inc., is a department store specializing in clothing and accessories. The budget director, Jillian Conti, prepared the following regression analysis of cash payments on purchases for the prior year, 19x1:

Regression Output
Standard error of Y estimated	$221
R^2	0.95142
Number of observations	12
Degrees of freedom	9

	Current	Last	Before Last
X coefficients	33.5%	45.8%	18.9%
Standard error of coefficient	3.0%	2.0%	2.8%

The budgeted purchases for the first quarter of 19x2 by month are January, $3,200; February, $3,600; and March, $3,800.

REQUIRED:
a. Interpret the meaning of the regression analysis.
b. Estimate the rate of average discount taken during 19x1.
c. Estimate the cash payments for merchandise for March 19x2.

PROBLEMS

15A–3. Multiple Regression of Cash Receipts.   Dravosburg Hospital had the following collections and billings for the last seven months of 19x5:

		Billings during Month		
	Receipts	Current	Last	Before Last
June 19x5	$ 5,729	$10,097	$ 8,474	$ 5,488
July	9,036	7,609	10,097	8,474
August	8,309	5,107	7,609	10,097
September	7,888	12,691	5,107	7,609
October	9,943	14,835	12,691	5,107
November	13,518	14,288	14,835	12,691
December	13,473	12,143	14,288	14,835

REQUIRED:

a. Prepare a multiple regression analysis of the cash receipts on the billings for:
   1. The current month and the last month.
   2. The current month and the prior two months.
b. Prepare an estimate of cash receipts for January 19x6 when billings are expected to be $11,000, using the results from:
   1. Two-month regression model.
   2. Three-month regression model.

15A–4. Multiple Regression of Cash Payments.   The Title XV fund of the Abbyton City School District has the following data on payments and purchases for fiscal 19x2:

	Payments	Purchases
June 19x1	$170,101	$187,836
July	173,706	72,905
August	112,215	79,261
September	86,236	129,769
October	96,131	67,028
November	115,875	208,499
December	126,573	86,844
January 19x2	171,910	202,483
February	132,433	113,501
March	147,939	135,312
April	122,899	122,198
May	126,284	119,513

The purchases during April 19x1 were $100,460 and during May 19x1 were $244,000. Title XV funds are used primarily to purchase equipment but may also be used for certain building improvements. Title XV funds have been continued in the amount of $1,660,000 by the state for fiscal 19x3.

REQUIRED:

a. Prepare a multiple regression analysis of the cash payments on the purchases during fiscal 19x2. Use three-month purchases in your analysis.
b. Estimate the Title XV cash payments for the first quarter of fiscal 19x3 given the following planned purchases by the school district:

June 19x2	$197,228
July	76,550
August	83,224

15A–5. Regression Analysis with Seasonal Patterns.   The Rocky Company sells ski equipment to retail stores and rental shops in the Rocky Mountain region. Both the purchases and payments are heavily seasonal in nature. Barny Aladen, corporate controller, has noticed that the payments during the months June through November are considerably slower than during other months.

	Receipts	Sales	Accounts Receivable
June 19x1	$ 24,202	$1,384,214	$1,383,145
July	117,416	1,050,975	2,308,767
August	460,014	2,040,591	3,876,254
September	577,462	1,512,055	4,796,318
October	1,065,109	2,521,009	6,235,764
November	1,260,139	2,528,791	7,482,137
December	2,791,185	1,231,205	5,889,202
January 19x2	3,229,736	2,598,307	5,210,120
February	2,161,633	665,630	3,679,129
March	2,264,787	915,068	2,308,138
April	1,688,248	685,783	1,273,844
May	1,748,047	770,632	280,347

Sales for March 19x1 were $820,400; April, $685,784; and May, $880,000. The June 1, 19x1, Accounts Receivable balance was $32,400.

REQUIRED:

a. Prepare a multiple regression analysis of the cash receipts on sales, using the current month and two prior months, for the six months ending:
   1. November 30,19x1
   2. May 31, 19x2

   (*Hint:* In these two regressions, allow for a constant amount because the Accounts Receivable balance increases during the first six months and decreases during the last six months of the fiscal year.)

b. Compute the amount of Accounts Receivable written off each month as either a discount taken or an uncollectible account.

c. Uncollectible accounts are written off during the third month after the sale. Discounts are taken on sales made during the current and prior months. Using multiple regression, estimate the rate of uncollectible accounts and discounts taken during the six months ending:
   1. November 30, 19x1
   2. May 31, 19x2

15A–6. Estimating Receipts Patterns with Regression. Charles Moores, Inc., manufactures wood and fiberglass speed boats. The boats are distributed through regional dealers in Arkansas, Louisiana, and Mississippi. Recent customer accounting activity data are:

	Sales	Receipts	Discounts	Write-offs
19x2 June	$135,895	$147,229	$ 1,789	$ 800
July	812,205	322,765	8,870	1,040
August	319,280	464,999	10,705	1,166
September	263,560	443,971	5,639	8,497
October	140,761	222,644	3,239	3,318
November	49,398	131,526	1,428	2,724
December	143,661	124,822	1,078	1,206
19x3 January	113,193	112,049	2,555	150
February	286,143	153,830	3,324	1,118
March	586,269	315,506	7,952	689
April	107,155	320,105	6,350	2,699
May	69,258	227,295	1,326	5,474
June	764,198	297,107	7,681	852
July	102,415	341,454	7,785	903
August	543,768	432,642	5,561	7,389

	Sales	Receipts	Discounts	Write-offs
19x3 September	$147,613	$267,784	$ 6,332	$ 559
October	133,409	244,443	2,800	5,787
November	84,634	104,634	1,561	1,377
December	81,005	89,323	848	964

The credit terms are 3/15, Net 60. Accounts are written off during the fourth month following sale, when unpaid accounts are sent to the collection agency.

REQUIRED:

Using multiple regression analysis, estimate rates for the following:

a. Collections on sales.
b. Discounts taken.
c. Write-offs.

APPENDIX 15B Budgeted Balance Sheet

LEARNING OBJECTIVES

After studying this appendix, you should be able to:

1. Determine the effect of the operations budget on balance sheet accounts.
2. Prepare a budgeted balance sheet.

One of the remaining steps in the preparation of the annual budget is the pro forma ("as if") preparation of the balance sheet for the end of the year. Exhibit 15B–1 presents a budgeted income statement and a balance sheet at the beginning of the fiscal year.[1] The beginning statement will have to be projected because the budget is prepared two to three months before the beginning of the year. We will present the effects of the operations projections on each line of the statement.

Computation of Account Balances

Worksheets, schedules, and other approaches can be used to arrive at the final numbers that will be displayed in the ending budgeted balance sheet. This section discusses where the numbers come from for a specific example.

Cash and Marketable Securities. The Cash and Marketable Security accounts reflect all the cash receipts from sales, payments for expenses, investment activities, and financing transactions. The account balances are also affected by the policies of management and loan agreements.

A large company has hundreds of checking and marketable security accounts with various financial institutions. Some of the checking accounts, especially the accounts of branches, maintain a zero balance, which is accomplished by electronically transferring required funds to clear checks presented each day. The projected ending Cash and Marketable Securities amounts can be found as the ending balance in the cash flow budget; for example, the ending balance in Exhibit 15–13 is $163.38 million.

Accounts Receivable. The projected balance in ending Accounts Receivable may be found by adding projected sales to the beginning balance and subtracting projected collections and adjustments. The beginning balance is $113.9 million, sales are estimated at $2,475 million in the budgeted income statement (Exhibit 15B–1), and collections were estimated in Exhibit 15–13 at $2,399.3 million. Assume that adjustments are expected to be $52.5 million and include cash discounts and uncollectible accounts. The ending balance may be estimated as:

Accounts receivable, 10/1/x8	$ 113.9	million
Plus: Sales	2,475.0	
Less: Collections	(2,399.3)	
Adjustments	(52.5)	
Accounts receivable, 9/30/x9	$ 137.1	

Inventories and Other Current Assets. The ending balance for Materials may be found by adding purchases to the beginning balance and subtracting issues to production:

Materials, 10/1/x8	$ 23.2
Plus: Purchases	313.3
Less: Issues to production	(317.9)
Materials, 9/30/x9	$ 18.6

---

[1] These data are from the Rapid Robotics, Inc., example in Chapter 14.

EXHIBIT 15B–1

RAPID ROBOTICS, INC.
Balance Sheet
September 30, 19x8
(in millions)
Assets

Cash and marketable securities	$ 72.0	
Accounts receivable	113.9	
Inventories: Materials	23.2	
Work in process	151.9	
Other current assets	58.2	
Total current assets		$ 419.2
Buildings, plant, and equipment	1,639.3	
Other assets	389.2	
Total fixed assets		2,028.5
Total assets		$2,447.7

Equities

Accounts payable	$ 15.5	
Notes payable	80.0	
Current taxes payable	50.0	
Other current liabilities	30.0	
Total current liabilities		$ 175.5
Long-term debt		450.0
		$ 625.5

Total Liabilities

Preferred stock	$ 350.0	
Common stock	331.6	
Other paid-in capital	613.2	
Retained earnings	527.5	
Total owners' equity		1,822.3
Total liabilities and equity		$2,447.7

Budgeted Income Statement
For the Year Ending September 30, 19x9

Sales			$2,475.0
Less: Sales discounts and allowances			(52.5)
Net sales			$2,422.5
Production costs			
Materials	$317.9		
Less discounts	(4.1)		
Direct labor	606.2		
Overhead	639.4	$1,559.4	
Plus: Beginning work in process		151.9	
Less: Ending work in process		(135.9)	
Cost of goods sold			(1,575.4)
Gross margin			$ 847.1
Sales and distribution		$ 78.4	
General and administrative		341.1	(419.5)
Income from operations			$ 427.6
Other income			2.0
Income before tax			$ 429.6
Income tax (Estimated at 52%)			(223.4)
Net income			$ 206.2

Note that this company treats the purchase discounts as a credit to Work in Process at the time they are taken. Thus, materials purchases and issues to work in process are recorded at invoice price. The example company chooses to credit Work in Process for discounts taken because (1) the clerks find the journal entries easy to prepare, (2) any inaccuracy caused by the approach is immaterial, and (3) the computerized accounting system was set up this way and is now difficult to change.

The ending Work in Process was estimated to be $135.9 million in the income statement. The other current assets, mostly Prepaid Expenses, are assumed to remain constant during the year at $58.2 million. (If this were not the case, adjustments to cash flows for changes in Prepaid Expenses would have to be made.)

Fixed Assets.   The ending balance for Plant and Equipment may be found by adding purchases and subtracting depreciation and the book value of equipment sold. The planned purchases of fixed assets are found in Exhibit 15–13 as $1,035.8 million. Depreciation in production overhead and expenses, found by examining the detailed accounts, is $144.8 and $66.0 million, respectively. The net book value of equipment sold will be $10 million for the year.

Buildings, plant, and equipment, 10/1/x8	$1,639.3
Purchases of buildings, plant, and equipment	1,035.8
Less: Depreciation ($144.8 + $66.0)	(210.8)
Book value of equipment sold	(10.0)
Buildings, plant, and equipment, 9/30/x9	$2,454.3

Other fixed assets include intangibles, such as patents or goodwill, and deferred charges. The detailed budgets must be examined for amortization of patents and goodwill. To compute the ending balance in other fixed assets, add purchases to the beginning balance and subtract the credits for amortization:

Other fixed assets, 10/1/x8		$389.2
Plus: Purchases (None planned)	0.0	
Less: Amortization of patents	$16.7	
Amortization of goodwill	6.0	(22.7)
Other fixed assets, 9/30/x9		$366.5

Accounts Payable.   The accounts payable ending balance may be found by adding purchases and subtracting estimated payments and discounts taken. Given a beginning balance of $15.5 million, purchases of $313.3, and payments of $305.7, and assuming adjustments of $4.1 million, the projected ending Accounts Payable balance will be:

Accounts payable, 10/1/x8	$ 15.5
Plus: Purchases	313.3
Less: Estimated payments	(305.7)
Discounts taken	(4.1)
Accounts payable, 9/30/x9	$ 19.0

Notes Payable.   Add the new loans for the year to the beginning balance of Notes Payable and then subtract the principal payments made. The short-term payments as found in Exhibit 15–13 are $75.5 million. Thus, the ending balance may be found:

Notes payable, 10/1/x8	$80.0
Plus: New loans (None anticipated)	0.0
Less: Estimated payments of principal	(75.5)
Notes payable, 9/30/x9	$ 4.5

The planned debenture issuance requires a major reduction of current liabilities to attain a current ratio greater than 4. Thus, a major reduction in short-term loans from $80 million to $4.5 million is planned.

Other Current Liabilities. Other liabilities include Expense Accruals, for example accrued salaries, interest, or taxes. For this example, the other liabilities are assumed to be about the same at the end of each month at $30 million. If the accrued expenses were expected to change, the cash disbursement required for expenses would be adjusted by an equal amount, and the ending cash balance would be adjusted by an equal amount.

Long-Term Debt. Long-term debt will start the year at $450 million. During the year, $10 million of serial debentures will be paid off and $50 million of new debt will be issued in August to end the year at $490 million.

Stock. Preferred stock issued and outstanding will stay the same throughout the year. During May, an additional 20 million common A stock shares will be issued for an expected $800 million. Common A stock has a $10 par value, which means that $200 million ($10 × 20 million shares) will increase common stock from $331.6 to $531.6 million. The paid-in excess will increase by $600 million ($30 × 20 million shares) from $613.2 million to $1,213.2 million.

EXHIBIT 15B–2

	Budgeted Balance Sheet **September 30** **(in millions)**			
	19x8		*19x9*	
Cash and marketable securities	$ 72.0		$ 162.8	
Accounts receivable	113.9		137.1	
Inventories: Materials	23.2		18.6	
Work in process	151.9		135.9	
Other current assets	58.2		58.2	
Total current assets		$ 419.2		$ 512.6
Buildings, plant, and equipment	1,639.3		2,454.3	
Other assets	389.2		366.5	
Total fixed assets		2,028.5		2,820.8
Total assets		$2,447.7		$3,333.4
Accounts payable	$ 15.5		$ 19.0	
Notes payable	80.0		4.5	
Current taxes payable	50.0		55.8	
Other current liabilities	30.0		30.0	
Total current liabilities		$ 175.5		$ 109.3
Long-term debt		450.0		490.0
Total liabilities		$ 625.5		$ 599.3
Preferred stock	$ 350.0		$ 350.0	
Common stock	331.6		531.6	
Other paid-in capital	613.2		1,213.2	
Retained earnings	527.4		639.3	
Total owners' equity		1,822.2		2,734.1
Total liabilities and equity		$2,447.7		$3,333.4

Retained Earnings.   In order to find ending Retained Earnings, add Net Income to the beginning balance and subtract the amount of Planned Dividends:

Retained earnings, 10/1/x8	$527.4
Plus: Planned net income	206.2
Less: Planned dividends	(94.3)
Retained earnings, 9/30/x9	$639.3

If we have done everything correctly, the balance sheet will now balance. If it does not balance, carefully go through the calculations and amounts for each reported amount and find the error.

Budgeted Balance Sheet

The final step in this phase is to prepare a complete comparative balance sheet as in Exhibit 15B–2. The chances that the final amounts in the actual balance sheet will be exactly these amounts are nil. The final amount for Cash and Marketable Securities may be between $100 million and $200 million and still be workable. As long as the current ratio stays above 4 and the minimum desired cash is kept, there can be some variation in its results. As the year progresses, the cash budget and budgeted balance sheet will be revised to reflect actual events.

REVIEW QUESTIONS

1. Why are the *beginning* balances for the statement of financial position most often on a pro forma basis?
2. If a zero balance account has no money in it, how are the bills paid through the account?

EXERCISES

15B–1. Pro Forma Current Asset Balances.   The Durango Print Shop has the following planned amounts for 19x3:

Sales	$2,300,000
Cost of goods sold	1,600,000
Collections on account	2,100,000
Purchases	1,500,000
Accounts receivable, 1/1	300,000
Inventory, 1/1	500,000

REQUIRED:
Prepare the following based upon the information above.
a. Accounts receivable, 12/31/x3.
b. Inventory, 12/31/x3.

15B–2. Pro Forma Current Liability Balances.   Murphy Mercantile has the following planned amounts for 19x3:

Purchases	$1,500,000
Payments on account	1,700,000
Loan interest expenses	50,000
Payments on loan principal	200,000
Additional loans	100,000
Accounts payable, 1/1	400,000
Loans payable, 1/1	300,000

REQUIRED:
Prepare the following based on the information above.
a. Accounts payable, 12/31/x3.
b. Loans payable, 12/31/x3.

PROBLEMS

15B–3. Pro Forma Financial Position. The Lamp Shop has the following statement of financial position for February 1, 19x1, and pro forma statement of operations for the year ending January 31, 19x2:

Financial Position, February 1, 19x1		**Operations**		
Cash	$ 32,000	Revenues		$900,000
Accounts receivable (Net)	105,000	Cost of goods sold		602,000
Merchandise inventory	340,000	Gross margin		$298,000
Furniture and fixtures (Net)	80,000	Salaries	$60,000	
Total assets	$557,000	Commissions, 3%	27,000	
		Rent	18,000	
Accounts payable	$120,000	Utilities	9,600	
Note payable	150,000	Depreciation	8,000	
Common stock	100,000	Bad debts	18,000	
Retained earnings	187,000	Interest	21,000	
Total equities	$557,000	Sundry	3,600	
		Total expenses		165,200
		Income before taxes		$132,800
		Income taxes (30%)		39,840
		Net income		$ 92,960

ADDITIONAL INFORMATION

The cash budget reveals that the expected ending cash is to be $51,560. Cash collections on account are $840,000, payments for merchandise are $580,000, and all salaries, commissions, utilities, sundry expenses, and taxes will be paid during the year. Additionally, $30,000 in payments will be made on notes payable (including the interest), and a $10,000 cash dividend will be paid. Finally, $52,400 in fixtures will be purchased and payments of $42,400 made, leaving a $10,000 note remaining. Accounts receivable in the amount of $22,250 are expected to be written off as bad during the year. Purchases will amount to $620,000.

REQUIRED:
Prepare a pro forma statement of financial position for January 31, 19x2.

15B–4. Pro Forma Financial Position. The Bellefonte Valve Company sells valves and valve parts for steam heat control. Stan Mitchell, controller, is nearing completion of the master budget and has finished all the schedules except for the pro forma statement of financial position. The beginning financial position, the annual planned operations, and the cash flows are presented below. All amounts are in thousands.

Financial Position, January 1, 19x4			
Cash	$ 693	Accounts payable	$ 1,402
Accounts receivable (Net)	2,402	Note payable	1,580
Inventories	3,223	Accrued expenses	126
Plant and equipment	7,442	Common stock	3,000
Total assets	$13,760	Retained earnings	7,652
		Total equities	$13,760

Planned Operations

Revenues		$42,400
Cost of goods sold		25,440
Gross margin		$16,960
Sales salaries	$ 260	
Commissions, 4%	1,696	
Bad debts	424	
Research	2,600	
Administration	5,200	
Depreciation	100	
Interest	237	
Total expenses		10,517
Income before taxes		$ 6,443
Income taxes (40%)		2,577
Net income		$ 3,866

Cash Flows

Cash receipts on sales			$40,280
Cash payments:			
Materials	$14,500		
Factory wages	4,834		
Factory overhead	3,300		
Sales salaries	260		
Commissions	1,696		
Research	2,500		
Interest	237		
Income taxes	2,300		
Administration	5,200	(34,827)	
Cash from operations		$ 5,453	
Dividends	$ 700		
Equipment purchases	1,300		
Note principal	200	(2,200)	
Increase in cash		$ 3,253	

ADDITIONAL INFORMATION

Materials purchases	$15,100	Materials used	$15,300
Factory depreciation	744	Conversion cost	8,868
		Cost of goods manufactured	$24,168

Work in process inventories are small and are ignored for planning purposes.

REQUIRED:
Prepare a pro forma statement of financial position for December 31, 19x4.

15B–5. Pro Forma Financial Position.   Mistel Latex Co. manufactures rubber gloves for medical and home use. The gloves are manufactured on seven automatic glove machines and are then sterilized. Pro forma data for the current year are presented below with all amounts in thousands.

Financial Position, January 1, 19x4

Cash	$14,600	Accounts payable	$24,827
Accounts receivable (Net)	25,260	Note payable	11,200
Inventories	25,260	Accrued expenses	1,490
Plant and equipment	43,100	Common stock	50,000
Total assets	$108,220	Retained earnings	20,703
		Total equities	$108,220

Planned Annual Operations		Cash Flows		
Revenues		$126,300	Cash receipts on sales		$116,196
Cost of goods sold		101,040	Cash payments:		
Gross margin		$25,260	Materials	$64,068	
Sales salaries	$ 3,448		Factory wages	21,016	
Commissions, 4%	5,052		Factory overhead	10,508	
Bad debts	758		Sales salaries	3,448	
Research	1,200		Commissions, 4%	5,052	
Administration	3,600		Research	1,300	
Depreciation	1,400		Interest	1,344	
Interest	1,344		Income taxes	3,106	
Total expenses		16,802	Administration	3,600	113,442
Income before taxes		$ 8,458	Cash from operations		$ 2,754
Income taxes (40%)		3,383	Dividends	$ 1,015	
Net income		$ 5,075	Equipment purchases	800	
			Note principal	2,000	(3,815)
			Decrease in cash		$ (1,061)

ADDITIONAL INFORMATION

Materials used	$63,049	Materials purchases	$62,067
Conversion cost	42,033	Factory depreciation	6,896
Cost of goods manufactured	$105,082		

Work in process inventories are considered immaterial and are excluded for planning purposes.

REQUIRED:
Prepare a pro forma statement of financial position for December 31, 19x6.

EXTENDED APPLICATIONS

15B–6. Comprehensive Master Budget. The Wiley Basket Company of Jacksboro, Texas, manufactures four sizes of baskets used for agricultural produce. The company is currently preparing the master budget for the coming year. The information on quarterly 19x2 unit sales was collected, and the projected growth by product was estimated by the sales manager (units in thousands):

	Quarter	Quart	Peck	Half-Bushel	Bushel
19x2	1st	750	1,250	1,000	2,000
	2nd	1,000	1,500	1,500	2,500
	3rd	1,250	1,750	2,000	3,000
	4th	1,000	1,500	1,500	2,500
	Price	$0.10	$0.175	$0.25	$0.30
19x3	Growth	3.00%	4.50%	5.75%	7.50%

Assume that sales will follow the same pattern as for 19x2 with an increase in units. The selling price is expected to stay the same for 19x3. Collections occur 75 percent during the quarter of sale, 22 percent during the following quarter, and 3 percent are uncollectible.

Selling and administrative expenses are planned with a flexible budget as a function of gross sales with the following form:

	Variable	Fixed
Commissions	6%	
Travel	10%	
Bad debts expense	3%	
Salaries		$205,416
Advertising		79,006
Depreciation		10,000
Other		47,404
Totals	19%	$341,826

Selling and administrative costs are paid 80 percent during the quarter incurred and 20 percent the following quarter.

Desired ending inventories of finished goods are 20 percent of the following quarter's sales. The December 31, 19x2, inventories were:

	Quart	Peck	Half-Bushel	Bushel	Total
Units	154,500	261,250	211,500	430,000	
Cost	$0.06	$0.10	$0.14	$0.17	
Inventory	$9,270	$26,125	$29,610	$73,100	$138,105

The production process is highly automated, and all labor is included in variable overhead costs. The following are planned unit production costs for 19x3:

	Quart	Peck	Half-Bushel	Bushel
Materials	$0.020	$0.050	$0.070	$0.090
Variable overhead	0.020	0.025	0.035	0.040

Materials are purchased as needed from a local supplier. Fixed factory overhead is $222,806 per quarter and is applied at the rate of 100 percent of variable overhead. Included in quarterly overhead is $22,000 of depreciation. Production costs are paid 75 percent during the quarter incurred and 25 percent the following quarter.

Selected account balances for December 31, 19x2, are as follows:

Cash	$ 10,000
Marketable securities	12,750
Accounts receivable	371,875
Allowance for uncollectibles	(44,625)
Finished goods inventories	138,105
Plant and equipment	900,000
Accumulated depreciation—Plant and equipment	(220,000)
Office building and sales equipment	280,000
Accumulated depreciation—Office and sales equipment	(80,000)
Total assets	$1,368,105
Accounts payable	$ 106,250
Accrued production liabilities	99,500
Accrued selling and general liabilities	66,413
Richard Wiley, capital	1,095,942
Total equities	$1,368,105

The company can borrow cash in increments of $1,000 at interest of 2.5 percent per quarter. Cash in excess of $10,000 may be invested in marketable securities that earn 1.75 percent per quarter. The minimum desired cash balance is $5,000.

(W. Baumgarter, adapted)

REQUIRED:
Prepare the following:
a. Sales revenue budget by product and by quarter.

b. Budgeted quarterly cash receipts from sales.
c. Planned production for 19x3 by product and by quarter.
d. Materials purchases budget by quarter for 19x3.
e. Overhead budget by quarter for 19x3.
f. Selling and general expense budget by account and quarter for 19x3.
g. Cash budget by quarter for 19x3.
h. Pro forma statement of operations by quarter for 19x3.
i. Pro forma balance sheet for December 31, 19x3.

15B–7. Comprehensive Budget.   Cohn, Inc., manufactures portable artificial respirators for use in emergency vehicles. The units are self-contained with power, oxygen, and pressure meticulously controlled. The units are manufactured to order with only an immaterial finished goods inventory. Recent months' data (in thousands) are provided for estimating receipts and payment patterns:

	Sales	Receipts	Purchases	Vendor Payments	Index of Sales Activity
July 19x1	$269	$244	$102	$ 90	
August	214	233	77	92	
September	240	226	86	83	
October	167	201	62	72	
November	176	185	66	67	
December	228	185	87	71	
January 19x2	197	201	74	73	78%
February	259	216	97	83	102%
March	269	243	95	96	106%
April	258	258	97	92	102%
May	227	241	80	91	90%
June	290	255	105	92	114%
July	287	266	109	98	113%
August	318	288	112	111	126%
September	249	283	94	103	98%
October	285	279	108	99	112%
November	194	243	76	90	77%
December	208	221	80	84	82%

The planned income statement and beginning balance sheet are expected to be:

COHN, INC.
Balance Sheet
For January 1, 19x3
(in thousands)

Assets

Cash and marketable securities	$ 70	
Accounts receivable	190	
Materials	50	
Work in process	200	
Other current assets	50	
Total current assets		$ 560
Tangible fixed assets	$2,000	
Accumulated Depreciation—		
Tangible fixed assets	(500)	
Other assets	200	
Total fixed assets		1,700
Total assets		$2,260
Liabilities:		
Accounts payable	$ 60	
Notes payable	50	
Current taxes	62	
Other liabilities	20	
Total current		
liabilities		$ 192
Long-term debt		200
Total liabilities		$ 392
Common stock	$ 600	
Retained earnings	1,268	
Owners' equity		1,868
Total liabilities and equity		$2,260

COHN, INC.
Planned Income Statement
For the Year Ending December 31, 19x3
(in thousands)

Sales		$3,500
Less: Sales discount (2.14%)		(75)
Net revenues		$3,425
Materials	$1,295	
Less: Purchase discounts	(17)	
Labor	454	
Overhead	680	
Plus: Work in process 1/1	200	
Less: Work in process 12/31	(150)	
Cost of goods sold		(2,462)
Gross margin		$ 963
Sales and distribution	125	
General and administration	280	(405)
Income from operations		$ 558
Other gains (Equipment)		10
Income before tax		$ 568
Income tax		(284)
Net income		$ 284

ADDITIONAL INFORMATION

Quarterly dividend beginning March 23	$ 20
Equipment purchases	240
Other fixed asset purchases (June)	30
Sales of Equipment (Net book value)	50
Accumulated depreciation on equipment sold	100
Gain on sale of equipment	10
Depreciation in overhead	100
Depreciation in general expenses	50
Amortization in general expenses	20

Notes payable require payment of $3,000 per month with interest expense of $5,000 for the year. Long-term debt requires an interest payment of $20,000 in November. The $25,000 of interest is included in general expenses. Equipment purchases and sales are spread evenly throughout the year. Production labor is 50 percent variable with sales. Labor-related costs make up 60 percent of projected overhead. The remaining overhead is fixed per month. Sales and distribution expenses are 75 percent variable with sales, and the remainder are fixed per month. General and administrative expenses are 25 percent variable with sales, and the remainder is fixed. Estimated income tax is paid quarterly beginning April 15.

REQUIRED:

a. Prepare a projection of sales by month using the index of sales activity column and the total sales estimate. Round the monthly estimates to the nearest $1,000 and adjust the highest activity month for any rounding error.

b. Using regression analysis on last year's data, prepare an estimate of the collection pattern.

c. Prepare projections of monthly cash receipts from sales (Round projections to the nearest $1,000):

	Current	*Last*	*Before Last*
1. Estimates from management	30%	40%	30%
2. Account analysis results	32.5%	38.3%	26.5%

3. Results of the regression analysis in (b)

4. Compare the projections based on management and account analysis with those based on regression analysis.

d. Prepare a projection of material purchases by month. Assume that Cohn, Inc., follows a just-in-time inventory policy. Thus, production and purchasing activity will coincide with sales. Round to nearest $1,000.

e. Using regression analysis, prepare an estimate of the vendor payment pattern.

f. Using the regression results, prepare monthly estimates of vendor payments. Round the final monthly payments to the nearest $1,000.

g. Prepare monthly estimates of labor and labor-related costs, overhead, sales and distribution expenses, and general and administrative costs. Remember to exclude depreciation and interest expenses.

h. Prepare a cash budget. Short-term borrowing up to $200,000 is available via a credit line from Western Commercial Credit. Assume that for now interest on this short-term borrowing is immaterial.

i. Prepare a budgeted balance sheet for December 31, 19x3. Assume that the other current assets and liabilities balances do not change during the year.

P A R T

V

Performance Measurement and Investigation

C H A P T E R

16

Variable Costing

■

MANIPULATING PROFITS THROUGH PRODUCTION

Everett Stetson had recently been appointed the division manager of the Conduit Pipe Division of LADO, Inc. He relocated to division headquarters in the small Illinois town of Centerville. The division was the town's largest employer, and the mayor, John Abrams, threw a welcome party for Stetson.

Everett is ambitious, cares little for the delights of small-town living, and wishes to be promoted to regional vice president as soon as possible. As regional vice president, he would live in Cincinnati, go to great restaurants, and generally live what he thinks is the good life. He knows that gaining the vice presidency requires showing immediate profits in the Conduit Pipe Division. Otherwise, he is stuck with Centerville and Mayor Abrams for the rest of the century. Showing profits will be a challenge. Last year the division lost over $800,000.

Conduit pipe is manufactured using metal sheets that are loaded into a large machine that continuously shapes, welds, and coats the pipe and then stacks it into bundles. A study of the product costs showed that about half of the total production costs are fixed. The costs of metal and coatings dominate the remaining costs. Half-inch conduit, a popular size for home use, is sold at a low price to develop business for the more profitable, larger sizes.

The division uses different machinery for various sizes and composition of pipe. The market for conduit pipe is directly related to construction, which has been slow recently. Substantial idle capacity exists in the company's facilities, and the plant operations have shown large losses. The Marketing Department is disheartened.

Everett Stetson asked for a special analysis of product profitability that compared revenue with traceable costs. He carefully studied the staffing of each department in the division. He then formed a strategy to get out of Centerville.

Over the next three years, Everett Stetson expanded the inventories, dramatically filling the surrounding fields with pipe. He ran the plant at capacity. He shifted people out of overhead areas and into producing areas. He reduced the management staff to a minimum and shifted former management people back into producing positions. Total sales dollars increased by about 22 percent, but this was mostly due to the reduction of certain prices that increased volume and an upturn in the economy; it was only partly due to improvement in sales efforts. However, profit increases were dramatic.

The division showed a profit of $1.2 million in his first year, $4.8 million in his second year, and, for the third year, an exciting $9.4 million. This brought him praise from the president and a pat on the back from the chairman. During the third year, he cut back substantially on maintenance personnel and drove the rest of the staff to their limits. He had fewer people doing more work. Fortunately, nothing major went wrong and high income was reported. In February of his fourth year, Mr. Stetson was promoted to regional vice president, and Mayor Abrams held a banquet in his honor at the Centerville High cafeteria.

After Mr. Stetson left, the Conduit Pipe Division experienced hard times. The sales declined somewhat, and the production was cut way back. The fields of inventory sold slowly, and production operations incurred large losses. The townspeople looked back with nostalgia to the times of Mr. Stetson and wondered where the "magic" had gone.

Everett enjoyed Cincinnati but occasionally had a guilty feeling about Centerville and sighed an "Oh, well . . ." on his way to yet another fine restaurant or his dearly loved Reds baseball games.

LEARNING OBJECTIVES

After studying this chapter, you should be able to:

1. Distinguish between variable costing and absorption costing.
2. Prepare a variable costing income statement.
3. Reconcile the differences between an absorption costing income statement and a variable costing statement.
4. Explain and compare the major arguments supporting both variable costing and absorption costing.

Mr. Stetson certainly used the cost accounting system to his own advantage. Although some people would question the ethics of his behavior, he did use valid tools in planning for the operations of the division.

His rapid expansion of production is where part of the problem lies. In running up the inventory, he was creating an illusion of profit for the division. The illusion comes from the substitution of current production for future production, which, by its very nature, will idle the plant in future years. Production cost accounting for external financial reports requires that fixed production costs be allocated to inventories, which defers some fixed costs to future years. A portion of the fixed costs of production becomes an asset and increases income by reducing the cost of goods sold. Further, costs related to the storage and the deterioration of the inventory are increased. Because the mistakes are concealed in inventory accounting, owners are misled and serious damage may be done to the future operations of the company. This is how Mr. Stetson used the accounting system for his purposes. We will study a method of cost accounting called *variable costing* that attempts to alleviate this problem.

Firing employees and discontinuing or deferring the maintenance of machinery during the third year were clearly poor management. The deterioration of equipment and employee morale will take its toll in later years. Stetson manipulated the system, and senior management was inept enough to reward him for it.

CHARACTERISTICS OF VARIABLE COSTING

Variable costing is an approach to the costing of production that allocates only variable production costs (materials, direct labor, and variable overhead) to items produced. Thus, product costs are limited to the variable production costs, and period costs include all fixed costs and nonproduction variable costs. **Absorption costing,** the method we typically use in accounting unless variable costing is specified, allocates all production costs (variable and fixed) to products. The following summary should highlight the single important difference in cost treatment between the two methods of costing products:

Cost Category	Variable Costing	Absorption Costing
Direct materials	Product	Product
Direct labor	Product	Product
Variable production overhead	Product	Product
Fixed production overhead ———————→	Period	Product ←———
Variable marketing and distribution	Period	Period
Fixed marketing and distribution	Period	Period
Variable general and administrative	Period	Period
Fixed general and administrative	Period	Period
Interest expense	Period	Period

The sole issue then is whether fixed production overhead is a product cost or a period cost.

Variable costing is also called *direct costing,* a term that is confusing at best. As you remember, direct costs are for the materials and labor that are directly traceable to a cost objective. Prior to about 1880, it was common practice to include only direct materials and direct labor in the cost of goods manufactured. However, as companies expanded their reliance on equipment, they found that excluding factory and equipment from costs resulted in what they interpreted to be an understatement of the costs of manufacturing the goods. Thus, in the early 1900s, production overhead was added to the cost of the product.

During the 1930s, a movement within accounting called *direct costing* invented anew the "old" cost accounting approach but added variable overhead to the direct materials and labor. Because accounting students are often confused with the meaning of the term *direct costing,* we will avoid this by adopting the term *variable costing* when referring to the costing method that includes variable production costs in product costs and specifically excludes fixed overhead.

Selecting one approach or the other has a bearing on inventory values and on periodic net income because costs excluded from inventory go directly against net income. Although net income can differ under the two approaches, variable-costing net income is not always higher or lower than absorption net income. The difference is determined by the relationship of production to sales. For example, consider the three possibilities:

1. *Production equals sales:* Absorption-costing net income equals variable-costing net income.
2. *Production greater than sales (building inventory):* Absorption-costing net income is higher than variable-costing net income.
3. *Production less than sales (liquidating inventory):* Absorption-costing net income is lower than variable costing net income.

The magnitude of any difference in net incomes is a function of the fixed manufacturing costs and the change in inventory levels.

PREPARING A VARIABLE-COSTING INCOME STATEMENT

The general format for a variable-costing income statement is a contribution format. The traditional approach of a functional income statement could be used as well, but the contribution format provides more useful information in view of having a separation of variable and fixed costs. An illustration of this format appears below:

DWYER PRODUCTS, INC.
Cosmetics Division
Income Statement (Variable Costing)
For the Month Ending June 30, 19x4
(in thousands)

Revenue	$300
Less: Variable costs	100
Contribution margin	$200
Less: Fixed costs	100
Income before taxes	$100

The variable costs represent a combination of the variable cost of products sold and variable marketing and administrative costs. More detail could have been given to show how the variable cost of goods sold is derived (beginning inventory plus cost of goods manufactured [or cost of purchases] less ending inventory), arriving at a manufacturing margin before subtracting the remaining variable costs. The thing to remember is that only variable production or purchasing costs are related to the products sold. Marketing and administrative costs, both variable and fixed, are still period costs.

Now that we have presented the general form, let us consider a specific case to show you what has to be done to prepare such a statement.

Analysis Setting

The Hyde Ski Company is a small producer of ski equipment. The company was started by students at the University of New Mexico in Albuquerque as a result of a proposal prepared for a graduate business course. The company now employs 12 people who work out of a small plant in the north valley of Albuquerque.

The Hyde ski wholesales for $60 and is allocated the following costs:

Materials	$12
Labor	4
Production overhead	12
Total production cost	$28

Fixed production costs are $6,000 per month, and fixed selling and administrative costs are $12,000 per month. Production overhead includes $10 ($6,000/600 = $10) in allocated fixed overhead. Variable selling and administrative costs are $2 per unit. The company sold 500 pairs of skis and produced 600 pairs during October 19x2.

Analysis with Variable Costing

Notice that the analysis setting gives the full or absorption costs rather than the variable production costs. Because of this, the first step is to find the variable costs of producing a unit of the product:

Materials	$12
Labor	4
Variable overhead ($12 − $10)	2
Total variable production costs	$18

Second, find the variable production costs for the 500 units sold: $18 × 500 = $9,000. Third, find the variable selling costs: $2 × 500 = $1,000. Finally, the variable-costing income statement may now be prepared using the standard format.

HYDE SKI COMPANY
Income Statement (Variable Costing)
For the Month Ending October 31, 19x2

Revenue ($60 × 500)		$ 30,000
Less variable costs:		
Production ($18 × 500)	$ 9,000	
Selling ($2 × 500)	1,000	(10,000)
Contribution margin		$ 20,000
Less fixed costs:		
Production	$ 6,000	
Selling and general	12,000	(18,000)
Income before tax		$ 2,000

An alternate, more detailed format makes a division of variable costs as follows:

HYDE SKI COMPANY
Income Statement (Variable Costing)
For the Month Ending October 31, 19x2

Revenue		$ 30,000
Less variable production costs		$ (9,000)
Manufacturing margin		$ 21,000
Less variable selling		(1,000)
Contribution margin		$ 20,000
Less fixed costs:		
Production	$ 6,000	
Selling and general	12,000	(18,000)
Income before tax		$ 2,000

The advantage to the greater detail is the ability to identify performance measures to evaluate managers. The manufacturing margin forms a basis to evaluate production managers. In a standard cost system, the manufacturing margin will be adjusted by variances for direct material, direct labor, and variable production overhead. The contribution margin will be used for evaluating marketing managers.

Comparison of Variable and Absorption Costing

Fixed production costs are included as part of the cost of the product under absorption cost accounting. The term *absorption costing* comes from the concept of absorbing all production costs into inventory.

Let us now prepare an income statement for Hyde Ski using the absorption-costing technique. First, find the cost of goods sold. The data in the case indicate that the production cost per unit is $28. Taking $28 times 500 results in a Cost of Goods Sold of $14,000. Variable selling and general costs of $1,000 plus the fixed selling and general costs of $12,000 result in total selling and general costs of $13,000. We are now ready to prepare the income statement:

HYDE SKI COMPANY
Income Statement (Absorption Costing)
For the Month Ending October 31, 19x2

Revenue	($60 × 500)	$ 30,000
Cost of goods sold	($28 × 500)	(14,000)
Gross margin		$ 16,000
Selling and general expenses		(13,000)
Income before tax		$ 3,000

Although this is the traditional format, we can expand the detail to include the variable and fixed cost separation, as follows:

HYDE SKI COMPANY
Income Statement (Absorption Costing)
For the Month Ending October 31, 19x2

Revenue		$30,000
Cost of goods sold:		
Variable ($18 × 500)	$ 9,000	
Fixed ($10 × 500)	$ 5,000	14,000
Gross margin		$16,000
Selling and general expenses:		
Variable ($2 × 500)	$ 1,000	
Fixed	12,000	13,000
Income before tax		$ 3,000

Why is income under absorption costing $1,000 higher than under variable costing? Is income really $3,000, or is it only $2,000? Where does this difference come from?

Reconciliation of Variable and Absorption Costing

All assets on the balance sheet must come from somewhere: borrowing, stockholder investment, or earnings of the entity. Absorption costing includes fixed overhead in ending inventories as an asset, and variable costing treats fixed overhead as an expense. The difference in assets between the two methods comes from a difference in earnings. The difference in accumulated earnings to date (i.e., retained earnings) will equal the difference in the amount of fixed costs in inventory.

During any given time period, the amount of fixed costs in inventory will increase or decrease because production differs from sales. As pointed out earlier in the chapter, if production is greater than sales, less fixed production costs will be expensed as part of cost of goods sold, and absorption-costing net income will be higher than variable-costing net income. Conversely, if sales are greater than production, more fixed production costs will be expensed through cost of goods sold, and absorption-costing net income will be less than variable-costing net income.

In the simplified case in which fixed overhead rates are the same in beginning and ending inventories, the difference between variable- and absorption-costing net income is exactly equal to:

(Change in inventory units) × (Fixed overhead per unit)

For the Hyde Ski Company, the change in inventory units is found by:

Units produced	600	
Less: Units sold	(500)	
Change in inventory	100	Increase

Either the fixed overhead per unit must be specified for the situation or the data must be presented to calculate the rate. Fixed overhead is given for Hyde Ski Company as $10 per unit. Putting the change in inventory units together with per unit fixed production costs results in a difference of $1,000:

$$100 \times \$10 = \$1,000$$

Whenever *inventory increases,* the absorption-costing net income must be *higher* than the variable-costing net income. This is the case for the Hyde Ski Company presented above. Whenever *inventory decreases,* the absorption-costing net income must be *lower* than the variable-costing net income. For example, if the Hyde Ski Company had produced only 400 skis during the month of October 19x2 with the rest of the data exactly the same, the absorption-costing net income would have been $1,000 lower than the variable-costing net income. Note that the production of 400 units would result in only $4,000 of the $6,000 in fixed overhead applied to Work in Process resulting in $2,000 being underapplied. The $2,000 would increase the cost of goods sold:

HYDE SKI COMPANY
Income Statement (Absorption Costing)
For the Month Ending
October 31, 19x2

Revenue	($60 × 500)	$ 30,000
Cost of goods sold	($28 × 500)	(14,000)
Underapplied overhead		(2,000)
Gross Margin		$ 14,000
Selling and general expenses		(13,000)
Income before tax		$ 1,000

Absorption-costing net income was $3,000 when production of 600 was set but decreased to $1,000 when 400 units were produced. The difference in income from variable costing is exactly $1,000 less. Inventory must decrease by 100 units if 400 are produced and 500 are sold. Reconciling the difference in income is:

(Change in inventory) × (Fixed OH rate) = (100) × $10 = ($1,000).

We have demonstrated the difference between variable and absorption costing using normalized overhead application. Some companies use actual overhead costs in calculating their ending inventories. As we will see, the conclusions with actual fixed overhead are similar to normal fixed overhead—only a few specifics change.

Reconciliation When Working with Actual Overhead

When actual overhead costs are used, the fixed overhead rate per unit goes up and down with changes in the volume produced. The higher the volume, the lower the fixed cost per unit and vice versa.

With wide shifts in volume, the cost of production has corresponding wide differences. Due to changes in the cost of goods produced, the effect of volume variation on income is partly determined by the inventory cost method chosen (FIFO, LIFO, or an average cost method). This complicates matters in practice because a company may use several cost-flow assumptions in accumulating the inventory costs of many products. For our purposes, assume that the company keeps all of its inventories on a first-in, first-out (FIFO) cost-flow assumption.

Analysis Setting. Assume the same data as in the original Hyde Ski setting except that the beginning inventory consists of 100 units and $3,400. The beginning inventory was manufactured when the fixed overhead rate was $16—the inventory cost includes $1,600 of fixed overhead.

The sales for the current period are 500 units. We will illustrate production at two different levels for the current period: (1) 600 pairs of skis—an inventory increase because production exceeds sales, and (2) 400 pairs of skies—an inventory decrease because production is less than sales.

Variable-Costing Analysis. The variable-costing analysis will be identical to the previous illustration. The beginning inventory will consist of 100 units at a variable production cost of $18 per unit. The current variable production cost is also $18 per unit. Because the variable costs for units sold and the fixed costs expensed have stayed the same, the variable-costing income will also remain the same at $2,000.

Absorption-Costing Analysis. For absorption costing, we must first calculate the cost of goods sold:

HYDE SKI COMPANY
Cost of Goods Sold—Actual Absorption Costing
For the Month Ending October 31, 19x2

	Production			
	600 Units		**400 Units**	
	Total	*Per Unit*	*Total*	*Per Unit*
Charges to Production				
Materials used	$ 7,200	$12	$ 4,800	$12
Labor	2,400	4	1,600	4
Variable overhead	1,200	2	800	2
Fixed overhead	6,000	10	6,000	15
Total charges	$16,800	$28	$13,200	$33
Beginning inventory	3,400	34	3,400	34
Goods available	$20,200		$16,600	
Ending inventory	5,600	$28	–0–	
Cost of goods sold	$14,600		$16,600	

The $2,000 difference in the cost of goods sold is due solely to the fixed costs allocated to different units produced—600 units in one case and 400 units in the other—while sales remain constant at 500 units.

Because variable costing uses the $18 unit cost, cost of goods sold will be $9,000 for either production level. How do you reconcile the difference between absorption-costing cost of goods sold and variable-costing cost of goods sold? Look at it in terms of flow of fixed costs as follows:

	600 Units	400 Units
Cost of goods sold—Absorption costing	$14,600	$16,600
Add: Fixed costs deferred in ending inventory (200 units × $10)	2,000	–0–
	$16,600	$16,600
Less: Fixed costs brought into period through beginning inventory (100 units × $16)	(1,600)	(1,600)
Less: Fixed costs of current period	(6,000)	(6,000)
Cost of goods sold—Variable costing	$ 9,000	$ 9,000

The income statement for Hyde Ski Company for sales of 500 units with both 600-unit and 400-unit production levels is:

HYDE SKI COMPANY
Income Statement (Actual Absorption Costing)
For the Month Ending October 31, 19x2

	Production	
	600 Units	400 Units
Revenue	$ 30,000	$ 30,000
Cost of goods sold	(14,600)	(16,600)
Gross margin	$ 15,400	$ 13,400
Selling and general expenses	(13,000)	(13,000)
Income before tax	$ 2,400	$ 400

In our earlier illustration, we calculated income before taxes for variable costing of $2,000. The reconciliation of absorption-costing income before taxes to variable-costing income before taxes follows essentially the same format as that used for reconciling cost of goods sold:

	600 Units	400 Units
Income before tax—Absorption costing	$2,400	$ 400
Add: Fixed costs brought into period through beginning inventory (100 units × $16)	1,600	1,600
	$4,000	$2,000
Less: Fixed costs deferred in ending inventory (200 units × $10)	2,000	–0–
Income before tax—Variable costing	$2,000	$2,000

Once again, the general conclusion holds: under absorption costing, the greater the increase of production over sales, the higher the reported income before taxes. This is true whether the overhead is applied on a normalized or an actual basis.

The same general results hold whether the company uses a FIFO, a LIFO, or an average cost-flow assumption. The calculations involved are more complex with LIFO and an average cost method. Therefore, we will not demonstrate them here.

In practice, a large majority of manufacturers use absorption costing for both internal and external financial reporting. As we have illustrated in this section, absorption-costing income changes as the production plans change.

SUPPORT FOR VARIABLE AND ABSORPTION COSTING

Do not be confused by arguments defending variable or absorption costing. These arguments are often based on different assumptions which, by the way, are often unstated or misstated in an attempt to sway attention one way or the other. The discussion below is an attempt to help you to understand and appreciate the arguments.

Arguments Supporting Variable Costing

Under absorption costing, fixed production costs are included in ending inventory in the balance sheet. If production is higher than sales, a higher amount of fixed production costs is allocated to ending inventories (an asset account) and a lesser amount to Cost of Goods Sold. The result is a higher net income. Managers should not be rewarded with higher net income for increasing inventory without increasing sales.

Because variable production costs are avoidable, they should be included in inventory. In the choice of how much inventory to hold to support sales, managers should focus on how much they have to invest in the inventory. The difference in cash requirements for investing in a large inventory versus a smaller inventory is only the variable costs of production. Managers may be misled as to the amount they have invested in inventory items by the amount of the fixed cost included in traditional accounting.

This overstatement of investment may also mislead the managers who use these costs as a baseline for assessing product pricing policies with a resultant move toward higher prices. Consequently, sales may be lost, especially to foreign competitors. Consider the example of computer-integrated chips. They require very little variable cost to manufacture but are recorded in inventory at a high cost because of the large plant and equipment required for production. This has misled an entire industry into overpricing their products and thus being less able to compete with Japan. Japanese industry uses a variable-costing approach and emphasizes a market share orientation. Under variable costing, the managers would clearly see that the chips require only pennies to produce, not dollars.

Another argument in favor of variable costing is the relationship between the direction of sales changes and that of net income changes. Most accountants and managers intuitively expect any increase (or decrease) in sales to result in an increase (or decrease) in net income. This happens under variable costing. With absorption costing, the direction and amount of change in net income depends on the difference between production and sales. It is therefore possible to have a sales increase but a net income decrease under absorption costing.

Arguments Supporting Absorption Costing

Traditions are difficult to change because they require unlearning the current system, which may be poorly understood, and then learning a new system. Managers now accept, even if they do not fully understand, the absorption-costing approach. The variable-costing approach would require a significant change in outlook and attitudes of managers and accountants.

Absorption costing is required for external financial reports and for compliance with federal income tax law. Because one set of records on an absorption-costing basis must be kept, another set of records on a variable-costing basis will have to be generated. This extra recordkeeping is not worth the cost. Further, having both accounting systems would be confusing to many managers.

Because senior management will be evaluated by investors using the external reports, management will naturally turn to reports based on external methods (i.e., absorption costing) in evaluating subordinates. Because people tend to respond to the reports on which they are evaluated, the subordinates will turn to the absorption-costing reports for their decision-making. Therefore, the only thing that implementing variable costing can accomplish is the employment of more accountants.

All costs are variable and avoidable at some level in the company and over a long enough time period. Arguments supporting variable costing use the time period of a month or a year in their examples because these coincide with the performance measurements of managers. However, performance evaluation of managers should be over a long time horizon—say three to five years—rather than one month or one year. The so-called fixed production costs allocated to products are a measure of the long-run costs of production.

The concept of variable versus fixed production costs is a fiction developed by economists for short-term analysis. Unlike textbook examples, labor and materials cannot be turned on and off like a water tap. Skilled factory workers are rarely let go under normal conditions—only a portion of direct labor is variable during the current month. Further, materials are often purchased on long-term contracts to get the best price. Contracts will specify the availability, volume, and cost of the materials. Thus, material costs are not completely variable. In the current production environment, factories are called upon to produce many goods with few people and fewer mistakes. This requires that managers focus more on capacities than flow. Managers should look at materials, jobs, equipment, and space as capacities that need to be simplified for the production of many products and services. Variable costs, per se, are virtually irrelevant. Instead, the manager should focus on capacity costs and utilization.

Variable- and Absorption-Costing Arguments

A case can be made for either variable or absorption costing. Although there are contradictions between and within arguments, the primary differences are:

1. *Short term versus long term.* Variable costers focus on the short-term consequences of accounting; the absorption costers assume that long-run performance is important.
2. *Behavior of managers.* Variable costers assume that managers can easily adapt to a new accounting method with little cost. They argue further that managers will be rewarded for playing games with absorption reports. Those who support absorption costing do not deny that an occasional short-term decision (i.e., amount of ending inventory to hold) will be made incorrectly. Over the long term, the mistakes will be more obvious and the ''games'' will be found out by competent superiors. The absorption costers might assert that incompetent managers cannot be suddenly cured by a change in accounting methods.
3. *Variable versus fixed costs.* Variable costers assume that costs can be easily and meaningfully divided into categories of variable and fixed. Absorption costers do not see this as important or meaningful for reporting purposes. Absorption costers also recognize the difficulty in making the separation.
4. *External versus internal reports.* Variable costers do not consider the external reporting approach to be important, or they argue that it is invalid. Absorption costers argue that the external approach will determine what is possible for internal reports. Adopting anything other than external reporting methods for internal reporting will be a harmful, futile exercise.

The different assumptions are neither correct nor incorrect. However, they are more or less consistent with the observed world of management. As a consequence, variable- and absorption-costing methods will be more or less useful in practice, depending upon how well the assumptions apply to a specific organization. In other words, in some companies a variable cost accounting system will be very useful and in other companies it will be a failure.

You should also notice that the difference between variable and absorption costing disappears if there is little or no inventory of work in process or finished goods. Thus, the arguments are of little consequence for service companies. Further, current movements to eliminate inventories also result in less difference in substance between the two methods.

SUMMARY

Variable costing includes only variable production costs as part of the cost of goods produced. The traditional method of accounting is called *absorption* (or *full*) *costing*, which includes fixed production costs as part of inventory cost. In comparing variable and absorption costing, we found that the relationship between production and sales (that is, inventory changes) has a bearing on the income differences of the two methods. Any time inventories are increasing, absorption costing yields a higher income; when inventories are decreasing, variable costing results in higher income. We presented arguments supporting each technique, formats for income statements, and the reconciliation of differences in income.

PROBLEM FOR REVIEW

The Congole Corp. makes high-precision rifles in its HPR Division in Butte, Montana. The rifles have the following normal price and cost structure:

Price		$150
Materials	$30	
Labor	20	
Overhead	40	90
Gross margin		$ 60

During the month of October 19x4, the HPR Division sold 10,000 rifles and manufactured 20,000. Variable selling costs are $10 per rifle, and fixed selling and general costs are $200,000 per month. The overhead application rate includes 50 percent fixed production costs. Total fixed production costs are $400,000 per month.

REQUIRED

a. Prepare an absorption-costing and a variable-costing income statement for the division.
b. Reconcile the difference in income.

SOLUTION

a. Absorption and variable costing.

CONGOLE CORPORATION
HPR Division
Income Statements
For the Month Ending October 31, 19x2

Variable Costing		*Absorption costing*	
Revenue	$1,500,000	Revenue	$1,500,000
Variable costs:			
Variable production	(700,000)	Cost of goods sold	(900,000)
Variable selling	(100,000)		
Contribution margin	$ 700,000	Gross margin	$ 600,000
Fixed costs:		Expenses:	
Production	(400,000)	Selling, variable	(100,000)
Selling and general	(200,000)	Selling and general	(200,000)
Income before tax	$ 100,000	Income before tax	$ 300,000

b.

Variable costing income		$100,000
Change in inventory	10,000	
Fixed overhead rate	$20	
Change in fixed overhead deferred		200,000
Absorption costing income		$300,000

KEY TERMS AND CONCEPTS

Variable costing (653)
Absorption costing (653)

ADDITIONAL READINGS

Ajinkya, Bipin; Rowland Atiase; and Linda Smith Bamber. "Absorption versus Direct Costing: Income Reconciliation and Cost-Volume-Profit Analysis." *Issues in Accounting Education*, Fall 1986, pp. 268–81.

Bruegelmann, Thomas W.; Gaile A. Haessly; Claire P. Wolfangel; and Michael Schiff. "How Variable Costing Is Used in Pricing Decisions." *Management Accounting*, April 1985, pp. 58–61, 65.

Chen, Joyce T. "Full and Direct Costing in Profit Variance Analysis." *Issues in Accounting Education*, Fall 1986, pp. 282–92.

Lere, John C. "Product Pricing Based on Accounting Costs." *The Accounting Review*, April 1986, pp. 318–24.

Schiff, Michael. "Variable Costing: A Closer Look." *Management Accounting*, February 1987, pp. 36–39.

Seed, Allen H., III. "Cost Accounting in the Age of Robotics." *Management Accounting*, October 1984, pp. 39–43.

REVIEW QUESTIONS

1. What is the basic difference between variable costing and absorption costing?
2. Explain how fixed production costs are shifted from one period to the next under absorption costing.
3. If production equals sales, which method would have the higher net income, variable costing or absorption costing? Explain.
4. If production exceeds sales, which method would have the higher net income, variable costing or absorption costing? Explain.
5. If sales exceed production, which method would have the higher net income, variable costing or absorption costing? Explain.
6. How is it possible to increase net income using absorption costing when sales are not increasing?
7. Can variable costing be used in an actual cost system as well as a normal cost system? Explain.
8. In what ways does the format of a variable-costing income statement differ from an income statement prepared under absorption costing?
9. What is the formula for the reconciliation of absorption-costing income with variable-costing income?
10. Where does the effect of absorption costing appear in the balance sheet?
11. Compare a contribution margin for variable costing with a gross margin for absorption costing.
12. List the arguments in favor of variable costing.
13. List the arguments in favor of absorption costing.

DISCUSSION QUESTIONS

14. A company had a highly labor-intensive manufacturing process. Recently, it implemented robotics and a number of other technology changes that made the process capital intensive. What impact would this change make on the inventory valuations for variable costing and for absorption costing?

15. Assume that you are using a standard cost system. Looking at two-, three-, and four-variance approaches, which variance(s) would you calculate for absorption costing that you would not calculate for variable costing?

16. How is it possible to show a profit under absorption costing but a loss with variable costing? Comment.

17. In actual settings, companies have hundreds or thousands of different products. Many production plants, warehouses, and sales districts are each evaluated by the accounting reports. Managers are monitoring operations via reports from remote locations. Describe the forces in this setting that tend to resist the adoption of a variable-costing approach.

18. In what ways might variable costing be better suited for managerial use in profit planning, control, and decision-making? In what ways might absorption costing be better suited for those purposes?

19. Organizations are currently attempting to be more cost competitive on world markets by simplifying their products, production processes, and organizational structures. They are dropping unprofitable products that are a lot of bother. At the same time, production plants are implementing computer-aided manufacturing that allows them to change from one product to another with no loss in production time.
    a. Discuss how these two movements can result in conflicts between the movement to reduce and simplify on the one hand and the movement to computerize and speed up changeovers on the other. (*Hint:* Remember your personal experiences with computers and changing technology!)
    b. Discuss how the two movements support each other.

EXERCISES

16–1. Variable/Absorption Costing. Leslie Moore Co. produces a single product, a vibrating sofa chair. During 19x4, the following activities and costs occurred.

Sales	75,000 units at	$	125.00
Units produced	100,000		
Costs per unit	Materials		16.75
	Labor		18.00
	Variable overhead		15.00
	Variable selling and administration		12.50
Fixed costs	Production overhead		1,000,000
	Selling and general		800,000

REQUIRED:
a. Prepare an income statement using the variable-costing format.
b. Prepare an income statement using the absorption-costing format.

16–2. Variable/Absorption Costing. Galvs Mine outside of Wind Town, Michigan, has the following information regarding the production of copper for May 19x3.

		Per Unit	*Fixed*
Sales	300,000 units at	$70.00	
Units produced	400,000		
Production	Materials	2.00	
	Labor	20.00	
	Variable overhead	20.00	
	Royalty	14.00	
	Production overhead		$4,000,000

Each unit consists of 100 pounds of copper molded into a cube for shipping. Other expenses associated with the mine are:

	Per Unit	*Fixed*
Variable selling and administration	$3.00	
Selling and general		$300,000

REQUIRED:

a. Prepare an income statement using the variable-costing format.
b. Prepare an income statement using the absorption-costing format.

16–3. Variable/Absorption Costing.   Jason Han Crystal Company produces a single product, Jasonium, a crystal used in the treatment of liver and related cancers. The crystals are grown from a special mixture in a highly automated plant in Brownfield, Texas. A partial income statement for 19x1 was:

JASON HAN CRYSTAL COMPANY
Income Statement
For the Year Ending December 31, 19x1

Revenues		$5,000,000
Cost of goods sold		3,000,000
Gross margin		$2,000,000
Selling expenses	$500,000	
Administrative expenses	800,000	1,300,000
Income before tax		$ 700,000

During the year, 100,000 units were sold and 200,000 were produced. The cost of goods sold includes $10 per unit variable costs and $20 per unit fixed costs. The selling expenses are all variable, and the administrative expenses are all fixed. There were no beginning inventories.

REQUIRED:

Prepare an income statement using the variable costing concept.

16–4. Contribution Margin.   Webber Manufacturing Company sold 130,000 units of product during the period at a price of $8 per unit. The variable production cost for the period totaled $340,000. The fixed production cost was $160,000. The variable selling and administrative expenses were $2 per unit sold. Fixed selling and administrative expenses were $80,000.

REQUIRED:

Prepare an income statement showing the manufacturing margin, the contribution margin, and net income.

16–5 Net Income Differences.   The president of Poage Enterprises has been examining past income statement data in an attempt to estimate net income expected for next year. Past data are given as follows:

	19x5	*19x6*	*19x7*
Number of units sold	8,000	10,000	7,000
Selling price per unit	$120	$120	$120
Variable cost per unit	$ 80	$ 80	$ 80
Fixed cost per unit	$ 15	$ 15	$ 15

The fixed cost per unit was computed at a normal operating level of 10,000 units. Actual fixed cost has equaled budgeted fixed cost for each of the three years and is expected to remain at the same level next year. The president estimates that 9,000 units will be sold in 19x8 with no other changes expected. Although normal capacity is at 10,000 units, production has been at 9,000 units for the three years and is expected to run at 9,000 units in 19x8.

REQUIRED:

a. Show the net income for each of the years 19x5, 19x6, and 19x7 using:
   1. Variable costing.
   2. Absorption costing.
b. Calculate the anticipated net income for 19x8 using:
   1. Variable costing.
   2. Absorption costing.

16–6. Variable Costing and Pricing Policy.   Karen Shaver has found that variable costing has helped her to price products. She knows that she can reduce prices to the point at which her store will recover more than the variable cost and that profit will increase when she gets more sales volume as a result of underselling the competitors. Data for the recent two years are below.

	19x8	*19x9*
Sales volume	50,000	80,000
Selling price per unit	$25	$20
Variable cost per unit	$15	$15
Total fixed costs	$300,000	$300,000

Next year, she plans to sell 120,000 units for $18 per unit. The cost structure is not expected to change.

REQUIRED:

a. How much net income was realized in each of the years 19x8 and 19x9, assuming variable costing?
b. How much net income can be expected in the next year, 19x0, assuming variable costing?
c. Comment on the policy Karen is following.

PROBLEMS

16–7. Variable/Absorption Costing.   CTC, Inc., assembles calculators from standard components. It has kept overhead and fixed costs very low by subcontracting all fabrication work. CTC grew rapidly during the past 15 years, but its growth has moderated during the past 3 years.

The calculator business is experiencing rapid change in technology. Thus, the company must continually develop new products and cut prices on old ones in order to maintain a competitive position. Management is currently considering the addition of lower-priced and higher-priced lines. Some basic data on the proposals include:

	Total fixed manufacturing	$336,000
	Total fixed selling	110,000

	Lower-Price (Proposed)	*Current Line*	*Higher-Price (Proposed)*
Volumes			
Normal volume	200,000	120,000	60,000
Expected 19x3 sales	180,000	115,000	72,000
19x3 planned units	190,000	135,000	77,000
Per Unit:			
Selling price	$5.00	$10.00	$15.00
Materials	2.00	4.00	8.00
Direct labor	0.30	0.50	0.80
Variable overhead	0.15	0.25	0.40
Fixed overhead	0.60	1.00	1.60
Variable selling	0.50	1.00	1.50
Fixed Costs:			
Traceable manufacturing costs	$ 4,000	$28,000	$26,000
Traceable selling cost	12,000	20,000	30,000

Mr. David Astab, president and CEO, likes this proposal because the current model will be more profitable and the product line will be broader. Without the two new product lines, the fixed overhead application rate would be $1.15 per unit on the current model. There are no beginning inventories. The traceable fixed costs are included in the total fixed costs applied to products.

(R. Gonzales; A. Chang; and H. Van Lare, adapted)

REQUIRED:

a. For the planned production and sales, prepare a pro forma statement of income assuming the variable-costing concept. (The report presentation need not include product-line performance.)

b. For the planned production and sales, prepare a pro forma statement of income assuming the absorption-costing concept. (The report presentation need not include product-line performance.)

16–8. Variable/Absorption Costing with Actual/Normal Costs.   The Martin Company has production and operation information for the year ending December 31, 19x7:

Sales	3200 units at	$250
Production costs:		
Direct materials	50 per unit	
Direct labor	36 per unit	
Variable production overhead	4 per unit	
Actual fixed production overhead (total)		$240,000
Selling and administrative costs:		
Variable selling costs	25 per unit	
Fixed (total)		160,000

Units produced for the year totaled 4,000. There were no beginning inventories.

(R. Sargent, adapted)

REQUIRED:

a. Using actual production costs, prepare an income statement under:
  1. Absorption costing.
  2. Variable costing.

b. Assume that planned fixed production costs were $240,000 and normal activity is 6,000 units. Prepare an income statement under:
  1. Absorption costing.
  2. Variable costing.

c. Summarize the effects of actual and normal costs on the difference between variable- and absorption-costing net income.

16–9. Variable/Absorption Costing.   The Seattle Pow Algon Division manufactures solid explosives used in large construction projects. The explosives are concentrated and very powerful. The product is produced on a highly automated line. A unit of the finished product consists of a 20-pound case containing 40 eight-ounce containers. The standard costs for a unit of the product are:

Materials	$ 85
Labor	22
Overhead	220
Total	$327

The overhead charge includes $160 in fixed costs for the production line. The standard was based on the production of 8,000 units of the product per month.

The product sells for $450 per 20-pound unit. Selling and general expenses associated with the product are $120,000 in fixed costs per month plus $50 in variable costs per unit. There are 4,000 units in beginning inventory. The company follows the policy of closing all standard cost variances to Cost of Goods Sold each month.

REQUIRED:
a. Given production of 7,500 units and sale of 6,000 units for the month of April 19x4, compute the income from operation using the absorption-costing method.
b. Given production of 7,500 units and sale of 6,000 units for the month of April 19x4, compute the income from operations using the variable-costing method.
c. Reconcile the difference between absorption and variable costing.

16–10. Variable/Absorption Costing. Whiteline Foamer Co. of Des Moines, Iowa, produces a concentrated liquid that foams when it is mixed with water. This white foam is used to mark the width of the fertilizer and chemicals applied to crops. Whiteline is in a competitive industry; its product is distinguished by the fact that the liquid, although more expensive, is four times more concentrated than others and the farmer needs to replace the canister only once per month.

Presently, the company uses the absorption-costing technique, but it is considering changing internal reporting to the variable-costing basis. During July 19x7, the company produced 20,000 canisters of Whiteline but sold 23,000. The beginning inventory was 6,000 units. The normal production volume is 22,000 units per month, and management has established the following standards:

Direct materials		$20
Direct labor		15
Factory overhead:	Variable	3
	Fixed	2
Total cost		$40

The variable marketing and administrative expenses are $1.80 per unit, and the fixed administrative expenses are $26,400. The selling price averages $50.

(C. Seely; A. Evans; and P. Anne, adapted)

REQUIRED:
Prepare projected income statements for July 19x7 under:
a. Absorption costing (assume beginning inventory is valued at $40 per unit).
b. Variable costing (assume beginning inventory is valued at $38 per unit).

16–11. Absorption and Variable Costing Reconciled. Mooney Company has just completed three years of operations. Valerie Mooney, president, has reviewed the audited financial statements for those three years and compared the results to the income statements prepared internally by the chief accountant. She notices a different net income figure for years 2 and 3 between the audited statements and the internal statements. The chief accountant told her the audited income statements were prepared under absorption costing and the internal statements were prepared under variable costing. Mooney has asked you to prepare a summary for the three years that reconciles the differences between the two costing methods.

The operating information for the three years is as follows:

Selling price per unit:		$14
Production costs:		
Direct materials cost per unit		$2.90
Direct labor cost per unit		$1.30
Variable overhead cost per unit		$0.60
Fixed costs		$144,000
Selling and administrative expenses:		
Variable costs		30% of sales
Fixed costs		$38,000

Units:	Year 1	Year 2	Year 3
Sales	50,000	40,000	60,000
Production	50,000	60,000	50,000

The company uses an actual cost system and assumes a FIFO method for costing inventories.

REQUIRED:

a. Prepare a three-year comparative income statement using absorption costing.

b. Prepare a three-year comparative income statement using variable costing.

c. Reconcile the net income figures of absorption costing and variable costing for each of the three years.

d. Plot on a graph the points for net income and sales units assuming absorption costing and then assuming variable costing. Explain why the absorption-costing net income does not vary in direct proportion to changes in sales units.

16–12. Net Income under Variable Costing.   The Southwest Center for Accounting Education conducts CPA review courses and markets a CPA review book. The book has been a real money-maker over the last few years. However, sales of the book have recently decreased noticeably. The manager is not certain whether the decrease is due to an economic downturn in the region or to dissatisfaction with the book.

The variable costs to produce each book are as follows:

Direct materials	$ 8.00
Direct labor	4.00
Variable overhead	6.00
Total	$18.00

Fixed overhead is $24,000 per year; selling and administrative expenses are $2.00 per book sold plus $12,000 of fixed cost per year. The selling price per book is $35. Actual data relating to inventories and sales for February, March, and April are below.

	February	March	April
Beginning inventory	–0–	2,000	3,000
Books printed	6,000	4,000	2,000
Books sold	4,000	3,000	1,000
Ending inventory	2,000	3,000	4,000

The company uses an actual cost system for recording costs of inventories.

REQUIRED:

a. Calculate the net income for the three months using variable costing.

b. Calculate the net income for the three months using absorption costing.

c. Prepare a reconciliation for the difference between the net income under each method.

16–13. Profit Planning.   Tony Ortiz is experienced in assembling IBM-compatible PC clones. He has decided to open his own business to supply computers to the expanding educational market. He has asked members of his family to join with him in this undertaking.

Tony has identified three configurations that seem to have the greatest possibilities in the marketplace. The prices and costs of the three models, together with assembly times, appear below:

	Models		
	PC–1	PC–2	PC–3
Unit selling price	$600	$1,100	$1,600
Unit variable cost	300	650	1,200
Unit contribution margin	$300	$ 450	$ 400
Assembly time per unit	$\frac{2}{3}$ hour	$1\frac{1}{2}$ hours	1 hour

Only 8,000 hours are available for productive operations. The fixed costs of production are estimated at $185,000 per year, and the fixed costs of selling and administration are estimated at $30,000 per year.

Market studies show that the company could sell 6,000 PC–1, 5,000 PC–2, and 4,500 PC–3 during its first year of operations. These quantities should grow by 10 percent in years 2 and 3. The costs to deliver each unit will amount to $25. Tony believes he can deliver or ship PCs as quickly as assembly is completed; no inventories of finished PCs are anticipated.

Tony is trying to complete his business plan so he can finalize the initial financing arrangements with his bank. As a part of this planning, Tony needs a profit plan that shows his expected operations for the year. An older brother suggests that in order to find the full unit cost of each PC, the fixed production costs must be allocated to the units produced at predetermined normal level of operation. A young sister states that this won't be necessary for profit planning. For this purpose, she said, it is more important to know how much each unit can contribute to the operation with fixed costs deducted in total.

REQUIRED:
a. How would you treat the fixed costs in this profit-planning situation? Explain.
b. For each of the three years, determine the optimal combination of PC–1, PC–2, and PC–3 that the company should produce and sell.
c. Using the variable-costing approach, prepare income statements for each of the three years.

16–14. Standard Variable-Costing Income Statement.   Bolin Company uses variable costing with its standard cost system. Karl Bolin, president, says the company can operate at 30,000 machine hours per month with the following standard costs for production:

Standard costs per unit:	
Direct materials	$ 2.00
Direct labor	8.00
Variable overhead (4 machine hours required)	4.00
	$14.00

Fixed production overhead is budgeted at $60,000 per month. Fixed selling and administrative expenses are budgeted at $10,000 per month.

During the month of August, the company sold 5,500 units of finished product at $40 each. Actual costs for the month are:

Direct materials used	$12,820
Direct labor	47,400
Variable overhead	25,300
Fixed overhead	60,000
Variable selling and administrative	30,780
Fixed selling and administrative	10,000

There were no inventories of work in process or finished goods at the beginning of the month. During the month, the company completed 6,000 units and had 200 units in ending work in process inventory. These partially completed units had all of their material costs and were 80 percent complete for conversion costs.

REQUIRED:
a. Calculate total variances for material, labor, and variable overhead.
b. Prepare an income statement using variable costing showing actual and standard costs with variances. (Indicate whether variances are unfavorable or favorable.)
c. Without preparing an income statement, show the amount of net income that would appear under absorption costing.

16–15. Profit Decrease with Sales Increase.   Sun Company, a wholly owned subsidiary of Guardian, Inc., produces and sells three main product lines. The company employs a standard cost accounting system for recordkeeping purposes.

At the beginning of 19x4, the president of Sun Company presented the budget to the parent company and accepted a commitment to contribute $15,800 to Guardian's consolidated profit in 19x4. The president has been confident that the year's profit would exceed budget target because the monthly sales reports that he has been receiving have shown that sales for the year will exceed budget by 10 percent. The president was both disturbed and confused when the controller presented an adjusted forecast as of November 30, 19x4, indicating that profit will be 11 percent under budget. The two forecasts are presented below:

SUN COMPANY
Forecasts of Operating Results

	Forecasts as of	
	1/1/x4	11/30/x4
Sales	$268,000	$294,800
Cost of sales at standard	212,000*	233,200
Gross margin at standard	$ 56,000	$ 61,600
Over/underabsorbed fixed manufacturing overhead	—	6,000
Actual gross margin	$ 56,000	$ 55,600
Selling expenses	$ 13,400	$ 14,740
Administrative expenses	26,800	26,800
Total operating expenses	$ 40,200	$ 41,540
Earnings before tax	$ 15,800	$ 14,060

* Includes fixed manufacturing overhead of $30,000.

There have been no sales price changes or product mix shifts since the 1/1/x4 forecast. The only cost variance on the income statement is the underabsorbed manufacturing overhead. This arose because the company produced only 16,000 standard machine hours (budgeted machine hours were 20,000) during 19x4 as a result of a shortage of raw materials while its principal supplier was closed by a strike. Fortunately, Sun Company's finished goods inventory was large enough to fill all sales orders received.

(CMA, adapted)

REQUIRED:

a. Analyze and explain why the profit has declined in spite of increased sales and good control over costs.

b. What plan, if any, could Sun Company adopt during December to improve its reported profit at year end? Explain.

c. Illustrate and explain how Sun Company could adopt an alternative internal cost reporting procedure that would avoid the confusing effect of the present practice.

d. Would the alternative procedure described in part *(c)* be acceptable to Guardian, Inc., for financial reporting purposes? Explain.

EXTENDED APPLICATIONS

16–16. Variable/Absorption Costing. Jack Stern is a successful investor whose specialty is revitalizing failed businesses. His goal is to maximize his profits within the limits of careful use of external financing, which usually means limiting growth rates and foregoing some potential profit. Stern believes this is the key to his success and that unlimited growth can easily lead to fatal financing problems. Stern is once again set to test his approach.

Five years ago, Robert West perfected a technique for joining the edges of laminated plastic parts so that the edges of subsurface layers were not visible. Since subsurface layers are a different color than the surface layer, West's edges greatly improved the appearance of the finished product. West then designed equipment that permitted large volume production of the edges. West's product was unique, and sales and production levels grew rapidly. Rapid growth, however, soon exceeded West's management ability and his ability to obtain financing. A few months ago, West's firm closed, leaving a regional bank holding the plant, equipment, and some inventory.

Stern believes that the product has sales and profit potential and has offered the bank $400,000 in cash plus assumption of the loan for the plant, equipment, and inventory. The bank accepted Stern's offer.

Stern has established Edge Company and contributed to it the acquired assets and $450,000 in cash. Edge Company's statement of financial position at the start of business is presented below.

THE EDGE COMPANY, INC.
Statement of Financial Position
As of January 1, 19x7
(in thousands)

Assets	
Cash	$ 450
Accounts receivable	0
Inventory	100
Plant and equipment	2,000
Total assets	$2,550
Liabilities and equities	
Accounts payable	$ 0
Current portion of long-term debt	90
Long-term debt	1,610
Common stock (no par value)	850
Retained earnings	0
Total liabilities and equities	$2,550

To implement his goal of making conservative use of external financing, Stern has established the following financial objectives:

- Paying no dividends, thus keeping all cash generated within the company.
- Issuing no additional capital stock.
- Incurring no new long-term debt while servicing current interest and $90,000 of principal annually on the existing bank loan.
- Keeping the cash balance at no less than $50,000.
- Taking advantage of supplier credit but not allowing accounts payable to exceed $100,000.

The bank's loan officer had commented that West was unable to control costs and working capital, and Stern agreed. He plans to hold variable costs at 75 percent of sales. Even though the existing plant and equipment have a capacity of $12,000,000 in annual sales, Stern's plan is to budget a lump sum of $500,000 per year for fixed costs, including both depreciation and interest. Depreciation of plant and equipment is $100,000 per year.

In making his plans, Stern has used 20 percent as the average income tax rate applicable to Edge Company. Because some of the firms he acquires have been in income tax trouble, Stern makes a point of keeping tax payments current and aims to finish each year with no tax liability on the books.

Customers for products of this kind are notoriously slow payers; however, Stern is confident that accounts receivable can be kept at 15 percent of annual sales. He also believes that inventories can be maintained at 20 percent of annual variable costs.

Some of West's former sales people have been rehired, and they feel that Edge Company's first year sales could easily reach $5,000,000. But Stern believes that managing growth is the most important part of the plan, and he plans to limit first year sales to $2,100,000.

(CMA, adapted)

REQUIRED:

a. Determine whether Jack Stern's financial objectives can be achieved by preparing a pro forma income statement in a variable (direct) costing format for the Edge Company for the year ending December 31, 19x7, and a pro forma statement of financial position for the Edge Company as of December 31, 19x7. Assume that Jack Stern's projections occur and sales are limited to $2,100,000.

b. Without prejudice to requirement *(a)* above, assume that the following results from the company's first fiscal year ending December 31, 19x7, occurred, and that Jack Stern's financial objectives were met.

- Sales: $2,000,000.
- Net income: $0.
- Cash balance at December 31, 19x7: $60,000.
- Accounts payable at December 31, 19x7: $100,000.
- Net working capital at December 31, 19x7: $470,000.

Compute the maximum amount by which Edge Company could increase dollar sales in its second year (ending December 31, 19x8) and still achieve Jack Stern's financial objectives.

Cost-Volume-Profit Analysis with Absorption Costing

After studying this appendix, you should be able to:

1. Prepare a cost-volume-profit analysis under an absorption-costing system.

The equation we presented in Chapter 4 for cost-volume-profit analysis was:

$$\text{Sales} - \text{Variable costs} - \text{Fixed costs} = \text{Income before tax}$$

From this equation we found that the formula for required volume was:

$$\text{Volume} = \frac{(\text{Fixed cost} + \text{Desired profit})}{\text{Contribution margin}}$$

This equation and formula have all of the key components used in the variable-costing method. We already know that when inventories do not change (i.e., production and sales volumes are equal), variable- and absorption-costing net incomes are equal. Thus, we were able to use the equation and formula with absorption costing by assuming that inventories did not change. This was convenient.

If sales do not equal production, the income statement equation and the required volume formula must be adjusted. With absorption costing, some current fixed production costs are placed into the Inventory account and are deferred to future years when ending inventories increase over beginning inventories. For an illustration, consider a specific setting.

Analysis Setting

Assume the same data for the Hyde Ski Company as for the example in the chapter. Based on that data, the contribution margin is $40:

Price		$60
Less variable costs:		
Materials	$12	
Labor	4	
Variable overhead	2	
Selling and administrative	2	(20)
Contribution margin		$40

Fixed production costs are $6,000 per month, and fixed selling and administrative costs are $12,000 per month. Further, assume that Hyde Ski has a required income before tax of $4,000.

Equation Method

When inventories are allowed to change, we shift the equation format to an absorption-costing income statement:

$$\text{Sales} - \text{Cost of goods sold} - \text{Expenses} = \text{Income before tax}$$

For convenience, we will shorten the equation to:

674

$$S - CGS - E = IBT$$

The cost of goods sold consists of variable costs of production, fixed production costs applied to sales, and underapplied (or overapplied[1]) overhead. Selling expenses include both variable costs for each unit and fixed costs. Letting Q be the volume measure, we convert the components to the following symbols:

$$S = SP \times Q$$
$$CGS = (VCMU \times Q) + (FCMU \times Q) + Und\ OH$$
$$E = (VCSU \times Q) + FSC$$

where

$$VCMU = \text{Variable cost of manufacturing per unit}$$
$$FCMU = \text{Fixed cost of manufacturing applied per unit}$$
$$Und\ OH = \text{Underapplied overhead}$$
$$VCSU = \text{Variable selling cost per unit}$$
$$FSC = \text{Fixed selling and administrative costs}$$

Our equation can now be expanded to:

$$(SP \times Q) - [(VCMU \times Q) + (FCMU \times Q) + Und\ OH]$$
$$- [(VCSU \times Q) + FSC] = IBT$$

This equation assumes that under/overapplied overhead is closed to Cost of Goods Sold.

For the Hyde Ski Company, the data can be substituted as follows:

$$(\$60 \times Q) - (\$18 \times Q) - (\$10 \times Q)$$
$$- Und\ OH - (\$2 \times Q) - \$12,000 = \$4,000$$

Simplifying this long equation and solving for Q:

$$(\$30 \times Q) - Und\ OH = \$16,000$$
$$Q = 533\ \tfrac{1}{3} + \left[\frac{Und\ OH}{\$30} \right]$$

Remember that the underapplied overhead will depend on the number of skis produced rather than sold. Thus, in order to find Q, we must know the production plans of Hyde Ski. If the company produces 400 pairs of skis, the underapplied overhead will be $2,000:

$$Und\ OH = \text{Fixed production cost} - \text{Applied (i.e., FCMU} \times Q)$$
$$= \$6,000 - (\$10 \times 400) = \$2,000$$

and Q will be 600 pairs:

$$Q = 533\ \tfrac{1}{3} + \left(\frac{\$2,000}{\$30} \right) = 600$$

Inventory will have to decrease by 200 pairs of skis, which is 400 produced minus 600 pair sold. The pro forma income statement would be:

---

[1] We use underapplied in the examples. If an overapplied condition exists, it can be used in the formulas with the opposite arithmetic sign to that of underapplied overhead.

HYDE SKI COMPANY
Pro Forma Absorption Costing Income Statement
For the Month

Sales	$60 × 600		$36,000
Cost of goods sold	$28 × 600	$16,800	
Underapplied overhead		2,000	
Adjusted cost of goods			18,800
Gross margin			$17,200
Selling and administrative expenses			
Variable	$2 × 600	$ 1,200	
Fixed		12,000	13,200
Income before tax			$ 4,000

If an inventory change is planned, production will be a function of expected sales. For example, if Hyde Ski desired the inventory to decrease by 200 pairs of skis, then underapplied overhead would be a function of sales:

$$\text{Und OH} = \$6,000 - \$10 \times (Q - 200)$$

Substituting this into the equation:

$$Q = 533\,\tfrac{1}{3} + \left[\frac{\$6,000 - (\$10 \times (Q - 200))}{\$30} \right]$$

Simplifying this equation results in:

$$Q + Q/3 = 533\,\tfrac{1}{3} + (200 - 200/3) = 800$$

Solving for Q:

$$Q = 800 \times \tfrac{3}{4} = 600 \text{ pairs of skis}$$

Thus, if Hyde Ski wanted to cut its inventories by 200 pairs of skis and earn its desired profit, it would need to sell 600 pairs of skis and manufacture 400. Any given number could be substituted for the inventory change and the required sales could be found.

We will now consider the formula method for fixed production plans and for planned inventory changes.

Formula Method—Fixed Production Plans

Under absorption costing, the fixed production costs included in adjusted Cost of Goods Sold during any period are the fixed production costs applied to sales plus any underapplied factory overhead. The total fixed costs expensed, FC′, also include any fixed selling and administrative expense:

Fixed production costs applied to units sold (FCMU × Q)
+ Underapplied overhead (Und OH)

= Fixed costs in cost of goods sold
+ Fixed selling and administrative costs (FSC)

= Total fixed costs expensed (FCE)

If we put this in a symbolic form:

$$\text{FCE} = (\text{FCMU} \times Q) + \text{Und OH} + \text{FSC}$$

Now, adjusting the formula that we used earlier, we have:

$$Q = \frac{(FCE + IBT)}{CMU}$$
$$= \frac{[(FCMU \times Q) + Und\ OH + FSC + IBT]}{CMU}$$

Solving this again for Q:

$$Q = \frac{(FSC + Und\ OH + IBT)}{(CMU - FCMU)}$$

This formula states that the contribution margin per unit less the fixed manufacturing costs per unit must be enough to provide for fixed selling and administrative costs, underapplied overhead, and the required profit.

The formula above can be used when the production plan is fixed in quantity and inventory is allowed to vary to absorb sales changes. If Hyde Ski sets the production plan at 325 pairs for the coming month, then it must sell 625 pairs of skis to earn the required profit:

$$Und\ OH = \$6,000 - (\$10 \times 325) = \$2,750$$

$$Q = \frac{[\$12,000 + \$2,750 + \$4,000]}{(\$40 - \$10)} = 625$$

Hyde Ski must have an inventory at the beginning of the month of at least 300 pairs because sales will exceed production by this amount. On the other hand, if Hyde Ski were to set its production plan at 625 pairs of skis, it would have to sell only 525 pairs:

$$Und\ OH = \$6,000 - (\$10 \times 625) = -\$250$$

$$Q = \frac{[\$12,000 - \$250 + \$4,000]}{(\$40 - \$10)} = 525$$

and inventory will increase by 100 pairs. Thus, the higher the planned production units, the lower the required sales to earn a given profit. Finally, if Hyde Ski were to set the production plan at 550 pairs, it would have to sell 550 pairs:

$$Und\ OH = \$6,000 - (\$10 \times 550) = \$500$$

$$Q = \frac{[\$12,000 + \$500 + \$4,000]}{(\$40 - \$10)} = 550$$

This is the required volume when there is no change in inventory.

Formula Method—Ending Inventory Fixed

Companies may set targets for either ending inventory amounts or inventory changes. The production plan is varied to meet the sales needs. Thus, the production plan is equal to the sales plus any inventory change. In this case, a formula very similar to the original one may be used.

The fixed costs expensed will equal the total fixed costs incurred less an adjustment for inventories. We start with the same fixed cost expensed as above:

$$FCE = FSC + (FCMU \times Q) + Und\ OH$$

The underapplied overhead is found by:

$$Und\ OH = FMC - (FCMU \times R)$$

where R is the number of units produced. R is always equal to the sales units plus any unit change in inventories:

$$\text{Und OH} = \text{FMC} - [\text{FCMU} \times (Q + \text{Change in inventory})]$$

Now that we have this, we substitute the underapplied overhead into the fixed costs expensed:

$$\text{FCE} = \text{FSC} + (\text{FCMU} \times Q)$$
$$+ [\text{FMC} - (\text{FCMU} \times (Q + \text{Change in inventory}))]$$

Simplifying the relationship results in:

$$\text{FCE} = \text{FC} - [\text{FCMU} \times \text{Change in inventory}]$$

In other words, this formula says that the fixed costs expensed are equal to the fixed costs incurred less the amount deferred in the Inventory Asset account. Because the change in inventories is set by policy, we can calculate the amount of the fixed costs to be expensed. The fixed costs are then plugged into the required volume formula.

As an application of the revised formulation, assume that Hyde Ski plans to increase inventory by 100 pairs. The adjusted fixed cost is then $17,000:

$$\text{FCE} = \$18,000 - [\$10 \times 100] = \$17,000$$

The required volume is then 525 units:

$$Q = \frac{(\text{FCE} + \text{IBT})}{\text{CMU}}$$
$$= \frac{(\$17,000 + \$4,000)}{\$40} = 525 \text{ pairs}$$

If the company sells 525 units and increases inventory by 100 units, production will consist of 625 units. Fixed overhead of $6,250 ($10 × 625) will be applied to production and overapplied overhead is $250. The fixed overhead expensed will be $5,000 ($5,250 for units sold less $250 for overapplied overhead).

If Hyde Ski planned to decrease inventory by 200 units, then the required volume would be 600 pairs:

$$\text{FCE} = \$18,000 - (\$10 \times (-200)) = \$20,000$$
$$Q = \frac{(\$20,000 + \$4,000)}{\$40} = 600$$

When Hyde Ski sells 600 pairs of skis and decreases its inventories by 200 pairs, the total fixed costs expensed will be $20,000, and it will earn the required profit of $4,000.

Complications with Inventory in Practice

We have ignored many cases of inventory complexities in practice because they would unnecessarily hinder the presentation. Inventory cost-flow assumptions, such as LIFO, FIFO, and the average costs methods, were not treated. These methods would affect both variable and fixed production costs in cost of goods sold. Dealing with the differences between costs incurred and expensed with the various inventory methods is possible but challenging. Changes in inventory dollar amounts are included in the formula as a policy amount or as a function of sales. In either case, the change in inventory dollars can be approximated.

The equations and formulae presented here assume that companies generally use normal costing with its fixed rate for overhead application rather than using actual costing. If the company uses actual costing, it will have no over- or underapplied overhead. Thus, the analysis would be altered because the production costs per unit will be a function of the production volume each period. This will have an effect on required volume only when there is a change in inventory.

REVIEW QUESTIONS

1. Why does absorption costing complicate cost-volume-profit analysis?

DISCUSSION QUESTIONS

2. Develop the formulae for cost-volume-profit analysis when income is calculated with actual absorption costs using the weighted average method.
3. Why might some managers be more interested in cost-volume-profit analysis based on absorption costing than one based on just variable costs?

EXERCISES

16A–1. Absorption CVP Analysis.   Marsha Lynn Enterprises produces engines used in stock race cars. The following data apply to the year 19x3:

	Per Unit	Fixed
Selling price	$22,000	
Variable manufacturing costs	$10,000	
Fixed manufacturing costs		$300,000
Variable selling and general	$2,000	
Fixed selling and general		$100,000
Planned production	55 engines	

Fixed overhead is applied at a rate of $5,000 per unit.

REQUIRED:
a. Compute the volume required to break even for 19x3 given the planned production.
b. Compute the unit volume required to earn $100,000 before taxes for Marsha Lynn Enterprises.

16A–2. Absorption CVP Analysis.   QCT, Inc., manufactures storage bins used for grain. An income statement for 19x8 is presented below.

QCT, INC.
Income Statement
For the Year Ending December 31, 19x8

Revenues		$3,000,000
Cost of goods sold	$2,000,000	
Underapplied overhead	200,000	2,200,000
Gross margin		$ 800,000
Selling expenses	$ 200,000	
Administrative expenses	300,000	500,000
Income before tax		$ 300,000
Income taxes		120,000
Net income		$ 180,000

During 19x8, QCT, Inc., manufactured 12,000 storage bins and sold 10,000 of them. Fixed overhead is applied at a rate of $100 per bin. Normal volume is 14,000 storage bins. Selling costs are one-half variable, and administrative costs are one-third variable. Production and costs for 19x9 are expected to be similar to those for 19x8.

REQUIRED:

a. Compute the volume required to break even for 19x9 given that the planned production is fixed at 12,000 units.

b. Compute the unit sales volume required to earn $300,000 after taxes for QCT, Inc., given production of 12,000 units.

16A–3. Absorption CVP Analysis.   John Ritter, president of Wood Products Co., wants to cut inventory in half during the year 19x4 but only if profits can be held at a reasonable level. Revenues and costs are as follows:

	Per Unit	Fixed
Selling price	$2.50	
Variable manufacturing costs	$0.20	
Fixed manufacturing costs		$500,000
Variable selling and general	$0.30	
Fixed selling and general		$200,000
Normal volume	500,000 units	

The 1/1/x4 inventory is 300,000 units at $1.20, or $360,000.

REQUIRED:

a. Compute the volume required to break even for 19x4 given that the inventories will be decreased to one half of the 1/1/x4 level.

b. Compute the unit sales volume required to earn $150,000 before taxes for Wood Products Co.

PROBLEMS

16A–4. Variable/Absorption Costing and CVP Analysis.   During the month of June 19x3, the Kenley Corp. has the following activity:

Sold 78,000 pond filters at $28.00 per unit	
Manufactured 72,000 units with costs of:	
Materials	$489,600
Labor	183,600
Variable overhead	90,000
Fixed overhead	270,000
Selling and general expenses:	
Variable	186,000
Fixed	380,000

REQUIRED:

a. Assume that the beginning inventory consisted of 12,000 units with materials of $84,000, labor of $24,000, and variable overhead of $15,000.
   1. Prepare a variable-costing income statement.
   2. Compute the sales volume required to earn $500,000 in income before tax under variable costing.

b. Assume that the beginning inventory consisted of 12,000 units with materials of $84,000, labor of $24,000, variable overhead of $15,000, and fixed overhead of $168,000.
   1. Prepare an absorption-costing income statement.
   2. Compute the sales volume required to earn $500,000 in income before tax under absorption costing.

16A–5. Absorption CVP Analysis. Refer to the data in problem 16–10 for the Whiteline Foamer Co.

REQUIRED:
a. Given absorption costing and planned production of 20,000 units, compute the sales volume required to earn $90,000 after taxes. Assume a 40 percent tax rate.
b. If management desires to reduce inventories by 3,000 units, compute the sales volume required to earn $90,000 after taxes. Assume absorption costing and a tax rate of 40 percent.

16A–6. Absorption CVP Analysis. The following data relate to the budgeted activity of Denzer Company and its single product:

Beginning inventory	60,000 units	$270,000
Selling price	$8.00	
Variable production costs per unit	4.00	
Variable selling costs per unit	1.00	
Fixed production costs		$ 50,000
Fixed selling and administrative costs		70,000

All of the fixed costs remain unchanged in the relevant range of 30,000 to 180,000 units of production or sales. Normal production volume is 100,000 units.

REQUIRED:
a. Given production of 100,000 units and the use of absorption costing by the company,
   1. Compute the sales volume required to break even.
   2. At the absorption break-even volume, prepare a variable-costing income statement. Why is this income not zero?
b. Given production of 120,000 units and the use of absorption costing,
   1. Compute the sales volume required to break even.
   2. At the absorption break-even volume, prepare a variable-costing income statement. Why is this income not zero?
c. If management wishes to reduce inventories by 20,000 units, what sales volume is required to earn $240,000 after tax? Assume a tax rate of 40 percent.

16A–7. CVP Analysis with Absorption Costs. Schoenberger Corporation has the following sales and production information for the year ending December 31, 19x0:

Selling price	$20	
Per unit costs:		
Direct materials	$ 5	
Direct labor	4	
Variable production overhead	3	
Variable selling	1	
Fixed costs:		
Production	$210,000	
Selling and general expenses	160,000	
Beginning inventories 50,000 units at $13.75		$687,500

REQUIRED:
a. If management plans to produce 120,000 units and uses actual absorption costing,
   1. Prepare an income statement for sales of 110,000 units.
   2. Compute the sales volume needed to earn $500,000 in income before tax.
b. If management plans to produce 140,000 units and uses actual absorption costing,
   1. Prepare an income statement for sales of 110,000 units.
   2. Compute the sales volume needed to earn $500,000 in income before tax.
c. If management plans to produce 120,000 units and uses normal absorption costing based on 140,000 units,
   1. Prepare an income statement for sales of 110,000 units.
   2. Compute the sales volume needed to earn $500,000 in income before tax.

CHAPTER

17

Segment Performance Reporting

SEGMENT PERFORMANCE PROBLEM

Clyde Holdorf and Mike White are sitting in the Library Lounge of Chicago's Union Club. They have been friends since they played football together in college. Clyde is a successful broker on the Chicago Board of Trade. Mike is the president of Clinton Machine Tools, which is a subsidiary of RFX, Inc., based in Delaware.

Mike: Do you remember Berney, the receiver who caught three passes for touchdowns in the game with State?

Clyde: Yes. He was the leading scorer that year. Wasn't he kicked off the team for flunking history?

Mike: You've got him. I now know how he felt. There he was doing everything the university seemed to care about and then "history" walks in and nails his blind side.

Clyde: You're leading up to something.

Mike: Yeah. I'll tell it to you straight. They're going to make it sound great with a bonus and a fancy title, but I'm expected to keep my mouth shut and take a big pay cut. B. R. [B. R. "Big Red" Mclintock, chairman of RFX, Inc.] told me in so many words to "step aside for a younger person." Come on! B. R.'s 12 years older than I am.

Clyde: Do you think he's getting heat from the board and he's using you?

Mike: Yeah. Income's been down for four years now and he's probably on his way out. When he goes, I go.

Clyde: How can that be? I thought your operation was the pride of the company. Didn't you have the highest return for several years running? What happened?

Mike: Used to be the best. Every year I showed the highest return and the best performance, and I expected to replace B. R. any year. But we are talking "history" now. The last two years my operation has flunked the history test. The market for machine tools is dead.

Clyde: So what happened? You saw that coming, didn't you?

Mike: Yeah! The market started getting soft on us about seven or eight years ago, but we were top of the line, the best. Old B. R. and the rest looked only at my rate of return in evaluating me. Nothing else seemed to be important. So I pushed sales and tried every gimmick to get orders. I pushed up prices to long-time customers. I cut back on everything: engineering staff, new products. Everything went that did not show an immediate high return. I even started giving easy credit to some Central American companies. There was nothing fancy about it—I just sold for as much as I could and cut expenses.

Clyde: I'm starting to get the picture.

Mike: My pride was at stake—I wanted to stay Number One on rate of return. I didn't buy much new equipment. I even cut maintenance. I used my connections with headquarters to force other subsidiaries to buy my products at an inflated cost plus a profit margin. This forced their profits down and mine up. You know how competitive I am—I just had to score the best.

About three years ago, headquarters started to pull in the reins. It started with a few rules and policies. Then there were more rules. Eighteen months ago they had control of everything. I had to ask permission to buy a machine, to hire a person, or to develop a new product. They clamped down on my pricing to other divisions. They left me no room at all.

Now I wish I'd gone for the best engineers, best MBAs, and pumped more money into new products before it was too late. There would have been more expenses, but I could have been out of machine tools and into something else by now and sitting strong. Instead, my operation is down to 1,800 people and falling. I have some plants that look like grave yards at midnight.

Clyde: What a shame. Do you have any immediate plans?

Mike: Yes. I have two tickets for the Michigan game. How are you set for Saturday?

LEARNING OBJECTIVES

After completing this chapter, you should be able to:

1. Distinguish between performance measurement and performance evaluation.
2. Distinguish between segment performance and manager performance.
3. Distinguish among the four traditional types of segments: cost centers, revenue centers, profit centers, and investment centers.
4. List and briefly discuss the long-term consequences of using short-term performance measures such as profit or return on investment.
5. Distinguish between decentralizing an organization's decision process and establishing profit or investment segments.

For control purposes, a **segment** of an organization is any portion whose performance is evaluated on a regular basis. Common segments are called *sections, groups, departments, branches,* and *divisions.* Large organizations segment their operations into subsidiaries, which are legally separate entities.

An organization employing 100,000 or more people would be unmanageable without segmentation. Segmentation breaks the organization down into manageable pieces with a person assigned to each piece. Performance measurement and evaluation are very important for purposes of controlling large organizations.

As illustrated in the introductory case, managers are very competitive people who keep score and like to win. Consequently, the manner in which performance is measured affects their choices and behavior.

SEGMENT PERFORMANCE MEASUREMENT

The numbers generated by an accounting system are used to evaluate the performance of individuals, segments, and entire organizations. The connection between accounting and performance evaluation is very important to accountants because it makes accounting systems indispensable to large organizations. The design, implementation, and maintenance of performance reporting systems provide many jobs for accountants.

Performance reporting systems should be **truth inducing** (promote honesty) among managers in reporting to their superiors. The importance of this is demonstrated in the following illustration. Consider the manager of a segment that sells and services automotive air conditioners on the Pacific Coast. The manager serves at the pleasure of the Western regional group vice president. This means that the group vice president can give the manager a raise, a bonus, or fire him or her at any time. Now suppose the company has no accounting system that reports achievement to top management on a monthly basis. Instead, the vice president calls and asks, ''How are things going?'' Now, how would the manager answer this question when the volume has been adversely affected by weather conditions? Does the manager tell the truth and possibly get fired, or lie and get by until the good months happen? The manager is not induced to tell the truth under these circumstances.

The circumstances should be arranged to encourage honesty; they should be truth inducing. For example, accounting and reporting systems that generate frequent reports, that are independent of the manager, and that are subject to periodic internal audit and external verification of performance data encourage managers to give truthful responses to questions from superiors.

Segment performance measurement is the process of accumulating and reporting data that relate to segment performance. As an example of a performance measurement, consider the report for the Pacific Coast Sales District in Exhibit 17–1. Notice that the performance report includes both financial data and operating statistics considered important to performance. In order to provide a basis for evaluation, the performance data also include an operations budget. A few performance reporting systems encourage managers to comment on unusual circumstances or new projects that are beyond normal operations.

Concepts of Traceability and Controllability

Periodic performance reports serve multiple purposes: measurement of the performance of the manager, the segment, and the organization as a whole. Exhibit 17–1 presents the performance of the segment and includes the traceable revenues and traceable costs of the segment as a whole. **Traceable costs,** also called *attributable costs,* are costs that are easily identified with the segment. The accountant must

EXHIBIT 17–1

PACIFIC COAST SALES DISTRICT
Report of Operations
For the Month Ending March 31, 19x1
(in thousands)

	Actual	*Budget*	*Difference*
Sales	$17,402	$18,000	$(592)
Cost of goods sold	12,340	13,000	640
Gross margin	$ 5,062	$ 5,000	$ 62
Controllable expenses	803	800	3
Controllable margin	$ 4,259	$ 4,200	$ 59
Committed Expenses	608	620	(12)
District margin	$ 3,651	$ 3,580	$ 71

	Month of March	
Operating statistics:	*19x1*	*19x0*
Sales unit volume	379,000	385,000
New customer accounts	46	37
Sales calls	3,407	3,480

Comments: A late winter storm delayed shipments from the Salt Lake City warehouse. As a consequence, a backlog of sales totaled $4.6 million at the end of the month. If the backlog could have been delivered, actual income would have been substantially above budget.

exercise judgment in deciding what is traceable and what is not. Traceable revenues and costs are useful for measuring the performance of the segment as an economic entity.

Another important purpose that should be considered in performance measurement is the performance of the person managing the entity. For this purpose, it is important to consider the activities over which the person has some control. That is, those costs controllable by the person should also be highlighted in the report as the controllable margin.

A **controllable cost** is one that the segment manager can influence during the current period. Most variable costs are controllable. Some fixed costs, such as advertising, travel, or small equipment purchases, may be controllable. A **committed cost** of the segment is one that is traceable to the segment but not controllable during the current time period. Depreciation, rent, and supervisory salaries are examples of committed costs.

Evaluating a manager's performance requires knowledge of controllable costs. Assessing the entity as an economic investment uses all traceable costs, both controllable and committed. A **common cost**[1] is one that is caused by a group of segments and relates to the assessment of the combination of segments as economic activity.

A segment manager's salary is controllable by top management, not by the segment manager. This is an example of a traceable but noncontrollable cost. Also, some overhead costs, such as insurance, property taxes, and depreciation on equipment, are due to past decisions. They can be identified as committed to the entity but are not controlled by that entity's manager. Home office costs are an example of a common cost.

---

[1] The common costs of several segments are not represented in Exhibit 17–1. These should be included on reports involving the combination of several segments.

EXHIBIT 17–2   Example Performance Evaluation

INTEROFFICE MEMORANDUM

To: Klaus Krogstad, Marketing Vice President   Date: April 18, 19x1
From: Bill Scarborough, Western Regional Group Vice President

Subject: Performance of Pacific Coast District Manager

Our promotion of Bollender to Pacific Coast District manager seems to be working out well. As you can see in the performance report [Exhibit 17–1], she has attained some sales dollar and profit growth in spite of difficult times. Her new customer sign up rate is good, and the sales calls have been maintained.

She handled the problem of blocked highways and slow deliveries with calm control. Her comment about the weather conditions in the region is really an understatement. In talking with the warehouse and trucking people, I learned that they found her easy to work with under tough conditions. She did not panic, just worked it through. In talking with several of her sales staff, I found them very supportive of her. The staff seems to like the changes she has made since taking over.

PERFORMANCE EVALUATION

Performance evaluation[2] is the judgment process of supervisors about the quality of the performance of subordinates. The results of performance evaluation are qualitative (also called *summative*) judgments such as outstanding, good, adequate, or poor. As an example of a performance evaluation, consider Exhibit 17–2 as the comments made by the Western regional group vice president regarding the Pacific Coast Sales District. The evaluation takes the form of a memorandum to the marketing vice president.

This memorandum is very important to Bollender's career. It will be filed and remembered by the marketing vice president. It will provide part of the basis for salary increases, bonuses, and future promotions.

The memorandum also reflects the performance of Scarborough in his role as regional vice president because performance evaluation is an important part of every manager's job. Specifically, the performance evaluation memorandum is evidence that Scarborough is doing his job in talking with people and seeing through the formal numbers to evaluate circumstances and specific behaviors.

Performance evaluation is strictly within the role of managers. Accountants are involved with the design of performance reporting systems, but accountants should not do performance evaluation (except for their own subordinates). This is an important distinction that should be kept in mind. Thus, accounting reports to managers should not include words such as *outstanding* or *poor* for performance. Further, an accountant should not argue with a manager as to what his or her evaluation should be. Evaluation is the manager's job. If a manager asks you what your beliefs are regarding the performance of another manager, use your judgment as to how to respond in the circumstances.

Performance measures are the relatively objective numbers resulting from a performance measurement system, and performance evaluations are the subjective judgments of managers. If the evaluations are fair and reasonable, there should be some correspondence between the measures and the judgments. Specifically, those people who have relatively high measures should have a good or outstanding evaluation rather than an adequate or poor one.

---

[2] This process is also called *performance appraisal* in related literature.

EXHIBIT 17–3   Types of Organizational Segments (for accounting performance measures)

Type of Segment	Common Examples	Financial Measures
Cost center	Production plant	Production costs
	Print shop	Cost per unit output
	Advertising department	Cost per hour
	Computer center	
Revenue center	Sales district	Revenue compared to budget
	Sales staff member	Unit sales
	Account executive	New account billings
	Sales branch office	
Profit center	Auto service department	Profit compared to budget
	Store department	
	Product line	
	Hospital pharmacy	
Investment center	Company division	Return on investment
	Store location	Residual income
	Subsidiary or affiliate	

A **performance history** is the accumulation of past performance measurements and evaluations. Organizations keep a file containing these documents for each of their employees. For example, early in your career, you should expect to have periodic (monthly or quarterly) reports and summative reviews of your performance as a staff accountant. This performance history is the basis for salary adjustments and promotions.

TYPES OF SEGMENTS

We will next consider the common types of segment used in organizations. A segment is classified by the type of financial performance measure that is commonly associated with it. The four basic types of organizational segments are cost or service centers, revenue centers, profit centers, and investment centers. Exhibit 17–3 presents some common examples of these types of center along with the common performance measures that are financial in nature.

Cost Centers

A **cost center** is a segment that provides services or products to other segments. Cost centers typically sell a low proportion, if any, of their services or products to outside entities. Common examples of cost centers include factory departments working directly on a product, a legal department, an accounting section, a computer repair group, the quality control center in a production plant, a company motor pool, a police department for a city, and a company print shop. Common names associated with cost centers include department, office, pool, service, shop, section, center, group, staff, function, and area. Preceding the common name is the service performed by the cost center, such as production, accounting, legal, executive, printing, safety, defense, welfare, food, or quality control.

The **cost center performance report** is typically a list of costs compared with a plan. Also, statistics typically indicate activity and/or quality along with comments explaining unusual conditions. The performance report for the Central Printing Department is presented in Exhibit 17–4.

The reason for the quality measures and for the commentary by the manager is to reduce problems associated with cost centers. If only the cost of the segment's

EXHIBIT 17–4

CENTRAL PRINTING DEPARTMENT
Report on Cost Performance
For the Month Ending November 30, 19x7

	Actual	*Planned**	*Difference*
Controllable Costs:			
Paper	$408,300	$406,000	$2,300
Wages and salaries	259,320	260,000	(680)
Employee benefits	101,135	98,800	2,335
Ink and supplies	86,400	92,600	(6,200)
Maintenance	36,400	35,000	1,400
Total controllable cost	$891,555	$892,400	(845)
Committed costs:			
Equipment depreciation	56,000	50,000	6,000
Supervision	6,000	6,000	0
Total department costs	$953,555	$948,400	$5,155

	For the Month of November		
	19x7	*19x6*	*Change*
Department Activity:			
Typesetting Hours	36,402	32,800	11.0%
Art Hours	4,907	5,230	(6.2)
Printing (in thousands)	16,400	13,408	22.3
Jobs completed	642	582	10.3
Jobs completed on time	626 (97.5%)	563 (96.7%)	
Jobs returned for rework	15 (2.3%)	10 (1.8%)	

Comments: The increase in equipment depreciation was due to a new press purchased last month. The new press produces high-quality output from a lower quantity of ink. Because the machinery has about 50 percent fewer moving parts, maintenance should be lower in the coming months. The new press is faster and increases our capacity to about 50 million pages per month.

* Planned amounts based on flexible budget.

activities is reported in the performance report, the quality of cost center performance is often inadequate. In such cases, staff members tend to become more concerned with the internal workings of their department than with their dealings with external users. Detailed rules are often set up to lower the total cost or cost per unit of the cost center. As a consequence, users encounter inconvenience to get the services that they need.

For example, a company print shop whose evaluation is based solely on costs may require that all work be hand carried with the proper work order form. Printing employees become preoccupied with their work and with each other rather than with pick-up and delivery services with rapid turnaround and friendly attention to detail. Errors in printing become common. This tendency toward low-quality service can be offset by a print shop performance report that includes measures of the proportion of jobs picked up and delivered on time, ratings by users, and proportions of jobs accepted by users as being correctly done.

Revenue Centers   A **revenue center** is an organizational segment that specializes in the sale of products or services. The function of a revenue center is to work with customers, keep them satisfied, and keep them buying. As the name implies, these segments are primarily evaluated on the basis of sales generated. The names for these segments include terms such as *branch, territory, line, region,* or *division.* The names often include a geographic name or general product type. For example, common names for revenue centers are Western region, consumer products division, industrial services line, Chicago branch, and chemical sales division.

Revenue center managers should organize and motivate their sales forces to sell as much as possible in their assigned markets. The sales force should build close relationships with existing customers, and it should also develop new customers. In building relationships with customers, it is important that promises on product quality, price, and delivery be kept and that the customer see a highly motivated, aggressive individual servicing the account year after year.

In order to build a satisfied customer base, the sales force will have to work smoothly with the production plant, warehousing and delivery people, and billing and administrative staff. Any one group can make customers unhappy and thus reduce revenue. Consequently, cooperative behavior among the segments is highly desirable. This cooperation is enhanced by the training of the sales force and the persuasion and leadership of revenue center managers. In general, rush orders, unusually low prices, and highly irregular special orders should be the exception because they make production difficult and reduce profitability. Customers should not be made unrealistic promises about quality or delivery time because such promises will harm long-run satisfaction and revenue. Costs associated with the generation of revenue should be kept within reasonable bounds.

On a short-term basis (a few months or a year), revenue center managers can pump up sales with extreme pressure on the sales force to perform, with promises for products that cannot be delivered on time, and with heavy verbal pressure on the credit staff to accept credit terms for risky customers. The sales force can be encouraged to overstep its market bounds and step on other segments' markets. These tactics reduce sales force morale, reduce customer satisfaction, and spoil relationships with the production plant, the warehouse, and the administrative staff. On the other hand, low performance expectations result in lackluster sales performance.

Thus, both desirable and undesirable behaviors of the revenue centers need to be evaluated by top management. The performance reporting system should be set up to measure events associated with these behaviors.

Example of a Performance Report for a Revenue Center. Exhibit 17–5 presents an example of performance measurement for a revenue center for a division that sells paper products, primarily boxes and copy paper. The performance evaluation of this segment and its manager would likely be carried out by the marketing vice president. In this evaluation, careful consideration should be given to both the improvement in revenues and the changes in the operating statistics. Although the performance appears to be much better than the budget indicates, there should be some concern with the slip in customer payment timeliness. As with all performance reporting systems, the marketing vice president should verify that the appearances are the reality.

The revenue center approach measures dollar sales, operating statistics, and various quality measures that relate to long-run performance. However, products with very low markups tend to be easier to sell and, as a consequence, generate high revenue. As a result, the product lines tend to become filled with low-profit products. Thus, performance based on sales will encourage the segment to focus on standard products sold in large volumes with low prices. This may or may not follow the strategy selected by top management.

High-profit products tend to be new or unusual in some way and may require extra effort to create a market for them. If the objective of top management is to

EXHIBIT 17–5

NORTHWEST SALES REGION
Performance Report
For Three Months Ending June 30, 19x3
(in thousands)

	Actual	*Budget*	*Difference*
Revenues			
Idaho	$ 3,000	$ 2,800	$ 200
Montana	2,600	3,000	(400)
Oregon	13,000	12,500	500
Washington	23,400	19,200	4,200
Totals	$42,000	$37,500	$4,500

Operating statistics:	*19x3*	*19x2*
Orders delivered on or		
before promised date	98.7%	96.3%
Order return rates	1.3%	1.4%
Operating costs (thousands)	$1,906	$1,820
New customer accounts	306	282
Calls on customers	30,307	26,305
Customer payments on time	92.2%	96.3%
Sales force turnover rate	10.3%	16.3%

Comments: 1. The new cardboard container design (product P4693) has sold specially well in Seattle for overseas shipments.
2. Sales staff morale has been helped substantially by a pay raise that puts the staff on par with our regional competitors and by the sales of new products.

expand new markets with new products requiring unusual sales efforts, the revenue center approach will not meet the objective.

Contribution Margin Center

The contribution approach to performance reporting focuses the short-run attention of segment managers on those products with high contribution in relation to sales efforts required. The commission rates and bonuses should be set higher for those products with higher contributions. In concept, the profits of the company will increase because profitable products are emphasized. The production plants will be filled with products that contribute substantially to profit. Managers will focus on and push the products that count in terms of net profit. Low-contribution products will gradually be reduced in importance.

As an example of a performance report based on contribution margin, we have reformatted the report for the Northwest Sales Region in Exhibit 17–6.

Notice that a different financial performance is implied by this report: even though the sales have increased by $4.5 million, the contribution has declined by $3 million. Consequently, both the segment manager and the marketing vice president will view the success of the segment less favorably. During the following quarter, the regional sales manager should respond by encouraging the sales force to change its emphasis to higher-contribution products. This may involve changes in alignment and compensation of staff, pricing, advertising, and promoting sales with customer incentives.

The contribution margin approach to performance measurement does have limitations. Top managers and management accountants should beware of a trap that is

EXHIBIT 17–6

NORTHWEST SALES REGION
Performance Report
For Three Months Ending June 30, 19x3
(in thousands)

	Actual	*Budget*	*Difference*
Revenues	$42,000	$37,500	$4,500
Variable cost of sales	26,600	19,200	(7,400)
Variable selling costs	1,200	1,100	(100)
Contribution margin	$14,200	$17,200	($3,000)

Operating statistics:	*19x3*	*19x2*
Orders delivered on or before promised date	98.7%	96.3%
Order return rates	1.3%	1.4%
New customer accounts	306	282
Calls on customers	30,307	26,305
Customer payments on time	92.2%	96.3%
Sales force turnover rate	10.3%	16.3%

Comments: 1. The new cardboard container design (product P4693) has sold specially well in Seattle for overseas shipments.
2. Sales staff morale has been helped substantially by pay raise that puts the staff on par with our regional competitors and by the sales of new products.

hidden in the contribution margin technique: all variable costs are "bad" because they decrease the contribution, and fixed costs are "irrelevant" or perhaps benign to the segment manager. Thus, in a choice involving a trade-off between fixed and variable costs, the marketing managers will support a plan that involves the decrease in variable costs because this increases the contribution margin.

For example, in a choice between building an automated production plant or keeping the old, high-variable cost plant, the sales manager will "sell" the new plant to top management. Because marketing people have the ability to sell concepts, the fixed costs tend to increase from year to year as the segments reduce their variable costs. Top management must counteract this tendency by approving and actively promoting long-term projects and programs that reduce total costs. Profit comes from the combination of high revenues, low variable costs, *and low fixed costs.* Otherwise, the company will become strapped with fixed costs and will incur large losses during poor sales years or when technology changes.

In summary, segments that specialize in the marketing function may be set up. Performance reporting for these segments should convey both short-term performance in revenue generated and long-term performance related to customer satisfaction. The sales force should be motivated to sell profitable products and expand markets.

Profit Centers

A **profit center** is a segment that generates both revenues and expenses. Profit centers are commonly called *divisions, branches,* and *centers.* Profit centers may be organized as separate corporations called *subsidiaries.* Exhibit 17–1 is based on the profit center concept.

A cost center may be changed into a profit center by changing the name of the unit, the title of the manager, and performance reporting system, and giving the manager responsibility for revenues. The form of the performance report is changed to an income statement plus operating statistics and comments.

In this changeover, more decisions regarding the sale and purchases of goods and services will be transferred from top management to segment managers; decentralization should occur. The profit center managers are told that they should run their operations as if they were separate entities and that the managers are primarily responsible for generating a profit.

In some circumstances, cost centers are shifted to profit centers without complete decentralization by the substance of the company policies surrounding the profit center.[3] For example, company policy may require that the profit center sell only to company segments and that company segments must purchase, where available, goods and services from other company segments. Prices may be set by company policy and purchases rigidly controlled through central purchasing and a strict budgeting process.

Why might top management choose to implement a profit center yet retain control over some decisions? This seems to be the manipulation of segment managers. It is the judgment of top managers that a profit center manager is more likely to focus on meeting the needs of users for the price charged rather than to focus strictly on efficiency. The segment manager should cooperate more with user segments. For example, top management might make the print shop a profit center in order to motivate the manager and printing staff to pay close attention to the printing needs of the other departments rather than minimizing cost per page printed.

Investment Centers

Investment centers are segments that are responsible for revenues, expenses, and investments. Some companies have found that cost, revenue, and profit centers do not meet their needs for encouraging specific behaviors related to investment in receivables, inventories, equipment, and buildings. Consequently, scarce capital is invested in existing projects when it could be more profitably used for new projects. For example, in order to increase revenue, credit may be extended on easy terms and late payers may not be pursued diligently. In order to attract new customers or increase sales from old customers, the inventory variety and availability may be increased. Finally, new, more efficient machines may be purchased and old, less-efficient machines may be allowed to sit idle. Although these investing behaviors increase income, millions of investment dollars are required. The result will often be an inadequate return on investment and disappointed stockholders.

One approach to handling the problem of the segment manager's investment behavior is to include return on investment as part of the performance report or report a residual income that allows for the required return. When this is done, an organization is said to be using an investment center approach to segmentation.

Return on Investment.   **Return on investment** (ROI) for a segment is the segment margin divided by the average investment in the assets associated with the segment:

$$\text{Return on investment} = \text{Segment margin} / \text{Investment}$$

---

[3] There is ongoing debate as to whether or not the creation of a profit center without complete decentralization of decisions affecting revenues and costs is an acceptable practice. However, recognize that there are many decisions with respect to revenues and expenses, each one of which may be wholly (centralization), partially, or not (decentralization) retained by senior management. Thus, the debate relates to whether partial decentralization is an acceptable practice. Pragmatically, the extent of decentralization is determined by the policies that senior management sets and by the latitude that it allows segment managers.

In concept, the manager is encouraged both to increase segment margin and to reduce investment, which are both worthy objectives. When ROI is included in the performance report, the segment manager should be more diligent with credit policies, reduce variety and quantity of inventory, and use machinery longer.

Exhibit 17–7 presents an example of a performance report based on the investment center concept.

The division manager obtained an ROI of 32.5 percent, which was 8.5 percent more than the 24 percent planned in the budget. This was obtained by increasing profits by $620,000 and decreasing investment by about $2.8 million.

ROI and related ratios.   ROI may also be considered as the product of the return on sales and investment turnover:

$$\text{ROI} = \text{Return on sales} \times \text{Investment turnover}$$
$$= \frac{\text{Segment margin}}{\text{Sales}} \times \frac{\text{Sales}}{\text{Investment}}$$

The planned results for the Pacific Coast Division included a return on sales of 12 percent ($4,320/$36,000) and an investment turnover of 2 ($36,000/$18,000):

EXHIBIT 17–7

PACIFIC COAST DIVISION
Report on Operations
For the Month Ending March 31, 19x1
(in thousands)

	Actual	*Budget*	*Difference*
Sales	$38,000	$36,000	$2,000
Cost of goods sold	24,700	23,400	1,300
Gross margin	$13,300	$12,600	$ 700
Controllable expenses	4,560	5,400	(840)
Controllable margin	$ 8,740	$ 7,200	$1,540
Committed expenses	3,800	2,880	920
Division margin	$ 4,940	$ 4,320	$ 620
Investment	$15,200	$18,000	
Return on investment	32.50%	24.00%	

Operating statistics:

	Actual	*Plan*
Sales unit volume	760,000	720,000
New product sales	$680,000	$650,000
New customer accounts	80	70
Customers paying on time	92%	96%
Sales return rates	2.1%	1.8%
Employee turnover	2%	2%
Return on sales	13%	12%
Investment turnover	2.5	2.0

Comments: A late winter storm delayed shipments from the Salt Lake City warehouse. As a consequence, a backlog of sales totaled $4.6 million at the end of the month. If the backlog could have been delivered, actual margin would have been substantially above budget.

$$ROI = 12\% \times 2 = 24\%$$

The actual results are a return on sales of 13 percent ($4,940/$38,000) and investment turnover of 2.5 ($38,000/$15,200):

$$ROI = 13\% \times 2.5 = 32.5\%$$

The actual results are better than those planned due to a 1 percent higher return on sales and better investment turnover ratio. The investment turnover ratio was improved by increasing sales by $2 million and by reducing investment by $2.8 million.

Measures of investment.   Several basic options are available for measuring the investment for the ROI calculation:

1. Net book values of assets.

2. Market values of assets.

3. Equities.

Net book value.   Most organizations interpret investment as accounting net book values, which is the original cost minus accumulated depreciation. These amounts are readily available in the accounting system and to the computer system that generates the performance reports. The data have been audited in the past and are subject to future audit.

As a practical matter then, segment managers are encouraged to reduce investment in net book assets and increase reported income. Old assets purchased at old prices have a relatively low net book value and low depreciation expense. If this old equipment were scrapped, there may be a loss on disposal. Thus, the segment managers are encouraged to keep the old plant and equipment running. Further, fully depreciated assets are "free" in terms of ROI. Thus, managers are encouraged to keep, or have transferred to them, assets that have been fully depreciated.

There will be competition to keep control over fully depreciated assets that generate some current income. Consequently, some divisions may report a good ROI and appear to have promising overall performance only to find later that they cannot survive the competition. Alternatively, other divisions may appear to have poor ROI performance but are building a chance to survive.

Some companies allocate the common investment in the headquarters assets, such as corporate cash or the building. In concept, this allocation has an effect similar to allocating common costs in that it encourages the segment managers to exert pressure for the reduction of the common amounts.

A few companies deal with the problems with net book values by using an average book value for all assets. The average is often approximated by dividing the original price for the equipment or building by 2.[4] The effect of this is to equalize all assets in terms of cost. However, newer equipment should be more efficient and require less maintenance cost and, thus, managers in this system are encouraged to purchase new equipment.

Market values and ROI.   Some companies deal with the problems with book values by using a market value measure of assets: either a replacement cost or the cash value

---

[4] This procedure approximates the net book value for assets at the midpoint in their depreciable lives. For example, a forklift with a $10,000 purchase price depreciated over four years will have net book values of $7,500, $5,000, $2,500, and $0 at the end of each of the four years, respectively. The net book value at the end of the second year, the midpoint, is $5,000, which is $10,000 divided by 2.

of the assets. This is appropriate when (1) there are relatively few assets, generally less than several hundred, (2) the prices are reasonably available, and (3) the prices are not subject to wide variations that are outside the control of the division manager. If there are thousands of assets or the prices are not readily available, the ROI calculation may become cumbersome or unreliable as a periodic performance measure.

Equities.   A few organizations treat investment as assets invested in the division less related liabilities. This encourages the division to borrow as much as possible from suppliers, which may be contrary to top management policy.

Problems with ROI in concept.   ROI is a short-term measure of performance. The performance measured is this period's segment margin divided by current investment. By specific decisions, a division manager may increase the ROI but decrease the long-run performance of the segment. For example, decreasing current research and development will increase current margin but reduce the number of future products or services. Similarly, forcing facilities and people beyond reasonable limits will increase current profits but will cause future personnel problems.

Because ROI is short run in nature, it is inconsistent with the long-run perspective needed for the selection and implementation of capital projects. Capital projects are selected on the basis of long-run promise and value rather than one-year performance. Normally a start-up period involves several years of cash outflows for new products or plants. During these loss years, the ROI performance will be low, even though the long-run performance is as expected. Thus, ROI penalizes managers for making long-run choices.

A second issue concerns ROI as a performance measure. Is an increase in a division's ROI always good? Is a decrease in a division's ROI always bad? Consider the Bat'n'Ball Company with the following two divisions:

	Slugger	*Bunt*	*Total Company*
Segment margins (in thousands)	$1,200	$ 200	$1,400
Assets invested (in thousands)	$4,000	$4,000	$8,000
Return on investment	30%	5%	17.5%

The Slugger Division is an ROI winner, and the Bunt Division is an ROI loser.

The Slugger Division has many products, programs, and activities that make it successful. Some projects have lower return rates than the 30 percent average, and others have higher return rates. Suppose that $2 million of the Slugger assets earn 20 percent. The manager can increase the average return by terminating this part of the division. What will be the effects of the termination on the Bat'n'Ball Company? Consider the following schedule:

	Slugger	*Bunt*	*Total Company*
Segment margin (in thousands)	$ 800	$ 200	$1,000
Assets invested (in thousands)	$2,000	$4,000	$6,000
Return on investment	35%	5%	16.7%

The Slugger Division's rate of return increases to 35 percent, which appears to be good in terms of the ROI. However, the overall corporate ROI declines as a result of the Slugger Division manager's choice.

Suppose instead that the Slugger Division manager decided to take on a $2 million opportunity that earns 20 percent. The following indicates what will happen to the division and the company as a whole:

	Slugger	*Bunt*	*Total Company*
Segment margin (in thousands)	$1,600	$ 200	$ 1,800
Assets invested (in thousands)	$6,000	$4,000	$10,000
Return on investment	26.7%	5%	18%

The division's ROI declines from 30 to 26.7 percent, and the overall corporate return increases modestly from 17.5 to 18 percent. Thus, the Slugger Division is penalized for doing something that is good for the company as a whole.[5]

In general, the ROI concept encourages profitable divisions to take only projects that have immediate, very high rates of return. Why will this occur? Nobody wants to mess up what appears to be a winner but only to make reported performance better by increasing the ROI.

Residual Income—Alternative to ROI.   As an alternative to the return on invesment measure, organizations occasionally adopt the residual income concept. **Residual income** is the income left after a charge is made for required return on investment. For example, assume that the Bat'n'Ball Company requires a return on investment of 10 percent. If we start with the original data on income and investment, we find residual income as follows:

		Slugger		*Bunt*		*Total Company*
Income after tax		$1,200		200		$1,400
Assets Invested	$4,000		$4,000		$8,000	
Required return	× 10%	400	× 10%	400	× 10%	800
Residual income		$ 800		($200)		$ 600

The residual income approach encourages managers to enter into and keep a project as long as it earns more than the required return. Both high return and low return segments are encouraged to expand their operations. Thus, the approach directly addresses one of the basic faults of the ROI measure. For example, if residual income is the performance measure, the Slugger Division manager would not drop the projects involving $2 million in assets and a 20 percent return. To do so would decrease residual income by $200,000 ($2,000,000 × (0.2 − 0.1)). The residual income approach would encourage the Slugger Division manager to take on projects as long as they earn more than the required return. Additionally, the approach would encourage the Bunt Division manager to drop products and activities with very small rates of return and thus come closer to the required return rates.

Like ROI, the residual income concept deals only with current performance and is subject to unethical behaviors. Similarly, the residual income measure penalizes managers for undertaking long-run projects that increase current expenses or investment.

Performance Evaluation of Investment Centers.   When top managers evaluate investment center performance, they must "see through" appearances and encourage the choices and behaviors that will increase the overall corporate ROI and long-run performance. Thus, high ROI segments should be encouraged to expand as long as each new project promises a return that is higher than the required return. Further, low ROI segments should be encouraged to drop products that do not earn the desired return.

---

[5] Additionally, it can be shown that the Bunt Division can increase its ROI by taking on projects that pay more than the 5 percent rate of return. However, unless the return rate is higher than the average return, the overall corporate return will decline.

The performance evaluation of investment centers should include consideration of the long-term effects of short-term decisions. As with cost, revenue, and profit centers, an investment center manager can get apparent performance by making short-term decisions that are harmful to long-run performance. Thus, in the short term, they can force more sales from the sales staff and less cost from production and administration. They can give liberal credit terms to risky customers. They can defer the maintenance of equipment. They can cut staff to the bare minimum. Research and development work can be cut to a minimum. These tactics work until a major crisis arises and then the investment center performance crumbles. During this time, collection rates decline, employee morale declines, plant and equipment deteriorate, customers become dissatisfied and stop referring their friends to the company, and new products are not developed.

This course of events is not inevitable. Top management can alter the attitudes and direction of segment managers with a well-timed performance review that lets them know that short-run tactics are unacceptable. To help top managers spot developing problems, the performance report should contain measures that indicate long-run performance: for example, collection rates, employee turnover, maintenance, new customer accounts, and new product sales.

In conclusion, top managers should not place undue emphasis on ROI as a performance measure. Heavy emphasis will distort the choices of segment managers and reduce overall return. Instead, performance evaluation emphasis should be placed on growth in high ROI segments and shifting of resources out of or changing the direction of low ROI segments. As with the performance of segments in general, the performance report for an investment center should contain longer-run measures such as employee turnover, new products developed, or new markets entered.

DECENTRALIZATION

The top managers of an organization have the responsibility and authority to make all decisions, no matter how the organization is organized. This responsibility includes all major and minor decisions regarding the organization. When the top managers fail to carry out this responsibility, the board of directors has the responsibility to replace them.

As a practical matter, top managers delegate the authority to make some decisions to lower-level personnel. For example, it is common to delegate specific purchase decisions to lower-level people. However, if the lower-level people make poor choices, the top managers are still fully responsible. **Centralization** is the extent to which the authority to make specific decisions is retained by the top management group. Many decisions need to be made regarding personnel (location, salaries, retention, and termination), financing, investment, credit, inventory, real estate, equipment, products, services, and pricing. Any one or more of these decision areas may be retained by top managers. With **decentralization,** one or more decisions are delegated to subordinates and segments. Some top managers strongly believe in the value of decentralization.

Advantages of Decentralization

Decentralization often results in better decisions because lower-level managers have better information or more time, or give more care to each choice. Decentralized decision processes tend to be more flexible and responsive to local differences. Bureaucratic behavior (behavior based on strict interpretation of rules and form rather than on substance) tends to decrease with decentralization of decisions.

With decentralization, the load of top managers is reduced and the decisions tend to be made more quickly. Thus, the organization may be more responsive to customer needs and changing conditions. Making decisions is good training for higher-level positions and tends to motivate managers.

In summary, decentralization often results in better decisions, better training, and more motivation. These factors should result in higher income in the long run.

Disadvantages of Decentralization

Lower-level managers do not consistently make choices that top managers want them to make. Segment managers lack the perspective of long-range plans and are less experienced than senior managers. They tend to make decisions in favor of their segment rather than the company as a whole, which is called **suboptimization.** They may not have the technical competence to make the decisions delegated to them.

The personal goals of lower-level managers (e.g., security, personal growth, compensation) will be different from the goals of top management (e.g., company growth, market penetration, strategic power). As with all human processes, there are differences among the goals of individual managers. The extent to which the goals between and within levels of management are similar is termed **goal congruence.** When decisions are decentralized, the lack of goal congruence becomes an important issue. Specifically, are choices being made that benefit the individual manager rather than the company as a whole? For example, consider the matter of perquisites.

Perquisites are the niceties that come with a position (e.g., plush office, company car, personal staff, club memberships, meals, time off, and travel). Many of these benefits are tax free and increase the quality of life for the manager. When managers of segments are given authority to hire people and spend money, the opportunity arises to increase perquisites. Excessive perquisites reduce profits.

Complete decentralization is not desirable because the entire corporation is legally responsible for each action of its segments. Thus, some laws make corporate officers responsible for specific criminal violations of subordinates, such as bribery of foreign officials. The pricing and contracting decisions of several segments for similar products can result in the violation of pricing or antitrust laws. The employment procedures of a segment may be substantially in violation of labor laws. A subsidiary may unknowingly issue securities in violation of securities registration requirements. Because of these legal problems, decentralization must occur within the context of general corporate policies.

Decentralization in Perspective

Although some disagreement exists in the matter, decentralization should not be viewed as patently good and centralization as bad or vice versa. Instead, both concepts are devices or tools for top management, who determines how much centralization of which decisions is currently appropriate. It is often productive (in terms of motivation, performance, and cost) to change the level of centralization of specific decisions. For example, one large chemical company might centralize its computer system in order to reduce costs at the same time that a similar company decentralizes its computer system for the same reason. How can both centralizing and decentralizing reduce cost? In the process of giving someone different a chance to make the decisions related to computer systems, top management often gets better choices and computer service per dollar expended. The new people are not bound by the choices and methods of the past.

Cooperation and Competition

In designing performance measurement systems, some consideration should be given to the extent to which top managers want segments to compete rather than cooperate with each other.[6] Measures that encourage competition place emphasis on individual segment performance. For example, a measure that ranks segments by sales will tend to make segments very competitive for sales. Managers like to be first—they prefer very much to win. Thus, getting the highest rank becomes a game, albeit a serious one, among segment managers, and seeing who wins this month or quarter becomes important for relative status.

The game becomes especially tense if bonuses and promotions are based upon relative sales rankings. In order to improve their ranking, segment managers may overstep their geographic or market boundaries. Cooperation among segments will become minimal. For example, some managers may use their influence with production supervisors or warehouse shipping clerks to get their shipments out ahead of other segments.

Measures that encourage cooperation place emphasis on group or overall performance. For example, the cooperation among sections of a factory might be encouraged by measuring performance based on high-quality output units that meet customer specifications with minimal inventories. In order for any of the sections to show good output, all sections must do quality work. When one section or department has a problem, the others are encouraged to pitch in and solve it. Cross-training is encouraged. Cooperation among departments is necessary to keep work in process inventories moving through production.

Unless carefully monitored, cooperative settings may result in complacency and letting other segments take the initiative. When poor output results, it can be difficult at times to trace causes. Further, some segments may not feel rewarded for cooperating. Poor attitudes and performance can result from lack of recognition for contributions made.

If an internal accounting and reporting system is implemented within the context of decentralization and competitive behaviors, the system should be supportive of that context. Therefore, the accounting system should be consistent with the extent of decentralization and competition desired by top management.

SUMMARY

Organizations segment their operations in order to gain effective control. Types of segment include cost, revenue, profit, and investment centers. Performance measurement is the relatively objective process of reporting short- and long-run measures of performance. Performance evaluation is the subjective process of judging the quality of performance and is performed by managers. Accountants are involved with setting up systems to measure performance.

Revenue centers specialize in the sale and delivery of products or services. These centers are evaluated on the basis of revenue generated. Long-term measures include new customers, new products, collection rates, staff turnover, and absenteeism. Cost centers produce a product or service and are evaluated on the basis of costs and long-term measures.

Profit centers both produce and sell. They may be set up in a decentralized or

---

[6] Keep in mind that competitive and cooperative behaviors are a function of hiring, training, compensation, and promotion policies in addition to how segment performance is measured and evaluated. However, as accountants, we have primary influence over the measurement system, so we will focus on that here.

centralized organization. The managers of profit centers often argue for decentralization of revenue and expense-related decisions.

Investment centers produce, sell, and invest in current and long-term assets. They are held responsible for maintaining an adequate return on investment (ROI). ROI should definitely not be the sole basis for performance evaluation because of the effects on manager decisions over time. Long-term performance is very important in evaluating an investment center.

Top management is in charge and is responsible for all choices and actions of the organization. It should decide the level of competitive and cooperative behavior that is currently appropriate for segments. It should also decide the extent to which choices will be decentralized to managers. These senior management decisions will change from time to time.

PROBLEM FOR REVIEW

Performance Measures. The Beberniss Company is a mail order company whose sales are based on catalogs mailed every two months. The company has the following costs for the Catalog Department for the two months ending April 30, 19x3:

Printing and postage	$480,000
Salaries	148,000
Computer cost	56,000
Department manager's salary	8,000
Administrative costs	86,000
Supplies	13,000
Depreciation	5,000
Rent	30,000
Total Catalog Department expenses	$826,000

Administrative costs represent an allocation of senior management expenses. Depreciation is for departmental equipment, and rent is an allocation based on floor space of the department. During the month, 72 employees were involved with the production of the April–May catalog, which was mailed to 800,000 addresses. It is estimated that 80 percent of the catalogs were delivered to the correct addresses. The remainder had an incorrect address and could not be delivered.

During April and May, $12 million in sales resulted from the catalogs shipped during April. The cost of goods sold averages 60 percent of the selling prices. Half of the cost of goods sold is variable cost. Variable delivery and administrative expenses are 10 percent of revenue.

REQUIRED

Compute the following performance measures:
a. Cost per unit for a catalog designed, printed, and mailed.
b. Cost per unit for a catalog delivered to a customer.
c. Revenue generated per dollar of Catalog Department cost.
d. Gross margin per catalog delivered.
e. Contribution margin per dollar of Catalog Department cost.

SOLUTION

a. Cost per unit for a catalog designed, printed, and mailed. The administrative costs are allocated common costs and are removed from the performance measure. The costs that relate to design, printing, and mailing as an economic activity are:

Total Catalog Department expenses	$826,000
Less: Common administrative costs	86,000
Traceable costs	$740,000
Divided by number of catalogs mailed	800,000
Unit cost	$0.925

b. Cost per unit for a catalog delivered to a customer. Only 80 percent of the catalogs were deliverable:

$$\text{Delivered unit cost} = \$0.925/80\% = \$1.16$$

c. Revenue generated per dollar of Catalog Department cost.

$$\text{Revenues per dollar of cost} = \$12,000,000/\$740,000 = \$16.22$$

d. Gross margin per catalog delivered.

$$\text{Gross margin per dollar of cost} = \$4,800,000/800,000 = \$7$$

e. Contribution margin per dollar of Catalog Department cost.

$$\text{Contribution margin per dollar cost} = \$7,200,000/\$740,000 = \$9.73$$

KEY TERMS AND CONCEPTS

Segment (684)
Truth inducing (684)
Segment performance measurement (684)
Traceable costs (684)
Controllable cost (685)
Committed cost (685)
Common cost (685)
Performance evaluation (686)
Performance history (687)
Cost center (687)
Cost center performance report (687)

Revenue centers (688)
Profit centers (691)
Investment center (692)
Return on investment (ROI) (692)
Residual income (696)
Decentralization (697)
Centralization (697)
Suboptimization (698)
Goal congruence (698)
Perquisites (698)

ADDITIONAL READINGS

Berg, P. "Telling It Like It Is: Effective Performance Appraisal." *CFO,* November 1987, pp. 97–100.

Berliner, C., and J. A. Brimson. "CMS Performance Measurement." *Cost Management for Today's Advanced Manufacturing: The CAM-I Conceptual Design.* Boston: Harvard Business School Press, 1989, Chapter 6.

Greenberg, R. "Generalized Multiple Criteria Model for Control and Evaluation of Nonprofit Organizations," *Financial Accountability and Management,* Winter 1987, pp. 331–42.

Howshower, L. B., and R. P. Crum. "Controlling Service." *Management Accounting,* November 1987, pp. 44–48.

Kaplan, R. S. "Measuring Manufacturing Performance: A New Challenge for the Managerial Accounting Research." *The Accounting Review,* October 1983, pp. 686–704.

Kaplan, S. E. "Improving Performance Evaluation." *CMA,* May–June 1987, pp. 56–59.

Keegan, D. P.; R. G. Eiler; and C. R. Jones. "Are Your Performance Measures Obsolete?" *Management Accounting,* June 1989, pp.45–50.

McNair, C. J., and W. Mosconi. "Measuring Performance in an Advanced Manufacturing Environment." *Management Accounting,* July 1987, pp. 28–31.

Odiorne, G. S. "Measuring the Unmeasurable: Setting Standards for Management Performance." *Business Horizons,* July–August 1987, pp. 69–75.

Richardson, P. R., and J. R. M. Gordon. "Measuring Total Manufacturing Performance."
Sloan Management Review, Winter 1980, pp. 47–58.

Santon, P. R., and A. D. Anderson. "Manufacturing Performance in the 1990s: Measuring
for Excellence." *Journal of Accountancy*, November 1987, pp. 141–47.

Steedle, L. F.; J. J. Darazsdi; and A. D. McCallion. "Measuring Productivity in an Integrated
Poultry Operation." *Journal of Accountancy*, June 1986, pp. 142–53.

Traska, M. R. "HMO Uses Quality Measures to Pay Its Physicians." *Hospitals*, 5 July 1988,
pp. 7–12.

Whitt, S. Y., and J. D. Whitt. "What Professional Service Firms Can Learn from Manufacturing." *Management Accounting*, November 1988, pp. 39–42.

REVIEW QUESTIONS

1. List four major types of segments.

2. Why is segmentation important to organizations?

3. Why is a performance reporting system important to inducing managers to tell the truth about performance?

4. Why is it important that companies know how each segment is performing on a regular basis?

5. What does it mean when it is said that managers "serve at the pleasure of senior management"?

6. List three common nonfinancial measures that are included on the performance report of a revenue center.

7. Distinguish between a controllable and a committed cost.

8. Who performs performance measurement and performance evaluation?

9. What is a performance history? Why is it important?

10. A cost center is appropriate for what type of organizational segment?

11. List five common names for cost centers.

12. Describe the format for a performance report for a cost center.

13. What is bureaucratic behavior?

14. Why do cost centers tend to become large and bureaucratic over time?

15. List three general problems with cost centers.

16. Why might some companies be moving away from cost centers to the concept of quality centers?

17. Why do companies set up revenue centers?

18. Why is it important that the sales force work smoothly with the factory, warehouse, billing, and administrative staffs?

19. List two tactics that revenue center managers can use to increase sales on a short-term basis but that have adverse long-term effects.

20. Briefly describe the general problem with revenue centers.

21. List two alternatives to using revenue to measure the performance of a marketing segment.

22. What is the difference between a profit center and an investment center?

23. Why might senior managers choose to implement a profit center yet keep control over many important decisions?

24. What procedural steps need to be taken to change a cost center into a profit center?

25. What is an investment center?

26. Under what circumstances might an increase in divisional return on investment not be good for the organization as a whole?

27. What is the problem with including old assets in the investment base?

28. Who has the primary responsibility to make decisions in all organizations?

29. What is decentralization?

30. Why might senior management want to decentralize certain decisions?

31. List three advantages to decentralization.

32. List three disadvantages to decentralization.

33. Why might senior managers change their minds on how much decentralization is currently appropriate?
34. Why will rules and policies be necessary in settings that encourage competitive behavior?
35. How might cooperation be encouraged with performance measures?

DISCUSSION QUESTIONS

36. It was noted that senior managers are held responsible for the performance of an organization by the board of directors and investors. What tactics might senior managers use to avoid this responsibility when profits are low?
37. Examples of performance reports with long-term, qualitative measures have been included in the chapter. Develop some qualitative measures for:
    a. A life insurance subsidiary.
    b. A retail chain store.
    c. The pediatric ward of a large hospital.
38. Why are comments on unusual occurrences important to a performance report?
39. Why is either cooperative or competitive employee behavior more productive than preoccupied or sullen employee behavior?
40. Both cooperative and competitive settings can result in the need for rules and policies. On the other hand, rules and policies tend to result in bureaucratic behaviors that reduce both cooperation and competition. What processes keep this from all getting out of control and becoming unproductive?
41. Why might senior management decide to change the extent of decentralization from time to time? Why change the performance measurement system in this process?
42. We have studied cost, revenue, profit, and investment centers. What might be the appropriate performance measures for projects, jobs, and contracts?
43. Managers with an internal locus of control believe that they are in charge and control events around them. Managers with an external locus of control believe that the environment controls them. How might the mix of managers in relation to locus of control change if senior management decides to centralize most major decisions?
44. Managers have different styles in dealing with their job. Some managers are concept and data oriented, and other managers are process and people oriented. How might performance evaluation by a concept-oriented manager differ from that of a process-oriented manager?
45. When senior management comes under fire for poor company performance, it looks for things to improve the company performance. Why might the performance reporting system be one of the things that changes?
46. List three long-term performance statistics for each of the following cost centers:
    a. Printing plant.
    b. Warehouse.
    c. Factory department producing a product.

EXERCISES

17–1. Segment Income Statement.   The Westerfeldt Division has the following data for the month of January 19x6:

	Actual	Budget
Sales	$140,000	$145,000
Cost of goods sold	91,000	89,900
Controllable expenses	14,000	14,500
Committed expenses	17,800	15,000

REQUIRED:
Prepare a divisional income statement with a difference column.

17–2. Return on Investment. The Stoker Company fabricates electrical parts in its plant in Chambersburg, Maryland. The following information summarizes the operations of the company for the year ending December 31, 19x4 (in thousands):

Revenues	$2,000
Cost of goods sold	1,000
Selling expenses	400
Administrative expenses	200
Net book value of assets	4,000

REQUIRED:
Compute the after-tax rate of return on net investment in plant. Assume a tax rate of 40 percent.

17–3. Residual Income. The Sacaw Department Store requires a 10 percent return for each department in the store. For the year ending January 31, 19x2, the following data are available (in thousands):

	Women's Wear	**Accessories**	**Shoes**
Income	$ 400	$ 380	$ 560
Investment	3,200	1,400	2,400

REQUIRED:
Compute the residual income for each department.

17–4. Segment Income Statement. The Saltfork Branch has the following data for the month of January 19x6:

	Actual	**Budget**
Sales	$200,000	$180,000
Cost of goods sold	130,000	111,600
Controllable expenses	20,000	18,000
Committed expenses	24,000	15,000

REQUIRED:
Prepare a divisional comparative income statement with a difference column expressed as a percentage of budget amounts.

17–5. Return on Investment. The Brausell Copper Company invested $280 million in a copper smelter in Texas City, Texas. The smelter has the following information for the year ending December 31, 19x2:

Tonnage produced	150,000 tons
Selling price per ton	$800 per ton
Ore purchase cost per ton of output	$320 per ton
Plant payroll	$ 5,000,000
Plant depreciation	$ 11,000,000
Other fixed costs	$ 3,000,000
Net investment	$258,000,000

REQUIRED:
Compute the after-tax rate of return on net investment in plant. Assume a tax rate of 40 percent.

17–6. Return on Investment and Residual Income. Selected information is provided below on four segments of Patterson Financial Services, Inc., for the year ending March 31, 19x4:

	Brownfield	*Caldron*	*Denver*	*Elder*
Net income	*a.*	$500,000	*e.*	$300,000
Investment	$1,500,000	*c.*	$2,000,000	$3,000,000
Return on investment	*b.*	20%	12.50%	*g.*
Required return	6%	18%	*f.*	*h.*
Residual income	$15,000	*d.*	($50,000)	$0

REQUIRED:

Provide the missing data indicated by the letters *a.* through *h.*

17–7. Performance Measurement and Evaluation. As a new staff accountant, you over-hear the following statements:

Manager A: The only thing I am evaluated on is the quarterly net income. The performance report is full of information, but my boss looks only at the income numbers. No credit is given for finding new customers, good employee morale, or developing new products.

Manager B: These accounting reports are not worth very much—just income statements and some ratios. I want the system to generate reports that tell me which of my subordinates are doing good work and which are doing poorly.

Manager C: There are a lot of rules around here. What right does Jake [Jacob Alastair, the new president] have to make all these changes to the way I set prices? We used to be free to do as we pleased as long as we showed a profit.

REQUIRED:

Comment on each statement.

17–8. Employee Turnover Rates. The segment performance measurement system at the Adalaide Company includes measures of employee turnover for each of the 40 final assembly plants. Three of the plants produce basically the same product but vary substantially in costs and quality of production. Employee turnover is computed by dividing the total number of employees leaving the plant for any reason by the average number of employees during the year. Normal turnover rates are considered to be about 10 percent of average work force. During 19x0, the following employee-related activity occurred at the plants:

Plant	*Beginning Employees*	*Newly Hired*	*Retirement*	*Fired*	*Resignations "Quit or Walk"*
Jeserve	3,640	795	36	546	73
Clinder	1,680	204	50	2	252
Grotun	2,410	287	145	24	48

The average is computed as the average of the beginning and ending employees.

REQUIRED:

a. Compute the employee turnover rate for each plant.

b. Comment on the employee turnover in each plant.

17–9. Contribution Margin Performance. The Sound Machine, Inc., has two major products with the following prices and contribution:

	Supreme	*Regular*
Price	$168.00	$120.00
Variable costs	84.00	74.00
Contribution per unit	$ 84.00	$ 46.00

The sales branches sell the products in varying proportions:

	Supreme	*Regular*	*Total*
Western branch	520	60	580
Central branch	300	450	750
Eastern branch	50	850	900

REQUIRED:

a. Compute the sales for each branch. If performance is measured by sales revenue, which branch will have the best revenue performance?

b. Compute the contribution margin generated by each branch. Which branch will have the best performance based on contribution margin?

17–10. Segment Performance Reporting.   The Louisiana Sugar Company has two divisions: Cane Division and Able Division. The divisions have the following information for 19x2 (in millions):

	Cane	*Able*
Revenues	$30	$20
Controllable fixed costs	5	3
Other traceable costs	3	2

Variable costs are 60 percent of revenue for Cane Division and 40 percent of revenue for Able Division. There were common costs of $10 million.

REQUIRED:

Compute segment income for each of the divisions of the Louisiana Sugar Company assuming that it is the company policy:

a. Not to allocate the common costs.

b. To allocate common costs on the basis of revenues.

PROBLEMS

17–11. Segment Performance Reporting.   MCT Delivery Company provides local delivery of circulars and packages. During 19x7, the service had total fixed costs of $4 million of which $2 million are traceable to the divisions. The circular division had $1.4 in traceable fixed costs of which half was considered controllable by the division manager. The package division had $.6 million in fixed costs of which one third was considered controllable. The circular division had $8 million in revenue with variable costs of $0.04 per item and a service fee of $0.08 per item. The package division had revenue of $6 million with a fee of $6 per item and a variable cost of $4 per delivery.

REQUIRED:

Prepare an income statement for each division for MCT Delivery Company. Do not allocate the common costs.

17–12. Establishing Performance Measures.   V. Dawn Addington was recently selected as the chief executive officer of NHA, Inc., which is a company specializing in medical products and providing health care. In the past, segment performance was measured strictly on total costs and profits. Ms. Addington requires implementation of a new system that takes a broader perspective on performance. Because the company has over 4,200 identifiable segments, this is quite a challenge. Samples of segments and of potential performance measures that might be applied to these segments appear on the top of the next page.

REQUIRED:

Select at least three measures of performance that would be reasonable to apply to each segment.

	Segment	Measures of Performance
_____ a.	Chain of drug stores	1. Collection rates
_____ b.	Credit department	2. Controllable margin
_____ c.	Hospital computer center	3. Cost per hour
_____ d.	Hospital design consulting group	4. Cost per unit
_____ e.	Large hospital laundry unit	5. Employee turnover
_____ f.	Maternity center in a hospital	6. Jobs completed on time
_____ g.	Purchasing department	7. Net income
_____ h.	Regional sales territory	8. New accounts opened
_____ i.	Small gift aisle in a drug store	9. Patient days
_____ j.	Subsidiary that constructs hospitals	10. Return on investment
_____ k.	Wheelchair production plant	11. Revenues
		12. Sales calls
		13. Total costs
		14. Units of activity

17–13. Revenue Center Performance. Millicent Jensen is the managing partner for Advant, Ltd., a partnership specializing in advertising and promotion. Ms. Jensen is reviewing the records on Patrick Kennedy, a midlevel account executive specializing in beverage accounts. Mr. Kennedy has recently had some personal problems that have interfered with his work. The agency earns its fees as a commission on advertising placed in various media. During 19x2, Mr. Kennedy placed the following advertising in the various media ($ in millions):

	Commission Rate	Billings
Television	8%	$10.5
Radio	10%	3.0
Newspaper	8%	4.0
Magazine	8%	8.0
Direct mail	10%	1.5
Total		$27.0

About 25 percent of each of the billings would occur each year without any effort by Mr. Kennedy. Account executives are paid a base salary of $40,000 plus 0.8 percent of the billings. The cost of producing the advertising is estimated to equal about one half of the commission rate. The cost of administering accounts is equal to about 1 percent of billings, but about one half of this is fixed costs. Additional costs associated with Mr. Kennedy include:

Fringe benefits	$ 38,400
Office	12,000
Secretary	17,500
Automobile	11,000
Travel	30,000
Entertainment	25,000
Client relations	12,000
Total	$145,900

The fringe benefits are a variable cost.

REQUIRED:
a. Compute the contribution of Mr. Kennedy to Advant, Ltd. (*Hint:* Be careful in computing the amount of traceable revenue for Mr. Kennedy.)
b. Compute the ratio of contribution to compensation.
c. Compute the ratio of contribution to fixed costs for which he is responsible.
d. Account executives are expected to contribute about twice their compensation and three times their fixed costs. Does Mr. Kennedy's performance meet these requirements?
e. During 19x3, Ms. Jensen expects Mr. Kennedy's billings to drop to about 80 percent of their 19x2 level. Compute the effect of this on his contribution and his ratios.

17–14. Segment Reporting.　The Givayarn Co. produces knit products in two segments: Georgia Division and Oregon Division. The following reports were available for 19x1 using absorption costing and full allocation of common costs (in thousands):

	Division	
	Georgia	*Oregon*
Sales	$2,800	$4,200
Cost of goods sold	2,000	3,000
Gross margin	$ 800	$1,200
Marketing and administrative	496	1,110
Operating income	$ 304	$ 90

V. J. Merton, the company president, wants to have better reporting of the contribution of each division to the company. He states, "The Oregon Division must be contributing more to the company than is being reported. I know Ron [Ronald Czecaki, division manager] is doing a better job than that."

　　Of the cost of goods sold for the Georgia Division, 60 percent is variable, 20 percent is controllable fixed costs, and 20 percent is traceable but not controllable. Marketing and administrative expenses are 7 percent of sales plus fixed costs of $300,000, of which half is controllable, $50,000 is traceable but not controllable, and the remainder is for common costs that have been allocated to the division.

　　For the Oregon Division, the cost of goods sold is 50 percent variable, 20 percent controllable fixed cost, and 30 percent traceable but not controllable. Marketing and administrative expenses are 5 percent of sales plus fixed costs of $800,000 of which $50,000 is controllable, $30,000 is traceable but not controllable, and the remainder is for common costs that have been allocated to the division.

REQUIRED:
Present the financial data for the division in a format that emphasizes the margin controllable by the division manager and the contribution of the segment to common fixed costs and profits.

17–15. Decentralization versus Centralization.　RNB is a bank holding company for a state-wide group of retail consumer-oriented banks. The bank holding company was formed in the early 1960s by a group of young investors who believed in a high level of consumer services. The number of banks owned by the holding company expanded rapidly. These banks gained visibility through their experimentation with innovations such as free-standing 24-hour automated banking machines, automated funds transfer systems, and other advances in banking services.

　　RNB's earnings performance has been better than most other banks in the state. The founders organized and continue to operate RNB on a highly decentralized basis. As the number of banks owned grew, RNB's executive management delegated more responsibility and authority to individual bank presidents. The bank presidents are viewed by RNB as a "linking pin" to its executive management. Although certain aspects of each bank's operations are standardized (such as procedures for account and loan applications and salary rates), bank presidents have significant autonomy in determining how each individual bank will operate.

　　The decentralization has led each of the banks to develop individual marketing campaigns. Several of them have introduced unique "packaged" accounts that include a combination of banking services. However, they sometimes fail to notify the other banks in the group as well as the executive office of their plans and programs. One result has been interbank competition for customers where the market areas overlap. Also, the corporate marketing officer had recently begun a state-wide advertising campaign that conflicted with some of the individual banks' advertising. Consequently, there have been occasions when customers and tellers have experienced both confusion and frustration, particularly when the customers attempt to receive services at a bank other than their "home" bank.

　　RNB's executive management is concerned that there will be a slight decline in earnings for the first time in its history. The decline appears to be attributable to reduced customer satisfaction and higher operating costs. The competition among the state's banks is keen. Bank location and consistent high-quality customer service are important. RNB's 18 banks are well located and the three new bank acquisitions planned for next year are considered to be in prime locations. The increase in operating costs appears to be directly related to the individual banks' aggressive marketing efforts and new programs. Specifically, expenditures increased for advertising and for the special materials and added personnel for the "packaged" accounts.

For the past three months RNB's executive management has been meeting with the individual bank presidents. The purpose of the meetings is to review RNB's recent performance and seek ways to improve it. One recommendation that appeals to RNB's executive management is to change the organization to a more centralized structure. The specific proposal calls for a reduction in individual bank autonomy and creation of a centralized Individual Bank Management Committee. The committee would consist of all bank presidents and be chaired by a newly created position, vice president of individual bank operations. The individual banks' policies, expected to conform to overall RNB plans, would be set by consensus of the committee. RNB's executive management feels that this participative management approach will be a "fair trade" for the loss of autonomy by the individual bank presidents.

(CMA, adapted)

REQUIRED:

a. Discuss the advantages attributed to a decentralized organizational structure.

b. Identify disadvantages of a decentralized structure supporting each disadvantage with an example from RNB's situation.

c. The proposed "more centralized" structure is said by RNB's executive management to include the "participative management approach."

    1. Define the concept *participative management*.

    2. Does RNB's recommended approach include participative management? Use information from the situation to support your answer.

17–16. Performance Measurement and Evaluation. The Motor Works Division of Roland Industries is located in Fort Wayne, Indiana. A major expansion of the division's only plant was completed in April of 19x4. The expansion consisted of an addition to the existing building, additional new equipment, and the replacement of obsolete and fully depreciated equipment that was no longer efficient or cost effective.

Donald Futak became the division manager of the Motor Works Division effective May 1, 19x4. Futak had a brief meeting with John Poskey, vice president of operations for Roland Industries, when he assumed the division manager position. Poskey told Futak that the company employed return on gross assets (ROA) for measuring performance of divisions and division managers. Futak asked whether any other performance measures were ever used in place of or in conjunction with ROA. Poskey replied, "Roland's top management prefers to use a single performance measure. There is no conflict when there is only one measure. Motor Works should do well this year now that it has expanded and replaced all of that old equipment. You should have no problem exceeding the division's historical rate. I'll check back with you at the end of each quarter to see how you are doing."

Poskey called Futak after the first quarter results were complete because the Motor Works' ROA was considerably below the historical rate for the division. Futak told Poskey at that time that he did not believe that ROA was a valid performance measure for the Motor Works Division. Poskey indicated that he would get back to Futak. Futak did receive perfunctory memorandums after the second and third quarters, but there was no further discussion on the use of ROA. Now Futak has received the following memorandum.

TO: Donald Futak, Manager—Motor Works Division   May 24, 19x5
FROM: John Poskey, Vice President of Operations
SUBJECT: Division Performance

The operating results for the fourth quarter and for our fiscal year ended on April 30 are now complete. Your fourth-quarter return on gross assets was only 9 percent, resulting in a return for the year of slightly under 11 percent. I recall discussing your low return after the first quarter and reminding you after the second and third quarters that this level of return is not considered adequate for the Motor Works Division.

The return on gross assets at Motor Works has ranged from 15 percent to 18 percent for the past five years. An 11 percent return may be acceptable at some of Roland's other divisions, but not at a proven winner like Motor Works—especially in light of your recently improved facility.

I would like to meet with you at your office on Monday, June 3, to discuss ways to restore Motor Works' return on gross assets to its former level. Please let me know if this date is acceptable to you.

Futak is looking forward to meeting with Poskey. He knows the division's ROA is below the historical rate but the dollar profits for the year are greater than prior years. He plans to explain to Poskey why he believes return on gross assets is not an appropriate performance measure for the Motor Works Division. He also plans to recommend that ROA be replaced with three measures—dollar profit, receivables turnover, and inventory turnover. These three measures would constitute a set of multiple criteria that would be used to evaluate performance.

(CMA, adapted)

REQUIRED:

a. On the basis of the relationship between John Poskey and Donald Futak as well as the memorandum from Poskey, identify apparent weaknesses in the performance evaluation process of Roland Industries. Do not include in your answer any discussion on the use of return on assets (ROA) as a performance measure.

b. From the information presented, identify a possible explanation of why Motor Works Division's ROA declined in the fiscal year ended April 30, 19x5.

c. Identify criteria that should be used in selecting performance measures to evaluate operating managers.

d. If John Poskey does agree to use multiple criteria for evaluating the performance of the Motor Works Division as Donald Futak has suggested, discuss whether the multiple criteria of dollar profit, receivables turnover, and inventory turnover would be appropriate.

17–17. Segment Reporting.   Music Teachers, Inc., is an educational association for music teachers that had 20,000 members during 19x5. The association operates from a central headquarters but has local membership chapters throughout the United States. Monthly meetings are held by the local chapters to discuss recent developments on topics of interest to music teachers. The association's journal, *Teachers' Forum,* is issued monthly with features about recent developments in the field. The association publishes books and reports and sponsors professional courses that qualify for continuing professional education credit. The statement of revenues and expenses for the current year is presented below.

MUSIC TEACHERS, INC.
Statement of Revenues and Expenses
For the Year Ended November 30, 19x5
(in thousands)

Revenues	$3,275
Expenses	
Salaries	$ 920
Personnel costs	230
Occupancy costs	280
Reimbursement to local chapters	600
Other membership services	500
Printing and paper	320
Postage and shipping	176
Instructors fees	80
General and administrative	38
Total expenses	$3,144
Excess of revenues over expenses	$ 131

The board of directors of Music Teachers, Inc., has requested that a segmented statement of operations be prepared showing the contribution of each revenue center (i.e., Membership, Magazine Subscriptions, Books and Reports, Continuing Education). Mike Doyle has been assigned this responsibility and has gathered the following data prior to statement preparation.

Membership dues are $100 per year of which $20 is considered to cover a one-year subscription to the association's journal. Other benefits include membership in the association and chapter affiliation. The portion of the dues covering the magazine subscription ($20) should be assigned to the Magazine Subscriptions revenue center.

One-year subscriptions to *Teachers' Forum* were sold to nonmembers and libraries at $30 each. A total of 2,500 of these subscriptions was sold. In addition to subscriptions, the magazine generated $100,000 in advertising revenue. The costs per magazine subscription were $7 for printing and paper and $4 for postage and shipping.

A total of 28,000 technical reports and professional texts was sold by the Books and Reports Department at an average unit selling price of $25. Average costs per publication were as follows.

Printing and paper	$4
Postage and shipping	$2

The association offers a variety of continuing education courses to both members and nonmembers. The one-day courses cost $75 each and were attended by 2,400 students in 19x5. A total of 1,760 students took two-day courses at a cost of $125 for each course. Outside instructors were paid to teach some courses.

Salary and occupancy data are as follows.

	Salaries	*Square Footage*
Membership	$210,000	2,000
Magazine Subscriptions	150,000	2,000
Books and Reports	300,000	3,000
Continuing Education	180,000	2,000
Corporate staff	80,000	1,000
	$920,000	10,000

The Books and Reports Department also rents warehouse space at an annual cost of $50,000. Personnel costs are 25 percent of salaries.

Printing and paper costs other than for magazine subscriptions and books and reports relate to the Continuing Education Department.

General and administrative expenses include all other costs incurred by the corporate staff to operate the association.

Doyle has decided he will assign all revenues and expenses to the revenue centers that can be:

Traced directly to a revenue center.

Allocated on a reasonable and logical basis to a revenue center.

The expenses that can be traced or assigned to corporate staff as well as any other expenses that cannot be assigned to revenue centers will be grouped with the general and administrative expenses and not allocated to the revenue centers. Doyle believes that allocations often tend to be arbitrary and are not useful for management reporting and analysis. He believes that any further allocation of the general and administrative expenses associated with the operation and administration of the association would be arbitrary.

(CMA, adapted)

REQUIRED:
a. Prepare a segmented statement of revenues and expenses that presents the contribution of each revenue center and includes the common costs of the organization that are not allocated to the revenue centers.
b. If segmented reporting is adopted by the association for continuing usage, discuss the ways the information provided by the report can be utilized by the association.
c. Mike Doyle decided not to allocate some indirect or nontraceable expenses to revenue centers because he believes that allocations tend to be arbitrary.

1. Besides the arbitrary argument, what reasons are often presented for not allocating indirect or nontraceable expenses to revenue centers?
2. Under what circumstances might the allocation of indirect or nontraceable expenses to revenue centers be acceptable?

17–18. Segment Reporting.   Caprice Company manufactures and sells two products—a small portable office file cabinet that it has made for over 15 years and a home/travel file introduced in 19x1. The files are made in Caprice's only manufacturing plant. Budgeted variable production costs per unit of product are as follows.

	Office File	Home/Travel File
Sheet metal	$ 3.50	—
Plastic	—	$3.75
Direct labor (at $8 per DLH)	4.00	2.00
Variable manufacturing overhead (at $9 per DLH)	4.50	2.25
	$12.00	$8.00

Variable manufacturing overhead costs vary with direct labor hours. The annual fixed manufacturing overhead costs are budgeted at $120,000. A total of 50 percent of these costs is directly traceable to the Office File Department and 22 percent of the costs is traceable to the Home/Travel File Department. The remaining 28 percent of the costs is not traceable to either department.

Caprice employs two full-time salespersons—Pam Price and Robert Flint. Each salesperson receives an annual salary of $14,000 plus a sales commission of 10 percent of his/her total gross sales. Travel and entertainment expense is budgeted at $22,000 annually for each salesperson. Price is expected to sell 60 percent of the budgeted unit sales for each file and Flint the remaining 40 percent. Caprice's remaining selling and administrative expenses include fixed administrative costs of $80,000 that cannot be traced to either file plus the following traceable selling expenses.

	Office File	Home/Travel File
Packaging expenses per unit	$ 2.00	$ 1.50
Promotion	$30,000	$40,000

Data regarding Caprice's budgeted and actual sales for the fiscal year ended May 31, 19x4, are presented in the following schedule. There were no changes in the beginning and ending balances of either finished goods or work in process inventories.

	Office File	Home/Travel File
Budgeted sales volume in units	15,000	15 000
Budgeted and actual unit sales price	$29.50	$19.50
Actual unit sales		
Pam Price	10,000	9,500
Robert Flint	5,000	10,500
Total units	15,000	20,000

Data regarding Caprice's operating expenses for the year ended May 31, 19x4, follow.

There were no increases or decreases in raw materials inventory for either sheet metal or plastic and there were no usage variances. However, sheet metal prices were 6 percent above budget and plastic prices were 4 percent below budget.

The actual direct labor hours worked and costs incurred were as follows.

	Hours	*Amount*
Office file	7,500	$ 57,000
Home/Travel file	6,000	45,600
	13,500	$102,600

Fixed manufacturing overhead costs attributable to the office file department were $8,000 above the budget. All other fixed manufacturing overhead costs were incurred at the same amounts as budgeted, and all variable manufacturing overhead costs were incurred at the budgeted hourly rates.

All selling and administrative expenses were incurred at budgeted rates or amounts except the following items.

(CMA, adapted)

Nontraceable administrative expenses		$ 34,000
Promotion		
Office files	$32,000	
Home/Travel files	58,000	90,000
Travel and entertainment		
Pam Price	$24,000	
Robert Flint	28,000	52,000
		$176,000

REQUIRED:

a. Prepare a segmented income statement of Caprice Company's actual operations for the fiscal year ended May 31, 19x4. The report should be prepared in a contribution margin format by product and should reflect total income (loss) for the company before income taxes.

b. Identify and discuss any additional analyses that could be made of the data presented that would be of value to Caprice Company.

EXTENDED APPLICATIONS

17–19. Return on Investment.   Senior management of Tuft Metals Company has asked you, as internal auditor, to review the operations of the Sitnam Division. Recent performance has been very poor, and senior management is considering liquidating the division. In preparation for making your detailed review of the division operations, you have gathered the following information for the past eight years ($ in thousands):

	Sales	*Income*	*Assets*	*Employee Turnover*	*R&D*	*Maintenance*
19x1	$6,200	$ 372	$3,100	5%	$500	$320
19x2	6,904	414	3,452	6%	520	350
19x3	7,720	772	3,860	22%	210	360
19x4	7,940	953	2,978	15%	28	80
19x5	8,203	1,148	2,871	30%	10	45
19x6	8,110	324	1,622	23%	0	50
19x7	7,200	(288)	1,610	15%	0	310
19x8	5,820	(524)	1,580	11%	0	560

During 19x2, the senior management of Tuft Metals Company was changed. The new CEO believed strongly in the value of decentralization. During 19x3, Joe Clossun was promoted to division general manager of the Sitnam Division and given free reign to make changes to bring the division up to expected profitability. Division managers are evaluated on the basis of return on investment. Even though Mr. Clossun received good pay raises every year, in March 19x6, he was hired away by a major competitor. Since then, the Sitnam Division has been declining rapidly.

REQUIRED:
a. Compute the return on investment for each year from 19x2 through 19x6.
b. Based on the objective evidence of the financial data and the measure of employee turnover, what are the apparent reasons for the change in ROI for each of the following years:

    1. 19x3   3. 19x5
    2. 19x4   4. 19x6

c. Comment on the reasons for the current operational problems of the Sitnam Division. Specifically, comment on what you expect to find in the general areas of new products, employee morale, and age and condition of equipment.

17–20. Segment Performance Reports.   The Computer Systems Department provides computer services to the 43 other departments, branches, and divisions of the Simkin Company. The Computer Systems Department had 210 employees at the beginning of the quarter and a quarterly expense budget of about $6.3 million. During the second quarter of 19x5, the department had actual expenses and a budget of the following:

	Actual	*Budget*
Salaries and wages	$1,630,200	$1,470,000
Employee benefits	521,664	411,600
Paper and supplies	1,892,000	2,241,000
Equipment rental	610,000	600,000
Software	628,200	620,000
Depreciation	915,400	803,400
Training and development	97,000	140,000
Total	$6,294,464	$6,286,000

	Actual	*Normal*
Activity		
Data entry (1,000 lines)	59,500	57,600
Printing (1,000 pages)	56,210	55,000
Terminal connect hours	559,060	526,000
Systems analysis and design hours	12,562	12,400
Programming hours	22,590	22,400

During the quarter, 18 new employees were hired, 28 employees quit, 4 were fired, and 1 retired. Normal employee turnover is 6 percent per quarter for computer departments.

REQUIRED:
Treat part *(b)* as independent from part *(a)*
a. Prepare a Computer Systems Department performance report assuming that the department is treated as a cost center. Display a difference column as a percentage.
b. The following transfer prices have been established based on budgeted cost, normal activity, and a 20 percent markup.

Data entry (1,000 lines)	$24.00
Printing (1,000 pages)	57.60
Terminal connect hours	1.20
Systems analysis and design	96.00
Programming	48.00

The department has assets of $8 million, and a tax rate of 40 percent applies.
1. Compute the total revenue to the Computer Systems Department from other segments.
2. Prepare a Computer Systems Department performance report assuming that the department is treated as an investment center. Display a difference column for each of the measures.
3. Compute the residual income for the Computer Systems Department assuming that a 10 percent after-tax rate of return is required.

17–21. Performance Measurement and Evaluation. The division general managers for Vralco, Inc., are meeting in Lexington, Kentucky. Vralco is a large, diversified company with 328 divisions and branches. The first day of the two-day training conference has been long and very windy. A full day was devoted to the new president's changes to the performance evaluation system.

Mack Robbins has entered the hotel lounge for a light snack in the late evening. Mr. Robbins has decided to retire after 35 years with the company. Thus, a conference on the performance evaluation system is about as exciting as 10 tons of snow in the driveway. (Right now he is dreaming about living full-time in the retirement home he built on St. Thomas Island.) Although he never finished college, Mr. Robbins worked his way up from the loading dock to general manager of the company's largest, most profitable division. He never seemed to be in a hurry to do anything but got things done. He survived six major shake-ups in top management and two mergers during his years. In the middle of his reverie, Mr. Robbins is joined by Jay Hoggenbak, an aggressive rival, who starts badgering Mr. Robbins as to how he was able to get high returns during the recent economic decline in the economy.

Hoggenbak: I see you have done it again, Mack. You're going out with a top-10 ranking of the 328 divisions. Now that you're retiring this month, could you give me any hints on how to run my division?

Robbins: Buy low, sell high.

Hoggenbak: Sure. And never take a wooden nickel. How have you been able to come up with such good products in your line? Your sales stay high and the prices hold. Your cost and income figures are unbelievable, and you have only a modest investment in assets to support a large volume.

Robbins: Win the war, not the battle. See the forest, not the trees. (Chuckles)

Hoggenbak: #$@&! Could you at least tell me why you buy all the old trucks and equipment from the other divisions? They must cost a bundle to maintain. That seems idiotic. How could we maintain our image with all that trash around?

Robbins: OK. That's good equipment that they were just going to throw away. They keep going after new equipment every few years and selling their old stuff for a dime. They want it to be shiny or "state of the art." That just increases their costs but doesn't provide products to customers. Image is expensive and doesn't impress our types of customer. I don't care about image, just profits.

Hoggenbak: Interesting. You never seem to dump people, even when top management insists. You fight for your people. The other managers think you're just soft or daft.

Robbins: That's my only regret in retiring. Losing those people. Good people are hard to find. I kept only the good ones and paid them well. Where do you think the new products and customers came from? That's profits. I drop unprofitable products rather than laying off good people. The next manager's probably going to mess it all up and treat them awful. It's up to the top, but I hope they appoint one of my assistants rather than some "fast track" whiz kid with an MBA.

Hoggenbak: Unusual viewpoint. Now I've got to know one last thing. Why did you never take the top position? I heard that you were given strong consideration. How can you turn down that much money?

Robbins: The board did approach me during the last shake-up. I was flattered, but I just couldn't take it seriously. The top is too far from what I know, and I've seen too many heads roll. All the board cares about is ROI and earnings per share. This "new" performance system is just more of the same old thing with fancy words around it. I know top management needs to look more deeply into each operation, but with the number of divisions we have, it will go crazy trying. I know I would. I was happy where I was, and I have made more money than I can possibly spend. Now if you will excuse me, I'd like to catch some shut-eye. I'm just an old man, you know.

REQUIRED:

a. Why does a system that rank orders 328 managers on the basis of ROI tend to make managers very competitive and secretive of their methods? Why would Mr. Robbins be unwilling to reveal his secrets and thoughts to a competitor?

b. Why did Mr. Robbins purchase old equipment from other divisions and branches?

c. What was Mr. Robbins' attitude toward new and innovative equipment? Would this attitude work in other industries, for example, a television network? Why was "image" unimportant to him?

d. How has Mr. Robbins connected the treatment of and personal loyalty toward his employees with his high ROI? Was he soft or daft as Mr. Hoggenbak seems to imply?

e. Why does Mr. Robbins believe that the top management of Vralco, Inc., faces an impossible assignment from the board of directors?

f. Would Mr. Robbins have been able to maintain his style in dealings with a new CEO who believed strongly in a centralized company? Comment.

17–22. Segment Reporting.   Thomas A. Krumwiede is the partner in charge of practice analysis for Mills, Moore & Co., which is a firm of certified public accountants with revenues of $2.3 billion. Mr. Krumwiede is reviewing the Construction Consulting Group (CCG). This consulting group specializes in designing accounting systems for construction companies to meet federal and state regulatory requirements. The practice group contains 38 professionals and 10 support personnel located in three regions. The partner in charge of the practice group, Clinton Abrams, is located in the Washington office. The billings of the unit have been disappointing during the two recent quarters but promise to increase in future years. The national board is considering disbanding CCG and merging its operations with the regional offices.

Mr. Abrams has explained that CCG's marketing efforts result in audit, tax, and other engagements for which the group gets no credit. Mr. Abrams comments, "Basicly, half of our time is spent in marketing the firm to the construction industry." For example, recent efforts gained the audit and tax work of JSC Construction, a company with $1.3 billion in assets. The audit group (with outside consultants) performed the systems consulting work and did not share the billings with the consulting group. Because Mr. Abrams believed that the audit group lacks sufficient expertise in construction regulatory work, the firm was unnecessarily exposed to risk. Mr. Abrams comments: "Frankly, Tom, JSC got a weak system, I lost $600,000 in billings, and our reputation for construction business is going down the drain."

Statements for the practice unit show the following amounts for the year 19x0 (in thousands):

Revenues			$8,967
Partners' compensation	3	$780	
Managers' compensation	12	432	
Consultants' compensation	23	989	
Outside consultants' fees		902	
Travel		820	
Professional liability insurance		836	
Professional—Memberships and library		114	
Office space and utilities		407	
Client development		960	
Training and seminars		119	
Support personnel	10	142	
Computer support		418	
Materials and supplies		23	
Central office		639	
Recruiting		646	
Total expenses			8,227
Net group margin			$ 740

Practice groups are required to generate a margin of 20 percent of billings in order to justify the investment in personnel.

Pure variable costs for CCG are the outside consultants, travel, and materials. Costs associated with professional liability insurance, office space and utilities, computer support, central office, and recruiting are allocated based on the number of professional staff. Training, professional expenses, and client development are discretionary expenses as planned by Mr. Abrams. He plans to have roughly one manager and two consultants for each $750,000 in revenues. Mr. Abrams agrees that the allocation of liability insurance and office space is reasonable. He disagrees with the computer support: ''All our work is done on client equipment.'' He also disagrees with the allocation of central office cost: ''If we traced costs for administration through the system, there would not be more than $100,000 that could be reasonably traced to our group.'' Finally, Mr. Abrams's group gets no value from the recruiting function: ''We have to hire our own people. Our consultants need 10 to 15 years of experience in the construction business.''

During 19x0, Mills, Moore & Co. had $212 million in billings to construction companies, of which 68 percent was for audit work, 22 percent was for tax work, and the remainder was for consulting work of all types. For the audit work, $11 million is for new work that Mr. Abrams can document as clients developed through CCG efforts. Further, $4 million in new tax billings and $2 million in new consulting billings (outside CCG) are traceable to CCG effort. However, Mr. Abrams does concede that about $1.5 million of his own billings relate to the efforts of other groups. Mr. Abrams estimates that about 70 percent of client development effort results in the billings that go to other practice units. Reasonable estimates of the contribution margins for additional work for each of the practice areas are:

Audit	36%
Tax	44%
Consulting (Other than CCG)	32%

REQUIRED:

a. Based just on the revenues billed by CCG:
   1. Prepare a contribution analysis of CCG.
   2. Compute the ratio of contribution to fixed costs.
   3. Compute the ratio of contribution to compensation of professional staff.
   4. What are the billings required to make a 20 percent contribution on revenues?
b. Based on the total revenues traceable to CCG efforts:
   1. Prepare a contribution analysis of CCG.
   2. Compute the ratio of contribution to fixed costs.
   3. Compute the ratio of contribution to compensation of professional staff.
c. Comment on the contribution of CCG to the firm and its relationships to other practice units.
d. Assume that audit and tax clients stay with the same CPA firm for an average of 10 years, but consulting engagements are only one-time events. Comment on the effect of this on the contribution of CCG to Mills, Moore & Co.

CHAPTER

Transfer Pricing

TRANSFER-PRICING PROBLEM

Robert Williams, 57, the Beth City Division manager, was concerned about his future. The division had shown little income during the past two years, and his performance evaluations have not gone well. The division produces packaging materials for the 38 plants of CTX, Inc. During each of the past two years, CTX, Inc. has changed the pricing approach for Beth City Division's products, and it has been a major adjustment each time. On December 21, 19x6, Williams received a memorandum from headquarters detailing the pricing approach to be applied in 19x7. Williams is speaking with the division controller, Michelle Robins:

Williams: Now headquarters wants us to split fixed and variable standard costs in setting prices? We get only a 20 percent margin over cost, instead of 30 percent. We just got our billing programs set up to run actual cost prices. What is this?

Robins: As close as I can tell from Lisa [a friend and accountant on the staff at headquarters], they now believe that if fixed and variable costs are split, they will get better decisions. Further, if prices are based on standard costs, then we will not be inefficient.

Williams: This is just another headache and another change to our computer system. Remember when they tried market prices two years ago? What a bother! Getting market prices on every unique package. Nobody else makes a lot of our stuff. Then, when that didn't work, they wanted us to negotiate prices for 580 packages with 38 divisions. That was a mess that took months to untangle. How are we supposed to split the $120,000 in monthly fixed costs among 38 divisions?

718

Robins: According to the memo, we're supposed to use the planned volume for the other divisions. I'll call headquarters and get the data for January. No problem on that issue.
Williams: OK, I guess that'll work.

On December 23, 19x6, Williams was talking with John Casion, an engineering staff member, on the final adjustments to standard costs for 19x7.

Williams: Because actual materials costs have gone up recently, I think we really need to adjust the materials standard for all 580 products.
Casion: OK, I'll run the programs this evening. How much should we increase them? 10 percent?
Williams: I think more like 30 percent would be reasonable under the circumstances.

LEARNING OBJECTIVES

After completing this chapter, you should be able to:

1. Compare cost allocation with transfer pricing.
2. Compute transfer prices for products or services based on cost concepts.
3. Discuss the limitations of each of the cost-based transfer-pricing approaches.
4. Compute transfer prices for products or services based on market price concepts.
5. Discuss the limitations of each of the market-based transfer-pricing approaches.

TRANSFER PRICE CONCEPT

A **transfer price** is the price set for goods or services transferred among profit or investment centers. Price is an issue only when transfers of products or services among segments are significant. Thus, the higher the proportion of transfers, the more important is the transfer-pricing method in measuring performance. In the introductory business problem, all of the output from the division was transferred to the other divisions. Thus, Mr. Williams was very much concerned about the transfer prices set. Top management changed the method of transfer pricing each year, and Mr. Williams has had to adjust the division's operation to match the pricing method.

The primary purpose for charging one segment for the use of products and services of another segment is to motivate the efficient and effective use of resources. If there were no charge for products or services, the tendency would be to use them inefficiently. For example, if packaging materials were not assigned a price, managers of the other divisions would ask for more expensive packing materials than they need to effectively protect product shipments. Additionally, as discussed in Chapter 16, charging user segments facilitates absorption or full cost accounting that is required by external financial reporting and tax reporting.

If a segment, for example Beth City Division, were organized as a cost center, the process of charging user segments for products or services is called a **cost allocation.** If the same segment were organized as a profit or investment center, the charges to users would be called a transfer price. Indeed, the transfer-pricing approaches of many companies bear a marked resemblance to cost allocation. The primary difference is that a transfer price often has a markup added to the cost to allow for a profit on the transaction. One important exception to this is in contracting with government agencies, in which case markups are not allowed on transfers among organizational segments.

Consider the effects of the transfer-pricing policy. The higher the price, the more the revenue there is for the selling division and the higher the seller's division income is. Similarly, the higher the transfer price, the higher the expenses are for the purchasing division and the lower the purchasing division income is. Because both the selling and the purchasing divisions are evaluated on the basis of profits, the divisions are keenly interested in the manner in which the prices are set.

Decentralization and Transfer-Pricing Policies

The policies for transfer prices are fundamental issues related to decentralization. These issues should be worked out between the profit center managers and top management. Although a case might be built for supporting one approach over others in specific settings, no one approach is intrinsically best in practical settings. Very practical considerations, such as the feasibility of implementing the policy among the divisions and the impact on the computerized accounting systems, must be considered in selecting a transfer-pricing approach.

A transfer price may be based on either costs or market price. Transfer prices based on cost are common for many organizations because cost numbers are available from the accounting system. A cost basis is appropriate when the company has numerous products and services or the product is highly specialized, such as research, design, or building construction. A cost basis is also appropriate when there is no intermediate market for the product or service.

COST-BASED TRANSFER-PRICING APPROACHES

The cost bases may include actual, normal, standard, or budgeted costs. Costs may be distinguished between fixed and variable, and the price may be based on actual or planned activity levels. Six common cost-based approaches to transfer pricing include:

1. Actual cost of actual usage plus a markup.
2. Normal cost of actual usage plus a markup.
3. Standard cost of actual usage plus a markup.
4. Budgeted cost at actual usage plus a markup.
5. Actual fixed costs allocated on planned usage and actual variable costs allocated on actual usage plus a markup.
6. Budgeted fixed costs allocated on planned usage and budgeted variable costs allocated on actual usage plus a markup.

Approaches involving variable and opportunity costs have also been suggested and will be discussed later in the chapter.

Example of Cost-Based Allocation

As an example of applying cost-based techniques, consider the following data for Beth City Division for the month of January 19x7:

	Actual	*Flexible Budget*
Materials	$150,000	$140,000
Wages and salaries	80,000	81,000
Employee benefits	28,500	27,000
Maintenance	15,600	15,000
Depreciation	40,000	38,000
Administration	5,000	5,000
Total division costs	$319,100	$306,000

Additional information will be used in computing transfer prices:

Division Activity	*For the Month of January*	
	Actual	*Planned*
Tonnage produced	3,000	4,000
Total variable costs	$189,600	$62 per ton
Total fixed costs	$129,500	$120,000

A markup of 20 percent is to be applied to each of the cost amounts in computing the transfer price. One customer, the Atlanta Division, planned to use 400 tons during the month but due to economic conditions, its actual usage was only 320 tons.

Under normal costing, the actual costs are accumulated for materials and wages, and then the remaining costs are applied at a rate of 120 percent of wages. Thus, normal costs are:

Materials	$150,000
Labor	80,000
Overhead applied $80,000 × 120%	96,000
Total normal costs	$326,000

For standard costing, assume a standard cost of $90 per ton.

Exhibit 18–1 presents the computation of the transfer price under each of the cost-based methods. The billing amount for products purchased by the Atlanta Division is also computed.

EXHIBIT 18–1

BETH CITY DIVISION
Computation of Cost-Based Transfer Prices
For January 19x7

Cost/Base	(1 + 20%) Transfer Atlanta Division = Cost × Markup = Price × Activity = Billing
1. Actual cost at actual activity:	$319,100/3,000 = $106.367 × 120% = $127.640 × 320 = $40,845
2. Normal cost at actual activity:	$326,000/3,000 = $108.667 × 120% = $130.400 × 320 = $41,728
3. Standard cost at actual activity:	[Given] $ 90.00 × 120% = $108.000 × 320 = $34,560
4. Flexible budget at actual activity:	$306,000/3,000 = $102.00 × 120% = $122.400 × 320 = $39,168
5. Actual fixed cost at planned activity:	$129,500/4,000 = $ 32.375 × 120% = $ 38.850 × 400 = $15,540
Actual variable cost at actual activity:	$189,600/3,000 = 63.200 × 120% = $ 75.840 × 320 = 24,269
	$39,809
6. Budgeted fixed costs at planned activity:	$120,000/4,000 = $ 30.000 × 120% = $ 36.000 × 400 = $14,400
Standard variable costs at actual activity:	$ 62.000 × 120% = $ 74.400 × 320 = 23,808
	$38,208

The billing for the Atlanta Division varied from $36,560 to $41,728, or a difference of about 14 percent. Over a year, this difference can have large effects on the performance report of the Atlanta Division. Which of the six transfer prices is correct? Because all six charging methods are acceptable in practice, all six amounts are technically correct. However, each method will have more or less desirable results when applied.

Concerns Regarding Cost-Based Transfer Pricing

Management Decisions.   Some managers manipulate transfer prices based on cost no matter which one is selected. They increase the cost basis to reflect the desired price rather than basing the price on cost. In many companies, this activity is considered unethical because the transfer price is based on deceit. Standard costs are supposed to be based on the concept of expected or currently attainable costs, rather than the desired transfer price. For example, in the introductory business problem, Mr. Williams manipulated the standard cost base by increasing the materials standard cost by 30 percent, which was much higher than the expected increase in actual materials costs.

Because setting standard costs involves detailed operating information, it will be to the advantage of the selling division to keep the standard-setting information private and increase the standard costs. This behavior is unproductive and perhaps unethical, but the behavior is rewarded with higher transfer prices and thus income for the division. Top management has to see through the manipulation and evaluate the substance of the profit center performance.

The Issue of Complexity.   Pricing approaches that separate fixed and variable costs as in approaches 5 and 6 in the example have appeal in concept. However, these pricing schemes become very complex in practice when there are many producing and purchasing segments and many products are being transferred. There are problems with maintaining agreements over time as to the proportion of capacity that is to be paid for by each user. Further, users' needs often change much faster than the profit center can change its fixed capacity. For a small number of users, say less than 10, this can be worked out, but with many users, the agreements are difficult or impossible to maintain over the life of fixed assets.

Motivation to Increase Costs.   All of the cost-based methods have the drawback of rewarding selling divisions for having high costs: the higher the cost, the higher the revenue. Consequently, higher costs result in higher profits. For example, assume that the selling division produces packaging with a cost of $100 per ton. The division markup allowed in internal sales is 20 percent, resulting in a price of $120 for a gross profit of $20 per ton. Now suppose the division manager has the opportunity to increase costs up to $120 by installing a new production line. The packaging material will be somewhat more reliable, and production is much easier. The new price will be $144 with a gross profit of $24 per unit.

Depending on the effects on volume of the higher price, the manager will be very tempted to recommend the new production process. Although this may be viewed by some as unproductive, unethical, or just wrong, the behavior is rewarded by a cost-based system. Senior management must counteract this in its review of capital projects and its performance evaluation of the division managers.

Fixed Costs and Transfer Pricing.   Transfer prices that include fixed costs based on actual activity are often considered unfair by purchasing divisions because the charge changes from period to period, depending on the activity of other divisions. These differences can be substantial and are totally uncontrollable. Thus, charges based on budgeted costs and actual activity to the Atlanta Division could go something like this for a three-month period:

	Cost/Base	Unit Cost × Markup	=	Price × Activity	=	Billing
January	$306,000/3,000 =	$102 × 120% =		$122.40 × 320 =		$39,168
February	430,000/5,000 =	$ 86 × 120% =		103.20 × 340 =		$35,088
March	275,000/2,500 =	$110 × 120% =		132.00 × 310 =		$40,920

A division manager might be led to believe that the more packaging materials he or she uses, the lower the cost will be. During other months, the reverse pattern could occur. The pattern depends on the activity in the other divisions in the company in addition to the activities of the Atlanta Division.

When actual volume is used to allocate fixed costs, the pattern of actual usage and of transfer prices during a year will be somewhat random. Consequently, if a selling division's costs are predominantly fixed, they should not be allocated on the basis of actual usage. Instead, planned or negotiated usage might be a more stable basis for determining the prices.

Standard Cost Pricing. Transfer-pricing policies based on the internal standard costs (approaches 3 and 6) encourage managers of selling divisions to increase standard costs. Instead of encouraging managers to set tight but attainable standards, the transfer-pricing policy encourages managers to set loose standards. The result is lower efficiency and less motivation to be effective, which is an undesirable consequence of a transfer-pricing approach. Some organizations impose the standards used for pricing from outside the selling division. This imposition reduces the decentralization of the organization.

External Sales and Purchases. To counteract the problem of increasing costs in selling segments, many companies allow purchasing segments to buy externally. The effect of this policy is to place the selling division managers in direct competition with external companies. The selling division manager can no longer increase income by increasing costs because buying divisions will shift their purchases to the outside companies. Thus, the tendency toward increasing costs can be counteracted by allowing purchasing divisions to buy from outside suppliers.

However, for strategic reasons involving trade secrets or market position, some companies cannot allow external purchases of certain parts or components. Those companies in defense or high technology may find that external purchases are highly risky or illegal.

Problems Related to Quality with Cost-Based Transfer Pricing. Transfer-pricing methods based on cost do not encourage the selling division to be both efficient and responsive. Because all costs are charged to buying divisions, there is little incentive to keep costs low or to provide outstanding service to purchasing segments. When selling divisions have captive customers, production tends to be of a lower quality than an external supplier might provide. The lower quality may be reflected in late deliveries, poor employee attitudes, or defective units. Consequently, companies that do not allow external purchases may shift the emphasis in the performance evaluation of selling divisions from profits to quality and cost measures. Thus, the selling division effectively becomes a quality/cost center. Timing of delivery, quality of units produced, employee turnover, and trends in production unit cost would appear in the performance report instead of the current profit numbers. In general, the problems with cost-based transfer pricing can be overcome in the performance measurement and evaluation process by the use of cost and quality measures.

Variable Cost–Based Transfer Pricing

Basic economic theory recommends that a company should produce and sell a product until the marginal revenue is equal to its marginal costs. The marginal cost is roughly equal to the variable cost of producing additional units of product or service. Transfer prices that are greater than marginal cost reduce the company's level of activity and profits. For example, assume that the selling division produces component C36 with a cost of:

Variable costs	$ 5
Allocated fixed costs	5
Total costs	$10

The purchasing division has the opportunity to sell 100,000 units of product P20 that includes component V36 at a price of $10 with other variable costs of $2 per product. If the transfer of C36 were priced at $10 full cost plus 20 percent profit, the selling division would have an increase in contribution of $700,000:

Revenues from C36	100,000 × $12	$1,200,000
Less variable costs	100,000 × $ 5	500,000
Contribution margin from transaction		$ 700,000

However, the purchasing division would suffer a loss of $400,000 on the sale of P20:

Revenues from P20	100,000 × $10		$1,000,000
Less variable costs:			
Purchase of C36	100,000 × $12	$1,200,000	
Other variable costs	100,000 × $ 2	200,000	1,400,000
Loss on transaction			($400,000)

Consequently, the purchasing division would not produce and sell the P20 and purchase the C36. This would be unfortunate because the transactions would net out to $300,000 in contribution for the company as a whole:

Revenues from P20	100,000 × $10		$1,000,000
Less variable costs:			
Selling division	100,000 × $ 5	$500,000	
Purchasing division	100,000 × $ 2	200,000	700,000
Contribution margin from transactions			$ 300,000

Because the purchasing division will not purchase the V36, the activity does not occur and neither division can benefit. In general, a transfer price at or near variable cost will increase the activity of purchasing divisions and thereby the activity of the selling divisions. Maximum activity and company profit will occur when the transfer price is set at variable cost.[1] However, more than the variable cost must be charged to the purchasing divisions or there will be practical dysfunctional consequences as described in the next section.

Limitations of Transfer Prices at Variable Cost. Three basic issues are associated with transfer prices set at variable costs:

1. Prices and bids of the purchasing divisions to external customers tend to be lower.
2. Over time, variable costs tend to decrease and fixed costs tend to increase in the selling divisions.

---

[1] Later in the chapter we will qualify this conclusion for the special circumstances when the selling division is operating at capacity and the units transferred are unique to the selling division.

3. Conflict among purchasing division managers over treatment by selling divisions tends to increase.

First, the prices and bids made to external customers by purchasing divisions are not independent of the costs paid for inputs. If all transfers were priced at variable cost, prices and bids set for sales made to outsiders tend to be lower. This may result in either increased profits or losses for the company as a whole, depending upon the reactions of customers and competitors. If losses in the selling division are not adequately offset by profits in the purchasing division, top management must counteract the effects on margins by insisting on higher external prices and profits in the purchasing divisions.

Second, charging through only the variable costs removes the pressure on the selling divisions to control fixed costs. Any proposal that reduces variable costs will find strong support from the purchasing division managers. Likewise, changes that increase variable costs will be opposed by the purchasing division managers. As a result, investment in equipment, fixed facilities, and salaries tends to increase. More costs tend to become fixed. After several years have passed, the company will have higher fixed costs and lower variable costs. Top management will have to counteract this tendency in the choices it makes in the capital project selection process.

Third, there is keen competition for favorable performance evaluations that result in salary increases and promotions. If the transfer price is set at variable cost, each transaction will benefit the purchasing segment in terms of contribution on external sales but will exclude the selling segment from sharing in the contribution and profits. Why should the selling segment manager cooperate with this process? Very few people are this charitable to their competitors for the limited number of promotions. Consequently, the selling division manager may place priority on that output that will benefit him or her the most in terms of salary and promotion. Low-priority (variable-cost) work may be performed later or given less quality effort. This can lead to conflicts among segment managers as to fairness of treatment by the selling division.

Opportunity Costing Approach

If the selling division is at capacity and if it is the sole producer of components, the production of the additional components requires giving up some production. For example, assume that component C89 with variable cost of $5 is placed into a product P16 that has a unit contribution margin of $100. Similarly, component C36 is used in production of P20, which has a contribution of $3 per unit. Now if an additional 100,000 of C36 were produced and sold to the purchasing division, the company has the opportunity to gain a contribution of $300,000 (100,000 units × $3 per unit) through the sale of P20, but it must give up the opportunity to produce C89 and earn $10,000,000 (100,000 units × $100 per unit) in contribution through the sale of P16. In these circumstances, economic theory recommends that the price be set at variable cost ($5) plus the contribution given up on the best alternative for the capacity. The price of the additional C36 would be $5 plus $100 in contribution given up for selling product P16. The price of additional C89s would be $5 plus $3 given up for sales of product P20. This is called the *opportunity-costing approach*.

Limitations of the Opportunity-Costing Approach.   The opportunity-costing approach rewards managers with higher revenue and income for being at capacity production when opportunity costs are high. Because a given selling division has many products, many inputs, many days, and many production processes, the very concept of *capacity* is subject to interpretation, differences of opinion, and some unethical behavior. If managers know that they will be rewarded with high transfer prices for producing at capacity, the selling division manager might arrange to produce at capacity during periods of high transfers. He or she could rearrange the production lines and plans to produce at capacity during those time periods in which large transfers are to be made. Inventories of low contribution products would increase during periods of low demand so these inventories would not need to be produced during high transfer periods. Then only high contribution (opportunity-cost) products need be manufactured during periods when many transfer items are to be produced. Consequently, transfers appear to result in high opportunity costs for the selling division.

In order to deal with the problems associated with all cost-based transfer prices, market-based prices have been suggested as a solution.

MARKET-BASED TRANSFER PRICING

A transfer price based on market prices is a workable approach when (1) the transferred products and services have published prices or (2) relatively few products and services are transferred. Thus, profit centers dealing with basic commodities, such as copper, petroleum, grains, or lumber, will have little problem in establishing a transfer price based on published amounts.

When market prices are readily available, the organization should use them to price transferred goods and services. The primary support for the use of market prices is that it encourages selling divisions to be efficient in their production and ethical in their behavior. The selling divisions are not encouraged to increase their cost bases or manipulate cost data.

Surrogates for Market Price

Many products and services do not have readily available market prices. Although some products may be found in catalogs from competitors, many catalogs do not list prices. Instead, the prices are listed separately on quote sheets that are available to only serious buyers. A large company will have thousands of transferred products and services of which only several hundred, depending on the industry, will have available market prices. Because of this, some companies have tried two surrogates for market price: bids and negotiated prices.

Prices Based on Bids.   A bid price is a formal, binding offer by an outside supplier to sell a given quantity and quality of an item at a stipulated price. The general approach is to gather bids from several qualified suppliers and then to establish the lowest bid as the transfer price. This approach is good conceptually, but in practice the bidders soon learn that they are not going to get the job and they either bid a high price or cease to bid at all. Some products have only a few qualified suppliers and they may be uninterested in bidding. However, when an order is placed, the suppliers will offer a price.

When technical information or trade secrets are involved, bidding may involve giving up important information. Getting reliable bids on thousands of products and services each year is a very cumbersome, error-prone process. Therefore, the bidding approach to approximating a market price is appropriate when there are relatively few nontechnical products transferred and there are many suppliers.

Negotiated Prices.   A second approach to approximating a market price is negotiation between the buying and selling divisions. The negotiation may be carried out in person, by telephone, or by memorandum. The segment managers may be directly involved, or the negotiation may be carried out by the purchasing and sales staffs. If both sides have similar negotiating power, the results will be satisfactory to both parties. In general, the buyers and sellers should be free to go to the outside with the transaction unless restricted for strategic reasons, and their future employment should not be threatened by the other party to the negotiation.

Negotiations take time and can be pleasant or unpleasant, depending on the personalities involved. Consequently, negotiated prices should be limited to relatively few important products or services.

Discounted Market Price

Some companies discount the transfer price from market for transfers. These companies argue that the internal production of goods and services should give the selling division a cost advantage over an external supplier. The selling division does not have to bear the risk of poor collections of accounts receivable and often does not have to pay a sales commission. Delivery costs are often low because of the company's location. In general, administrative and selling costs should be less for transferred goods and services than for external sales. Because of these cost differences, some companies take a percentage off the market price. For example, a company may take 10 percent off the market price for electrical components purchased from other segments. Because the purchasing segments receive a discount, they are encouraged to purchase from the selling segments. Thus, the discount encourages cooperative behavior from the purchasing segments.

If the discount rate on transfers is reasonable (approximates cost differences), the selling segment should not object to the transfer price and it will cooperate in meeting the needs of purchasing segments. The buyers will respond positively to the 10 or 20 percent discount of regular market prices. Consequently, both sides of the transaction will respond positively to the arrangement and try to keep the good relationship going.

If the discount is too steep (say 30 percent or more), the selling segment will be motivated to favor external sales, not to be cooperative with purchasing segments. As an illustration of this, consider the effects of a 40 percent discount on the scheduling of a company printing plant. Assume that the plant is working very hard to meet deadlines and that it has two orders for printing, both of which have a normal market price of about $300,000. One of the orders is for 800,000 copies of the spring catalog for the company's marketing division; the other order is for an external customer. The printing plant manager can choose to do the printing work for the outside customer immediately for revenue of $300,000 or do the spring catalog for the inside customer for a 40 percent discount, or $180,000. The plant manager estimates that the effect on plant income from immediately doing each order is:

	External Order		Internal Order	
Revenue		$300,000		$180,000
Printing costs	$170,000		$165,000	
Selling and administration	40,000	210,000	5,000	170,000
Impact on plant income		$ 90,000		$ 10,000

The printing plant manager will be motivated to put off printing the spring catalog for a week or two in favor of doing the external work. The marketing vice president will not be thrilled by having the catalog delayed so that the printing plant manager can show $80,000 more income. Consequently, company policies will have to be set to force the printing plant manager to give priority service to internal work.

If the discount is set very low, the selling segments should be highly motivated to make internal sales because they are less costly to service. Because internal sales will be more profitable than outside sales, selling segments should provide service and actively lobby to increase the internal demand for their products. However, the purchasing divisions often become uncooperative and purchase from outside suppliers. In the competitive game of who wins the favor of top managers for bonuses and promotions, purchasing segments do not want the selling segments to get a big advantage from very profitable internal sales. Company policies will have to force user segments to buy internally. In summary, the following expected results occur from setting the discount rate from market prices:

Discount	Selling Segment	Purchasing Segment
Low or no discount	Very cooperative	Uncooperative
Reasonable discount	Cooperative	Cooperative
Steep discount	Uncooperative	Very cooperative

Judgment is required to distinguish among low, reasonable, and steep discount rates.

The policy on discount rates is a matter of decentralization. Thus, some companies set the discount rate by central policy for all segments, say at 10 or 20 percent. Other organizations strongly encourage negotiation of the discounts among segments. Finally, decentralized organizations allow the selling segments to set their own discount rates and are unconcerned whether transactions occur internally or externally as long as all segments show good profits and growth. In general, the policy on discount rates from market prices should be consistent with senior management's general strategy on centralization and decentralization.

SUMMARY

When products or services move from one segment to another, a cost or price is attached. If the selling segment is a cost center, the amount is called a *cost allocation*. If the segment is organized as a profit center, transfers are accounted for with a *transfer price,* which often includes a profit margin.

The pricing of transfers may be an issue if transfers are large in proportion to selling division sales. Transfer-pricing methods include those based on cost, which is similar to cost allocation, or market. Cost bases for allocation to other segments include actual cost, normal cost, standard cost, and budgeted cost. The fixed and variable costs may be accounted for separately. Prices may be determined on the basis of actual volume or planned volume.

Market prices are often discounted to encourage cooperation by both selling and purchasing segments. Market prices may be approximated using bids from potential suppliers or negotiation between purchasing and selling divisions.

PROBLEM FOR REVIEW

The Printing Division of CTX, Inc., prints all forms and stationery used by each of the 22 other divisions plus the headquarters. During February 19x7, the division had the following costs and activity:

	Actual	Flexible Budget
Materials	$200,000	$210,000
Wages and salaries	40,000	38,000
Employee benefits	20,000	20,000
Maintenance	20,000	15,000
Equipment rental	10,000	10,000
Supervision	10,000	7,000
Total division costs	$300,000	$290,000

	For the Month of January	
	Actual	*Planned*
Division Activity		
Pages produced (in thousands)	50,000	58,000
Total variable costs	$240,000	$4.00 per 1,000
Total fixed costs	$ 60,000	$ 58,000

One customer, the Chicago Division, planned to print 2 million pages during the month but due to market conditions, its actual output was only 1,200,000 pages. For normal costing, the actual costs are accumulated for materials and wages and then the remainder of the costs is applied at a rate of 140 percent of wages. Thus, normal costs are:

Materials	$200,000
Labor	40,000
Overhead applied $40,000 × 140%	56,000
Total normal costs	$296,000

For standard costing, assume a standard cost of $5.00 per 1,000 copies. Standard variable costs are $4 per 1,000 copies. The company uses a 30 percent markup over cost in its transfer pricing.

REQUIRED

Compute the billing to the Chicago Division assuming each of the following cost bases:
a. Actual cost of actual usage plus a markup.
b. Normal cost of actual usage plus a markup.
c. Standard cost of actual usage plus a markup.
d. Budgeted cost at actual usage plus a markup.
e. Actual fixed costs allocated on planned usage and actual variable costs allocated on actual usage plus a markup.
f. Budgeted fixed costs allocated on planned usage and budgeted variable costs allocated on actual usage plus a markup.

SOLUTION

		Cost		Price		
		×		×		
Cost/Base	=	*Markup*	=	*Activity*	=	*Billing*

a. Actual cost at actual activity:

$300,000/50,000 = $6.00 × 130% = $7.800 × 1,200 = $ 9,360

b. Normal cost at actual activity:

$296,000/50,000 = $5.92 × 130% = $7.696 × 1,200 = $ 9,235

c. Standard cost at actual activity:

[Given] $5.00 × 130% = $6.500 × 1,200 = $ 7,800

d. Flexible budget at actual activity:

$290,000/50,000 = $5.80 × 130% = $7.540 × 1,200 = $ 9,048

e. Actual fixed cost at planned activity:

$60,000/58,000 = $1.035 × 130% = $1.345 × 2,000 = $ 2,690

Actual variable cost at actual activity:

$240,000/50,000 = $4.800 × 130% = $6.240 × 1,200 = 7,488

$10,178

	Cost/Base	=	Cost × Markup	=	Price × Activity	=	Billing

f. Budgeted fixed costs at planned activity:

$$\$58,000/58,000 = \$1.000 \times 130\% = \$1.300 \times 2,000 = \$\ 2,600$$

Standard variable costs at actual activity:

$$\$4.000 \times 130\% = \$5.200 \times 1,200 = \underline{\quad 6,240}$$
$$\underline{\$\ 8,840}$$

KEY TERMS AND CONCEPTS

Cost allocation (719)   Transfer price (719)

ADDITIONAL READINGS

Agami, A. M. "How to Choose Transfer Prices for FSCs." *Management Accounting,* May, 1986, pp. 48–50.

Benke, R. L., and A. C. Bishop. "Transfer Pricing in an Oligopolistic Market." *Journal of Cost Analysis,* Fall, 1986, pp. 69–81.

Benke, R. L., and J. D. Edwards. *Transfer Pricing: Techniques and Uses.* New York: National Association of Accountants, 1980.

Casey, M. P. "International Transfer Pricing." *Management Accounting,* October, 1985, pp. 31–35.

Cassel, H. S., and V. F. McCormack. "Transfer Pricing Dilemma—and a Dual Pricing Solution." *Journal of Accountancy,* September, 1987, pp. 166–75.

Cats-Baril, W.; J. F. Gatti; and D. J. Grinnell. "Transfer Pricing in a Dynamic Market." *Management Accounting,* February, 1988, pp. 30–33.

Eccles, R. G. "Analyzing Your Company's Transfer Pricing Practices." *Journal of Cost Management for the Manufacturing Industry,* Summer, 1987, pp. 21–33.

Harris, D. R. "Artificial Transfer Prices and Foreign Captives." *Management Accounting* (England), April, 1986, p. 43–44.

Hoshower, L. B. "Transfer Pricing Policies of Diversified U.S.–Based Multinationals." *International Journal of Accounting Education and Research,* Fall, 1986, pp. 51–59.

Keegan, D. P., and P. D. Howard. "Making Transfer Pricing Work for Services." *Journal of Accountancy,* March, 1988, pp. 96–103.

Kimball, R. C. "Trends in Funds Transfer Pricing." *Bank Accounting and Finance,* Summer, 1988, pp. 19–25.

Lococo, L. J. "Selecting the Right Transfer Pricing Model." *Management Accounting,* March, 1983, pp. 42–45.

Mays, R. L. "Divisional Performance Measurement and Transfer Prices." *Management Accounting,* April, 1982, pp. 20–24.

Scarpo, J. A. "Auto Dealers Lag in Transfer Pricing." *Management Accounting,* July, 1984, pp. 54–56.

Terbrueggen, J. E. "Can a Central Cash Pool Work for Transfer Pricing?" *Management Accounting,* July, 1986, pp. 31–33.

REVIEW QUESTIONS

1. What is the name of the process that charges users for the output of cost centers?
2. Why is the method of pricing the cost center outputs important to users?
3. Why should the volume measure for cost centers be closely related to outputs provided by the center?
4. List six cost bases for the pricing of cost center outputs.

5. What is the problem with pricing cost center outputs based on actual costs? Standard costs? Actual volume?

6. What is the problem with pricing schemes that allocate fixed costs and variable costs separately?

7. How are cost allocation and cost-based transfer prices very similar? What is the difference between them?

8. Why is the method of transfer pricing important to profit center managers?

9. Why are market prices not used for all transfers?

10. Why are market-based transfer prices often discounted in practice?

11. In what setting might it be appropriate to use negotiated transfer prices? Prices based on bids?

DISCUSSION QUESTIONS

12. Under some circumstances, a segment is allowed to purchase items that are produced externally; in other circumstances, they are not. List the conditions in which:
   a. Segments should be forced to purchase internally.
   b. Segments should be allowed to purchase externally.

13. What is the effect of the capacity of the producing segment on the pricing of transfers?

14. What is the increase or decrease in profits to the company as a whole when the transfer price is changed assuming that:
   a. The volume of activity does not change.
   b. An increase in transfer price decreases volume and vice versa.

EXERCISES

18-1. Applying Transfer Price Methods. The Scotch Division produces component XV-102 with the following costs per unit:

Materials	$ 4.00
Labor	1.50
Variable overhead	2.50
Fixed overhead	3.00
Total cost	$11.00

During January 19x7, the Liggen Division received 12,000 units of XV-102 from the Scotch Division. Assume that materials are a variable cost and that labor is a fixed cost.

REQUIRED:
Compute the amount of the billings from Scotch to Liggen, given that the prices are based on the following transfer-pricing policies:
a. Full cost plus 20 percent markup for profit.
b. Variable cost plus 50 percent markup for profit.
c. Variable cost plus a negotiated fee of $40,000 per month.

18-2. Impact of Transfer Prices on Segment Margin. The Chicago Solder Division, a segment of MAS Techtronics, Inc., manufactures flow solder used in the production of integrated circuit boards. During August 19x1, the division manufactured and shipped 500,000 pounds of solder of which 40 percent went to other divisions of MAS Techtronics. Sales to outside customers were at a price of $3.00 per pound with variable production costs of $1.20 per pound and variable selling costs of $0.40 per pound sold to outside customers. Fixed costs of production were $350,000, and administrative costs were $100,000. Sales to other divisions of MAS Techtronics involve a variable selling cost of $0.20.

REQUIRED:

a. Compute segment margin if transfer prices are set at the variable cost plus a 20 percent markup for transferred units.

b. Compute segment margin if transfer prices are set at the selling price to outside customers less the savings in variable selling costs.

18–3. Applying Transfer-Pricing Methods.

The Walls Parts Division fabricates air conditioner parts for the Thompson home air conditioner. Half of the parts are sold to the Thompson Assembly Division. The other half of the parts manufactured are sold to the Services Division that repairs the air conditioners after sale. During the month of June 19x8, the Walls Parts Division manufactured 40,000 condensing pumps at the following costs:

Materials	$ 600,000
Labor	300,000
Variable overhead	150,000
Fixed overhead	240,000
Total cost	$1,290,000

Overhead is assigned on the basis of direct labor. Assume that all material and half of labor costs are variable costs. Similar pumps can be purchased from other suppliers at a price of $50.

REQUIRED:

Compute a transfer price for the pumps based on:

a. Variable cost plus a 20 percent markup.

b. Full cost plus a 10 percent markup.

c. Market price less a 20 percent discount.

18–4. Actual, Budget, and Normalized Cost Transfer Pricing.

Triants, Inc., is a defense contractor located in the Los Angeles, California, area. One segment of the company is the Systems Consulting Group consisting of 18 professionals with four clerical staff. The actual expense and current budget for the group include costs for 19x4 (in thousands):

	Actual	*Budget*
Salaries and benefits	$670	$700
Computer time	90	100
Travel and training	90	100
Other costs	50	60
Total costs	$900	$960

During 19x4, the F22V7 project required 6,200 actual hours of consulting. During the year, the Systems Consulting Group worked 27,000 chargeable hours but had planned to work 32,000. Because this is a government contractor, markup is not appropriate on transferred work.

REQUIRED:

Compute the amount of systems consulting to be charged to the F22V7 project using each of the following charging policies:

a. Actual cost is allocated on the basis of actual hours.

b. Budgeted cost is allocated on the basis of actual hours.

c. Normalized rates (budgeted cost divided by planned hours) are charged to actual hours.

18–5. Impact of Transferring or Selling Outside.

The Frendson Division of Cripts, Inc., manufactures sheet aluminum with the following costs per unit:

Material	$9.00
Labor	0.50
Variable overhead	1.00
Fixed overhead	1.50

The aluminum sheets are sold regularly for $17 per unit, and variable selling costs are $0.40 per unit. The Frendson Division currently manufactures and sells 1 million units per month, which is the capacity of the plant. Fixed general and administrative costs of the division are $500,000 per month.

Cripts, Inc., recently purchased the Eastern Cola Bottling Division. It is the policy of Cripts, Inc., to require transfers at full cost plus a 10 percent markup. Eastern Cola Bottling requires 500,000 units per month. Variable selling costs are expected to be $0.10 per unit on the transfers.

REQUIRED:

a. Compute the monthly income of Frendson Division assuming that all sales are made to outside customers.
b. Compute the monthly income of Frendson Division assuming that the 500,000 units are sold to the Eastern Cola Bottling Division and the remainder is sold to outside customers.

18–6. Fixed and Variable Costs. The Pacific Construction Division of Fulton Stores constructs retail shopping stores. During 19x5, Pacific Construction had the following costs (in millions):

Material	$120.00
Labor	48.00
Overhead	40.00

In addition, variable administrative costs were $200,000, and fixed administrative costs were $100,000. All of the materials, half of the labor, and 30 percent of the overhead are considered variable costs.

One of the projects, Westwood Mall in Las Vegas, Nevada, required $24 million in materials, $6 million in labor, and $8 million in overhead. Variable administrative costs of $40,000 can be identified with the Westwood Mall project.

REQUIRED:

a. Assume that it is the policy of Fulton Stores to set a transfer price at 20 percent above full cost. Compute the transfer price for Westwood Mall.
b. Assume that it is the policy of Fulton Stores to set a transfer price at 40 percent above variable costs. Compute the transfer price for Westwood Mall.

18–7. Discounted Market Prices. MCC, Inc., of Kalamazoo manufactures replicas of vintage automobiles. It specializes in pre–1920 vehicles for six passengers or less. The tires for these vehicles are made by the South Side Tire plant of MCC and transferred to the North Side Assembly plant. The tires may also be purchased from two other companies in the United States and one in Germany. For March 19x2, the full actual cost per CV24X4 tire was $26, of which $20 was variable cost including $0.50 in shipping. During March, 1,000 CV24X4 tires were used. The prices for competitive CV24X4 tires during March were:

	Invoice	*Shipping*	*Total*
Tritanic	$38	$2	$40
Critendum	$41	$1	$42
UDV (Germany)	108 marks	6 marks	114 marks

During March, the average currency price was three German marks per one U.S. dollar. MCC, Inc., follows the policy of basing transfer prices on average market price when possible.

REQUIRED:

Compute the transfer price, gross profit and contributing margin to the South Side plant for the sales of CV24X4 tires during March under the following discount policies:
a. No discount is required from average market price.
b. A 20 percent discount is required from average market price.
c. A 50 percent discount is required from average market price.

18–8. Dual Prices.   The Printing Division of Sunny General Hospital prints forms, brochures, and manuals for the hospital. During the past three years, the following actual costs per 1,000 sheets of printing have been observed:

	19x3	*19x4*	*19x5*
Materials	$4.00	$5.50	$7.00
Labor	1.00	1.20	1.60
Overhead	0.50	1.00	1.20
Total	$5.50	$7.70	$9.80
Units printed (thousands)	4,000	4,800	5,000

The hospital follows the policy of dual transfer pricing with the selling division receiving credit for actual cost plus 20 percent and the buying divisions being charged the price of lowest local market minus 10 percent. The average market prices for 19x3, 19x4, and 19x5, respectively, are $11.00, $11.50, and $10.50 per unit. All of the labor and 70 percent of the overhead are considered fixed but could be eliminated if printing were all done outside.

REQUIRED:

a. Compute the revenue, cost of goods sold, and gross margin for the Printing Division for 19x3, 19x4, and 19x5.

b. Compute the total printing charges to the hospital for the years 19x3, 19x4, and 19x5.

c. Comment on the impact of the dual pricing policy on actual printing costs.

PROBLEMS

18–9. Cost Allocations and Transfer Prices.   The Granite Construction Company builds and repairs highways in North and South Carolina. One of the major materials used in road construction is crushed rock of various sizes. The actual costs of running the rock-crushing unit and the flexible budget amounts for September 19x9 are:

	Actual Cost	*Flexible Budget*
Wages	$ 495,580	$ 452,500
Fuel	1,038,202	805,000
Supervision	63,858	45,250
Depreciation	110,000	110,000
Maintenance	402,000	385,000
Administration	83,000	65,000
Total	$2,192,640	$1,862,750
Total fixed costs	$ 320,000	$ 300,000
Total variable	1,872,640	1,562,750

The actual volume was 805,000, but the planned volume was 900,000.

The Road Repair Division agreed to 100,000 cubic yards for the month but, because of weather conditions, was able to accept delivery on only 60,000 yards. Crushed rock normally sells commercially for $6 per yard for large quantities delivered less than 100 miles. The standard cost per yard is $2.20. For normal costing on government contracts, the overhead is applied at a rate of 50 percent of actual wages and fuel. Granite Construction Company follows the policy of including markups in transfer prices but eliminating them at the time of billing governmental units.

REQUIRED:

a. Apply each of the six cost-based transfer-pricing schemes presented in Exhibit 18–1 using a markup of 20 percent above cost. Compute the amount to be billed to the Road Repair Division.

b. Compute the transfer price and billing to the Road Repair Division assuming actual quantities are priced at:
  1. Market price.
  2. A 20 percent discount from market price.
  3. A 50 percent discount from market price.

4. An outside bid of $5.50 per yard that has been received.
5. A negotiated price of $5 per yard.

18–10. Transfer Pricing and Special Orders.   Bohn Division manufactures a component that is used by the Odom Division in the production of a finished product. The component has a competitive outside market—Bohn Division can sell all its production to the outside and Odom Division can buy all it needs from outside suppliers. Bohn Division is using the market price of $25 as its transfer price. Its variable cost is $15, and it is producing at full capacity.

   Odom Division has just received a request for a special order on its product but must give a discount on the regular selling price. Because it is operating at 50 percent of capacity, the division would like this order. The costs for the finished product are:

Variable production costs:	
Component from Bohn Division	$25
Other production costs	30
Fixed costs (at normal capacity)	15
Total production costs per unit	$70
Variable selling and administrative	5
Total costs per unit	$75

The purchaser is expecting a discount, and the sales people at Odom Division believe that a price of $62 will get the order. The manager of Odom Division has asked Bohn Division to reduce its transfer price to variable cost of $15 so that the total cost can be reduced to near the proposed selling price.

   Bohn Division has capacity to manufacture 100,000 of the components. The special order is for 40,000 units, and Odom Division has sufficient capacity to fill the order.

REQUIRED:
a. Calculate the change in operating income for Bohn Division if it reduces the transfer price to $15 for this one order of 40,000 units.
b. Calculate the change in operating income for Odom Division if it takes the special order at a selling price of $62 and pays a transfer price of $15. (Remember that the application of overhead to production will reduce the underapplied overhead by $15 per unit, which will decrease adjusted cost of goods sold by an equal amount.)

18–11. Transfer Pricing and Segment Reporting.   DePaolo Industries manufactures carpets, furniture, and foam in three separate divisions.

ADDITIONAL INFORMATION
   Included in Foam Division's sales revenue is $500,000 in revenue that represents sales made to the Furniture Division that were transferred at manufacturing cost.
   The cost of goods sold comprises the following costs.

	Carpet	*Furniture*	*Foam*
Direct material	$ 500,000	$1,000,000	$1,000,000
Direct labor	500,000	200,000	1,000,000
Variable overhead	750,000	50,000	1,000,000
Fixed overhead	250,000	50,000	–0–
Total cost of goods sold	$2,000,000	$1,300,000	$3,000,000

Administrative expenses include the following costs.

	Carpet	*Furniture*	*Foam*
Segment expenses			
Variable	$ 85,000	$140,000	$ 40,000
Fixed	85,000	210,000	120,000
Home office expenses (all fixed)			
Directly traceable	100,000	120,000	200,000
General (allocated on sales dollars)	30,000	30,000	40,000
Total	$300,000	$500,000	$400,000

Selling expense is all incurred at the segment level and is 80 percent variable for all segments.

John Sprint, manager of the Foam Division, is not pleased with DePaolo's presentation of operating performance. Sprint claimed, "The Foam Division makes a greater contribution to the company's profits than what is shown. I sell foam to the Furniture Division at cost and it gets our share of the profit. I can sell that foam on the outside at my regular markup, but I sell to Furniture for the well-being of the company. I think my division should get credit for those internal sales at market. I think we should also revise our operating statements for internal purposes. Why don't we consider preparing these internal statements on a contribution approach reporting format showing internal transfers at market?"

(CMA, adapted)

DePAOLO INDUSTRIES
Operating Statement
For the Year Ended December 31, 19x3

	Carpet Division	Furniture Division	Foam Division	Total
Sales revenue	$3,000,000	$3,000,000	$4,000,000	$10,000,000
Cost of goods sold	2,000,000	1,300,000	3,000,000	6,300,000
Gross profit	$1,000,000	$1,700,000	$1,000,000	$ 3,700,000
Operating expenses				
Administrative	$ 300,000	$ 500,000	$ 400,000	$ 1,200,000
Selling	600,000	600,000	500,000	1,700,000
Total operating expenses	$ 900,000	$1,100,000	$ 900,000	$ 2,900,000
Income from operations before taxes	$ 100,000	$ 600,000	$ 100,000	$ 800,000

REQUIRED:

a. John Sprint believes that the intracompany transfers from the Foam Division to the Furniture Division should be at market rather than manufacturing cost for divisional performance measurement.

1. Explain why Sprint is correct.
2. Identify and describe two approaches used for setting transfer prices other than manufacturing cost used by DePaolo Industries and market price as recommended by Sprint.

b. Using the contribution approach and market-based transfer prices, prepare a revised operating statement by division for DePaolo Industries for 19x3 that will promote the evaluation of divisional performance.

18–12. Overhead and Transfer Prices.   IC Systems Division of Inforce, Inc., manufactures computer chips in a large plant in San Francisco, California. Although there are many types of computer chips, this problem concentrates on R36000 and R38000, which have the following standard costs:

	R36000	R38000
Materials	$0.80	$0.30
Labor	0.10	0.30
Overhead	1.00	3.00
Total cost	$1.90	$3.60

The overhead rates are based on direct labor, and the total overhead is 80 percent fixed. The chips are sold to four divisions and to other manufacturers at the following percentages:

	R36000	R38000
Inforce Mainframe Division	–0–	10
Inforce PC Division	10	10
Defense Systems Division	10	65
Service Division	10	10
Outside manufacturers	70	5
Total	100	100
Unit volume for the year (in millions)	20	30
Market price of chips	$5.50	$3.80

Defense contracting regulations do not allow markup to be included in transfer prices among divisions of a contractor. Thus, it is the policy of Inforce, Inc., to transfer all products at full standard cost, which is consistent with industry practices.

REQUIRED:

a. For product R36000:
1. Compute revenues from sales to divisions and outside manufacturers.
2. Compute the cost of goods sold.
b. For product R38000:
1. Compute revenues from sales to divisions and outside manufacturers.
2. Compute the cost of goods sold.
c. Based on your analysis in parts (a) and (b), compare the profitability of the two products for IC Systems Division.
d. After a careful review of the operations, you determine that 75 percent of the total overhead for the two products relates to R36000. Recompute the total cost per unit and revise the analysis in parts (a) through (c) to reflect this new information regarding fixed costs.
e. Comment on the effects on transfer prices caused by changing the allocations of fixed overhead.
f. When IC Systems Division is producing R36000, the direct labor efficiency variances are highly unfavorable. When the division is producing R38000, the labor efficiency variances are highly favorable. Because there is only one efficiency variance account, these variances net out at the end of each year. Why might the standard costs have been set so that this pattern occurs?

18–13. Transfer Pricing. Kent, Inc., has 28 divisions. Four of the divisions—three subassembly divisions (Dolan, Olson, and Grant) and one final assembly (Combo) division—manufacture related products. Combo Division produces a powered remote-control helicopter, the Combo, for hobbyists. Combo Division purchases an equal number of parts from each of the subassembly divisions.

The following products are produced by each of the divisions:

		Assets	Prices		
Division	Product	(in thousands)	Market	Transfer	Capacity
Dolan	Motor	$ 600	$ 50	$40	10,000
Olson	Frame	750	$ 70	$50	10,000
Grant	Guidance	1,500	$ 80	$60	10,000
Combo	Helicopter	375	$250		5,000

All divisions are operating at capacity and will continue to operate at this level for the foreseeable future. All divisions can sell all of their production to the outside market. Combo Division can purchase subassemblies from the outside market, but they are not consistently of the superior quality required by the Combo helicopter. If the subassemblies from the other divisions are not available, Combo Division produces another helicopter, the Junior, that sells for $140 and has total variable costs of $100. Combo Division could produce and sell 9,000 of the Junior helicopters with the current capacity.

The following additional information is available:

	Product			
	Motor	*Frame*	*Guidance*	*Helicopter*
Variable costs:				
Production	$ 10	$ 15	$ 20	$ 160
Selling	5	10	10	15
Fixed costs:				
Production	100,000	50,000	100,000	200,000
Administration	50,000	50,000	50,000	50,000

The $160 in variable costs for the helicopter in the Combo Division includes:

Motor from Dolan	$ 40
Frame from Olson	50
Guidance from Grant	60
Other materials	2
Labor and overhead	8
Total variable	$160

Assume that the variable production costs are the same for internal and external sales, but that the variable selling costs are 40 percent less for transfers.

A proposal to change all company transfer prices to market price is before the senior managers of Kent, Inc. The managers of the subassembly divisions strongly support this proposal, but the division manager for the Combo Division is strongly opposed to it. Kent, Inc., has an effective tax rate of 40 percent.

(W. Baumgarten, adapted)

REQUIRED:

a. Prepare a divisional income statement with columns for each division assuming the current transfer prices, costs, and sales to external customers. Include an after-tax rate of return for each of the divisions. Rank order the divisions by rate of return.

b. Prepare a divisional income statement with columns for each division assuming the proposed transfer prices at market prices. Include an after-tax rate of return for each of the divisions. Rank order the divisions by rate of return.

c. Would the Combo Division be better or worse off to produce and market the Junior helicopter assuming the following:
   1. Current transfer prices?
   2. Proposed transfer prices?

d. Which transfer-pricing policy seems to be best for this company taken as a whole?

e. To what extent would the recommended transfer-pricing policy be affected by the drop in external demand for production to only 50 percent of capacity for each division?

18–14. Service Costs and Transfer Pricing.   Scripts-Johnson Hospital is a 1,500–bed teaching hospital with many programs and activities. The hospital is financially secure with a large endowment and a high occupancy rate. One service department that is critical to the functioning of the hospital is the Surgical Blood Test Laboratory (SBT Lab). The SBT Lab performs all blood tests prior to and during major surgery. (All other blood work is performed in another lab or sent out to external labs.) For fiscal 19x7, the budgeted and actual costs for the unit were:

	Planned	**Actual**
Laboratory technicians	$ 312,000	$ 309,880
Employee benefits	156,000	162,198
Supervisor	38,900	38,900
Materials and supplies	210,000	192,000
Conferences and training	20,000	20,000
Equipment depreciation	100,000	100,000
Occupancy	153,000	159,000
Insurance	230,000	340,000
Miscellaneous	43,000	23,000
Administrative expenses	104,000	284,000
Total budget	$1,366,900	$1,628,978

Tests performed for:	**Planned**	**Actual**
Emergency surgery	12,000	13,920
Thoracic surgery	24,000	40,600
Cancer surgery	18,000	9,280
General surgery	66,000	52,200
	120,000	116,000

All costs are fixed except for materials and supplies. For purposes of billing patients, the hospital must base the pricing of lab work on its planned cost or on external prices. Waiting for actual costs to be known would be very impractical.

REQUIRED: `
a. Assuming that the hospital establishes a price of planned full cost per test plus 30 percent:
   1. Compute the price per test.
   2. Compute the actual departmental revenue.
   3. Compute the actual departmental income.
b. Assume that the hospital establishes a two-part price that allocates fixed costs in proportion to planned activity and variable cost on the basis of actual activity. A markup of 50 percent is allowed on variable costs.
   1. Compute the two-part price.
   2. Compute the actual departmental revenue.
   3. Compute the actual departmental income.
c. Assume that the hospital establishes a price based on market price and that average market price for each of the types of blood tests is:

Emergency surgery	$47.00
Thoracic surgery	$28.00
Cancer surgery	$42.00
General surgery	$18.00

The prices were determined by obtaining the price list from six commercial laboratories in the city and averaging the results. The prices were a weighted average of the specific laboratory tests performed during the previous year for each category of work. For this pricing approach:
   1. Compute the actual departmental revenue.
   2. Compute the actual departmental income.
d. Comment on:
   1. The relative ease of implementing each of the pricing policies.
   2. The appearance of contribution of the SBT Lab under each of the pricing approaches.
   3. The purpose of the SBT Lab. (*Hint:* Can surgery be performed at the hospital without this lab?)
   4. Your recommended pricing approach.

EXTENDED APPLICATIONS

18–15. Transfer Pricing, Performance Measures, and Taxation. Four Sixes Petroleum, Inc., has four subsidiaries associated with petroleum products:

Subsidiary	ID	Primary Function
Six Fields, Inc.	SFI	Oil field production
Niven Pipeline Co.	NPC	From field to refinery
Bay City Refineries	BCR	Petroleum products produced
Four Sixes Service	FSS	Service stations

The stream of production goes in the order presented. Thus:

$$SFI \rightarrow NPC \rightarrow BCR \rightarrow FSS \rightarrow Consumer$$

The operations are not fully integrated because Four Sixes was formed by the purchase of four independent companies. Senior management follows a policy of decentralization. Each subsidiary is free to purchase products from outside companies and to sell to outside companies. The purchases and sales among subsidiaries for 19x2 are as follows (in millions):

	Inputs Purchased from		Outputs Sold to	
	Inside	Outside	Inside	Outside
SFI	$ –0–	$ –0–	$ 5,340	$ 3,560
NPC	5,340	25,068	10,860	25,340
BCR	10,860	13,280	14,200	14,200
FSS	14,200	14,780	–0–	34,500

Financial reports for 19x2 included the following information (in millions):

	SFI	NPC	BCR	FSS
Revenues	$ 8,900	$36,200	$28,400	$34,500
Production costs:				
Purchases	–0–	30,408	24,140	28,980
Variable production	3,071	2,534	2,272	–0–
Fixed production	510	820	950	–0–
Gross Margin	$ 5,320	$ 2,438	$ 1,038	$ 5,520
Variable selling	89	362	284	2,029
Fixed administration	50	30	40	2,488
Operating income	$ 5,181	$ 2,046	$ 714	$ 1,003
Income taxes	2,279	552	257	492
Net income	$ 2,901	$ 1,494	$ 457	$ 511
Total assets	$13,620	$ 6,510	$ 3,967	$ 5,686

The effective tax rates on the operations differ by subsidiary. Because of various provisions, the effective tax rates on wells and service stations are somewhat higher than those on pipelines and refineries.

The following capacities are being utilized:

Unit	Current Production
SFI	Wells are all pumping at 100 percent of field capacity.
NPC	The lines are moving oil at about 80 percent of peak load.
BCR	The refineries are working at 60 percent of capacity.
FSS	Service stations could sell 20 percent more for each 5 percent drop in prices up to 200 percent of the current sales.

Senior management of Four Sixes, Inc., follows a decentralized transfer-pricing policy. Each division contracts independently with prices approximating average market prices. Assume for simplicity that income taxes paid for 19x2 for each subsidiary represent the marginal tax rate on additional income. Assume that 19x3 will be similar to 19x2.

REQUIRED:

a. Compute the return on investment in each of the operating companies.

b. Compute the effective tax rates on each of the subsidiaries.

c. Suppose that a transfer-pricing policy was adopted that decreased the before-tax operating income of Six Fields, Inc. (the oil wells), by $800 million. The effect of the policy is that more of the pipeline capacity is used and this increases the before-tax income of Niven Pipeline Co. by $1 billion.

　1. What would be the operating income, taxes, and net income for Six Fields, Inc., and Niven Pipeline Co.?

　2. What would be the return on investment for Six Fields and Niven Pipeline under the new policy?

d. Independent of part (c), suppose that $16 billion in sales by Niven Pipeline is directed to Bay City Refineries rather than to outsiders. Niven Pipeline offers a 6 percent credit from contract market price in order to induce the refinery to purchase the petroleum. Niven Pipeline's operating expenses would stay about the same. The income before tax for the Bay City Refinery would increase by $1.994 billion.

　1. What would be the operating income, taxes, and net income for Niven Pipeline Co. and Bay City Refineries?

　2. What would be the return on investment for Niven Pipeline Co. and Bay City Refineries?

18–16. Performance Measurement, Segment Reporting, and Transfer Pricing.　Sonar Calibration Unit (SCU) is a service group that provides precision adjustment and repair to sonar equipment. SCU is a segment of CA, Inc., which manufactures and services maritime sonar units. The active sonar units on surface ships are useful for navigation through shallow and otherwise difficult areas that involve danger to the ship and crew.

　Senior management at CA, Inc., is reviewing the performance report for the SCU for the year 19x1:

SONAR CALIBRATION UNIT
Operations Report
For the Year Ending December 31, 19x1
($ in thousands)

	Actual	Budget	Variances
Service revenues	$9,100	$9,020	$ 80
Materials	$ 273	$ 271	$ 2
Wages and salaries	2,184	1,984	200
Travel	2,920	2,600	320
Employee benefits	655	595	60
Occupancy	728	722	6
Insurance	800	450	350
Marketing expense	1,092	752	340
Administrative expenses	480	397	83
Total expenses	$9,132	$7,771	$ 1,361
Income from operations	$ (32)	$1,249	$(1,281)
Income tax (40%)	(13)	500	(513)
Net income	$ (19)	$ 749	$ (768)
Assets	$2,111	$1,810	
Return on investment	−0.9%	41.5%	−42.4%

After reviewing the report, Les Sczceny, president, commented to Johann Vrill, chairman of the Board:

Sczceny:　We may have to find a new skipper for SCU. This performance report is terrible. The only thing that he's been able to do right is in the billings area.

Vrill: I quite agree. Terminate Mr. Jasie-Qua [SCU manager] immediately. His promotion from senior calibrator is an obvious mistake because he just cannot keep SCU profitable. There is no way we can let this poor performance continue. We need at least a 20 percent ROI on all of our units.

SCU works out of small dispatch offices in 22 ports throughout the world. Two to five calibrators are in each office. The calibrators spend about half their time waiting for and going on calls from ships with sonar trouble in their part of the world. On a regular basis, they service equipment that is in port, but this requires only about 20 percent of their time.

SCU unit provided significant service (about 30 percent of the calibrators' time during 19x1) to CA, Inc., for which there is no charge. For example, SCU must provide free repair and calibration for all CA, Inc., units that are less than four years old. Further, the calibrators are all highly experienced sonar operators who provide training to the crews of merchant ships that purchase a CA, Inc., unit. About 40 percent of the materials and travel costs during 19x1 related to this nonrevenue service. The budget was estimated under the assumption that nonrevenue activities would be 20 percent of the time and 25 percent of the materials and travel costs for the calibrators.

Materials, wages and salaries, and travel were all accounted for as direct costs of the unit. Employee benefit costs were traced to units by applying a rate of 30 percent of unit wages and salaries. This closely approximates actual cost. Occupancy costs, primarily depreciation and utilities, are allocated on the basis of square footage of the space used by the unit. To this allocation was added the $228,000 in local occupancy paid by SCU. (SCU rents its facilities in every port and pays its own utility and costs.) The insurance expense is allocated on the basis of ships serviced by SCU. Insurance contracts are negotiated by the home office. The insurance is a function of ships serviced, and rates per unit increased 50 percent above those planned for 19x1. About 40 percent of the insurance cost relates to nonrevenue work performed.

Marketing and administrative expenses are allocated on the basis of revenues. Even though the revenues of SCU are up from last year, the total revenues of the company have fallen $10 million short of the $50 million planned, which is primarily due to a temporary drop in the sales of new CA units during 19x1. SCU service is prominently displayed in all literature to potential customers. As one sales agent commented, "We could sell no equipment without SCU. It's doing a great job and every captain and builder around knows it." About $100,000 of the administrative expenses can be traced to SCU. The remainder is allocated common costs.

The net income of CA, Inc., for 19x1 was $4.4 million, which represented a 25 percent return on assets. SCU has $320,000 in assets, primarily equipment, parts, and office furniture, plus an allocated share of the home office.

REQUIRED:
a. For each line in the SCU operations report, indicate:
1. To what extent can Mr. Jasie-Qua control the item?
2. To what extent is the line traceable to SCU?
b. For the budgeted costs:
1. Determine the costs that are traceable to the revenue and nonrevenue work. Assume that all of the waiting time relates to revenue-producing calls. Allocate on the basis of planned work rather than actual work.
2. If senior management were to allow a billing of traceable cost plus 10 percent for the nonrevenue work, what would be the total transfer price?
c. For the actual costs:
1. Determine the costs that are traceable to the revenue and nonrevenue work. Assume that all of the waiting time relates to revenue-producing calls. Allocate on the basis of actual work performed.
2. If senior management were to allow a billing of traceable cost plus 10 percent for the nonrevenue work, what would be the total transfer price?

    d. Using the results from part *(c):*
        1. Compute an estimated ROI for 19x1.
        2. What percentage of the total profits can be reasonably traced to SCU?
    e. Based on your analysis:
        1. Comment on the following: The president and chairman have decided to fire Mr. Jasie-Qua on the basis of the annual performance report. Mr. Jasie-Qua has held this position only for the past year.
        2. If your analysis had shown that SCU contributes very little to the profits of CA, Inc., would you recommend that the unit be dropped?
        3. As the chief financial officer for CA, Inc., you are responsible for the performance reporting system. You know that Mr. Jasie-Qua has worked very hard to motivate the calibrators and hold together SCU. What actions might you take to save the career of Mr. Jasie-Qua?

CHAPTER

19

Profit Analysis

■

WHAT FACTORS CAUSED PROFITS TO DIFFER FROM PLANS?

One of the major product lines manufactured by Eakin Manufacturing Company is a computerized machine control system, the NC–5000 series. The first products in the series are the 5000L for lathes and the 5000MC for machining centers. The system extends processing capability through the use of a distributed microprocessor system and a dual bus structure for maximum speed and accuracy. The architectural concept allows the machine tool builder and machine tool user full access to the central processing unit of the control. A high level of reliability is achieved by having fewer components and less circuit board surface area. From the user's point of view, the control has been designed for ease of programming, operation, and maintenance.

Eakin Manufacturing has an incentive program for managers based on the monthly divisional and departmental performance reports. It pays a bonus to any divisional or departmental manager whose profit performance is better than that budgeted. Michelle McQueen, marketing manager for the NC–5000 series, is pleased with the incentive program because she has been named manager of the month several times and has received substantial bonuses. One of the company's goals is customer satisfaction. Michelle is known for exceptional service to customers. She has received several new orders and has rushed to fill others when competition has refused to do so. In the most recent month, her profit performance was favorable as shown below:

Master budget	$252,000
Flexible budget performance	260,000
Actual performance	264,000

Ron Hicks, manager of the Assembly Department for the NC–5000 series, is unhappy with the incentives. Last month, for example, he operated near capacity and completed all orders within the promised delivery schedule but had excessive costs. He can show that the labor efficiency variance, which was unfavorable by 2,500 hours, would have been favorable by 750 hours if he had been able to produce at the scheduled production level without the interference of rush orders. His profit performance for the month was:

Master budget	$378,000
Flexible budget performance	442,000
Actual performance	453,000

Although many factors are involved in performance within Eakin Manufacturing Company, more detail is needed to pinpoint the reasons for actual performance differing from planned performance. Planning and control cannot function properly within an organization if the analysis stops with the overall comparisons shown above.

LEARNING OBJECTIVES

After completing this chapter, you should be able to:

1. Explain the purpose of profit analysis for a period.
2. Define gross profit and contribution margin.
3. Identify the components of a sales price variance, cost variance, sales volume variance, sales mix variance, and sales quantity variance.
4. Calculate the variances of gross profit analysis when budgets and standards are the base, and when the previous period is the base.
5. Identify and calculate the operating expenses variances.
6. Explain the difference in gross profit variances if a contribution margin approach is used.

A principal function of comparing results with plans is to help explain the what, why, and how of any differences. This explanation helps managers to see the impact of key variables on the actual results, focus on areas that deserve more investigation, and assess the changes necessary for future planning and control. We looked at determining variances for direct material, direct labor, and production overhead in Chapters 12 and 13. In this chapter, we extend the variance analysis concepts to gross profit analysis, to operating expenses (also called *nonproduction costs*), and to contribution margin analysis.

PROFIT ANALYSIS

Top management wants to know why a division or department is not performing according to expectations. These expectations are tied to performance measures typically related to profitability. Adequate answers usually require an investigation into the causes of variations in the components of the performance measure. Therefore, net income is always one of the numbers dissected and reviewed. The analysis yields more specific variances, which lead to areas that may require investigation. The level of detail needed in decomposing profit variances depends on individual situations,

EXHIBIT 19–1   Decomposition of Profit Variances

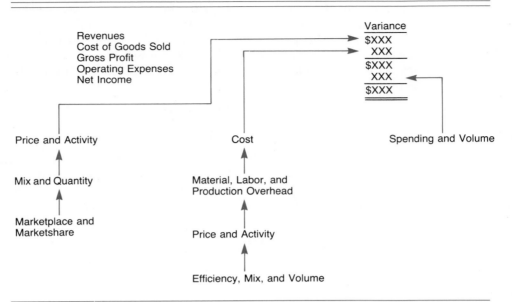

but each new layer is tied to some aspect of an income statement format: (1) revenue, cost of goods sold, gross profit, and operating expenses or (2) revenue, variable costs, contribution margin, and fixed costs.

For example, the variances for a typical income statement are shown in Exhibit 19–1. The revenue variance can be decomposed into price and activity factors. If a multiproduct environment exists, activity can be further analyzed into sales mix and quantity changes. Otherwise, activity is for volume only. Changes in volume can be further analyzed in terms of changes in the marketplace and market share if companies have the data for such changes. Variances for cost of goods sold and operating expenses can likewise be separated into potentially useful components. Cost of goods sold can, for instance, have variances traced to material, labor, and overhead. Each of these can be subdivided into price and activity variances. The activity variances can then be further analyzed into efficiency, mix, and volume variances. Another level of detail is provided when variances are identified with specific departments or areas of responsibility.

One useful technique that will help to explain changes in revenue and cost of goods sold is called **gross profit analysis. Gross profit** (or **gross margin**) is the excess of sales revenue over the cost of those sales. This differs from the **contribution margin,** which is the excess of sales revenue over all variable costs (including variable production, marketing and distribution, and general and administrative costs). Analysis of gross profit is made in a manner similar to the analysis of standard cost variances, although standards are not essential for the analysis. The factors we will emphasize in the analysis are changes that result from one or a combination of the following:

1. Changes in selling prices (sales price variance).
2. Changes in volume sold as reflected in the number of units sold (sales quantity variance) and in the sales mix (sales mix variance).
3. Changes in the cost elements in cost of goods sold (cost variance), such as direct materials, direct labor, and production overhead.

Later in the chapter we will look at variances for the operating expenses. Then we will present an analysis of an income statement prepared under the contribution format.

Single Product Case

The easiest illustration of gross profit analysis is for a single product. For example, the gross profit data for Willhite Corporation is as follows (in millions):

	Master Budget	Actual	Variance
Sales	$150	$126.5	$23.5
Cost of goods sold	120	112.7	7.3
Gross profit	$ 30	$ 13.8	$16.2
Units of product sold	30	23	7
Selling price per unit	$ 5.00	$ 5.50	+ $0.50
Cost per unit	$ 4.00	$ 4.90	+ $0.90
Gross profit per unit	$ 1.00	$ 0.60	− $0.40

Gross profit was $16.2 million lower than anticipated. Revenues were $23.5 million lower on a volume decrease of 7 million units even though the unit selling price was higher. Cost of goods sold was lower in total, but the per unit cost was higher. These changes can be analyzed in terms of a sales price variance, a cost variance, and a volume variance. There is no mix variance because we have only one product. We could split the volume between sales and cost of goods sold, but the source of the variance is a change in sales volume, not production volume.

The **sales price variance** is the change in gross profit due to a difference between budgeted and actual selling price per unit. Its computation is based on this formula: (actual unit selling price − budgeted unit selling price) × actual units sold. For the above data, the variance is ($5.50 − $5.00) × 23 million = $11.5 million favorable. In other words, the gross profit increased by $11.5 million due to a price increase. One strategy that marketing managers pursue is to increase revenues with higher selling prices while accepting reduction in volume. If the strategy works, the unfavorable volume variance will be less than the favorable price variance.

The **cost variance** is the change in gross profit resulting from an increase or decrease in unit cost. The computation is (actual cost per unit − budgeted cost per unit) × actual units sold. For our example, the cost variance is $20.7 million unfavorable [($4.90 − $4.00) × 23 million]. Production managers' failure to maintain control over direct materials, direct labor, and production overhead increased costs and reduced gross profit by $20.7 million.

A **sales volume variance** is the increase or decrease in gross profit resulting from the difference between the planned and actual number of units sold. The variance is computed by this formula: (actual unit sold − budgeted units sold) × budgeted gross profit per unit. For the above data, this variance is (23 − 30) million × $1.00 = $7 million unfavorable. Comparing this with the price variance, we see that a higher selling price increased gross profit by $11.5 million, but the decrease in volume reduced gross profit by $7 million, a net increase of $4.5 million. We could say that if management was following the strategy of increasing prices while accepting a reduction in volume, it may have worked in this case.

The total change in gross profit in the illustration was $16.2 million unfavorable. A summary of the three variances can now be shown to equal that total:

Sales price variance	$11.5 Favorable
Cost variance	20.7 Unfavorable
Sales volume variance	7.0 Unfavorable
Change in gross profit	$16.2 Unfavorable

Gross Profit Analysis for Multiproducts

Most manufacturing companies make more than one product, and the sales, cost of goods sold, and gross profit can vary widely among the products. Therefore, we approach the analysis knowing that a mix of products, sales revenues, and costs exists. In making the analysis, it is necessary to have a baseline for establishing a variation. The examples in this section assume the use of budgets. The chapter's problem for review is based on the previous year's data. A modification for standard costs will be explained later.

Consider the data for the Lemaree Manufacturing Company, which produces and sells three automotive products: KarKare, VacPak, and WaxEasy. In the gross profit analysis, we compare the actual results for 19x9 and the budgeted amounts established for the year.

	Master Budget	Actual	Variance
Sales	$6,480,000	$7,100,000	$620,000 F
Cost of goods sold	4,368,000	4,970,000	602,000 U
Gross profit	$2,112,000	$2,130,000	$ 18,000 F

The company planned for a gross profit of $2,112,000, but actual performance realized $2,130,000. At the same time, the total units declined from 480,000 planned to 466,000 actual. Actual data on sales and costs are:

	19x9 Sales			Cost of Goods Sold	
Product	Units	Price	Amount	Cost	Amount
KarKare	120,000	$ 7.50	$ 900,000	$ 5.25	$ 630,000
VacPak	90,000	12.00	1,080,000	8.40	756,000
WaxEasy	256,000	20.00	5,120,000	14.00	3,584,000
	466,000		$7,100,000		$4,970,000

Average selling price: $7,100,000 ÷ 466,000 = $15.23605
Average cost: $4,970,000 ÷ 466,000 = $10.66524
Average gross profit per unit: $15.23605 − $10.66524 = $4.57081

The detail about budgeted sales and costs for the year are:

	Budgeted Sales			Cost of Goods Sold	
Product	Units	Price	Amount	Cost	Amount
KarKare	144,000	$ 7.00	$1,008,000	$ 5.00	$ 720,000
VacPak	96,000	12.00	1,152,000	8.00	768,000
WaxEasy	240,000	18.00	4,320,000	12.00	2,880,000
	480,000		$6,480,000		$4,368,000

Average selling price: $6,480,000 ÷ 480,000 = $13.50
Average cost: $4,368,000 ÷ 480,000 = $9.10
Average gross profit per unit: $13.50 − $9.10 = $4.40

We could calculate three variances for sales and another three for costs each based on price, mix, and quantity. Because the source of mix and of quantity differences associated with gross profit is in the number of units sold rather than production,[1] mix and quantity variances are calculated in terms of gross profit rather than revenues and costs. Therefore, we compute four variances instead of six: sales price variance (change in selling price per unit), cost variance (change in cost per

---

[1] Mix and yield variances directly related to units produced were discussed in the appendix to Chapter 12. In the context used here, mix and quantity relate to the sales mix and the total units sold.

unit), sales mix variance (based on gross profit), and sales quantity variance (based on gross profit).

Sales Price Variance.   When selling price per unit changes, total sales revenue will change and so will gross profit. The sales price variance is calculated for each product by this formula: sales units × (actual selling price − budgeted selling price). This calculation for the example is:

Product	19x9 Sales Units	Difference in Prices	Variance
KarKare	120,000	($ 7.50 − $ 7.00) = $0.50	$ 60,000 F
VacPak	90,000	($12.00 − $12.00) = $0.00	–0–
WaxEasy	256,000	($20.00 − $18.00) = $2.00	512,000 F
			$572,000 F

The variance is favorable because the actual selling prices are higher than budgeted selling prices, with the exception of those for VacPak. Therefore, higher selling prices increased gross profit by $572,000.

An alternate approach to putting the numbers together compares 19x9 actual sales with 19x9 units at budgeted prices:

Product	19x9 Sales	19x9 Units at Budgeted Prices	Variance
KarKare	$ 900,000	120,000 × $ 7.00 = $ 840,000	$ 60,000 F
VacPak	1,080,000	90,000 × $12.00 = 1,080,000	–0–
WaxEasy	5,120,000	256,000 × $18.00 = 4,608,000	512,000 F
	$7,100,000	$6,528,000	$572,000 F

The sales price variance may be caused by changes in the marketplace, in pricing policy, or in allowable discounts at the discretion of salespeople. The actual cause is detected through investigation, not through variance analysis. Once causes are isolated, management must correct something or must determine that the informal policies and procedures underlying performance are acceptable and should be formally adopted, or conclude that the causes are not controllable at present. Should management not investigate variances because the amounts are insignificant, the variances can continue to appear in the future.

Cost Variance.   The formula for a cost variance uses the same factors as the sales price variance, except the cost per unit replaces the selling price.[2] For our example, the calculations are:

Product	19x9 Sales Units	Difference in Costs	Variance
KarKare	120,000	($ 5.25 − $ 5.00) = $0.25	$ 30,000 U
VacPak	90,000	($ 8.40 − $ 8.00) = $0.40	36,000 U
WaxEasy	256,000	($14.00 − $12.00) = $2.00	512,000 U
			$578,000 U

With actual costs per unit higher in 19x9 than the budgeted costs for all three products, the variances are unfavorable. The higher costs will drive down the 19x9 gross profit by $578,000. A favorable variance on individual products would occur if an actual cost per unit were less than a budgeted cost per unit.

An alternate approach is similar to the sales price variance. Insert unit costs for sales prices and the calculation is:

---

[2] The cost variances may be further analyzed into materials, labor, and overhead variances as presented in Chapters 12 and 13.

Product	19x9 Costs	19x9 Units at Budgeted Costs	Variance
KarKare	$ 630,000	120,000 × $ 5.00 = $ 600,000	$ 30,000 U
VacPak	756,000	90,000 × $ 8.00 = 720,000	36,000 U
WaxEasy	3,584,000	256,000 × $12.00 = 3,072,000	512,000 U
	$4,970,000	$4,392,000	$578,000 U

The difference between actual and budgeted cost per unit is a composite of a number of factors in production associated with direct material, direct labor, and production overhead variances. These factors must be identified and investigated when appropriate.

Sales Volume Variance. As in the single product case, the sales volume variance measures the increase or decrease in gross profit resulting from changes between the planned units and the actual units sold. This variance is measured as the difference in units multiplied by the budgeted gross profit, as follows:

Product	19x9 Units at Budgeted Gross Profit	Budgeted Units at Budgeted Gross Profit
KarKare	120,000 × $2.00 = $ 240,000	144,000 × $2.00 = $ 288,000
VacPak	90,000 × $4.00 = 360,000	96,000 × $4.00 = 384,000
WaxEasy	256,000 × $6.00 = 1,536,000	240,000 × $6.00 = 1,440,000
	$2,136,000	$2,112,000

Product	Variance
KarKare	$48,000 U
VacPak	24,000 U
WaxEasy	96,000 F
Sales Volume	$24,000 F

In the multiple product situation, this variance is difficult to interpret because it combines the interaction of changes in the mix of products and changes in the quantities. It is customary, therefore, to analyze the sales volume variance in terms of sales mix and sales quantity. These variances are discussed in the following sections.

Sales Mix Variance. A **sales mix variance** measures the impact on gross profit of shifts in sales units toward the more profitable or less-profitable products. A favorable variance occurs when a company either (1) sells fewer units of less-profitable products, or (2) sells more units of more profitable products. An unfavorable variance occurs when a company (1) sells more units of less-profitable products, or (2) sells fewer units of more profitable products. Whether a product is considered more or less profitable is determined by comparing the individual gross profit per unit with the average gross profit per unit for all units combined. If the individual gross profit per unit is greater, the product is more profitable. The opposite is true for the less-profitable product. The average gross profit per unit is calculated as a weighted average, weighted by the total quantity and the mix. For example, 480,000 units were budgeted for 19x9 with revenues of $6,480,000 and costs of $4,368,000, which results in gross profit of $2,112,000. Those numbers are a function of the 480,000 units budgeted and the sales mix for 480,000 units. The weighted average gross profit per unit is $2,112,000 ÷ 480,000 units = $4.40.

The sales mix variance is the difference between the actual units and actual mix and the actual units restated into the budgeted mix with that difference multiplied by the difference between the budgeted gross profit and the weighted average gross profit. The budgeted mix is:

		Product	Units	Budgeted Mix Percentage
		KarKare	144,000	30
		VacPak	96,000	20
		WaxEasy	240,000	50
			480,000	

Now we restate the 466,000 units actually sold during 19x9 to the 19x9 budgeted mix as follows:

Product	Total Quantity × Mix Percentage
KarKare	466,000 × 30% = 139,800
VacPak	466,000 × 20 = 93,200
WaxEasy	466,000 × 50 = 233,000
	466,000

Now compare the 19x9 units with the restated mix and multiply the difference in units by the difference in budgeted unit gross profit and average budgeted gross profit. This results in the following:

Product	Actual Units at Actual Mix	Actual Units Restated	Difference	Budgeted Gross Profit	Average − Budgeted Gross Profit	Variance
KarKare	120,000	139,800	(19,800)	($2.00 −	$4.40)	$47,520 F
VacPak	90,000	93,200	(3,200)	(4.00 −	4.40)	1,280 F
WaxEasy	256,000	233,000	23,000	(6.00 −	4.40)	36,800 F
	466,000	466,000				$85,600 F

The sales mix is important because some products contribute more to profit than others; they have a greater gross profit. Because changes in sales mix can change total gross profit, managers need to know when a change in the mix occurs and how to assess its impact on gross profit. The sales mix variance gives us this measure. In the situation above, the shift in mix was toward the more profitable WaxEasy (favorable variance) and away from the less profitable KarKare and VacPak (favorable variances). The effect of the shift will increase gross profit by $85,600.

Sales Quantity Variance.   The sales quantity variance occurs when total actual sales units differ from the total budgeted sales units. The calculation of the variance is a comparison of total actual sales units stated at the average budgeted gross profit per unit and the budgeted units stated at the average budgeted gross profit. This gives, in simplified form (466,000 − 480,000) × $4.40 = $61,600 unfavorable. The sales quantity variance is unfavorable because the total units sold were less than the total units budgeted.

The quantity variance is usually considered only in total. However, some managers want a quantity variance for each product or product line. Because of the effects from sales mix changes, the quantity variance on a product basis is not the same straight forward calculation as that for the total variance. We use two components in the calculation: (1) the difference between the actual units and the budgeted units multiplied by the average budgeted gross profit; and (2) the difference between the actual units stated at the budgeted mix and the budgeted units multiplied by the difference between the budgeted gross profit per unit and the average budgeted gross profit.

This latter component is to adjust for the impact of sales mix on quantity. The following calculations give the amounts for each component:

Product	Actual Units at Actual Mix	Budgeted Units	Difference	Average Budgeted Gross Profit	Component (1)
KarKare	120,000	144,000	(24,000)	$4.40	$105,600 U
VacPak	90,000	96,000	(6,000)	4.40	26,400 U
WaxEasy	256,000	240,000	16,000	4.40	70,400 F
					$ 61,600 U

Product	Actual Units Restated	Budgeted Units	Difference	Difference in Budgeted and Average Gross Profit
KarKare	139,800	144,000	(4,200)	($2.00 − $4.40)
VacPak	93,200	96,000	(2,800)	($4.00 − $4.40)
WaxEasy	233,000	240,000	(7,000)	($6.00 − $4.40)

Product	Component (2)
KarKare	$10,080 F
VacPak	1,120 F
WaxEasy	11,200 U
	$ 0

Now combining the two components, we get the following variances:

Product	Component (1)	Component (2)	Sales Quantity Variance
KarKare	$105,600 U	$10,080 F	$95,520 U
VacPak	26,400 U	1,120 F	25,280 U
WaxEasy	70,400 F	11,200 U	59,200 F
	$ 61,600 U	$ 0	$61,600 U

Because the second component is adjusting the quantities for the changes in sales mix, it will always total to zero. Consequently, the adjustment is only necessary when identifying a sales quantity variance with individual products.

The sales quantity variance can be caused by many factors such as unanticipated changes in general economic conditions, differences in the effectiveness of salespeople or the advertising program, or the changes in credit policy. As with all variances, management will want to investigate the cause of significant amounts.

In large companies, a sales quantity variance is isolated separately for each distribution channel, for each geographic region, and possibly for each product line. Reporting by channel of distribution indicates whether the variance occurred in wholesale or retail divisions. A geographic identification helps to show where the activities need investigation. A separation according to product line directs the investigation to the product lines that were causing the sales quantity variance. Not only will separation help to be more precise in identifying sources of variation, but also it permits performance reporting along the lines of accountability according to responsibility accounting.

Recapitulation of Gross Profit Variances. The four variances identified above are summarized as follows:

Sales price variance	$572,000 F	
Cost variance	578,000 U	
Sales mix variance	85,600 F	
Sales quantity variance	61,600 U	
Change in gross profit	$ 18,000 F	

Even though some variances were unfavorable, the changes resulted in increasing the gross profit during 19x9 over the budgeted gross profit.

Modification for Standard Costs

When a standard cost system is in place, the cost of goods sold is stated at the standard cost per finished unit. That means the actual results will be sales at actual selling prices and actual quantities sold with cost of goods sold stated at actual quantities sold at standard costs. This is reasonable because units produced are transferred from Work in Process Inventory to Finished Goods Inventory at standard costs. Any difference between actual costs and standard costs has already been isolated during production. Those variances are treated in Chapters 12 and 13. The following summary is for the Lamaree Manufacturing Company, assuming that the budgeted cost data used earlier for 19x9 are based on standard costs:

	Master Budget	Actual	Variance
Sales	$6,400,000	$7,100,000	$700,000 F
Cost of goods sold	4,320,000	4,392,000	72,000 U
Gross profit	$2,080,000	$2,708,000	$628,000 F

The actual amounts show sales at actual units and prices and cost of goods sold at actual units and standard costs. These data appear as follows:

Product	Actual 19x9 Sales			Cost of Goods Sold	
	Units	Price	Amount	Cost	Amount
KarKare	120,000	$ 7.50	$ 900,000	$ 5.00	$ 600,000
VacPak	90,000	12.00	1,080,000	8.00	720,000
WaxEasy	256,000	20.00	5,120,000	12.00	3,072,000
	466,000		$7,100,000		$4,392,000

This approach changes the gross profit analysis in only one respect: it eliminates the cost variance calculation. With standard costs per unit identical between actual and budgeted amounts, the cost variance is always zero. Therefore, the $72,000 of change in gross profit related to cost of goods sold above is due only to mix and quantity considerations. Calculating sales price, sales mix, and sales quantity variances using the formulae as we did before gives the following results:

Sales price variance	$572,000 F	
Sales mix variance	85,600 F	
Sales quantity variance	29,600 U	
Change in gross profit	$628,000 F	

A FRAMEWORK FOR ANALYSIS

Too often the computation of variances appears as just so many formulae. There is, however, a logic to them; each one is a piece of the total change. In the case of gross profit, the total change is the difference between actual and budgeted gross profit. Sales price, cost, sales mix, and sales quantity variances are parts of the overall change, and none of the variances overlap, although boundaries between each one may appear fuzzy. The conceptual relationships between the variances are presented in Exhibit 19–2.

Essentially, gross profit is made up of three factors: unit gross profit, a mix, and a quantity level. The variances are isolated by changing one or two factors while holding the other two factors constant. In the price/cost variances, for example, the unit gross profit changes from actual to budget while the mix proportions and quantity level are held constant at actual.

As the exhibit indicates, three variances (price/cost, mix, and quantity) can be computed using the unit gross profit in the calculations. In most cases, additional information can be obtained by looking at the changes in selling prices and costs

EXHIBIT 19–2   Framework for Gross Profit Analysis

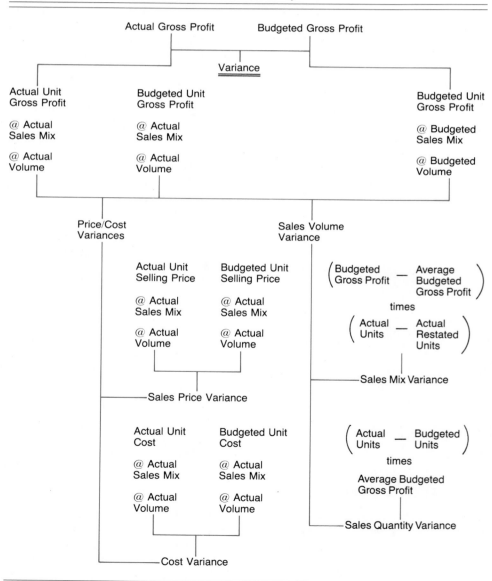

separately. Therefore, a sales price variance and a cost variance are individually computed; the net of the two variances is the same as using the unit gross profit amounts.

Gross Profit Analysis Based on the Previous Period

Some companies do not use budgets or standards but instead use results of the previous period as their baseline. The approach to the gross profit analysis will not change. The results of the previous period are utilized in a manner similar to the budgeted information for purposes of computing sales price, cost, sales mix, and sales quantity variances.

Using the previous period as the baseline is not the ideal approach if budgets or standards are available because we must assume that nothing has changed from the previous period. That is, we will do things in exactly the same way this period as we did last. Therefore, excessive costs and inefficiencies of the previous period are assumed to continue and are hidden in the analysis of gross profit. Budgets and standard costs eliminate this problem and permit a realistic assessment of actual performance against expectations.

If people outside the company are analyzing income statement data, they will not have access to budgeted or standard cost information. But the prior period's results are available. An analysis of changes between the two periods can then be made.

Uses of Gross Profit Analysis

The gross profit analysis identifies weak spots in performance for the period. The preceding summaries and analyses provide ample motivation for management to initiate a variance investigation leading to possible corrective actions. Because gross profit is the joint responsibility of the marketing and production functions, the gross profit analysis brings together these two major functional areas. The marketing function must explain the changes in sales prices, the shift in the sales mix, and the decrease in total units sold. The production functions must explain the increase in costs.

Not all changes in the gross profit have the same degree of significance. For example, an increase in sales revenue as a result of price increases may be less desirable than an increase generated by sales volume. Or, decreases in unit fixed costs traceable to increases in the volume of production activity mean less than lower unit costs achieved through more efficient use of direct material and direct labor or through a savings in some area of production overhead.

Responsibility for gross profit changes resides with different managers within the organization. Sales managers typically cannot be held responsible for sales price increases, but volume increases and decreases rest with them. Increases in selling prices are in the domain of top management decision making. A production manager cannot control cost increases from decreased activity attributable to a lack of sales orders. However, production managers can be held accountable for cost increases caused by inefficient production operations or excessive spending.

Limitations of Gross Profit Analysis

Useful though it is, gross profit analysis suffers from three limitations. First, although we have defined variances in a specific way, the boundary between one variance and another is fuzzy when it comes to interpreting the amounts. Therefore, variances can be regarded as providing only an order of magnitude and direction. They cannot be interpreted literally. Second, the budget plan for the period and the actual results do not necessarily represent what the manager should have been able to accomplish during the period, given the conditions that actually prevailed. In other words, as conditions changed, did the manager respond to those changes in an optimal way?

This is not measured. The third limitation is more fundamental. The analysis does not indicate why the sales price variance is as large or as small as it is, or why volume failed to meet the budgeted level, or why the mix of products changed from the budgeted mix. In fact, the variances may even be interdependent. Volume may be down because price is too high, the mix may be good because the more profitable product is underpriced, and so on.

The variance analysis is nothing more than a series of computations that yield amounts we identify as favorable or unfavorable. All any variance analysis can do is provide a convenient summary of symptoms. Identification of the underlying causes is left to the manager. The technical breakdown is useful in identifying areas that should be investigated. If the analysis shows, for example, that the main problem seems to be the sales mix, management is closer to finding a solution than if this information were not available.

VARIANCES FOR OPERATING EXPENSES

Operating expenses (sometimes called *nonproduction costs*) encompass marketing and distribution expenses, and general and administrative expenses. For our purposes in this section, we will use the terms *marketing expenses* and *administrative expenses*.

Administrative expenses are often the hardest to manage because they are not engineered. That is, the beneficial/causal relationship between input and output is not well defined. Administrative costs are usually budgeted with a discretionary cost budget, which places a ceiling on costs for a particular set of tasks. Although discretionary budgets can provide a ceiling for expenditures, they do not provide a good baseline for measuring performance. If there is no measure of output, there is no measure of input-output relationships, and ascertaining the proper level of costs is quite difficult. These difficulties must be weighed when evaluating an administrative cost variance.

From an income statement point of view, the difference between actual and budgeted operating expenses will be isolated as two variances: spending and volume. These variances are depicted schematically as follows:

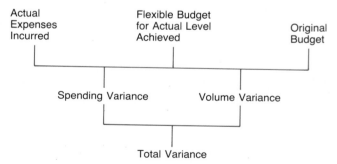

At the end of the period, a flexible budget is calculated for the actual level of operations achieved. The **spending variance** is the difference between the actual expense and the flexible budget calculations. It is the difference between what was actually spent and what should have been spent at that same level of activity. A **volume variance** is the difference between the flexible budget and the original budget. It is due to preparing a budget for one level of sales activity and then not operating at that level.

Returning to Lemaree Manufacturing Company, assume the company had the following information about operating expenses:

Budget for the year	$1,500,000
Actual expenses incurred	1,990,000
Total variance	$ 490,000

The budgeted amount is based on 5 percent of budgeted sales ($6,400,000) plus $1,180,000. Actual sales for the year totaled $7,100,000. A flexible budget would show a total of $1,535,000 ($1,180,000 fixed plus 5 percent of $7,100,000). We do not have a breakdown of the actual variable and fixed costs. However, the segregation is not necessary for the following analysis. This information is summarized as:

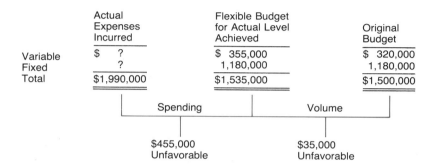

	Actual Expenses Incurred	Flexible Budget for Actual Level Achieved	Original Budget
Variable	$?	$ 355,000	$ 320,000
Fixed	?	1,180,000	1,180,000
Total	$1,990,000	$1,535,000	$1,500,000

Spending: $455,000 Unfavorable

Volume: $35,000 Unfavorable

These variances relate in part to the variable and fixed nature of the operating costs. A spending variance consists of both variable and fixed costs, and the volume variance consists only of variable costs. This differs from the volume variance for production overhead, which consists of only fixed costs. The spending variance is controllable; the volume variance is the result of whatever factors produced the increase in sales.

The spending variance is the result of the responsible manager's efforts to keep spending in line with the amount expected at that level of activity. Besides estimating errors in specifying fixed and variable cost components, this variance includes price and quantity differences identified with individual expense categories within the operating expenses.

The volume variance is the difference between two budget calculations made at two different levels—the actual level and the originally planned level. It is the result of whatever factors produced the change in sales. The reasons for not operating at the originally planned level could be the result of random economic events, but more than likely, one or more identifiable factors are related to the marketing function or the marketplace.

CONTRIBUTION MARGIN ANALYSIS

A contribution approach is popular in some companies for profitability and performance reporting. The basic format of the report shows revenues less variable costs to equal a contribution margin. From that, fixed costs are deducted to arrive at operating income. Gross profit is not a component of the contribution approach, yet the techniques of gross profit analysis can be applied to a contribution margin. There are still sales price, cost, sales mix, and sales quantity variances, although some of the dollar components of the variances differ from those of a gross profit.

Looking at the functional costs and their variable and fixed categories, we have an income statement as follows:

Sales		$558,200
Less variable costs:		
Variable cost of goods sold	$245,920	
Variable marketing costs	46,110	
Variable administrative costs	15,370	307,400
Contribution margin		$250,800
Less fixed costs:		
Fixed production costs	$ 90,100	
Fixed marketing costs	10,600	
Fixed administrative costs	5,300	106,000
Operating income		$144,800

The differences between a contribution margin and gross profit should be emphasized. Variable operating costs (marketing and administration) are combined with variable cost of goods sold and will be included in the contribution margin analysis. Fixed production costs are now treated as operating expenses with the fixed marketing and administrative costs.

How will these differences affect variance analysis? Let's look first at the fixed costs. Treated as operating expenses, the fixed costs would be analyzed as spending and volume variances. Because, as noted in the earlier discussion on operating expenses, a volume variance for operating expenses consists only of variable costs components, there will be no volume variances for any of the categories of fixed costs. Therefore, only spending variances are identified for costs below the contribution margin. Variable costs are above the contribution margin and would be included in a contribution margin analysis. The variable marketing and administrative costs would have dollar amounts appearing in cost, sales mix, and sales quantity variances.

We noted earlier that a significant amount of the marketing and administrative costs are discretionary fixed costs. One could, therefore, assume that the variable operating expenses are insignificant and that a contribution analysis will be influenced by variable production costs only. If this is the case, the contribution margin can be treated as sales revenue less variable cost of goods sold and the cost, sales mix, and sales quantity variances would not reflect the variable marketing and administrative costs.

This means that some companies treat all operating expenses as fixed, which leaves variable production costs as the only variable cost component of contribution margin. Consequently, a contribution margin differs from a gross profit only in the treatment of fixed production costs. If variable operating expenses are significant, investigation of variances must cover all functions. The cost variance in this case is a combination of variances that occurred in production, marketing, and administration. It is common practice to separate and report separate expense variances for each function. For example, separate variances would be likely for significant other areas such as research and development or personnel. To avoid having to repeat the same analysis for many different functions, the data in this section combine production, marketing, and administration.

In the example below, we assume variable production costs and variable operating expenses are in the contribution margin. Because fixed costs have only a spending variance, our analysis covers only those items included in the contribution margin. Kermit Products, Inc., produces and sells three products that are purchased by several other manufacturers as components for major defense weapon systems. Budgeted and actual costs and pricing data for the quarter are:

Product	Budgeted Sales Units	Price	Amount	Variable Costs Cost	Amount
R-Module	1,200	$100	$120,000	$50	$ 60,000
Laser cone	2,800	60	168,000	40	112,000
O-Ring	4,000	45	180,000	20	80,000
	8,000		$468,000		$252,000

Product	Actual Sales Units	Price	Amount	Variable Costs Cost	Amount
R-Module	1,500	$98	$147,000	$46	$ 69,000
Laser cone	3,200	57	182,400	42	134,400
O-Ring	5,200	44	228,800	20	104,000
	9,900		$558,200		$307,400

This information is summarized in a comparison in which changes in contribution margin are related to sales and variable costs:

	Master Budget	Actual	Variance
Sales	$468,000	$558,200	$90,200 F
Variable costs	252,000	307,400	55,400 U
Contribution margin	$216,000	$250,800	$34,800 F

The average contribution in the budget is $27 ($216,000/8,000).

What are the causes of the $34,800 increase in the contribution? Answering that question begins with an analysis of the contribution margin in terms of sales price, cost (variable cost in this case), sales mix, and sales quantity variances. Using the techniques we have learned with gross profit analysis, we calculate the variances for the contribution margin.

Sales Price Variance

The sales price variance occurs when the actual sales price differs from the budgeted sales price. The formula for each product is actual sales units × (actual sales price − budgeted sales price). For Kermit Products, Inc., the variance is:

Product	Actual Sales Units	Difference in Price	Variance
R-Module	1,500	($98 − $100) = − $2	$ 3,000 U
Laser cone	3,200	($57 − $ 60) = − $3	9,600 U
O-Ring	5,200	($44 − $ 45) = − $1	5,200 U
			$17,800 U

All three products have an unfavorable variance because their prices decreased. The cause of those decreases can be determined and assessed only after further investigation.

Cost Variance

The variable costs can consist of the variable costs of production, marketing, and administration. If all three are present, there may be situations in which a separate cost variance is calculated for each of three functions. A combined variance is calculated here. The formula for doing so is the same as for the price variance except that cost is substituted for product prices. The calculation is:

Product	Actual Sales Units	Difference in Cost	Variance
R-Module	1,500	($46 − $50) = − $4	$6,000 F
Laser cone	3,200	($42 − $40) = $2	6,400 U
O-Ring	5,200	($20 − $20) = $0	–0–
			$ 400 U

One product had a decrease in variable costs but another product realized increased costs. The net effect is an unfavorable cost variance of $400; the cost increase for laser cones had a greater impact on the contribution margin than did the cost savings on the R-Module.

Sales Mix Variance

The sales mix variance measures the change in the contribution margin due to a shift in the mix of products sold. The budgeted mix is:

Product	Units	Budgeted Mix Percentage
R-Module	1,200	15
Laser cone	2,800	35
O-Ring	4,000	50
	8,000	

Restating the 9,900 units actually sold in terms of the budgeted mix gives the following:

Product	Total Quantity × Mix Percentage
R-Module	9,900 × 15 = 1,485
Laser cone	9,900 × 35 = 3,465
O-Ring	9,900 × 50 = 4,950
	9,900

Comparing the actual units with the restated mix and multiplying by the difference in budgeted contribution margin and average contribution margin yields the sales mix variance:

Product	Actual Units at Actual Mix	Actual Units Restated	Difference	Budgeted Contribution − Average Budgeted Contribution	Variance
R-Module	1,500	1,485	15	(50 − 27)	$ 345 F
Laser cone	3,200	3,465	(265)	(20 − 27)	1,855 F
O-Ring	5,200	4,950	250	(25 − 27)	500 U
					$1,700

The shift in the mix moved toward the more profitable products resulting in a $1,700 increase in the contribution margin.

Sales Quantity Variance

The change in the contribution margin due to quantity is related to the difference between the total actual units sold and the total units budgeted. We already know from the earlier data that the total units sold for the quarter exceeded the budgeted units. Therefore, the sales quantity variance is favorable. The dollar amount attached to that favorable variance is calculated as: $(9,900 - 8,000) \times \$27 = \$51,300$ F.

Should the company want the sales quantity variance by product, a separate calculation can be made. Since that calculation was illustrated earlier, it is not repeated here.

Recapitulation of Variances

The four variances that identify major areas that will help explain the increase in contribution margin are summarized as follows:

Sales price variance	$17,800 U
Cost variance	400 U
Sales mix variance	1,700 F
Sales quantity variance	51,300 F
Change in contribution margin	$34,800 F

The major factors affecting the change in contribution are changes in sales prices and an increase in the number of units sold.

SUMMARY

Profit becomes part of most performance measures used to evaluate division or department managers. Any time actual performance varies from expectations, explanations for the differences are sought. Once reasons for or causes of variations are identified, changes can be made in the future through the planning process or the use of control mechanisms. Common categories of variances are usually isolated as a first step in looking for explanations.

Gross profit analysis is one approach to look at where changes that result in increases or decreases in gross profit have occurred. A sales price variance indicates differences caused by changes in sales prices. A cost variance isolates the dollar amount associated with changes in costs of products sold. A sales quantity variance measures changes due to higher or lower total units sold than expected. If a company has multiple products, a sales mix variance identifies the change in gross profit due to shifts in the sales mix of the products.

A baseline is necessary to compare actual performance with planned performance. Budgets or standards are preferable because they indicate what was planned (the goals and objectives for the period of performance).

Operating expenses can also be analyzed into variances. Spending and volume variances are the two common ones calculated. A spending variance shows the difference between actual expenses and a flexible budget for the level of activity achieved. The volume variance is the difference between the flexible budget and the budget for the original level planned; it consists only of variable costs. Spending is usually considered more significant than volume.

Gross profit analysis and variances for operating expenses can also be applied when the income statement is prepared in a contribution format. The variances for a contribution margin are sales price, cost (variable only), sales mix, and sales quantity. For the fixed costs, the only variance is a spending variance.

PROBLEM FOR REVIEW

Assume that the Lemaree Manufacturing Company, which produces and sells three automotive products, KarKare, VacPak, and WaxEasy, compares the actual results of the previous year with actual results of the current year. The gross profit for the two years is summarized as:

	19x8	19x9	Variance
Sales	$6,300,000	$7,100,000	$800,000 F
Cost of goods sold	4,320,000	4,970,000	650,000 U
Gross profit	$1,980,000	$2,130,000	$150,000 F

The actual sales and cost data for the two years are:

	19x8 Sales			Cost of Goods Sold	
Product	Units	Price	Amount	Cost	Amount
KarKare	150,000	$ 6.00	$ 900,000 *	$ 4.80	$ 720,000
VacPak	100,000	9.00	900,000	6.00	600,000
WaxEasy	250,000	18.00	4,500,000	12.00	3,000,000
	500,000		$6,300,000		$4,320,000

Average selling price: $6,300,000 ÷ 500,000 units = $12.60
Average cost: $4,320,000 ÷ 500,000 units = $8.64
Average gross profit per unit: $12.60 − $8.64 = $3.96

	19x9 Sales			Cost of Goods Sold	
Product	Units	Price	Amount	Cost	Amount
KarKare	120,000	$ 7.50	$ 900,000	$ 5.25	$ 630,000
VacPak	90,000	12.00	1,080,000	8.40	756,000
WaxEasy	256,000	20.00	5,120,000	14.00	3,584,000
	466,000		$7,100,000		$4,970,000

Average selling price: $7,100,000 ÷ 466,000 = $15.23605
Average cost: $4,970,000 ÷ 466,000 = $10.66524
Average gross profit per unit: $15.23605 − $10.66524 = $4.57081

The gross profit increased in spite of a decrease in the total units sold. You are asked to analyze the gross profit and to identify the potential sources of variation in gross profit.

REQUIRED

a. Calculate the following gross profit variances:
   1. Sales price variance.
   2. Cost variance.
   3. Sales mix variance.
   4. Sales quantity variance.
b. Prepare a summary that recapitulates the variances in such a way that the net of all variances equals the change in gross profit.

SOLUTION

a. 1. Sales price variance.

Product	19x9 Sales Units	Difference in Prices	Variance
KarKare	120,000	($ 7.50 − $ 6.00) = $1.50	$180,000 F
VacPak	90,000	($12.00 − $ 9.00) = $3.00	270,000 F
WaxEasy	256,000	($20.00 − $18.00) = $2.00	512,000 F
			$962,000 F

In this case, the variance is favorable because the 19x9 selling prices are higher than the 19x8 prices, which brings in higher revenues. Thus, gross profit is increased.

An alternate way to calculate the sales price variance is to compare 19x9 actual sales revenue with 19x9 sales units priced at 19x8 prices:

Product	19x9 Sales	19x9 Units at 19x8 Sales Prices		Variance
KarKare	$ 900,000	120,000 × $ 6.00 =	$ 720,000	$180,000 F
VacPak	1,080,000	90,000 × $ 9.00 =	810,000	270,000 F
WaxEasy	5,120,000	256,000 × $18.00 =	4,608,000	512,000 F
	$7,100,000		$6,138,000	$962,000 F

a. 2. Cost variance.

Product	19x9 Sales Units	Difference in Prices	Variance
KarKare	120,000	($ 5.25 − $ 4.80) = $ .45	$ 54,000 U
VacPak	90,000	($ 8.40 − $ 6.00) = $2.40	216,000 U
WaxEasy	256,000	($14.00 − $12.00) = $2.00	512,000 U
			$782,000 U

Because costs per unit were higher in 19x9 than in 19x8, the variances are unfavorable. The higher costs drive down the 19x9 gross profit.

An alternate approach for calculating the cost variance is the same as that used for the sales price variance. Insert unit costs where we used sales prices, and the calculation is:

Product	19x9 Costs	19x9 Units at 19x8 Unit Costs	Variance
KarKare	$ 630,000	120,000 × $ 4.80 = $ 576,000	$ 54,000 U
VacPak	756,000	90,000 × $ 6.00 = 540,000	216,000 U
WaxEasy	3,584,000	256,000 × $12.00 = 3,072,000	512,000 U
	$4,970,000	$4,188,000	$782,000 U

a. 3. Sales mix variance.
The 19x8 mix is:

Product	Units	Percentage
KarKare	150,000	30
VacPak	100,000	20
WaxEasy	250,000	50
	500,000	

Now we restate the 466,000 units in 19x9 to the 19x8 mix as follows:

Product	Total Quantity × Mix Percentage
KarKare	466,000 × 30 = 139,800
VacPak	466,000 × 20 = 93,200
WaxEasy	466,000 × 50 = 233,000
	466,000

Putting actual and restated units together, we calculate the mix variance as follows:

Product	Actual Units	Actual Units Restated	Difference	Budgeted Gross Profit	Average Budgeted Gross Profit	Variance
KarKare	120,000	139,800	(19,800)	($1.20 −	$3.96)	$ 54,648 F
VacPak	90,000	93,200	(3,200)	(3.00 −	3.96)	3,072 F
WaxEasy	256,000	233,000	23,000	(6.00 −	3.96)	46,920 F
						$104,640 F

a. 4. Sales quantity variance.
Multiply the difference between the 19x8 and the 19x9 quantities by the 19x8 average gross profit per unit. This gives (466,000 − 500,000) × $3.96 = $134,640 U. The sales quantity variance is unfavorable because the total number of units sold in 19x9 was less than the total number of units sold in 19x8.

If the sales quantity variance is needed for each individual product, it would be calculated as follows:

Product	19x9 Units at Actual Mix	19x8 Units	Difference	Average 19x8 Gross Profit	Component (1)
KarKare	120,000	150,000	(30,000)	$3.96	$118,800 U
VacPak	90,000	100,000	(10,000)	3.96	39,600 U
WaxEasy	256,000	250,000	6,000	3.96	23,760 F
					$134,640 U

Product	Actual Units Restated	Budgeted Units	Difference	Difference in Budgeted and Average Gross Profit
KarKare	139,800	150,000	(10,200)	($1.20 − $3.96)
VacPak	93,200	100,000	(6,800)	($3.00 − $3.96)
WaxEasy	233,000	250,000	(17,000)	($6.00 − $3.96)

Product	Component (2)
KarKare	$28,152 F
VacPak	6,528 F
WaxEasy	34,680 U
	$ 0

Now combining the two components, we get the following variances:

Product	Component (1)	Component (2)	Sales Quantity Variance
KarKare	$118,800 U	$28,152 F	$ 90,648 U
VacPak	39,600 U	6,528 F	33,072 U
WaxEasy	23,760 F	34,680 U	10,920 U
	$134,640 U	$ 0	$134,640 U

b. Recapitulation.

The four variances identified in the above computations are summarized as follows:

Sales price variance	$962,000 F
Cost variance	782,000 U
Sales mix variance	104,640 F
Sales quantity variance	134,640 U
Change in gross profit	$150,000 F

The net variance of $150,000 favorable is the net of the favorable and unfavorable variances. Even though some variances were unfavorable, the changes resulted in increasing the gross profit during 19x9.

KEY TERMS AND CONCEPTS

Gross profit analysis (746)
Gross profit (gross margin) (746)
Contribution margin (746)
Sales price variance (747)
Cost variance (747)
Sales volume variance (747)

Sales mix variance (750)
Sales quantity variance (751)
Operating expenses (756)
Spending variance (756)
Volume Variance (756)

ADDITIONAL READINGS

Bastable, C. W., and D. H. Bao. "The Fiction of Sales-Mix and Sales-Quantity Variances." *Accounting Horizons,* June, 1988, pp. 10–17.

Boer, Germain. "What Gross Margins Do Not Tell You." *Management Accounting*, October, 1984, pp. 50–53, 91.

Brayton, Gary N. "Productivity Measure Aids in Profit Analysis." *Management Accounting*, January, 1985, pp. 54–58.

Chow, Chee W.; Howard R. Toole; and Adrian Wong-Boren. "Make Better Decisions: Divide and Conquer." *Management Accounting*, August, 1986, pp. 41–45.

Enrick, Norbert L. "Using Sales Equivalency as a Cost Saving Tool." *Management Accounting*, February, 1985, pp. 46–50.

Govindarajan, Vijay, and John K. Shank. "Profit Variance Analysis: A Strategic Focus." *Issues in Accounting Education*, Fall, 1989, pp. 396–410.

Lawler, William C., and John Leslie Livingstone. "Profit and Productivity Analysis for Small Businesses." *Journal of Accountancy*, December, 1986, pp. 190–96.

Sprohge, Hans, and John Talbott. "New Applications for Variance Analysis." *Journal of Accountancy*, April, 1989, pp. 137–41.

REVIEW QUESTIONS

1. What is the difference between gross profit and contribution margin?
2. What are the principal factors influencing gross profit for single products? For multiple products?
3. What are the formulae for the following variances in the single product case: (a) sales price, (b) cost, and (c) volume?
4. Explain why a single product firm will not have a sales mix variance in a gross profit analysis.
5. Sales price variances are excluded from all calculations of sales mix and sales quantity variances. Explain how this happens.
6. What are the formulae for the following variances when there are multiple products? (a) sales price, (b) cost, (c) sales mix, (d) sales quantity.
7. Cite three examples of possible sources of variances that will be reflected in a sales price variance.
8. Explain where cost variances come from.
9. How do changes in the sales mix affect profits?
10. A company sells a variety of products with different gross profit margins. Explain how it is possible for gross margins to move in an opposite direction from sales revenue even though selling prices and unit costs remain the same.
11. When is it appropriate to compute a sales mix and a sales quantity variance rather than just a single sales quantity variance?
12. Explain how a sales mix variance differs from a sales quantity variance.
13. What effect do changes in selling prices and costs have on the change in gross profit attributable to the volume factor?
14. How are variances from standard costs used in gross profit analysis?
15. Explain why a cost variance will not appear in a gross profit analysis when cost of goods sold is based on standard costs.
16. At a recent luncheon, a product line sales manager stated: "The sales variances of price, mix, and quantity are given the same weight in our performance evaluation because all of them are important." Do you agree that all sales variances are equally important? Explain.
17. Identify three limitations of gross profit analysis.
18. The bright young assistant controller said in a staff meeting, "The flexible budget amounts for operating expenses will be different from the master budget amounts for operating expenses at exactly the same number of units sold." Explain why the assistant controller is or is not correct.
19. What are the components of a spending variance for operating expenses? How does a volume variance differ from a spending variance?

20. Analysis of gross profit changes requires a different approach than the one used for contribution margin analysis. Do you agree? Explain.
21. If variable operating expenses are significant, how are they included in a contribution margin analysis? Explain.

DISCUSSION QUESTIONS

22. We normally assume that the production function does not influence sales price, mix, or quantity variances. The responsibility for these variances usually rests with the marketing function. How could the production function have a direct impact on sales mix or sales quantity variances?
23. Any production variances isolated in a standard cost system must be disposed of by the end of the period. Significant variances are prorated to appropriate inventory accounts and cost of goods sold. Insignificant variances are closed to cost of goods sold. Explain how the disposition of variances affects the analysis of gross profit. How would the recapitulation of variances for reporting purposes change?

EXERCISES

19–1. Gross Profit Analysis—Single Product. The following single product information is for the month of July for a small manufacturing company in the Southeast:

	Sales		Cost of Goods Sold	
	Price	Amount	Cost	Amount
Budgeted	$8.00	$20,000	$6.00	$15,000
Actual	7.50	22,500	6.50	19,500

REQUIRED:
As the accountant for the company, you have been asked why the budget for the month was not met. Using a gross profit analysis, show all details to explain why budgeted and actual gross profit differ.

19–2. Contribution Margin Analysis–Single Product. Amy Fire Prevention manufactures an auto fire extinguisher. During May, the company sold 2,500 extinguishers for $30,000 and actual variable costs totaling $24,375. The budget for the month called for sales of 3,000 units at $14.00 each and variable costs of $9.50 per unit.

REQUIRED:
a. Calculate the contribution margin for the fire extinguisher.
b. What are the contribution margin variances? Show your calculations.

19–3. Gross Profit Analysis on Single and Multiple Products. Zielke Creations has two major products that it has been selling through retail distributors in the Chicago area. Wholesale data for 19x2 are as follows:

Product	Units	Sales Price	Cost/Unit
Imagic	200,000	$5.00	$3.20
Creatif	300,000	6.00	3.00

For 19x3, the comparable data appear below:

Product	Units	Sales Price	Cost/Unit
Imagic	150,000	$5.25	$3.15
Creatif	400,000	6.00	3.20

REQUIRED:

a. Calculate the change in gross profit for each product and in total between 19x2 and 19x3.

b. Calculate the gross profit variances for each product individually. Use 19x2 as though it were the budget.

c. Perform a gross profit analysis for the two products combined. Use 19x2 as though it were the budget.

d. Reconcile the results in *(c)* above with those of *(b)* above. What is the source of any difference?

19–4. Sales Mix and Quantity Variances.   Next year's budget for Eldon Sweat, Inc., a multiproduct manufacturer, is given below:

	Product Lines		
	ME2	*RT*	*U2*
Sales	$1,488,000	$1,200,000	$1,318,800
Less: Variable costs	868,800	900,000	1,108,800
Fixed costs	210,000	225,000	136,950
Operating income	$ 409,200	$ 75,000	$ 73,050
Units	240,000	150,000	210,000

The actual results for the year show that the sales price, unit variable costs, and total fixed costs were exactly as budgeted. However, the units sold were as follows:

Product Line	*Units*
ME2	255,000
RT	140,000
U2	205,000

REQUIRED (using contribution margin analysis):

a. Calculate the sales quantity variances that apply to individual product lines.

b. Calculate the sales mix and quantity variances that apply to the total of the product lines.

c. Reconcile your answer in *(b)* to *(a)*.

19–5. Gross Profit Analysis in Budgeting.   Romano Shirts sells two highly sought-after shirts for businessmen. The trimline retails for $26.00 and has a cost of $15.00. The professional deluxe line retails for $35.00 with a cost of $20.00. During September, Romano expects to sell 1,200 trimline shirts and 800 professional deluxe shirts. Terry Broadman, marketing supervisor, has found data that suggest if Romano would decrease the price on the trimline by $6.00, unit volume would increase by 20 percent. On the other hand, increasing the price of the deluxe model to $40 would decrease the unit volume 10 percent. Romano is trying to decide whether to make the price changes in both shirts, only in one of the shirts, or in neither shirt. He has asked your advice.

REQUIRED:

a. Compute the gross profit for the September budgeted data.

b. Perform a gross profit analysis on the following three alternatives:

  1. Make the price changes in both shirts.
  2. Make the price change in the trimline but not in the deluxe.
  3. Make the price change in the deluxe but not in the trimline.

c. What is your recommendation for Romano?

19–6. Operating Expense Variances.   Patterson Enterprises produces airplane parts for Davis Aircraft Division of McDougal, Inc. The following information pertains to one of the product lines, MD–1011:

	19x6	19x7
Sales	$200,000	$180,000
Cost of goods sold	125,000	135,000
Gross profit	$ 75,000	$ 45,000
Operating expenses	40,000	32,000
Operating income	$ 35,000	$ 13,000

The average selling price per unit increased from $50.00 to $60.00 from 19x6 to 19x7.

REQUIRED:
Calculate any appropriate variances for the operating expenses.

19–7. Operating Expense Variances. Chee Company has selling and administrative expense behavior as follows:

Fixed	$10,000
Variable	5% of sales

Sales were budgeted at $100,000. Actual sales and selling and administrative expenses were as follows:

Sales	$110,000
Selling and administrative expenses	$ 19,250

REQUIRED:
Compute the following selling and administrative expense variances, indicating whether favorable or unfavorable.
a. Spending variance.
b. Volume variance.

PROBLEMS

19–8. Profit Analysis with the Contribution Approach. The Walker Hydrant Company produces and sells three types of hydrants. The following data were obtained from the company's records:

	19x8	19x9
Industrial Hydrant		
Sales	$500,000	$540,000
Variable costs	$300,000	$379,200
Quantity sold	10,000	12,000
Commercial Hydrant		
Sales	$750,000	$760,000
Variable costs	$498,000	$543,750
Quantity sold	12,000	12,500
Classic Hydrant		
Sales	$600,000	$625,000
Variable costs	$480,000	$500,000
Quantity sold	6,000	5,000

REQUIRED:
a. Compute the following variances based on contribution margin:
　1. Sales price variance.
　2. Cost variance.

   3. Sales mix variance
   4. Sales quantity variance.
b. Show that the sum of these variances accounts for the change in contribution margin from
   19x8 to 19x9.
c. Calculate the variances assuming that each hydrant is a single product. In what ways will
   the variances be different from those in *(a)* above?
d. Would you approach your variance analysis differently if 19x8 data were budgeted and
   19x9 data were actual? How would the variances differ?

19–9. Variances for Single and Multiple Products.   Daniel Manufacturing Company produces wedding accessories. Its main products are invitations, napkins, and albums. Perry, the
company's accountant, has been asked to perform a gross profit analysis on these products
for the fiscal year just ended. Although the information is not complete, Perry has come up
with the following:

(D. Washburn, adapted)

	Budget	*Actual*
Invitations		
Sales	$200,000	$225,000
Cost of sales	120,000	187,500
Sales price per unit (25)	?	?
Cost per unit (25)	12.00	12.50
Napkins		
Sales	$ 75,000	$ 72,000
Cost of sales	41,250	40,000
Sales price per unit (100)	10.00	9.00
Cost per unit (100)	?	?
Albums		
Sales	$ 90,000	$ 88,000
Cost of sales	66,000	55,000
Sales price per album	15.00	?
Cost per album	?	10.00

REQUIRED:
a. Determine, from the data available, the amounts represented by the question marks in the
   data above.
b. Assume that each product is independent. Calculate the following variances for each product:
   1. Sales price variance.
   2. Cost variance.
   3. Sales quantity variance.
   Summarize the variances to see if they equal the change in gross profit.
c. Assume that the products are sold in a mix. Calculate the following variances for the
   combination of the three products:
   1. Sales price variance.
   2. Cost variance.
   3. Sales mix variance.
   4. Sales quantity variance.
   Summarize the variances to see if they equal the change in gross profit.
d. Explain the difference in the variances between the single product case and the multiple
   product case.

19–10. Computation of Variances for Multiple Products.   Ellis Corporation produces four
commercial varieties of chemical cleaner. The salespeople have considerable flexibility in
setting selling prices. A standard variable costing system is used in production. The variable
operating expenses are recorded at actual. The operations for May resulted in the following:

	Galaxy	Cleanet	Stripper	Maxiclean
Sales (in units)	500	300	400	800
Sales (in dollars)	$5,000	$4,500	$4,800	$7,200
Variable production costs at standard	3,000	3,600	2,400	2,000
Variable operating expenses	1,000	600	800	1,200
Contribution margin	$1,000	$ 300	$1,600	$4,000

The June operations are complete, but the results do not appear to be as good as those for May. The data for June are below:

	Galaxy	Cleanet	Stripper	Maxiclean
Sales (in units)	700	300	500	600
Sales (in dollars)	$6,300	$4,800	$6,500	$6,000
Variable production costs at standard	4,200	3,600	3,000	1,500
Variable operating expenses	1,400	900	1,000	3,000
Contribution margin	$ 700	$ 300	$2,500	$1,500

REQUIRED:
a. Calculate the change in total contribution margin that took place from May to June.
b. Analyze the total contribution margin to find the following information:
   1. Sales price variance.
   2. Cost variance due to operating expenses.
   3. Sales mix variance.
   4. Sales quantity variance.
c. Summarize the variances and ascertain that the variances explain the change in contribution margin.

19–11. Profit Analysis with Standard Variable Costs.   Diamond Electronics produces two electronic organizers: Executive and CEO. The organizers are sold to chain stores and independent distributors. The Executive has a standard wholesale cost of $90; the CEO, $100. The budget for 19x1 called for production and sales of 50,000 units of the Executive and 40,000 units of the CEO. Actual sales for the year were 52,000 units of the Executive and 41,000 units of the CEO, with the following results:

	Executive	CEO
Sales	$4,600,000	$3,895,000
Variable cost of goods sold	$2,265,000	$1,695,000
Production variances	75,000	(14,000)
Variable cost of goods sold at standard	$2,340,000	$1,681,000
Contribution margin	$2,260,000	$2,214,000
Common fixed costs:		
Production costs		$2,050,000
Selling and administrative expenses		1,400,000
		$3,450,000

Standard production costs are variable costs only and were set as $45 for the Executive and $41 for the CEO. The fixed production costs are common to both products and were budgeted at $2,160,000 for the year. All selling and administrative expenses apply to both products.

They are fixed costs in total. The selling and administrative expenses were estimated at $1,550,000 for the year.

REQUIRED:

a. Prepare contribution income statements for 19x1 for budgeted and actual results.
b. Perform a contribution margin analysis by calculating all appropriate variances that relate to the contribution margin.
c. Calculate variances for fixed production costs and selling and administrative expenses.
d. Without calculating variances, explain how the variances in a gross profit analysis would differ from the variances you have calculated above.

19–12. Comprehensive Variance Report. The controller of West Virginia Distributors reported the following information to the company's president for January:

	Budget	*Actual*	*Variance*
Sales in units	12,500	10,000	(2,500)
Sales in dollars	$100,000	$120,000	$20,000
Cost of goods sold	50,000	62,000	12,000
Gross profit	$ 50,000	$ 58,000	$ 8,000
Expenses:			
Supplies	$ 2,000	$ 1,900	$ (100)
Salaries	12,000	13,700	1,700
Utilities	1,600	1,400	(200)
Depreciation	7,000	7,000	–0–
	$ 22,600	$ 24,000	$ 1,400
Net income	$ 27,400	$ 34,000	$ 6,600

REQUIRED:

Compute all gross profit variances and operating expense variances necessary to explain the difference between budgeted net income and actual net income.

19–13. Comprehensive Operating Expense Variance Analysis. The budget for the McMannis Company for the month of February included sales estimates of 100,000 units at a selling price of $15 and a cost per unit of $7.50. The company's flexible expense budget shows the following budget formulae for the operating expenses:

Administrative salaries: $50,000 + ($0.06 × units sold)
Depreciation: $62,000
Sales salaries: $20,000 + ($0.05 × units sold)
Supplies: $0.10 × units sold
Taxes: $10,000
Travel and entertainment: $1.05 × units sold
Utilities: $11,000 + ($0.20 × units sold)

At the end of February, the records show that McMannis Company had sold 115,000 units for a total of $1,610,000 and that the cost of goods sold was $862,500. Actual costs for the operating expenses were:

Administrative salaries	$ 57,100
Depreciation	62,000
Sales salaries	25,000
Supplies	12,300
Taxes	10,200
Travel and entertainment	115,750
Utilities	35,000
	$317,350

REQUIRED:

a. Prepare an income statement for February showing budgeted and actual amounts.
b. Calculate a spending variance for each of the individual operating expense items.
c. Calculate a volume variance for each of the individual operating expense items.
d. What conclusions can you reach about the type of cost behavior that appears in the spending variance? In the volume variance?

19–14. Contribution Margin Analysis. JK Enterprises sold 550,000 units during the first quarter ended March 31, 19x1. These sales represented a 10 percent increase over the number of units budgeted for the quarter. In spite of the sales increase, profits were below budget as shown in the condensed income statement presented below.

JK ENTERPRISES
Income Statement
For the First Quarter Ended March 31, 19x1
(thousands omitted)

	Budget	*Actual*
Sales	$2,500	$2,530
Variable expenses		
Cost of goods sold	$1,475	$1,540
Selling	400	440
Total variable expenses	$1,875	$1,980
Contribution margin	$ 625	$ 550
Fixed expenses		
Selling	$ 125	$ 150
Administration	275	300
Total fixed expenses	$ 400	$ 450
Income before taxes	$ 225	$ 100
Income taxes (40%)	90	40
Net income	$ 135	$ 60

The accounting department always prepares a brief analysis that explains the difference between budgeted net income and actual net income. This analysis, which has not yet been completed for the first quarter, is submitted to top management with the income statement.

(CMA, adapted)

REQUIRED:

Prepare an explanation of the $75,000 unfavorable variance between the first quarter budgeted and actual before-tax income for JK Enterprises by calculating a single amount for each of the following variations:

a. Sales price difference.
b. Variable unit cost difference.
c. Volume difference.
d. Fixed cost difference.

(CMA, adapted)

19–15. Contribution Margin Analysis. Allglow Company is a cosmetics manufacturer specializing in stage makeup. The company's best-selling product is SkinKlear, a protective cream used under the stage makeup to protect the skin from frequent use of makeup. SkinKlear is packaged in three sizes—8 ounces, 1 pound, and 3 pounds—and regularly sells for $21.00 per pound. The standard cost per pound of SkinKlear, based on Allglow's normal monthly production of 8,000 pounds, is as follows.

Cost Item	Quantity	Standard Cost	Total Cost	
Direct materials				
Cream base	9.0 oz.	$0.05/oz.	$0.45	
Moisturizer	6.5 oz.	0.10/oz.	0.65	
Fragrance	0.5 oz.	1.00/oz.	0.50	
				$ 1.60
Direct labor*				
Mixing	0.5 hr.	$4.00/hr.	$2.00	
Compounding	1.0 hr.	5.00/hr.	5.00	
				7.00
Variable overhead†	1.5 hr.	$2.10/hr.		3.15
Total standard cost per pound				$11.75

* Direct labor dollars include employee benefits.
† Applied on the basis of direct labor hours.

Based on these standard costs, Allglow prepares monthly budgets. Presented below are the budgeted performance and the actual performance for May 19x6 when the company produced and sold 9,000 pounds of SkinKlear.

Contribution Report for SkinKlear
For the Month of May 19x6

	Budget	Actual	Variance
Units	8,000	9,000	1,000 F
Revenue	$168,000	$180,000	$12,000 F
Direct material	$ 12,800	$ 16,200	$ 3,400 U
Direct labor	56,000	62,500	6,500 U
Variable overhead	25,200	30,900	5,700 U
Total variable costs	$ 94,000	$109,600	$15,600 U
Contribution margin	$ 74,000	$ 70,400	$ 3,600 U

Barbara Simmons, Allglow's president, was not pleased with these results; despite a sizeable increase in the sales of SkinKlear, there was a decrease in the product's contribution to the overall profitability of the firm. Simmons has asked Allglow's cost accountant, Brian Jackson, to prepare a report that identifies the reasons that the contribution margin for SkinKlear has decreased. Jackson has gathered the following information to help in the preparation of the report.

May 19x6 Usage Report for SkinKlear

Cost Item	Quantity	Actual Cost
Direct materials		
Cream base	84,000 oz.	$ 4,200
Moisturizer	60,000 oz.	7,200
Fragrance	4,800 oz.	4,800
Direct labor		
Mixing	4,500 hr.	18,000
Compounding—manual	5,300 hr.	26,500
Compounding—mechanized	2,700 hr.	13,500
Compounding—idle	900 hr.	4,500
Variable overhead		30,900
Total variable cost		$109,600

While doing his research, Jackson discovered that the Manufacturing Department had mechanized one of the manual operations in the compounding process on an experimental basis. The mechanized operation replaced manual operations that represented 40 percent of the compounding process.

The workers' inexperience with the mechanized operation caused increased usage of both the cream base and the moisturizer; however, Jackson believed these inefficiencies would be negligible if mechanization became a permanent part of the process and the workers' skills were improved. The idle time in compounding was traceable to the fact that fewer workers were required for the mechanized process. During this experimental period, the idle time was charged to direct labor rather than overhead. The excess workers could either be reassigned or laid off in the future. Jackson also was able to determine that all of the variable manufacturing overhead costs over standard could be traced directly to the mechanization process.

(CMA, adapted)

REQUIRED:

a. Prepare an explanation of the $3,600 unfavorable variance between the budgeted and actual contribution margin for SkinKlear during May 19x6 by calculating the following variances.
  1. Sales price variance.
  2. Material price variance.
  3. Material quantity variance.
  4. Labor efficiency variance.
  5. Variable overhead efficiency variance.
  6. Variable overhead spending variance.
  7. Contribution margin volume variance.

b. Allglow Company must decide whether or not the compounding operation in the SkinKlear manufacturing process that was mechanized on an experimental basis should continue to be mechanized. Calculate the variable cost savings that can be expected to arise in the future from the mechanization. Explain your answer.

EXTENDED APPLICATIONS

19–16. Developing a Computer Model for Variance Analysis. Jennifer Campbell is a product manager at Twin Sisters Hospital Supply. On this particular day, she was busy working on employee performance evaluations, which were due in Personnel two weeks ago. Carla, the Business Office manager, had given Jennifer some information on three medical products the hospital administrator was concerned about. Jennifer used the information given her by Carla to do a gross profit analysis. Jennifer spent several hours preparing the analysis and was due to present the results to the hospital administrator in one hour. Carla's presence at this moment was most unfortunate because she was the bearer of anything but good news. She advised Jennifer that the computer must have messed up because the original numbers given her for analysis were incorrect. She then handed Jennifer the corrected data, as follows:

Product	Total Sales	Total Cost	Budgeted Sales	Budgeted Cost	Actual S.P./Unit	Budgeted S.P./Unit
TEMP 03	$ 9,900	$ 8,100	$10,000	$ 9,000	$11.00	$10.00
LIST 43	22,500	18,000	15,000	15,000	7.50	7.50
SLO-D7	10,000	11,000	12,000	10,000	5.00	6.00

Carla wished she had a computer spread sheet model that could perform the gross profit analysis with the correct data. That would also help her in future analyses.

(P. Hutchison, adapted)

REQUIRED:

Prepare a computer spread sheet model that will perform a gross profit analysis using the above data as input. This model should automatically generate the following items once the input is entered:

a. Sales price variance.
b. Cost variance.
c. Sales mix variance.
d. Sales quantity variance.
e. Recapitulation of gross profit variances.
f. Total actual and budgeted gross profit in dollars and percentages.

19–17. Profit Analysis of an Annual Corporate Report.   International Networks, Inc., is a holding company with a number of wholly owned domestic and foreign subsidiaries. The company represents an international distribution network for computers and computer-related products. It has agreements with a number of computer, peripheral, and software manufacturers to supply the company's outlets. The consolidated statements of operations for fiscal 19x2 and 19x1 appearing in the 19x2 annual report are as follows:

	Year Ended September 30,	
	19x2	*19x1*
	(000 omitted)	
Net sales	$471,106	$403,911
Other income	7,249	4,592
	$478,355	$408,503
Costs and expenses:		
Cost of products sold	$268,174	$225,721
Selling, general and administrative expenses	213,536	174,057
Depreciation and amortization	7,758	6,444
Foreign currency transaction (gains) losses	(5,119)	(3,271)
Interest expense	6,891	7,828
	$491,240	$410,779
Loss before income taxes	$ (12,885)	$ (2,276)
Provision (benefit) for income taxes	(282)	2,330
Net loss	$(12,603)	$ (4,606)

A discussion of the consolidated operations gives selected details of happenings over the two years. They are summarized below.

Net sales. The consolidated net sales of International Network, Inc., increased by $67,195,000 to $471,106,000 from the prior year. The major factor in sales increases in fiscal 19x2 was an increase in volume in existing stores. However, sales were influenced by the addition of 92 company-owned retail sales outlets. A total of 75 company-owned stores was closed during this fiscal year, for a net increase of 17 stores. Sales were also enhanced by the introduction of new products.

Other income. Other income includes various items related to normal business operations. Included in this category are gains or losses on disposition of fixed assets, computer training income, repair income, contract service income, and various smaller items. Repair income and contract service income were the largest components of the total, and both categories increased in fiscal 19x2 due to expansion of these programs and a larger store base.

Gross profit and cost of products sold. Gross profit as a percentage of sales was 43.1 in fiscal 19x2 and 44.1 in fiscal 19x1. The change in gross profit percentage for fiscal year 19x2 was primarily due to the reduction in carrying value of slow-moving inventory items, particularly computer products, and the third quarter reduction in gross profit as a result of the closure of 31 company-owned retail outlets in Germany and the related discounted selling price of this German inventory.

In fiscal year 19x1, gross profit as a percentage of sales was 44.1, primarily due to the increased cost of merchandise in Canada and Australia, to general market conditions, and to local competition in Europe. Additionally, during the fourth quarter of fiscal 19x1, the company recorded adjustments that in the aggregate approximated $2.5 million. These adjustments principally consisted of inventory write-downs and other adjustments to inventory carrying costs resulting from management's revisions in the net realizable value of certain inventory categories.

Selling, general, and administrative expenses. Selling, general, and administrative expenses increased $39,479,000 during fiscal 19x2. Following are the main components that compose selling, general, and administrative expenses.

Payroll expense is the largest component of selling, general, and administrative expenses. The amounts totaled $89,754,000 in fiscal 19x2 and $72,542,000 in fiscal 19x1. One factor contributing to the increase in payroll expense this year is the third-quarter severance pay charge of approximately $1 million related to the closure of all company-owned retail sales outlets in Germany and the termination of approximately 40 related support personnel in Belgium. Another factor contributing to the increase was the accrual, in the fourth quarter, of vacation pay that resulted in a charge of approximately $2,700,000. New retail store additions in the United Kingdom and France, which generally carry a higher than average payroll as a percentage of sales until the stores mature, also contributed to the increase. Additionally, a provision of approximately $500,000 has been made for the severance pay associated with a small joint venture in France, which the company has decided to close.

Advertising expenditures include costs for advertising in newspapers and magazines, on television and radio, and in other media. The preparation, printing, and distribution of the various country catalogs and other printed material are also a component of advertising expense. Advertising costs totaled $35,705,000 in fiscal 19x2 compared with $33,067,000 in 19x1. These amounts do not include salaries and various other overhead expenses incurred by the company's advertising departments located in most of the countries in which the company operates. The increase in advertising expenditures in 19x2 was mainly due to the higher advertising budget allowed by a greater number of retail locations. An increased amount of television advertising in Canada, which was very effective, also contributed to the increase. Advertising expenditures as a percentage of sales have declined each of the last three years due to economies of scale related to adding new store outlets in markets already served by the company's advertising.

Rent expense totaled $29,709,000 in fiscal 19x2 and $22,323,000 in 19x1. Several factors have contributed to this increase. During 19x2, the company closed certain computer outlets in the United Kingdom, Belgium, and Holland. In addition, all company-owned outlets in West Germany were closed in March 19x2. The future rent payments, net of estimated future sublease income, at time of closure, aggregating approximately $3,850,000, have been included in 19x2 rent expense. Also, the company is expanding its number of outlets, particularly in the United Kingdom and France. These new stores initially have a higher rent as a percentage of sales than do fully mature stores of one year or more.

The company leases rather than owns most of its facilities. Retail space is generally leased because store locations are in major shopping malls, shopping centers, and other retail spaces owned by other companies or individuals. Five warehouses are located in Canada, the United Kingdom, Belgium, France, and Australia.

Taxes (other than income taxes) were $16,989,000 in 19x2 compared to $13,056,000 in 19x1. The majority of these are payroll and property taxes. These amounts increased due to payroll cost increases and additional store locations.

Other selling, general, and administrative expenses were $41,379,000 in fiscal 19x2 and $33,069,000 in 19x1. These other expenses include such items as employee benefit plans, bad debts, postage, utilities, telephone and telex expenses, office supplies and printing, insurance, and other items.

REQUIRED:
a. An outsider does not have all of the data available to perform a gross profit analysis that an insider does. Describe how you would approach a gross profit analysis and an expanded profit anlysis for International Network, Inc.
b. Using your approach, perform an analysis generating appropriate variances. Explain your variances in terms of the information contained in the discussion of the consolidated operations.

Reports for Variance Investigation

■

MISLED BY ACCOUNTING REPORTS

Chris Frescoln is the new plant manager for the Levelland plant of Conington Electronics, Inc. The Levelland plant, which produces parts and subassemblies for medical equipment, employs 542 people in 124 production processes that are organized into 16 departments. The plant began operations in 1976. During recent years, production costs have mounted while quality has dropped to mediocre.

During his first tour of the plant, Mr. Frescoln observed a number of things. Assembly areas were filled with thousands of parts awaiting assembly and hundreds of partially completed products; thousands of completed assemblies were stacked in aisles, under stairwells, and in any other available space. Everyone seemed busy moving materials and products around. Parts fabrication had large storage areas for raw materials and wide aisles for the movement of completed components. Everyone seemed busy. The quality control department with 22 employees tested every product. This department was so busy that products often waited a week for testing. The backlog required a well-organized holding area next to the inspection area. The warehouse was filled with finished subassemblies and assemblies ready for shipment. Overall, the plant had ample inventory, employees were working hard, and team spirit was high. All available space was used, and no one seemed to waste time.

On returning to his office, Mr. Frescoln began a review of various production reports. The weekly materials reports showed price and usage variances for each of the 630 raw materials. The weekly labor reports gave labor efficiency variances for all labor categories in 124 production processes. In addition, labor rate variances were reported by department. Mr. Frescoln noticed that six of the production departments had unfavorable labor efficiency variances greater than $100 for the past week. A monthly report on overhead showed variances by department. He noticed a $3,000 favorable indirect labor variance in the maintenance shop on one of these reports. He found a total of 14,208 variances to consider for a month's production.

Mr. Frescoln wanted more information about overhead because 57 percent of total cost was production overhead. However, because the data on materials and labor were readily available, he decided to start working on material and labor usage in assembly departments. Production overhead would come later.

Chris Frescoln was about to be misled by the accounting reports. The information indicated several conditions that resulted in high overhead costs: (1) excessive inventories, (2) excessive space allocated to current production, (3) long lag times between production steps, and (4) excessive movement of products around the plant. Although Mr. Frescoln should have been concerned with overhead because of its significance to total cost, he allowed the production report to direct him to material and labor usage variances. Although materials and direct labor were important in general, the variances described were not significant. What misled him?

LEARNING OBJECTIVES

After completing this chapter, you should be able to:

1. List and describe the limitations managers have in identifying variances for investigation.
2. Discuss the strengths and weakness of the four variance presentation approaches that indicate a need for investigation:
   a. Physical.
   b. Images of physical variances.
   c. Graphs (of numerical variances).
   d. Columnar reports (of numerical variances).
3. Compare the approaches used by different levels of management to identify variances that should be investigated.

Managers and supervisors and, in some cases, production workers investigate variances. Accountants design and implement variance reporting systems that help the line people identify variances that need investigating. In this chapter, we will discuss ways to design reporting systems that support variance investigation. We will start with the limitations of managers in investigating variances.

LIMITATIONS OF MANAGERS IN VARIANCE INVESTIGATION

The ability of managers to perceive data and numerical relationships is limited. Because they focus primarily on what is reported formally and because they have patterned responses to variances, managers have difficulty with reports containing many numbers. This section discusses these limitations and suggests potential remedies in the reporting systems.

Limits on the Number of Variances Perceived	Most people can focus on only a few items of data (5 to 9) at any one time. For example, at a ball game or a social function, try to observe more than 10 people at one time. In large groups, observers tend to lose the significance of the individual and establish relationships by size or location, and observe people in groups of perhaps five to nine. The same thing happens with numbers. If managers receive reports with 50 variances (or 20-page reports with 1,000 variances), they cannot distinguish individual items. Instead, they look for patterns and relationships in the numbers. Studies indicate that people can see patterns in any list of numbers, even purely random ones. Therefore, the patterns managers identify in long lists of variances may not be real.

Accountants should avoid designing reporting systems that report long lists of numbers. Additionally, the report formats should build in the patterns and relationships for the managers. For example, variances can be reported from large to small and by time. Large variances can be highlighted in some way to distinguish important from insignificant items. An image or graph of key variances across time also helps managers perceive patterns with less effort.

Focus on Formal Reports	Managers tend to focus on what is formally reported rather than to search for detailed information on their own. This is especially true for people new in a position and who have not been able to test the validity of the formal reports. Thus, if the accounting system generates weekly labor variance reports, managers and supervisors will focus on these reports whether they should or not. Consequently, these reports substantially influence the direction and nature of any investigative action.

In the changing manufacturing environment that focuses on automation and integration of production processes, direct labor cost loses its significance because it is often less than 10 percent of total cost. However, direct labor variances are easy to calculate and report. Production overhead cost is much more important in these innovative production changes, but variances are difficult to track daily or weekly. Variances in production overhead cost are generally reported monthly. Unfortunately, the daily and weekly reports of labor efficiency variances convey an importance to managers that causes them to act to eliminate the reported variances. Therefore, managers concentrate on the insignificant and take actions that can, in the long run, increase production costs. Because the system does not focus on overhead variances, managers can easily get priorities mixed up. Consequently, care must be taken as to which variances are reported and the frequency with which they are reported.

Many formal accounting reports of variances contain only quantitative data such as units and cost measures. Managers are likely to investigate the quantitative factors and ignore important qualitative issues (for example, employee morale, product design, or customer satisfaction with services performed). Unit and cost variances are often short run in nature, and qualitative measures more often relate to long-run performance. Therefore, qualitative issues should be addressed in formal reports in order to bring balance to managers' investigations and subsequent decisions.

Perception Patterns of Managers	People tend to react to data with patterned perceptions and memory; different people react differently. Consequently, with the receipt of new data, they may react too much or too little, or may perceive cause and effect relationships incorrectly.

Some managers tend to recall only the most recent events (**recency**) and have difficulty placing variances in a longer-run context. For example, if sales have been down for the past week or costs are up, managers conclude that the business is in a downturn. These managers tend to overreact to insignificant and even random events. They are always trying to fix things that are not broken.

Other managers recall only the long-run performance (**anchored**) and discount current variances as only passing events. They change very slowly to new conditions. They tend to let things "ride" as they are until the problem is very large or obvious to others.

Still other managers perceive patterns in data and act without investigation or perform only superficial investigations. They jump to conclusions. These managers view patterns of variances as **representative** of certain problems. For example, one manager might conclude that all labor variances result from scheduling problems. With appropriate investigation, the manager might find that the problems relate to employee morale and the quality of supervision. Such people tend to fix the wrong problems.

Managers who follow recency or anchored patterns will be helped if reports show variances over a longer time period than a day or a week and show comparative variances over time. Graphic presentations can also be helpful for this presentation. Managers who follow representative patterns or stereotype situations are not helped with reports that present a pattern of variances over time. Such reports only reinforce their tendency to stereotype because variance reports reflect results rather than causes. Written comments and explanations of variances might help this type of manager go beyond stereotypes. Reports that include qualitative measures may help this type of manager see the effects on long-run performance from making changes. Be warned that managers with a strong representativeness perception pattern are only moderately affected by changes to the reporting system.

PRESENTATION OF VARIANCES FOR INVESTIGATION

There are four basic formats for presenting variances for managers: (1) physical, (2) images of a physical variance, (3) numeric graphs, and (4) columnar reports of numeric variances. Each of these approaches is discussed in this section.

Physical Items to Represent Variances

A **physical variance** is represented by physical objects that are set aside, marked, or tagged in some way to indicate that they are unexpected. For example, products rejected due to poor quality during production can be stacked within a painted red square on the floor. If the workers and managers want to know how many units have been rejected this shift, they just look in the red square area. Nothing has to be written down; no one has to wait for a computer report. When there is a problem, everyone can see it. If a manager chooses to find the source of the problem, he can do it right away.

As another example, low or high utilization is an important variance for service companies. For a hospital, the utilization can be represented by the number of beds with patients. The observable empty beds represent the variance in utilization. Further, each empty bed can be represented by an empty patient record slot on the door to the room or at the nurse's station. Thus, if floor supervisors want to check the number of empty beds on their floor, they scan the doors down their hallway or record slots at the nurse's station. Similarly, extra or overflow patients can be set up in one side of the recovery area, which is normally in use only during the late morning after surgery. Thus, a positive variance will show up as occupied beds in the recovery area. This variance is observable without the need for a computer report of utilization.

Another example can be found in a grocery store. When customers are frustrated with the selection, display, or prices in a grocery store, they often walk out leaving partially filled grocery carts in aisles. The number of full carts near checkout counters can also indicate the frustration customers have in waiting for the cashier. Each cart left partially full represents a failure in expected performance. Finding one unattended cart is of some concern, but finding 15 or 20 abandoned carts during the day is a variance that indicates real problems. Likewise, the variance for spoilage in a grocery store can be seen as a pile of spoiled and dated items in the "spoiled" bin.

Physical variances are effective for managing a process "here and now." These variances are simple and require little or no documentation; often the variance can be seen as it happens. Because of its simplicity, the physical variance approach results in little or no increased cost. It is preferred whenever feasible.

On the other hand, physical variances are not effective in representing past periods because the items involved take up space or they change with time. It makes no sense to keep past spoiled production in a factory, filled shopping carts or spoiled food in grocery stores, or empty chart boxes in a hospital. Physical variances, in themselves, do not help the manager consider how the current situation fits into the patterns of the past and where the process is going. Because senior managers must adopt a longer-run perspective, the physical variance approach is more appropriate for lower-level supervisors.

Images of Physical Items to Represent Variances

Photographs and videotapes can record the physical variance for later comparison. As long as the date and place are noted, the image can provide a reasonable record of unexpected performance. Photographs are particularly useful for variances that are very large (such as excess corn dumped in a parking lot in Des Moines, Iowa) or move (like a crowd hoping for tickets to a sold out Super Bowl or a herd of yearling steers waiting for a train in Boise, Idaho). The pictures can be saved and compared over time to help managers compare current with past variances. For example, a shop supervisor can quickly review the trends in spoilage for the past month by scanning small photographs pinned to a calendar.

The basic strength of images is that they are easy to understand and can be compared over time. The approach does not require computer equipment, systems analysts, or clerks. Although not all important characteristics can be captured in a photograph or videotape, many types of physical variance can be documented by this method. If the use of physical image to represent a variance is appropriate, pictures can communicate the variances quickly and are easy to compare. Videotapes and pictures are quick to produce, are not error prone, and are inexpensive relative to graphic or columnar formats. The picture (or tape) can be duplicated and sent over distances with little error and misunderstanding. Finally, a picture or videotape can be scanned for input to computer processing should that additional step be needed. There is some cost associated with the image approach.

The image approach cannot be used for conglomerate or overall variances, such as variances in prices, revenues, administrative expenses, or short-term borrowing. Further, images of physical objects do not lend themselves to abstract characteristics such as income, morale of the work force, or sales to new customers.

Graphics Formats to Represent Numerical Variances

A graph or chart is almost as good as a picture in communicating variances to managers. A graph can represent changes across time or across departments better than the physical item or image methods. The graph represents a measure or characteristic by size or height of lines. For example, a graph can represent weekly total sales for a merchandiser for the past year. Variances can be represented as amounts above or below a specified line.

Graphs can provide valuable supplemental information in describing quantities and qualities across time or products. The preparation of graphs does, however, result in a time lag of several hours to a month or more. In addition, graphic methods often require additional equipment, space, and cost.

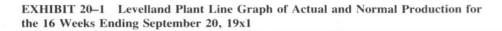

EXHIBIT 20–1   Levelland Plant Line Graph of Actual and Normal Production for the 16 Weeks Ending September 20, 19x1

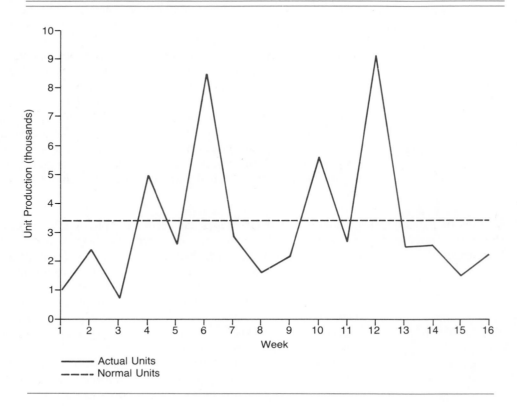

Graphs are excellent for representing the relationships among abstractions such as expenses, borrowings, or cash flows, which cannot be represented by physical items. If the manager can understand the variance being represented, the graph will help him or her understand changes over time and the relationships among variances. For example, Exhibit 20–1 presents a line graph of units produced compared with normal volume for the past 16 weeks. This graph should help a plant manager understand variation and trends in plant output. The graph helps the plant manager to see that production has been below normal for the past four weeks. Because very low and very high volumes are unusual, the manager might decide to investigate why output was so high during weeks 6 and 12 followed by several weeks of below-normal volume.

If the manager does not understand the variance, the graph will not be effective. For example, Exhibit 20–2 presents the same circumstances as Exhibit 20–1, but presents the information in terms of fixed overhead volume variances.[1] Although an accountant knows the meaning of an overhead volume variance, it is a relatively difficult concept for many plant managers to understand. The plant manager is more

---

[1] As presented in Chapter 13, the overhead volume variance is equal to: Budgeted Fixed Overhead − (Fixed overhead rate × units produced). The overhead volume variance has an inverse relationship to units produced.

EXHIBIT 20–2   Levelland Plant Line Graph of Overhead Volume Variances for the 16 Weeks Ending September 20, 19x1

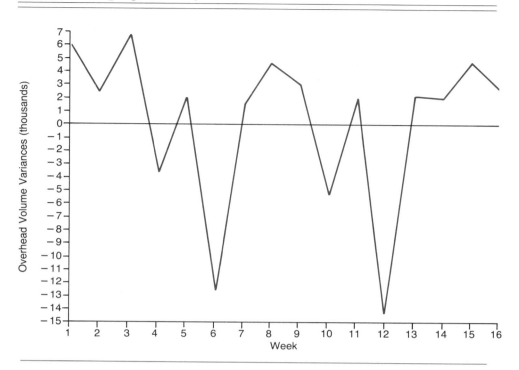

likely to accept data in a concrete form such as units of product, as shown in Exhibit 20–1, than in an abstract form as the overhead volume variance in Exhibit 20–2.

Assume that a manager at the Levelland plant is trying to cut overhead costs by reducing the product flow time of one of its products, a specialized circuit board. The manager would like to ship on the day that an order is received but keep minimal finished goods inventories. **Product flow time** is the clock time it takes for an average unit to go from the beginning of the production process to completion and shipment. Product flow time is equal to productive time plus wasted time (moving, waiting, and setting up). The Levelland plant has seven departments that work on the specialized circuit board starting with a Solution Department and ending with a Packing and Shipping Department. Assume that the accountant has gathered the data in Exhibit 20–3 on a recent week's product flow time and wishes to prepare a meaningful graph for the plant manager.

The majority (64 percent) of the time that the product is in the plant is wasted time. The plant manager wants a weekly report that can be quickly and easily understood. Using a spread sheet program, the accountant generates two prospective report formats as presented in Exhibits 20–4 and 20–5. The plant manager likes both formats. The bar chart in Exhibit 20–4 provides a visual comparison of wasted time with productive time among departments. The pie chart in Exhibit 20–5 also clearly shows that the Fabrication, Subassembly, and Finishing departments are causing the majority of the time required for the product flow. The manager will ultimately select one or the other format as his preference. In addition, the numbers in Exhibit 20–3

EXHIBIT 20–3   Levelland Plant Specialized Circuit Board No. 4039 Average Product Flow Time **(in minutes)**

Production Department	Time in Department	Productive Time	Move, Wait, Setup Time	Wasted Time
Solution	162	107	55	34%
Extrusion	20	5	15	75%
Fabrication	235	61	174	74%
Subassembly	205	43	162	79%
Assembly	58	35	23	40%
Finishing	161	60	101	63%
Packing and shipping	57	15	42	74%
Total minutes in plant	898	326	572	64%
Hours in plant	14.97	5.43	9.53	64%

EXHIBIT 20–4   Levelland Plant Bar Chart of Productive and Wasted Flow Time for the Week Ending September 20, 19x1

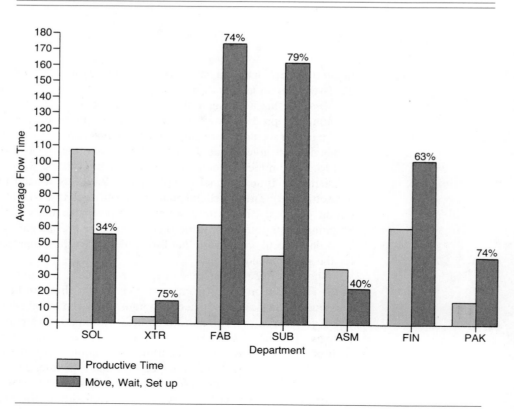

EXHIBIT 20–5   Levelland Plant Pie Chart of Wasted Flow Time by Department for the Week Ending September 20, 19x1

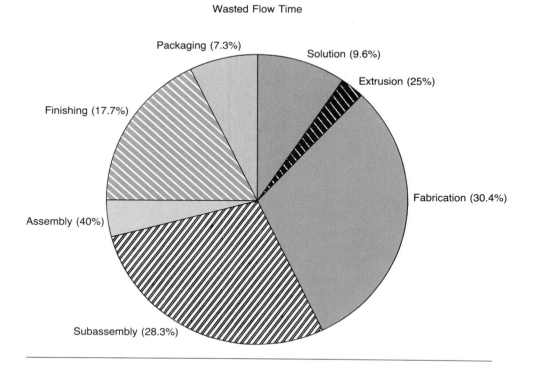

Wasted Flow Time

Packaging (7.3%)

Solution (9.6%)

Extrusion (25%)

Finishing (17.7%)

Fabrication (30.4%)

Assembly (40%)

Subassembly (28.3%)

are provided as a supporting schedule just in case something attracts the manager's interest and he wants more details.

Line graphs are useful for presenting variances that span many time periods; bar charts are useful for reporting several variances across segments; and pie charts are useful for presenting a single type of variance across segments.

Columnar Formats to Represent Numerical Variances

A **columnar report** is a standard report with columns and rows. It is much easier for accounting systems to produce than a graph. The columnar format can be used for the presentation of all numerical variances. Hundreds or even thousands of variances can be presented in one report. Once programmed, the format requires little attention by the accounting or computer staff. In short, creating this variance report form bothers the staff very little.

As discussed earlier, a list of many numbers is relatively difficult for managers to perceive. Data accumulation is also expensive. Both measurement and entry require people and time, and people can make errors either in measurement or in data entry, or in both. As a rule, computer facilities are required for data manipulation. Once the system is set up, it is relatively difficult and very slow to change. Because of the nature of data processing for columnar printouts, variances for relatively few periods (perhaps only two or three) are easily presented. Written comments on the variances represented are generally not included with a columnar report because comments are more complex to process than numbers and are inconvenient to gather and edit.

However, few managers are really aided by just a listing of so many numbers. If such reports are to be useful, they must be streamlined and simple.

The general approach is to present a format with time going across the page from current to old, as in the following data:

	19x8 January	19x7 December	19x7 November	19x7 October
Units produced	1,490	1,610	1,260	1,120

The manager must approximate differences by subtracting from right to left, which is difficult to do. However, most managers will find it somewhat easier to perceive trends in the same data using the following form:

	Units Produced
October 19x7	1,120
November 19x7	1,260
December 19x7	1,610
January 19x8	1,490

Although this may seem to be a minor change in format, it is very important in improving the clarity of the information presented.

In summary, we have presented four formats for displaying variances to managers for investigation. In order of preference for vividness and communication, the formats are use of physical items to indicate variances, use of images of physical items representing variances, use of graphs, and use of columns of numbers. The images of physical variances and graphing methods are better at helping managers understand a variance across many days, weeks, or months. We have noted some strengths and limitations of each format.

LEVELS OF MANAGEMENT AND VARIANCE INVESTIGATION

We now focus on variance investigation by the various levels of management: senior managers, middle managers, supervisors, and workers.

Variance Investigation of Senior Managers

Senior managers are interested in the big picture and how the current performance fits into the company's past, present, and future. Their focus tends to be on overall summaries of data from both external and internal sources. For financial information, they concentrate on income statements and balance sheets. In their evaluations and investigating decisions, they are concerned about both short-term and long-term performance.

An indicator of short-term performance, for example, is how well the actual income statement compares with the planned income statement. Senior managers ask questions about current operations: Are sales better (or worse) than planned? How do production costs and output compare with the plan? What are the recent trends? Does anything need to be adjusted in plans or controls, or are operations meeting expectations? At this level, variances are broad indicators of performance. The basic question is whether the broad strategies adopted in the past are working now or should be changed.

Senior managers are also interested in the long-term performance of the company. For example, market share, new products, product promotions, personnel recruiting and retention, employee absenteeism, and new customer accounts are indicators of long-term performance. Each industry has certain factors, called **critical success factors,** that are critical to its survival. These are activities that the company must do well or characteristics it must have in order to survive. An airline, for instance, must have a high percentage of passengers filling the available seats on each flight, must follow departure and arrival schedules, must have an excellent safety record, must have a good record of aircraft maintenance, and must develop well-trained personnel and new routes. Senior airline managers have goals and objectives that relate to each of these areas. A consumer products company differentiates its products through advertising and promotion, maintains specific market shares, has strong relationships with retailers, researches and develops new products, delivers orders quickly to retailers, maintains an even quality of product, and keeps production costs low.

Variance investigation for senior management occurs as the year unfolds. Its form of investigation is often verbal in nature—asking managers to explain variations in weekly sales numbers, production cost figures, or employee retention. Its investigations focus on people, segments, processes, products, or services. A staff study with official reports and recommended courses of action is occasionally requested. Managers, accountants, engineers, or other staff may be called upon to assist in these special analyses. Senior management's emphasis shifts fluidly as the situation demands. For example, it might want to investigate weekly (or cumulative) sales by product line for the current year compared with the last year. Such investigations are performed quickly because the president or the board is demanding an explanation for the variance.

Because senior managers should receive explanations and take needed action during the year, the final results should hold no surprises. All corrective actions necessary would have been taken.

In large organizations, senior managers are divided into two levels: corporate and group or divisional. For example, subsidiaries and divisions are grouped by product or geographic area with a vice president in charge of each group. The group vice president performs the senior management functions for that group and reports to someone at the corporate level. Because distance may separate corporate managers from group or divisional managers, corporate managers may find some surprises when final reports are submitted.

Variance Investigation by Mid-Level Managers

Mid-level managers include anyone below the senior management level to whom lower-level supervisors report. For example, mid-level managers may include managers of individual divisions or segments, plants and chain stores.

Division and segment managers are similar to senior managers in their approach to investigating variances. Their focus is narrower and they do not emphasize the broad strategies. These managers are primarily concerned about profitability and its interaction with sales, production, and expenses. Consequently, division managers review and investigate variances related to the monthly income statement. In addition, they often have 5 to 10 indexes of activity that they follow closely. For example, they may closely follow units sold, new customer accounts, collection rates, major contracts signed, or similar measures. They investigate and act as variances in these indexes occur.

A plant manager has narrower concerns than a division manager. The plant manager is concerned with maintaining low cost and production of the right products with the right quality. This requires constant monitoring of materials quality and variety, output quality, and time to complete customer orders. The plant manager must maintain adequate but minimum inventories. Excesses here are a major cause of overhead cost increases. Thus, the plant manager's investigations often include variations in total quantity produced, total work force in plant, product rejection or spoilage rates, customer orders delivered late, and increases in materials or work in process inventories. Although plant managers develop their own variances and investigation methods, they limit the variance amounts and number of indexes in order to reduce perception problems.

Accountants are often involved with helping mid-level managers set up and maintain systems that aid in monitoring and investigating variances. These systems range from the informal to the complex. The informal may be as simple as calendars or wall charts; the complex involve large computer systems with extensive data bases. Timeliness, understandability, and ease in changing the approach to meet the changing situation are most important. However, it is important that the manager be able to compare the data with the past in order to place them in perspective. For example, weekly reports that present line graphs are useful for presenting the data to a plant manager.

Part a of Exhibit 20–6 presents line graphs that relate units shipped with production and inventory levels. There is a large variability in the units shipped, and production closely follows units shipped. The desired level of unit sales is indicated by the straight line at about 3,400 units per week. The general pattern of units produced and shipped indicates that they follow each other very closely, which is exactly what the plant manager wants. Of course, the plant manager would be concerned by the drop in shipments during the past four weeks. The bottom line is an index of total inventories that the plant manager wants to keep as low as possible.

Part b of Exhibit 20–6 contains three qualitative measures that the plant manager believes are important: absenteeism, spoilage rates, and late deliveries. The top line is absenteeism, which is a general measure of employee morale—how happy employees are with working conditions. The absenteeism rate has been going up during the past 16 weeks, which indicates that something is out of line and the problem is growing. The plant manager had thought absenteeism related to summer vacations, but the summer vacations are over and employees should now be back at work. Instead, they are calling in sick or taking personal leaves. The plant manager must investigate and locate the problem.

Late deliveries lead to lost sales, so the plant manager follows them very closely. He has been successful in getting the late delivery rate down from about 12 percent to about 2 percent during the past 18 months, with the past two weeks being less than 1 percent. He is currently working with an industrial engineer to rearrange the production process so that there will be no late deliveries.

The reject or spoilage rate has a large effect on the level of overhead costs. The plant manager has been successful in lowering the reject rate from about 5.5 percent to about 1 percent during the past 18 months. He has instituted a zero defect, total quality control program by involving the workers in production planning and product improvement. However, recent spoilage rates have started to go up again. He will investigate this if the problem continues in future weeks.

Exhibit 20–7 presents an example of financial information that might be useful to a plant manager. Part a of the exhibit indicates that total weekly revenues, cost of goods sold, and plant profits have been quite erratic. Most of the plant's profits for the year to date have been the result of sales made in just four of the weeks: 4, 6, 10, and 12. Little plant profit has been made during the past four weeks. There is a problem building here somewhere that needs investigation.

Part b of Exhibit 20–7 presents the average price, cost per unit, and unit profit margin. The top line is selling price, which is determined by the corporate staff on the basis of market prices. The plant manager can see that this has been slipping slightly during the past 16 weeks. The manager can do nothing about prices, except

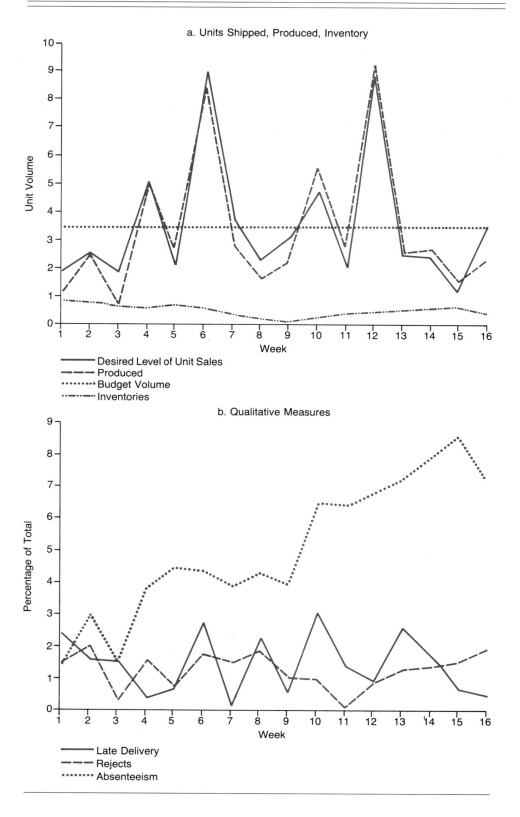

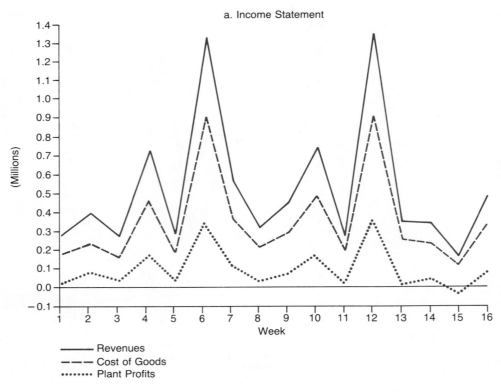

a. Income Statement

— Revenues
--- Cost of Goods
..... Plant Profits

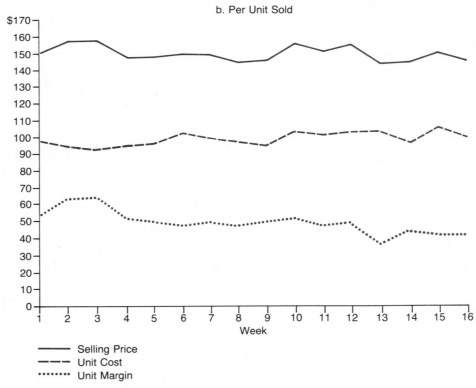

b. Per Unit Sold

— Selling Price
--- Unit Cost
..... Unit Margin

EXHIBIT 20–7   *(concluded)*

c. Summarized Financial Performance

This Week

	Actual	Planned*	Variance
Revenues	$ 488.2	$ 513.9	($25.7)
Cost of goods	340.7	342.6	(1.9)
Gross margin	$ 147.5	$ 171.3	($23.8)
General expenses	70.1	75.0	(4.9)
Operating income	$ 77.4	$ 96.3	($18.9)

Year-to-Date

	Actual	Planned	Variance
Revenues	$8,396.4	$8,222.4	$174.0
Cost of goods	5,601.8	5,481.6	120.2
Gross margin	$2,794.6	$2,740.8	$ 53.8
General expenses	1,217.2	1,200.0	17.2
Operating income	$1,577.4	$1,540.8	$ 36.6

* Planned amounts in this column are from the master budget. In detailed cost schedules used for the performance evaluation and controlling detailed expenses, the planned cost amounts are based on a flexible budget for each segment as discussed in Chapter 17.

complain at the next meeting of plant managers. The middle line is the cost per unit produced. The plant manager can see that this has been going up slightly for the past 16 weeks. He had gotten the cost per unit down from about $120 to about $90 by redesigning the product and production process and working with employees directly. Now it is creeping back up over $100. He will definitely investigate this further.

The bottom line of part b is the unit profit margin. This has slipped from about $60 per unit to under $50. The drop is due to the decrease in price and increase in costs. This indicates that a problem is worsening.

Part c of Exhibit 20–7 contains some summarized financial data. The profits for the current week are $18,900 below planned performance, but the year-to-date financial performance compares favorably. Thus, the plant and its manager are performing at or exceeding the budget performance required. However, most of the profits have come from just four weeks of sales. With sagging profit margins and employee morale, the manager should investigate and act immediately.

Variance Investigation by Supervisors

Supervisors do very specific jobs. For example, consider the following supervisor positions:

- A floor supervisor in the pediatric ward of a hospital.
- A district sales manager for an agricultural chemical company.
- A night shift foreman in a frozen foods warehouse.
- The supervisor of security for a shopping center.

The job of the supervisor is to see that the department works during its shift. Employees must show up and work. The supervisor will do whatever is necessary to get the work done.

Variances must be investigated and responded to immediately in order to keep the work going out. If there is a problem with production, supervisors must know about and fix the problem here and now, *not* later. Thus, these managers investigate daily or hourly variances. Only the here and now is important. Last month is old, and last year is ancient.

Accounting systems often report variances to supervisors that relate to events for last month or last quarter. These variances are almost irrelevant to current operations and in some cases may be harmful. Although some supervisors become confused and try to investigate variances from six weeks or three months ago, more experienced supervisors ignore these reports. They concentrate on correcting today's problems.

Useful variance reports for supervisors must be daily, hourly, or even continuous. Physical presentation of variances should be used when possible because of the immediate perception of problems. Images of physical variances for this week may be useful for placing the variances in context. Graphs and charts are often helpful provided the data relate to the here and now. Thus, product quality variances, production time variances, worker attendance, job orders, and line stop data need to be for today or this week, not last month or the last three months. Timeliness is absolutely critical.

Variance Investigation by Workers

In current production settings, workers are taking a more active role in responding to problems that arise. Each worker is expected to think and continuously improve the product and the production process. The job of the shift supervisor and the worker may have little distinction in this situation. For example, if a worker fails to show up or becomes ill, the supervisor, along with other workers, must fill in. Both supervisor and laborers work on the line; the supervisor is there to train and encourage.

Physical, image, and graphic variance presentations should be used with workers. Workers should not be expected to deal with complex abstract concepts such as profit, liabilities, and expenses. Instead, variances must relate directly to the product or service they are producing or providing during the current shift or week. Measures of the product or service quality and quantity are very important.

As an example of worker investigation, consider fabrication workers who shape parts for later assembly. Fabrication workers might find feedback of variances useful provided the data relate to their own (or their unit's) production, as reported directly to them. More specifically, an operator fabricating parts with a large metal press would find it useful to know immediately that pressed parts are not meeting quality standards. Perhaps the press needs minor adjustments or maintenance that can solve the problem. For this worker, a useful device would compare the pressed parts with "ideal" parts and give an indication of any variance. For example, an image on a computer screen could indicate symbols for too thick, too thin, wrong shape, or cracks forming along edges. The press operator should then investigate and take action to correct the problem. Quite obviously, quality variances that are reported the next day do not help the worker right now.

Many production machines come equipped with gauges, graphic devices, and computer input devices that aid the workers in their jobs. For example, in chemical processing, most contemporary equipment continuously monitors heat, acid levels, and pressure. The data are input into a computer and it signals the workers when a variance occurs with a specific machine or process.

SUMMARY

Because managers are limited in the quantity of items they can perceive, they often limit themselves to formal reports and perceive data in patterns. Managers can perceive and compare only 5 to 9 numbers at one time. Reporting numerous variances on a page without perception aids such as sorting by size or providing emphasis to large items should be avoided. Graphics can help make numbers clearer. Because managers, especially new ones, focus on formal reports, those reports should include only the quantities and qualities that senior managers want controlled. Because many managers follow a recency or anchored perception pattern, the presentation should allow for comparison across time. Those following a representativeness pattern may be moderately helped with written comments.

In presenting variances, abstract concepts should not be used when concrete objects are available. If at all possible, images should not be substituted for physical objects, graphs should not substitute for images, and columnar reports should not be used for graphs. The four formats for the presentation of variances are physical, image, graph, and columnar report. A physical system uses the actual object to represent the variance. This format is simple, inexpensive, and easy for everyone to understand; it involves little overhead cost or error.

An image system represents a variance with a picture or videotape of the object. The approach is generally clear and inexpensive, and the image of the variance can be stored and compared across time.

A graph system represents variances as bars or lines. A computer and support personnel are required to produce the graphs, which results in both overhead cost and possible errors. Graphs can present data across time and across many departments. Many graphs are easily understood.

Columnar reports use numbers down a column to represent variances. Such reports are easy to generate, can present many variances in one report, and are moderate in cost. However, there may be errors in data entry, and columnar reports can be difficult to understand.

Senior managers, mid-level managers, supervisors, and workers perform variance investigation. Senior managers investigate current performance of the entity as a whole and place strong emphasis on long-term, qualitative performance. The investigation is sometimes made by staff departments, one of which is accounting. Mid-level managers investigate variances on a short-term basis, with moderate emphasis on qualitative measures. They often limit themselves to 5 or 10 measures that they follow closely. Supervisors and workers investigate variances in the here and now. Old variances and accounting reports are irrelevant for them. Physical variances, images, and limited graphics are most effective for supervisors and workers.

PROBLEM FOR REVIEW

As one of the assistant controllers of St. James Fashion Products, you have been asked to help Ms. Totterdane, the new Brunswick plant manager, with a report design that will meet her needs. You have gathered the following data for the nine weeks ending March 2, 19x3, that may be helpful in your presentation (all amounts in thousands except for workers):

| | *Week* | | | | | | | | |
	1	*2*	*3*	*4*	*5*	*6*	*7*	*8*	*9*
Output units	130	129	145	128	126	155	163	167	171
Shipment	143	139	156	139	134	164	172	176	177
Late shipments	3	4	13	8	14	14	2	12	1
Workers in attendance	399	386	397	386	382	397	385	377	387
Spoilage	4	7	5	3	1	9	6	3	4
Total flow hours	157	153	204	170	165	176	208	244	293
Revenues	$532	$517	$553	$494	$464	$561	$611	$622	$634
Cost of goods sold	351	331	372	320	295	386	403	410	421

The budget was based on the assumption that the average selling price will be $3.90 per item and that cost of goods sold will be 60 percent of normal selling price. The planned shipments are 160,000 units per week. The total plant work force is 408. The inventory at the beginning was 210,000 units. The desired production is 10,000 units below sales until inventory declines to 80,000 units. The standard production time is 48 minutes per unit.

The following normal rates have been estimated:

	Absenteeism	Spoilage	Late Shipment	Wasted Flow Time
Normal rates	4%	3%	2%	30%

REQUIRED

a. Prepare a line graph of:
1. Units shipped, produced, and in inventory.
2. Unit variances from desired levels for shipments and production.
3. Revenue, cost of goods sold, and gross margin.
4. Selling price, cost per unit, and unit margin.

b. For absenteeism, spoilage, late shipments, and wasted flow time:
1. Present the variances from normal in a columnar report.
2. Present a graph of the variances.
3. Express each of the measures as a rate and graph the rates.
4. Express each measure as a percentage of normal and graph the results.
5. Which of the report formats will communicate most effectively to Ms. Totterdane?

SOLUTION

a. 1. Line graph of units shipped, produced, and in inventory. First, compute the level of inventory at the end of each week:

	1	2	3	4	5	6	7	8	9
Beginning inventory	210	197	188	177	166	159	150	141	132
Plus: Production	130	129	145	128	126	155	163	167	171
Less: Shipments	(143)	(139)	(156)	(139)	(134)	(164)	(172)	(176)	(177)
Ending inventory	197	188	177	166	159	150	141	132	126

Next, graph production, shipment, and inventory units.

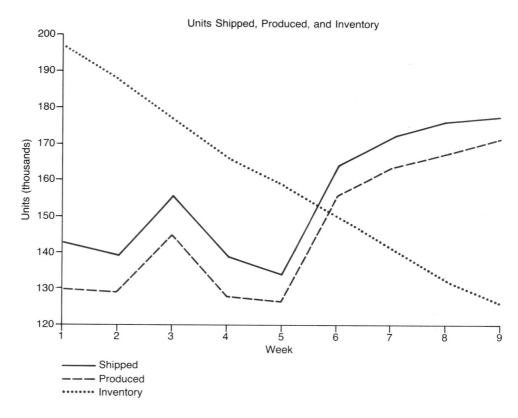

2. Line graph of unit variances from desired levels for shipments and production. First, compute the variances for shipments from 160,000:

	1	*2*	*3*	*4*	*5*	*6*	*7*	*8*	*9*
Shipment	143	139	156	139	134	164	172	176	177
Planned level	160	160	160	160	160	160	160	160	160
Variance	(17)	(21)	(4)	(21)	(26)	4	12	16	17

Next, compute the desired level of production as 10,000 less than shipments and subtract this from actual production:

	1	*2*	*3*	*4*	*5*	*6*	*7*	*8*	*9*
Actual production	130	129	145	128	126	155	163	167	171
Desired production	133	129	146	129	124	154	162	166	167
Variance	(3)	0	(1)	(1)	2	1	1	1	4

Finally, graph the variances:

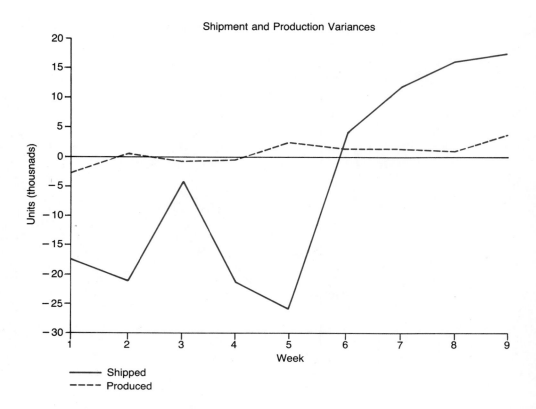

Shipment and Production Variances

3. Line graph of revenue, cost of goods sold, and gross margin.
   Revenue and cost of goods sold are given in the problem. The gross margin is the
   difference:

	1	2	3	4	5	6	7	8	9
Gross margin	181	186	181	174	169	175	208	212	213

   Next graph the results.

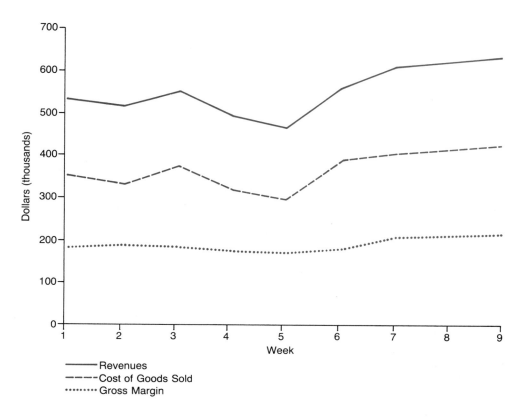

4. Line graph of selling price, cost per unit, and unit margin.
First divide revenues, costs, and margin by unit shipment:

	1	*2*	*3*	*4*	*5*	*6*	*7*	*8*	*9*
Selling price	3.72	3.72	3.55	3.56	3.46	3.42	3.55	3.53	3.57
Cost per unit	2.45	2.38	2.39	2.31	2.20	2.35	2.34	2.33	2.37
Unit margin	1.27	1.34	1.16	1.25	1.26	1.07	1.21	1.20	1.20

Next graph the results.

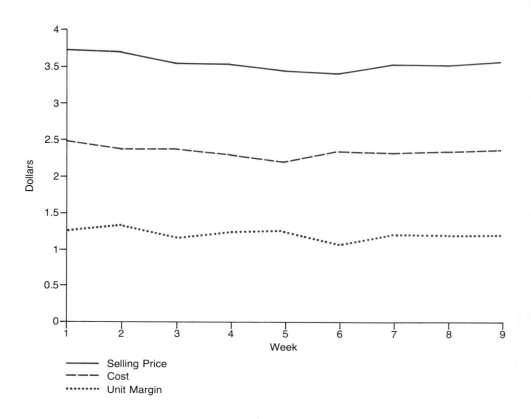

b. For absenteeism, spoilage, late shipments, and product flow time:
1. Present the variances from normal in a columnar report. First, compute the variances from normal for each of the qualitative measures:

	1	2	3	4	5	6	7	8	9
Actual absences	9	22	11	22	26	11	23	31	21
Normal absences (4%)	16	16	16	16	16	16	16	16	16
Variance	(7)	6	(5)	6	10	(5)	6	14	4
Actual spoilage	4	7	5	3	1	9	6	3	4
Normal spoilage (3%)	4	4	4	4	4	5	5	5	5
Variance	(0)	3	1	(1)	(3)	4	1	(2)	(1)
Actual late shipments	3	4	13	8	14	14	2	12	1
Normal late shipments (2%)	3	3	3	3	3	3	3	4	4
Variance	0	1	10	5	11	11	(1)	8	(3)
Total flow time	157	153	204	170	165	176	208	244	293
Productive hours	104	103	116	102	101	124	131	134	137
Normal wasted hours (30%)	31	31	35	31	30	37	39	40	41
Variance	22	19	53	37	34	15	38	70	115

Next we prepare the columnar report of these variances with time going down the page to make it easier for Ms. Totterdane to understand relationships across time.

St. James Fashion Products, Inc.—Brunswick Plant Variances for
Qualitative Measures For the Nine Weeks Ending March 2, 19x3

Week	Absenteeism	Spoilage	Late Shipments	Wasted Flow Hours
1	(7)	(0)	0	22
2	6	3	1	19
3	(5)	1	10	53
4	6	(1)	5	34
5	10	(3)	11	34
6	(5)	4	11	15
7	6	1	(1)	38
8	14	(2)	8	70
9	4	(1)	(3)	115

2. Present a graph of the variances.

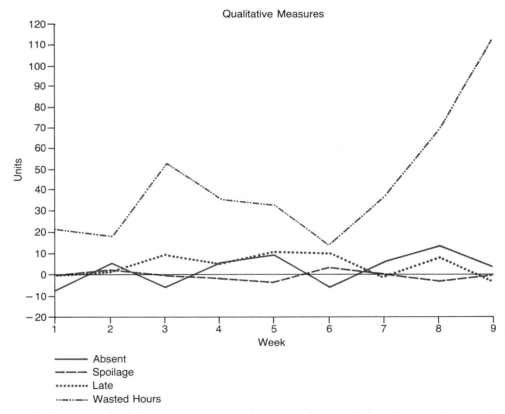

Qualitative Measures

Legend:
— Absent
--- Spoilage
.... Late
.—..—. Wasted Hours

3. Express each of the measures as a variance rate above or below the normal rate and graph the rates.

	Normal	1	2	3	4	5	6	7	8	9
Absenteeism	4%	−2%	1%	−1%	1%	2%	−1%	2%	3%	1%
Spoilage	3%	0%	2%	0%	−1%	−2%	3%	0%	−1%	0%
Late shipments	2%	0%	1%	6%	4%	8%	6%	−1%	5%	−2%
Wasted flow time	30%	4%	3%	13%	10%	9%	−1%	7%	15%	23%

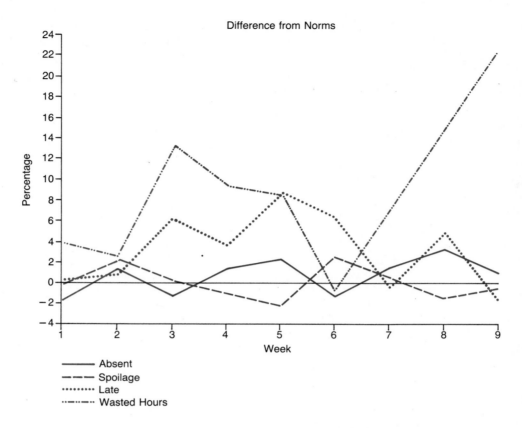

4. Express each measure as a percentage of normal and graph the results.
   First, compute the variance as a percentage of normal:

	1	2	3	4	5	6	7	8	9
Absenteeism	−44%	35%	−34%	34%	59%	−33%	39%	87%	27%
Spoilage	−5%	74%	9%	−30%	−72%	89%	14%	−48%	−17%
Late shipments	11%	38%	320%	182%	418%	323%	−29%	242%	−81%
Wasted flow time	71%	61%	154%	118%	110%	38%	96%	175%	279%

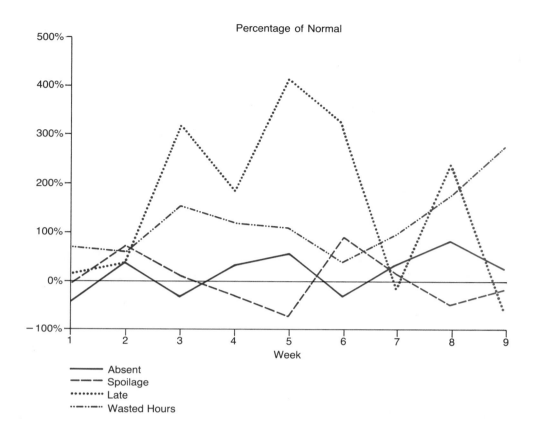

Percentage of Normal

Week

——— Absent
- - - Spoilage
········· Late
·—··—· Wasted Hours

5. The choice of report format is somewhat subjective. We expect graphics to communicate more effectively than columnar reports, but the choice among graphic forms is also somewhat subjective because they all communicate the same facts but in different forms. We prefer the presentation in part 3 because it is less abstract than part 4. We prefer the graph in Part 3 because in it the large numbers in the units of wasted flow hours completely overshadow the other variances in part 2.

KEY TERMS AND CONCEPTS

Recency (779)
Anchored (779)
Representative (780)
Physical Variance (780)

Product flow time (783)
Columnar report (785)
Critical success factors (786)

ADDITIONAL READINGS

Anderson, A. V. *Graphing Financial Information—How Accountants Can Use Graphs to Communicate.* New York: National Association of Accountants, 1983.

Baiman, S., and Joel Demski. "Variance Analysis Procedures as Motivational Devices." *Management Science,* August, 1980, pp. 840–48.

Douglas, Patricia P., and Teresa K. Beed. *Presenting Accounting Information to Management.* New York: National Association of Accountants, 1986.

Dudick, Thomas S. "Productivity Trend Control Reports." *Journal of Accountancy,* December, 1985, pp. 147–50.

Edwards, James B. *The Use of Performance Measures*. New York: National Association of Accountants, 1986.

Fertakis, J. P. "Reporting the Cumulative Variance." *Cost and Management*, November–December 1981, pp. 38–40.

Liao, W. M. "Performance Reports in Profit Planning and Control." *Managerial Planning*, January–February 1979, pp. 29–31.

Morse, Wayne J.; Harold P. Roth; and Kay M. Poston. *Measuring, Planning, and Controlling Quality Costs*. New York: National Association of Accountants, 1987.

Murdick, R. G. "Development of a Structure of Reports." *Journal of Systems Management*, January, 1980, pp. 36–41.

Taylor, Barbara G., and Lane K. Anderson. "Misleading Graphs: Guidelines for the Accountant." *Journal of Accountancy*, October 1986, pp. 126–35.

Wiseman, Bennett. "Better Looking Graphs with Lotus 1–2–3." *Business Software*, December 1987, pp. 64–68.

REVIEW QUESTIONS

1. What is the primary role of accountants in the variance investigation process?
2. List the four levels of personnel that perform variance investigations.
3. How many persons, places, or things can people easily compare and evaluate at one time?
4. Why should we avoid long lists of numbers in the design of internal reporting systems intended to support investigation?
5. What is the consequence for accountants in the statement, "Managers focus on data reported to them"?
6. List three qualitative production measures.
7. What is a recency perception pattern?
8. What is an anchored perception pattern?
9. What is a representative perception pattern?
10. How can managers who follow a recency or anchored perception pattern be helped by the variance system?
11. How can managers who follow a representative perception pattern be helped by the variance system?
12. Why is there less overhead cost associated with a physical variance reporting format?
13. Give two examples of a physical format to represent a variance.
14. Give two examples of the use of images of physical items to represent variances.
15. List the advantages and disadvantages of using images of physical items to represent variances.
16. Why should a graph not be substituted for an image of a physical variance?
17. What are the strengths of graphs for presenting variances?
18. Why should an abstract concept (overhead volume variance) not be substituted for a concrete concept (units produced) in preparing a graphic presentation for a manager?
19. What is product flow time?
20. Why will reducing product flow time cause a reduction in work in process inventories?
21. What is a columnar report of variances? List the strengths and weaknesses of a columnar report.
22. Give two examples of short-term measures that are important to senior managers.
23. Give two examples of long-term measures that are important to senior managers.
24. For small companies, why should there be no surprise when actual results are compared with the plan at the end of the year?
25. For very large companies, why might there be some surprise in the accounting numbers at the end of the fiscal year?
26. Briefly define the role of accountants in senior management investigations.
27. How does variance investigation by mid-level managers differ from that of senior managers?
28. Describe the level of investigation required by production supervisors.

29. What type of variance reporting is most useful for production supervisors?
30. List three qualitative measures that might be useful for a plant manager.
31. Why are reports of variances for the past month or quarter considered ancient by production supervisors?
32. What types of variance approach might be useful for line workers?

DISCUSSION QUESTIONS

33. In the introductory business problem, Chris Frescoln was led astray by the accounting system. What was there about Mr. Frescoln or about the situation that led him to be misinformed by the accounting system?
34. Why would it be undesirable to present to supervisors monthly variance reports that take the form of long lists of overhead budget and volume variances?
35. How might a new manager learn about the process by investigating many variances?
36. If variance reports give only results rather than causes, of what use are they to anyone except for creating jobs for accountants and clerks?
37. Give some examples of physical variances for:
    a. A university registration process.
    b. A retail clothing store.
    c. The production of parts for the space shuttle program.
38. How might qualitative measures and variances differ for:
    a. A service company.
    b. A merchandising company.
    c. A manufacturing company.
39. Under what limited circumstances might it be useful to translate images of physical variances into graphs of numeric variances?
40. Discuss ways in which product flow time may be reduced.
41. Why do senior managers change their approaches to investigating variances from one circumstance to the next?
42. What types of surprises might the senior managers of very large companies have in the review of the final financial reports?

EXERCISES

20–1. Limitations of Managers. Among the limitations of managers in variance investigation are:

1. Number of variances.
2. Focus on formal reports.
3. Recency Pattern.
4. Anchored pattern.
5. Representativeness pattern.

REQUIRED:
For each of the following statements, indicate the limitation(s) that the manager is exhibiting:

_____ a. Purchasing manager: "Jorgenson, Ltd., has been a great supplier of bolts for our company for 83 years. Its current delivery and quality problems are unimportant."

_____ b. Company president: "Why am I getting this detailed report on labor variances for each item produced in 48 plants? This report is just a waste of my time."

_____ c. Plant manager: "I want our actual cost per unit to equal the standard cost in our report to headquarters. Otherwise, someone will be out looking for a job."

_____ d. Shop supervisor: "We've always produced the best bearings around. Sure, we've had some quality problems the past few weeks, but that's only a temporary situation that will go away on its own. It's nothing really."

_____ e. Medical doctor: "Last month was great, but this month is a disaster. Our billings are down by $300,000 and only a few patients are on the surgery schedule. Should we change our location? Be open more hours? How are we going to make payroll?"

_____ *f.* Plant manager: "I don't want to adopt just-in-time production right now. Its adoption will mean that I'll have to shift 200 people to new jobs. My variance report will be shot for two or three months with the labor efficiency variances as people learn their new jobs."

_____ *g.* Department store manager: "Sales for men's clothing are down this month. I think we need to hire a new department manager. This one is not working out."

20–2. Selecting Variance Presentation Approaches.   For each of the following variances, select the variance presentation format that would best present the variance to managers.

1. Physical   3. Graph
2. Image   4. Tabular

	Variance	**Reported to**
_____ *a.*	Spoiled production for one 8-hour shift in a clothing factory.	Shift supervisor
_____ *b.*	Difference between actual and planned materials inventories by division for 218 divisions.	Senior management
_____ *c.*	Variance between actual and planned sales by week for the past year.	President
_____ *d.*	Remaining unsold tickets/seats for one college football game.	Ticket clerks
_____ *e.*	Unclaimed baggage for an air terminal by day for the past month.	Baggage supervisor
_____ *f.*	Cash above minimum balance by day for the past 10 days.	Treasurer
_____ *g.*	Number of back-ordered units by day for the past month.	Plant manager

20–3. Matching Variance Reports to Managers/Workers.   For the following variances, select the type(s) of person who would most likely receive (or observe) the variance report.

Person/level that should receive (or observe) a report

1. Senior management   4. Plant manager
2. Division manager   5. Supervisor
3. Sales manager   6. Worker

	Variance	**Format**
_____ *a.*	Corporate monthly income less planned income amounts for current year.	Graph
_____ *b.*	A report of errors made by machine operators.	Tabular
_____ *c.*	Overtime worked by department in a factory.	Tabular
_____ *d.*	Spoilage of production units in a fabrication department.	Physical
_____ *e.*	Employee turnover by division for 15 divisions.	Graph
_____ *f.*	Customer satisfaction measure by quarter for the past three years.	Graph
_____ *g.*	The theft of merchandise as recorded by a movie camera in a retail department store.	Image
_____ *h.*	The detailed report of the crash landing of a large aircraft at DFW International Airport.	Images

20–4. Graphing Variances.   The Hadstew Company has the following four overhead spending variances by department and by quarter for 19x3:

	Department	
	Heat	*Mixing*
1st	$22,000	$15,000
2nd	7,000	17,000
3rd	25,000	19,000
4th	8,000	22,000
Totals	$62,000	$73,000

REQUIRED:
a. Prepare a bar chart of the variances by department.
b. Prepare a line chart of the variances by department.

20–5. Graphing Variances. Hearington Works, Ltd., manufactures pottery of various types. Breakage in handling and shipment is a major cost. For the two months ending February 28, 19x0, the breakage on three selected pot styles has been:

	Breakage		
Pot Style	*January*	*February*	*Total*
A–306	70	50	120
B–045	90	150	240
F–002	220	140	360
Total	380	340	720

REQUIRED:
a. Prepare a pie chart of total breakage by pot style.
b. Prepare a bar chart of total breakage by month.
c. Prepare a line graph of breakage by style and month.

20–6. Measure of Employee Turnover. The Diamond Mountain Works processes ore from the Diamond Mountain Mine. Data from two recent months (with some missing amounts) are listed below:

	February	*March*
Beginning workers	320	*c.*
Quit during month	*a.*	40
Hired during month	28	*d.*
Ending workers	316	330
Employee turnover	*b.*	*e.*

Employee turnover is computed as the ratio of employees quitting during the month to the average of beginning and ending workers.

REQUIRED:
Find amounts *a* through *e*.

20–7. Variance Report. The Cincinnati Division of Bunker Enterprises produces a line of children's toys under the name The Batboy Collection. The following variance report was issued November 14, 19x3, for production during the preceding September.

Variance Report, Robin Line

Sales variances	$1,500 F
Production variances:	
Material quantity variance	$ 300 F
Labor rate variance	200 U
Fixed overhead volume variance	400 F
Material price variance	100 U
Variable overhead spending variance	500 F

Labor efficiency variance	$ 800 U
Fixed overhead spending variance	1,000 U
Variable overhead efficiency variance	600 U

REQUIRED:

Comment on the report and make recommendations as to how you would improve the report.

PROBLEMS

20–8. Qualitative Variance Reports, Employee-Related Measures. The Skulkyl plant prints, binds, and packages small books on a job order basis for numerous publishers. The plant employs 600 people in various tasks and operates three shifts per day, five days a week. The plant manager has noticed that the total payroll has been down during the past three weeks and has asked you to compute employee turnover, absenteeism, and tardiness. Data for the three weeks ending June 28, 19x2 are:

	For the Week Ending		
	June 14	*June 21*	*June 28*
Beginning workers	600	596	586
Quit during week	16	26	44
Hired during week	12	16	26
Ending workers	596	586	568
Absent 1 or more days	26	44	56
Late 1 or more days	44	56	70

REQUIRED:

a. For each week, compute the following ratios (using the average of beginning and ending workers as a base):
  1. Employee turnover.
  2. Employee absenteeism.
  3. Employee tardiness.
b. Present a line graph of employee turnover, absenteeism, and tardiness ratios.

20–9. Developing a Reporting Format. Utah Grain and Feed, Inc., buys various grains from farmers and mixes the grains according to selected recipes. The grains are packaged in 50 lb.- and 100 lb.-bags for shipment. The company has processing plants scattered throughout Utah, Idaho, Oregon, and Washington.

The Alpine plant is currently reviewing its reporting system with plans to redesign it. Of particular importance is the development of critical performance factors for management review. The plant manager wants an overall report of grains and conversion costs that are under her control. Plant managers do not have control over the price and quantity of grains purchased, but two key elements the plant managers can control are the use of grains and the packaging. The measures for these elements are dollars of grain lost in production and the dollars of packing materials lost in production. The plant manager can also control labor and overhead costs.

Cost data were gathered for several periods on each of the three areas. The following is a summary of the actual data and the plans for next year:

Year	*Grains Lost in Production*	*Packaging Lost in Production*	*Labor and Overhead*
19x2	$4,260,000	$305,000	$2,540,000
19x3	4,190,000	300,000	2,530,000
19x4	3,240,000	295,000	1,970,000
19x5	3,780,000	380,000	2,510,000
19x6	3,540,000	310,000	2,530,000
19x7 (Planned)	3,530,000	300,000	2,540,000

REQUIRED:

a. Through various graphic approaches, show different ways to present the above data to the plant manager so that she will quickly identify those areas that need her attention.

b. Select one of the graphs and explain why it has advantages over the remaining graphs.

c. Suppose you had additional data about production that you could draw on. What data would you like to have that would make the reports in *(a)* above more meaningful? Explain your rationale as to why that data would be helpful.

20–10. Cost Center Labor Variances.   Aerospace Fabricators, Inc., has its Orange County, California, plant organized into 15 cost centers, each with three categories of labor skill. Each week, the plant manager receives a report on each cost center that shows labor rate and efficiency variances by labor category. The plant manager received the following labor report for last week's performance:

Cost Center	Labor Skill 1		Labor Skill 2		Labor Skill 3	
	Rate	*Efficiency*	*Rate*	*Efficiency*	*Rate*	*Efficiency*
1	208 U	1,219 U	389 F	755 U	220 U	1,262 F
2	153 F	777 U	318 F	1,012 U	197 U	885 U
3	270 U	1,407 U	305 F	800 F	232 F	1,180 U
4	252 U	631 F	185 F	765 F	327 F	1,234 U
5	171 F	814 F	266 U	944 U	289 U	1,219 U
6	225 U	866 U	274 U	664 F	308 F	940 U
7	267 F	734 F	163 F	1,197 U	324 U	860 U
8	159 U	913 U	354 F	983 F	295 F	1,181 F
9	247 U	1,224 F	337 U	1,297 F	176 U	928 U
10	157 U	1,120 F	246 U	718 F	205 F	1,207 F
11	223 F	1,141 U	271 F	692 U	369 F	855 F
12	194 U	990 U	109 U	908 U	329 F	1,353 F
13	220 U	985 U	329 U	974 F	204 U	608 U
14	172 F	1,016 U	315 F	598 U	304 F	1,333 U
15	222 F	718 F	204 F	1,076 F	168 U	1,102 U
Totals	724 U	4,073 U	943 F	1,171 F	791 F	4,431 U

REQUIRED:

a. Comment on the effectiveness of this report at the plant manager level.

b. Demonstrate how line graphs, bar graphs, and pie charts could be used to report effectively the same information. Remember, you want the plant manager to identify areas that may need further investigation.

20-11. Form and Format of Report.   Each month the department heads of the National Association of Trade Stores receive a financial report of the performance of their departments for the previous month. The report is generally distributed around the 16th or 17th of the month. Although the association is a not-for-profit trade and educational association, it does attempt to generate revenues from a variety of activities to supplement the member dues. The association has several income-producing departments: research, education, publications, and promotion consulting services. As a general rule, each department is expected to be self-supporting, and the department head is responsible for both the generation of revenue and the control of costs for the department.

   As an example of the monthly department report, the March 19x7 report of the education division is presented as follows, with the comments of the accounting department:

NATIONAL ASSOCIATION OF TRADE STORES
Education Department
Report for the Month of March 19x7

	Budget			Actual			Variance		Variance as a % of Budget	
	Person Days or Units	$	%	Person Days or Units	$	%	Person Days or Units	$	Person Days or Units	$
Revenue										
Week-long courses	1,500	$225,000	71.4%	1,250	$187,500	66.4%	(250)	$(37,500)	(16.6)%	(16.6)%
One-day seminars	50	15,000	4.8	17	5,100	1.8	(33)	(9,900)	(66.0)	(66.0)
Home-study courses	1,000	75,000	23.8	1,100	89,700	31.8	100	14,700	10.0	19.6
		$315,000	100.0%		$282,300	100.0%		$(32,700)		(10.4)%
Expenses										
Salaries		$174,000	55.2%		$167,000	59.1%		$ 7,000		4.0%
Course material		35,500	11.3		34,670	12.3		830		2.3
Supplies, telephone, and telegraph		4,000	1.3		4,200	1.5		(200)		(5.0)
Rent, utilities, and janitorial service		7,000	2.2		7,000	2.5		—		—
Equipment depreciation		700	.2		700	.2		—		—
Allocated general administration		5,000	1.6		5,000	1.8		—		—
Temporary office help		5,000	1.6		3,750	1.3		1,250		25.0
Contract employees		15,000	4.8		18,500	6.6		(3,500)		(23.3)
Travel		12,000	3.8		11,500	4.1		500		4.2
Dues and meetings		500	.2		500	.2		—		—
Promotion and postage		32,000	10.1		36,500	12.9		(4,500)		(14.1)
Total expenses		$290,700	92.3%		$289,320	102.5%		$ 1,380		0.5%
Contribution to the Association		$ 24,300	7.7%		$ (7,020)	(2.5)%		$(31,320)		(128.9)%

Comment: The department did not make its budget this month. There was a major short-fall in the week-long course revenues. Although salaries were lower than budget, this saving was entirely consumed by overexpenditure in contract employees and promotion. Further effort is needed to increase revenues and to hold down expenses.

The annual revenue target that becomes the revenue budget is established by the executive director and the association's board of directors. The annual and monthly expenses budgets are then developed at the beginning of the year by the department heads for all costs except Rent, Utilities, and Janitorial Services; Equipment Depreciation; and Allocated General Administration. The amounts for these accounts are supplied by the Accounting Department. The monthly budget figures for revenues are also determined by the department heads at the beginning of the year. The monthly budget amounts for revenues and expenses are not revised during the year.

For example, the following changes in operations have taken place, but the monthly budgets have not been revised: (1) a new home-study course was introduced in February, one month earlier than scheduled; (2) a number of the week-long courses were postponed in February and March and rescheduled for April and May; and (3) the related promotion effort—heavy direct-mail advertising in the two months prior to a course offering—was likewise rescheduled.

(CMA, adapted)

REQUIRED:

Identify and briefly discuss the good and bad features of the monthly report presented for the Education Department as a means of communication in terms of

a. Its form and appearance in presenting the operating performance of the education department.

b. Its content in providing useful information to the department head for managing the education department.

Include in your discussion the changes you would recommend to improve the report as a communication device.

20–12. Modifying Performance Report.   Denny Daniels is production manager of the Alumalloy Division of WRT, Inc. Alumalloy has limited contact with outside customers and has no sales staff. Most of its customers are other divisions of WRT. All sales and purchases with outside customers are handled by other corporate divisions. Therefore, Alumalloy is treated as a cost center for reporting and evaluation purposes rather than as a revenue or profit center.

Daniels perceives the Accounting Department as a historical number-generating process that provides little useful information for conducting his job. Consequently, the entire accounting process is perceived as a negative motivational device that does not reflect how hard or how effectively he works as a production manager. Daniels tried to discuss these perceptions and concerns with John Scott, the controller for the Alumalloy Division. Daniels told Scott, ''I think the cost report is misleading. I know I've had better production over a number of operating periods, but the cost report still says I have excessive costs. Look, I'm not an accountant, I'm a production manager. I know how to get a good quality product out. Over a number of years. I've even cut the raw materials used to do it. But the cost report doesn't show any of this. Basically, it's always negative, no matter what I do. There's no way you can win with acounting or the people at corporate who use those reports.''

Scott gave Daniels little consolation. Scott stated that the accounting system and the cost reports generated by headquarters are just part of the corporate game and almost impossible for an individual to change. ''Although these accounting reports are pretty much the basis for evaluating the efficiency of your division and the means corporate uses to determine whether you have done the job it wants, you shouldn't worry too much. You haven't been fired yet! Besides, these cost reports have been used by WRT for the last 25 years.''

Daniels perceived from talking to the production manager of the Zinc Division that most of what Scott said was probably true. However, some minor cost reporting changes for Zinc had been agreed to by corporate headquarters. He also knew from the trade grapevine that the turnover of production managers was considered high at WRT, even though relatively few were fired. Most seemed to end up quitting, usually in disgust, because of beliefs that they were not being evaluated fairly. Typical comments of production managers who have left WRT are:

- ''Corporate headquarters doesn't really listen to us. All they consider are those misleading cost reports. They don't want them changed and they don't want any supplemental information.''

- ''The accountants may be quick with numbers but they don't know anything about production. As it was, I either had to ignore the cost reports entirely or pretend they are important even though they didn't tell how good a job I had done. No matter what they say about not firing people, negative reports mean negative evaluations. I'm better off working for another company.''

A recent copy of the cost report prepared by corporate headquarters for the Alumalloy Division is shown below. Daniels does not like this report because he believes it fails to reflect the division's operations properly, thereby resulting in an unfair evaluation of performance.

(CMA, adapted)

ALLUMALLOY DIVISION
Cost Report
For the Month of April 19x0
(thousands omitted)

	Master Budget	Actual Cost	Excess Cost
Aluminum	$ 400	$ 437	$ 37
Labor	560	540	(20)
Overhead	100	134	34
Total	$1,060	$1,111	$ 51

REQUIRED:

a. Comment on Denny Daniel's perception of:

1. John Scott, the controller.
2. Corporate headquarters.
3. The cost report.
4. Himself as a production manager.

Also discuss how his perception affects his behavior and probable performance as a production manager and employee of WRT.

b. Identify and explain three changes that could be made in the report presented to the production managers that would make the information more meaningful and less threatening to them.

20–13. Cost Report.   Berwin, Inc., is a manufacturer of small industrial tools with an annual sales volume of approximately $3.5 million. Sales growth has been steady during the year, and there is no evidence of cyclical demand. Production has increased gradually during the year and has been distributed evenly throughout each month. The company employs a sequential processing system. The four manufacturing departments—Casting, Machining, Finishing, and Packaging—are all located in the same building. Fixed manufacturing overhead is assigned using a plant-wide rate.

Berwin has always been able to compete with other manufacturers of small industrial tools. However, its market has expanded only in response to product innovation. Thus, research and development is very important and has helped Berwin to expand as well as maintain demand.

Carl Viller, controller, has designed and implemented a new budget system in response to concerns voiced by George Berwin, president. An annual budget that has been divided into 12 equal segments has been prepared to assist in the timely evaluation of monthly performance. Berwin was visibly upset upon receiving the May performance report for the Machining Department (reproduced below). Berwin exclaimed, ''How can they be efficient enough to produce nine extra units every working day and still miss the budget by $300 a day?'' Gene Jordan, Machining Department supervisor, could not understand ''all the red ink'' when he knew the department had operated more efficiently in May than it had in months. Jordan stated, ''I was expecting a pat on the back and instead the boss tore me apart. What's more, I don't even know why!''

Similar performance reports are prepared for the other three departments.

(CMA, adapted)

BERWIN, INC.
Machining Department Performance Report
For the Month Ended May 31, 19x4

	Budget	Actual	(Over) Under Budget
Volume in units	3,000	3,185	(185)
Variable manufacturing costs			
Direct material	$24,000	$ 24,843	$ (843)
Direct labor	27,750	29,302	(1,552)
Variable factory overhead	33,300	35,035	(1,735)
Total variable manufacturing costs	$85,050	$ 89,180	$(4,130)
Fixed manufacturing overhead			
Indirect labor	$ 3,300	$ 3,334	$ (34)
Depreciation	1,500	1,500	
Taxes	300	300	
Insurance	240	240	
Other	930	1,027	(97)
Total fixed overhead costs	$ 6,270	$ 6,401	$ (131)
Corporate costs			
Research and development	$ 2,400	$ 3,728	$(1,328)
Selling and administration	3,600	4,075	(475)
Total corporate costs	$ 6,000	$ 7,803	$(1,803)
Total costs	$97,320	$103,384	$(6,064)

REQUIRED:

Review the May performance report for the Machining Department of Berwin, Inc. Based upon the information presented in the report:

a. Discuss the strengths of the new budget system in general.

b. Identify the weaknesses of the performance report and explain how the report should be revised to eliminate each weakness. Specifically consider the role of the Machine Department supervisor.

20–14. Performance Report for Service Department.   The Argon County Hospital is located in the county seat. Argon County is a well-known summer resort area. The county population doubles during the vacation months (May–August), and hospital activity more than doubles during these months. The hospital is organized into several departments. Although it is a relatively small hospital, its pleasant surroundings have attracted a well-trained and competent medical staff.

An administrator was hired a year ago to improve the business activities of the hospital. Among the new ideas he has introduced is responsibility accounting. This program was announced along with quarterly cost reports supplied to department heads. Previously cost data were presented to department heads infrequently. Excerpts from the announcement and the report received by the laundry supervisor are presented below.

> The hospital has adopted a "responsibility accounting system." From now on you will receive quarterly reports comparing the costs of operating your department with budgeted costs. The reports will highlight the differences (variations) so you can zero in on the departure from budgeted costs. (This is called "management by exception.") Responsibility accounting means you are accountable for keeping the costs in your department within the budget. The variations from the budget will help you identify what costs are out of line, and the size of the variation will indicate which ones are the most important. Your first such report accompanies this announcement.

(CMA, adapted)

ARGON COUNTY HOSPITAL
Performance Report—Laundry Department
July–September 19x3

	Budget	Actual	(Over) Under Budget	Percent (Over) Under Budget
Patient days	9,500	11,900	(2,400)	(25)
Pounds processed—Laundry				
Costs	125,000	156,000	(31,000)	(25)
Laundry labor	$ 9,000	$12,500	$(3,500)	(39)
Supplies	1,100	1,875	(775)	(70)
Water, water heating and softening	1,700	2,500	(800)	(47)
Maintenance	1,400	2,200	(800)	(57)
Supervisor's salary	3,150	3,750	(600)	(19)
Allocated administration costs	4,000	5,000	(1,000)	(25)
Equipment depreciation	1,200	1,250	(50)	(4)
	$21,550	$29,075	$(7,525)	(35)

Administrator's Comments: Costs are significantly above budget for the quarter. Particular attention needs to be paid to labor, supplies, and maintenance.

The annual budget for 19x3 was constructed by the new administrator. Quarterly budgets were computed as one fourth of the annual budget. The administrator compiled the budget from analysis of the prior three years' costs. The analysis showed that all costs increased each year with more rapid increases between the second and third year. He considered establishing the budget at an average of the prior three years' costs hoping that the installation of the system would reduce costs to this level. However, in view of the rapidly increasing prices, he finally chose 19x2 costs less 3 percent for the 19x3 budget. The activity level measured by patient days and pounds of laundry processed was set at 19x2 volume, which was approximately equal to the volume of each of the past three years.

(CMA, adapted)

REQUIRED:
a. Comment on the method used to construct the budget.
b. What information should be communicated by variations from budgets?
c. Does the report effectively communicate the level of efficiency of this department? Give reasons for your answer.
d. List and briefly describe additional performance measures that might be used relative to the Laundry Department.
e. Recommend changes to the investigation of performance by the hospital administrator at Argon County Hospital.

20–15. Evaluation of Performance Measures. In late 19x1, Mr. Sootsman, the official in charge of the State Department of Automobile Regulation, established a system of performance measurement for the department's branch offices. He was convinced that management by objectives could help the department reach its objective of better citizen service at a lower cost. The first step was to define the activities of the branch offices, to assign point values to the services performed, and to establish performance targets. Point values, rather than revenue targets, were employed because the department was a regulatory agency, not a revenue-producing agency. Further, the specific revenue for a service did not adequately reflect the differences in effort required. The analysis was compiled at the state office, and the results were distributed to the branch offices.

The system has been in operation since 19x2. The performance targets for the branches have been revised each year by the state office. The revisions were designed to encourage better performance by increasing the target or reducing resources to achieve targets. The revisions incorporated noncontrollable events, such as population shifts, new branches, and changes in procedures.

The Barry County branch is typical of many branch offices. A summary displaying the budgeted and actual performance for three years is presented below.

Mr. Sootsman has been disappointed in the performance of branch offices because they have not met performance targets or budgets. He is especially concerned because the points earned from citizens' comments are declining.

REQUIRED:

a. Does the method of performance measurement properly capture the objectives of this operation? Justify your answer.

b. The Barry County branch office came close to its target for 19x4. Does this constitute improved performance compared to 19x3? Justify your answer.

c. Describe changes that would improve the reporting system.

(CMA, adapted)

Barry County Branch Performance Report

	19x2		19x3		19x4	
	Budget	Actual	Budget	Actual	Budget	Actual
Population served	38,000		38,500		38,700	
Number of employees						
Administrative	1	1	1	1	1	1
Professional	1	1	1	1	1	1
Clerical	3	3	2	3	1½	3
Budgeted performance points*						
1. Services	19,500		16,000		15,500	
2. Citizen comments	500		600		700	
	20,000		16,600		16,200	
Actual performance points*						
1. Services		14,500		14,600		15,600
2. Citizen comments		200		900		200
		14,700		15,500		15,800
Detail of actual performance*						
1. New drivers licenses						
a. Examination and road tests (3 pts.)		3,000		3,150		3,030
b. Road tests repeat—failed prior test (2 pts.)		600		750		1,650
2. Renew drivers licenses (1 pt.)		3,000		3,120		3,060
3. Issue license plates (.5 pts.)		4,200		4,150		4,100
4. Issue titles						
a. Dealer transactions (.5 pts.)		2,000		1,900		2,100
b. Individual transactions (1 pt.)		1,700		1,530		1,660
		14,500		14,600		15,600
5. Citizen comments						
a. Favorable (+.5 pts.)		300		1,100		800
b. Unfavorable (−.5 pts.)		100		200		600
		200		900		200

* The budget performance points for services are calculated using 3 points per available hour. The administrative employee devotes half time to administration and half time to regular services. The calculations for the services point budget are as follows:

19x2: 4½ people × 8 hours × 240 days × 3 pts. × 75% productive time = 19,440 rounded to 19,500
19x3: 3½ people × 8 hours × 240 days × 3 pts. × 80% productive time = 16,128 rounded to 16,000
19x4: 3 people × 8 hours × 240 days × 3 pts. × 90% productive time = 15,552 rounded to 15,500

The comments targets are based upon rough estimates by department officials.

The actual point totals for the branch are calculated by multiplying the weights shown in the report in parentheses by the number of such services performed or comments received.

CHAPTER

21

Models for Process Control

PROBLEM OF CONTROLLING MACHINE OUTPUT

For the past six months, Jaine Phillipe has been a production supervisor at Englese Processing Plant in Southern California. The plant processes fruits and vegetables in frozen or canned forms in mass quantities. Ms. Phillipe supervises 60 pack-and-fill machines that automatically pack plastic bags with fruits or vegetables and seal the bags for quick freezing. A work center with 10 machines is operated by one person who troubleshoots the process. Ms. Phillipe oversees six such work areas.

The machines can be set for 16-, 24-, or 32-ounce bags. About 72 percent of the production cost is the food; the remainder is treated as production overhead. Less than 4 percent of the total cost relates to labor. The plant runs continuously from May through November with one 8-hour maintenance shift per week. When one machine goes down, the work is shifted to the other machines until it can be repaired by the operator or a machine specialist.

Vegetables and fruit vary in density and composition, making it difficult for the machinery to pack exactly the correct weight in each package. Because of various state and federal regulations, the package must have at least the weight printed on the label. On average, more than 16 ounces must be packed to be sure to achieve a minimum of 16 ounces. When the machines are off or the food density is off, more than standard material has to be used because a bag that is underweight is treated as a spoiled unit. The standard allows for an average 10 percent overfill to keep the minimum weight. The machines operate at a rate of one 16-ounce bag filled per 2 seconds.

Older machines are more difficult to control and have more variation in weight. Thus, older machines require a higher than average pack weight to assure the minimum package weight.

■

LEARNING OBJECTIVES

After completing this chapter, you should be able to:

1. Explain and apply the approaches to the investigation of single-period variances: investigation of every variance, only large variances, and the costs and benefits.
2. Apply quality process control charts to a production process.
3. Apply three approaches to the variance investigation decision over multiple periods.

A sudden failure in the oxygen system for an 800-bed hospital at 2 A.M. resulted in the use of 104 canisters of bottled oxygen at a cost of $2,080, plus calling in 20 additional nurses on an emergency basis at a cost of about $2,000. Most of the patients slept through the occurrence, but the nurses and supervisors were shaken. The system was reset and was running again by about 5:30 A.M. If the oxygen system had failed during surgery (7 A.M. until 12 noon), several lives would have been lost. Is this failure of the oxygen system worth investigating?

The most beneficial investigations are those that result in identifying something that can be fixed. Of course, this variance in the oxygen system *must* be fixed. If it is not, some patients might die or additional costs might be incurred. In cases of wrongful death, other hospitals have had to pay judgments of $2 million and higher. The hospital did investigate and, after much effort, found the problem in a cracked circuit board in a control panel located in the basement. A slight moisture buildup had caused the circuit board to overheat and fail temporarily. The hospital paid $3,800 to an oxygen system expert to find the problem after its own efforts failed. The control panel had to be relocated to a drier place and rewired at a cost of $18,000. In addition, the hospital invested $80,000 in a backup control panel with an automatic cut-over switch in case of failure of one panel. Therefore, the variance was fixable.

Other variances result from circumstances that cannot be changed because they are caused by uncontrollable random events. For example, the monthly patient and surgery variances in a medical practice are not controllable. The variance in monthly volume can be 50 percent above or below average. Some months the practice is cash poor and has to borrow money for payroll and payments to creditors. In other months, it has excess cash. There is no predictable pattern from year to year, other than that the elderly are ill more frequently during winter months and youth have more injuries during the summer.

With this uncertainty, the physicians need to keep a positive attitude, maintain technical skills, give personal treatment to each patient (make them believe that their doctor cares), and present a professional image in both staff and office appearance. Medical practices change slowly over many years. People generally stay with the same physician for many years. During some months, few patients come in, but in other months, the practice is very busy. Almost nothing can be done on a month-to-month basis to change the inflow of patients. Thus, the signal that patient flow is up or down has little meaning with regard to a fixable problem. Investigating a variance in patient flow may even be harmful because it can generate negative attitudes about uncontrollable events.

The models for deciding when to investigate variances are classified as single-period models or multiple-period models. We look first at the single-period models.

SINGLE-PERIOD MODELS FOR INVESTIGATING VARIANCES

A variance in a process is the result of either a fixable or an unfixable problem. A **fixable problem** is one that the manager can do something about by taking a corrective action. An **unfixable problem** is one for which no corrective action is currently available. Distinguishing between problems that can be fixed and those that cannot is a matter of judgment. Those problems deemed currently unfixable, for example the variation in pack fill in a food processing line, must still be examined periodically to determine if corrective solutions might be available at a reasonable cost.

The decision to investigate must involve three factors: the cost of investigation, the cost of correcting a fixable problem, and the benefits to be received if corrective action is taken. Three single-period approaches are available: investigation of all variances, investigation of only large variances, and cost-benefits.

Investigate All Variances

One approach to variances is to investigate all of them. This means that every variance is considered a surprise that requires investigation and that has potential correction. Stopping production processes for every variance and acting on every customer complaint are examples of this approach. The benefits from correcting problems and finding opportunities for improvement are assumed to cumulatively outweigh the costs of interruption and the costs of correction.

This approach might apply to the production of a concert, a movie, or a sports event. An outstanding director or coach drills the actors or players until they produce perfectly. Mistakes cannot be tolerated, and rehearsals and drills are designed to eliminate them. Actors or players who do not show the needed improvement are dropped early. Only outstanding performance can win an Academy Award, a standing ovation, or a championship trophy. If the director or coach accepts mediocrity from some players, the combined performance tends to be inadequate. Therefore, performing artists and athletes must seek perfection in order to be adequate. They can never accept anything less than their best performance. All variances must be investigated and corrected or they become habits that make the cumulative performance unacceptable. Even favorable variances, for example a brilliant play, indicate that there are opportunities for improving the production and should be studied.

Investigating every variance is useful for improving quality in many manufacturing processes in which a tolerance for production variances results in poor attitudes by workers and each worker's performance is just good enough. The cumulative result of everyone's performance being just good enough is a product that is *not* competitive.

If we accept that bad days occur on Monday, Friday, or around a holiday, poor production happens on those days. On the other hand, if we always investigate the causes for every variance, fewer bad days tend to occur. Thus, some companies have concluded that the primary benefit of investigating every variance is in preventing problems before they arise.

As another example of this approach, consider relationships with suppliers. If we expect suppliers to deliver high-quality parts just in time for production, they tend to accommodate. For example, when we demand an explanation immediately for untimely deliveries or shoddy materials, suppliers in a competitive environment will make maximum efforts to deliver quality materials on time. On the other hand, when we accept some late or poor-quality deliveries, suppliers will continue to exploit that. Suppliers who cannot meet timing and quality standards should be dropped from the list of qualified suppliers.

Another advantage of investigating every variance is that previously unfixable problems may now have a solution. Processes change over time, and creative people are always finding new ways to do things. New solutions are always becoming available to correct previously unfixable problems.

The major disadvantage to investigating every variance comes in situations in which random occurrences exist. Investigating every variance is not cost effective and can result in poor attitudes and demoralizing behavior. This is generally true because the variance is not controllable by the actions of employees. For example, baseball is a game of skill, probabilities, and personal psychology. Outstanding hitters with averages of .350 or above still strike out. The strike outs are not necessarily caused by the quality of the hitter's swing but by the variation in the quality of pitching. Making batters explain every time they strike out will make them lose confidence, which in turn leads to lower hitting averages. Coaches must therefore balance their demand for high-quality batting every time with the variation in the quality of pitching.

Similarly, the sale of products involves customers who do not cooperate by placing the same sized order every week. Sometimes sales are lower than expected, and at other times, sales are higher. Investigating every staff member with sales below weekly expectations can eventually affect their attitudes. They will hold back sales orders during good weeks and release them during poor weeks. This behavior builds a time lag into the system, resulting in slow deliveries and customer dissatisfaction.

Randomness in a process should not be taken for granted. Processes that appear to be random may be controlled with creative approaches. Thus, every process should be examined periodically to determine whether a new solution exists to achieve more consistent activity.

In summary, investigating every variance is a reasonable approach to apply to a process that is or can become closely controlled. However, investigating every variance for a process with significant random components may not be worthwhile or may be harmful. Judgment is required to distinguish when a process can be controlled very closely and when it cannot. Technology changes and employee relations are important in making this judgment.

Investigate Only Large Variances

In order to deal with random processes, some supervisors investigate only variances that are large enough. A **screen** is a rule or policy that a manager might use to determine which variances are large enough to warrant consideration. A screen that might be used in the pack-and-fill line example from the introduction is to investigate all machines that fill bags more than 10 percent above the desired weight or that pack bags lower than the printed weight. Using this screen, the pack-and-fill line supervisor would not investigate variances occurring within the acceptable range. These screens may also be stated in dollar terms. Such a screen for machine maintenance might be to investigate any machine that requires more than $5,000 in unplanned maintenance during a month. Qualitative factors can also be an important consideration. Thus, screens may involve the qualitative aspects of a process, such as: Investigate employee morale when either employee absence or tardiness is greater than 2 percent.

Screens are convenient devices because they can be computerized and work automatically. Thus, screens may free supervisors and managers so that they can consider other aspects of their jobs, such as training new employees, planning, or motivating employees by personal interaction.

Investigating only large variances makes sense when managers must review daily or weekly variances related to production processes with high variety. For example, consider a manager who has to review daily reports containing variances related to usage of 173 materials and components, daily time variances on 27 small orders, and weekly overhead variances involving 36 accounts, or 1,436 variances per week. Screens that select or emphasize no more than 10 of the largest variances will substantially simplify this supervisor's job. Similarly, a supervisor with 60 machines operating does not have time to investigate every variation that can be identified with operations. Supervisors and managers cannot seriously consider every variance but instead must be selective and investigate only those most worth the effort.

We now present a single-period approach that explicitly considers the costs and benefits of investigation.

Cost-Benefits Investigation

We stated earlier that any approach that helps a manager decide whether to investigate a variance should consider three critical factors: the cost of investigating and correcting a problem and the benefits of correction. The **cost-benefits approach,** which looks for benefits exceeding costs, explicitly includes these critical factors. The reason for including them is simple enough. If we investigate and find nothing, we have wasted our time and money. If there is a problem but we do not investigate, we have lost the benefit from fixing the problem.

We can summarize these concepts as:

	Circumstances	
Choice	*No Fixable Problem*	*A Fixable Problem*
Investigation	Wasted investigation costs	Costs of investigating and fixing problem
No investigation	Nothing lost	Benefit lost from not fixing the problem

We can model this with the variables:

I = Cost of *I*nvestigating the variance.
F = Cost of *F*ixing a problem that is found with a process.
B = *B*enefit lost if problem is left uncorrected.
p = *P*robability that a fixable problem exists with this process.

In general, the approach indicates that we should investigate the variance when the expected benefit $(p \times B)$ is greater than the cost of investigating (I) plus the expected cost of fixing the problem $(p \times F)$:

$$p \times B > I + (p \times F)$$

For example, let us set the cost of performing an investigation at $100, the cost of fixing a problem at $500, the benefit of correcting it at $3,000, and the probability that there is a fixable problem at 20 percent. Now, applying the heuristic, we find:

$$0.2 \times \$3,000 > \$100 + (0.2 \times \$500)$$
$$\$600 > \$200$$

The expected benefit is $600 and the expected cost is $200. Therefore, we should proceed with the investigation.

Limitations of the Approach.   Although the cost-benefits approach provides some guidance in deciding whether to investigate, it is limited in practice. First, real life can be messy. In order to know the costs and benefits of a fixable problem, we need to know what that problem is. However, before we know what the problem is, we must perform an investigation. Thus, there may be one or more problems, but whether they are fixable or not, as well as the costs and benefits of fixing them, cannot be known prior to investigation. For example, assume that high employee absenteeism is observed. Without an investigation, we have little idea what the problem is, the costs of fixing the problem, or the benefits of fixing it. However, we may be able to guess, based on past experience, that there is a strong likelihood (p of about 0.8) that a fixable problem indicated by the absenteeism exists. A second limitation to the cost-benefits approach is that it requires that someone estimate the costs, the benefits, and the likelihood of fixing the problem for every variance. This is expensive and certainly not practical for small variances. Finally, the model assumes a single-time period, but real processes extend for many periods.

Usefulness of the Approach.   The cost-benefits approach is useful for accountants who are examining alternative variance-reporting systems. It is especially useful for highly repetitive processes in which the nature of the problems with the process is known. For instance, in our pack-and-fill example 60 machines are working continuously for six months per year. Each machine has a history of certain types of problems.

In selecting among variance-reporting models, the size of the variance is important. Assume that the accounting staff is considering three plausible screen sizes for a variance-reporting system: 1, 3, and 5 percent. Based on past experience, the staff has gathered the following simplified data:

	1%	*3%*	*5%*
Number of investigations	1,000	100	10
Cost per investigation	$50	$75	$100
Number of fixable problems	100	20	4
Average cost per problem fixed	$200	$600	$1,000
Average cost saving (benefit)	$500	$1,500	$3,000

The variance-reporting system costs $2,000 per time period, whichever screen is used. Notice that a smaller screen results in numerous investigations, which find many small problems. Because the problems are small, they cost less to fix and provide less benefit. The solution according to this approach involves the calculation and comparisons of totals:

	1%	*3%*	*5%*
Total cost savings expected	$ 50,000	$ 30,000	$ 12,000
Less: Cost of investigations	(50,000)	(7,500)	(1,000)
Cost of fixing problems	(20,000)	(12,000)	(4,000)
Benefit (loss)	$(20,000)	$ 10,500	$ 7,000

On the basis of this comparison, the 3 percent screen appears to be most beneficial. The $2,000 systems cost for variance reporting should be subtracted from the $10,500 highest benefit to find the value of the variance system, which is $8,500.

MULTIPLE-PERIOD APPROACHES FOR INVESTIGATING VARIANCES

The time and money required to investigate variances are limited. Every manager has experienced the frustration of investigating a variance only to find that it was the result of an unusual set of circumstances that could not have been prevented and will likely never be repeated. The investigation of variances can provide new managers a worthwhile training exercise because they will learn much about the process and the types of events that lead to variances. However, an established manager knows the processes and wants to investigate only those variances that are likely to lead to a fixable problem.

Several approaches to multiple-period analysis exist. The following section will discuss quality control charts and costs, statistical process control, "wait and see" approaches, and other miscellaneous approaches.

Investigate Quality Control Charts and Costs

The control of random production processes over multiple periods involves controlling the quality and quantities of inputs, labor, and technical processes. Quality varies to some extent. For example, the quality and size of unprocessed fruits and vegetables vary substantially from small low-grade to large premium-grade. Even for a given grade, flavor and density vary. In addition, workers vary in their ability and judgment in controlling equipment. Stable quality materials, well-trained and motivated employees, and equipment kept in good repair are necessary for a controlled process.

Set quantities are also needed to effectively control a production process. For example, one quantity that should be controlled in the packaging of food is the weight of the food in the final product. The food industry is highly regulated by state and federal agencies. Weight is a specific element that is carefully monitored. Thus, a package with less content than the label states cannot be sold without certain penalties or fines. Underweight packages must be either repackaged or disposed of. On the other hand, overweight packages involve higher costs. Food-processing lines are highly automated with only a few workers monitoring many machines. The packaging machines have various manual and computer controls to set food size and average weight. The resulting food weight is a function of the food density and the ability of the equipment to compensate for differences in the weights of food chunks.

A **quality control chart** is an approach to multiple-period variance investigation that involves charting the quantity or quality that must be controlled over a period of time and examining the resulting pattern. A perfect machine would place exactly the correct weight in every package. Because of variation in the raw material and the machine, extra material must be placed in each package to make certain that it holds the minimum weight indicated on the package. The difference between the total packaged product cost and the ideal cost of the product is attributed to the variation in the quality of the production process, an important element in total quality cost.[1]

High and low control limits can be set to determine the points at which the equipment controls should be reset or the machinery should be repaired. Thus, the machinery is assumed to be performing adequately unless the measures go outside a control limit. Control charts for various aspects of production can be automated and displayed to workers and supervisors on monitors in the production area. Exhibit 21–1 presents an example of a control chart for three pack-and-fill machines in a food-processing operation. Each control chart represents the 14 hours of production from 8 A.M. to 10 P.M. for each of the machines. The lower control limit has been set by management policy at 16 ounces, and the upper desired limit is set at 19 ounces. In Exhibit 21–1, Panel A represents machine no. 9, a moderately controllable machine that has some periods of instability that require worker intervention. In general, the machine can be kept within the control limits by the machine operator. The average weight of the packaged material is set at 17.5 ounces in order to keep all packages

---

[1] Total quality costs include all costs involved in developing quality products, maintaining quality control programs, fixing internal quality problems, and responding to quality problems after the sale of the product.

EXHIBIT 21–1   Quality Control Charts with Policy Set Limits

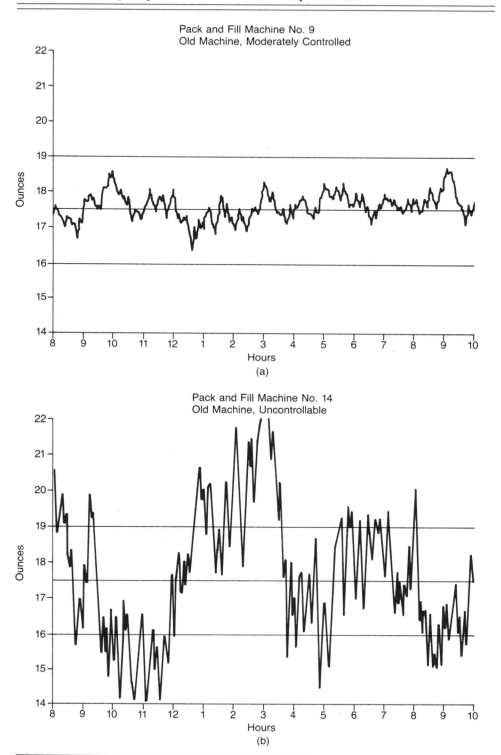

Pack and Fill Machine No. 9
Old Machine, Moderately Controlled

(a)

Pack and Fill Machine No. 14
Old Machine, Uncontrollable

(b)

EXHIBIT 21–1   *(concluded)*

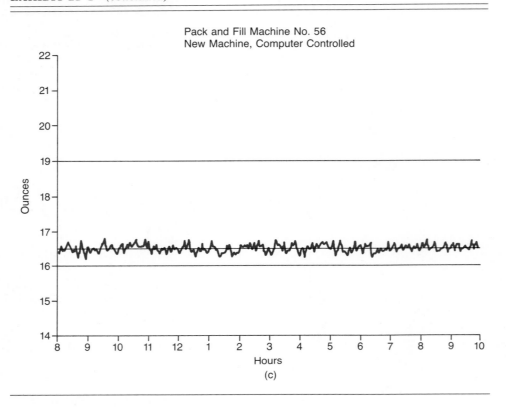

Pack and Fill Machine No. 56
New Machine, Computer Controlled

(c)

above 16 ounces. For a one-hour period, the machine produced 1,200 package of product and used 1,312.5 pounds (17.5 ounces $\times$ 1,200 packages/16 ounces per pound) of food. Thus, because of the quantity requirements, this machine must use an extra 112.5 pounds (1,312.5 $-$ 1,200) of food per hour. This extra food must be purchased, processed, frozen, warehoused, and shipped. Assume average total costs of $0.40 per pound. The hourly process quality cost for machine no. 9 is:

$$112.5 \times \$.40 = \$45 \text{ per hour}$$

For a 26-week food-processing season, this machine has process-related quality costs of $196,560:

$$\$45 \text{ per hour} \times 24 \text{ hours} \times 7 \text{ days} \times 26 \text{ weeks} = \$196,560$$

Machine no. 14 in panel B is unstable and went well outside the control limits, and the worker was unable to control it. Although the controls were constantly adjusted by the worker, the machine was unable to handle unusual material or hold its settings. For example, at about 8 A.M., the machine started overfilling the packages, and after the worker tried to adjust the machine, it started underfilling the packages at about 8:40 A.M. Another adjustment resulted in overfilling, and then from 9:30 A.M. till about 12 noon, the packages were underfilled. The worker could not pull the machine back into control. At the 4 P.M. shift change, a new worker was just barely able to pull the machine into control. The machine started having problems again at about 8 P.M. For the past month, machine no. 14 has averaged only 1,000 good packages

EXHIBIT 21–2   Table of Likelihood for a Run Due to Random Chance

Length of Run	Pr.*
1	1.0000
2	0.5000
3	0.2500
4	0.1250
5	0.0625
6	0.0313
7	0.0156
8	0.0078
9	0.0039
10	0.0020

* The exhibit should be read as the likelihood that a run this long or longer is due to chance. The run is assumed to be part of a large number of possible runs with each observation having an equal chance of being above or below the mean. Thus, no drift is assumed in the random process.

per hour using 1,283 pounds of material. This machine has process-related quality costs of $113.20 per hour [(1,283 − 1,000) × $.40], or $494,458 per season:

$113.20 per hour × 24 hours × 7 days × 26 weeks = $494,458

Illustrated in panel C of Exhibit 21–1, machine no. 56 is a newer computer-controlled machine that is very well maintained. The machine produces within the control limits with a very narrow band of variation in output weight. The average weight of the packages is 16.5 ounces, and all of the variation is between 16.3 and 16.7 ounces. The machine is fast (2,400 packages per hour) and requires 2,475 pounds of input (16.5 ounces × 2,400 packages). It uses 75 pounds of extra material per hour, which translates into $30 per hour cost (75 pounds × $0.40) and $131,040 per season.

Statistical Process Control Approaches

The **statistical process control** approach uses time-series statistics to indicate when processes are likely to be in or out of control. In the simplest form, the standard deviation is used to set control limits; the process is assumed to be in control until the process falls outside the limits. Standard practice uses either two or three standard deviations as the limits.[2]

If a process is in control, the variations should be random. As a process drifts out of control, the measures stay above or below the average for some time or show wild gyrations in the pattern. Various tests determine how many observations must be found above or below an amount before the process is considered out of control. A *run* is the term for two or more observations above or below the expected value and the length of a run is the number of variances in the run. Exhibit 21–2 presents a table of likelihood that runs of a specific number of observations are due to a random process. There is a 50–50 chance that a run with two variances in the same direction will be due to chance or indicate an out-of-control machine. However, there is only a 0.2 percent chance that a run of 10 variances in the same direction is due to chance. The average length of a run should be two for a random process that returns to the average after each trial. A computer model can be developed to highlight runs that

---

[2] One standard deviation contains about two thirds of the observations. Therefore, only one third of the variances would be investigated. Two standard deviations contain about 95 percent of the observations. Only 5 percent of the variances would be investigated. Three standard deviations cover more than 99 percent of the observations. That means less than 1 percent of the variances would be investigated.

are highly unlikely, that have less than 1 percent chance, so that the worker can adjust the machine. The computer can automatically adjust computer-integrated machines up or down, according to the direction of the run.

Various tests determine whether a time series is random or not. Some tests involve counting the number of runs above or below an expected value during a time period and then comparing this with the expected number of runs. Other tests involve counting the number of positive variances during a time period. Exhibit 21–3 presents a test that determines for a given time period whether the number of observations above the long-run average is too high (indicating an increase in the average) or too low (indicating a decrease in the average). If there are too many or too few positive variances, the machine needs adjustment. For example, assume that a machine is

EXHIBIT 21–3   Control Limits for the Number of Deviations above the Average

Production Rates per Period	Expected* above Average	Standard Deviation	95% Confidence Interval	
			Lower	Upper
10	5	1.6	1	9
20	10	2.2	5	15
30	15	2.7	9	21
40	20	3.2	14	26
50	25	3.5	18	32
60	30	3.9	22	38
70	35	4.2	27	43
80	40	4.5	31	49
90	45	4.7	36	54
100	50	5.0	40	60
200	100	7.1	86	114
300	150	8.7	133	167
400	200	10.0	180	220
500	250	11.2	228	272
600	300	12.2	276	324
700	350	13.2	324	376
800	400	14.1	372	428
900	450	15.0	421	479
1,000	500	15.8	469	531
2,000	1,000	22.4	956	1,044
3,000	1,500	27.4	1,446	1,554
4,000	2,000	31.6	1,938	2,062
5,000	2,500	35.4	2,431	2,569
6,000	3,000	38.7	2,924	3,076
7,000	3,500	41.8	3,418	3,582
8,000	4,000	44.7	3,912	4,088
9,000	4,500	47.4	4,407	4,593
10,000	5,000	50.0	4,902	5,098

* These amounts are based on a binomial distribution with $p = 0.5$. The average of such a distribution is equal to:

$$\text{Average} = np$$

where n is the number of observations. The standard deviation is equal to:

$$\text{Standard deviation} = \sqrt{np(1 - p)} = 0.25/n$$

The confidence interval for less than 100 is approximated with a t-distribution. Above 100, the distribution is approximated with a normal distribution.

operating at a rate of 100 packages for five minutes and that it has 70 packages in excess of the long-run average weight. Because 70 exceeds the tolerance limit of 60 for 100 observations, the machine should be adjusted somewhat to fill the packages less. After the adjustment, the process should be observed for another five minutes to determine whether the machine is working properly.

"Wait and See" Approaches

Some positive or negative variances are more or less likely to occur 50 percent of the time. The manager has limited information on exactly how likely these variances are. However, the manager should have some conception as to whether a specific variance may be described as occurring rarely, infrequently, half the time, frequently, or very frequently. For example, the processing of cash receipts is often done on a batch basis with hourly deposits. It is possible, with adequate procedures, to control cash very closely. Thus, missing cash should be a rare event, and any such occurrence would indicate that an investigation or correction is in order. Waiting for a second occurrence of missing cash has only a slight effect on the likelihood that a variance is random. Therefore, the manager will investigate immediately.

Exhibit 21–4 presents a line graph representing the hypothetical likelihood of variances due to the process being out of control. The numbers can be only roughly approximated by the manager, but they are useful for illustrating changes in beliefs about variances over time. The vertical axis is the likelihood that the variance indicates a fixable problem, and the horizontal axis is the number of variances that have occurred. The top line relates to the variance of cash missing.

The second line down in the exhibit is for the variance absenteeism. The first variance indicates that there may be a problem (40 percent chance), but it is more likely (60 percent chance) that it is just a random occurrence due to illness or personal problems. On the second day, the variance indicates more certainty (60 percent) that there is a problem and less certainty (40 percent) that it is a random occurrence that will reverse itself. By the fourth occurrence, the manager becomes fairly certain (roughly 95 percent) that there is a problem. Waiting longer will not change the manager's mind very much about the existence of the problem and may make the problem more expensive to fix.

The bottom line in Exhibit 21–4 relates to sales. Sales is a fairly random process, the investigation of which can be time consuming and potentially damaging. The manager knows that, if every low sales week is scrutinized in detail, the sales staff will start hiding sales orders during high sales weeks and placing them during low sales weeks. Thus, immediate investigation builds in a sales lag and unethical behavior. The observance of one low sales week indicates little (10 percent chance) likelihood of a fixable problem but high likelihood (90 percent chance) that the drop in sales is a random occurrence. The manager knows that an investigation would be wasted or harmful. However, after four weeks of low sales, the manager will be fairly sure (90 percent chance) that there is a problem. Waiting longer will be expensive because the variance now indicates that sales revenue is being lost.

Other Multiple-Period Approaches

Several additional approaches deal with the multiple-period setting. Here we consider three approaches:

1. Wait until fairly certain that the variances indicate a fixable problem.
2. Apply the single-period, cost-benefits model to the approximations and investigate when the expected benefits are large enough to merit investigation.

EXHIBIT 21–4   Likelihood Estimates by Type of Variance

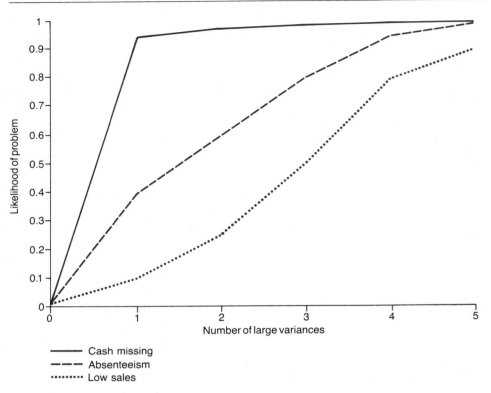

Cash missing
Absenteeism
Low sales

Basic Data

	Variances	*Cash Missing*	*Absenteeism*	*Sales*
		Likelihood Estimates		
	0	0.010	0.010	0.010
	1	0.950	0.400	0.100
	2	0.980	0.600	0.250
	3	0.990	0.800	0.500
	4	0.995	0.950	0.800
	5	0.999	0.990	0.900
	Additional Data			
Investigation cost	*(I)*	$ 8,000	$15,000	$ 75,000
Cost of fixing problem	*(F)*	50,000	30,000	200,000
Benefits from fixing	*(B)*	500,000	60,000	400,000
Dollar value of variance	*(V)*	10,000	5,000	30,000

3. Wait as long as the expected cost of investigation is greater than the expected variance that will result from waiting.

We will apply each of these heuristics to the data in Exhibit 21–4.

Wait until Certain.   Assume that the manager is fairly certain that a problem exists when the likelihood is 90 percent. Go down the likelihood column in the exhibit until the manager's likelihood estimate is equal to or higher than the required amount. This results in the following:

	Cash Missing	Absenteeism	Sales
Investigate after variance	1	4	5

This approach is easy to apply. The only estimation required is the manager's estimate of likelihood. Specifically, the costs of investigation, fixing the problem, and benefits may be unknown. However, it is assumed that the benefits are larger than the costs. No computation is required, no data are written down, and, thus, the potential overhead cost of the technique is low. If the required likelihood is set very high, the costs of investigation are low, but the cost of the variances observed is high.

Apply the Single-Period Cost-Benefits Model. Apply the standard rule of

$$p \times B > I + (p \times F)$$

and investigate when p increases to a point where

$$p > \frac{I}{(B - F)}$$

Using the approximations in Exhibit 21–4 results in the following:

		Cash Missing	Absenteeism	Sales
Investigation cost	I	$ 8,000	$15,000	$ 75,000
Cost of fixing problem	F	50,000	30,000	200,000
Benefits from fixing	B	500,000	60,000	400,000
$p = \dfrac{I}{(B-F)}$		$\dfrac{8}{(500-50)}$	$\dfrac{15}{(60-30)}$	$\dfrac{75}{(400-200)}$
Threshold likelihood		0.02	0.50	0.38

Go down the likelihood column until the manager's likelihood estimate is higher than the required amount. The results of this will be:

	Cash Missing	Absenteeism	Sales
Investigate after variance	1	2	2

This approach generally results in more investigations and fewer variances than the first approach. The major drawback is that data must be approximated for investigating, fixing, and the benefits to be achieved from fixing a problem.

Wait until Cost of Investigation Exceeds Variance. The general approach is:

$$(1 - p) \times I > p \times V$$

Where V is the dollar equivalent value of the variance. Solving for p results in:

$$p > \frac{I}{(I + V)}$$

This approach is applied to Exhibit 21–4 data:

		Cash Missing	Absenteeism	Sales
Investigation cost	I	$ 8,000	$15,000	$75,000
Variance	V	10,000	5,000	30,000
$p = \dfrac{I}{(I+V)}$		$\dfrac{8}{(8+10)}$	$\dfrac{15}{(15+5)}$	$\dfrac{75}{(75+30)}$
Threshold likelihood		0.444	0.750	0.714

The results of applying these threshold likelihoods are:

	Cash Missing	Absenteeism	Sales
Investigate after variance	1	3	4

This approach requires the estimation of investigation and variance costs. The specific amounts for benefits and fixing costs need not be known. It is assumed that the benefits are greater than the costs of investigating and fixing the problem. This approach will result in fewer investigations and more variances than the second approach.

SUMMARY

The decision to investigate a variance may be based on single-period approaches (investigate every variance, only large variances, or costs-benefits) or on multiple period approaches (use quality control charts and costs, time-series statistics, the wait until certain, the single-period cost-benefits, or the wait until investigation cost exceeds variance cost). Investigating every variance makes sense for those processes that are (or can be) closely controlled. For processes with many variances and some random elements, investigating large variances rather than every variance is appropriate. The single-period, cost-benefits approach bases the decision on those that have an expected benefit greater than the costs of investigating and fixing the problem. Although conceptually correct, the single-period, cost-benefits approach is difficult to apply in practice because it requires that the benefits and costs be estimated before the nature and extent of the problem are known. Also, the approach is single-period in nature.

The multiple-period approaches to investigating variances allow the manager to have more information about the process and change likelihood estimates as variances are observed. Quality control charts are useful for investigating production processes that involve mass production. Three multiple-period approaches and their strengths and weaknesses were also presented.

PROBLEMS FOR REVIEW
PROBLEM A

Bakersfield Refinery currently sells three grades of unleaded gasoline: regular, medium, and premium. The medium and premium grades differ in the quantity of a blending agent that increases the octane rating. The amount of blending agent added to unleaded gasoline to make medium and premium grades is controlled by a valve that releases the blending agent at the end of the refining process. The problem the company can have in the medium-grade process is that a malfunctioning valve can turn a batch into premium unleaded instead of medium unleaded. The market is not as good for the premium as for the medium; therefore, it is hard to sell any unintended premium quantities. Experience indicates that when additional quantities of premium occur, the refinery cannot sell them for more than the medium-grade unleaded. Consequently, the cost of the extra blending agent is lost. Once the blending process has started, it must continue until 100,000 gallons of fuel have been processed.

Cost data for the medium-grade process are as follows:

Cost per gallon of the unleaded fuel	$0.80
Cost per gallon if proper amount of blending agent is added	$0.05
Cost per gallon if higher amount of blending agent, resulting in premium grade	$0.12
Cost of checking the valve	$1,200
Cost of adjusting valve	$600

Data from past experience indicate that the valve is in adjustment 70 percent of the time. Hence, the probability that the valve is out of adjustment is 30 percent.

a. Given a variance in the fuel, should the refinery investigate the valve? Show computations to support your answer.
b. At which probability would the refinery be indifferent about whether to investigate?
c. Assuming the original probabilities, at which cost of checking the valve would the refinery be indifferent about whether to investigate?

Before addressing the requirements to the problem, it is necessary to quantify the variables:

I = Cost of investigating the variance
  = $1,200
F = Cost of adjusting the valve if it is not adjusted properly
  = $600
B = Benefit lost if problem is left uncorrected
  = (100,000 gallons at $0.12) − (100,000 gallons at $0.05)
  = $12,000 − $5,000 = $7,000
p = Probability that a fixable problem exists with this process
  = 30 percent or .30

a. We now apply $p \times B > I + (p \times F)$

$$0.30 \times \$7,000 > \$1,200 + (0.30 \times \$600) \rightarrow \$2,100 > \$1,380$$

b. The indifference point occurs by finding the p value that makes the following equality true: $p \times B = I + (p \times F)$. We can solve for p and get: $p = I/(B - F)$. Therefore,

$$p = \$1,200/(\$7,000 - \$600) = \$1,200/\$6,400 = 18.8\%.$$

c. The indifference point occurs by finding the I value that makes the following equality true: $p \times B = I + (p \times F)$. We solve for I and get: $I = (p \times B) - (p \times F)$. Therefore,

$$I = (0.30 \times \$7,000) - (0.30 \times \$600) = \$2,100 - \$180$$
$$= \$1,920.$$

PROBLEM FOR REVIEW PROBLEM B

Scott Andresen is manager of the Grinding Department for Fowler Fabrication Company. In last week's production reports, he noticed an unfavorable labor efficiency variance (V) of $2,000. The cost to investigate (I) the variance is $800. The cost to correct (F) the process if it is out of control is estimated at $1,000. The estimated benefit (B) from fixing the variance is savings of $30,000. Scott does not want to investigate every variance unless he believes he is justified in doing so. He has estimated the likelihood of the process being out of control as follows:

Number of Variances	Likelihood Estimate
–0–	0.01
1	0.15
2	0.40
3	0.70
4	0.95
5	0.99

REQUIRED

Help Scott Andresen decide when to investigate by calculating the following:

a. Where the value of p is high enough to make the benefits of investigation worthwhile.

b. Where the value of p is high enough to suggest that the expected cost plus the expected variance make investigation worthwhile.

SOLUTION

a. Expected benefits are sufficiently large.

Investigation cost (I)	\$ 800
Cost of fixing problem (F)	1,000
Benefits from fixing (B)	30,000
$p = I/(B - F)$	\$800/(\$30,000 − \$1,000)
Threshold likelihood	0.028

Conclusion: Investigate with every variance.

b. Costs of investigation and variance make investigation worthwhile.

Investigation cost (I)	\$ 800
Variance (V)	2,000
$p = I/(I + V)$	\$800/(\$800 + \$2,000)
Threshold likelihood	0.286

Conclusion: Investigate when the second variance occurs.

KEY TERMS AND CONCEPTS

Fixable problem (816)   Cost-benefits approach (818)
Unfixable problem (816)   Quality control charts (820)
Screen (817)   Statistical process control (823)

ADDITIONAL READINGS

Dittman, David, and Prem Prakash. "Cost Variance Investigation: Markovian Control Versus Optimal Control." *The Accounting Review*, April, 1979, pp. 358–73.

Duvall, Richard M. "Rules for Investigating Cost Variances." *Management Science*, June, 1967, pp. 631–641.

Howell, Robert A., and Stephen R. Soucy. "Operating Controls in the New Manufacturing Environment." *Management Accounting*, October, 1987, pp. 25–31.

Jensen, R. E., and C. T. Thomas. "Statistical Analysis in Cost Measurement and Control." *The Accounting Review*, January, 1968, pp. 83–93.

Kackar, R. N. "Off-Line Quality Control, Parameter Design, and the Taguchi Method." *Journal of Quality Technology*, October, 1985, pp. 176–88.

Kaplan, Robert S. "The Significance and Investigation of Cost Variances: Survey and Extensions." *Journal of Accounting Research*, Autumn, 1975, pp. 311–37.

Wheelwright, Steven C., and W. Earl Sasser, Jr. "The New Product Development Map." *Harvard Business Review*, May–June 1989, pp. 112–27.

REVIEW QUESTIONS

1. Why is a variance not always an indication of a fixable problem?
2. What distinguishes a fixable problem from one that cannot be fixed at any cost?
3. In what circumstances is investigating all variances appropriate?
4. In what circumstances is investigating only large variances appropriate?
5. What is the formula for the single-period, cost-benefits approach for the decision on variance investigation?

6. What are two practical limitations to using the single-period, cost-benefits approach?
7. List the three approaches for investigating multiple-period variances.

DISCUSSION QUESTIONS

8. What is the relationship between each of the limitations to managers' perception of variances and the practical application of the single-period, cost-benefits approach?
9. What relationships are there between the attitudes and behavior of lower-level personnel and the approach taken by management in the investigation of variances? Why does this occur?
10. In what ways can the investigation of every variance help in a company's search for excellence? In what ways might it be harmful?
11. In what ways might investigating only unfavorable variances influence the attitudes and behavior of subordinates?
12. In what ways might investigating only large variances influence the attitudes and behavior of subordinates?
13. How can we know the benefits of fixing a problem and how much it will cost to fix it before we know what the problem is?
14. How can we know the likelihood of a fixable problem and the cost of performing the investigation before we investigate?

EXERCISES

21–1. Estimating Investigation Cost.   The County Welfare Department for Harris County is responsible for handling applications for those who apply for county support payments and medical care. Investigation of support payments requires eight hours of a case worker's time, 30 miles of driving and $3 in materials. Investigation of an application for medical services requires four hours of time, 20 miles of driving, and $2 in materials. Case workers are paid $1,500 per month plus 30 percent of salary in benefits. Mileage is reimbursed at a rate of $0.25 per mile. Each investigator has office space that costs $150 per month. An investigator is scheduled for 150 hours of work per month.

REQUIRED:
a. Estimate the cost of investigating a support payment case.
b. Estimate the cost of investigating a medical services case.

21–2. Single-Period Variance Investigation Decision.   Given the following data for the Rendell Co. for the week ending July 12, 19x9:

	Symbol	*Sales Volume*	*Late Delivery*
Investigation cost	*I*	$4,000	$ 3,000
Fixing cost	*F*	1,000	6,000
Benefit lost	*B*	8,000	18,000
Probability of problem	*p*	40%	70%

REQUIRED:
a. Should the sales volume variance be investigated?
b. Should the late delivery variance be investigated?

21–3. Single-Period Variance Investigation Decision.   The state tax authority processes monthly sales tax returns for the 48,320 businesses in the state. The decision to investigate a return is up to the Compliance Office. In regard to sales tax license 140222, Consolidated Cleaners, Inc., the compliance officer makes the following estimates:

	Symbol	*No. 140222*
Investigation cost (10 days at $480)	I	$ 4,800
Cost of tax refiling/correction	F	$ 180
Expected underpayment of taxes + penalties	B	$16,000
Probability of underpayment	p	40%

REQUIRED:
Is this sales tax return worth investigating? Explain.

21–4. Control Limits.   Carl Elkins, controller of Utah Valley Metal Works, Inc., established a good statistical correlation between the cost of fuel used and the weight of metal charged in the furnaces. A regression line has been computed for various weights, and the standard error of the estimate was computed as $180. The data for this statistical analysis are as follows:

Weight (in tons)	*Projected Fuel Costs*
50	$ 600
60	690
70	780
80	870
90	960
100	1,050
110	1,140
120	1,230

REQUIRED:
a. Establish the control limit for fuel cost at each weight, assuming the company uses plus or minus one standard error of the estimate as the limit.
b. If the actual cost at 110 tons turns out to be $1,380, should the variance be investigated? Explain.
c. If the actual cost at 90 tons was $1,140, should the variance be investigated? Explain.

21–5. Control Limits.   Lionel Chavez, supervisor of the repair and maintenance department at Spanish Designs Company, has found that the cost to investigate a variance from a projected average cost is relatively high, and he is reluctant to investigate unless there is a strong probability that the variance is not due to random factors. The projected average cost is based on a regression line developed from data that had a standard error of the estimate of $145. Lionel believes he can use this information to develop a system to indicate when to investigate variances.

The following data on repair and maintenance costs and production hours are given for a 12-week period. The data include the hours of operations, the projected average cost, and the actual cost.

Hours of Operation	*Projected Average Cost*	*Actual Costs*
800	$4,200	$4,200
1,000	5,000	5,200
1,500	7,000	5,200
1,200	5,800	5,900
900	4,600	4,400
1,800	8,200	8,400
2,000	9,000	9,300
1,400	6,600	6,500
1,700	7,800	7,700
1,600	7,400	7,600
1,300	6,200	6,200
1,100	5,400	5,500

REQUIRED:

a. Calculate the control limits for each level of operation assuming one standard error is the limit. Which variances would be investigated under this rule?
b. Calculate the control limits for each level of operation assuming two standard errors is the limit. Which variances would be investigated under this rule?
c. Calculate the control limits for each level of operation assuming three standard errors is the limit. Which variances would be investigated under this rule?
d. Comment on what happens as the control limits are increased.

21–6. Identifying Patterns.   Refer to the data in Exercise 21–5. Plot the data on a graph so that a visual pattern can be viewed.

REQUIRED:

a. Describe what you think is happening in the process. Is it in or out of control? Explain.
b. How many runs can you identify? What do they signify?

PROBLEMS

21–7. Multiple-Period Variance Investigation.   The plant manager for PLC, Inc., has the following estimates of likelihood that consecutive unfavorable variances in product quality are due to a problem that can be fixed:

Consecutive Variances	Likelihood Estimate	Described by the Plant Manager as
0	0.05	"Remote."
1	0.25	"Might find a fixable problem."
2	0.50	"About half the time we will find a fixable problem."
3	0.75	"Likely that a fixable problem can be found."
4	0.95	"We are confident that we have a problem with quality."

Additional data available based on past averages:

Cost of investigating product quality	I	$ 5,000
Cost of fixing product quality problems	F	$ 2,000
Benefits from fixing product quality problem	B	$10,000
Average cost per variance	V	$ 800

Assume the following in the analysis:

1. The costs and benefits are independent of the size of the product quality variance and the number of variances that have occurred.
2. The likelihood estimates are independent of the size of the product quality variance.

REQUIRED:

How long will the manager wait under each of the following independent decision approaches?
a. The manager waits until he is fairly certain that there is a quality problem before investigation occurs.
b. The manager waits until the expected benefits are greater than the expected costs of the investigation.
c. The manager waits as long as the expected cost from useless investigations are greater than the expected variance.

21–8. Likelihood, Costs, and Benefits of Variance Investigation.   Consumer Affairs Department of ISC International, Ltd., has investigated every customer complaint for the past two years. The following summary has been reported to senior management:

	Product Line	
	Cosmetics	*Hair Dryer*
Valid complaint with product:		
Product quality	12,208	5,194
Verified allergic reaction	3,052	
Invalid complaint, nothing wrong with product:		
Misunderstanding of product feature	38,659	3,246
Needs help using product	10,173	1,082
Just felt like complaining	12,208	1,298
Total complaints received	76,300	10,820

If a complaint is not investigated, the customer is given a certificate to receive another product of equal value. If a complaint is investigated and found to be invalid, the customer must be notified by letter or telephone in a very diplomatic manner so that future sales are not lost.

REQUIRED:
a. For each of the products, estimate the likelihood that a customer complaint received is invalid.
b. In concept, what are the costs of fixing invalid complaints that have been found?
c. In concept, what are the benefits of finding and fixing invalid complaints?

21–9. Estimating Costs for Investigation.   Paul Hardt is executive director of the National Hobby Association, a nonprofit, educational association. The association currently has about 100,000 members, but membership has declined during the past two years by about 5,000 per year. This drop occurred in spite of gaining 3,000 new members per year. Prior to two years ago, the association had always increased in membership. Each member pays $20 in dues, and the variable cost of having a member is $10 for the quarterly journal and administrative costs.

Mr. Hardt is considering three methods for investigating the drop in membership with related expected response rates:

Method	*Response Rate*
1. Personalized letter to former members for past two years with a questionnaire and return envelope.	40%
2. Form letter to former members for past two years with a questionnaire and return envelope.	20%
3. Journal insert to all existing members with questionnaire and return envelope.	15%

Additional Data

	Investigation Method		
	1	*2*	*3*
Cost of developing and testing the questionnaire	$ 500	$ 500	$ 800
Costs per survey:			
Letter	0.35	0.04	
Questionnaire	0.15	0.15	0.15
Envelope going out with address	0.05	0.12	
Business reply envelope	0.03	0.03	0.03
Postage going out	0.12	0.11	
Total	$0.75	$0.45	$0.18
Postage on return	$0.40	$0.40	$0.40
Processing of returns	0.80	0.80	0.80
Cost of returned questionnaires	$1.20	$1.20	$1.20

REQUIRED:
a. How many members quit the association for each of the past two years?
b. Compute the expected total cost for the first method of investigating the drop in membership.
c. Compute the expected total cost for the second method of investigating the drop in membership.
d. Compute the expected total cost for the third method for investigating the drop in membership.

21–10. Estimating the Costs of Investigating Variances.   Laute Works produces lamp shades of various styles and sizes in a highly automated plant. Among the 528 products is the A–100 series of small shades for desk lamps. Data on production and units rejected for the week ending April 5, 19x2, are:

Product	Unit Production	Rejections	Rejection Rate	Number of Rejections > 4%	Number of Rejections > 8%
A–100	5,004	252	5.0%	52	–0–
A–110	7,610	265	3.5%	–0–	–0–
A–120	9,795	229	2.3%	–0–	–0–
A–130	819	158	19.3%	126	93
A–140	5,997	129	2.2%	–0–	–0–
A–150	5,348	214	4.0%	–0–	–0–
A–160	6,509	250	3.8%	–0–	–0–
A–170	2,590	339	13.1%	236	132
A–180	4,328	344	7.9%	171	–0–
Total	48,000	2,180		585	225

Laute Works management estimates that the cost of investing rejections for a product is $35 plus $1 per rejection investigated.

REQUIRED:
a. Estimate the cost of investigation of variances for each of the following screens:
   1. Investigate all rejections.
   2. Investigate only those rejections that are more than 4 percent of production.
   3. Investigate only those rejections that are more than 8 percent of production.
b. The variable cost of producing each of the shades is about $2 per unit. Assume that fixing a problem reduces the rejection rate to 4 percent for up to 10 weeks. For each of the products, compute the expected benefit from the reduction of rejections from the current rate.
c. The cost of fixing the production process increases with the size of the problem. Management estimates that it costs $200 plus $3 per rejection above 4 percent to fix problems that have been discovered. For each of the products, estimate the cost of fixing problems with the production.

21–11. Investigating Large Variances.   Ginder Products Corp. has the following sales revenues, unit sales, and average selling prices for the 13 weeks ending March 30, 19x9:

Week	Revenues	Units Sold	Average Price
1	$22,995	2,190	$10.50
2	19,448	1,700	11.44
3	20,631	2,300	8.97
4	21,979	2,280	9.64
5	20,157	2,270	8.88
6	22,003	2,170	10.14
7	20,102	2,150	9.35
8	15,098	1,770	8.53
9	24,388	2,290	10.65
10	18,271	1,950	9.37
11	18,218	1,690	10.78
12	15,325	1,780	8.61
13	22,841	2,190	10.43
	$261,456		
Averages	$ 20,112	2,056	$ 9.79

The budgeted revenue is $20,000 per week with an average selling price of $10 per unit and 2,000 units sold.

REQUIRED:

Management desires to investigate variances in revenues, volumes, and prices when they are large. Using each of the following approaches, during which weeks should management investigate the variance?

a. Management desires to investigate revenues when they are more than 10 percent above or more than 5 percent below budget.

b. Management desires to investigate all variances in revenues that are more than $2,200.

c. Management desires to investigate when volume or price is more than 10 percent below planned amounts.

d. Management desires to investigate when both volume and prices are more than 10 percent below expected.

21–12. Single-Period Variance Investigation Decision.   The managers of Conover, Inc., are considering whether to stop production of their candy and investigate for potential problems. Based on past experience and the variances presented, the managers estimate that there is a 40 percent chance of a problem with the production line. However, in the past, only half of the problems could be solved, and the remainder were due to difficulties that could not be changed. Stopping the production process will result in $100,000 in spoilage cost, $100,000 in lost contribution from candy not produced, and $50,000 in start-up costs. It will cost $100,000 to perform the detailed investigation required. If a correctable problem can be found, it will cost about $500,000 to correct the production process. However, if the problem can be fixed, $2,000,000 in benefits is expected.

REQUIRED:

a. Using the single-period cost-benefits approach, compute the expected net benefit (loss) from the decision to investigate.

b. Should management investigate the candy production line?

c. Now assume that there is a 5 percent chance of a major problem with the candy line that could result in food poisoning after consumption of the candy. Food poisoning will result in closing the line by regulators and changes involving $20 million in costs and lost contribution. How would this affect your analysis in parts (a) and (b)?

21–13. Single-Period Costs and Benefits.   Vince Johannesen is the vice president in charge of equipment maintenance for Big C Airlines. Aircraft maintenance is a critical function in providing for passenger safety. Regulations require standard maintenance of all systems every 100 flying hours and complete overhaul of motors, pumps, and hydraulics every 1,000 flying hours. Careful analysis of the wind surfaces for cracks and warpage is done at the 1,000-hour checkup.

The maintenance vice president has a report from a pilot that plane 3682 is handling "funny" on landing and takeoff. (The plane banked left 5 degrees on takeoff, but all other gauges read normal.) The variance was most likely caused by an unregistered wind gust in which case nothing is wrong with the aircraft. In checking the maintenance file, the codes indicate that 3682 is five years old, has 880 flying hours since its last complete overhaul and 80 hours since its last routine maintenance. Mr. Johannesen has the option to:

1. Leave the plane in service for 20 more hours until normal maintenance.
2. Have routine maintenance performed on the plane at a cost of $40,000.
3. Have a complete overhaul performed at a cost of $1,400,000.

Maintenance cost is $18 million over budget for the month to date, and Mr. Johannesen is evaluated on the basis of controlling maintenance costs and of the safety record. The nature of the problems, likelihood of occurrence during 20 hours given the pilot's statement, cost for a one-time repair, and savings on occurrence from repair are:

In-Flight Problem	*Likelihood*	*Cost to Repair (millions)*	*Savings (millions)*
Structural warpage	2%	$2.50	$ 0.20
Left engine failure	3%	0.30	1.00
Fuel balance off	1%	0.10	0.10
Hydraulic failure	1%	0.40	580.00

The first three in-flight problems are unlikely to cause a crash, but they could complicate flight and landing. Warpage and fuel balance can be adjusted by the pilot, but they are an inconvenience and increase fuel usage. It is possible that engine failure on takeoff could cause a serious situation, but the likelihood is extremely remote because the plane has three engines. On the other hand, the hydraulic system controls all surfaces, and if it fails during operation, the aircraft is at risk of an uncontrolled crash landing. The benefits from not crashing are substantial: about $240 million in payments to heirs of crash victims plus the $40 million cost of the plane, plus about $300 million in lost contribution due to the publicity. There is a 100 percent chance that all of these problems will be found on a complete overhaul. Although the 100-hour maintenance will certainly catch the first three problems, maintenance has only an 80 percent chance of finding the hydraulic problem.

Mr. Johannesen asks you, as an assistant controller, to prepare for him an analysis of the economics of this situation to provide input into his final decision.

REQUIRED:
The variance in this circumstance is the report by the pilot. Apply the single-period, cost-benefits approach to this problem treating both the 100- and the 1,000-hour maintenance as two methods of investigating the variance.
a. For each of the in-flight problems, indicate whether the problem should be fixed if it were known to exist.
b. Estimate the expected benefits and costs for the 100-hour maintenance. Accumulate the expected benefit across the in-flight problems that will be fixed if they are discovered.
c. Estimate the expected benefits and costs for the 1,000-mile overhaul. Accumulate the expected benefit across the in-flight problems that will be fixed if they are discovered.
d. Comment on the effect the fact that Mr. Johannesen and other senior managers dislike risk very much might have on the choice between the 100-hour maintenance and the 1,000-hour overhaul.

21–14. Estimating Parameters for a Single-Period Model.   Jill Dvorcak is the plant controller for Yellowhouse Motor Company. The plant manufactures electric motors in sizes from 1/3 to 5 horsepower. During the past two years, Ms. Dvorcak has collected data on the benefits and costs of investigating variances in materials handling costs. During the two-year period, there were 15 investigations with the following variances, costs, and benefits from cost savings:

Investigation ID	Materials Handling Variance	Investigation Cost (I)	Fixable Problem (1 = Yes)	Cost of Fixing (F)	Benefit Cost Saving (B)
1	$ 16,694	$ 4,755	1	$ 20,070	$ 97,264
2	11,781	3,961	1	13,318	52,126
3	10,262	4,012	–0–		
4	40,603	7,241	1	35,971	250,442
5	15,906	5,067	–0–		
6	8,646	3,489	–0–		
7	11,717	4,260	1	19,673	102,400
8	39,379	7,119	1	34,498	274,872
9	50,880	8,333	1	37,974	292,000
10	5,129	3,434	–0–		
11	17,569	4,710	1	16,071	135,322
12	5,856	4,072	1	17,834	4,812
13	19,804	5,067	1	24,178	135,202
14	18,865	5,371	–0–		
15	27,859	5,673	1	26,297	180,236
Totals	$300,950	$76,564	10	$245,884	$1,524,676
Averages	$ 20,063	$ 5,104		$ 24,588	$ 152,468

Ms. Dvorcak notices that smaller variances tend to result in fewer fixable problems and that the costs and benefits are less. Likewise, large variances are more likely to indicate a fixable problem and the costs of investigation, fixing the problem, and cost savings are all larger.

REQUIRED:

a. The likelihood, p, of a fixable problem may be estimated by dividing the number of fixable problems by the number of investigations. Estimate the likelihood that there is a fixable problem for a variance:
1. Less than $20,000.
2. Greater than $20,000.

b. Ms. Dvorcak estimated the cost of investigating (I) as a function of the variance size and found:

Regression Output

Constant	$3,015
Standard error of Y estimated	$258
R^2	97.05%
Number of observations	15
Degrees of freedom	13

X coefficient(s)	$0.10414
Standard error of coefficient	$0.00503
t-statistic	20.7

Using this analysis, estimate the cost of investigating:
1. A $15,000 variance in materials handling costs.
2. A $40,000 variance in materials handling costs.

c. For the 10 investigations that resulted in finding a fixable problem, Ms. Dvorcak estimated the cost of fixing the problem, F, as a function of the variance size with a regression, and found:

Regression Output

Constant	$10,992
Standard error of Y estimated	$3,001
R^2	89.71%
Number of observations	10
Degrees of freedom	8

X coefficient(s)	$0.56153
Standard error of coefficient	$0.06725
t-statistic	8.3

Using this analysis, estimate the cost of fixing a problem, given that a fixable problem has been found, associated with:
1. A $15,000 variance in materials handling costs.
2. A $40,000 variance in materials handling costs.

d. For the 10 investigations that resulted in finding a fixable problem, Ms. Dvorcak estimated the cost savings or benefits, *B*, as a function of the variance size with a regression and found:

Regression Output

Constant	$762
Standard error of Y estimated	$24,222
R^2	94.33%
Number of observations	10
Degrees of freedom	8

X coefficient(s)	$6.26515
Standard error of coefficient	$0.54285
t-statistic	11.5

Using this analysis, estimate the cost savings, given that a fixable problem has been found, associated with:
1. A $15,000 variance in materials handling costs.
2. A $40,000 variance in materials handling costs.

e. Estimate the expected benefit and expected total cost from investigating:
1. A $15,000 variance in materials handling costs.
2. A $40,000 variance in materials handling costs.

f. Is a $3,000 variance worth investigating?

g. At what variance level would the company be indifferent as to investigating? (At this level, the expected benefit will equal the expected cost.)

21–15. Estimating Benefits and Costs from Investigating Variances.   Lifetime, Inc., photographs and prints elementary school pictures in the New England states. During a normal year, the company photographs 8 million children with half of them purchasing prints. The average print revenue is $12 per sale for an average of 18 prints. Production costs are expected to average $0.10 per print, and handling costs are $1 per order. The cost of the sitting is expected to be about $0.50 per student, including a daily wage of $75 for photographers. Photographers are also paid a commission of 3 percent of revenues.

Not all photographers are equally capable, nor are they consistently capable of taking a high-quality child's photograph. Technical skill is important, but personality, charm, and tact are also needed. The quality of the photographer's work can result in a sales rate as low as 20 percent or as high as 70 percent with an acceptable level of 50 percent. A photographer will do one school per day (about 750 children) with excellent work resulting in at least a 60 percent sales rate and revenues of $6,300 with 20 prints per sale. A photographer having a poor day (or a poor photographer) will result in sales to 150 students with revenues of $1,500. It is critical that Lifetime, Inc., find out early who needs help and who should be terminated.

The company keeps 400 photographers on staff with about 10 percent turnover per year. For the 19x8–x9 school year, 40 new photographers were hired. Listed below are basic data for 10 of the new hires for the month of September 19x8:

Employee ID	Schools Visited	Students Sittings	Number of Sales	Sales Rate	Revenues	Revenue per Sale
2209	18	17,393	12,090	69.5%	$130,858	$10.82
2210	17	8,750	3,415	39.0%	44,931	13.16
2211	18	15,346	10,004	65.2%	126,299	12.62
2212	17	15,819	7,988	50.5%	96,300	12.06
2213	18	14,888	3,320	22.3%	46,125	13.89
2214	17	15,879	8,579	54.0%	103,120	12.02
2215	20	16,821	6,685	39.7%	71,036	10.63
2216	18	12,423	9,092	73.2%	114,014	12.54
2217	17	12,506	7,472	59.4%	100,440	13.52
2218	17	6,260	2,872	45.9%	34,407	11.98
Totals	177	136,085	71,472	52.5%	$867,529	$12.14

The home office schedules the school visits, and the photographer has no control over the number of students in each school. There is wide variation in school size. Only those photographers who have attained the expected revenue performance for the year will be retained for the following school year.

REQUIRED:

a. The investigation of a variance in a photographer's revenues requires the skills of an excellent photographer. This results in the loss of two days' work for the excellent photographer who must be paid expenses of about $100 plus regular salary and commission. Compute an estimate of the cost of investigating a revenue variance for one new photographer. (Include the impact of the lost contribution of the sales of the excellent photographer.)

b. About 70 percent of the time, the excellent photographer decides that the new photographer cannot be helped because of personal characteristics. The other 30 percent of the time, the excellent photographer can spend about four days working with the person and as a result bring him or her up to the expected level of sales per sitting (50 percent rate with $12 revenue per sale). Estimate the cost of fixing the problem with revenues for a new photographer.

c. Dana Clariss, senior marketing manager, judges that six months' expected activity (October through March) should be used to compute the expected benefit from having an excellent photographer work with a poor one. For each of the new photographers who are below expectations on sales rate or revenue per sale, estimate the benefits from correcting the problem. During the six months, assume that each photographer will be at 18 schools per month with an average of 750 student sittings per school.

d. For each of the new photographers who are below expectations on sales rate or revenue per sale, compute the expected benefits. Which new photographers should be investigated?

EXTENDED
APPLICATIONS

21–16. Designing a Variance Decision System, Selecting a Screen.   L-Mack Department Stores, Inc., has 240 department stores located in the Western region. The company has 4 million active charge accounts, which are billed monthly. These accounts have an average of three purchases per month and an average balance of $200. During the month, there is an average of 150,000 data entry errors to the accounts of which 98 percent are detected and corrected by automatic controls included in the applications programs.

For a retail department store, charge accounts are an important part of the service, and errors should be kept to a minimum. The basic nature of some errors, for example amounts billed to the wrong account or errors corrected improperly, cannot be found by the computer system and can be found only by chance or by customer complaint. When a customer complains about a billing error, L-Mack has two options:

1. Adjust the account balance down immediately by the amount of the complaint and lose the revenue (operating income).
2. Investigate the billing complaint in detail and adjust the account balance only if the complaint is valid. L-Mack has to bear the cost of investigating complaints and responding to customers.

L-Mack has about 3,000 billing errors per month that escape the system. Of these errors, 40 percent, or 1,200, result in complaints from customers. Most of the remaining errors are in favor of the customer and rarely involve complaints. Customers file an additional 4,800 billing complaints that are mostly related to the customer's arithmetic, oversight, lack of communication between spouses, poor memory, and occasionally to cranks or fraud. Thus, of the average 6,000 complaints received per month, only 20 percent relate to a valid error on the part of the billing system. If all of the complaints are investigated, many of the invalid complaints will be discovered and corrected with the customer. On the other hand, if only large complaints are investigated, many small invalid reductions in account balances will occur each month. Some future revenue and contribution will be lost as the result of each investigation because customers do not like to be questioned. Thus, the benefit of the investigation is in the savings related to not reducing customer account balances for invalid complaints. The cost of fixing an invalid complaint includes the cost of responding to the customer and the expected loss of future contribution from the loss of the customer. When the monthly complaints are analyzed by size and validity, the following results are found (on average):

	Size of Complaint			
	< $10	$10 to $99	> $100	Totals
Valid	1,000	120	80	1,200
Invalid	3,000	1,380	420	4,800
Total	4,000	1,500	500	6,000
Average cost	$7.00	$44.00	$148.00	$28.00
Total cost	$28,000	$66,000	$74,000	$168,000

Below are data related to three suggested screen sizes for the investigation of billing complaints on a per month basis:

	Screen size		
	I	II	III
Investigate billing complaints	> $0	> $10	> $100
Number of investigations	6,000	2,000	500
Cost per investigation	$10	$15	$20
Invalid complaints discovered	2,400	1,400	400
Average cost per invalidation	$6	$6	$6
Future contribution lost per invalidation	$10	$17	$31
Average size of the complaint investigated	$28	$70	$148

REQUIRED:
a. If all complaints are investigated (screen I),
   1. What is the likelihood that an investigated complaint will be found invalid?
   2. How much investigation cost per month should be planned?
   3. How much cost should be planned for responding to customers with invalid complaints?
   4. How much future contribution is expected to be lost?
b. If only complaints greater than $10 are investigated (screen II),
   1. What is the likelihood that an investigated complaint will be found invalid?
   2. How much investigation cost per month should be planned?
   3. How much cost should be planned for responding to customers with invalid complaints?
   4. How much future contribution is expected to be lost?
c. If only complaints greater than $100 are investigated (screen III),
   1. What is the likelihood that an investigated complaint will be found invalid?

2. How much investigation cost per month should be planned?
3. How much cost should be planned for responding to customers with invalid complaints?
4. How much future contribution is expected to be lost?

d. Assuming that the fixed budgeted costs for investigating billing errors are $2,000 per month, prepare an analysis of the three proposed screens for billing system error investigation.

21–17. Multiple-Period Costs and Benefits Analysis.   VBS, Inc., is a television network with 80 affiliated stations. Television networks earn revenue by selling national advertising and by receiving a share of local advertising. The price for advertising depends primarily on the number and type of viewer audience. Thus, it is critical that each of the 80 affiliated stations maintain and develop as large a viewer base as possible.

The development of cable television networks has substantially increased the competition for audience, and the general networks are doing their best to compete. Variation in audience share is normal from week to week. The quality of local programming, primarily local news and sports, influences audience share. In addition, audience share can be affected by local entertainment and events outside the control of the affiliate.

The investigation of drops in local affiliate market shares can be carried out with the following approaches:

1. *Staff Study.* This type of study involves analysis of the local station through reports submitted on topics such as population changes and through tapes from the local stations and competitors. This study usually involves two weeks of staff study by two to five people along with a mail survey of viewers in the market.
2. *National, on-Site Study.* With this approach, a team of up to eight people is sent from the national studios to study local operations and markets. The study takes 5 to 10 days and involves intensive interviews of audience, employees, managers, and local sponsors. The local competition is also studied intensely.
3. *Consulting-Firm Study.* This in-depth investigation is performed by a major independent consulting firm on television marketing. It requires up to two months' effort by as many as 15 people.

Senior management has different levels of confidence that an investigation will find local problems to correct. A large part of the judgment involving the effectiveness of the investigation depends upon the size and the number of weeks of the audience drop.

Cost to investigate. The cost to investigate depends upon the proportion of the drop, the size of the market, and the type of investigation:

$$\text{Type 1} = \$2,000 + \$30,000 \times (\text{Drop} \times \text{Weeks}) + \$0.01 \times \text{Size}$$
$$\text{Type 2} = \$10,000 + \$60,000 \times (\text{Drop} \times \text{Weeks}) + \$0.04 \times \text{Size}$$
$$\text{Type 3} = \$50,000 + \$90,000 \times (\text{Drop} \times \text{Weeks}) + \$0.02 \times \text{Size}$$

where
Drop = Proportion from 0 to 1.
Weeks = The number of weeks with a drop.
Size = The population from 100,000 people up.

Likelihood. The likelihood that an investigation will identify enough of the problems so that the station can regain the market share depends on the drop in share and the length of time involved. This is presented in the following table:

	Weeks of Drop											
Drop	*Staff Study*				*National on-Site*				*Consulting-Firm*			
Rate	*1*	*2*	*3*	*4*	*1*	*2*	*3*	*4*	*1*	*2*	*3*	*4*
2%	0.05	0.15	0.25	0.35	0.10	0.25	0.40	0.55	0.25	0.40	0.55	0.70
4%	0.10	0.20	0.30	0.40	0.15	0.30	0.45	0.60	0.30	0.45	0.60	0.75
6%	0.15	0.25	0.35	0.45	0.20	0.35	0.50	0.65	0.35	0.50	0.65	0.80
8%	0.20	0.30	0.40	0.50	0.25	0.40	0.55	0.70	0.40	0.55	0.70	0.85
10%	0.25	0.35	0.45	0.55	0.30	0.45	0.60	0.75	0.45	0.60	0.75	0.90

Cost of fixing problems. The costs to fix the problems with an affiliate depend upon the size of the market, the amount of drop in market share, and the duration of the drop:

$$F = \$30,000 + \$0.30 \times (\text{Drop} \times \text{Size} \times \text{Weeks})$$

Benefit. The benefit from fixing the local problems with an affiliate are a function of the market size and the drop in market share to be recovered:

$$B = \$5 \times (\text{Drop} \times \text{Size})$$

The policy of VBS, Inc., is to investigate a drop in affiliate market with the method that maximizes the expected benefits minus the expected costs.

REQUIRED:
a. The Chicago affiliate has had an 8 percent drop in market share for the past two weeks. Assume that the size of the Chicago market is 10 million people.
   1. For each of the investigation methods, compute the expected benefit and expected cost of the investigation.
   2. Which, if any, of the investigation methods should be used with this affiliate?
b. The Winston-Salem affiliate has had a 4 percent drop in market share for the past three weeks. Assume that the size of the market is 800,000 people.
   1. For each of the investigation methods, compute the expected benefit and expected cost of the investigation.
   2. Which, if any, of the investigation methods should be used with this affiliate?
c. The New York metropolitan market has had a drop of 8 percent for one week. The size of the New York market is 20 million people.
   1. For each of the investigation methods, compute the expected benefit and expected cost of the investigation.
   2. Which, if any, of the investigation methods should be used with this affiliate?
d. The policy of management maximizes the single-period benefits from investigation. Discuss alternatives that management might have to this policy. Assume that the variance in operating income as a result of the drop in viewers is equal to:

$$V = \$0.11 \times (\text{Drop} \times \text{Size})$$

for each week that the drop continues.

PART

VI

Decision Support Processes

22

Product-Related Decisions

23

Strategy and Investment

24

Capital Project Design Concepts and Techniques

CHAPTER

22

Product-Related Decisions

■

PRODUCT DECISION PROBLEM

John Gamble is the controller for Fiesta, Inc. The company manufactures and promotes recreational products. For example, it manufactures hot-air balloons and sailboats. One of its newer products is a wind sailboat for sailing on lakes. The company also sells a line of sportswear with the Fiesta brand name. Annual revenues of the company have increased to about $45 million, and net income is an adequate $4 million, mostly from the clothing line.

Several of the products appear not to be profitable, especially the Fiesta line of hot-air balloons. The owners, two well-known movie actors, have asked the president to review the balloon line for anything that can be improved. The president asked John Gamble and Reine (''Rennie'') Klingsdorn from marketing to review the hot-air balloon product line.

John and Rennie first studied the standard product line income statements in Exhibit 22–1. The statement indicated that the balloon line was losing $800,000 per year. However, it did not seem right to drop the balloon. Hot-air balloons were the original product of the company when it started in 1968. Today, the Fiesta balloon is among the largest selling balloons with annual sales of 885 units. Because of strong name identification, dropping the product would have a negative effect on the sales of sportswear.

Rennie talked with the sales staff and found that many customers associate the sportswear with hot-air ballooning and sailing. In fact, dropping hot-air balloons would probably cut sales of sportswear by at least 20 percent. Furthermore, senior

EXHIBIT 22–1   Standard Product Line Income Statements

FIESTA, INC.
Product Line Report
For the Year Ending March 31, 19x9
(millions)

	Fiesta Sportswear	Hot-Air Balloons	Other	Total
Revenue	$23.2	$14.2	$8.1	$45.5
Cost of goods sold	11.1	12.8	4.7	28.6
Gross margin	$12.1	$ 1.4	$3.4	$16.9
Selling expenses	2.5	1.5	0.9	4.9
Administrative expenses	2.1	1.3	0.7	4.1
Income before tax	$ 7.5	$ (1.4)	$1.8	$ 7.9
Income tax (45%)	3.4	(0.6)	0.8	3.6
Net income	$ 4.1	$ (0.8)	$1.0	$ 4.3

sales people emphasized that dropping hot-air balloons would demoralize the sales staff, who were highly valued balloon enthusiasts representing the company at various balloon festivals in their region. The sales staff enjoys selling at balloon festivals, and the commissions are enough to be interesting (3 percent or $480 per balloon sold).

John reviewed the cost records and found that the cost of goods sold for the hot-air balloons included $7.3 million in overhead. This seemed out of proportion in comparison with the other costs:

	Total (in millions)	Per Unit
Materials	$ 2.2	$ 2,500
Labor	3.2	3,600
Overhead	7.3	8,250
Total	$12.8	$14,350

The balloons were manufactured in the Muncie plant, which was mainly idle. Of the overhead costs, $6 million appeared to be fixed, including a large product liability insurance policy that costs $2 million per year. Increasing the selling price from an average $16,000 to $17,500 could drop sales volume by about 4 percent, or 12 percent with an increase to about $19,000.

■

LEARNING
OBJECTIVES

After studying this chapter, you should be able to:

1. Prepare a contribution analysis.
2. Prepare an analysis of the effect of dropping a product or service.
3. Prepare an analysis of the effect of adding a product or service.
4. Prepare a cost-based or market-based price change report.

Product-related decisions such as the one faced by Fiesta, Inc., require careful analysis. These decisions relate to adding products, dropping products, and changing prices. The product line and the production mix determine the company's revenues and the majority of its costs. Thus, income is closely tied to the contribution of the product or service to the organization.

THE ANALYSIS OF CONTRIBUTION

The basic question in product-related decisions is "How much does the product or service contribute?" **Contribution analysis** of a product or service involves the comparison of revenues generated with the avoidable costs of the product or service. **Avoidable costs** are those costs that would decrease if activity related to the product were reduced or terminated entirely or that would be incurred if the activity were undertaken. Thus, the activity or creating capacity to perform the activity of producing and marketing the product causes the cost.

The accountant must exercise judgment in deciding what is avoidable cost and what is not. The most frequent problem concerns handling costs that are common to several entities. For example, when analyzing the contribution of each of several products produced on the same machine, how should the fixed costs of operating the machine be treated? Because the fixed costs of the machine do not change when production ceases for one of the two products, these costs are not avoidable in the decision to add or drop one of the products. However, the decision to drop both of the products results in the fixed cost of the machine becoming avoidable because in that case the machine could be completely shut down and sold.

The Cost of Complexity and Trouble

Some products or services are more trouble to deal with than others. Even the best products or services occasionally have a problem. If everything went right in companies all the time, the companies would need far fewer people. Problems develop and people are hired to solve those problems—they "make it work" when things go wrong. An **expediter** is a person whose primary task is to handle problems as they arise. Some employees spend all their time expediting; others spend only a small portion of their time in this activity. Most supervisors and some managers spend much of their time handling activity-related problems. Thus, part of the cost of having individualized or complex products and services is that more people are needed. Products and services are costly to produce and market when they are hard to understand and/or have many unique parts. Therefore, products that are easy to understand, that use generic pieces, and that are simplified should cause few problems, need fewer people, and be less costly to produce.

The accountant should carefully analyze how much of the total costs are being caused by the complexity of the products under consideration. For example, a company manufactures thousands of parts for automobiles. It found that 80 percent of the parts generated much less than 20 percent of the revenue and no profits. One specific part that caused many manufacturing problems generated very few sales. After detailed analysis, the company found that competitors purchased about one third of the product, painted it a different color, and relabeled it as their own. The competitors wanted to stock the part for their customers but did not want the aggravation of manufacturing it. The company found that the part was generating over $150,000 in avoidable costs and less than $40,000 in revenues. After increasing the selling price of this product by 400 percent, demand fell and this product created fewer production problems.

General Format for a Contribution Analysis

A contribution analysis follows the form presented in Exhibit 22–2. Fiesta Travel, a division of Fiesta, Inc., provides packaged tours related to ballooning in addition to general travel services. One of its main tours is the European Grand Tour held each July.

EXHIBIT 22–2   Example Contribution Analysis

FIESTA TRAVEL DIVISION
European Grand Tours
Contribution Analysis
For July 19x2

Revenues	$800,000
Variable costs	500,000
Contribution margin	$300,000
Avoidable fixed costs	200,000
Contribution to common costs and profit	$100,000

The format of the contribution analysis looks very much like an income statement, but there are important differences. First, variable costs are subtracted from revenues to yield a contribution margin as in the variable costing income statement (Chapter 16). However, the emphasis is only on avoidable costs. It includes only those fixed costs that are avoidable if the product or service were dropped. Variable costs are generally assumed to be avoidable. For the European Grand Tour, variable costs would include such items as airfare, meals, lodging, entrance fees to balloon festivals, and tips. Avoidable fixed costs for the European Grand Tours would include costs related to promotion, guides, entertainment arrangements, ground security, and some transportation costs.

DROPPING AND ADDING PRODUCTS

The decision to drop or add products or services should be based on their contribution to common costs and profit. Due consideration must be given to the impact on all revenues and costs, both those directly related to the product and those indirectly related. Consideration should also be given to whether changing the product or service frees up (or uses) valuable limited resources, for example management time or shelf space in a grocery store. Thus the potential impact on other products should be analyzed. The analysis should be supplemented with a discussion of the qualitative issues involved with the decision. If the product or service contributes to the organization as a whole, it should be kept or added.

Fixed Capacity and Fixed Cost Allocations

Many product additions or deletions can be made with only minor changes to facilities and a nominal change in investment. Services can often be changed by retraining the staff and providing them with different tools. However, if major changes must be made to inventories or facilities, such as the purchase of new equipment, the product addition is a capital project that requires additional analysis.[1]

Some products or services appear to be unprofitable because the methods of allocating the costs load either common or unrelated costs onto the product. For example, the Fiesta Balloon product line was charged with the full cost of the Muncie plant, even though the plant was mostly empty and the balloons could be manufactured elsewhere. Further, $2.8 million in administrative and marketing costs were allocated based on balloon revenues. These two allocations make the balloon line appear unprofitable.

---

[1] See Chapters 23 and 24 on Capital Project Analysis.

Dropping a Product

Dropping a product or service is a serious matter. Customers rely on the company as a supplier and can be inconvenienced in a major way. If the company drops a product as a result of temporary circumstances or a misunderstanding, it can not easily start selling the product again when the circumstances change. Therefore, the accountant should carefully analyze any proposal to drop a product.

In the introductory business problem, the hot-air balloon line had a reported loss of $800,000 per year. A contribution analysis of the hot-air balloon product line is presented in Exhibit 22–3. The hot-air balloon line made a $3.5 million contribution to Fiesta, even in its oversized production plant. Because the $3.5 million in contribution is 44.3 percent of the overall company profit before tax, the product line should definitely be kept.

Notice that some of the direct labor is listed as an avoidable fixed cost. Many of the workers are highly skilled at balloon-making and would be laid off only if the balloon line were dropped completely. Thus, the categorization of a portion of direct labor as a fixed cost reflects the intent of management. Also notice that the effect of a 20 percent reduction in sportswear sales is reflected in the analysis.

A product should be dropped only if the product has a negative contribution that is expected to continue for some time or if there is an alternative use for the facilities and people that promises to contribute more.

The accountant must use judgment in relating avoidable costs to the decision at

EXHIBIT 22–3   Example Contribution Analysis

FIESTA HOT-AIR BALLOONS
Contribution Analysis
For the Year Ended March 31, 19x9

Revenues		$14.2
Variable costs:		
Materials	$2.2	
Direct labor	1.2	
Variable overhead	1.3	
Commissions	0.4	
Total variable		5.1
Contribution margin		$ 9.1
Less avoidable fixed costs:		
Fixed direct labor	$2.0	
Overhead	4.0	
Liability insurance	2.0	
Total avoidable		8.0
Direct contribution to Fiesta		$ 1.1
20% of sportswear sales	$4.6	
Less: Variable costs (48%)	2.2	
		2.4
Total contribution before taxes		$ 3.5

Comments: The fixed labor and overhead can be reduced only if production is halted completely. If the Muncie plant were shut down and balloon operations moved to Seattle, the overhead could be reduced from $4.0 to $1.8 million.

The liability insurance can be reduced only if the sale of hot-air balloons is dropped completely.

hand. Some fixed costs may be unavoidable for a one-month period but may be cut entirely over a one-year period. If the company is considering dropping the product line, most of the fixed costs related to it can be avoided. Facilities can be sold or altered in use and the workers can be transferred to other facilities.

Costs that have been arbitrarily allocated, such as the $2.8 million in marketing and administration, can not be avoided and would have to be reallocated to the other product lines if the balloon line were dropped. An **arbitrary allocation** is a cost allocation based on convenience or precedent rather than an allocation based on the decisions that caused the cost.[2]

Product Additions

A product addition analysis is similar in form to the analysis for dropping a product, except that less reliance can be placed on the estimates. New products and services tend to show a favorable contribution margin because of overoptimism. The possible actions of competitors are often not considered. Production complexity and problems are often underestimated. Thus, the estimates tend to be biased upward for revenues and downward for costs. The revenue and cost estimates for a new product are more uncertain than for an existing one. Consequently, new products have a high rate of failure.

One approach to developing new products that counteracts the optimism involved with them is called the *target concept*. Companies have noticed that as soon as a new product is introduced, competitors introduce an enhanced version of the product at a lower price. Therefore, to maintain a competitive advantage, a company must introduce new products in an enhanced version at a price that will maintain market share after competitors have reacted. The target product is the version of a new product that contains enhancements that the competition's product is likely to include. The target price is that price that should maintain market share after competitors enter the market.[3]

Generally, new products or services that are marginal should not be accepted because they use money and people and can damage company prestige. A marginal product should be seriously considered only if it opens important markets, keeps a promising market position, or results in use of employee skills that clearly will pay off in other areas.

Qualitative Issues

Qualitative issues involved in product addition and deletion analyses include customer loyalty, competitive position, alternative use of facilities, and future opportunities.

Customer Loyalty.   Some products or services may be kept for the purpose of maintaining or building customer loyalty. For example, department stores generally provide gift wrapping at a low price in order to encourage customers to shop in their store. Banks often provide low-cost checking accounts to get customers to bank with them. Equipment manufacturers often provide new customers with low-cost starter units to help develop brand recognition.

Companies also build customer loyalty to their products by providing high-quality service at a low price. If the service segment were analyzed independently, its contribution would be inadequate. Of course, the customer loyalty generated by the costly service must be demonstrated with market share and profitability for the other products. Without this, the expensive service can not be justifiable.

---

[2] See Chapter 25 on cost allocation for more complete development of this concept.

[3] The target cost is the difference between the target price and a normal profit margin. The production process is then designed to meet the target cost objectives.

Competition.   Companies that provide subsidized products or services in order to build customer loyalty may find their strategy undermined by competitors. Competitors market directly competing products for the high-priced products and ignore the low-priced products or services in the full line. These competitors can afford to price their products low because they do not offer the low-priced products in the line, or the quality service. Because they concentrate on fewer products, they can often achieve both higher quality and lower unit cost.

Facilities Usage.   The impact of a new product on the facilities should be considered. For example, thousands of new products require grocers to allot shelf space. Cloth manufacturers can make hundreds of different colors and textures on computer-controlled weaving machines. The question is which colors and textures can be handled efficiently. Similarly, many more syndicated columnists write for newspapers than can be included in any one newspaper. Many more movies are produced each season than can be shown in first-run movie theatres.

No attractive use for a facility may be available. For example, if a city loses its baseball team, it can do little with a specially designed baseball stadium. Similarly, train tracks age whether they are used or not. The resale value of specialized facilities, such as baseball stadiums or train tracks, tends to be relatively low and thus the avoidable fixed cost will be low. As long as some contribution can be generated by a product or service, the facility with no alternative value should be utilized.

Future Opportunities.   Finally, product and service changes made today affect future opportunities for products or services. New opportunities to which management would like to respond will arise in the future. Adding products today may open new markets in the future and provide productive skills that are valuable. Likewise, dropping products may close off markets or production skills that will be needed in the future.

We will next deal with a special case concerning services. In this special case, the person filling the role of service provider makes a major difference to the consumer. Thus, the service is different depending on who provides it.

SERVICE ADDITIONS

The service provided by one physician or ball player is different from that provided by others. Analyzing the contribution of a physician, an athlete, or an actor to an organization depends on the specific service provided, which is a personal performance. The analysis includes the estimated audience or clientele generated by the presence of a person in a specific role. Avoidable costs are negotiated in the employment contract between the service provider and the organization.

Although the service provider has an initial asking price, everything is negotiable. If the person is right for the role and has a demonstrated or potential clientele, the negotiations will commence because the performer needs to work and the organization needs the unique service. We will use the following example to illustrate the analysis of service contribution.

Service Contribution Analysis Setting

John Sean is the casting director for Mega Films. He has just auditioned over 600 people for various parts on the new movie *Michelle,* an epic romance mixed with action placed in early 19th century Atlanta. The actress who is best for the leading role is Felicity Mauris, who has appeared in several starring roles during the past three years. She has had a large stable audience of about 20 million for each of the past three movies, in which she had similar roles. She asks for a $2 million fixed fee, 15 percent of gross billings received by the studio above an audience of 10 million, and no more than three months of filming time.

Mr. Sean could also go with an unknown face for a small fee of $200,000 and still hold a base audience of 10 million. Harvey Matlock, the producer, estimates that the variable costs of distribution will run 35 percent (excluding any payments to Ms. Mauris) and other fixed costs of production and distribution will be about $6.7 million. The studio receives 30 percent of the revenue from ticket sales in theaters or about $1.50 per patron. If Ms. Mauris is offered the part, promotion costs will increase by $500,000. Also, it will cost about $1 million extra to speed up rehearsing and filming the epic from the normal six months to a rushed three months.

Mr. Matlock told his accountant, Shawn Hevron, to prepare an analysis of this data for him. "Will Felicity contribute enough to the picture? Every star should contribute more than the fixed costs they cause and more than their personal compensation."

Contribution Analysis

Shawn studied the estimates carefully; then he started with an estimate of revenue. Ms. Mauris would add an audience of 10 million to the film (her 20 million less the base of 10 million). This estimate is considerably uncertain because the 10 million increment is an informed guess based on past films. The expected revenue from this would be $15 million:

$$\text{Revenue} = \text{Added audience} \times \text{revenue per patron}$$
$$\$15 \text{ million} = 10 \text{ million} \times \$1.50$$

Avoidable costs include variable costs of 35 percent plus the film royalty to Ms. Mauris of 15 percent:

$$
\begin{aligned}
\text{Avoidable variable costs} &= 35\% \times \$15 \text{ million} = \quad \$5.25 \\
\text{Royalty payments} &= 15\% \times \$15 \text{ million} = \quad \underline{2.25} \\
\text{Total avoidable variable costs} & \qquad\qquad\qquad\qquad\quad \underline{\$7.50}
\end{aligned}
$$

Shawn then studied the fixed costs. Ms. Mauris wants a $2 million fixed fee. This would add $1.8 million to fixed costs (as compared to going with the alternative). Distribution will cost $.5 million more, and production costs will be $1 million more. Thus, the avoidable fixed costs (in millions) are:

Actress fixed fee	$1.8
Production	1.0
Distribution	0.5
Total avoidable fixed costs	$3.3

Shawn then found Ms. Mauris' contribution to the film by subtracting the avoidable costs from the revenues:

Revenues		$15.0 million
Avoidable costs:		
Variable	$7.5 million	
Fixed	3.3	
Total costs		10.8
Contribution to the film		$ 4.2 million

The estimated contribution to the studio of $4.2 million was above the fixed costs of $3.3 million added by Ms. Mauris. Shawn then estimated the total expected

EXHIBIT 22–4   Service Personnel Analysis

To: Mr. Matlock
From: Shawn Havren
Regarding: The Contribution of Ms. Mauris to *Michelle*

I have analyzed the data on Ms. Mauris. The contribution seems reasonable except for the ratio to compensation. Any one of several options seems feasible:

A. Negotiate with Ms. Mauris for a lower royalty percentage rate—perhaps 14 percent.

B. Negotiate for a longer shooting schedule so that fixed cost may be reduced and increase the contribution—perhaps five months.

C. Lower the fixed fee—perhaps to $1.8 million.

Mega Films Production of **Michelle**
Contribution Analysis of Ms. Felicity Mauris

		(Thousands)	
Audience increment		10,000	
Revenue		× $1.50	$15,000
Avoidable variable costs:			
Variable costs	35%	$5,250	
Star movie royalties	15%	2,250	(7,500)
Contribution margin			$ 7,500
Avoidable fixed costs:			
Actress		$1,800	
Production		1,000	
Distribution		500	(3,300)
Contribution to film			$ 4,200
Total expected compensation for Ms. Morris:			
Fixed fee total		$2,000	
Film royalties		2,250	
Total compensation			$ 4,250

Ratio Analysis

Contribution to fixed costs	$4,200/$3,300 = 127%
Contribution to compensation	$4,200/$4,250 = 99%

compensation of Ms. Mauris. He added the required fixed payment of $2 million to the estimated 15 percent film royalties of $2.25 million and found total expected compensation of $4.25 million. The margin for the studio was less than the total compensation, which Shawn knew would concern Mr. Matlock. However, the numbers were very close.

Then Shawn prepared a memorandum and a summary of his analysis for Mr. Matlock (see Exhibit 22–4). The analysis indicates that the expected contribution of Ms. Mauris is marginal and additional negotiations are appropriate.

In the next section, we will consider issues that concern the accountant regarding product pricing.

PRODUCT PRICING

Organizations and industries vary in the approach they take to setting prices. Some organizations change their prices once a year (for example, hospitals and ski slopes), others once a season (for example, department stores), others when profits are down (equipment manufacturers), and still others quote daily prices (basic commodity and security dealers). Some organizations set prices with no negotiation allowed (grocery stores), and others leave some negotiation or bid leeway in the price (auto dealers). Some organizations set their prices first and see how competitors react (automobile service stations), and others wait for competitors to move before they change their prices (fast food franchises). Some organizations set their prices strictly on the basis of costs (parts manufacturers), and others consider the prices of comparable products (for example, consumer goods).

Some organizations base their prices on market-oriented strategies. For example, the strategy of **market penetration** involves pricing below the competition. The strategy of **skimming a market** involves pricing high and waiting for the competitors to enter the market. Other organizations might segment their market by geographic area, customer type, or product line and then pick a pricing strategy to fit each market segment.

In some industries (for example parts manufacturers, wholesale distributors, industrial product manufacturers, and equipment manufacturers), prices are not listed and are rarely quoted over the telephone. Thus, pricing information is treated as privileged information available only to customers who place a current purchase order. Competitors are specifically excluded from finding out what the real prices are.[4]

Some Legal Background

The pricing of products and services is regulated by both state and federal law. We will first deal with U.S. federal statutory law and legal precedent. The Robinson Patman Act (1936), which amended the Clayton Act (1914), requires that any differences in prices among customers in direct competition with each other must be cost justified at the time the prices are set. Thus, cost records must support a difference in manufacturing, sales, or shipping costs for particular customers. Therefore, the price that a company sets must be the same for competing customers unless a different price can be specifically cost justified before the Federal Trade Commission and in federal court. Triple damages are awarded for judgments under the act. The only defense for the differences in prices is based on cost. Accountants are involved with preparing the support for the defense against charges by groups of customers or the Federal Trade Commission.

The Consumer Goods Pricing Act (1975) prohibits agreements among producers and retailers that fix the prices of products or services at specific amounts. Thus, producers can suggest retail prices, but local retail franchises and distributors may set their own prices.

Regulated Prices.   Many organizations provide services that are regulated by a state or federal agency; examples are telephone, electric power, and natural gas companies. Prices for these companies are set by a public regulatory agency, commission, or board. Accountants are involved in preparing cost estimates for the price-setting hearings. The resulting prices may be arbitrary and bear little relationship with the cost, but this is the natural result of having prices set by political appointees. For example, the commercial telephone and electric power rates are often two or three times higher than residential rates. Rural rates for service delivery (mail, electricity, telephone) are similar to municipal rates, even though the cost of providing the service is much higher.

The regulation of prices has changed in recent decades. For example, the trucking and airline industries have been generally deregulated as to pricing. Long distance

---

[4] The real prices may be hidden in various discounts from listed or posted prices and incentives, such as free product service, given.

telephone rates have become competitive. However, health-care rates have become more regulated with charges being fixed (for federal programs) by the Health Care Finance Administration. The cost-based pricing by defense contractors became more controlled with the regulations set by the Cost Accounting Standards Board.

International Issues. Pricing of goods that are sold outside the boundaries of the country is regulated by antidumping laws. The laws were originated to protect local industry and jobs from "predatory" foreign competition. In many countries, selling a product for any amount less than the price quoted to regular customers is considered "dumping" the product. The consequences for a company normally include losing the right to sell products in that country. Further, double or triple damages may be imposed. Therefore, pricing products across national boundaries should be approached very carefully.

Price Fixing. A series of laws relates to consulting with competitors to set prices. This is called **price fixing.** It is illegal for private companies to fix prices. Price fixing of work for a government agency may result in jail sentences. Doctors, hospital administrators, financial managers, real estate brokers, and others occasionally discuss rates and prices over the telephone or at professional meetings, but they must be very careful that this activity is not considered price fixing.

Any action or process that restrains trade, including setting prices, is potentially illegal under the Sherman Antitrust Act (1890), Clayton Act (1914), or Department of Justice rulings. The organization's attorneys should be consulted for specific legal advice. Generally, prices should be set on the basis of internal information plus anything available from public sources. Organizations may consult published catalogs, price lists, and advertisements. The amount of bids made on public contracts, unless specifically protected, may be requested under the Freedom of Information Act.

Cost-Based Pricing For **cost-based pricing,** an organization finds the cost of the product or service from its cost accounting records and adds a percentage markup to the cost. Each category of goods or service often has a different markup rate.

This approach to pricing is most appropriate for unique goods for which no market is established. For example, each construction project is unique. The bid price is based on estimated costs plus a markup. If contractors want to be competitive, they must estimate the minimum markup that provides for administrative costs and an adequate profit margin. During difficult economic times, some contractors bid the minimum possible price (generally materials, direct labor, and variable overhead) in order to keep their organization active.

Cost-based pricing also is appropriate when the products or services are so numerous that it is not beneficial to search out information about competitors' prices for each product. For example, some manufacturers produce over 100,000 products and parts; seeking competitors' prices is an unreasonable task. Because companies keep cost records for control and evaluation, the application of a cost-based pricing approach requires little additional human effort. Judgments are required periodically, however, regarding the appropriate markup rates for each category of goods.

Cost-based pricing can result in odd prices, such as $321.03. Minor adjustments may be made to get a price that is perceived as more acceptable by customers. For example, a retail furniture store might have a general markup set for sofa chairs of 80 percent over cost. A particular sofa has a cost (with shipping) of $178.35. Applying the formula of $178.35 × 180 percent results in $321.03. To make the price more appealing to the retail customer, the final price might be set at $319 or $324.99. As another example of prices accepted by customers, this textbook was developed on a computer purchased for $1,299, stored on a hard disk drive retailing for $499, with word processing software retailing for $399, and rough drafts were printed on a $99 printer on paper retailing for $21.98 a box.

Caution on Cost-Based Pricing.   Care must be taken with cost-based pricing. The cost base includes the fixed production cost, which increases per unit with declines in units sold—the lower the volume, the higher the price. Thus, when the demand is down, the price rises. The demand will likely decrease again as a result of higher prices. Sales will continue to decline until the pricing approach is altered. Conversely, when demand rises, the price falls, which further expands demand until facilities are overloaded.

In concept, the fixed costs should be included only to the extent that the fixed costs are avoidable by dropping the product. Further, some short-term losses should be accepted until the volume increases to the point that avoidable fixed costs are covered.[5] In practice, organizations rarely distinguish between avoidable and arbitrarily allocated fixed costs in cost-based pricing.

Cost-based pricing does not pressure the production process to be efficient. If production is inefficient, the prices are increased to reflect the increased costs. From basic economics, the demand for the product or service should go down as customers shift to competitors. However, the danger with cost-based pricing is that the organization will not know that its costs are too high but will try to pass the inefficiency on to customers who respond by purchasing less or going to competitors for better prices.

Special-Order Pricing

Customers will always prefer a price that is lower than the price a company can afford to offer. The customer's own profits or welfare will be higher if he or she can get the same or similar product for less. Thus, customer purchasing agents, depending upon industry practice, make serious offers to purchase goods or services for a low price. Should such an offer be accepted or a counteroffer be made? The general rule for this decision is as follows: Accept the offer provided that (1) the price is greater than avoidable variable and fixed costs, (2) capacity is sufficient to cover the production, and (3) the offer will have little or no effect on the market for regular production.

During slow economic periods or when customer demand is down for various reasons, there will be significant excess production capacity and the special order will be attractive. The item produced should be different from regular production for both legal and economic reasons. The Robinson Patman Act requires that all differences in prices offered to competing customers for the same products must be cost justified. If the special-order product is exactly the same as regular products, regular customers will have legal recourse. Further, when regular customers hear about the price cut given on the special order, they will seek similar low prices for themselves. Thus, total revenue may decline because of the special order.

Market-Based Pricing

Under **market-based pricing,** the company first consults the publicly available information about prices for a particular good or service. Only secondary reference is made to the costs of producing the good or service. Organizations define what their market is—a city segment, state, region, or class of customer. Organizations may

[5] For analyses of this type, the absorption cost-volume-profit techniques from the Chapter 16 appendix are useful.

price above, near, or below "the market." Their prices may be inconsistent with some above the market and others below. The price may vary in its relation to the market during the year or the business cycle.

Market-based pricing is appropriate when relatively few products and publicly available prices can be found. The accountant's role in setting market-based prices is limited. The data input is external, and marketing managers often must use judgment in applying the pricing approach. The prices are taken as a given by the accountant. However, if managers set prices below reasonable estimates of variable costs, the break-even point is impossible to achieve. The prices also can shift the product mix toward low-contribution products or services that are difficult and thus costly to produce. Temporary situations of this sort are acceptable to gain customer loyalty or hold eroding markets. Occasionally, managers ask accountants to analyze the effects of price changes on company profits or cash flow given certain assumptions about changes in demand.

Demand Estimates

An analysis using either cost- or market-based prices involves estimates of the effect of the proposed prices on demand. The marketing staff should provide these estimates. Some companies pilot test the effects of price changes in a representative market. The pilot test provides some confidence as to the magnitude of the change before it is implemented in the entire market.

Providing a sensitivity analysis of the impact of errors in their estimates on profits would be helpful to managers. Thus, the accountant may calculate income with estimate volumes that are higher and lower than those made by the manager. The report to managers should compare the current income with income under the proposed prices and demand. The sensitivity analysis should be a supplement to this report.

Example Price Analysis

In the Fiesta, Inc., example, the controller considered an alternative price of $17,500, which was 9.4 percent higher than the current price of $16,000. He received an estimate of a 4 percent decrease in volume from marketing. Why not consider a price of $17,000 or $18,000? How do the controller and the marketer know the volume will decrease exactly 4 percent?

The $17,500 price sounded like a good number to the controller and the marketer. A large number of prices are possible between $16,000 and $20,000—far too many to consider. Instead, the controller and marketer picked one number and analyzed the plausible effect of that price on profits. This simplified and reduced the report for senior managers:

	(in millions)
Revenues ($17,500 × 849)	$14.9
Variable costs	4.8
Contribution margin	$10.1
Avoidable fixed costs	8.0
Direct contribution to Fiesta	$ 2.1

No one knows if the volume reduction for a $17,500 price will be 4 percent or 3 percent or 5 percent. The 4 percent volume reduction is an experienced guess by the marketing staff.

For supplemental purposes, a more complete analysis of the effect of a price change could follow a format similar to the one presented in Exhibit 22–5. The report includes estimates for a price range from $16,000, the current price, to $19,000. Further, the sensitivity of the contribution to the error in the estimates of the demand reduction is also given.

EXHIBIT 22–5   Example Price Change Report

FIESTA HOT-AIR BALLOON
Contribution Analysis with Proposed Prices
For the Year Ending March 31, 19x9 (Pro Forma Basis)
(revenues and costs in millions)

	Price					
	$16,000		**$17,500**		**$19,000**	
Units sold (approximate)		885		849		785
Revenues		$14.2		$14.9		$14.8
Less: Variable costs						
Materials	$2.2		$2.1		$2.0	
Direct labor	1.2		1.1		1.0	
Variable overhead	1.3		1.2		1.1	
Commissions	0.4		0.4		0.4	
Total variable		5.1		4.8		4.5
Contribution margin		$ 9.1		$10.1		$10.3
Less: Avoidable fixed costs						
Direct labor	$2.0		$2.0		$2.0	
Overhead (See comment)	4.0		4.0		4.0	
Liability insurance	2.0		2.0		2.0	
Total avoidable		8.0		8.0		8.0
Direct contribution to Fiesta		$ 1.1		$ 2.1		$ 2.3

Comments:
1. This analysis assumes that the only change made to the hot-air balloon line is the price. Thus, production is assumed to be in the Muncie plant. In addition to direct contribution, there is $2.4 million in indirect contribution from sales of sportswear.
2. If the production were to occur in the Seattle plant, fixed overhead would be $2.2 million less and contribution would be higher by an equal amount.

Sensitivity Analysis

	$16,000	**$17,500**	**$19,000**
Contribution if the volume reduction from 885 were 50% more.	$1.1	$1.9	$1.6
Contribution if the volume reduction from 885 were 50% less.	$1.1	$2.3	$3.0

The contribution to common fixed costs and income is highest at the $19,000 price, which would favor that price. However, the sensitivity analysis indicates that at the $19,000 price, the contribution is more sensitive to demand estimates than at the $17,500 price. The sensitivity analysis also indicates a higher contribution from increasing the price, even if demand reduction estimates are off by as much as 50 percent. Therefore, the price should be increased from the current $16,000 per unit.

The report comments indicate that $2.2 million in potential overhead reduction would occur if the Muncie plant were sold and production of hot-air balloons moved to the Seattle plant.

SUMMARY

Contribution analysis of a product involves the comparison of revenues related to the product with avoidable costs. Avoidable costs are those costs that would be eliminated if the product were dropped or would increase if the product were adopted.

A product should be dropped only if its contribution is inadequate to cover its avoidable costs, giving due consideration to qualitative issues. Product-related decisions should consider the qualitative factors of customer loyalty, competitive position, alternative use for facilities, and future opportunities. Temporary price declines should not result in dropping products. Products should be added only if the contribution promised is enough to cover its avoidable costs (including the costs of problems the product will cause). The quality of data for product additions tends to be poorer than that for deletions.

Pricing products and services is restricted by industry customs and by federal and state laws. Only internal and public data should be consulted in establishing a price. Prices may be based on costs or on published market data. Cost-based prices are appropriate when there are many unique or low-cost items. Market-based prices are appropriate when there are relatively few products or services and published prices are available.

PROBLEM FOR REVIEW

Matt St. John has been asked to review several products at the Consumer Products Division of VRG, Inc. The Consumer Products Division has over 8,000 active products in its catalog. They are produced at 17 plants and distributed through eight regional warehouses. Matt was asked to review 21 of these products, which are all comparable consumer products such as irons, toasters, and mixers with the Happy Home brand name. Senior management is concerned about sales volumes and profitability for some of the products. In reviewing the files on product sales for the fiscal year ending June 30, 19x7, Matt has found the following data for the product line:

Product	Costs per Unit Variable	Fixed	Total	Price	Volume	Revenue
Premium Happy Home						
32604	$ 5.65	$ 3.77	$ 9.42	$18.80	3,180	$ 59,784
32607	5.21	3.47	8.68	17.30	113	1,955
32610	4.87	3.25	8.12	16.20	3	49
32613	3.56	2.37	5.93	11.80	65	767
32616	2.92	1.94	4.86	9.70	547	5,306
32619	7.09	4.73	11.82	23.60	1,222	28,839
32622	9.32	6.21	15.53	31.00	135	4,185
32625	9.91	6.60	16.51	33.00	3,075	101,475
32628	3.90	2.60	6.50	13.00	1,200	15,600
Economy Happy Home						
33018	14.29	1.58	15.87	19.00	164,512	3,125,728
33022	11.50	1.27	12.77	15.30	112,043	1,714,258
33032	7.75	0.86	8.61	10.30	229,857	2,367,527
33037	15.38	1.70	17.08	20.50	126,725	2,597,863
33046	8.66	0.96	9.62	11.50	43,991	505,897
33052	3.95	0.43	4.38	5.20	30,768	159,994
33060	10.73	1.19	11.92	14.30	160,556	2,295,951
Classic Happy Home						
33502	3.50	8.17	11.67	35.00	8	280
33504	1.26	2.95	4.21	12.60	1	13
33508	5.28	12.34	17.62	52.80	48	2,534
33512	4.90	11.43	16.33	49.00	6	294
33514	3.57	8.34	11.91	35.70	2	71
Totals					878,053	$12,988,368
Average for product						$618,494

Matt obtained the variable and fixed costs per unit from the standard cost file for each product. Fixed costs are estimated on the basis of normal volume for each product group. Thus, a low-volume group will have a very high fixed cost per unit. The price comes from the prices file used to generate customer invoices. The volume data are summarized from the cumulative year's sales file. The markup percentages for these products have not been changed for four years.

The report for product line performance for management is summarized as:

HAPPY HOME PRODUCT LINE
Product Group Performance Report
For the Year Ended June 30, 19x7

	Premium	Economy	Classic	Totals
Sales	$217,960	$12,767,216	$3,192	$12,988,368
Cost of goods	109,114	10,656,911	1,065	10,767,090
Gross margin	$108,846	$ 2,110,305	$2,127	$ 2,221,279
Selling and general	43,592	2,553,443	638	2,597,674
Profit before tax	$ 65,254	$ (443,138)	$1,489	$ (376,395)

Senior management is very unhappy about the performance of the economy Happy Home line. The premium and classic lines appear to do well enough, but their volumes are too low. Selling and general expenses are allocated on the basis of revenues. About 30 percent of the selling and general cost relates to the number of products in each product line rather than the sales revenues. The remainder is either fixed or very closely related to sales dollar volume. About half of the production fixed costs allocated to product groups is considered avoidable if the entire group is dropped.

REQUIRED

a. How are the prices being set in the three product groupings?
b. Compute the percentage of fixed cost to total unit cost for each product grouping.
c. What was the effect of volume on cost per unit? On prices?
d. Compute the contribution of each of the product groupings assuming that the selling and general cost avoidable to the product is $3,000 per product in the group plus 8 percent of sales revenue. Further, assume that half of the production fixed costs assigned to a product could be avoided if the product line were dropped. Should the economy line be dropped based on this analysis? Assume that there is no other use for the production facilities.
e. Matt asks marketing to generate estimates of the effects of price changes on demand. He receives the following estimates for each product grouping:

	20% Increase	20% Decrease
Premium	−40%	40%
Economy	−8%	40%
Classic	−50%	200% at least

Assuming that 19x8 will be like 19x7, prepare an analysis of the effects of these prices on contribution for the three product groups. Which alternative prices generate the most contribution?

SOLUTION

a. From the wording of the problem, we can state that the company is setting its prices by marking up some type of cost number. If we review the cost and price columns, we notice that the markup for the premium line is higher than that for the economy line and lower than that for the classic line. By computing a ratio of price to cost, we find that totals are:

	Premium	Economy	Classic
Revenue	$217,960	$12,767,216	$3,192
Cost of goods sold	109,114	10,656,911	1,065
Ratio	1.9975	1.1980	2.9972

The prices appear to be rounded down to the nearest $0.1. Thus, the markup applied will be higher than a strict percentage calculated. By applying ratios of 2, 1.2, and 3, we find that the these ratios exactly fit the data. We conclude then that the markups are 100, 20 and 200 percent.

b. Percentages of fixed costs to total for each product group:

	Premium	Economy	Classic
Product	32604	33018	33502
Fixed cost	$3.77	$1.58	$8.17
Total cost	9.42	15.87	11.67
Ratio	40.02%	9.96%	70.01%

c. As stated in the problem, the higher the normal or expected volume, the lower the fixed cost per unit because standard fixed costs are set on the basis of normal volume. Because the pricing approach marks up fixed costs, the price charged will be inversely related to normal volume. Thus, the lower the expected volume, the higher the prices charged.

d. Analysis of product groups for dropping:

	Premium	Economy	Classic
Revenue	$217,960	$12,767,216	$ 3,192
Production variable costs	(65,475)	(9,595,055)	(319)
S & G variable costs (8%)	(17,437)	(1,021,377)	(255)
Contribution margin	$135,048	$ 2,150,784	$ 2,618
Avoidable fixed costs:			
Production (50% × Fixed cost)	(87,294)	(530,928)	(373)
Selling & administration ($3,000/Product)	(27,000)	(21,000)	(15,000)
Contribution of product line	$20,754	$1,598,856	($12,755)

Based on this analysis, the economy group should not be dropped, but the classic group should be considered further for discontinuance.

e. Price change analysis report:

	Premium	Economy	Classic
No change in prices			
Contribution margin (from (d))	$135,048	$2,150,784	$2,618

Increase prices by 20 percent

	Premium	Economy	Classic
Old revenue	$217,960	$12,767,216	$3,192
Price factor (1 + Price change)	120%	120%	120%
Volume factor (1 + Volume change)	60%	92%	50%
New revenue (Old times factors)	$156,931	$14,095,007	$1,915
Production variable costs	(39,285)	(8,827,450)	(160)
S & G variable costs (8%)	(12,554)	(1,127,601)	(153)
Contribution margin	$105,092	$ 4,139,956	$1,603

Decrease prices by 20 percent

	Premium	Economy	Classic
Old revenue	$217,960	$12,767,216	$3,192
Price factor (1 + Price change)	80%	80%	80%
Volume factor (1 + Volume change)	140%	140%	300%
New revenue (Old times factors)	$244,115	$14,299,282	$7,662
Production variable costs	(91,664)	(13,433,077)	(958)
S & G variable costs (8%)	(19,529)	(1,143,943)	(613)
Contribution margin	$132,921	$ (277,737)	$6,091
Apparent choice on prices	No change	Increase	Decrease

Note: The avoidable fixed costs are the same under each alternative.

KEY TERMS AND CONCEPTS

Contribution analysis (849)
Expediter (849)
Avoidable costs (849)
Arbitrary allocation (852)
Skimming a market (856)

Market penetration (856)
Price fixing (857)
Cost-based pricing (857)
Market-based pricing (858)

ADDITIONAL READINGS

Barkman, A. I., and J. D. Jolley, II. "Cost Defenses for Antitrust Cases." *Management Accounting,* April, 1986, pp. 37–40.

Dudick, T. S. "Pricing Strategies for Manufacturers." *Management Accounting,* November, 1989, pp. 30–37.

Ekstein, H. C. "Pricing Your Product—What Should You Sell It for" *CPA Journal,* April, 1987, pp. 76–79.

Lee, J. Y. "Developing a Pricing System for a Small Business." *Management Accounting,* March, 1987, pp. 50–53.

Lere, J. C. "Product Pricing Based on Accounting Costs." *The Accounting Review,* April, 1986, pp. 318–24.

Malloy, J. "Making Pricing Decisions in Small Business." *Management Accounting,* December, 1984, pp. 50–52.

Marvel, H. P.; J. M. Netter; and A. M. Robinson. "Price Fixing and Civil Damages: An Economic Analysis." *Standford Law Review,* February, 1988, pp. 561–75.

"McDonnell Douglas Grabs a Piece of China's Sky." *Business Week,* August, 1987, p. 35.

Runk, R. C. "Controllers on the Firing Line." *Management Accounting,* November, 1989, pp. 38–42.

Schneider, A. "Pricing and Indirect Cost Allocation—A Note." *Accounting and Finance,* May, 1987, pp. 49–54.

Sharav, I. "Cost Justification under the Robinson-Patman Act." *Management Accounting,* July, 1978, pp. 15–22.

Sias, R. G. "Pricing Bank Services." *Management Accounting,* July, 1985, pp. 48–49, 59.

Thomas, A. R. "DCF: How a Small Company Outbid Its Competition." *Management Accounting,* March, 1989, pp. 115–18.

REVIEW QUESTIONS

1. What is the general analysis for dropping or adding a product or service?
2. What is the effect of a scarce, fixed resource used by a product or service?
3. Why should the cost allocations be carefully reviewed in the analysis related to dropping (or adding) a product or service?
4. List four qualitative factors that should be considered in the analysis for product additions and deletions.
5. Why might an organization provide customers with a product or service at below cost?
6. In what ways might dropping (adding) a product or service today influence future opportunities?
7. Why is an analysis related to dropping (adding) a product or service always incomplete?
8. What is an arbitrary cost allocation and what effect should it have on product addition or deletion decisions?
9. List two reasons that estimates related to new products tend to be more biased and uncertain than estimates related to dropping existing products.
10. If a company wants to charge customers different prices for the same product, what is required by the Robinson Patman Act?

11. List two settings in which cost-based pricing is appropriate.

12. List two problems associated with cost-based pricing.

13. Under what circumstances is it reasonable to use market-based prices?

DISCUSSION QUESTIONS

14. A few managers (and professors) argue with the theory that selected products and services should be provided at below cost in order to build customer loyalty or sales of other products. Opponents of this theory believe that it leads to lost profits and reputation because the poor products and services are a waste of management time and productive facilities. How might these pricing approaches differ from those presented in the chapter materials?

15. Temporary price declines should not trigger the immediate dropping of a product or service. How can we tell the difference between a temporary decline and a permanent decline in the price of a good or service? Use as an example airline fares between New York and Los Angeles.

16. Why is it difficult to drop and then bring back a product some time later? Use as an example a favorite breakfast cereal.

17. Respond to the statement: "Companies should set all their prices for services, parts, and products strictly on the basis of the market."

18. Managers of private businesses may go to jail or pay a large fine for collusion in price fixing, but governmental agencies see no problem with fixing the prices for hospital, mail, telephone, natural gas, or electric services. Comment.

19. Governments set their prices (taxes and fees) in a complex negotiation among voters, legislators, and executives. One basic component in the price negotiation is the cost of providing government services. Discuss other influences on government prices in addition to the cost of providing the service. Use a local school district as an example. Its revenues primarily come from property taxes on real estate in the district. Also, districts are subsidized by the state and federal government under various programs.

EXERCISES

22–1. Contract Contribution. The General Quaramics Corporation is trying to evaluate the contribution of the XR1–9A project based out of the Maryland Defense Contract Unit. The contract has a fixed price of $29 million for the coming year, but $6 million of that is being held up by Senator Jiles due to an alleged deficiency in the program and will probably never be paid. Costs expected on the contract for the year are:

Salaries	$13 million
Materials	3
Overhead	10
Total	$26

About half of the overhead relates to unavoidable fixed costs of the Maryland Defense Contract Unit plus an allocation of the Georgia headquarters cost.

REQUIRED:
Prepare a contribution analysis of the XR1–9A project to the Maryland Defense Contract Unit.

22–2. Sales Contribution. Jane Shaw, Eastern regional sales manager for CST, Inc., is analyzing the contribution of a sales staff member, William Jizmaticek. During 19x3, William sold $3 million in industrial products. He is paid $40,000 plus a 3 percent commission. Other avoidable costs related to William are fixed costs of $20,000 for automobile and office expenses. Variable cost of goods sold is 50 percent of sales, and other variable costs are 20 percent of revenue.

PART VI DECISION SUPPORT PROCESSES

REQUIRED:

a. Prepare an analysis of the contribution of William Jizmaticek to CST, Inc., during 19x3.

b. Compute the ratio of contribution to compensation.

c. CST, Inc., requires that all sales personnel each contribute four times as much as the total compensation of the salesperson. Is the continued employment of Mr. Jizmaticek justified?

22–3. Product Analysis. Jein Vickery, a marketing manager for World Toymakers, Inc., is reviewing the contribution of Wetten Wonder, a doll. The doll wholesales for $12 with a variable manufacturing cost of $3. The variable cost of marketing and shipping the doll is $1 per unit. Other costs that are avoidable and related to the toy are $30,000 in fixed manufacturing costs and $10,000 in marketing costs. Common costs allocated to the product are $3 per unit for manufacturing and $2 per unit for sales and administration. During 19x9, 19,400 units of the doll were sold.

REQUIRED:

Compute the contribution of the doll to World Toymakers, Inc.

22–4. Product Deletion. Bonita, Cocha & Co. produces two food product lines: Cocha Salza and Cocha Cheese. Cocha Salza is simple to produce, but the Cocha Cheese line involves complex processes and involves risk due to bacterial contamination. Both processes are highly automated. A statement of operations for Bonita, Cocha & Co. is as follows (in millions):

BONITA, COCHA, & CO.
Statement of Operations
For the Year Ending August 31, 19x2

	Cocha Salza	*Cocha Cheese*	*Total*
Revenues	$6.0	$7.0	$13.0
Cost of goods sold	4.8	3.2	8.0
Gross margin	$1.2	$3.8	$ 5.0
Selling and general expenses	1.8	2.1	3.9
Income from Operations	$ (.6)	$1.7	$ 1.1

The cost of goods sold includes equipment and product insurance costs that have been allocated based on pounds produced. If the Cocha Salza line were dropped, the total cost of goods sold would decrease by $3.2 million. The selling and general expenses are allocated on the basis of revenues. If the Cocha Salza line were dropped, the total selling and general expenses would decrease by $1.4 million.

REQUIRED:

Should the Cocha Salza line be dropped for 19x3? Support your judgment with analysis.

22–5. Service Unit Avoidable Costs. The Selisonga County Hospital Board is evaluating the EEG (electroencephalographic) unit for phaseout. The unit has revenues of $1,120,000 and the following costs:

a.	Staff salaries	$420,000
b.	Supplies	95,000
c.	Equipment depreciation	88,000
d.	Occupancy charge	195,000
e.	Staff training	25,000
f.	Administrative expense	120,000
g.	EEG equipment maintenance	12,000
h.	Malpractice insurance	280,000

The equipment is outdated and can no longer be sold. The occupancy charge is for building depreciation and general maintenance. The hospital building is currently 28 percent vacant. Administrative expense is a share of general hospital expenses and has been allocated to the

EEG unit based on number of staff. About 40 percent of administrative expense closely relates to the number of staff for each unit. The malpractice insurance is the premium on a specialized policy that covers only the EEG unit for one year.

REQUIRED:
For each cost of the EEG unit, determine the percentage that the cost should be considered avoidable upon its complete shutdown.

22–6. Product Addition.   The Wizard Company of Kansas City, Missouri, is considering the production and sale of a new line of coffee mugs based on popular cartoon characters. Wizard Company must pay a 15 percent royalty on cash received to the cartoon originators for the use of the cartoon logo and characters. The following are the estimated costs for 1,000 mugs:

Materials	$200
Direct labor	600
Overhead	800

The mugs will be manufactured during the slow season when the direct labor would otherwise be idle. The overhead is about 25 percent variable cost and the remainder is fixed. The mugs will use standard molds and standard glazing processes. The mugs will be listed in the extensive *Wizard Wholesale Catalog*. Only the master images will distinguish the cartoon mugs from thousands of others that the company makes. The master images will cost $120,000 and can be used indefinitely unless broken by rough use.

Mugs will be sold in cartons of 12. The following wholesale prices have been proposed along with estimates of unit sales:

Wholesale Price per Carton	Cartons Sold
$24.00	37,500
36.00	20,000

REQUIRED:
a. Compute the projected net contribution of the product at each of the wholesale prices proposed.
b. Should the new product be added? If so, at which price?

22–7. Product Deletion.   Three shoe models are being considered for deletion by the Selma Shoe Company. Listed below are the data for 19x2, the most recent year:

		Unit Costs		Unit	Avoidable
Model	Price	Variable	Total	Volume	Fixed Costs
4282	$4.20	$1.80	$3.50	40,000	$ 90,000
5065	4.60	1.95	4.60	250,000	120,000
5120	6.40	1.00	3.50	20,000	150,000

Overhead is allocated on the basis of direct labor. The avoidable fixed costs are for a one-year period and are independent estimates based on the complexity and difficulty in manufacturing each product.

REQUIRED:
a. Compute the gross margin generated by each product.
b. Compute the contribution margin for each product.
c. Compute the contribution margin net of avoidable fixed costs.

22–8. Service Addition.   Coach Ott, Inc., provides services to telecommunications networks. The company is considering the following line service procedures for addition during the 19x4 fiscal year:

Service	Price	Unit Costs Variable	Fixed	Unit Volume	Avoidable Fixed Costs
A202	$39.00	$18.50	$8.50	200,000	$1,800,000
A466	22.50	9.25	8.60	500,000	3,500,000
B599	29.00	12.00	6.50	250,000	5,500,000

Overhead is allocated to services on the basis of labor charges. Service B599 is highly complex, will be difficult to perform, and requires additional unique machinery and support personnel. Unfortunately, the prices reflect competitive pressure and cannot be increased.

REQUIRED:
a. Rank the services by the total gross margin.
b. Rank the services by the total contribution margin.
c. Rank the services by the total contribution margin net of avoidable fixed costs.

22–9. Product Deletion.   The sales manager for Ring Toys, Inc., recommends that the Fita Hoveraft product be disbanded. Product sales have been disappointing, and prices have fallen. The current price for the toy is $20 with manufacturing costs of $18 per unit, shipping costs of $2 per unit, and administrative costs of $1 per unit. The manufacturing costs consist of:

Materials	4
Direct labor	2
Production overhead	12

Sales for 19x8 consisted of 25,000 units.

The manufacture of toys is highly automated with long production runs. Production overhead is allocated on the basis of machine hours plus setup time. The Fita Hoveraft is manufactured in short runs as a filler in the production schedule to keep otherwise idle machinery and workers busy. A total of $15,000 in overhead costs could be avoided if the product were dropped. All of the shipping costs plus half of the allocated administrative costs could be avoided if the product were dropped.

REQUIRED:
a. Compute the total costs that could be avoided by dropping the toy.
b. Should the Fita Hoveraft be deleted for the product line? Explain.

22–10. Cost-Based Pricing.   S & J Construction Co. is preparing a bid for the construction of a bridge over Interstate 80 due for completion on October 29, 19x8. The estimated cost of materials and labor for the bridge are (in millions):

Materials	$2.4
Direct labor	3.8

S & J applies overhead on the basis of 40 percent of materials handled and 50 percent of direct labor. Approximately half of the overhead and three quarters of the direct labor are variable costs. The controller prepares the following bid range for government-related work:

Low bid:	Variable cost + 20 percent markup
High bid:	Full cost + 15 percent markup

The general manager, consulting with the supervisors and controller and giving due consideration to the competition, then selects a final price that is in the bid range.

REQUIRED:
a. Compute the low bid price.
b. Compute the high bid price.

22–11. Cost-Based Pricing.   Tippa, Inc., of Boston specializes in the development and installation of guidance systems for cargo jet aircraft. Every contract requires significant engineering and development to meet unique customer requirements. R. J. Nolan, guidance systems manager, is preparing the bid for a contract of 20 planes to be built by Power Jet, Inc., to be used by European Overnight Express. The following direct costs are estimated to complete the contract (in millions):

Direct engineering	$2.4
Direct materials	2.0
Direct labor	1.4

Production overhead is applied at a rate of 80 percent of direct engineering, 15 percent of materials, and 60 percent of direct labor. About 70 percent of the production overhead is variable. Only about 60 percent of the direct engineering and 70 percent of the direct labor are avoidable if the contract is not awarded to Tippa, Inc.

REQUIRED:
Compute a bid price assuming that Tippa, Inc., follows a pricing policy of:
a. Full cost plus a 10 percent markup.
b. Avoidable cost plus a 50 percent markup.

PROBLEMS

22–12. Service Contribution.   Archie Zeph is the producer and business manager for the 29th Annual Mountain Music Festival to be held in July 19x9 at Midway, Colorado. The three-day festival has an expected attendance of 40,000. Mr. Zeph is reviewing the potential contribution of the muscial group, Cattle Car, to the festival. The group, which would perform on Friday evening, is expected to add 6,000 to the 40,000 festival attendance. The group is asking for $30,000 plus 4 percent of the ticket sales of the entire festival. Tickets for the festival are $30, but a $3 commission is paid to ticket sales agents. If Cattle Car is chosen, additional promotion costs of $15,000 would be incurred. An alternative to Cattle Car is Roy Subbs, who would contribute no additional audience, but who requires only a $5,000 fee for the evening performance and 1 percent of festival revenues. Because a Friday evening performance is a must, either Cattle Car or Roy Subbs will be contracted.

REQUIRED:
a. Prepare an analysis of the contribution of Cattle Car to the 29th Annual Mountain Music Festival.
b. Compute the ratio of contribution to compensation.
c. Compute the ratio of contribution to avoidable fixed costs.

22–13. Product Deletion.   Elyria Pen Co. has run out of room at its Systol Felt plant. At the Systol location, standard felt tip pens and specialty pens are produced. The following product line information is available (in millions):

	Standard		*Specialty*	
Revenues		$15.0		$10.0
Direct materials	$3.0		$1.0	
Direct labor	2.0		1.0	
Production overhead	6.0		3.0	
Selling and general costs	1.8	12.8	1.2	6.2
Operating income		$ 2.2		$ 3.8

About 40 percent of the production overhead is variable as to units. Only 10 percent of the total overhead could be avoided if the standard pen were moved, but 80 percent of the total overhead could be avoided if the specialty line were moved. The selling and general costs are allocated on the basis of revenue, but only 20 percent of these costs are variable and only 10 percent could be avoided if either of the products were moved to another plant.

If standard pens were moved, the production of specialty pens could be expanded by 50 percent. If the specialty pens were moved, the production of standard pens could be expanded by 400 percent.

REQUIRED:

a. Given the current operations, compute the contribution of standard pens to the Systol Felt plant operating income.
b. Given the current operations, compute the contribution of specialty pens to the Systol Felt plant operating income.
c. If standard pens were moved from the Systol Felt plant, compute the contribution of specialty pens.
d. If specialty pens were moved from the Systol Felt plant, compute the contribution of standard pens.
e. What is your recommendation to the senior management of Elyria Pen Company? Explain with references to parts *(a)* through *(d)*.

22–14. Product Addition. Cal Lewis, the acquisitions editor at Triple Knight Publishing, was very excited. He was close to signing James Lauton-Smith, the mystery writer, for publication of his new work, *The Unlimited Affair*. Lauton-Smith's recent works have each sold over 10 million copies worldwide. *The Unlimited Affair* reads very well but will need the standard editorial work before publication. Publishers receive 60 percent of the normal retail price for volumes sold. Film rights are negotiable with producers. The author normally receives a 15 percent royalty on all cash received by the publisher. However, important authors negotiate their own rates. For *The Unlimited Affair,* Lauton-Smith is asking $4 million for signing plus a 20 percent royalty on book sales and a 40 percent royalty on movie rights. All the reviewers agree that the book will sell about 10 million volumes.

The president of Triple Knight is cautious. Publishing a book of this type will require $1 million in development costs and another $500 thousand in promotion. If the book is picked up, the film rights will be about $2 million. The cost of printing and distributing the book is $1.90 per volume. Of the printing costs, $0.40 is fixed (all allocated common cost). The projected retail price will be $4.95.

REQUIRED:

a. Prepare an analysis of contribution for the Lauton-Smith book. Assume that the film rights will be sold.
b. Prepare a contribution analysis assuming that only 6 million volumes are sold and that no producers want the film rights.

22–15. Sales/Product Line Analysis. Millicent Jensen is the managing partner for Advant, Ltd., a partnership specializing in advertising and promotion. Ms. Jensen is reviewing the records on Patrick Kennedy, a mid-level account executive specializing in beverage accounts. He has recently had some personal problems (a divorce and the death of a twin brother) that have interfered with his work. The agency earns its fees as a commission on advertising placed in various media. During 19x2, Mr. Kennedy placed the following advertising in the various media ($ in millions):

	Commission Rate	*Billings*
Television	8%	$10.5
Radio	10%	3.0
Newspaper	8%	4.0
Magazine	8%	8.0
Direct mail	10%	1.5
Total		$27.0

About 25 percent of each of the billings would occur each year without any effort by Mr. Kennedy. Account executives are paid a base salary of $40,000 plus 0.8 percent of the billings. The cost to produce the advertising is estimated to equal about one half of the commission rate. The cost to administer accounts is equal to about 1 percent of billings, but about one half of this is unavoidable fixed costs. Avoidable costs associated with Mr. Kennedy include:

Fringe benefits	$ 38,400
Office	12,000
Secretary	17,500
Automobile	11,000
Travel	30,000
Entertainment	25,000
Client relations	12,000
Total	$145,900

The fringe benefits are a variable cost and are 15 percent of compensation.

REQUIRED:
Hint: Be careful in computing the amount of revenue added by Mr. Kennedy.
a. Compute the contribution of Mr. Kennedy to Advant, Ltd.
b. Compute the ratio of contribution to compensation.
c. Compute the ratio of contribution to fixed costs that he causes.
d. Account executives are expected to contribute about twice their compensation and three times their fixed costs. Comment on Mr. Kennedy's contribution.
e. During 19x3, Ms. Jensen expects Mr. Kennedy's billings to drop to about 80 percent of their 19x2 level. Compute the effect of this on his contribution and his ratios.

22–16. Product Distribution.   J. R. Matoney, the marketing vice president of URI, Inc., is reviewing the contribution of marketing through specialty shops to the company. URI, Inc., sells specialized attire and footwear for long-distance running. URI has three channels of distribution: specialty shops, running magazines, and catalog sales. Product line statements for 19x4 are (amounts in millions):

	Specialty Shops	*Running Magazines*	*Catalog Sales*
Revenues	$20.00	$10.00	$8.00
Cost of goods sold	14.00	4.00	3.20
Gross margin	$ 6.00	$ 6.00	$4.80
Selling and general	5.00	2.50	2.00
Income from operations	$ 1.00	$ 3.50	$2.80

Given the amount of sales to specialty shops, Mr. Matoney did not believe that the effort was being rewarded with sufficient profits. Mr. Matoney asked Terri Shein, controller, to study the specialty shop contribution very carefully for possible change. If specialty shop sales were dropped, about 30 percent of those sales could be retained through catalog sales, which have a higher markup.

Ms. Shein found that half of the cost of goods sold was for fixed manufacturing costs. After talking with the plant manager, she estimated that the fixed manufacturing costs could be cut by $2 million if the sales were cut by $10 million or more. Selling and general expenses have been allocated on revenues. About half of the selling and general expenses are fixed. If specialty store sales were dropped, the total selling and general expenses could be cut by only $2.5 million. (Remember that catalog sales will increase at the same time.)

REQUIRED:
Prepare an analysis of the contribution of sales through specialty shops to URI, Inc.

22–17. Product Deletion and Special Order.   SpeedByke, Inc., manufactures high-quality bicycles. Its product line presently includes three different models that they wholesale through bicycle dealers and racing clubs. The least expensive model, the Cruiser, is designed for the occasional weekend rider or commuter. The middle-priced model is the Flyer, which is capable of matching the speed of any racing bicycle in the world on level terrain. The most expensive model, the Climber, is designed specifically for hill races and has 18 speeds and can match the speed of the Flyer on level ground.

The company controller, Antonio Bista, has the following information on the three models:

	Cruiser	Flyer	Climber
Selling price	$135	$190	$235
Unit variable cost	$ 80	$120	$155
Inventory units, 1/1/x8	100	40	20
Production units 19x8	2,500	700	400
Units sold 19x8	2,450	740	300
Estimated unit sales 19x9	2,500	1,100	300
Machine hours per unit	7	9	10
Avoidable fixed costs	$10,000	$15,000	$18,500

Total fixed costs are $150,000 per year; 28,000 machine hours are available for production. SpeedByke would like to have a 19x9 ending inventory of 50 bicycles per model.

The Bucaneers of Florida, a club based in Miami, has offered to purchase a minimum of 50 or as many as 200 stripped-down versions of the Flyer for $165 per unit. The bicycles would be unpainted and without the extras but would have all of the speed of the Flyer. SpeedByke estimates that this bicycle would have variable costs of $100 per unit to manufacture and ship and would require eight machine hours.

SpeedByke, Inc., has the option to allow all of the production and sales of Climber to be licensed to Arizona Bicycles, Inc., for a licensing fee received of $1,000 plus $10 per unit sold. Under this option, total sales are expected to increase to 500 units per year.

(E. Templer, adapted)

REQUIRED:

a. Compute the net contribution of Climber to SpeedByke, Inc., during 19x8.

b. Compute the net contribution of Climber to SpeedByke, Inc., assuming that it is licensed to Arizona Bicycles during 19x9.

c. Assuming that the Climber model is retained in its current form, comment on the problems that SpeedByke will face in meeting its 19x9 production needs and make sales as planned. Compute the contribution per machine hour for each model and comment on which model should be reduced in the production schedule.

d. Assuming that the Climber model is licensed to Arizona Bicycles, Inc., how much, if any, of the order for Bucaneers of Florida should be accepted? Show computations.

e. Comment on the legal issues surrounding acceptance of the price for the Bucaneer order. In your judgment, recognizing that legal counsel would be consulted in a real situation, is there a problem with accepting the Bucaneer order? Show an analysis with normal markup of 35 percent in defense of your judgment.

22–18. Product Addition.   Flatland Power Company is an electric utility serving the Oklahoma panhandle. Flatland owns and operates two power plants, Plant No. 1 (coal fired) and Plant No. 2 (natural gas fired). During times of high natural gas prices, Plant No. 2 is operated at the minimum level and Plant No. 1 generates the bulk of the power required to serve regular customers. However, both plants are much more efficient if they are operated on a steady basis. It is very expensive to start up and shut down units in each plant, especially in Plant No. 1. For this reason, unexpected periods of high and low demand are very costly.

Plant No. 1 requires approximately $400 in coal plus $500 in allocated overhead to generate a megawatt of electricity for one week. The plant has $39 million in production overhead per year of which $26 million relates to fixed costs. Plant No. 1 has a generating capacity of 1,500 megawatts; it is always operated at or near full capacity. Plant No. 2 has a 2,500-megawatt capacity and requires approximately $700 in gas and $400 in overhead to generate a megawatt of electricity for one week. The plant has $31.2 million in production overhead per year, of which $23.4 million relates to fixed costs. Current demand for electricity in the Flatland service area averages 2,000 megawatts with normal seasonal peaks at 2,500 megawatts. Only very rarely during mid-summer will the local demand exceed 3,000 megawatts. Local power rates have been set to average $1,200 per megawatt per week.

Flatland is a member of the Southwest Grid Power Pool. This is a service through which utility companies can contract to purchase and sell power within the grid area on a short-term basis of 12 hours to several weeks.[6] Power companies opt to buy power on the local grid to get through high demand periods. Power is bought and sold at the "spot" price that reflects local supply and demand. Prices on the spot market vary from $300 per megawatt up to $1,100 with an average of $700 per megawatt for one week. In addition, a local grid fee of $2.16 per megawatt for a half day transmission is paid for any movement across the local grid. The local grid fee is used to maintain the grid connections across power companies within the region; the fee applies only to local purchases and sales.

Power that is sent across regional grids is termed *wheeled power;* it can be sold on a week-to-week or a longer-term basis. The average fee for sending electricity across a grid is set at $50 per megawatt entering the grid per week (or major fraction thereof). The power sent across a grid is very high voltage and low amperage, which results in relatively little power loss. Only about 5 percent of the power sent is lost going across each grid. For example, 100 units of power placed in a grid on one edge will result in an average of 95 units of power on the other edge. Flatland has not previously dealt in wheeled power, which is a new product to consider. Flatland has dealt within the local grid market and has found it useful for smoothing out production at Plant No. 2. However, the board of directors is concerned that Plant No. 2 consistently operates at 60 percent of capacity or less.

The Purchasing Department has been offered the unusually low price of half the usual price from the Luca Pinto Gas Field. Under the offer, Flatland must take the gas for at least five years with options to continue. Unfortunately, Flatland has already contracted for all the gas it needs to meet local needs. The Luca Pinto natural gas would be enough to generate 1,000 megawatts of power per week.

Middle California Power Company has offered to purchase up to 2,000 megawatts of power wheeled across the New Mexico grid and the Arizona grid to the California border. The contract offered is for a one-year period at a price of $900 per megawatt. The minimum electricity supplied must be a constant 800 megawatts of power. The contract may be continued for up to five years at a price escalating at 6 percent per year.

(R. Gilliland and K. Mackey, adapted)

REQUIRED:
Assume that there are exactly 52 weeks in the contract year.
a. Compute the variable and full cost of generated power at each of the plants under the existing fuel contracts.
b. Compute the contribution margin per unit and the net contribution for each plant for the year under the existing fuel contracts.
c. Compute the variable cost per megawatt hour delivered from converting the Luca Pinto natural gas to electricity and then wheeling it to the California border. Allow for the spoilage or reduction that occurs in movement across the two power grids.
d. Should the Middle California Power contract be accepted and, if so, for how many megawatts? Show analyses to support your conclusions.

22–19. Use of Scarce Facilities. OSC, Inc., produces a line of pipe-cutting templates, called *One-Step*. The Engineering Department has just developed Kut-Shur, a sleeve system for pipe cuts. The Kut-Shur line is best suited for repetitive cuts, and the One-Step templates, which contain a variety of cut patterns, are more cost effective for jobs that involve a variety of cuts.

Management believes that the established One-Step distribution channel will be suitable for Kut-Shur, but commitment to the product will require an increase in fixed factory overhead of $50,000 per month. Now producing 280,000 One-Step templates, the plant is at full capacity. Any Kut-Shur production will require the reduction of One-Step volume. The plant can produce

---

[6] Assume that the power lost on movement within local grids is immaterial for purposes of this problem.

seven One-Steps in the time it takes to produce four Kut-Shurs. Projections for 19x8 assuming that only one of the products is produced are as follows:

	One-Step		Kut-Shur	
	Unit	*Total*	*Unit*	*Total*
Revenues	$15.95	$4,466,000	$39.95	$6,392,000
Cost of goods sold	9.89	2,768,920	28.04	4,486,920
Gross margin	$ 6.06	$1,697,080	$11.91	$1,905,080
Selling and general expenses		933,390		1,125,390
Income from operations		$ 763,690		$ 779,690

Estimated cost of goods sold and expenses include:

	One-Step	Kut-Shur
Materials	$1,288,000	$ 960,000
Direct labor	784,000	1,440,000
Variable factory overhead	420,000	1,760,000
Fixed factory overhead	276,920	326,920
Variable selling and administrative expense	488,000	640,000
Fixed selling and administrative expense	485,390	485,390

The sales manager has argued that the company should produce all the Kut-Shur it can sell because of the more favorable income from operations based on full capacity. However, the production manager points out that if both are produced, the total capacity can be 25 percent higher because of the more effective utilization of machinery. The sales manager then states that "at least 70,000 units of One-Step or 40,000 units of Kut-Shur must be sold to have a viable marketing effort. We can't mount an effective marketing campaign for just a few units."

Senior management has requested a comparison of the best use of the production facility based on the following capacity utilization:
1. One-Step, 50 percent and Kut-Shur, 50 percent
2. One-Step, 40 percent and Kut-Shur, 60 percent
3. One-Step, 70 percent and Kut-Shur, 30 percent

(A. Gregory, adapted)

REQUIRED:
a. Prepare a contribution analysis for each capacity utilization by product and in total.
b. What other capacity utilizations should be considered?
c. What is your recommendation to senior management regarding the best use of the facilities?

22–20. Product Processing, Prices, and Volume Analysis.   Simone Virgil, Inc., grows cucumbers. Simone has developed a hydroponics process to grow the cucumbers year round in a converted warehouse. She can select the size and growth rate through genetic control, light source, and nutrients. The operation employs 115 people and has the capacity to produce 18,000 bushels of raw cucumbers per month.

Raw cucumbers have been selling for $13.50 per bushel in the recent past, but the price has just fallen to $10.50 due to competition from the California Growers Association. Because Simone Virgil's cucumbers are of consistently high quality, she can sell as much as she produces as long as she accepts the market prices quoted. Due to the recent price drop, Simone is considering selling fewer cucumbers and producing pickles.

If Simone chooses to process pickles, the pickling will take up space and time needed for growing cucumbers. The pickle processing takes months for curing, and each bushel of processed pickles would use the space and time required to grow 1.5 bushels of raw cucumbers. However, processing pickles requires little additional variable cost because it does not need light, uses few materials, and requires little labor.

The variable cost of producing and selling a bushel of cucumbers is $7.50; the avoidable fixed costs associated with this production are $15,000. The current selling price of processed pickles is $17.50 per bushel and the additional variable costs are $1.50 per bushel. Each bushel of cucumbers results in one bushel of processed pickles. The avoidable fixed costs associated with pickle production are $10,000 per month.

(K. Bogdon, adapted)

REQUIRED:

a. Consider the $13.50 for raw cucumbers:
   1. What are the break-even volume and maximum profit from selling all cucumbers?
   2. What are the break-even volume and maximum profit from processing all cucumbers into pickles?
   3. Should any of the cucumbers be processed into pickles?
b. Consider the $10.50 current price for raw cucumbers:
   1. What are the break-even volume and maximum profit from selling all cucumbers?
   2. What are the break-even volume and maximum profit from processing all cucumbers into pickles?
   3. Should any of the cucumbers be processed into pickles?

22–21. Product Decisions, Special Orders, and Pricing. Colorado Trout Division is a commercial trout operation located near Colorado Springs, Colorado. It is a division of NBR Grain Products, Inc., of Omaha, Nebraska. By mixing combinations of cold water from a stream with naturally hot spring water, Colorado Trout can keep an optimum water temperature year round (58 to 62 degrees Fahrenheit). Oxidation units keep the water at the correct oxygen saturation point. Electricity is required to run the three large pumps and oxidation unit.

Colorado Trout is not a hatchery but instead purchases 1-inch fry or hatchlings from local suppliers. As they grow, the trout are categorized as follows and require the percentage of total feed indicated:

Size	Stage	Proportion of Total Feed
1″ to 4″	Fingerling	10
4″ to 8″	Growing-out I	20
8″ to 10″	Growing-out II	30
10″ to 12″	Near market	40

The trout are ready for market at the 12-inch size. Larger fish lose prime market value and require much more feed for growth.

Trout production is a protein feed-intensive business. Most of the labor is involved with hauling, mixing, and spreading the tons of feed in the 1,000 acres of trout ponds and runs. Minor labor is also involved in maintaining waterways and piping. The labor involved with harvesting and processing is relatively minor compared with feeding and tending the ponds and runs.

Unlike shrimp and catfish, trout require an extremely high mix of protein in the feed and relatively few carbohydrates. The nutritional value of the feed must be within very close tolerances. Every month 25,000 fry are placed into the process and begin their growth through stages. Any higher number of fry in the current acreage would result in stunted growth and increased mortality. The young fish are fragile and subject to stress and genetic problems. Mortality from all causes is about 20 percent in the fingerling stage, 15 percent in growing-out I, and 6 percent in growing-out II. Losses after the 10-inch size are negligible if the water temperature and feed are correct. Each month the 12-inch size fish are processed and quick frozen for market. The average market size is 12 ounces of processed fish. The current contract price is $3,800 per 1,000 pounds of processed fish. Due to continuing strong demand from wholesalers, Colorado Trout is able to sell its full monthly output at the quoted prices.

The current operation is at capacity and has the following annual expenses:

Stock	$ 48,048
Feed	178,274
Direct labor	89,101
Power	11,039
Transportation	4,015
Communication and marketing	9,032
Management	30,000
Property taxes	30,491

The stock, feed, and direct labor are considered variable costs, and the remainder is fixed costs.

Colorado Trout has received an offer from Continental Divide Fishing Club. The club has purchased a large steam-fed lake and would like to begin a stocking project. For a one-year period, the club would like to purchase batches of 4-inch fingerlings at the price of $600 for 1,000.

(S. Greer, adapted)

REQUIRED:
a. Compute the variable cost of 1,000 pounds of processed fish.
b. Compute the variable cost of each batch of 1,000 4-inch fingerlings.
c. If instead of selling it to Continental Divide Fishing Club, the batch of 1,000 four-inch fingerlings is grown to market size:
   1. Compute the variable cost of growing the batch from 4-inch size to market size.
   2. Compute the revenue from the sale of the batch once it has reached market size.
d. Should the offer from Continental Divide Fishing Club be accepted? Support your judgment with numerical analysis.
e. At what selling price would Colorado Trout be indifferent between sale to the Continental Divide Fishing Club and growing the fish to market size?

22–22. Special Orders and Legal Issues.   Canine Homes, Inc., specializes in the production of dog houses for the pampered pets of the affluent. Canine Homes normally sells its products through veterinarians and specialty pet shops. During 19x6, a recession resulted in a lull in its business activity. D. L. Mashion, the president of Canine Homes, is concerned about covering operating costs and keeping the production workers active. He considers all direct workers as highly valued people who have been with the firm for years and will not be terminated or furloughed.

Canine Homes, Inc., has received an offer from Dr. Lin Yuang "Doc" Sun, chief veterinarian of a large group practice and popular television personality in Southern California. The offer is for 100 large dog houses at $600 each per month for 12 monthly purchases. However, this is much below the production cost of $828:

	Fabrication	*Finishing*	*Total*
Direct materials	$220	$ 80	$300
Direct labor	70	200	270
Overhead applied	90	168	258
Totals	$380	$448	$828

The offer for this special sale is also below the normal $1,000 price for this product. The controller estimates that 20 percent of applied production overhead per unit could be eliminated for each unit not produced. The sales manager estimates that accepting the order will drop sales through regular channels by 25 units per month.

(K. Mackey and R. Gilliland, adapted)

REQUIRED:
a. Identify the production costs that are avoidable in the decision to accept or not accept the special offer.

    b. Prepare an analysis of the contribution from acceptance of the special order.
    c. Acceptance of the special order might be in violation of the Robinson Patman Act.
        1. What circumstances indicate a potential violation of the Robinson Patman Act?
        2. Can Canine Homes justify the difference in price based on differences in costs and normal markup?
        3. Compute the potential liability if Canine Homes is found in violation of the Robinson Patman Act. Assume that triple damages would apply.

22–23. Service Prices and Value Added.* Johnson, Atkinson, & Co. is a regional CPA firm that has adopted a value billing concept in service pricing. For average service in audit, tax, or consulting, the staff charges an average hourly rate. For services in which there is extra value, for example cost savings, financial advice, or large purchase decisions, the rate is higher. The price charged for services depends on the quality of the work performed, the value added by the work. Johnson, Atkinson & Co. has the following standard hourly rates:

Partners	$200
Managers	150
Staff seniors	100
Staff accountants	60

In addition, the firm bills a rate of 3 percent of value added for advice of a valuable nature. The value added is estimated for the subsequent year.

    The audit of Klinderstruk, Inc., required 2 partner hours, 8 manager hours, 16 staff senior hours, and 48 staff accountant hours. Charles Dross, the audit manager for the Klinderstruk account, observed that the production plant was paying to dump scrap in a land fill instead of selling the scrap. The plant manager agreed that this was a significant opportunity being lost and decided to change the practice. The plant produces 4,000 tons of scrap per year, which it was paying $10 per ton to dump. The scrap can be sold for $12 per ton.

REQUIRED:
Compute the price for the Klinderstruk audit including the value-added portion.

22–24. Service Pricing. Systems Planners Institute (SPI) is a professional educational association for systems analysts and programmers. The organization has approximately 50,000 members.

    SPI holds an annual convention each October, and planning for the 19x6 convention is progressing smoothly. The convention budget for such items as promotional brochures, fees, and expenses for 20 speakers, equipment rental for presentations, the travel and expenses of 25 staff people, consultant fees, volunteer expenses, and so on, is $330,000. The amount does not include any of the hotel charges for meeting rooms, luncheons, banquets, or receptions.

    SPI has always priced each function at the convention separately (i.e., members select and pay for only those functions they wish to attend). For each registered function, a member receives a ticket that is surrendered at the function. If members attend the convention, they must pay a registration fee that allows them to attend the annual reception and the annual meeting at no additional charge.

    The Annual Convention Committee, consisting of volunteer members of SPI, has recommended that SPI consider setting a single flat fee for the entire convention. The fee would entitle a registered member to attend all functions at the convention. Entrance to each convention function would be permitted if the member displayed the official convention badge that would be issued only to persons paying the fee.

    Listed below are data on convention functions, including the price that SPI would charge if priced separately:

---

    * This problem is based on concepts in S. F. Jarrow, ''Value Billing,'' *Practicing CPA*, November, 1987, pp. 1–2.

Function	Percentage Participation	Price	Hotel Charges
Registration fee	100	$50	None
Wednesday reception	100	Free	$25/attendee
Annual meeting	100	Free	$2,000 for room
Keynote luncheon	90	$40	$25/attendee
Concurrent sessions (6)	70	$60	$1,200 for 6 rooms
Plenary session	70	$50	$2,000 for room
Workshops	50	$100	$1,200 for 6 rooms
Banquet	90	$50	$30/attendee

The hotel package of services to SPI and the convention attendees is as follows:
- Three free rooms for convention headquarters and storage.
- Discount of 20 percent on posted room rates for all convention attendees who stay in the hotel during the three-day convention. The types of rooms, posted rate, and the proportion of reservations of each type of room taken by attendees are as follows:

Single	$100	10%
Studio	105	10%
Double	125	75%
Suite	200	5%

Attendees are to make room reservations directly with the hotel, and all hotel room charges are the responsibility of the attendees.
- SPI is given credit for one double room for three days for every 50 convention registrants who stay at the convention hotel. The credit will be applied to the room charges of staff and speakers.
- Meeting rooms and halls are free if food is served at the function.
- Meeting rooms and halls are free if 1,000 members are registered at the hotel.
- Meal costs given above include all taxes and gratuity.
- The hotel receives all revenue from cash bar sales at the reception and before the luncheons and banquet. The hotel estimates that the average consumption at each of these functions will be one cocktail per attendee at a contribution of $1.50 per cocktail.

If SPI continues to price each convention function separately, the prices given in the prior table will apply. Estimated attendance under this type of pricing would be 2,000. The annual convention committee has estimated the convention attendance for three different single, flat-fee structures as follows:

Fee	Attendees
$325	1,600
300	1,750
275	1,900

SPI estimates that 60 percent of the persons who attend the convention will stay in the convention hotel. Furthermore, convention attendees will each require a separate room and stay an average of three nights.

(CMA, adapted)

REQUIRED:
Assume that the same proportion of attendees will attend each function under each of the pricing approaches.
a. Compute the contribution margin for each of the following pricing approaches:
   1. Separate pricing approach.
   2. Flat fee of $325

    3. Flat fee of $300.

    4. Flat fee of $275.

b. What intangible considerations should be discussed by SPI regarding the pricing approach?

c. SPI wants to maximize its contribution from its annual convention. Recommend whether SPI should price each function at the convention separately or charge one of the three single flat fees for the convention.

22–25. Special Orders.   RexRobin, Inc., manufactures two types of copying machines. The DR model has standard features; the DC model has extra features that make it more costly to manufacture. During 19x8, the company had a production and sales level of 80 percent of capacity. This level is expected to be achieved during 19x9. The statement of operations for 19x8 was:

REXROBIN, INC.
Statement of Operations
For the Year Ending December 31, 19x8

Sales	$32,200,000
Cost of goods sold	23,797,000
Gross margin	$ 8,403,000
Selling and general expenses	2,625,000
Income from operations	$ 5,778,000

For 19x8, the following data were available:

	Model DR	*Model DC*
Units sold	25,000	30,000
Selling prices	$520	$640
Direct materials	$105.10	$ 79.10
Direct labor hours	5	7
Machine hours	15	18

Direct labor is charged to production at the rate of $13.50 per hour. Fixed production overhead costs are 75 percent of cost of goods sold. Variable selling and general costs are 4 percent of sales revenues. Overhead is charged to production on the basis of machine hours, which closely approximate the actual relationship between the production of units and the variable portion of production overhead cost.

(D. Ripple, adapted)

REQUIRED:

a. Shawnda's Copies, a national chain, offers a price of $575 for 13,000 of the DC model copiers. Shawnda's is not a regular customer so this sale would be in addition to sales to regular customers. However, Shawnda's Copies is in direct competition with other customers served by RexRobin. The machines would carry the RexRobin brand name and be shipped from RexRobin facilities. What would be the contribution from accepting this order?

b. R. C. Benjamin, Inc., a supplier to universities, requested an order of 10,000 DR model copiers and offered $420 per unit and also asked for a $50 trade-in for each of its 5,000 old machines. These old machines have no net value to RexRobin, Inc. This order would involve an additional $8 per unit cost to customize the machines with the R. C. Benjamin name and color. The machines would be shipped in bulk to R. C. Benjamin, which would ship them to customers from its facilities at a savings in selling and general costs of $12 per unit for RexRobin. RexRobin does not currently serve the university market. What would be the contribution from accepting this order?

c. Review the potential legal complications related to accepting each of the offers in requirements *(a)* and *(b)*.

**EXTENDED
APPLICATIONS**

22–26. Product Performance, Absorption Costing, Special Orders.   Limestone Division
of STM, Inc., produces two types of chalk at the Slender Creek plant: chalkboard and industrial.
For 19x9, 12,500,000 boxes of chalkboard are expected to be sold through various channels
of distribution. The plant plans to produce 15,000,000 boxes of the chalkboard during the
year. The plant also plans to produce and sell 1,400,000 sacks of industrial chalk. The total
fixed costs of the plant are $2,800,000. The total fixed costs of plant marketing and admin-
istration are $300,000.
   The variable cost of producing a box of chalk is $0.18. Fixed costs are applied to production
at a rate of $0.0875 per box. The variable distribution costs are $0.02 per box. Although
prices vary by the size of the order and bidding processes, the average price in the past has
been $0.33 per box. Normal production volume is set at 16,000,000 boxes.
   Industrial chalk is produced in 100-pound sacks. Each sack sells for $4 and has a variable
cost of $2 ($1.50 production and $0.50 marketing and administrative) and fixed manufacturing
costs applied of $1 per sack. Normal production volume is set at 1,400,000 sacks. Of the
total fixed manufacturing costs, $500,000 are avoidable for chalkboard chalk and $280,000
are avoidable for industrial chalk with the remainder as common to both products. Of the total
fixed marketing and administration costs, $100,000 are associated with chalkboard chalk,
$50,000 are related to industrial chalk, and the remainder is common to both products.
   Of the division headquarter's costs, $100,000 are caused by the Slender Creek operations.
In addition, the division allocates headquarters common cost at a rate of 8 percent of plant
revenues.

(S. Manchanda, adapted)

REQUIRED:
a. Prepare an analysis of the contribution of the sales of chalkboard chalk to the Slender
   Creek plant for 19x9.
b. Prepare an analysis of the contribution of the sales of industrial chalk to the Slender Creek
   plant for 19x9.
c. Prepare an analysis of the contribution of the Slender Creek plant to the Limestone Division
   for 19x9.
d. Prepare a pro forma Slender Creek plant income statement under absorption costing for
   19x9.
e. The division is considering a contract to sell 250,000 boxes of chalk to New York Public
   Schools. Because of the nature of the order, the shipping costs will be only $0.01 per box.
   The marketing manager estimates that this contract can be won at a bid price of $60,000.
   The cost of administering the order is expected to be $1,000. How much would this order
   contribute to the division?

22–27. Product Additions, Contribution, and Absorption Costing.   CTC, Inc., assembles
calculators from standard components. It has kept overhead and fixed costs very low by
subcontracting all fabrication work. CTC grew rapidly during the past 15 years, but its growth
has moderated during the last 3 years.
   The calculator business is experiencing a rapid change in technology. Thus, the company
must continually develop new products and cut prices on old ones in order to maintain a
competitive position. Management is currently considering the addition of a lower-priced and
a higher-priced product line. Some basic data on the proposal include:

Total fixed manufacturing (Including avoidable)	$336,000
Total fixed selling costs (Including avoidable)	110,000

	Lower Price (Proposed)	Current Line	Higher Price (Proposed)
Volumes:			
Normal volume	200,000	120,000	60,000
Expected 19x3 sales	180,000	115,000	72,000
19x3 planned units	190,000	135,000	77,000

	Lower Price (Proposed)	Current Line	Higher Price (Proposed)
Per unit:			
Selling price	$5.00	$10.00	$15.00
Materials	2.00	4.00	8.00
Direct labor	0.30	0.50	0.80
Variable overhead	0.15	0.25	0.40
Fixed overhead	0.60	1.00	1.60
Variable selling	0.50	1.00	1.50
Avoidable Fixed costs:			
Manufacturing costs	$ 4,000	$ 28,000	$26,000
Selling cost	12,000	20,000	30,000

Mr. David Astab, president and CEO, likes this proposal because the current model will be more profitable and the product line will be broader. Without the two new product lines, the fixed overhead application rate would be $1.15 per unit on the current model. There are no beginning inventories. The avoidable fixed manufacturing costs are included in the total fixed costs applied to products.

(R. Gonzales; A. Chang; and H. Van Lare, adapted)

REQUIRED:
a. For the lower-priced product:
   1. Compute the contribution of the product to CTC, Inc.
   2. Compute the ratio of contribution to avoidable fixed costs.
b. For the higher-priced product:
   1. Compute the contribution of the product to CTC, Inc.
   2. Compute the ratio of contribution to avoidable fixed costs.
c. For the planned production and sales, prepare a pro forma statement of income assuming the variable costing concept. (The report presentation need not include product line performance.)
d. For the planned production and sales, prepare a pro forma statement of income assuming the absorption costing concept. (The report presentation need not include product line performance.)

22–28. Service Unit Deletion, Detailed Product Line Analysis.   Timothy Krumwiede is the partner in charge of practice analysis for Mills, Moore & Co., which is a firm of certified public accountants with revenues of $2.3 billion. Mr. Krumwiede is reviewing the Construction Consulting Group (CCG). This consulting group specializes in designing accounting systems for construction companies to meet federal and state regulatory requirements. The practice group contains 38 professionals and 10 support personnel located in three regions. The partner in charge of the practice group, Clinton Abrams, is located in the Washington office. The billings of the unit have been disappointing during the two recent quarters but promise to increase in future years. The national board is considering disbanding CCG and merging its operations with the regional offices.

Mr. Abrams has explained that CCG's marketing efforts result in audit, tax, and other engagements for which the group gets no credit. Mr. Abrams comments, "Basically, half of our time is spent in marketing the firm to the construction industry." For example, recent efforts gained the audit and tax work of JSC Construction, a company with $1.3 billion in assets. The audit group (with outside consultants) performed the systems work and did not share the billings with the consulting group. Because Mr. Abrams believed that the audit group lacks sufficient expertise in construction regulatory work, the firm was unnecessarily exposed to risk. Mr. Abrams comments: "Frankly, Tim, JSC got a weak system, I lost $600,000 in billings, and our reputation for construction business is going down the drain."

Statements for the practice unit show the following amounts for the year 19x0 (in thousands):

Revenues			$8,967
Partners' compensation	3	$780	
Managers' compensation	12	732	
Consultants' compensation	23	989	
Outside consultants' fees		902	
Travel		820	
Professional liability insurance		836	
Professional—Memberships and library		114	
Office space and utilities		407	
Client development		960	
Training and seminars		119	
Support personnel	10	142	
Computer support		418	
Materials and supplies		23	
Central office		639	
Recruiting		646	
Total expenses			8,527
Net group margin			$ 440

Practice groups are required to generate a margin of 20 percent of billings in order to justify the investment in personnel.

Pure variable costs for CCG are the outside consultants, travel, and material. Costs associated with professional liability insurance, office space and utilities, computer support, central office, and recruiting are allocated based on the number of professional staff. Training, professional expenses, and client development are discretionary expenses as planned by Mr. Abrams. Mr. Abrams plans to have roughly one manager and two consultants for each $750,000 in revenues. Mr. Abrams agrees that the allocation of liability insurance and office space are reasonable. He disagrees with the computer support: "All our work is done on client equipment." He also disagrees with the allocation of central office cost: "If we traced costs for administration through the system, there would not be more than $100,000 that could be reasonably assigned to our group." Finally, Mr. Abrams' group gets no value from the recruiting function: "We have to hire our own people. Our consultants need 10 to 15 years of experience in the construction business."

During 19x0 Mills, Moore & Co. has $212 million in billings to construction companies, of which 68 percent was for audit work, 22 percent was for tax work, and the remainder was for consulting work of all types. For the audit work, $11 million is for new work that Mr. Abrams can document as clients developed through CCG efforts. Further, $4 million in new tax billings and $2 million in new consulting billings (outside CCG) are related to CCG effort. However, Mr. Abrams does concede that about $1.5 million of his own billings relate to the efforts of other groups. Mr. Abrams estimates that about 70 percent of client development effort results in the billings that go to other practice units. Reasonable estimates of the contribution margins for additional work for each of the practice areas are:

Audit	36%
Tax	44%
Consulting (Other than CCG)	32%

REQUIRED:
a. Based just on the revenues billed by CCG:
   1. Prepare a contribution analysis of CCG.
   2. Compute the ratio of contribution to fixed costs.
   3. Compute the ratio of contribution to compensation of professional staff.
b. Based on total revenues related to CCG efforts:
   1. Prepare a contribution analysis of CCG.
   2. Compute the ratio of contribution to fixed costs.
   3. Compute the ratio of contribution to compensation of professional staff.

c. Comment on the contribution of the CCG to the firm and its relationships to other practice units.

d. Assume that audit and tax clients stay with the same CPA firm for an average of five years, but consulting engagements are one-time-only events. Comment on the effect of this on the contribution of CCG to Mills, Moore, & Co.

CHAPTER

23

Strategy and Investment

■

THE CAPITAL INVESTMENT PROBLEM

Robert Jefferson and Donald Keys are sitting in the Old House Coffee Shop in Butte, Montana. Robert is division general manager for the Minerals and Exploration Division of CSV, Inc., a Delaware company. Donald is the manager for the Butte Mine, which mines and smelts lead and copper ore. The CSV, Inc., board of directors has indefinitely deferred a proposal by Robert and Donald to sink a new mine shaft about six miles from the current site. The ore at the proposed site is high grade, and the $6 million investment in the new shaft promises substantial returns over the next 15 years. It should pay for itself in three years and have an average return of 30 percent, a net present value of $10 million, and a discounted rate of return of 24 percent—all of which are well above the stated requirements for capital projects.

Donald (upset and irritated): Tell me again. After all our work in negotiating leasing rights, fights with environmentalists, test drillings, projections of volume, technical drawings, equipment bids, engineering studies, and financial analyses out the kazoo, why did the board just say, "Wait"? Four years to put this thing together and they want us to wait! I'm tired of waiting.

Robert: Don, I doubt they will ever give us the go ahead. The board is not pleased with our division's performance; our growth and cash flow have been low for some time. Some of our mines have been losing money for three years now and the market for basic minerals is shaky at best. They might not believe our numbers.

Donald: How can we grow? They're just draining us.

> **Robert:** The news may be worse than you think. It's just a guess, but I think the real reason they're holding off on all of our projects is because we are about to be sold. I'm more worried about my job than I am about a new shaft for the Butte Mine.

■

LEARNING OBJECTIVES

After completing this chapter, you should be able to:

1. Distinguish between capital projects and other projects.
2. Distinguish between capital budgeting and strategic planning.
3. Identify the motivation for and risks of undertaking a capital project for both the company and the proposer.
4. Compute cash flows for a project given the estimates and assumptions.
5. Compute financial report-based measures of return and risk: average return on investment, impact on sales, income, earnings per share, and payback.
6. Compute net present value, discounted rate of return, discounted payback.

BASIC CONCEPTS

Capital projects are projects that require a relatively large investment in assets for more than one year. Capital projects are also known as *investment projects, investment proposals, plant acquisitions, equipment purchases,* and *development projects.* These projects often involve the purchase of buildings, machinery, computers, or software. Such projects result from the introduction of new products, services, production methods or technology, or acquisition of another company. Some projects involve the routine replacement of fixed assets as they wear out or become obsolete.

The length of time (more than one year) and the size of investment in assets distinguish capital from other projects. A typical example of a capital project might be a proposal for Bear Country, a high-energy candy line by the Consumer Products Division. The candy line is made from honey, strawberries or blackberries, assorted nuts, and grains. The Bear Country product line has been test marketed and has projected sales of $1,200,000 per year for 10 years. The proposed product requires a $300,000 processing line, $50,000 in inventories, $13,000 in start-up manufacturing costs, $8,500 in assorted government fees for food inspection, and $120,000 in start-up marketing costs. The project will add six people to the payroll: three in production and one each in marketing, order entry, and the warehouse. Assets are required for this project (processing line and inventories), and the sale of the product is projected over 10 years. Thus, the Bear Country product line proposal is a capital project.

If the Bear Country product line could be produced on existing equipment with only a minimal investment in inventory and start-up costs, the new line would be treated as a part of the operations plan rather than as a capital project.[1] Additional proposals that would *not* be capital projects include:

- Advertising campaigns for existing products are typically for less than one year and do not result in a separate asset that can be sold.

---

[1] Short-term decisions of this nature are more easily handled through cost-volume-profit analysis or an appropriation process within budget approvals. The set of criteria for accepting/rejecting a short-term decision differs from those for capital projects.

- Personnel programs, such as training or safety, do not develop a separate asset that can be sold.
- Small acquisitions, such as the purchase of a file cabinet or a tool set, are not treated as capital projects because too little money is involved to merit analysis. Instead, small acquisitions are treated within the annual operations plan.

Strategic Planning

Senior management evaluates capital project proposals from the perspective of its strategic plan. **Strategic planning** is the planning of broad strategies to attain the goals and objectives of senior management. Although the corporate staff may help with specialized aspects of strategies, the strategic plan itself is strictly within the jurisdiction of the senior managers. The goals of senior managers for the organization are general concepts involving, for example, growth, position in the industry, income, return on investment, flexibility, and capacity to survive change. Objectives are more specific with numbers or rates attached: 10 percent growth in sales, first in the industry in terms of market share, income per year of $500 million, or 15 percent after-tax return on investment.

Strategies to achieve these objectives are general activities that are expressed in phrases such as: "expanding defense-related divisions through acquisitions of other companies," "slowing the growth in lower-margin consumer products," "getting out of the transportation business," and "increasing the emphasis on biomedical research." These strategies, together with the goals and objectives, give direction to the organization.

The strategic plan is negotiated among the executives and changes with time and experience. The plan is never fully revealed to others in the organization; individual strategies are partially made known to lower-level managers only on a need-to-know basis. Revealing strategies outside the executive group can create real difficulties for a company. For example, if competitors were to find out IBM Corporation's strategies, they could alter their own strategies to take advantage of IBM. In another case, worker motivation would be substantially reduced if the employees of a division became aware that their division is to be liquidated soon.

Senior managers have broad latitude in defining their strategies. They can follow growth, medium quality, and very low prices or high return on investment, slow growth, and an image of high quality. They can buy other companies or emphasize growth from within. They can develop products or services or copy the products of competitors. They can follow a set strategy in a highly ritualistic manner, or they can improvise as opportunities arise. As long as senior management retains control of the company, it can pursue whatever objectives and strategies that it has the will and determination to pursue.

The **required return** is the profit that senior managers desire from capital projects. A required return becomes a threshold or screen that filters out unpromising projects before much effort is wasted on them. Thus, senior management should see only promising project proposals. The required return may be considered a fixed rate, for example 20 percent after tax, or it may vary by project or division, especially by the amount of risk or size of investment. The required return may be conceptualized by senior managers as a function of the **cost of capital,** which is often defined as the weighted-average, after-tax cost of all debt and equity sources. However, senior managers are quite free to define the required return as broadly or as narrowly as they choose.

A capital project proposal that is inconsistent with the long-range strategies of senior management will not be accepted, even though it exceeds the stated required return. For example, the proposal to dig a new mine shaft at the Butte Mines location of the Minerals and Exploration Division will be given a low priority if senior management plans to sell the division. Similarly, a project to develop a new software product may be given little priority if senior management plans to purchase a software company that produces similar products. Alternatively, a project to open automobile leasing franchises in Georgia will be given a high priority if one of the strategies is to expand consumer franchising. Note that these three proposals might have exactly the same promised earnings, but some are accepted and some are rejected.

Senior managers are not mindless computer programs that pick one project over another based on rates of return or net present values. Nor are they necessarily being capricious, playing favorites, or being personally vindictive. Instead, senior managers evaluate capital projects in the context of their objectives and strategies for the entire organization.

Normal Sequence of Approval

Capital projects come in all sizes. The system for the control of capital projects includes a normal sequence for obtaining approval starting with lower-level managers and proceeding to upper levels. Thus, each level of management must approve a project before it is submitted to a higher level in the organization. This process screens projects that either will not work or do not meet specified criteria.

Approval levels will also be established. Small projects may be approved at lower levels and large projects must be reviewed in detail by the board of directors. For example, the approval levels might be stated as:

Funding Level	*Detailed Review and Approval Required*
Less than $1,000	Department manager
$1,000 to $10,000	Division manager
$10,000 to $100,000	Vice president
$100,000 to $400,000	President
Over $400,000	Board of directors

Approval levels such as these are effective in limiting the number of projects that each level of management must consider in detail. If the board of directors had to seriously consider every small project, little time would be available to evaluate more important matters. Instead of considering every project, senior managers consider large projects in detail, and smaller projects are grouped together by type or segment. Thus, a company with three divisions might have a capital budget presented to senior management as in Exhibit 23–1.

EXHIBIT 23–1   Capital Project Requests

	(*millions*)
Projects for review	
Acquisition of Berry, Inc.	$25.6
Construction of Beaverton Plant	18.0
New main shaft at Butte Mine	6.0
Consumer products candy line	.4
Division-level projects:	
Medical Products Division	2.0
Consumer Products Division	.6
Mining and Exploration Division	3.4
Total requested	$56.0

Because large proposals commit the organization to considerable risk, they should be given detailed review by the board. Thus, the board should give close attention to the acquisition of Berry, Inc., the construction of a new plant, and the mine shaft at the Butte Mine. The board decides to go ahead with the Berry acquisition and the Beaverton plant. It defers the mine shaft because the board has decided to sell the Mining and Exploration Division in order to help fund the Berry acquisition. The candy line is considered by the president; it did not require detailed review by the board.

The amounts proposed for the divisions will be evaluated and discussed in light of strategic plans, and adjustments will be made as needed to meet these plans. For example, the amount proposed for the Mining and Exploration Division might be cut to zero because of a prior, but unannounced, decision to liquidate it.

Economic Feasibility

The **economic feasibility** of a capital project is the extent to which it meets the economic objectives of senior management. Economic feasibility is measured using criteria such as net present value, rates of return, and risk measures. However, economic feasibility is not the only consideration necessary for project selection. There will also be marketing, engineering, personnel, architectural, logistical, legal, and other technical analyses of feasibility.

Given the estimates of investment cash flows, staff analysts apply the economic criteria. Although analysts must be careful in applying concepts, the availability of electronic spread sheets has reduced the mechanics of analysis to a challenging exercise rather than a formidable task.

Most of the effort in an economic feasibility study is in developing the estimates of the impact of a project on financial reports and cash flows, not in applying the criteria. Engineering drawings, parts lists, time studies, equipment and construction bids, and personnel requirements are studied carefully. The estimates of knowledgeable people are gathered and organized. Then the implications of these estimates on cash flows and financial position must be carefully judged. Only after all of this effort and judgment can the criteria be applied.

Capital Budget

The **capital budget** is a summary of capital project proposals that have been presented to senior management and the board of directors for action. Each project in the capital budget is carefully reviewed by the staff of senior management for accuracy of the calculations and reasonableness of the assumptions underlying the project. The capital budget includes a summary of each project, the amount of investment required, summary results of the economic criteria applied, and the proposed method for financing the project. The capital budget is supported by the detailed capital project proposals.

Accountants' Role in Capital Project Analysis and Design

Accountants are an integral part of the system for project analysis and design. They help set up systems of paper flow within and between divisions and with senior management. They establish standard procedures, provide supporting analytical tools to design teams and managers, consult with managers on the effects of projects on cash flows, gather facts, and organize figures. Because the accountant understands systems and has the ability to connect physical flows with estimates of cash flows and income, he or she is uniquely qualified to analyze the effects of a project on a division's financial reports and performance measures. The accountant's detailed knowledge of document flows and accounting systems permits evaluation of the effects of project alternatives on the accounting system and the effects of the accounting system on the project. The accountant also reviews and recommends internal controls for the preparation, selection, and implementation of capital projects.

After a proposal has been prepared, senior staff accountants review the estimates for reasonableness and the calculations for accuracy. After project implementation, division staff accountants support the gathering of project results and summarize them in a final implementation report for senior management. Internal auditors review project results after implementation. Thus, accountants provide support to various levels of management in preparing, selecting, and reviewing capital projects.

Accountants, especially those with product-costing experience, should be involved during the project design because choices made in the detailed design lock in 75 to 85 percent of both investment and the subsequent cost of products or services. As the engineers and marketing people consider alternatives, the accountant should model the consequences of the alternatives on cost, volume, and profits.

Before discussing selection criteria, we will consider the motivations and risks involved in the submission of a project proposal.

MOTIVATION AND RISK RELATED TO PROJECT PROPOSAL

Organizational Motivation

On the simplest level, the primary reason for organizations to undertake a capital project is to increase future profits, thus, the wealth of their owners. This wealth is realized through growth in resources, information, and position in important markets.

On another level, senior management views capital projects as developing the company's movement toward its goals. For example, the changes brought about by projects may be used to challenge the employees to improve their performance and to keep them interested in their work. New products, production methods, or sales territories give senior managers the opportunity to rearrange the people and job content to meet changing conditions. Without challenge and change, people become bored and inflexible, which reduces the ability of the organization to survive a sudden change. Thus, capital projects allow senior managers to improve both the performance of employees and the survivability of the company.

Organizational Risk

The most obvious risk is that a capital project will have to be abandoned and, as a direct result, the organization incurs financial losses. Abandonment is a real risk because the majority of new products introduced each year are abandoned, and thousands of plants are closed and bankruptcies declared every year. For example, in the early 1980s, many computer companies introduced brands of personal computer. Although much of the hardware was technically sound, the products were unsuccessful because of the strategies undertaken by the IBM Corporation, which overwhelmed the competition with brand name, marketing, and the availability of software and service. As a consequence, many of the computer companies had to withdraw from the market, and a large number of them declared bankruptcy.

During each year, an organization has available only so many resources, whether in money, people, markets, production facilities, distribution channels, information, or management skill. The undertaking of promising projects now commits current and future resources that would otherwise be available for other projects. Consequently, only a limited number of projects can receive a commitment of resources while other projects must wait until additional resources become available or current projects are completed. Thus, part of the risk of a given project is the deferral of future opportunities.

Proposer Motivation

Division general managers and others propose capital projects for several reasons. First, managers propose projects in an attempt to gain a promotion or an increase in compensation as a result of increasing their division's profits. These are tangible rewards for successful projects. To gain these rewards, the managers do what is expected of them: they generate new ideas, defend those ideas to senior management, and then see that those ideas work.

Second, the division manager submits proposals because there is competition for funding. Many managers are naturally competitive and will play the project-funding game because it is challenging. Getting a project accepted by senior management and the board of directors is like winning at a high-stakes game. It is intrinsically rewarding to win.

Finally, the submission of a capital project proposal distinguishes a general manager who wants to have the image of a mover, not a caretaker. The movers get the attention of senior management, and the caretakers get left out. Because it is better to have the image of a mover rather than a caretaker, successful projects are evidence that the managers have merit.

Proposer Risk

After a proposal has been funded, it must be implemented successfully. The proposer must make the project happen through personal initiative. Large projects can take all of the manager's time and energy, which leaves little for managing the division. This situation can result in the neglect of other important activities.

An unsuccessful project is a major setback in the credibility and performance record of a manager. A major failure results in a loss of confidence by senior management and reduces the likelihood that future proposals by the manager will be accepted. Consequently, a manager's self-confidence and sense of creditability suffer.

CRITERIA FOR SELECTING CAPITAL PROJECTS

Selection criteria are included in the policies and procedures for capital projects. The purpose of the criteria is to encourage managers to submit only promising proposals. Meeting these criteria requires gathering and reporting information that is important to senior managers in their decision process.

Relationship of Strategy and Criteria

Capital project criteria result from the strategies adopted by senior management. The strategies often go beyond plans to increase current cash flows and income, or to improve financial position. Because strategies are not often communicated outside of the executive group, the formal criteria may be developed by executives with limited input and analysis. This can result in quasieconomic or even uneconomic actions. Quasieconomic actions are those that change revenues or improve future market position but that do not create wealth and profits. Uneconomic actions reduce wealth and profits. The following are three situations where quasieconomic or uneconomic criteria can influence decisions.

Dominant Market Position.   Whether for personal ego or company image, certain executives must have the dominant position in some of the markets in which they operate. They will give up current income by sharply reducing prices to attain or maintain a dominant market position. They drive their competitors out of the market with low prices and high quality. Thus, product proposals must either support an existing market share or promise to open a new market and eventually dominate it. Market dominance may or may not be intended to create future profits.

Personnel-Related Considerations.   Some senior managers enjoy moving people or seeing them develop in some direction. Thus, projects may be required to meet criteria for minimum training, a percentage of change in personnel, or an improved level of management-worker interaction. These requirements may or may not be intended to increase future profits.

Projects with No Economic Return.   Organizations undertake some projects for their image or public relations value even though no economic return is expected. Criteria for this type of project often include measures of the number of people affected or the cost per person helped by the project. For example, unused land or depreciated buildings might be set aside as a camp or for meeting space to benefit local youth groups. Companies often donate to local charities, which is socially responsible, but such donations reduce income with no promise of future returns.

External Reporting-Based Criteria

Several criteria are related to the return and risk of a project. We will use the following analysis setting to apply the criteria.

Analysis setting: JMV, Inc., is considering a major modification to the plant and equipment in order to produce a new product, a condensing pump for automobile air conditioners. The company has the following balance sheet:

JMV, INC.
Statement of Financial Position
January 1, 19x4
(in thousands)

Cash	$ 1,000	Current debt	$ 2,000
Accounts receivable	2,500	Long-term debt	5,000
Inventories	4,500	Common stock ($10 par)	1,500
Current assets	$ 8,000	Paid-in excess	3,000
Non current assets	12,000	Retained earnings	8,500
Totals	$20,000		$20,000

The current income is $6 million per year on sales of $30 million with a stable 4 percent growth in the market. The income tax rate is 40 percent.* Senior managers require a 10 percent return on investment, payback within two years, and a growth in sales of 10 percent per year.

The proposed project requires inventories of $2 million and equipment and start-up costs of $6 million, which will be depreciated over four years on a straight-line basis. By the end of the first year, accounts receivable will increase by $500,000. The project will be financed by a current bank note payable for $1 million, a four-year loan from an investor for $2 million, and sale of 500,000 shares of stock for $3 million; the remainder will come from current operations as they become available.

There is some uncertainty about selling prices, costs, and unit volumes. The managers of JMV agree that the following estimates are reasonable (amounts in thousands except price and variable cost):

Selling price		$ 4.00
Fixed costs		$4,000
Variable costs		$ 1.50
Sales units year	1	3,000
	2	5,500
	3	5,000
	4	2,500

---

* A complex maze of laws passed by Congress and rules and regulations set by the Internal Revenue Service to implement those laws determine income tax rates. Because Congress tends to change tax laws in each congressional session, tax rates and circumstances for application can be different each year. Rather than discuss all of the different rates and the circumstances to which they apply, we use a specific rate throughout this chapter so you know that tax implications must be analyzed as a part of an investment proposal.

Average ROI.   The **average return on investment** (ROI) is the average income over the life of the project divided by the average investment:

$$ROI = \frac{Average\ (Income)}{Average\ (Investment)}$$

In order to calculate ROI, we must first calculate the average income over the four years of the project. This is computed as $2.7 million per year in Exhibit 23–2 along with the cash flows. The **average investment** in most instances is found by adding the nondepreciating investment (inventories) to the average depreciating investment:

$$Average\ investment = Average\ (Inventories + Depreciable\ property)$$

The average depreciable property is found by dividing the investment by 2, which assumes straight-line depreciation and no salvage value at the end. For this example, assume that inventories stay at $2 million throughout the life of the project until the last year, when they are sold. The average investment will be:

$$\$2,000,000 + (\$6,000,000/2) = \$5,000,000$$

Based on this estimate,

$$Average\ ROI = \frac{\$2,700}{\$5,000} = 54.00\%$$

The impact of the project on net income is the most likely effect on income stated as a proportion. The calculation uses average income because the first year's income is often low and not representative

Exhibit 23–2   CMV, Inc. (calculation of net income and cash flows)

Year	Revenues*	Costs†	Deprec.‡	Taxes§	Net Income	After Tax Cash Flow‖
1/1/19x3						$(8,000)
19x4	$12,000	$ 8,500	$1,500	$ 800	$1,200	2,700
19x5	22,000	12,250	1,500	3,300	4,950	6,450
19x6	20,000	11,500	1,500	2,800	4,200	5,700
19x7	10,000	7,750	1,500	300	450	1,950
Averages	$16,000				$2,700	

Computation Notes:

   * Revenues are estimated by taking the price of $4 times the volume for each of the four years. For year 19x4, this is $4 × 3,000 units = $12,000.

   † Costs are estimated by adding the $4 million fixed costs to $1.50 times annual unit volumes. For 19x4, this is:

$$\$4,000 + \$1.50 \times 3,000 = \$8,500.$$

   ‡ Depreciation is found by dividing $6 million by 4 and assuming no salvage value at the end of year 19x7.

   § Taxes are 40 percent of income before tax.

   ‖ The after-tax cash flow is approximated here by adding back the depreciation to net income. However, in a practical setting, some of the expenses will be deferred (i.e., taxes, some employee-related costs, and some purchases of materials will not be paid until a later time period). If these costs are material, allowance should be made for them by increasing the current net cash flows. Similarly, some of the revenue will not be collected until later; in this problem, $500,000 in uncollected revenue accumulates during the first year. If material, adjust the cash flows by decreasing the first year by this amount and then adjust each subsequent year by the expected change in accounts receivable balance.

of the project. This impact on income is interpreted by many organizations as the total growth in income as a result of the project. The increase in income for CMV, Inc., is:

$$\text{Average impact on income} = \frac{\text{Average income}}{\text{Current income}} = \frac{\$2,700}{\$6,000} = 45.00\% \text{ increase}$$

Another growth measure that is important to some senior managers is the growth of the total sales. The sales growth may be found by dividing the average change in sales by the current sales:

$$\text{Sales growth} = \text{Average project sales / Current sales}$$
$$= \$16,000 / \$30,000 = 53.33\%$$

Still another measure of growth is the impact of the project on earnings per share (EPS). The financing of the project includes the issuance of 500,000 shares of stock. Assuming that the shares are issued at the beginning of the year,[2] the calculations on a pro forma basis will proceed as:

EPS (Before)	$6,000,000 / 1,500,000 shares =	$4.00
Impact of project	2,700,000 500,000 shares	
EPS (After)	$8,700,000 / 2,000,000 shares =	4.35
Increase in EPS		$ .35 8.75%

For many senior managers this is a critical calculation because their cash bonus and stock option plans often depend upon growth in the reported earnings per share. Senior managers with such compensation plans often require that a project *not decrease EPS during its first year*. For this project, the first year (19x4) EPS promises to be:

Net income/Shares

EPS (Before)	$6,000,000 / 1,500,000 shares =	$4.00
Impact of project	1,200,000 500,000 shares	
EPS (After)	$7,200,000 / 2,000,000 shares =	3.60
Decrease in EPS		($ .40) 10%

Thus, the project will cause a decline in earnings per share of 10 percent during the first year. Some senior managers would react negatively to the proposal because of the first-year decline.

The calculation of EPS growth is very sensitive to the number of shares issued. Thus, senior management will be pleased or displeased with the impact of a project on EPS depending upon how many shares are in the financing plans, for example:

Assumed Issuances	Calculation	EPS	Growth
–0–	$8,700,000 / 1,500,000	$5.80	45.00%
250,000	$8,700,000 / 1,750,000	4.97	24.25%
500,000	$8,700,000 / 2,000,000	4.35	8.75%
750,000	$8,700,000 / 2,250,000	3.87	(3.33%)

The break-even share issuance is 675,000.

Payback Period Method.   The **payback period** is the length of time required for the cash flows from operations to accumulate to the amount of the investment. The longer a project takes to pay for the initial investment, the riskier it is because of

---

[2] Shares issued midyear technically require the calculation of the equivalent shares for the year. Because the calculation is for the entire life of the project, this requirement is often immaterial.

changing circumstances and the poor quality of estimates about the distant future. The payback period is found by accumulating the sum of the cash flows and interpolating between years:

	Cash Flows	*Cumulative*		*Years*
Investment	$(8,000)	$(8,000)		
19x4	2,700	(5,300)		1.00
19x5	6,450	1,150	$5,300/$6,450	.82
Payback years	=			1.82

This project promises to pay for itself in a little under two years. Many companies have a three- to five-year limit on payback because, after five years, there is considerable risk to product markets. Payback indicates that the project is not very risky.

The payback method places a major focus on return *of* investment rather than return *on* investment; survival or recoupment takes a higher priority than profitability. The payback method ignores cash flows beyond the payback point, which makes comparing several projects difficult. However, the payback method is useful as a screening device to narrow projects for consideration when many projects have been proposed. Payback may also be a critical element as the riskiness of the project increases.

Liquidity and Solvency Effects.   These criteria measure the effect of the project's financing on the financial risk of the company. The effects are the changes in common financial ratios for liquidity and solvency. **Liquidity** is the ability to pay current liabilities as they are due. **Solvency** is the ability to make long-run repayment of all debt and interest as it falls due. Common ratios of liquidity and solvency are:

$$\text{Quick ratio} = \frac{(\text{Cash} + \text{Marketable securities} + \text{Receivables})}{\text{Current liabilities}}$$

$$\text{Current ratio} = \text{Current assets} / \text{Current liabilities}$$
$$\text{Debt/Equity ratio} = \text{Total liabilities} / \text{Total equities}$$

If we apply these three ratios before and after the acceptance of this proposed project, the following results will occur:

	Before Project	*After Project*
Quick ratio	(1,000 + 2,500)/2,000 = 1.75	(1,000 + 3,000)/3,000 = 1.33
Current ratio	8,000/2,000 = 4.00	(8,000 + 2,500)/3,000 = 3.50
Debt/Equity	7,000/20,000 = 0.35	(7,000 + 3,000)/26,500 = 0.38[3]

These ratios show that the company will be less liquid and less solvent after this project is financed and the investments in inventory and equipment are made. Senior management could choose to reduce this risk by issuing more stock; however, this would decrease the 8.75 percent expected increase in earnings per share.

Criteria Based on Discounting

Money received today is worth much more than money to be received in 10 years. Therefore, money has a time value that the foregoing methods have ignored. Because of this value, money to be received many years from now must be discounted by an interest factor to determine its value in present dollars, called the **present value.** In this section, we discuss four of the most common methods involving present values.

---

[3] Total equities here are approximated on a pro forma basis. Because $2 million is going to be financed from current operations, it will be some months before the final investments can be made without draining the cash account. The impact of this assumption on the solvency measure is very small ($<.01$).

Net Present Value. The **net present value** is the present value of future cash flows discounted at the required rate of return minus the initial investment.[4] The net present value at a 10 percent rate is computed by arranging the data as follows:

Time Period	Cash Flow	10% Discount Factor	Discounted Cash Flow
1/1/19x4	$(8,000)	1.0000	$(8,000)
19x4	2,700	0.9091	2,455
19x5	6,450	0.8265	5,331
19x6	5,700	0.7513	4,282
19x7	1,950	0.6830	1,332
		Net present value	$5,399

The discount factors come from the 10 percent column of Table 23–A at the end of this chapter. The calculation assumes that the cash inflows occur at the end of each year.

The net present value format presented above is a format that assumes a hand calculator is used. Electronic spread sheets commonly have present value functions built into the commands. For this example, the spreadsheet command[5] is similar to:

$$@NPV(0.10,CASH\ INFLOWS) - INVESTMENT$$

where

$$0.10 = Required\ return$$
$$CASH\ INFLOWS = Locations\ of\ cash\ flows\ for\ 19x4–19x7$$
$$INVESTMENT = Location\ of\ the\ \$(8,000).$$

The interest factor used is the minimum desired rate of return. Any project with a positive net present value has an excess of the minimum return. A zero net present value indicates that the return from the project is equal to the minimum return. If the net present value is less than zero (negative), the project is not expected to earn the minimum return. Only those projects that meet or exceed the minimum return are acceptable.

Discounted Rate of Return. The **discounted rate of return** is the rate at which the net present value is zero. The manual approach to finding a solution is to search with higher and lower rates until the net present value approaches zero. Thus, for our example, we would start with a 10 percent rate[6] and find a net present value of $5,399. Because the net present value is positive, we would try a high rate, for example 50 percent, which results in a negative net present value of $(1,259). Thus, 50 percent is too high. If we try a 30 percent rate, the net present value is $1,171. Performing a linear interpolation between these amounts for the zero present value results in:

---

[4] The detailed concepts and calculations of present value are treated in basic accounting, finance, marketing, and economics courses. Therefore, the calculations are not presented here.

[5] The spread sheet commands illustrated here are for LOTUS 1–2–3 and compatible packages. Consult user manuals for detailed application requirements for other packages.

[6] One starting point is to use the average return on investment. It is a rough approximation of the discounted rate of return, and its use should reduce the iterations necessary to arrive at a final number.

Rate	Net PV	Interpolation	Estimate
50.00%	(1,259)	(1,259)/(1,259 + 1,171) × 20% =	−10.4% + 50% = 39.6%
30.00%	1,171	1,171/(1,259 + 1,171) × 20% =	9.6% + 30% = 39.6%

This approximation will have some error, but it will be within 1 or 2 percent of the true rate.

Finding the true discounted rate manually is tedious. On an electronic spread sheet, the form of the discounted rate function is:

$$@IRR(0.10,CASH\ FLOWS)$$

where

0.10 = Starting estimate for the iterations
CASH FLOWS = Location for the cash flows arranged in one column of numbers.

Be sure to have the investment input as a negative number and the cash inflows as positive numbers. For the example data, the discounted rate of return is computed as 38.40 percent, which is 1.2 percent below the interpolated rate from the manual calculation.

The discounted rate of return method considers cash flows over the entire life of the investment as does the net present value method. The discounted rate of return method therefore is potentially useful in comparing competing proposals and, where necessary, ranking proposals. This method provides a measure of profitability that can be compared with a minimum desired rate of return. On the negative side, this method is more complicated to use than the net present value method.

Discounted Benefit-Cost Index.   The **discounted benefit-cost index** (also called the *present value index* or *profitability index*) is the ratio of the discounted present values to the original investment cost.

$$DBC\ index = \frac{\text{Present value of cash inflows}}{\text{Investment}} = \frac{\$13,399}{\$8,000} = 167\%$$

An index above 100 percent indicates that the project meets the criterion of the required return rate.

The discounted benefit-cost index becomes useful when ranking several investment proposals with different initial investments, project lives, and cash flow streams. It demonstrates where the greatest return for the dollar is.

Discounted Payback.   Managers who want to emphasize the payback period but also want to incorporate the time value of money concept use a discounted payback method. The **discounted payback method** is a variation on payback. It discounts the cash flows and uses the present value of cash flows in the payback computation:

	Cash Flows	10% Discount Factor	Discounted Cash Flow	Cumulative Cash Flow	Years
Investment	$(8,000)	1.0000		$(8,000)	
19x4	2,700	0.9091	$2,455	(5,545)	1.00
19x5	6,450	0.8265	5,331	(214)	1.00
19x7	5,700	0.7513	4,283	4,069 214/4,283 =	0.05
					2.05

Payback Years.   The discounted payback period will be slightly longer than the undiscounted payback period. For payback periods of less than three years, the approximate discounted payback period equals:

$$\text{Undiscounted payback} \times (1 + \text{Required return})$$

For our example, this is:

$$\text{Approximate discounted payback} = 1.82 \times (1 + .10) = 2.002$$

SUMMARY

Capital projects are large projects that require investment in assets for more than one year. Other projects are either small, do not involve assets, or are short in time period. Strategic planning is determining methods to use to attain the goals and objectives of senior management. Capital projects must be consistent with the strategic plans, which include exceeding a minimum required return.

A normal sequence of approval is set for capital projects, starting with lower-level managers and moving up the hierarchy. Approval levels are designed such that each level of management may give the final detailed review and approval to a specific-sized project.

The economic feasibility of a capital project, along with the other feasibility studies, is demonstrated with measures such as net present value or rates of return. Much effort and judgment are required in developing the estimates that are inputs to the economic feasibility analysis.

Organizations are motivated to implement projects by profits, growth, information, and market position. New projects often result in improvements in employee performance and the survivability of the company. Managers submit proposals in order to gain salary raises and promotions, or because they are highly competitive people who like the challenge of getting a project funded and implemented. Additionally, the submission of proposals creates an image of the manager as a mover. However, submitting proposals involves risks to a manager. The amount of time and attention required to supervise a proposal or funded project often leaves little time or energy for regular activities, which may result in a drop in short-run profits. A large unsuccessful project may doom the career of the proposer.

Capital project criteria are the results of senior management strategies, which may be only partially revealed. Thus, some quasieconomic or uneconomic objectives, such as dominant market position, employee development, or projects with public relations value may be included in project selection criteria.

Criteria for selection of capital projects may include measures of return and risk based on changes to the external financial report. The economic feasibility of the project may be measured by the average return on investment or change in income, sales, and earnings per share. Risk measures include the payback period and changes in liquidity and solvency measures, and the discounted payback.

Other selection measures include the net present value and the discounted rate of return methods. The net present value is the present value of cash flows minus the initial investment. The discounted rate of return is the rate that discounts the cash flows to zero. Closely tied to the net present value method is the discounted benefit-cost index, which is the ratio of the present value of cash inflows to initial investment. This index is useful in ranking projects when limited funding exists.

PROBLEM FOR REVIEW

Midland Oil Services Company is a contract oil and gas drilling company that operates out of West Texas. One of the supervisors has indicated the need to acquire a new piece of drilling equipment. The equipment will cost $70,000 and has an estimated useful life of seven years.

At the end of the useful life, the salvage value is expected to equal disposal costs. The straight-line depreciation method will be used for the equipment. The after-tax cash flows estimated by the controller appear below:

Year	Cash Flow
1	$ 25,000
2	21,000
3	17,000
4	13,000
5	12,000
6	11,000
7	9,000
	$108,000

Note: Because the cash flows are stated after tax, there is no need to make any adjustments to the above amounts.

REQUIRED

a. Compute the average return on investment.
b. Determine the payback period.
c. Compute a discounted payback assuming a 12 percent discount rate.
d. Assuming an annual minimum desired rate of return of 12 percent, determine the net present value.
e. Calculate the discounted benefit-cost index.
f. Determine the discounted rate of return. How does this rate compare with the minimum desired rate of return of 12 percent?

SOLUTION

a. Average return on investment.

$$
\begin{aligned}
ROI &= \text{Average income/Average investment} \\
&= (\$38,000/7)/(\$70,000/2) \\
&= \$5,429/\$35,000 \\
&= 15.5\%
\end{aligned}
$$

b. Payback period.

	Cash Flows	Cumulative		Years
Investment	$(70,000)	$(70,000)		
1	25,000	(45,000)		1.00
2	21,000	(24,000)		1.00
3	17,000	(7,000)		1.00
4	13,000	6,000	$7,000/$13,000 =	0.54
Payback years				3.54

c. Discounted payback period.

	Cash Flows	12% Discount Factor	Discounted Cash Flow	Cumulative Cash Flow	Years
Investment	$(70,000)	1.0000	$(70,000)	$(70,000)	
1	25,000	0.8929	22,323	(47,677)	1.00
2	21,000	0.7972	16,741	(30,936)	1.00
3	17,000	0.7118	12,101	(18,835)	1.00
4	13,000	0.6355	8,262	(10,573)	1.00
5	12,000	0.5674	6,809	(3,764)	1.00
6	11,000	0.5066	5,573	1,809	
				3,764/5,573 =	0.68
Discounted payback period					5.68

d. Net present value.

	Cash Flows	12% Discount Factor	Discounted Cash Flow
Investment	$(70,000)	1.0000	$(70,000)
1	25,000	0.8929	22,323
2	21,000	0.7972	16,741
3	17,000	0.7118	12,101
4	13,000	0.6355	8,262
5	12,000	0.5674	6,809
6	11,000	0.5066	5,573
7	9,000	0.4524	4,072
Net present value			5,881

The computer spread sheet calculated net present value as $5,878.

e. Discounted benefit-cost index.

$$\text{DBC} = \text{Present value/Investment}$$
$$= (\$70,000 + 5,879)/\$70,000 = \$75,879/\$70,000$$
$$= 108\%$$

f. Discounted rate of return.
1. By interpolation.

Rate	Net PV	Interpolation	Estimate
14%	2,201	$2,101/(2,101 + 1,358) \times 2\% = 1.2\%$	
		$1.2\% + 14\% =$	15.2%
16%	(1,358)	$(1,358)/(2,101 + 1,358) \times 2\% = -0.8\%$	
		$-0.8\% + 16\% =$	15.2%

2. By computer spread sheet calculation.
   15.2%

KEY TERMS AND CONCEPTS

Capital projects (885)
Strategic planning (886)
Required return (886)
Cost of capital (886)
Approval levels (887)
Economic feasibility (888)
Capital budget (888)
Average return on investment (895)
Average investment (895)

Payback period (893)
Liquidity (894)
Solvency (894)
Present value (894)
Net present value (895)
Discounted rate of return (895)
Discounted benefit-cost index (896)
Discounted payback method (896)

ADDITIONAL READINGS

Hendricks, James A. "Applying Cost Accounting to Factory Automation." *Management Accounting,* December, 1988, pp. 24–30.

Howell, Robert A., and Stephen R. Soucy. "Capital Investment in the New Manfuacturing Environment." *Management Accounting,* November, 1987, pp. 26–32.

Mulder, H., Jr. "Project Approach to a Global Change Process in High Technology Manufacturing and Distribution." *Production and Inventory Management Journal,* First quarter, 1988.

Myers, S. C. "Interaction of Corporate Financing and Investment Decisions." *Journal of Finance,* March, 1974, pp. 1–26.

Richards, Archie M., Jr. "How to Use Internal Rate of Return to Evaluate Investments." *The Practical Accountant*, April, 1987, pp. 66–71.

Richardson, P. R., and J. R. M. Gordon. "Measuring Total Manufacturing Performance." *Sloan Management Review*, Winter, 1980, pp. 47–58.

Singhvi, Surendra S., and Robert J. Lambrix. "Investment versus Financing Decisions." *Management Accounting*, March, 1984, pp. 54–56.

Skinner, W. "Manufacturing—Missing Link in Corporate Strategy." *Harvard Business Review*, May–June, 1969, pp. 136–45.

———. "The Focused Factory." *Harvard Business Review*, May–June 1974, pp. 114–21.

Spiller, Earl A., Jr. "Capital Expenditure Analysis: An Incident Process." *The Accounting Review*, January, 1981, pp. 158–65.

Taggart, R. A., Jr. "Capital Budgeting and the Financing Decision: An Exposition." *Financial Management*, Summer, 1977, pp. 59–64.

REVIEW QUESTIONS

1. How does a capital project differ from other projects proposed by management?
2. List three projects that will not be considered capital in nature.
3. Who performs strategic planning? What are a goal, an objective, and a strategy?
4. Give three examples of a strategy.
5. Give two reasons for not writing strategic plans and distributing them to employees and investors for approval.
6. Why might a project with a high promised rate of economic return be rejected by senior management?
7. Why do many corporations have lower-level managers approve projects before the project may be considered by the senior management?
8. Why do many corporations establish approval levels for the funding of projects? Why not have the board of directors review in detail all projects instead of just large ones?
9. Why is economic feasibility important?
10. What is the capital budget? How does it differ from a capital project proposal?
11. Give three reasons for involving accountants in capital project analysis and control.
12. Why do senior managers want to fund capital project proposals?
13. What risks are there to funding a large number of capital projects in one year?
14. Why would an unsuccessful project tie up resources?
15. Give three reasons that a division manager might want to submit a capital project proposal.
16. What risks do managers face when they submit a capital project proposal?
17. Give an example of a quasieconomic strategy and an uneconomic strategy.
18. How is the average investment computed for the average ROI criterion? What assumptions are made?
19. In what way is the payback period a measure of risk?
20. How does the funding of a capital project affect the liquidity and solvency of a company?
21. Define net present value and discounted rate of return.
22. Describe the discounted benefit-cost index and explain its usefulness.
23. Define and compare the payback method and the discounted payback method.

DISCUSSION QUESTIONS

24. Which capital product criteria can be applied to projects that do not require any initial investment?
25. How might a project with little initial investment but an extremely large termination cost be analyzed? Consider a project that involves handling nuclear material for a medical company that requires only a modest initial investment in equipment but an extremely expensive decontaminating process after 25 years.
26. Why should corporate strategies be set by senior managers? Why not have all the workers and investors vote on the best strategies to ensure the future profitability of the company?
27. What would motivate a division manager to be certain that a proposed project exceeds

all stated financial criteria? Why would the manager design the project to exceed stated criteria and drop all concepts that could not be so designed?

28. Why can senior managers presume that all of the calculations involving cash flows and investment have been made correctly in proposals? Why might they question the assumptions, estimates, and judgments on which the calculations are based?

29. Some authors argue that because accounts receivable balances increase as the result of capital project acceptance, receivables should be included in the investment base. Other authors argue that no investment occurs with accounts receivable because accounts receivable is just future cash inflow. How would you support each viewpoint?

30. Why is it important to make explicit as many assumptions involving investment and cash inflows as possible?

EXERCISES

23–1. Discounted Payback, NPV, and IRR.   Cloudcroft Resorts is evaluating a capital investment proposal that has the following predicted cash flows:

Initial investment	$44,590
Salvage value at disposition	–0–
Net operating cash inflows:	
Year 1	17,400
Year 2	25,600
Year 3	19,500
Year 4	8,100

REQUIRED:
a. Determine the discounted payback, assuming a 14 percent discount rate.
b. Determine the net present value, assuming a minimum desired rate of return of 14 percent.
c. Determine the discounted rate of return (internal rate of return) for the proposal.

23–2. Payback, NPV, and IRR.   Midway Airport is considering a proposal for the addition of a new piece of traffic control equipment. The anticipated cash flows are as follows:

Initial investment	$51,670
Savings in operating costs:	
Year 1	18,900
Year 2	25,800
Year 3	29,700
Year 4	16,600
Year 5	8,500

The salvage value at the end of five years is expected to equal the costs of disposition.

REQUIRED:
a. Calculate the payback period.
b. Calculate the net present value, assuming a 10 percent discount rate.
c. Determine the internal rate of return.

23–3. Ranking Investment Proposals.   Hubble Paints is considering changing its product containers from stainless steel to either plastic or aluminum. The machinery needed to handle plastic containers costs more than that for aluminum containers but it offers greater opportunities for operating cost savings. The cash flow information is presented below:

	Plastic	*Aluminum*
Initial investment	$85,000	$72,000
Annual operating cost savings	$36,000	$31,000
Salvage value end of six years	$ 7,000	$ 8,000
Useful life	6 years	6 years

The company has a minimum desired rate of return of 12 percent.

REQUIRED:
a. Determine the net present value for each alternative.
b. Determine the discounted benefit-cost index for each alternative.
c. Which alternative would you select? Explain.

23–4. Impact of Discount Rate on NPV.   Wellington Industries is evaluating two projects with three-year lives. Each will require a $10,000 initial investment. The annual cash flows are below:

Year	Project 1	Project 2
1	$9,000	$ 3,000
2	7,000	6,000
3	4,000	11,000

REQUIRED:
a. Calculate the net present value for each project, assuming a 10 percent discount rate.
b. Calculate the net present value for each project, assuming an 18 percent discount rate.
c. Explain the difference in the results of the two discount rates.

23–5. Payback Converted to Discounted Rate of Return.   Stacie Spa and Fitness Center is considering a project with a 20-year life and uniform cash inflows throughout the project's life. The total investment is required at the start of the project. The payback has been calculated at 5.1 years.

REQUIRED:
Determine the discounted rate of return for this project.

23–6. Acquisition of a Company.   Katherine Perez, president of Innovative Oil Exploration, Inc., wants to expand operations by acquiring the assets of Kennon Gas Processing Company. Kennon processes the gas from oil wells into natural gas, butane, and propane. Last year, Kennon showed revenues of $18,000,000 with operating expenses of $16,000,000. Included in the operating expenses is depreciation of $1,200,000. This level of earnings will continue for five years, at which time a new processing technology must be installed and the old assets will have no salvage value. The investment would cost Innovative $10,000,000 up front. In addition, the operating profits of the acquired company would be subject to a federal and state income tax rate of 40 percent.

REQUIRED:
a. Determine the after-tax cash flows for each year of the five-year period.
b. What is the discounted rate of return on this investment?
c. Calculate the payback period.

23–7. Changes after Investment Made.   Duncan International has made investments in small companies and properties in the United States and several foreign countries. Four years ago, it invested $1,000,000 in a small venture in Mexico. The investment was estimated to have a 10-year life with annual cash returns of $250,000. The investment returned $250,000 for four years. However, conditions in Mexico have changed, and the revised estimate for the annual cash return is only $150,000, which will continue for seven years. Because of a special tax status for this investment, there are no tax effects on current or future income.

The investment can now be sold for $540,000, and Duncan International is considering selling. At the present time, a minimum desired rate of return of 18 percent is necessary for an investment.

REQUIRED:
Should the investment be sold for $540,000? Make this determination by calculating the following:

    a. Discounted rate of return.

    b. Net present value.

23–8. Fill in the unknowns marked by letters below:

	Project 1	Project 2	Project 3
Initial investment	$60,000	$80,000	$260,000
Annual cash flow	$10,000	$20,000	*f.*
Project life	*a.*	9	10
Payback period in years	*b.*	*d.*	*g.*
Discounted rate of return	4%	*e.*	14%
Net present value at 5%	*c.*	$86,590	*h.*

PROBLEMS

23–9. Comparison of Evaluation Methods.   Scott Lieberenz, chief financial officer of Orosco High-Tech Products, Inc., has received four investment proposals from his staff. Each proposal requires an initial investment of $10,000, but the annual cash flows and the project lives differ. The cash flows for an eight-year span follows:

Year	Project 1	Project 2	Project 3	Project 4
1	$5,000	$1,000	$1,000	$1,000
2	4,000	2,000	1,000	2,000
3	3,000	3,000	2,000	4,000
4	2,000	4,000	8,000	4,000
5	1,000	5,000	6,000	3,000
6				2,000
7				2,000
8				1,000

Lieberenz wants to evaluate each of these proposals using the various evaluation methods before deciding which alternative he will support and then recommend to the top management team. He knows that the desired rate of return is 10 percent.

REQUIRED:

a. Calculate the following for each of the four projects:
    1. Payback period.
    2. Net present value.
    3. Discounted rate of return.
    4. Discounted benefit-cost index.
    5. Discounted payback.
    6. Average return on investment.
b. Identify which project is best for each of the six evaluation methods above.
c. Which project would you recommend that Lieberenz support to the management team? Why?

23–10. Investment Choices.   Beaver Company is faced with four mutually exclusive investment choices. The proposal preparation staff has labeled these potential projects as PDQ, FYI, VISTA, and SIERRA. The appropriate cash flow for each is as follows:

	PDQ	FYI	VISTA	SIERRA
Investment	$10,000	$10,000	$10,000	$30,000
Cash inflow year 1	7,500	12,000	–0–	16,800
Cash inflow year 2	6,000	–0–	14,400	22,000

The minimum desired rate of return for Beaver Company is 10 percent.

REQUIRED:
a. For each investment alternative, calculate the:
   1. Discounted rate of return.
   2. Net present value.
b. For each of the following pairs of investments, pick the better of the two:
   1. PDQ and FYI.
   2. PDQ and VISTA.
   3. PDQ and SIERRA.
   4. FYI and VISTA.
   5. FYI and SIERRA.
   6. VISTA and SIERRA.

23–11. Plant Closing Decision.   Abilene Cottonseed Oil Company has been losing money over the past few years. The unprofitable operation is the Big Springs plant. The accounting records show the plant is losing $250,000 a year in net cash flow. The plant income statement shows losses per year of $450,000. Because of economic conditions in the area and nationwide, the company believes the cash losses will continue for the next 10 years.

The company president wants to close the plant, but to do so will result in accounting write-offs that will generate $6,250,000 in accounting losses. In addition, a union contract requires a termination payment to employees that totals $2,500,000 in a one-time payment.

Another option is to modernize the plant and restructure the organization. This would cost approximately $3,000,000 immediately but would eliminate the cash loss of the past. Annual net cash inflows for each year over the next 10 years would be $600,000. The desired rate of return is 15 percent, and there are no tax effects.

REQUIRED:
a. Determine the net present value of each alternative (stay open or close down).
b. If the company could negotiate a better settlement with the union, what payment would make the company indifferent to whether it closed the plant or made the investment to modernize?

23–12. Various Minimum Desired Rates of Return.   Danielle McWilliams has just inherited $60,000 that she would like to invest. After much advice and research, she has identified two mutually exclusive options. The first option yields $13,000 a year after-tax annual cash flows for 10 years. The second option yields a one-time after-tax cash flow of $190,000 at the end of 10 years.

REQUIRED:
Develop a spread sheet for the following:
a. Prepare a table that shows the present value of future cash flows of each investment option at interest rates from 4 percent to 24 percent in increments of 1 percent.
b. Prepare a graph that presents the foregoing table with lines for each investment option. The vertical axis is the amount of present value and the horizontal axis is the minimum desired rate of return (interest rate).
c. Identify the range of interest rates over which the investment option would be preferable to Danielle:
   1. For investment option 1.
   2. For investment option 2.
d. At which interest rate would Danielle be indifferent as to the better investment option?

23–13. Expansion of Business.   Town & Country has several convenience stores with a self-serve gasoline station. One of the largest operations is at what city officials consider the busiest intersection in the city. The district manager would like to add an automatic car wash at that location because of the traffic pattern and the availability of space on company property. The car wash equipment would require an initial investment of $75,000 and have a 10-year life with no salvage value. The equipment would be depreciated on a straight-line basis for tax purposes. Estimated operating information for the expansion is as follows:

1. Annual cash operating costs:

Salaries	$19,200
Water	2,800
Other utilities	3,600
Repair and maintenance	6,400
Miscellaneous supplies	1,000

2. Annual cash revenues $55,000
3. The tax rate is 40 percent.

REQUIRED:

a. Compute the annual cash flows after tax.
b. Compute the following for this investment to the nearest two decimal places:
   1. Average return on investment.
   2. Payback period.
   3. Discounted rate of return.
   4. Net present value.
   5. Discounted payback.
c. Assuming that Town & Country established the following cutoff points for proposal acceptance, should the company expand to the carwash?
   1. Average return on investment of 18 percent.
   2. Payback period of three years.
   3. Discounted rate of return of 16 percent.
   4. Positive net present value at 16 percent.
   5. Discounted payback of five years.

23–14. Ranking Investment Alternatives. The board of directors for Caldwell Engineering, Inc., decided to increase its research and development efforts in the future. It earmarked $2.1 million for new research and development projects in the upcoming fiscal year. A number of potential projects have surfaced and are shown below with their net present value:

Project	Investment	Net Present Value
1	$500,000	$80,000
2	430,000	60,000
3	420,000	42,000
4	210,000	4,000
5	500,000	70,000
6	300,000	12,000
7	380,000	(21,000)
8	200,000	14,000
9	400,000	36,000
10	275,000	–0–

These net present values were computed using a minimum desired rate of return of 14 percent.

REQUIRED:

a. Calculate the discounted benefit-cost index for each project and rank from high to low in order of the index calculated.
b. Identify those projects that should be accepted, given the limited funds available.
c. If less than the entire amount of available funding is invested in research and development projects, what is the opportunity cost of the unused funds?
d. Is there any other combination of investments that will yield a higher total net present value than that combination shown in *(b)* above? Explain.

23–15. Company versus Division Rates of Return. Cluff Computer Software is organized into three divisions: retail sales, computer repairs, and training seminars. Computer repairs is looking at the possibility of opening a facility at another location. Space is available for lease, but remodeling costs and equipment will require an initial investment of $210,000. Although the property is available for a long-term lease, the current option is to take five years. At that point, the company will know better which direction its businesses should take.

The projected operating performance for the five-year period is summarized below:

Year	Revenues	Expenses*
1	$172,900	$101,000
2	182,000	121,000
3	193,800	130,500
4	206,400	132,500
5	219,816	132,500

* Includes lease payments but does not include depreciation or income tax expenses.

Depreciation of remodeling, fixtures, and equipment will be on a straight-line basis with no residual value. Federal and state income taxes are 40 percent. Cluff Computer Software has a minimum desired rate of return of 12 percent. However, the computer repairs division has been earning no less than 16 percent on its investments.

REQUIRED:
a. Compute the average rate of return for the expansion proposal.
b. Determine the annual after-tax net cash flows for the expansion proposal.
c. Determine the discounted rate of return.
d. Calculate the net present value for the investment at each of the following rates:
   1. Minimum desired rate of return of 12 percent.
   2. Minimum desired rate of return of 16 percent.
e. Is the division manager for computer repairs motivated to accept the expansion proposal? Explain.

23–16. Equipment Replacement.   UIL, Inc., manufactures electronic control devices for commercial and military aircraft. The company is considering replacing one of its computer-controlled machines. A new unit sells for $30,000 delivered. Installation costs will add another $2,000 to the costs to be capitalized and depreciated. The new equipment has an estimated useful life of 10 years. At the end of that time, the salvage value will equal the costs to remove and dispose of the machine. Depreciation will be on a double-declining basis over 10 years.

The old equipment could easily be used for another 10 years if the company wants to incur high repair and maintenance costs. A new machine would have lower repair and maintenance costs and would free workers who normally monitor the current machine. The estimated annual cash savings of the new machine will be $10,000.

The company's minimum desired rate of return is 12 percent and the tax rate is 40 percent.

REQUIRED:
a. Determine the annual after-tax net cash flow for the 10-year period.
b. Calculate the net present value of acquiring the new machine.
c. Assuming the new machine will be depreciated only over five years for tax purposes (salvage value at the end of 10 years remains the same), calculate the following:
   1. Annual after-tax net cash flows.
   2. Net present value.
d. What is the difference in net present value that can be attributed to the tax treatment of depreciation?

23–17. Various Minimum Desired Rates of Return.   Kaylene Investments, Inc., is considering several real estate investment opportunities. The profitability of each alternative depends on many factors, two of which are annual cash flows and interest rates. Because Kaylene will select only one of the alternatives, it is important that she select the best one. The following are the anticipated after-tax net cash flows from each alternative over an eight-year life:

Year	Property 1	Property 2	Property 3	Property 4
1	$ 100,000	$ 450,000	$ 100,000	$ 200,000
2	150,000	400,000	200,000	400,000
3	200,000	350,000	300,000	400,000
4	250,000	300,000	500,000	100,000
5	300,000	250,000	500,000	100,000
6	350,000	200,000	300,000	300,000
7	400,000	150,000	200,000	500,000
8	450,000	100,000	100,000	200,000
Investment	$1,100,000	$1,400,000	$1,300,000	$1,200,000

REQUIRED:

Develop a spread sheet for the following:

a. Prepare a table that shows the net present value of cash flows of each property at interest rates from 4 percent to 24 percent in increments of 1 percent.

b. Prepare a graph that presents the foregoing table with lines for each property. The vertical axis is the net present value and the horizontal axis is the interest rate.

c. Identify the range of interest rates over which each property would be preferable to Kaylene.

d. Identify the range of interest rates over which the following properties would be preferred to one another:
   1. Property 1 and property 2.
   2. Property 1 and property 3.
   3. Property 1 and property 4.
   4. Property 2 and property 3.
   5. Property 2 and property 4.
   6. Property 3 and property 4.

23–18. Ranking Competing Proposals.   Baze Corporation is in the final stages of its annual capital budgeting cycle. Of the many proposals generated in the various departments, only six have survived the review and approval process at the lower management ranks. Top management is currently making its final review of the proposals and assessing what resources will be available to fund any or all of the proposals. Partial details for these proposals are below:

Proposal	Initial Investment	Annual Operating Cash Flows	Net Present Value of Operating Cash Flows
1	$680,000	$185,000	$125,676
2	520,000	165,000	105,515
3	400,000	160,000	107,200
4	300,000	120,000	154,920
5	200,000	60,000	61,300
6	160,000	55,000	48,505

A 10 percent minimum desired rate of return was used in computing the net present values of operating cash flows.

REQUIRED:

a. Determine the expected life assumed in each of the proposals.

b. Rank the proposals on the basis of the following criteria:
   1. Payback period.
   2. Discounted payback.
   3. Discounted rate of return.
   4. Net present value.
   5. Discounted benefit-cost index.

c. Assume that $1.2 million is available for new capital proposals. How would you allocate the available funds to the six proposals? Explain what considerations you assessed in allocating the funds.

d. Comments on any concerns management should have when allocating funds to competing proposals with unequal lives.

EXTENDED
APPLICATIONS

23–19. New Product Introduction. Ohio Instruments, Inc., is evaluating a proposal to expand production with a new product, called Solar Lite. The proposed project requires inventories of $1.5 million and equipment and start-up costs of $5 million, which will be depreciated over six years on a straight-line basis. By the end of the first year, accounts receivable will increase by $500,000. The increase in accounts receivable and inventory will be financed from current operations. The rest of the project funding will come from three sources: (1) a one-year note payable with the bank for $1.2 million at 8 percent; (2) the sale of 500,000 shares of stock for $2.5 million; and (3) a five-year loan from a commercial investor for $1.3 million at 10 percent in annual payments of $342,937.

Although some uncertainty exists about selling prices, costs, and unit volumes, the managers have agreed that the following estimates are reasonable:

Selling price	$24.00
Variable costs per unit	$ 9.00
Fixed costs (excluding depreciation)	$4,000,000
Sales volume by year	
Year 1	500,000
Year 2	900,000
Year 3	1,000,000
Year 4	800,000
Year 5	400,000

During 19x5, Ohio Instruments, Inc., had operating income of $6 million on revenues of $30 million, with a stable 4 percent growth in the market. Depreciation expense is currently $2 million per year. The combined federal and state income tax rate is 40 percent. Top management requires a 10 percent return on investment, payback within three years, and a growth in sales of 10 percent per year. The balance sheet as of January 1, 19x6, is as follows:

OHIO INSTRUMENTS, INC.
Statement of Financial Position
January 1, 19x6
(in thousands)

Assets

Current assets:		
Cash	$1,200	
Accounts receivable	2,600	
Inventories	4,900	$ 8,700
Property, plant, and equipment		19,300
		$28,000

Liabilities and Stockholders' Equity

Current liabilities	$ 4,000
Long-term liabilities	15,000
Common stock ($1 par value)	3,000
Paid-in capital in excess of par	2,400
Retained earnings	3,600
	$28,000

REQUIRED:
a. Calculate the annual after-tax cash flows for the proposal.
b. Compute the following for the proposal:
   1. Average return on investment.
   2. Payback period.
   3. Discounted rate of return.
   4. Net present value.
   5. Discounted payback.

c. Prepare pro forma balance sheets for each of the five years in the period to reflect the financial effects of the investment. The company pays no dividends at this time.

d. Assess the impact of this investment on the financial position of the company in the following areas:

1. Income.
2. Growth.
3. Earnings per share.
4. Liquidity.
5. Solvency.

e. Should the company expand to the new product? Give your rationale for your recommendation.

23–20. Plant Rearrangement.   While visiting during a coffee break, a group of workers for a small defense subcontractor, Tripplet Corporation, complained about the inefficient layout of equipment on the production floor. They thought a lot of wasted time could be eliminated if equipment were arranged for an orderly flow from one machine to another without criss-crossing several cost centers. Later in the day, one of the workers told a supervisor about the conversation. The supervisor, looking for ways to improve her performance rating, outlined a proposal and passed it on to upper management. The suggestion finally reached the president. He thought the idea was worth considering and asked for a staff review and a capital project proposal.

The capital project proposal estimated $500,000 to make the necessary arrangements, which would have an estimated useful life of five years. Rearrangement costs would be amortized on a straight-line basis over the five years. The salvage value at the end of five years is estimated at $30,000. The elimination of wasted time will increase production capacity and sales units as follows:

Year	Sales Production without Rearrangement	Sales Production with Rearrangement
1	50,000	55,000
2	60,000	66,000
3	70,000	77,000
4	75,000	77,000
5	75,000	77,000

The rearrangement will result in cost savings in several areas. Direct labor costs will be reduced by $1 per unit in years 1 and 2. Because of learning curve effects, that savings will increase to $2 per unit in years 3 through 5. Variable overhead costs will be reduced by $1.50 per unit immediately. The need for one supervisor is eliminated at a savings in fixed costs of $16,000. Accounts receivable are expected to increase at the end of each year by 10 percent of the increase in sales volume. Accounts payable are expected to increase at the end of each year by 5 percent of the increase in sales volume. Inventories will increase at the end of the first year by $200,000 and remain constant at that level throughout the five-year period.

The contribution margin per unit is $200 before adjustments due to the rearrangement; the contribution margin ratio is 40 percent. Net income before taxes has been averaging 12 percent of sales revenue each year. The average income tax rate is 35 percent.

The original investment in rearrangement must be financed from a five-year bank loan with interest at 8 percent and payments due at the end of each year. The increases in current assets and current liabilities will be financed out of current operations. Depreciation expense is $800,000 per year.

The company has a stock purchase plan for employees through which they can purchase shares from the treasury at $2 per share. Employees have typically purchased 20,000 shares each year. This program is expected to continue during the next five years. No other issuance of capital stock is anticipated during the investment period.

The audited balance sheet at the end of the year, just before the rearrangement takes place, is below:

TRIPPLET CORPORATION
Statement of Financial Position
December 31, 19x0
(in thousands)
Assets

Current assets:
    Cash .... $ 384
    Accounts receivable 2,130
    Inventories .... 3,060 ..... $ 5,574
Property, plant, and equipment 8,418
                                                             $13,992

Liabilities and Stockholders' Equity

Current liabilities:
    Accounts payable $1,637
    Other current liabilities .... 1,243 ..... $ 2,880
Long-term notes payable 3,500
Stockholders' Equity:
    Capital stock ($1 par value) $1,800
    Paid-in capital in excess of par 3,600
    Retained earnings 2,512
                                    $7,912
Less: Treasury stock (150,000 shares) 300 7,612
                                                               $13,992

TABLE 23–A   Present Value of $1

n	1%	2%	3%	4%	5%	6%	7%	8%	9%	10%
0	1.0000	1.0000	1.0000	1.0000	1.0000	1.0000	1.0000	1.0000	1.0000	1.0000
1	0.9901	0.9804	0.9709	0.9615	0.9524	0.9434	0.9346	0.9259	0.9174	0.9091
2	0.9803	0.9612	0.9426	0.9246	0.9070	0.8900	0.8734	0.8573	0.8417	0.8264
3	0.9706	0.9423	0.9151	0.8890	0.8638	0.8396	0.8163	0.7938	0.7722	0.7513
4	0.9610	0.9238	0.8885	0.8548	0.8227	0.7921	0.7629	0.7350	0.7084	0.6830
5	0.9515	0.9057	0.8626	0.8219	0.7835	0.7473	0.7130	0.6806	0.6499	0.6209
6	0.9420	0.8880	0.8375	0.7903	0.7462	0.7050	0.6663	0.6302	0.5963	0.5645
7	0.9327	0.8706	0.8131	0.7599	0.7107	0.6651	0.6227	0.5835	0.5470	0.5132
8	0.9235	0.8535	0.7894	0.7307	0.6768	0.6274	0.5820	0.5403	0.5019	0.4665
9	0.9143	0.8368	0.7664	0.7026	0.6446	0.5919	0.5439	0.5002	0.4604	0.4241
10	0.9053	0.8203	0.7441	0.6756	0.6139	0.5584	0.5083	0.4632	0.4224	0.3855
11	0.8963	0.8043	0.7224	0.6496	0.5847	0.5268	0.4751	0.4289	0.3875	0.3505
12	0.8874	0.7885	0.7014	0.6246	0.5568	0.4970	0.4440	0.3971	0.3555	0.3186
13	0.8787	0.7730	0.6810	0.6006	0.5303	0.4688	0.4150	0.3677	0.3262	0.2897
14	0.8700	0.7579	0.6611	0.5775	0.5051	0.4423	0.3878	0.3405	0.2992	0.2633
15	0.8613	0.7430	0.6419	0.5553	0.4810	0.4173	0.3624	0.3152	0.2745	0.2394
16	0.8528	0.7284	0.6232	0.5339	0.4581	0.3936	0.3387	0.2919	0.2519	0.2176
17	0.8444	0.7142	0.6050	0.5134	0.4363	0.3714	0.3166	0.2703	0.2311	0.1978
18	0.8360	0.7002	0.5874	0.4936	0.4155	0.3503	0.2959	0.2502	0.2120	0.1799
19	0.8277	0.6864	0.5703	0.4746	0.3957	0.3305	0.2765	0.2317	0.1945	0.1635
20	0.8195	0.6730	0.5537	0.4564	0.3769	0.3118	0.2584	0.2145	0.1784	0.1486
25	0.7798	0.6095	0.4776	0.3751	0.2953	0.2330	0.1842	0.1460	0.1160	0.0923
30	0.7419	0.5521	0.4120	0.3083	0.2314	0.1741	0.1314	0.0994	0.0754	0.0573
50	0.6080	0.3715	0.2281	0.1407	0.0872	0.0543	0.0339	0.0213	0.0134	0.0085
60	0.5504	0.3048	0.1697	0.0951	0.0535	0.0303	0.0173	0.0099	0.0057	0.0033

The president has a 15 percent minimum desired rate of return on new capital projects, but he also wants to maintain a growth pattern in both earnings and earnings per share. The company pays no dividends at this time.

REQUIRED:
a. Calculate the annual after-tax cash flows for the proposal.
b. Compute the following for the proposal:
   1. Average return on investment.
   2. Payback period.
   3. Discounted rate of return.
   4. Net present value.
   5. Discounted payback.
c. Prepare pro forma balance sheets for each of the five years to reflect the financial effects of the investment.
d. Assess the impact of this investment on the financial position of the company in the following areas:
   1. Income.
   2. Growth.
   3. Earnings per share.
   4. Liquidity.
   5. Solvency.
e. Should the company make the investment in the rearrangement? Give the rationale for your recommendation.

11%	12%	13%	14%	15%	16%	17%	18%	19%	20%	24%
1.0000	1.0000	1.0000	1.0000	1.0000	1.0000	1.0000	1.0000	1.0000	1.0000	1.0000
0.9009	0.8929	0.8850	0.8772	0.8696	0.8621	0.8547	0.8475	0.8403	0.8333	0.8065
0.8116	0.7972	0.7831	0.7695	0.7561	0.7432	0.7305	0.7182	0.7062	0.6944	0.6504
0.7312	0.7118	0.6931	0.6750	0.6575	0.6407	0.6244	0.6086	0.5934	0.5787	0.5245
0.6587	0.6355	0.6133	0.5921	0.5718	0.5523	0.5337	0.5158	0.4987	0.4823	0.4230
0.5935	0.5674	0.5428	0.5194	0.4972	0.4761	0.4561	0.4371	0.4190	0.4019	0.3411
0.5346	0.5066	0.4803	0.4556	0.4323	0.4104	0.3898	0.3704	0.3521	0.3349	0.2751
0.4817	0.4523	0.4251	0.3996	0.3759	0.3538	0.3332	0.3139	0.3538	0.3332	0.3139
0.4339	0.4039	0.3762	0.3506	0.3269	0.3050	0.2848	0.2660	0.2487	0.2326	0.1789
0.3909	0.3606	0.3329	0.3075	0.2843	0.2630	0.2434	0.2255	0.2090	0.1938	0.1443
0.3522	0.3220	0.2946	0.2697	0.2472	0.2267	0.2080	0.1911	0.1756	0.1615	0.1164
0.3173	0.2875	0.2607	0.2366	0.2149	0.1954	0.1778	0.1619	0.1476	0.1346	0.0938
0.2858	0.2567	0.2307	0.2076	0.1869	0.1685	0.1520	0.1372	0.1240	0.1122	0.0757
0.2575	0.2292	0.2042	0.1821	0.1625	0.1452	0.1299	0.1163	0.1042	0.0935	0.0610
0.2320	0.2046	0.1807	0.1597	0.1413	0.1252	0.1110	0.0985	0.0876	0.0779	0.0492
0.2090	0.1827	0.1599	0.1401	0.1229	0.1079	0.0949	0.0835	0.0736	0.0649	0.0397
0.1883	0.1631	0.1415	0.1229	0.1069	0.0930	0.0811	0.0708	0.0618	0.0541	0.0320
0.1696	0.1456	0.1252	0.1078	0.0929	0.0802	0.0693	0.0600	0.0520	0.0451	0.0258
0.1528	0.1300	0.1108	0.0946	0.0808	0.0691	0.0592	0.0508	0.0437	0.0376	0.0208
0.1377	0.1161	0.0981	0.0829	0.0703	0.0596	0.0506	0.0431	0.0367	0.0313	0.0168
0.1240	0.1037	0.0868	0.0728	0.0611	0.0514	0.0433	0.0365	0.0308	0.0261	0.0135
0.0736	0.0588	0.0471	0.0378	0.0304	0.0245	0.0197	0.0160	0.0129	0.0105	0.0046
0.0437	0.0334	0.0256	0.0196	0.0151	0.0116	0.0090	0.0070	0.0054	0.0042	0.0016
0.0054	0.0035	0.0022	0.0014	0.0009	0.0006	0.0004	0.0003	0.0002	0.0001	—
0.0019	0.0011	0.0007	0.0004	0.0002	0.0001	0.0001	—	—	—	—

Capital Project Design
Concepts and Techniques

■

THE PROBLEM OF ESTIMATING INVESTMENT
AND CASH FLOWS*

John Calloway is the Foods Division general manager for CSV, Inc. John has held this position for two years and has had a good start at turning the division into a profitable enterprise. He has reduced production costs by 13 percent per unit and administration costs by 17 percent while increasing sales by 16 percent. John has also placed over $200,000 of the operations budget into product development and is now considering whether to propose a new product line to senior management.

The new product is a high-energy candy called Bear Country. The candy line is made from honey, strawberries or blackberries, assorted nuts, and grain. The Bear Country product line with six products has been test marketed and found to be promising with projected sales of roughly $1,200,000 per year. Because existing production lines are full, the proposed product requires a new production line at a cost of about $300,000.

This is John's first capital project proposal, and he wants to be careful in developing the proposal package. He asks the division controller, marketing manager, and plant manager to study the new candy line in detail according to the guidelines sent by central headquarters. If the project requires less than $400,000 investment, only the president needs to approve it. John would like to avoid going to the board of directors

* This problem is a continuation from Chapter 23 and is concluded as extended problem 24–20.

for approval, so the project must be kept under $400,000 in investment. He also wants to have precise estimates for investment and cash flow in which he can have confidence before he sends the proposal to the president.

LEARNING OBJECTIVES

As a result of studying this chapter, you should be able to:

1. Apply techniques for determining estimates of cash flows.
2. Identify investment elements and calculate the total amount of investment.
3. Compute sensitivity to assumptions.
4. Compute loss on abandonment.

CAPITAL PROJECT DESIGN

Capital project design is a process that takes a rough concept to a detailed design in the development of a capital investment proposal. Design includes identifying and specifying the project's physical characteristics: function, location, size, shape, production process, number of parts, suppliers, equipment, and number of workers. Design involves the skills of the engineering, marketing, purchasing, financial, legal, and other specialized staffs. Because of the complexity introduced by the many physical characteristics and skills, large projects go beyond one or two individuals and require project teams. The target concept is an example of a successful approach to project design.

Target Concept

The target concept is really a strategy. It requires designing expected competitive enhancements into new products and services from conceptualization through production development. Many companies have noticed that soon after they enter a market, competitors react by offering an enhanced version of the product or service at a lower price. With such competitive pressures, the large profits projected in capital project proposals seldom materialize. Most people easily recognize that the loss of anticipated market share for the new product is one reason for lower than expected profits. However, a greater impact on profits comes from the costly redesign, retooling, and relearning that takes place after product introduction but while current production continues. In this case, management operates under the aura that it is aiming at a target that the competition keeps moving. In management's attempt to recapture or maintain its market position, it frequently makes costly mistakes in the rush to change the product design, the production process, and the marketing strategy. The natural consequence is generally poor quality and service, which leads to customer dissatisfaction, and that results in lost profits.

The **target concept** is a strategy for designing, marketing, and pricing that involves anticipating the reactions of the competition. The first step is to estimate the eventual price that competitors will likely charge for their products and to design an enhanced version of the product that can be sold at the competitor's price and that has the features that the competition will likely place in their products. In this process, prices should be set assuming that the learning curve (see the appendix to Chapter 7) exists in the production process. The objective is to reduce to zero, if possible, the number of changes that will have to be made to the product and its distribution and prices during the start-up of the product.

Once a target price has been established, a total cost target is set by subtracting a normal profit margin from the target price. This total cost target[1] is then apportioned to production, marketing, and administration costs. Within production, target costs are set for materials, labor, and overhead for each production process (such as fabrication and assembly). The accountant builds a cost-volume-profit model (as in Chapter 4) that can reflect the financial impact of each change in the proposed product design, production flow, marketing method, and distribution method. The results of a cost-volume-profit analysis become part of the capital project proposal and will be subject to the evaluation process. It is at this point that the criteria required by senior management—payback, average rate of return, net present value, and discounted rate of return—are applied to the proposal.

The accountant's role is to gather the financial estimates associated with the project, model the alternatives, organize the results in the required format, and apply the appropriate decision criteria. This often involves assisting managers in developing estimates for all factors necessary to complete planning decisions.

Techniques for Assisting Estimation

Managers have different abilities to estimate costs due to a wide variety of perceptions, cognitive ability (the way thoughts and perceptions are processed), and attitudes (likes and dislikes). Some managers think quantitatively and can estimate easily, but others need assistance. Still others are optimistic and give high estimates of revenue and low estimates of cost, and others are pessimistic and give conservative estimates of both. Some managers may be strongly biased by their preference for (or against) a project. Still others are not accustomed to committing themselves; they wait for someone else to commit to an estimate first. Finally, some managers make estimates based on what they think senior managers want to hear. Therefore, the leader of the project proposal must use good judgment in selecting people for the team and in determining which estimation technique is appropriate for the situation.

Estimates Based on Historical Data.   Many managers are interested in estimates based on historical information. In this form of estimation, the manager gathers data from situations similar to the current project. Either by adjusting the average of past data, or by using regression analysis (as in Chapter 3) and making projections, they prepare an estimate of the expected amounts. This estimate should be based on a consideration of learning curves (as in Chapter 7), changes in technology, and production methods.

Historical analysis is often the technique with which the accountant feels most comfortable. However, basic assumptions that may not be correct are built into the analysis. Such assumptions are that (1) the future will be similar to the past and (2) the situations selected are equivalent to the project proposal. If these assumptions are wrong, the estimates from past data could be seriously biased.

Estimates based on historical evidence are useful in gathering information from managers who are unable to easily form a quantitative estimate or who are overly optimistic or pessimistic. The historical quantitative data give managers the numbers to question and to adjust.

Estimates Based on Individual Manager Judgment.   Managers who have quantitative facility can give straightforward estimates given reasonable assumptions. For example, the sales manager might be asked to estimate sales quantities at two prices assuming that a specific product is introduced next year. Further, assume that the product has good production quality and marketing efforts:

	Selling Price	
	$2	$4
Year 1	2,000	500
Year 2	4,000	2,000
Year 3	3,000	2,000
Year 4	1,000	300

If the manager making the judgment is knowledgeable, it will be moderately reliable for analysis. The technique also has the advantage of requiring relatively little time to gather numerous estimates.

Estimates Based on Group Average.   One method of improving individual management judgments is to take an average of the estimates from a small but knowledgeable group. The group need not be large because the average estimate from 3 or 4 managers is only somewhat less accurate than the average estimate from 10 or 20 managers.

The Delphi Estimation Technique.   Another version of the group average technique is called the **Delphi technique.**[2] In this technique, the manager first obtains initial estimates from each of a small group of knowledgeable persons. The results of the first estimates are reported back to all members, and then revised estimates are obtained. This process is repeated until the project leader is satisfied that the individual estimates will change little. The final results are then summarized as an average estimate.

The Delphi technique is often more accurate than the average of group estimates because it allows each person to carefully think through the judgment and experience of others. It takes more time and can be cumbersome when many estimates are involved. Thus, the technique should be used for relatively few, perhaps less than 10 or 20, critical estimates.

Estimating Amounts with Odds.   This is a technique for increasing the accuracy of individual estimates. Starting with a high number, estimates should be picked until the manager is willing to accept equal odds that the actual result will be either above or below the estimate. Thus, the manager would accept a bet paying $1 if the actual amount falls below this number or receiving $1 if the actual amount is higher than the estimate. The result is an estimate of the median or midpoint.

This technique can be used for estimating a few items, say up to 10, but is time consuming and boring when dealing with hundreds of items. When the items to be estimated are numerous, they should be aggregated in some way, or the estimates may reflect fatigue or boredom rather than knowledge. Further, the results will be somewhat biased, high or low, depending on the risk aversion of the manager—how much the manager likes or dislikes taking risks. Some managers are, for personal reasons, opposed to betting in any form. Other managers argue that either the quantity will happen or it will not, and taking odds on it is nonsense. The straightforward, judgment technique should be used with the latter managers.

---

[2] Delphi was the ancient Greek site of the Temple of Apollo. In the temple was Pythia, an Oracle, who spent most of her time uttering sounds that were supposedly the words of Apollo. Temple officials conferred among themselves to develop a common interpretation of Pythia's utterances. The common interpretation was then reported to the king.

Estimating Risk with Odds.   Our estimates to this point represent means (averages) or medians (midpoints). Now we are interested in obtaining some measure of the risk associated with those estimates and identifying odds of such risks. This section presents common techniques used.

Estimating quartiles.   One technique for assessing risk is to divide the range of possible estimates into quartiles. Quartiles are the points that divide the range into quarters. Given a median, quartiles, and extreme points of the range, it is possible to estimate a variance. The process for doing this is described below.

The first step is to divide the range from the median to the upper extreme. This is done subjectively by asking the manager to put odds on successively increasing amounts until the manager will just accept one chance in four (25 percent) that the actual quantity will be above the estimate. For the lower quartile, the same process is followed downward. Starting with the median, the quantities are successively decreased until the manager will just accept one chance in four that the actual quantity will be below the estimate.

The next step is to get estimates of very high and very low points. The manager should give a low number with only 1 chance in 20 (5 percent) that the actual amount will be below that number. Then the manager should give a high number such that there is only 1 chance in 20 that the actual amount will exceed that number. The highest number plausible is interpreted as only 1 chance in 20 that the actual amount will be above the high number.

One final set of numbers is necessary before we can make appropriate calculations: extremely high and extremely low amounts. These numbers are remotely possible but highly unlikely. *Highly unlikely* is interpreted as less than 1 chance in 100 (less than 1 percent). Care should be taken not to be too extreme because this will inflate the estimated standard deviation we will calculate from the foregoing numbers.

As an illustration, assume that you obtained the following estimates for the cost of a particular material next year, say A grade lumber, from a manager:

Median	$100
Upper quartile	140
Very high	200
Lower quartile	90
Very low	86

We have to use our judgment to pick an extreme low and extreme high cost. In this case, we select $40 as the extreme low and $260 as the extreme high. Because of the manner in which all of the above numbers were selected, percentages are automatically assumed as follows:

Extreme low to very low	5
Very low to lower quartile	20
Lower quartile to median	25
Median to upper quartile	25
Upper quartile to very high	20
Very high to extreme high	5

Now we combine this information into a calculation technique to give an estimate of the standard deviation for the price we build into our capital investment proposal. Exhibit 24–1 presents a summary of the calculations.

EXHIBIT 24–1   Technique for Approximating an Average and Standard Deviation
(from quartiles and very high and low estimates)

	Prices *Step 1*	*(X)* *Mid-points* *Step 2*	*(p)* *Prob-* *abilities* *Step 3*	*Average (X)* *p × (X)* *Step 4*	*Variance* *p × (X-$120)²* *Step 5*
Extreme low	$ 40				
Very low	86	63	5%	$ 3.15	$ 162.45
Lower quartile	90	88	20%	17.60	204.80
Median	100	95	25%	23.75	156.25
Upper quartile	140	120	25%	30.00	0.00
Very high	200	170	20%	34.00	500.00
Extreme high	260	230	5%	11.50	605.00
Totals			100%	$120.00	$1,628.50
Standard deviation (square root of variance)					$40.35

The technical procedures outlined in the exhibit are labeled steps in each heading. These steps are explained as follows:

Step 1   *Basic Estimates.* Arrange the estimates from very low to very high.

Step 2   *Midpoints.* Compute the midpoints between each of the estimates. The midpoint is equal to the sum of each two points divided by 2. For example, the first midpoint is $(40 + 86)/2 = 63$.

Step 3   *Probabilities.* Arrange the probabilities as described in the example data. For this technique, they will always be the percentages listed in the example.

Step 4   *Average.* Compute the estimate of the average by multiplying the midpoints times the probabilities and summing the column. The result is $120 for the example.

Step 5   *Standard Deviation.* Multiply the probability times each deviation (midpoint minus the average) squared:

$$p \times (X - \bar{X})^2$$

Sum the column and take the square root of the total. This result is an estimate of the standard deviation, which is $40.35 for the example. *Note:* there will be error in this estimate due to error in the original estimates, judgments on extreme points, and the approximation built into the technique.

Once a standard deviation has been calculated, it can be used to establish a risk for the amount that will actually happen. For example, the probability of the actual amount falling within plus and minus one standard deviation of the average (mean) is approximately 68 percent; or 95 percent for plus and minus 1.96 standard deviations. Therefore, we could have the following ranges for our probabilities:

> 68 percent—Upper price is $120 plus $40.35, or $160.35
> —Lower price is $120 minus $40.35, or $79.65.
> 95 percent—Upper price is $120 plus (1.96 times $40.35), or $199.09.
> —Lower price is $120 less (1.96 times $40.35), or $40.91.

Sensitivity analysis (as discussed later in the chapter) can be applied to these ranges to assess the sensitivity of these risks in the evaluation technique (payback, net present value, etc.) used for the capital investment proposal.

Estimates of risk with scenarios.   When many estimates are required, the estimation with odds technique can be too time consuming and perhaps inaccurate due to fatigue on the part of the estimators. Another technique is to ask the manager to describe three scenarios:

> *Most Likely.* "What do you expect to be the most likely set of events to occur in relationship to this project?" Have the manager describe the sales and costs that will happen if the project is accepted.
> *Pessimistic.* "What would you expect to be the worst sales and costs that will occur after the acceptance of this project?" Interpret pessimism as only a 1-in-20 chance (5 percent) that things could get worse.
> *Optimistic.* "What would you expect to be the best set of events to occur after the acceptance of this project?" Interpret optimism as only a 1-in-20 chance that things could get better.

The most likely estimates are the person's estimates of most common results, which are technically called the mode. For data on costs, prices, and volume, the mode will be less than the median (midpoint in the distribution), and the median will be less than the average because cost, price, and volume cannot be negative numbers, but the high side is unlimited. For example, the price of a barrel of oil next year could be estimated as most likely being $18 and possibly being as low as $10 or as high as $60, depending on the vagaries of war and international diplomacy. A median expected oil price might be $22; an average oil price would be $24.

For illustrative purposes, assume that you are analyzing a project that requires barrels of crude oil for input. You have obtained the following long-range estimates from the purchasing agent who is considered most knowledgeable about the purchase price of oil:

	Pessimistic	*Most Likely*	*Optimistic*
Prices	$46	$18	$9

In the pessimistic scenario, there is substantial war damage in the Middle East and shipping is very unreliable. General inflation heats up, and supplies of oil are hoarded for speculative reasons. In the most likely scenario, the supply situation stays at current levels. In the optimistic situation, shipping is resumed at above-normal levels, and the Organization of Petroleum Exporting Countries loses substantial control of production volume. Exhibit 24–2 presents a technique for roughly approximating the

EXHIBIT 24–2   Technique for Estimating Average and Standard Deviation from Scenario Estimates

	Prices *Step 1*	*(X)* *Mid-points* *Step 2*	*(p)* *Prob-abilities* *Step 3*	*Average (X)* $p \times (X)$ *Step 4*	*Variance* $p \times (X\text{-}24.75)^2$ *Step 5*
Low possible	$ 4		5%	$ 0.33	$ 16.65
Optimistic	9	6.5	40%	5.40	50.63
Most likely	18	13.5	50%	16.00	26.28
Pessimistic	46	32	5%	3.03	63.90
High possible	75	60.5			
Totals			100%	$24.75	$157.46
Standard deviation (square root of variance)					$12.55

average and standard deviation from these estimates. These computations are similar to those in Exhibit 24–1. As with the earlier example, it is necessary to use your judgment to pick a lowest possible and highest possible value for oil prices. These values should be remotely possible, but unlikely. Again values that are too extreme will inflate your estimate of the standard deviation.

The technical procedures outlined in the exhibit are labeled steps in each heading. These steps are explained as follows:

Step 1   *Basic estimates.* Arrange your estimates from low to high.

Step 2   *Midpoints.* Compute the midpoints between each of the estimates. The midpoint is equal to the sum of each two points divided by 2. For example, the first midpoint is (4 + 9)/2 = $6.50.

Step 3   *Probabilities.* Arrange the probabilities as above. For this technique, the middle two probabilities are judgments by the estimator but must add up to 0.90. The first and last probabilities are similar to the earlier example and are stated at 0.05. Remember, these probabilities are subjective in nature.

Step 4   *Average.* Compute the estimate of the average by multiplying the midpoints times the probabilities. Sum the column. The result is $24.75 for this example. The average will always be greater than the most likely estimate.

Step 5   *Standard deviation.* Multiply the probability times each (midpoint minus the average) squared:

$$p \times (X - \bar{X})^2$$

Sum the column and take the square root of the total. This result is an estimate of the standard deviation, which is $12.55 for the example. *Note:* there will be error in the estimate due to error in the original estimates, your judgments on extreme points, and the approximation built into the technique.

We can subsequently use the standard deviation as a measure of risk.

ESTIMATING INVESTMENT AND CASH FLOW

In the previous sections, we discussed issues relating to estimating in general. Within the capital investment proposal, estimates are necessary to establish the required investment and the cash flows that will occur throughout the life of the investment. Now we discuss the specifics of estimating these two critical areas.

Estimating Investment

Project investment refers to the assets that are committed to the project up to the point of normal operation of the project. The estimation of investment follows the detailed engineering design plans for the plant and equipment, the marketing plans for the promotion and distribution of the new product, and the administrative plans for paperwork flow and product management. Thus, a capital project involving new products requires the following types of investment:

1. Purchase price of production machinery, equipment, and tools for both production and maintenance. Shipping and delivery charges should be included in this amount.
2. Preparation of production plant and equipment setup, which will involve construction or modification of appropriate space to place the equipment.
3. Project start-up costs that include inspection costs, testing fees, process engineering, worker training, and similar setup costs.
4. Raw materials, work in process, and finished goods inventories.
5. Initial marketing, distribution, and administrative setup costs.

Projects *not* involving new products (e.g., equipment replacement) may involve very little of types 4 and 5 investment.

In some organizations, only the direct investment in productive equipment and the preparation of the production plant (items 1 and 2) are included as investment. This definition understates the amount of resources committed to a project. Because the investment is understated and unseen, it is not controlled. Although this practice might be expedient, it may result in *overinvestment* in project setup, inventories, marketing, distribution, and administration. As a consequence, the production and administrative overhead costs may increase without warning as a result of accepting a project.

As with decisions discussed in Chapter 22, the concern is for the differential or net investment, that is, the net additional outlay of cash required to obtain the future cash flows. In most cases, the net additional outlay or net investment is the net outflow of cash or increase in asset levels to support a capital investment. Assume, for example, that equipment with a net book value of $100,000 will be sold if a certain capital investment proposal is accepted. The investment in the new proposal must reflect the impact of the sale of the equipment (gain or loss as adjusted by income tax effects) to arrive at a net proposal investment.

Estimating Cash Flows

Estimating cash flows from a project involves the same techniques as estimating cash flows from operations (as in Chapter 15). However, the estimates relate to many future years instead of just one year. Further, some projects change both revenues and costs (a new product or service), and others change only the expected costs (e.g., a new production method or machine).

In estimating the cash flows by time period, a number of factors must be considered.

The items to be considered for cash flows are as follows:

1. Income generated by projects increases cash inflows.
2. Cost savings are treated as increases in cash inflows.
3. Disposal values of depreciable or amortizable assets and cash values from nondepreciable assets increase cash flow in the period when released from the project.
4. Depreciation and amortization create a tax shield, which refers to the taxes saved because of the deductibility of depreciation and amortization.

When estimating cash outflows, consideration should be given to the following:

1. Recurring costs of operation for assets invested in the project increase cash outflows.
2. Direct costs of projects, such as costs of developing, designing, engineering, market testing, and so forth, increase cash outflows.
3. Identifiable indirect costs of projects, such as production overhead, support costs, and administrative costs, increase cash outflows.
4. Income taxes due on net cash flows, before consideration of the tax shield created by depreciation and amortization, are costs that increase cash outflows. These amounts are typically treated as reductions of cash inflows after tax.

In some companies, the approach to estimating cash flows is first to estimate the sales revenues and costs for each year of the project. Next, arrange the estimates in pro forma income statements and compute income taxes. Then convert the income statements to a cash basis using the standard techniques of:

1. Adjusting revenues by the expected changes in receivables balances.
2. Adjusting cost of goods sold by the expected changes in inventories,[3] plant and equipment depreciation, depletion of natural resources, amortization of patents, and the change in accounts payable.
3. Adjusting expenses:
    a. Taking out marketing/administrative depreciation.
    b. Reflecting changes in prepayments and accrued liabilities.
4. Adding back the start-up costs to the first year's income in computing cash flows. Line start-up costs are included in the investment and are expensed during the first year. Because they are included in the cash outflow for the investment, they should not also be treated as a cash outflow for operations.

It is important to make clear as many of the assumptions as possible in estimating cash flows. Be as specific as possible in stating the assumptions. For example, receipts assumptions might include a 20 percent share of a total product market growing at 8 percent per year with 4 percent inflation. The market growth and share might be based on the assumption of an annual $6 million promotion campaign to retailers on a national basis supported by an $18 million advertising campaign to consumers.

Assessing Risk of Cash Flows

Risks are involved in capital projects, and a proportion of the best plans will fail. We discussed risk measures earlier, but now we want to present an example of sensitivity analysis and look at one new risk measure.

Analysis Setting. The following analysis setting is summarized and extended from Chapter 23:

JMV, Inc., is considering a major modification to the plant and equipment in order to produce a new product, a condensing pump for automobile air conditioners. The company has the following balance sheet:

JMV, INC.
Statement of Financial Position
January 1, 19x4
(in thousands)

Cash	$ 1,000	Current debt	$ 2,000
Accounts receivable	2,500	Long-term debt	5,000
Inventories	4,500	Common stock ($10 par)	1,500
Current assets	$ 8,000	Paid-in excess	3,000
Noncurrent assets	12,000	Retained earnings	8,500
Totals	$20,000		$20,000

The current income is $6 million per year on sales of $30 million with a stable 4 percent growth in the market. The income tax rate is 40 percent. Senior managers require a 10 percent return on investment, payback within two years, and a growth in sales of 10 percent per year.

The proposed project requires inventories of $2 million and equipment and start-up costs of $6 million, which will be depreciated over four years on a straight-line

---

[3] During the last year of the project, all inventories should be used up. As a consequence, the last year's cost of goods sold will be higher than cash payments by the amount of inventory liquidated. Therefore, inventories must be added to income plus depreciation for the last year's cash flow.

basis. By the end of the first year, accounts receivable will increase by $500,000. The project will be financed by a current bank note payable for $1 million, a four-year loan from an investor for $2 million, and sale of 500,000 shares of stock for $3 million; the remainder will come from current operations as they become available.

There is some uncertainty about selling prices, costs, and unit volumes. The managers of JMV agree that the following estimates are reasonable (amounts in thousands except price and variable cost):

		Pessimistic	Most Likely	Optimistic
Selling price		$3.00	$4.00	$5.50
Fixed costs		$5,000	$4,000	$3,500
Variable costs		$1.65	$1.50	$1.35
Sales units year	1	1,500	3,000	4,500
	2	2,750	5,500	8,250
	3	2,500	5,000	7,500
	4	1,250	2,500	3,750

If the project were abandoned at the end of the first year, the investment could be salvaged for about $5.6 million.

Sensitivity Analysis. **Sensitivity analysis** is a "what if" technique that looks at how a result will be changed if assumptions change or original estimates are not achieved. We used the technique in conjunction with cost-volume-profit analysis (Appendix 4A). In the example used there, we applied sensitivity analysis by changing the estimates in increments of plus and minus 10 percent and recomputing the results. Because we have already shown that use of sensitivity analysis, we show here another approach that ties in with the pessimistic, most likely, and optimistic estimates.

Using the data of the analysis setting above, we will calculate the cash flows under the most likely assumption. Applying the most likely sales price, fixed costs, and variable costs to the most likely volumes for the four years, we obtain the following (in thousands):

	Revenues	Costs	Depreciation	Taxes	Income	Cash Flows*
1/1/19x4						$(8,000)
19x4	$12,000	$ 8,500	$1,500	$ 800	$1,200	2,700
19x5	22,000	12,250	1,500	3,300	4,950	6,450
19x6	20,000	11,500	1,500	2,800	4,200	5,700
19x7	10,000	7,750	1,500	300	450	1,950
Average income					$2,700	

* The cash flows are calculated as the sum of income plus depreciation.

Various evaluation techniques as we presented in Chapter 23:

Average project ROI $2,700/($8,000 ÷ 2) = 67.6%
Earnings per share ($6,000 + $2,700)/2,000 = $4.35
Payback period   = 1.82 years
Net present value at 10%   = $5,399
Discounted rate of return   = 38.40%
Discounted benefit-cost index   = 167%

The next step is to assume the pessimistic estimates and recompute the results to see the impact of changes. Using the pessimistic estimates, we obtain the following cash flows:

	Revenues	Costs	Depreciation	Taxes	Income	Cash Flows
1/1/19x4						$(8,000)
19x4	$4,500	$7,475	$1,500	$(1,790)	$(2,685)	(1,185)
19x5	8,250	9,538	1,500	(1,115)	(1,673)	(173)
19x6	7,500	9,125	1,500	(1,250)	(1,875)	(375)
19x7	3,750	7,063	1,500	(1,925)	(2,888)	(1,388)
Average income					$(2,280)	

Various evaluation techniques:

Average project ROI $2,280/($8,000 ÷ 2)   = −57.00%
Earnings per share ($6,000 − $2,280)/2,000 = $1.86
Payback period   = Never
Net present value at 10%   = ($10,449)
Discounted rate of return   = Undefined
Discounted benefit-cost index   = −31%

The pessimistic set of assumptions results in a decrease in net income, a negative average return on investment, a decrease in earnings per share, and the project never being able to pay back the original investment. In addition, the project has a negative net present value, an undefined discounted rate of return, and a negative discounted benefit-cost index. This would be a highly unsatisfactory scenario for senior management to consider.

Now, turning to the optimistic side, here are the cash flows assuming the optimistic set of numbers:

	Revenues	Costs	Depreciation	Taxes	Income	Cash Flows
1/1/19x4						$(8,000)
19x4	$24,750	$ 9,575	$1,500	$ 5,470	$ 8,205	9,705
19x5	45,375	14,638	1,500	11,695	17,543	19,043
19x6	41,250	13,625	1,500	10,450	15,675	17,175
19x7	20,625	8,563	1,500	4,225	6,338	7,838
Average income					$11,940	

Various evaluation techniques:

Average project ROI $11,940/($8,000 ÷ 2) = 298.50%
Earnings per share $17,940/2,000   = $8.97
Payback period   = 0.82 years
Net present value at 10%   = $34,817
Discounted rate of return   = 154.16%
Discounted benefit-cost index   = 535%

Under this scenario, the income almost triples from the current level, ROI is more than 100 percent, EPS more than doubles, and payback is less than one year. Net present value, discounted rate of return, and discounted benefit-cost index are all extremely positive.

Looking at all of the evaluation results, we must conclude that this project is risky. If the pessimistic assumptions prove true, the result will have a large impact on earnings. If the optimistic assumptions prevail, the earnings will be high.

Project Abandonment Ratio.   When a project is terminated early, the investment must be salvaged as effectively as possible. The basic concept for estimating abandonment or termination value is the "next best use of the assets." Rely on the judgment of management as supported by the engineering staff in determining the next best use. Some of the assets will be transferred to other projects, some will be held for future use, and the remainder will be sold. In general, only plant, equipment, and inventories are salvageable for cash. The remaining investment in project setup costs is lost.

Special-purpose plant, equipment, and inventories have very low salvage values. For example, a blast furnace in a steel mill is constructed in place, cannot be moved, is used only to produce steel, and has very little salvage value. On the other hand, general purpose items, such as a truck, a computer-controlled drill press, or lumber, have a ready market.

The investment cost less the abandonment or salvage value is equal to the loss on abandonment. Some organizations require that the potential loss on abandonment of the prospective project be no greater than some proportion, say 50 percent of investment. Other organizations will risk on abandonment no more than some proportion of retained earnings or total owners' equity on a specific project, say no more than 25 percent of equity.[4]

Under the pessimistic assumptions in our example, abandonment will occur at the end of the first year. The accumulated cash lost after the abandonment would be:

Pro Forma Project Net Cash Losses
For the Pessimistic Scenario
For the Year Ending December 31, 19x4

Investment cash outflow	$(8,000)
Cash flow (Income + Depreciation)*	(1,185)
Cash termination value at end of 19x4 given as	5,600
Tax effects 40% × ($8,000 − $1,500 − $5,600)	360
Net cash lost	$(3,225)
Lost investment ratio ($3,225/$8,000)	40.31%

> * This amount comes from the first row of the pessimistic assumption sensitivity analysis. Under the pessimistic assumptions, JMV, Inc., would likely cut its losses and abandon the product after the first year.

In proportion to January 1, 19x4, retained earnings, the net cash lost from abandonment, would be $3,225/$8,500 = 37.94 percent. If the project must be abandoned after the first year, relatively large cash losses will be realized with a material reduction in retained earnings due to the project. This measure indicates that the project is risky.

INCOME TAX EFFECTS

Before any capital investment proposal is finalized, the impact of income taxes on the investment and future cash flows should be explored. Where possible, after-tax cash flow amounts should be used. Because the tax laws are complex and ever changing (congressional tinkering every session), tax rates for various circumstances are easily outdated. Therefore, we explore the areas in which income taxes influence the amounts of cash outflow and inflow. If we need an income tax rate for an example, we simply assume a rate to illustrate the impact of income taxes.

Income taxes can affect the amount of the initial investment and the cash flow of future periods in several areas. These areas are summarized below.

---

[4] In the abandonment of the Edsel in the 1950s, the Ford Motor Company lost much of its retained earnings from the previous year.

Gains or Losses from Disposition of Old Assets

In some capital investment proposals, assets must be released as a part of implementing the proposal. The tax effect of any gain or loss on disposition adjusts the cash flow from disposition. For example, the tax rate times the gain reduces the proceeds of disposition, which increases the incremental investment for the project. The tax rate times the loss is a cost savings that increases the proceeds. The higher amount reduces the incremental investment for the new project.

Capitalization/ Expense Policy

The policy for capitalizing or expensing items that might be purchased initially or during the life of the proposed project influences the amount of taxes paid or saved during the period of acquisition. Any items capitalized are subject to depreciation or amortization, and items expensed show up as cash outflows in the period purchased. The amount of taxes saved as a result of expenses is measured by the tax rate times the expense. For proposal purposes, we use the after-tax expense, which is (1 − tax rate) × cash expenses.

Inventory Cost Methods

If inventory levels must be increased as a result of the current capital investment proposal, the inventory costing method used (first-in, first-out; average costs; or last-in, first-out, for example) affects cash flows in the period of buildup and the period in which inventory is released from the project.

Depreciation/ Amortization Methods

Because they are noncash expenses, depreciation and amortization provide a tax shield—taxes that are saved. The tax shield is measured by the tax rate times the amount of depreciation or amortization. This amount is then treated as a cash inflow or a reduction in cash outflows. The amounts for depreciation and amortization are determined by the method used. Depreciation is commonly calculated on either a straight-line basis or on some form of a declining balance basis. Amortization is straight line. Under present value concepts, a declining balance method is usually preferred because it results in the greatest tax shields in the early years of the capital investment.

After-Tax Cash Flows

We are looking for after-tax cash flows for evaluating the acceptability of any capital investment proposal. After-tax cash inflows are calculated as (1 − tax rate) times cash inflows. After-tax cash outflows are determined in a similar manner: (1 − tax rate) times cash outflows.

SUMMARY

Capital project design is the highly detailed projection of the capital project's characteristics. The project design requires the skills of many staff areas, such as the engineering, marketing, financial, and legal staffs. The target concept is a strategy for designing and marketing new products to meet the responses that will be made by competitors.

Accountants help managers in recording estimates with calculations based on historical data, individual manager judgment, and group averages. In certain circumstances, estimates can be enhanced using the Delphi technique, betting techniques, or estimating the distribution of plausible outcomes. The distribution may be represented with quartile data or with optimistic and pessimistic scenarios.

The financial investment in a project includes the delivered cost of hardware, preparation of plant, setup and training costs, inventories, and marketing and administrative setup costs. Cash flows are calculated from estimates of revenues and expenses. All assumptions should be stated. Project abandonment value should be estimated on the basis of tangible assets that can be sold. Setup costs are lost. Special-purpose plant, equipment, and inventories have very little value.

Through the use of sensitivity analysis and abandonment losses, the risks of any capital investment project can be assessed.

The impact of income taxes must be explored because income taxes often make or break the proposal. After-tax cash flows are essential in proposal evaluation, and they must be determined for all elements of the investment and future cash flows.

PROBLEM FOR REVIEW

4B Corporation has developed a new product with an estimated life cycle of six years. Management is now trying to decide whether it should be produced. Estimated product demand and price are as follows:

	Product Demand			
Year	Pessimistic	Most Likely	Optimistic	Price
1	5,500	6,000	6,500	$10
2	7,250	8,000	8,750	11
3	9,000	10,000	11,000	12
4	6,000	7,000	8,000	11
5	5,000	6,000	7,000	11
6	3,500	5,000	6,500	10

The most likely variable costs associated with this product are:

Direct material	$2.00
Direct labor	1.50
Variable production overhead	1.50
Selling and administration	0.50
Total variable costs	$5.50

The engineering department has given the following distribution on variable costs that will remain throughout all six years:

	Variable Costs	Midpoint Probabilities
Low possible	$4.40	
Optimistic	5.00	5%
Most likely	5.50	60%
Pessimistic	6.20	30%
High possible	7.00	5%

Producing the product requires new equipment costing $71,000 that has a useful life of six years with no salvage value. Depreciation will be under the double-declining balance method. Warehousing space that is currently leased for $3,000 per year must be expanded. The new lease costs are $8,000 per year. Like the former lease, payments are due at the beginning of the year. If the project is terminated at the end of the first year, the equipment could be sold for $35,000, and the lease could be terminated by making a regular $5,000 lease payment at the end of the first year plus a penalty of $6,000.

Fixed costs, without consideration for depreciation, will also increase. Production will add $4,000 per year to fixed production overhead. Advertising and other marketing fixed costs will increase by $2,000 per year.

The tax rate is 40 percent. An after-tax minimum rate of return for accepting capital investment projects is 13 percent.

REQUIRED

a. Determine the investment amount for the project. This is the amount of cash outflow at point zero.
b. Calculate the average variable costs and their related standard deviation.
c. Determine the after-tax net cash flows for each uncertainty level:
   1. Pessimistic for revenues/plus one standard deviation for costs.
   2. Most likely for revenues/average for costs.
   3. Optimistic for revenues/minus one standard deviation for costs.
d. For each of the three uncertainty levels, calculate the:
   1. Average rate of return.
   2. Payback period.
   3. Net present value.
   4. Discounted rate of return.
   5. Discounted benefit-cost index.
e. Calculate the abandonment ratio at the end of the first year, assuming the pessimistic level (pessimistic for revenues/plus one standard deviation for costs) was realized.

SOLUTION

a. Project investment.

New equipment		$71,000
New leasing costs ($8,000 − $3,000)	$5,000	
Less tax shield ($5,000 × 0.40%)	2,000	3,000
		$74,000

b. Average and standard deviation of variable costs.

	Variable Costs	(X) Mid-points	(p) Prob-abilities	Average (X) p(X)	Variance p(X-5.47)²
Low possible	$4.40				
		4.70	5%	$ .235	$0.0296
Optimistic	5.00				
		5.25	60%	3.150	0.0290
Most likely	5.50				
		5.85	30%	1.755	0.0433
Pessimistic	6.20				
		6.60	5%	0.330	0.0638
High possible	7.00				
			100%	$5.47	$0.1657

Standard deviation (square root of variance) $0.41

c.1. After-tax cash flows for pessimistic/plus one standard deviation.

Year	Volume	Selling Price	Variable Cost
1	5,500	$10	$5.88
2	7,250	11	5.88
3	9,000	12	5.88
4	6,000	11	5.88
5	5,000	11	5.88
6	3,500	10	5.88

Year	Revenues	Variable Costs	Fixed Costs	Leasing	Depreciation	Net Income before Tax	After-Tax Cash Flow
0	Investment						$(74,000)
1	$ 55,000	$32,340	$6,000	$5,000	$23,667	$(12,007)	16,463
2	79,750	42,630	6,000	5,000	15,778	10,342	21,983
3	108,000	52,920	6,000	5,000	10,519	33,561	30,655
4	66,000	35,280	6,000	5,000	7,012	12,708	14,637
5	55,000	29,400	6,000	5,000	4,675	9,925	10,630
6	35,000	20,580	6,000	–0–	3,117	5,303	6,299
							$59,832

2. After-tax cash flows for most likely/average.

Year	Volume	Selling Price	Variable Cost
1	6,000	$10	$5.47
2	8,000	11	5.47
3	10,000	12	5.47
4	7,000	11	5.47
5	6,000	11	5.47
6	5,000	10	5.47

Year	Revenues	Variable Costs	Fixed Costs	Leasing	Depreciation	Net Income before Tax	After-Tax Cash Flow
–0–	Investment						$(74,000)
1	$ 60,000	$32,820	$6,000	$5,000	$23,667	$ (7,487)	19,175
2	88,000	43,760	6,000	5,000	15,778	17,462	26,255
3	120,000	54,700	6,000	5,000	10,519	43,781	36,787
4	77,000	38,290	6,000	5,000	7,012	20,698	19,431
5	66,000	32,820	6,000	5,000	4,675	17,505	15,178
6	50,000	23,350	6,000	–0–	3,117	13,533	11,237
						$105,492	

3. After-tax cash flows for optimistic/minus one standard deviation.

Year	Volume	Selling Price	Variable Cost
1	6,500	$10	$5.06
2	8,750	11	5.06
3	11,000	12	5.06
4	8,000	11	5.06
5	7,000	11	5.06
6	6,500	10	5.06

Year	Revenues	Variable Costs	Fixed Costs	Leasing	Depreciation	Net Income before Tax	After-Tax Cash Flow
–0–	Investment						$(74,000)
1	$ 65,000	$32,890	$6,000	$5,000	$23,667	$ (2,557)	22,133
2	96,250	44,275	6,000	5,000	15,778	25,197	30,896
3	132,000	55,660	6,000	5,000	10,519	54,821	43,411
4	88,000	40,480	6,000	5,000	7,012	29,508	24,717
5	77,000	35,420	6,000	5,000	4,675	25,905	20,218
6	65,000	32,890	6,000	–0–	3,117	22,993	16,913
						$155,867	

d. Evaluation criteria at levels of uncertainty.
1. Average rate of return.
(Average net income after tax)/Average Investment or
(Average net income before tax × 60%)/Average Investment

Pessimistic: ((59,832/6) × 60%)/(71,000 ÷ 2) = 16.9 percent
Most likely: ((105,492/6) × 60%)/(71,000 ÷ 2) = 29.7 percent
Optimistic: ((155,867/6) × 60%)/(71,000 ÷ 2) = 43.9 percent

2. Payback period.

Pessimistic: 3.34 years
Most likely: 2.78 years
Optimistic: 2.48 years

3. Net present value.

Pessimistic:	$(3,198) rounded
Most likely:	$14,578 rounded
Optimistic:	$34,125 rounded

4. Discounted rate of return.

Pessimistic:	11.2 percent
Most likely:	20.4 percent
Optimistic:	29.1 percent

5. Discounted benefit-cost index.

Pessimistic:	(NPV + Investment)/Investment = 0.957
Most likely:	1.197
Optimistic:	1.461

e. Abandonment ratio.

Investment cash outflow	$(74,000)
After-tax cash flow, year 1	16,463
Cash termination value of equipment	35,000
Lease termination penalty	(6,000)
Before tax loss	$(28,537)
Tax effect at 40%	11,415
Net cash loss	$(17,122)

Lost investment ratio: $17,122/$74,000 = 23.1 percent.

KEY TERMS AND CONCEPTS

Capital project design (913)   Delphi technique (915)
Target concept (913)   Sensitivity analysis (922)

ADDITIONAL READINGS

Bennett, Robert E., and James A. Hendricks. "Justifying the Acquisition of Automated Equipment." *Management Accounting,* July, 1987, pp. 39–46.

Fairchild, Keith W., and Dennis Bline. "Capital Investment Analysis: The Index Method." *Issues in Accounting Education,* Spring, 1988, pp. 72–78.

Gonzalez, Jose A., and Gary J. Saunders. "Using Lotus 1–2–3 to Perform Net Present Value Calculations." *Computers in Accounting,* January–February, 1988, pp. 52–61.

McGrath, Jack. "Calculating a Discount Rate for Present Value Analysis." *CFO,* April, 1986, pp. 55–59.

———. "Lease or Buy?" *Business Software,* December, 1987, pp. 54–58.

Moyle, James H. "Justifying Retrofit Projects." *Management Accounting,* April, 1987, pp. 59–61.

Spiller, Earl A., Jr. "Return on Investment: A Need for Special Purpose Information." *Accounting Horizons,* June, 1988, pp. 1–9.

REVIEW QUESTIONS

1. How does the target concept reduce the need for price and engineering changes?
2. List three reasons that the estimates made by managers tend to be more or less accurate.
3. Why does a group average tend to be better than individual estimates?

4. List the steps used in the Delphi technique.
5. In estimation using a betting technique, what odds should be given for estimating the
   a. Median?   *b.* Lower quartile?   *c.* Upper quartile?
6. List five costs that should be included in project investment.
7. Why will special-purpose plant and equipment have a lower abandonment value than general-purpose equipment?

**DISCUSSION
QUESTIONS**

8. Managers vary in their ability to make accurate estimates. What can be done to counteract the fact that some managers are optimistic but others are pessimistic?
9. Why should the abandonment losses of a project be considered?
10. Why should the potential impact of the abandonment of a very large project be considered before that project is funded?

EXERCISES

24–1. Estimating Selling Price through Quartiles.   Brenda Products, Inc., plans to introduce a new product. The production people have good numbers on production costs, and sales volumes are reasonable. However, the selling price is subject to a good deal of uncertainty. The marketing manager was asked to estimate prices at various levels. The estimates are below:

Extreme low	$ 45
Very low	75
Lower quartile	80
Median	90
Upper quartile	130
Very high	190
Extreme high	220

REQUIRED:
a. Using the probabilities relating to the estimated quartiles method, determine the:
   1. Average selling price.
   2. Standard deviation of the selling price.
b. Determine a range of selling prices that will include a 95 percent probability that the actual selling price will fall within the range.

24–2. Investment Calculation.   Ramirez Company is considering the replacement of a bar code–sorting machine. The old machine was purchased several years ago for $50,000. It has been depreciated to its salvage value of $4,000. A new bar code sorter has a purchase price of $90,000. Because Ramirez Company has been a good customer over the years, the vendor is willing to extend a 10 percent discount to the purchase price, plus give a $6,000 trade-in allowance on the old machine. If the new machine is not purchased, $30,000 will be spent immediately to repair the old machine.

Gains and losses on trade-in transactions are not subject to income tax. The cost of repairs can be deducted in the first year for computing income taxes. The appropriate tax rate is 40 percent.

REQUIRED:
Compute the net investment if the new machine is purchased.

24–3. Calculation of Cash Flows.   Timbercreek Manufacturing has estimated the sales volume of a potentially new product according to pessimistic, most likely, and optimistic levels for the next four years:

Year	Pessimistic	Most Likely	Optimistic
1	30,000	60,000	70,000
2	35,000	70,000	90,000
3	45,000	80,000	100,000
4	20,000	40,000	60,000

Selling prices and various production and marketing costs have also been estimated. These prices and costs are expected to remain constant over the four-year period:

	Pessimistic	Most Likely	Optimistic
Selling price	$ 14.00	$ 18.00	$ 20.00
Variable costs	10.00	9.00	8.00
Fixed costs (without depreciation)	60,000	55,000	50,000
Annual depreciation	40,000	40,000	40,000

The tax rate is 40 percent.

REQUIRED:
Calculate the after-tax net cash flows for each year for each of the following levels:
a. Pessimistic.
b. Most likely.
c. Optimistic.

24–4. Abandonment Ratio.   Ribbon-Matic makes computer printer ribbons for a wide variety of makes and models. At the beginning of the year, the company installed some robotic equipment that it hoped would save operating costs. The equipment cost $50,000 installed and had a five-year useful life due to technological obsolescence. It would be depreciated over the useful life on a straight-line basis. The appropriate tax rate was 40 percent. Information on the annual cash operating savings is as follows:

	Annual Cash Operating Savings
Pessimistic	$10,000
Most likely	16,000
Optimistic	18,000

The pessimistic condition was realized during the first year, and the company is trying to determine if it should abandon the investment. At the end of the year, the equipment could be disposed of for $35,000.

REQUIRED:
a. Calculate the after-tax cash flow for the first year assuming the pessimistic condition.
b. Determine the amount of any loss if the investment were abandoned at the end of the first year.
c. Determine the abandonment value and abandonment ratio.
d. What factors would you recommend the manager consider to finalize the decision of whether to abandon the investment?

24–5 Probabilities and Investment.   Marconi Powder Company has decided to purchase a new machine that will replace an older, obsolete machine. The anticipated purchase price is $80,000. The installation costs are subject to uncertainty. Information on installation is as follows:

	Costs	Midpoint Probabilities
Extreme low	$ 3,000	
Very low	3,600	5%
Lower quartile	4,200	20%
Median	5,000	25%
Upper quartile	6,000	25%
Very high	8,000	20%
Extreme high	10,000	5%

A metal scrap dealer is willing to pay $2,500 for the old machine; the removal costs are estimated at $1,000. Income taxes are ignored.

REQUIRED:
a. Calculate the average and standard deviation for installation costs.
b. Determine the net investment that will be made in the new machine.
c. Compute a range of values for the net investment in which the probability is 95 percent that the actual net investment will be within the range.

24–6 Equipment Purchase Decision.   Customers of Variety Meats of Santa Fe, New Mexico, are complaining that the beef is too tough. The tenderizer machine the company is currently using is not doing the job, and it should be replaced. Two good machines that will meet the company's standards are available. The Beat-It machine costs $50,000 installed, and the Choppin Block machine costs $75,000 installed. Both machines have a 10-year life with no salvage value and will be depreciated using the straight-line method. The company's tax rate is 40 percent.

Although the revenue generated from using either machine is estimated at $100,000, there is considerable uncertainty about the operating expenses of the machines. The chief accountant has reviewed all of the literature on each machine, has talked to various owners who have had experience with the machines, and has provided the following estimates of operating costs:

(Miller and Highlander, adapted)

	Beat-It	Choppin Block
Low possible	$11,000	$11,000
Optimistic	16,000	13,000
Most likely	20,000	15,000
Pessimistic	25,000	18,000
High possible	30,000	22,000

Probabilities are:

	Beat-It	Choppin Block
Low possible/Optimistic	5%	5%
Optimistic/Most likely	35%	45%
Most likely/Pessimistic	55%	45%
Pessimistic/High possible	5%	5%

REQUIRED:
a. For each machine, calculate the average cost of operating it and the standard deviation.
b. Determine the annual after-tax net cash inflows for each machine, using the average cost of operating the machine.
c. Calculate the following:
  1. Payback period.
  2. Net present value. Assume a 12 percent minimum desired rate of return.
d. Which machine should the company purchase? Explain.

24–7. Sensitivity Analysis.   CPAs International is considering whether to computerize its billing and collection procedures. The necessary equipment, peripherals, and software will be depreciated over five years on a straight-line basis. The firm requires a 12 percent minimum desired rate of return; the tax rate is 35 percent. The investment in the system and the savings in operating costs contain some uncertainty. A systems consultant has given the following estimates:

	Investment	Annual Cash Operating Savings
Pessimistic	$150,000	$40,000
Most likely	120,000	55,000
Optimistic	90,000	62,000

REQUIRED:

a. Calculate the average return on investment for pessimistic, most likely, and optimistic uncertainty levels.
b. Determine the after-tax net cash savings for pessimistic, most likely, and optimistic uncertainty levels.
c. For each of the uncertainty levels (pessimistic, most likely, optimistic), calculate the following:
   1. Payback period.
   2. Net present value.
   3. Discounted rate of return.
   4. Discounted payback.
d. What conclusions can you draw about how risky this investment is?

24–8. Management Judgment on Estimates. CAR-TOP Enterprises is looking at the possibility of introducing a new automotive product. Marketing managers have estimated that sales will either be 50,000 units or 80,000 units for the year. If sales are at the lower level, the selling price is $8 per unit; at the higher level, $6 per unit. Production managers estimate variable costs at $4 per unit. However, fixed costs, without depreciation, will be $22,000 at the lower sales level and $33,000 at the higher sales level. Equipment modifications to produce this new item will cost $40,000 for the lower sales level and $48,000 for the higher sales level. These modification costs will be depreciated over five years on a straight-line basis. The income tax rate is 40 percent. A minimum desired rate of return is 14 percent.

REQUIRED:

a. Calculate the relevant annual after-tax net cash flows over the five-year period for each sales level.
b. Compute the following for each sales level:
   1. Payback period.
   2. Net present value.
   3. Discounted payback.
   4. Average return on investment.
c. If there were a 70 percent chance of achieving the lower sales level and a 30 percent chance of achieving the higher sales level, would you recommend introduction of the product?

24–9. Uncertainty of Salvage Value. Satellite Research Associates develops prototypes of components for space satellites. The company has contracted with the Department of Defense to produce 10 special components for experimental satellites at a price of $1,000,000 per component. Production costs before depreciation of special tooling and equipment are $600,000 for each unit. The government knows it wants the 10 units sometime over the next three to five years. If three years is the time period, the distribution of units among the years is in the order of one, four, and five. For four years, the distribution is one, two, three, and four. A five-year period will give a distribution of one, one, two, three, and three.

The special tooling and equipment will cost $400,000 and be depreciated over the life of the contract on a straight-line basis, assuming no salvage value for tax purposes. However, any salvage value realized on disposition will be taxed at the ordinary rate of 40 percent. If the contract covers only three years, the salvage value of the equipment will be $150,000; at four years, the salvage value will be $80,000; and at five years, the salvage value will be $30,000. The minimum desired rate of return is 10 percent.

REQUIRED:
a. Determine the annual after-tax net cash flows for this contract assuming the following:
    1. Three years.
    2. Four years.
    3. Five years.
b. Calculate the net present values for each of the three possibilities in *(a)* above.
c. Which has the greater impact on net cash flows? The change in time from three to five years, or the change in salvage values?

PROBLEMS

24–10. Selecting Depreciation Methods.   Adelphi Property Management has just acquired a new building that costs $8.1 million. The building will be depreciated over 15 years for tax purposes. No salvage value is expected. Depreciation methods available for this type of property are 150 percent declining balance and the straight-line method. The tax rates that will be available are uncertain because Congress is tinkering with them. Also, economists are projecting changes in the interest rate structure. The experts have estimated the following possible tax rates and interest rates:

	Tax Rates	Midpoint Probabilities
Low possible	25%	
Optimistic	28%	5%
Most likely	35%	30%
Pessimistic	40%	60%
High possible	45%	5%

	Interest Rates	
Low possible	8%	
Optimistic	9%	5%
Most likely	11%	70%
Pessimistic	13%	20%
High possible	15%	5%

REQUIRED:
a. Determine the before-tax depreciation charges under the 150 percent declining-balance method and the straight-line method for this property.
b. Calculate the average and standard deviation for tax rates and interest rates.
c. Using the average tax rate, calculate the after-tax savings from each of the depreciation methods.
d. Using the average interest rate, calculate the present value of tax savings under each depreciation method.
e. Determine the present values of the tax savings under each depreciation method, assuming the following conditions:
    1. Optimistic tax rate and optimistic interest rate.
    2. Pessimistic tax rate and pessimistic interest rate.

24–11. Make-or-Buy Decision.   Carrollton Manufacturing Company currently purchases a subassembly used in the production of residential security systems. The company purchases 40,000 subassemblies a year at a unit cost of $20.70. Jennie Elliott, a production engineer, believes the company would be better off over the next five years if it manufactures the part. To help evaluate the option of bringing the subassembly production in-house, she has gathered the following information.

1. Variable production costs per unit, all out-of-pocket costs, are estimated at three different levels of uncertainty:

Pessimistic	$20.40
Most likely	19.50
Optimistic	18.60

2. One of the machines needed is currently held in stand-by status. It was purchased three years ago for $40,000 and is being depreciated on a straight-line basis at $5,000 per year. It has no salvage value.

3. A second machine is needed and must be purchased. The best available machine will cost $50,000 installed and will last five years. This machine has an estimated salvage value of $5,000 at the end of five years. For tax purposes, salvage value is ignored and the full cost of the machine is depreciated on a double-declining basis. At the end of five years, the salvage value will be realized through sale and taxed at ordinary tax rates.

The controller indicates that a 15 percent minimum after-tax rate of return is appropriate for this investment. The tax rate is 40 percent.

REQUIRED:

a. Calculate the relevant after-tax net cash flow of the make alternative for the five years under each of the following production cost estimates:
  1. Pessimistic.
  2. Most likely.
  3. Optimistic.
b. Determine the net present value of the cash flows in (a) above.
c. Compute the net present value of continuing to purchase the subassembly from an outside source.
d. Should the company make or buy the subassembly? Explain.

24–12. Expanding to Different Locations.   One-Stop Truck Stops, Inc., owns and operates over 120 truck stops on major highways throughout the United States. Ric Franchetti, president, has become aware of two potentially lucrative truck stops that could be available on 10-year leases. Because of the increasing dependence on foreign oil, Franchetti is concerned about overextending the operations only to have a foreign cartel control oil prices and cut into profits significantly. He believes the company could expand to one more location without increasing its current debt load. Therefore, he would be interested in adding the better of the two locations to the truck stop network.

Both truck stops are similar in operations and revenue/cost structures. For operations, the convenience stores and repair shops are under one roof, a concept Franchetti believes is compatible with the company's operating philosophy. Nonfuel items are sold in the truck stop part of the outlet. Sales in both the convenience store and repair shop vary directly with the number of trucks that stop to buy fuel. Accounting has found that it can relate revenues and costs of a location to the gallons of diesel fuel sold. The revenue/cost structure for all but the diesel fuel is:

	Nonfuel Items Truckstop	*Convenience Store*	*Repair Shop*
Sales revenue	$0.04/gal.	$0.05/gal.	$0.10/gal.
Variable costs	65% of sales	60% of sales	70% of sales
Fixed costs	$10,840	$37,050	$63,100

Rental fees at each location are $50,000 plus 0.05 percent of total revenues. If the diesel fuel sales exceed 2.75 million gallons per year, the fees increase to $70,000 plus 0.05 percent of total revenues. The company has kept statistics on fuel purchases per truck and finds the following distribution:

	Diesel Fuel Gallons/Truck	Midpoint Probabilities
Low possible	30	
Pessimistic	100	5%
Most likely	120	35%
Optimistic	130	55%
High possible	170	5%

One location is a truck stop located on Interstate 25 just north of Cheyenne, Wyoming. The annual truck market on this part of the interstate is about 220,000 stops. The marketing department believes the company will attract 8 percent of the market during each of the first two years of the lease, 9 percent during each of the next three years, and 10 percent for each of the final five years. The market price for diesel fuel will run $0.90 per gallon for the first three years and then increase to $1.00 per gallon for the remaining life of the lease. Diesel fuel has consistently cost the company 90 percent of the selling price.

The second location is on Interstate 10 near Baton Rouge, Louisiana. The truck market there is 300,000 stops per year. Because this location is in "gasoline alley" and must compete with several other companies, marketing estimates a 6 percent market share during the first two years, increasing to 7 percent during the next four years, and 8 percent in the final four years. Market research shows the market selling price per gallon of $0.85 for the first two years, $0.90 for the next four years, and $0.96 for the remainder of the lease. The company estimates that diesel fuel will cost it $0.09 less than the market selling price.

Leasehold improvements at the Wyoming location are expected to be $400,000 and at the Louisiana location the improvements are $320,000. Leasehold improvements are amortized on a straight-line basis over the life of the lease.

Franchetti wants a 16 percent after-tax minimum rate of return. The tax rate is 40 percent.

(Smith and Hayden, adapted)

REQUIRED:
a. Determine the average gallons per truck together with a standard deviation.
b. Using the average gallons per truck, determine the annual after-tax net cash flows for each location over the 10-year lease.
c. Calculate the following for each alternative. Consider all after-tax cash outflows at the beginning of the first year as the investment.
   1. Net present value.
   2. Discounted rate of return.
d. Explain how you would use the standard deviation of the gallons per truck to help determine the riskiness of each alternative.

24–13. New Product Proposal.   Slip-On, Inc., is looking for new markets to tap. Management has become aware of the concern health-care workers have for potential AIDS infection. Workers fear exposure to the virus, and workers who have been exposed have filed lawsuits against their employers. Consequently, hospital officials are looking for solutions to stop the threat of AIDS contamination.

Jack Steele, president of Slip-On, Inc., met with Jason Kleen of All-American Hospitals, a corporate hospital chain. They pursued different approaches to solving the problem. After a great deal of experimentation, Slip-On developed a new technique to manufacture metal-mesh hospital gloves. Jason likes the gloves so well that he wants a proposal from Slip-On for a price based on the following potential purchase volumes per year over the next five years: pessimistic volume, 35,000 pairs per year; most likely volume, 50,000 pairs per year; and optimistic, 60,000 pairs per year.

Mesh-Tec is the name of the new product. It is a metal-mesh hospital glove designed to be worn over rubber surgical gloves. The pliable material used in the glove has thin nickel-plated brass rings, protecting the fingers. Mesh-Tec is designed to prevent accidental needle sticks, scalpel cuts, and other accidents. The cloth-like material requires a special alloy that costs $207 per pair of gloves. This cost is expected to increase 15 percent every year after the first year. Direct labor is estimated at $3.00 per pair and will increase by 10 percent each year, as specified by the union contract. Variable production overhead is $1.68 per pair and will increase at 5 percent per year. Fixed costs other than new investment-related costs are $36,100 for the first year. They are expected to increase at 5 percent per year. The tax rate is 40 percent.

To manufacture the gloves, Slip-On needs more space and additional equipment. The company can lease space in an adjacent building for $48,000 per year for five years, with payments due at the beginning of the year. The special equipment can be leased at $150,000 per year. A maintenance contract on the equipment is available for $12,000 per year. The lease payments on both the equipment and the maintenance contract are due at the first of each year.

Slip-On usually requires a minimum rate of return of 16 percent. But in this case, management believes the market potential is great enough that prices should support either 18 percent or 20 percent.

(R. Pineda, adapted)

REQUIRED:
a. Calculate the annual after-tax cash flows over the five-year period assuming 50,000 pairs per year. There are no revenues at this point.
b. Using net present values, establish a minimum selling price per pair of gloves for 50,000 pairs per year under a rate of return of:
   1. 16 percent.
   2. 18 percent.
   3. 20 percent.
c. Given the selling price determined at 18 percent, calculate the break-even volume for each of the five years.
d. Repeat (a) and (b.2) above for 60,000 pairs per year. What is the break-even volume for each of the five years?
e. Compare the break-even volumes in (c) and (d) above. Comment.

24–14. Ranking of Investment Proposals. Golden West Printing & Publishing is a partnership formed by three brothers. Daryl is president and handles marketing duties; Todd is in charge of operations; Brian serves as the chief financial officer. Brian is currently evaluating three different capital investment proposals: a major plant expansion, a rearrangement of current plant layout, and acquisition of a new press that utilizes current technology. The plant expansion and rearrangement alternatives are mutually exclusive. A new press is dependent on available funds, if this alternative is an acceptable one.

The plant expansion alternative involves construction of a new wing on the main plant, which will permit work on several jobs simultaneously. The volume of orders for business printing, calendars, books, and offset advertising material has been rising steadily over the last three years. All indications point to a continuation of the trend. Recently, the company lost several very profitable contracts because it did not have enough capacity to do the work in the short time the customers required. The investment would be $2,000,000 with the following annual after-tax net cash flows for each of the next 10 years:

Pessimistic	Most Likely	Optimistic
$230,000	$270,000	$320,000

The rearrangement alternative involves moving some walls and rearranging some of the operations in the present printing plant. The company gains extra room and more efficient flow through operations. The modifications would be extensive, and business will be lost during renovation. Amounts identified as the investment in rearrangement total $600,000. Annual after-tax net cash flows for the next five years are:

Year	Pessimistic	Most Likely	Optimistic
1	$120,000	$180,000	$210,000
2	210,000	270,000	300,000
3	250,000	310,000	340,000
4	210,000	270,000	300,000
5	90,000	150,000	180,000

The new press will allow the company to move into the high-resolution color segment of the marketplace. However, space is needed for the new press. Therefore, either the plant expansion or the rearrangement must prove worthwhile for this alternative to be considered. The press will cost $1,200,000 and will generate annual after-tax net cash flows over the next 10 years of:

Pessimistic	Most Likely	Optimistic
$210,000	$300,000	$375,000

The company has a minimum desired rate of return of 15 percent for accepting investment projects.

(W. Maxwell, adapted)

REQUIRED:
a. Calculate the net present value for each of the three alternatives at each uncertainty level:
   1. Pessimistic.
   2. Most likely.
   3. Optimistic.
b. Which projects are acceptable at the 15 percent level? How do you arrive at this decision when the three levels are considered?
c. Should the company entertain the expansion or the rearrangement alternative?
d. Combine the investment in the new press and the related annual cash flows with each of the other two alternatives so that there are really only two options of which the new press is a part. Perform the same analysis in (a) through (c) above, assuming these two alternatives.

24–15. Lease or Purchase.   Loco Coco, Inc., is in the business of making frozen pina colada mix for a vast U.S. market. Although it is a relatively small firm, it has about 40 percent of the market. The headquarters and plant are located on St. Thomas in the Virgin Islands.

On this particular day, Boris Lejewski, president, was informed that the major coconut-splitting machine had broken down and could not be repaired. This necessitated purchasing a new machine quickly. He asked his executive assistant, Jamie Thoreau, to gather data about the options for leasing or purchasing a new machine. If the machine is to be purchased, the company must borrow $3.8 million on a five-year, 10 percent note with equal payments due at the end of each year. The remaining cash needs can be met from cash reserves. Lejewski requires a 12 percent minimum rate of return on all investments. The company's average tax rate is 35 percent.

If purchased, the machine would have a five-year useful life with the 150 percent declining-balance method for depreciation. It will cost $5 million delivered and installed. Although salvage value is ignored in determining depreciation for tax purposes, the estimated salvage value at the end of five years is uncertain but is expressed as follows:

	Salvage Values	Midpoint Probabilities
Low possible	$250,000	
Pessimistic	350,000	5%
Most likely	500,000	60%
Optimistic	550,000	30%
High possible	600,000	5%

A salvage value will be taxed at 35 percent. A maintenance contract is available for $250,000 per year, payable at the beginning of each year. The company wants the maintenance contract if the lease is taken.

A five-year lease requires annual payments of $1,375,000 at the beginning of each year. The lessor will maintain the equipment. At the conclusion of the five years, the machine will be returned to the lessor.

REQUIRED:
a. Determine the annual after-tax net cash flows for each alternative:
   1. Purchasing alternative—use an average salvage value as determined by the assigned probabilities.
   2. Leasing alternative—the first lease payment, net of tax, could be treated as an investment or as a cash outflow at point zero.
b. Calculate the net present value for each alternative.
c. Compute the standard deviation for the salvage value and assess at which point the amount of salvage value would influence whether the company should purchase or lease the machine.

24–16. Evaluating New Technology.   Fiber Fluff, Inc., is a technology-driven producer of residential and commercial thermal and acoustical fiberglass insulations. Fiberglass production may be thought of as being similar to making cotton candy. However, unlike cotton candy, fiberglass insulation requires a bonding agent that will make the individual fibers of glass adhere to one another. This bonding agent is called a *binder;* it is mixed at a mixing station and then transferred through flow meters to binder application pumps. The application pumps apply the binder to the spun fiberglass during production.

The Jones facility presently uses six high-pressure binder application pumps, and the Angora facility employs two low-pressure application pumps. Development of the low-pressure technology was considered a technological breakthrough. The Angora facility is using this technology at significant savings. The company would like to replace the six high-pressure application pumps at the Jones facility with two low-pressure application pumps.

With two low-pressure pumps, the amount of normal spinner machine downtime would be reduced by two thirds. The current six machines have experienced different levels of downtime for spinner hours. The optimistic level is 81 hours of downtime per year; most likely level is 102 hours; pessimistic level is 135 hours. One spinner hour of downtime produces $255 of wasted material.

Each high-pressure pump requires 7.5 horsepower (hp) per hour to operate; each low-pressure pump uses 1.5 hp per hour. At the Jones facility, a kilowatt hour (kwh) will most likely cost $0.038 (there are 0.746 kwh per hp). The pessimistic estimate is $0.045, and the optimistic estimate is $0.03. Either process must be up and running a minimum of 8,322 hours (i.e., all machines in the process must run the 8,322 hours).

The investment in new equipment for two low-pressure pumps is $55,000 for equipment, $2,000 for delivery charges, and $8,000 in installation costs. The investment will be depreciated over five years with no salvage value on the basis of 150 percent declining balance. The existing equipment has been fully depreciated and can be sold for scrap at $3,000, all of which represents a taxable gain.

Because the total revenue on sales will remain the same, the savings in operating costs and the tax shield on depreciation represent the annual returns. The tax rate is 40 percent. In accepting capital investment proposals, the company has the following policy:
1. If the net present value is greater than or equal to zero at 18 percent for the most likely amounts, the proposal is accepted and funding is provided.
2. If the net present value is greater than or equal to zero at 15 percent for the most likely amounts, the proposal must be reevaluated for the worst possible scenario. If the worst scenario yields a net present value greater than or equal to zero at 14 percent, the proposal will be funded.
3. If the net present value is greater than or equal to zero at 14 percent, the proposal will be included in a pool of proposals that must wait to see if funds will be available. The proposals are ranked, and available funds are rationed according to the ranking.

4. No proposals are acceptable if the net present value is less than zero at 14 percent for either the most likely or the worst scenario amounts.

(A. Gould, adapted)

REQUIRED:
a. Calculate the savings in material cost from downtime and savings in energy costs with the two low-pressure pumps.
b. Determine the investment for the two low pressure pumps.
c. Find the net present value for each of the following interest rates:
   1. 18 percent.
   2. 15 percent.
   3. 14 percent.
d. Apply the company's decision policy and make a recommendation about whether to invest in the two low-pressure pumps.

24–17. Comparison of Equipment Alternatives. In the 90s, space is money. So to save both, manufacturers are revamping packages: getting rid of air, concentrating contents, and cramming more containers into the same area. Compact Designs, Inc., has developed a variety of interlocking plastic containers that can fit twice as much liquid into the same space as conventional bottles. The stack packs save space in the warehouse, in transit, and on the market shelf. They encourage consumers to buy two bottles rather than one and lend themselves to complementary products. Compact Designs, Inc., is licensing the technology.

Rocky Mountain Manufacturing wants to use the stack packs technology and has identified two machine setups that are compatible with the technology. Each machine will last eight years with no salvage value. Machine 1 will cost $500,000 installed and machine 2 will cost $600,000 installed. The estimated annual after-tax cash benefit of each machine is below:

	Machine 1		Machine 2	
Year	Average	Standard Deviation	Average	Standard Deviation
1	$130,000	$2,000	$ 60,000	$ 500
2	130,000	2,500	85,000	600
3	130,000	3,000	95,000	700
4	130,000	3,500	125,000	800
5	130,000	4,000	155,000	1,000
6	130,000	4,500	200,000	1,600
7	130,000	5,000	300,000	2,000
8	130,000	5,000	400,000	2,500

Rocky Mountain requires an after-tax return of 10 percent.

REQUIRED:
a. Using the average amounts for each machine, calculate the following:
   1. Payback period.
   2. Discounted rate of return.
   3. Net present value.
   4. Discounted payback.
   5. Discounted benefit-cost index.
b. Based on the results of the above analysis, which machine is preferable? Explain.
c. Repeat (a) above by using the cash benefits for each machine at:
   1. Plus one standard deviation.
   2. Minus one standard deviation.
d. Based on these results, which machine is preferable? Explain.

EXTENDED APPLICATIONS

24–18. Market Expansion and Growth Rates. Roger Coen, president of Perdenales National Bank, is looking at the possibility of installing automatic teller machines in five new shopping centers that are under construction around the metropolitan area. The bank has never used automatic teller machines and is facing increased competition from other banks that are using such devices. Coen assigned Curtis Fowler, the bank's marketing director, the task of identifying feasible options and gathering data to evaluate those options. Coen wanted something that would last for five years because in that period, technology and trends will change and the bank will have to pursue other strategies. Fowler visited a number of manufacturer's representatives, telephoned several companies, and talked to banks in other cities. He soon had four good options and relevant data to help Coen reach a decision.

Option 1. The bank would purchase five Docutel drive-through automatic teller machines. Perdenales would build five drive-through stations on purchased sites at the new shopping centers. These stations would be open to the public 24 hours daily. The total purchase price for all five Docutel machines would be $175,000 with installation costs of $17,500. Five 20 × 30-square-foot lots would be purchased on the grounds of each shopping center at a total cost of $100,000. Five drive-through stations would be constructed at a total cost of $50,000. Additional working capital of $45,000 would be needed to implement the system. First-year operating costs include the following:

Security	$25,000
Insurance	16,500
Repair and maintenance	5,000

Anticipated first-year revenues resulting from these stations are $200,000.

Option 2. The bank would purchase five NCR walk-up exterior teller machines. Perdenales would locate these machines on the front exterior wall of the five new HEB supermarkets being constructed in the shopping centers. These stations would be open to the public 24 hours daily. The total purchase price of the five NCR machines would be $120,000 and would cost an additional $12,500 to install. The space for the automatic teller machines would be leased from HEB supermarkets at a cost of $25,000 annually. Additional new working capital of $30,000 would be needed to implement this project. First-year operating costs beyond the lease costs include the following:

Security	$10,000
Insurance	15,000
Repair and maintenance	4,000

Anticipated first-year revenues resulting from these stations are $190,000.

Option 3. The bank would purchase five Burroughs enclosed walk-up automatic teller machines. Perdenales would build five enclosed walk-up facilities on sites purchased in the new shopping centers. These stations would be open to the public 24 hours daily. The total purchase price of the five machines would be $150,000 and would cost an additional $16,500 to install. Five 20 × 30-square-foot lots would need to be purchased in the shopping centers at a cost of $100,000. The five walk-up stations could be constructed at a cost of $75,000, and additional net working capital of $48,000 would be needed to implement the project. First-year operating costs include the following:

Security	$25,000
Insurance	20,000
Heating, cooling, and lights	15,000
Repair and maintenance	7,500

Anticipated first-year revenues resulting from these facilities are $190,000.

Option 4. The bank would purchase five Mosler interior automatic teller machines. Perdenales would locate these machines on the inside of the five new HEB supermarkets being constructed in the shopping centers. These indoor facilities would be open to the public during regular store hours of 6 A.M. to 12 A.M. daily. The total purchase price of the five Mosler machines would be $110,000, with an additional $10,000 to install. The space for the tellers would be leased from HEB supermarkets at a cost of $25,000 annually. Additional working capital of $28,000 would be needed to implement the project. First-year operating costs beyond the lease costs include the following:

Security	$10,000
Insurance	5,000
Repair and maintenance	2,500

Anticipated first-year revenues resulting from these machines are $130,000.

The growth in the annual operating costs of all options is subject to some uncertainty. The lease costs of options 2 and 4 will remain fixed over the life of the project. All other cash operating costs would increase at some rate. Fowler's information suggested the following possibilities on growth percentages:

	Cost Growth	Midpoint Probabilities
Extreme low	6%	
Very low	8	5%
Lower quartile	9	20
Median	11	25
Upper quartile	12	25
Very high	13	20
Extreme high	14	5

All physical structures and equipment were estimated to have a five-year useful life; depreciation is on a straight-line basis. No salvage value is assumed for tax purposes. This is true of the five tellers, but the structures in options 1 and 3 will have a disposal value equal to 10 percent of their cost (before installation costs).

Revenue growth, like growth in operating costs, is uncertain. Fowler was able to piece together economic forecasts that gave the following information on growth:

	Revenue Growth	Midpoint Probabilities
Low possible	3%	
Pessimistic	4	5%
Most likely	6	30
Optimistic	7	60
High possible	8	5

Coen usually requires a 15 percent minimum rate of return on investments. The bank's tax rate is 40 percent.

(Nichols, adapted)

REQUIRED:
a. Determine the total investment cost of implementing each option at the beginning of year 1.
b. Determine the annual after-tax net cash flows of each option for each of the five years, using the average growth rates for revenues and cash operating costs.
c. Calculate the following for each option:
   1. Payback period.
   2. Discounted rate of return.
   3. Net present value.
   4. Discounted payback.
   5. Discount benefit-cost index.
d. Assess the sensitivity of growth rates for revenues and costs on the net present value. For this purpose, use the standard deviations that can be calculated from the probability distributions.
   1. Recalculate everything in (b) above assuming plus and minus one standard deviation away from the average.
   2. Recalculate everything in (b) above assuming plus and minus 1.96 standard deviations away from the average.
e. Assess the sensitivity of growth rates for revenues and costs on net present value by using

the pessimistic and optimistic estimates. Use the upper quartile as pessimistic and the lower quartile as optimistic costs.

f. Which option should the bank pursue? Explain.

24–19. Capital Rationing. MasterCare is a small medical supply company located in a Dayton, Ohio, suburb. MasterCare's products include syringes, laboratory control equipment, and packaging for various chemicals. Its customers include hospitals in the surrounding Miami Valley region, minor emergency clinics across the midwestern United States, and pharmaceuticals manufacturers in Cincinnati. The historically strong company has been able to increase its cash position while holding debt to a minimum.

MasterCare has budgeted a maximum of $300,000 to fund new projects during the current year. These funds will be spent only if enough acceptable projects are available. Any excess moneys will be invested elsewhere. The minimum desired rate of return is 12 percent after tax; the tax rate is 40 percent. Currently, three proposals are before the capital budget committee.

Alternative 1. An independent marketing agency has submitted a proposal to handle the promotion of a MasterCare product, the C–6 lab tube, for five years. The C–6 aids in testing urine samples for the presence of illegal drugs. The tube provides no improvement in the accuracy of a test, but it offers added convenience for the technician. The marketing firm believes that sales may be increased from the current 80,000 units per year by 20 percent each year through the next five years. MasterCare's management believes the growth rate is overly optimistic and has identified the following distribution:

	Sales Growth	Midpoint Probabilities
Low possible	8%	
Pessimistic	10	5%
Most likely	15	50
Optimistic	18	40
High possible	20	5

The firm believes the growth could be maintained with an increase in the average selling price of $0.15 per unit. That would yield a new selling price of $4.20.

In return for the promotion, MasterCare must pay the firm an initial fee of $250,000 plus $0.10 per unit of C–6 sales in excess of the current 80,000 units per year. The current variable costs are $2.65 per unit. However, the added volume will introduce a few economies that will reduce the variable costs: the pessimistic reduction is $0.05 per unit; the most likely reduction is $0.08; the optimistic reduction is $0.12.

Alternative 2. Another of MasterCare's products is a small sterilization machine, or autoclave. The principal precision machinery used to make the autoclave was installed only two years ago at a cost of $81,000 and was being depreciated on a straight-line basis over 10 years with no estimated salvage value. Recently, MicroTool, Inc., developed a device incorporating miniature robotics. If MasterCare acquired the new device, it would have to redesign the autoclave housing. The design change would result in a direct materials cost savings of $18 per unit. Additionally, supervision costs in the assembly area could be reduced by $18,000 per year.

The new system would require retooling and cleaning in the third and sixth years of the estimated eight-year useful life. The retooling is a unique and expensive process costing $40,000 in year 3 and $50,000 in year 6. The system can be purchased and installed for $170,000. The old machine can be sold for $40,000. Any gain or loss is subject to the ordinary tax rate.

Demand for the autoclaves has been running about 1,000 units per year. This is expected to continue for the next three years. MasterCare believes demand will jump to a new level for the fourth through sixth years. The most likely new demand level is 1,400 units. Pessimistic and optimistic estimates are 1,100 and 1,500 units, respectively. The company expects a 10 percent growth rate in the seventh and eighth years.

Alternative 3. The chemicals-packaging division produces packaging for pharmaceuticals and special casings. Products include the protective sleeves for x-ray film and canisters used in laboratory chemicals storage. Inherent to this production is testing the effects on the chemicals of materials in the packaging.

MasterCare must take steps to assure that the materials used will in no way alter the product to be stored. The division's testing process emits small amounts of chemical into the air. Although these emissions are not radioactive and do not result in as much air pollution as that released by a nearby auto factory, MasterCare would suffer a loss of reputation if the release of the chemicals were publicized.

Under new regulations, MasterCare must stop emitting these chemicals or be fined $12,000 for each year in which emissions occur. SAFE Petroleum Company has developed a system that could be used to restrict and contain the emissions. The system would cost $64,200 installed. It would be effective for 10 years; straight-line depreciation with no salvage value will be used. Although maintenance costs for the system are unknown, the engineers have projected the following annual maintenance costs:

	Annual Costs	*Midpoint Probabilities*
Extreme low	$ 400	
Very low	600	5%
Lower quartile	800	20%
Median	900	25%
Upper quartile	1,200	25%
Very high	1,400	20%
Extreme high	1,600	5%

In developing annual after-tax cash flows for all alternatives, the company uses the average amounts for a year when probabilities are available. Otherwise, the most likely estimates are used. If results are marginally good, standard deviations and pessimistic amounts are evaluated to assess the alternative's risk.

(S. Warkentin, adapted)

REQUIRED:

a. Compute the following for each alternative, assuming the use of averages and most likely amounts:
   1. Payback period.
   2. Net present value.
   3. Discounted payback.
   4. Discounted benefit-cost index.
b. Based on your results in *(a)* above, rank the three alternatives in order to ration the available funds.
c. Reevaluate the alternatives using the lower limits of standard deviations and pessimistic amounts. Then compute the following:
   1. Payback period.
   2. Net present value.
   3. Discounted payback.
   4. Discounted benefit-cost index.
d. Do the results of *(c)* suggest a different ranking for the alternatives in *(b)*?

24–20. New Product Introduction.   John Calloway is the Foods Division general manager for CSV, Inc. He is considering a proposal for a new high-energy candy line.

The initial estimate of $300,000 investment is very rough. Food production lines require substantial setup time and careful testing. Price estimates for the equipment ranged from $220,000 for the basic unit up to $380,000 with all the options. A $300,000 model that had most of the options was available. Because he could do more with the $380,000 model, the plant manager would like very much to get that model. Shipping and installation fees would be about $11,000. Prior to installation of the equipment, some existing equipment would have to be moved at a cost of $1,000, the power supply would have to be augmented at a cost of $8,000, the air handler boosted at a cost of $1,500, and some production patterns rearranged, which would cost $2,500. Federal and state inspection fees required would be about $8,500. Training would cost $3,000, production start-up would involve materials of $6,200, direct labor of $2,800, and overhead applied at a 100 percent rate. Finished goods inventories are estimated at $42,000 based on historical data; materials inventories are $5,100. The initial promotion campaign would cost $120,000.

Only modest changes to the administration of the division would be required as a result of the new product line. For example, some forms would have to be reprinted and seven computer programs adjusted. A few new accounts would be required, and the formats of several reports would have to be changed. The estimated cost of this is minimal at $1,000.

Food products have a history of growth that follows a slow start, a rapid buildup, a stable position in the market for a time, then a modest decline as competition enters the market. Thus, the pattern of sales was estimated at $250,000 for year 1, increasing to 1,100,000 in year 2 and peaking at $1,800,000 in year 3. After year 3, the sales estimates decline at about 20 percent per year. This revenue reflects an assumed price of $0.25 per unit. About 2 percent uncollectible is expected, and the collection period is one month. The project is assumed to terminate normally after 10 years. For purposes of sensitivity analysis, the marketing manager estimated a pessimistic pattern as sales of $200,000 in the first year followed by $100,000 in year 2 and abandonment at the end of year 2. The price will be dropped to $0.22 per unit early in year 1. At the end of year 2, the value of the abandoned inventories and depreciable plant and equipment will be about 60 percent of cost. The optimistic sales are expected to be 50 percent higher than the most likely pattern with an expected selling price of $0.30 per unit.

The controller prepared the following break-even analysis for the first year, assuming most likely costs:

Sales price		$0.250
Materials	$0.103	
Labor	0.016	
Variable overhead	0.005	
Variable marketing	0.005	−0.129
Contribution margin		$0.121
Fixed overhead	$ 22,500	
Depreciation	40,500	
Fixed marketing	50,000	
Writeoff of start-up costs (year 1)	144,300	
First-year fixed costs		$ 257,300
Break-even volume		2,126,447 Units

This analysis assumes that the $380,000 production line is purchased with about $25,000 in delivery and setup costs. For the pessimistic scenario, the variable costs are 20 percent higher and the fixed costs are 10 percent higher, except for depreciation, which is the same. For the optimistic scenario, the variable costs are 10 percent lower and the fixed costs are 5 percent lower, except for depreciation. Required return after tax is 15 percent, and the tax rate is 40 percent.

CSV, Inc., has total expected sales of $20 million with expected net income of $2,000,000. The project will be financed from current cash and the issuance of a $250,000 long-term note.

CSV, INC.
Statement of Financial Position
January 1, 19x1
(in thousands)

Cash	$ 300		Current debt	$ 400	
Accounts receivable	500		Long-term debt	1,000	$1,400
Inventories	2,200		Common stock ($1 par)	$ 500	
Current assets		$3,000	Paid-in excess	500	
Noncurrent assets		2,000	Retained earnings	2,600	3,600
Totals		$5,000			$5,000

REQUIRED:[5]

a. Prepare an estimate of the investment required assuming that:
   1. The plant manager requires the $380,000 model.
   2. The plant manager requires the $300,000 model.

b. The division manager was most unhappy with the investment estimates found in *(a)*. He decided that $40,000 of the initial advertising can be deferred for six months and be included as part of the other advertising for the division. Further, finished goods inventories must be cut to $22,000, although that level might be too low to support sales. Further, the plant manager agreed that he could live with the $220,000 model line, but this would require about 50 percent more production training and start-up cost. Finally, the administrative item was deleted as immaterial. Prepare a new estimate of the required investment.

   Irrespective of your answer obtained in part (b), make the following assumption in the remaining requirements: The required investment was estimated at $390,000 of which $248,000 is depreciable over 10 years, start-up costs of $114,000 are expensed in year 1, and the remainder consists of inventories of $28,000, which are liquidated during year 10.

c. Estimate the pattern of sales, the cash receipts, and the unit volumes for each of the 10 years for:
   1. A pessimistic scenario.
   2. The most likely scenario.
   3. An optimistic scenario.

d. Estimate the variable cost per 1,000 units and the fixed costs for years 1 and 2 under the:
   1. Pessimistic scenario.
   2. Most likely scenario.
   3. Optimistic scenario.

e. Compute the income after tax for each of the 10 years for the:
   1. Pessimistic scenario.
   2. Most likely scenario.
   3. Optimistic scenario.

f. Compute the cash flow for each of the 10 years for the:
   1. Pessimistic scenario.
   2. Most likely scenario.
   3. Optimistic scenario.

g. Compute the measures of return and risk based on the financial report:
   1. Average return on investment.
   2. Average change in income and sales.
   3. Average impact on earnings per share.
   4. Payback period.
   5. Sensitivity of the measures to the assumptions.
   6. Effect on liquidity and solvency.
   7. Abandonment loss and ratio to investment and retained earnings.

h. Compute the return and risk measures based on discounted values:
   1. Net present value.
   2. Discounted rate of return.
   3. Discounted benefit-cost index.
   4. Discounted payback period.
   5. Sensitivity of discounted measures to the scenarios.

---

[5] Because of the volume of calculations, an electronic spread sheet should be used for solution.

Concepts for Designing Cost Systems

CHAPTER

25

Concepts of Cost Allocation

ALLOCATION PROBLEM

Sheryn and Bryan Glazer founded Glazer Technology, Inc., about 18 months ago. Sheryn is president and her husband, Bryan, is vice president. Both of them earned degrees in engineering and computer science. After graduating from college, Sheryn and Bryan worked for Systems Consulting, Inc. (SCI), as computer programmers, systems analysts, and software designers. After seven years of experience with SCI and a contract from the Department of Defense (DOD), the Glazers stepped out of SCI and into their new venture.

Glazer Technology, Inc., specializes in adapting computer mainframe software applications to minicomputers and, when possible, to networked personal computers. The specific software applications are simulations such as those used in war games, airplanes, and tests of major weapons systems. Sheryn prepares the conceptual and detailed design and Bryan implements that design in the programming. At present, the company has no other employees. Instead, the Glazers contract some of their programming work to approved subcontractors.

DOD awarded a $300,000 contract to Glazer Technology for a war game package. That contract is about complete. Sheryn is now in the process of submitting two proposals on additional contracts for software packages, one for DOD and one for a commercial airline. A cost accounting system was not needed for the original contract because all costs incurred related to the single contract. Now a cost allocation structure is needed because several contracts will be worked on simultaneously. Sheryn and Bryan have no concept of how to structure a cost accounting system. The requirements for defining direct and indirect costs, cost pools, and allocation bases do not mean much to them. The Glazers know that the cost accounting practices used to estimate the costs of defense contracts must be consistent with the required practices for accumulating costs and charging them to contracts.

■

LEARNING OBJECTIVES

After studying this chapter, you should be able to:

1. Identify and describe the three key facets of cost allocation.
2. Explain how the degrees of remoteness relate to distinguishing between direct and indirect costs.
3. Describe and apply the four primary purposes for cost allocations.
4. Identify and apply the criteria for selecting an allocation base.

The cost allocations of an organization are the result of choices made regarding product costing, performance measurement, and information needed for decision-making. Similarly, the choice made as to cost allocation influences product costs, performance measures, and information for decision-making. In almost every line of work that an accountant pursues, cost-allocation issues arise. This chapter presents the critical conceptual issues related to cost allocations and identifies the purposes cost allocations serve. Special emphasis is given to the concepts required in cost accounting systems approved for accumulating costs related to government contracts.

DEFINITION OF COST ALLOCATION

The term *cost allocation* does not have one definition that includes meanings for all uses. Accountants cite a number of diverse situations that represent cost allocations. Examples are depreciation of property, plant, and equipment; amortization of bond discount; charging freight for a shipment received to the individual units in the order; or assigning costs, revenues, and profits to segments as a part of financial reporting. Terms used as synonyms for cost allocation include *proration, assignment, distribution, application, absorption,* and in some cases, *charge.* The most frequent interpretation of cost allocation is tied to indirect costs—costs that cannot be specifically traced.

In defining a cost accounting practice for government contracts, the Cost Accounting Standards Board (CASB)[1] identified and defined three important terms: measurement, assignment to periods, and allocation to cost objectives. **Measurement** encompasses defining cost components and determining the basis for cost measurement.[2] For example, measurement addresses what goes into the cost of an hour of labor, or a unit of product; whether to use standard or actual costs; or under what conditions present values will be used. **Assignment** concerns determining the amount of cost to identify with individual cost accounting periods.[3] This is where depreciation

---

[1] The Cost Accounting Standards Board is the agency of the U.S. government responsible for promulgating cost accounting standards as they apply to contracts with the federal government. See Appendix 25A for further discussion of the CASB and details on the current standards.

[2] *4 Code of Federal Regulations,* 331.20(k) (1).

[3] *4 Code of Federal Regulations,* 331.20(k) (2).

and amortization fit. The whole purpose of accrual accounting deals with placing costs into accounting periods. According to the CASB, **allocation** refers to identifying costs with cost objectives of the period. The allocation process encompasses the accounting methods and techniques used to[4]:

1. Accumulate cost.
2. Determine whether a cost is to be directly or indirectly allocated.
3. Determine the composition of cost pools.
4. Determine the selection and composition of the appropriate allocation base.

Measurement, assignment, and allocation are three steps in a process to identify costs with cost objectives. First, boundaries should be put on the cost under consideration. Second, the cost should be identified to a period of time. And third, the cost should be charged to the cost objective within that time period. We will use cost allocation to refer to the process of tracing, directly or indirectly, an item of cost or a group of costs to one or more cost objectives for a period of time.

FACETS OF COST ALLOCATION

To this point, we have used terms and concepts related to cost allocation but have not developed its conceptual facets. The main ideas are presented in the following sections.

Interrelationship of Three Facets of Cost Allocation

The three key facets of cost allocation are (1) selecting one or more cost objectives, (2) choosing and accumulating (pooling) the costs that relate to those cost objectives, and (3) establishing a method for identifying the accumulated (pooled) costs with the appropriate cost objectives. Given a cost objective and a total cost or cost pool, the problem is to choose a means to link the cost to the cost objective. The link should represent a measure of the relationship between cost and cost objective. Exhibit 25–1 depicts the relationship among the three facets.

Cost Objective.   A **cost objective** is any object for which a cost is measured. A manager would measure costs of activities, functions, cost centers, divisions, groups, departments, operations, processes, products, jobs, or projects. However, a cost objective can be a vacation trip to some exotic place, a planned elementary school construction, a political advertising campaign, the operations of a tour bus, or a fundraising program. An individual determines the object of interest. The cost objective is the primary facet of cost allocation because the definition of the cost pool and the identification of relationships are dependent on the cost objective.

Cost Pool.   A **cost pool** is a grouping of costs. When the cost object is a unit of material, the cost pool may be its purchase price or may be extended to include all costs associated with the material, such as purchase price, freight-in, insurance while in transit, adjustments for cash and other discounts, warehousing, materials handling, and interest charges on carrying the material in inventory. Therefore, a cost pool may have a single cost element or several cost elements.

Measure of Relationship.   Not every element in a cost pool will have the same relationship to the cost objective, but each element contributes to an average rela-

---

[4] *4 Code of Federal Regulations*, 331.20(k) (3).

EXHIBIT 25–1   Facets of Cost Allocation

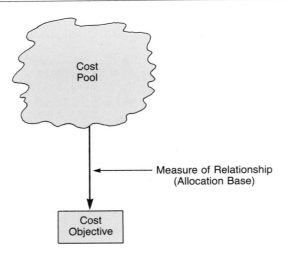

tionship that relates to all cost elements taken as a whole. This "averaging process" is at the heart of homogeneity, which was discussed in Chapter 8.

An **allocation base** is the measure that links cost objectives with the cost pool. In concept, the existence of the cost objective should be the dominant factor causing the incurrence of the costs. That is, if the cost objective were not present, there is no reason to incur the cost.[5] A global example is a business. Without products or services, the business would have no reason to incur the costs of property, plant, and equipment, or of administration of the organization. Although some accountants would call this a cause-and-effect relationship, we hesitate to go that far because cause and effect can not be clearly demonstrated for some of the costs typically classified as administrative costs.

The general procedure for identifying a relationship is to examine first the potential allocation bases that have measures in the cost objective, such as machine time, labor time, total cost input, or square footage. Selection of an appropriate allocation base is made after considering the following issues:

1. The allocation base should be a measure of activity that relates the cost pool with the cost objectives. Typical measures of activity are quantity, time, or dollars.
2. The clerical costs and effort incurred in making use of a particular allocation base. Accumulating the allocation base may be costly in itself, and the costs necessary to implement an allocation base may not be worth the benefits that base yields.
3. If the differences among allocation bases are immaterial, the least costly allocation base will be appropriate.

The general view is to select an allocation base that reflects an important aspect of activity. For example, if a fabrication operation is organized around machine centers, activity is often measured by machine time. On the other hand, if the company

---

[5] This is the concept of avoidability as developed in Chapter 22 related to product decisions.

specializes in products that are very difficult to manufacture, a measure of "the difficulty in manufacture" might be an appropriate allocation base.

In the next section, we will present more formal criteria for selecting among allocation bases.

CHOOSING AMONG ALLOCATION BASES

Management should establish reasonable and appropriate criteria and select allocation bases that meet those criteria. Some of the conceptual criteria suggested are included in the categories beneficial or causal, independence of cost objectives, equity or fairness, and ability to bear.

Beneficial or Causal Criterion

The Cost Accounting Standards Board defines allocations in terms of determining a beneficial or causal relationship rather than distinguishing between demand (benefits received) and supply (causal activities).[6]

Benefit.   One criterion for choosing an allocation base is to allocate costs among cost objectives in proportion to the benefits that the objectives receive from the costs incurred.[7] The benefit received should result in a demand for the product or service by those responsible for cost objectives. Thus, the more benefit received, the more demand there should be for the services that result in cost. However, benefit depends on judgment in most cases, and the criterion becomes increasingly difficult to apply as the services become more remote from the cost objectives. Benefit is a viable criterion when the connection between the cost and the cost objective is easily seen in the form of a physical good or measurable service. For example, there is little disagreement that factory departments benefit from a power plant in proportion to their consumption of power. However, there is little agreement as to how much each department benefits from the factory manager's office staff.

Cause.   Another criterion in choosing among allocation bases is to allocate costs in proportion to the factor or factors that cause those costs.[8] If those causal factors are clearly identifiable with the cost objectives to which the allocation is to be made, the causal relationship between the cost object and the costs incurred should be clear. For example, the cost of operating a financial institution is clearly related to the thousands of transactions that the institution must process. Thus, it would be reasonable to allocate the processing costs on the basis of the number of transactions related to the cost objective.

Cause is attributed to and is often measured by input activity, such as transactions.

---

[6] As with the economics for external markets, the amount of the internal product demanded and supplied and of the cost incurred is a result of interplay among the customers and the suppliers. Looked at dynamically, the relationship is constantly shifting as capacities are increased or decreased. Therefore, neither benefit received nor causal activity is a complete solution to the allocation of internal resources and subsequent costs.

[7] For example, see R. Nolan's compelling arguments for the allocation of computer costs based on benefits received by user departments: "Controlling the Costs of Data Services," *Harvard Business Review,* July–August, 1977.

[8] Emphasis in the current literature on cost drivers is an example of application of the causal criterion. Questions such as What is driving the cost? or What is causing the transactions that are driving costs? are causal in concept. In his retrospective, Gordon Shillinglaw strongly supports the concept of cause. See "Managerial Cost Accounting: Yesterday and Today," *Journal of Management Accounting Research,* Fall, 1989, pp. 33–46.

In concept, the cause is attributed to the number of units of activity or capacity that is supplied to each cost objective. Attribution requires judgment, which can be made with less and less confidence as the relationship between cost objective and cost pool becomes more remote.

Independence of Cost Objectives Criterion

Independence of cost objectives asserts that the allocation method should be designed so that the amount of cost allocated to one cost objective is not affected by actions or events in other cost objectives. In concept, this criterion attempts to separate causes among cost objectives. This is a criterion that is particularly important when the purpose of the cost allocation is measurement of performance.

Cost allocations that consist of both variable and fixed costs and that have an allocation based on activity create a dependency for the fixed cost part of the allocations. That is, the amount of fixed cost allocated to one cost objective is dependent upon the volume level in another cost objective. One solution is to segregate variable and fixed costs and use a separate allocation basis for fixed costs based on planned activity. A similar situation occurs when an allocation is based on actual costs incurred. This can be rectified by establishing allocation methods based on budgeted costs rather than on actual costs.

Equity or Fairness Criterion

The **equity or fairness** criterion refers to allocating costs to cost objectives based on what is "fair" to managers of those objectives. In concept, this criterion is an application of the benefit criterion with different terminology. The difficulty with this criterion is its inherent subjectivity; fairness is in the eye of the beholder. An allocation base that is fair to one manager is often viewed as detrimental to another manager. For example, allocating utilities costs on the basis of peak demand is fair to the division manager who operates at or near peak demand most of the time. However, a manager whose department hits peak demand only once a month will consider that allocation unfair, unreasonable, and biased.

Ability to Bear Criterion

According to this criterion, costs are allocated in proportion to a cost objective's **ability to bear** the charge for those costs. Often those cost objectives are presumed to be more able to bear the cost in some way because they either benefited more from or caused more of the cost. This criterion often leads to an allocation based on some measure of the size of the cost objectives. Examples of allocation bases representing ability to bear are those related to revenues (sales or net sales, and cost of sales) and those related to asset levels. The number of employees is an example of an allocation base that represents both a measure of ability to bear measure and a causal relationship for employee-related costs.

In the next section, we will discuss two characteristics of the relationship between the cost objective and the cost pool: the purpose for the allocation and the degree of remoteness.

CHARACTERISTICS OF ALLOCATION

Different concepts of allocation result from the several purposes for which the allocation is performed and the degree of remoteness of the cost object from the cost pool.

Purpose of the Cost Allocation

Cost allocations are made because someone perceives a need for them. The accounting literature suggests four common purposes for preparing cost allocations: financial reporting, planning and decision-making, pricing and cost recovery, and control and performance measurement.

Financial Reporting.   Financial reporting is the periodic preparation of financial statements in accordance with generally accepted accounting principles (GAAP), or principles of some regulatory agency (such as the Internal Revenue Service) for use by parties external to the reporting organization. Cost allocations are important in financial reporting in asset valuation and income determination.

An example of cost allocations in financial reporting is segment reporting. Statement of Financial Accounting Standards No. 14, ''Financial Reporting for Segments of a Business Enterprise,'' requires the reporting of operating profit or loss and, in some cases, asset dollar amounts for ''reportable segments.'' Allocation concepts apply anytime common costs and common assets must be allocated to various segments. Many administrative costs are common costs that must be allocated to individual segments. If a segment benefits from a cost or an asset, an allocation to that segment is required. The method of allocation is not, however, prescribed.

Planning and Decision-Making.   Some accountants maintain that cost allocations of indirect costs are not useful for planning and decision-making. However, this is not necessarily correct. Suppose a company is considering the expansion of its materials handling and warehousing operations. The costs of these operations (typically considered indirect costs) are tax deductible by way of flowing costs through inventories. Therefore, the question of tax consequences requires an assumption about inventory levels and periods when inventory levels fluctuate. The tax consequences require assignment to periods and then allocation to inventories.

Another example is a commercial building contractor who is planning work for the coming year and uses the percentage-of-completion method for contract accounting. The work plan is influenced by the profit picture of ongoing contracts, which in turn is influenced by the estimated costs to complete, which involve cost allocations that are affected by volume of activity.

Pricing and Cost Recovery.   Cost-based pricing occurs whenever prices of products and services are based either wholly or substantially on the seller's costs. The subjective nature of this pricing process is a reflection of management's goal to recover costs and generate a profit rather than a desire to obtain precise unit costs. Therefore, pricing in cost recovery and management will be concerned about recovering certain costs in the short run and all costs in the long run. An imperfectly competitive marketplace creates those situations where cost-based pricing is popular and will flourish. In many cases, the parties to sales contracts will go so far as to mutually agree on which costs will be used to justify the price. Thus, cost allocations are important to pricing issues.

Control and Performance Measurement.   The method of cost allocation influences performance measures and thus the behavior of managers. For example, a large company has acquired a computer system with a local area network. To encourage each segment to start using the system, the company makes no charges for usage. As demand increases, users are encouraged to think about restricting their needs. As a result of allocating some of the computer cost to each user department, the computer costs will appear in user performance reports and therefore usage will be reduced. Thus, the allocation of computer cost will influence the performance of users.

Whether cost allocations of indirect costs are useful in stimulating managers to control costs and in evaluating performance is controversial. There are those who argue from the supply side that allocations are not useful. They believe that control should be exerted over the costs in the responsibility center in which the costs are initially incurred—the supplying segments. These accountants support their position with cause-and-effect arguments.

The opposing argument is based on demand-side concepts (beneficial relationships). These accountants argue that cost control requires that management be aware of all the demands they place on resources. This requires that indirect costs be allocated to cost objects. Managers must be aware that indirect costs exist and must be covered by the direct profit contributions of their segments. In this way, managers are encouraged to use resources to the extent of a positive cost/benefit position. If managers believe that costs are out of line, they should seek to control indirect costs by putting pressure on the managers of the supply that results in costs being out of line.

Degrees of Remoteness

A continuum of relationships[9] called the **degree of remoteness** exists between cost objects and cost pools. Because a cost allocation requires a measure of relationship between cost pool and cost object, that relationship influences the allocation base selected. Beckett recognized three methods of cost allocation based on the degree of remoteness[10]:

1. The first method is used when a demonstrable and immediate relationship exists between the cost and the object to which the cost is being allocated.
2. The second method is used when a demonstrable relationship exists between the cost and the object to which the cost is being applied, but the relationship is not determinable with absolute accuracy or "rightness." It is clear, however, that a definite and fairly close relationship exists, but the nature of the relationship is somewhat subjective.
3. The third method pertains to circumstances in which no convenient relationship exists to rely upon, yet costs must be assigned. The relationship between the cost pool and the cost objective may be described as remote.

The degrees of remoteness are depicted as follows:

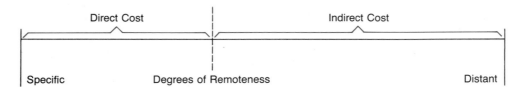

On one end of the continuum, the relationship is specific. The characteristic of costs at this end is that an individual cost can be easily traced to and specifically identified with a given cost objective. These costs are referred to as direct costs. At the other end of the continuum, the relationship is distant and the costs are called indirect costs. As the relationship changes from specific to distant, there is an in-between area where

---

[9] Some accountants firmly believe that all cost allocations are arbitrary and, thus, intolerable. The perceived arbitrariness of cost allocation arises from the belief that, because no single method of cost allocation is absolutely "right," all cost allocations are wrong and should not be attempted. Further, people with diverse interests in the outcome of an accounting measurement may prefer one allocation method over another. We counter this with the philosophical tenet that all measurement systems, whether weight, distance, mass, or allocation, are human inventions, not discoveries, and thus can never be proven correct. Even though discovery of a "true" system can never be achieved, weights, distances, masses, and allocations must still be measured for practical purposes.

[10] John A. Beckett, "A Study of the Principles of Allocating Costs," *The Accounting Review,* July, 1951.

EXHIBIT 25–2   Product Costing and Degree of Remoteness

Cost	Relationship
Direct materials	Specific
Direct labor	
Indirect materials	
Indirect labor	
Other variable overhead	
Selling expenses	
Distribution expenses	
Machinery and equipment	
Plant building	
Division administration	
Corporate administration	Distant

the relationship loses its specificity or directness and the costs move into the indirect area. Exhibit 25–2 gives examples of costs along the continuum, assuming a product is the point of reference for assessing whether a cost is direct or indirect.

COST ALLOCATION APPLICATIONS

Typical Allocation Bases

Exhibit 25–3 gives examples of typical allocation bases used for indirect costs labeled under several categories of costs: people related, material related, machine related, space related, service related, and transaction related. A careful review of this table should give an appreciation for the diversity of cost allocation bases.

Multiple Allocation Rates

In situations in which a responsibility center is used for cost pool definition and cost accumulation, more than one dominant relationship may exist between the cost pool and the cost objectives. Some companies fragment the pool and treat it as two or more pools, each with a single allocation base rather than use a single cost pool with multiple bases.

For example, Wetzel Enterprises built a power plant capable of generating 5,000,000 kilowatt hours of electricity per year. Three of its departments are expected to use the following electricity: Sewing, 2,500,000 kilowatt hours; Pressing, 2,000,000 kilowatt hours; and Packaging, 500,000 kilowatt hours. Actual consumption of electricity for the year was Sewing, 1,500,000 kilowatt hours; Pressing, 1,800,000 kilowatt hours; and Packaging, 700,000 kilowatt hours. The costs of the power plant consisted of $800,000 variable costs and $1,200,000 fixed costs. How should the power plant costs be allocated to the departments?

Three allocation methods are possible for this situation: (1) budget capacity, (2) actual capacity, and (3) variable costs based on actual capacity with fixed costs based on budget capacity.

Using budget capacity, the rate per kilowatt hour is $0.40 ($2,000,000/5,000,000 kilowatt hours). This method gives the following cost allocations:

Sewing:	$0.40 × 2,500,000 =	$1,000,000
Pressing:	$0.40 × 2,000,000 =	800,000
Packaging:	$0.40 × 500,000 =	200,000
Total		$2,000,000

EXHIBIT 25–3   Typical Allocation Bases for Selected Indirect Costs

Category	Indirect Cost	Typical Allocation Base
People-related	1. Supervision	Number of employees, payroll dollars, or labor hours
	2. Personnel services	Number of employees
	3. Pension costs	Payroll dollars, factor on which pensions are based
	4. Group insurance	Payroll dollars, number of employees, factor on which insurance is based
Material-related	1. Materials handling	Quantity or value of material
	2. Indirect materials	Value of direct materials
Machine-related	1. Depreciation	Machine hours, equipment value
	2. Maintenance	Number of machines, machine hours
	3. Taxes on equipment	Value of equipment
	4. Insurance on equipment	Value of equipment
Space-related	1. Depreciation	Space occupied
	2. Building rental	Space occupied
	3. Building insurance	Space occupied
	4. Heat and air cooling	Space occupied, volume occupied
	5. Interior maintenance	Space occupied
	6. Concession rental	Space occupied weighted by desirability of location
Service-related	1. Cafeteria	Number of meals, number of employees
	2. Laundry	Weight processed
	3. Janitorial	Hours worked, square footage
Transaction-related	1. Billing and accounting	Number of documents
	2. Production engineering	Number of change orders
	3. Production scheduling	Number of production orders
	4. Purchasing	Number of purchase orders, number of line items

Actual capacity used as the basis for cost allocation results in a rate per kilowatt hour of $0.50 ($2,000,000/4,000,000 kilowatt hours). Under this method, the costs allocated to each department would be as follows:

Sewing:	$0.50 × 1,500,000 =	$ 750,000
Pressing:	$0.50 × 1,800,000 =	900,000
Packaging:	$0.50 × 700,000 =	350,000
Total		$2,000,000

The third method recognizes that fixed costs provide capacity, and variable costs relate to the volume of usage. Therefore, the fixed costs are allocated based on budget capacity and variable costs on actual capacity used. This allocation results in rates of $0.24 per budget kilowatt hour for fixed costs ($1,200,000/5,000,000 kilowatt hours) and $0.20 per actual kilowatt hour for variable costs ($800,000/4,000,000 kilowatt hours). This results in the following cost allocations:

Sewing:	Fixed	$0.24 × 2,500,000	=	$600,000	
	Variable	$0.20 × 1,500,000	=	300,000	$ 900,000
Pressing:	Fixed	$0.24 × 2,000,000	=	$480,000	
	Variable	$0.20 × 1,800,000	=	360,000	840,000
Packaging:	Fixed	$0.24 × 500,000	=	$120,000	
	Variable	$0.20 × 700,000	=	140,000	260,000
Total					$2,000,000

The third method is more appropriate for control and performance evaluation because it separates the variable costs from the fixed costs that provide capacity.

Multiple Factors in Allocation Base

Some costs have a relationship to cost objectives so that more than one factor is necessary to determine the allocation base. An example of this is the residual home office expense allocation covered by Cost Accounting Standard 403. The standard gives a three-factor formula consisting of:

1. The percentage of payroll dollars in each segment to the total payroll dollars of all segments.
2. The percentage of sales revenue in each segment to the total sales revenue in all segments.
3. The percentage of average net book value of tangible assets of each segment to the total net book value of tangible assets in all segments.

These factors come from the assumption that corporate headquarters is responsible for people, volume, and investment. The standard assumes that home office expenses are people-related, volume-related, and investment-related in equal proportions. Because the relationship of cost pool (home office) to cost objectives (divisions) is multifaceted, the allocation base must incorporate those factors in some manner.

Assume that a company has $600,000 of residual corporate headquarters costs that it wants to allocate to the Eastern, Central, and Western divisions. The following information about payroll dollars, sales revenue, and tangible assets is taken from the divisional records (dollar amounts in thousands):

Division	Payroll Dollars	Payroll Percentage	Sales Revenue	Sales Percentage	Net Book Value Tangible Assets	Net Book Value Percentage
Eastern	$1,500	30	$ 7,500	50	$6,300	70
Central	1,200	24	3,000	20	900	10
Western	2,300	46	4,500	30	1,800	20
Total	$5,000	100	$15,000	100	$9,000	100

The factors are weighted to arrive at an average:

Eastern:	(0.30 + 0.50 + 0.70)/3	= 50%
Central:	(0.24 + 0.20 + 0.10)/3	= 18%
Western:	(0.46 + 0.30 + 0.20)/3	= 32%

The residual home office expenses would be allocated to the three divisions as follows:

Eastern:	50% × $600,000	= $300,000
Central:	18% × $600,000	= 108,000
Western:	32% × $600,000	= 192,000
Total		$600,000

Prices Based on Full Cost

Care must be exercised in using full-cost allocations for pricing. Assume that a company produces only one product and that the cost structure is as follows:

Material costs—Variable	$10
Labor costs—Variable	6
Other variable costs	2
Total variable costs	$18
Fixed overhead and other fixed costs	$200,000

In order to determine the full cost per unit, it is necessary to select a specific number of units over which to allocate the fixed costs. The fixed cost per unit decreases as the number of units increases. If the company has a price policy of marking up 10 percent based on full cost, the prices shown in the following table are possible, depending on the decision about volume.

	Number of Units (in thousands)				
	50	*100*	*150*	*200*	*250*
Variable cost per unit	$18.00	$18.00	$18.00	$18.00	$18.00
Fixed cost per unit	4.00	2.00	1.33	1.00	.80
Total full cost per unit	$22.00	$20.00	$19.33	$19.00	$18.80
10% markup	2.20	2.00	1.93	1.90	1.88
Selling price	$24.20	$22.00	$21.26	$20.90	$20.68

If 100,000 units are selected as the number of units over which to allocate the fixed cost, the profit per unit is $2.00. Should any other number of units be sold, the profit per unit would not be $2.00, but the total fixed costs would still be $200,000. Therefore, the question arises as to the validity of allocating fixed costs in a pricing decision. When fixed costs are included, a manager must exercise caution in selecting the volume level that determines the fixed cost per unit.

Allocation in Stages

Cost allocations typically occur in stages with a hierarchy of cost pools and cost objectives. For example, in allocating costs to the services provided by a hospital, it is typical to perform the cost allocations in stages. If the primary cost objective of concern were the cost of an X ray in the radiology department, the cost of an X ray includes more than the direct costs of the radiology department. Therefore, all costs of administration, centralized services, and other costs benefiting radiology must first be allocated to the radiology department. That is the first stage of an allocation. The second stage involves allocating all costs accumulated in the radiology department to X rays produced. Chapter 8 explains the methods for allocation for a production process in more detail.

IMPACT OF RECENT PRODUCTION TECHNOLOGY CHANGE

U.S. industry is changing as a result of a shifting competitive balance between domestic and foreign producers. The changes have resulted in higher quality, lower inventory, flexible flow lines, increased automation, shift to product-line organization, and effective use of information. Together, these changes reflect management's commitment to produce high-quality goods on time at the lowest possible cost. These changes have an impact on the cost allocation process.

Automation and increasing reliance on "information workers" (the high incidence of computer usage) are shifting the emphasis from labor to equipment. As a result, direct labor costs are decreasing while production overhead costs are increasing. Because many companies still apply overhead on the basis of direct labor, overhead rates have increased dramatically. Thus, allocation methods must give greater recognition to activities that are different from the incurrence of labor hours.

The proportion of variable costs, which are directly identifiable with products, is decreasing with an associated increase in fixed costs. A greater need now exists to distinguish between contribution margins and full-cost profit margins. Consequently, more emphasis will be placed on separating the variable and fixed cost components and identifying cost allocation methods for each category.

The shift from functional production organizations to product lines or cellular manufacturing changes the nature of the traditional cost pools. The product-line orientation allows direct identification of many overhead costs to the product line and thus reduces the allocation problem across departments. However, the ability of production processes to produce diverse products, especially fabrication processes, increases the problem of cost allocation to the products flowing within a given production process.

The drive toward higher quality causes companies to more tightly control all aspects of their production operations. To achieve this, knowledge of quality costs is critical.[11] Thus, there is the need to accumulate and separate all quality costs such as design, scrap, rework, product warranty, field service, and other costs. This accumulation results in new cost objectives with different relationships to new cost pools. Thus, a redefinition of relationships and even of cost pool construction is important.

SUMMARY

Cost allocations are common in financial accounting and cost accounting. The phrase *cost allocation* does not have a definite meaning for all uses. Other terms used for cost allocation are *proration, assignment, distribution, application,* and *absorption.* The Cost Accounting Standards Board defined a cost accounting practice by including three aspects related to costs: measurement, assignment to periods, and allocation to cost objectives.

The three key facets to cost allocation are cost objective, cost pool, and allocation base. They are interrelated in that the identification of one or more specific cost objectives directly determines how cost pools should be established. The allocation base is a measure of the relationship between a cost pool and its cost objectives. Degrees of remoteness in this relationship exist. At one extreme, costs have a *direct* relationship. Moving along a continuum, the relationship becomes *indirect.*

Cost allocations are made because someone perceives the need for them. The primary purposes of cost allocations have been identified as financial reporting, planning and decision-making, pricing and cost recovery, and control and performance measurement. Cost allocation methods depend on one or more purposes served. Therefore, it is important to know beforehand how the results of cost allocations will be used.

Choosing among allocation bases involves both conceptual and practical considerations. Conceptual considerations include equity or fairness, ability to bear, benefit,

---

[11] Quality costs include the costs of all aspects of quality from initial design through production to final customer usage and product disposal.

cause, and independence of cost objectives. They give guidance on a conceptual level. Practical considerations for selecting an allocation base include the nature of cost pools, the purpose of the allocation, the cost versus the benefits of the allocation, and the technological change involved.

KEY TERMS AND CONCEPTS	Measurement (950)	Allocation base (952)
	Assignment (950)	Independence of cost objectives (954)
	Allocation (951)	Equity or fairness (954)
	Cost objective (951)	Ability to bear (954)
	Cost pool (951)	Degree of remoteness (956)

ADDITIONAL READINGS

Anthony, R. N. "Cost Allocation." *Journal of Cost Analysis,* Spring, 1984, pp. 5–15.

Baumol, W. J. "How Arbitrary Is Arbitrary?—or, Toward the Deserved Demise of Full Cost Allocation." *Public Utilities Fortnightly,* September 3, 1987, pp. 16–21.

Blanchard, G. A., and C. W. Chow. "Allocating Indirect Costs for Improved Management Performance." *Management Accounting,* March, 1983, pp. 38–41.

Haskins, M., and R. P. Crum. "Cost Allocations: A Classroom Role-Play in Managerial Behavior and Accounting Courses." *Issues in Accounting Education,* 1985, pp. 109–30.

Kaplan, R. S. "One Cost System Isn't Enough." *Harvard Business Review,* January–February, 1988, pp. 61–66.

Mackey, J. T. "Allocating Opportunity Costs." *Management Accounting,* March, 1983, pp. 33–37.

McLaughlin, J. K., and A. Farley. "Resolved: Joint Costs Should Be Allocated (Sometimes)." *CPA Journal,* January, 1988, pp. 46–53.

Miller, B. L., and A. G. Buckman. "Cost Allocation and Opportunity Costs." *Management Science,* May, 1987, pp. 626–39.

O'Neal, J. "Allocating Interest Associated with Mixed-Purpose Loan." *CFO,* April, 1989, pp. 51–59.

Schneider, A. "Pricing and Indirect Cost Allocation—A Note." *Accounting and Finance* (Australia), May, 1987, pp. 49–54.

Skinner, R. C. "Cost Allocation in Management and Financial Accounting." *International Journal of Accounting, Education and Research,* Spring, 1986, pp. 91–107.

Sourwine, D. A. "Does Your System Need Repair." *Management Accounting,* February, 1989, pp. 32–36.

REVIEW QUESTIONS

1. Explain measurement, assignment, and allocation as defined by the Cost Accounting Standards Board.
2. The allocation process, according to the Cost Accounting Standards Board, encompasses methods and techniques that accomplish four things. What are those four things?
3. What are the three key facets of cost allocation?
4. "A cost objective is the most important of the facets in cost allocation." Comment.
5. What is the importance of the cost objective to cost allocation? Give three examples of cost objectives.
6. Describe a cost pool. Give two examples of a cost pool.
7. What is the major reason for having a cost allocation base?

8. ''Remoteness means distant from the known and usual or common.'' Does this definition apply to cost allocations? Comment.

9. Cost allocations may differ depending on the purpose for which they are prepared. Briefly explain the four primary purposes for cost allocations.

10. How are allocations used in segment reporting, other than for inventories?

11. Explain which costs are important in choosing cost allocations for planning and decision-making.

12. Control might be called *obtaining the desired motivation*. What is the relationship between cost control and cost allocation?

13. How might a cost allocation influence the behavior of a manager? Give an example.

14. Ability to bear may not be an equitable or fair way to allocate costs in specific circumstances. Comment.

15. Distinguish between benefit and cause as a criterion for selection of an allocation base.

16. Relate the criterion of equity or fairness to independence of cost objectives in selection of an allocation base.

17. From a practical point of view, list the items that should be considered in the selection of an allocation base.

18. Explain how current technological changes impact on the cost allocation process. Use the example of direct labor as an allocation base.

19. When might it be appropriate to use machine time as an allocation base for product costing?

DISCUSSION QUESTIONS

20. Fairness, ability to bear, benefit, and independence of cost objectives are criteria for selecting an allocation base. They initially appear independent when in fact they interrelate or overlap. Explain how these criteria interrelate.

21. In earlier chapters, we argued that plant-wide overhead rates are not as good as departmental overhead rates. The reason relates to the concept of homogeneity of the cost pool. If you were in a position to quote a price for products and later compare actual costs with those costs you estimated when quoting the price, would you prefer more or fewer cost pools? Justify your position.

EXERCISES

25–1. Cost Pools and Allocation Bases. On July 1, 19x3, Paula Drevcek started as the new assistant controller for the Black Hills Division of Womble Enterprises. During the first month in the Black Hills Division, she was asked to find the cost of:

a. Plastic intrusion sleeve, #582, size 4 inches (This part is produced on a completely automated machine #90–2, which produces 10 different parts on a regular basis.)

b. Units spoiled in the Assembly Department on July 5.

c. Disposal of the highly toxic waste VOX20 during July (The division pays a substantial fee for disposal of all its toxic wastes; VOX20 is particularly dangerous.)

d. Cleaning one of the six division offices for the month.

e. Installation of one part of the new computer system.

REQUIRED:

For each cost objective *a.* through *e.*, suggest to Ms. Drevcek
1. The appropriate cost pool.
2. An allocation base.

25–2. Cost Cause, Objectives, Purpose, and Control. The executives of Grotis Stores are very concerned about the increase in costs related to information processing and systems. For the past three years, such costs have totaled (in millions):

19x3	$2.3
19x4	3.9
19x5	6.2

J. W. Vriblett, president, stated to the executive committee: ''This computer cost has gotten out of control. I want the cost to decrease to about $4 million in 19x6.'' The vice president of finance responded: ''J. W., the cost would be controllable if we charged the stores for the computer services they are using.'' After some discussion, the executive committee approved a project to charge all computer costs to the stores.

REQUIRED:
a. What is the purpose of considering the cost?
b. What is the cost objective to which costs are to be allocated?
c. List three cost elements that would be included in the cost pool for the cost objective.
d. What was the stated reason for allocating the cost to the cost objective?

25–3. Cost Pools and Allocation Bases.   Listed below are cost pools and allocation bases:

	Cost Pool	*Allocation Bases*
_____ *a.*	Janitorial	1. Number of employees
_____ *b.*	Personnel	2. Machine hours
_____ *c.*	Materials handling	3. Space occupied
_____ *d.*	Heat and air cooling	4. Materials
_____ *e.*	Purchasing	
_____ *f.*	Group insurance	
_____ *g.*	Machine maintenance	
_____ *h.*	Building rental	

REQUIRED:
For each cost pool, select the most likely allocation base.

25–4. Selection Criteria.   Listed below are five cost pools, allocation bases, and cost objectives:

	Cost Pool	*Allocation Base*	*Allocation to*
a.	Public school district	Property value	Property owners
b.	Printing press	Pages printed	Books
c.	Materials handling	Weight	Materials
d.	Home office expense	Revenue	Divisions
e.	Shopping mall parking lot	Square feet	Retail stores

REQUIRED:
Using the responses ''yes,'' ''no,'' or ''to some extent,'' indicate whether the allocation base meets each of the following criteria:
1. Benefit received.
2. Causal relationship.
3. Ability to bear.
4. Fairness.
5. Independence of cost objectives.

25–5. Allocation Bases and Profit Sharing.   Congottle Associates, Inc., is a consulting group that performs accounting systems consulting and sells software. During 19x2, the following occurred:

	Consulting	*Software*
Revenues (000s)	$2,772	$1,628
Space requirements (square feet)	1,980	1,620

The total of all expenses for 19x2 is $3.4 million. There are six consulting partners and four software partners. The partners share their respective area profits equally.

REQUIRED:
Compute the profit share for consulting and software under each of the following independent allocation bases for the total expenses:

a. Revenues

b. Traceable costs allocated directly and the remainder allocated on space requirements. (The traceable costs for consulting are $1,800,000 and for software are $455,000.)

25–6. Ability to Bear versus Beneficial Relationship. Creibon Financial, Inc., is an integrated financial services organization providing loans, investments, and insurance. One primary cost of the organization is data processing, which was $15.4 million during 19x4. The following data are available regarding the three activities:

	Loans	Investments	Insurance
Revenues (millions)	$80	$320	$500
Number of transactions (000s)	1,200	600	200

REQUIRED:

a. Allocate the data processing cost on the basis of
   1. Revenues.
   2. Number of transactions.

b. Comment on the differences between the allocations based on revenues and those based on transactions.

25–7. Cost Recovery and Pricing. Flotta County Hospital, as with most designated county hospitals, must provide care to the indigent with little hope of collecting the full amount for services rendered. Indigent care is more expensive to provide than regular patient care because of complicating factors, such as poor nutrition, poor sanitation, drug abuse, and physical abuse. During 19x1, Flotta County Hospital had the following costs that could be directly traced to the Pediatric Care Unit:

	Number of Cases	Direct Cost per Case
Regular	4,000	$ 800
Indigent	1,000	5,000

In addition, indirect costs of about $200 per patient are related to medical records and case administration. The county and state will pay only $1,200 per indigent pediatric case. Virtually all regular pediatric care patients are fully covered by health insurance.

REQUIRED:

a. Assuming that 19x2 will be similar to 19x1, what price should be charged to regular pediatric patients during 19x2 to recover the full costs of the Pediatric Care Unit?

b. Is this pricing approach based on equity, fairness, ability to bear, beneficial relationship, or causal relationship? Comment.

25–8. Selecting Allocation Bases. The records of Fairfield Fabricators, Inc., show a department for general administration, five service centers, and four producing departments. The controller is in the process of selecting the basis for allocating service center costs to other service centers, general administration, and producing departments. The service centers are personnel, cafeteria, building and grounds, repairs and maintenance, and power. The producing departments are cutting, grinding, assembly, and finishing. The controller has reduced the allocation bases to four types: number of employees, square meters of floor space, hours of service, and kilowatt hours of power. She is now trying to decide which base goes with which service center.

REQUIRED:
For each service center, give your rationale for which allocation base would be most appropriate for allocating the costs of that service center to other service centers, general administration, and the producing departments.

PROBLEMS

25–9. Cost Allocation Bases and Planning. The cost of copying materials for Moore, Lehman, Black & Co, Attorneys at Law, includes copy machine rental, paper, labor, space, and repairs. A portion of the copies made are at the discretion of the attorneys working on each case. In planning copying costs for 19x4, Mr. Moore estimated that the total costs would be the following if revenues, planned usage, and actual usage are the bases selected:

Allocation Basis	Planned Cost
Revenues	$400,000
Planned usage	350,000
Actual usage	320,000

During 19x4, the following occurred:

	Moore	Lehman	Black
Revenues (000s)	$820	$600	$580
Planned usage (000s)	800	650	550

REQUIRED:
Consider the following requirements independently.
a. Allocate the planned copy cost of $400,000 on the basis of revenues.
b. Allocate the planned copy cost of $350,000 on the basis of planned usage.
c. Assume that Mr. Moore chose to allocate on the basis of actual usage. Subsequently, the number of copies (in 000s) actually incurred was 760 for Moore, 480 for Lehman, and 360 for Black. Allocate the copy cost of $320,000 on the basis of actual usage.

25–10. Independence, Beneficial, and Causal Relationship. Sampton Paint Stores, Inc., has three paint stores in one city. After discussion with store managers, Bill Sampton, the company president, makes the decisions with regard to the city-wide advertising over television and radio and in newspapers. During the month of June, 19x2, Sampton placed $20,000 in city-wide advertising for a special sale at all the stores. Sales activity for June at the three stores was:

Location	Actual	Planned	Difference
Eastside	$ 90,000	$ 50,000	$ 40,000
Westside	110,000	100,000	10,000
Southside	350,000	200,000	150,000
Totals	$550,000	$350,000	$200,000

The planned revenues were based on normal June sales without consideration of the special city-wide advertising. The store managers agree that the difference in revenue is predominantly due to the special advertising. The store managers are paid a salary plus a bonus equal to 20 percent of store profits before the bonus.

REQUIRED:
a. Allocate the city-wide advertising cost over the three stores on the basis of:
   1. Actual sales.
   2. Planned sales.
   3. Difference in sales from plan.
b. Which, if any, of the three allocation bases from requirement (a) results in allocations to stores that are:
   1. Independent of activities that occur in other stores during the month?
   2. Related to the benefit received from the advertising by each store?
   3. Related to the amount of advertising cost caused by each store?

25–11. Causal and Beneficial Relationships. The state auditor questioned the allocation of engineering costs made by the Jarson Construction Company during August 19x6. Jarson's Engineering Department had the following time percentages on projects during August 19x6:

Project Type	Actual	Normal
State related	30	50
County related	30	30
Commercial	20	20
Idle time	20	0

The normal time reflects long-run experience. As a result of this time analysis, Jarson charged the state government $300,000 of a total of $800,000 in engineering costs. The state auditor's report included two specific statements of cost allocation concepts:

1. Half of the state-related time was due to work on options for changes to the Colt River overpass that were requested by the state highway department. Because the original engineering drawings were retained without change, this work provided no benefit to the state. The taxpayers should not pay when there is no benefit received.
2. Because 20 percent of the engineering time was idle, $160,000 (20 percent of $800,000) should be charged to overhead, not directly charged to the state because the state receives no benefit from idle engineers.

REQUIRED:

a. Based on the state auditor's concept statements, recompute the allocation to state-related engineering costs to be directly charged.
b. Comment on the state auditor's two cost allocation concepts using the causal relationship concept.

25–12. Allocation of Travel Costs.   Yvonne Carroll is a consultant specializing in government contract accounting with offices in Dallas, Texas. On Sunday evening February 2, 19x3, she traveled to Long Beach, California, to perform regular consulting work with a client for three days. On Wednesday night, she flew to Chicago to spend two days as an expert witness for a client there. She returned to Dallas Friday evening. Ms. Carroll bills for her time at a rate of $1,500 per day for regular consulting and $2,250 per day for expert witness time. In addition, clients generally agree that they should pay their share of out-of-pocket costs but would disagree with being billed for more travel costs than incurred. Yvonne is faced with how to allocate the costs incurred during the week to the two clients. The actual expenses for the week were as follows:

Airfare: Dallas/Long Beach/Chicago/Dallas	$1,452
Mileage: Round trip to airport from office (80 miles at $.25)	20
Airport parking in Dallas ($7 per day or $28 per week)	28
Hotel: Long Beach	354
Hotel: Chicago	194
Rental car: Long Beach	123
Limo service: Chicago	80
Meals: Long Beach	91
Meals: Chicago	65

Regular round-trip fares from Dallas to the two locations are as follows:

Long Beach	$980
Chicago	770

REQUIRED:

a. Compute the amount of expenses that is traceable to each client and the amount of expenses that is common to both clients.
b. Allocate the common costs on each of the following allocation bases:
    1. Billings for time with the client to the maximum of the regular round-trip airfares.
    2. Days spent with each client to the maximum of the regular round-trip airfares.

3. Fair share based on the regular round-trip air fares. (This is the most common allocation basis in practice.)
4. Amount "caused" by each client. The Los Angeles client's work has been scheduled for many weeks. The Chicago client was scheduled last week.

c. Comment on whether or not the common (joint) cost of travel should be allocated to the two clients.

25–13. Selecting Allocation Bases. Slegton Community Hospital was paid $2,240 for delivery room and pediatric charges related to the birth of Delma Ross on July 6, 19x8. In computing the actual cost related to this delivery, the assistant controller found costs associated with the following items:

a. Surgical supplies
b. Hospital occupancy
c. Nursing staff—Obstetrics
d. Laundry
e. Computer system
f. Oxygen handling system
g. Laboratory
h. Supervision—Obstetrics
i. Building security
j. Billing and insurance—Clerical
k. Hospital malpractice insurance
l. Supplies—Nursery
m. Hospital administrator
n. Janitorial
o. Parking lot
p. Fetal monitors
q. Nursing staff—Newborn nursery
r. Hospital legal department
s. Pharmacy

REQUIRED:
For each cost, indicate an appropriate allocation base in computing the actual hospital cost related to the birth of Delma Ross.

25–14. Beneficial Relationship. Murghi Power Company is required to maintain capacity to meet peak load demand for consumer power in the Murghi Valley area. In order to meet peak load demands, the company maintains two power plants with the following planned costs:

Plant	Fixed Costs (per month)	Variable Cost (per megawatt hour)	Average Capacity (megawatts)
Vindaloo	$3,000,000	$40	150
Goa	4,500,000	30	250

Vindaloo plant is consistently run at full capacity, which meets the Murghi Valley area needs 50 percent of the time. Goa plant was recently added to meet local needs for the foreseeable future. The current plan calls for half of the capacity to be reserved to meet the needs of Murghi Valley and the other half to be sold at a rate of $75 per megawatt hour. During May 19x6, the Goa plant was actually used as follows:

20 percent to meet local needs.
50 percent for sales to other power companies.
30 percent idle capacity.

The Vindaloo plant generates an average of 108,000 megawatt hours per month (150 average megawatt hours × 24 hours × 30 days). The company has made an investment of $10 million in the Vindaloo plant and $20 million in the Goa plant.

Under state law, a power company is allowed rates on local service equal to actual total cost of providing the service plus a 1 percent per month return on plant investment. The state regulatory board is currently reviewing the allocation of the Goa plant costs to the local power pool cost. Two proposals base the allocation for the Goa plant on

Plan A: Total cost allocated on current actual usage. Investment is allocated on current actual usage.

Plan B: Fixed costs allocated on reserved capacity and variable costs allocated on actual activity. Investment is allocated on reserved capacity.

REQUIRED:
a. Compute the expected total cost of operations for June 19x6 at the
   1. Vindaloo plant.
   2. Goa plant.
b. Compute the total cost allocated to power for the Murghi Valley for May 19x6 under
   1. Plan A.
   2. Plan B.
c. Compute the amount of investment base used to generate power for the Murghi Valley during May 19x6 under
   1. Plan A.
   2. Plan B.
d. Comment on whether or not any portion of the fixed costs of the Goa plant should be allocated to the cost of supplying power to the Murghi Valley.

25–15. Allocation Base Criteria.   Surgical Associates, Ltd., is a group surgical practice with three physicians. The practice maintains offices for the physicians and support staff, an examining room, a waiting area, a records and insurance room, and a general area. The office has a total of 4,000 square feet. Expenses relate to support personnel, insurance, equipment, and other. During 19x6, the total practice expenses, excluding the physicians' salaries, were $880,000. The three physicians had the following activity and space:

	Miller	*Ozchek*	*Lota*
Number of patients seen	1,800	1,200	3,000
Office space (square feet)	800	600	800
Total billings	$540,000	$360,000	$600,000
Traceable expenses	$150,000	$100,000	$150,000

The physicians receive total compensation equal to the difference between total revenues and total expenses, excluding their salaries.

REQUIRED:
Compute the amount of the compensation for each physician under each of the approaches suggested:
a. Dr. Ozchek suggests that the fairest division of expenses would be in proportion to revenues.
b. Dr. Lota suggests that the fairest approach would be to divide all the expenses equally.
c. Dr. Miller suggests that the expenses should be allocated on the basis of what caused the cost. Thus, the traceable expenses should be allocated to each physician. Of the remainder, one half should be allocated on the basis of office space and the other half should be allocated in proportion to patient visits.

25–16. Allocation Base Criteria.   The Civil Court at Eagleton, Tennessee, has total planned operating costs of $2,400,000 for 19x4. Approximately 50 percent of the costs relate to time spent in session and another 25 percent relate closely to the number of pages of documents filed in each case. All costs are charged to cases and are called *court costs*. Listed below is a sample of the types of cases the court handles.

4–3092   Mabelle Johnson, suit for wrongful death of husband George Johnson, who died while employed at Eagleton Lumber Yard. (There are six children and Mrs.

Johnson has no means of support. Case was dismissed after start of trial due to an error committed by plaintiff's attorney.)

4–3093   Melton H. and Julie V. Jackson, divorce suit.

4–3094   Weilton, Inc., suit for contract breach against Memphis Iron and Supply. (Weilton is bankrupt due to the alleged actions of Memphis Iron and currently has assets of $2 million and debts of $10 million.)

The following information is available regarding these three cases (dollar amounts in millions):

Case No.	Suit Amount	Settlement/ Judgment	Court Time	Pages Submitted	Defendant Equity
4–3092	$ 4	$ 0	38	380	$184
4–3093	$ 16	$16	2	120	16
4–3094	$100	$ 4	360	35,500	200

REQUIRED:

Allocate the court costs to the case types based on the:

a. Benefits received (use the settlement or judgment). Would this seem fair to the plaintiffs? Comment.
b. Costs caused (allocate the page variable costs on number of pages submitted and the remainder on the basis of court time). Would this seem fair to all plaintiffs? Comment.
c. Ability to bear (allocation base is the net equity of the plaintiff). Would this seem fair to all plaintiffs? Comment.
d. Ability to bear (allocation base is the net equity of whoever loses the case). Would this seem fair to all plaintiffs? Comment.
e. Of the allocation bases proposed in requirements (a) through (d), which, if any, meets the requirement for independence of cost objectives?

25–17. Allocation of Service Costs.   Triple A Machining has repair and maintenance costs for two machine centers. The variable costs of repair and maintenance are budgeted and allocated at a rate of $0.50 per labor hour of repair and maintenance worked in a machine center. The fixed costs of repair and maintenance, budgeted at $8,000 per month, are allocated on the basis of machine-hour capacity in each machine center. Under this arrangement, Machine Center A is 40 percent and Machine Center B is 60 percent of total capacity. The budgeted and actual times for each machine center are as follows:

	Machine Center	
	A	B
Budgeted maintenance labor hours	1,000	2,000
Actual maintenance labor hours	1,200	2,100
Budgeted machine hours	4,000	6,000
Actual machine hours	4,500	5,500

REQUIRED:

Assume that actual variable costs per maintenance labor hour and the actual fixed costs equaled the budgeted amounts.

a. Allocate the repair and maintenance costs on the basis of budgeted amounts.
b. Allocate the repair and maintenance costs on the basis of actual maintenance labor hours and actual machine hours used.
c. If you were the manager of Machine Center B, which of the foregoing methods of allocation would you prefer? Comment.

25–18. Cost Pools and Allocations.   One of the major costs for LLB Construction is project engineering design. During April 19x9, the firm had six projects in the design phase and had the following actual and planned design costs:

	Actual	Planned
Hours of activity	1,950	2,000
Salaries—Design	$48,735	$45,500
Benefits—Design	12,400	11,900
Travel—Design	15,300	15,600
Supplies—Design	4,600	5,000
Miscellaneous—Design	3,400	2,000

The travel and supplies are considered variable costs. In addition to the direct costs listed above, the design staff actually used 30 percent of the computer system capacity even though only 25 percent was planned. Further, engineering design staff occupied 25 percent of the office building. The total building contains 16,000 square feet of which 10 percent is used for the computer system. The costs of occupancy and the computer system are considered fixed in nature. The following actual and planned amounts were found in the records for the month:

	Actual	Planned
Utilities—Building	$11,200	$12,200
Janitorial—Building	17,000	18,000
Depreciation—Building	10,000	10,000
Rental—Computer	12,000	12,000
Salaries—Computer	22,000	21,000
Benefits—Computer	8,000	7,500
Supplies—Computer	10,000	9,500

During the month, the engineering design staff worked on several designs, one of which was the South River Bridge project, which actually required 700 hours of design time even though only 650 hours were used to bid the design. Bids are based on planned full costs plus a 20 percent markup.

REQUIRED:
Compute the actual cost and the planned cost for each of the following cost objectives for April 19x9:
a. Office space per square foot.
b. Computer service in total.
c. Engineering design per hour (full cost).
d. South River Bridge project (full cost).

25–19. Allocating Departmental Costs. Two years ago, Messer Products, Inc., built its own electrical generating unit, which supplies all of the electrical power for the entire plant. The costs of the generating unit have been allocated to the three operating departments on the basis of actual relative use. The managers of the operating departments are unhappy about the impact such allocations have on their performance measures. They have asked the controller to devise a better method for allocating the power costs.

Variable costs of generating electricity are about $0.02 per kilowatt hour (kwh), and monthly fixed costs are about $420,000. The generating plant has monthly capacity of 600,000 kwh. The actual usage for June 19x0, the six-month average usage, and the maximum monthly usage are as follows:

	Operating Departments		
	Foundry	Machining	Finishing
Actual June 19x0 usage	190,000	150,000	80,000
Six-month average usage	210,000	180,000	60,000
Maximum monthly usage	220,000	190,000	90,000

The managers of the operating departments are willing to have charges for variable costs based on the actual usage. The question is how to allocate the fixed costs.

REQUIRED:

a. Determine the amount of monthly fixed costs that would be allocated to the operating departments based on each of the following allocation bases:

1. Actual monthly usage.
2. Six-month average usage.
3. Maximum monthly usage.

b. Explain the advantages and disadvantages of each of the three bases.

c. Which of the three bases would you recommend? Give your reasons for the selection.

25–20. Uncompensated Overtime.   On February 1, 19x1, Energy Technology, Inc., entered into a contract with an agency of the federal government to produce certain rubber-based extruded parts on a cost-plus contract. Each part required that a unique design be prepared and implemented. Because the agency needed the parts by February 20, significant overtime was required by all staff of Energy Technology. Although the long, extra hours caused noticeable strain in normal working relationships, the contract was forced through on time.

At the conclusion of contract performance, the company billed the federal agency as follows:

Material costs	$ 675,880
Labor costs	340,000
Overhead	442,000
Total costs	$1,457,880
Profit at 20%	291,576
Total billing	$1,749,456

The government auditor reviewing the billing with Energy Technology personnel found several items that needed adjustment and correction:

1. Labor costs included 4,000 hours for salaried professional and technical people who worked on the contract. These charges for all overtime hours were not actually paid to the salaried employees. The costs included were determined by dividing an employee's annual salary by 2,000 hours and applying that rate to the hours worked on the contract. Thereby $68,000 of labor costs were charged to the contract for labor costs that were never paid to the employees.

2. Overhead is allocated on the basis of labor dollars charged to contracts at the rate of 130 percent. The amounts applied to the current contract included the labor costs not paid to employees.

3. Uncompensated overtime hours and dollars are not included in bids and proposals for fixed-price contracts. They are included only in bids and proposals for cost-plus contracts.

REQUIRED:

a. If the uncompensated overtime dollars were not included in the labor costs, what impact would this have on the total billing? Show computations.

b. Discuss the conceptual issues involved with an inconsistent treatment of the uncompensated overtime between fixed-price and cost-plus contracts.

c. Discuss the fairness and equity of charging a contract for costs that were never paid.

d. Discuss the concept of benefit received from the work performed during uncompensated overtime.

e. The auditor involved with this case stated: "It would have been very different if the cost-plus contracts were completed during regular working hours and the fixed-price contracts were completed during uncompensated overtime." Comment on the conceptual basis for this statement.

f. What changes would you suggest that the company make in its allocations to incorporate the time worked on contracts but exclude the amounts that employees were not paid?

25–21. Determining Allocation Bases.
Bonn Company recently reorganized its computer and data processing activities. The small installations located within the accounting departments at its plants and subsidiaries have been

replaced with a single data processing department at corporate headquarters responsible for the operations of a newly acquired large-scale computer system. The new department has been in operation for two years and has regularly produced reliable and timely data for the past 12 months.

Because the department has focused its activities on converting applications to the new system and producing reports for the plant and subsidiary managements, little attention has been devoted to the costs of the department. Now that the department's activities are operating relatively smoothly, company management has requested that the departmental manager recommend a cost accumulation system to facilitate cost control and the development of suitable rates to charge users for service.

For the past two years, the departmental costs have been recorded in one account. The costs have then been allocated to user departments on the basis of computer time used. The detailed costs and charging rate for 19x5 are as follows:

(1)	Salaries	$ 622,600
(2)	Supplies	40,000
(3)	Equipment maintenance contract	15,000
(4)	Insurance	25,000
(5)	Heat and air conditioning	36,000
(6)	Electricity	50,000
(7)	Equipment and furniture depreciation	285,400
(8)	Building improvements depreciation	10,000
(9)	Building occupancy and security	39,300
(10)	Corporate administrative charges	52,700
	Total costs	$1,176,000
	Computer hours for user processing*	2,750
	Hourly rate ($1,176,000/2,750)	$428

*Use of available computer hours:	
Testing and debugging programs	250
Setting up jobs	500
Processing jobs	2,750
Down time for maintenance	750
Idle time	742
Total hours	4,992

The departmental manager recommends that the department costs be accumulated by five activity centers within the department: Systems Analysis, Programming, Data Preparation, Computer Operations (processing), and Administration. He then suggests that the costs of the Administration activity should be allocated to the other four activity centers before a separate rate for charging users is developed for each of the first four activities.

The manager made the following observations regarding the charges to the several subsidiary accounts within the department after reviewing the details of the accounts:

1. Salaries and benefits—records the salary and benefit costs of all employees in the department.
2. Supplies—records paper costs for printers and a small amount for miscellaneous other costs.
3. Equipment maintenance contracts—records charges for maintenance contracts; all equipment is covered by maintenance contracts.
4. Insurance—records cost of insurance covering the equipment and the furniture.
5. Heat and air conditioning—records a charge from the corporate heating and air conditioning department estimated to be the incremental costs to meet the special needs of the computer department.
6. Electricity—records the charge for electricity based upon a separate meter in the department.
7. Equipment and furniture depreciation—records the depreciation charges for all owned equipment and furniture within the department.

8. Building improvements—records the amortization charges for the building changes required to provide proper environmental control and electrical service for the computer equipment.
9. Building occupancy and security—records the computer department's share of the depreciation, maintenance, heat and security costs of the building; these costs are allocated to the department on the basis of square feet occupied.
10. Corporate administrative charges—records the computer department's share of the corporate administrative costs. They are allocated to the department on the basis of number of employees in the department.

(CMA, adapted)

REQUIRED:

a. State whether or not each of the 10 cost items should be distributed to the five activity centers, and for each cost item that should be distributed, recommend the basis upon which it should be distributed. Justify your conclusion in each case.

b. Assume that the costs of the Computer Operations (processing) activity will be charged to the user departments on the basis of computer hours. Using the analysis of computer utilization, determine the total number of hours that should be employed to determine the charging rate for Computer Operations (processing). Justify your answer.

Classification and Summary of Cost Accounting Standards

After studying this appendix, you should be able to:

1. Describe a cost accounting standard as defined by the Cost Accounting Standards Board.
2. Identify and explain the five groupings of cost accounting standards.

The Cost Accounting Standards Board

The original Cost Accounting Standards Board (CASB) existed from 1970 to 1980. It consisted of representatives from the accounting profession, industry, and government. The CASB was responsible for developing cost accounting standards designed to achieve uniformity and consistency in the cost methods utilized by defense contractors on government contracts. During its lifetime, the CASB published 19 cost accounting standards that have the full force and effect of law.

In late 1988, President Ronald Reagan signed a law that reestablished the Cost Accounting Standards Board as part of the Office of Federal Procurement Policy. The CASB will amend current standards and issue new ones in the future.

What Is a Cost Accounting Standard?

A cost accounting standard, according to the CASB, is a formal statement that it issues.[1] This statement may be general or specific, as the CASB sees fit, but it will accomplish one or more of the following: (1) enunciate a principle or principles to be followed, (2) establish practices to be applied, or (3) specify criteria to be employed in selecting from alternative principles in estimating, accumulating, and reporting costs of contracts. The CASB gave itself wide latitude in setting out the areas to be covered by cost accounting standards.

Classification of Standards. A person can remember cost accounting standards more easily if some association of the standards is made. Grouping or classification is one such association. Therefore, the standards are grouped as follows, recognizing that in reality there can be overlaps—one standard can properly apply to more than one group.

1. Consistency in cost accounting practices: CAS 401 and 402.
2. Allocation concepts: CAS 403, 406, 410, 418, and 420.
3. Fixed asset accounting: CAS 404, 409, 414, and 417.
4. Compensation of personnel: CAS 408, 412, 413, and 415.
5. Other standards: CAS 405, 407, 411, and 416.

The sections below provide summaries of all standards.

Consistency in Cost Accounting Practices. The two standards in this group deal with the consistent use of cost accounting practices in estimating, accumulating, and reporting costs, and in classifying costs as direct and indirect. The standards provide broad principles for implementing concepts but do not address the cost accounting treatment of specific functions, elements of cost, or cost pools.

---

[1] Cost Accounting Standards Board, *Restatement of Objectives, Policies and Concepts*, May, 1977, p. 1.

CAS 401, "Consistency in estimating, accumulating and reporting costs."   This standard requires a mutual consistency between cost accounting practices used in estimating costs and cost accounting practices used in accumulating and reporting actual costs. Consistency in reporting costs is not addressed specifically by the standard but is included with accumulating costs. Practices relate to the classification of elements or functions of cost as direct and indirect, the indirect cost pools to which each element or function of cost is charged or proposed to be charged, and the methods of allocating indirect costs to contracts. Costs estimated for proposals must be presented in such manner and detail that any significant cost can be compared with the actual cost accumulated and reported for the contract.

The CASB also issued an interpretation of this standard. It requires that a contractor support the percentage factors used in estimating the direct material costs to cover expected material losses such as those occurring when items are scrapped, fail to meet specifications, are lost, are consumed in the production process, or are destroyed in testing and qualification processes. The factors may be supported with accounting, statistical, or other relevant data from past experience, or by a program to accumulate actual costs for comparison with such percentage estimates.

CAS 402, "Consistency in allocating costs incurred for the same purpose."   This standard requires that each type of cost be allocated only once and on only one basis to any contract or other final cost objective. In other words, all costs incurred for the same purpose in like circumstances must be treated either as direct costs only or as indirect costs only in making allocations to final cost objectives. The standard is directed to those circumstances in which contractors (1) charged items to contracts as direct costs, even though those or similar items were customarily accounted for as indirect costs; and (2) allocated cost items directly to a final cost objective without eliminating like cost items from the indirect cost pools, which are also allocated in some form to that final cost objective.

The CASB issued an interpretation for this standard that covers the costs of bids and proposals. Generally, bid and proposal costs are indirect costs to a contract. The interpretation says, in effect, that if a contract requires a proposal for a follow-on contract, the costs of preparing that proposal are direct costs of the current contract.

Allocation Concepts.   Standards in this area deal with the cost accounting treatment of specific pools of cost. The standards establish criteria for accumulating costs within the pools, with particular attention to ensuring the homogeneity of the pooled costs. The standards also establish acceptable allocation bases or criteria for base selection, in accordance with the beneficial or causal relationships between the pool and the cost objective. CAS 418 provides principles and/or criteria for formation of an indirect cost pool and its proper allocation.

CAS 403, "Allocation of home office expenses to segments."   This standard recognizes that home office expenses are not an amorphous mass of cost to be allocated over a single allocation base. Rather, many home office expenses benefit, or are caused by, certain segments and should be allocated to such segments as nearly as possible on the basis of such beneficial or causal relationships. Therefore, the purpose of this standard is to establish criteria for allocating home office expenses to the segments of an organization.

The standard requires that home office expenses be allocated directly to segments to the maximum extent practical. This means that those home office expenses that benefit or are caused by a particular segment must be allocated only to that segment.

Of course, there are many elements of home office expenses for which no direct relationship to particular segments exists. The standard requires the grouping of these expenses into logical and homogeneous expense pools. To accomplish this, the standard suggests appropriate groups and possible allocation bases. The standard also gives a hierarchy of preferable allocation techniques that represent beneficial or causal relationships. Home office expenses that do not fall into one of the groupings are classified as a residual expense. The standard gives the rules for allocating residual expenses to segments.

CAS 406, "Cost accounting period."   This standard establishes the general rule that the cost accounting period used for contract cost estimating, accumulating, and reporting is the contractor's fiscal year—the period of performance of a contract may not be used. It requires the contractor to follow consistent practices from one cost accounting period or periods to another in which any type of cost and any type of adjustment are accumulated and allocated. It also requires that the period used for accumulating costs in an indirect cost pool coincide with the period used for establishing the pool's allocation base. The standard, in effect, rules out the use of monthly or quarterly indirect cost rates for allocations; an annualized rate must be used.

CAS 410, "Allocation of business unit general and administrative expenses to final cost objectives."   The purpose of this standard is to provide criteria for the allocation of business unit general and administrative (G&A) expenses to final cost objectives based on their beneficial or causal relationships. These expenses represent the costs of the management and administration of the business unit as a whole. The base for allocating the G&A expense pool to final cost objectives is a cost input base representing the total activity of the business unit for the period. The cost input base may be (1) total cost input, (2) value-added cost input, or (3) single-element cost input. The standard also provides criteria for the allocation of home office expenses received by a segment to the cost objectives of that segment.

CAS 418, "Allocation of direct and indirect costs."   The three major purposes of this standard are to provide (1) consistent determination of direct and indirect costs, (2) criteria for the accumulation of indirect costs, and (3) guidance for selection of allocation measures based on the beneficial or causal relationship between an indirect cost pool and its cost objectives. To achieve these purposes, the standard gives an overall framework for accounting for, and allocating, direct and indirect costs.

The most significant requirement of the standard is probably that each business unit must have and consistently apply a written statement of accounting policies and practices for classifying costs as direct or indirect. The standard does not provide specific criteria for making the distinction between direct and indirect costs. Each contractor, rather, is required to set forth his or her own criteria for distinguishing between direct and indirect costs; that is, the policies and practices for classifying costs as direct and indirect. Once a cost meets the contractor's criteria for a direct cost, the standard governs the accounting for those costs.

Regarding indirect costs, the standard sets forth requirements governing the composition and number of indirect cost pools, the types of allocation measure available, and the cost objectives to receive the allocations from indirect cost pools. For example, because the standard requires accumulating indirect costs in homogeneous cost pools, it defines the characteristics of "homogeneous." In addition, it states that the allocation from cost pools to cost objectives should be in reasonable proportion to the beneficial or causal relationship between the costs and the cost objectives.

The standard explains the type of allocation bases that may be used for overhead pools and for service centers (also support functions). In the case of overhead pools, conditions are given under which a contractor may use a direct labor-hour base, a direct labor-cost base, a machine-hour base, a units-of-production base, or a materials cost base. Service centers must be allocated on the specific indentifiability of resource consumption with cost objectives by means of one of several bases. These are (1) a resource consumption measure (input measure), (2) an output measure, or (3) a surrogate that is representative of resources consumed. Because the CASB believed that these allocation measures were essential for good cost accounting, it included criteria for determining the appropriate use of them.

CAS 420, "Accounting for independent research and development costs and bid and proposal costs."   The purpose of this standard is quite simple: to accumulate and allocate the independent research and development costs and bid and proposal costs. To accomplish this purpose, the standard gives details for cost measurement, assignment to cost accounting periods, and allocation to cost objectives. Allocation procedures are defined for cost pools at the home office level, segment level, and the business unit level.

Fixed Asset Accounting.   Standards dealing with fixed asset accounting address the issues of what assets must be capitalized and a depreciation policy that reflects physical use of the asset. In addition, two standards provide a new allowable cost consisting of the imputed cost of interest on capital invested in tangible assets.

CAS 404, "Capitalization of tangible assets."   This standard requires the contractor to have and apply a written policy on tangible asset capitalization that designates the economic and physical characteristics on which the policy is based. According to the standard, any tangible asset with minimum service life of two years or more and a cost of $1,500 must be capitalized. The standard also provides that constructed assets be capitalized at amounts that include a full share of indirect costs, and that donated assets be capitalized at their fair value.

CAS 409, "Depreciation of tangible capital assets."   This standard requires that the cost of a tangible capital asset, less its estimated residual value, be assigned to the cost accounting periods representing its estimated life in a manner that reflects the pattern of consumption of service over the life of the asset. The estimated service lives must be reasonable approximations of the asset's expected actual periods of usefulness. Evaluating service life is based on the records of either past retirement or withdrawal from active use for like assets used in similar circumstances. Then a contractor may modify those lives by specifically identified factors expected to influence future lives. Estimated service lives for which the contractor has no data available, or no prior experience for similar assets, will be established based on a projection of the expected actual period of usefulness until the contractor is able to develop estimates supported by personal experience.

Gains and losses on disposition of tangible capital assets are generally considered as adjustments of depreciation costs previously recognized and are assigned to the cost accounting periods in which disposition occurs.

CAS 414, "Cost of money as an element of the cost of facilities capital."   The purpose of this standard is to establish criteria for the measurement of the cost (imputed interest) of capital committed to existing facilities of a contractor. The cost of money rate for any cost accounting period is the arithmetic mean of the interest rates specified by the secretary of the Treasury. Provisions in the standard explain the proper criteria for allocating the imputed interest to the final cost objectives.

CAS 417, "Cost of money as an element of the cost of capital assets under construction."   The essential requirement of this standard is that a contractor include the cost of money in the acquisition costs of assets under construction. The rate applied is an average rate, determined by any acceptable method, based on the same interest rate used for purposes of CAS 414. This is an imputed interest instead of actual interest paid. Once a contractor measures the cost of money, that cost is part of the cost of those capital assets to be spread over the assets' anticipated useful life.

The standard also defines *assets under construction,* which includes tangible and intangible capital assets being constructed, fabricated, or developed for a contractor's own use. The term is broader than what some accountants refer to as *self-constructed assets.*

Compensation of Personnel.   These standards concern the costs of compensation of personnel in money, with something of value other than money, or through the rendering of other benefits. These standards deal only with the peripheral aspects of compensation, not with the direct compensation paid for work performed on a regular basis. The standards do not cover all types of compensation paid to personnel, nor do they establish rules regarding whether specific compensation should be treated as a direct cost or an indirect cost. Rather, the focus is on how to treat the costs in the company's cost accounting practices.

CAS 408, "Accounting for the costs of compensated personal absence."   This standard puts the accounting for costs of sick leave, vacations, holidays, jury duty, military training, or other personal activities on an accrual basis. The basis for recognition is the concept of entitlement, which is an employee's right to receive a determinable amount of compensated personal absence, or pay in lieu thereof. The standard states that these costs are assigned to the period in which entitlement is earned and then allocated pro rata on an annual basis among the final cost objectives of that period.

CAS 412, "Composition and measurement of pension cost."   This standard provides guidance for determining and measuring the components of pension costs and assigning those costs to appropriate cost accounting periods. It deals with defined-benefit pension plans, defined-contribution pension plans, and pay-as-you-go plans.

CAS 413, "Adjustment and allocation of pension cost."   This standard provides guidance for adjusting pension costs by measuring actuarial gains and losses and assigning such gains and losses to cost accounting periods. The standard also provides criteria for allocating pension costs to each segment of the company having participants in a pension plan.

CAS 415, "Accounting for the cost of deferred compensation."   This standard provides criteria for the measurement of deferred compensation, such as stock options and cash awards, and the assignment of its cost to cost accounting periods. The measurment of the amount of deferred compensation is the present value of the future benefits to be paid by the contractor. The standard provides the instructions for calculating present value whether or not an interest rate is attached to the future benefits. The cost of deferred compensation is assigned to the cost accounting period in which the contractor incurs an obligation to compensate the employee. The standard defines the conditions under which that obligation exists.

Other Standards.   Standards here deal with the definitions and cost accounting treatment of individual classes, categories, or elements of cost that do not fit more logically in one of the previous groupings.

CAS 405, "Accounting for unallowable costs."   The purpose of this standard is to facilitate the negotiation, audit, administration, and settlement of contracts by establishing guidelines covering (1) identification of costs specifically described as unallowable, and (2) the cost accounting treatment to be accorded such identified unallowable costs.

   Unallowable costs are typically identified in the government regulations or are included in contract provisions. Examples of unallowable costs include charity contributions, lobbying costs, entertainment costs, and bad debt expense.

CAS 407, "Use of standard costs for direct material and direct labor."   This standard states that standard costs may be used for estimating, accumulating, and reporting costs of direct material and direct labor if (1) standard costs are entered in the books of account, (2) standard costs and related variances are appropriately accounted for at the level of the production unit, and (3) the practices with respect to setting and revising standards, use of standard costs, and disposition of variances are stated in writing and are consistently followed. It also specifies that material variances and direct labor variances should be allocated at least annually to cost objectives in a way that adjusts the cost objectives to actual costs of materials and labor used. Bases for such allocation are specified.

CAS 411, "Accounting for the acquisition costs of material."   Most material used on government contracts subject to these standards is purchased specifically for and charged directly to the appropriate contract. This standard permits direct charging of such costs provided the specific contract was identified on the purchase order at the time of purchase or production of the units. Some materials, of course, are drawn from existing inventories. Such materials may be priced into contracts using one of the following methods consistently applied: (1) the first-in, first-out (FIFO) method; (2) the moving average cost method; (3) the weighted average cost method; (4) the standard cost method; or (5) the last-in, first-out (LIFO) method.

   Contractors are required to have and consistently apply written statements of accounting policies and practices for accumulating material costs and allocating them to cost objectives. The cost of materials that are used solely in performing indirect functions or that are not a significant element of production cost maybe charged to an indirect cost pool and allocated as part of the item.

CAS 416, "Accounting for insurance costs."   This standard provides criteria for measuring insurance costs, assigning them to cost accounting periods, and allocating them to cost objectives.

   A company may cover its exposure to risk of loss either by purchased insurance, by a trusteed fund, or by a self-insurance program. Under any of these alternatives, the amount of insurance cost assigned to a cost accounting period is the projected average loss for the period plus insurance administration expenses of the period. The projected average loss is represented by the premium for purchased insurance plans and by payments to the fund for trusteed plans. The standard contains the criteria for determining the projected average loss for self-insurance programs.

REVIEW QUESTIONS

1. What are the three things a cost accounting standard may accomplish?
2. Which two cost accounting standards are classified as consistency standards? How do those two standards differ?
3. Cost accounting standards provide a framework for cost allocations. Identify the cost accounting standards that relate to cost allocations.
4. What is the relationship between CAS 418 and the three cost accounting standards 403, 410, and 420?
5. How does CAS 409 apply depreciation that may be different from practices in financial reporting?
6. What is unique about CAS 414 and 417?

CHAPTER

26

Designing Management Accounting Systems in a Changing Environment

◼

MANAGEMENT ACCOUNTING SYSTEMS CHANGE PROBLEM

Jan Holladay is the chief financial officer (CFO) for Teletech, Inc. As the CFO, she is responsible for the internal financial reporting system, but she is somewhat limited by the accountants and their computer systems. Because she was trained as an accountant and rose through the ranks, she knows that the Accounting Department would not move rapidly in the development of a new management reporting and cost system to meet competitive requirements facing Teletech, Inc. The president, chairman, marketing vice president, and vice president of manufacturing have decided on a strategy to reduce overhead of all types: manufacturing, marketing, and administration. One objective is to cut overhead by 40 percent during the next four years.

Overhead costs are for the support people and the facilities that they use. Thus, meeting the objective requires cutting 40 percent of the accounting, computer systems, clerical, treasury, and similar staffs. Additionally, both expensive computer hardware and highly sophisticated software costs must be evaluated in the light of needs versus the cost reduction program. The current internal reporting system is frustrating because it includes the most modern hardware but the programs always are two or more years out of date.

As the chief financial officer, Jan is responsible for the internal reporting system. Through subordinates, such as the controller and budget director, she modifies this system to reflect the strategies of the senior management.

◼

LEARNING OBJECTIVES

After studying this chapter, you should be able to:

1. Distinguish among strategic planning, management control, and operational control.
2. Distinguish between control and controls.
3. List and give examples of sources of change to management accounting systems.
4. List and define the constraints that a chief financial officer (CFO) faces in changing a management accounting system.
5. Give examples of areas of choice for the CFO in performance measurement, operations planning, product costing, internal system compliance, decision support, personnel, and structure.

STRATEGIC PLANNING, MANAGEMENT CONTROL, AND OPERATIONAL CONTROL[1]

Strategic planning was defined (Chapter 23) as the planning of broad strategies for attaining the goals and objectives of senior management. **Strategies** are the broad activities that senior managers choose for the organization; for example, strategies might include getting out of the steel industry, increasing genetic research contracts, or expanding operations through acquisition of competitors. **Goals** are general concepts that describe the desires of senior management; for example, goals might include growth, obtaining a high ranking in industry, return on investment, or developing the capacity to survive. **Objectives** are specific requirements that relate to the goals of senior management, for example, a 10 percent growth in revenues or a 20 percent return on investment. Strategic planning is performed by senior management and is supported by its staff. The management accounting system should reflect the strategies, goals, and objectives of senior management.

Management control refers to the system that assures that resources are obtained efficiently and used effectively in the attainment of senior management's objectives. This is a very broad activity and includes much of the effort of a management accountant. Management control is related to, but is not limited to, the following processes:

1. Planning (Chapters 3, 4, and 12 through 15).
2. Performance measurement and evaluation (Chapters 12, 13, 16, 17, 18, and 20).
3. Short-term decision-support (Chapters 3, 4, and 21).
4. Long-term decision-support (Chapters 23 and 24).

Reports that summarize costs of producing goods and services (Chapters 2 and 5 through 13) aid in management control. In addition, general internal controls support management control. For example, company organization, separation of duties, employment policies, accountability for assets, and documentation all support management control. Mid-level managers (plant managers and division managers), accountants, and other staff carry out management control.

---

[1] These concepts were first presented by Robert Anthony in *Planning and Control Systems: A Framework for Analysis* (Homewood, Ill.: Richard D. Irwin, 1965). The concepts were the result of Harvard Business School faculty discussions on the role of control in organizations as reported in R. N. Anthony, ''Reminiscences about Management Accounting,'' *Journal of Management Accounting Research*, Fall, 1989, pp. 1–20.

Operational control is the highly detailed process of assuring that specific tasks are carried out efficiently and effectively. Operational control occurs within the context of management control. Operational control is supported by detailed records of cash accounts, accounts receivable, job order cost sheets, process cost records, finished goods records, equipment maintenance records, shipping documents, payroll records, and other detailed records that comprise the accounting system. Operational control is carried out by supervisors and employees and is supported by clerical staff and detailed computer files.

Controls versus Control[2]

Hundreds of controls could be implemented in an internal accounting system. However, implementing all of them in one company would be both very costly and unproductive. Too many controls result in bureaucracy and rules—everything that needs to be done "right now" must be delayed because of some rule or permission requirement. In addition, otherwise good managers blame the complex rules and procedures for poor performance rather than finding creative solutions to challenges. It is ironic that the more controls implemented beyond the practical and necessary, the more inefficiency and ineffectiveness there is. Therefore, too many controls cause poor management control.

The necessary controls must be chosen with common sense and intelligence. Implementing, supervising, and supporting each control within the accounting system is costly. Every control should be evaluated on a cost-benefit basis. Thus, no list of 100 controls will result in optimal management and operational control. Instead, judgment is necessary in selecting the controls that are appropriate for the setting.

Change outdates controls. One of the roles of the accountant is to keep the accounting system current and responsive to changes. In the next section, we will discuss the sources of change to management accounting systems.

SOURCES OF CHANGE TO MANAGEMENT ACCOUNTING SYSTEMS

There is an expression, "The only constant is change itself." We should appreciate that change is positive rather than negative because change creates accounting jobs. Specifically, if circumstances were to stay the same for most companies, ideal internal accounting systems could be designed to meet the requirements of both management and external parties. Then the majority of accountants, as well as managers, engineers, attorneys, and other staff, would be redundant and have to find another line of work.

It is important that the CFO and the controller understand the sources of change to the management accounting system. The primary sources of change as summarized in Exhibit 26–1 come from changes to products, processes, and structures; external reporting requirements; personnel turnover; and fads and human foibles.

Products, Processes, and Structure

As the external markets for goods and services change, their sale, prices, and marketing must change. As products are dropped and added and/or marketed in a new form, the internal accounting system must adjust. Further, the management accounting system should support the change in products and production processes by providing the capacity for special analyses of these decisions. New production processes and plants also create the need for changing the internal accounting system. Periodic reports are added, and report lines are added or deleted. As a consequence, the detailed files and procedures must change.

---

[2] The concepts in this section follow Anthony Hopwood, "Controls," *Accounting and Human Behavior* (Englewood Cliffs, N.J.: Prentice-Hall, 1976).

EXHIBIT 26–1   Sources of Change to Internal Accounting Systems

Sources of Changes	Result in Changes to
Products, processes, and structures	
New product additions	Internal reports
	Detailed forms, procedures
Old product deletions	Internal reports
New production processes	New accounts
	New reports
	Planning, decisions
Plant closings	Records, accounts, reports
Change in organization	Reports, accounts
External reporting requirements	
Financial accounting standards	Internal records
	Accounting methods
	Reports
Tax reporting requirements	Internal records
	Accounting methods
	Planning, decisions
Securities and Exchange Commission	Internal records
	External reports
Personnel turnover	
Senior management	Performance measurement
	Planning, decision processes
Lower management	Training, errors
Fads and human foibles	
Performance	Performance measures
	Reports, files, accounts
Accounting system	Hardware and software purchases

Changes to the organizational structure affect the management accounting system. Addition or deletion of segments, moving of products, changes in reporting relationships (who reports to whom), and significant changes in responsibilities must be reflected in the management accounting system.

External Reporting Requirements

The Financial Accounting Standards Board (FASB) and the Securities and Exchange Commission (SEC) annually issue pronouncements that change external reporting and thereby change requirements for internal accounting systems. There are numerous complex rules regarding accounting for pensions, leases, earnings per share, taxes, and consolidated earnings. Each statement of financial accounting standard must be reviewed to determine the extent to which the system reporting to management must be changed.

Federal, state, and even foreign government legislatures have the authority to tax companies and regulate reporting. The legislative process is political, rather than logical, and results in many complex, conflicting rules. Because each legislature can change the existing rules, periodic changes are made to the rules and procedures. This creates numerous job opportunities for accountants as internal accounting systems must be adjusted to meet the legislated requirements. For example, a corporation files periodic tax and information returns for sales, employment, pensions, production, transportation, purchases, inventories, real estate, franchises, and income. In spite of the periodic change and potential confusion about rules, the company must respond in a timely manner to each taxing authority.

**Personnel
Turnover**

Senior managers retire or step aside to consulting positions. Midlevel managers move on to better opportunities or are transferred. Supervisors are promoted or quit. Competitors periodically raid companies of their best personnel in engineering, marketing, and administration. Employee disability due to accidents, health problems, or alcohol or drug abuse also causes turnover. Divisions expand or contract. Plants and warehouses are expanded or closed.

New senior managers have different goals, objectives, and strategies than the prior senior managers. Consequently, new managers often change the management control and operational control. Thus, with a change in senior management, modifications will be made to planning, performance measurement, decision approaches, and capital project control. The details of operational control will change as a result of changes to management controls.

Changes in supervisors and workers will have relatively little effect on the accounting system. A high employee turnover rate will result in hiring new employees who require training and who will input more errors into the system.

Changes in accounting personnel also occur. Staff turnover results in lost skills and knowledge but has only a limited effect on the content of management accounting. Staff turnover results in higher recruiting and training costs.

**Fads and Human
Foibles**

New concepts and theories of management are often faddish. New theories come into style and are implemented by companies. Some of the new concepts survive, but others are dropped when they fail to live up to their promise. These new concepts often affect job content, reporting relationships, approaches to performance measurement or evaluation, production, marketing, product evaluation, and similar management control issues.

New concepts are often presented as panaceas for operating losses. Thus, managers are told that their companies will earn more income if they follow the theory recommended by a consultant or by one of the senior managers. For example, companies might be told to lease all their fixed assets, enter into leveraged buyouts of competitors, centralize all their information processing, or use a consultive leadership style. Although these concepts are often good, each new one involves a change to the management control system.

Humans have shortcomings. For example, some people have strong egos or are somewhat jealous, untruthful, vindictive, or manipulative. Other people are bumbling, indecisive, or easily influenced by any strong person around them. These people will make changes to management or operational control for reasons that are not appropriate, and their motivations will often be disguised. Similarly, some people are fascinated by new hardware and flashy gimmicks. They recommend that the management accounting system be modified so that it can take advantage of a new technology, such as a laser printer, telecommunications network, memory device, or graphics terminal. Whatever their motivations, these people and the changes they implement will affect the management accounting system in diverse ways.

In the next section, we will present the limitations that the CFO faces in changing a management accounting system.

**Structural
Limitations on
Management
Accounting
Systems**

Although the pressure for change may be urgent, the CFO and controller cannot change the management accounting system rapidly. There are structural limitations to the changes that can feasibly be made.

Accounting Is Administrative Overhead.   All staff and management functions are administrative overhead and thus are a drain on the profits of a company. Accounting is no exception. The costs of accounting, including personnel, personnel-related costs, space occupancy, computer systems, software packages, training, and audit fees, are all administrative overhead. Specifically, accountants do not produce a product or service that is sold to external customers. Therefore, the expense of accounting and accountants must be cost justified on the basis of benefits received from the following:

1. *Filing external reports.* Investors, lenders, taxing authorities, and regulatory agencies require an audited external financial report.
2. *Supporting cash inflow transactions.* Support is given by collecting receipts on account through the billing and accounts receivable systems. Also, support is given to sales and delivery of products.
3. *Controlling expenditures.* Payments to vendors and employees must be controlled through the budget, payables, and payroll systems. Division of duties and required approvals can help prevent fraudulent expenditures.
4. *Decision-making.* Decisions concerning performance, investment, products, and operations must be made.
5. *Preparing special analyses.* Support of highly specific decisions, such as mergers or in support of litigation, must be provided.

Large companies often have 500 members or more on the accounting staff. Assuming salaries averaging $30,000 per year and 50 percent in support costs, accounting staff budgets could start at about $22.5 million ($30,000 × 150 percent × 500). This expenditure should be justified as part of the annual operating budget (as in Chapter 14). Changes to accounting systems are very expensive in terms of employee time and dollar cost. Because the budget is limited, the amount of change in any year must be limited.

Computerized Systems Are Fragile after Change.   Most accounting systems are computerized because of the volume of transactions handled. Computerized accounting systems for applications, such as product costs or performance measurement, typically involve between 30 and 200 programs. These programs involve between 10 thousand and 2 million lines of computer language code. Programmers understand the general outline of the programs, but they understand the specifics of only a few programs. Thus, the total computer code of a management accounting system is beyond the comprehension of any one programmer.

Programs must be updated to meet current requirements. Each change makes the programs more susceptible to error, more complex, and less flexible in handling unusual transactions. As a consequence, systems analysts and programmers may become reluctant to change the system for fear that any changes will make it inoperable because of errors.

As systems become relatively old (i.e., five to eight years old), they become fragile for several reasons. First, the inevitable staff turnover results in having few systems analysts or programmers who understand the original logic, language, and assumptions on which the old systems were built. Second, old systems have been moved to new computer hardware but have not been redesigned to reflect assumptions in the new hardware regarding data transmission, storage, and processing procedures. Consequently, the capabilities of the old hardware have to be simulated on the new hardware, which is very inefficient in terms of speed and is subject to error.

Finally, programmers vary substantially in their abilities, logical processes, and motivation. Although some programmers are extremely good, others seem to "think with their elbows and type with their feet." As a result, the quality of the system changes will vary and will depend on the quality of other parts of the system.

New Systems Are Costly.   With all of these problems regarding old accounting systems, why not just implement a new management accounting system every five years or so? New accounting systems require between one and three years to design and fully implement. A complete accounting application requires up to 2 million lines of source language code. A good programmer can code, debug, and test an average of 10 to 50 lines per work day (2,500 to 12,500 lines of new code per work year).[3] A large accounting system requires between 50 and 100 programmers and a year's time. A programmer costs about $30,000 per year. Consequently, the programming of a new accounting system is expensive and very slow.

Software Vendors Are Unwilling to Adapt.   Accounting systems can be purchased from an outside vendor. Vendor packages are leased on an annual basis. When software is leased from a vendor, the company must conform its administrative procedures and concepts to meet the vendor's design assumptions. Thus, the clerical procedures, the terms, the report formats, and all concepts come prepackaged in the system as purchased. Vendors are rarely willing or able to customize their systems. Further, vendors rarely, if ever, provide source code statements so that the software can be modified by the company's programmers. For most companies, the changes required to implement the new system are similar to fitting size 10 feet into size 5 shoes: the surgery is painful, but once the toes are cut off, the company can hobble along fairly quickly on the crutches. After two years, they do not miss the toes very much.

Therefore, rapid changes to old computer systems are difficult and costly, and new systems require years to implement. Purchased systems require changes to operations and organization. These limitations effectively curtail rapid change to the management accounting system.

Resistance to Change.   People have various capacities to learn and change with a company. Those with very little capacity tend to strongly resist changes. Thus, changes made to a management accounting system will result in some resistance by managers, accountants, and other employees. A large number of changes in a short time period tend to be highly resisted either:

1. **Actively.** As an example of active resistance, consider the following response to a proposed change: "We will not adopt the new report requirements as stated in your proposal. Instead, we propose the attached requirements, which retain the very valuable parts of the old system."
2. **Passively.** As an example of passive resistance, consider the following brief response to a proposed change in accounting system: "We don't understand the full effects of this change on our operations. Let's have a joint task force review the proposal before it is implemented. We will get in touch with you soon for your recommendation for who should serve on the task force."

Forceful support of a new system by senior management overcomes most resistance, whether active or passive. However, forceful pressure from senior management should be reserved for major management accounting changes because it may reduce morale among lower-level managers and staff. The effect of resistance to change is to limit the size and number of changes that are possible in any one time period without heavy pressure from senior management.

---

[3] Brilliant programmers can work much faster than this, but these people are rare and are not usually working on accounting applications.

Attitudes and Aptitudes of Managers.   Part of the resistance to change among managers is their attitude toward and aptitude for accounting. Some managers have poor general attitudes toward accounting and accountants. They view accounting as an evil to be endured rather than encouraged. They require accountants only to record the transactions and prepare the financial reports and tax returns. This attitude limits the opportunities for the accountant to act.

The CFO should follow the strategy of marketing the accounting function and, thus, justifying its existence beyond recordkeeping. The CFO should emphasize the benefits of management accounting in planning, performance measurement, and decision-making. The attitudes of managers can be changed with sufficient effort, but there are limits to what can be accomplished because of aptitudes.

Some managers have little aptitude for accounting or understanding the financial consequences of their actions. They may be excellent engineers, chemists, inventors, production managers, or personnel managers, but they will never grasp the meaning of expense, asset, liability, equity, or cost. Unfortunately, the aptitudes of specific managers cannot be improved. Thus, their understanding of accounting will always be limited. The CFO must recognize that managers with little aptitude are a limitation to the development of the management accounting system.

Attitudes of Accountants.   Some accountants restrict their viewpoint to the numbers and controls required for external financial and tax reports. They are very involved with changes to the myriad of financial reporting requirements and the tax code. They have little competence or interest in topics outside this narrow focus. They provide only limited help to management in such areas as performance measurement, cost control, or planning. These accountants limit the development of the management accounting system. It is the challenge of the CFO and the controller to broaden the horizons of these people through education and job assignments. Selective hiring and placement in the mix of accountants can also influence the attitudes of the group.

In conclusion, the CFO is *not* free to change the management accounting system as he or she desires. Exhibit 26–2 summarizes the limitations on change to management accounting systems. The system constantly is being adapted to small changes in external and internal requirements. Because large changes require persuasion and

EXHIBIT 26–2   Limitations to Management Accounting System Change

Limitation	*Consequence*
Accounting is administrative overhead.	Costly changes are difficult to justify.
Old systems are fragile after change.	Only certain changes are feasible to an existing system.
	Reluctance to make changes leaves some changes in midstream.
New systems are costly, time consuming.	Rapid change is expensive and is not often feasible.
Software vendors are unwilling or unable to customize software.	Purchase of software results in changes to procedures and organization.
Change is resisted.	Resistance limits the size and number of changes possible.
Attitudes and aptitudes of managers are limiting.	It limits the scope of management accounting.
Attitudes of accounting staff are limiting.	Attitudes limit the scope of management accounting but can be influenced by CFO.

some use of raw power and are costly and time consuming, they must be carefully considered. A successful management accounting system is one that achieves management and operational control given all its limitations.

CFO CHOICE IN MANAGEMENT ACCOUNTING SYSTEMS

The choices made by the CFO should be consistent with the strategies adopted by the other senior managers. Thus, if senior management decides on a strategy that involves decentralized decision-making, the management accounting system should be set up to be consistent with this strategy. Although we cannot elaborate on all of the choices that the CFO should consider in changing management accounting systems, we will present some of them next.

Simplify Accounting Systems[4]

A general philosophy of less is better should be adopted for management accounting systems. Because all of accounting is administrative overhead, its cost should be reduced and its effectiveness increased per dollar spent. The accounting system, along with all of the administrative structure, must be as simple as possible. Thus, complex accounting systems are costly and should be discouraged. Where appropriate, local processing of data should be encouraged with minimal forms and data required for transmission. As discussed in Chapter 20, variances should be reported to production areas in simple physical forms (for example, rejected products placed in red squares) rather than in time-consuming printed reports. Paperwork associated with production should be kept to a minimum.

The simplification of accounting systems can be accomplished by a zero-based review of the management accounting system:

1. Eliminate detailed reports that are not critical for running the business. This results in the elimination of the detailed files needed to produce the reports and reduction in the clerical support necessary to maintain the files.
2. Make every regular cost report be justified with the question: "Why does it (the cost objective or cost variance) need to be accounted for?" Some costs can be effectively analyzed on an annual or special basis rather than be accounted for on a daily or weekly basis.
3. Reduce the number of vendors, number of times per year they are paid, number of times per year employees are paid, number of employees, amount of travel, number of plants, and similar numbers. As a result of this reduction, fewer transactions need to be accounted for.
4. Reduce the number of systems by requiring that each system be justified on a cost-benefits basis. The more internal accounting systems there are, the more complex the maintenance and correction of errors.
5. Use cost allocation as little as possible in regular product costing, performance measurement, and operations planning. Reserve complex allocation to cost objects for special cost analyses. Allocation leads to complexity in the normal transaction processing because of errors and changes to the production process over time.

The simplification of internal accounting systems and redirection of accountants often involves a reduction in personnel. Many CFOs adopt an attrition policy rather

---

[4] This section on simplification is based on extensions of the concepts in J. M. Juran, *Juran on Leadership for Quality* (New York: Free Press, 1989), and on M. V. Tatikonda, "Just-in-Time and Modern Manufacturing Environments: Implications for Cost Accounting," *Production and Inventory Control Journal*, First quarter 1988, pp. 1–5.

than a termination policy to reduce staff. An **attrition** policy involves not replacing staff as turnover occurs. A **termination** policy immediately cuts staff to the required level. An attrition policy supports better morale than does a termination policy. A termination policy can adversely affect the attitudes of the close associates of those fired. Terminations should be made within federal labor laws; care should be taken so that employees terminated are not of the same age, sex, or national origin. Because managers and officers are given little protection under labor laws, they can generally be terminated more easily than clerical staff.

Concepts of Performance Management

Performance reporting is a very important function of internal accounting systems. Simple performance reporting systems are an offshoot of gathering transactions for external reports and, thus, have very little incremental cost. A simple system has only one financial performance measure, for example, net income with budgets set autocratically. Each addition to a simple system increases the cost to develop, implement, and maintain. The maintenance costs for a complex system are high because it has to be changed more often than a simple system to meet changing circumstances. Potential changes to the basic performance reporting system include multiple measures, qualitative measures, participation, and mentoring performance.

One versus Many Measures. The performance reporting system may have one measure, for example, segment profit or return on investment. Alternatively, the reports may have several measures, for example, profit, plant maintenance, and research and development expenditure.

Financial versus Qualitative Measures. Performance reports may include only financial numbers or they may include qualitative measures in addition to numbers. Qualitative measures include such items as employee turnover, new customer accounts, and new products developed.

Level of Participation. The standards for performance measures may be set autocratically by senior management. Or the standards may be negotiated between each manager and his or her supervisor. Management by objectives (MBO) implements the concept of participatively set objectives and measures. According to the MBO approach to setting performance standards, each manager negotiates objectives (financial and/or qualitative) with his or her supervisor. The objectives are specific, such as a 4 percent increase in sales in the Cincinnati district. Performance evaluation is then based on the extent to which the objectives are met.

Mentoring Performance. The performance of managers may be negotiated as in the MBO concept or it may be developed by a manager who takes a personal interest in the career of a new employee, as in mentoring. A **mentoring** program assigns each new employee an experienced employee who recommends to that person training opportunities, career path choices, performance efforts, and similar activities. New employees are then evaluated on the extent to which they develop through the years of the program.

Approaches in Implementing the Planning System

The CFO is responsible, through subordinates, for the financial planning of the organization. Several basic choices must be made in implementing a planning system.

Fixed versus Flexible Budgets. The budget for revenues, costs, and expenses may be set for each time period (fixed budget), or the budget may be increased or decreased with the level of activity (flexible budget).

Level of Participation.   The budgeted amounts may be set by senior managers in an autocratic fashion or negotiated among the levels of management. The degree of participation in planning the budget may vary from very low to very high involvement of lower-level staff.

Product Cost Measurement

The costs of products affect pricing, planning, performance measurement, and income. The CFO is responsible for making choices regarding absorption and variable costing; actual, normal, and standard costing; and allocation bases and cost pools. Each of these choices affects product cost.

Absorption versus Variable Costing.   As discussed in Chapter 16, the costs of a product may be based on absorption costing, the traditional requirements, or variable costing. The difference is in the treatment of fixed manufacturing costs. If the internal records are based on variable costing, additional calculations must be performed to translate the report totals to absorption costing amounts for external reporting.

Actual, Normal, and Standard Cost Bases.   The costs for a product may be based on the actual cost of material, labor, and overhead. The flow assumption built into the actual cost may be LIFO, FIFO, weighted average, or a modified approach. In normal costing, the actual cost of materials and labor is used, and the production overhead is averaged over a time period, usually a year. LIFO, FIFO, and weighted average may also be applied to inventories costed with normal overhead. In standard costing, the prices and usage of materials, labor, and overhead are set in advance, usually once a year for each product. Normal and standard costs may be based on theoretical perfection, currently attainable, long-run average, or annual expected costs.

Allocation Bases and Cost Pools.   Production overhead is often allocated on one measure, such as direct labor hours or production time, with only one cost pool for the entire production area. Alternatively, overhead may be allocated according to several bases for each department or process. As was demonstrated in Chapter 8, having a cost pool for each production process and having more than one allocation basis results in a more accurate cost measure in terms of cause and effect. However, the additional cost pools and allocation bases increase the cost of developing and maintaining the accounting system.

Extent of Internal Compliance with External Requirements

Most companies keep one set of detailed transactions and then modify these records to meet the requirements of both external reporting and internal management. Alternatives to this procedure are sometimes followed.

Exact Correspondence.   The company may choose to base its internal records on the requirements of the Internal Revenue Code. The external financial report is compiled to correspond with the tax return. Management, more or less, operates the company according to the tax records and reports. This reporting alternative is used by some small companies.

Financial Report and Tax Differences.   Some of the requirements of the Internal Revenue Code are not generally accepted accounting principles for large companies. For example, expensing goodwill and certain life insurance premiums is not acceptable for tax purposes but must be done for financial reporting purposes.[5] A company must reconcile all differences between income for the financial report, called *book income*, and taxable income. The corporate records may be kept on a tax basis with separate worksheets resulting in numbers for the financial report, or the records may be kept on a financial reporting basis with tax worksheets.

Management Accounting Regarding Financial Report Differences.   If the financial records are not kept on a basis consistent with generally accepted accounting principles for external financial reports, the accountants must reconcile the differences. For example, if inventories are kept on a realizable value basis (for management accounting purposes) that is higher than cost, the accountants must construct an accepted cost basis (that is, LIFO, FIFO, or weighted average) for the inventory. This requires additional accounting records on inventory cost. Similarly, if all costs (development, production, sales, and administration) are allocated to products and services, the costs must be reclassified for the financial report and the tax return. For financial reporting, only the production costs apply to products; the remainder applies to expenses.

The CFO chooses the extent to which the management accounting reports and system may vary from that required for external reporting and tax returns. The cost of varying relates to the cost of reconciling the reports and maintaining the capacity to issue them on different bases. Large differences may be difficult for the external auditor to understand and may require that the audit procedures be complex and expensive. Using different bases results in increased accounting cost, which is administrative overhead.

Extent of Decision Support

The management accounting system can more or less support management decisions for planning, pricing, and performance evaluation.

Periodic Reporting and On-line Access.   Decision support may be in the form of periodic reports or on-line access or both. The management accounting system provides periodic reports in a predetermined format. The files are updated as often as the reports are issued (weekly, monthly, quarterly, or annually). In addition, the system may provide on-line access to detailed transaction files (inventories, accounts receivable, cost records). On-line access requires special programs, communications devices, phone lines, terminals, and space. If files are to be accessed, they must be updated continuously and kept available. A system based on on-line access is far more complex than one based on periodic reporting. Thus, an on-line system results in costs for hardware purchase and maintenance, software lease and maintenance, collection of data, data entry, internal audit, error correction, space for equipment and people, and processing of more transactions than a periodic reporting system.

Special Analyses.   In addition to periodic reports and on-line access, the management accounting system may have the capacity to issue special reports and analyses. Issuing such reports is usually a labor-intensive process because the programs must be manipulated in some way. The data from the system plus external data are combined

---

[5] Intermediate financial accounting textbooks deal with this topic, often called *tax allocation*. There are many highly specific areas of difference: depreciation methods, useful lives of assets, depletion of natural resources, interest income on certain securities, dividends from certain stocks, and so forth.

in a report that often includes discussion and recommended actions. A trained staff must be available to support special analyses of decisions, which is an additional expense.

Personnel and Structure of Management Accounting Function

The CFO should adopt an accounting personnel strategy that is consistent with the strategic plans of senior management. For example, the CFO should address questions such as: "How many highly intelligent, motivated, decisive accountants do we need over the next 10 years to meet the senior management objectives for growth and earnings?" If senior management plans involve rapid expansion in financially oriented industries (banking, insurance, or real estate), many excellent accountants will be needed. If senior management plans to stay in the same industry with limited growth, the CFO should develop enough people to maintain the current group.

Design of Jobs and Development.   Any task is boring if it is performed repetitively. Boredom is a major cause of stress, poor performance, and burnout. Most jobs are routine. Performing routine tasks for 30 years does *not* prepare a person for a controllership or a high-level position. One basic principle in job design is to maintain the variety and challenge of a job through the two to five years that a person will fill the position. Variety should be in the tasks performed, the location in which they are completed, and the people with whom the employee interacts. A second principle is that employees must perceive that they are developing skills that could help them gain promotions. Aspirations are very important in maintaining performance and morale. Thus, the training received while performing job duties should prepare the accounting staff for the next higher level, and that training should eventually qualify staff members for a controllership or senior management position. A third basic principle in job design is to promote a sense of fairness and equity in treatment. Thus, the accountants should agree with the statement: "If I work hard and achieve, I will be rewarded with a good salary and a promotion."

Clerical Tasks.   Another part of the management accounting function is to determine the extent to which a position involves performing mundane tasks versus the extent to which it involves managing resources and providing knowledge. Use of college-trained accountants to perform many routine tasks is inefficient and perhaps ineffective. If accountants repeat mundane, uncomplicated tasks, for example, cost allocations or product costing, weekly or monthly, their profession skill will not grow.

Accountants should be designers of approaches and systems rather than performers of clerical tasks. Most routine accounting functions should be performed by computers, clerks, or paraprofessionals.[6] However, this is an ideal situation for two reasons. First, not all accountants are capable of developing into designers of systems and approaches. Second, some tasks for example, the pro forma calculations related to a prospective merger, are too complex for clerks or computer programs to perform correctly. Thus, the CFO should develop tactics to make the accounting staff as productive as is realistically possible while recognizing the constraints of individual aptitudes and the complexity of tasks.

---

[6] A paraprofessional is a person who is trained in the performance of tasks, such as a person with a trade-school background. A paraprofessional knows how to perform procedures but not necessarily why they are performed or how the procedures would be changed to meet new circumstances.

Extent of Decentralization. The CFO has a choice as to the extent to which management accounting activities are decentralized. A decentralized accounting staff is consistent with a senior management strategy of decentralization of general management. In a decentralized structure, it is more difficult to develop staff through training and rotation. The decentralized staff has primary allegiance to its division managers instead of to the CFO. With decentralization, each segment will have its own management accounting system instead of the company as a whole having one. With decentralization, the CFO loses some management control and most operational control over the management accounting system.

Current Changes to Manufacturing Environment

The CFO should make choices that are consistent with current changes in the manufacturing environment: reduction of inventory, elimination of support services, change in technology, and planning to meet capacity.

Inventory Reduction and Accounting Systems. When inventories are reduced substantially, they become immaterial to the financial report. Inventories can be combined with "other" current assets in the financial report and have an immaterial effect on net income. Although product costing is still important for pricing, cost control, product decisions, and general decision-making, it is irrelevant to income determination. Cost-flow assumptions of FIFO, LIFO, and weighted average are irrelevant to income. Further, the distinctions between variable and absorption costing (Chapter 16) are irrelevant for financial reports. In such circumstances, the accounting system for a factory can be simplified with all costs of production charged to Cost of Goods Sold accounts. Thus, Cost of Goods Sold rather than Work in Process is the control account for production costs.

Support Services. When the workers in each production area perform most of their own support services, the departmental cost pools include almost all of the costs associated with production. This eliminates the need for service department cost allocation (Appendix 8A), which simplifies the accounting. Costs still need to be allocated from the production area to the product on some basis.

Technology. For industries that require expensive technology, the production overhead is many times the amount of the direct labor. For example, a $20 million computerized wind tunnel with annual operating costs of $4 million is operated by a person making $40,000 in salary. Charging on the basis of the operator's time is almost meaningless. Instead, charging should be based on technology usage.

Planning of Operations. When a manufacturer has very little inventory, planning operations is essentially the same as the planning function in the service industry. Thus, capacities should be planned to match expected demand to achieve a high load on facilities. Load is the ratio of productive time sold to productive time available. Developing products to use the available capacities and marketing plans is very important to maintaining a high load factor. The projection of customer demands and the development of productive capacities to meet customer requirements is critical to planning.

Exhibit 26–3 summarizes the strategies and choices available to the CFO in developing a management accounting system.

EXHIBIT 26–3   Choices in Management Accounting Systems Change

Topic Area	Choices
Simplify	Reduce detailed reports
	Justify all reports
	Reduce number of transactions
	Reduce number of systems
	Allocate less
Performance measures	One versus many
	Quantitative versus qualitative
	Level of participation
	Mentoring performance
Planning	Fixed versus flexible budgets
	Level of participation
Product costs	Absorption versus variable costing
	Actual, normal, and standard cost bases
	Allocation bases and cost pools
Internal compliance	Exact correspondence
	Financial and tax report differences
	Management accounting and financial reports differences
Decision support	Periodic and on-line access
	Special analyses
Personnel and structure	Design of jobs
	Clerical tasks
	Extent of decentralization
Production changes	Inventory reductions and accounting
	Support service accounting
	Technology
	Planning of operations

SUMMARY

The chief financial officer provides direction for management accounting system development in order to be consistent with strategic planning, provide adequate management control, and support operational control. Strategic plans are the broad strategies for attaining the goals and objectives of senior management. Management control is the assurance that resources are obtained efficiently and used effectively. Management control includes planning, performance measurement and evaluation, short-term decision-making, and capital project control. Operational control is the highly detailed process of assuring that specific tasks are carried out efficiently and effectively.

Changes to management accounting systems come from new products, production processes, organizational structures, personnel turnover, external reporting requirements, and fads and human foibles. Although management fads will always arise, some will be more useful than others. Human foibles can be difficult.

All accounting activity is overhead because it does not generate a product or service that is sold to outside customers. Accounting expense can be justified because of its contribution to the company: ensuring that external requirements are met, facilitating cash inflows, controlling expenditures, supporting decision-making, and preparing special analyses. Computerized accounting systems become fragile with age because the changes made over time vary in quality, and the changes interact in unpredictable ways. Completely new accounting systems are very expensive and take some time to become fully operational. Purchased software is difficult to change and, thus, the company often has to change to fit the software. Rapid change will be resisted by different segments and by individual employees. Accountants often restrict their viewpoint to numbers for external reports. Some managers have poor attitudes toward and aptitude for accounting.

Performance measurement can be based on one or many measures, on financial or qualitative measures, on autocratically or participatively set standards, and with or without mentoring. Planning may result in fixed or flexible budgets for months, quarters, or years on an autocratic or participative basis. Allocations may be based on one measure or many measures. The internal accounting system may be set up to meet management requirements, financial report requirements, or tax requirements. The accountant must be able to reconcile between these requirements. The CFO may decide to have only periodic reports, allow on-line access to files, and/or provide special analysis reports. The CFO may choose to design jobs in certain ways to encourage growth and retention or in other ways to encourage attrition. Accountants should not perform clerical tasks although some do. The CFO may centralize or decentralize the accounting staff.

The CFO should consider the effects of current changes in the manufacturing environments. When there is little inventory, product costing has little effect on reported income but is still important for control, pricing, and decision-making. With little inventory, the system will require less service department allocation. Direct labor should not be used for allocation of the costs of technology. Capacity should be planned to meet customer demand.

KEY TERMS AND CONCEPTS

Strategies (983)
Goals (983)
Objectives (983)
Management control (983)

Operational control (984)
Attrition policy (991)
Termination policy (991)
Mentoring (991)

ADDITIONAL READINGS

Ballew, V. B., and R. J. Schlesinger. "Modern Factories and Outdated Cost Systems Do Not Mix." *Production and Inventory Management Journal*, First quarter, 1989, pp. 19–23.
Berlinger, C., and J. A. Brimson, ed. *Cost Management for Today's Advanced Manufacturing: The CAM-I Conceptual Design.* Boston, Mass.: Harvard Business School Press, 1989.
Brimson, J. A. "How Advanced Manufacturing Technologies Are Reshaping Cost Management." *Management Accounting*, March, 1986, pp. 25–29.
Capettini, R., and D. K. Clancy, ed. *Cost Accounting, Robotics, and the New Manufacturing Environment.* Sarasota, Fla.: American Accounting Association, 1987.
Cooper, R. "You Need a New Cost System When, . . ." *Harvard Business Review*, January–February, 1989, pp. 77–82.
Edwards, J. B., and J. A. Heard. "Is Cost Accounting the No. 1 Enemy of Productivity?" *Management Accounting*, June, 1984, pp. 44–49.
Howell, R. A., and S. R. Soucy. "Major Trends for Manufacturing Accounting." *Management Accounting*, July, 1987, pp. 21–27.
Johnson, H. T., and R. S. Kaplan. *Relevance Lost: The Rise and Fall of Management Accounting.* Boston, Mass.: Harvard Business School Press, 1988.

Juran, J. M. *Juran on Leadership for Quality.* New York: Free Press, 1989.

Keegan, D. P.; R. G. Eiler; and J. V. Anania. "An Advanced Cost Management System for the Factory of the Future." *Management Accounting,* December 1988, pp. 31–37.

Lammert, T. B., and R. Ehrsam. "The Human Element: The Real Challenge in Modernizing Cost Systems." *Management Accounting,* July, 1987, pp. 32–37.

Mackey, J. T. "11 Key Issues in Manufacturing Accounting." *Management Accounting,* January, 1987, pp. 32–37.

McIlhattan, R. D. "How Cost Management Systems Can Support the JIT Philosophy." *Management Accounting,* September, 1987, pp. 20–26.

Neumann, B. R., and P. R. Jaouen. "Kanban, Zips and Cost Accounting: A Case Study." *Journal of Accountancy,* August, 1986, pp. 132–41.

O'Connell, J. F. "How We Simplified Administrative Tasks." *Management Accounting,* December, 1984, pp. 40–44.

Schonberger, R. J. *Japanese Manufacturing Techniques—Nine Hidden Lessons in Simplicity.* Falls Church, Va: Association of Production and Inventory Control Society, 1982.

Tatikonda, M. V. "Just-in-Time and Modern Manufacturing Environments: Implications for Cost Accounting." *Production and Inventory Control Journal,* First quarter, 1988, pp. 1–5.

REVIEW QUESTIONS

1. Who is responsible for changes to the management accounting system?
2. Define strategic planning, management control, and operational control.
3. What functions are included in management control?
4. What is the danger with trying to gain control by implementing many controls?
5. List sources of change to external reporting requirements.
6. What effects do changes in organization structure have on the management accounting system?
7. Why will turnover of senior managers affect the management accounting system?
8. How do management fads affect the management accounting system?
9. How might foibles and human failings affect the system?
10. Why should all of accounting be considered administrative overhead?
11. What reasons can be used to justify the existence of the accounting system?
12. Why are computerized accounting systems fragile after many changes and years have passed?
13. Why is purchasing vendor software a limitation? Why is it often the least expensive alternative?
14. Compare active with passive resistance to change.
15. Why might the attitudes and aptitudes of managers limit the ability to change management accounting systems?
16. List several examples of choice with respect to performance measurement.
17. List several examples of choice with respect to product cost measurement.
18. If a management accounting system does not exactly comply with external reporting requirements, what must the accountants be able to do?
19. What decision support alternatives does the CFO have with respect to the management accounting system?
20. Why is job design important to accounting positions?
21. Why should accounting systems be simplified? What is wrong with a complicated accounting system?
22. Why is an attrition personnel reduction strategy often considered better than a termination strategy?
23. Why will there be less service department cost allocation in the new manufacturing environment?

GLOSSARY

ABC analysis and classification: A technique for inventory management in which inventory items are categorized in classes A, B, and C in terms of relative value to the business. This value may be expressed in dollar amounts or in terms of how critical the material is to production, or a combination of the two. A is considered most valuable and C is least valuable. After categorizing items into the three classes, management selects appropriate management tools, techniques, and procedures that are cost-effective for each class. (Chapter 6a)

Abnormal spoilage: Any spoilage in excess of normal spoilage. (Chapter 11)

Absorption costing (or full costing): A costing methodology that classifies all production costs as product costs. Marketing and distribution expenses, and general and administrative expenses are period costs. (Chapters 2, 8, 16, 26)

Account analysis: A cost estimation technique in which variability of a particular cost is estimated directly from information obtained through (1) an inspection of the historical activity of the cost and (2) an interpretation of managerial policies with respect to the cost. (Chapter 3)

Activity measure (*see* Measure of activity.)

Actual costing: A cost identification technique that recognizes the actual costs of direct material, direct labor, and production overhead in accumulating the costs of work in process. (Chapters 2, 26)

Allocation: The process of identifying costs with cost objectives of the period. (*See also* Cost allocation.) (Chapter 25)

Allocation base: The measure of activity that links cost objectives with cost pools. (Chapters 8, 25, 26)

Analytic production process: A production process in which raw materials are broken down into multiple products with some products more valuable than others. Processing and extractive operations are examples of this type of process. (Chapter 10)

Arbitrary allocation: A cost allocation based on convenience or precedent rather than an allocation based on the decisions that caused the cost. (Chapter 22)

Assembled products: Products for which parts and subassemblies are brought together and assembled into a final product; each product passes through the same assembly operations. (Chapter 5)

Assembly plant: A facility that presses, welds, bolts, or wires parts together. Its direct materials are the outputs of processing and fabrication plants. (Chapter 2)

Assignment: The process of determining the amount of cost to identify with individual cost accounting periods. (Chapter 25)

Autocorrelation: A condition in which successive observations of the dependent variable are not independent over time. This is also called *serial correlation*. (Chapter 3)

Average investment: The average inventories plus average depreciable property. The average depreciable property is found by dividing the investment in depreciable property by 2. (Chapter 23)

Average return on investment: The ratio of the average income over the life of a project to the average investment. (*see also* Return on investment) (Chapter 23)

Avoidable cost: A cost that would decrease if activity were reduced or terminated entirely or a cost that would be incurred if the activity were undertaken. (Chapter 22)

Break-even volume: The units or sales dollars at which there is no profit or loss; total revenue exactly equals total cost. (Chapter 4)

Budget: A quantitative expression of a plan of action. It is an aid to coordinating and implementing the actions by responsible management. (Chapters 1, 14)

Budget variance: The difference between actual overhead costs incurred and the flexible budget for actual units produced. Sometimes called the *controllable variance*. (Chapter 13)

Budgetary slack: The excess in a budget above the minimum necessary to run an efficient operation. This excess is expressed in higher estimates for expenditures or lower estimates for revenues. (Chapter 14)

Bureaucratic behavior: The strict adherence to rules and standardized operating procedures. The environment is one in which rules become more important than economic substance, and standard procedures replace rational thought. Creativity is stifled and opportunities are lost. Rigid budgets and performance goals are a symptom of bureaucratic behavior. (Chapters 14, 18)

By-product: An output from a joint process that has a relatively minor total sales value when compared with joint products. The sales value can be influenced by either a minor quantity or a minor sales price per unit. (Chapter 10)

Capacity costs: The fixed costs incurred to provide capacity to render a service or make a product. These costs refer to costs related to the people who form the basic organization, the equipment to perform operations and processes, and the buildings to house the people and equipment. (Chapter 3)

Capital project: A project that requires a relatively large investment in assets for more than one year. A capital project may also be known as an *investment project,* an *investment proposal,* a *plant acquisition,* an *equipment purchase,* or a *development project.* (Chapter 23)

Capitalized cost (*see* Unexpired cost)

Carrying costs: The costs related to having quantities of material available. These costs are (1) out-of-pocket costs associated with the physical presence of the inventory and (2) the cost of capital or money tied up in inventory rather than in other income-generating assets. Out-of-pocket costs include such items as insurance on the value of the inventory, inventory taxes, storage facilities, inspections and physical inventory counts, obsolescence, breakage, handling, and pilferage. Cost of capital is the weighted average of the cost to obtain funds from the various equity sources. (Chapter 6a)

Cellular manufacturing (or group manufacturing): A production concept in which products are grouped together and manufactured in one area of the plant. The concept works well when the product mix is stable but has some problems when the product mix changes, leaving some cells idle and others swamped. The concept may be applied to final products, subassemblies, or groups of parts. (Chapter 5)

Centralization: The extent to which the authority to make decisions is retained by the top management group. (Chapter 17)

Chain joint production: A production process in which at least one output from a joint process becomes an input for another joint process. (Chapter 10A)

Chief financial officer: The member of the management team who is primarily responsible for setting financial goals, evaluating alternatives, acquiring capital, managing cash, and establishing financial controls. The title is CFO or vice president of finance. (Chapter 1)

Coefficient of determination: A measure of association between the dependent and independent variables. It represents the proportion of total variation in the dependent variable that is accounted for (or explained) by the variation in the independent variable. (Chapter 3)

Commingled products: Products for which individual units are not distinguishable until contained in some way. A pound of flour in a bin, for instance, cannot be distinguished from any other pound of flour in the bin until the flour is taken out and packaged. (Chapter 5)

Committed cost (or committed fixed cost): A fixed cost arising from the possession of property, plant, and equipment and a basic organization. The level of such costs is primarily affected by management's long-run decisions regarding the desired level of capacity. These costs are usually not controllable during the current period. (Chapters 3, 17)

Common cost: A cost of shared facilities, products, or services. (Chapter 17)

Compensated personal absence: Compensation for absences from work such as vacations, holidays, sick days, personal leave, jury duty, military training, or civic functions. Such compensation does not represent value-added work, but it is necessary for the morale, health, and welfare of employees. (Chapter 7)

Composite unit: A combination of units of individual products in proportion to their normal sales volume. It is also called a *package unit, basket unit,* or *sales mix.* (Chapter 4)

Computer-aided design: The use of high-quality computer graphics and software to design new products or change existing products. The software has the capacity to enlarge or reduce the product in size, do cross-sections through the product at various lines, print out part specifications, and print final blueprints for the entire product. (Chapter 5)

Computer-aided manufacturing: A process in which machines or entire production lines are run by computers. It allows setup times for machines to be reduced from hours to seconds with considerable accuracy. One worker can oversee the activities and maintain 3 to 10 production stations simultaneously. (Chapter 5)

Contribution analysis: The comparison of revenues generated with the avoidable costs of the product or service. (Chapter 22)

Contribution margin: Revenue less variable cost. The variable cost includes the variable component of production, marketing and distribution, and general and administrative costs. A contribution margin increases and decreases in proportion to changes in volume. (Chapters 4, 16, 19)

Contribution margin formatted income statement: An income statement format in which all variable costs are subtracted from revenues to determine a total contribution margin. Then all fixed costs are deducted from the contribution margin to determine profit. The format is very useful for analyzing the impact of volume changes on profits. (Chapter 4)

Contribution margin per unit: The selling price per unit less variable cost per unit. (Chapter 4)

Contribution margin ratio: The contribution margin expressed as a percentage of revenues or selling prices. (Chapter 4)

Control: The process of measuring costs incurred by management's actions and comparing the results against plans. It is a process of monitoring the specific steps taken by management to achieve the organization's goals and objectives and to use resources effectively and efficiently. (Chapter 1)

Controllable cost: A cost that the segment manager can influence during the current period. (Chapter 17)

Controller: The financial officer responsible for all accounting activities within the organization. This individual is primarily responsible for the design and operation of the accounting system, tax planning and accounting, budgets and budgetary control, internal auditing, and a periodic review of operations. (Chapter 1)

Conversion cost: An input cost into a production process that consists of direct labor and production overhead. It is the cost incurred to convert raw materials to a completed product. (Chapter 9)

Conversion ratio: The ratio of outputs to inputs. (Chapter 9a)

Cost: An exchange price, a foregoing, or a sacrifice made to obtain a benefit. It is the cash or cash equivalent value required to attain an objective such as acquiring the goods and services used, complying with a contract, performing a function, or producing and distributing a product. (Chapter 2)

Cost accounting: The branch of management accounting that provides internal, primarily financial, information for the management of a company. It not only includes finding the costs of products and activities but also

encompasses financial planning, controlling operations, and investment topics. (Chapter 1)

Cost allocation: The distribution of accumulated costs to specific cost objectives. It is normally considered the process of identifying an organization's costs with products and services although other cost objectives are also involved. Other terms for this process are *assign, charge, apply,* and *distribute.* (Chapters 2, 8, 18)

Cost-based pricing: Setting prices of products and services when the prices are based either wholly or substantially on costs. The typical approach is to add a percentage markup to the cost of the products and services. The approach is appropriate when the products or services are so numerous that it is not beneficial to search out information about competitors' prices for each product. (Chapters 22, 25)

Cost center: A segment that provides services or products to other segments and is evaluated on the basis of cost performance. (Chapter 17)

Cost control: A process of comparing actual performance with the standard (or budgeted) performance, analyzing variances to identify controllable causes, and taking action to eliminate inefficient performance in the future. (Chapter 12)

Cost determination: The process of finding the costs of something, either products or services. The process seeks the costs directly traceable to or specifically identifiable with the object of interest plus a share of the other related costs. (Chapter 1)

Cost driver: The activity or event that is the reason for cost incurrence. (Chapter 8)

Cost estimation: The process of estimating a cost relationship with activity for an individual cost item or grouping of costs. (Chapter 3)

Cost management: The process of managing the activities that cause costs in organizations. The primary purpose of cost management is to maintain, meet, or beat the competition on selling price and profits. The emphasis is on measuring, planning, and evaluating activities that cause or drive costs. (Chapter 1)

Cost objective: Anything for which we want to measure costs. Cost objectives include products, services, processes, departments, and many other objects. Identification of a cost objective is a key factor in selecting appropriate allocation methods and techniques. (Chapters 2, 8, 25)

Cost of capital: The weighted average of the cost to obtain funds from the various equity sources (short-term and long-term debt financing, capital stocks, and retained earnings) of the company. (Chapters 6A, 23)

Cost-of-living allowance: The additional compensation

due to the inconvenience of a temporary move or a higher cost of living in a new area. (Chapter 7)

Cost of production report: A summary report form for a department using a process cost system that shows the flow of physical units and the flow of dollars through the department. (Chapter 9)

Cost pool: A grouping and accumulation of costs under a common designation. (Chapters 2, 8, 25, 26)

Cost reduction: A philosophy of decreasing the costs of operations through improved methods and procedures, better selection of resources (people and materials), or capital investments. (Chapter 12)

Cost variance: The change in gross profit (or contribution margin) resulting from an increase or decrease in unit costs. This variance is decomposed into a number of variances that relate to materials, labor, and overhead, and, in the case of contribution margins, marketing and distribution, and general and administrative costs. (Chapter 19)

Cost-volume-profit analysis: The study of the impact of changes on and interrelationships among revenue, costs, profits, and volume. (Chapter 4)

Currently attainable standard: A cost for material or labor that should be incurred under forthcoming efficient operating conditions. (Chapter 12)

Decentralization: The extent to which the authority for one or more decisions is delegated to subordinates and segments. (Chapter 17)

Defective units: Outputs that do not meet quality standards and can be sold as second-quality goods ''as is'' or can be reworked and sold as first- or second-quality goods. (Chapter 11)

Degrees of freedom: A statistical concept necessary for calculating certain statistical measures relating to a set of observations. It is calculated as the number of observations reduced by the number of parameters that must be estimated in the regression equation. (Chapter 3)

Degrees of remoteness: The continuum of relationships from specific to distant that exists between a cost or grouping of costs and cost objectives. (Chapter 25)

Delphi technique: An estimation technique in which a manager first obtains initial estimates from each person in a small group of knowledgeable persons. The results of the first estimates are reported back to all members and then revised estimates are obtained. This process is repeated until the project leader is satisfied that the individual estimates will change little. The results are then summarized as an average estimate. (Chapter 24)

Dependent variable: Represents the costs to be estimated

from the budget equation for cost estimation. In formula form it is the Y term in the equation. (Chapter 3)

Direct allocation: A cost allocation process in which individual costs or groups of costs are identified specifically with or traced to individual cost objectives. As a rule, such cost allocations are based on a measurement of the specific usage of a cost objective. Such allocations usually occur when the usage is easy and economical to measure and trace to the cost objective in question. (Chapters 2, 8)

Direct cost: A cost that can be specifically identified with or traced to a cost objective. (Chapters 2, 25)

Direct costing (*See* Variable costing.)

Direct labor: Refers to employees who work directly on the product or service and whose efforts can be economically identified with or specifically traced to a product or service. (Chapters 2, 7)

Direct materials: Quantities of material that can be identified with the production of a specific product, that can be easily and economically traced to that product, and whose cost represents a significant part of the total product cost. (Chapter 6) They are the primary raw materials, unassembled parts, and subassemblies purchased for use in producing the company's finished products. (Chapter 2)

Direct method: A method of allocating support and service department costs in which the costs are allocated directly to production departments in proportion to activity performed for the production departments. No attempt is made to recognize the reciprocal services among the support and service departments. (Chapter 8a)

Discounted benefit-cost index: The ratio of the discounted present values to the original investment cost. It is also called the *present value index* or *profitability index*. (Chapter 23)

Discounted payback: The length of time required for the present value of cash flows from operations to accumulate to the amount of the investment. (Chapter 23)

Discounted rate of return: The rate at which the net present value is zero. This can also be interpreted as the rate at which the present value of future cash flows equals the investment. Another term is *internal rate of return*. (Chapter 23)

Discretionary fixed cost: A fixed cost that arises from the periodic, usually annual, appropriation decisions that directly reflect management's short-term policies on capacity levels. Management can react quickly to increase or reduce this cost. Other terms used are *managed* or *programmed fixed costs*. (Chapter 3)

Economic feasibility: The extent to which a capital project meets the economic objectives of senior management. It is measured using criteria such as net present value, rates of return, and risk measures. (Chapter 23)

Economic order quantity (EOQ): The purchase order quantity or production order quantity that minimizes the total annual costs of maintaining an inventory of the item in question. This order size occurs when order costs and carrying costs are equal. (Chapter 6a)

Effectiveness: The measurement of whether an objective was achieved or not. (Chapter 1)

Efficiency: The measurement of how much resources were used to achieve the objective. (Chapter 1)

Efficiency variance: The difference between the flexible budget for actual hours worked and the flexible budget for standard capacity allowed. Because fixed overhead costs are identical in both budgets, the efficiency variance consists only of differences in variable overhead costs. An alternate calculation is the difference between actual capacity and standard capacity allowed multiplied by the variable overhead rate per unit of capacity. (*see also* Labor efficiency variance) (Chapter 13)

Engineering approach: A cost estimation technique that uses analysis and direct observation of processes to identify the relationship between inputs and output and then quantifies an expected cost behavior. (Chapter 3)

Equivalent units of production: The theoretical number of units that could have been produced had the resources been applied only to starting and completing units. (Chapter 9)

Excess capacity: Capacity that is greater than can normally be used in the near future. It represents specific plant and equipment that are not being used or are being used only partially. (Chapter 8)

Expected actual capacity: Management's estimate of capacity utilization for the upcoming period, or the productive capacity needed to meet market demand and inventory needs. It is a short-run concept. (Chapter 8)

Expenses: Expired costs. (Chapter 2)

Expired costs: Costs whose future benefits have expired. They then appear in an income statement. (Chapter 2)

Extractive companies: Companies that start with mineral rights, labor, and equipment to produce an ore or material product that is normally the input to a processing plant. (Chapter 2)

Fabricated products: Products for which production involves reshaping a material through a cutting, stamping, or molding operation with every unit coming off the line in the same way. (Chapter 5)

Fabrication plant: A facility that shapes, treats, or cuts the materials. (Chapter 2)

FIFO equivalent units: Equivalent units of production calculated under a first-in, first-out product flow concept. It considers work effort to complete the units in beginning inventory and the units started and completed, and the work effort in the partially completed units in ending inventory. (Chapter 9)

Financial accounting: The branch of management accounting that comprises the preparation of financial reports for nonmanagement groups such as shareholders, creditors, regulatory agencies, and tax authorities. Its primary purpose is to provide information to outsiders on (1) the results of company operations and (2) the company's financial position. (*see also* Financial reporting) (Chapter 1)

Financial reporting: The periodic preparation of financial statements in accordance with generally accepted accounting principles (GAAP), or principles of some regulatory agency (such as the Internal Revenue Service) for use by parties external to the reporting organization. (Chapter 25)

Finished goods inventory: The account in which costs are recorded for goods that are completed and ready for sale or ready for shipment to customers. It represents the accumulated costs through the final stage of production. (Chapter 2)

Fixable problem: A problem in a process about which the manager can take corrective action to eliminate variances. (Chapter 21)

Fixed budget: The plan of operations that is fixed at the beginning of the year with no changes in amounts depending upon activity levels. It is also referred to as a *static budget*. (Chapters 14, 26)

Fixed cost: A cost that remains constant in total as the level of activity changes. Although fixed costs remain constant in total, the cost per unit decreases as volume increases. That is, the fixed cost per unit is inversely related to changes in the activity base. These costs are also known as *capacity costs* because an organization incurs fixed costs to provide the capacity to render a service or make a product. (Chapter 3)

Fixed overhead spending variance: The difference between actual fixed overhead costs incurred and the budgeted fixed costs. Sometimes called *fixed budget variance*. (Chapter 13)

Flexible budget: A budget that is adjusted to the amount of the activity that actually occurs. (Chapters 14, 26)

Flexible manufacturing: A concept of production that emphasizes increasing the variety of products that can be produced on a given machine or group of machines. The purpose is to reduce space and costs associated with the machinery. (Chapter 5)

Flexible overhead budget: A budget based on a formula

that expresses the budgeted production overhead at any point within the relevant range of activity. (Chapter 13)

Focused production: A process of reducing the variety of products produced or services rendered and concentrating efforts and resources on fewer products or services that have the highest contribution margins. (Chapter 5)

Full costing (*see* Absorption costing)

Functional budget: A budget that represents expected amounts for functional departments or responsibilities. Each department or responsibility is a line item in the overall budget for the total function. It is also called an *activity budget*. (Chapter 14)

Further processing decisions: Decisions in which management considers whether to sell a product now or process it further to generate a higher selling price. The decision is based on a comparison of the incremental revenues and the separable costs to generate those revenues. (Chapter 10)

General and administrative expenses: The costs of managing the general activities of the company. They are the costs that cannot logically fit under either production costs or marketing and distribution costs. (Chapter 2)

Goals: General concepts that describe the desires of senior management. They might include growth, obtaining a high ranking in industry, a high return on investment, or developing the capacity to survive. (Chapter 26)

Gross profit (or gross margin): The excess of sales revenue over the cost of those sales. (Chapter 19)

Heteroscedasticity: A condition in which the spread of observations around the regression line is not constant throughout the entire range of observations. (Chapter 3)

High-low point method: A cost estimation technique that utilizes the high and low activity levels to estimate the variable cost and fixed cost portions of an individual cost or a grouping of costs. (Chapter 3)

Homogeneity: The condition of sameness or being alike. In cost allocation homogeneity means that the relationship between the costs in a cost pool and the cost objective is the same or similar. (Chapter 8)

Homoscedasticity: A condition in which the spread of observations around the regression line is constant throughout the entire range of observations. (Chapter 3)

Hybrid cost system: A cost system in which either job order or process costing is used for one or more segments of a production process and another costing system is used for the remaining segments of a production process. (Chapter 9b)

Ideal capacity (*see* Theoretical capacity)

Ideal standard: A standard cost based on level of performance that allows for no work interruptions (machine breakdowns, for example) and calls for a level of effort that is achieved only by the most skilled and experienced workers operating at peak efficiency 100 percent of the time. Also referred to as a *perfection*, *maximum*, or *theoretical standard*. (Chapter 12)

Idle capacity: Capacity represented by the temporary nonuse of facilities resulting from a decrease in the demand for a company's products or services. (Chapter 8)

Incentive wage plan: A compensation plan employed by a company as a means to motivate workers. It is an exchange of additional compensation for greater productivity. The plan may apply to individuals, groups, or an entire facility. (Chapter 7)

Incremental budget: A budgeting process in which the budget for the upcoming period is adjusted by an incremental amount over the previous period to reflect changes in operations and inflation. (Chapter 14)

Independent variable: For cost estimation refers to the one or more predictors in the budget equation that represent measures of activity. In formula form it will be the one or more X terms in the equation. (Chapter 3)

Indirect allocation: A cost allocation process in which individual costs or groupings of costs must be allocated to two or more cost objectives. As a rule, such cost allocations are based on a measurement of an approximated usage. Such allocations usually occur when the usage is difficult and uneconomical to measure and trace to individual cost objectives. (Chapters 2, 8)

Indirect cost: A cost that can be attached to a cost objective only through allocation. (Chapters 2, 25)

Indirect labor: Labor that is not readily traced to a product or service. Indirect workers supervise, repair, manage, purchase, inspect, record, advise, or otherwise support the direct workers. In most cases indirect workers are nonvalue added. (Chapter 7)

Indirect materials: All materials and supplies that become part of the product or are consumed otherwise in production of the item that are not classified as direct materials. (Chapter 6)

Internal rate of return (*see* Discounted rate of return)

Investment center: A segment that is responsible for revenues, expenses, and investments. (Chapter 17)

Job cost sheet: A record in a job order costing system that is used to accumulate the costs of material, labor, and production overhead associated with each job or batch of units. This record gives a cost summary for the entire production of the job, even if it spans more than one accounting period and many producing departments. Also referred to as a *job cost card, job cost record,* or *job detail file.* (Chapter 5)

Job order costing: A cost accumulation system that charges the costs of materials, labor, and production overhead to the specific jobs when those costs are incurred. It is generally used when products are manufactured or services rendered in identifiable lots or groups, or when products are manufactured or services rendered according to customer specifications. (Chapter 5)

Joint costs: Materials, labor, and production overhead costs incurred during the processing of inputs before the point at which joint products become individually identifiable. (Chapter 10)

Joint products: The outputs of a process for which common resources are the inputs and the individual products are indistinguishable prior to a split-off point during or at the end of the process. The products are so related that one cannot be produced without producing the others, each having relatively substantial value. (Chapter 10)

Just-in-time inventories (JIT): A zero-stock concept in which materials arrive just in time for production, move from one work-in-process department to another just in time for the needs of the next department, and enter finished goods just in time for sale. All production facilities are viewed as a pipeline, and all movement of goods between facilities is viewed as a uniform flow of materials, component parts, and subassemblies. This reduces, or potentially eliminates, inventory carrying costs. (Chapter 6a)

Labor: The physical or mental effort expended in manufacturing a product or rendering a service. (Chapter 7)

Labor cost: The price paid to employees in the form of wages and salaries. (Chapter 7)

Labor efficiency variance: The difference between the actual hours worked and the standard hours allowed for the final product output. It is calculated as standard rate per hour × (actual hours worked − standard hours allowed). (Chapter 12)

Labor rate variance: The difference between the actual labor rate and the standard labor rate paid to a worker. It is calculated as (Actual rate per hour − Standard rate per hour) × Actual hours worked. (Chapter 12)

Labor-related cost: An expenditure made by an employer on behalf of employees in addition to the wages and salaries. It may be for incentive pay for performance above minimum levels, payroll taxes, or fringe benefits. (Chapter 7)

Lead time: The interval between the time an order is placed and the time the items are received and placed into inventory. (Chapter 6a)

Learning curve: Refers to the fact that as experience is gained through repetition of a task, workers take less time to complete it, make fewer mistakes, and increase units of output. The rule is that when the quantity of units produced doubles, the cost per unit declines by a constant percentage. This constant percentage identifies the degree of cost decline or learning experienced. (Chapter 7a)

Line stop: A production system technique for quality control that requires stopping the entire production cell when a poor-quality product is discovered anywhere in the cell. All workers gather around to discover the cause and fix the problem if they can. Only if workers cannot fix the problem are outside engineers or managers consulted. (Chapter 5)

Linear regression: A statistical tool for describing the movement of one variable based on the movement of another variable. (Chapter 3)

Liquidity: A measure of the ability to pay bills as they become due. (Chapters 15, 23)

Loose or lax standard: A standard cost for material or labor that is an average of previous actual costs. (Chapter 12)

Machine loading file: A file in a production information system that contains the status of each machine used in production, including operations completed and operations scheduled on production orders in process. Because the file is organized by work centers, it also reflects the activity status of each work center. (Chapter 5)

Major (or main) products: Joint products that have relatively substantial value at the split-off point in the process. (*see also* Joint products) (Chapter 10)

Make-or-buy decision: A decision situation in which an organization evaluates whether to purchase component parts, subassemblies, or assemblies from the outside or produce them internally. (Chapter 6)

Management accounting: The process of identifying, measuring, accumulating, analyzing, interpreting, and communicating financial information used by management to plan, evaluate, and control within an organization and to assure appropriate use of and accountability for its resources. Management accounting also comprises the preparation of financial reports for nonmanagement groups such as shareholders, creditors, regulatory agencies, and tax authorities. (Chapter 1)

Management by exception: A management reporting principle based on reporting only those items that permit management to focus on situations that need investigation. In the case of cost variances, only those variances are included in management reports that fall outside of an acceptable range. (Chapter 12)

Management control: The control of the day-to-day activities of the organization with respect to obtaining and using resources effectively and efficiently. This process is usually carried out by the middle levels of management. (Chapters 1, 26)

Margin of safety: The difference between the expected volume (or actual volume) and the break-even volume when volume can be measured in units or sales dollars. This difference is usually expressed as a percentage of the expected volume. It represents the percentage that sales can drop from the expected volume before the break-even point is reached. (Chapter 4)

Market-based pricing: An approach to pricing products and services that utilizes the prices in catalogs, price lists, brokerage quotes, and so forth that are publicly available. (Chapter 22)

Marketing and distribution expenses: The costs of securing customer orders and getting the company's products or services to the customer. They are incurred from the time the production process is complete through delivery to the customer. (Chapter 2)

Master budget: An overall plan of operations for a specific time period at a certain level of activity. It consists of a planned income statement, statement of cash flow, and a balance sheet. These are supported by schedules that reflect the estimates of each manager in the organization. (Chapter 14)

Material price variance: The difference between the actual price per unit of material and the standard price. The variance is calculated as (Actual price − Standard price) × Actual quantity purchased. (Chapter 12)

Material quantity variance: The difference between the actual quantity of material used in production and the standard quantity allowed for the final units of output. The variance is calculated as Standard price × (Actual units used − Standard quantity allowed). (Chapter 12)

Material requirements planning (MRP): A production management system that starts with a master production schedule and designates the requirements for raw materials, component parts, and all subassemblies and assemblies for the individual products. The system automatically identifies when a job is to be performed and how much and when raw materials need to be purchased or parts and subassemblies acquired from subcontractors. (Chapter 6a)

Materials inventory: The account in which to record the

costs that represent the materials stored and ready for production but not yet released to the production floor. (Chapter 2)

Materials inventory master file: A master file in a production information system that contains the material records showing receipts, issues, open orders, and on-hand balances of raw materials and purchased parts and subassemblies. It may also contain purchase or manufacturing lead times and order quantities; it is the subsidiary ledger supporting the Materials Inventory account in the general ledger. (Chapters 5, 6)

Materials-related costs: Costs closely related to the acquisition and issuance of materials but considered indirect costs because they cannot be economically and feasibly identified with the materials costs. They are incurred in the activities from purchasing through the time materials enter production. They include costs for such activities as purchasing, receiving, receiving inspection, storeroom costs prior to materials entering production, and issuance and movement of materials to the production area. (Chapter 6)

Materials requisition: A document or computer output that authorizes the storeroom to issue specific quantities of materials to the authorized production orders. (Chapters 5, 6)

Maximum capacity (*see* Theoretical capacity)

Measure of activity: The measure selected to represent the work performed. The best measure is the one that most closely relates to cost changes as activity increases or decreases. (Chapters 8, 13, 17)

Mentoring: A program in which new employees are assigned to someone in the organization with maturity and experience who can recommend to the new employee training opportunities, career path choices, performance efforts, and similar activities. (Chapter 26)

Method of least squares: A method used in cost estimation in which a regression line is fitted to the data by simultaneous equations. The line is determined so that the algebraic sum of the squared deviations from that line is at a minimum. (Chapter 3)

Mix variance: The cost change that results from combining quantities of materials and labor in a ratio that differs from standard specifications. It comes from changing the recipe or formula. It is measured as the difference between the actual mix of materials or labor used in production and the standard materials or labor that should have been used. (Chapter 12a)

Mixed cost (*see* Semivariable cost)

Modified cost system: A cost system that has one or more cost elements on a job order system and the remaining one or more cost elements on a process order system, or where some but not all of the cost elements are present. (Chapter 9b)

Multicollinearity: The existence of a very high correlation between two or more independent variables. The variables move together so closely that the regression analysis cannot tell them apart. (Chapter 3A)

Multiple regression: An extension of simple linear regression used in cases in which a significant functional relationship exists between two or more independent variables and the dependent variable. (Chapter 3A)

Multiple split-off points (*see* Chain joint production)

Net present value: The present value of future cash flows discounted at the required rate of return minus the initial investment. (Chapter 23)

Net realizable value method (By-products): A method of valuing the by-product of a joint process. The net realizable value of the by-product becomes the inventory value until additional costs are incurred. The amount of net realizable value is deducted from the joint costs. (Chapter 10)

Net realizable value method (Joint products): A method of allocating joint costs to joint products based on the relative net realizable value of each product to the total joint products at a split-off point. A net realizable value is used at the split-off point because the products cannot be sold at that point and must be processed further. A sales price is not available at the split-off point, and the net realizable value is an approximation. (Chapter 10)

Normal capacity: An average utilization of plant, equipment, and people over several years to even out the swings in market demand. It is a long-run concept. Three to five years are considered the common period for establishing this average. (Chapter 8)

Normal costing: A cost identification technique that recognizes the actual costs of direct material and direct labor but applies production overhead on the basis of one or more predetermined overhead rates in accumulating the costs of work in process. (Chapters 2, 26)

Normal spoilage: The minimal level of spoilage expected to occur under efficient operations and as an inherent result of the process. (Chapter 11)

Normality: A statistical quality in which the residuals follow a normal distribution with a mean of zero. (Chapter 3)

Objectives: Specific requirements that relate to the goals. An example is a 10 percent growth in revenues or a 20 percent return on investment. (Chapter 26)

Open production orders file: A file in a production information system that contains information on production orders still in process. Each production order has a number and space is provided to record the progress of the order through individual production steps in the process. It is therefore a status file for each order. (Chapter 5)

Operating control: The process of monitoring individual jobs, tasks, or projects to assure that they are carried out within a specified framework. It is usually performed by the lower levels of management. (Chapter 1)

Operating expenses: A global term for nonproduction costs that include marketing and distribution expenses and general and administrative expenses. (Chapter 19)

Operating leverage ratio: The ratio of the contribution margin to net income before taxes. It measures the effect of percentage changes in sales volume on percentage changes in net income before taxes. The ratio has an inverse relationship to margin of safety. (Chapter 4)

Operational control: The highly detailed process of assuring that specific tasks are carried out efficiently and effectively. It is usually carried out by supervisors and employees and is supported by clerical staff and detailed computer files. (Chapter 26)

Operations file: A file, usually a computer data file, that specifies the sequence of operations to be performed in shaping, fashioning, and assembling raw materials component parts, subassemblies, and complex final assemblies required for specific products. It may include the work centers at which the operations take place as well as machine requirements. It is also known as a *routing file*. (Chapter 5)

Order costs: The managerial and clerical costs to prepare the purchase order to a vendor or a production order to a manufacturing operation. The order costs for a purchase order are the incremental costs of identifying and issuing an order to a single vendor, the cost for computing each line item on a single order, the costs to receive and inspect the goods as received, and the cost to process accounts payable and cash payments. Also included are the costs related to the people, facilities, equipment, and supplies needed to maintain an ordering system.

Order costs for production are called *setup costs*. These are the costs involved in obtaining the necessary materials, arranging specific equipment setups, filling out the required papers, appropriately charging time and materials, and moving out the previous stock of material. These costs may also include the costs of hiring, training, or laying off workers and idle time or overtime. (Chapter 6a)

Output decisions: Regarding joint products, decisions in which management must decide whether to produce a product group or to increase or decrease the volume of a specific product group. The physical characteristics of the joint products in the group require that all products in the group be produced. Depending on the production process, the products within any group may be in fixed proportions or in variable proportions. (Chapter 10)

Overhead efficiency variance (*see* Efficiency variance)

Overhead spending variance (*see* Spending variance)

Overhead volume variance (*see* Volume variance)

Overtime premium: The extra compensation paid for hours worked in excess of 40 per week or on holidays or Sundays. (Chapter 7)

Parallel process flow: The processing of parts or subassemblies in two or more departments at the same time. (Chapter 9b)

Payback period: The length of time required for the cash flows from operations to accumulate to the amount of the investment. (Chapter 23)

Payroll master file: A master file in a computerized system that contains the earnings records for each employee. This file includes accumulated earnings to date plus all of the key information necessary for payroll preparation. Also included are the number of withholding exemptions, any special shift premiums, and wage rates. The file is used to prepare payment to each employee (usually a check), a payroll register of each paycheck issued, summary journal entries, and various control and management reports. (Chapter 7)

Performance evaluation: The judgment process of managers and supervisors about the quality of the performance of subordinates. (Chapters 14, 17)

Performance measurement: Feedback from the accountant to management that provides information about how well the actions represent the plans; it also identifies where managers may need to make corrections or adjustments in future planning and control activities. The measurements of activities appear in performance reports that show comparisons of actual with budgeted results and variances. (Chapters 1, 17)

Period cost: A nonproduction cost that has been incurred, is not an asset, and becomes an expense of the period. (Chapter 2)

Periodic (or physical) inventory system: A procedure for tracking inventory costs in which the cost of materials issued for the period is determined by subtracting the Ending Materials Inventory from the sum of the Beginning Inventory and Purchases. A physical count of materials on hand must be made in order to determine the costs in the ending inventory. The procedure is performed only periodically, and costs of issues and ending inventory are not determined after each transaction. (Chapter 6)

Perpetual inventory system: A procedure for tracking inventory costs that requires an ongoing record of receipts and issuances and associated costs. The cost of materials issued to production is charged to the job or department at the time materials are issued. Any balance in the Materials Inventory account is the cost of materials still available for use. Both the cost of materials issued and the ending balance in the Materials account can be directly ascertained after each transaction. (Chapter 6)

Physical measures method: A method of allocating joint costs to joint products that is based on the relative quantities of each product to the total joint products at a split-off point. (Chapter 10)

Physical variance: Physical objects that are set aside, marked, or tagged in some way to indicate that they are unexpected. (Chapter 20)

Plan of operations: A description of the desired activities for a period of time within an organization. (Chapter 14)

Planning: The formulation of short-term and long-term goals and objectives, predictions of potential results under alternative ways of achieving them, and decisions as to how to attain the desired results. (Chapter 1)

Practical capacity: The level of activity at which a facility can operate if demand for its product or service is high enough for the facility to produce all it can. It is theoretical capacity less unavoidable interruptions and delays, such as holidays, vacations, time off for weekends, machine breakdowns, material and labor shortages, and rest breaks. (Chapter 8)

Predetermined overhead rate: An overhead rate determined in advance for a period of time and calculated by dividing the budgeted (estimated) overhead costs for the period by the budgeted (estimated) activity for the same period. (Chapter 8)

Present value: The value of money today that will be received or paid at some future date. (Chapter 23)

Price standard: A price for materials or a rate for labor that represents how much a unit of quantity or a unit of time should cost. It represents the sum of those cost elements management decides to call *the price* or *rate*. (Chapter 12)

Pricing (*see* Cost-based pricing and Market-based pricing)

Prior department costs: The costs associated with units in a process cost system that are the output from one department and the input to a subsequent department. (Chapter 9)

Process costing: A cost accumulation system that charges the costs of materials, labor, and production overhead to departments or other work center for a period of time. It is generally used when products or services are indistinguishable, mass produced, or otherwise homogeneous. (Chapters 5, 9)

Processing companies: Companies that start with natural materials to form their products or change the natural materials in some way to generate other products. (Chapter 2)

Product cost: Any cost element that is included in production costs. (Chapter 2)

Product flow time: The time it takes to convert raw inputs into the final products sold to a customer. Flow time comprises productive time, move time, and wait time. (Chapters 8, 20)

Product structure file: A file, usually a computer data file, that provides the part numbers of the components of each manufactured item. The relationships of all parts to each other are organized into a tier of inventory items in a hierarchy rising from the simple raw materials to component parts, to subassemblies, and to complex final products. Bills of material, which are lists of parts requirements, for any product can be retrieved from this file. (Chapter 5)

Production costs: All costs necessary to get a good or service ready for sale. They include the costs of people, materials, equipment, and space. (Chapter 2)

Production department: An organizational unit most closely tied to the productive effort that results in products or services to customers. (Chapter 8a)

Production information system: A management information system that identifies production costs with work performed and provides management with information that assists in planning and controlling physical activities and cost elements and in measuring the performance of departments or other activity centers within the operations. (Chapter 5)

Production overhead: The production costs that cannot be specifically identified with or traced directly to individual units of the finished product or the service. It may also include some costs that might be directly traceable, but it is uneconomical to trace them to the unit. Production overhead is generally referred to as *all production costs other than direct materials and direct labor.* (Chapters 2, 8, 13)

Production overhead cost (*see* Production overhead)

Production schedule file: A file in a production information system that contains the assigned priorities for each open production order, the scheduled start date, and the anticipated completion date for each operation. (Chapter 5)

Profit center: A segment that generates both revenues and expenses. The profit center is commonly called a *division, branch,* or *center.* An incorporated segment is called a *subsidiary.* (Chapter 17)

Profit margin: The profit expressed as a percentage of sales revenue; also called *return on sales.* It can be determined as the product of the contribution margin ratio and the margin of safety. (Chapter 4)

Pseudoparticipation: An environment in which top management seeks the input of lower management in the budget process but ignores the input when it is given. (Chapter 14)

Pull production system: A production system in which parts are produced only if they are needed by and a signal is received from subsequent operations. If the customer operations is next to the supplier operation, the signal can be verbal or can be indicated by an empty designated area. If the operations are separated, the signal is a document or computer output that authorizes movement or production of parts. (Chapter 5)

Purchase order: A written request to a vendor for specific goods at an agreed-upon price. It usually stipulates terms of delivery and payment and authorizes the vendor to deliver goods and submit an invoice. (Chapter 6)

Purchase requisition: A document that represents a written request to the Purchasing Department for the acquisition of materials. This document provides the Purchasing Department with an authorization to act. (Chapter 6)

Quantity standard: The unit of material or the task or activity that represents amounts that should be used in producing good units of output. In establishing such quantities, management considers the type of corporate philosophy, size, and structure of the organization, and actual or desired state of efficiency. (Chapter 12)

Reasonableness of relationship: A concept that says that a reasonable explanation should be given as to why and how the independent variable (activity) causes the dependent variable (cost). (Chapter 3)

Receiving report: A physical document generated by the receiving department for both the storeroom and accounts payable that indicates that the goods were received and the quantities counted. (Chapter 6)

Reciprocal (linear algebra) method: A method of allocating support and service department costs in which simultaneous equations are used to allocate reciprocal services to the appropriate support and service departments prior to allocating departmental costs to production departments. It specifically recognizes the reciprocal services among the support and service departments. (Chapter 8a)

Regression analysis: A statistical procedure to determine the relationship between variables. In the case of cost estimation, the relationships will be identified as variable and fixed. (Chapter 3)

Regression line: A line fitted to a set of data that represents a series of conditional averages given activity levels. The line is computed to minimize the squared differences from the line. (Chapter 3)

Relevant range: The range of activity over which the definitions of fixed and variable costs are valid. (Chapter 3)

Reorder point: The quantity level of inventory that triggers the placement of a new order. It is usually calculated as the quantity demanded during the lead time. If safety stocks are maintained, it is the quantity demanded during the lead time plus the safety stock level. (Chapter 6a)

Representative points approach: A cost estimation technique that is used when actual cost information for anticipated activity levels do not exist. Managers use their knowledge of operations and costs to estimate the costs of two activity levels. These estimates are used in the same manner as the high-low point method to obtain an estimated cost formula with variable and fixed cost components. (Chapter 3)

Required return: The profit that senior managers desire from capital projects. A required return becomes a threshold or screen that filters out unpromising projects before much effort is wasted on them. (Chapter 23)

Required volume: The units of sales dollars at which the required return is earned. Because a profit level is required for maintaining an investment in assets, the required volume is greater than break-even volume. (Chapter 4)

Residual income: The income left after a charge is made for the required return on investment. (Chapter 17)

Return on investment (ROI): Profit expressed as a percentage of the investment. It is also expressed as the product of the profit margin and the investment turnover. (Chapters 4, 17)

Revenue center: An organizational segment that specializes in the sale of products or services. These segments are primarily evaluated on the basis of sales generated. The names for these segments include *branch, territory, line, region,* or *division.* (Chapter 17)

Rolling budget: An annual budget prepared by quarter or month. Then each quarter or month, a new period is added and the others are changed to reflect new information. Also called a *continuous budget.* (Chapter 14)

Safety stock: The extra inventory carried to act as a buffer to protect against increased demand, delays in delivery, or other conditions that might create an out-of-stock condition. (Chapter 6a)

Salaries: A fixed periodic payment (weekly, biweekly, semimonthly, or monthly) paid to employees. They are fixed costs. (Chapter 7)

Sales mix: A combination of units of individual products in proportion to their actual or expected sales volume. (Chapter 4)

Sales mix variance: The impact on gross profit of shifts in sales units away from the budgeted sales mix. It is a comparison of (Actual units and Actual mix × Budgeted gross profit) and (Actual units restated into the budgeted mix × Budgeted gross profit). (Chapter 19)

Sales price variance: The change in gross profit due to a difference between budgeted and actual selling price per unit. Its computation is based on the formula: (Actual unit selling price − Budgeted unit selling price) × actual units sold. (Chapter 19)

Sales value method: A method of allocating joint costs to joint products that is based on the relative sales value of each product to the total joint products at a split-off point. The sales values can be measured at the split-off point because the products can be sold at that point. (Chapter 10)

Sales volume variance: For a single product this variance is the increase or decrease in gross profit resulting from the difference between the planned and actual number of units sold. It is computed as (Actual units sold − Budgeted units sold) × Budgeted gross profit per unit. For a multiple product situation the variance relates to changes in total actual sales units and total budgeted sales units. The variance is computed as (Actual sales units stated at the budgeted mix × Budgeted gross profit) − (Budgeted sales units stated at the budgeted mix × Budgeted gross profit). (Chapter 19)

Scattergraph and visual fit method: A cost estimation technique that requires plotting all observations of costs on a graph and fitting a line to the data by visual and judgmental means. (Chapter 3)

Scrap: A material input residual that has a recovery value significant enough to measure. It may be sold in some outside market or reused in a production process. (Chapter 11)

Segment: An organizational unit whose performance is evaluated on a regular basis. (Chapter 17)

Segment performance measurement: The process of accumulating and reporting data that relate to segment performance. (Chapter 17)

Selective process flow: A production process in which the sequencing of operations and the type of operations vary by the desired final product. (Chapter 9b)

Semivariable cost: A cost that has both fixed cost and variable cost portions. The fixed cost portion is the minimum cost required if some activity takes place, but as activity increases, total costs increase above this minimum at the proportionate rate. (Chapter 3)

Sensitivity analysis: The study of how important results such as profit, volume, or rate of return change with changes in estimates. Sensitivity analysis may be applied to any analytical technique. (Chapters 4a, 22, 24)

Separable costs: The costs of additional processing for individual products after the split-off point in a joint process. These are the costs necessary to put the products in a form or condition to sell. (Chapter 10)

Service department: A special type of department that provides support services for producing departments and customer service for outside customers. (Chapter 8a)

Setup time: The time required between jobs to gather the materials, tools, machinery, people, and work space required to perform the next job. (Chapter 5)

Shift premium: The extra compensation for working less desirable times, such as evening or night shifts. (Chapter 7)

Solvency: The ability to make long-run repayment of all debt and interest as it falls due. (Chapter 23)

Spending variance: When used with production overhead, the difference between actual overhead costs incurred and the budget for actual activity. This variance includes both variable and fixed costs. For nonproduction costs it is the difference between the actual expenses and the flexible budget for the same level of activity. (Chapters 13, 13a, 19)

Split-off point: The point at which joint products become individually identifiable. (Chapter 10)

Spoilage: Units of output that do not meet quality standards and no amount of rework can make the units salable as firsts or seconds. The units may be partially or fully completed. (Chapter 11)

Spurious relationship: A relationship between a dependent variable and an independent variable in which measures of the association between the variables are high but the variables are not directly related. (Chapter 3)

Standard cost: A cost for a product that consists of a price standard (price for materials, rate for labor) and a quantity standard (quantity for materials, time for labor). (Chapter 12)

Standard cost sheet: A summary for an individual product that shows the various categories of direct materials used and their standard costs, the direct labor operations employed and their standard costs, and the departmental production overhead costs to support operations. (Chapter 12)

Standard costing: A cost identification technique that uses predetermined rates for recognizing the costs of direct material, direct labor, and production overhead in accumulating the costs of work in process. (Chapters 2, 26)

Standard error of the coefficient: The ratio of the residual squared errors in the dependent variable to the square root of the mean square error of the independent variable. (Chapter 3)

Standard error of the estimate: A measure of the average deviation between the actual observations of the dependent variable and values predicted by the regression equation. (Chapter 3)

Step cost: A cost that increases or decreases in lumps of cost with changes in activity. A given amount of cost will sustain some increase in volume without any increase in cost. At some point the cost must go up like a stair step in order to increase volume. (Chapter 3)

Step (sequential) method: A method of allocating support and service department costs in which the departments are arranged in a sequence and their costs allocated one after the other. It is an attempt to recognize the reciprocal services among the support and service departments. (Chapter 8a)

Stockout costs: The costs of having demand for an item exceed the units in inventory or exceed the ability of the company to meet delivery schedules. A customer order for the item must either wait until the stock is replenished or be canceled. The common measurable costs are the additional administrative effort required to process a back order and the contribution margin lost if the customer goes elsewhere without waiting for the back order. Another important cost is the loss of goodwill because the customer may not return and may convey dissatisfaction to others. (Chapter 6a)

Strategic planning: The process of deciding on organizational goals and objectives and identifying the direction an organization will take to achieve them and how resources will be allocated. It is usually carried out at the top management levels. (Chapters 1, 23, 26)

Strategies: The broad activities that senior managers choose for the organization. Strategies are developed once senior management establishes its goals and objectives. (Chapter 26)

Support department: An organizational unit that provides supporting services that faciliate the activities of the production departments. It generally does not engage directly in productive effort on final products or services to customers. (Chapter 8a)

Synthesis production process: A production process in which raw materials and component parts are assembled to build the final product. Fabrication and assembly operations are examples of this type of process. (Chapter 10)

Target concept: A strategy for designing, marketing, and pricing a product that involves anticipating the reactions of the competition. The first step is to estimate the eventual price that competitors will likely charge for their products and to design an enhanced version of the product that can be sold at the competitor's price and that has the features that the competition will likely place in its products. Once a target price has been established, a total cost target is set by subtracting a normal profit margin from the target price. This target cost is apportioned to production, marketing, and administration. From this a cost-volume-profit model is developed to reflect the financial impact of each change in the proposed product design, production flow, marketing method, and distribution method. (Chapter 24)

Theoretical capacity: The productive activity under perfect conditions. Plant, equipment, and people operate at a peak efficiency in an engineering sense. It does not allow for unavoidable but expected interruptions. (Chapter 8)

Time-and-motion study: A technique used to estimate the amount of time required for the tasks to be performed within each process. Such studies identify the most efficient manner to complete a task by eliminating unnecessary motion or waiting and then measuring the amount of time needed to complete the task. (Chapter 3)

Total quality control: A production system concept that assumes that all units produced will be good with no spoilage, or that no defective units will be considered acceptable. The emphasis is on doing whatever is necessary to satisfy customer needs and doing the work right the first time. (Chapter 5)

Traceability: The characteristic associated with a cost that can be specifically identified with or traced to a cost objective. (Chapters 8, 17)

Transfer price: The price set for goods or services transferred from one segment to another. It can be a cost allocation for a cost center or a cost-based or market-based price for a profit center and an investment center. (Chapter 18)

Transfer pricing: The process of setting prices for goods

or services transferred from one segment to another. (Chapter 18)

Transferred-in cost (*see* Prior department cost)

Treasurer: The financial officer responsible for all money management functions and activities. The major areas of responsibility are for capital, investor relations, short-term financing, banking and custody, credits and collections, investments, and insurance. (Chapter 1)

Unexpired costs: Costs related to future benefits and classified as assets. (Chapter 2)

Unfixable problem: A problem in a process for which the manager cannot eliminate variances by taking corrective action. (Chapter 21)

Value added: A concept in the new manufacturing environment in which activities that add value to the product or service are those activities that transform materials into final product. Activities that must be reduced or eliminated are those required to move, inspect, or store a product. (Chapter 5)

Value-added cost: A cost associated with activities that add value to the product or service and relate only to good units produced or services rendered. (Chapter 11)

Value-added direct labor: That portion of direct labor that changes raw material into a finished product or service that is delivered to a customer. (Chapter 7)

Value-added direct labor ratio: The ratio of value-added direct labor to total direct and indirect labor. The ratio can use either number of employees or dollars of cost. (Chapter 7)

Variable cost: A cost that changes in total in direct proportion to changes in the activity base. Once the variable cost per unit of activity is established, it is constant per unit throughout a relevant range. (Chapter 3)

Variable costing: A cost methodology that classifies as product costs only those production costs that increase or decrease with production volume (direct material, direct labor, and variable production overhead). This means that fixed production costs are treated as period costs. (Chapters 2, 8, 16, 26)

Variable overhead spending variance: The difference between actual variable overhead costs incurred and the variable overhead costs for the flexible budget at actual hours worked. (Chapter 13)

Vice president of finance (*see* Chief financial officer)

Volume variance: When used with production overhead, the difference between the flexible budget for the actual units produced (or standard capacity allowed for the actual units produced) and the amounts applied to work in process. This variance consists only of fixed costs and can also be measured in one of two other ways: (1) the difference between budgeted fixed costs and fixed costs applied to production or (2) [Normal production (or normal capacity) − Actual units produced (or standard capacity allowed for the actual units produced)] × Fixed overhead rate. In the case of non-production costs, this variance is the flexible budget for the activity level achieved less the original budget. (Chapters 13, 19)

Wages: Payments to employees based on hours worked or pieces produced. They are variable costs. (Chapter 7)

Waste: Material that is lost, evaporates, or shrinks during a production process or is a residue. (Chapter 11)

Weighted average equivalent units: Equivalent units of production calculated under a weighted average product flow concept. It considers work effort to complete the units finished and the work effort in the partially finished units in ending inventory. Beginning inventory units are assumed to be started and completed during the current period. (Chapter 9)

Work in Process Inventory: The account in which costs are accumulated during the time products pass through the production process. It covers the stages of the total process between the time materials are released to pro-duction and the time the goods are moved to a finished goods warehouse. (Chapter 2)

Work in Process Inventory file: A master file in a production information system that contains the important data for each open production order identified by product number. It summarizes the cost elements for materials, labor, and overhead costs. This file is the subsidiary ledger supporting the Work in Process Inventory general ledger account. (Chapter 5)

Yield variance: The cost change that results from an actual yield of finished product that is different from the standard quantity of product established for a given input of materials or labor. A variance occurs when the output from production, given a specific amount of material or labor input, differs from the output established as the standard yield. It is measured as the difference between the actual quantities of material or labor used in production and the standard quantities allowed for the completed product times an average standard price. (Chapter 12a)

Zero-based budget: Budgets that require all of the expenditures for a function to be justified from the base level up. It is also called a *sunset review*. (Chapter 14)

INDEX